With wit and wisdom, K.
ONLY A MOTHER CAN... P9-DUZ-867
HAVING A BABY:

HUSBANDS: "I can certainly sympathize with a father who is frightened by hospitals and wary of birth: all that blood and gore! And I believe him when he says he doesn't know the first thing about caring for a baby. That's exactly how most mothers feel. The difference is, most mother's don't have a choice."

CHILDBIRTH: "The truth is that childbirth in America is getting more *un*natural every day...even a 'natural' birth often means that the mother is merely 'awake' for the proceedings. Never mind that she's strapped down, numb below the waist, electronically monitored, chemically induced and intravenously fed!"

LABOR: "A labor bed is no place to worry about proper etiquette. One doctor pointed out that a laboring woman may become 'very cross and ill-tempered, shrewish and cantankerous.' I don't wonder. Who wouldn't become ill-tempered during transition? One woman I knew threw a lemon at her husband."

K.C. COLE

WHAT ONLY A MOTHER CAN TELL YOU ABOUT HAVING A BABY

BERKLEY BOOKS, NEW YORK

This Berkley book contains the complete
text of the original hardcover edition.
It has been completely reset in a typeface
designed for easy reading and was printed
from new film.

WHAT ONLY A MOTHER CAN TELL YOU
ABOUT HAVING A BABY

A Berkley Book / published by arrangement with
Doubleday & Company, Inc.

PRINTING HISTORY
Doubleday edition published 1980
Berkley edition / September 1981

ISBN: 0-425-11232-2

A BERKLEY BOOK ® TM 757,375
Berkley Books are published by The Berkley Publishing Group,
200 Madison Avenue, New York, NY 10016.
The name "BERKLEY" and the "B" logo are
trademarks belonging to Berkley Publishing Corporation.

PRINTED IN THE UNITED STATES OF AMERICA

10 9 8 7

For Baby Whosis,
who became my son,
Peter

Contents

Preface

K. C. Cole's book provides the reader not only with an in-depth portrayal of one woman's experience in childbirth but also with exposure to the possible varieties in childbirth through post-birth interviews with other new mothers.

This book is representative of an ever-growing new trend toward recognition of the totality of childbirthing. Childbirthing is neither a purely physical nor a specific isolated act. Rather, it is part of a nine-month continuum that can have important ramifications in the subsequent development of a new family unit. It has great emotional significance both for the woman and for the family to which she belongs. Surely, physical factors and safety are of primary concern in the choice and provision of childbearing services. However, with these factors accounted for, it then becomes important for each individual and family to determine and arrange for the preferred type of birthing format. This requires education and investigation into what modes are available and the subsequent communication to health-care personnel of desired procedure.

At this time, the American College of Obstetrics and Gynecology has stated that archaic rules that interfere with family-centered birth but do not threaten physical safety of the child and mother should be eliminated. It is my belief, in keeping with Ms. Cole's discussion of the varieties possible in safe childbirth, that every woman has the right to expect, seek out, and receive childbirth services geared to supply the optimum not only in physical care but also in psychological support.

Family involvement should be considered an integral part of the childbirth experience. Thus it should be promoted and included in operational procedures available to expectant mothers and their families.

—Dr. Alvin Donnenfeld

Introduction

This book is the product of pure frustration. The frustration of a mother who read every preparation-for-pregnancy book on the market—and still found herself totally unprepared for the experience of having a baby. At times, I was pleasantly surprised. And at other times, I was most unpleasantly surprised. But I was almost always surprised. The more I read, it seemed, the less I knew.

Of course, nobody can tell you how to have a baby. Or what it's like. Especially not a male obstetrician who has never felt a labor pain or strained to see his toes. Pregnant women have always found solace and sound advice in the company of other women: their friends, mothers, sisters, aunts, and even mothers-in-law. But today it's getting harder. Today pregnant women are increasingly isolated. As apartment walls replace backyard fences, as women go to work, as families disintegrate, or move away, or get smaller. As women have fewer children.

Four years ago, I found myself in the ridiculous position of being the only pregnant person I knew. Or had ever known, for that matter. A dozen or so friends had a small party for me. All were attractive, articulate, heterosexual women between the ages of twenty-eight and thirty-five. Not one was a mother. I was left quite alone in my childbirth adventure. For company, I turned to books. But among my friends I remained a curiosity. A pioneer. The hardest part was not having anyone "like me" to talk to.

Many young mothers have friends who are also young mothers, but that doesn't mean they talk or share experiences. Sometimes they are too busy. And sometimes they are afraid to say what's on their minds. Often there's an unspoken understanding that "baby talk" is, well, babyish. That grown women should have more "interesting" topics to share. Now even pregnant women who know each other are finding it harder and harder to talk to each other. That's one reason they flock to Lamaze classes and La Leche groups. To learn, but also to talk. And to listen.

Their only alternative is how-to-have-a-baby books with their unrealistic advice and often condescending tone. Or obstetricians, who mete out a reluctant ten minutes a month. The same obstetricians who write the books. It's not surprising that the obstetricians don't know what women really want to know about being pregnant because women don't talk to obstetricians. They talk to other women. When they can.

And so I set out to discover what mothers had to say about the process of motherhood. I wanted to let women speak for themselves about pregnancy and childbirth, to exchange their uniquely feminine perceptions, to share secrets, to learn from one another.

I began by getting groups of women together. Three or four or five at a time. I'd turn on a tape recorder and pass around wine or cookies and coffee and try to get a conversation going. It was almost always difficult. The mothers would protest that they didn't remember what it was like to be pregnant, and that their experiences were so unique that they wouldn't apply, and that they really didn't have anything to say anyway. But they always did, and they always remembered, and nobody was as unique as she had thought. And three or four hours later, I'd always have trouble terminating the interview. Everybody wanted to go on, and on, and on.

As a supplement, I sent out several hundred questionnaires to mothers in Massachusetts and Vermont and North Carolina and other areas I didn't have a chance to visit. I tried to balance my selection of mothers geographically, educationally, professionally. I didn't want all Lamaze mothers, or all housewives. I wanted a representative sample. In all, approximately 200 mothers contributed their experiences and insights to this book. Career mothers and home mothers, old mothers and young mothers, modern mothers and old-fashioned mothers.

Surprisingly, they usually formed a consensus. It's true that better-educated mothers tended to favor natural childbirth and nursing; but on most topics, the same ideas were echoed again and again. There is a wide range of things, it seems, that nobody ever tells you about having a baby. Things that only mothers know. And while we often disagreed as to whether it was a good idea to know the "truth," we seldom disagreed on what the "truth" was.

This book is not only *for* mothers, it is also *by* mothers. As such, it relies heavily on quotes. The quotes were selected from hundreds of hours of taped interviews. Most of the time, they were selected because they were typical of a certain set of ideas. I may have chosen the words of the mother who said something best, but that mother is almost always speaking for many other mothers who said almost exactly the same thing. The quotes are representative, not unique. They are examples, not isolated incidents.

As a book *by* mothers, this book is necessarily limited. It does not discuss nursing or home birth or obstetrical problems in detail. In part, because there are many other fine books on these subjects. In part, because the mothers I interviewed simply weren't knowledgeable on these subjects. By chance, I didn't interview a single mother who had her baby at home, or who had a woman obstetrician, or who was not married to the father. Therefore, these topics are not covered. I did, however, interview two cesarean mothers who had ruptured uteruses, and one mother who had a Leboyer birth; so these subjects are covered. In general, the subjects covered are those which came up. Most are subjects which came up repeatedly.

Above all, this book presents a perspective, not a total body of knowledge. This book should be read *in addition to* traditional books on nursing and Lamaze and pregnancy and childbirth in general. A pregnant woman needs all the information she can get. This book is meant to supplement—not supplant—other childbirth literature. But it *is* different. That's why I wrote it.

Most how-to-have-a-baby books are just that. How-to books. And telling a woman how to have a baby is about as futile as telling her how to feel about sex. Whatever the rules, each woman is bound to be the exception. Childbirth is much too individual and personal an experience to condense into a few chapters on diet, morning sickness, and labor. Most childbirth books sound artificial because they *are* artificial. The women they speak to and about are hypothetical women, "average" women—conglomerate patients compiled from the files and memories of obstetricians. They lack life, which is what childbirth is all about.

The books are therefore often misleading. "Average" women have "average" feelings and experiences. Books that concentrate on the average woman can't and don't illuminate the wide range of physiological and psychological changes that pregnancy can bring. Even a woman who has read every book—as I did—can find herself unprepared. The average woman portrayed in childbirth books can't stop eating, is always tired, and suffers from hemorrhoids; otherwise, she has a "normal" delivery, uncomplicated by anything more serious than stretch marks. Real mothers rarely follow such predictable scenarios. The misleading message of the childbirth books can frighten and confuse them.

Books written by a single author also tend to be contradictory. Readers have a hard time separating the reality from the author's personal rhetoric. One author might insist that a successful pregnancy depends on strict obedience to the obstetrician, a weight gain of less than fifteen pounds, and minimal travel and exercise. Another might have a laissez-faire attitude toward nutrition, insist on vigorous exercise, and denounce obstetricians as greedy male-chauvinist incompetents. What's a pregnant woman to believe?

Women talking about their own experiences in pregnancy and childbirth have no ax to grind: no particular propaganda to sell. They can and do talk freely about what happened to *them*.

Sometimes I may sound as if I have a particular platform of my own. But it is almost always based upon the hundreds of interviews, upon hearing the same thing over and over again. And even then, I am not always convinced. I thought I was convinced that excessive anesthesia almost always makes childbirth more difficult. I had just finished making that point rather strongly when I had to quit writing to go to the dentist to have a tooth pulled. It was a simple extraction, and I had not expected any anesthesia. But when the doctor asked me if I wanted to be knocked out, I almost said yes. It is always hard to say no to something called a "pain killer"—even though I knew it would result in more pain.

In the same way, it is always easy to give advice. It is much more difficult to take it—even when the advice is your own.

I'm not trying to win converts, I'm trying to share what I learned from talking to hundreds of mothers. And I'm hoping that the reader—and the author—will gain something from the experience. Whether or not we can act on what we learn is another matter.

So You're Pregnant:

Getting and Giving the News

It all seems so simple. A shot in the dark. A close encounter of the most permanent kind. A classic tale of egg meets sperm. Within minutes, the intricate process of long division begins. Before you know it, you're buying baby clothes, orthodontia, college tuition. How did it happen?

The phrase "I'm pregnant" is undoubtably the most loaded—not to mention the most pregnant—in the English language. Never do two little words mean so much. I remember the joke we used to tell about getting pregnant in high school. Question: What takes fifteen minutes and lasts nine months? Answer: A Toni Home Permanent.

Of course, there's more than one way to start a child. And there's more than a semantic distinction between being "pregnant," "knocked up," and "with child."

"Knocked up" is what happens to high school girls with tight sweaters and loose morals, like the unfortunate member of the Pink Ladies gang in *Grease*. "There are worse things I could do," she sang, but not according to the standards of the fifties. The only good news about getting "knocked up" comes when you finally get your period. The only "happy event" is *not* being pregnant.

"With child," on the other hand, is what happens to the mommie models on the Ivory Snow commercials. Two hours after they miss a period, they're on the phone to their husbands:

"Darling! I have the most wonderful news!"

"You don't mean . . . ? !"

"You're going to be a father!"

Followed by tears, pledges of love, and dinner at the fanciest place in town (and, of course, a dozen long-stemmed red roses).

"Getting pregnant" is what happens to the rest of us. We may know it immediately, or not for months. It may bring us agony or ecstasy, make us giggle or gasp. We may shout it to the world from the highest hill, or keep it under our skirts as long as loose-fitting clothes allow. But few women react to the news with simple delight or dread. After all, getting pregnant signals perhaps the most important event in your life. It's not surprising that feelings are mixed, potent, and changeable.

ARE YOU OR AREN'T YOU?

To your doctor, discovering that you're pregnant is a matter of simple science. His examination will probably turn up such tell-tale signs as enlarged breasts, bluish discoloration of the vulva and vagina, and softening of the uterus and cervix. A sample of your urine will contain certain hormones associated with pregnancy. In years past, countless frogs and rabbits sacrificed their lives in the service of detecting those hormones. Today chemical tests can identify them in a matter of minutes. Other signs and symptoms are so obvious that your doctor could probably diagnose your pregnancy based on them without even looking at you. If you've been missing periods, throwing up, and craving asparagus ice cream, chances are you're pregnant.

No doubt there is some proper etiquette for responding to the doctor's announcement: "You're pregnant." My own performance was less than sterling. I had a pretty good idea that I was pregnant before I ever saw the doctor, but I wasn't prepared for the waiting room full of big-bellied women—

looking like so many characters out of Dr. Seuss. The thought that I might become one of them filled me with nothing but dread. Then, the nurse's leaving me lying undressed under a sheet for fifteen long, cold minutes, failed to improve my frame of mind. The strange doctor who confirmed the "good news" was greeted not with kisses, but with a blank stare. He waited, then whispered, "You *do* want the baby, don't you?"

Like many women, I didn't react to the news of my pregnancy with joy or tears or terror or sighs. I just didn't react. The news was as numbing as a shot of Novocaine. I didn't know what to think. How can you think about the unthinkable? Women who get pregnant for the second or third or fourth time know what's to come. But I couldn't conceive of what it meant even to be pregnant, much less to have a baby. Some doctor in a white jacket was telling me that I was something called "pregnant," but I felt and looked the same as I did last month or last year when I wasn't pregnant. Who's pregnant? What baby?

And this was the enthusiastic response of a woman who was *trying* to get pregnant. It must have been hard to distinguish from the reactions of women who were trying not to.

Despite much mythology to the contrary, shocked silence is perhaps the most common reaction to getting the news. This doesn't strike me as especially strange—not when you consider that the doctor who tells you you're pregnant is often a complete stranger. That's not the sort of person you normally jump up and throw your arms around—especially not when he (she) is facing you from the end of a cold narrow table and you're lying prone covered only by a white sheet. If you did want to hug him (her), you'd probably have to use your feet.

But doctors have expectations, too. Specifically, they expect their patients to react—somehow—to the news. If you don't, the doctor may assume that you're thinking things over. (How is he to know that you're just dumbfounded?) He may try to be helpful, spark a conversation. Like "Do you want to keep the baby?" Or "You'll have to decide what you want to do about the pregnancy."

These remarks come off as callous, at best. But the doctor may not know you're happy. And indeed you might be thinking about abortion. In fact, the doctor may be just as dumbfounded as you are. So if he (she) says something that sounds a little strange, it may be because you didn't say anything at all. Come to think of it, the best solution might be for doctors not to say anything at all.

Of course, there are women who yell and scream and jump up and down and hug everybody when they hear the news. One woman's doctor told her to settle down; he was afraid she might have a miscarriage. Almost inevitably, these are women who have been trying to get pregnant for some time and who have been going to the same doctor for some time. Why so many women first seek out an obstetrician or seek out a new one when they get pregnant remains a mystery. But it does put a damper on the ideal doctor-patient relationship outlined in the books. (See Doctor, Doctor.)

Women's intuition seems to play almost as large a role in determining pregnancy as do the doctor's instruments. Patrice told her doctor she was pregnant. The doctor said the tests were negative. Two weeks later, Patrice proved to be right. The world is full of pregnant Patrices.

Not all is intuition, of course. Much is just plain common sense. "Joan came into my office," remembered her friend Lee, "and we were talking about the extra bedroom in her apartment. I was sort of fishing as to whether she was going to fill it with a baby, because it was on my mind. Then we started talking about the blue veins on our tits, and I was hoping I was pregnant and so was she. Finally we both went to the same doctor to get tests at the same time. Hers was positive and mine was negative, so that same night that she was so excited, I was absolutely disheartened. But Joan said, 'Those blue veins didn't come from nowhere. If you have blue veins on your tits, you're pregnant.' And I was."

A surprising number of women say they experienced conception on the spot. Whether this is wishful thinking, Sunday-morning-quarterbacking, or some special sensitivity, many mothers seem to know the exact moment their child was conceived:

"I knew right away," said Candy. "I said, 'You *bastard!*' I had my IUD taken out because of heavy periods, so we were going to use all these store-bought contraceptives. Sometimes we used the store-bought things, and sometimes we didn't. And I said, 'Stop Right Now, You're Making Me Nervous!' And he kept saying, 'Don't worry, I'm going to get up in a minute.' I mean, it wasn't even a completed act!"

Of course, finding out is only the first step. More reactions begin to surface as the idea sinks in: relief and remorse, anxiety and accomplishment, ebullience and stark terror. It all depends on you—and on your situation. Not a few newly pregnant women find themselves crying one minute, giggling the next.

THE GOOD NEWS

You're supposed to be happy when you find out you're pregnant because being pregnant means you're going to have a baby. But there are other reasons to rejoice. Marilyn was happy because being pregnant meant "we didn't have to use a rubber anymore." I was happy because it meant at least a brief respite from a job I couldn't stand. And Martha was happy because she'd been trying for so long: "It was like Christmas. I felt so good that all my efforts weren't wasted." Too bad about all those wasted efforts.

I'm not being cynical. For most women, the "baby" part of having a baby doesn't become real for a long time. Pregnancy at this point often seems a technicality, a tale told by a urine test. If you have detailed visions in your dreams about what it's going to be like to have a baby in the house, then you can be happy that your visions are finally going to come true. But if you don't have any notion at all, you may still be happy for other reasons. And there's a wide range.

For all the women who are happy to be pregnant because they tried so long and so hard, for example, there are just as many who are happy because they didn't try at all.

Gene found it ironic that she had to wait so long to get pregnant. "Isn't that the pits? Here you go around college worrying that you're going to get pregnant. Then you want to get pregnant, and you don't get pregnant for a whole year."

What she was in such a hurry about, I don't know. Getting there is half the fun of it. Still, many women are happy when they manage to plan their pregnancies down to the millisecond, so the baby can be born the same day as their mother-in-law, or on Christmas, or so they can avoid going into labor during a heat wave or a blizzard. ("I'm going to get pregnant this month, or that's it until next year," one woman told me.) Still others revel in getting pregnant spontaneously because they think it's romantic. A love child. "Trying" makes it too mechanical.

Either way, not having to wait means not having to say you're sorry every month when you get your period.

Personally, I don't believe in the joy of spontaneous—or meticulously planned—conception. I think it's got to be fun to try a little. I don't know because I didn't get the chance. I felt cheated on that one—and so, I found, did a lot of women. Trying seems to make succeeding all the more rewarding. Even women who desperately want to get pregnant don't always want to get pregnant so fast.

Some miss the anticipation; others feel they would appreciate a pregnancy more that didn't come so easily; still others need time to get used to the idea. Lee said, "I figured if I'm not totally resolved to have a child, I've got a whole year to get pregnant. My husband kept saying, 'Nobody gets pregnant right away.' And then I got pregnant in three days. It's one thing to say, 'Okay, let's have a baby.' It's another thing to deal with the reality of being pregnant—especially when it happens so fast."

And then there's always the sneaking suspicion that what was too easy this time around might also be too easy the next time, and the time after that. Anne said, "I was upset for my husband because he was the baby of eight children, and I had this whole frightening vision that this would keep happening and we would keep making babies. The most frightening part to me was that I didn't seem to have control over my body. I felt as though, wow, this is so easy. What's going to happen a year from now? Bunnies?"

The happiest pregnant woman in the world is the one who tries for five years and then conceives twins.

I got pregnant in five days. But besides feeling cheated out of the fun of trying, I was still very happy. I now realize that I was happy, in large part, because I was relieved. Relieved that I really *could* get pregnant. I never doubted it—not consciously, anyway. But I think I *must* have worried about it. Otherwise, why would I have been so relieved to find out my worries were unfounded?

Sally said much the same thing: "It was a tremendous relief to find out that all systems were operational. I had never been pregnant before, and I thought maybe I couldn't. I was thrilled to know I could produce. To get over the fear that I would surely be sterile. And I was surprised at how important I felt about simply joining the millions of women who'd been pregnant before."

Anxious relatives tend to intensify the fears of women who are afraid they might be sterile—and also to add to the relief that follows when they find out they're not. "I had been married for ten months already, and I wasn't pregnant, and everybody wondered what was the matter," said Barb. "I was trying to prove myself—to prove that I wasn't like the aunt everybody said I was like who could never have babies. So I was very happy, very relieved." Barb went on to have six babies in short order.

I felt that my parents were somewhat anxious, too—not that I couldn't have children, but that I wouldn't want them. And I was a little anxious about this, too. As my twenty-ninth birthday approached, I got more anxious than ever. At this point in my life, getting pregnant was a big decision and a difficult one. So I was happy and relieved when the decision was made, the die was cast, the baby was already in the oven. It was a wonderful feeling. Like last summer at the beach when I was invited for a dawn swim and the water was cold and I had a hangover and I really wasn't at all sure that I wanted to take the plunge. But once I was in, the water felt just great.

THE BAD NEWS

Getting pregnant—even when you're glad about it—isn't always a bed of baby showers. Many women react to the news with outright terror—and they aren't all insane. After all, who wants to look forward to nine months of throwing up, losing your figure and possibly your freedom, with labor, childbirth, poverty, and the need to grow up looming in the future. It's not for nothing this book contains a whole chapter about fears—there's a lot to be afraid of.

The initial reaction to pregnancy is most often bad news when the pregnancy itself is a matter of bad timing. When I first started interviewing mothers for this book, I would go around the room, asking each to tell her first reaction to the news that she was pregnant. The very first mother answered, "I must say the news wasn't great because I wasn't married, the baby's father was in Iowa, and I was in Stockholm."

Getting pregnant isn't great news if you're moving to Morocco or you and/or your husband is unemployed or you've got German measles or you just got a job that involves commuting cross-country twice a week. Sometimes the timing is so bad that even very good news temporarily becomes bad news. Linda's was a classic case.

"We had been trying to have children for a couple of years, so we decided to adopt. We were at the end of the adoption process, so we had to have physicals. My physical showed I was pregnant. We were in such a state of shock that we went back to the adoption conference and we didn't even tell them. We just said yes, we were very excited about the adoption. Then we drove from one place to another. Finally, the next day, we called and put off the adoption."

The shock of getting pregnant when you least expect it can be downright scary. Barbara found out that she was five months pregnant while rock climbing in Maine. She had conceived in Africa's Kalahari Desert. "I had never thought I could have children because I'd always had trouble with my period. They used to give me hormone injections to bring it on, and my ovaries were six times the normal size. They were always telling me that something was wrong with me. So I didn't think there was anything unusual that I wasn't getting my period. I thought it was the excitement of being in Africa. My husband and I were both sick, but I thought it was from the food we were eating. Toward the third or fourth month, I started to worry, but I was afraid to face it. My husband thought I had a tumor or something. Then we went to Maine. I wasn't feeling well, so I went to the doctor that night. I was really scared. The doctor said. 'You're pregnant.' I couldn't believe it. I didn't think I could give birth to anything."

If shell shock stops many women from jumping with joy when they find out they're pregnant, it's not surprising how many don't jump. Indeed, the number of women who get pregnant in the first place isn't surprising when you consider the number who don't seem to know how they got that way. "I don't remember not using protection" seems to be as common a statement as "It's a girl."

"At Christmas my mother said, 'I bet you're pregnant,'" said Joan. "I said, 'I couldn't be pregnant.' We didn't screw that much. My husband was away all the time. So when was I getting pregnant? So I said, 'Oh, Ma, I'm not pregnant.' And

I must have been two weeks pregnant—already I was throwing up."

BREAKING THE NEWS

My sister-in-law called me a few months ago to say she was expecting a baby in December. That was in April. Her period was two days late. I thought she was crazy. In fact, she was pregnant.

The baby books say you shouldn't tell anyone that you're pregnant until you're three months along, just in case you should have a miscarriage. Three months turned out to be my mother's birthday, so I gave her a birthday card signed "Baby Whosis—see you in six months." She got the message right away. My father didn't get it at all. Finally she said to him, "Don't you remember Theopolis?" Theopolis was my parents' pet name for my brother—the fetus—before he was born.

Aside from my parents, however, I didn't break the news to anyone until I could no longer get away with the excuse that I was just putting on weight. I kept my secret for almost seven months. I loved having this little friend to carry around whom nobody at the office knew about but me. I was also afraid that I might lose promotion opportunities at work if my employers discovered my condition—and also vacation time. I spent most of my sixth month on vacation in Brazil. By the time I got back, I didn't have to break the news to anyone.

Most women want the world to know when they're pregnant. But at the same time, they like to keep it a secret. Instead of breaking the news, many women leak it out a little at a time, prolonging the pleasure. It's fun every time you tell someone; and the more shocked they are, the better. I'll never forget the look on my neighbor's face when I told her: she had come over to ask me to speak at our local public library on "The Case for Remaining Childless."

But there's another reason for keeping you pregnancy to yourself, I now realize. The reason is fear. If you lose the baby and nobody knows you had a baby to lose, then maybe you can pretend it never happened. I was still trying to pretend I wasn't pregnant when I was three months from delivery. At the time, I thought I was being clever. Looking back, I realize I was just plain scared. If I'd had my way, I wouldn't have told a soul I was pregnant until I had seen the baby and counted his toes.

I watched recently, fascinated, as my ballet teacher triple-pirouetted her way through all nine months of pregnancy. Never once did she acknowledge her condition. Never once did she seek advice or comfort from the many mothers in the class. When I asked one of the other students why, she said she was scared. This strong, vital woman was afraid to acknowledge to anyone—even to her husband, it seemed—the fact that she was about to have a baby at any minute.

Husbands of course are usually the first to get the good news—but not always. "I told everyone *except* my husband," said Lee. "I was furious because he was away on business at Christmas. So when he called, I thought, 'I'll be damned if I'm going to tell him.'"

But husbands have other ways of knowing. As one baby-book author put it: "If he comes home night after night and has to set fire to your bed to get you up to defrost his dinner— or if he finds that you spend all your waking hours in the bathroom vomiting, he should be able to figure out that something unusual is going on."

Breaking the news is best when you're carrying the first grandchild. It's worst when your relatives have funny ideas about what it means to get pregnant:

"My mother looked like I had just told her I had syphilis," said Ellie. "Her face dropped. My mother had a big sexual problem, and having a baby meant you had sex. It also solidified my relationship with my husband, whom she didn't like. And my mother gave birth under the worst circumstances, so she viewed pregnancy as a very serious sickness. Then she told me not to tell my father, because it meant that you had sex or something. You didn't even use the word 'pregnant' in my house. You said 'in a family way.' My mother-in-law said the same thing: 'Don't tell Papa.'"

ABORTION

There's nothing funny about abortion. And nothing easy. It's a shame when women who support the *right* to abortion are depicted as being in *favor* of abortion. Virtually no woman is. And yet many, many women, for almost as many reasons, find themselves at one time or another considering ending their pregnancy before it really gets underway.

Mary, a Catholic, was pregnant for the fourth time when she considered having an abortion. "I felt there was no way this baby could come into our lives without being a drain on the other three children and on me. I felt logically that it did not make any sense to have this baby at this time, that there was no reason I couldn't get pregnant again. I thought about abortion almost every day for three months, until the legal cut-off. I couldn't quite totally express to my husband how much I wanted an abortion. If he had said, 'Gee, why don't you?' I think I would have considered it more seriously, but I just couldn't bring myself to do it."

Sometimes thinking about abortion is a way out of thinking about the reality of pregnancy, a way of putting it off. "We sat down and my husband said, 'You'd better decide,'" Nancy said. "He said, 'I want the baby, but more important, I want you to be happy.' And at that point I said to myself, 'Okay, stop playing around with the idea. If you want an abortion, do it. If not, don't.' Then I knew I wanted the baby. It was like my body was ready for the baby before my head was."

Circumstances can make it even more difficult to go through with the already difficult decision. For example, insensitive hospital personnel. "The nurses looked at me like I was a freak," said Anne of her one abortion. "They said, 'Oh, dearie, are you sure you know what you're doing? How many children do you have?'" Anne had two children. And six months after the abortion, she was pregnant again. "This time I figured, if somebody up there wanted me pregnant that badly, I would go ahead."

Even the most liberated women find it hard to have abortions—and feel guilty when they do. Holly tells how the abortion she'd had years earlier affected her next pregnancy:

"It's not even a lesser of two evils, it's more like pick your evil. I have never felt comfortable about what I did, and yet anything else I would have done under the circumstances would have been equally disastrous. But it does mean I have to go through the rest of my life feeling kind of haunted. When I was six months pregnant with Cassie, I started to bleed a little, and I was rushed to the hospital and prepped for a cesarean. It turned out to be nothing—everything was fine. But in the weakness of that emotional state, lying on my back and holding on to her, feeling her kick through my body and just crying and sobbing and wanting her to live so terribly badly, all the guilt of the abortion came back. It doesn't make any sense, but I felt that this was being visited on me because I had killed my other child."

Happily, abortion is only a last resort. Most women who start a pregnancy stick with it. For them, finding out that they're pregnant is only the beginning.

There's no such thing as an unusual reaction to the news. Indeed, the people you tell you're pregnant will probably react with the same range of feelings you do. Some (mostly relatives and other mothers) can be so excited for you that you feel all warm and tingly in spite of yourself. Others (like some bitter divorcees I ran into) may make you cringe: "What did you go and do a stupid thing like that for?" And finally there will be those (like my single career-woman friends) who are merely puzzled and uncomfortable. It's as if somebody suddenly died, and they don't know exactly what to say. I guess it served me right for not knowing exactly what to say myself.

Emotional Ups and Downs:

The Secret World of You and Baby Whosis

"What does it *really* feel like to be pregnant?" friends continually asked me. "Great," was my honest reply. "Whaaa?" was their ever-surprised reaction. But if my friends were surprised, I was shocked. The baby books had led me to expect "many moods" during pregnancy. Bad moods. I certainly wasn't prepared for being in such a *good* mood most of the time.

But each to her own illusions. Mothers-to-be who spent too much time in the pages of women's magazines got their own misimpressions. They expected expecting to live up to the advertisements: blond mommie model in flowing $600 negligee; hands folded on ample belly, fingering forget-me-nots; eyes misty; gaze distant; Mona Lisa smile. She looks so contented she could almost moo.

By and large, the literature on the emotional aspects of pregnancy boils down to "the blues." The books tell us, for example, that women are "emotional creatures" who (or that?) are likely to go through "emotional storms during pregnancy. Most of these storms consist of depressive interludes." The author goes on to mention anxieties, physical discomfort, apprehension, crying spells, and marital problems. Not a hint that there might be a *good* mood hidden in there somewhere.

Yet another book strips the rich emotional fabric of pregnancy to a paragraph on "moodiness." An excerpt: "Obstetricians frequently hear that a patient has become irritable or depressed. This information is sometimes volunteered by the patient; more often, it emanates from the husband." Indeed!

One of the most popular books on the subject suggests that pregnant women combat their bad dispositions with tranquilizers, "excellent morale boosters," and then reassures the reader that "after delivery, the stable, sweet and tranquil dispositions of the patients return unvarnished." In researching this book, I interviewed scores of women who felt sweet and tranquil during pregnancy, but not one who felt that way when she had a new baby on her hands.

A good part of your emotional state during pregnancy may depend on the state of your sex life; this is one of the "moods" baby books rarely discuss at all—despite the curious finding that pregnant women are surprisingly often "in the mood." In fact, the only one of four popular pregnancy books to mention Sexual Intercourse at all (which is not the same as sex, anyway) sandwiches the section between "Teeth" and "Immunizations"—and I'm still pondering the significance of that.

Of course, books also talk at length about the "fetus"—which one expecting couple dubbed "fo-ee-tus." Most of this talk is in terms of weeks and cells and grams and inches, but it's interesting nonetheless. I especially liked the description of a three-month-old fetus as "about as big as a large rosebud," and such tidbits as "tail of embryo is quite long" at the sixth week.

However, none of this even suggested the very special (not to mention inseparable) relationship I would have over the next nine months with the fetus my husband and I called "Baby Whosis." When I was "with child," I really felt I was "with child." And so, I found, did most women.

In short, pregnancy is perhaps the most emotion-packed experience in a woman's life. She feels scared and happy and womanly and awkward and proud and shy—probably all at the same time. It's a time for thinking and dreaming and hoping and planning—and, yes, for crying and worrying. But to condense all that into a matter of "moods" is missing the point.

IT'S NOT HAPPENING TO *ME*

Ellie said, "I was twenty-two at the time and my husband was a musician and I was a singer and we traveled around a lot. The thing that struck me was that I don't remember not using protection, and I just couldn't understand how I got pregnant. And when the doctor said I was, it was like a wonderful secret. I just felt marvelous. I felt, God! I can do that! I had no doubts whatsoever that everything would be perfect; I never gave a thought to counting fingers and toes. And people would talk about oooh and whatever, and I would get into the drama of the whole thing, but never once would I relate it to myself. Not until he was born. The instant he was born . . . it was, like, soooo heavy. . . ."

Like Ellie, many women don't really accept the fact that they're carrying a baby until they see it for themselves. Pregnancy seems to have little connection with childbirth, especially in the beginning. You may feel a little tired, nauseous, or sore (and big) in the bust, but somehow it all seems very remote. Like it's really happening to someone else.

Being "with child" seems to have even less to do with children. No matter how many times I watched the Lamaze films of natural childbirth, I was surprised—every time—to see a baby come out. I don't know what I was expecting. But certainly not a squiggling, squealing real-live person.

Pregnancy is like waiting for something. But I never seemed to know what I was waiting *for*. I used to spend hours staring at the empty bassinet in the baby's room, trying to imagine a baby in there. I could spot a pregnant woman a mile away, but I couldn't conjure up a baby.

"It's like when you look in the women's magazines," said Janis. "Even when you're pregnant, you see babies and you just flip right by. But then you have your own and you stop at each one and say, 'Oh, isn't she adorable?' Because now you can relate to it. The whole time I was pregnant, I didn't relate to a baby."

A feeling of detachment from babies when you're pregnant doesn't mean you'll feel detached from your baby when it's born—it's just that pregnancy is one process and having a baby's is another. And while the two are biologically connected, emotionally they may have nothing in common at all.

I vividly remember the first time I held a young baby—a baby boy about one month old. I was seven months pregnant at the time, and very excited about getting a chance to hold a real-live baby. But my feelings changed when I found this insubstantial blob of blue fuzz on my lap. His wobbly, hairless head kept nodding onto his chest. He smelled funny. His face was all pinched, his eyes closed. He didn't seem to take to me any better than I took to him. Finally his mother grabbed him back from me with obvious doubts about my mothering instincts.

Curiously, this uncomfortable encounter in no way intruded on the fun of my pregnancy. After all, my baby was still two months away.

Sometime later, when I was two weeks overdue, I was running around to various obstetricians' offices writing an article on cesarean sections. Whenever I got the chance, I sneaked into the hospital nursery for a glimpse of what was to come. As I gazed at those pink and blue bundles, I had no motherly feelings. Only vague disconnectedness and worry about whether I really wanted one of those squinty-eyed prune-faces in my life.

My own squinty-eyed prune-faced baby made me misty-eyed from the start. And for months after he was born, I seemed to see newborns everywhere I went. And all of them were beautiful—just as when I was pregnant I thought pregnancy was a state of grace. And just as when my child was one, there was nothing more adorable than a one-year-old.

I'm feeling a little differently these days. My brother's newborn baby boy looked to me like a funny squinty-eyed prune, and pregnant women look funnier to me still. I can barely imagine what it's like to be pregnant or to have a newborn in the house. On the other hand, I can't imagine why anyone would want to call my charming and energetic son a "terrible two."

It has been said that the nine months of pregnancy are designed to give a woman time to get used to the idea of having a baby. Somehow, nine months just doesn't seem to be enough. But it doesn't seem to matter. On one of my hospital interviews. I saw a mother nursing her newborn baby and I broke into tears. I realized then that maternal instinct wasn't a matter of babies. It was a matter of mothers and babies together.

FEELING GREAT

"I absolutely adored my pregnancy," said Barbara. "I thought it was the best time of my life. Everyone said that I would feel self-conscious about getting fat, that I would feel ugly. And my whole life I have always thought, 'Oh boy, am I going to feel ugly when I'm pregnant.' But I didn't, and I was delighted. The fatter I got, the happier I was. This was incredible. I never never dreamed this would happen to me. And my husband would say, 'My! It's a big belly!' And I'd say, 'Isn't it gorgeous?' It was like the reversal of everything I'd ever heard in my life. I stuck out my stomach as far as I could every place I went, and I felt really terrific and had a lot of energy. I was never sick a day after I found out I was pregnant."

Never feeling nauseous or succumbing to any of the other minor and major bodily complaints does tend to paint pregnancy with a rosy hue. But almost everybody finds some aspects of pregnancy to enjoy. Laura found that the "nausea thing" really got her down at first, but after that she went into what she called the "honeymoon stage—before you get too big to be comfortable. You don't have to worry about contraceptives, so sex is better. And once you get past that first shock of, oooops, there goes the figure, you start enjoying your tummy. You're having fun buying maternity clothes, all the little cutesy things, planning for the baby, thinking of names, looking forward to Lamaze classes, reading all the books. It was so much fun at that point."

Baby showers are fun, too. And so is the extra attention most pregnant women get. I loved being a curiosity among my mostly single career-minded friends. Other women get a lift out of doing what all their friends are doing, comparing notes and baby names and remedies. Pregnancy is the only time during parenthood when you can wish whatever kind of baby you like: a girl today, a boy tomorrow. It's a time that's ripe for daydreams and making plans that may never come true, but it really doesn't matter.

There's also a tremendous psychological high that seems to come from being "in gear," as one woman put it. I knew exactly what she meant. It was the revved-up feeling that all this intricate equipment I'd been carrying around ever since puberty was finally being put to use. And it worked! After suffering though that first menstrual period, the too-large (or too-small) breasts, the pimples and cramps, it was all for a purpose. Of course, I had always known that having periods had something to do with having babies, and that you didn't menstruate when you were pregnant. But none of it seemed real. It didn't connect. And now, here was everything speeding along at full throttle: the ovaries laid the egg, the uterus was occupied, the hormones were humming—even the breasts were good for something other than sex. One of the most thrilling moments came when a tiny drop of fluid leaked out of one breast and I thought, "My God! They work, too!" I couldn't believe how proud I was for achieving such a common biological condition.

Almost every mother I interviewed mentioned how pregnancy made her feel good to be a woman. How special she felt to carry around inside her something that most people didn't have. And how feminine, in a strange way. Feminine and powerful. A virtual magician. A baby growing inside! Now, that's some trick! That's something to feel very proud and very special about.

No wonder so many pregnant women have a feeling of accomplishment. "For the first time in my life," said Marilyn, "I felt like I was doing something important. Today, the hell with it, I'd rather be writing a Pulitzer Prize-winning story. But at that point, I felt very accomplished."

Marilyn was first a mother, then a writer. I spent ten years concentrating on my career before even considering motherhood. But our feelings about pregnancy were quite the same. There's something about having a baby growing inside you that makes all those other things that seem so important now seem not so important. Now I know where Mona Lisa got that contented smile: she was probably pregnant.

Indeed, while pregnancy does make most women feel more feminine, it also made me even more the feminist. I don't know a single man who could do what I have done. I gained a new respect for mothers in general and for women in general. Suddenly I had something in common with millions of people I never knew before. That gave me a tremendous feeling of confidence.

Perhaps that's why for all the tension and turmoil associated with pregnancy, many women find it refreshingly peaceful, an oasis of calm in an otherwise active, if not turbulent, life. "It was the one period in my life when I wasn't in tremendous turmoil over ego accomplishments or all kinds of psychological traumas," Lee said. "It's almost as if everything had been taken care of. I could push it off and say, 'I'm never going to think about those things again,' even though I knew they were going to come back. I just had such a *clarity* then."

During my own pregnancy, I felt so calm and confident that I traveled by subway all over New York City—sometimes to areas I would have normally avoided. My belly was my passport to safety. Who, after all, would harm a pregnant woman? It wasn't until after I gave birth that I was told that pregnant women are prime targets of muggers.

FEELING LOUSY

"Say 'boo' to me and I was hysterical," said Martha. "If somebody turned around and said something not really nasty, but curt and to the point, I'd say, 'We'll leave now, thank you.' I would cry very easily. My husband would tease me by getting me a tissue before the TV show started so he wouldn't have to get up in between. He knew that I'd cry at the drop of a hat. I was so embarrassed to say anything to anyone because they'd think, 'Oh, this lady is really whacko.'"

Crying seems to be as much a part of pregnancy as constipation. Even the happiest pregnancy is likely to be tainted by tears. Some of that, no doubt, is just hormones. But most of it comes from the release of tensions that go hand in hand with carrying a child. Often, the worst saves itself for the end.

"Last night I got into bed and I cried," said Sheryl, who was expecting her second child at any moment. "Yesterday I went to the doctor, and he said I had started to dilate. And I said to myself, 'I don't really want the baby. I enjoy my first child. I'm having fun with her. Why do I have to share that now?'"

Sheryl wasn't alone. Toward the ninth month, I, too, felt that I had made a terrible mistake. I was out on the sun porch, rocking back and forth in an old wicker chair and feeling like Grandma Moses. I held onto the baby in that huge belly and cried, "Why did I ever do this? Nobody loves me. Nobody loves the baby. What am I going to do now?" That evening,

I got a condolence call from a mother who had just given birth to her seventh child. "Didn't anyone ever tell you about the ninth-month blues?" she asked.

The blues can hit you at any time; they can range from a slight feeling of sadness to severe depression. They may alternate with periods of profound happiness and boundless energy, which can make the pregnant woman think she's a manic-depressive. But she's hardly crazy. Having a baby isn't a matter of "for better or for worse." It's a matter of for better *and* for worse.

Deep down inside, every pregnant woman knows that a baby is going to make big changes in her life—probably drastic ones. It's going to mean more responsibility and less money, and a restructuring of her relationship with her husband. It's going to mean saying good-bye to the person she was before and will never ever be again. There's a lot to look forward to, but also a lot to leave behind.

I get much the same feeling every time I take a trip. I'm excited about the anticipated arrival, but always a little sad about the departure. (And terrified about what's in between.)

Working women, especially, often find it hard to adapt a baby into the way they think about their lives. I adapted by vowing to get right back to work as soon as the baby was born. And I did. Now I think I was being somewhat silly, overreacting to the fear that I might not do anything but mother again, that that other part of me would be lost irretrievably. Today I tell pregnant women who want to go straight from the hospital to the office to take it easy if they can, to not worry so much that they can't take some time to enjoy the baby. But I know they worry anyway.

"I worked into the ninth month because I wanted to," said Linda. "I had worked for eleven years before I had Danny, and I loved my job. In the ninth month, we bought a house and we moved and I stopped working. I stopped the job I loved. I had thought that looking forward to the baby and getting ready would be enough. And I'm not a particularly moody person. But in the ninth month I went into a terrible depression. My husband didn't know what to do with me. I'd cry all the time. If I found out that people were planning a shower for me, I'd become hysterical and call them up and say I couldn't come. It was awful. I'd keep saying to my husband, while I was crying, 'I'm so happy about having the baby. I love you so much.' But he couldn't help my mood. I think that leaving the job was just too much."

I'd venture that any woman who doesn't feel a bit sad at some point during her pregnancy is probably hiding something from herself. That's hardly healthy, especially now. Nor is it a good idea to dismiss the blues as a matter of hormones or the natural emotional excesses of mothers-to-be. Having a baby is a serious matter. It's a time to take your feelings seriously. After all, the ups and downs of pregnancy merely reflect the ups and downs of having a child. Analyzing how you feel might not make you feel any better now, but it might help you handle what's to come.

Many women handle the future by postponing it—by trying to hang onto pregnancy forever. I know I did. After all, pregnancy is a great deal. It means having a baby without ever having to change a diaper. You can have all the maternal feelings of motherhood without having to cope with being a mother. You can sleep through the night and shop for baby clothes during the day. You can nurse yourself instead of the child.

Pregnant women aren't emotional, they're just foresighted. No wonder some of them want to hold onto pregnancy as long as they can.

"From my fourth month on, pregnancy was just fabulous," said one mother. "I worked, I took a dance class, I exercised, I felt wonderful. Then, when I went into the ninth month, I remember panicking. I thought, 'Do I really want this?' And when they finally said, 'You're fully dilated—let's get you down to delivery,' I just kept thinking that all the fun was over."

All things must end, and pregnancy ends in childbirth—and motherhood. Most women are glad when it does.

"I wanted to hold onto that baby forever and ever," said Barbara. "I never wanted it to end, except for that night in the hospital. Whenever anyone came by, I would shout: 'When will it be over? Enough, already!'"

SEX AND THE PREGNANT WOMAN

I was cooking hamburgers in the backyard, about nine months pregnant and looking like I had just swallowed the Goodyear blimp, when my downstairs neighbor appeared, appraised me, and said, "Pregnant women are so sexy; they really turn me on."

Sexy? What's sexy about a blimp, I wondered?

Several weeks later, my agent explained that when she was pregnant, strange men would make passes at her, giving the excuse that "pregnant women are sexy." A man told me that he found pregnant women very seductive; he had even had dreams of making love to them. Almost every woman I interviewed mentioned how surprised she was that men seemed to be turned on to them sexually.

Whatever it is about blossoming motherhood that gets the juices flowing in so many men seems to affect women as well. "I loved sex with no pressure or worry," said one woman, typically. "I was horny all the time. Being pregnant 'frees' you for sex somehow."

Ellie asked her doctor if it was all right to have intercourse when she was eight months pregnant, because, she said, "I really wanted it more. And he explained that the baby was positioned thus and so, and the pressure was there, and the labia were stretched and so on."

Probably as much a force as physical factors is the special closeness that many women feel with their husbands during pregnancy, and also that charged-up femininity that makes them feel more like women than ever before. There's a lot of attention to the body now, especially the sexual parts. And, for many women, good feelings about what's happening to them.

Indeed, there's a curious relationship between having 'children and having sex based on the hormone oxytocin. Oxytocin seems to precipitate labor contractions, along with breast milk release, and orgasm. Nursing mothers often find that orgasm brings on an abundant flow of milk. Orgasm has even been said to precipitate labor.

"My sex life with my second pregnancy was absolutely marvelous," said Cathy. "I had sex four hours before I left for the hospital, and the doctor was horrified. We precipitated labor. I know it because I felt it. We made love and I had an orgasm, and while we were lying there, I started to feel the contractions. I've even heard that sometimes when labor stops, they bring the husband into the hospital to get it going again."

Needless to say, heated testimonials from women who enjoyed sex all through pregnancy don't do much for those women who found sex cumbersome, painful, or just plain funny.

"It just didn't feel right, and we wound up laughing when we tried it," Joan said. "He was uptight, I was uptight, and it wasn't working. Then I went to my natural-childbirth class, and the teacher talked at great length about these pelvic exercises, and how if we did them during intercourse, your husband would know if you were doing them right. And I was looking around the room at everyone, thinking: 'Is everybody doing it but me? Am I the only one that's backward, or what?'"

One woman said that making love while pregnant was like "having another person in bed with you." Another found that the presence of the fetus added "humor" to the situation, which added to her enjoyment.

Many other women just aren't interested.

And if you aren't interested, it isn't any more abnormal than being turned on or turned off. Sex, like pregnancy, is intensely personal. To say the two are interrelated is an understatement: after all, sex is what made you pregnant. But *how* they are related varies with the person, the time, the mood. Some women find themselves in a constant state of ambivalence.

"My body seemed to be trying so hard to protect itself," said Lee. "All the things that would be terribly exciting before, any stroking or touching, I hated it. It felt like a tremendous intrusion. If he could get inside, beyond that, then it was all right. But the whole outside had erected barriers."

Sometimes husbands erect barriers themselves. Afraid of damaging the baby, they are afraid to have sex at all. Wives often pick up their fears. Of course, there's nothing to be afraid of—not unless there's bleeding or other indications to put a stop to sex. Some husbands wise up after the first time and come back with renewed vigor the second time around. Sheryl said, "During my first pregnancy, my husband could just as well have been sleeping at his mother's. But the second time . . . I finally had to call him off."

NESTING

Janis should have known she would deliver the next day. At 6 P.M., her husband called to invite her out to dinner. "I can't," she said. "I have to clean the shower curtain."

The day before Cathy delivered, she was up at 7 A.M., cleaning. "I cleaned the whole day, and at four-thirty in the morning I just finished polishing all the silver." Just in time to go into labor.

What is it that transforms otherwise perfectly normal pregnant women into white tornadoes? Whence this strange urge to nest, to clean, to make order? Janis and Cathy seem to have succumbed to the classic "burst of energy" that so many women experience before labor—energy which, in their case, released itself in scrubbing sinks.

Many women want to put their houses in order before the new addition arrives. Some are concerned about the company that inevitably comes with a new baby, and they want their homes to shine. (Perhaps they're afraid that *they* won't be so sparkling.) Others seem to feel that this is their last chance to "clean up" before fifteen years of spit-up and grubby fingers and dirty boot tracks make it all but impossible.

But others seem afflicted by a more primal mothering urge.

Like the mother bird who carefully constructs her twig nest for the long period of sitting and hatching, the human mother readies her ranch house for long periods of baby-sitting. She may scrounge around at garage sales, refinishing an old crib here, picking up drapes and pillows there. Or she may give her house a complete make-over, buying out Bloomingdale's in an attempt to make every room look as through it came out of *Better Homes and Gardens*. She'll do whatever she can to make herself feel settled because there's something about having a baby that seems to mean getting settled, settling down, settling in. The presence of children changes a couple into a family, a house or apartment into a home.

And, practically speaking, new babies do tend to tie mothers to their nests for a while. That so many women try to make that nest a nice place to roost isn't just a matter of hormones. After all, the bed she remakes is the one she'll be sleeping (and not sleeping) in for a while.

I never experienced nesting myself, so I'm not writing from experience. Many women never do. In our case, I think our nest was too small to bother with, or perhaps just too temporary. We seem to change nests so often that settling in seems beyond all hope. I also think that I'm somehow not ready to settle in just yet—baby or not.

But I interviewed many women whose pregnancies seemed

to center on nesting. Rachael was just one of them. When I spoke to her, she was due in two weeks.

"The one thing that has carried through my whole pregnancy, and has become especially tense during the last couple of months, is this obsession with my apartment," she said. "I can't stand anything that is undone about it. I get home at night and I'm in a fine mood. Then my husband comes in, and I say, 'What have you done about the apartment?' I spend every free minute taking off at him about the apartment. I've been through every designer showroom in town. I know all about mirrors and wallpaper and carpenters. It's tearing me up emotionally, and I want it over with, so that when the baby comes I can just relax. But it's not going to be finished. Who knows? Maybe a miracle happens and afterward it doesn't bother you—you're so absorbed in the baby that you don't worry that the rug hasn't come. But right now I feel terrible about it. It's the one thing that fuels me during the day."

In Rachael's case, a miracle didn't happen. A year after her baby was born, she's as obsessed with her apartment as ever—and I'm as nonchalant. Which leads me to believe that pregnancy only intensifies feelings which are there in the first place. Nesting doesn't materialize from nowhere anymore than do the other emotions of pregnancy. And it's just as unlikely to disappear when pregnancy is over.

BABY WHOSIS

Oscar. Rover. Becky (who was a boy). Frebitz. X. Junior. Fred. Gambino. Bratnick. Laetrile. Cholorine. Twinky. Fo-eetus. Max. The Elephant. Freddy Fetus. Theopolis. Baby Whosis. These are some of the fetuses I have known. (Most not until after they were born.)

It's funny how a name can stick. The mother who called her fetus Bratnick found that she and her husband continued to call it Bratnick out of habit after it was born. Finally she had to say to her husband, "Hey, the baby has a name." My own Baby Whosis didn't become Peter until almost a month after his birth.

Of course, a fetus is not a person. But it may be closer to you than any person in your life. Inevitably, most women develop a strong relationship with their inseparable sidekick.

I took mine swimming in Ipanema to give him a feeling for making waves. I played Bach concertos to seduce him (unsuccessfully) to come out. He kicked me under my desk when I was editing a book on working mothers.

Pregnant women who seem to be talking to themselves are actually talking to their fetuses.

Cathy said, "I was shopping the night before Thanksgiving. I was in Bloomingdale's, and I had to get things for the table, and I started to get a kind of cramp. So I said, 'Don't start now, kid. Please, I want to do a little shopping. Give me a break.'"

Barbara was firm with her fetus. "I said, 'Look, I don't like to be sick, and we are not going to vomit. Do you understand? Otherwise, you're going to pay for it. I just do not handle vomiting well.' And I never did vomit."

It's tempting to say that Barbara was really just talking to herself; that her positive, determined attitude helped her to avoid getting sick—not her conversation with her fetus. But it's nicer somehow to think that she did actually communicate something to the little person-to-be inside. And even if she didn't, it's enough that she may have thought she did.

For the fact is, having a fetus as a friend can be fun.

One mother I know relied on her fetus's moral support to win a bicycle race. A man riding on a five-speed passed her on her ten-speed. So she said to her fetus, "Come on, Max, let's pass him." And she did—on an uphill. And all she wanted to do when she won was to turn around and yell: "Hey, I'm pregnant! There's *two* of us!"

Some fetuses, like Twinky Morgenstern, get valentines from friends and grandparents on Valentine's Day. A fetus named Rover (a girl) was serenaded by her father in utero. Daddy massaged Mommy's belly and sang and played the guitar. Both parents felt that the fetus might absorb some of the good vibrations. Friends and neighbors thought the parents were crazy. But they didn't care what the neighbors thought. They said the fetus was "life."

Are mothers who talk to their fetuses mad? Should fathers who sing to them be put away in a safe place? My brother tried to teach his unborn son the fine points of Monday-night football, and I know he's on the strange side—but that's all in the family.

Many people, including many pregnant women, do view

people who have feelings for fetuses as slightly off their rockers. To them, a fetus is an "it." Some women even regard it as a parasite: a little devil inside who gives you heartburn and saps your energy and makes you throw up. Most of these women love babies; they just don't care much for fetuses.

But by and large, mothers tend to dote on their better (if smaller) halves. Watch how often a pregnant woman will absently stroke her belly, or cover it with a protective hand. Not unlike a person sitting by a fire, absently stroking his golden retriever behind the ears. A pregnant woman is never really alone. If only subconsciously, she always has the feeling that she has company.

If you love that feeling, as I did, then the whole nine months of pregnancy becomes a fantasy land, a dream world where you carry your best friend around with you everywhere you go. It's as close as any friend can be. You talk to it on the bus. Or it kicks you while you're riding in an elevator, and you start to laugh. You have secrets and feelings and experiences that you share with no one else. It's your own private universe.

This doesn't necessarily mean that you think of your fetus as a person. A fetus alone can be enough to make you fall in love.

"I didn't have a baby, I had a fetus," said Holly. "It annoyed me when people referred to the creature as a baby. It will be a baby when it's born. And yet, even in its present condition, there was such an affectionate feeling. I had this wonderful little creature to cuddle up to. I loved that creature as it was, and not just as the potential of what it was going to be."

The fetus tends to take on a personality as soon as it begins to move. For most women, this is the biggest thrill of pregnancy. But how do you know when it happens? The feeling was variously described in baby books as resembling "gas" and "angel's wings." I half-expected an angel with gas. When he finally did move, it felt more like someone very small turning somersaults in my belly—which he probably was. Other women described fetal movements that felt "like a wave," "like a big worm twisting around," "like a ballon," "like fluttering," "like tapping inside"—and my favorite: "like a full tank of fish."

As the fetus grows, the twitches and twinges turn into thumps and jabs. You may get a punch in the bladder or a kick in the ribs. And it may hurt. "At first it felt like a tapping inside," said one woman. "Then the movement became more deliberate, and finally it was like a person trapped inside a bag too small to allow any change in position."

Sometimes you can make out an elbow or a knee (or think you can). Sometimes your whole stomach moves from one side to another, like shifting sand. Or maybe you have the quiet kind of fetus who sits contently sucking his thumb.

One way to set a fetus in motion is to give it a gentle prod. Don't be surprised if it pokes you back. My childbirth instructor told us that fetuses respond to warm baths and music. And it's true that Baby Whosis never lay still the night we went to the opera.

Even if they don't quite qualify for personhood, fetuses have personalities too. Baby Whosis hiccuped a lot. The doctor said it was because he was a big drinker. I used to try to figure out if he was a boy or a girl by calling him by name. At the time, we had decided on either Karen or Christopher. I'd call: "Christopher? Karen? Kick twice if you can hear me." He didn't answer because he knew all along his name would be Peter.

My mother still accuses me (as a fetus) of kicking books off her stomach. Now I know why. We still don't agree on reading matter.

Many women say that their fetuses have been as individual as their children. Stephanie said, "I could always tell the difference. I could tell their personalities before they were born. Jennifer was a twitchy fetus, and she turned out to be a twitchy kid."

In recent years, there's been much new research on the development of the fetus—on what its own world is like and on how much of the outside world it can respond to. But only a mother knows what it feels like to have a fetus inside. It's wise to remember that this is a transitory relationship; you two will never be as close again. So enjoy it if you can—while you can.

Of course, something as thrilling as a baby moving inside is something most women want to share. But as every pregnant woman finds out, it can also be very frustrating. All you have to do is call your husband from the next room and say "Come feel it! It's moving!" for your fetus to stay perfectly still. And all your husband has to do is walk out again for the fetus to start up its antics all over again.

Your fetus may tell you something about itself by the way it behaves during pregnancy. In the same way, your feelings about your fetus—like all your feelings during pregnancy—can tell you something about yourself. Like a barometer, they can forecast the emotional weather ahead. So it's important to listen to them, to listen to yourself.

You may experience strange new feelings during pregnancy, but it's unlikely that they sprang out of thin air. Rather, pregnancy gives old feelings a new and special tone. During pregnancy, you may discover feelings you never knew you had, or discard some that aren't useful anymore. But you're not becoming a new person. You're just adapting to motherhood in your own special way.

Perhaps that's what the feelings of pregnancy are all about. More than "ups and downs," they seem to be important indicators. Your senses are more attuned to yourself and to the world around you than ever before. Pregnancy gives you a kind of extrasensory perception. It's a unique state of mind as well as body—one that mothers tend to remember long after the pains of labor and the morning sickness are forgotten. When mothers talk about pregnancy, it's the feelings they remember. It's the feelings that make women say they'd like to be pregnant again—even when they don't want to have another baby.

Fears:

Nightmares and "The Guilties"

Who's afraid of having a baby? Just about everyone. Some women hide their worries under their maternity clothes, and others let them all hang out. But I'll venture there isn't an obstetrician in the country who doesn't spend half of his or her time telling patients, "There's nothing to worry about."

Pregnant women should know better—and they do. Thalidomide was something to worry about, and so is rubella (German measles), and smoking, and kitty litter, and a whole plethora of dangers we don't even know about yet. Assuring women that most babies are born beautiful is justifiable and true. Telling them there's "nothing to worry about" is misleading. It can—and often does—lose doctors the confidence of their patients.

One of the most worrisome aspects of pregnancy is that the child you carry is hidden—a mystery package tucked away in a secret compartment. You can feel it kick, but you can't lift the cover and count fingers and toes. For all you know, you could be carrying a football with feet. And so we worry: "Is the baby okay?"

A small preventive dose of worry is probably good for you, as long as it doesn't project itself into paranoia. Who would have suspected that common aspirin posed dangers to unborn children? Or so many other over-the-counter drugs? Too many doctors don't warn pregnant women to watch what they eat and drink. A little worry never hurt if it helps you to give up smoking (whatever), or to drive more carefully, or to cut down on cocktails.

Pregnant women worry about other things, too. The responsibilities of parenthood. The pain of labor. The prospect of giving up a job or gaining a permanent midriff bulge. The intrusion of a third party into the cozy "two's company" of your marriage. The financial burdens of a baby's care and feeding, intensified when a two-family income is suddenly split in half.

Mary was worried that colleagues at work would laugh at her pregnant figure when she walked down the corridor. Karen worried that the baby would have her father-in-law's nose. "I can remember lying in bed one night in hysterics, saying to my husband, 'What if the baby has your father's nose and my feet?' I went down the whole list of all the little and big defects on both sides of the family, saying, 'What if?'"

Many women—and some doctors—are wary of activities such as driving. "Your hormones are in such havoc when you're pregnant. I remember driving somewhere once and I don't remember how I got there," said one woman. "I remember my mind was not on it—I was always thinking about the baby. And when I got to where I was going, I said, 'I'd better not drive anymore.'" Her doctor agreed with her.

Another woman was frightened because her marriage was shaky. "My husband and I fought a lot. And I used to think, 'Oh God, here I am pregnant, and what if this isn't the right thing? We shouldn't have gotten married. He could just take off, and here I'd be with a kid.'"

In short, pregnant women worry because they have a lot to worry about. The fears are not unfounded. Pregnancy produces the biggest change in your life, and you have nine long months to fret about the fruits of your labor—to fantasize about what it's going to be and how it's going to affect you. Nine months of day-dreams and nightmares.

"I was never really terrified," Susan said, "but I remember being surprised that these thoughts crossed my mind so often. I thought, 'This is a joyful time, and I shouldn't be thinking about things like this.'"

Everybody accepts that mothers worry about their children. Why shouldn't mothers-to-be? Pregnant women often assume a motherhood mentality. If the baby is kicking constantly, you think, "My God, am I carrying a hyperactive child? What's wrong with him?" Then, when he isn't kicking you think, "What's happened to him?"

Just like a mother.

Sometimes the motherhood mentality affects you subconsciously. When I was about eight months pregnant, I remember buying lumber for a new deck. I started to reach for the roof of the car to steady a heavy plywood plank. But my arms didn't move. My motherhood mentality was protecting my baby even before he became a baby or I became a mother.

The first time I became consciously worried was when I read in a book that women taking the pill should wait for several months before becoming pregnant; the incidence of malformed children increased slightly when they didn't. But instead of waiting several months, I got pregnant in several days. And I worried.

Three obstetricians told me there was nothing to worry about. Three others have since said it would have been better to wait. But there's still no consensus among doctors, so women who conceive within days of abandoning their pills or IUDs often worry. "My doctor told me to wait three months after I had my IUD taken out to let my body get back to normal," said Rosalie. "But I skipped only one month. And I was scared, because I said to myself, 'My body's not ready yet.'"

If I hadn't read that book, I wouldn't have worried. Some pregnant women stop reading altogether, in hopes that they'll stop worrying. But it doesn't always work.

Linda said, "I didn't read at all. Then one day my mother called and talked to my husband. She wouldn't even let me talk on the phone. She said, 'Send Linda into the other room. Now, I don't want you to have her cleaning out the kitty litter. I just read this article that said it's very dangerous. But don't tell her about it either, because she's going to get worried.'"

My doctor had already warned me about kitty litter. (There

is a statistically rare but still real chance that contact with kitty litter can transmit a particularly frightening disease to the fetus.) No matter—I don't even have a dog. My doctor also steered me away from, of all things, raw meat. But he never said a word about aspirin, and he prescribed barbiturates without restraints or restriction. These dangers (however rare they may actually be) I read about in the newspaper. I have never forgiven him for those omissions. Women who don't read newspapers wouldn't have been as well informed.

"I wouldn't read articles about things like that," said Barb. "I avoided the outside world. I mean, you put yourself in this little padded world, and then when someone does confront you...I mean, when you do see a retarded child, you walk away very fast. I was reading *The Grapes of Wrath,* and my girlfriend grabbed the book away and said, 'Don't read that!' And she took it away. I would never go to a violent movie because I was afraid it would affect the baby."

My next serious scare came during Lamaze class. We were practicing the art of relaxation in preparation for labor. The ability to relax some muscles while tensing others was crucial to a controlled labor. And suddenly I remembered all those years of ballet lessons, my teacher yelling "Relax! Relax!" I never could manage to do a plié without my eyes popping out, or to relax my face and shoulders while every other muscle in my body was screaming with tension. And I knew right then that I would flunk labor, too.

GIVING BIRTH

Lots of women are afraid of labor and birth. They're afraid of the pain, afraid of being alone, afraid of doctors and hospitals and medications. Childbirth classes often help—sometimes in strange ways: One woman found her childbirth classes so boring that she totally lost her terror.

But, for most of us, the fear goes beyond the superficial, even beyond the pain. A deep-seated fear of the unknown lies lurking behind the worried brow of every pregnant woman. What's it like to give birth? How much does it hurt? How long will it take? How will I perform? Will the doctors/nurses stay with me, tend to me? How will my husband react? What's going to happen to me?

And beneath it all is the fear of being vulnerable; of strange people and strange places and strange sensations.

"I was especially afraid of being in that kind of position in a hospital," said one woman, typically. "I was afraid of being vulnerable to people who were sticking things into me and tying me down and things like that. That scared the hell out of me. Everybody I spoke with said, 'Get knocked out.' But my greatest fear was to get put out. I would have done anything to hold onto reality, to stay with it. I didn't necessarily think the birth would be natural, but I wanted to be in complete control throughout labor. That was my one desire: not to be a screaming maniac. I was not going to lose control."

No wonder pregnant women all over the country are crowding natural-childbirth classes—or, more precisely, "prepared-childbirth" classes. Prepared is the point. And the more prepared you are, the less worried you are apt to be.

Of all the fears and worries associated with childbirth, this is one that you can do something about.

Of course, not all fears about having a baby are as serious. Some are downright silly. One woman was worried because her baby was four weeks late and her doctor told her that she had already begun to dilate. So she was afraid that the baby might somehow just "fall out" in the middle of the A&P or running for a bus. She tried to walk with her legs crossed just in case the baby should drop out in the frozen-foods section.

Other women are afraid—really embarrassed—at the prospect of breaking their water at an inconvenient time or place. At a party perhaps. Our Lamaze instructor suggested that if we broke our water in Macy's, we should look disapprovingly at the woman standing next to us. But, as my husband pointed out, what if the person standing next to you is a man?

It's pointless to tell women not to worry about giving birth: they worry anyway. It's even okay to worry about silly things as long as you know they're silly. Serious worries warrant more serious attention.

One way to ease your mind may be to talk to a number of mothers about their experiences. They can give you an idea of the range of things that might happen to you—and you'll get the idea that there *is* a very broad range. The more experiences you hear about, the more you'll be prepared for whatever experiences may befall you.

One caveat: Listen carefully to what mothers say, but don't

believe everything you hear. If you do, you might wind up more worried than before. Just as men tend to exaggerate war stories, mothers often embellish the perils and pains of labor for dramatic effect—not to mention the hours. If there were as many thirty-six-hour labors as some mothers claim, we'd all stop having babies.

Try to listen to the advice that lies behind the bravado. If the woman had a bad experience, was it preventable? Most of the time, you'll find that a little knowledge would have gone a long way toward an easier labor.

Beware equally of mothers who tell you they casually delivered their babies in the bathroom after five minutes of labor. Two-hour labors are as rare as thirty-six-hour labors. And remember that pain is in the mind of the beholder. The mother who prepares for an excruciating labor and has a normal one will perceive little pain; but if you have preconceptions that labor is painless, your perceptions might be quite the opposite.

Still, a lot can be learned from talking to mothers. Specifically, they can tell you about the quirks of hospitals and doctors and nurses and about the many forms and faces of labor and childbirth. They may even give you some advice on how to deal with them. That's the reason I wrote this book.

A wise mother will tell you to expect the unexpected. That labor can be easy or hard, long or short, painful or less painful. You can prepare for anything, but you can't prevent or predict. So read up and relax. No matter what happens to you, you can bet your baby it's happened to hundreds of other mothers before you. And if you've had the opportunity to talk to a mother who had a similar experience, so much the better: you'll know what to expect.

I doubt that pregnant women will ever learn to stop worrying and love labor. But at least we can learn to stop worrying quite so alone.

MEDICATIONS AND DRUGS

If you are what you eat, that goes double for what you drink or smoke or swallow when you're pregnant. Almost everything crosses the placenta from mother to baby. What you eat affects not only you, but your baby, too.

Which is why so many mothers-to-be worry so much about

what they take in the form of pills and prescriptions. What crosses the placenta never seems to stop crossing the mind. Many doctors do warn pregnant women not to take anything they don't have to. But others don't. And those who do are too often ignored by their patients. Or else they tell us too late—or the damage is done before the pregnancy is apparent. And so we worry.

"The whole time I was pregnant, my husband wanted me to get this test where they stick the needle in your stomach (amniocentesis)," said Vicki. "When we were younger, we both did our share of drugs and stuff, and he was just afraid. You hear of so many kids being born deformed. But neither of us had done anything like that in a long time. I talked to the doctor about it. I told him I had tripped but I don't know exactly on what. And he said that if your chromosomes do get damaged by LSD or something, they repair themselves in several months, so he didn't feel that the test was necessary. But my husband was driving me nuts with it. I would calm him down, and then I would be nervous that if anything was wrong with the baby, then it would be my fault. If I had found out five months ago, we could have stopped it—or at least been prepared for it."

It doesn't take LSD to put a pregnant woman into a dither over drugs. Antibiotics, antihistamines, and even aspirin have their effects on fetuses. So do marijuana and tranquilizers. A small dosage of drugs doesn't necessarily result in a deformed baby. But it does often result in worry.

Elisabeth swore that she would never smoke marijuana again the night she had her IUD taken out. "Then we had this terrific party—just the two of us—and we got absolutely stoned. I still don't know whether or not the baby was conceived that night. The doctor was very casual about it. But I was worried. Today I won't even go into a room where people are smoking. I'm afraid it will contaminate the baby."

Another mother took one Librium (a tranquilizer) and became an instant emotional wreck. For the rest of her pregnancy, she was convinced she had brain damaged her child.

Sometimes worry is more dangerous to your health than the drug itself. Angela had what she described as a "terminal case of the flu" through her whole ninth month. Her doctor insisted that she take some medication so that she'd be in better condition for labor. But Angela refused. "I figured I'd gone this far, I could stand the discomfort."

A pregnant woman's attitude toward drugs depends largely on her experience. If she has a friend who took ten aspirins a day while pregnant and gave birth to a genius, she's not going to worry much. But this can lead to dangerous assumptions—like women who say, "Well, my mother smoked two packs a day while she was pregnant with me, and *I'm* fine." That may be true, but smoking poses a statistically proven risk for fetuses. If you want to take that risk, that's up to you. But don't deny that it's a risk.

Other women have opposite experiences and wind up worrying too much. Cindy, a nurse, took a certain kind of cold medicine before she knew she was pregnant. Then she remembered delivering a patient who had taken the same cold medicine and gave birth to a baby with only four fingers. That vision never left her mind.

How can you tell whether a drug is going to permanently affect your child? You can't. But you can become as well informed as possible. You can ask your doctor—but don't ask *only* your doctor. Doctors don't tell you everything.

Indeed, avoiding worry may be as good a reason for not taking drugs as avoiding damage to your baby. If any kind of medication is going to make you worry excessively, it's probably better not to take it—on that basis alone. Obstetricians and pediatricians often go too far in telling you not to to worry because they worry about worry, too. And because medications are sometimes necessary. But mostly because they, like you, have no way of really knowing the answers.

Gene was very sick with a virus and high temperature before she knew she was pregnant. She was on antibiotics for two weeks. Then she missed a period. "I thought, 'Oh God!' and I went to the doctor, and sure enough I was pregnant. So I thought, 'What do I do?' The doctor said, 'Don't worry, dear, if there's anything wrong with the fetus, you'll have a miscarriage.' And I said, 'Well, how can you explain all the malformed babies that are born?' That didn't wash. But the pediatrician told me the same thing."

For roughly the same reasons, Ellie stopped taking medications designed to *prevent* a miscarriage. "Suddenly I got very very frightened, and I said to my hsuband, 'I'm not taking these anymore. If this baby is due to abort, nature will do that.'"

GUILTY

Women who take drugs and medication or expose themselves to disease during pregnancy are prime candidates for "the guilties," as one woman called them. The guilties rarely result from an accidental dose of a medication you didn't know was dangerous, or that you knew was dangerous but didn't know you were pregnant. The guilties is what you get when you know it's dangerous, but you do it anyway.

Joan felt guilty because she didn't give up smoking: "I kept saying to myself, 'What if something's wrong with the baby? Then it is totally my fault, and I can't blame it on God or chance.'"

If something goes wrong, we seem to have a need to pin the blame on someone. It's nice if we can blame a doctor or nurse or fate or God. It's awful when we have to blame ourselves. I'm convinced that's why so many women give birth in hospitals even though 95 per cent of them could probably deliver just as safely—if not more safely—at home. If something goes wrong with a hospital birth, there are scores of people to share the blame. If something goes wrong at home, it's all yours.

Still, almost every pregnant woman blames herself for something. I remember getting panicked over a yoga exercise I tried a couple of times. Come to think of it, I haven't tried yoga since.

Many mothers feel guilty about painting—even though redoing rooms and moving to new houses seems synonymous with having babies. Sarah's feelings were typical: "We had just moved into a new house, and I had read that there are always warnings about painting while you're pregnant. And yet we had to paint. Or so we thought. Of course, we could have waited a year. We tried to use latex paint, and we would keep the windows open, but I still remember feeling this terrible guilt."

Sometimes well-meaning friends and relatives make you feel guiltier than you need to be: "A friend told me that lifting heavy things would make you strangle you baby," said Betty.

"And here we had this sofa bed and I was folding this damn thing up every day, and suddenly somebody tells me that! I freaked out! I strangled my baby!"

The cure for the guilties is much the same as the cure for worries in general: know as much as possible what is dangerous and what isn't. Don't do the former and don't worry about the latter. (P.S. sofa beds and latex paint aren't dangerous if used in moderation. Neither is yoga.)

A DAMAGED CHILD

Few pregnant women are worried about dying from an overdose of aspirin, or from lifting a love seat. What they *are* worried about is damaging their unborn child. Lingering in every pregnant woman's mind is the question: "Is this going to be a normal child?" And the even more important corollary question: "What if it isn't?"

Nobody is more attuned to children than pregnant women. And nobody is more attuned to children who aren't quite "normal." Even a strawberry mark on a friend's baby can make a pregnant woman panic. Even an ugly baby. I remember being depressed for a whole day after seeing an unattractive infant in a clothing store. What if mine turned out like that? And this is nothing to say of real handicaps.

It's bad enough when a pregnant woman hears of—or, God forbid, runs into—a damaged child. It's that much worse if the handicap runs in the family.

"My sister was born with a harelip," said Carol. "I know it wasn't the most terrible thing—there are a lot worse things. But that was the most terrible thing that could have happened to me, I thought. I know it's hereditary. Why did this happen to our family? I know everybody worries, but we were doubly worried because we had already seen something go wrong."

I suspect fear of birthing a damaged child is like fear of flying in an airplane. If you're at the airport every day and watch plane after plane take off and land without problem, you're unlikely to suspect problems with your own flight. But if the airline you're flying had a crash yesterday, you think twice before you get on board. Obstetrical nurses and female obstetricians—like flight attendants—seem to have the same degree of fear as the rest of us. They see the worst, but they also see that most of the time, everything turns out fine.

Linda was in the peculiar position of seeing *only* the worst. "I was the head of a nursery for handicapped children, and I was really scared. I was surrounded by handicapped kids all the time, and I just had this feeling that I was going to be blessed with a handicapped baby. I thought it was going to be a cleft palate, which to me was the hardest of all the different handicaps to work with because I'm a speech therapist. I remember going for a walk with my husband and saying, 'I feel I can handle my own retarded child, and I feel I can handle an emotionally disturbed child,' and I listed all these kinds of children that I thought I could handle. But I said that if the child has a cleft palate, I just didn't know what I was going to do. And that was the first thing I wanted to see when they brought the baby to me."

Spending your pregnancy surrounded by handicapped children is certainly not ideal. But running away from them isn't a great idea, either. If you're going to have a baby, you might as well accept the possibility that that baby might have a problem. Perhaps even a serious one. As long as you don't get morbid about it, it's probably not a bad idea to think about it. Some mothers-to-be think that giving birth to an imperfect child would be the end of the world. But look around at mothers who did. It doesn't have to be.

Many couples ask their obstetricians about options if they should produce a damaged child. Most who do ask think they're the only ones to broach such a bothersome subject. Of course, they aren't. In truth, obstetricians and pediatricians have few options themselves. What they do is determined by the dictates of medicine and law. Your husband doesn't have to tell your doctor: "If it comes to a choice, save my wife first." The doctors will try to save both of you, and chances are unlikely that anyone will need to be saved at all.

And while you're talking to your doctor, be sure to talk to your husband. He's probably just as concerned as you. Even if you don't share the same feelings, you should know what each other's feelings are.

"It's the one thing we really worried about," said Cathy, "because if we ever had a deformed child or a retarded child, we disagreed on what we would do. We were afraid because I had a cat and there was a big scare about kitty litter. I felt that a damaged child was something you had to accept. But my husband felt I probably wouldn't be able to handle it because I'm sensitive. If something was wrong with the baby and it died, then I would think it was God's blessing."

STILLBORN

The specter of a stillborn child doesn't seem to haunt half as many mothers-to-be as does the thought of a damaged one. Still, many women walk around with vague fears that they won't be bringing a baby back home from the hospital. This isn't so much a fear that the baby will be born dead as the difficulty of grasping the idea that it will come home at all.

Women often cope with these fears by refusing to prepare for the baby they're not sure will come. They order baby clothes and cribs and changing tables but leave them in the stores until it's time to deliver—both. They may decorate a baby's room, but always in such a way that it would also make a nice sewing room. They purchase little and bring home nothing. They don't go to baby showers, even at the risk of alienating friends. "My family believes in having showers *after* the baby is born," Joan said.

Pregnant women sometimes avoid buying maternity clothes until the last possible minute. They call it vanity and complain about the construction and style of the clothes. But they really want to wait and see that everything's all right before they go around parading it in front of everybody. I know, because I did it myself. When you *really* need maternity clothes, then you're *really* pregnant.

What we're talking about is simply superstition. If you're superstitious in general, you'll undoubtedly be superstitious with child. And there's little remedy for that. However, you might keep in mind that while anticipation brings worry, it can also be a lot of fun. If you don't prepare for the baby at all, you can miss one of the best parts of pregnancy. You might also create serious emotional problems and have trouble adjusting to the baby when it *does* come. Postponement can also be hard on your husband. After all, he's the one who'll have to buy all the baby things and make a home in the three days before you both get home from the hospital.

THE END OF INDEPENDENCE

Toward the end of my pregnancy, I had a sudden, desperate desire to see all my friends "one last time." I needed, almost compulsively, to get in touch with everyone I knew while I was still myself. That is, before I became a mother; before my life was irrevocably altered. I don't know why I thought that motherhood would be some kind of isolation chamber. But I know I worried a great deal about it at the time.

And I wasn't alone.

Betty said, "I remember one day when the baby first started moving, and I realized that there was something really *in there*, something I was going to be responsible for. I was sitting in the den having some wine. The fire was going. The baby kicked, and I thought, 'My God! This is all going to change!' That was all I could think of. I turned to my husband and said, 'What have I done?' We used to sit here so calmly and relax. Now there's going to be someone else, and I won't be able to sit here calmly and relax."

Betty was right. Having a baby means no more Sunday mornings lying in bed with fresh bagels and the *Daily Bugle*. No more quiet evenings at home or candlelight dinners for two. No more going out whenever you want to on the spur of the moment. So enjoy the life you have now while you have it. Then get ready to enjoy the new life you'll have when the baby comes.

Of course, the idea of motherhood as banishment from society is a myth. Mothers get around a lot more these days than they ever did before; now they bring baby to work and parties and trips. I took my son to California when he was three weeks old, even though it wasn't easy. And the idea that motherhood isn't going to change your life at all is as much a myth as the idea that it's going to change it completely.

Once you have a baby, motherhood is with you for a long time to come. Many women are bothered not so much by the responsibility of parenthood as its longevity. Or, as Lee told me: "My mother and I were walking around the apartment trying to figure out a place for the baby, and the obvious place was the office next to our bedroom. I said, 'We'll put up a partition.' And my mother said, 'That's impossible—the baby needs the room. He is going to be in it for eighteen years.' For some reason, that sentence about eighteen years kept going around and around in my mind. I could break out in tears over that—the thought of eighteen years."

Take it one step at a time.

NIGHTMARES

Freud said that our worries show themselves in dreams. After all, worries are the stuff that dreams are made of. So it shouldn't come as a surprise to anyone that pregnant women sometimes have strange dreams. When I was pregnant, I dreamt that I gave birth to a beagle with a long pointy nose. Looking back, I think it was the combination of fears that the baby would have my husband's patrician nose and his constant joking that what he really wanted was a golden retriever.

Most pregnancy dreams are right out of *Rosemary's Baby*. Women dream about giving birth to kangaroos, babies with hideous faces, babies that are born dead. Anne dreamt about having a monster child that she could never see. "There was something horribly wrong with this child and the doctors would never tell me what it was. Once I heard the doctor say, 'What a shame. It has two heads.'"

Another woman told me she often dreamt about giving birth to a full-grown person—possibly a secret desire to avoid diapers and the terrible twos. Some of us visualize our worries in dreams; others solve them.

I often dreamt about doctors and hospitals. Scary dreams that my doctor wouldn't recognize me or that the hospital wouldn't know what I was there for or that they would take away my baby. None of this turned out to be too far from reality, so perhaps I was more prepared for what happened. But that's for another chapter.

Even men have pregnancy dreams—often when they're going through a life change, a new job, a move, a marriage. It's normal to dream about what you're worried about. When you're pregnant, you're worried about having a baby. So much for psychology.

But worrying through pregnancy doesn't have to be a nightmare—not if you realize that every pregnant woman worries, always has, and always will. This gives you a tremendous resource to turn to if your worries get out of control. And it is important that they don't. Worry in and of itself can be something to worry about. It can prolong labor, hinder childbirth, and perhaps even affect the fetus in utero. So if you think your worries are getting out of bounds, talk to a friend. If that doesn't work, talk to a doctor. Above all, remember that if fears during pregnancy are sometimes a nightmare, it's only because (at the risk of sounding corny) having a baby is a dream come true.

Your Body/Yourself:

Big Bellies and Hemorrhoids and Pickles and Ice Cream

The beginning of this book has dealt with the parts of pregnancy that go on in your head. Of course, a great deal more goes on in your body.

Pregnancy is nothing if not physical. It is a physical condition completely unlike any other: a state that is supposed to be normal, but which every pregnant woman knows is not.

The graphic illustrations passed around in childbirth classes tell you all you need to know about your body during pregnancy. One look, and you should never again wonder why you have heartburn or can't breathe well or have to go to the bathroom every five minutes.

In the "before pregnancy" illustration, your intestines spread themselves out comfortably throughout your lower abdomen, resting on your bladder and colon. The stomach floats on top, just below the diaphragm and lungs.

During pregnancy, the space formerly occupied by your internal organs is taken over by a growing baby. You don't have to be a doctor to understand that this makes for a conflict of interests. Your insides are pushed out by the fetus and its environment. Your once ample bladder is now a puny pocket; your colon is condensed into a state of constant constipation. Your intestines are squashed up into your stomach; your stomach is squashed into your chest. As one pregnancy book put it, your stomach becomes "a very ineffective repository for food."

No wonder you live on Maalox and prune juice.

In addition to sharing your belly, you and your fetus also share the functions of your circulatory system. Before you were pregnant, your heart pumped blood to every bone in your body—from the top of your head to the tip of your toes. Now it has to concentrate its pumping toward your active uterus to feed the creature inside. It's not surprising that your own circulation suffers in the process. Consequently, pregnant women are prone to fainting, dizziness, varicose veins, hemorrhoids, and puffy ankles.

And that's to say nothing of hormones. To produce a healthy baby, your body produces a whole arsenal of special hormones. Some of these hormones can make you quite sick—especially, it seems, in the morning. They can also give you a moustache, acne, and make your hair fall out.

"I've never felt such ill health in my life," said Joan, eight months pregnant and counting. "Every paragraph in the books that begins 'Some women might . . .' and I've got it. Barfing twenty-four hours a day. I said to my husband last week, 'John, I made it through hemorrhoids.' So this week I got hemorrhoids. I wouldn't have minded if I'd expected it. But I expected to feel great. So I thought I must be dying—you can't feel this rotten and be pregnant. Because that's the hype. Look at any magazine with a pregnant woman in it. She's got on the long flowing gown and the long blond hair, and she's patting her belly. She's not running to the bathroom. She's not green."

Of course, not all women get green with pregnancy. But most suffer from something sometime—even though later they tend to forget. Most of the women I interviewed for this book were mothers. Only a few were mothers-to-be. It was startling how the pregnant ones could jar the long-locked memories of mothers with babies only two or three months old, including myself. I had totally forgotten about trudging to the bathroom three times a night to empty what was left of my bladder; about the cute little night light in the hall. I had forgotten about the twitches and pulls and pains that I always mistook for imminent miscarriage. One new mother told us she even forgot about the 3 A.M. charley horses:

"This is fascinating," said Nancy, listening to a group of pregnant women compare battle scars, her own son only six weeks old. "I can't tell you how many of the things you're talking about I had forgotten. I used to get up so many times in the middle of the night with a horrible, horrible pain in the back of my leg. I would wake up screaming, and my husband would think I was in labor. I couldn't even move. He had to throw my legs over the side of the bed so I could get down and knead my foot. And now it's as if it never happened."

Recently I refreshed my own memory when I picked up a pamphlet on the "minor discomforts" of pregnancy in an obstetrician's office. I remember reading such a list in a pregnancy book when I was first pregnant. I felt positively queasy at the thought of what was in store. And who wouldn't? Among the common physical symptoms of pregnancy, from head to toe, are:

Loss of hair. I went to a new hairdresser about six weeks after my son was born. Naturally, I told her I had recently had a baby. She said, thumbing pensively through my hair, "That's very unusual."

I said? "What's unusual?"

She said: "You still have your hair."

Of course, this doesn't happen to everyone. But if you feel yourself getting thin on top, don't be surprised.

Headaches.

Dizziness.

Fainting. It had never happened before in my life, and I pray it will never happen again. I was eating dinner in a fancy hotel restaurant, just digging into the main course, when I suddenly had to leave the table. I made it as far as the elevator before I then blacked out. I thought I was dying. I was so happy to wake up alive in my husband's arms that I went right back to the dinner table to celebrate—despite the stares of other diners, not to mention the elevator operator. In the movies, fainting always seems so romantic. But to me, it turned out to be terrifying.

Nosebleeds.

Runny noses, colds. Our Lamaze instructor told us that we all had the sniffles because the linings of our nostrils were made out of the same kind of tissue that lined the uterus. That has always made me think twice before blowing my nose.

Salivation. This may be "so profuse," according to one source, "that the woman cannot manage to swallow all of it, so she must continually expectorate."

Inflammation of the gums.

Mask of pregnancy. Yellowish brown patches on the skin. While I did manage to avoid getting a moustache, I didn't escape the thin dark line that runs down the middle of your belly, dividing you in two. Other women notice darkening of the aureola around the nipples or blotches on their face. Fortunately, all these badges of pregnancy go away.

Vascular "spiders." Tiny red raised lines on the face, neck, and upper arms. They go away, too.

Acne.

Swelling, tenderness of the breasts. Also blue veins. Also itching, pain, lumpiness. One woman who didn't know she was pregnant thought she was getting breast cancer. Small-breasted women often love pregnancy because it makes them voluptuous. I remember trying to squeeze into a small bikini about three months along. The rest of me was normal, but you could tell I was pregnant just by the breast. If they jiggled, they hurt. The changes in the breasts during pregnancy are what make them droop later, so don't decide not to breastfeed your baby because you think it will ruin your figure. The stretching that can lead to sagging happens *now*.

A thick yellowish fluid may come out if you squeeze them (or even if you don't). This can really be a turn-on if you plan to breastfeed. Otherwise, it's just plain messy.

Ribs. The rib cage has to expand to make room for baby. Sometimes ribs even separate from the breastbone. This pulling can be very uncomfortable. It can also have permanent results. It is not at all unusual for a woman to jump one or even two bra sizes in the process of having a baby.

Gas.

Heartburn. (See above, also below.)

Heart palpitations.

Nausea. "Morning sickness" should be a chapter in itself, since it seems to be synonymous with pregnancy. I never had it for a minute. Some pregnant women have it all the time. It does seem to have some relation to diet, in that pregnant women who followed strict health habits seemed to have less of it than those who were more casual. Several women reported being sick during one pregnancy, but not another—and all attributed the difference to a different diet. But this is hardly a scientific survey.

Other women felt nauseous and gassy as a result of all the vitamins and iron they took during pregnancy. They do produce a kind of foul gas. However, since the incidence of morning sickness is decreasing while the incidence of vitamin taking is increasing, I doubt that there's any direct correlation.

Meanwhile, about half of all pregnant women feel nauseous during the first few months of pregnancy, although they don't necessarily feel that way only in the morning. Some women don't actually vomit at all; they simply gag at the sight or smell (or even suggestion) of certain foods. Others find that "morning sickness" is a mild kind of nausea, the kind that "just comes up pretty easy," as one woman put it. "I'd just hurry up and get it over with. It wasn't overwhelming."

She was one of the lucky ones. In fact, "overwhelming" was precisely the word used by less fortunate mothers to describe their experiences with morning sickness. Two women I interviewed found it overwhelming enough to get an abortion. Half a dozen said it made them vow never to get pregnant again.

When morning sickness really makes you sick, it can be a constant kind of seasickness. It can mean spending most of the morning and maybe the evening in the bathroom—no small problem for a working woman or a mother with toddlers at her feet. You may feel sweaty and/or dizzy or even "paralyzed with nausea," in the words of one sufferer.

Few doctors (I hope) still say that morning sickness is a psychological illness. This sort of diagnosis doesn't sit well with women who are "'Chucking up an awful lot of stuff that sure isn't psychological." Instead, the theory seems to be that morning sickness is caused by the hormones of pregnancy. The standard remedy is dry crackers before you get out of bed and keeping something in your stomach at all times. While this can help to keep your food down, it might not help keep your weight down. Gene had a fairly typical case of morning sickness:

"I was working at the time, so I would eat the crackers in bed, get up, eat breakfast, then get on the subway downtown. On my way, I had to walk past the vendors with the sauerkraut and hot dogs. I didn't think I would make it. My doctor told me to always keep something in my stomach. So as soon as I got to work, I'd have coffee and a danish. Then I'd have lunch. Then at three o'clock I'd be sick again so I'd eat again. Then I'd have dinner, and then I'd have an after-dinner snack. I gained thirty-seven pounds that way. Twenty pounds in three months."

Striae. Known to mothers as stretch marks. They don't go away. Some women are ashamed of them, and shun bikinis for the rest of their days. Others consider them badges of motherhood, to be proudly displayed. If you want to coat your belly with cocoa butter, go ahead. It probably won't help, but it certainly won't hurt.

Groin pains. Caused by stretching of the ligaments attached to the uterus. They can be achy and/or painful. I also found them scary. It's not normal to feel those ligaments stretch— but then, you aren't normally pregnant. The unexpected pulling in such an unexpected place leads many women to assume that something is wrong. It isn't.

Frequency of urination. Some say it's hormones; others say it's the pressure of baby on your bladder. Either way, everybody seems to get it, especially during the first few (and last few) months. You need to know the location of every bathroom in town—just like a toddler getting toilet trained.

Flatulence. Not socially acceptable, so not much discussed. Common advice is to stay away from beans and cabbage, but chances are you figured that out for yourself. I like the description of this symptom in one book as "the frequent desire to pass flatus."

Of course, heartburn, gas, and flatulence are simply different aspects of the same problem. To relieve it, you can eat sensibly and take certain over-the-counter drugs. But, as all doctors should warn you, stay away from anything that contains sodium bicarbonate. The sodium in the compound is a component of salt. And salt in excess is harmful to pregnant women. (And to any one else, for that matter.) (See Diet.)

Backache. For obvious reasons.

Constipation. Bran in the morning and prunes at night.

Hemorrhoids. Related to above. Common advice is "don't strain at stool," whatever that means. One doctor recommended lying on your back "with hips slightly elevated and apply to the rectal region a washcloth or piece of cotton which has been soaked in ice water—or, better yet, witch hazel."

Still, hemorrhoids are no joke to the pregnant woman who gets them. Especially postpartum. (See Postpartum.) "The first time I ever saw my doctor, he never noticed my face, he just noticed my hemorrhoids," Martha said. "I was on the table in his office, and as soon as he opened the door, that's what he saw. They were as big as grapefruits. And from then on I was Martha-with-the-hemorrhoids."

Vaginal discharge.

Varicosities of the vulva. Poor circulation results in all kinds of varicosities; including hemorrhoids, which are varicosities of the rectum. Few doctors mention varicosities of the vulva, but I had them and so did several women I interviewed. They aren't serious, but mine tended to bleed from time to time and caused me worry. Another woman said the condition made her feel as though she was about to give birth for the last four months of pregnancy. She found the pressure quite uncomfortable.

"Dislocated" hips. A hormone that relaxes the ligaments around your pelvis and hips may cause you to feel as if your hips are coming out of their sockets. I interviewed only one woman who had this problem, and from her description, I'm glad it's an uncommon affliction: "I can handle delivery, I can handle the child, but I couldn't handle being pregnant again. I have this thing where my hips seem to disconnect totally. When I sit on the sofa, people have to lift my legs up so I can lie down. I feel like I'm going to come apart and the rubber bands are all stretched out."

Varicose veins. The good news is that not everybody gets them. The bad news is that they get worse with each subsequent pregnancy.

Leg cramps. Especially at night.

Swollen ankles. I flew to Brazil when I was seven months pregnant, and when I arrived in São Paulo twelve hours later, I didn't have any ankles. My legs were formless blobs. It took two days of keeping my feet up before the swelling entirely went down. Of course, any kind of abrupt or prolonged swelling of ankles, face, or fingers could be serious, so see your doctor. But if you've been on your feet all day or in a car or in a plane, or it's ninety-plus degrees outside, it's probably normal.

Other symptoms of pregnancy may or may not be primarily

physical, but they do have physical consequences. Insomnia, for example. One mother speculated that insomnia during pregnancy was nature's way of letting you know you're not going to get any sleep from now on. I'm not even sure that it's nature who's giving you the message, but the fetus inside. After all, it's his kicking that keeps you awake. His very bulk makes it hard to snuggle down to a comfortable position. Some women reported sleepwalking during pregnancy. Others said they dropped things or lost their memory. One woman wrote in a questionnaire: "My husband said I lost my memory, but I don't remember."

Lethargy. Pregnant women are notoriously tired all the time—also boundlessly energetic. Like your moods, your physical condition seems to swing from high to low, rarely stopping in between. Mothers-to-be like myself who felt mostly great during pregnancy also not surprisingly had a great deal of energy. "There are periods in the day when I feel like I've taken an upper or something." "I had so much vigor and I got so much done." "I felt revved up, ready for anything."

Contrast these statements with the tale of tired old Mary: "When I wasn't driving the car pool, I fell asleep. They had to wake me up when we got to work. I had a ten o'clock coffee break and dozed off for the whole fifteen minutes, head on the desk. I slept through lunch. I slept through my three o'clock coffee break. Back in the car at five o'clock, and I'd sleep until I got home. Then I was back on the couch until six, and in bed by nine."

Pregnancy manuals often tell about the burst of energy that women feel during pregnancy, often just before the onset of labor. "I kept waiting and waiting for the burst of energy," said Sally, who had her baby three months ago. "I'm still waiting."

Some women use the same tactic for coping with the physical aspects of pregnancy that they use for the emotional symptoms—denial. Ignore your condition and it will go away. Denial works well as long as you feel well. It's fine to keep up all your non-pregnant activities as long as you're up to them. It's not so fine if you don't feel up to it. Or if the only reason you're still playing volleyball or working a twelve-hour day is because your sister Sally did.

Your pregnancy is as individual as you are. Listen to the signals from your body just as you should heed the thoughts in your head. Do what comes naturally—to you. If you get every symptom in the book, you don't have to be a martyr about it. There's no law that says you have to suffer in silence. Take it easy if you can. Pamper yourself while you can. It won't be long before all you're Pamper-ing is a baby.

The physical effects of pregnancy are ironically unpredictable. I've interviewed weak, sickly women who bloomed with good health throughout their pregnancies. I've interviewed others who were never sick a day in their lives *until* they were pregnant. "I couldn't believe that I—me—Marilyn—had heartburn! I never got *anything*. I was never even late for *school*. I read about these things, but I always thought they were for other people."

There's no point in worrying about what might not happen. There's also no point in worrying because the little (and big) aches and pains you feel are so strange. Of course they seem strange to you. You've never been pregnant before. The aches don't feel normal because pregnancy isn't your normal state. Pregnancy has its own special set of symptoms. If you haven't been pregnant before, then you probably haven't experienced thes symptoms before.

Even if you have been pregnant before, you may be in for some surprises. Like snowflakes, no two pregnancies are ever alike—even your own. Indeed, mothers with two or three children often say that while handling birth and babies is easier the second time around, pregnancy can be harder; the novelty has worn off, and your body is more worn out. But other mothers suffered through a first pregnancy only to sail through the second. So much for predictions.

YOUR BELLY / THE PREGNANT LOOK

The most obvious physical symptom of pregnancy is that bulge in your belly; the protuberance that makes you proud; that potbelly that makes you waddle like a duck; the mound that moves you in the middle of the night; the shelf where you rest your hands.

You may detest it, but you can't dismiss it. Most mothers miss it when it's gone. Suddenly there's no place to put your hands. "It was relaxing to sit down with that thing," said one mother. "You feel protected, you know, what could hurt you?"

One mother-to-be painted a jack-o'lantern on her belly for Halloween. (Of course, it had a beard.) Many mothers (or fathers) take snapshots of the growing belly just as they later take pictures of the growing baby. They keep a record on film as the belly grows from a gentle mound into a veritable mountain. I have a picture of myself sunbathing at nine months. Looking at the pictures today, I think I look silly. But then, I thought I was beautiful.

In truth, it may have been the bathing suit that looked more silly than me. During my vacation in Brazil, I learned that pregnant "girls from Ipanema" don't wear "maternity" suits. They wear bikinis, as always. And they look surprisingly lovely.

"I was almost nine months pregnant," remembered Sharon, "and we went to this nude swimming hole up in Massachusetts somewhere. I didn't go in nude, of course. But there was another pregnant woman there, and she was absolutely magnificent. Suntan from the tip of her hair to the tip of her toes. And she looked so fabulous I couldn't believe it."

Bellies can be beautiful. Or at least they can make the rest of you feel beautiful. Having a belly is not the same as getting fat. It sticks out only in front. From the behind, you may look like everybody else. In fact, pregnant women sometimes want their bellies to be as big as possible so that it's the baby who's putting on weight, not the mommie.

The pregnant look, if you like it, is made even more appealing by the large bust, the sparkle in your eye, the glowing skin, the nice, thick hair. When it works, it works wonders.

"All of a sudden I just felt different and looked different," said Mary. "Even my facial contours changed. I was absolutely radiant. My hair got thicker. People said my eyes sparkled. I remember making shorts and a top for a company picnic, and I was surprised at how beautiful I looked in them, because I don't even sew that well. But I thought to myself, 'Damn it, you're eight months pregnant, and you look really good.' My legs were thin. I was really beautiful."

Or at least that's what happens to some of us. Other mothers don't remember company picnics. Instead, they remember forgetting what their feet looked like, and not being able to tie their shoes, or bend over for a book, or even get up from a chair. They tell about feeling as if their belly is going to burst, about the protruding navel that pops out and shows through their clothes, about the general bulkiness and awkwardness of it all.

"My husband would say to me, 'Aren't pregnant women supposed to be radiant? When are you going to be radiant?' And I'd say, 'When I stop throwing up.' I did not feel womanly. I did not feel motherly. I felt like a neuter. Like an incubator. Did you try to get into a sexy nightgown at nine months? You can't. My breasts weren't even breasts, they were mammaries. They flop on top of your belly and get blue veins. Your belly button pops out. It's disgusting."

Misery loves company. Pregnant women who are ambivalent about their looks often seek solace in the sight of other pregnant women. They may still feel awful, but at least they don't feel so odd. On the other hand, nothing makes a mother-to-be feel worse than a room full of size 7s—even if she was feeling beautifully maternal in the first place.

"Sometimes I thought I looked pretty cool," said Ellie. "My husband sort of liked the round look. I was always so skinny. I had a particularly nice nightgown that was really flowing, and I would stand sideways in the mirror and just take in that whole look. But then I remember going to a big party. I got myself a really good maternity dress and I thought I looked pretty nice—until I got there. There were all these women who were small and small-waisted and tan. I can remember my husband talking to one of them. He was a little drunk, and he put his hand around her waist. And it was instant pain. Because if I had not been big like that, I would have gone over to another man and done my number. But I felt I wasn't attractive. And I was dancing with these guys who were trying to make themselves concave."

Ellie felt great about herself until she saw the size 7 in the sequined dress. So do we all. A pregnant woman doesn't need competition from someone with a twenty-three-inch waist. Still, Ellie shouldn't have tried to compete with the sequined dress on her terms. She should have thought of herself as "special," not odd; as maternal, not awkward. After all, lots of women wear size 7s. But only you have your belly. You can't try to hide it, but you can try to use it. So if you can't bring yourself to feel "attractive," at least think of yourself as unique.

WHAT GOES IN / YOUR DIET

No matter what shape your belly's in, you'll undoubtedly be worried about the size of it. Diets and pregnancy seem to go together like pickles and ice cream.

"A doctor knows from years and years of frustrating experience just how much mothers tend to shovel in," writes the author of one popular birth and baby book. "What is so horrible about being a little hungry once in a while?" asks another. Most obstetricians and the books they write are rife with rules and regulations pertaining to diet, with "ideal weights" and "permissible" weight gains. They all talk about the "natural tendency" of pregnant women to eat "too much."

My question is, if the tendency is natural, why fight it? Of course, no one wants to go back to the old days when pregnant women spent most of the day seated in front of the refrigerator, "eating for two" and gaining sixty or so pounds in the process. Fat is unhealthy for anyone. The last thing a pregnant woman needs is unnecessary pounds—and unnecessary burdens on her heart and lungs.

But it also seems unnecessary to starve. Too many mothers' most vivid memories of pregnancy revolve around stepping on scales, doctors' threats, and nurses' stares. And the damage is more than psychological. Indeed, so much has been written recently about the hazards of low-birth-weight babies that obstetricians have begun to change their tune. The "permissible" weight gain in obstetrical circles has been revised up dramatically in the past several years—from about fifteen pounds or less to twenty-five pounds or more. But even these numbers are based on "ideal" weights for "average" women. Few of us are either average or ideal.

The solution is using your common sense. Yes, you are eating for two. That doesn't necessarily mean increasing the quantity of food you eat, but it does demand that you increase the quality. Junk food and greasy food and sugary food are bad for your baby. They are also likely to make you sick. It's hard to live in this country today and not know that fruit and vegetables and nuts and whole-grain breads and fish and chicken are better for you than fatty red meat or white flour or sugar and salt. All this goes double when you're pregnant.

Some doctors tell you to drink a quart of milk a day. Others say it doesn't make a difference as long as you eat a balanced diet—which would probably include cheese and/or yogurt anyway. Most doctors say something about salt. Salt makes you retain fluids. Excessive fluid retention can result in toxemia—which is dangerous to mother and baby and can even be fatal. Your doctor watches your diet for good reason.

Yet it does seem unreasonable for obstetricians to put perfectly healthy women on a totally salt-free diet. Salt-free means virtually no canned or packaged foods. Almost all of them contain salt—look at the labels. Some authorities say that too little salt can be as dangerous as too much. Obviously, you shouldn't sprinkle salt on foods or eat bacon, ham, or potato chips. But there's no reason to cut out salt completely. Pregnancy has problems enough.

I didn't know much about pregnancy and nutrition when I got pregnant. But I did sense that something was wrong when my obstetrician tried to put me on a very restricted diet with a weight-gain limit of only fourteen pounds. And I was slim to begin with. He didn't remain my obstetrician for long. I gained a total of about twenty-five pounds and never put on an ounce of fat. The twenty-five pounds was gone in about a month. Many other mothers shared my experience.

So if you think your doctor has put you on a diet that's unworkable or unhealthy, don't be afraid to modify it—reasonably—to suit you. Or, if you're unsure, ask another doctor. Obstetricians have a notoriously bad record when it comes to diet. Many older mothers I interviewed had taken diet pills while pregnant, or diuretics, or both. The result was unhealthy babies. And very unhappy mothers.

Of course, it would be unfair to blame obstetrics alone. Until recently, even those of us who tried to eat well were doing it all wrong. Nobody knew about cholesterol in 1965, or the benefits of fiber and the hazards of fat. We don't know everything about nutrition now. But it is confusing when you're raised to eat three meals of red meat every day, only to find out that red meat isn't good for you after all. Or when all the convenience foods that make eating so easy also make eating healthy so hard.

But we can try. Good nutrition is good nutrition, pregnant or not. It's just more important when you're pregnant.

It's silly to follow rules and regulations that don't make

sense. One mother stopped for ice cream every night on her way home from work, then felt so guilty that she drowned her sorrows in her mandatory quart of skim milk. (Skim milk is ice cream without the cream and sugar.)

Of course, using your common sense isn't good advice to follow if you're not knowledgeable, or if you're not good at using common sense. If you don't know anything about nutrition, plan your diet by the book—a doctor's book. Don't—like one mother—eat pastries all day to try to bolster your energy. Eating sugar doesn't give you added energy, just added pounds. And if you experience sudden weight gain or puffiness, see your doctor right away.

Curiously, many of the foods that turn your stomach while you're pregnant are the very ones that don't belong there. And many pregnant women develop cravings for foods that are good for them—like peanuts or fruit juice or even lobster and ice cream (in moderation). Vast numbers of pregnant women develop automatic aversions to alcohol, cigarettes, greasy foods, meats, and/or coffee. Perhaps our stomachs are trying to tell us something.

PICKLES AND ICE CREAM

"I'm a real food freak when it comes to pregnancy," said Karen. "There was this market around the corner that made the most fantastic potato salad, and the first clue I had that I was pregnant was when I realized that I was spending $12 a day in that market. I would get cravings and just go. We were in San Francisco at the time, and they had fabulous Chinese places or health food stores. I had an avocado every day. But they had no Jewish delis. One time I searched the whole damn city for a kosher pickle. Finally, I found one place and gorged all day on pickles and sauerkraut."

Mary craved gefilte fish and lox and bagels even though she was Italian. Carrie went on a tomato juice kick. Susan ate a whole chocolate cake. And Carol couldn't stay away from Baskin-Robbins. "Every time I'm getting my period, I have a craving for ice cream. And when I was pregnant, I had it all the time. That was really funny."

Do pregnant women really crave pickles and ice cream? According to some sources, they have been known to crave everything from chalk to turpentine and Vaseline. However, among the mothers I interviewed, cravings during pregnancy seemed to be simply an extension of normal cravings. After all, it isn't really unusual to crave ice cream or a good kosher pickle or broiled lobster. Perhaps pregnancy makes our cravings more conspicuous while giving us an excuse to indulge.

At the least, pregnancy makes our stomachs more discriminating. The things you usually love like morning coffee or cold beer can suddenly make you queasy. I'm sure I wasn't the only person to get sick from Thanksgiving dinner. Rich fowl seems to be a prime offender—especially with stuffing. The only other time I got "morning sickness" was the night of my baby shower, which none of us had the sense not to have at a restaurant called The Duck Joint.

"My husband took a liking to Japanese food when I was pregnant with my second child," said Lynn. "I was huge and bulky and it was February, so I had to wear this big old wool coat over my big old wool dress. It was a horrible cold day. My husband pranced me into this little Japanese restaurant, with a little chair and a little table and the little Japanese lady bowing to my husband. I was trying to be such a good sport and be the nice little wife. So I said that of course I'd try the sushi and sashimi. Now, to me, raw tuna fish is what comes out of a can. But this was raw bass and raw octopus with the tentacles. When they put it in front of me, I started to cry. I had to go to the ladies' room."

Pregnancy makes you more sensitive to everything—including tastes and odors. One pregnant woman described herself as "radar nose. I can tell by smell what everyone down the hall is having for dinner." Another couldn't stand toothpaste and had to brush her teeth with salt. Many, many women get sick at the smell of cigarette smoke—even if they had been heavy smokers before. "That is one of the great things about being pregnant," said Laura. "You can stand there with your big belly and tell somebody, 'Please stop smoking or I'm going to throw up all over you.' Nobody buys that when you're not pregnant."

Do the cravings and aversions last? My mother couldn't stand coffee all the while she was pregnant. But the first thing she wanted after delivery was a cup of hot coffee. Many mothers who can't stand smoke start puffing again as soon as they get home from the hospital.

But others are different. I couldn't tolerate cigarettes or alcohol during pregnancy, and I still can't today. For me, pregnancy was Alcoholics Anonymous and Smoke-Enders in one. Other women find they retain aversions to things like grease or frying bacon—not exactly "health foods" either.

In general, the cravings and aversions of pregnancy seem to make sense. So unless you have uncontrollable cravings for turpentine or chalk, eat what makes you happy and don't eat what makes you sick. Who knows? Maybe pickles and ice cream has untold health benefits for the pregnant woman.

THE NINTH MONTH / YOUR ELEVENTH HOUR

During the ninth month, your thoughts and your body turn from pregnancy to the business of preparing for birth. At this point, almost everybody wants to get it over with. I remember being furious that I could no longer run for the train. As a commuter, running for the train is as much part of my life as brushing my teeth. Enough of this damned stomach. My big beautiful belly had turned into The Incredible Hulk. I wanted to take it off, put it aside for a while, anything. One obstetrician used to tell his patients to be grateful they weren't elephants; they're pregnant for eighteen months.

And so you wait for signs of birth. One sign that I waited for in vain was the so-called "lightening," when the baby's head settles down in your pelvis. Our Lamaze instructor told us to expect this to happen about six to two weeks before delivery. Most baby books say it happens several weeks to several days before labor. Nobody says it doesn't happen at all. Only when my baby was two weeks overdue and still hadn't engaged in the pelvis did my obstetrician say, "Oh, don't believe that old saying that babies who don't engage are always cesareans." I, for one, had never heard that saying. And of course I was, in the end, a cesarean.

Lightening, when it happens (which is most of the time—*not* all of the time) makes you breathe easier and go to the bathroom more. There's more room for your lungs, but less for your bladder.

Once the baby is engaged and ready to go, all you have to do is wait for him/her to come out. This is undoubtedly the worst part of pregnancy. The phone calls from well-meaning friends and relatives asking. "Why aren't you in the hospital yet?" The jumping up at every little ache and pain, being sure that this time it's labor—and then it isn't.

Too many obstetricians still induce babies they think are due—either for their convenience or for the mother's. The trouble is that the baby might not be ready to be born. If it isn't, it can develop a life-threatening lung deficiency. Amniocentesis can test for lung maturity, but the test itself carries risks. Thus it's wise to wait a reasonable period before rushing in to induce a reluctant fetus. Maybe it's not coming out for a good reason.

On the other hand, very late babies run the risk of "postmaturity"—the placenta stops functioning, and the baby can die. You and your doctor have to use some discretion. If your normal menstrual period is longer than twenty-eight days, some doctors say you can expect your baby a few days later. Even with normal periods, two weeks late isn't considered "late" yet. So sit tight, wait, and discuss strategy with your doctor.

Sometimes labor starts "early" or "late" not because the baby is premature or postmature, but because you calculated your due date wrong. The way to avoid this is to keep track of your menstrual periods. As one author/doctor put it, "Do not tell the doctor that your last menstrual period was just before the Delta Epsilon door-to-door campaign for Distressed Daughters in Delaware." Some people just love to keep records. Most of us keep careful track of periods only when we think we're pregnant or hope we aren't. It's probably not even practical to advise women to pinpoint every period to the day. I can't imagine many men who would do that. But it certainly should be a goal if you're even thinking of the possibility.

The physical aspects of pregnancy are just as complex as the emotional ones. A detailed knowledge of them requires a medical degree, which is why we turn to doctors when we run into trouble or out of knowledge. Yet it's not fair to yourself or to your baby to abdicate all responsibility for your well-being to a doctor. You know yourself better than he or she does. And doctors don't know all the answers. As one obstetrician told me, "When twins are born, one-fourth of the time the obstetrician doesn't know it's going to happen. That's the state of the art."

So take care of yourself—just as you always do, only more

so. And remember that nine months really isn't very long in the scheme of a lifetime. If you can enjoy pregnancy, great. If you're green all the time, try to bear with it for just a few more months.

Perhaps by coincidence, the women I interviewed who had the most difficult pregnancies breezed through labor and delivery. In my case it was vice versa. Maybe there is justice after all.

FOOTNOTE / WHEN SOMETHING GOES WRONG

This is a book about women's reactions to pregnancy—not a medical encyclopedia. It is written from the mother's point of view, not the doctor's. Thus, this is hardly the place for a long list of possible complications or tips on how to tell if you're about to have a miscarriage.

Frankly, I was disappointed that pregnancy books written by doctors didn't have more on these subjects. I felt it would be reassuring to know what the symptoms of disaster are; then, if I didn't have them, I would know I was okay. But many women don't want to read about the complications. What I would find "informative," they would find "depressing."

Still, I think it's worthwile to know how women react when something goes wrong. What is it like to have a miscarriage? Or a stillborn child? One out of every ten pregnancies ends in "spontaneous abortions." Yet we hear very little about it.

"You never know how many miscarriages there are in this world until you have one," said Marilyn. "Then you find out that Aunt Sadie had one, and Cousin Sally, and that seventeen friends had them, and that miscarriages are very common. Once you know they're common, I don't think they are as traumatic. But I thought I was the only one."

Miscarriage usually happens during the first three months. Marilyn had already "felt life" when her fetus suddenly stopped moving in the beginning of the fifth month. A fetus that dies after the fifth month is generally considered stillborn. This is far more rare than early miscarriage.

Whenever it happens, we know how miscarriage affects the fetus. But how does it affect the mother? Most doctors take pains to point out that no harm befalls a mother who loses a baby this way. But mothers tell a different tale. Even though the physical complications may be minimal, psychological wounds may take a long time to heal.

Mothers who miscarry often feel guilty or inadequate. Faced with an inexplicable loss, they look nonetheless for explanations. Since the cause of miscarriage is generally thought to be malformed eggs or sperm or both, a miscarriage is the kind of accident that happens on purpose. Still, mothers tend to blame themselves.

"It was a personal failure," said Sheryl. "It was as if I failed to produce a normal egg—I couldn't produce a normal child." Nancy even blamed herself for an "ectopic" pregnancy—where the fertilized egg begins to develop in the fallopian tube. "I felt it was my fault that it got stuck in the tube instead of getting into the right place."

Other mothers blamed something they ate, or a rough road trip, or the time they cleaned the oven. Yet all were somehow reassured by the thought that the baby probably wasn't meant to be born. That whatever happened was meant to happen. That if the fetus was healthy to begin with, horseback riding or a whiff of Easy Off wouldn't be enough to kill it.

Janis' baby was born stillborn at term (nine months):

"I knew when I was in the delivery room because of the way they were rushing around and doing things. I sensed. Nobody told me. During my labor that day, I felt that something was wrong. I had excruciating pains right away. It didn't build up. I was at a Memorial Day parade, and suddenly I buckled over. I didn't tell anybody, but I thought to myself, 'Something is wrong with me—something is odd.' The baby was alive during delivery. It died while it was delivered. It weighed seven and one half pounds. The doctor said it had a rare brain disease and wasn't viable outside the womb—that I should have lost it at four months. He said it was a freak of nature. And somehow I never felt as if I had lost a *baby*. I felt as if I had a miscarriage. I don't know why. I accepted it right away. The doctor came in right away and said she was stillborn. This is why. You can have more children—that's what I was concerned about. I knew I lost the baby before he walked in."

Among the complications I encountered while interviewing mothers for this book were ruptured uteruses (from previous cesareans), one calcified placenta (the mother needed seventeen transfusions), and other conditions ranging from strange body rashes to breech births. The first two complications could have been fatal. Yet these women were fine, and so were their babies.

Of course, that doesn't mean they weren't scared. It also doesn't mean that pregnant women—like other women—don't occasionally die from heart attacks or strokes or other conditions. Pregnancy and childbirth have their own complications which add to the risk of having a baby—just as cancer poses a risk to being alive. But few women would give up their lives—or their children—to avoid the risk that something might go wrong.

"By this time, I was beginning to regret the whole thing," said a woman with a history of complications when talking about the birth of her second child. "I was beginning to think, 'Okay, kid. You might end up in a wheelchair for the rest of your life. You made a stupid mistake not getting an abortion six months ago.' But ever since then, every time I look at my daughter, I'm so glad I didn't."

Getting Around:

Working and Traveling in the Outside World

Pregnancy is essentially a private matter. It affects both your internal organs and your internal thoughts. Yet your condition is conspicuous externally. And while so much is going on in your insides, you also spend a great deal of time in the outside world. Often the needs of your inside world and those of the outside world conflict. In more ways than one, being pregnant can turn you inside-out.

Not so many years ago, pregnant women didn't have to worry about insides and outsides. A pregnant woman's place was in the home. Pregnancy was simply not the sort of thing one talked about—much less displayed—in polite society. Pregnant women were expected to keep their condition to themselves. They were pretty much confined to quarters for the duration.

Today pregnant women are everywhere on the job and on the go. Hardly shrinking violets, they parade themselves proudly. Instead of hiding their pregnancies, they advertise them—wearing T-shirts that spell out "BABY" or "UNDER

CONSTRUCTION." Just in case you didn't notice.

As women have become more liberated, pregnancy has begun to come out of the closet. If you run into a pregnant woman in the doctor's office today, she's as likely to be the doctor as the patient. Pregnant women are ballerinas, teachers, doctors, lawyers, students, reporters, volunteers for Planned Parenthood. You see them at the opera, on the beach, on TV talk shows, on the A train to Brooklyn or the flight to Rio. Just as their being women no longer confines them to certain attitudes and roles, neither does their being pregnant.

So they get around. People notice. A pregnant woman does not easily fade into the woodwork. She tends to get a lot of attention—friendly and otherwise. Some people find the presence in public of a pregnant woman offensive; they look away, as if embarrassed. Others may think you belong in a hospital, where nurses and doctors can look after your "fragile" condition. Still others view you as an affirmation of life; the mere sight of you is enough to make their day.

When your pregnancy goes public, it not only affects the people around you, it touches on your life, too. What was once strictly a private matter is now in the public interest. Complete strangers feel free to make friends and to make comments. Depending on whom you talk to, this is one of the nicest or the most upsetting parts of being "with child."

Working "with child" keeps you in day-to-day contact with other people. The presence of pregnant women in offices is turning heads everywhere—and creating new problems and possibilities in the process. Nobody seems to know how to treat pregnant working women, and I'm not sure pregnant women know themselves. If special treatment means a longer coffee break or a more convenient parking spot, then I'm all for it. If it means getting fired, then pregnant women should fight every effort to treat them as "special." Indeed, only recently airline hostesses and schoolteachers had to go to court to win the right to stay on the job past the fifth month.

Attitudes toward pregnancy are changing so fast that doctors' advice is often contradictory. Take travel. Some obstetricians still tell you not to travel outside a 100-mile radius at any time; others permit any kind of travel until the seventh or eighth month. Sometimes pregnant women are advised to travel as much as possible—because they won't be getting around much once the baby comes.

But if the advice you get is sometimes contradictory, so are your feelings. You may want to tell the world you're pregnant—and at the same time keep it to yourself. You want to share, but you want secrets, too. You want to get around, but you also want to stay home and "nest." You don't want special treatment, but you do appreciate special favors. You want your privacy and your public exposure, too. I've often wondered: is it worse when everybody on the bus stares at you—or when nobody notices you at all? Such is the price of celebrity.

Pregnancy is a very private matter that you parade before the whole world. Never has the outside world been more irrelevant—or more important.

THE OTHER PEOPLE IN YOUR LIFE

When I was pregnant, we lived in a small Italian neighborhood. The community was close-knit, without much interest in outsiders. I don't think I ever struck up a conversation with a neighbor, or they with me. Until I was pregnant. As soon as my belly started to bulge, I became a member of the family almost overnight—and a very proud family at that.

As I walked down the street, the old women on the stoops would nod in approval. Little girls on bikes would come up and say, "I hope it's a boy." Women came out of the woodwork everywhere, giving advice and making predictions. The men who never smiled before were suddenly full of questions about the "bambino."

Pregnancy can be a lovely experience to share with someone else—even if that someone else is a total stranger. My favorite characters were the two brothers who ran the fruit stand. They would give me slices of watermelon "for the baby," and they marked his estimated date of arrival on a big calendar behind the cash register. They wanted to know all the details of my condition every time I came by. They became closer to me than my doctor. By the time the baby came, it was as if they had a hand in it.

"I had a tremendous sense of finally having entered the mainstream of American life," said Anne. "I was working longer than I should have and I didn't get married until I was thirty. And suddenly here I was sharing. I enjoyed it tremendously.

"All these characters would talk to you and all the little concerns that you sort of get bogged down in would go away. I even had friends at college—people who had been aloof for years—who suddenly started being my best friend when they heard I was pregnant. I thought it was very peculiar. I guess they really didn't know how to relate to someone who didn't have a child. I guess they thought we'd have nothing to talk about."

The prospect of becoming a parent automatically gives you something in common with literally millions of people you never knew before. Suddenly strange men approach you—not to pick you up, but to show you pictures of their babies, or even of their wives giving birth. Everybody is a potential friend, helpmate, midwife. A photographer I worked with told me I'd be three weeks late. (I was.) The mailman told me I'd have a girl. (I didn't.) The man in the garden store warned me not to feed the roses, and my editor urged me to walk a mile every day without fail.

The women I interviewed shared their pregnancies with strangers, too: "Other women would look at you and smile. And because I felt good about myself I'd smile back." "You feel like a million dollars. You feel like you didn't do much to deserve all this attention." "I loved when the people in the office called me Mom. It made me feel very up because they were so up about me. Their excitement was contagious." "I loved when people treated me as if I were carrying precious cargo. I loved the phone calls, the showers."

At times, it seems as if the whole world loves a pregnant woman. Packers in the supermarket pack the bags lightly—and may even offer to carry them outside. People open doors for you, give up their seats on the bus. Curiously, I noticed that women were far more apt to defer to a pregnant woman than were men. And that strangers are sometimes more solicitous than husbands. "My husband never catered to me," said Janis, among others. "That made me appreciate the attention I got from strangers all the more."

Of course, what the strangers cater to is your pregnancy, not you. You may be going into the same shops or offices for years, and never even get a nod unless you're pregnant. It still upsets me today that the people in our old neighborhood don't seem to remember who I am. Or at least they're not talking. Whatever made me so special, I don't have it anymore. All those special smiles and added attention came with the belly—and too often tend to leave the minute the belly is gone.

"It pisses me off that I have no identity other than being a mother," said Jean, about ready to deliver. "I'm sick and tired of having pregnant women smile and talk to me like it's one big sorority. I was at the airport in Tulsa and this woman not only smiled at me, but she started to talk to me, and I hate that. I'm not that friendly to begin with. It's like automatically because you both have bellies, you have something in common. Nobody knows Jean Barberry Smith. Nobody knows what I do and what I think. When you walk down the street, nobody even looks at your face. They just look at your stomach."

So there's a dark side to the silver lining. Many women, in fact, hate the forced intimacy that pregnancy brings. The too-easy acquaintances with strangers, the too-familiar stares and questions. Good intentions are had by all—but even good intentions don't always lead to good feelings.

"I found it incredibly offensive when I was pregnant that men, in particular, acted like your stomach was free access. They would just come over and pat your belly. I felt that was an invasion. They wouldn't normally come over and pat my stomach, but now somehow they thought it was okay."

Often, it's not the strangers, but the relatives who can get too familiar. Just because you're in a family way doesn't mean you want your pregnancy to be a family affair. Janis said, "I was at my mother-in-law's house, and she suddenly pulls down my pants to see my stomach. She says, 'Oh, your belly button is gone. Isn't that nice? You're going to have a girl.' And there was my brother-in-law and the man from across the street who I've met twice in my life. I thought, 'How dare you?' It was almost funny."

There's a fine line between the right amount of friendship and too much familiarity. Between getting attention and getting taken for granted. Between caring and invasion of privacy. The terms change both with the woman and with the mood. A gesture perceived as warm one minute may be unwanted the next. What one woman sees as companionship, another perceives as prying. One mother who was repulsed by familiarity from men said she "sort of liked it when women came over and poked my belly. It was kind of nice."

Contradictions seem to go with the condition. I felt especially ambivalent about my status because I was a pregnant woman among single career-minded friends. I wasn't only "special," I was a downright oddity. A freak. None of us had even known a pregnant woman before, much less been one. So while it was nice to be a pioneer, it wasn't so nice to be an outcast. And while I loved being unique, I hated being lonely.

I think that's why you notice other pregnant women more when you're pregnant yourself. The camaraderie is welcome even if it's only at a distance. Somehow the knowledge that so many other pregnant women exist is in itself comforting. Pregnant women often seek each other out, full of questions and chatter and comparing notes. Deep down inside, I think that's why so many women flock to natural childbirth classes: they want someone to talk to. Someone like themselves.

The other side of the companionship coin is the very desire for uniqueness that sets you apart. "I resented other pregnant women because I wanted all the attention," said Nancy. "I wanted to be the only one. Every time someone said, 'Oh, you're pregnant. Let me tell you about my labor,' I'd cringe. I didn't want to know. I was the only pregnant person in the world. I didn't want to know about them, or their labor, or anything else."

Mothers who like to keep their maternity to themselves think that others should offer the same courtesy. In the same way that they don't want strangers picking up their blouses to peer at their bellies, they don't like to see other people's pregnant bellies exposed on the beach. Women often feel about other pregnant women much as they feel about their pregnant selves. And vice versa.

Before I became a mother myself, I viewed the pregnant bellies in my gynecologist's office with great alarm. Embarrassed at the shameless display, I'd stare out the window or at my feet or at a magazine—anything to avoid coming eyeball-to-belly with tumescent motherhood. Once pregnant myself, I was sure that my single friends viewed me with much the same mixture of curiosity and repulsion.

"I feel very embarrassed around other women because I would never look at a pregnant woman until I got pregnant," said a very-pregnant Lee. "I've always been terribly uncomfortable around them. So if I meet a single woman, or a married woman who doesn't have children, I feel that I make her uncomfortable, too."

Still, pregnancy can form a bond among women that lasts long after birthing is through. When I see a pregnant woman today, I feel an instant recognition, a camaraderie that makes me want to tell her what to expect, to tell her, "I know what you're going through. Isn't it awful? Isn't it great?" Sometimes I'm jealous of them and hope they're loving it as much as I did. And sometimes I'm sorry for them and glad it's not me.

As you get around in the world, it's probably not a good idea to expect consistent reactions—either from yourself or from the people around you. You'll learn to take the sweet with the sour, the stares with the smiles. But you may as well expect to attract attention because you undoubtably will. Pregnancy is special even for people who aren't pregnant. It's not surprising that they should want to share.

WORKING "WITH CHILD"

Pregnancy and working go together like oil and vinegar—you have to keep shaking things up to get them together. For whatever reason, the vast numbers of pregnant working women have had scant impact on the world of baby books and childbirth classes. The hospital where I delivered typically offered courses on breastfeeding and on infant care—both in the middle of the day. At first I thought I was the only one who had trouble getting off from work. Then I asked my pregnant classmates how many of them still held jobs. All thirty raised their hands. (Of course, the Lamaze classes for husbands are at night.)

Baby books tell you to exercise three times a day, or to take naps whenever you feel tired. That's difficult if not impossible on a nine-to-five schedule. Like books on parenthood, books on pregnancy often assume that it's easy to get part-time work. Unfortunately, most jobs are all-or-nothing propositions; so the problem becomes one of blending work and pregnancy, rather than balancing them.

Should you work while you're pregnant? For most women, this is a moot question. Either they have to work to bring in the money for baby, or they already have babies at home—which is work enough. The question is not whether you should work, but whether you should work at home or at the office—or, as is often the case, both. Some women have been liberated from scrubbing floors so that they can scrub for surgery. But they are working nonetheless.

Obstetricians seem to be of two minds on the work question—and often it's the same obstetrician who has the two minds. One writes: "Most types of female employment are well tolerated by the expectant mother." Then, in the same paragraph: "My wife, a practicing attorney, went into labor in the subway coming home from work." Another doctor, almost echoing the first, assures the reader that "no harm will come to you from washing the dishes or taking dictation." Then he describes how one of his classmates in medical school raised a child at home, commuted to school, and attended all classes through the ninth month. "She then disappeared from a lecture one day and had her second baby an hour later."

What are they trying to tell us? That we should aspire to nothing more strenuous than "female employment"—dictation and dishes? Or that we should keep up our medical/law practices right until delivery? This presented me with a serious image problem. I don't practice dictation *or* law. Not only was the advice not applicable, it was not palatable either way.

My own obstetrician was no less cryptic. He said I could work until the end if I wanted to, but he recommended that I take three months off and "sleep late and have lunch with the girls." That was not my idea of how to spend three months of my time. But the only other model I had was a lawyer I knew and admired who did practice practically through labor. I tried to emulate her, and I was sorry. Somewhere there has to be a middle ground.

I'm still looking for that middle ground. I can't seem to find it because there are so many considerations to consider, so many variables to vary. For example, is it more exhausting to go to the office or stay home with a terrible two? Which is worse: being bored at home or tired at work? Why am I really working? Because I want to and/or need the money? Or because I want to live up to the lawyers and medical students?

"The baby was due April nineteenth so I was going to work until April eighth," said Nancy, a TV producer. "But by the beginning of March, I was wiped out, absolutely exhausted. So I stopped working. But it was very hard for me. I felt, 'What's wrong with me? Why can't I work up until the end, like everyone else?'"

I felt much the same way. My ego told me to live up to the

lawyers and stay; my body told me to lie down and leave. Toward the end, I realized that my body was right. I should have planned to take a few weeks off. Then, when my baby was three weeks late and I had a taste of what it was like to stay home, I almost wished I were back at the ofiice. (Almost.)

Women who love puttering around the house and preparing for baby will enjoy a month or so off to do so. Workaholics need projects—reading *War and Peace,* perhaps—to help them over the what-will-I-ever-do-at-home-for-two-weeks hump. Part-time work is nice if you can get it. But everybody needs to follow their own instincts when it comes to working—not the instincts of somebody you heard of or read about in a book. Only you know whether a week at home calms you down or drives you crazy. Whether you're happier on the job or on the couch. Just how much you need those extra two weeks' salary—or those extra two weeks' rest.

My favorite advice from an obstetrician on working is "No matter what you do or plan, don't forget your eight hours a night sleep plus adequate rest or nap times during the day." Then, a few pages later: "Keep working as long as you can function as a homemaker, wife and companion to your husband." All that plus working and eight-hours-sleep and naps. Right.

I came across very few women who stayed home for their entire pregnancy. But those who did loved it. Martha had been working since she was fourteen years old, with no summers or weekends off. At age twenty-five, she got pregnant. After eleven years on the job, she figured she deserved a little vacation. She enjoyed every minute.

Many women see their nine months of pregnancy as the last chance—ever—to completely relax. To do what they want, to go with the flow, without responsibility and without pressure. To indulge themselves in the deliciousness of having nothing to do.

"I had been teaching for five years, and I didn't really like it," said Barbara. "I quit so that I could have the whole year off while I was pregnant. I figured that would be the last year off I would ever have. So I did a lot of nice things. I took courses, and sewing lessons, and went out to lunch. It was a beautiful year. It can be a lot of fun being able to read, to go out shopping. There's all that nice kind of stuff you don't know about because you've never done it. Like not having to get up in the morning. Last week, it was my son's first birthday, and I said to myself: 'A year ago today is the last time I slept late.'"

I get jealous just listening to her.

But I know the nirvana she's outlining isn't for me. Even when I hate my job, I like my work. At home, I'm sure I would have gone crazy after the third novel. Even Nancy, who threw in her typewriter at eight months, found she was very bored at home. Some people just don't know what to do with free time on their hands. Somebody should give us lessons. But meanwhile, we extol the benefits of working.

"I worked up until two weeks before I delivered, and it helped a great deal," said one woman. "My pregnancy went very fast. I think if I was home, it really would have dragged. I would have gotten depressed. I was also afraid that I'd just have more time to be nervous, to get scared. Working kept my mind on something other than myself."

Working can be fulfilling, but so can staying home. Working can be tiring—and so can staying home. Staying home can be boring, and so can working. Staying home can be a challenge to your ingenuity. And so can working.

I asked Joan, who had morning sickness morning and night, how she managed to pull off a full-time job. No problem, she said. "I'd just go to the bathroom and flush the toilet so no one would know I was vomiting."

Pregnant women can be remarkably adaptable. One woman realized that she was getting tired and "discombobulated." But that didn't stop her from working. "I wasn't able to keep my mind on priorities and organization, and my energy level was way down. So when I went to work in the morning, the first thing I'd do was to make a little pile so that if I got tired, which happened maybe once or twice a week, I had something to take home with me so I could nap and work later."

I napped during lunch hour in the ladies' room, to the sounds of flushing toilets. I also did Lamaze exercises in the ladies' room—the most remote one I could find. Occasionally, I got caught practicing Phase II breathing or massaging my tummy; generally, people were too embarrassed to ask what all the panting was about.

Even if you don't get caught in the ladies' lounge practicing Lamaze, you're bound to get some curious looks. But given time, almost everybody gets used to your presence and your habits. "I think once they accept that you are really going to stick it out until you have the baby, then they get over the staring," said Gail.

You can (usually) cope with the conditions of work and pregnancy. You can learn to prop your feet up under your desk; to nap at your desk and ignore the stares (and the noise); to find a ladies' room or take long walks at lunch for exercise—even if you just walk up and down the corridors. You can even cope with throwing up.

Harder to handle are the prejudices some people still harbor against working pregnant women. Many men, for some reason, seem to think that being eight months pregnant means calling a doctor every time the fetus rolls over. They seem to think you're going to deliver on the spot, or rather, on the floor. Right there in the Xerox room. And that they're going to have to deliver. Clearly, these sorts of people don't like having you around, and they usually find ways to make it clear to you. I know because my employer was one of them. So was my husband's boss. He used to view my belly like a case of nitroglycerin; as if at any moment it would surely go off.

"People would say, 'Oh, my God, Nancy, do you think you should work another week? Don't you think you should go home?' They thought I was going to have the baby right there."

"That's just what I've been getting," said Joan. "People say, 'You're quitting only the week before? Why don't you quit two weeks before?'"

I found this phenomenon rather funny. I plotted to go into a "false" labor before I left, just to see the expression on my boss's face. But I knew he'd run so fast in the other direction that I'd never even get to see the results.

Not so funny are the attitudes that employers (and colleagues) can take when you're sick. Other people get sick because they got a bug. You get sick because you got a baby. Even if you've got pneumonia, people assume you're out because you're pregnant, not ill. And if you're out at all, it only goes to prove that pregnant women shouldn't work because they're sick all the time.

Of course, I'm not speaking for all employers. But I am speaking, alas, for too many of them. "My boss was overprotective in a phony kind of way," said one woman, typically. "He was nice, but condescending. Still suffering from the attitude of 'Hire a woman, she goes and gets pregnant.'"

It is now illegal for an employer to fire you just for getting pregnant. If he or she tries to pressure you, you can take your case to court. Of course, that won't do much for your promotion prospects, so you may have to walk a fine line between fighting for your right to work (and to be sick occasionally) and your desire to maintain friendly relations for the future.

If possible, find out all you can about your employer's policy toward pregnancy *before* you get pregnant. Or at least before you make your pregnancy public. That way, you can plan your strategy in relative secrecy. It may seem a little sneaky, but it may be a matter of survival.

In my case, it was just a matter of a two-week vacation I really wanted to take. I was on the verge of telling my employer that I was pregnant at about five months when something (or somebody) told me that I wouldn't get my vacation if my employer knew I wasn't planning to work the full year. So I bought some tent dresses and complained about how I was getting fat—until I got back from vacation. It wasn't the way I would choose to conduct myself, but then, I didn't much care for my employer's conduct either.

Other circumstances may compel you to keep your pregnancy under wraps. Kay kept her condition a secret until her temporary typing job was made permanent. "I knew they wouldn't take me seriously if they knew I was pregnant," she said. She was undoubtably right. Discrimination against pregnant women in promotion and hiring is probably as inevitable as it is illegal. If you can't do anything about it, at least you can know about it.

Looking back, I must have seemed somewhat ludicrous, running around at six or seven months pregnant looking for a job that would have meant long hours and lots of responsibility. But if I wasn't taken seriously by others, I was very serious myself. I assumed that the fact of my pregnancy was irrelevant to the prospect of my employment. But I'm sure it was irrelevant only to me.

Indeed, to me, pregnancy seemed the perfect time not only to end an old job, but to start a new one. The baby was a job in itself, but it seemed to bring with it an urge for renewal, for starting over, for a new life. My friend Lee felt much the same way, even though her motivations were more negative. "I'm afraid that if I don't do it now, I won't ever make a move. After the baby comes, there'll be too many excuses. I'll be too depressed or too tired."

Some employers don't think twice about sending a pregnant woman on assignment or giving her a promotion. Most think about it all the time. Some bend over backward for you, and some are just plain backward. Some are accommodating, and some are awful. If you don't know how pregnant women are treated at your office, ask a new mother. She's the only one who can tell you what to expect.

Matters of maternity leave and maternity pay are unresolved in the courts and often unresolved within companies. You may have a case for a sex-discrimination suit if your employer's medical plan pays for vasectomy but not maternity. But the legal rights of pregnant women—like those of all women—are in great flux. Meanwhile, the pregnant woman in the working world is still somewhat of a pioneer. And while the frontier may be rough at times, it can also be exciting.

Special circumstances make working "with child" especially, well, special. One woman got a lot of comments because she was pregnant while working at Planned Parenthood. Another was a maternity nurse. She said that for the first time, the doctors she worked with acted like gentlemen. I wrote an article about cesarean sections when I was several weeks overdue. In every obstetrician's office I visited as a reporter, I was received as a patient. The confusion was compounded because I used my maiden name and introduced myself as "Miss."

Kathy taught elementary school during her pregnancy: "Some people obviously thought I shouldn't still be working. Some parents were resentful that you didn't deliver the baby on the last day in June. That your timing wasn't perfect, you know. Others told me it was very exciting to be part of a birth, and they thought it was exciting for the children. But the most interesting part was the reaction of the children themselves. You could just see them in the lunch line, whispering about how much bigger I was getting. Some of the children were really frightened that something would happen to me. They verbalized their fears, and I think it helped the whole class when we talked it out."

Whatever job you're in, working "with child" means day-to-day contact with other people—for better or for worse. Their reactions can enrich your experience, just as your presence enriches theirs. Sometimes I think "a pregnant woman in every office" should be somebody's campaign slogan, if not a law. A pregnant working woman is a constant reminder of the human condition in conditions that are seldom human. And even when she makes people uneasy, she probably does them some good.

Pregnant working women are inevitable. Sooner or later, they'll be acceptable, too.

The truth is that pregnant women *can* use their heads and pat their bellies at the same time. It's a shame that in order to be accepted in the "normal" world, you so often have to renounce the very feature that makes you special. Just as women who want to make it in a man's world so often must become "like a man." Femininity never subtracted from competence. And neither did pregnancy. Ideally, a pregnant working woman should be able to display her condition along with her skills; her belly should be viewed as a complement, not an encumbrance; and just because she needs to lie down once in a while, it doesn't mean she's lying down on the job. A pregnant woman in the office is not just "one of the boys." The lady's having a *baby*.

TRAVEL, TENNIS AND THE PURSUIT OF PLEASURE

"My doctor said that as long as I felt well, I could continue to play tennis twice a week. Then, at the ninth month, he realized that I was still playing, and he said 'Stop!' He was panic stricken. He suddenly realized that we were not just popping the ball back and forth at a tea party. He realized what kind of game I play."

There is tennis, and there is Tennis, just as there is skiing and Skiing, or walking and Walking. A tour of Europe can mean a week in luxury hotels or an arduous hike up the Alps. Sailing in a Sunfish is not a cruise on the *QEII*. So before you ask your doctor what you can do while you're pregnant, ask yourself what you *really* have in mind. If you're planning to paddle across the English Channel, don't ask him / her if you can go for a little swim.

One day the women in my Lamaze class started comparing their doctors' advice on vacations and leisure activity. The doctor who skied said it was okay to ski, but not to drive a car. The tennis-playing doctor nixed skiing, but okayed three sets of singles a day. Sedentary doctors were afraid of travel, while world travelers urged their patients to see the world.

Most such restrictions are a matter of opinion. However, two general rules emerge from the confusion. For a change, both seem to synchronize the advice of doctors, the tales of women, and the needs of your body.

Rule #1 is a matter of timing. The middle three months of pregnancy are probably your best, and thus by far the best time to travel. There's little chance of miscarriage (as in early pregnancy) or of a premature arrival. Morning sickness and advanced lethargy are usually over, but hemorrhoids and that huge feeling haven't yet set in. If you're planning a world cruise, do it now.

Rule #2 is a matter of transportation. Walking is the best way to get around—but impractical if you want to visit relatives 3,000 miles away. Second best is air travel, and worst is car or train. Ask any woman who's been cramped in a car for ten hours, having to stop at every rest area, about the joys of motoring on bumpy roads. Besides, as one obstetrician said, airline stewardesses make better midwives than gas station attendants. I know I'd certainly rather go into labor on the flight to Boston than on Interstate 22.

Traveling is an adventure, and so is being pregnant. Put them together, and it can be the best vacation you ever had. Or at least the most memorable. One woman was in Italy in the middle of a cholera epidemic when she ate something that didn't agree with her. She thought she was going into labor; her Italian hosts were afraid she had cholera. Either way, she got a lot of attention.

Another woman won the Ping-Pong tournament on the ship coming to America: "Let me tell you that ship gave me a standing ovation. I beat the men's champion, who was Japanese. I was six months pregnant. You know how you grow in stages? Well, one day I was not very big at all, and that's how I came aboard that ship. I wore very loose clothes, but not really maternity clothes. But by the time they were giving out the awards, I somehow swelled about five inches. I was dressing for the captain's dinner, and the only thing I could squeeze into was a maternity dress. So when I went to get my Ping-Pong award, I stuck out a mile. The guy who was the men's champion was mortified. Not so much that a woman had beaten him, but that a pregnant woman had beaten him. And the people just roared. It was one of the proudest moments of my life."

Pregnancy is a universal language. It can help you feel not so much of a stranger in a strange land. Even in your own country, it can be a ticket to a better seat at the ball park or a suitcase to sit on in the airport. The whole time I was in Brazil, I thought the good times I was having might rub off on the baby—or perhaps he would be born speaking Portuguese. I used to lift up my T-shirts so he could peep out my belly button at the view. I don't know if he really enjoyed the trip. But I do know that his being there made me enjoy it all the more.

In fact, I enjoyed most aspects of being a pregnant woman in the public eye. I liked having the privilege of being special and the prerogatives of doing what I liked. My one frustration was that I had to try so hard *not* to be special in order to keep on with my job and with my life. I would like to see the day when I could integrate both sides of me: the official and the maternal, the ambitious and the amorous, the lady-with-the-baby and the lady-with-the-career. Or as the real estate saleslady told me: "I don't care what those women's libbers say. I think having a baby is the most wonderful thing a woman can do." So do I. And I didn't even cancel my subscription to *Ms*.

I have the feeling that the presence—and power—of pregnant women is about to be felt in our society as never before. And I think it's about time. After all, pregnancy *is* beautiful. If you've got it, flaunt it.

Be Prepared:

Lamaze and Other Sources of Advice and Discontent

Anybody can learn how to have a baby, I thought. All you need is a good teacher, some informative books, and the advice of your doctor, friends, and relatives. I had always been a good student in school. Surely I could learn to excel at childbirth just as I had learned to excel at math. At worst, I could cram in enough to earn a comfortable C. And if I studied harder and practiced more diligently, I would do even better. I certainly had the motivation and the confidence to succeed. So I read every book I could buy or borrow; I talked to everybody who would talk to me; I attended every childbirth and baby class offered at the hospital; I read magazines, newspapers, barraged my doctor with questions. By the time I went into labor, I was feeling so well prepared that it took months before I realized just how ill prepared I had been.

Never before has the pregnant woman been offered such a cornucopia of instructional materials. Bookstores are already stacked to the brim, and still every obstetrician I know is writing a book. TV specials bring birth into our living rooms.

Magazines and newspapers sing the praises of Lamaze, La Leche, and Leboyer. Almost every major hospital offers courses in preparation for childbirth. Mothers and fathers take a six-week course in birthing that includes homework in the form of rigorous exercise and practice. Surely by the time delivery rolls around, they know everything there is to know about having a baby.

Or do they?

Of course, you can never know *everything* about having babies. Even obstetricians don't know that. But it is disappointing when you seem to know so much, only to realize that you've learned so little. I think the reasons for the disappointment are twofold:

First, our expectations have run far ahead of reality. We've come from a time when women were expected to know next to nothing about the business of birthing to a time when they are demanding to know almost everything; from a time when women had no control to a point where they want all the control. We have come so far so fast that it seems women must by now know everything they ever wanted to know about giving birth. But they don't. Not by a long shot.

Second, "prepared" childbirth is a reaction to the unsavory circumstances in which our mothers gave birth. Ignorant and frightened, the only preparation they received was from each other—mostly in the form of old wives' tales and agonizing accounts of labor, which served only to frighten more. Fear breeds bad experiences, which in turn breed more fear. Prepared-childbirth classes try to reverse that cycle by eschewing the negative in favor of the positive. Labor "pains," in a master PR stroke, are today called "contractions." All this is well and good and helpful and necessary. But often the result is that something very properly called "labor" comes off looking like a bed of roses. And a lot of women come through the experience wondering what hit them.

If the first source of disappointment is a matter of perspective, the second is a matter of context. It isn't so much that preparation for childbirth may fall short of your expectations, it's more that your expectations may be unrealistically high.

"Prepared childbirth" has become almost synonomous with "Lamaze." The Lamaze method is only one of several ways to prepare for childbirth. But it is so far and wide the most popular that most people have come to use the terms interchangeably.

People also tend to confuse the terms "prepared childbirth" and "natural childbirth." Here the distinction is more than semantic. Natural childbirth means childbirth without pain medication. It is much easier if you are also prepared. Prepared childbirth takes place with or without medication, but the goal is to reduce the amount of medication as much as possible. This is because pain medication (1) is bad for the baby, (2) isn't very good for you, and (3) may slow down—or even stop—labor, so that in the end it becomes more painful than it would have been without painkillers. (More on this under Anesthesia.)

The Lamaze method is supposed to train you for childbirth much as Dr. Pavlov trained his salivating dogs. At the sound of the bell (or your husband's voice, in this case), all your muscles immediately relax to let the labor contractions proceed more easily (and thus with less pain). This is made difficult because one of your major muscles—your uterus—is straining to push the baby out, no small feat. Relaxing under these circumstances is like trying to pat your head and rub your stomach at the same time when you can't control one of your hands.

Lamaze teaches you *about* birthing, as well as how to do it. You learn to recognize your pubic bone and the three stages of labor. You get advice on how to ease leg cramps and how to deal with your mother-in-law. You learn calisthenic exercises to keep you strong and breathing exercises to keep you under control. There is deep breathing for early labor, short pants for "serious" labor, pant-and-blow combinations for the really rough stuff. The breathing helps you to concentrate, relax, and distract you from the pain.

But Lamaze is far more than a course of study. It has become almost a cultural phenomenon. Like jogging and Bloomingdale's, it implies a state of mind—even a social status. The image of Lamaze is young, hip, and beautiful—just like the people who participate in it. It is a promise not only of an easy labor, but also of friendship and camaraderie. It is, in short, the "in" thing to do. And it was something I was about to miss.

My first impression of Lamaze was bellies: a room full of people who looked exactly like me! In all, some thirty students sit around a large room on folding chairs. Half of them have roughly the same shape—like so many bowling pins. The other half are husbands. They seem, in face, to look remarkably like their wives. Now I know why people say that married couples look alike. I can almost tell what the baby will look like by studying the parents. I wonder if the fetuses inside know the company they're in. I wonder if they can communicate.

Our instructor is Fritzie: blond, pretty, and full of giggles. She is nothing if not a male chauvinist. We are to go around the room each in turn saying why we want to study Lamaze. I speak, but Fritzie is more interested in what my husband has to say. By the time we get to the third couple, *only* the husbands are speaking. "Hi, I'm Steve, and I'm here because I want to make an informed decision about how I'm going to have my baby." Another father is a cop. Once he had to deliver a baby in a patrol car. Next time, he wants to know what he's doing.

Fritzie gives us a reading list:

"I think a lot of the men will like this book because it's a little more scientific. . . . In the end there's a section on the enema, skip it. . . . This book may be a little overenthusiastic. If you ladies think your husbands won't like it, give him something else."

Each week we have a lesson, along with a review and a quiz. "Now what's this little bone here?" asks Fritzie, pointing to the big diagram on the board. "What's the first stage of labor?" Naturally, a man answers. Fritzie tells us what happens to our "oodles of intestines." She inquires about our complaints. "Who's having discomforts? Nobody? Ha. Ha. Now, gentlemen, look at this. All these pregnant women and no complaints. Ha. Ha. Not a peep. I know something *everybody* has. Ha. Ha."

We learn about effacement and dilation (the first stages of labor) and about transition, the "horrible part."

"What do you mean by 'horrible'?" a woman asks.

"It hurts like hell," Fritzie answers.

We practice panting and blowing, but my husband jokes that I look like a fish, so I can't concentrate. We put pillows on the floor and kick into the air like a prone chorus line of Rockettes. We grunt like bears and practice pushing the baby out. We watch movies of Lamaze births, advertisements for the method. I've seen these films before. The shot of the baby's head coming out still makes me gasp. Like those little wooden Russian dolls—one inside the other. The birth always makes me cry. It also scares the hell out of me. The mother in the movie was three weeks late going into labor. Everybody wants to know why.

One of the women in our class wants to know about the Leboyer method. Leboyer is a romantic approach to birth, with soft lights, quiet whispers, and a soothing hot bath for the baby after it's born. Fritzie obviously loves this question: "You'll notice that the doctor gets his kicks, but there's no role for the father."

Everybody in the class objects. Why couldn't the father give the baby a bath? "Fathers don't want that responsibility."

By the fifth session, we are down one couple. They are in another part of the hospital, in labor. Suddenly it's all very exciting. This is the first indication that all our schooling leads to something real. There is a party atmosphere—like a graduation. In a continuing game of muscial chairs, our circle shrinks slowly. On the wall someone has posted a sign: "I'm selling my $47.50 credit at Lady Madonna maternity boutique for $40."

The last session turns out to be a harbinger in more ways than one. A new father and former classmate comes to tell us what it was really like. Fritzie does the introductions: "This is Chris Brody, who delivered on Monday." Then Chris tells his tale:

"I guess we were about two centimeters dilated when we arrived," he reported. "We pushed from a quarter to eleven until a quarter to two. The baby's head was in a funny position. They had to use forceps, and I had to leave. It's a real downer to find out you have to leave. It's confusing. I made the mistake of counting on being there."

There are murmurs all around.

Chris goes on: "The forceps marks lasted for two days. She had a little scar right here below the eye."

Fritzie interrupts. "It's not a *scar*, it's a *scratch*."

Later we pass around a baby bottle and some nipples for inspection. What a strange contraption! I wonder how it works. What part did she say to boil? For how long?

Fritzie gives us a short course in baby care, including admonitions against sharing a room with the child, or taking it to crowded places. Her final advice is appropriate: "After two weeks, we think you owe it to your husband to get out for a night."

Like all good little Lamaze pupils, I practiced at home almost every night. Cross-legged on the bed, clock in hand, I timed and breathed and panted. I got my husband to practice about twice. Some couples are the opposite. The husband practices diligently, and the wife has to be dragged along.

Panting is not the same as simple breathing. It takes a lot of practice, and it can be a rather subtle technique. After you almost pass out the first couple of times, you understand why they ask you to bring a brown bag to blow in, in case you should hyperventilate. You also learn why you're supposed to bring lip balm and breath spray in your bag: panting makes you parched. Out of all the books I read, only one warned that it takes at least a full week to learn how to pant correctly. Even that may be an understatement.

One reason expectant parents don't always practice their Lamaze breathing is that they feel foolish. This is not surprising. Who wouldn't feel foolish staring at a spot on the wall for sixty seconds while you pant and slowly rub your stomach?

In order for the Pavlovian conditioning to work, your muscles must learn automatically to respond to the words: "Contraction begins." It is the job of your husband or coach to know when the contraction begins and to tell you. However, you must say "Contraction begins" even if you're practicing by yourself and even if you have no notion of how a contraction would feel—much less begin. If you want to see how blowing works during delivery, you can try this graceful exercise proposed in a book: "[Sit] in a chair or on the toilet with your feet flat on the floor, straining downward as if you were constipated and trying to have a bowel movement, and then quickly blowing out."

Lamaze is not always aesthetically pleasing, but it can be extremely effective. Indeed, most women who delivered naturally say they couldn't have done it without Lamaze. "It kept you busy," said Laura. "You had all these terrible pains, it was something to do—something to concentrate on besides the pain." In the best of circumstances, there isn't that much perceivable pain: "In my first pregnancy," Anna said, "I used the Read method, which is basically just going along with the contractions. And I can remember experiencing pain. But the second time I used Lamaze, and I can't use the word 'pain.' I was always on top of it. I'll use 'discomfort'—it was an uncomfortable feeling. But pain, no."

Many women discover that Lamaze breathing is useful for other kinds of pain as well. One Lamaze father now uses it in place of anesthesia when he goes to the dentist. My attorney (also a Lamaze mother) suggested that I try Phase I breathing to keep calm during a deposition.

Of course, a labor that is merely "uncomfortable" is about as rare as steak tartare. And Lamaze works *only* if conditions are right. As one woman put it: "Lamaze is realistic only if you are determined to do it. If you practice, if you have a good, knowledgeable coach, and if you can relax." Those are a lot of "ifs." Unfortunately, even the best husbands don't always make good coaches. And while good labor nurses are invaluable, they are not always available. (More on that under Labor and Husbands.)

Lamaze has uses apart from pain control. Even if you don't learn to achieve a "natural birth," you will still learn much that is helpful if not essential. "I liked learning what was happening to my body chemistry," said Susan, typically. "I learned about how the baby comes down, what the birth canal is, what's transition, what's a contraction, what's this and that. The course gave all the emotions that a woman is going through, what to expect. It really made living together easier. When I had crabby moods or when I was tired, it kind of helped me along. Instead of getting mad at me for being a crab, my husband would understand."

The best advertisements for Lamaze are the mothers who gave birth to their children naturally and loved every minute. However, it can be dangerous to take them as models. Indeed, obstetricians often warn Lamaze mothers not to feel like failures if they don't get through labor without a shot or a squeak. In my case, I didn't feel as if I'd failed. I felt as if I'd been cheated.

The trouble is that Lamaze, at its worst, can be misleading. The picture of an average labor that it paints is real enough in statistical terms, but not necessarily in human ones. The diagrams in the books, the charts in class, all map out labor like a flight plan or so many plays in a football game. For six to ten hours (they say) you will experience light contractions from thirty to sixty seconds in duration. They will occur at five- to twenty-minute intervals. You will rub your tummy and knit, chat with your husband, read a book, wash your hair. For the next two to five hours, you will feel stronger contractions lasting exactly sixty seconds and recurring every one to three minutes. If you're tired, you can sleep in between pains. However, you must be awake in time to catch the contraction before it starts, pant your way through, then relax. The next hour consists of very strong contractions sixty to ninety seconds long, occurring every minute or so. You want to push the baby out, but you shouldn't, so you blow. You may vomit. You feel confused, mad at your husband. The final hour is for pushing. This feels great. You expel the baby and everybody lives happily ever after.

This is what happens in the Lamaze movies and books. Sometimes it even happens in real life—but not that often.

"I'm sure if I've heard one woman talk about Lamaze, I've heard a hundred," said Holly. "And I've gone through it myself. Don't get me wrong—I think it's great. But it's left me with a certain bitterness. Too many women have been led to believe that normal labor is like x, y, and z. And everybody seems to come out with a gut feeling that you have failed if you did not run down the x, y, and z—the Lamaze description of delivery. I know my bitterness isn't rational because Lamaze just tries to give you an idea of what a normal delivery is like, what the stages are. And yet, I've yet to meet anybody who experienced labor in exactly that way."

Any Lamaze instructor would argue with Holly. He or she would say that Lamaze is meant only as a guide, not as a model. But either some Lamaze instructors aren't making that point clear, or the mothers aren't listening. No doubt, it's a combination of both. But no matter what the instructor says, the ubiquitous charts and graphs give you the impression that labor is somehow predictable; they can't help but lead you to expect a certain sequence of feelings and events. The point of Lamaze is to prepare you to deal with all the variations of a normal labor. But if you aren't expecting the variations, you won't be very well prepared.

Another aspect of Lamaze that many women find less than honest is the perception of pain. Of course, if Lamaze is accidentally misleading on the subject of pain, it's misleading accidentally on purpose. A fear of pain makes it impossible to relax, and without relaxation Lamaze is impossible. Moreover, "labor pain" wasn't a very descriptive term. It's much more useful to call a contraction a contraction. That is, after all, what it is. It's nice to know what's hurting and why. But it's also helpful to know that it *is* (probably) going to hurt.

Here's the description of labor à la Lamaze offered in a popular how-to manual: "An untrained woman going into labor interprets her contractions as 'pains.' . . . An educated woman learns that contractions are the mechanism by which the cervix is opened and her baby is expelled. She looks forward to each contraction as a step further in the progress of the birth of her baby."

I interviewed at least a dozen women who had successful Lamaze births. Not a single one reported "looking forward to" the next contraction.

"I think I expected labor to be utterly painless, as Dr. Lamaze would have it," Mary said. "I was surprised at the pain, as I'm sure others must have been. The worst part about the books and the classes was their optimistic attitude. No where can you find anything that talks of the discomfort and pain, both mental and physical, that you may encounter. It's nice to think of the positive aspects of childbearing, but it's also nice to know that you are not the only one who may not be having everything quite as rosy as depicted. Lamaze films tend to glamorize birthing, and to gloss over the nitty-gritty painful part. No one ever said that the pain of childbirth is like no other. It's not 'uncomfortable'—that word keeps popping up—in the colloquial sense. No one ever really said, 'It hurts like hell.' After I had my baby, I would mention that to other women. They would smile and respond with that knowing look—as if it was information privy only to a mother. Even Lamaze classes don't play this part honestly."

Of course, Lamaze doesn't pretend to offer you a painless labor. Or at least it shouldn't. But most women—including myself—still somehow expected one.

Other misconceptions and disappointments about Lamaze run the gamut from the traumatic to the trivial. Some osbtetricians or Lamaze instructors will advise women to "try" Lamaze techniques for a while during labor, as if they were sampling chocolates. This rarely works. To some extent you should be "psyched up" to go all the way, as one mother put it. It still might not work for you, but at least you'll have a chance. If you're vacillating even before you start, it will be easy to vacillate yourself right into a medicated birth.

Second, Lamaze mothers are *not* all brave and strong. They do not attempt natural childbirth because they like pain. On the contrary. The whole point of taking Lamaze is to *avoid* pain. "There is a hole in that theory that women who have Lamaze are brave," said Cathy. "I was certainly not brave. And certainly not unafraid of pain. I can't even stand to have a needle in my mouth when I go to the dentist. I never would have gone through Lamaze if I thought I was going to suffer."

And there's no doubt that Lamaze mothers seem to suffer far less than mothers who were totally unprepared.

Another myth is that Lamaze is somehow only for feminists or revolutionaries or people who are anti-medicine. Fritzie was anything but. Indeed, she often sent out mixed signals. For example, praising the benefits of panting while at the same time raving about wonder drugs that let you witness the birth of your child while avoiding any sensation of pain. This was not only misleading, but also confusing.

Some women get the impression that loving Lamaze means you have to hate your doctor:

"I had a great doctor and I loved Lamaze, but I had great anxieties because the class was so vehement about all the things you would have to fight your doctor for," said Cheryl. "Like you had to demand to have your husband there while you were being prepped. I can't imagine why. It was really not necessary for him to be there at that point. They also made a big deal about taking a pillow with you into the delivery room. But I didn't remember half that stuff, and they already had pillows there. It wasn't that you had to have an argument for it. But I was so keyed up and defensive. I remember discussing it with my doctor while I was in labor. He said, 'Yes, well, that's one of the problems with Lamaze. You're paying $700 to the obstetrician and you are paying $60 to some nurse, and who are you going to listen to?' But the nurse was very helpful, too. It was a very good experience. Both Lamaze *and* my doctor."

Lamaze is not necessarily an "us against them" situation. It is certainly more rewarding to undergo Lamaze with the cooperation of your doctor. And it is much more difficult to cooperate with your doctor in the birth if you haven't had Lamaze.

Similarly, no doctor or nurse or anybody else is going to

call you a failure if you need medication. Some women find that certain kinds of medication can relax them just enough to stay on top of their contractions. Lamaze is not a test of your physical or mental powers. It is a way to have a baby in the easiest, healthiest way possible. But sometimes Lamaze gets the image of being a trial or contest. And few women want childbirth to turn into a competition.

"The first time I saw my doctor, I said, 'If you're one of those doctors who shoves natural childbirth down my throat, we are not for one another. If I can do it, fine, but if I can't, I'm not going to feel like a failure.' I know some women who are bent out of shape about it. I know a woman who had breeched twins, and God forbid they should give her any medication. Sometimes I think it's getting really sick." (The woman who said those words eventually had a totally natural birth.)

The couples in the Lamaze movies always seem to become fast friends. Perhaps you, too, will make lasting friendships with your classmates. Like the "movie" couples, you might share secrets and even get together for birthdays for years to come. On the other hand, you might not. My class was a case in point. The prospective parents came to learn the techniques of childbirth, not to make friends. The group was certainly not hostile, but it was not particularly warm either. Somehow, I had expected that it would be. So had Laura:

"I remember thinking that the people in our Lamaze course were very uptight. We figured everybody would get in touch with everybody else to find out what they had, but nobody was interested. They were so unenthusiastic. I guess they just weren't talkers."

You should also realize that not all of Lamaze is to be taken literally—and not all the techniques work for everybody. If they don't work for you, you haven't been "tricked," even though it may feel that way.

"Another lie they told in Lamaze class was that the breathing would take away the pain," Barbara said. "They had this little trick—I don't know how they did it—but you did your breathing and your husband pinched you on the thigh real hard, and you couldn't feel it. I thought that was how labor would be. You would be in great pain, but with the breathing, you wouldn't feel it. Lies! Lies!"

Among the techniques that sometimes don't work is the gentle tummy massage called effleurage. Many women find it irritating; they can't stand to have anyone touch their stomachs during labor. Others find that their husbands are embarrassed to do it. Or aren't very good at it. "I had so many people touching my stomach that I couldn't find a place to effleurage," said Sally. It's also not easy to effleurage if you have a fetal monitor strapped around your belly.

Indeed, some of the best Lamaze techniques may be subverted by hospital policy. For example, your brown Lamaze "goodie bag" is supposed to contain lollipops for you to suck during labor. But many hospitals don't allow it. Mine didn't even allow ice chips. One manual advises changing your position as often as possible to avoid "getting bored." Getting bored generally isn't a problem during labor, but changing positions *is* a good idea. It can be difficult, however, when you are strapped to a fetal monitor and hooked up to an IV. That goes double for "urinating as frequently as you need"—unless you use a bedpan.

Finally, Lamaze takes a great deal of energy. Or rather, labor takes a great deal of energy. It's much harder if you have either a very long labor or very little sleep the night before.

In short, while Lamaze may well be the best available method of preparing for childbirth, it makes no guarantees. Lamaze is a method, not a promise. It can't account for your physical or mental condition, for the actions of your doctor, for the rules of your hospital. It should try to stress the wide range of variations that occur in labor, but it can't cover every one. It has to walk a fine line between preparing you to have your wits about you during labor without scaring you out of your wits. It can't tell you how long or how severe your labor will be because your instructor doesn't know. If you expect Lamaze to birth your baby for you, you will certainly be disappointed.

You should listen as closely as possible to what your Lamaze instructor has to say, but you should not take it as gospel. Sometimes this is easier the second time around:

"I found that the first time I took my teacher very literally," said Stephanie. "I hung on her every word. And I was very disappointed and shocked that my labor was so erratic and strange. I kept thinking, 'She didn't tell me this.' But the second time I took the course—I don't know if she had changed or if I had changed—but I felt a lot looser. I got the impression this time that all kinds of things were presented as possible and normal, and that this might happen or that might happen. I don't know if I just didn't hear that the first time, or if she didn't say it."

Women who take Lamaze classes tend to be educated, curious, somewhat self-confident. They want to know exactly what's going to happen to them and why. Sometimes this leads to great frustration—because, of course, they can't always know what or why. However, they do have a certain sense of control, of participation, that is both satisfying and assuring.

"I wanted to know what was happening so I wouldn't be scared," Joan said. "Nothing can prepare you for the pain, but you can be in control. When I have that pain I want to know what it is, and the scientifically proven best method to deal with the pain. You can't remove it, but you can know what to do with it. And if something terrible is happening—if I need a cesarean or whatever—I want to know that the professionals are doing the best thing. I want to be the one to make the decisions. Because I know that, for example, I would probably have a bad reaction to certain kinds of anesthesia. So I wanted it to be my decision if something went wrong."

Some mothers are even more adamant: "Doctors have been duping women for long enough. We deserve to know what's going on. It's my baby."

On the other end of the spectrum are mothers who don't want to know anything. They wish to remain in what they think is blissful ignorance. Or at least, they want to know only selectively.

What women often don't want to hear is horror stories—especially if they're trying to nurture a positive attitude about childbirth. Like the ostrich, they think if they don't see it, it won't hurt them. And they aren't entirely wrong. Confidence is one of the best midwives you can have. If not knowing certain things makes you more confident, then don't listen.

"Yes, it was harder than I imagined, but I don't think you want to convey that pain to other people," said Irene. "I don't know how you can sit down and say to a pregnant woman, 'Listen, I'm going to tell you exactly how bad labor is.' Because you're running a fifty-fifty chance that their labor will not be that bad, and you're going to scare the hell out of them for nine months for nothing. But it's a dilemma. I had a girlfriend who delivered in September, and in August she would come and visit me to see my new baby. She had this big belly and she was feeling great. She was so cool and comfortable, and I was half dead taking care of the kid. And every time she came over, I would call my mother beforehand and say, 'Should I tell? Should I tell?' And my mother would say, 'Don't tell.' And I never told. Well, when I went to see her in the hospital, she said, 'Why didn't you tell me?' And she was dying, the pain, everything. And nobody told her. I should have told her. I felt bad about that."

Even if Irene had told her friend, she might not have listened. Mothers who are determined to make childbirth a positive experience simply stay away from negative impressions. The same is true about motherhood.

"I found that when I was blunt, pregnant women didn't want to hear it," Karen said. "They didn't want to know. When I told them you are going to be awake a lot of nights and you are going to be tired, they just didn't want to hear. They were so used to hearing all the fairy tales, or wanted to believe the fairy tales, that they weren't ready to face the truth."

Horror stories on any aspect of childbearing are counterproductive. But that doesn't mean that ignorance is bliss. At the very least, most mothers want to know the "technical" aspects of labor, birth, and babies. And they should. Because—horror stories aside—the more you know about what's going to happen, the more familiar it will seem and the less frightening. You've got enough to cope with during labor and childbirth without having to figure out what's a centimeter or a contraction or where's the bathroom. The more you understand, the less you have to be afraid of. The more you know, the less you fantasize. The more that's in your head, the less that will be on your mind.

"I do think it's better to know some things," said Marge, who had never taken a Lamaze class or read a book and didn't particularly want to. "I think you should at least tour the hospital and know what to expect, where you're going, what are they doing to me, and why can't I see my husband. They should show you what the showers look like, or show you, 'This is a sitz bath.' I think girls now should be more enlightened about what takes place in a hospital birth. You can't explain everything, but you can learn about the whole setup, the technicalities. Like, are you allowed in the nursery? What happens if you have a premie baby? What the delivery room looks like, and the labor room. And, yes, you are going to have stitches and, yes, it is going to hurt, depending on how many. And if your uterus doesn't contract, yes, they are going to put ice packs on. I would rather have been more alerted. I would rather have somebody tell me, well, your bottom feels like it's going to fall out. Even books don't tell you these things."

Marge wouldn't have touched a Lamaze class with a ten-foot pole, despite her eagerness for knowledge. Like other women, she did not see herself as a Lamaze "type." Lamaze was something for women's libbers, for health nuts, for the sort of people who watch public television. Unfortunately, the same "in" quality that turns some people on to Lamaze tends to turn others off.

But Lamaze is not all it's cracked up to be—for better or for worse. There's certainly no reason to be intimidated by it. And if—for whatever reason—you still don't care for Lamaze, remember it's only one of several ways to "prepare" for childbirth. Your hospital (or your telephone directory) will tell you what other kinds of courses are available in your area. If you can't find a class, you can always read books. Even television can prepare you. One woman I interviewed seemed particularly knowledgeable despite her claim that she never attended a single class or read a single word. She said she learned everything she knew from watching TV soap operas.

However you do it, though, do be prepared. Just because books and Lamaze classes may be misleading doesn't mean that you shouldn't use them to your advantage. And I don't know of any mother who took a Lamaze class who doubts that advantage. Even if you plan on leaving everything in the hands of your doctor. Even if you want to be "knocked out" the minute you enter the hospital. You never know when you'll give birth in the taxi, or your doctor won't make it, or you won't be *able* to take medication. If you wind up not using your Lamaze training during childbirth, it still won't be a total loss. You can always use it the next time you go to the dentist.

SUGGESTION AND SUPERSTITION

"Drink Marsala wine and egg in the morning for good health and a rosy complexion."

"Don't take a bath. Don't reach for anything—the cord will

get wrapped around the baby's neck."

"At dinner, the pregnant woman must always be served first."

"If you have a craving, you must eat whatever you crave. If you don't satisfy the craving and you have an itch, wherever you scratch the baby will have a birthmark in the shape of the food you craved."

Pregnant women are always getting advice—much of it silly. This sort of advice is called "old wives' tales"—presumably because it comes from old wives. Many of those old wives may be your own relatives.

Other advice you get may be sterling. This advice usually comes from close friends. Rarely do pregnant women seek advice from their own mothers. Indeed, of all the women I interviewed, only a handful even knew what their mothers' labors were like. Those who did tended to know much that was horrible, but little that was really helpful. Of course, mothers have changed mightily in the last generation. So has childbirth.

"My mother delivered me during the war years," said Uta, "so the only help she got during labor was a rosary. It was a terrible experience, and I got a pretty negative view from her. But then I talked to my friends and read some books, and I got a lot of positive feedback. So I thought, 'Wait and see what happens. A lot of it depends on me and how I look at it. If I expect it to be a bed of roses, it might not be. But it might not be horrible, either. So I'll just have to wait and see.'"

The best source of advice for a pregnant woman is a friend who has just given birth. Her experience won't be exactly like yours, but it's likely to be somewhat similar. More important, she'll be able to answer your questions based on firsthand—and fresh—experience. I thought Cheryl got the best advice of all:

"One of my closest friends had a baby two weeks before my son was born. I spoke to her husband on the phone the day after her delivery, and he said, 'Cheryl, just remember to take one contraction at a time.' And I remembered that one thing all through labor. It was the biggest help of all."

I asked all the mothers I interviewed to rate the advice they received; to tell which kind of advice was the most useful, which was the least useful. Invariably, doctors' advice was on the botom of the list. Friends' advice was on the top. Books and Lamaze classes fell somewhere in between. But no matter how good the advice you get, you still can't know what it's like to have a baby until you do it. Not really. Not any more than you can know what it's like to go to the moon.

Carol said, "In spite of all the friends and Lamaze and books and everything, it was so much more real than I had expected. There was a lot more pain, but also a lot more emotion and a lot more excitement and a lot more everything than you could get out of a book."

Even this book, I might add. I could no more describe what it's like to have a baby than I could describe what it's like to be born. Or to die. Or to fall in love for the very first time. And childbirth is nothing if not a labor of love. The emotions are simply too powerful for the printed page—perhaps even for the artist's palette.

The closest thing in my experience to giving birth was hiking down (and up) the Grand Canyon. It was exhausting and exhilarating, terrifying and thrilling, frustrating and satisfying—all at the same time. And my advice to anyone attempting the canyon would be the same as to someone attempting birth: Bring the right equipment (water/boots or husband/lip gloss); savor every minute that you can (you won't be traveling this road many times in your life); be prepared for anything (from cesareans to mules). And above all, as Cheryl said, remember to take one step at a time.

Labor:

The Beginning, and the End

Labor is the hard part. Pregnancy is packed with promises, and birth is a cause for celebration. But labor is pure effort. This is not to say that labor isn't promising or even can't be exhilarating. But nobody ever said it was easy—at least, not anybody I ever met.

Strangely, nature has contrived things so that most women actually look forward to labor. After nine months of carrying around a baby on the inside, you are more than ready to see what it looks like on the outside. Pregnancy seems to get unbearable just in time to make labor come with a sigh of relief. After weeks of rushing to the telephone every time you feel a cramp, or checking three times a day for signs of the "bloody show," you know you're ready—psychologically, at least—for labor.

Technically, the term "labor" encompasses the birth as well as the afterbirth. Colloquially, most women think of labor as the time leading up to the birth—and that's how the term will be used in this book. Since the physical and mental aspects of birth and labor are quite different, it seems artificial to group them together. Still, they are clearly all part of the same process—with a beginning, middle (birth), and end (afterbirth). In this chapter, we will begin at the beginning.

Labor gets your body ready to deliver your baby. In order to do so, your uterus, which has closed so tightly around the fetus, must now thin out and open up to allow the baby space to get through. The thinning out is called effacement. This part of labor is often so mild that most women don't even know it's happening. The opening up is called dilation. You may be as much as two centimeters (finger-widths) dilated before you even go into labor. However, it normally takes hard, active labor of several hours beofre the cervix (opening of the womb) is dilated enough to let the baby's head pass through. This happens at ten centimeters.

Next to her husband and the clock on the wall, nothing is so important to a laboring woman as her centimeters. The best part of labor is when the doctor tells you that you've dilated three more centimeters in the past hour. The worst is when he or she tells you that you haven't dilated at all in the past six hours. I should know. The day before I went into labor, the doctor told me I was dilated three centimeters. After five hours of labor, he told me I had progressed backward to two.

Between dilation and birth (termed "expulsion"), comes a tricky stage of labor known as "transition." Transition is what Fritzie called the "horrible part." It is the time for losing control, yelling at your husband, vomiting, shaking and otherwise having a hell of a time. The good news is that transition signals the end of labor. It is also supposed to last only a few minutes—at maximum, an hour. But note that I said "supposed to." Some women don't seem to experience transition at all. Others are astonished at how long a "few minutes" can last.

THE FIRST SIGNS

The two most frequently asked questions about labor are: How much will it hurt, and how will I know when it starts? It is possible, though highly unlikely, that your labor will not hurt at all. It is also possible—and far more likely—that it will not start. In this case, it will be induced by the doctor. But either way, labor patterns are as unpredictable as weather patterns.

The best you can do is know what has happened to others before you.

Labor can begin in almost as many ways as it can end. The three traditional landmarks of labor are the "bloody show"— when the plug of mucus that has been bottling up the cervix comes out; the breaking of waters—when the amniotic sac surrounding the fetus bursts under pressure; and, of course, those characteristic contractions.

However it happens, the onset of labor (as it's called) is almost always a happy occasion: "I couldn't believe how lucky I was," said Nancy. "I was due on the nineteenth, and this was the twentieth, and here I was ready to go. And I thought, 'Wow! It's really going to happen. This is really neat. Finally, after all this, we're going to have a baby.'"

The onset of my labor was signaled not by nature, but by the fact that my doctor was going on vacation the next day. True, the baby was already three weeks late. But it's also true that my doctor was leaving on Thursday, and while I was in his office, I distinctly heard him tell his secretary: "Okay, you can go ahead and set up another induction for Wednesday." When he waved good-bye in the recovery room, he had a suitcase in hand.

Be that as it may, I never experienced spontaneous contractions or bloody show or ruptured membranes. But I didn't miss out on the excitement. The night before our baby was "due," my husband and I sailed into the sunset in our small sailboat and feasted on cold cuts and beer. (I wasn't allowed to eat after midnight—at which point I officially turned into a patient.) We were both so excited that we could barely speak. We certainly couldn't sleep. (A good argument against induced labor.) And all I could think of was 'No matter what happens tomorrow, at some time during the day I'm going to have a baby.' I pondered my belly and wondered what was inside— for the last time. Before I finally drifted off for a few hours, I patted it and said, "This is it, kid."

A great deal of attention is given in baby manuals to knowing when labor begins, and beyond that, when to go to the hospital. I have heard of women with labor pains so imperceptible that they practically gave birth in the toilet, thinking merely that that "funny feeling" meant they had to move their bowels. However, labor contractions usually exert their presence far more forcefully. And it doesn't usually take much deliberation to decide when it's time to head for the hospital.

Candy's labor was over almost before she knew it had begun:

"I felt something like gas pains a little before 1:00. At 1:00 I woke my husband. I said, 'I think this is it.' He said, 'Well, then I'll go back to sleep now.' Because that's what they told us in the Lamaze class: When labor begins, try to get some sleep because you'll need it.

"I sat on the edge of this captain's chair and waited, and read a book for a few minutes and put on makeup. And then at 1:10 I went back to him and said, 'No, you don't understand. You have to get up now and help me with the contractions.'

"By the time he came up the stairs to our bedroom, I was paralyzed with pain. I said, 'Something is wrong.' But I was still feeling the movement of the fetus, so I was convinced that it wasn't labor. Still, every time I moved, there would be a contraction. Very erratic. There was no constant timing. So I said, 'Call the doctor, call the hospital, call my mother. We have to go.' And my husband said, 'Shouldn't we wait? Don't we have to time the contractions for an hour first?' And he was getting his stopwatch, his pencils, his legal pads. And I was saying, 'You don't understand, I have to go to the hospital.'

"By 1:20 I was desperate, begging him to make the calls. By the time my mother got there, I was hanging on the sink, my water was breaking, and things were happening fast. I told my mother it really hurt, and I didn't know whether I was going to make it. I was turning purple. And my husband was trying to do everything normally. He was carefully packing the bag, getting the tape recorder, the lemons, the lollipops.

"When we got to the hospital, I couldn't even get out of the car. They wanted to know my name, social security number, and so on. I said, 'Here's my wallet.' Then they gave me a nurse who had never been on the maternity ward. She said, 'I'm not quite sure where it is.' And I said, 'Turn left here.' I was trying to be cool. She was a kid, and I didn't want to freak her out. So I told her where to go, and when I saw another nurse, I said, 'I don't think I'm going to be able to do this.' and the nurse said, 'Oh, you'll go quickly.'"

Less than two hours after Candy felt her first "gas pain," she gave birth to a baby boy.

One excellent indication that you might be in labor is a wet bed.If you're nine months pregnant and you suddenly wake up in a swamp, it's probably a good time to call the hospital:

"I woke up at 7:30 and I was a fountain—literally," said Holly. "It must have been shooting two feet in the air. It just gushed. I couldn't get dressed because there was water, water, water everywhere. How can you get dressed? Ten thousand Tampax, fifty Kotex, nothing would have stopped it. I had to use three towels. I thought breaking my water would be a kind of trickle. Instead, it was like bursting a balloon. It felt great. I was so big and there was so much pressure. Then I heard the sound—just like a balloon breaking—and it was so refreshing, a great relief. It lasted for fifteen or twenty minutes, and then I really started going into labor."

Holly had expected her membranes to rupture in a gentle trickle. Kathy expected a gush. When she woke up in the morning to a slow drip, she couldn't understand what was happening. "I thought I was losing control of my kidneys. I went to the bathroom, but the water just came trickling out. I said to my husband, 'What am I going to do? I can't go to work like this.' So we thought the worst that could happen would be that I'd have to take the day off until it stopped."

Of course, it didn't stop. It started her labor.

OFF TO THE HOSPITAL

According to the book(s), the start of labor is supposed to be a time to wash your hair, read a book, go to a movie—do anything but go to the hospital. I remember having lunch one day at a restaurant near our hospital when I was expecting any day. A very pregnant woman and her husband were sitting at the next table. He kept a sharp eye on his watch while she rubbed her tummy and panted with as much dignity as possible in a public place. She was clearly distressed. Finally, the man came over to me and said, "My wife's been having contractions two minutes apart for almost an hour, but the Lamaze class told us to put off going to the hospital as long as possible. Do you think it's time?"

Some women take the time before the trip to the hospital to dress up for the main event. They wash their hair, shave their legs, paint their toenails, pluck their eyebrows—all in hopes that if the outside looks good, the inside will perform accordingly. If this gives you a lift, fine. But don't expect your hair spray to hold through transition.

"I broke my water at 7:00 and called my doctor," said Ilene. "He said, 'Come right over to the hospital.' I said, 'Can I take a shower?' He said no. I hung up the phone and looked at my husband. I was filthy; I'd been cleaning all day. He said, 'Take a shower.' So I washed, dried and set my hair, put on makeup, and dressed to look gorgeous. When we got to the hospital, my doctor said, 'You look gorgeous. What do you think you're here for? You're going to have a baby.' By the time I finished, I looked awful."

Never eat before going to the hospital. Vomiting is common during labor and is dangerous if for some reason you should require anesthesia. The body seems to want to clean itself out before giving birth. For this reason, the traditional hospital enemas are often redundant: many women seem to get severe diarrhea as soon as they go into labor. Others throw up.

"At lunch that day, everybody was urging me to eat," said Martha. "They said, 'You need your strength.' I didn't feel like eating, but I ate anyway. So I spat up all the way to the hospital, going over potholes on Fifty-ninth Street."

Of course, it's a fine idea to put off the trip to the hospital as long as possible. You will be much more comfortable at home—and much more distracted by a good movie. The longer you stay home, the less time you'll spend attached to an IV or a fetal monitor; the more time you'll have to walk around; the more chances you'll have to use your own toilet instead of a cold bedpan, and so on. But when you really think it's time to go, it's not the time to stand on ceremony. It's time to get in the car.

"My folks were supposed to come over and take care of my daughter," said Mary. "And you'd think they would have known that things were serious when I called at 6:00 in the morning. But I didn't want to scare my father. So I said to him, 'Well, I think I'll go to the hospital now. Why don't you come over? But don't kill yourself.' I didn't want him to have an accident on the highway. So, of course, he took his time. He took two hours to get here, and I was about to have the baby in the kitchen sink. Sometimes I'm really a schnook. If there was ever a situation when you should think about yourself, this is it. But here I was trying to be Mr. Nice Guy. By the time they got there, I tore out of the door. And I made it to the hospital just in time."

FALSE LABOR

You may get to the hospital just in time to be told to go home again. This is known as false labor. It always sounded singularly traumatic to me: the idea of going into labor, only to be told you aren't really in labor; of preparing for the arrival, only to be faced with a premature departure. But it's more likely to be embarrassing, amusing or matter-of-fact—depending on your own sense of the situation.

Lynn was embarrassed:

"Two days before the baby was born, I tooled up to the hospital and was all set to go. Then they examined me and sent me home. You just want to die. You've called your mother and your sister and your mother-in-law. Now you have to call them again and say it was all a big mistake. About forty-eight hours later, I started to get the contractions again. But now I was afraid to call the doctor. Finally I called him and said, 'I think it's for real.' And he said, 'Are you sure?' And we kept going back and forth like that for hours. Neither of us wanted to go through that again."

False labor is no reason to be embarrassed in front of your doctor or your relatives. It's certainly not a reason not to tell your doctor if you think you're in labor. Better to make the trip to the hospital twice than not make it at all. The easiest way to avoid calling your relatives twice is not to call them in the first place. Some of the best advice I got in Lamaze class was not to call anybody until you've already *had* the baby. Calling on the way to the hospital only results in delay (on your part), pacing (on theirs) and embarrassment (if you aren't really in labor). What your mother-in-law doesn't know can't disappoint her.

Sometimes *you* may know you're not in labor, but nervous relatives may force you to go to the hospital anyway.

Evelyn said, "My back hurt, so my mother said, 'Call the doctor, call the hospital.' I said, 'I'm not in labor.' But they kept bugging me to call. Five hours of this, and finally I called and packed my suitcase. I was laughing because my husband was running all the red lights, and I wasn't even in pain. But I thought, 'We're only going to get to do this once—let him enjoy it.' When we got to the hospital, the doctor said, 'You're in false labor.' I said, 'I thought so.' And we went back home.

"The next night, the pains started getting very close together and very strong, so I called him again. He said, 'Look, I really think you are imagining things. Just go back to sleep.' As soon as I hung up, I got the worst contraction in the world. After that, every one was like that. So I called him again and said, 'Look, this time I know I'm not imagining. If I have to stand this any longer, I'm going to go bananas.' And he said, 'Now I believe you.'"

False labor isn't a figment of your imagination. It may not be the real thing, but it is practice for the real thing. And it's those practice contractions that can get you dilated to two or three centimeters before you actually go into labor. During one of my last doctor visits, the nurse put her hand on my belly and said, "you're having a contraction." This news was both encouraging and discouraging. Encouraging because if labor was like this, I knew it would be a breeze. Discouraging because I had read over and over again that such "practice" or "Braxton-Hicks" contractions would give me an opportunity to practice my Lamaze training. But how was I to practice if I couldn't feel them? Try as I might, I couldn't tell when my uterus was contracting (hard and tight), and when it wasn't (relaxed). It felt hard as a rock all the time.

Some women feel false labor quite strongly—strongly enough to make them think it's the real thing. False labor is probably the truth behind the stories of three- and four-day labors that we hear so often from our mothers. On the other hand, a three-day labor wouldn't be allowed today. It would be terminated in cesarean section. (See Birth.)

False labor can also be real labor that comes to a halt when a women enters a hospital. Such cases of what one mother called her "sudden rigor mortis" are surprisingly common—not so surprising, I suppose, given the tension associated with hospitals in general. But there's something about walking into one that seems to stop even labor in its tracks. Childbirth-at-home advocates say that's one good reason to have your baby someplace else. Of course, it's not necessarily the hospital that stops your labor. It's your own (not insignificant) feelings and fears about hospitals. In some cases, it may even be simple coincidence: your false labor may suddenly happen to end just as your trip to the hospital begins.

The one sure way to tell false labor from true labor is that true labor invariably gets worse.

PREMATURE LABOR

Labor comes as more of a surprise when it comes early—especially as much as a month early. Babies born more than four weeks before they're due are termed "premature." And prematurity is one of the leading causes of infant death and disease. That's why you're likely to hear so much about cigarettes and junk food during pregnancy. Both smoking and nutrition are directly related to prematurity.

Approximately one in ten babies is born premature. Most of them wind up as well and healthy as their later-arriving counterparts. Still, don't be surprised if your hosptial tries to stop a premature labor—either with drugs or with that more common household drug, alcohol. Indeed, I remember Fritzie advising a hot bath and a stiff drink to take the sting off Braxton-Hicks contractions. (Those you can feel, that is.)

You should also be aware that premature labor usually precludes the use of pain medications. Because premature infants are more likely to have underdeveloped lungs, they can ill afford the depressant effects of most anesthetics.

Beyond that, though, there's little you can do and less to worry about. The good news is that you've just missed out on the last long month of pregnancy. The bad news is that you've also probably missed the last crucial four weeks of Lamaze training.

"About six weeks before I was due," said Carol, "we had a party for ten people and we were up cleaning until 3:00 A.M. Then I woke up around 6:00 A.M. the next morning, and I thought I had wet my bed. I thought I had had too much to drink. I thought, 'This is ridiculous, Carol. At your age!'

"Then I got out of bed and I knew that my water had broken. I woke up my husband and said, 'Honey, guess what?' And he said, 'No, it can't be, absolutely not.' But it obviously was. So we called the doctor, and he was as surprised as we were.

"Now the problem was, we had gone to only two Lamaze classes. We had the introductory stuff, but not one lesson on how to do it. So when we got to the hospital, my husband brought along one of the books, and he was reading to me and I was trying to guess what stage I was at. The doctors decided that they wanted the baby not to be born, if that were possible.

They wanted to put me on my back for the next six weeks, which was the worst thought in the world. They gave me a sedative, but it didn't work.

"It was very disconcerting that we hadn't been through the Lamaze. A woman was screaming in the other room, and I was unnerved by the noise. I thought, 'This is what it is really going to be like.' So we were watching the clock, looking at the minute hand going around, and we were counting, and my husband was reading from the book, and this woman was screaming and I had the monitor on, and they were trying to stop the labor, and meanwhile I was anticipating six weeks flat on my back.

"The pains were getting much more painful and coming much faster. The nurse said she didn't want to disturb anything or look and see if the baby was coming because they didn't want to cause an infection. But I knew I was going into another stage. I kept wishing I had gone to the classes. Finally the nurse came back, took one look, and said she could already see the baby coming out. So much for stopping the labor."

A LOT MORE THAN MENSTRUAL CRAMPS

What does labor feel like? That is the question. The only answer I have ever read in a book is "like strong menstrual cramps." Most mothers respond to that description with cynical smiles. Not only because it is misleadingly mild, but also because it is too specific, too localized, too detached. It lacks the grandeur of labor; it belittles the awesome power of that seldom-used monster muscle, your uterus; it is too meager to describe such a momentous event. As one mother put it, labor is a "total body pain." It has nothing in common with breaking an arm or getting your teeth pulled. It can be easier or harder, depending on your particular proclivities for pain. But it certainly is something else.

"What does labor feel like?" is truly a question that only a mother can answer. I'm not a particularly good candidate because I didn't have a particularly normal labor. I had induced labor, back labor, what turned out to be very unproductive labor that ended in cesarean section. Moreover, the mechanics of my labor were overshadowed in my mind by the hospital mileu. (More about that later.)

I do remember that the beginning seemed remarkably easy. The doctor broke my water with a long orange stick, and slowly, almost imperceptibly, I began to feel some dull aches in my lower abdomen. A nurse came in and told me I was doing great. I was feeling very proud. But I also knew I was cheating: it was easy to control contractions you could barely feel.

As the pain increased, my control deteriorated and my frustration mounted. A string of mostly strange doctors came in every few hours to report on my progress. I started at three centimeters, went down to two, up to five, down to three, up to seven, down to five—until nine hours later, when they finally decided to do a cesarean, the doctors still couldn't decide if I was at nine or seven. I understand, of course, that doctors differ in their interpretations, and also that the degree of dilation changes with the state of your contracting uterus. But somehow I had been led to expect steady, if slow, progress. I had not prepared to spend labor on a seesaw.

Labor itself was painful but not excruciating. I moaned (says my husband), but I didn't feel like screaming—except at the doctors. The clock on the wall moved like molasses. When the doctor said he'd be back in an hour, an hour seemed like an eternity, I remember literally trying to crawl out of the pain, out of my uterus, to leave it to do its thing while I went out for a cup of coffee, for a rest.

My biggest surprise was the nature of the contractions themselves. They were not at all what I had had in mind—much less what I had been practicing for these last three months. They did not, as far as I could tell, slowly crest and then subside like the neat diagrams in the books. They seemed instead to shoot up suddenly and stay there—for long minutes at a time. I remembered the advice that you could talk or joke with your husband or read or sleep between contractions; that you were really only in labor for a few hours if you subtracted the time you got in between contractions for rest. And I wondered why I wasn't getting a break. The pain started and didn't stop: there was no rest, no pit stop, no jokes, no time out at all.

And I wasn't the only one:

"I never experienced a predictable sequence of contractions," said Judy. "In that sense, Lamaze was unrealistic. I was not prepared for the unrelenting pain, the five-minute-long contractions, and the pain that did not go away in between. I thought, 'My God, this is not in the book!' How was I to pant for five minutes? I couldn't do it."

It can be much harder than advertised to tell when your contractions are coming and going—a major problem with the Lamaze technique. If you don't begin the Lamaze breathing at the beginning of the contraction, it's hard to make use of it at all. Many women suddenly find themselves in the middle of a painful contraction before they even know it's started. Perhaps the solution is to practice harder—to concentrate more—on the early contractions. Some women say they learn to ride out the contrations while they are in labor—and that therefore labor gets easier as it goes along—but it's hard to see how to practice much beforehand.

"I went through the entire process of birth thinking I was having thirty-second contractions, and that was my main problem," said Holly. "I could really see my stomach mound up fifteen seconds on either side of what I thought was the peak. And I wouldn't start the breathing until I felt it mound. But now I know I was wrong. It was starting to mound fifteen seconds before I realized it—and continuing to subside for fifteen seconds after I thought it was over. That's why I could never get on top of them, and also why I felt that continuous pain. Instead of starting from the beginning of the contraction and letting it build, I came in right in the middle."

Even if the sequence of contractions is fairly predictable, the intensity is almost always a surprise—especially if you've been hearing a lot about menstrual cramps. "It was like being run over by something," Susan said. "I couldn't even think where the pain was coming from. It's a pain that takes over your body. It has control over your body—this muscle or organ is going its own way. I remember I was on my hands and knees trying to crawl right off the bed. And they said, 'Where are you going?' And I said 'I don't know—it really hurts.' Six months after I gave birth, I broke my arm pretty severely. The doctor asked me if I wanted something for the pain. And I said, 'Pain? Are you kidding? I gave birth six months ago.'"

Even Laura, who had what she described as a "very good, very constructive" labor, was surprised by its force:

"There was a time when I got into active labor when I was really fighting against my urge to run around and scream bloody murder. I was thinking, 'My God! This is really something.

I can't go back. I'm stuck in the middle of this.' My husband says I was calm and cool through the whole thing, but in my head I was panicking. And I thought of what would have happened if I hadn't had Lamaze. It would have been a terrifying experience. I realized that I should have taken certain things in the course more seriously. There was a point where I remember thinking vividly: 'My God, this is really—you know—a lot more than menstrual cramps!' "

Other women I interviewed described labor variously as "a vise," "like taking a rubber lip and pulling it over your head," and like having am IUD put in: "I backed off the table when I had the first one. I almost fainted." Many women get depressed that they are dilating so slowly. Invariably, they think they are further along than they really are. Labor can feel like it's never going to end. That's when the strongest of us say, "Give me something. Take away the pain. Do anything. Do a cesarean. Get me out of this."

Still, labor isn't all bad news. Indeed, some women are surprised by the nice aspects of labor that they hadn't considered or expected. Some, I have to admit, even said they were surprised by its mildness; that it did really feel like menstrual cramps—"only ten times worse." This seemed to be true especially toward the beginning, but was sometimes true almost up to the end.

Moreover, if your labor goes according to the book, even the quality of the pain has its compensations. "It's not a searing constant pain. At least you have a chance to catch your breath," said Joan. "I think this is the part of labor that isn't emphasized. When the pain came, you knew it would eventually go away again. That you would have a few minutes of nonpain. When you're coming to the crest of the contraction, you know it's going to diminish, and psychologically that is a very strong factor in not making it seem so bad."

In addition to getting a breather from labor, you also get a baby. And a baby provides more motivation than a root canal or cap. If the effort is that much greater, so is the reward. Labor pains, like pregnancy, are for a purpose—a thought that certainly helps to take the sting off.

Indeed, sometimes I think I may be doing a disservice by writing about "pain" at all. It's certainly out of fashion. I do believe it's a far better thing to be prepared for labor, even if you're prepared for the worst. But being prepared is counterproductive if the only result is fear. Fear can keep you from doing all you can to minimize the pain you do feel. And you can do a lot. As one Lamaze book put it wisely, preparation can't take away the pain of labor, but it can take away the unnecessary pain. Better to be busy with your breathing than petrified with fear.

The question is: How much pain can you prepare for without getting petrified in the process?

"I never realized that the actual childbirth and labor would be so long and painful," said Melissa. "And I resented other women for not telling me. But now that it's in my past, I realize that emphasizing the pain to a pregnant woman is not the answer. Building up fear would do no good. It's hard, but it's bearable."

However, it's hard to escape the conclusion that it's better to be prepared than surprised. Better to be a little apprehensive before labor than to freeze with fright when it turns out to be more than you bargained for. Better that labor be a pleasant surprise than a rude shock. In fact, women who experience a lot more pain than they expect tend to come to one of two conclusions (or both): first, they may think, "I can't control this; if I didn't read about it in the book, I'm not prepared for it. I can't go through with it." In truth, some of the mothers who spoke most eloquently about the pain of labor had totally natural births—and were glad they did. Just because contractions are intense doesn't preclude an intensely satisfying experience. Pain is not always an indication to ask for anesthesia. On the contrary: the most harrowing tales of labor usually come from heavily sedated mothers.

Second, mothers may conclude that if the pain is unexpected, something must be wrong. Some women even fear that they—or their babies—are dying. They may become very afraid at the symptoms of what might be a very normal labor. The fear and tension produced only precipitate the pain that speaking in terms of "contractions" is supposed to avoid. To speak of a labor pain as a contraction is to give a more accurate description; it is not to say that it doesn't hurt.

Of course, pain of any kind is nearly impossible to describe—much less predict how it will pertain to another person. The perception of pain is always personal, always subjective, never taken out of context. How much "pain" does a ballerina happily endure, or a boxer, or even a sailor from the rope burns on his or her hands? Pain in the pursuit of pleasure becomes secondary, maybe even imperceptible. It is said that labor requires the energy (and perhaps the pain) of a twelve-mile hike. Both, I think, can offer ample rewards.

TRANSITION, BACK LABOR, INDUCED LABOR AND OTHER PITFALLS TO PREPARE FOR

For a good four hours, I was trembling uncontrollably, sweating profusely, vomiting, and experiencing totally erratic, almost continuous, contractions. These are the traditional signs of transition. The only trouble is that they traditionally last for a few minutes to an hour.

Uncontrollable trembling—"the shakes"—is common both during labor and after. It is not, as one nurse told one mother, a matter of nerves. It is your body's response to the shock of what's happening to it. Therefore there's no reason to be afraid, or to apologize. Even in the operating room, as the doctors were delivering my baby by cesarean, I was shivering like crazy. Teeth chattering. Hands out of control. Unable to stop. And all the while I was apologizing. I still don't know why. But almost every woman I know who got tremors during labor felt that she had to say she was sorry.

Of course, it's highly unlikely that I or anyone else was in transition for four hours. I may not have been in transition at all. I did, however, have back labor—which may have accounted for some of the symptoms. Back labor is that often-feared but seldom-described labor that comes from a baby in a posterior presentation. The labor nurses call this brand of baby "sunny-side up." Instead of emerging nose to your backside, he comes out facing up—with his bony skull pressing all the while against your spine. Back labor seems much more difficult to control than normal labor. Whether the contractions are more intense or more erratic or just different, they do seem to be harder to ride out. More like a bucking bronco than an ocean wave.

The best remedy for back labor is a hot or cold compress—or both. We brought an ice pack, but found that we needed two: one for my back, and one to keep in the hospital freezer, at the ready. (Fortunately, the hospital was better prepared than we were.) Other women have reported getting relief from the pressure of tennis balls on the small of their backs, or of their husband's fists. We brought the tennis balls, but never figured out how to use them. Besides, I wouldn't let them take away the ice pack long enough to try.

A final circumstance of labor that can throw a curve into the best-laid plans is induced labor. One obstetrician wrote that induced labor is good for natural childbirth because it makes labor shorter. It is far more accurate to say that it telescopes labor—making it shorter, yes, but also much harder and without the slow buildup that allows you to practice riding the contractions. I've also heard proponents of induced labor say that parents who plan their deliveries in advance can be "well rested" for the event. My experience was to the contrary. Indeed, most mothers with a birth to look forward to the next morning are unlikely to get much sleep the night before. They are far more likely to be "rested" if they wake up spontaneously in a wet bed. And fatigue is a handicap you don't need.

Be that as it may, lack of sleep is the least of the problems associated with induced labor. Years ago, it was commonplace to induce babies so that they would be born on Aunt Minnie's birthday or when Daddy had a week off or the day before the doctor was going on vacation. Today, obstetrical circles have officially frowned on the practice of "elective" induction—that is, of inducing a baby for a nonmedical reason. If your baby is three or four weeks overdue, then that might be a medical reason. If it's one week overdue, it might not.

What's wrong with induction? First, the baby might not be ready to be born, in which case he or she might develop a life-threatening lung disease. Prematurity and induced labor often go hand in hand. Second, the drugs used to induce labor can be extremely potent. If your cervix isn't ready to dilate, the contractions only serve to pound the baby's head against the hard muscle. The result can be brain damage or worse. Indeed, many obstetricians even oppose artificially "breaking the water" to induce labor because they say the amniotic sac protects the baby's head during labor.

Even if your labor isn't induced and your contractions begin spontaneously, your labor may be "stimulated" at some point—either by breaking the water or by administering an oxytocin. An oxytocin is a hormone (real or synthetic) that stimulates uterine contractions (and milk flow). The most common oxytocin is pitocin. Some obstetricians estimate that it may be used to speed up labor up to 60 per cent of the time. Some hospitals administer it routinely. It drips into your arm along with the "sugar water" in your IV. You may or may not be able to do anything about this, but you should at least know about it. It can seriously affect the course of your labor.

In short, stimulated and induced labor is faster, stronger, and harder to control than natural labor. My four-hour "transition" was as likely the result of induction as of a baby too big to come out. Mothers who are administered pitocin almost immediately experience more pressure, longer contractions, and less time between contractions.

There are many medical situations which may warrant stimulation of labor to save you or your baby. There are also many nonmedical situations. Either way, if you are prepared for the effects on your contractions, you will be much better able to deal with them. If you aren't, you might wind up very unhappy with your doctor—and possibly with yourself.

Marilyn had induced labor when her spontaneous labor stopped:

"I got to the hospital, and my labor stopped entirely," she said. "So they stuck the pitocin in my arm. I wish I had known that it would increase the intensity of the contractions. The doctor knew that I wanted to have natural childbirth. He should at least have said to me: 'You're going to have a shorter and harder labor.' But they never do. And I felt the greatest sense of failure because I asked for anesthesia."

You should also know that induced labor doesn't always work. Just as drugs can't always stop labor once it's started, they aren't always successful in bringing out a baby who isn't ready to be born. Cathy was two weeks overdue when her doctor tried to induce her reluctant child: "I got these mild kind of contractions, and I kind of practiced a little bit, and it did not work. The doctor came in to tell me that I had to go home. He was very embarrassed. He said, 'I hate to tell you this, but it isn't working.' And I said, 'You're telling me?'"

ALONE

"I didn't know where anybody was, you know. I had no doctor. My husband wasn't there. I was in severe pain, and nobody was saying anything to me. I was becoming crazy. Even if the man who mopped the floor had been there to talk to me, it would have been better. I had this ripping pain in my back, and I was sure that something was wrong. But nobody was helping me. It was terrifying."

With all the talk of Lamaze and husband-coached childbirth, a distressing number of women are still alone during labor. Distressing for me, more distressing for them. Women may vary widely as to how they want to cope with labor: awake or asleep, medicated or "natural," prepared or head-in-the-sand. But nobody wants to be alone. Solitude may be the most painful part of labor. And it's totally unnecessary.

Most hospitals today allow husbands at least in the labor room. But the conditions vary, and you should be aware of them. For example, your husband may be required to attend Lamaze classes, or he may have to leave if you require medication. You may not think you want your husband with you now, or he may think he doesn't want to go. But it's foolish to limit your opportunities later by not taking a few classes now. This way, you can change your mind if you want to later. And you probably will.

It is most unfortunate that husbands are so often banned in the presence of anesthesia. That's precisely when you may need them most. You are even less in control, less aware, less able to fend for yourself. More than ever you need somebody to fend for you. Even if your husband isn't the fending type, his mere presence will be a comfort to you. If only subconsciously, you will know that someone is looking out for you and your baby when you can't really look out for yourself. And if you should need help—or a lollipop—he'll be there to give it to you. Husbands are the greatest innovation in childbirth since maternity boutiques.

At the time, of course, you may not feel that your need for your husband is as great as your need for medication: Jill said, "By the time the doctor got there, I was in such agony that I was yelling at him, 'Give me something for this pain, goddammit.' And he was yelling back at me, 'If I give you something for the pain, your husband can't come in.' And I said, 'My husband can go to the moon. I want something for the pain. That's all I care about.'"

Some husbands refuse to participate in labor—even as spectators. Usually, a Lamaze class or two is enough to convince even the most stubborn holdouts. For hundreds of years, fathers have been left out of childbirth—so it's not surprising that they should feel left out, perhaps permanently. When they come to see that their role is more than superficial and that birthing isn't necessarily the horror they had heard it was, they're likely to at least test the waters. And of those who try it, most like it.

If your husband still feels strongly that labor is woman's work, don't resign yourself to muddling through alone. Bring a friend, bring your mother, hire a midwife. Labor nurses can be great when they're around, but they aren't always available; so be prepared to bring somebody who has no other job than to look out for you. First, check to see what or whom your hospital allows. If it doesn't allow you to bring anybody, find a hospital that does.

LONG LABOR

Being in labor for a long time is bad enough in itself. To complicate matters, long labors tend to come with their own set of extenuating circumstances. Some of these conditions are the causes of long labors; others are the results. None is particularly serious, and all are relatively common. The less that comes as a surprise to you; the more you will be prepared to cope with in your own eleventh hour:

Hyperventilation: The Lamaze bag has a reason. If you hyperventilate from doing your breathing either incorrectly or over a prolonged period of time, you can breathe into the bag to restore the proper oxygen balance in your blood. If that doesn't do it, a little something to relax you might be required:

"I had a long labor with my second child and I began to hyperventilate," said Anne. "That means, with the breathing techniques, you let in too much oxygen, and you begin to get numb. Up to that point I had not had any medication. But I was afraid that when it came time for pushing, I might be numb all the way up, so I began to get a little bit alarmed. I blew into the bag, but it didn't help much. So the nurse said she'd just give me one little shot to relax me. And I said, 'Okay, but I worked so hard I don't want to be knocked out.' And she worked with me and everything worked out fine. I just needed to relax a little bit."

Fatigue: If normal labor is a twelve-mile hike, abnormally long labor is hiking down and up the Grand Canyon in a single day. It's not only hard work, it's tiring. Indeed, after twelve hours or so of active labor, many women find that it isn't the pain that gets them down, but the fatigue. That's one reason that practicing Lamaze breathing techniques is so important. It takes energy both to concentrate on the breathing and to execute it. It's much easier when you've got the panting down pat.

Fatigue is a frustrating liability. If you've worked well for many hours to see the birth of your child, it's especially difficult to throw in the towel—or washcloth, as the case may be—at what might be the very end. The best antidote for fatigue is a tireless husband or labor nurse who substitutes his or her own energy when yours starts to fail. Even then, fatigue may take you out of the game before you reach your goal.

Cathy said, "We went through Lamaze because my husband wanted to be part of it, and also because I wanted to see my baby being born. I could handle the pain. It was excruciating, but the desire to see the baby born was overwhelming. The problem was that I had been up until 4:30 A.M. the night before. I was exhausted. The breathing exercises that I learned were very, very helpful. They made the contractions milder. But I was out of breath. I couldn't do them anymore. I was pooped. So I asked the doctor, how long do you think it will be? I was dilated seven centimeters. And he said it could be anywhere from ten minutes to two hours. So I figured I'd wait. Then— it seemed like two hours but it must have been five minutes— I said, 'Just put me out.' I woke up in the recovery room. They put me out at 2:30 and I had the baby at 4:04. But as much as I wanted to see that baby born, I couldn't have held out."

Anesthesia: Pain medication can be both a cause and an effect of prolonged labor. So when labor gets to be too much for you to take, remember that taking the medication may mean taking the pain for that much longer.

"I was in labor for twenty-six hours," said Vicki. "At first it was so easy that I thought, 'Wow! If this is labor, what are all these women complaining about?' They kept telling me I'd deliver before midnight, but it went on and on. They kept giving me Demerol, and I cried all night long. The baby wasn't born until late the next day. And all the while I was crying and getting more Demerol. I know that every nurse in the place must have hated me."

Would Vicki's labor have been short and sweet without so much Demerol? It's impossible to say. But it's *probable* that the labor would have been much shorter, and possible that if she'd been more in control, she would have experienced less pain. Medication can make it harder to control contractions; it can increase the pain and lead to the need for more medication. All the while, the medication might be slowing down the labor, requiring a drug like pitocin to speed it up again—which increases the pain even more. A vicious circle can be set up in which more pain medication simply leads to more pain. Sometimes pain medication can take the edge off a long labor; other times, the medication can create the long labor in the first place. (See Anesthesia.)

Disproportion: Disproportion occurs when babies and mothers are wrong for each other-fitwise. For whatever reason, the baby's bony skull can't make it through the bones of your pelvis. One or both of you may be the wrong shape, or the wrong size. Posterior and breech babies need more room than others; and disproportion during a pregnancy that produces a ten-pound baby won't necessarily be repeated if the second child is a more manageable size.

If you have a long labor and your doctors suspect disproportion as the cause, you might be wheeled down to X-ray for a pelvic series. Indeed, you may have had your pelvic series weeks before the birth—if the doctor suspected a breech birth or a too-large baby, or if the baby was late and hadn't engaged.

I was especially pleased with the results of my pelvic series, taken several weeks before the day of induction. My doctor said I had plenty of room despite the baby's posterior presentation; he said the chances of my having a cesarean were practically nil. When it came time to do the cesarean, he whisked my husband down the hall to have a look at the X-rays. "As you can see, there is very little room. It was an iffy proposition all along." So much for the interpretation of X-rays.

Many, many mothers have X-rays taken during labor to check for possible disproportion. Most of them deliver their babies vaginally. So don't regard the trip to the X-ray room as a sentence to cesarean. It may even save you from an unnecessary cesarean.

GOODIE BAGS AND OTHER SOURCES
OF AMUSEMENT DURING LABOR

Everybody should bring a Lamaze goodie bag to the hospital, if only because they are so much fun to pack. The basic ingredients are champagne, washcloths, breath spray, lemons, lollipops, tennis balls, ice packs, sandwiches for "the coach" (your husband), and whatever other security blankets you may want to bring along. You also need a "spot" picture or object to focus on during your breathing. I couldn't decide between a pair of booties (for motivation) or a red rose from the garden. We wound up bringing both, but I don't remember using either. Some women never forget: "I'll keep that image of that purple and orange and yellow flower as long as I live," said one mother. Another brought a small mobile: "Ironically, it was the same mobile that we hung in the baby's room. So every time I go in there, I'm reminded of my labor."

During my cesarean, I remember asking my doctor when I could have my champagne. He obviously thought I needed my head examined along with my uterus. But how was I to know that I wouldn't be able to eat or drink for days after major surgery? And I had so been looking forward to that celebratory drink! That and a Big Mac and a milkshake.

Don't expect to use everything you bring in your bag, even if you don't have a cesarean. The highest praise goes for lip balm and breath spray (and ice packs if you have back labor). Lollipops may bring you relief or heartburn, and sour ones are recommended over the sweet types. But be aware that your hospital may not allow you to have either.

Among the items you will most probably *not* need are cards, books, games, and knitting. "They say in Lamaze to bring a book so you won't get bored," said Mary. "Afterwards I thought, 'You have to be kidding!' It cracked me up. I remembered how they told us that in between contractions you would doze off or play cards with your husband. Oh, brother! Hell's fire and damnation! There was no way in the world that I could ever forget about the next contraction or the last one and doze off. No such animal. I brought a deck of cards. That was funny. I broke out in a sweat. I was shivering like crazy. And we were supposed to be playing honeymoon bridge?"

COMPORTMENT DURING LABOR

A labor bed is no place to worry about proper etiquette. One doctor pointed out that a laboring woman may become "very cross and ill-tempered, shrewish and cantankerous." I don't wonder. Who wouldn't become ill-tempered during transition? One woman I know threw a lemon at her husband.

"It was a pretty good shot," she said. "He reached out to touch my hand. He was urging me to relax or something. And I screamed, 'Don't touch me.' But he did. So I threw the lemon."

Lamaze classes tell you to expect this sort of behavior. They tell the husbands not to walk out just because their wives tell them to get lost. But I feared deep down inside that mine would do precisely that. Fortunately, I didn't tell him to, and he didn't.

Some women are stoics during labor. Others are screamers. If screaming makes you feel better, go ahead. But it probably won't. Screaming takes energy away from the more important business of controlling your contractions. Mothers who are medicated and/or alone are likely to scream most of all. Sometimes they aren't even aware of what's happening:

"My first labor was totally under the influence of drugs, so I really didn't feel anything," said Gene. "I can remember hearing this ungodly shrill scream and then realizing it was me, and hearing somebody say, 'Give her more gas.' Something was registering that it hurt, and something was coming out of my mouth. And that scared the daylights out of me."

I once read in a book that "vanity and modesty are instinctively shed by the woman in labor." I think this is wishful thinking on the part of some doctors. The truth is that vanity and modesty are *impossible* during labor. But that doesn't mean they are forgotten. Stoics or screamers, women *do* care about how they act during labor and about how others perceive them. Considering what they go through, I think most of them hang onto as much etiquette as does anybody taking a twelve-mile hike. And hikers, as a whole, are celebrated for their courtesy.

BLESSED FORGETFULNESS

Thirty years ago, the most popular way to go through labor was in "twilight sleep," which meant you experienced all the pain but forgot about it. Most women go through modified twilight sleep today—even with natural childbirth. Labor seems to be as easily forgotten as yesterday's mail. This is indeed fortunate for young children who want brothers and sisters. Only when the end of the second pregnancy draws near do mothers seem to remember the perils of the first:

"I put it out of my mind entirely until the next time I was in the labor room," Maureen said. "Then I thought, 'Oh my God, here I am again. Why did I do this? Why didn't I learn the first time?'"

Of course, the reason women go through labor a second time is to have a second baby. When labor comes again, so does the stork. In the end, it's the fruits of our labors that make us forget how difficult they were in the first place:

"It was awful when it happened, but right afterwards you forget because it brings you so much happiness," said Vicki. "I'll never forget when the nurse first showed him to me— before I could even touch him or nurse him or anything. You can't even begin to compare the pain to that kind of happiness."

In the end, you will survive labor, and you may even learn to like it. One mother stashed away the time sheets she and her husband kept while clocking her contractions, and looks at them from time to time with fond memories: "We giggled a lot when we did these. I guess I was lucky, but everything just worked out perfectly. Even labor."

If you don't get through labor with happy memories, at least you will have your war stories to compare with other mothers. If boot camp separates the men from the boys, labor separates the girls from the mothers. Years later, you'll still be comparing pains and hours, doctors and hospitals. Half the fun of labor is telling about it when it's over—even if you do exaggerate a bit.

Labor is the end of pregnancy and the beginning of birth. It's the part of having a baby that almost everyone fears, but also looks forward to. Like yourself, it is unpredictable, sensitive to many factors, and works best in the company of those you love. So hope for the best, expect the worst, prepare for everything, and remember that almost anything that happens during labor is "normal."

Birth:

An Act of Creation

Birth is what it's all about. For the past nine months, you've nurtured an embryo, then a fetus, who is now a baby, ready to be born. For the past two or twenty hours, you've labored with contractions designed to open up your body, to let the rascal out. Now it's time for that magic moment when you become the two of you. When a pregnant woman metamorphoses into a mother. When Baby Whosis becomes Sam or Sally or Betty Lou.

No matter how many children a woman has, birth never ceases to be a surprise. A miracle, new every time. No matter how many labors, how many pregnancies, how many moments of birth, we still wind up asking: How did it happen? A minute ago I was me, and now I'm me plus somebody else. A minute ago, this person wasn't in the world, and now he or she is. A minute ago, I had a fetus inside, and now I have a baby outside—a brand-new person, somebody I need to get to know.

I had fantasied introducing myself to my baby as soon as it was born: "Hello there, I'm Mommie. Who are you?" To which it would reply (somewhat sleepily): "I'm Sylvester (or Mary), and I like dolls and baseball and playing the violin."

Birth is what makes the baby. You are a mother from the moment of conception, but a baby isn't a baby until it's born. And from the way some of them go about getting born, you'd think they wanted to stay right where they are. Others seem so anxious that they practically break in the door.

My own baby was yanked into the world by cesarean section, so I did not experience birth as I had learned it in Lamaze. But I did at least have a chance to say a brief hello.

We, or rather I, was separated somewhat below the neck by blue surgical draperies. I could not see the birth, but I could hear the strange deep-throated gurgle of a visitor arriving from another world. I could hear the doctor exclaim about his big shoulders—and later wait anxiously to learn his weight, as if he were an angler who had just landed a prize fish. I caught only a glimpse of that puzzled prune face before it was whisked off to be bathed and swathed in sterile sheets. But it was a look that would last me a lifetime. Cesarean or not, I wouldn't have missed it for the world.

PUSHING AND BLOWING

Birth à la Lamaze is different. I was merely a spectator; Lamaze mothers learn to participate, to push their babies out. I had looked forward to that moment when the passive pain of labor turned into the productive "urge to push." I practiced lying on the floor with my feet in the air, sucking in my breath and pushing for all I was worth. I also practiced blowing in short, hard puffs—the Lamaze strategy for holding off the "urge to push" until the time (and you) are ripe—until the cervix is fully dilated, open and ready for delivery. I blew myself blue in the face, but to no avail. I never felt the urge to push or the need to stop it.

Pushing is usually promoted as the good part of labor. Not only an overwhelming urge, but also a great relief. Now that the waiting is over, the work can begin. At last you can actively contribute, cooperate, even control. No longer do you merely "ride out" contractions, letting your uterus boss you around. Now it's time to take the reins and push together with the natural needs of your body, time to match the strength of your pushing with the strength of your contractions to make it the last mile to motherhood.

Many women positively revel in pushing:

"That was the beginning of the beautiful part. I was in the middle of a contraction, doing my Lamaze. It hurt, but I was semi-resigned to it. And all of a sudden, without any warning, I heard myself grunt and push as hard as I could. And the nurse yelled, 'Don't do that—you could hurt the baby's head!' But there was nothing I could do to stop it. It was absolutely marvelous. And the thing that was most glorious about it was that the minute I started to push, not only did all the pain go away, but there was absolutely no discomfort whatsoever. Nothing. All the pain—even the mildest twitch—completely disappeared. All the way to birth.

"The nurses were concerned that I was pushing too soon, but then my doctor came in and said that I was more than ready. He took one look at me, grabbed my foot, and said 'Go!' And I'd push, and he'd pull the other foot, and I'd push again. And it was beautiful. They wheeled me into the delivery room and painted me with iodine, which looked so strange. I had my legs up in stirrups with all these funny things draped over them. I had brought a big pillow with me—a big wedge— and it was a great help, so that when I fell back, I didn't fall back flat. But the pushing urge was so strong. I really felt elemental. I mean it felt beautiful when I was pushing—the urge was really glorious. And the noise you make! That bearing down growling animal-like noise. I loved it. And my husband laughed right out loud."

The most consistent complaint about pushing and blowing is how difficult it is *not* to push. When the urge overtakes you, it is apparently overwhelming. Especially when the end is so near:

"They were wheeling me down the hall, and I was yelling, 'I have to push; I have to push.' And my husband was blowing in my face, telling me to blow, too. The doctor was snapping at the nurses because I wasn't painted and draped. And I was trying not to push. But it was coming so fast that I was pushing from flat on my back. I couldn't even get up because I had to push so hard. In the classes, they tell you just to blow until the doctor tells you to push. Well, try blowing. It's almost impossible. There was almost no way I could keep from pushing."

Blowing is a great improvement over the old-fashioned way of keeping the baby from birthing until the doctor came—namely, crossing the mother's legs. And it does seem to work—given enough practice and willpower. Why bother to blow? First, because if you aren't fully dilated, it may be bad for the baby to try to push his head through the too-small opening. Second, because it might be bad for you. The more the baby's head has a chance to mold and the more your tissues have a chance to stretch, the less likely you'll be to tear. Most doctors in this country perform episiotomies (small incisions) to prevent vaginal tears. But natural-childbirth advocates say that we wouldn't need incisions if we learned how to "ease" the baby out.

One of the ironies of anesthetized childbirth is that the pain-killing often doesn't really begin until the pain is almost over. Many women decide to have spinal anesthesia for the final hours of pushing only to find that labor was the hard part—that pushing can be a relief. They work all through the preliminaries only to be absent for the main event. They labor without their just reward. The part they dread—the birth—turns out to be the easiest.

Still, pushing, like the first stages of labor, is often more than it's cracked up to be. Women who expect some kind of passive pain relief are in for a big surprise. Pushing can be positive, but it's also very strong. Participating is rewarding, but also demanding. Pushing out a baby takes a great deal of effort over several hours. Nobody ever said labor wasn't a lot of work.

Women who aren't prepared for the power of pushing can be overwhelmed, and sometimes terrified—especially if they've been anesthetized for delivery before. Most drugs designed to kill pain also eliminate the sensation of pushing. You push not on the basis of an urge, but on doctor's orders. After that kind of experience, the demands of your own body can seem strange and scary:

"With my first two children, I had a caudal (a spinal-type anesthesia), so the doctor had to tell me when to bear down. I would say, 'Do you mean like going to the bathroom?' And he would say yes. And I'd say, 'Oh, good. I'm good at that because I'm always constipated.' And I was good at that kind of pushing. But this time, it was the weirdest feeling. All of a sudden, when you're ready, your body automatically pushes down. You felt like you had to shit a watermelon. Nobody was with me, so I started grunting and pushing and the nurse came in and said, 'What are you doing?' And I thought I was being so good. I wasn't yelling and screaming. But I was scared, I thought something was wrong. I could feel it coming down. It felt like a volcano. It was painful and very hard to take. It was like the push wouldn't end, and what was supposed to come out wouldn't come out. And I dreaded the next push. It was a very weird sensation. I was scared stiff."

Like everything else in labor, your reaction to pushing will depend on where—or what—you're coming from. If your first-stage contractions are mild or you are anesthetized, pushing may come as a rude shock. But if your contractions are hard and painful, pushing is more likely to signal relief.

BIRTHING

Birthing a baby requires that a rather large object—the baby—pass through a rather small opening—your vagina. Of course, the baby's head molds to fit the space, and the tissues of your vagina stretch to accommodate him, but the passage can still be uncomfortably tight. For all the women who said they were surprised at how "easy" birth was compared to labor, there were almost as many who found it surprisingly hard. Mothers often said they felt like they were being "torn apart" or "ripped open" or "like your whole insides are trying to come out." This is more likely to happen if the birth is especially fast or the baby especially large. One mother said she thought she paid for her two-hour labor with a particularly painful birth: "I knew that he was going to rip me to pieces, so I tried to slow things down. I felt that the head was huge, the opening was tiny, and behind it was this big thing. And he wanted out and I knew it. It was like a big trap and I had no choice—he had to come out. The pressure to birth him was enormous. But in the end, I think he birthed himself."

Strangely, birthing mothers are often so preoccupied with pain or pushing that thoughts of the new baby are temporarily set aside. Who can look in the mirror when your eyes are shut in an effort to bear down? Who cares if it's a boy or a girl when birth itself requires your total concentration?

Many women wind up licking their wounds after delivery

instead of looking after the new born. Even without fear or pain, childbirth can be exhausting. The new mother may want to collapse instead of cuddle. As a consequence, she may feel guilty. But just because you don't feel like celebrating doesn't mean you'll make a bad mother. It may simply mean you're pooped.

"I had been looking forward to this as a big spiritual experience, and all through my pregnancy whenever I would think of the minute of birth I would absolutely cry, just thinking how fantastic it would be. But when I gave birth I thought I must be an awful person inside. Because I have to confess that I couldn't care less whether she was dead, alive or what sex she was. All I knew was that she was out of me and that's all I cared about.

"When she started to come out, I heard these funny noises, and I thought it was me. But it was her. As soon as her little nose cleared me she started to breathe, and the funny noises that I heard were her taking her first breaths even before the head was out. And then, when she got out altogether, she was completely purple. She looked like a purple rubber doll and she looked like she was dead—not that I gave a shit at that point. And then she did this bursting-forth-like-a-flower business. She gave this tremendous kick, and she was so slippery that she slipped right out of the doctor's hands, and he had to catch her again.

"I made a big deal when I was pregnant about asking the doctor if I could nurse on the delivery table. And I couldn't have cared less. And I thought it was nice that he didn't make a big deal about it."

Technically, birth is only the second stage of labor. The third and final stage is the delivery of the placenta, which generally is accomplished in the next one or two contractions. The contractions may be stimulated synthetically with injected or intravenous oxytocins, or naturally by the hormones you produce when you nurse your baby. Or a nurse may push on your abdomen to push the placenta (and sometimes the baby) out. If the placenta should tear, it may have to be delivered manually. In this case, the afterbirth may be more painful than the birth. Several mothers who delivered too quickly to make use of their Lamaze breathing found it a godsend when delivering a torn placenta.

In more ways than one, labor, birth, and afterbirth are part of the same process. Certain symptoms such as tremors or chills may appear during any one or all three. Even uterine contractions stay around long after labor is over. Indeed, you may feel them for months to come—especially if you're nursing.

Birth has its own special afterglow—or depression, as the case may be. (See Postpartum.) The aftermath depends largely on the birth itself. Even when it doesn't matter medically how your baby is born, it may matter a great deal emotionally. That's why natural-childbirth mothers tend to be so cocky after birth, floating around on their own natural high. And why some other mothers sometimes feel disappointed, depressed, or downright bitter—especially mothers who had counted on natural childbirth and got knocked out (voluntarily or otherwise) or were delivered by cesarean.

Barbara was given a general anesthetic—against her will— just minutes before her baby was born. "When I woke up in the delivery room, I was hopping mad. I was awake for two hours and nobody came. I felt so weak, and I was too dazed to call out. Finally the doctor came up and told me I had a girl. And all I could think was, 'Boy, I really screwed this up. I disappointed my husband because he wanted a boy, and because he wanted to be there for the birth, and he lost out on both.' And I had the most bizarre, the most traumatic experiences and feelings for months afterwards. I'm not the kind to get shook up easily, but I was extremely upset about it. I couldn't wait to get pregnant again so that I could have another baby and do it the right way."

I, too, felt bitter, disappointed, and cheated after my cesarean. It was hard to listen to the natural-childbirth mothers recount the joys of being there at the moment of birth. In a way, it still is. And in a way I'd like to have another baby just to share in that special experience I've been hearing so much about.

Of course, it's unrealistic to expect that every mother can, or wants to, or should participate in her baby's birth. In fact, the number of women who do deliver naturally is extremely small—probably less than 5 per cent. If we expect birth always to be just like it is in the (Lamaze) movies, some of us are bound to be disappointed. But there's nothing wrong in knowing how wonderful birth *can* be—and working toward that goal.

What's so great about natural childbirth? Mothers who experience it say it is perhaps the most profound moment of a lifetime. To be present at the creation of a new person, your child. To witness life spring from life. To watch the dime-sized opening between your legs reveal a patch of matted hair, then a quarter's worth, until the head finally crowns. From then on it's pure science-fiction—and for the moment you are a two-headed mother/woman. Seconds later, pop goes the baby. A new person has arrived in the world. (Hello!)

"The thing I most remember is the shock of a real live person springing forth from between my thighs. The overwhelming and surprising surge of motherly love. I can't imagine doing it any other way. The actual deliveries both times were probably the most exciting and elevating experiences of my marriage. It had to be one of the nicest experiences we've ever shared. And afterwards, I felt so accomplished. If I'd sedated myself, it might not have been such a high."

"The nurse told me the head was coming, and that I could watch in the mirror. But I said, 'No, no, I'm busy.' I kind of started to look up, and from that moment on it was incredible. And what was most incredible to me was that if you have a normal delivery, the doctor doesn't do anything. I mean it's all there—the baby just does everything. Nature is just taking care of everything so beautifully. To this day I can't watch a natural childbirth without going through the whole emotional experience myself, and crying because it's such a celebration. I don't think I've ever experienced anything that put me so in touch with life."

This is birth at its best. In between the best and the worst are the mixtures of highs and lows, ups and downs, that characterize most deliveries. Among the factors that may influence your delivery are a host of hospital procedures—including IVs, fetal monitors, forceps, and the curious probings of medical students. Anesthetics and analgesics may help or hurt. Your husband or your doctor play pivotal roles. All these variables are discussed in the following chapters.

One kind of birth possibility that bothers almost everyone is a breech. There's something intriguing and also a bit worrisome about a baby who decides to come out feet first. Indeed, breech births do involve risks to the fetus—although not generally to the mother. In a normal headfirst delivery, the baby's largest part—the head—molds gradually to fit through the pelvic bones. In a breech, the largest part comes last—with no chance to accommodate the head to the small passage. Therefore there's a greater risk that the head won't fit—and that's not the sort of thing you want to find out at the last minute.

If there's any chance of disproportion, a cesarean is done before labor begins. Indeed, today cesareans are done almost routinely in cases of breech birth—and some medical schools aren't even teaching the technique of birthing breech babies naturally. One obstetrician told me: "In the old days, you'd be proud to deliver a breech baby. Today, if there's even the slightest irregularity, everybody wonders why you didn't do a cesarean."

A vaginal breech birth generally means natural childbirth—whether you like it or not. It's another good reason to be prepared:

"My second labor made my first one look easy because it was a breech birth. His head was down until an hour before delivery. Then he turned at the last minute. The nurse came in to examine me and said, 'I feel feet!' Up until then, I had counted on getting an epidural. I didn't take childbirth classes or anything. But being a breech, they don't like to give you any kind of drugs. They need your breathing and your pushing and your relating to the doctor to get the baby out properly. I was in a state of shock. It was such a surprise when the doctor said I couldn't have any medication. He wanted me to do the whole job. But he gave me a lot of confidence; he was very supportive. Then he raced off—he didn't realize everything was going to happen so fast. So he came back and we raced down to the delivery room. Everything was so exciting and so fantastic, it's really very hard for anybody to describe what that experience is all about."

Breech babies also tend to get wrapped up in their umbilical cords, cutting off their oxygen supply. This is another reason to avoid anesthesia, and also another frequent indication for cesarean: "I went in and the membranes had ruptured and labor didn't start. We knew that she was a breech. And the doctor knew how much I wanted to have natural childbirth, so he tried to mildly induce. But at the slightest contraction, her heart rate jumped way up and then down again. So they knew there was fetal distress. They went right in and got her. The cord was around her neck twice, so she couldn't have made it through labor anyway."

CESAREAN BIRTH

Cesareans are increasingly the answer to every obstetrical problem from breeches to long labors. Indeed, the national cesarean section rate has more than quadrupled in the last ten years—with many hospitals averaging rates as high as 25 per cent.

I can still remember when Fritzie told our Lamaze class that four of us (out of twenty) would deliver by cesarean. Nobody else seemed particularly surprised, but my husband and I were shocked. Indeed, when I first started writing stories on the rising cesarean rate, most nonmedical people were inclined not to believe me. ("Oh, you must be talking about forceps deliveries," they'd say.) Since that time, the "section" rate has continued to rise—precipitously.

Why so many cesareans? The reasons are as controversial as they are complex. On the positive side, cesareans are more common because they are safer than ever before. Anesthesia is better; scars are smaller; recovery is faster. On the negative side, cesareans are overused and abused. In some hospitals, during some months the rates climb as high as 35 or 45 per cent. A classic case of defensive medicine, cesareans are an "easy out" used to prevent the possibility of fetal brain damage and also of malpractice suits. (Or, as one doctor told me, "If the child doesn't excel in nursery school, the parents can't come back and sue you for not doing a cesarean." Some obstetricians say that even normal labor can be dangerous for a baby because it pounds the head against the not-fully-dilated cervix.)

Traditionally, of course, a cesarean section was an emergency measure. Today it is almost routine. The most common indications include disproportion (and long labors which may be the result of disproportion); medical complications (such as premature separation of the placenta, which can deprive the baby of oxygen); maternal indications (such as diabetes, high blood pressure, previous cesarean, or even old age); ruptured membranes (if your water breaks and labor doesn't begin in twenty-four hours, some doctors fear that infection might set in); breech and transverse (sideways) presentations, and fetal distress.

"Fetal distress" applies to almost anything that could endanger a baby. In the old days (five or ten years ago), a nurse monitored the baby's condition by listening to his heart with a fetuscope; today, electronic fetal monitors do much the same thing—without, of course, the bedside manners. Monitors can save lives. But they are also easy to misinterpret. And the misinterpretation of fetal monitors—perhaps more than anything else—has led to the rapidly increasing cesarean rate.

Are so many cesareans good or bad? If you have a cesarean because you need one to save your baby, of course it's good. If you have an unnecessary cesarean, it's very bad. Any major operation entails risk, and a cesarean is a major operation. Ask any cesarean mother. The trouble is that it's very difficult to know with any certainty when you really need a cesarean and when you don't. Thus most doctors (and mothers) are inclined to do them "just in case." To this day, I still don't know whether I really needed that operation. And neither—I'm sure—does my doctor.

Still, arriving at the hospital pregnant but not in labor can be funny—if not necessarily fun. You arrive to be induced or sectioned (as they say), and you are the only woman in the admitting office who isn't huffing and panting or moaning. The admitting nurse wants to know why you're there, and you say you're going to have a baby. But you're not really sure. After all, you're not feeling a thing.

I knew I was being induced, but I never thought I would have a cesarean. Still, when the time came, I was more than ready. Unfortunately (or fortunately) a C-section may seem to be an easy out for the mother as well as the doctor. For hours my contractions had been getting longer and more painful, but less productive. Finally, a staff doctor studied my "monitor readout" and announced that I hadn't had a decent contraction in hours. (Thanks for telling me *now!*) Clearly, it was time to take matters in hand. Or at least I hope it was. The trouble is, you never know for sure.

The anesthesiologist went about the business of inserting a catheter in my back—all the while instructing a young medical student on the fine points of epidural anesthesia. I felt an immediate and welcome cessation of sensation. Unfortunately, it lasted only for about five minutes, and the pains came back stronger than ever. The anesthesiologist and his charge tried and tried again. I was sitting on the edge of the bed, hunched over, bear-hugging a friendly nurse for support, begging them to hurry up. And I wasn't the only one. Suddenly my doctor appeared in the hallway, shouting, "We've been scrubbed for an hour! Where the hell have you been?"

All the way to the delivery room, I kept wishing I would feel that urge to push. And kept wondering: Why was this happening to me?

Of course, I know some of the reasons. I had a nine-pound, eleven-ounce baby. He was posterior (sunny-side up). Perhaps even my age (thirty) had something to do with it. One mother was told that she needed a cesarean because her uterus was too old and tired out to deliver a baby:

"I didn't sound so bad at the time. There are some advantages to a cesarean when labor is getting hard and the doctor walks in and says he's going to do a section. I felt like I was going to be there forever. The doctor said I had an old uterus, and that I should have been doing this when I was eighteen, and here I was thirty-one. I had been on pitocin all day from noon to 7:00 P.M. and nothing was happening. I had dilated only three centimeters. And so—you know—it was Saturday night—I think that had something to do with it—and they were sitting and hanging around all day waiting for me, and it just didn't seem worth it."

Another mother—a veteran of four cesareans—said she could feel that the baby wasn't coming down by itself, until the last moment: "You can feel that you're having these horrible contractions and nothing's happening. When they finally decided to do the section, it was so long and so late that I figured either me or the child was just not going to make it. They ran down the hall and I just could feel that the baby was starting to come out. If they'd only waited ten more minutes. But you have to make a judgment. There's no way of knowing. If they had waited ten more minutes, I might have died or the child might have died."

Once the decision to "section" is made, many women find that they are in store for several surprises. Cesareans are rarely talked about in natural-childbirth classes—or anywhere else, for that matter. And yet, one-fourth of all new mothers will be cesarean mothers. There's a lot they need to know.

About anesthesia, for example. Fortunately, I knew that I could have a local, or spinal-type anesthesia (epidural) that would leave me numb below the waist but awake and aware to greet my child. One of the cesarean mothers I shared a room with (we were three C-sections out of four mothers) didn't know about epidurals. She labored for thirteen hours hoping for a natural birth and was sorely disappointed that she missed the main event—no matter how unnatural it might have been.

What I didn't know was that an epidural doesn't numb you completely. I could feel the doctors poking and prodding; I could even feel the baby being pulled out. This was disconcerting, to say the least. Later, I found out that spinal-type anesthesia *should* leave you with some sensation while taking away the pain.

One mother didn't lose her sensitivity to touch *or* pain. "The worst thing about an epidural is that you have to keep your face normal because you're not all doped up. I felt them poking around every time. They don't always wait for the drugs to take effect. Once I screamed so loud—I had heard about cases where they went ahead without anesthesia—because I could feel myself being cut. I thought if I didn't scream, they wouldn't know. I was embarrassed because it's not my personality to carry on in a public place. But I screamed and screamed and they said, 'What is the matter with you?' And I said I could feel them cutting my stomach. So the doctor tapped my stomach with his fingers and said, 'What am I doing?' And I said, 'You're tapping my stomach with your fingers.' And they put a mask over my face and I never felt another thing."

This sort of thing seems to happen uncomfortably often. So if you feel pressure, fine. If you feel pain, for heaven's sake, speak up. Generally, local anesthesia is safer than general anesthesia because the mother can breathe on her own. But it's a tricky procedure that's not available in every hospital. Whether or not you can have it depends entirely on the skills of the anesthesiologist. If you're interested in an epidural, ask around. (Your best bet is a major teaching hospital.)

Of course, being awake means being aware of all the operating-room activity. Here you are awaiting perhaps the most important moment of your life, and here are the doctors and nurses discussing tonight's dinner or yesterday's football game. And then there's that sinking feeling when you hear the doctor say, "Ooops!" Several parents' groups throughout the country are lobbying to get husbands into the operating room for cesarean births—and I hope they succeed soon. Meanwhile, at least request that your husband be present. If the hospital still says no, find someone's hand to hold. But be prepared to face the consequences: "Every time in the operating room I'd pick out some poor guy and ask him to hold my hand," said one mother. "Then I'd see him the next day, and I'd be so embarrassed." Of course, there's no need for you to be embarrassed—and you can be sure that he isn't, either. Chances are, he's held many hands before.

Anesthesia isn't the only thing that's improved about cesareans in recent years. Long, disfiguring scars that run vertically up the abdomen have been replaced by the barely noticeable "bikini" cut—a small, low, horizontal incision just below the bikini line. Not only are "bikini" cuts more aesthetic, many doctors say they're safer, too. Still, some obstetricians are set in their ways and won't do bikini cuts. Ask your doctor about his preferences in surgery and anesthesia if you think you have any chance of becoming a cesarean mother—and remember that nationally your chances are one in four.

"I'm such a fanatic on clothes and bathing suits," said one pretty young cesarean mother. "I needed an operation like that like a hole in the head. That morning, the baby was in the right position. I was doing Lamaze. I was feeling terrific. Then, at the last minute, she turned breech. She got all crunched up. Poor baby. When she came out, her legs didn't fall for hours afterward. But I would have broken both the doctor's legs if he hadn't given me that bikini scar. When I first looked for it, I asked, 'Where is it?' It was just a little thing, like a little smile. I don't understand how they got the baby out of there."

The worst part of a cesarean delivery is the recovery—especially if you've been counting on going right back to work or to the tennis courts or on a long-planned vacation. Recovery is almost always rougher than mothers think. Of course, they should expect all the major and minor problems of major abdominal surgery, because that's what a C-section is. But few of us do. And the postpartum letdown can lead to postpartum depression. While the typical hospital stay is only four to eight days, full recovery takes at least six weeks—and sometimes much longer.

The cesarean mother is a conspicuous figure in the maternity ward. She walks stooped in the characteristic "cesarean shuffle," pushing her IV pole in front of her. Among the discomforts she can expect are abdominal pain, gas, constipation, fever. The first few days she'll sip fluids, and maybe Jell-O, and build up her diet from there. While most obstetricians advise her to get up and around the day after surgery, it isn't always easy.

One mother said she felt as though she "had been hit by a train," and I knew exactly what she meant. Weeks later, I was stooped over from pain, soothing my poor violated belly with heating pads, but unable to take pain medication because I was nursing. A cesarean may be a relatively simple surgical procedure, but it's still major surgery—with all the attendant after-effects.

Recovery depends on many factors, including the mother's general recuperative powers and the length of her labor, if any. The longer the labor, the more chance of infection, of stomach distention, of fever. I've frequently heard veteran cesarean mothers say that the operation is far easier the second—or third—time around: in part because it's less a shock to their systems, and in part because they know what to expect and are better prepared.

Few mothers are prepared for the postpartum fever that so often comes with cesarean births. In most hospitals, the fever means you can't see your newborn baby. And that can be the rudest shock of all. I'll never forget when the nurse came in and delivered all the other infants to their mothers for feeding—but not mine. She said I couldn't handle him until I was without fever for twenty-four hours. That turned out to be three days. But I've spoken with mothers who didn't see their babies for a week or more. Nursing cesarean mothers who are isolated from their babies should request breast pumps to keep up their milk supply. (More on infant-maternal separation under Hospitals.)

Cesarean mothers who deliver under general anesthesia often feel a sense of separation from their newborn babies—even when they aren't separated physically. "I had this feeling that I really hadn't birthed it," said one mother. "It's like I hadn't done any work to get the child, and I'd just look at her and sort of say, 'How did you get here?' It was about a week and a half before I really felt that she was my baby. Because I was expecting to see the process of birth, and I didn't."

Perhaps the most radical innovation in the cesarean business is the loosening of the once-ironclad rule: once a section, always a section. This is especially true if the conditions that indicated the first cesarean don't exist the second time. For example, if the first baby was too large for the mother's pelvis, but the second baby is small. Or if the first baby was breech. At at least one major teaching hospital, 20 per cent of cesarean mothers have normal vaginal deliveries the second time around. However, it's not the sort of thing you should attempt in an ordinary hosptial. It should be in a complete medical center with all facilities.

In a recent "trial labor" study in San Antonio, half of 526 cesarean mothers had safe vaginal deliveries on subsequent births, according to *The New York Times*. However, the women who did require repeat cesareans had a much higher rate of complications than do cesarean mothers who don't attempt labor. Trial labor assures that the baby is delivered when it's due. But it also poses the risk of uterine rupture, with its potentially deadly results. Still, many doctors think it's worth trying under the right conditions. After all, there is a certain incidence of death from cesarean section alone. You and your doctor have to balance that against the risk of uterine rupture.

Indeed, an old uterine scar can rupture long before labor— during the last weeks of pregnancy. (This is not the scar you see on your abdomen, but the one inside, on your uterus.) Uterine rupture is a very rare—but also very real—risk associated with all cesareans. Usually the baby dies. Sometimes the mother dies, too. However, I spoke with two cesarean mothers who suffered ruptured uteruses—and both they and their babies were doing fine:

"It happened in the middle of the night a few weeks before the baby was due. I was beside myself, having very sharp pains. I called the doctor, and he told me to take an aspirin and call him in four hours. I right away tried the Lamaze breathing, thinking it was just a kick or something. I tried to calm myself down, but the pain didn't go away. I knew there was obviously something very wrong. I thought maybe it was food poisoning because we had just had a big dinner. And there was no bleeding or anything. Nobody had ever mentioned the possibility. Afterwards, I read all the books to see if anyone ever mentions the possibility of uterine rupture, and none did. It's evidently quite rare.

"We knew the doctor was wrong just to prescribe aspirin, but we didn't know what to do. I couldn't really talk, and I couldn't tell my husband how to get to the hospital we were supposed to go to. So finally we went to a nearer hospital— a small hospital not really prepared for emergencies. But fortunately there were a number of obstetricians on that night. None of them had ever seen me before. It took about an hour for them to figure out what had happened, to get my blood type, to try to figure out how pregnant I was, to call a pediatrician, to call the obstetrician who had told me to take the aspirin, and then to call the obstetrician who had made the original cut, to find out what kind of cut it was. Evidently I was in shock, so I don't remember too much. But I was awake when she was born. They told us before we went to the delivery room that the baby was dead because there was no heartbeat."

Against all odds, both mother and baby made it, although they didn't know the final outcome for many days.

Of course, no one can predict how a cesarean will affect you. I interviewed one mother for this book while she was pregnant, and she listened as we told her horror stories of our cesarean births. When it came time for her own cesarean, she was so well prepared that it didn't mar her motherhood experience in the slightest—even though she was in labor for twelve hours before the operation, and even though a fever kept her isolated from her baby for ten days. I don't think I've ever seen a happier or healthier mother.

Now that cesareans have become more safe and more efficient, perhaps they can become more humane, too. Medical reasons rarely prevent a mother from holding and feeding her infant as soon as it's born, but hospital rules often do. Fathers in the operating room provide welcome support, but they are rarely allowed. (Some fathers become depressed after cesarean births because they feel they have been cheated out of their roles.) A C-section does not have to be a denial of the birth process—and that includes watching the baby come into the world, nursing, bonding and sharing with a partner. It involves two people. It's still a baby birth.

Indeed, no matter what the circumstances of your delivery—cesarean or otherwise—the result of your labors is perhaps the most precious gift on earth: a new baby. The birth may or may not be a celebration in itself, but the outcome surely will be. And that simple inarguable fact turns every delivery into a joyous occasion.

It is predicted that some 3 million babies will be born in the United States this year. That means 3 million different reactions from 3 million different mothers. Each birth experience will have much in common with all the others, and each will be special and memorable in its own right. There's nothing as universal as childbirth—and nothing as individual. So welcome to motherhood. It's the largest sorority in the world. And also the nicest.

Hospitals:

Technological Childbirth Comes of Age

Birth, curiously, is one of the most hotly debated subjects in our society today. And the reasons rest squarely with the American hospital. If childbirth has become controversial, it is because hospitals have injected the birthing process with a huge dose of technology that can be as dangerous as it is lifesaving—as frightening as it can be comforting.

The alternative to hospital birth is home birth—equally comforting to some, equally dangerous to others. Home birth is not discussed in this book because out of 150 women interviewed, not one had her baby at home.* Like it or not (and most of us don't), more than 95 per cent of American women give birth in hospitals.

Between home and hospital are birth centers and midwife programs and a host of other alternatives that try to take the best of both worlds—to try to humanize the hospital experience. The Leboyer soft-lights and warm-bath "romantic" method of birth has enjoyed much publicity, but much less practice. Unfortunately, the medical establishment is slow to innovate, slower still to compromise.

*Alice Gilgoff's *Home Birth* (New York: Coward, McCann & Geoghegan, 1978) is one of several enlightening books on the subject.

Left in the middle of all this is the mother. She has two unpleasant alternatives: unsupervised home birth or oversupervised hospital birth. Neither is particularly safe or satisfying. But rather than drawing together, the two sides of the controversy are pulling increasingly apart. The course of American childbirth is headed simultaneously in two strongly opposing directions: total technology and no technology. And because most of us are afraid of no technology, total technology usually wins.

This may seem surprising. After all, everybody's read about the "natural childbirth" revolution. All over the country, it seems, women are giving birth in homey hospital settings, huffing and puffing their way through labor without a hint of anesthesia, delivering their babies into the supportive hands of their husbands or a midwife.

But despite all the media attention to Lamaze, La Leche and Leboyer, the truth is that childbirth in America is getting more *un*natural every day. A woman expecting her first baby today has a 25 per cent chance of delivering by cesarean. Even a "natural" birth often means that the mother is merely "awake" for the proceedings. Never mind that she's strapped down, numb below the waist, electronically monitored, chemically induced, and intravenously fed. "Natural childbirth" mothers use some form of anesthesia up to 75 per cent of the time. In some hospitals, they are hooked up to fetal monitors and a variety of intravenous fluids and drugs 100 per cent of the time.

Some medical schools don't even teach aspects of "natural" birth anymore. Breech births, for instance. Today's obstetrician can take technology or leave it; tomorrow's may not have a choice. "The present-day obstetrical resident is an electronic wizard," one obstetrician told me. "You go into conference with them, and nobody knows if the patient drinks or smokes or fights with her husband. But they know all about her A Scan and her B Scan. You get the feeling you're in a NASA conference about to be shuffled off to Mars."

Indeed, as evidence seems to accumulate in favor of leaving nature alone, the new technology threatens to take over the birthing business. Where technology is indicated, it often saves lives; but it's most often used "just in case" it's indicated—which means all the time. And the forces pushing it are powerful: fear, malpractice suits, and slick merchandising. One obstetrician went so far as to call this the Chef Boyardee syndrome—a reference to the purchase of a large fetal-monitor company by American Home Products, which also makes Chef Boyardee foods. According to him, it was no concidence that once a sharp marketing team like AHP bought a monitor company, suddenly hospitals started buying monitors.

Clearly, there's nothing babyish about the battle over childbirth. Pediatricians, obstetricians, and patients often find themselves at odds with each other, often bitterly: "I don't pay much attention to what obstetricians say because they make their money off it," a respected pediatrician told me. "The incidence of complications of hospital births is 99 per cent. The incidence of complications of home births is 1 per cent."

On the other side of the delivery table is the chief of obstetrics at a major New York teaching hospital. "Babies die from natural childbirth," he said. He pointed out that in 1930 one in 150 mothers died in childbirth. "Going back to natural childbirth will reverse us to this."

Nobody disputes the fact that infant mortality in this country has been steadily declining—a powerful argument for technology. On the other hand, the United States still ranks only about fifteenth in infant mortality among all countries—a common theme of home-birth advocates. They say American hospital procedures are at fault.

What bothers me and many others is the lack of objectivity, the rigidity, on both sides. Many doctors and mothers find themselves emotionally in sympathy with natural childbirth. They would like to see technology used in a more humane way. But they are distressed by the back-to-nature movement. When things go wrong, they can go wrong very fast. In that case, it's better to be in a hospital—assuming, of course, that the hospital didn't cause the problem in the first case.

What's a mother to do? She wants "natural childbirth." But she also wants the best modern medicine has to offer. If she doesn't get it, she might sue the doctor—which puts more pressure on him or her to use technology whether the mother wants it or not.

Natural-childbirth advocates say the answer is to screen out those women who probably will need the technology from the 95 per cent who probably won't. Inevitably, they say, if there is a high-powered instrument in a hospital, it's going to be used on a healthy woman. So the best control is to keep healthy women out of hospitals. Routinely giving everything to everyone is causing more and more iatrogenic (doctor-caused) ill-nesses.

But screening doesn't always work. Home-birth centers se-lect a very low-risk population, and still some mothers get transferred to hospitals during labor. So problems aren't always predictable. Natural-childbirth advocates would counter that doctors don't know how to screen because they have a vested interest in *not* learning. Medical schools don't teach screening. Perhaps if they did, it wouldn't be such an iffy proposition.

The home-versus-hospital controversy is fueled to a large extent by the new childbirth technology. Ironically, as more hospitals use technology routinely, more women choose to have their babies where most doctors would least like to see them—at home. Few doctors—or patients—like the alternatives. If the choice is between an IV and a home delivery, and the mother chooses a home delivery, then the hospital is partly responsible.

My own experiences and research into this matter have helped me come to my own conclusions—and they are uncom-fortably inconclusive. I know that hospital procedures are al-most always uncomfortable, often unnecessary, sometimes dangerous. They certainly were in my case—and also in the cases of the vast majority of the mothers I interviewed. And yet I know that without the hospital I might have lost my baby and perhaps even my life. This is the dilemma that most mothers face. In the long run, the answer is for home and hospital to cooperate in the birthing process. In the short run, however, it behooves every mother to bone up on the procedures in use at her hospital today. If she arrives for the delivery and hasn't ever heard of a fetal monitor or an IV, she's going to be in for a big surprise.

Of course, hospitals mean more than technology. They mean nurses and residents and interns (the "house staff") and nurs-eries filled with babies and labor rooms filled with women having babies. The quality of your hospital stay may hinge as much on the quality of your relationship with these people as it does on the quality of your medical care.

It's difficult to generalize about hospitals; they come in so many sizes and shapes. Teaching hospitals usually boast the most sophisticated technical gadgetry—and also the greatest number of inquiring medical students and student nurses. (They have to practice on someone, don't they?) A smaller community hospital might be a more homey place to give birth, but it might not provide you with the best care in an emergency. The best guide to hospitals in your area is the advice of mothers who recently have delivered in them. You should also take a hospital tour, ask as many questions as possible, in as much detail as possible—both of the hospital staff and of your own doctor. The more you know before you go in, the less you'll be disappointed afterward.

My own experience was not atypical for a large sophisticated teaching hospital. I escaped the enema and shave (the "prep"), but almost immediately was attached to an IV and a fetal monitor. Attached to the monitor for the duration was a young East Indian technician who clearly regarded my attempts at Lamaze breathing as the crazed behavior of a mental-ward escapee. Three times I asked her please to stop staring at me, and three times she (unsuccessfully) tried.

Labor rooms weren't built to accommodate husbands, much less technicians and technology. So we were rather crowded. We had a sink, a bed with bars, and chairs for my husband and the technician. We also had a wonderful labor nurse for a few hours, but we soon lost her to the lady laboring alone next door. Occasionally, an intern or resident would come in to check my dilation, but they never stayed to chat.

Several weeks before, my husband and I had been on a hospital tour, along with the rest of our Lamaze class. Two things had struck me at the time. One was the delivery room. Not the room itself exactly—which was nondescript (a table with stirrups surrounded by a lot of cabinets). But the rows of tiered seats at one end. There was room enough for twenty or so medical students to watch the proceedings from an uncomfortably close perspective—or at least that was my feeling. Several of my Lamaze colleagues must have felt the same way, for they asked Fritzie whether we could refuse the pleasure of the medical students' company if we wished. Fritzie replied that, of course, we could ask them to leave. But she was clearly surprised at the thought that anyone would want to.

The second surprise came when Fritzie discussed the relative arrangements for nurseries, rooming-in, private rooms, and sharing a room with other mothers. A pregnant classmate noted that her best friend had delivered in the same hospital only two weeks before, had "reserved" a private room on the rooming-in ward, and had received neither privacy nor room-in. It quickly became obvious that reservations were a matter of what was available. Even if you reserved a rooming-in arrangement months before the baby was due, you wouldn't get rooming-in unless space was available on the day of delivery. Many hospitals spell out this warning explicitly. But wherever you plan to give birth, you should understand that most hospitals can reserve anything only up to a point.

In the end, I missed out on the delivery room (because of my cesarean). Instead, I was wheeled down to an operating room. Here, the rows of seats for the medical students were high above me, behind great glass windows. The room itself was a huge (it seemed) amphitheater, and I was (or should have been) the main attraction. In the glass panes above, I could see my own reflection: a bulbous yellow belly, which a nurse was scrubbing down with yellow soap and a big brush. I thought for a moment that I would be able to see the whole operation, but I no sooner thought it than they cut off my head (from the rest of me) with a blue surgical sheet. From then on, I saw only the lights on the ceiling, the clock, and heard the operating-room chatter—most of it about how everybody wanted to get home.

After it was over, I asked my husband again and again what had happened. My own memory was foggy, at best. I remember being wheeled past the nursery window so that I could catch a glimpse of my son in his Plexiglas case, but he seemed faraway and unfamiliar. I remember the nurses in the recovery room talking—again—about going home. I remember shaking uncontrollably, and my doctor coming in to say good-bye, suitcase in hand, off on his own vacation. I remember him saying, "I'm sure glad I consulted the other doctor. I was going to give you pitocin, which would have been a disaster."

And then I remember some grumblings about finding me a bed, but it didn't matter much at that point. All I wanted was sleep.

The next morning I awakened from my stupor enough to realize what had happened. Not only was there no rooming-in (so I could see my baby as much as I wanted), there was no room in the maternity ward at all. I couldn't see my baby at all. I was certainly in no condition to travel up two floors to the nursery, and he wasn't permitted to travel down to visit me. It was just rough luck.

Fortunately, my husband cornered Fritzie, who managed to get me a bed on the maternity ward. At noon I nursed my son for the first time. An incomparable thrill. I was groggy and stuck with IVs like a voodoo doll. so it was awkward. But an awfully nice nurse helped. I couldn't wait to nurse him again. At 4:00 P.M., the nurses brought in the babies for feeding one by one. But not mine. "It's hospital policy," I was told. "You can't have him until your temperature goes down." No exceptions, no explanations, no apologies.

The next day, my fever was worse. I could feel it. I asked the nurse for an aspirin. She said she was allowed to give me only painkillers or enemas. I said I didn't want an enema or a painkiller. I had a fever. She said she'd have to note on my chart that I'd refused all medication. My husband tried to find me a doctor. Mine was on vacation. Of his two associates, each thought the other was "covering" the hospital. None of the nurses at his office seemed to know what was going on. We waited.

Hours later, a resident showed up. I said I was hot; I wanted some aspirin. He said I was hysterical. I sure was. An hour later, the nurse took my temperature with her computerized, digital thermometer and confirmed that it was rising. So I got another IV. I had an IV for five days. It fell out five times. Later, when the nurse came around with her thermometer, I asked how I was doing. (I wanted to see my baby.) She said she wasn't allowed to tell me my temperature. I wonder why Kafka never wrote a book on hospitals.

By the fourth day, my husband and I decided we couldn't be any *worse* off at home, so we called the associate doctor. He appeared, telling us in great detail about the dinner he'd left getting cold on his plate at home. We sympathized. He prescribed that I watch TV and move into a private room. What I wanted, I said, was an aspirin and the opportunity to see my baby. He finally agreed to let my husband bring me aspirin.

The next morning, my temperature was down and my baby was back. The day after that, we went home. I realized only when we got there how much I had feared that we would never be a family again. I cried with relief. But my tears were also bitter and angry. And they would be for a long time to come.

For too many women, the hospital is the worst part of having a baby. "I never worried about the birth until I got to the hospital," said a mother who had given birth to her first child in Europe. "There was so much hysteria attached to it. In Sweden you get laughing gas, but the general feeling is you can manage. In that hospital, we sat around and played honeymoon bridge and drank beer. It was so completely different."

Of course, some mothers thoroughly enjoy their hospital stays. To them it's a vacation. A time to be waited on hand and foot. A time when they don't have to do dishes or clean house or cater to anyone but themselves. "I liked the feeling of being with lots of other people who were doing the same thing," said one mother.

A particularly nice nurse or a favorite intern or resident can make the difference between good memories and bad ones. Even the technology can be welcome: "I like the security of knowing good medical care is nearby if needed. I feel secure in a hospital."

And the experience of giving birth to one baby won't necessarily be repeated the second time around—even in the same hospital. "The first time was horrible: women were screaming, and the nurses were totally indifferent. The second experience was beautiful. The nurses were trained in Lamaze, and the atmosphere was calm and quiet."

But you'll be able to put your hospital stay in better perspective if you realize that hospitals are made for doctors, not patients. And even when they're wonderful for sick people, they may not be appropriate to the needs of a woman having a baby. Listen to this obstetrician's description of what a hospital provides its patients: "Sometime during the last month of pregnancy, every woman seems mysteriously compelled to pack a bag. This is an instinctive compulsion which baffles most men, including me. . . ." The hospital, he explains, will provide everything you need. Hospital gowns are "much more practical" than your own nightie. (Just what you want to wear to greet visitors in.) He writes that there's no need to bring your own cosmetics when the hospital can supply you with a "limitless supply of soap, sheets, and sanitary napkins." The doctor concludes that hospitals are really a lot like hotels, catering"to the simplest and most exacting tastes." The doctor obviously never spent much time as a patient in a maternity ward.

I doubt that the doctor was being callous. Indeed, from a purely medical point of view, it may not matter whether you have your favorite nightie, or if you look attractive for visitors or feel comfortable in your surroundings. Some hospitals are beginning to make concessions. One mother reported that the hospital piped Christmas music into the labor room. (She delivered on December 19.) But by and large, if you want a homey atmosphere, you'd better bring it with you.

One thing you might just as well leave at home is your independent spirit. When you're in a hospital, you do things their way. You might get lucky and run into a warm and sympathetic staff—just like in the Lamaze movies. Then again, you might not. But either way, you're playing by their rules. The hospital dictates when (and if) you can see you husband and child—or other children. It dictates what you wear and what you eat and when and how you have your baby. If you're the type who likes to control things, either be prepared—or stay away.

Indeed, the most bitter protests about hospitals come from women who felt they were victims of an uncaring bureaucracy:

"This sounds like a small thing, but I really wanted to see the birth, and they took my glasses away. I can't see anything without them. I wasn't going to smash them into my eyes. They take all the control. The procedures are very degrading. Even by the time I reached the labor room I was a nervous wreck. I'd like to bomb that place."

"When it came time for the afterbirth, I was so well prepared with Lamaze that I was waiting for the doctor to say "Push," so I could deliver it. But instead he turned to a nurse and said, "Okay." And she pounded—boom!—on my stomach. And it hurt, and I was very angry. I could have delivered without any of that stuff. I was fully in control."

"They put me in stirrups with the sheet over me and they left me. You're so totally vulnerable. The clean-up man came in and was looking in on the whole thing. I felt so totally a victim."

Nature doesn't always fit neatly into hospital routines, which can cause endless conflict. If the baby's ready but the doctor isn't, a mother may be told to cross her legs. (Although this is far less common than it once was.) The procedure is inhuman for the mother as well as the baby. It's not like waiting for the next gas station.

Moreover, doctors and nurses who consider themselves "professionals" sometimes don't like to listen to what a mere mother has to say. Even if what you have to say is that you can feel your baby coming out—or that you have to go to the bathroom—or that you hurt. Don't be surprised if someone disagrees with you.

"A woman was wheeled into the room next to me, and she was saying, 'I'm having this baby, I'm ready to have this baby.' And the nurses were saying, 'Oh no, Mrs. So-and-So, you're not ready yet.' And the woman screamed, 'Will somebody please listen to me? I've had seven children—I know the baby is coming.' So an older nurse whipped on some gloves and got over there just in time to catch the baby."

In short, if you keep in mind what a hospital is and who it's primarily for (very sick people), you won't be so put off by what you might find there. Even the "homiest" hospitals have to abide by state and federal health regulations. They have to provide the best possible care for the greatest number of people in the safest possible way. So don't be offended if you—as an individual—somehow get lost in the shuffle. You're there in case of an emergency—in which case you will probably get perfectly appropriate care. If you don't have an emergency, the care might not be so appropriate, but it's still better than having an emergency—and at least you'll understand why you're being treated so strangely.

THE DELIVERY ROOM

Delivery rooms differ—but the main difference seems to be in the eye of the beholder. Here's an obstetrician's description of a delivery room: "Most modern delivery tables these days are as shiny and complex as a modern automobile, each wheel and lever enabling the delivery-room staff to add to your protection and comfort."

Now a mother's view: "I was frightened by all the delivery-room paraphernalia. All that stainless steel and drab green is depressing. I remember stiff bedclothes, being cold, and wishing I were home."

Still another mother was disappointed because the delivery room wasn't automated *enough:* it wasn't as fancy as the ones she had seen on TV.

"In the movies, they've got all this beautiful equipment, with curtains on the windows. I figured it was going to be more modern, more new, more elaborate—with a bigger mirror to see your baby being born."

One thing all mothers agreed on was that the mirror was too small. It's usually a dinky arrangement, not much larger than the rearview mirror on a car. But then, mirrors in delivery rooms are new enough innovations that doctors might be wary of what a mother might see in them—especially if something goes wrong. Also, a small mirror can be pushed out of the way faster if something *does* go wrong.

The most important equipment in the delivery room is the people—the atmosphere that surrounds the birth of your child. You might find yourself attended by a friendly and supportive staff, by screaming women and sadistic nurses (or doctors), or left totally alone.

"The worst thing about not being medicated is that you can hear all the conversations of the doctors and nurses from outside the room, and they're joking and clowning while you're in this room experiencing all this uncomfortableness," said Jane. "I was really resentful because I was kind of nervous about the whole thing and my doctor, the anesthesiologist, and the nurses were talking about the fertilizer they were putting on their lawn. But the worst part was being alone—waiting on the delivery table to deliver while the doctor chatted with the nurses. All by myself in this huge room with all this equipment."

Ellie, on the other hand, had more delivery-room company than she bargained for:

"They put me in with four women with sheet partitions in between. And I could hear the sounds of a table being wheeled in next to me, a woman screaming, and a doctor saying, 'Come on, come on, come on, come on, good, good, good. Okay, okay, okay, that's a good mother, come on, come on.' And then I'd hear 'Waaaaaaaa!' And there would be the sound of wheels again. That went on for hours.

"Finally it was my turn. My doctor took that thing they use to break the waters and then connected me to the IV—and the pains started coming like unbelievable. I couldn't stand it. And then I noticed that there was another woman delivering right beside me. It was like a great big factory. And the anesthesiologist would put a mask on me and then run over to the other woman. I couldn't believe it. I was pleading. 'Please don't go. Wait a minute.' And he's say, 'Just hang in there—

I'll be right back.' So finally, I could see a baby being slapped on this woman's stomach, and I yelled, 'Bring him back!' And he came running.

"Later I arrived in my room, and guess who was my room-mate? That woman. And she said, '*I* heard you tell him not to come to me. You witch! You didn't want to share him with me!' I told her that I thought we should share his bill."

One of the nicest innovations on the delivery scene is the birthing room, or Lamaze room, or birthing/labor bed. It means you don't have to change beds in the middle of your birthing efforts. You don't have to take that frantic last-minute trip down the hall from the labor room to the delivery room—grabbing your pillow and your husband as you go. Instead, you stay in one place, in one bed, in a room with all the necessary equipment, and at least some of the comforts of home. More and more hospitals now have such arrangements for Lamaze mothers, so be sure to ask if one is available in your area.

Indeed, some women are pleasantly surprised by what they find even in old-fashioned delivery rooms:

"I thought it would be a serious place, but the nurse and anesthesiologist were friendly and funny. The anesthesiologist was Italian, and I had a boy, so he was telling me to name the baby after him. It was all very pleasant."

Another mother found that her doctor's presence was enough to take the chill off an otherwise cold situation: "The delivery room is basically a very sterile place, but my doctor exerts such warmth and personality that it didn't seem so bad."

Other women find comfort in the company of their hus-bands.

You may not even notice much about the delivery room. Or even about the people around you. You may be too busy delivering your baby to notice much of anything. But it's a good idea to go on a hospital tour just so you won't be totally surprised. Just remember: things do look different from a prone position.

THE ENEMA

I still remember the woman who first introduced me to the then-shocking notion of natural childbirth. One of the most shocking and puzzling aspects (to me) was her adamant refusal to have an enema while she was in labor. Why, I had asked, would anyone want to give a laboring woman an enema? "So you don't have a bowel movement in the doctor's hands," she explained. "But I figure, that's why they wear gloves."

Since then, I've learned that enemas are a cause célèbre in the natural-childbirth movement. And for good reason. An enema for a laboring woman can be a humiliating, usually unnecessary, and often painful experience:

"To me that was the most ignominious part. First of all, it hurts like hell. Then you don't know whether you are having a contraction or whether you are going to the bathroom. You don't know whether you're going to drop the baby in the toilet or what. I spent most of labor on a bedpan. And I never could tell where the pressure was coming from."

"I must have turned pink, purple, and every color because I was mortified that this was happening to me. You're on your side in a kind of fetal position, and they pump a whole bucket full of soapsuds into you. So you're having contractions and you're miserable and you're walking around holding your rear end tight so you don't push all the solution out. I started to walk across the hall to the bathroom, but the nurse said, no, I had to walk around more. But I just couldn't hold it anymore, it was coming out. And she said, 'Okay, honey, just take deep breaths.' I was mad and annoyed, and finally I just flew into the toilet. I sat there and ached, my stomach ached, and I said, 'Please leave me alone so I can get this out of me.' So she left and left the door wide open. I could hear doctors walking by and everyone can hear you, and meanwhile all this garbage is pouring out of you. It's a relief, but it's mortifying."

However horrible, an enema can improve your control during labor. It removes some of the pressure and makes it easier to keep track of your contractions. Nature usually provides her own enemas by giving mothers a strong dose of diarrhea in the early stages of labor. If you do have diarrhea, be sure to tell the hospital staff so you won't have an enema, too. Still, don't be surprised if they give the enema anyway. (Rules *are* rules.)

Doing without an enema almost assures that you will deliver some feces along with your baby. This is perfectly normal and expected—and it happens even with enemas, since the baby's head pushes out everything in its path. However, if a bowel movement on the delivery table is going to make you unduly embarrassed, or take away from the birth experience, by all means have an enema. Ideally, enemas—like other hospital procedures—would be matters of personal choice rather than "hospital policy." Only a mother can weigh the indignity and discomfort of an enema with the possible drawbacks of passing one up. Only a mother knows whether she's had diarrhea at home. It's precisely the kind of decision that only a mother should be allowed to make; instead, she's rarely even consulted.

THE SHAVE

The enema is part of what is commonly called "prepping," in hospital terms. The other part of prepping is the shave. Hospitals have traditionally shaved a mother's pubic hair to avoid potential infection. Recently, however, more and more obstetricians are conceding that razors probably provoke more infections than they prevent. And so, today many women receive "mini shaves"—also known as the "French poodle cut." Or no shave at all, if the doctor is particularly progressive. Pubic shaves aren't "horrible," as enemas can be, but they are, as one mother put it, "just another awkward thing you don't need."

"It was a total shame. It is so undignified to have all your pubic hair shaved off, and you look down and there's this little-girl vulva looking at you, and a baby coming out of it. It's just so ludicrous. I hate it. And then when it grows back, there's all that itching. It's dreadful."

"You're so vulnerable. The nurse whipped in and said, 'Oh, spread your legs. Put your heels together and draw them up toward your stomach.' And the she goes lather, lather, lather, whip, whip, whip. Like she was going to cut me. I was scared to death. But I felt sorry for the nurse, too. I thought. 'What a way to make a living!'"

Ask your obstetrician if he or she will spare you the experience of prepping. If you are refused, try to grin and bear it. At least you know that enemas and shaves won't unduly harm either you or your baby. And if you voice your opinion strongly, perhaps some future mother will be rewarded by a more relaxed hospital policy—even if you still have to abide by the rules.

THE FETAL MONITOR

The fetal monitor is an "electronic nurse"—and as such it is undoubtably the most controversial piece of equipment on the American hospital scene. It consists of a large box (or boxes) which stand vigil at the laboring woman's bedside. (Sometimes displacing her husband.) Electronic bleeps and blinking lights keep time with the fetal heartbeat. A stylus draws graphs of the mother's contractions on a moving strip of paper. Her belly is encircled by a heavy strap and is attached with suction cups to a plastic box. Sometimes, electrodes are implanted in the baby's head through her vagina.

Monitors are standard at most major hospitals today. Indeed, in many cases, they are installed on the advice of hospital attorneys who recommend that they be required on all patients to avoid the risk of malpractice suits. But recently strong evidence has surfaced against monitors—mainly because they are so easy to misinterpret. And so mothers, doctors, and hospitals find themselves in a quandary. They don't want to be without monitors, but they're not sure they like living with them either.

Before monitors came on the scene, a nurse would watch a woman in labor carefully. She'd listen to the baby's heartbeat with a special stethoscope called a fetuscope. "It was a good procedure because the nurses were so good," a prominent newborn specialist told me. "Today's nurses are good at looking at monitors, but not very good at listening to fetal hearts. And people say that the old technique is terrible. Well, maybe . . ."

Studies on the use of monitors have shown that they can save babies' lives—usually by signaling the need for a cesarean section. Almost every modern obstetrician has seen a baby who was saved who might have been stillborn if the monitor hadn't warned of trouble.

On the other hand, misinterpretation of monitors is easy. They are, as one baby-book author stressed, merely "gadgets" and "not perfect"—but doctors and nurses tend to over rely on them, forgetting their long years of training in the face of impressive technology.

One result is that some early supporters of monitors (including their inventors) have come out against them because of the way they've been abused. And because they are inextricably linked with the rising cesarean rate. Some obstetricians have taken to calling them "feeble monitors."

Still, studies show that monitors are safer. The question is: safer than what? If the mother is left alone, without a well-trained nurse, without a caring obstetrician, with drugs, then she's probably better off with a monitor. Monitors plus bad obstetrics is better than bad obstetrics alone.

On the other hand, a monitor can create the very kinds of problems it's designed to detect. It interferes with the normal process of labor by forcing the mother to lie prone and virtually immobile. Sometimes the monitor will detect an irregularity in the fetal heartbeat which is caused by the prone position itself—and which could be corrected if the mother could get up or roll over. But she can't roll over if she's wearing a monitor. "It was a very strapped-down kind of feeling," said one mother. "I hated that belt across my waist. I felt I could have just ripped it off." I shared her feelings exactly.

Moreover, monitors can be frightening—especially if nobody's watching the machine, and if the only medical company you keep during labor is the "bleep bleep" of your electronic nurse. Of course, doctors and nurses are supposed to monitor the monitor. But sometimes they don't. In my case, nobody looked at it for eight hours except the technician who came attached to it. Other mothers have had to send their husbands out into the hall to fetch a doctor or nurse when the monitor acted up—or even shut off.

"They kept putting this machine on me, and the machine was not working properly. I thought there was something wrong with the baby because all these people were coming in and looking at the monitor and whispering to each other. I didn't know what the hell was going on. I thought the baby was dead because I couldn't hear the heartbeat. Instead, it was just the machine that was no good. But they didn't tell me any of this. They just kept whispering and looking at the monitor."

Like other aspects of hospital technology, monitors are only as good as the people who use them. They are useful tools, but they can't be substituted for good care. And certainly not for any care at all.

Still, many mothers find the monitors comforting. They can't imagine not taking advantage of the very latest that modern obstetrics has to offer. And in some respects they're right. Certainly, strong drugs like pitocin would be even more dangerous without monitors to keep track of their effects on the fetus.

At its best a fetal monitor can even be an aid to "natural" childbirth:

"I felt secure with the monitor because my water broke suddenly. The labor got very strong, and I was really worried about the baby. My husband would look at the monitor, and he would know from that when a contraction was about to start. And he'd say, 'Get ready.' And I could see how long the contraction was going to last. I'd know I'd have two minutes, or however long it was, and then I could tell when it would peak. And I could say, 'Well, it's peaking now.' And knowing that you're at the top and coming down was very helpful psychologically."

In the end, it's often the mother who opts for the monitor "just in case" and also who agrees to the cesarean section "just in case" the signals from the monitor are serious.

"It's very hard for a woman in labor to be natural with a monitor," said one obstetrician. "It shows a little abnormality, and everybody comes in. Then she has to make the decision: Does she want to have a section? Or risk damage to the baby's brain? She always says no. They always twist these poor things' minds around—even the strong-willed ones. Then the baby turns out fine, and she doesn't know if she needed that cesarean after all."

THE IV

IVs, like monitors, are now standard procedure at most major hospitals. And many obstetricians think they're overdone. Women who are up and around immediately after childbirth are sometimes still attached to IVs. Cesarean mothers may have IVs many days after surgery—even though they may be sitting up and asking for a cup of tea. Women in labor are attached to IVs the minute they enter a hospital.

Doctors and hospitals often insist on an "intravenous line" to offer them ready access in case the mother should need emergency anesthesia to perform an emergency cesarean. IVs also provide the mother with fluid and a source of energy (glucose) during labor. Hospitals that routinely require IVs don't allow mothers to eat or drink—just in case she should need emergency anesthesia, vomit, and choke. My hospital didn't even allow lollipops or ice chips.

But IVs are hardly conducive to "natural childbirth." They anchor a woman to the bed—and also to the bedpan. The flow of fluids make the mother want to urinate, but the IV prohibits her from going to the bathroom. None of this does much for her confidence or her positive attitude toward childbirth. Of course, you can always ask not to have an IV. But then your doctor might say he can't—or won't—treat you. Nurses have been known to argue with mothers who protest IVs: "What's wrong with you? You want to kill your baby?"

And so IVs, like the rest of the hospital hardware, are hard to reject—and equally hard to accept. "They made me feel as though I were sick," said one mother. "Like something was wrong with me." Other mothers said that IVs made pushing difficult, and that being tied to the bed was "torture." Many mothers experienced problems:

"I was surprised that I had to have an IV, and I hated it. It hurts like hell, it's scary, and it's uncomfortable. Something went wrong with mine, and my hand swelled up and hurt for days afterward."

The scariest thing about an IV is that you never know what's in it. It could be sugar water, or it could be pitocin or a variety of other drugs. Fooling around with Mother Nature is hard to stop once started. And once you get an IV, there's a tremendous temptation to inject intravenous drugs. Most of those drugs affect the fetus, which means it's probably prudent to get hooked up with a fetal monitor—just in case.

Technology fuels its own chain reactions.

If you give birth in a modern hospital, you probably won't have much to say about whether or not you have an IV. But you can at least try to find out what it's pumping through your veins. If it's just glucose, fine. But if you're getting a dose of pitocin or Demerol, knowing what to expect can help you to control your labor.

THE LITHOTOMY POSITION

In layman's terms, this means lying flat on your back—the position in which most American women give birth. It's hard to see why hospitals insist on this position—except that of course it's conducive to IVs and fetal monitors and episiotomies and the teaching of medical students. The most "natural" position for birth is the one that suits you best. But you probably won't have a choice. Women in other countries often squat to give birth—in order to give gravity a chance to help pull the baby down—or else lie on their sides—to reduce pain and pressure. But American women lie flat on their backs, legs in the air—like overturned beetles.

(The prone position is more than merely uncomfortable. It can increase the pressure on the blood vessels running along your back, interfering with your circulation, and also your baby's.)

One reason hospitals insist that you lie on your back is so that they can fit your legs into stirrups. Your hands might be strapped down, too. Most mothers balk at being all buckled up for delivery, but again, the choice is not usually theirs to make. ("I hated it. All of a sudden, you don't have control over your own body.")

Once the hospital staff has you safely secured, the nurses can paint you with an antiseptic solution. Then they drape you with sterile sheets, so that all that shows is your gaping vagina. The doctor gets in position to perform the episiotomy. Needless to say, a mother who was heavily drugged would have to be tied down for such procedures. (Or perhaps it's the *awake* mothers that they have to tie down!) But most normal mothers would prefer to retain some shreds of dignity.

"That was a weird sensation, when they slop you with that cold solution. All of a sudden you feel that slop on you, and then they drape the sheets over you. When I had my second child, they threw it on me because she was coming so fast. The nurse took the can and just threw it on my crotch, like she was putting out a fire."

Recent improvements in obstetrical gadgetry have produced ways to tie you down that aren't quite so medieval. And if you're lucky, you might find yourself fitted into a softer kind of stirrup.

"It wasn't like a stirrup. You laid on the table and they put your legs on some kind of pads. And they closed with some kind of fuzzy stuff. It was the sensation of being warm on your legs—not of being strapped in."

You probably can't do much about being strapped down or on your back. But you don't have to take it lying down. Bring along some large pillows (and your husband) to prop you up for the pushes. Most mothers say this helps immeasurably.

THE EPISIOTOMY

The episiotomy is what doctors call a "relaxing incision." It allows the baby's head to be born without tearing vaginal tissue. The neat cut of the scalpel is easier to repair than the jagged wound that might result naturally. One mother in our Lamaze class had given birth once before without an episiotomy and vowed that she would never do it again. However, whether or not you need an episiotomy depends entirely on your physical and psychological state, your doctor, the size and position of your baby, and what sort of anesthetics and/or stimulants you've had during labor.

The objection to episiotomies is that they are routinely performed on all women all the time—in this country, not in Europe—regardless of whether or not they need them. A properly prepared mother should be able to ease the baby out without tearing tissue. Of course, if labor is speeded up by pitocin, the tissues don't have a chance to gently stretch to accommodate the baby. Forgoing an episiotomy requires that the mother be well trained in blowing—and that the doctor be well trained in waiting. It also helps if the mother isn't lying in the beetle position. Episiotomies are always required if forceps are used—or if the baby's simply too big to fit.

An episiotomy can be a four-inch-long incision, requiring regional anesthesia, and dozens of stitches. Therefore, it's not the sort of surgery you want performed unnecessarily. At best, if takes the bloom off the rose of motherhood, when you can't sit down for a week and have to inch around the maternity ward to avoid pulling your stitches. If sloppily performed, it can seriously hinder your sex life. So ask your doctor if you can try to deliver without an episiotomy—or at least with as small a one as possible.

My main objection to episiotomies is the scare stories doctors tell to talk women into having them. Tales of protruding bladders and rectums, inside-out vaginas and prolapsed uteruses. Undoubtedly it happens. But it also sometimes happens even with episiotomies. Episiotomies are not the cure for all female ills.

ISOLATION

Nothing takes a bloom off the rose like being separated from your baby. Isolating the mother when she runs a temperature "just in case" she should transmit something to the baby is also becoming standard hospital procedure. And it's running right in the face of evidence that maternal-infant bonding is too important to sacrifice for just-in-case medicine. Here are two prominent obstetricians' views:

"If anything has been demonstrated scientifically beyond a doubt, it's the bonding technique. Children who are held immediately by their parents have higher IQs, better vocabulary, better growth patterns, decreased infection rates."

"With all this bonding baloney, I don't see where it's prevented divorce or decreased juvenile delinquency. I have two of the most wonderful children in the world—they're bound to me like glue—and I nursed them myself on a bottle."

The conditions that can cause a mother's temperature to rise after childbirth include bladder infections (perhaps from a catheter), breast engorgement (when her milk comes in), cesarean section and normal aftereffects of labor and delivery. Most conditions that cause fevers are innocuous.

The problem is telling which is which. If the mother has a strep infection and it gets to the baby, it can cause serious complications, even death. So hospitals tend to cast a very wide net—even at the expense of maternal-infant contact. Some neonatologists (newborn specialists) say that the proof that mothers transmit infections to babies is absolutely zero. Indeed, some specialists say that holding a baby as soon as it's born is a good way to expose it to the mother's germs on purpose, so it can begin developing immunities in the safest possible way. A nursery full of other babies and nurses is a great deal more dangerous. (Nurses have sick children at home, too.)

Naturally, nursing mothers suffer most because separation from the baby interferes with milk production—and sets off another cycle. If the mother's running a temperature because her milk is coming in and she can't nurse her child, her temperature will go up even more. Therefore nursing mothers should be sure to request breast pumps to keep the milk flowing until they get their babies back.

Even if you have the most marvelous obstetrician in the world, he may not be able to do much to reunite you and your baby—not if isolation is a strict hospital policy. The best you can do is to remember that while bonding is important, it isn't going to make or break your relationship with your child. And just because he or she gets a couple of bottles of formula isn't necessarily going to mean that she isn't going to nurse. So take a little R and R and do everything possible to get your temperature down. This might mean cooling your temper for a while, too. But you're less likely to get hot under the collar if you are at least prepared.

Isolation, like episiotomies, enemas, and shaves, are unlikely to cause serious consequences for you or your baby. At most, they can damage your morale—which itself is no small factor. IVs, fetal monitors, drugs, and the beetle position can lead to cesarean section or the need for even more drugs which can adversely affect both your labor and your baby.

Unfortunately, there isn't usually much you can do to avoid many of these procedures. And it does little good to enter the hospital—or your doctor's office—with your dukes up, looking for a fight. You probably won't win anyway. And you might make things much more unpleasant than they have to be.

The best attitude, I think, is one of cautious optimism, constructive criticism, and calm acceptance of what you can't avoid. After all, it's a challenge to remain cool and dignified in the face of all that. Perhaps you can even retain your sense of humor—the greatest antidote of all. The more you are awake and aware, the more you will be able to control all aspects of your birth and labor. The better you are prepared, the more you will know what to expect, and what you think you can legitimately object to. A supportive husband never hurt either.

Hospitals differ, of course. So find out as much as possible about your hospital's procedures *before* you are admitted. Then, if you have strong objections, ask you doctor if the rules can be waived. Be sure to write the chief of obstetrics at the hospital, too. If hospitals don't know what women want, they won't know how to change to accommodate them.

NURSES

Almost without exception, the mothers I interviewed who had good childbirth experiences were attended by good nurses.

Nurses are the heartbeat of the hospital. They are everywhere, taking care of everything. A nurse will check you in and check out your baby's heartbeat. She'll give you your enema, shave, and medications. She'll wipe your brow and clean up your bedpan. It is not the ideal circumstance under which to make friends.

In some sense I am always amazed that nurses are *ever* pleasant, considering the work they do, and the pay they get to do it. Nurses do the dirty work of doctoring. At about one tenth the salaries doctors make. And yet, surprisingly, mothers reserve their highest praise for labor nurses—with little left for their obstetricians.

Perhaps this is a matter of misplaced expectations. We don't expect all our nurses to be Florence Nightingale, so we are pleasantly surprised when a total stranger takes a personal interest in our affairs. On the other hand, we've paid our doctor a pretty penny to take a personal interest. If he doesn't, we're deeply disappointed.

I don't remember having a particularly nice nurse—or an especially bad one (except the one who offered me the enema for a fever—and even she was more harried than horrible). I did, for a short while, have a very supportive labor nurse. Perhaps if she had been able to stick around, I would have had stories to tell like so many mothers I talked to:

"The nurses there make you feel as if you are the first one who ever had a baby there. A few of them stayed over their shift to see if I had a boy or a girl. One of them was my 'special nurse'—she stayed with me throughout labor. She was fantastic. She put me in a trance and made me relax. She made natural childbirth a reality for me."

"I think my greatest savior was that nurse because I went in there, and I was a wreck, and I said, 'I can't pull this off.' I was pleading with her to give me some medication. And she said, 'Get in control, get a grip on yourself.' And she went right down next to my ear and started with the breathing, and she got me back on my rhythm."

"I give all the credit to the Lamaze nurse who gave me the course. Because she really prepared me for what was going to happen and for taking charge. I did not lie down for pushing. I asked for pillows and sat up. And I never let them examine me during a contraction because she had warned me that was the most painful part. So I was fully prepared. She told me exactly what I needed to know."

Many mothers tell of being taught Lamaze right on the spot by supportive nurses. Or of watching nurses teach other mothers how to breathe properly—even mothers who had never heard of Lamaze or who didn't speak English. ("Watching them reminded me to keep control.") Of course, your nurse's attitude toward Lamaze—and her competence to teach it—depends not only on her personality, but also on hospital policy. She can't teach you a method she hasn't been taught, or isn't encouraged to use.

Indeed, some mothers felt their nurses were *too* insistent on Lamaze. They resented being "told what to do."

"I had to do it their way. And I didn't think it was right that they discouraged me to the point of threatening. They kept telling me that my baby would come out sleepy if I took any medication at all. One particularly rotten nurse—I had asked for medication because the pain was particularly bad—said, 'What do you expect? You're having a baby.'"

A nurse is there to serve you—but not to be your servant. If you treat her with respect, she'll probably return the favor. If not, then remember that the good news about nurses is that they always change with the next shift. If you get a nasty nurse for the beginning of labor, Florence Nightingale might just show up in time to help you through the end.

THE HOUSE STAFF

Needless to say, as long as you're in a hospital, you're going to have dealings with a lot of doctors. Most often, the doctor who cares for you won't be your personal physician, but rather one of the residents or interns or attending physicians who come with the hospital. Indeed, many women wonder after a hospital birth why they bothered to have a private doctor in the first place. Most of the time they are treated by the "house staff."

What this means for the birthing mother may be a lot of strangers poking and prodding—and also strangers controlling the circumstances of birth. You may have spent hours explaining to your private doctor about your preferences for anesthesia or nursing or Lamaze, but it won't do any good if he or she isn't there to implement the order. Many private doctors instruct the house staff not to call them until the mother is almost ready to deliver. If the house staff misjudges, then the doctor may not get there in time.

"I was very upset because I did not have my own doctor. The hospital doctors would come in and say, 'Oh, you're doing fine. Your doctor is on his way.' They said that at 6:15 and again at 7:45. So finally I said, 'Look, you have been telling me he's on his way for an hour and a half. I live ten minutes from here and he lives five minutes from me. So don't tell me he's on his way.' So finally they told me that he'd be there at 8:00. And I knew then they hadn't called him. I delivered at 8:03, and he was nowhere to be seen. The next day, he chewed out the resident because he hadn't called him."

Before you go into labor, try to pin down your private doctor as much as possible as to when he will come and how long he will stay with you. But still don't count on anything. My doctor, like others, promised to be around for at least the last few hours of labor. But he showed up only for the last five minutes—just in time to do the cesarean.

Meanwhile, being treated by many different doctors isn't necessarily harmful to your health, but it does break your sense of continuity. Especially if they each have different ways of counting centimeters—and different ideas of how well you're progressing. For that reason alone, having a string of strangers take care of you can be disconcerting. When those strangers are simply along to "observe" instead of to help, it can be downright offensive. My experience with the East Indian technician was not by any means unique:

"It was like the United Nations. First there was the Indian man. Up goes the sheet. Then there was the Chinese woman. One of them told me I had been pregnant for ten months. At one point a resident came in with four interns. He thought I would be an interesting 'case.' And the second resident with him was a woman—I'll never forget it. And she said, 'There's no way you're going to let all those people examine that girl. She's having a baby. This isn't all for the benefit of your education.' She was a real women's libber. And my doctor, of course, was over in his office on Park Avenue."

Whereas you pay your doctor to provide personal attention, the house staff has a full house of patients to take care of. Sometimes that care is good and sometimes it isn't. But either way, the house staff is hardly in a mood to listen to your personal complaints. More than private doctors, house physicians are bound by the book. They follow the rules—even when the rules might not apply to you. In a sense, interns and residents are still students. You may wind up as someone's guinea pig in a botched attempt to learn how to insert an IV:

"After I had Jamie, I had very high blood pressure, so they had to give me an intravenous. Now, nobody came in and told me I had high blood pressure; nobody told me I had to have an IV. This woman I never saw in my life walked in and gave me an intravenous and I started to go crazy. It didn't work right. The fluid started to come down very fast. And I was saying to her, 'I can't breathe.' And she completely ignored me. My husband called my doctor. He said that some of the new interns just didn't pay attention. They went by the rules and ignored you. So finally I screamed and a resident came in and ripped it right out of my arm. He said to the woman, 'What do you think you're doing?' He threw a fit at her. And afterwards, my doctor threw a fit at the resident. Because the resident insisted on telling me that it was all my imagination. After it was over, I apologized to the resident for panicking. But I really couldn't breathe. And he said, 'It was your imagination. I've never heard of that.' So later I asked my doctor, 'Have you ever heard of someone not being able to breathe? I'm getting a complex around here.' And he said, 'Of course.'"

I remember a very similar experience. A strange woman in a white coat came in the middle of the night to insert a new IV. (What a way to wake up!) Suddenly I was sweating profusely, clammy, and quite uncomfortable. A nurse came to the rescue. She said the IV was dripping much faster than it should have been. I was glad I spoke up; I thought I had become seriously ill.

It's frustrating enough when doctors do something obviously wrong. It's even more frustrating when they don't agree on what's wrong and right. One of my absent doctor's associates would tell me to stay in bed and drink fluids to bring down the fever. Five minutes later, the other doctor would arrive, wondering why I wasn't up walking around. He said that drinking fluids would only increase abdominal pain.

Nurses can disagree, too:

"It was in the middle of June, and I was dying of the heat. Finally I got this nice nurse to get me a fan. Two minutes later, another nurse walks in and turns it off. She says, 'You can't have that thing blowing on you!' I was going out of my mind."

Nobody wants to argue with someone wearing a white

coat—even if they aren't all good guys. But if you don't speak up when you think something is wrong, nobody's going to come around to right it. The more you understand about how hospitals birth babies, the more you'll be able to demand your rights without becoming a royal pain in the neck. If you sit back and say nothing, you not only may lose your mind—but your husband as well:

"My husband was supposed to be with me, but he was waiting for the nurse to call him in. I waited over an hour. Finally, another nurse went to get him. And thirty minutes later, he still wasn't there. Finally I had to get up and go out into the hallway and fetch him myself."

Some women love the attention they get from a large hospital staff. They like the distraction, the company, the extra care extra people can provide. "During a Leboyer delivery, I looked over and there were four or five people standing in the doorway, but that was okay. It was beautiful at that point."

Other women are amused by interns and student nurses. They enjoy being part of the teaching process. Sometimes they sympathize so much with the struggles of a student to help at her first birth or insert her first IV that they forget their own troubles in the process.

"One student nurse revealed by her expression that she was having trouble detecting the heartbeat. She silently left and returned with her instructor, who demonstrated the correct procedure. I thought it was funny. And I found myself trying to put *her* at ease."

In short, doctors and nurses, like patients, are only human. If you can't do anything about the sometimes inhospitable atmosphere in hospitals, it doesn't help to contribute to it either. It doesn't mean you should let incompetent or inconsiderate doctors walk all over you; it just means you shouldn't—unnecessarily—walk all over them. If you're well and healthy, you don't need to be in a hospital anyway. So bring along your husband and your teddy bear, and try to pretend you're at home.

THE MOTHERS

You may feel as if you're the only woman in the world who's ever had a baby—but of course you're not. And your stay in the hospital may make this uncomfortably clear. You'll labor with other women, deliver with them, and recover in their company. Depending on when and where you deliver, you may see only one or two other mothers, or you may begin to think that having a baby is a group activity. Either way, the presence of other mothers can be comforting. It can also drive you right up the proverbial wall. The last thing a mother attempting Lamaze needs is a laboring women who's screaming her head off next door:

"I told one of the nurses, 'I hurt, too, but I'm not screaming my brains out like that other woman. Would you please shut her up? She's not helping me one bit. If I can hold it down, so can she.'"

Sometimes another woman's screams can be just the extra incentive you need to help you concentrate on your contractions:

"I heard this woman in the background yelling, 'Kill me! Somebody please kill me!' It was the most bloodcurdling, spine-chilling thing I ever heard. I turned around to my husband and I said, 'Thank God I took Lamaze.' That convinced me not to take any drugs—I didn't want to wind up like her."

You may hear other kinds of screaming in the hospital halls: doctors screaming at nurses, nurses screaming at mothers, mothers screaming at doctors. And depending on your personality, it may distract you, amuse you, or drive you crazy.

Whether or not you keep company during labor may not be a matter of choice. But whether you want to share a room afterward usually is. In most hospitals, you can reserve either a private room or semiprivate facilities—a large room with two or four mothers. (Just remember that your reservation is a request and not a guarantee.)

I'm normally a loner, but when it came to having a baby, I figured I could use all the help I could get. I opted for sharing my room with three other women. The arrangement had its pros and cons.

Cons, because when you're isolated from your baby, it doesn't feel very good to look on as three other mothers feed and fondle theirs. For three days I hid behind my curtain, glowering at my breast pump and at anything or anybody else who dared to venture inside. On the third day, I made a tentative re-entry into the world—only to discover that two of my roommates were cesarean mothers themselves. Indeed, it was they who told me that fevers are common after sections. (They both had fevers with their first births.) And they who encouraged me to cool down and wait it out.

In some ways, it's hard to predict whether or not you'll want to share a room. If you have an easy delivery, you might just want the company of other women. If you're sick or have had a cesarean, you might want to be left alone to lick your wounds. So you have to follow your instincts—and your pocketbook. Private rooms are much more expensive then semiprivate rooms or wards. And they are not generally covered by health insurance.

THE BABIES

Rooming-in means having your baby with you in the hospital most of the time. And like everything else associated with childbirth, it is a matter of opinion:

"I loved it," said one mother. "I loved having my new doll with me to cuddle and play with."

"I would hate it," said another. "I can't stand the aquatic sounds babies make."

Rooming-in is best when it's your first baby. Worst when it's your third, you have two toddlers at home, and this might be your last chance to rest for a year. Obviously, rooming-in, like sharing a room, works better when you're feeling better. I desperately wanted rooming-in in spite of my cesarean, but perhaps I would have been better off taking advantage of the rest. Indeed, I used to think I was superior to mothers who risked bonding with their new baby in order to speed their own recuperation. ("Why do I need to care for the baby full-time in the hospital? I'll be caring for her full-time for the next fifteen years.") Now I know better. There is a legitimate case for wanting to be left alone.

Still, it takes two to room-in. Before you abandon the idea, think about what it means to abandon your baby to his Plexiglas cradle and the irregular care of busy nurses. At least *you* can call for a nurse to come and change your IV—but your baby can't call for someone to come and change his or her diaper— or to give her a cuddle or something to eat. All she can do is add her cries to those of her swaddled companions in the nursery. If a hospital is a strange and forbidding place to you, just think what it's like to a newborn child.

Of course, as long as you're in the hospital, the hospital will set certain restrictions as to when and how you can see your baby—even if you are rooming-in. Don't be deceived into thinking that mere maternity gives you maternal rights. The baby is really yours only when you get it home. Before then, everything goes by the clock and by the book. I've known some nursery nurses who should have been sentries guarding the crown jewels.

"I went down to the nursery, and the head nurse saw me and let out a yell—like I was a fox in the henhouse."

One morning a platoon of white-coated men spent almost an hour examing my poor Peter. Pediatricians, I later learned. He had an adverse reaction to the silver nitrate they put in all babies' eyes. (The reaction is common.) But would anybody tell me why my baby was suddenly a subject for medical school? No way. I learned what the fuss was about only when I left. When the nurse at the desk chased us halfway down the hallway yelling, "Mommy! (That's what they call you in the hospital.) You forgot the prescription for the baby's eyes!"

It is probably obvious by now that I am not a great fan of the American hospital as a place to birth babies. The reader may wonder, then, why I'm not promoting home birth. In part this is because I'm confused—like everybody—about the statistics. Studies that show home births are safer are contradicted by studies that show hospitals are safer—and vice versa.

On balance, the risks are probably about equal—assuming that the mother at home has adequate care and has been properly screened. Still, I'd be afraid to have a baby at home for one ill-conceived (no pun intended) reason: I'm chicken. Not that I'm any *less* afraid of hospitals. But if something goes wrong, I'd rather blame somebody in a white coat than keep it on my own conscience. Which, I know, is lousy logic. By that reasoning, I should feel just as guilty if something went wrong in a hospital and I chose not to have the baby at home. But I fear this is not an issue that lends itself well to logic—lousy or otherwise.

Unfortunately, even the most modern mothers have few viable options. Midwives or obstetricians who will deliver at home are as hard to find as homey hospitals. But they are—increasingly—around. So before you resign yourself to the rigors of a traditional hospital birth, ask around about birthing rooms and Lamaze rooms and hospitals that don't put a lot of technical paraphernalia on perfectly healthy mothers who don't want it. Maybe if enough mothers ask, the hospitals will begin to get the message. Everybody wants the technology around when they need it. Nobody wants the technology to be the main event.

Pain Relief:

Knocking Yourself Out to Have a Baby

Pain has always been a part of labor. Pain relievers are a far more recent discovery. Queen Victoria was the first mother to ease the pain of labor by inhaling ether (or chloroform, depending on who you read) to deliver her son Edward. And until the time our mothers bore us, the art of anesthesia had remained essentially Victorian.

Today we know that drugs like ether and chloroform and morphine often produce dangerously drugged babies. In their place, modern mothers turn either to the increasingly intricate forms of anesthesia administered only in modern hospitals. Or to no drugs at all—the "psychoprophylactic" pain relief provided by Lamaze training.

Indeed, today's mother has a veritable drugstore of pain relievers to choose from. The various compounds may be inhaled or injected or dripped into her veins or spinal fluid through intravenous catheters. They can numb part of her or all of her. They can ease the pain of birth, or of labor, or both. They "relax" her, "put her to sleep," or "knock her out."

Surprisingly, few mothers know exactly what anesthetic agent was used to dull their senses during childbirth. (Except Lamaze mothers, of course.) Fewer still are prepared for the consequences. One reason is that terms like "knocked out" and "relaxed" often mean nothing of the kind. Because the terms are misleading, the mother is misled. In the same way, it is misleading to describe as "sleepy" a baby who is hard to resuscitate because the mother was overmedicated. "Sleepy" and "drugged" are not the same thing at all.

Fritzie (our Lamaze instructor) first developed a credibility problem when she told us that too much Demerol during labor might produce a "sleepy" baby. I knew that drugs like Demerol often produced babies who had trouble breathing. But "sleepy"? It was the first (but not the last) time I heard that word used in that context.

I was further confused when Fritzie advertised the advantages of spinal-type anesthesia to "take a rest" during labor. First, I was surprised to find a Lamaze instructor waxing so enthusiastic about wonder drugs. Second, because a classmate suggested that it might be difficult physically and psychologically to suddenly find yourself in active labor after such a "rest." Fritzie said it wouldn't be. But not ten minutes before, she had said that induced labor was difficult for precisely that reason—because the mother didn't have a chance to "get used to" labor in a gradual way.

I had every intention of going through labor with no anesthesia at all—mainly because I couldn't stand the thought of needles and gas masks and intravenous injections. Many mothers share my fears. Like me, they need to be practically put out to have a tooth pulled. (We are not a brave bunch.) But they fear injections and IVs, and most of all the thought of being unconscious while others do with you what they will.

Nevertheless, about eight hours into labor I succumbed to the thought of how nice it would be to have just a little something to take the edge off the pain. Only to be told no. No? I protested. What do you mean no? Whatever happened to all those marvelous painkillers and relaxers and being "knocked out"? But it was nothing doing. An hour or so later, I got a small shot of Demerol. Almost immediately, labor went from bad to unbearable. At first I thought it was mere coincidence. But having talked to many mothers, I'm convinced it was the Demerol itself. Demerol can take away your control, your confidence, and your ability to ride out contractions. But it can't take away pain. The combination can be harder to handle than the contractions themselves.

Only when the time came to do the cesarean did I experience real "pain relief": when the anesthesiologist showed his student how to give me an epidural injection. It lasted about five minutes. They talked golf while I tried desperately to convince them that the injection wasn't working. Finally they tried again. Eureka! Blessed relief!

I didn't feel so blessed after I woke up. And I was surprised to learn that much of the abdominal pain I was experiencing came not from the surgery, but from the pain reliever itself.

"Usually, if you have an operation, you don't see yourself recovering from the anesthesia because you're also recovering from this far more overwhelming thing, the surgery," said Holly. "But when I had an abortion, I realized how bad the anesthesia was. It was just a little peanuts operation. But I was knocked out for it—and I spent two days recovering from the anesthesia."

Anesthesia is strong stuff.

It is also dangerous stuff—which is why obstetricians won't always allow you to have as much as you might like. No, Virginia, there is no such thing as being "knocked out" for labor. Mothers who ask, "Just put me to sleep" are asking for a big surprise.

Obstetricians rarely discuss anesthesia more than superficially. Even if you ask, you won't get the right answers unless you know the right questions. If your question is vague ("What about the epidural?"), you're likely to get an equally vague answer—usually in the nature of how it works and how long it lasts. More often, the obstetrician merely tells you what kind of anesthesia you're going to get. Rare is the obstetrician who presents options. Rarer still the one who discusses how a pain-killer will affect (and aftereffect) you. Almost nonexistent is the one who warns of effects on your baby.

(*All* painkillers and relaxers affect the baby to some degree. None is "perfectly safe." This isn't meant to scare mothers away from accepting painkillers. It is merely to state the facts. Of course, some drugs are much more harmful than others— and it behooves you to know which is which.)

Why don't doctors discuss options in anesthesia? One reason is that they often don't have options. Obstetricians like to use the kinds of anesthesia they are familiar with. Just as their preference to perform vertical as opposed to "bikini" cuts for cesareans depends largely on what they've been practicing in the past. Not every obstetrician (or anesthesiologist) knows how to administer every kind of painkiller. Moreover, not every hospital has available every kind of anesthetic apparatus. Or the personnel needed to administer them. If your obstetrician tells you you can't have a certain (or any) kind of anesthesia, he may really be saying, "You can't have any of the anesthesia I have available here."

Granted, the hows and whys of modern painkilling agents are not always easy to explain or understand. As techniques and drugs have proliferated, so has their complexity. But this does not mean you should abdicate all decisions to your doctor. And even if he or she does make the final choices, you will have to live with the consequences. If you are ill-informed, you will be ill-prepared to cope.

DEMEROL: Just a Little Something to Relax You

An invention of modern medicine, Demerol is a synthetic narcotic. It makes a mother sleepy, dreamy, numb. In the process, it slows down labor and can even stop it. It affects your respiratory system as well as your nervous system—indeed, it slows down all your systems. Most important, it slows down the immature respiratory system of your unborn child—making it more likely that he or she will be born with breathing difficulties ("sleepy").

It does everything but take away the pain:

"The Demerol calmed me down. If someone had been talking to me, I'm sure I sounded like I was half-gone. I remember everything being very slow. My mouth was dry. I felt like everything was very numb. Except the pain. No matter how much they gave me, the pain didn't go away. Everything was going so slowly. I just wasn't dilating. They kept giving me more and more, and they'd put it right through the IV. And each time I could feel it taking effect. But it just didn't do anything for the pain."

"You don't have control with Demerol unless they are very sensitive as to how much they give you. It relaxes your muscles, and you can still sort of hear what they are saying, but you're sort of out of control. The nurses had to wrap my arms up tight so they didn't go flying all over because I was struggling to deliver the baby, but I was not in control. The nurses were really working with me to push the baby out, but I don't think I was doing it right. It's humiliating because you're so out of it."

Demerol is the "little something to relax you" that laboring women hear so much about. The shot in the arm that gives you a second wind for a long labor. And sometimes it works well. Especially if the mother is nervous or breathing too fast (and hyperventilating) or just plain scared.

"I was able to handle it better because the Demerol acted like a tranquilizer. I feel I would have shorted out without it. It did not help the contractions at all, which is something I understood about Demerol anyway. But it did allow me to relax in between. And I think just being able to nod off between the contractions really gave me a second wind."

Unfortunately, the disadvantages of Demerol often outweigh the advantages—especially if it's given in too large a dose—which it too often is. (One sound piece of advice I got from Fritzie was to specifically request a small dose of anything. Then you can see how it affects you and proceed from there. Also, be sure to tell the anesthesiologist and/or nurse if you are particularly tired or particularly susceptible to drugs. There's no guarantee that they'll pay attention, but it's well worth trying.)

Demerol is only one of many kinds of narcotics and tranquilizers that relax you and sometimes "take the edge off" the pain. All go directly to the baby. They are not anesthetics, but rather analgesia—which reduces pain, but doesn't obliterate it. (Aspirin is analgesia.) Anesthetics numb you or knock you out. (Novocaine is an anesthetic.) Of the former, Demerol is by far the most popular.

What's wrong with "a little something to relax you"? Most important, if it's any more than a very little, it's going to relax your baby right into a "sleepy" state. But it can also have ill effects on you. The one I experienced was what I've come to call the "alarm clock" effect—a phrase I borrowed from one of the mothers I interviewed:

"I was doing this on three hours' sleep, and the Demerol did allow me to sleep between contractions, but all of a sudden you would find yourself in the middle of this pain. I mean, an alarm clock is bad news, but this is ridiculous. It's a hell of a way to wake up."

Because Demerol often makes you sleep between contractions, you may be unconscious of the one- or two-minute rest in between. The result is that labor might feel like one continuous contraction.

"I had no respite. It was a contraction, and then I would nod off, but I didn't know I had nodded off. And then when I came crashing awake with the next contraction, it was like one big long contraction. I found it very disconcerting. There was no rhyme or reason to it."

I, too, remember being barely able to lift my head up, so sleepy was I from the Demerol. The world around me seemed hazy, blurred, semiconscious. The only thing that was in focus was the pain. But instead of being in control of my faculties so I could stay on top of my contractions, my faculties were numbed. My contractions were controlling me. Indeed, I didn't even perceive them as contractions, but as one unrelenting ache. And I was at the mercy of that ache. It was a helpless, hopeless feeling—like a drunk trying to rally himself to come in out of the cold.

Like booze, Demerol can put you literally out of your senses. It may throw off not only your physical balance, but your emotional stability as well. One mother blamed Demerol for letting loose her fears that she had damaged her unborn child by taking antibiotics while she was pregnant:

"I was dilated almost completely. And then I said, 'It's getting a little uncomfortable.' So they gave me some Demerol in the rear end. And something in my brain clicked. I guess the stuff was working. It brought out my subconscious fear that the baby was not going to be normal. Therefore I was not certain I wanted him to come out. It took many more hours of them giving me all sorts of stuff. I was terrified. I was in agony. And the doctor kept saying, 'But dear, you're not even having a contraction.' And it was the most ripping agonizing pain ever. The labor was not so bad until I got the drugs. Then it was my subconscious that took over and made it so horrible."

My own (new) obstetrician warned me recently that Lamaze teachers and doctors are setting up a dangerous situation when they recommend Demerol as a relaxant. Dangerous for babies and dangerous for mothers, too. "It dulls their reflexes, and it dulls their minds," he said. "The price they pay for taking the edge off the pain is losing control. From then on, everything gets worse. From then on, the obstetrician has to take control. It's a form of brainwashing."

So before you take a little something to relax you—whether it's Demerol or another similar drug—remember that it may make your labor worse. It will almost certainly make it longer. If you must have something, ask for just a little bit—half the normal dose. And try if you can to rely on the much more effective medicine contained in the loving care of a good doctor, a supportive nurse, and your ever-helpful husband.

EPIDURAL: The Ace in the Hole

How would you like to be awake and aware for the birth of your child and yet not feel an iota of pain? How would you like an anesthetic that numbs you completely, but is completely safe for your baby? The answer, of course, is: "Who wouldn't?"

No wonder so many women consider the epidural their "ace in the hole."

The epidural is a type of spinal anesthesia that seems to be getting more popular every day. It is a modification of the spinal—or saddle block, as it's also known. Spinals go directly into the spine and are notorious for producing violent headaches. Epidurals go into a layer of nerves just outside the spinal canal. Therefore (if properly administered) they don't cause headaches. The epidural anesthetic can be administered through a catheter in the mother's back and provides continuous, total relief.

"Once they gave me the epidural, I was out. I would have swept the floors for them. It was terrific. My doctor said, 'You know, you sure rallied at the end.' And I said, 'Sure, I rallied. It didn't hurt anymore. Once it stopped hurting, I was terrific.'"

"What's nice is that you can start off Lamaze, and then if you need something, it doesn't have to be total. Even if you don't do Lamaze, you can be awake for the birth. My girlfriend got an epidural right away. She felt great through the whole labor. She was awake, aware, her husband was there, they saw the delivery, she felt super. I didn't have an epidural until the end, but it was very important for me to know that when I wanted something—when I felt I couldn't handle it—I could get something. Everybody I know who had an epidural says childbirth is the most wonderful experience in your life."

Hospital-based Lamaze classes often promote the epidural as the "easy out" when the going gets rough. If you can't make it all the way on Lamaze, don't worry. We'll give you an epidural. It won't hurt your baby and it won't knock you out. It isn't even like getting a drug.

The trouble is, epidurals *are* drugs. And they have effects many mothers don't prepare for. The most serious is that the mother is insensitive not only to labor pains, but also the spontaneous signals from her uterus that tell her it's time to bear down to help the baby out—the urge to push. The result is frequent use of forceps and a higher rate of cesarean sections.

An epidural—like Novocaine—leaves you numb, a feeling that may last for hours after labor is over. Some mothers say it makes their legs feel heavy and puffy, like "lead cotton candy." Others say their legs feel disembodied, as if they belong to someone else. They try to wiggle their toes only to feel for the first time what a "paralyzed" person feels like.

But epidurals don't really paralyze you. Spinals, on the other hand do—which is why they are a much more "serious" kind of anesthesia. Spinals block the nerves going both to and from the affected areas. The mother couldn't push if she wanted to. Epidurals block only the nerves coming *from* the areas—in other words, the sensation of pain or the urge to push. But the mother is not paralyzed. She can push on the doctor's command if she's been practicing diligently and if the doctor knows how to direct her. Unfortunately, neither mothers nor doctors are always well trained.

(Interestingly, I found out that Fritzie herself had an epidural during childbirth some years after she taught our Lamaze class. She herself was not prepared for pushing on command. And she herself finally had a forceps delivery.)

Forceps are not necessarily a cause for feeling the delivery is a failure. On the contrary. And an obstetrician who is skilled with a forceps will not harm your baby. However, he or she will have to perform a larger episiotomy on you. And your husband will probably have to leave the room and miss the birth. (Ask your doctor and hospital about their policy on husbands and forceps.)

Another disadvantage of epidurals is that they can be administered only for the final hours of labor. For many mothers, this means laboring without anesthesia until they are almost ready for pushing—the "good" (or at least productive) part. An epidural administered too early can stop labor completely, so cautious obstetricians tend to postpone it as long as possible. If you've been counting on the epidural as your ace in the hole and therefore haven't bothered to learn Lamaze breathing, you're going to find yourself with no recourse for the long first stages of labor. You can probably have Demerol, but that will make the labor even longer.

"He said they can't give it to you until the second stage of labor, which is the least painful. It's almost like Catch-22. I felt the baby's head coming out before I was given the epidural. It was not given until I started to push. I still felt the episiotomy, and I felt the baby come out. Next time I want to go natural because I was so close that I don't think I really needed it at all."

Epidurals don't have to be given at the last minute. They can be given as soon as you are really in active labor. But since no one—much less interns and residents—wants to take the chance that you aren't, they wait until you are a predetermined number of centimeters dilated. A skilled obstetrician would be able to establish that it could be administered sooner, but those kinds of skills are rare.

Indeed, many, many hospitals don't do epidurals because they consider them too dangerous, too risky. Inserting the needle in just the right place is a tricky procedure; it involves a tremendous amount of training and skill. Hospitals tend to give epidurals almost all of the time—or almost none of the time. It depends entirely on the skills of the attending anesthesiologists. (Two teaching hospitals within twenty miles of each other—both affiliated with the same medical school—perform epidurals for cesareans 5 per cent of the time and 95 per cent of the time, respectively.) If your hospital doesn't do epidurals frequently, it may not be a good idea to have one done there.

A "caudal" is the same as an epidural, only it's given lower. It's rarer, trickier, and better still. The anesthetic effect travels feet first directly to your cervix and vagina. Epidurals fan out in both directions from the belly button. Thus caudals get to the painful spots faster and more effectively.

The cloud in the caudal lining is that it's even more difficult to administer than an epidural. A badly administered caudal or epidural often results in an inadvertent spinal. That's why women frequently say they got violent headaches from "epidurals." What they really had was an epidural that went wrong—and wound up as a spinal.

"They gave me an epidural. And after a while that wore off. So they gave me another one. But he gave it to me wrong, and it went up to my brain. I had a huge enormous headache. My head was throbbing. I didn't even feel the labor pains. And my doctor was nowhere to be found. He was off delivering someone else."

Another mother got her headache—and worse—the day *after* delivery:

"The first day I was fine. I was walking around. But by four o'clock in the afternoon the next day, I couldn't pick up my head because I had this incredible headache. The next thing I knew, I had a stiff neck. And it was downhill for two days. I was totally paralyzed. I couldn't move. I couldn't even get my head up from off the pillow."

An epidural administered too high can even hit the mother's lungs or heart. And despite frequent claims to the contrary, recent studies by a Dr. John Scanlon have shown that the epidural anesthetic does show up in the babies' bloodstreams. It also shows up in their behavior, producing "floppier" newborns. (Although the harmful effects on babies of regional, spinal-type anesthetics are far less than those of systemic drugs like Demerol or general anesthetics.)

Finally, epidurals tend to get mothers caught up in the hospital-technology spiral. If an epidural stops labor, pitocin is used to start it up again. The mother needs an IV, a fetal monitor, a spinal catheter, probably forceps, and perhaps a cesarean. So before you get the cycle going, at least be aware of where it may take you.

Another type of regional anesthesia that mothers often confuse with spinals and epidurals and caudals is the paracervical block. This is administered by a long "scary" needle through the vagina to the nerves leaving the uterus. It numbs the cervix and uterus completely (labor pain) but not the vagina or perineum (birth pain). You can't have an episiotomy with a paracervical, and it doesn't relax the muscles of the birth canal, but for some mothers, it's a perfect solution.

"I was a Lamaze patient, so they called down the anesthesiologist and gave me a paracervical. And he said it was a local, and it could only be given at the end when you are almost ready to deliver, and it would last only an hour. He said I would not feel the contractions, but when I started pushing, it has nothing to do with that. I would feel everything. And within two minutes after he gave it to me, I felt nothing. And it was weird because I could have walked around. It doesn't paralyze you. It's not like an epidural where you can't feel the pushing. Because even though it hurts like hell, I want to feel that. To me, that is the birth."

For the same reason that mothers might like it (that they can feel the birth), the paracervical block is not as medically useful as are epidurals. Indeed, epidurals are the preferred form of anesthesia for breech and premature births. The absence of pain in the birth canal allows the mother to relax completely. This allows for an easier passage (for the baby) and makes it easier for the doctor to use forceps if necessary to speed things along even faster. General anesthesia would also relax the mother's muscles, but is too readily transmitted to the baby. A paracervical block wouldn't relax the vaginal muscles at all because the mother can still feel pain there.

In short, epidurals and caudals and even paracervicals *can* be your ace in the hole. But it's foolish to count on it. It's more foolish still to forgo Lamaze training in the belief that epidurals promise painless labor. They don't. When they work (and they don't always), they can give you a painless birth. Consider your options carefully, based on what your obstetrician and your hospital offers. And then be prepared to labor on your own until the final stages, to push on command from your doctor, and to have a forceps delivery if the pushing isn't effective enough. If you know what to expect, you won't be disappointed. You may even have a "beautiful birth experience" with an epidural. But it still isn't "natural childbirth." Which isn't wrong or right, it just isn't. Being "awake" is better than being asleep. And being a spectator at your child's birth is in some ways a spectacular achievement. But being a participant is even better.

KNOCKED OUT: I Didn't Feel a Thing, Doctor

Knocking yourself out to have a baby is the hard way. What's more, it's a deception. You know those women in the labor room who are screaming hysterically? Those are the ones who've been "knocked out." Indeed, using the expression "put to sleep" to describe what happens to a mother during a medicated birth is about as accurate as using "put to sleep" to describe what happens to your dog on his final visit to the vet.

Nevertheless, myths die hard—especially this one. I cringe when I hear mothers say, "I knew I would need medication because I hate pain." Or "My doctor tries to push you to have natural childbirth, but I just can't see why I should have to feel pain if I don't have to." Or "I just want to be put to sleep for the whole thing. Tell me when it's over."

Unfortunately, the truth is that *nobody* gets knocked out for labor. If you did, labor would come to a halt. Not to mention your baby's vital signs. Why, then, do so many women say that they "didn't feel a thing" during labor? That they woke up after it was all over and asked the doctor, "When will I have my baby?" Not because they didn't *feel* their labor, but because they *forgot* their labor. They *felt* every probably very painful minute.

Scopolamine, my obstetrician tells me, was developed by the Nazis in World War II concentration camps. I don't doubt it. The so-called "twilight sleep" method of childbirth involves injecting the laboring mother with this powerful amnesiac so that she forgets the entire birth experience. But scopolamine is also a stimulant. It makes the mother hyperactive, so she needs Demerol and other drugs to calm her down. She may also get a variety of other narcotics and tranquilizers that can be extremely dangerous for her baby. Of course, the doctor doesn't *have* to give her any painkillers at all. She can writhe and scream for hours of uncontrolled agony—only to wake up the next morning and say, "Thank you, Doctor. I didn't feel a thing."

"I went twilight, and I had a beautiful trip. Twilight is an amnesiac. What it does is, you're really awake, but you don't remember it. At least you're not supposed to remember it. But I can remember yelling and sobbing and screaming, and I didn't know if it was a dream or if it wasn't a dream. I snapped to at one point, and the doctor was pushing on my stomach hard as hell, and I was saying to him, 'Give me something, please give me something.' And I remember saying, 'You sent my husband away, so give me something.' And he said, 'No, you're going to help me have this baby, damn it.' And when I woke up I had this horrible sore throat for a whole day. I didn't want to hold the baby because I thought I was sick. But it was just because I was screaming and screaming."

"I was a labor nurse, which is why I had a midwife when I had my own baby. If you knock them out right away, the labor stops. So you give them pitocin. And with every contraction, they're crying and screaming, but they don't even know they're screaming. One woman woke up black and blue—she was fighting so hard, and they had to tie her down. And when she woke up, she didn't even remember it."

Fortunately, scopolamine is slowly going the way of concentration camps. Today good obstetricians use it only in unusual cases—for example, if the mother is very young and plans to give up her baby for adoption.

In the absence of an amnesiac, getting "knocked out" means getting a general anesthetic for the birth itself. You can't get it much before the last minute because the depressing effects of the drugs (gas or injection) are much too dangerous for your baby. They are also dangerous for you. Regional anesthesia, such as the epidural, numbs you only below the waist. But you can still breathe on your own. Under general anesthesia, the mother may not breathe normally for many hours after delivery. During delivery, she may vomit, inhale food, and develop pneumonia. This is the single most common cause of maternal death.

Why is general anesthesia used at all then? It's used when epidurals aren't available, or for emergency cesareans, or in other cases when the mother (or doctor) demands a completely unconscious patient. But whatever you may get *before* delivery, you won't get the general anesthetic until the beginning of the actual birth. Which means, in effect, that you've suffered through all the bad part only to be knocked out for the good part.

This usually comes as news to mothers. Indeed, several malpractice cases have been brought by mothers who had counted on being knocked out for childbirth, then sued their doctors when they didn't get *enough* medication. The mothers didn't know (because the doctors didn't tell them) that they still had to go through those early stages of labor.

"I always thought that not having natural childbirth meant that somebody gave you a shot and you went bye-bye for the whole thing. But it was absolutely horrendous."

Other mothers feel like suing because they got cheated out

of the birth experience, having already paid the price of labor. If they had known that knocking out was a last-minute thing, they wouldn't have wanted to be knocked out at all:

"I had wanted natural childbirth, but I couldn't find a doctor to do it. Then, to add insult to injury, they gave me pitocin, which meant my labor was forty-five minutes long. And so when I said, 'I think I need something for the pain,' the doctor, instead of saying, 'Stick with it, you'll have the baby in five minutes,' just stuck that thing in my arm, and I woke up sick. And for five minutes more I could have done it, but nobody ever told me I was so close. The only way I knew what happened was that I saw the clock on the wall and I saw the birth certificate. My baby was born five minutes after I asked for anesthesia."

Before you get the general anesthetic, you'll be asking for and getting Demerol and other analgesics. You won't get as much as you'd like—but you will get enough to prolong your labor significantly. One obstetrician writes that it takes about twice as long to deliver drugged as it does au naturel. So be sure to balance that against the benefits of painkillers. This explains some of the three- and four-day labors our mothers tell about. In some cases, the women were simply so overmedicated that they couldn't produce the child.

"My sister was in labor for something like thirty-six hours. I mean, it was absolutely insane. They would give her a shot of something, and it would put her to sleep. And labor would stop. And then she'd start all over again, and then it would hurt and they'd put her to sleep again. And they did that over and over. Today she still has nightmares about it. She wakes up screaming, and her husband tells her that she was delivering a baby."

The effects of being "put to sleep" stay with you in more ways than one. Even if scopolamine has made you forget everything. Freud would have had a field day uncovering the damage done to a woman's subconscious by the effects of a semiconscious labor. Indeed, *not* remembering labor may simply be another way to prolong it. That's why you have nightmares.

Medicated mothers and babies also have more traditional sorts of hangovers. You may wake up with headaches or nausea or breathing problems or just plain feeling dopey. Whatever it is, it doesn't feel good, and it doesn't do you much good either. Alka-Seltzer doesn't help.

"They gave me Demerol and the stuff that makes you forget, but they gave me too much. After it was over, I kept waking up and saying, 'Did I have a baby?' And they'd say, 'Yes, you had a son.' And I'd go back to sleep, and I'd wake up and ask again, 'Did I have a baby?' And that's my son Robbie, who I have so many problems with."

Robbie's problems may or may not be related to his birth experience. But his mother thinks they are, which is a problem in itself. Indeed, the problems associated with knocked-out deliveries seem to far outweigh any possible benefits. And while I've talked to mothers who raved about epidurals or para-cervical blocks or Leboyer or Lamaze, I never once met a mother who had anything good to say about a knock-down-drag-'em-out-birth. However you look at it, it's a disappointment.

Of course, I don't pretend to know all the ins and outs of anesthesia. Few people do. Not obstetricians. Not mothers. It's a specialty that takes years to learn, decades to master. And I've heard a lot of tales from mothers that I still don't fully understand. For example, of how husbands are often asked to leave if even the slightest bit of medication is given. Or of being knocked out immediately *after* the birth—perhaps so that the doctor can sew up the episiotomy. Sometimes these procedures are the results of sound medical reasoning, sometimes a doctor's personal preferences, sometimes time-honored (and ironclad) hospital policy. Mothers often wake up unaware not only of what happened to them, but also of how and why. Only your anesthetist knows for sure.

But even if you can't predict exactly what anesthesia will do for you (or to you) during labor, you can know what it *can't* do. What it *can't* do is put you to sleep for the duration. You may as well make up your mind that you're going to be around for most of the birth experience. Having gone that far, it's probably worth your while to stick around for all of it.

EVEN WITHOUT LAMAZE

If you can't count on an epidural, and if anesthesia to "put you to sleep" won't, then what's a mother to do? Well, she can always try Lamaze. But the statistics show that a very small percentage of mothers are even preparing for natural childbirth, much less going through with it. Does this mean that they're doomed to drugs?

Not at all. Indeed, mothers have been having babies long before Lamaze was around. Lamaze was a reaction to the horrors of drugged deliveries. Before drugs, childbirth was completely natural (if also very dangerous). But the anesthetics were fairly effective: they consisted of support from friends and relatives and a knowledgeable midwife (or witch doctor).

Which is only to say that you can't prescribe a particular pain remedy for everyone. Whether it's a prescription for drugs, or a prescription for breathing. Some people have adverse reactions to drugs. And some have adverse reactions to huffing and panting. Many mothers steer clear of Lamaze simply because they don't like the tone of the books, or because they don't want to go to "classes" to learn how to have a baby, or because they want to keep their pregnancies private.

But dropping out of your Lamaze course is a poor excuse for turning to drugs. In the first place, non-Lamaze birth alternatives abound—from hypnotism to husband-coached. Second and more significant is that most mothers—given a maximum of support and a minimum of medication—seem to figure out the breathing all by themselves. Natural childbirth often seems to come naturally. You go with the flow. Like sailing or riding a bike, it's something you learn by feel. And many mothers seem to learn it remarkably well. I can't count how many non-Lamaze mothers have told me that they didn't take drugs because they didn't feel they were necessary. Or that labor without medication hurt a great deal less than labor with medication. And these are mothers who never took a breathing lesson in their lives.

So even if you're without training, without preparation, without your husband and even without lollipops, you still may do a whole lot better without drugs.

THE PUSHERS

More than anything, childbirth is a state of mind. You have to have your wits about you to handle it. It's all too easy to succumb to the temptation of drugs. But I often think we wouldn't succumb so easily if we weren't tempted so often.

If there is one common complaint among mothers about

hospital births, it is how often they are stuck with injections that they didn't want. Or tempted with drugs that they just as well could have done without:

"I hated that they would not listen when I told them I did not need whatever it was that they were putting on my face. I told them I didn't want anything unless there was some kind of complication, but they just snuck up on me. And all those drugs go directly to the baby. With Tracy, it took them a long time to slap her around."

"My mother had four kids, and on the last one she went in the hospital at 7:30 and my sister was born at 8:00. And she said to the nurse, 'I'd like to see this one.' And the nurse said, 'Oh, Laura, it's not glamorous—you don't really want to see it.' And she had gone through the entire day in her gentle way, shaving her legs, bathing, preparing the other children, so that she had been through the entire labor and was ready to deliver when they put her out."

"I wanted to have natural childbirth, and my doctor finally said, 'Okay, okay, yeah, yeah, yeah,' in a very condescending way. So when I went into labor, I called him and started doing my exercises. And I arrived at the hospital and he said to me, 'You're hyperventilating. You're getting a shot.' And I said, 'No I'm not. I don't want a shot.' And he said, 'Well, you're getting one. Nurse!' And she gave me a shot and I went out and I did not wake up for nine hours. I woke up vomiting. It's a very babyish state they reduce you to. I crawled out of my bed and into the hall, and I said, 'Will somebody please tell me: do I have a baby or not?' And they came running down the hall, yelling. 'Get her back into bed!' And I pleaded, 'Somebody please tell me!' And finally somebody told me, 'Yes, you had a baby.'"

"They gave me sugar water or something to induce the labor. And I didn't want to take any kind of drugs, even though I hadn't had any classes. I just didn't want any. My doctor told me that the baby's head was coming out, and he wanted me to take something. I said I didn't want to, that I had already gone this far. But in the meantime I was in great agony. It was easy to give in. I was extremely torn because my husband was upset. He wanted to be there at the birth. And the doctor said, 'Look, why don't you wait and have natural childbirth with your second child.' I remember him saying those exact words. Since I had the baby approximately twenty minutes later, I obviously could have done without drugs.

"Since then, I've talked to a lot of other mothers who really began to figure out in labor these breathing techniques themselves, and get the rhythm of it. And they wouldn't even ask for medication. But on a regular basis a nurse would come in and shoot them up anyway. And with each shot they would lose more and more control. And then at the time of birth, the pain would really let up, and they really wouldn't want to be knocked out. But they got put out anyway."

All this undoubtably sounds strange—if not downright demented—to a mother who kept begging for more anesthesia and didn't get it. But of course, that mother may have been begging in the first place because of the effects of drugs she had already received—be they narcotics or stimulants. (There's nothing like pitocin to make you beg for Demerol.)

And it's easy to say after it's all over that you really didn't want those drugs after all. I'm certain that an obstetrician would insist that it's really mothers who demand anesthesia.

But all those qualifications aside, there's something about the mere availability of drugs in a hospital that makes it all the harder to pass them up. Like walking by the pastry shop at lunch hour and not stopping for just a nibble—even though you know you can't stop at just a nibble. If the chef comes out and says, "Wouldn't you like just a little prune danish to take the edge off your hunger?" Well, so much for willpower.

It's easy to understand why a woman would want a medicated birth. (She thinks it will hurt less.) It's harder to understand why hospitals and doctors so often push drugs on the unwilling. Or offer them to the weak-willed. One reason is certainly that doctors and hospitals are accustomed to controlling things. And an unmedicated mother is in control of herself.

Another reason is that unmedicated childbirth—in recent history—is relatively new. Some doctors still don't believe it "works." So they don't see the point in really trying.

It's also important to understand that doctors and hospitals are in the business of practicing medicine. Prescribing a drug is medicine. Patting you on the shoulder and saying, "Stick with it" isn't medicine. So, if you're in a hospital, you're likely to see much more of the former than of the latter.

Writing this, I can't help wondering how many of my warnings about anesthesia will go unheeded. Too often I've heard mothers tell harrowing tales of medicated births, only to say that if they had it to do over, they'd be medicated again—because they "can't stand pain." I'm not sure I'm not listening with only half an ear myself.

I suppose it's not so strange. After all, we regularly ignore warnings that cigarettes cause cancer and that speeding causes car accidents—even when our best friends are killed by cars or cancer. But at least we receive some immediate gratification from smoking or from racing a car. Whereas "pain medication" in childbirth is often a total deception. The drugs may induce more pain. So it isn't as if we're giving up long-term benefits for short-term relief; we're giving up everything for nothing.

I feel a little foolish (not to mention guilty) urging mothers to avoid pain relief for a condition (labor) that I know can cause a lot of pain. I wish I could come up with a more tangible alternative than a supportive doctor or a husband who knows how to nurse.

But I know from listening to mothers that those who used anesthesia well also used it wisely. They expected what they got and got what they expected. Demerol relaxed them a bit; it did not take away the pain. Epidurals gave them painless births (not labors), possibly with forceps and sometimes cesarean deliveries. General anesthesia knocked them out only for the moment of birth. Twlight sleep erased their memories, not their labors.

So if you are tempted to opt for anesthesia, don't be fooled by false promises. In the end, babies and mothers would both be better served if we all had a little less faith in modern medicine—and a lot more faith in modern mothers.

It's a Baby!:

Greeting the New Arrival

Birth always signals an arrival. The Easter chick tapping its way out of its shell. The butterfly slithering out of a cocoon. The new sprout unfurling from the spring sod.

Baby births are more like volcanic eruptions. For nine long months the pressure builds inside, culminating in the explosive, expulsive efforts of labor. And then, as suddenly as it started, it's over, bringing with it the unbelievable yet unmistakable confirmation that that bulge in your belly was really your child. That somebody was really at home. Lo and behold, it's a baby!

Newborn babies are produced at the rate of some 3 million a year—in this country alone. And yet they are as precious as rainbows. As awe-insiring as shooting stars. As fleeting as reflections. They are somehow both more and less than real. Marvelous in the science-fiction sense. One look is enough to dissolve a grown man into a puddle of tears. To give a strong woman weak knees. To turn the most crotchety mother-in-law into one long contented coo.

The newly arrived, like the newly departed, fill us with emotions we don't clearly understand. I think that's why they both make us cry.

I still cry sometimes, thinking of my newborn son. Maybe mothers always do. Maybe that's why I hated the hospital so much for taking him away. When they finally gave him back, I would watch him for hours as he slept in his see-through crib, smothering him with my stares, violating his private dreams with my curious love. One day a pregnant woman caught me in the act. She was visiting with her Lamaze class, much as I had done—it seemed like so many years before. I saw her looking at me and she saw me looking at him. And we both got weepy-eyed. And that room was so saturated with emotion that you could have sopped it up with a sponge.

Babies are built for mother love. Nothing fits into your arm so neatly, or fills your heart so completely. A wobbly little half-awake head burrows into your shoulder. The muffled movements feel like the flutter of a small bird in your hand. The smell is pink and new and clean and so delicious you can almost drink it. The sounds are soft tentative gurgles. Nothing makes you feel so grand, or so humble. So needed and so inadequate. This brand-new person who can take a perfectly normal confident woman and by the mere act of birth turn her into an emotional wreck.

This is your baby.

Of course, a baby is what you've been expecting, isn't it? I mean, after nine months, you didn't expect to get a basketball or a fox terrier, did you? Why is having a baby so hard to believe?

"The funny thing is I looked into the mirror and I guess it was adjusted wrong, because I saw myself, and I said, 'Oh, I look awful!' And then all of a sudden the baby came out. And she started crying, because the head came out before the rest of her—just like in the movies. And Sam and I were standing there like two nitwits, saying, 'I can't believe it, I can't believe it.' And the doctor looked up and said, 'It's a girl!' And I looked, and said, 'It's a baby!' And everybody laughed, and my husband said, 'Well, what did you expect? A watermelon?'"

"I was just incredulous. They brought the baby in, and every inch of me just turned to jelly. I was enthralled. I was amazed. I couldn't find the adjectives. It came out of me! It's a baby!

I was bonkers! I was so awed that I could have done that that I had trouble relating the baby to me. I was so shocked that something alive had actually come out of me that I couldn't touch her. I had never thought that we would go in as one and come out as two. I have never duplicated that experience in my life. To this day, my husband and I sometimes stand at her crib at night before we go to bed and we look at her and say, 'You know. I just can't believe that's really ours.'"

"The first thing I reacted to emotionally was her smell. Her mouth was open and I could see in her little mouth, and I could smell her. And I remember feeling this is what a virgin person smells like that has been out of the inside for such a short period of time. I felt like I could smell all her brand-new organs inside. And then I started to laugh, but I was also shaking so much that I wanted to touch her but I couldn't touch her. So I was laughing and shaking all at the same time."

"Jennifer was born with a smile on her face, and they put her on my breast, and I was just crying and crying, the whole thing was so overwhelming. My husband was crying, the baby was crying, everybody was crying. Crying and giggling and relieved all at the same time. And I said to her, 'Stop crying now. You're out now. This is Mama.'"

THE GENERAL ASSESSMENT: Counting Fingers and Toes

Baby books constantly warn new mothers not to expect too much in the looks department. And most new mothers don't. After all, what can you expect from someone who's been pickled in amniotic fluid for nine long months, without so much as a haircut or manicure? Especially considering that he or she has just been squeezed out of a warm womb bath into a cold green world—compressed through a small hole like toothpaste coming out of a tube. None of us look our best when we first wake up in the morning, or when we first step, soaking, out of the tub. And so it is with babies.

I must admit that I thought my baby was beautiful from the start. The illusion was enhanced by my semiconscious state, and also by my mother, who of course confirmed that he was by far the most well-formed baby in the nursery—already sitting up and saying his alphabet. Everybody said he was beautiful, and so I thought he was. Until three months later, when a friend came to visit, and said, "My, he's really improved, hasn't he?" I was insulted, but also curious. I checked his early baby pictures. Sure enough, his face was squashed, and his head was pointed, and he had a real shiner on his right eye. But he still looked like Burt Reynolds to me.

I'm not the only mother who wears blinders as far as her baby is concerned:

"The first thing they said was, 'Mrs. S., say goodnight to your daughter.' And it was like something out of a fairy tale. There was this little pink face looking at me from the green sheet. So I said, 'Goodnight.' I thought she was neat. I stuck my finger in her hand and she grabbed it. She was a big baby, fat cheeks, just beautiful. And the doctor kept saying, 'Isn't she beautiful?' So when my husband came in, I said, 'Don't you think we've got the most beautiful baby in the world?' And he said, 'Oh, sure, she's pretty.' And then about a week later I heard him talking to some guy, and he said, 'Oh God, I couldn't believe how ugly she was.' And it hurt me so. And I said, 'How could you say that and not tell me?' And he said, 'She looked so red, she looked like a little monkey. I didn't want to hurt your feelings.'"

Mothers who are more objective describe their babies variously as looking like "an old lady," "a prune," "an embryo," with a head "shaped like a football," " a real banana head," "red and wrinkled," and "scrawny and ugly.... Everybody else's baby came to them beautiful, and ours looked like a plucked chicken. I didn't want to take him home and say, 'This is my kid.' We nicknamed him 'the Chicken,' and we called him that for the longest time."

"The Chicken" was a premature baby, weighing in at only about four pounds. Premies are not renowned for their appearance. They have more than their usual share of wrinkles and less than their share of baby fat. Forceps babies, on the other hand, are likely to come out looking as if they've just been on the losing side of a barroom brawl:

"Dennis had forceps marks on his cheeks, and it just looked like he had been in a big fight. I was so happy he was a boy because he looked so ugly. I thought, 'Oh God, if you were a girl and had to go through life like that!'"

The best-looking babies are usually cesareans, because their heads haven't been misshapen by the long squeeze though the birth canal. (This doesn't apply if your baby has also gone through a long labor—as mine did.) Late babies tend to be better formed, and also lacking the thick white layer of vernix that can make a newborn look like a newly opened package of cream cheese. But whatever your baby's appearance, his looks won't necessarily determine whether it's love at first sight. Indeed, some mothers seem to love ugly babies more—because they feel so sorry for them. And because they seem so obviously in need of a mother's loving care.

"My husband had warned me that the baby was kind of ugly. So we went down to the nursery and there was this one baby who was just so gorgeous, full and big and nice and round and ruddy. So I looked at this baby and said, 'That baby is gorgeous. How can you say it's ugly?' And my husband said, 'That's not our baby—it's the one next to it.' So the nurse comes out with this tiny thing. She was so pathetic looking. She had a horrible gash on her head from the forceps, and lumps and bumps over her eyes. I wasn't going to nurse her, but when I saw that she looked so puny, I changed my mind. And the nurse was shocked. She had never seen a mother change her mind about nursing in ten seconds flat. But I felt so sorry that poor thing had suffered so much, I felt it was the least I could do."

Pink and plump or red and wrinkled, a baby's first looks are transitory. Even the scrawniest ones fill out in a few weeks, and the scars of birth slowly fade. Few children arrive for the first day of school with wrinkles or pointy heads. (Damage from drugs may be permanent, of course. And even the evidence of a badly wielded forceps may last for years. But that's not the norm.)

Far more important than surface beauty is general health. There's probably not a mother alive who hasn't rushed to tally up fingers and toes—and eyes and noses and all the other standard newborn equipment. It can be distressing if you don't have the opportunity; when your child is whisked away to be weighed and washed and tested before you even have a chance to check him or her out.

But don't be too impatient. Often it's necessary to resuscitate a newborn, to put scary-looking tubes down its throat to help it breathe if it's swallowed a lot of fluid, to suck out the mucus, or to administer oxygen. All this can be worrisome to watch. It can take time. And the doctors and nurses may be too busy to explain. But try to take it in stride. That sort of fussing around is relatively normal.

Obviously, some hospitals like to fuss around more than others. Sometimes the fussing means there's a problem; sometimes it's more a matter of hospital policy. I had wanted to nurse on the delivery table—something that was encouraged by the nurse who taught the breastfeeding class at the hospital. But then my obstetrician objected, saying that the baby's "sucking reflex" would have to be tested first. Since then I've talked to many other obstetricians and pediatricians who never heard of "testing the sucking reflex." Sometimes these things are extremely arbitrary. So what happens to your baby when he's born will depend not only on your hospital, your obstetrician, and your pediatrician, but also on a host of unpredictable factors including the mood of the nurses and the number of other new arrivals that day. If you have specific requests such as nursing on the table, be sure to make them known. (And don't necessarily give up after the first person says no.)

While you're assessing *how* your baby looks, you'll also have an eye to *whom* he or she looks like. Indeed, before the new arrival has been around for twenty-four hours, there'll undoubtably already be a consensus as to whether he has Aunt Millie's nose or Uncle Arthur's ears. Even today, people feel required to say my son looks like either me or his father (depending on who's in the room) even though he really doesn't remotely resemble either of us. I feel similarly obliged, meeting a new baby, to remark that he looks just like whoever-first-comes-to-mind.

Of course, most new babies have a lot more in common with other new babies than they do with any adult. And it's hard to categorize a nose after it's been squashed through fifteen hours of labor. But it pleases most of us to do so. After all, it's rather flattering to think that someone decided to be born looking just like you. Sometimes we have to remind ourselves that we're having children, not clones. That just because they don't look like us isn't a good reason to throw them back.

Peter has the sort of face that goes with everyone, so when he was born, I diligently called all the relatives with assurances that he looked just like them. Then I felt terribly pleased when someone said he looked just like me. I've come to see him since as an original. Sometimes I seem to see myself in his glance, or he'll flash a certain smile that mirrors his father, or my grandfather. But it's more a kinship of expression than of ears or a nose. Which isn't to say that some babies don't emerge as Xerox copies of your second cousin twice removed. It's just that most of them don't.

"My first reaction was, 'My God, it doesn't look like me, and it doesn't look like Paul.' For some reason when I turned to look at him I expected to see Paul's exact face, or my exact face, but he just looked like himself. It was fantastic."

A baby who looks like you at least makes identification easy. You don't have to worry that a nurse mixed up the bracelets—or worse, the babies. If the baby she brings you is plump and you're thin, or he's dark and you're fair, then you may wonder whether it's really yours. And sometimes you might be right:

"They brought me this baby and I had her for a full fifteen minutes. I never thought to look at the tag on the arm. And I kept saying to myself, 'Now don't be critical'—because this was really an unattractive baby. I went through the whole thing: 'You've got to accept it. Whatever it looks like, it's yours. You'll learn to love it.' And it wasn't mine. It was horrible. It wasn't mine at all."

It's easier to tell who's who if you're aware of what's what during the birth. Fear of mistaken identity is a problem Lamaze mothers don't have. When you see it come out of you, you can't deny that it's yours. One cesarean mother was grateful she had an epidural just so she wouldn't be tempted to disown her own child.

"My first reaction to the baby was that I was glad I wasn't knocked out beause I never would have chosen him out of a group of babies. I never expected him to look like that. He didn't bear the slightest resemblance to either me or my husband or anyone else in the family."

Many mothers say that being wide awake to greet your new child is one of the best reasons for not being medicated. To be able to look your mystery child in the eye—and to be the first thing it sees with its own brand-new eyes. A baby can't really "see" much for several weeks after it's born. But right away, it knows who's Mama. Even mothers who insist on totally medicated births often wish there were some way they could come to for the welcoming of the baby:

"The biggest disappointment was that I had so much medication that I was still tripping when I first saw the baby, and I didn't really appreciate it. The nurses brought her in and waited around for me to oooh and aaah, but I must have disappointed them, because I just wanted to go back to bed. I was too dopey to hold her, and she was too dopey to nurse anyway. When it was time to go home, I wasn't really sure it was the same baby. I felt like I was stealing a baby. It was a very strange experience."

Being dopey isn't the only reason you may not recognize your baby. You or the child may be isolated—either because you have a fever or because the baby has a problem. Premature babies are often kept in special "premie" nurseries. And although you may be allowed to visit, you may feel more like a visiting nurse than a mother:

"It was very strange because we had to wear masks and sterile gowns. I would go in and pick her up and change her diaper, and they showed me how to take her temperature. But all the while you feel like you're taking care of somebody else's kid."

Even under the best of circumstances, the hospital is not home. Your mothering may be restricted to certain hours and certain settings. Much of the time you may have to content yourself with getting acquainted through the nursery window. Waving "Hi! It's me! Mommie!" And hoping that the right baby responds. The newborns are kept behind the counter like prize paintings, on display for the visiting public. Look, but don't touch. And just when you think you can't take this whole nursery business for one more minute, something so nice will happen that it will throw you totally off guard. The nursery nurses in one hospital gave an exasperated mother the best present ever:

"I was beside myself with interest to see him. I had to wait fourteen hours, and at the 6:00 A.M. feeding they didn't bring him to me because they said he was sleeping. I was furious. I begged them to bring him to me, but they said I had to wait until 10:00 A.M. And then he came in with a little sticker on his T-shirt, in a heart-shape, and it said 'Happy Mother's Day.' I was so touched, I forgot how mad I was."

BONDING: Love at First Sight?

Bonding is one of the nicest new words in the parenting vo-cabulary. It signifies the emotional glue that holds you and your baby together—and the latest research indicates that it's quite important for you to get together right away. Before the glue has a chance to dry, so to speak.

Bonding means looking your baby right in the eye as soon as he's born. Letting him know he's loved by you—the same set of skin and organs he's been so close to for so many months. The heartbeat he knows by heart. The sounds and smells he takes as his own. When you bond with your baby, you provide a soft cushion for his harsh entry into the world.

The benefits of maternal-infant bonding have been proven in a wide range of studies. Everybody's heard of the baby monkey deprived of its mother who bonded instead to a terrycloth substitute. And of the mommie mammals who reject their newborns if they aren't given a chance to lick them right after birth. Bonding in humans is said to enhance not only emotional ties, but also the emotional health of both mother and child, and even physical development.

Some mothers (and doctors) pooh-pooh bonding. They say it takes time to learn to love your baby. "To get it through your head that it's really yours." Especially if the mother's been heavily medicated. Or separated from her baby because of a fever, or because the baby's premature or has other problems. But bonding is designed to prevent just this kind of alienation. And a mother is much more likely to be cool on contact with her infant if she hasn't tried it.

Thus mothers who don't put much stock in bonding often don't. And mothers who do, do. The mother who doesn't want to see her baby born and doesn't want rooming-in and doesn't want to nurse usually doesn't care much about bonding either—even though it would benefit her baby most. on the other hand, the Lamaze nursing mother is too often panic-stricken if she doesn't get her licks in right away—even though she'll more than make up for it later. Just because bonding is beautiful doesn't mean that if you don't see your baby in the first twelve hours, you'll be beating it two years later. Conversely, just because you aren't big on bonding doesn't mean you're a bad mother. It just might mean you're missing one of the nicest parts of having a baby:

"I think you develop an immediate love for the baby while you are still carrying it. But the baby books and the Lamaze classes prepare you not to love your baby right away. They say you can't expect to love it until it starts turning into a person, until you start caring for it. So I prepared myself for two things. First, I prepared to think the baby was ugly, because that's what the books said. Second, I prepared not to feel any overwhelming love. And then when I looked at him I couldn't believe it. I thought he was beautiful from the moment I laid eyes on him, and my heart just filled with him. It was love at first sight. And even though I didn't feel he knew who I was, I had the feeling that he knew all the things that I was doing for him."

Bonding is also a family affair. Indeed, many mothers say that the most beautiful part of childbirth is seeing, not the baby for the first time, but rather father and baby together for the first time. "My most vivid memory of the whole experience is when my husband held her up in the delivery room. He was in awe of her. And he cried. He was so happy, and it was so nice to have the three of us finally together."

Lots of daddies cry. I don't know what my husband did because he wasn't allowed in the operating room. I do know that up until the last moment he had disapproved of naming a boy baby after himself. And that after father and son got together, the latter was suddenly Peter, Jr.

The family reunion can be less than ecstatic if there's a sex problem. That is, if everybody wants a girl and it's a boy. Or vice versa—which, even in this day of women's liberation, is far more common. You'd think this sort of thing went out with bound feet, but it's a distressingly familiar scene. Indeed, I remember calling up a friend on the birth of her second child, only to hear her say, "I can stop now. I had the male heir."

Relatives and hospital staffers don't always realize the pressures that pushing for boys puts on a mother. Of course she can't control the sex of her baby. And she herself was once a girl. So what's the big deal about having boys? It's often the mother who (sometimes secretly) wants a girl. But she pushes her preference aside to please everybody else:

"I really wanted a boy. No, I wanted a girl, but my husband wanted a boy, so I wanted a boy for him. When my daughter was born, I was so disappointed. I didn't want a second-class citizen. And my husband said, 'It's a nice baby, but it would have been better if it was a boy.'"

Few are so callous. Still sometimes relatives make their feelings known in more subtle ways. Like husbands who tease, "It better be a boy, or I won't bring you home from the hospital." Those words keep coming back. One older mother I know had amniocentesis, a prenatal test that tells the sex (and other characteristics) of the unborn child. She was terrified to get the results. She feared that if the baby was a girl, her husband would lose interest even before she was born. Often women say they cried from happiness when their first son was born. It might be more accurate to say they cried from relief.

Of course, it seems innocent enough to want a son to take over the family business, or a girl to doll up in fancy dresses. But sex discrimination aside, it just doesn't pay to put all your hopes on one or the other. The consequences of trying can be long-term guilt.

It's worse when the pressure comes from outsiders:

"I had always wanted girls. Our fourth child was a boy, and he died when he was three days old. At that point, I had three children and they were very close. We didn't feel that it was such a terrible thing that it was a boy who died. But the people in the hospital had a thing about males. And when the baby died, they thought it such a terrible catastrophe. And I said, 'But I have three children at home.' And they said, 'But they're girls!' Even today people come up to me and say, 'Don't worry. The next one will be a boy.'"

It's probably unnecessary to say that you shouldn't listen to talk like that. Or perhaps you should—and talk back. If people weren't so ignorant of a mother's (and father's) feelings, perhaps they wouldn't be so insensitive. Meanwhile, if you do have a girl, you should be doubly delighted: someday she'll grow up to be a mother.

There's one more thing that might put a wrinkle into your relationship with your new baby. Fear.

"The nurse came down the hall handing out babies, yelling, 'Babies! Babies!' She handed mine to me and I said, 'Don't leave me! What do I do?' And she showed me. You put this here, you take the bottle, you do this. And it was terror, sheer terror. I thought I was going to kill the kid. I felt that I was going to drop her, that she was like a beautiful doll, and she would break into a million pieces."

Of course, there's nothing to be afraid of—yet. In the hospital you have lots of help on hand in the form of nurses and other mothers. If you feel inadequate now, wait till you get home. I've always felt that babies, like horses, seem to know instinctively who knows how to handle them and who doesn't. For the former, they're kind and gentle. For the latter, they kick and scream, trying to throw you off. But your child is hardly so calculating. If you don't know what she wants, chances are she doesn't know either. You will learn these things together. And the more you handle your child in the hospital—where there's help around—the better you'll be able to handle her at home—where it counts.

The first encounter with your new baby is the most important meeting you'll ever attend. Don't let anything interfere. It's a moment of a lifetime: His, hers, and yours. It's something you'll carry with you wherever you go. And whenever you remember it you'll get that warm funny feeling all over again. That's one advantage of living in New York: If you start to get tear-eyed on the subway, everybody assumes it's the soot.

Postpartum Recovery:

It's a Long Road Back to a Size 10

One of the things nobody ever tells you about having a baby is what happens *after* you have the baby. I knew that recovering from a cesarean was bad. But I had no idea that "natural child-birth" mothers suffered postpartum problems, too.

Looking back, I should have taken the hint when I called a La Leche League mother for help when Baby Whosis (as we still called him) was about ten days old. I felt run-down, wrung out, and I didn't know what hit me. A flailing fragment of my former self. She couldn't understand what I was so upset about: "It always takes me six months or so to feel myself after a baby is born." Six months! I didn't think I could last six minutes.

If I hadn't been so immersed in my own problems, I might have been even more surprised by the other meaning in her message. I should expect to feel awful. I had major surgery. But the woman who had just told me it took her six months to recover from a baby birth had virtually "ideal" deliveries. No medications, no problems—the last baby was born at home. Where did someone like that get off taking six months to recover? According to my calculations, she should have been back to normal in a matter of days.

Indeed, when I started interviewing mothers for this book, I didn't even bother to ask noncesarean mothers about recovery. The last thing I wanted to listen to was their accounts of how great it was to be up and around with the new baby, pushing the pram in the park, entertaining relatives, playing tennis, and lying on the beach in a bikini: happy, healthy—I hated them. Imagine my surprise when a mother who delivered vaginally interrupted our cesarean complaint chorus to comment: "Yeah, the recovery is worse than the labor."

You, too?

Or as another mother put it:

"The first time I went to the bathroom, I came back hysterical. The nurse wanted to know what was wrong. I said, 'What did I do to my poor body? My poor little body?' I was overwhelmed by the fact that I hurt. They had never mentioned that in the books. I couldn't move, I couldn't sit down, I couldn't get up, I couldn't do anything. Whoever tells you that your stomach is still tender? Now with a cesarean you expect that because you had an incision. But even without it—your tummy is still hanging there, it's not where it should be, it's like your insides aren't functionng. Whoever talked about the terrible pain of episiotomies? Of stitches? Whoever mentioned catheters, or that they wouldn't let you out of the hospital until you went to the bathroom? You suddenly realize that you've gone through hell and back, and suddenly you've got to recover from this horrible thing."

With three years of hindsight to help me, I can't help wondering how we could be so naïve. It's the same mentality that deludes my husband into thinking he can shed five years of inactivity by running around the block. The twenty pounds that took two years to accumulate won't be lost in two weeks. And the damage that nine months of pregnancy does to your body doesn't disappear in a day.

When you think about it, nothing abuses your body (and mind) quite like having a baby. For nine months you play hostess to a parasite who makes you sick in the morning and sleepless at night and has a powerful mood-altering influence on your thoughts. Your efforts to expel it are enormous. You virtually rip yourself open in the process. And then you expect to wake up the next morning as if nothing had happened.

Postpartum problems are almost always a surprise. Perhaps, because pregnancy is a time of unprecedented self-absorption. You cater to your needs, pamper your body, immerse yourself in books and chatter and daydreams about all these fascinating things that are happening to *you*. Every feeling, every physical change, comprises a chapter in a book. You practice your concentration, time your contractions, anticipate your pain. Your every ache is cause for calling the doctor.

Birth makes you irrelevant. Now the subject of everyone's affections and attentions is the new baby. Not that nobody cares about you. Of course they do. But you're no longer the main attraction. The trouble is that the body and mind you've been nursing so carefully for so many months hasn't gone away. And it still has a lot of recovering to do.

The belly that has been bloated by nine months of carrying a baby isn't going to flatten overnight. The stretch marks don't vanish, and neither do the hemorrhoids. In addition, birth and hospitalization have left you with a whole new set of scars. An episiotomy and stitches (in the most inconvenient place). Anesthesia gives you a headache. IVs and injections make you sore (in more ways than one). Your breasts are engorged. You can't urinate or defecate. Everything either hurts or is out of order.

Come to think of it—if labor is a twelve-mile hike—that's pretty much how we felt when we climbed out of the Grand Canyon.

Perhaps the reason we don't hear a lot about the postpartum problem is that the silver lining obscures the cloud. As well it should. You've got everything to be on Cloud Nine about. A new baby. Lots of attention. A day filled with flowers and phone calls and visits from friends. You have announcements to write, baby-bathing classes to attend. Some mothers find themselves on a permanent postpartum high. Stitches? What stitches?

But postpartum problems are more than skin deep. Licking your wounds after labor is more than a physical need. In some ways, the end of pregnancy is like waking up after a long period of insanity. For nine months you've floated on a very special kind of cloud. When you come out of the fog, you expect to come down where you started from. Instead, everything has changed. Like the morning after a long liquid party when you suddenly realize that on top of your hangover and your hurting head and sick stomach, the place is a total wreck. Somebody has rearranged the furniture and strewn stuff all over the floor. And you've got company coming in two hours. And if that isn't enough, there's this BABY, crying for attention. What are you supposed to do now?

Most important, who *are* you now? You aren't your pregnant self, but you aren't who you were before either. Your body isn't familiar, and neither are your feelings. Suddenly you're a mother. Suddenly there's a family. It's like finding yourself in a strange place and not really knowing how you got there. Like the first days in a foreign country. (What's the currency exchange rate? What's the word for "bathroom"?) You've woken up in a strange house, and you're always making wrong turns or bumping into something unexpected. It's the first day of school, and you're excited and scared and a little more grown up than you'd like to be.

I might have forgotten what it felt like to exist on the foggy bottom of recovery but for a few notes I took the night I left the hospital. They were the only notes I took during the entire experience. I guess I must have had a premonition that someday I would want to look back, to repenetrate the postpartum state. But I do so only as a visitor. I certainly wouldn't want to live there:

"My last night at the hospital. I'm so teary. So much immense love for Baby Whosis. Such a life transition. So afraid of the constant care he needs. Peter is clumsy with the diapers—as clumsy as I am. Neither of us can get his hands through the armholes of the T-shirt. How do we dress him when we get home? Baby cries and cries. We try cotton balls to wipe tears from his eyes, like nurse said. I get too much water—his face is all wet. Peter uses too little water, leaves tufts of cotton stuck to his eyes. Can't comfort him. He's fed, burped, changed, cuddled. I try to remember that he's only five days old. So young. Life is so different, so difficult, for him, too. I just stare at him and love him. I'm so tired.

"Last night, got him for the first time. Fed him until 10:00 P.M., went to sleep at 11:00. But doctor and nurse fooled around with my IV until 12:00. Up at 2:00 A.M. to nurse. Sweating because of intravenous. Nurse him again at 6:00 A.M. Zonk out at 7:00. Doctor comes at 8:00. Take shower. Eat breakfast. Nurse again at 10:00 A.M. Barely finish in time for baby-care class at 11:00. I can't even sit in a chair for an hour! Have lunch. Take one phone call. Go to bathroom. Pooped, but now need to feed the baby. Rush to breastfeeding class at 2:00. So, so exhausted. Peter comes at 3:00. Get some rest. Lie down to read at 4:30. Brought two books and haven't opened either one. Dinner comes, but baby needs to eat, so I have to push my dinner aside. Wow. Just can't comfort him and eat dinner at same time. Peter comes again. Barely time to hold him, feed him, change him, burp him, wash face. We don't even have time to wrap him up before nurse comes to take him away.

"I'm so tired, need to rest, but also need to file baby's nails.

"Last five days have been like months. Nightmarish quality. I'm really scared that somehow Whosis and I will never leave here alive. That they'll find something to keep us here. (One degree temperature?) Look out window. Seems weird. River, traffic. Get shivers. Think of driving to doctor visits. Can't imagine that expressway will ever look the same again. Peter talks about thunder showers and I have to try to think hard to remember what that is. Can't focus on conversation about outside world. Can't believe I'll ever be *out there* again. Can't believe Baby Whosis and I can exist outside hospital. That he'll sleep in his bassinet. That I'll ever sleep in my own bed again with Peter.

"A Lamaze class comes by. A woman stares in at me and Whosis. She wipes tears from her eyes. I remember seeing a mother and child in the same situation, having same tears, when I was pregnant—so, so long ago. All those pregnant bellies and slightly puzzled, slightly scared, excited faces. Like it happened to me five years ago. I want to say something to them, but I don't know what."

The pregnant woman and the new mother may as well exist on different planets for all they have in common. The space that divides them is not outer space, but inner space. And yet it's quite a chasm. Crossing it is probably the biggest step you'll ever take.

Why is arriving at motherhood so often accompanied by such a bumpy landing? I've come up with many reasons, and I'm sure there are many others. One thing I know for certain is that postpartum problems are no more a case of simple "blues" than is the rich emotional fabric of pregnancy. It's true that some women feel a slight letdown after the baby comes. Like Christmas morning, after all the presents are open. Maybe this is the "blues." But the special postpartum state of mind and body is much more than a matter of raging hormones. It's a matter of adjusting to a new life. Two new lives, in fact. And that's where the problems begin:

"Before I got pregnant, I had this terribly impacted wisdom tooth removed. And I was in terrible pain every time I tried to open my mouth. And I really took care of myself. I stayed in bed and sipped soup and let people wait on me. Now having a baby is a similar kind of thing. The episiotomy is surgery. I had stitches. And every time I went to move, it hurt. It wasn't my mouth, but it was somewhere else that I had to use all the time. But this time I couldn't pamper myself. The baby kept me up all night and I was exhausted. I had to ignore my own problems to take care of him."

The double-headed nature of the postpartum problem makes it doubly difficult to deal with. Both you and your baby are in need of loving care. Maybe even intensive care. And there's only so much to go around. Suddenly the invalid is called on to get up and play nurse—whether she's up to it or not.

It's curious how few mothers put these pieces together *before* they have their babies. We may read baby-care books that certainly hint at the amount of work and worry involved in the care and feeding of a child. We read childbirth books that suggest we might not feel so hot ourselves after delivery. But somehow we don't get the idea that these adjustments are simultaneous. They're not even different chapters, much less different books. No wonder you're a mess.

In addition, the hospital experience can be traumatic in itself. At the very least, it's very strange. So in addition to strange feelings, a strange baby, and unexpected aches and pains, you have to cope with a strange bed, strange food, strange medicines, strange hours, and lots of strangers. The experience can be so intense that it can shake you loose from your safe home mooring. You may feel permanently dislodged.

"I had a nightmare that I couldn't shake for two weeks. The world was coming to an end, and no one else knew it. I had the nightmare over and over again, day after day, and I was afraid to go to sleep because I was afraid I wouldn't wake up. I didn't sleep at all for many nights. If I had been able to get out of bed, I would have gone down the hall to ask the nurse if I could see a psychiatrist, but I couldn't get out of bed because of the pain. I was convinced I would never get out of the hospital. And I lay awake thinking of ladies who had babies who had gotten out of the hospital, and I couldn't think of any. It was like they had all disappeared."

Will life ever get back to normal? You're not really sure.

Moreover, most women carry into motherhood some of the fears and worries that haunted them during pregnancy. Sure, you know the baby's okay now. And so are you. But you can't calm down nine months of anxiety and anticipation just by having a baby. The effects linger. Just as when you've had a fright, your heart keeps right on fluttering even when there's no longer anything to fear.

Having a baby takes a lot more than nine months. Pregnancy, labor, and childbirth are only the beginning. Now your mind and your body both need to begin the slow process of healing and adjustment. It took you nine months to get where you are, so don't be surprised if it takes you nine months to get back where you started.

SHOTS AND STERILE WIPES

Your labors are over, the battle of birth won. Now it's time to assess the damages. If you're like some mothers, you're so buoyed by the baby that nothing can bring you down. If you're still dopey on drugs, you may not *know* what's coming down. By the time they wake you up, it's almost time to go home:

"They kept smacking me, trying to wake me up, but I was very comfortable sleeping. The nurses kept coming in to give me this little test. They would ask, 'What did you have?' When I answered, 'A girl,' then they knew I was awake. They wheeled me past the nursery, but I couldn't care less. I only wanted to sleep. My roommate was from my Lamaze class, and she wanted to talk, but I fell asleep on her, too. Even when my husband came in and wanted to talk about the baby, I only wanted to tell about my latest dream. I think I slept through the entire hospital stay."

If you're awake enough to notice, however, you might find yourself being used as a human pincushion or punching bag. The first business of recovery is promoting healing of the uterus. The faster it returns to its normal size, the less chance of hemorrhage. You'll get a shot of pitocin to speed this process along. You might also find a nurse's fist pressing into your tender belly. The massage helps the uterus to contract even more. (As if labor contractions weren't enough.) And if that doesn't do it, you'll be packed with ice until the brunt of the bleeding stops.

Meanwhile, you'll be getting a series of shots. Pitocin for your uterus. IVs to bring the fever down. Painkillers. Sedatives. Sleeping aids. Maybe a shot to stop the milk flow if you're not nursing. (If you *are* nursing, don't take anything you don't want the baby to have, too.) Either way, your breasts will become engorged with milk—so you might wind up packing them in ice, too. Or binding them so they can't move around. You look like Mae West, but you feel like someone who just grew boulders on her chest. Engorgement can hurt. It can also give you a fever.

You'll be bleeding, so you'll be wearing a sanitary napkin for many weeks. ("First you change the baby's diaper, then you change your own," said one mother.) The "lochia" or reddish discharge is supposed to gradually subside in a month or so, but "gradually" seems to take interminably long. You still have to be careful about infections, so going to the bathroom becomes a major production. Along with your Kotex and sterile wipes (just like baby), you take along a squirt bottle of soapy water for cleansing the vaginal area. A portable douche. Transporting all this to the toilet is quite a trick if you need one hand to push the IV pole.

And all the while, you can feel the uterus contract in a series of small, painful cramps. It contracts harder and faster if you're nursing. Actually, I found these "afterpains" quite comforting—especially when nursing. I felt I was finally helping to "heal thyself"—or myself, as the case may be.

But these are just the preliminaries. Still to come are:

CATHETERS AND COCKTAILS

First the catheters. It may take several days before you can even urinate on your own—either because a long labor has left your bladder muscles weak, or because you're too dopey, or because the stitches from the episiotomy make it hurt too much. Fortunately, catheters aren't more than merely "uncomfortable." But they do often come as a surprise. They can also cause infections. (Another source of the fevers that keep the baby away.) Still, if you haven't passed water in a day or so, and you feel this strange excruciating pain, do ask a nurse if you shouldn't be catheterized. It's better than the alternative.

The entire area that includes your vagina, perineum, and anus has taken quite a beating in the last few days. Hemorrhoids don't help:

"They are so awful! You cannot even go to the bathroom. I had to smear my rear end with Vaseline. You're in such excruciating pain that tears are just streaming down your face. I couldn't sit for three weeks. I could barely get out of bed. I remember sitting on the couch and nursing at an angle because I couldn't sit. Eating on an angle. I did everything on an angle for weeks."

You needn't be ashamed of your hemorrhoids. Everybody knows that new mothers have them. Especially since hemorrhoid preparation commercials on TV have begun featuring happy new mothers just home from the hospital.

Some women never get hemorrhoids. Some have them and don't notice:

"When the nurse was prepping me, she said to ask the doctor to take care of my hemorrhoids while I was on the delivery table. So he cut them or sewed them or something, and I never even knew I had them."

There's only one real cure for hemorrhoids. And the cure can be more painful than the problem. Somehow or other over the next four or five days, you've got to resume your "regularity," as they say in the laxative commercials: you've got to have a bowel movement. It's no small task considering what's been happening to your bottom recently.

"They let me out after two days because they gave me milk of magnesia. When I got home, the nurse kept saying, 'Take everything you can think of that will make you go.' Finally I went and I burst a stitch. The pain was unbelievable."

No self-respecting hospital would have let that mother leave with a mere helping of milk of magnesia. Most keep you hostage until they're sure you've moved your bowels. And they'll do everything possible to help you along. Childbirth seems to begin and end with enemas. If the enema doesn't work, you'll get a special concoction called "the cocktail"—guaranteed to clear out anybody:

"There's this chocolate thing that they make you drink, but it's horrible. They call it the cocktail, because it literally hits you like a Molotov cocktail. All of a sudden you get up and you realize you've got to go to the bathroom. But the bathroom is too far away. I didn't make it to the bowl. That's how fast it acted. And it was just the most incredible, embarrassing thing. I stood there in my condition trying to do something about this mess."

No wonder so many women lie to the nurses about the status of their bowels. It's better than getting a good-bye cocktail. Or at least it is if you can use gentler methods to move things along. You aren't doing yourself a favor if you get home only to burst a stitch.

SEX, STITCHES, AND SITZ BATHS

Most obstetrician-written baby books seem to be particularly callous on the subject of stitches. One doctor writes that mothers often want to know how many stitches were taken, but that the "doctor is too busy to count them." Another complains that women "overprotect" the stitched-up perineum because it is in "such a delicate area." At the risk of sounding like a disgruntled female chauvinist, I can't help but wonder if the doctor wouldn't "overprotect" the twenty stitches that somebody took in his penis. He'd certainly know how many there were.

An episiotomy can be much more than a "small, relaxing incision"—especially if you have a forceps delivery, or a breech birth, or a very big baby. It can require a great number of stitches, both inside and out. The pain can be disabling both physically and emotionally:

"I felt horrible for about two months. The episiotomy must have been two feet long. I remember being very excited about the baby and feeling it was the greatest high of my life. I couldn't wait to get out and push the pram in the park, like I'd always dreamed of doing. And here I could hardly walk. I would take a pillow to the park and sit precariously on the bench. But it was a big disappointment because I was physically so uncomfortable."

"I had a gaping hole because my daughter was a breech. I got this little tube to carry around with me, and I had to bring it to the office. Now it's my daughter's dolly tube, and she takes it to the beach. But here I was the dignified director of public relations, sitting on this little tube. I was so embarrassed."

Some women are afraid that the episiotomy and subsequent stitches can leave their sex life permanently impaired. It shouldn't, if you've been stitched up by a skilled doctor. But it may feel that way at first. Many mothers said that intercourse after childbirth was like intercourse for the very first time. Many more said they just weren't in the mood. Especially nursing mothers: "You feel like too many people are trying to share your body at once."

Between the hemorrhoids and the stitches, the catheters and the cocktails, you might feel pretty tender for quite a long time. You can cut your recovery time by exercising your vaginal muscles as you learned in Lamaze. If you haven't had Lamaze, just squeeze—as if you're trying to "hold it in." Do this slowly, about twenty times per session, several times a day. It's an excellent exercise, and no one will ever know you're doing it. Yes, it will hurt. But it will also help you get better faster in the long run.

A hot tub also helps. Most hospitals have portable plastic "sitz baths" that fit into the toilet. You fill one with warm water, sit down and soak. A bathtub serves the same purpose— to bring blood to the perineal area to help it heal.

The hospital will also have available a great variety of pain-killers to ease the aches of episiotomies or headaches or even engorgement. Non-nursing mothers can take them as needed and prescribed. Nursing mothers, however, will have to rely on the healing powers of time. (And also of nursing—which helps healing, too.)

CESAREAN RECOVERY

Recovering from a cesarean is like recovering from vaginal childbirth—only more so. You won't have an episiotomy, of course, but you will have stitches in your belly. If these are the "clamp" variety, they will have to be pulled out before you leave the hospital. Anesthesia is not used. This is a good time to put your Lamaze breathing into practice.

Cesarean mothers are spared the pushing that so often produces hemorrhoids. However, you will not have an easier time having the first obligatory bowel movement. Indeed, your whole abdominal area remains effectively out of order for at least several days. The result is painful gas and cramps. Don't rush to eat anything (even if they let you) because you can't digest it anyway. A heating pad on the tummy helps.

Meanwhile, you'll be urged to walk around and to "stand up straight." This is harder than it looks. As one mother put it, "It felt like my navel had been stitched to my knees." This posture produces the characteristic cesarean shuffle. With your IV pole, you look like an old witch pushing a portable broomstick. When somebody says, "Oh, there's another section," they're not talking about grapefruit. They mean you.

ISOLATION

Your one source of comfort during recovery is your brand-new baby. What makes recovery unbearable is when they take your baby away. This happens not only to cesarean mothers, but to any mother whose temperature rises for any reason—whether it's contagious disease or simple breast engorgement.

I'm convinced that isolation is a major cause of postpartum depression:

"I had every intention of rooming in, and then I had him for one feeding and they took him away. I didn't get him back for eleven days. I used to lie on that bed and cry because they would bring the babies to the rest of the women on the floor and I'd hear the babies crying and I couldn't have my baby. Those were the most horrible days of my life."

"My depression was related to the circumstances in the hospital because my baby was in the premature lab, and everybody else's little baby came down at feeding time except her. I was the only kid on the block with this four pound fourteen ounce pint-sized little thing that was inside a glass case, and it was so awful. I cried all the time and walked up and down the hall with tears streaming down my face."

"They took away Dennis, and I thought there was something wrong with him. I had a fever and they wouldn't give him to me, and I'd count the minutes until the nurse came around with the babies again. But then I'd still have the fever, so I couldn't have mine. Right away I panicked. He was nine pounds three ounces. I couldn't imagine what was wrong. But I was so worried. I cried all day long until I got him back."

The stories never end. Indeed, maternal isolation is far more common than most people think. And far more damaging to the mother's emotional health. (Possibly the baby's, too.) Isolated mothers often have severe postpartum problems when they get home. It's not surprising: what they labored for so long, and looked forward to so much, is denied them. It is a sad and lonely fate to be the only mother in the maternity ward without a baby. Watching a strange nurse feed your newborn infant through the nursery window. Waiting and hoping that the baby won't mistake the nurse for his mother, and that he'll still nurse after so many days on a bottle. Birth should be a cause for celebration, but you don't feel like celebrating under the circumstances.

The only consolation is the certain knowledge that the hospital will return your baby eventually. They always do. Just don't let anybody tell you that your hormones are raging because you're crying for your baby. Your baby is also crying for you.

THE BIG SQUEEZE BACK INTO SIZE 10

As if everything else wasn't enough, your figure's not what it used to be either. Not what it used to be when you were pregnant. And certainly not what it used to be *before* you started to blow up like a balloon. Indeed, the postpartum figure is quite similar to a popped balloon: torn, wrinkled, flabby, and deflated.

About two weeks after delivery, I remember resigning myself to the thought that I'd never wear my prematernity clothes again. The extra two inches around my waist seemed depressingly permanent. And yet, six months later, I was a thin shadow of my former self. Nursing and no sleep do wonders for helping you lose weight.

Still, it was quite a shock that second day in the hospital when I stepped on the scale and saw that I'd lost only three pounds. I made the mistake of asking a passing doctor what was wrong. And he said something cute about cutting down on chocolate sundaes. But it wasn't very funny because I was really worried. By the next morning, I had dropped another fifteen pounds, and learned from a nurse that most of the excess was water weight. (My dear old IV.) It's probably better not to get on the scale at all for several weeks because the results are usually deceptive.

Still, you're only deceiving yourself if you think your hospital "going-away" outfit can be the same size 10 you wore before you got pregnant. The best thing to wear home is what you wore to be admitted. That's right, maternity clothes. Or at least, large loose clothes with elastic or drawstring waists. This may be the most painful part of recovery of all.

"It seems like it's going to be forever before you can wear normal clothes. You've been wearing those awful maternity things for so long. So you go out and buy a special outfit to wear home. The same size you used to be, or maybe a little bit looser. And then my husband tells me I look like a Forty-second Street hooker because everything was skintight. I couldn't even zip up the pants. It was like I was still six months pregnant. That was the most depressing of all."

You can tone up and trim down faster if you exercise—which, needless to say, few postpartum mothers are in the mood for. Nevertheless, some hospitals pass around pamphlets encouraging their patients to start modified situps in bed. When I was still pregnant, I thought the idea of starting to shape up while still in the hospital seemed like a sensible idea. When I realized I would be hardly able to walk, the same idea seemed quite insane. Indeed, the postpartum exercise books are a source of substantial amusement to many new mothers. (They don't laugh too loud because they might burst a stitch.) Pushing yourself out of bed is hard enough without attempting pushups.

Sooner or later, however, exercise is going to be the surest road back to your old shapely self. The sooner you tackle those accumulated bulges, the sooner they will go away. How long is "sooner" depends entirely on you. It may be six months or six weeks. Some mothers take months to resume their shapes after the first child, but only weeks after the second. Others shape up almost immediately after the first, but never quite recover from the second.

For a while, I was thoroughly intimidated by new mothers who wore bikinis a bare few weeks after delivery. But I consoled myself by thinking that my cesarean made me a special case. I joked about my doctor's wasted efforts in slicing me a thin smile of a bikini cut. My belly was in no shape to wear a bikini. But then I saw some new cesarean mothers who did their bikini cuts proud, and I felt more depressed than ever. Indeed, it now turns out that cesareans may be a plus: my new obstetrician tells me if I ever go through this again, he'll take a tuck in the tissue that will restore my flat stomach to its prematernal state.

Other postpartum physical changes are more permanent. Stretch marks, for example, although they do tend to fade with time. (Or maybe you just forget about them.) Your chest measurement (not bust measurement) may bring you up a bra size or two. And some women find that their feet get bigger. (I went up a half size.) Scars from cesarean incisions may be visible for years, and the area around them may feel numb. It's been about three years now since my operation, and I can hardly find a trace of my bikini scar. My figure is back to normal (although it's three years older). And I still haven't lost my hair.

POSTPARTUM DEPRESSION

Postpartum depression is the sum of its parts. And the primary parts are discussed above. They include confusion about your new status; the responsibility of caring for a new baby coupled with the necessity to heal yourself; a dramatic life change that produces intense internal turmoil; an overwhelming amount of work to accomplish on drained energy resources; the end of anticipation, followed by the harsh reality of coming home; the lingering effects of a sometimes traumatic hospital stay; and—most of all—fatigue.

This is not, by any stretch of the experts' imagination, a simple case of "blues." It is not an "emotional problem" that suddenly appears for no reason around the third postpartum day and "disappears just as promptly as it appeared"—in the words of one popular pregnancy manual. It is a very real response to a very real set of problems. And nothing makes it worse than when somebody dismisses it as "the blues."

"I resent all this attention that's given to postpartum depression. I know that many people suffer from it, but it seems to me that the people are really suffering from the reality of what having a baby is. And this gets termed depression. It's a lovely way to castrate you. You come home, you're up all night, you hurt all over, the baby doesn't stop crying, and people say you're upset because of your hormones or something."

Calling depression "the blues" is more than a case of simple misunderstanding. It can have serious consequences for the mother—perhaps propelling her into a real clinical depression which requires psychiatric care. Postpartum mothers often feel isolated and alone—partly because they can't communicate their feelings to someone who has the attitude: "Oh well, she's just got the postpartum blues, and she'll be over it in a day." That leaves her more alone than ever:

"I'm not sure what they mean by depression. I think it's more tiredness and confusion and how am I going to cope with the baby. It was an inability to understand what it was all about. It's like my whole body, my whole world, everything in my universe changed. Everything hurt, everything was different— and here you expect me to react the same way, to be the old me. And I just kept crying all day, trying to explain to my husband, 'You don't understand. You don't understand.' And I felt so stupid because they make so light of the so-called 'baby blues.' You feel you are really queer because here you are falling into all the set patterns, feeling blue and tears running down your face. But it's much more than that. It's real. It's very real."

What's so depressing about having a baby? It's not the baby that's depressing, but the series of unpleasant surprises that often come with the baby. And the fact that friends and relatives and doctors and husbands don't seem to understand the extent of the strain you're under. But when you think about it, how could they? Understanding comes from experience. You can't learn to swim if you don't go near the water. Only you yourself experience what it's like to have a baby. Not your husband, and not the doctors who write the books. Before you give birth, you're every bit as ignorant of postpartum problems as your relatives remain afterward. You can read in a book that babies cry for several hours a day "without reason." Or that you're going to be physically debilitated and tired. But it doesn't really *mean* anything until you've lived through it. Not to you, and not to those around you.

"I hated myself. I don't know if you call that depression. They don't tell you that your stomach is still fat when you get out, and besides you can't walk anyway. They don't even wheel you out of the hospital, even though you feel worse than you did when you came in. They just say, 'Here, you're on your own, get out, good-bye.' There was nobody even to carry the baby for me, and I was getting really faint. So I got in the car and went home and that was it. And I couldn't even cry because all my in-laws were there. I don't think they realized how keyed up I was. I didn't fall asleep for three days. And then my sister-in-law started a big argument over the godmother thing. The next day, the baby and I had a crying session together."

Babies also bring big responsibilities. And for all the talk about "parenting," in most families it's still mothering that's counted on to care for the child. Twenty-four hours a day, seven days a week, with no time off for good behavior—or even for nervous breakdowns. Experts can write all the books they want about postbaby burdens, but only a mother knows what it's really like:

"I remember feeling an awesome sense of responsibility— this little thing is dependent on *me!* I got some violent headaches right out of the hospital because of all the pressures that suddenly fell in on me. They call it the baby blues, but I think it's more a combination of the letdown and the unrelenting responsibility. You've got this baby, you're tired, your metabolism is off, and all of a sudden, whammo! Noon and night, this kid is your responsibility. When I came home I was definitely secondary. It wasn't like before, when if I was sick, I just stayed home from work. Well, you can't stay home from work when you have a baby. You come second. I had to hold off all my aches and pains. And then I had all this company to deal with. Everyone else comes first."

Babies, of course, grow up to be children who eventually grow up to grown-ups. But not for a long time. For a long time the responsibility will remain primarily yours. I had thought that thinking in terms of six months was an eternity. Some mothers think in terms of six or more years. This is one time when long-term planning can plunge you into a full-scale panic:

"The permanence of it was the worst. There was no getting out for me, and my life was scripted at least until the kid got out of nursery school. I kept thinking, 'My God, this is my life, and there's no getting out of it. My life is ruined for the next eighteen years.'"

Sometimes postpartum depression is deadly serious. Mothers have been known to commit suicide, or even murder their own children, in cases of severe untreated depression. I know more than one mother who told her husband to watch her carefully during the first couple of months after the birth and if anything seemed strange or wrong, to call a doctor right away. This kind of depression is likely to be signaled by neglect of the baby, or of yourself, or true inability to cope with day-to-day life.

A more common kind of postpartum depression doesn't show itself as depression at all. The mother feels content and confident with her new baby. But she may not feel like going out or is unexplicably anxious or can't sleep even when the baby does. She may experience a gnawing nervousness or a sudden sadness. She doesn't connect these feelings with the baby because the baby is her one source of total contentment. Also because the baby may be as much as eight months old; she thinks she's sailed through the three-day "blues" unscathed.

By the time Baby Whosis (now known as Peter) was six weeks old, he was sleeping soundly through the night. But not his mother. I would lie awake into the wee hours waiting for him to wake up. Or else I would sleep for an hour or two only to arise wide-eyed at the crack of dawn. Eventually I began to get quite depressed. Not about the baby, but about my inability to sleep.

So I went to the doctor. The doctor said that insomnia was a classic symptom of depression. I protested. I wasn't depressed, I just needed some sleep. Desperate, I asked my obstetrician what to do.

He, too, pointed out that insomnia was a sure sign of depression. (Sleeping pills only make it worse.) And again I insisted that I was perfectly happy. I loved my baby, I enjoyed my job. If I was depressed, it was because I was getting desperate for some sleep.

When my son was about nine months old and I was on the verge of a permanent panic, my obstetrician talked me into seeing a psychiatrist who specialized in depression. And yet again I insisted that I didn't feel depressed. To my great surprise, he agreed with me. Indeed, he told me that most mothers who suffer from postpartum depression *don't know* they are depressed. And that depression often shows itself instead in characteristic symptoms—such as insomnia. The shrink said I didn't need my head shrunk at all, and that what I was going through was fairly common.

On my son's first birthday, the whole problem disappeared just as suddenly as it had appeared. I think it took me that long to become convinced that my baby was okay and that the hospital wasn't going to take my baby away again. One solid year.

Since then, countless mothers have confessed to me that they suffered from serious insomnia and anxiety well into the first year after their babies were born. Not one equated their problem with "postpartum depression," primarily because what they experienced bore no resemblance to the "baby blues" they had read about in books. And also because the "third-day blues" often didn't hit until the baby was three or six or even nine months old.

Recently, a mother of an eight-month-old girl asked me if I had ever had trouble sleeping after my son was born. (Did I!) She couldn't understand what had hit her, seemingly out of the blue. All of a sudden she was sleeping only two or three hours a night. And was miserably tired all day. When I told her what I had learned about depression, she insisted that she wasn't depressed. I almost wanted to laugh—except I knew that it wasn't funny.

Often, postpartum depression is a delayed reaction to something that happens during or after the birth, and that doesn't register until months after the fact. Perhaps because it doesn't have a chance to. You're too occupied with too many other things.

In my case, the hospital experience obviously left depression in its wake. Other mothers thought that worries about the baby during pregnancy (especially if the mother had taken dangerous drugs) might have taken that long to surface. Gwen thought it was her experience with a live-in nurse.

"The nurse totally took over the baby," she said. "At times, I feared she would run away with her while I was asleep. She wouldn't let me give her a bath, and I had to almost fight to feed her. But I was too tired and intimidated to protest. And I think it took four or five months for my fear and resentment to really surface."

Between suicidal depression and depression that just leaves you awake nights are the more common variations of depression brought on by isolation, confusion, physical fatigue, and emotional strain. Or a combination of all.

The best cure, I'm convinced, is the company of other mothers who share your worries and concerns—even if you don't know you have worries and concerns. In fact, Elizabeth Bing, renowned preparation-for-childbirth educator and author of many books on pregnancy and birth, recently turned her attention to the postpartum period. New mothers, experience taught her, need to get together in groups to work out their problems as much as—if not more than—pregnant women. And her new mother groups are now as popular as her Lamaze classes. Indeed, throughout the country, women with new babies are banning together in "mother share" groups to compare common problems, to gain strength in numbers. Many of these groups are Lamaze classes or La Leche League chapters that don't end when pregnancy or nursing does. If you're looking for kindred maternal spirits, this is a good place to start.

The postpartum problem is all the more perplexing because with the depression comes an almost delirious happiness. This is precisely why depression goes so often unnoticed. Your baby fills you to the brim with love and warmth and contentment and accomplishment and so many good feelings that there simply doesn't seem to be room for the bad ones. But it's the combination of both that gets you. The wonder of it all plus the worry of it all. The agony and the ecstasy.

Perhaps in the end postpartum depression is simply too much of a good thing. The new mother is plugged into eight emotions at once. But she's also suffering from an energy shortage, so she short-circuits. She still can't stop because she's got that baby to take care of—blackout or not.

What she *can* do is cut down on all the nonessentials. Conserve power. Don't plan on dinner for twenty. Don't entertain too many relatives that are a drain on you. Don't—as I did— fly out to Santa Barbara for a week with a three-week-old baby. Don't try to prove that having a baby isn't going to make a difference in your life. It is.

In short, the postpartum period is both the best and the worst. The most grueling and the most gratifying. It's like being up and down on the seesaw at the same time. To float on Cloud Nine and always carry a little dark cloud over your head. Be prepared to be ecstatic and exhilarated and a little sore and shell-shocked at the same time. Just because you're overworked and overwrought doesn't mean you'll miss out on participating in your baby's first precious months. You won't. You're as likely to overdose on love as on lack of sleep.

It is a time of much ado about everything.

Father Figures:

The Myth of the Heroic (or Helpless) Husband

When it comes to having babies, nobody needs an equal rights amendment more than fathers. Equal responsibilities, too. For too long, fathers have been having it both ways. And getting it from both sides. On the one hand, they are often excluded from a process in which they have as much a birthright as anyone: The father figure in the delivery room is not Daddy, but Dr. Obstetrician. Even though your husband may be the most important person around, he will be treated as the most irrelevant. He may even be thrown out.

On the other hand, there are those fathers who feel that labor and childbirth and babies are women's work. I can certainly sympathize with a father who doesn't want to be a witness to the pain of labor or who is frightened by hospitals and wary of birth: all that blood and gore. I absolutely understand why he would want to avoid dirty diapers. And I believe him when he says he doesn't know the first thing about caring for a baby.

That's exactly how most mothers feel. The difference is, most mothers don't have a choice.

Lamaze training has introduced a new kind of father figure into the labor room. This husband starts out totally untutored (as do we all). He doesn't know a menstrual cramp from a labor contraction. But give him six weeks of Lamaze classes, and suddenly he's as expert as any obstetrician. His bedside manner is beyond reproach. When his laboring wife pelts him with lemons, he offers her lollipops. He mops her brow, times her contractions, monitors her monitor. They should rent this kind of father out in hospitals by the hour. In a way, they do. That is, many hospitals seem to labor under the assumption that a Lamaze-trained father is a satisfactoy substitute for a labor nurse: if you bring the father, you often can forget the nurse. This way the hospital saves money. This may be the greatest single disservice to women wrought by Lamaze.

You can tell that the obstetricians who write the baby books are fathers. For example, one warns that husbands should participate in childbirth only when they want to, because, after all, some husbands "get sick." So, he neglects to mention, do some wives.

Another doctor suggests that a wife might want her husband in the labor room to "witness her suffering." He recommends that if the husband finds labor too hard to take, you should "let him off the hook; let him go home." I think this is a great idea—for mothers. When labor gets too hard to handle, the obstetrician "lets her off the hook" and sends her home.

When husbands aren't being expected to do too little, they are often looked to with expectations that are highly unrealistic. If not downright insane. No wonder most mothers find that fathers don't live up to the story-book pictures painted of them. A father (according to one book) must "manifest just the right combination of husbandly attentiveness, masculine reserve, paternal devotion and scientific curiosity." All that and he looks like Robert Redford, too.

Here's another of my favorites: A husband should give his wife sympathy and "show a philosophical acceptance of the situation. . . . Be aware of her moods and concerns. . . . Explore them as to their source and truth. Reassure her with facts, but present them in acceptable ways."

I know doctors with dozens of years of medical training behind them who don't begin to do that.

And then there's Daddy as the fumbling fool. This is the Daddy who paces impatiently in the waiting room wondering whether he's having a boy or an elephant. This father doesn't opt out of childbirth because he lacks the interest. He's dismissed as a dithering dolt. What can a mere father know about having babies? He probably thinks they fall out of trees. Or come by stork. To the extent that these husbands really exist, they need as much pampering during pregnancy as do their wives. It is callous and condescending to suggest (as does one book): "If your husband seems too wretched, buy him a teddy bear."

The three faces of fatherhood during pregnancy and childbirth, then, are: Macho-man, who thinks baby-business is woman's work; helpful hero (Lamaze variety) who could practically have the baby by himself (and often wants to); and the foolish fumbler, who's so helpless that he gets lost on the way to the hospital. Sometimes Macho-man pretends he's a foolish fumbler to avoid getting involved. (This applies not only to childbirth, but also to cooking, laundry, hanging pictures, and other household tasks.) And sometimes the heroic Lamaze husband fails to live up to his billing and falls apart just when you need him—even though he may still think he's terrific. And finally, the old foolish fumbler himself may surprise everyone (especially himself) by turning out to be the best labor nurse of all.

Fathers, that is to say, are only human. If we allow them to be. And require them to be. Just to put my personal prejudices out front, I don't believe that anybody has the right to deny a father his proper participation in the process of birth. And I also don't believe that a father has the right to deny the mother of the child he has, after all, fathered, to labor alone. If he's in on the conception, he should be there at the creation, too.

But I also think we must be fair with fathers. Let's face it: when it comes to childbirth, husbands are sometmes called upon to perform Herculean tasks. They have to be strong and steadfast even when their wives are falling to pieces—even when they themselves may feel like falling to pieces. They are expected to excel at what they can never understand, to appreciate what they can never experience. Of course, we pay high-priced obstetricians to do the same thing all the time. But somehow even though we expect more from our doctors, we accept less. Husbands, on the other hand, *have to* be there when we need them. They must respond to the *urgency* of the appeal, even when they don't understand its meaning. And in tackling the often intangible, some of them do remarkably well:

"My husband isn't at all into pregnancy and birth; he's kind of befuddled, not interested, not involved. But when I got hit with this sudden postpartum depression—thinking nobody cared about me—I called him in his office and said if he didn't get here in half an hour, our marriage was over. Boom. And he came."

"My husband has never come home from work because of something at home. But when I found out I was pregnant, I don't know why, but I called him and burst into tears. And he came right home. In a minute."

"If he was nervous on the outside, he was very calm with me. Driving to the hospital, saying, 'We'll get there, don't worry. Let's stop and get some gas.' He saw the babies (twins) before I did because they took me to the recovery room. And he said to me, 'Now don't get upset, because the babies have all kinds of hookups, but they're fine, don't worry, they have oxygen masks, don't worry, they're in an incubator, don't worry, they look a little small, but they're the biggest in the premie nursery.' In a way it was very condescending, but he didn't want me to be upset when I saw them. Then later I realized how upset *he* must have been when he saw them. I don't know how he acted so calm."

Not all husbands turn into towers of strength. Some simply bolt—as fast and as far away as possible. When you're lying in the hospital all alone, it doesn't help to understand that your husband isn't there because he's afraid of what he might see. You're probably afraid, too. But it might make you a bit more sympathetic to know (as if you didn't already) that mothers are sometimes stronger in these matters. Perhaps because they have to be. So perhaps you can find it in your heart to take pity on the weaker sex.

"John came only at night, just before the baby came out. And I said, 'Why don't you come sooner? All the other fathers come in the afternoon. Sometimes they pop in in the morning.' I was almost hysterical. After all, I had a cesarean. My husband had to take a special course just to be able to come and visit me whenever he wanted to. And then he never came. I think they're afraid—afraid of hospitals."

My husband, like most, was a mixed bag. He didn't really participate in pregnancy, and he slept through most of labor, but he received an A in recovery. When I couldn't nurse my baby because of the fever, my husband showed up to bottle-feed him morning, noon and night. (If my child wasn't going to know who his mother was, I was *determined* he'd know his dad.) To be at my bedside, my husband crossed picket lines, cursed out doctors, jeopardized his job. He was a gem. The star of the maternity ward. I was the only mother there with a husband in almost constant attendance—even in my baby's absence. Some husbands are tigers at timing contractions, and others get turned on by pregnant wives. I guess the man I married is simpy better at sickness than at health.

But no husband can be expected to excel at all aspects of childbirth. Parents (as we well know) are never perfect. Not mommies, not daddies. Not during pregnancy, or childbirth; not training toddlers or teaching the facts of life to teens. So I figure if a father performs well on one part of the birthing process, he should make any mother proud. Or at least content. Come to think of it, those aren't bad standards to apply to our performance, either.

THE PREGNANT HUSBAND

Everybody's heard of the husband who gets morning sickness or sympathetic labor pains or even heartburn and hemorrhoids. One husband put on forty pounds during pregnancy. Another felt fatigued during the first three months:

"My husband is terrific—he really identifies with pregnancy. He gets on the couch and falls asleep before I have a chance to. He has all the symptoms."

Some husbands get so excited they want to carry the baby themselves. They bother their wives for every little detail: What does it feel like? What did the doctor say? What's the baby doing now? In a scientific sense, they want to experience this strange new sensation. (And are jealous that they can't.) In an emotional sense, they're simply exultant:

"I can't describe how happy he was. He wanted to be pregnant, too. He couldn't wait for delivery. He was so excited about an offspring of ours that he wouldn't have minded if I'd grown a beard."

For husbands, as for wives, the happiest parents-to-be are often those who have been trying the longest and hardest. And among the most delirious daddies I've known are former priests, or husbands who thought they were sterile, or who were convinced for whatever reason that their wives could never conceive. These husbands are the biggest belly-patters and most avid baby-book readers around. They are proud and sometimes sheepish and almost always aggressively attentive. They don't let their wives sleep in the subway or go out in the rain. Sometimes they don't let them out of the house. For some happy fathers, pregnancy is a reaffirmation of their faith in family life and the renewal of life itself. For others, all it renews is their masculine pride:

"I don't think my husband was even aware that I was pregnant in the beginning. He was peripheral; it was the woman's thing. And then one day he had a reaction that really stunned me—even in my nonfeminist days. I was trying on maternity clothes—my mother was putting in hems—and suddenly my husband just glowed! You could see him thinking, 'Wow! You're going to get a big belly in that!' And what he was really saying was, 'Wow! Now the whole world is going to know that I can really get it up. I can get you pregnant!'"

Most husbands are pleased when they get pregnant. But that doesn't mean he's going to bring you roses every night. Unfortunately, our own preconceived notions coupled with Madison Avenue advertisements lead us to expect more than any expecting mother could hope for. Who could forget Paul Anka's poignant (and putdown) ode to motherhood: "You're Having My Baby" (Sedaka). The point of the song is that the woman gets placed on a pedestal because she's pregnant with the man's child. Never mind that she's carrying her own child, too. Those of us who take this kind of literature literally are bound to be disappointed.

"You always see the advertisements of a man and woman walking on the beach. He's looking so lovingly at his wife, who is pregnant. And I thought my husband was going to be like that. He was very helpful, of course. He took in the groceries. But he didn't get into 'Oh, you're carrying my kid' kind of thing. But because I saw it in the advertisements, I expected it."

Alas, most men are more matter-of-fact. What they relate to is not some ethereal aesthetic of childbirth, but rather to the mundane manifestations of impending motherhood, like aches and pains and the need for some help to get out of bed in the morning. Frequently, the primary contact between husband and wife during pregnancy centers on the wife's ailments. Your husband may not be able to understand what it's like to carry a child, but he can relate to heartburn. He knows what it's like to be nauseous. Still, you shouldn't let your husband's own down-to-earth mentality bring your own head out of the clouds. He's just doing what he knows best. Even if it is bringing you Maalox at three o'clock in the morning.

At times, almost every pregnant marriage can tap new depths of mutual understanding and touch both partners in unexpected, exciting ways. The thought of making a baby together may or may not strike you as transcendental, but it is almost certainly thrilling. A special experience that only the two of you can share. The family that labors together . . . well, labors together. There's no guarantee that sharing a baby birth will cement your marriage, but as an activity to engage in together, it sure beats tennis or bridge.

"We joked together the entire time. Somebody gave us a baby carriage, and my husband brought in these two Siamese cats. And it was so funny and embarrassing to see these big cats sitting there in the carriage. We did things like that all the time."

"My husband went on a research trip for his dissertation, and I was living in this house with some other people. Even though I was away from him, I felt very close to him. It was a tremendous time for us. We wrote a lot of very close letters, and we had a very alive feeling."

Devoted or indifferent, your husband will no more fit into a mold during pregnancy than you will. And if your pregnancy doesn't go by the book, neither will his. He will be himself, only more so—or perhaps less so. Just like you. His strengths and weaknesses may take on new dimensions. You may even find facets of his personality that you never noticed before. But don't expect him to develop a whole new set of attributes over night. If he does, heed them as harbingers of what is to come. Perhaps he's finally found himself in prospective fatherhood. In that case, be prepared to step aside while he stays home and plays full-time parent. Or perhaps he's confused and more concerned than the situation calls for. Or even angry and withdrawn. All these signs signal his future feelings about becoming a father. It behooves you—and him—to find out what they are.

Everybody talks about husbands getting sympathetic labor pains, but nobody talks about husbands who "get the blues."

He may need love and care and understanding as much as you do. And if nothing else works, he may even need that teddy bear.

THE BIRTH OF A FATHER

I had a curious conversation with my older brother the other day. About five months ago, he watched as his first child was born. Actually, he didn't watch. He said he couldn't bear to. Indeed, he said he found the whole experience upsetting, even frightening. "You can tell that having a baby is a very dangerous thing," he said. "If it wasn't, they wouldn't have all those doctors and nurses running around."

Fathers, like mothers, an be put off by the vast array (sometimes disarray) of hospital paraphernalia and personnel. For some reason, I had assumed they were immune. I guess because the fathers in the Lamaze movies seem to be so stoic, to take it all in stride. But the cold and clinical approach to delivery *can* leave a father feeling that birth is cold and clinical itself. Something for doctors and nurses and technicians and machinery. A delivery room is a dangerous place to be. There's definitely no room for Daddy.

Of course, this has been the traditional role of fathers when it comes to babies. If fathers often express little interest in pregnancy or childbirth, it is because they have for so long been excluded. Women have tended to be cliquish about childbearing, "While the males sort of stand in the background, pawing the ground or something," said one mother.

No wonder so many husbands have to be roped into Lamaze training. Once you get them in the corral, you hope that they'll see it isn't as horrible as they had thought; and that they'll understand that they do have an important role. But Lamaze has a lot to overcome:

"My mother-in-law instilled in my husband that this was horrible, gruesome, painful and miserable. I had to try to convert him along the way. But he was scared. He had the gunsmoke image of blood and gore and screaming and biting into the bedposts and everything. And when he found out it wasn't like that, I think his relationship with his mother went down the tubes."

Lamaze prepares prospective fathers to participate in birth

as a beautiful experience. The trouble is that Lamaze—like mothers-in-law—can be misleading. (If I'm beginning to repeat myself, it's not unintentional. Some things bear repetition.)

The husband gets geared up for being an "important person" in the birth process, for helping and coaching and cheering you on from his ringside seat. He's expecting to be a welcome member of the team that delivers the baby. If he finds that the only place for him to sit is the commode (as did my brother), or that he's made to feel otherwise uncomfortable and out-of-place, he may be sorely disappointed. he's all dressed up in his sterile gown with nowhere to stand and nothing to see. If he's disappointed enough, the first trip to the delivery room may be his last: "My husband tried to be interested for my sake. So I finally convinced him to watch the birth. He did, but disliked it so much that he flatly refused to watch the second time around."

More common, of course, is the husband who has to be led by the hand into birth, then likes it so much he can't wait to do it all over again. This is the father who faints during the blood test for the marriage license, but sticks it out for delivery because he gets so totally involved. He's a convert. But in a way we've more or less come to expect.

The husband who encounters unpleasant surprises is a more serious problem—for both of you. So beware of painting too bright a picture just to get your husband into the labor room. The reality may be so disillusioning that you'll defeat your own purpose, not to mention his. It doesn't hurt, while you're packing your own Lamaze goodie bag, to pack something pleasant for him, too. You may not be able to bring him a comfortable chair, but you can always find room for a cold beer and a corned beef sandwich. He'll need his strength, too.

Writing this, I suddenly realize why my husband wasn't more excited about watching the birth of our own child. He had witnessed one natural birth already—that of his daughter by a previous marriage. Having experienced the excitement of the first, I thought he would be ecstatic about the prospect of a second. But he said he hadn't felt that he'd ever really belonged. And then when we reached the labor room ourselves, he had to squeeze himself into a small uncomfortable chair. For eleven hours. Nobody exactly went out of their way to make him feel at home. I'm not really surprised that I didn't take notice. Like most mothers in labor, I had more pressing problems on my mind. But his attitude is not so difficult to understand. Hospitals can be hard on husbands, too:

"I was nine centimeters dilated, and they knocked me out and sent my husband away. And he was so furious that he went home. He said, 'This is ridiculous. That creep sent me away. I'm not going to hang around this place.' So he went home, but then he changed his mind. 'I can't do this—my wife's having a baby.' So he went to a friend's house, a girl who had been through natural childbirth three weeks before us, because he was so incredibly upset about being sent away. So they talked to him and sort of simmered him down. And then the doctor called and told him that I had the baby. And my husband really told him off. He said that he felt it was so cruel and unjust to send him home, to put me out when I was doing so well, when I hadn't even requested it. It was really a heavy experience for him."

Of course, it's hard to know the right mix of reality and pretty rhetoric to use to get a reluctant husband over his hesitancy about participating in the birth. With some husbands, the more they know, the less they want to hear—no matter what you tell them.

"My husband is going to classes only because I want him to. He doesn't want to be there, and he told me that right off, from the beginning. He is so afraid of pain. Not for himself so much, but for me. He doesn't want to see me in pain. I thought seeing the Lamaze movie would make him feel better. And he said, 'Are you crazy? You thought I was going to feel better after that? I don't want to see you in that kind of pain!'"

The only thing to tell a husband like this is how much you need him. And to explain that labor isn't so much pain as very hard work. And that you can't do it without his help. Perhaps then he'll put aside his preoccupation with pain and think more about his obligations as husband and father. Birth is a job that needs doing. Like moving the furniture or changing the tires or helping you put in the screens. He isn't there to watch you suffer, he's there to help you *not* suffer.

Some husbands don't have to be convinced to participate in childbirth at all. The moment you get pregnant, they're ready to take control. They love Lamaze because it allows them to play the role of drill sergeant. They're tyrants when it comes to timing contractions, and if you don't do your exercises right, they'll stay on you until you do. One husband even told his wife that he thought she was "rather weak in not resisting the pain any better than I did. He was probably right." No, he was probably wrong. And anyway, it's easy to say someone else is weak when you're not going through it yourself. Husbands are there to help, not judge. Make sure yours remembers this.

Or perhaps your husband is the strong silent type. He may be so stunned by the whole process that he doesn't know what to say. Or he may by training or by nature be the sort of person who doesn't let his insides show on the outside.

"My husband just isn't the type to jump up and down or cry or show he's scared or whatever. The whole time I was in labor, his expression never changed, even when I was literally squeezing the blood out of his fingers. I think it must have been hard for him to watch me go through that, but he never let it show."

No matter what your husband says or shows, he's probably very worried about you. If he tells your doctor twelve times during labor to "save my wife before the baby," he's actually acting normally. (Even though you may be extremely embarrassed.) After all, the baby is still a stranger—especially to him. You're the one he knows and loves and may be very afraid to lose. That's one reason that he may want to be with you in the hospital wherever you go. Not because he particularly wants to particpate in your labor. But because he wants to look out for your welfare. And when you're helpless in the hospital yourself, it certainly doesn't hurt to have somebody else to go to bat for you.

Indeed, if your husband doesn't get a little hysterical, you may even be disappointed:

"The interesting thing about my husband is that he grew up on a farm, and so this was the most boring of all births to him. He delivered goats and he delivered cows at all hours of the night from the time he was about one year old. She he wasn't awed or worried by the birth process at all. I remember at one point thinking that he really should be a little more awed."

I'll never forget the husband in our Lamaze class who came to tell us about the birth of his baby—the one that he missed at the last moment because the baby had to be delivered by forceps. My husband reacted strongly to his story—and so, I think, did most of the other men in the room. No matter what you think about birth, if you're counting on being there to watch or help or even hide under the covers, it can be a terrible letdown to miss out at the last minute:

"My husband was so enthusiastic that if he could get up on the delivery table and have a baby himself, he would do it tomorrow. And so it was one of our biggest disappointments that he didn't make it for either birth. The first time when he left they put me out, and he kissed me and said, 'I know I have to go now, but I'll see you soon. Maybe next time you can be awake and I can see the birth, too.' And I felt so bad that he missed it. I think it hurt him even more than me."

So no matter how your husband approaches the moment of birth, be sure that he—like you—is prepared for all possibilities. If you are knocked out or deliver by cesarean or for whatever reason have the type of birth that your husband can't attend, he'll still probably see the baby before you do. It isn't like being present at the creation, but at least it's some consolation.

FATHER AS COACH

The Lamaze father is a special case. Not only is he expected to be husband and helpmate and source of strength, but he's also called upon to coach. Fathers are often recruited in later years to coach Little League baseball teams and the like. But the presumption is that they know something about playing baseball. Few fathers practice playing childbirth games when they are little boys—at least not the type that would help them learn anything about labor. The job of labor coach is one for which most fathers are totally unprepared. A trained labor nurse takes many years to absorb enough expertise to help you deliver your baby; your husband is expected to become an expert in just six weeks.

Labor training starts in Lamaze class. Your husband's attitudes (and abilities) toward birth may hinge on how well he likes going to school. He probably won't like it much at all if he's not comfortable in groups. Or if he's put off by practicing panting in front of large numbers of people. Or if your instructor is especially silly and makes him (and everybody else) feel as if he's in second grade. If your husband doesn't like to help you practice your exercises, there may be a good reason. Nobody wants to make a fool of himself. Or herself.

Lamaze training and exercises should be taken very seriously. If your Lamaze class doesn't get this message across, you'll have to carry it yourself. You might even find that books alone are better, if the class really turns your or your husband off. What you want to look for is the learning method that's most informative—and least condescending. And that gives you the most motivation to practice and learn.

Of course, some people put on a better public face than others, and many households participate freely in class only because it's less embarrassing than *not* participating. But don't let that fool you into thinking you've got the only husband on the block who doesn't practice regularly at home. It only looks that way.

"You know how they tell you, you're supposed to rub the tummy, rub the legs. John never touched me. In the classes, I'd say, 'John, you're supposed to be doing this now, and he'd say, 'No, not in front of everybody.' And he didn't do it when we were in the labor room either. But he held my hand until it almost broke. Afterwards, he admitted that he adored the experience, especially the delivery room. But he wasn't as good a coach as I would have liked because he didn't like the classes, and never helped me with my exercises. I always felt like I was pestering him."

If you have to pester, pester. If you don't do the exercises together, you're not going to be prepared. And if you're not prepared, you're going to have a problem.

Even with the best preparation, coaching is not always easy. My husband offered strong psychological support, but little practical assistance. Not that he has anything against contractions—it's just that I'm the one who's naturally interested in things medical and scientific, and he's just naturally not. He never really knew whether the contractions were coming or going, which meant he wasn't much good at timing them. He was so tired that at one point he even nodded off. Of course, I would have been lost without his continual encouragement—but I also could have used a labor nurse.

"The one thing that I did not like about this hospital was that they didn't stay with me, they left it up to my husband, who was not up to handling the situation. And I never got any attention from a nurse, which I needed. He was not cluing me into when the contractions were coming, and he threatened to leave me. I told him to watch the monitor, but he didn't know what to make of the monitor because he'd never seen one before."

One pregnancy manual reminds fathers that their most important functions is to keep their wives apprised of every sign of progress. This assumes he knows what progress is. Your husband doesn't examine you, and can't tell about your centimeters, and doesn't know whether you're ready to deliver or not. Or whether you should be pushing or panting or blowing or getting prepped for a cesarean. One father unknowingly stepped out to lunch at the worst possible time:

"Almost as soon as he left, the doctor came in to examine me. And he said, 'Okay, we are ready for delivery. Where's the husband?' And the nurse said, 'He's out to lunch. Somebody go and get him.' And later in the recovery room I heard two doctors walk by saying, 'Hey, did you hear about the husband who went out to lunch?'"

A father can't do it all. And he shouldn't be expected to. If you need help, you might try to specifically request a labor nurse or doctor to help your coach coach you. This isn't an admission of defeat on his part or yours. It's simply accepting that Lamaze training doesn't substitute for nursing school. I doubt that your husband would be offended if you wanted to bring in an assistant. He would probably be relieved:

"David was so glad that he really didn't have to do anything. He didn't have to time me, he didn't have to rub anything, he didn't have to give me lemons, so he went around giving out lemons to all the people in the hospital."

Coaching is a big responsibility. It involves study and practice and most of all not being out of town on a business trip when the time arrives. This often produces problems. My husband wanted to fly out to his daughter's junior high school graduation in California two weeks before our son was due to be born. I certainly didn't want to be a spoilsport and say no. But I wasn't every enthusiastic about "yes" either. If the baby had come two weeks early instead of three weeks late, and my husband had been 3,000 miles away at the time, I would have faced labor alone. And if I were he, I wouldn't have wanted to face me when he got home.

"Of course, I knew my husband had to travel a lot when

I married him, but this is ridiculous. He's away all the time, and here I am six weeks from my due date. I could go at any time. I tell him that any other woman would nag him to death and divorce him for going away. What do you think, I'm a woman of steel? If I go into labor, I'm going to have to get some bum and give him a bottle of Gallo and make him come and be my coach."

Coaching also involves a certain amount of tact. When the coach sees a contraction coming on the monitor, it's not tactful to say, 'Get ready, you're going to have a real awful contraction any minute now, it's really going to hurt.' Unfortunately, some husbands really love machines. Instead of worrying about you, they get totally tied up in the monitor. He winds up cheering for the contractions instead of for you. Whose side is he on, anyway?

Fetal monitors may send other husbands into a panic. If he runs out into the hall screaming for a doctor every time the little light goes on he, isn't going to help your concentration. (The light is *supposed* to go on. It shows that the baby's heart is beating.) If you're going to share your labor room with a fetal monitor, be sure to get someone to explain it to both of you as soon as you're plugged in.

Indeed, the only thing worse than an apathetic coach is an overenthusiastic one. He takes total control to the point where you and your contractions become almost irrelevant. Power corrupts. You have to keep reminding him: "Hey, remember me? I'm the one who's having the baby."

"I'm afraid my husband will get so into it that I will be raving in pain on the table, and my doctor will say, 'Joan, would you like an epidural?' And my husband will say, 'No, she's fine' He just loves stopwatches. He can't wait to time the contractions. There's no way he'd let me take medication. It's like that part in the Lamaze movie where the wife is losing control of her breathing, and the husband says to her, 'Come on, shape up, what's the matter with you?' I couldn't believe he said that. But I know my husband would be just the same."

In the end, it's personality that's of prime importance. A husband's character may account for whether he's just plain bored with labor (and falls sleep) or whether he's so fascinated that he wants to do everything himself. And, of course, what you need in a coach depends on your personality, too. You may need someone who takes command, or you may resent someone who tries to tell you what to do. You may want one kind of coach at some times, and another at others. All of which places a tall order on your husband—one he may not be able to fulfill:

"My husband was a hundred per cent cooperative and everything, but he wasn't able to help me during labor because he just gets overwhelmed. He's very good in day-to-day things, which is when I really fall apart. But I'm good in a crisis, and he's not. I think with natural childbirth it is very important to have somebody around who can take control in a crisis, and Paul is not the sort of person who can do that."

Sometimes the requirements are more psychological:

"Whenever John is exceedingly nice to me is when I am always my bitchiest. So if he said, 'Joan, stop messing around and do your breathing,' I'd be less apt to step on him. I make him sound like this creep, but I think it's a master-slave thing, and I think I'll be good as long as he's the master and I'm the slave because unless he really is master I'm not going to listen to him."

What's a father to do?

The best he can do is try his best. He can't change his personality just because your going to have a baby. But you both can recognize what are likely to be his strengths and weaknesses beforehand. That way, you won't be surprised or unduly disappointed. You have every right to ask your husband to be around and be prepared and be adequately informed about what's going to happen. You can't ask him to be someone he's not. Don't be upset by stories (even the true ones) about husbands who are Mr. Wonderful during labor, mopping the brow and keeping track of every contraction. If this doesn't sound like the man in your life, don't worry. Let the hospital know that you can't get along without a good labor nurse. And remember: just because he isn't a great coach doesn't mean he won't make the team as a father.

IT'S A FATHER!

A man I once knew used to say that he liked children well enough, but he just couldn't relate to what he called "wobbly-headed jobs"— i.e.,babies. There's a myth going around that men for some reason don't relate to newborns as well as women. It isn't a myth that men can be wary of small babies. It's a myth that women aren't wary, too.

Still, when they pass out the babies in the hospital, its somehow less acceptable for a mother to say she's afraid to hold the baby, and would the nurse mind taking care of it until it gets a little older. Fathers do this all the time: "They had a father's hour in the hospital. And the nurse came in and said to my husband, 'Would you like to hold the baby?' And he said, 'Oh no, I'll hold it when it comes home. It's much too little now.'"

Girls do baby-sit more than boys, and that gives (some) women a headstart when it comes to baby care. But it also seems that many mothers have a connection with newborns that some fathers don't. After all, the baby came out of her body. A child is as much a father's eight pound of flesh as the mother's, but the demonstration isn't as undeniable or graphic. Moreover, if a mother is nursing or for whatever reason has the primary responsibility for feeding and caring for the baby, she may feel a closer connection at first. We've all spent some time in our childhood playing with dolls—something that boys are only beginning to do. The mother may find that the baby is almost exclusively *hers* in the beginning—and the father's only later.

"As supportive as he was all during my pregnancy, once the baby arrived, it was *mine* and it stayed that way for a long time. The first year, I was the one who took care of her, and the whole thing was mine. He just couldn't relate to that little thing. And then once she started responding and coming around as a human being, the whole thing changed. Now it's like she's *his* child even more than mine."

It isn't necessarily wrong for a father (or mother) to be more attuned to taking care of an infant or a toddler or a teen-ager, as long as they don't abrogate their responsibility. Your child needs you at all ages, no matter what your personal proclivities. If you aren't into babies, you shouldn't have one. That means fathers, too.

Fortunately, it's become an accepted part of our popular culture for fathers to love little babies now—to feed them and change them and cuddle them just as much as mothers have always done. Fathers are finally finding out what they've always been missing. And most of them are glad they did:

"My husband was apprehensive that he wouldn't love the

child, that he wouldn't be a good father. But when he saw the baby, he cried with joy. He was really moved. Now, when the baby cries, he always picks her up first. He holds the baby like this, with one hand under her head and one hand supporting her rear end, and he marches her around and sings a marching band song. Ba dum ba dum. And the baby just beams. And I know it gives my husband a great sense of satisfaction knowing he can make the baby so happy. I think sometimes he's closer to her than I am."

Husbands can be helpful, too. Indeed, many baby books advise against having any help around the house other than your husband when the baby comes home. This is good advice if your husband is truly helpful, and a disaster if he isn't. By the time you get home from the hospital, it's too late to teach him how to run the washer and cook the meals and take care of your toddlers—so be sure to make an accurate appraisal beforehand. That isn't to say that he won't try to help under any circumstances. It's simply to say that he might not succeed.

"My husband took a week off from work after my second baby was born, and it was the worst experience of my life. My mother had to come over daily to cook his meals. And after spending all day with my eighteen-month-old, he was a wreck. I lined up sitters so he could visit me every night. And he would come in looking so awful, dressed in dirty khakis, crummy shirt, hadn't shaved. Moaning, 'Oh, I'm so tired.' And he would turn on my television and get in my hospital bed and tell my mother and me to go and look at the baby while he slept. And I did not want to leave the hospital to go home. I stayed for five days and tried for a sixth."

This is the stereotypical situation-comedy husband. But among the women I interviewed, he turned out to be not very typical. More and more husbands are becoming more and more helpful in every sense, even though it's sometimes hard for them (and us) to cope with all that's involved. Like long nights up with the baby, and long days changing diapers and doing laundry. But it seems that husbands are increasingly willing. even happy—to do their share. One husband hand-washed the baby's clothes every night when he came home from work. (The baby had a rash, so his clothes had to be washed in special soap.) Another was so helpful the first week at home that the mother never even changed a diaper. Then, when he went back to work, she was the one left not knowing what to do. All she'd done was breastfeed. He'd even taken care of the burping.

"It really makes you love him, doesn't it?" these mothers say again and again.

Indeed, you might be doing your husband a favor by making him help out a little more than he'd like to, especially if he is hesitant or unsure. This doesn't mean that you should depend on his help totally if he's not the dependable type. This is a time when you need to think of yourself and your baby first. But don't cut him off completely. You'll be doing both him and yourself a disservice:

"I never left him with the first two babies, and I wish now that I had. Just leave him and walk out of the house and make him cope. But I was afraid of being irresponsible to the baby. And yet my husband needed it, because he never would have taken over by himself. And the baby needed it—to be with his father. And I needed it. My mother used to say that she'd leave us with my father when we were babies, and she'd come home and the diapers would be on upside-down. Well, with the third baby, I didn't care if the diaper was upside-down or inside-out as long as I got my relief and he was with the baby. He had to learn as well as I did. No matter how much you read before, you suddenly become a mother and you have to learn it, so you do. And so did he. And it was the best move I ever made. For all of us."

The things that people don't like to do are often the things they don't know how to do. Whether it's fixing the car or changing a diaper. Some people don't understand math, and others are bored by Bach and some "don't know the first thing about" babies. So they avoid them. But the only way to enjoy something is to understand it, and the only way to really understand something is to do it. To do it often, and to do it well. That's where the sense of satisfaction comes from. The sense of accomplishment. And that's why I think it's important for fathers to care for infants. And for mothers to care for cars.

YOUR MARRIAGE

And baby makes three. But baby can also wreak havoc with the comfortable two's-company of your marriage. I was recently at a meeting of the Professional Women's Association of my college. We were asked to draw little diagrams of how we spent our time. Not surprisingly, almost everybody carved out the lion's share for her career. A small circle was set aside for the child. But the husband's place was definitely on the periphery. A tiny speck shoved in here or shunted off to the side there. Not that we didn't all love our husbands; we just couldn't find time for them.

"Somebody has to do the shopping and the laundry and the cooking and take care of the baby and we just never saw each other. I mean, it's hard to have anything left by nine o'clock when everybody is finally bedded down and you are finished in the kitchen and you sit down with *The New York Times*. You just don't feel that close together. You can barely make it to page two."

Working mothers aren't the only ones whose marriages suffer. Babies take time—no matter what else you do with your life. And that time has to come from someplace. Or someone. No matter how strongly you and your husband feel about sharing the responsibility of a baby, he easily can feel displaced by this new rival for your time, attention, and energy. Your new baby can't do anything for himself or herself—walk, talk, eat, even sleep. You're going to be exhausted. If that doesn't take away your sexual interest, it will certainly take away your stamina.

A baby is supposed to give you and your husband something to share. And it does. But in doing so it may eliminate all the things you used to share before you became parents. Now it's you do something while he watches the baby, or he does something while you watch the baby. The first few months (years, to be perfectly honest) don't leave much time for the two of you together. That's a long time to be separated from someone you were very close to. To say that husbands often feel neglected is a gross understatement.

"There's definitely a feeling of resentment and competition. There has to be. Before there were just the two of you, and now all your time is taken up with an infant. One day I looked over at my husband, and he was sort of sitting there like a forlorn puppy. And I said, 'Okay, you really feel you're being ignored, don't you?' And he said yes. And he looked like he was going to cry. He said, 'You have no time to even talk to me, you're so busy with the baby.' And I *was* happy being with the baby. In a way, he was right."

Baby books say that husbands should always come first.

But husbands can feed themselves and change their own diapers. The baby has to take precedence—in the allocation of your time, if not of your affections. And often the latter is also true. Let's face it. Your husband has been around for a while. Your baby is new and different and irresistibly cuddly and cute.

Your husband may be cuddly, too, but when a baby is born, a bit of the romance in your marriage is bound to temporarily die. Facing your husband over a changing table is just not the same as looking into his eyes over dinner by candlelight. You can't party until two in the morning because somebody has to be up at six. And there's not much point in putting on your prettiest outfit just to get drooled on.

"Some of the caring does go to someone else, and I feel very guilty about that. I did not expect children to interfere with the romantic aspects of our marriage. But I found I couldn't stand to have sex when there was even the possibility of Cynthia crying. I see some childless couples, and they seem so close. I feel I've lost something so special."

Remember, too, that you are more immediately prepared for all of this than is your husband. He has certainly noticed by now that you've been looking and acting strangely for the past nine months. It isn't as though he wasn't expecting a baby, too. But he hasn't actually been carrying the child around with him; he hasn't been keeping company with it in the same way you have. It still may come as somewhat of a shock. Here's this package home from the hospital. And it's threatening to replace him. Suddenly, he's obsolete.

Suddenly he's also a father. And you're a mother. No longer primarily husband and wife, you're now Mom and Dad. This is more than a matter of semantics. It's a whole new relationship. You may find that even when you do have time together, you spend it talking about the child who is (finally) asleep. You may also find that you have something brand-new to fight about.

"My husband and I never fought before the baby was born. Now we fight all the time. Mostly about the fact that we never have any time together. But also about how to do this or that, or who's going to change the next diaper. If he cries at night, we always argue about whether to let him cry or pick him up. And we never—once—argued about anything before."

The very thing that is keeping you apart can also bring you

together. Specifically, caring for baby. But it takes a lot of time and maturity to learn how to concentrate on the together side and ignore or at least put aside the forces that tear you apart. For example, if you're home all day with the baby, you may be glad and grateful when your husband walks in the door at night. But you may be too frazzled and tired to let him know. This can be a fatal mistake. Hire a sitter, take a bath, take a few minutes off. Anything so that you can *share* your day with your husband when he gets home, not dump it on him. (This goes double for husbands who get frazzled by a long day at work and come home to dump all their problems on their weary wives.)

Remember that vow in your marriage service, "for better or for worse"? This may be what the "worse" was all about. Frankly, you don't have the energy for fighting, so you may as well learn to lean on each other instead. You both need the support. And when you can overcome all the (not insubstantial) obstacles that a baby brings to marriage, you may find yourselves with more reasons to love each other than ever before.

"Our relationship has gotten so much richer. We have an additional bond between us that wasn't there before. We've worked out our lives so that we make sure we have time alone together—and that's been very important. But just sharing the baby—and knowing that it's something we did together—has made us so much closer."

Unfortunately, happy families don't always come naturally. If you see that your marriage is being neglected because of the baby, do something about it. Take the time to spend with the (other) one you love. Or at least tell him how much you miss him, and *wish* you had the time to spend with him. He isn't going to know telepathically. Remember, your marriage is what brought you your baby. Don't let your baby break it apart.

WHAT THE FATHER'S ROLE MEANS TO MOTHER

This chapter is supposed to be about fathers only, but the part your husband plays in childbirth can itself play a pivotal role in your own experience. A father's involvement may mean a great deal to him. It may mean even more to you. Indeed, mothers whose husbands haven't participated have considered that to be one of the major disappointments of having a baby.

"I would say to my husband, 'Do you want to feel the baby kick?' And he'd say, 'No, not particularly.' And it was just so disappointing. I didn't have that sharing experience that so many women seem to have, and it was very hard for me because I wanted the Lamaze birth, I wanted the pregnancy to be all that it could be. I was very interested in all the biological drawings of the baby growing, all the little charts, and I thought about it all the time. But I was the only one thinking about it. I wanted it to be special, but it was special to me alone."

Many mothers experience this disappointment to some degree. We want our husbands to be every bit as interested as we are. And often they're not—for the simple reason that we're carrying the baby and they're not. Pregnancy is really about woman's body, woman's mind, woman's hemorrhoids. We are involved by definition. Husbands have to try a little harder sometimes. And yet, we expect every father to live up to the Lamaze ideal. Reading every book, practicing every exercise, listening for the baby's heartbeat with a kitchen cup pressed between your belly and his ear. When this doesn't happen, we feel we've lost something. And we're right. When it does happen, it's as precious as pregnancy itself.

"I really had such a lovely pregnancy, mainly because my husband was so interested and tender—which was surprising because he is not a demonstrative person in general and usually jokes about everything. But he took a sabbatical that semester, and when the president of his college asked him what he was going to do, he said, 'Well, I'm going to study very early child labor.' And we had such a lovely time together. We traveled a lot. And he was with me the whole time. Really. I mean not just physically with me, but emotionally, too. And I think that says a lot for him."

This is the husband every woman wants. And I think all mothers can have a piece of him, to some degree. The important thing is to remember that all of us bring a great deal of excess baggage to childbirth—husbands and wives alike. All the fears and taboos and feelings of being irrelevant and out of place. Try to find out what the bad feelings are, to dispel those you can, and to ignore those you can't. Because whatever his hang-ups, his help is important to you. A husband who can participate during pregnancy, labor and birth is the greatest gift of all. Ask any mother:

"One of the things I can't fathom is that all our mothers had children without their husbands with them. I just can't picture having had the child without Lou being next to me. That was the greatest medicine in the world."

"It was really my husband who delivered the baby. He was helpful, interested, loving. In fact, so helpful that I had no need for a labor nurse or doctor or anything. I felt we could have done it alone. I consider him irreplaceable in my memories of both deliveries."

"I was never mad at my husband the way they tell you you're going to be. I was so sweet to him because I was so glad to have him there. The poor guy was so tense that I think if anything had gone wrong, he would have thrown up in his goodie bag. But at least I wasn't lonely. And that's a long time to be alone."

In the end, the father may be the essential ingredient that flavors your childbirth experience, sweet or sour. Keep him with you if you can, and if you can't, try to forgive whoever or whatever keeps him away. Whether it's the hospital, or factors pertaining to your health, or your husband's disinterest. It's especially important not to blame him if his hesitancy is the reason you're not together. And even more important not to blame yourself if the reason pertains to you. You can live up to some of your ideals all the time, and all of your ideals some of the time, but nobody's personality is perfect for every situation. Fathers, like mothers, are people, too.

Doctor, Doctor:

Everybody in a White Coat Isn't the Good Humor Man

I had a nightmare recently that pretty well sums up how I feel about physicians in general. Obstetricians in particular. I was sitting at a large table with several official-looking women in white dresses. (Nurses? Lawyers?) We were in the middle of a malpractice proceeding: I was suing my obstetrician for negligence. Every time I tried to make my case using one of my battery of big words—like "malpresentation" or "disproportion"—they'd respond with a battery of bigger ones. The louder I talked, the less they listened. The more convinced I was that I was right, the less they were.

Then my obstetrician joined us: white coat, white hair, white teeth. Suddenly I was a simpering child, soliciting his approval. I smiled prettily and pulled out my baby pictures. His mere presence was enough to make me defer to him. Self-confident and determined a moment ago, I was now confused and coy.

In short, I feel about doctors roughly the way I feel about airline pilots and nuclear power plant operators. I know that among their ranks are those who are negligent, ignorant, ma-

levolent. Even mad. But I'm forced to believe in them. I can't
afford not to. I can't afford to confront the very real possibility
that they don't know what they're doing. So even when the
evidence is indisputable: Three Mile Island. A DC-10 crash.
A $48 million malpractice suit. I still disregard my better judg-
ment to defer to those in authority. Especially when their authority is over my life.

However, I did *try* to be objective.

My search for an obstetrician started in an office with wall-
to-wall women and piped-in music. I filled out a form that
asked for my husband's or father's occupation. The first time
I saw the doctor, it was feet first, naked on the table. Hi, how
do you do? I told him a little bit about myself. He forgot all
of it by the time it was my turn to enter his office.

He told me that I was pregnant, that I should gain no more
than fifteen pounds, avoid all canned fods and most meat. He
said there was "no difference" between natural childbirth and
the knocked-out kind. He told me to come back in a month.

When I made the follow-up appointment, the nurse set me
up with another doctor. Indeed, she said I would have to "rotate
through" five doctors before I was done. I felt like a revolving
door. This wasn't private practice, it was a medical merry-go-
round. The second doctor was outright rude. Besides, I was
planning a trip to Brazil, and he forbade all long-distance travel.

So much for doctors number 1.

I already had an ob/gyn I liked in the city, but that was
twenty miles of bumper-to-bumper traffic away. So before
making the trek, I checked up on him. The friendly physician
who advised me said my doctor was dangerously "unorthodox."
(I later learned this meant he believed in natural childbirth.)
But I took the advice of the man in the white coat and went
to some friends of his with a practice right next door. I have
never regretted a decision more in my life.

By all accounts, I was now hooked up with one of the best
obstetrical practices connected with one of the finest maternity
centers in the country. I'm not sure what the implications are
of that. I'm not sure I want to think about it.

The beginning was uneventful. Except that the doctor did
mistakenly triple the prescription for prenatal vitamins (the
druggist caught it), and twice weighed me wearing boots. At
first I'd get chastised for gaining weight, and then (with boots
off) for losing it.

Meanwhile, Fritzie had some advice for our Lamaze class on dealing with doctors. She said we should be careful to tell the doctor everything we thought was important because "many things go unnoticed when you're in and out of the office in five minutes." She also told us that our doctors would "love to communicate with you if they thought you knew anything. You can imagine how awful it must be for the doctor to see fifty ladies in one morning and have to say 'everything's fine' to all of them." Fifty ladies! No wonder my doctor couldn't seem to remember me from one appointment to the next.

Late in my pregnancy, I started to bleed a bit. I tried to call the doctor, but I couldn't get through the nurse. She'd ask, "Is this an emergency?" I didn't know. I didn't even know how I was supposed to know. Look it up in a book?

Eventually, the doctor sent me in for a sonargram ("Have you ever heard of sonar?"), which is an ultrasound picture of the baby. The results would tell him if the placenta was in the wrong place, or if there were other problems. Sonargrams are also required of patients undergoing amniocentesis. It is not a painful procedure, but it can be uncomfortable—mainly because you have to fill your bladder to the bursting point, then lie flat on a table for a long time while a specialist runs a kind of microphone back and forth over your well-oiled belly.

Fortunately, the test showed nothing wrong. But just in case, I was given an appointment for the following week—this time with another doctor in the practice. Playing musical chairs outside his office (one woman in the examining room, one in the green chair outside his office, one changing, one in his office), I counted his appointments on the calendar for that day. Altogether, there were twenty-eight names. Fritzie wasn't so far off. I wondered how many patients a clinic doctor sees in a day. And calculated how much extra we were paying for the privilege of "private" care.

Anxious after my bleeding episode, I asked doctor #2 when I could start exercising again. "Who told you to stop exercising?" he said. He knew nothing about the bleeding, the test, the results. My chart held not a hint. So much for intra-office communication.

By week 37, we were getting pretty excited about the delivery itself. I was writing an article about the high rate of cesarean sections, so my doctor gave me some background. Including the information that more cesareans were being performed because more women were demanding "perfect babies." And that a baby delivered after a long, hard labor "might be smart enough to be President of the United States, but not President of Harvard." He also said he didn't heed the warnings of so many other obstetricians that epidurals could dull the urge to push, thus leading to more cesareans. "Don't worry about that," he said. "I'm a good man with a forceps." When I asked who would do the surgery, if necessary, he answered, "I do whatever relates to having the baby. I do forceps. I do cesareans. I take out your uterus." I'd just as soon keep my uterus, thank you.

Two weeks later, my doctor had totally forgotten our previous conversation. He even told me the President-of-Harvard joke again. This visit gave me nightmares. (Literally.) First, because I realized that the doctor hadn't measured my uterus for three visits. Second, because I was suspicious about his procedure for checking the fetal heart. He never listened very long or took note of a number. A nice nurse had let me listen to the heartbeat myself that day, and we found it on the "lower right." We had looked on "lower left," but all we heard there was the swooshing of the placenta. The doctor listened for a moment to the lower left and pronounced everything "fine." Perhaps he was listening for the placenta. Or perhaps . . . anything. But he still made me nervous.

Meanwhile, the baby had not yet "dropped," or engaged. I asked what would happen if labor was late. My doctor explained that two weeks after D-day, we would make an appointment for a cesarean—provided there was no dilation and the baby still hadn't dropped. This put me in a panic. I thought I was familiar with most indications for cesarean section, and postmaturity per se was not one of them. I was also uneasy because:

—How could he be so sure of the due date? My brother, for example, was born "three weeks late."

—The doctor himself had said to expect the baby to be two weeks late. Was two weeks late "late"? Or normal?

—The sonargram showed that the baby really wasn't due until a week later than we had thought.

—Why wasn't the doctor measuring the baby? Or trying to determine in some other way whether he was "ready" to be born?

—Finally, the doctor had prescribed phenobarbital during

my pregnancy for fear of flying—the airplane kind. I had since read that this was dangerous for nursing mothers. Had my doctor ever asked me if I was nursing? No. Indeed, he had never asked me or warned me about medications of any kind.

That night I went home in a cold sweat. I dreamt that I showed up at the hospital to have the baby, and that my doctor couldn't remember who I was or what I was there for.

By a week before D-day, I had determined that my doctor visits were dangerous to my health. I could feel my blood pressure rising even before I got out of the car. When it was over, I was done for the day. This time:

—We had determined that the bleeding was probably due to varicosities of the vulva, and nothing internal. The doctor had asked if I thought the bleeding was related to intercourse, and I said no. This visit, he said, "Oh, you're the one who thought the bleeding was related to intercourse." Next time I'll bring along the minutes of our previous conversation.

—While I lay spread-eagled in the examining room, I could hear the doctor make two personal phone calls, both about a dinner engagement that night.

—This was the second time I had brought my husband in to meet the doctor, and he said, "Nice to meet you." The first time never registered.

—The doctor insisted that breastfeeding on the delivery table was forbidden by the hospital—even though three hospital nurses had insisted to the contrary. Even Fritzie said it was allowed, though "uncomfortable."

—He interrupted our conversation to talk to his insurance agent. When he put the phone down, he told us his unhappy tale: One of his patients was suing him. He had discharged her after she complained of high back pain. It turned out to be a pulmonary embolism. (Blood clot in the lung.) No doctor ever examined her, but a hospital resident had (sight unseen) prescribed Valium. "I don't know what the hell she's complaining about. I didn't even see her until two days later. Now you see what we poor doctors have to put up with."

To make the rest of my long story short, some highlights from my final visits:

—I found a moldy urine sample in the ladies' room. The nurse said, "I have no idea who that belongs to."

—The doctor was out delivering a baby, and the nurse said he'd be back in less than an hour. An hour seemed awfully short. He had promised *me* to attend during at least the last few hours of labor. The nurse, mistaking my puzzled look, explained: "Oh, it doesn't take that long to deliver the baby. But it does take him about a half an hour to sew up the episiotomy."

—During an internal exam, the nurse said, "You forgot..." He said, "Oooops, yeah, I forgot..." Nurse: "You always forget that." What did he forget?

—The doctor was due to go on vacation that Friday. That Tuesday he made the decision to induce. "Okay, Debbie," he shouted to his secretary. "Set up another induction for Wednesday."

My other uncomfortable encounters with the best modern medicine has to offer are related elsewhere in this book. Indeed, things went from uncomfortable to catastrophic when he waved good-bye in the recovery room—leaving both doctors #2 and #3 under the impression that the *other* was responsible for my postpartum care.

But that's beside the point.

The point is that I and many other mothers approached labor with a complete lack of confidence in our medical care. I'm not at all sure that encounters with obstetricians are always healthy for pregnant women. And I'm not at all sure that it's the obstetricians' fault. I think our hopes get shattered because they are often too high in the first place. Whoever said your doctor needed to know the intimate details of your baby's heartbeat or of your day-to-day life? Whoever said he had to join your husband's bowling league to prove he cared? For that matter, whoever said he had to know your name? (Lamaze classes and baby books—that's who.)

Perhaps in the end it was my fault that I went into labor shaky instead of strong. Perhaps I expected too much—or the wrong things—from my obstetrician. But whatever the cause, the result was a loss of faith I could ill afford. The best prescription for a good labor is confidence. All I had was false hope.

GREAT EXPECTATIONS

Somebody once devised a formula for calculating fulfillment on vacation. "Satisfaction equals Reality divided by Expectations." If Expectations are high and Reality low, then Satisfaction will be very small. If the forecast is rain, however, and you're surprised by sunshine all week, you're going to be satisfied no matter what else happens.

The same goes for obstetricians. How happy you are depends on what you get divided by what you expected.

Unfortunately, we've all been brought up on soap-opera stereotypes that make the best real doctors look bad by comparison. And it isn't only the patients who are misled. Marcus Welby's patients don't demand to have their husbands in the operating room. They don't ask endless questions about anesthesia or read up on their operations in books. If your obstetrician expects you to know nothing, you might be insulted. But if he assumes you know everything, you won't get all the information you need. One doctor writes in a pregnancy manual that obstetricians "don't expect to be called for every trivial complaint." The question is, what's trivial? And how's a mother to know?

Expectations are easily satisfied when they're relatively simple:

"My doctor assumed that either I was too dumb to know anything or that I had read up and knew everything. It didn't bother me though, because I knew when I went to him that that was his attitude. I went to him because he is a fabulous surgeon. That's what I expected, and that's what I got."

Most mothers expect more. Especially if they consider childbirth to be more than a medical matter. And a doctor-patient relationship to mean more than paying a bill.

"When you get through going through seven months of examinations, and you share that special moment with him, I mean you just want to hug him. It would be nice to have a relationship with your doctor on a different level. I always wished that the doctor could share in this sort of spiritual celebration of birth. Wow, this is wonderful. You know, when my husband and I yelled and screamed, I wanted him to scream, too."

Some Lamaze mothers say they don't need this sort of emotional reinforcement from their doctors. That they get enough of it from their husbands. With husband as companion and coach, the obstetrician can concentrate on the emergencies and complications he or she was trained for.

Indeed, it's often when the obstetrician is asked to practice *more* than medicine that the mother is disappointed. The patient-doctor relationship often smacks of unrequited love. The patient falls in love, but the doctor doesn't. To the patient, the intimacy of sharing a pregnancy is special. To the doctor, it's routine. Still, many pregnant women "fall in love" with their obstetricians. Husband or not, that second level of involvement seems to be significant. And at least one mother who missed it with her obstetrician transferred her feelings to her pediatrician: "He's the one who gave me my baby, the same way the obstetrician did the first time around."

Of course, the obstetrician doesn't make the baby—although you'd sometimes think that was the case, from listening to mothers and doctors alike. You and your husband are the parents; you deliver the goods. You shouldn't ever sell your role in childbirth short. Especially not when it means you expect almost everything of your doctor, and nothing of yourself. It's hard *not* to defer to your doctor, God knows, when he's wearing the white coat and you're naked on the table—when you call him "Doctor" and he calls you "Dearie." But it's distressing when women become so intimidated by their obstetricians that they don't call them even when there's an emergency. Even when that "emergency" is labor:

"I felt guilty about wasting his time, about calling him. That's why I had only forty-five minutes to spare when I got to the hospital. It was very hard for me to get over this godlike image. I was embarrassed about having to wake him at that hour of the morning. Which is totally ridiculous, because he was getting paid a hell of a lot of money for that."

Money plays a part in expectations, too. It's foolish to think that you're going to get more out of your obstetrician just because you've paid more for him. As my own experience proved, it is sometimes precisely the most highly paid and highly praised doctors whose practices are overloaded. Yet, when you've shelled out $1,000 for obstetrical care, you expect $1,000 worth of service. Contrast this with the clinic patient who pays almost nothing and may with luck run into "the most wonderful resident in the world." S equals R/E.

What mothers expect of obstetricians also has changed with time. As women have gained more self-confidence and more self-knowledge, they're asking more questions and demanding more answers. Now that childbirth is more a matter of choice, mothers and doctors are looking at each other in new ways.

"When I had my first baby, I trusted my doctor so much that I didn't want to think that anything could possibly go wrong. You just tend to put yourself in their hands and go through the mechanics. But I must say if I had a baby tomorrow, I would question everything. I think I was basically very naïve."

Most obstetricians don't know yet what to make of today's mothers. Indeed, most obstetricians know precious little about Lamaze, Leboyer, or other modern birthing methods (except the technical ones). Expecting them to is bound to lead to disappointment. What you should expect from your obstetrician is good medical care. Period. Everything else is gravy. You just might be lucky enough to get a doctor who is husband/companion/labor nurse/coach. But you might not. It's better to be pleasantly surprised than bitterly disappointed.

THE PERSONALITY FACTOR

Obviously, the type of obstetrician you prefer will depend on your personality. And his. It will depend on whether you are twenty or forty-two. On whether your husband is planning to be your partner. On whether you're the type who likes to take control or leave everything to the experts.

Just because a doctor's personality fills you with confidence doesn't mean he's medically competent. Or vice versa. You may have to choose which is more important to you: His bedside manner or his surgical skills. Many times, mothers put up with all manner of personality flaws because they believe in their doctor's ability to intervene in an emergency. (After all, that's what he's there for.)

The most skilled surgeon may be something of a "cold fish," though. To this kind of doctor, babies mean business. He'll handle your strictly medical needs, but anything in the psychological support department is up to you. And your husband:

"You think you're special. But they don't. They just didn't seem very friendly, or as concerned about my baby as I was. You come in, they check you, close the door, in comes the other girl, they check her. You're nothing. You're just another body. But I knew that the doctors were very competent, and that they would be marvelous if you ever had a problem. So when I went to them I sort of expected that. I would have liked a little more sympathy and support, but it was not essential because my husband was there. And I think in the long run I would go back to them. Because of their reputation."

Cold fish are innocuous enough if you know what you're getting into. "Father figures" are popular among women who feel they need strong men to boss them around. But few women like to be abused:

"I had a father figure. I wouldn't stand for it today. He called me 'Marilyn' and I called him 'Doctor somebody.' He was a real egomaniac. Forceful and strong and pushy and continually laughing and sneering. I would ask about certain things. Like, I would feel a sort of lump, and I'd say, 'Is that the head?' And he'd say, 'The head? What is the matter with you?' He always made me feel like such a blithering idiot about my own body. I hated it. But I didn't know I hated it. He seemed so strong. He told me everything to do. And I thought that was what I needed."

Of course, medicine is supposed to have a human side. Your body is more than a clockwork orange. Bedside manner is more than a psychological crutch. It can have real medical consequences. That's why it's so nice when a doctor offers more than the minimum. When he's your friend as well as your physician. Most obstetricians harbor some sentiment toward delivering babies—and almost all have a human side. In some doctors, it's well hidden. In others, it's big enough to embrace the whole world:

"When I found out I was pregnant, my doctor was so thrilled that he came in and gave me a big hug and a kiss. And after the baby was born, he took out his Polaroid camera and took a picture of my husband and me and the baby. And I asked him to take another picture with the intern who helped out. The intern looked so panicked, and he still does in the picture. That was really so special. I even wrote a nice letter to the hospital about the whole experience."

"My obstetrician was married to a pediatrician, and between them they had ten children. So when I got pregnant with my third baby, I was worried because the children would only be about eighteen months apart. So I called the doctor and told him I thought I was pregnant. And he said, 'Wonderful, wonderful!' And I said, 'But they're so close together!' And he said, 'Oh, my goodness. Eighteen months is the biggest space we have between any of our children.' But the most important thing was the warmth in his voice when he said he was so thrilled for us. I believed him."

Mothers often love their obstetricians with good reason. One doctor held onto his patient for a whole hour while the anesthesiologist tried to thread the catheter for the epidural. Another nursed a slightly soused husband through labor one New Year's Eve. And even the doctor I deserted because he told me to gain only fifteen pounds has the loveliest way of singing "Happy Birthday" to all the new babies as soon as they're born. Many mothers love their doctors simply because they never seem too busy to be bothered.

"He was always available. I mean, I'd get all these funny pains and I'd be in the middle of nowhere—I'd be in an outboard motorboat in the middle of Buzzard's Bay—and I'd pull into a place and say I'm dying and leave a message with the answering service. And he'd call back in two minutes."

Your own obstetrician is likely to have some personality traits that you like and others that you don't. Before you get too deeply involved with him or her, make sure that your personalities mesh—at least minimally. If you're an accepting sort of person, perhaps you can put up with almost anything so long as the medical care is good. But if you need to think your doctor loves you, you'd better look around for a loving type. You don't want to have your heart broken just because your expectations were based on fairy tales.

THE INSENSITIVE OBSTETRICIAN

More than any other class of doctors, obstetricians are open to the charge of being insensitive. This is not surprising. They are a largely male practice catering to a completely female clientele. Being sensitive means being attuned to somebody else's needs. Most obstetricians aren't even in the right sex, much less the right ball park. Often, they don't know what offends women. Sometimes, they don't care. Not because they are necessarily "mean," but because it's not medically "significant"

Women's liberation has muddied the waters even more. What was expected yesterday is not even accepted today. Today's indignity was yesterday's everyday occurrence. Who cared even five years ago that he was "Doctor" and you were "Dear"? But today the patient is as likely as not to be a forty-year-old professional herself. And if she's a housewife, she's more likely to look on herself as a grown woman rather than a little girl. It's silly—not to mention insulting—if she has to call him "Dr. Smith" and he gets to call her "Sally." In general, the older mothers get, the less they like to be treated like children. The more they know about childbirth, the less they allow doctors to condescend.

And so, whether or not insensitivity among obstetricians is gaining, it's certainly more apparent. And a lot of it seems to have to do with sex. I remember being shocked when my obstetrician, after my six weeks' postpartum checkup, nudged me in the ribs and suggested that a "little lovin'" would fix me right up. Maybe that was his way of being nice—or of looking out for what he thought were my husband's interests. But frankly I felt it was overstepping the bounds of an intimacy we never established.

"He always called me 'Honey.' And then one time the embryonic fluid leaked after we had intercourse. And I called the doctor because I was worried that something was wrong. And he went into this whole number about 'acrobatics on the bed.' He said, 'You don't go in for any of this perverted stuff, do you?' And it cut off the conversation right there. And yet I worried about it for the rest of the pregnancy."

Obstetricians are often insensitive to a mother's feelings about childbirth itself. And again, this isn't really surprising. Until recently, women weren't expressing their feelings about birth. They weren't even around for it. (Consciously, that is.) The mother was put out, the doctor delivered, and that was that. Birth was an ugly, painful process and everybody was glad when it was over.

Now, many women look forward to birth as a creative and rewarding experience. What they used to want to be knocked out for is now something they don't want to miss. It's no wonder that some doctors are still wondering what hit them. But it's still no excuse. When giving birth is something you hold sacred, a doctor who talks about it in callous terms can hurt:

"I had my first baby by Lamaze, so I assumed I would have the second the same way. But the doctor took one look at me and said, 'You couldn't give birth to a squirrel.' And he did a cesarean." Perhaps the mother did have an unusually small pelvis. But the first time around, she did give birth to a *baby*.

Speaking of sensitivity, one of the first things you learn in Lamaze is that the peak of your contraction is the most painful time for an internal examination. Surely obstetricians must know this. And yet they often don't pay attention:

"He didn't come until the very end. And when he did it was like God had walked though the door. He did not say anything, he did not ask me anything. He started to examine me and I said, 'No, please wait. I'm in a contraction. I'm trying to do my breathing.' But he did it anyway, and I thought I'd go through the sky, he was so damn rough. It hurt like hell. I figured he had taken his time to get there, he could have waited another thirty seconds."

This is not a time for begging favors. it's a time for demanding rights. Husbands, by the way, come in very handy when it comes to holding off hurried obstetricians.

A doctor who doesn't value birth as an experience isn't going to encourage you to stay awake for it. And if he's not used to watching a mother labor without drugs, he may misinterpret your efforts as pure agony. That's one reason that doctors often arbitrarily announce that a mother has "suffered enough" and put her out. Such a doctor isn't necessarily being malicious. He's just doing what he knows best, what he's used to. But that's all the more reason to have your own advocate in the labor room to argue your case.

If your obstetrician seems always insensitive to your needs, he may not know what your needs are. Try to explain them as thoroughly and explicitly as you can. If something he says offends you, tell him. (Nicely.) Don't be surprised if he seems angry or bewildered. Obstetricians have been placed on a pedestal by women for a long time. If they think they're gods, it's at least in part because that's how we've treated them. So give him credit for trying. Coming down off a pedestal isn't easy for anyone. If he insists on being insensitive, however, you either have to learn to live with it now—or start shopping around for another doctor.

PLEASE, DOCTOR: LAMAZE

Dr. Lamaze was an obstetrician himself, but many of today's obstetricians still look on the Lamaze method with disdain. At best, they think Lamaze is silly. At worst, a waste of time. One popular pregnancy manual says the effects of Lamaze are mostly psychological: "The ritualistic performance of these exercises amounts to a form of self-hypnosis." (The implication is that you're only fooling yourself.) Another book gives the impression that the aim of Lamaze is to make you a model patient: "Prepared childbirth classes . . . are good for any pregnant girl. She is taught what to expect during labor, how to relax, how to cooperate with her obstetrician." Lamaze does do that, of course. But that's hardly the point. The purpose of the exercise is to train you physically and mentally to go through labor yourself. Many doctors seem to think it's an exercise in self-deception. Or even masochism.

"My doctor's attitude was more or less, 'Well, we'll start out and you'll try your Lamaze, and then when you start to scream, we'll knock you out.' Even when I first mentioned to him that I wanted my husband there, he said, 'Why do you want him there to see all the blood and feces?' And my insides just shriveled up. I cried. So finally he relented. But I had that pressure on me the whole time. And then he'd come in during labor and say, 'Oh, are you still huffing and puffing?' I could feel him, just figuratively tapping his foot and waiting for me to say, 'Yes, I'll have an injection.' So I did. And I went out. And the baby was born ten minutes later."

Why are obstetricians so often reluctant to try Lamaze? Cynics would say that it's because they are trying to protect their practices. And that when women discover they can deliver babies by themselves, they'll stop going to doctors. I'm sure this is occasionally the case. But more often obstetricians, like the rest of us, are simply suspicious of what they don't understand. They can't be advocates of something when they're not sure that it works. Or how it works. It's totally outside their medical training.

Indeed, one of the biggest mistakes mothers make in preparing for childbirth is counting on their doctors to get them through a Lamaze labor. Few obstetricians are even familiar with Lamaze techniques. Even those who favor natural childbirth and disdain drugs leave most of the laboring to you. Lamaze is something that happens between you and your husband and your labor nurse. Your doctor's part comes later. And until delivery, chances are he won't even be involved.

Some mothers say that getting doctors involved is the surest way to change their minds. And that once they really participate in a Lamaze birth, they can't help but become true believers:

"The nurses and mothers had been fighting to allow Lamaze

in that hospital for years, but the head doctor just wouldn't go along with it. Then one day he was in the room when a Lamaze mother delivered a breech baby without so much as an aspirin. He could not believe the cooperation that took place. And he said, 'Okay. I'm convinced.' And that's what changed the policy at that hospital."

WHAT YOU GET

Certain services you expect from an obstetrician. Others you get. These may or may not be the same, and to the extent that they aren't, you will be disappointed. Therefore it's nice to know what mothers say you can realistically expect from your doctor. Of course, obstetricians vary. So do mothers. So do pregnancies, hospitals, fathers, the coming of the full moon, and other factors affecting childbirth. But in general, the mothers I interviewed agreed on the following guidelines:

Don't expect your obstetrician to know the details of Lamaze techniques; don't expect him or her to be particularly enthusiastic about them, either.

Don't expect your obstetrician to tell you everything you need to know about diet, drugs, and health. You have to use your head, too. And read up.

Don't expect your obstetrician to care about your pregnancy as much as you do. Or about you, for that matter.

Don't expect your obstetrician to let you listen to the baby's heartbeat every time you come into his office. Certainly don't expect him or her to offer. Don't expect him to be overjoyed when you plug in the tape recorder. (I know, they do this in Lamaze movies all the time, but it's rare in real life.)

Don't expect your doctor to remember everything about you every time you come in. If you have a continuing problem, remind him. By all means, make a list of questions that concern you. Don't be afraid to pull them out of your purse. Don't leave until he's answered every question.

Don't be surprised if your doctor groans when you pull out your list.

Do expect your doctor to be available for phone calls at any time of day or night. Do call him or her about anything that really worries you.

Don't expect him to manage your labor. In most hospitals,

labor is left to husbands, labor nurses, and occasional visits from the house staff. You can expect your obstetrician to pop in and out. But you can't expect him to mop your brow for ten hours. *Do* expect him to be there for the delivery.

Don't rely on your obstetrician to be a "source of confidence and trust as well as information and guidance," as one author put it. He may be, but don't count on it. "I would have preferred not to have doctors around during both deliveries," said one mother, not atypically. "I was well prepared because I myself took the initiative," said another. "I have no patience with women who rely totally on doctors and then wonder what went wrong."

Expect to pay a lot for a private obstetrician. Estimates are impossible because of regional differences. But a doctor with a private practice on Park Avenue in New York can cost as much as $1,000 for an uncomplicated delivery. That's not including the hospital. So poke around before you plop down your money and try to determine whether it's money well spent. If you are going to pay the price of private practice, try to find a doctor who gives truly personal service.

Expect your doctor to pull you through in an emergency. That's what doctors are trained to do. (Indeed, that's often what they *like* to do.) Expect him or her to be competent in assessing your medical state and in prescribing medical care. If he's not so competent when it comes to Lamaze breathing or tact, turn to your husband or labor nurse. Fortunately, doctors tend to excel when you need them most and fall short in areas where others can take over. And that's better than the other way around.

THE GROUP

Expect your doctor to practice in a group. (My new obstetrician doesn't, which I write as a warning against generalizations. But he's rare.)

Group practice makes sense from the doctor's point of view. He can keep regular hours—"shifts" if you will—trading off with others in the practice so that everybody's off every other weekend, or whatever. Baby books say that "the abilities of each doctor are invariably similar to those of his partners." But mothers know better. In fact, most mothers come to adore one of their doctors and avoid the others like German measles.

"The practice had one doctor I liked, one I was in fear of because he was so incompetent, and two new guys who were unknowns. So that was three out of four that I didn't want near me. When I went into labor, it was in the morning, and I went to the hospital for a checkup. And it was the doctor who I knew was incompetent. So I said, 'Well, how long are you going to be here?' And he said, 'I'll be here until seven o'clock, when Dr. Smith takes over.' Well, Dr. Smith was the one I liked. So I went home and the contractions came on and off until seven o'clock. Then, boom, I was in labor again. And I know that I suppressed that labor for the whole day just to avoid that doctor."

Doctors *are* different. And often mothers dread that a particular one will be on duty the day they deliver. But there's usually nothing they can do about it. "Love me, love my partner" is the normal group-practice policy. The doctor on call is the doctor who delivers your baby. You can't request your favorite. (For obvious reasons, I think.) But there's always the chance that you may be pleasantly surprised:

"It really bothered me at first. I really liked this one doctor, and he said I would have to rotate through his two partners. And I said that I didn't want a strange man delivering. And he said they wouldn't be strange, that I'd have a chance to meet them. And that anyway I didn't have a choice. It really bothered me that every time you go in, it's a different guy. My initial reaction was that they should distribute pictures so if you delivered early, everybody would know who everybody was. But then it turned out that one of the other doctors did deliver. And I loved him. He was wonderful. And I've been going to him ever since."

I suppose there's something to be said for group practice in that you're less likely to fall in love with five doctors. And you're certainly less likely to get false impressions of what to expect. After all, how much "personal" attention can you expect from a group? In that sense, group practice puts a pregnant woman in her place. As a patient. And it puts the doctor in his place, too. As a medical mechanic. Of course, a doctor on a "shift" doesn't normally make for a particularly personal childbirth experience. But it's an important reminder that the quality of your childbirth experience shouldn't depend on your doctor, anyway.

THE DOCTOR'S ADVICE

"Doctors were no help at all," said one (but by no means the only one) of the mothers I interviewed. "I even had to ask him whether I could take antihistamines for allergy. He should have warned me that common medications might be harmful. But the only thing that interested him was my weight. It was the only subject he ever brought up."

Clearly, pregnancy is a time when you need sound advice on scores of matters. Yet doctors' advice seems distressingly arbitrary or absent. Thumbing through some popular pregnancy manuals and comparing notes from women, I get the uncomfortable impression that there's no real consensus on anything. One doctor says drink milk, the other says don't. Sometimes a single doctor will warn against aspirin one day (or on one page), only to prescribe it the next. After my cesarean, I had one doctor urging me to get up and walk around, another chastising me for being out of bed. One mother with painful hemorrhoids got advice that went to extremes: she was on ice packs one day, in hot tubs the next, depending on which doctor was on duty.

Here's a sampling of doctors' advice from three popular pregnancy books:

"If you are concerned about the color of the little things you are knitting, use green or yellow yarn."

"Avoid contagious disease."

"A daily bath is a good idea."

"Eat three meals a day."

"Continue your outside interests."

"Don't forget the care of your teeth."

"Throughout the day I hear...excuses given by mothers as they try to slither out of their weight problems. Instead of excuses,...you can try tidbits or tears. A moist eye is hard to level with—and so is a moist homebaked brownie."

One kind of advice doctors are good at giving is the kind that says "Don't worry." Which is all some women ever hear. Of course, I couldn't condone a doctor who *did* encourage worrying, but that and a pat on the head won't get you through pregnancy. Besides, you worry anyway. Telling you to not can only make it worse. When the doctor warns you not to worry, you may think he's only hiding something. And so you'll only worry more.

It's too much to expect every obstetrician to repeat every piece of advice for every pregnant patient. But they certainly can be expected to distribute lists or pamphlets detailing common things to avoid and remedies for common problems and symptoms. I suppose that's why so many obstetricians seem to write books. But if they rely on written materials for advice, then at least they should make them required reading.

Ideally, midwives or nurse practitioners (nurses-plus) could manage the uncomplicated pregnancies and labors while doctors could stand by for emergencies. That way, pregnant women wouldn't have to worry that they were using up a precious extra minute of the obstetrician's time. They could linger for a while to talk over their concerns with someone with a sympathetic ear—not to mention someone of a sympathetic sex. The practice of using nurse practitioners is spreading rapidly in pediatrics. Perhaps someday it will spread to obstetrics as well.

Meanwhile, it's important for you to get as much advice as possible from as many sources as possible—not only from your doctor. Then you can sort out what you've learned using your own common sense. Don't do anything that sounds silly or dangerous—even if it does come from a man wearing a white coat. Maybe he's only the good humor man.

TALKING TO YOUR DOCTOR

Talking to doctors can be frustrating—especially when they don't talk back.

"You really have to press for every item of information. I always wished that my doctor would tell me things instead of me always having to ask. But they tend not to treat you like intelligent human beings. They treat you like children. I had to do all my own reading, and I always brought in a list of questions. But his answers were very vague and full of jargon. I would trace a question so far, and when I left, I knew that I didn't have the whole answer. So finally I said, 'The hell with it.' It just wasn't worth talking to him."

Silence is especially sinister when you have reason to believe that something is wrong. And especially infuriating when you're in labor and eager for every ounce of available information:

"I was perfectly conscious throughout labor, but they treated me like I was doped up and couldn't understand. He kept saying, 'It's anterior, it's posterior, it's interior.' And I kept saying, 'What does that mean? What are you talking about?' And he would say nothing to me."

Doctor-patient communication is always nice. During childbirth, it's essential. You have to know where you are and where you're going or you won't be able to get there. Only your doctor can tell you if you're anemic or if you baby is posterior or if you're dilated two centimeters or six. Only your doctor can tell you his preferences for anesthesia or induced labor or his criteria for cesareans. Thus, you have to be able to talk to him even if he doesn't want to talk to you. Different mothers resort to different methods to get through to their doctors. Some obstetricians require that you use every method in the book.

Above all, to get the right answers, you have to know the right questions. Read up before you even enter his office. That way he won't be able to put you off with six-syllable words. And that way you'll know the proper follow-up questions to ask so you won't be left with half an answer. If he's inconsistent or confusing, keep asking until you pin him down. The information is too important to let your own insecurities get in the way.

You can also try infecting your doctor with some of your own enthusiasm. Just because obstetricians have been around childbirth all of their careers doesn't necessarily mean they're immune to it. Perhaps you can restore some of his lost wonder of the birth process itself.

"I found it helpful to keep saying to the doctors, 'Don't you just love doing this? Isn't this exciting?' And that attitude would carry over into the delivery room. I think they caught some of my own good feelings."

The best doctors do supply their own dose of enthusiasm. But not every obstetrician is a great conversationalist. He may simply be shy or reticent or reluctant to give you a lot of information "you won't understand." So make sure he knows that you *do* understand. And that you are interested in details. And that you want to learn—not teach *him* a lesson. When possible, cooperation is always the best policy. And often it comes remarkably easily:

"He'd just say, 'Get dressed and come in and let's talk for a while.' He always invited me to stay as long as I liked and ask as many questions as I liked. It made it so easy for me. And I never realized how unusual he was until I heard other women's experiences."

If you find a doctor like this, hold on to him. Until birth do you part.

SHOPPING AROUND

"There is nothing to be gained, and both time and money to be lost, by shopping for a doctor," writes one obstetrician. I couldn't disagree more. Obviously, it's a lot harder to muster the courage to change doctors when you're sixteen than when you're thirty-six. Harder when you're six months pregnant than when you're three. But if something really gets you the wrong way about the situation, you should get yourself out of it before it's too late. Not "too late" in the sense that something horrible is going to happen to you. It probably won't. But you might miss out on the wonderful thing that *can* happen when your doctor is more wonderful himself.

One warning: Look carefully at the reasons you want to leave your doctor before you start looking for another. You may find yourself in a worse situation the second time around. Be realistic. A good obstetrician doesn't have to live up to the soap-opera stereotypes. And if he doesn't exactly inspire complete confidence, remember that for the most part you're going to have to rely on yourself anyway. Only when the differences are truly irreconcilable should you consider going through with the separation. Then do what has to be done quickly. And without guilt. The worst thing you can do—for both of you—is to waver.

MOTHER KNOWS BEST

Obstetricians invariably tell you not to listen to your mother's advice in preference to theirs. But your mother is, after all, a mother. And so are you—or about to be. There are many things that only a mother can know about having a baby. It's always infuriating when someone thinks they know you better than you know yourself. It can also be dangerous:

"My first baby suddenly stopped kicking at about five months, and I told my doctor I had not felt life for several weeks, to please tell me if anything was the matter. And he said nothing was the matter. He didn't even use a fetuscope to listen. I hadn't gained weight in four weeks, and I hadn't felt any life. I knew that the baby was dead. I told him that. But it took me four weeks even to get him to take an X ray. And the baby had died."

"My doctor insisted I take phenobarbital throughout my pregnancy because he said I had high blood pressure. But the only time I had high blood pressure was when I was in his office. I was still teaching at the time, and every day I'd have my blood pressure taken by the school nurse. And it was fine. But every time I was in the doctor's office, he'd say it was elevated. And he never told me how elevated. I told him to call the nurse and check, if he wanted to. But he wouldn't believe me."

If your doctor doesn't listen to you, you're just going to have to talk louder. If he still doesn't pay attention, and you think what you have to say is important, start shouting. Don't let him intimidate you into doubting what you know for certain. Doctors may be authorities when it comes to pregnancy per se, but nobody knows your own pregnancy like you do. So if he says, "It's nothing," but you think, "It's something," don't give up until you get through. Even if you have to use Western Union.

I'll never forget the frustration of lying in the hospital with a fever and being offered an enema by the nurse. And of being told by the resident that I was hot because there was a heat wave outside. I thought my husband and I raised a pretty big ruckus at the time, but if I had it to do over again I'd raise an even bigger one. There's nothing illegal about insisting that somebody take your temperature or check a fetal heart. It reminds me of all the mothers who know they're about to give birth, only to be told "You're not ready yet"—as the baby spurts forth from between their legs.

In sum, obstetricians can be sources of great comfort, or of great distress. Some mothers remember their doctors as the nicest part of having a baby. Some as the worst. But whatever your doctor does, it's up to you to ensure the safest, happiest, healthiest passage to life for your unborn child. The responsibility is really yours. So even if you have the most wonderful obstetrician in the world, don't expect him to do everything. It's your baby.

Coming Home:

You're Really a Mother Now

You can tell a new mother a mile away. She's the one with the hair that hasn't been washed for a week and the eyes that haven't closed for a month; the one with the permanent white spot on her shoulder, the brown one in her lap. She wears a Mona Lisa smile that says she's floating in a special space, thinking secret things. She wheels that carriage as if its cargo were eight pounds, twelve ounces of eggshells—all solid gold. If you nod at her, she'll answer with a look that says, "Isn't this heaven?" And at the same time: "How am I ever going to live through this hell?"

The baby's all yours now. You've finally got an infant to go along wth the infant seat and the crib with the mobile and the Pampers and stuffed toys. The picture's complete. Except it isn't quite like the one you've been watching on TV. Your baby isn't cooing, she's crying you don't look so great yourself. In fact, you're a wreck.

"I spent the first four months without ever putting any clothes on. The baby just nursed all the time. So I'd go to sleep without brushing my teeth, just living in such a weird sort of state. That's one reason I can't imagine having anybody else around. The thought of having to put on a bathrobe to go from one room to the next would have been an overwhelming burden."

I've heard it said that women with new babies sometimes "let themselves go." This is like saying that an airplane that's lost all four engines "lets itself" fall to the ground. Neither has much choice. When your goal is simply to get through the day, everything that isn't essential is eliminated. Sometimes even that.

Having the baby all to yourself has its highs, too. You can admire her in private and show her off in public. You can snuggle up to her softness whenever you please and look on proudly as you pass her around for others to hold. But don't think that's all there is to coming home with a baby:

"I wanted everything to be baby blue and nice, and it wasn't. He was crying all night, and I couldn't get it together. I'd sit and hold the crying baby and cry myself because he wouldn't stop crying. And then my husband would get irritated because I wasn't an expert, and say things like, 'You're the baby yourself.' I felt awful. I felt inadequate. Not only does your physical appearance deteriorate, your self-confidence goes with it. Your self-image is so low because you can't accomplish the job that all the baby books say you should be doing. And you're the only one who's not doing it well."

Of course, you're not the only one, but that's something only another mother can tell you. Indeed, other mothers probably already have, but you were probably so puffed up on pregnancy that you didn't listen. Still, there's no reason to think you're all alone just because that lovely little baby is making you into a monster. Welcome to the club.

"THE WHOLE WORLD WOULD BE ALL RIGHT IF I COULD JUST GET ONE NIGHT'S SLEEP"

Bringing home a new baby is like being on a treadmill. It's a marathon race against the strength of your own resources. Like the old-time obstetrician, you're constantly on call. If there isn't a diaper to change, there's a bottle to warm or a baby to comfort. Twenty-four hours a day. If you sleep, it's on the baby's schedule, not yours. If you can't adjust, you don't sleep at all. Sometimes you don't sleep at all anyway.

"In the beginning, Cassie never slept more than six hours in any twenty-four-hour period and that would be in ten- to fifteen-minute stretches, with her getting up fully in between. So for the first four months it was sort of an interesting period if you look at it clinically. You can see what happens when you are exhausted for such a long period. First you get the fatigue and the mouth poisoning and the numbness. And then it progressed through all these different stages. Eventually I started to hallucinate. It was terrifying."

I interviewed another mother whose two-year-old son was still waking up three times a night. Horror stories abound.

So do tales of babies (and mothers) who seem to have no trouble sleeping through the night from the moment they hit home. I remember feeling falsely superior to a mother I met who claimed her baby slept through from the start, because I assumed he was bottle feeding. (Everyone knows that breastfed babies don't sleep through the night for months.) But no, she was nursing, too.

In a way, it's lucky for all of us that we can't predict which babies will sleep through at two weeks and which will be keeping us up at two years. What keeps you going is the hope that yours will be one of the "good" ones. To boost your chances, you can play him Bach while he's in your belly and otherwise try to promote good vibes. But in the end you have to prepare for anything. The problem is, *how* to prepare? Nobody gives Lamaze classes in coping with the "night shift."

"All my kids were born in October, so the first three months it was freezing cold, and you're sitting there watching 'The Cisco Kid' at four o'clock in the morning trying to get a burp out of this kid. And it's dark and cold, and you look out the window, and there are no lights on. Everyone else is asleep. So you have to cope. There is no one else to turn to. Like, who are you going to call at four o'clock in the morning?"

I was prepared to get up every few hours to nurse. But I was also prepared to get down again quickly. What I had expected was that Peter would cry, and I would nurse him, and then we'd both go back to sleep. But that isn't what I got.

Once he was up, Peter wanted to play. And for some reason, it took me totally by surprise that he couldn't understand that his hours were inappropriate. Didn't he know that daytime was playtime? That nights were for sleeping? Waking Mommie up because you're hungry is one thing. Waking her up just to fool around isn't in the books. But it is related to something else that isn't in the books: Breastfed babies especially often have loose, messy bowel movements while (or shortly after) they nurse. By the time you change the diaper, change the crib, and wash off the walls, you're almost guaranteed to have a wide-awake baby. Not to mention a wide-awake mother.

Sometimes I wonder why lack of sleep seems to be such a problem. It wasn't in school, when we stayed up all one night to study for exams—then stayed up the next night to celebrate when they were over. Of course, that was by choice. And when it was over, we could hit the sack whenever and for as long as we wanted. But what about women who have their babies one day and are back working in the fields (or in the courtroom) the next? What's their secret source of stamina? Perhaps necessity is the mother of that, too.

You can try to catch up on your sleep *before* the baby comes home by letting the nurses take care of the night feedings in the hospital. But don't be misled: even if you do nurse your baby at night from the start, the nurses bring her to you only in four-hour shifts. That doesn't mean that's the schedule you'll be on at home:

"It was a great shock. I thought in the hospital that Noah was a gret sleeper, because I only got him at ten, two, and six. And then I got home and this little brat was up every two hours, and he was hungry, and I thought, 'Gee, that's unusual.' I mean nobody told me they always do that."

Most babies finally do sleep through the night after several weeks—or at least after several months. Indeed, many mothers are convinced that babies somehow sense when you just can't take it one more night. Or perhaps that's just wishful thinking.

Unfortunately, exhaustion doesn't end even when night feedings do. It just changes shape:

"Yesterday I really felt miserable, and I sat down and computed how many pounds I push when I pedal a bicycle with my ten-month-old son, and I figured out it was about 190 pounds. I thought, no wonder I get tired. My house is never in order. Sometimes I think I should have done this ten years ago. But I imagine no matter what your age, it's overwhelming."

I remember wondering, when Peter was a mere but barely

manageable ten pounds, how mothers of toddlers lugged around thirty-pounders all day with such seeming ease. Now, of course, I know. But strangely, carrying Peter doesn't seem such a heavy burden anymore, even though he is almost forty pounds. Perhaps I've grown stronger. Or more confident. Or just accustomed to his weight. In many ways, we've grown stronger together. And sleeping through the night hasn't hurt, either. But in the end, being tired is a part of motherhood that almost everybody has to live through. The good news is, everybody does.

TWO'S COMPANY

Company can be the best part of coming home. Everybody ooohs and aaahs over the baby, while you oooh and aaah over the gifts and cards and flowers. The excitement alone is enough to keep you going for a while. Or at least keep you awake. There's certainly nothing boring or humdrum about it.

But beware: this sort of medicine is helpful in small doses only.

"I thought it would be great having help around. I thought my mother could take care of the baby while I slept during the day, but of course I never slept because people kept coming over to see the baby, and anyway I don't get to see my mother that often. So when I do, I like to sit down and chat and have a cup of coffee. Then, meanwhile, I had my mother-in-law, my sister, my other sister, my brother-in-law, and my two sisters-in-law. They try to be helpful, but you have to make lunch for all these people, make them this and that. You want your house to look nice, so you vacuum, and then you try to look nice yourself. Then you have to change the baby, get the bottles. And they say, 'Here, let me show you how to wrap him.' And you think, 'Please, show me next week.' I had company like that for a month."

I can still remember our first visitor—the friend who brought our baby's first doll. (A Cookie Monster.) It was so reassuring to visit with an emissary from the outside world. To think of things other than feedings and diapers and sleep. But it was also nice to say good-bye. To take the phone off the hook and take five for myself. And maybe nod off for a minute or two, just in time to hear "Waaaaaa!" And start all over again.

TENSION / RESPONSIBILITY / WORRY: EXCEDRIN HEADACHE NUMBER 29

As if you didn't already have enough things to lose sleep over, there's your concern about the baby. And about your own ability to care for her:

"I saw the baby as a totally dependent thing that would die because I was inadequate. I kept thinking, 'What if this baby stops breathing?' I wasn't at the hospital. I couldn't buzz the nurse. I didn't know how to give artificial respiration. The first night she came home, we were so scared that the baby slept with us in our bed. She was crying and we couldn't get her calmed down, no matter what we did. So that whole night we just kept this little blob—six pounds five ounces—in between us."

Even if you don't succumb to full-scale panic, you're bound to nurse a nagging kind of worry. The kind of worry that makes you stay up and watch the baby sleeping—even though that's just when you should be getting some sleep yourself. You worry when she's sleeping and when she's not. If she's sleeping too long, or too little. If she makes funny noises in her sleep, or no noise at all. After trying for two hours to get the baby down, you can't wait to get her up again:

"I was always anxious for Michael to go to sleep because I just wouldn't believe he would go for his nap, and then I would get all my paints and everything and turn on the music and just get covered with turpentine, and then he would nap for such a long time that I would watch him, and I would get so anxious for him to wake up so I could communicate how sorry I was that I had been angry and tense with him when he was awake—anxious for him to go to sleep. So I'd wait for him to wake up, and as soon as he woke up, I would get tense again."

Some babies make you more tense than others. Like those who don't sleep well, or don't eat well, or take to projectile vomiting. Some babies' chins quiver when they cry, which is normal, but scary. Others may have a bit of blood in their stool. ("I thought, 'Oh God, he inherited my hemorrhoids!'") Some are convulsants who get 106° fevers and make you think they're dying. None of this helps to settle your nerves.

Neither do worries about your marriage. The demands of a new baby can create cracks in the strongest marital bonds. Surviving this period can make your marriage much stronger, closer, more mature. But it may not seem that way at the time.

The result of all this tension may bring you to the breaking point:

"It's horrible the way you get shorted out. I remember holding one of my kids and shaking him. Looking at this infant and saying, 'What's wrong with you? I'm doing everything I can! I just can't do anymore!' I always had this feeling that I could get rid of him so easily because he was so small and vulnerable, and I'd picture myself throwing him out the window. And I was really scared that I would do that. He was making my life miserable. He was so demanding. I found myself sympathizing with these poor women who do in fact throw their babies out of windows."

Just because you shake your baby or yell at her doesn't make you a candidate for child abuse. But it does tell you something about what tension is doing to you. It's a warning that's important to heed. A clear signal that says, "Hire a sitter. Get out for a while. Relax."

After all, worrying about children is what mothers (and fathers) are for. There's nothing wrong with a little worry as long as you don't let it get out of control. And you may as well get used to it, because it's something you'll be doing for a long time to come. You don't stop checking on your sleeping child just because she's two or three or even six. If you think you're worried now, wait till you have a toddler on your hands. Or a teenager.

TAKING CARE OF BABY

For nine months now, you've been reading baby books that tell you how to give an infant a bath and a bottle, how to feed and change and care for a child under any circumstances. Here are some of the things the books *don't* tell you:

The thought of giving a new baby a bath strikes fear in the heart of every new mother. It doesn't help that the baby often seems to have roughly the same reaction. I remember when the nurse at the hospital gave a demonstration bath on a "volunteer" baby. The baby howled all the way through, which didn't bother the nurse a bit. But it certainly bothered me. And it bothered his mother. And I knew right then that there was no way my baby was going to get a daily bath if he acted like that.

I have since met many other mothers who cheated on the daily bath routine. One delivered at a hospital where giving your own baby a bath before leaving is mandatory, but she evaded even that. Of course we all still feel guilty about our sins of omission. And of course it is a good idea to keep the baby clean. But he isn't going to die if you don't give him a full tub bath every day. So if it's killing you, and you don't always bother, don't worry.

Caring for baby can call for much more difficult (and more important) procedures than giving baths. I had to squirt medication three times a day into Peter's eye—which would have been almost impossible even if I hadn't been terrified. And then there are umbilical cords and circumcisions to care for. Whoever trains a mother for that?

"Caring for the baby in the hospital is deceptive because they bring you this neat, clean bundle and you feed it or diaper it, and it's sweet and happy and you send it back and it's like a dry cleaner. You send it away dirty and it comes back clean. The nurses do all the dirty work, but you don't know that. My baby never cried in the hospital. We weren't home ten minutes when he started. And he didn't stop."

Not only is more involved in baby care than you ever imagined, it takes more time. No matter how well organized you've been before, you just can't manage everything now. You're lucky if you find time to eat, sleep and breathe. Forget amenities like showers or brushing your teeth. If you wonder where the times goes, look back at my account of the first few days under Postpartum Recovery. And that was in the hospital—with a full staff to help out.

One thing that eats up a lot of time is feeding. Breastfed babies sometimes nurse every two hours or less—but what's more, they nurse for twenty or thirty minutes at a stretch. That gives you just one-and-one-half hours to change her and get her down before she's up again for the next feeding.

Bottle babies—and even breastfed babies—sometimes don't want to suck. Sometimes they don't know how. You have to *teach* them, but who ever tells you that?

"I didn't know that babies sucked too much and started to

choke on it, or sucked too hard and couldn't get it out of the bottle. I'd give the baby an entire bottle of milk and he'd throw it up almost immediately and ask for more. How was I to know to give him a pacifier? The instructions tell you to feed them every four hours, and if they cry after three-and-a-half hours, to give them water. But they don't tell you that sometimes the baby's going to cry twenty minutes after you put him down."

I'll never forget when Peter's pediatrician said he was finally ready for cereal and fruit. I thought she meant corn flakes and sliced bananas. Who ever said anything about *baby* cereals?

Pacifiers are mainly for mothers, I think, but it takes some skill to use one. I don't know why they bother to put those little rings on the end, since little babies who really need the sucking can't grasp them anyway. You put the pacifier in, and the baby spits it out. So you keep popping it back in again, or *hold* it in, until he finally knocks off to sleep. Or you do. In which case, the pacifier promptly falls out again and the baby cries and wakes you up. Some mothers I know have resorted to Scotch tape.

My biggest disappointment was the other mothers I sometimes turned to for help. Unfortunately, I didn't know many other mothers with children Peter's age, but I figured any mother would do. I was wrong. Give mothers six months, and they manage to forget everything there is to know about caring for small babies. I used to think they were avoiding me, but they really didn't know. Even now, I haven't any idea of what to do with a crying three-month-old. It must be some sort of automatic protective reaction that immunizes old mothers against the new—that blocks out all memory of early motherhood. It makes us forget so that we all won't stop procreating altogether.

"I was always calling my friends up asking what do you do now, and what happens when they do such-and-such, and what does this mean? And they would never know. They would never remember. There was a woman next door who had eight children, and she didn't remember anything. It was like she never had any children at all."

CRYBABY

The biggest piece of baloney about baby care is the idea that a mother somehow has an automatic instinct for knowing what her baby is crying about. You will soon learn to discriminate, the books tell you, between your baby's "hungry cry," his "tired cry," his "wet cry," and assorted other cries. Like a scientist sorting out the calls of dolphins, you are supposed to be able to decipher one howl from the next. Without a single lesson, you are supposed to be fluent in baby talk. As one mother put it, "That's another myth perpetrated by male doctors who never got up in the middle of the night to take care of a baby."

A baby's cries are insistent and irritating and easily heard, but not so easily understood. And even when you've absolutely decided that you're going to pick the baby up everytime she cries (or that you're not), there are times (most times) when you simply won't know what to do. Deciding whether or not to pick up a crying baby is the roughest decision a mother has to make. And she has to make it some two dozen times every day. And night:

"I just couldn't stand to listen to the crying. It drove me out of my mind. I wanted to put cotton in my ears, but I was afraid I wouldn't be able to get it out. I remember listening to music to drown it out, or turning on the vacuum cleaner, and you know damn well they're crying, but you don't know why. I used to take a shower—it was so relaxing—just to shut out the noise. I still do that with the kids."

Another mother was so worried about her baby's cries and purple complexion that she called the pediatrician. His advice: "Don't worry if the baby's purple. Worry if he's green. He's supposed to be red from crying."

For the truth is that babies cry. Sometimes for no discernible reason. Sometimes for hours on end. Sometimes for days. The best we can do is to try to comfort them. It's got to be hard to be such a small person, so new in the the world. Maybe they're trying to cry themselves back into the womb, where life was warm and quiet and not so complicated. I don't blame them. But as low as your resources may be at this point, you're still stronger than your baby. One of you has to comfort the other, and your infant isn't about to comfort you. So hang on.

Mothers can cry, too, remember. And often do. Often with a baby in their arms, who is also crying, which is why the mother is crying. Crying together beats crying alone, any day. And sooner or later you'll both dry your eyes and cheer up. For babies, this takes about three months. Many mothers remain misty-eyed forever.

CONFINEMENT

Sometimes coming home with a baby is like doing six months in solitary confinement. Not that you're alone. On the contrary, you have constant company. The constant company (the baby) is the problem. Indeed, it seems silly to call pregnancy confinement when it's really what comes after that locks you up and throws away the key.

A new mother's world is a very special place. So special that it admits few visitors. Friends may come into your house, but they can't step into your situation; they can't share what you're going through. It can get lonely—especially if you don't know other new mothers to talk to. You may feel as if you've been isolated permanently from the outside world. Barred from the human race for a crime you never committed.

"For me, the worst part was when my husband left me and went back to work and I stayed home by myself. I remember standing there at the door in my robe with the baby in my arms, the dirty breakfast dishes behind me, and saying good-bye, and thinking, 'He's really going to desert me. I have to stay here and take care of this baby all day long and be by myself, and he's going out into the world.' And after that he'd come home and I'd be hungry for every bit of information: What did he have for lunch? Were the buses still running? He was my only tie with the real world. I had this incredibly trapped feeling because before I had led such a busy, active life myself."

Your new baby is totally dependent on you, and that takes away whatever independence you may have had yourself. Of course, you can always hire a sitter. Or bring in Grandma. But the fact is that few mothers do. Especially not during the first crucial months—when they need you the most, and when you need to get out the most. The more independent you were, the more being dependent will bother you. If you were working, and stopped, you'll miss your friends, your freedom, and the dollars that once filled your pocketbook. You may have been worried before about how the lack of an independent income was going to affect your independence, but it doesn't hit home until it happens.

"I was working for six years, and I just couldn't wait to stop and stay home. But then I had to sell my brand-new

Triumph Spitfire to buy carpeting for my son to crawl on. To me, my car was my baby. Then the baby came, and the car said good-bye."

There's nothing that says you can't keep on working. Many (perhaps even most) mothers have to. And they usually aren't the ones in the glamour jobs or the flexible jobs that let them work half-time or at home. There's a myth that says work—any kind of work—is more intellectually stimulating, more liberating, than motherhood. Never mind that work for many women means licking envelopes and fetching coffee. It's as easy to get tied down to a job as it is to a baby.

Still, I have to admit I'm paranoid about being "only a mother." I'm convinced that whenever someone finds out I'm a mother, they automatically deduct fifty points from my IQ. At work recently, someone asked, "How's the baby?" I said, "Who knows? I'm so busy doing other (read: more interesting) things that I never have the chance to see him."

Of course, I was lying. And afterward, I felt awful. But the experience told me something about my self-image as a mother. Deep down inside, I think women who spend their lives locked up with babies are trapped, boring, dumb. And so I work eight hours a day just to prove how liberated I am.

There's more than one kind of trap.

Whether or not you go back to work (and when) has to depend on the requirements of both your pocketbook and your personality. Working "with child" (pregnant) and working with child (alive and kicking) are subjects that often lend themselves to the same questions. And sometimes the same answers. If you hate to cook and sew and can't stand to be housebound and love your job, you'll obviously hate to stay home—during pregnancy or motherhood. But that doesn't mean that you have to be back in the office the first day you're back home from the hospital. When possible, you should feel your way slowly. One tentative toe at a time. Remember, this is new territory.

"When I stayed home, I was really climbing the walls. I thought I would sew and cook, but I really don't like to sew and cook. I'm not the sort of person to sit around and drink coffee. Now that I'm working, it's like my son and I have a love affair. We go out on the bike, or we'll go to see his friends. And if I say to the other mothers, 'Let's take the kids to the park,' they always say, 'No, I'm really into doing the wash or the cleaning,' and they let the kids play alone. But I do everything with him because I have such a limited time.

For me, working made me a better mother."

On the other hand, I know a lot of workaholic mothers who became homebodies as soon as their babies were born. They thought they wouldn't like home life partly because they'd never tried it. They'd never tried motherhood before, either. That, too, came as a pleasant surprise. Some mothers who think they aren't the mothering type turn out to be the most maternal of all—especially those who think careers are "stimulating" but babies are boring. Often they find the reverse is true.

Either way, it's nice to have a choice.

It's also nice to have the company of other mothers during your stint in solitary. Mothers to call up (even at four o'clock in the morning) to confer with, compare with, and complain to. The happiest mothers I know are those with friends with babies. They admire each other's children, share each other's problems, take part in each other's successes and celebrations. And now that it's Okay to admit that new mothers *do* sometimes have problems, mothers are getting together in groups (formal or otherwise) more often than ever before. It wasn't always that way:

"I never knew that everybody else was going through the same stuff. It was like all the other secret things that people carry with them. I thought nobody didn't love every minute of motherhood but me. People like to live up to the premise of the books, and they're not about to admit that they aren't. The same way they don't admit that anything's wrong with their marriage."

Almost every community today has some kind of "mother-share" group. Often, they grow out of La Leche or Lamaze groups. Hospitals and day-care centers are also good places to look around. Or just place an ad in the newspaper. Mothers in my community do it all the time.

And next time you see a mother who seems to have it all together—her career, her kids, her marriage—the type who never looks harried or has a hair out of place, look closer. Everybody has to give in or give up somewhere. It's just a matter of where.

"I had this friend, Marisa, who was always so calm. Who got everything done. She always had time to sit in the park with her baby. She never looked tired. And here I was a wreck. So one day I went to her house to see what she was doing.

And her house was filthy. It was a sty. And so I said, 'Okay, so *that's* how she does it.'"

So if you feel trapped or lonely or overwhelmed by the burdens of a new baby, talk to another mother. And make sure she tells you the truth.

MY MOTHER / MY CHILD

Coming home is time to face another potential problem of motherhood: your own mother. Should she be around to help out when you come home? Should you hire a nurse? What about your mother-in-law?

Often it is assumed that the new grandma will take a hand in helping out the new mother. Often it is also assumed that she will take over. Baby books are full of advice on how to thwart your mother's efforts to push you out of the picture. "Returning home is an event to be shared and cherished with your husband—and no one else," warns one author. Another writes off mothers entirely as sources of strength or advice during pregnancy, admitting that his advice may "seem cruel." He then goes on to solicit Grandma's help with the "cooking and dusting" when you get home. But remember, "it's *your* baby." In other words, hands off, Grandma. No wonder some grndmothers aren't exactly eager to help. Who wants to get stuck with all the cooking and none of the cuddles?

You can avoid the mother problem altogether simply by hiring a nurse or a housekeeper. And for some new mothers, this works out beautifully. They can come and go as they please, leaving the baby in trusted hands—and they don't have to worry about "imposing" or hurting anybody's feelings. The nurse is a hired hand.

Of course, you won't warm up to a nurse if you don't like the idea of having "a stranger" in the house (although some women put their mothers in the same category.) And remember that a nurse—unlike your mother—is not a known quantity. You might not get to know the nurse well until you start working together—and that may be too late. Your mother comes with a familiar face. And familiar foibles. You know if she's a help or a nuisance, if your chemistry is hot or cool, if she'll cheer you up or wear you down. You also know whether your mother is the takeover type. Some nurses like to take over, too. If your mother tries it, at least you'll be prepared.

But then again, you may always be surprised:

"My mother and I never got along. We fight after we're together for twenty minutes. But she was fabulous. This is the one time in my adult life that I remember getting along with my mother. Absolutely incredible. My mother was there for ten days, and not a harsh word was spoken."

"I get along very well with my mother. But she drove me and my husband nuts. We had big arguments, which we never do. I wasn't home from the hospital an hour when she was screaming at me, which she never does. I wound up making lunch while she played solitaire. And I said, 'Mother, what is going on? This is all wrong.'"

Still, your mother's been your mother for a long time, and you should have some idea by now of what kind of mother she is. If you do get along, by all means invite her to stay. And listen to what she has to say—she's done this before. Of course, she might be wrong, but that doesn't mean you have to turn a deaf ear. There's a germ of truth in the worst old wives' tales. Above all, let her take a hand in handling the baby. She isn't there only to wash the dishes.

Some mothers are almost angelic. I used to think that nobody could help you with night feedings if you were nursing, but I heard of at least one grandma who brought the baby to the nursing mother, then stayed up burping and changing the baby while the mother went back to sleep. Other grandmas clean and cook and shop and launder and rock the baby during his "fussy" (i.e., crying) periods while you take a nap. (Mine did.) You may be so wiped out that you don't even notice. And only later wonder why the house is so clean, or who cooked the casserole, or why the baby slept so well in the afternoons while your mother was there. (He wasn't sleeping; you were.)

Many young mothers find that having their own mothers at home is a way to establish a new kind of closeness. To share a personal experience, perhaps for the first time. To exchange childbirth stories and childrearing techniques. Several mothers said their own mothers felt cheated out of the experience of natural childbirth after talking to them. It made the new mothers all the more grateful. And all the more appreciative of having a husband's hand to hold during labor.

Some grandmothers, however, are strictly for laughs.

"My mother's kind of dippy, like Edith Bunker. She always makes me laugh. She's loose. So she wasn't scrubbing the floors. She slept until eleven. But she kept me company. And a couple of times when I was crying and saying, 'What did we get ourselves into?' she'd turn to my husband and say, 'You know, it's a good thing you're cute, because she would have sold you long ago.' I just needed someone there to make me laugh."

If your mother is good company, or a good cook, or just a good friend, now is the time for a nice long visit. Be prepared to panic the moment she leaves, because as long as she's around, you won't have a true taste of being a mother by yourself. But at least she'll get you on your feet.

There are times when a mother is a true necessity. If you have a cesarean, for example. And if you're nursing, it's important to make sure that someone feeds you a warm meal every now and then or you won't have anything to feed the baby. Nursing and non-nursing mothers agreed that the single most helpful thing their own mothers brought them was food. Things haven't changed a bit. After all, who gave you milk and cookies when you came home from school?

Still, it sometimes happens that you have to say no to your mother. And a surprising number of new mothers are doing just that. As fathers participate more in housework and baby care, grandmothers are needed less. Many mothers want to share those special first weeks with the baby only with their husbands—especially if they've just shared a birth with him. Others would rather recuperate before having company—even when the company is family. And some simply don't get along well enough with their mothers to have them around during a time that is trying enough. If you don't feel comfortable with your mother, you don't want her around now. If she isn't totally supportive, she'll have to move over for someone who is.

But if your mother is counting on coming, how do you say no?

Obviously, it is not a nice idea to tell her you simply don't want her around. Better to spell out your motivations as precisely as possible. You're going to hurt her feelings anyway, so you might as well be honest about it. Take it as an opportunity to open up new channels of communication—to get to know each other a little better. In the end, it wll probably benefit both of you. So if you really don't want your mother around, tell her now. And tell her why.

"My mother wanted to come, and it was very difficult to tell her not to. Yet I knew that this just had to be a special time for me and my husband, so the way we put it was that I wanted to be feeling better when she was there, and could she come in a month or so. And she finally accepted it, and she did come later, and it was better because the baby was a little older, too. And I had the chance to treasure those first few weeks alone. You know, if I couldn't diaper the baby, I wanted to deal with that problem myself."

Another mother put the blame on herself. She said she was too hard to live with and would probably be impossible during the first few weeks with the baby. But what she was really afraid of was that she would wear herself out catering to her mother—not because she had to, but because she wanted to. Indeed, if you like to entertain your mother when she's around, to present her with a clean house and a prepared dinner, then you don't want her around now. Have her come later, when you're up to entertaining.

You might also consider some other questions: If your mother's up cooking and caring for the baby, are you going to feel too guilty to really rest? Is your mother a nervous person who will make you more nervous yourself? How do your mother and your husband get along? Does *he* want her around? Needless to say, all of this goes for mothers-in-law, too. One way to fend off all unwanted company is simply to say, "Even my mother isn't coming." Then people will know that you really want to be alone.

If your mother does come, don't be surprised if she doesn't live up to your expectations. I was appalled that my mother didn't know how to put on a Pamper—never mind that she had her last baby thirty years ago. I sent her scurrying all over town in search of Nuk nipples, and was horrified when she came back with another brand. Didn't she know that was the only kind the Lamaze nurse allowed? Where had she been, anyway?

Where she had been, of course, was not being a mother for a long time—at least, not a mother of infants. In a way, having a baby was as new an experience to her as it was to me:

"The only person who was more terrified of the baby than

me was my mother. She was scared stiff to go near him. And lots of my friends have said the same things about their mothers. They couldn't believe it. I mean, my mother had three children, and yours had two, and you certainly would think that they would feel comfortable around babies. Yet we all got this feeling that we're not even really sure they want to hold the babies. It's funny."

It's not so funny if you've been counting on your mother as a full-time baby-sitter—only to find out that she doesn't know the first thing about babies. Or doesn't want to. Many grandmothers have put in too many years as mothers themselves to want to do your mothering, too.

Indeed, it's a myth that a mother's life is over when her children leave the nest. And it's unlikely that yours has been withering on the vine waiting for you to present her with grand-children. So don't be surprised if she's too busy to baby-sit because she has a date or a yoga class or an assignment to finish for the Famous Writers' School. "My mother is finally free after having kids in the house for thirty years," said one new mommie. "And she looks ten years younger."

Mothers, like children, never stop getting better.

LADY MADONNA, BABY AT YOUR BREAST

The only thing that didn't surprise me about having a baby was nursing. It was every bit the high that I had heard about. Like most mothers, I wanted to nurse because I knew it was better for the baby. But it turned out to be a privilege for me. Nine months later, I still couldn't bring myself to wean him. To break the connection, to lose the physical contact, to give up the intimacy we established when he stared me right in the eye. Eventually, he weaned himself.

There's probably no doubt that, medically speaking, nursing is better for both of you. It's a thrill to feel your uterus contract in tiny twinges as you feed your baby. You can almost feel yourself getting better—feel nature taking care of herself. It also makes sense that mother's milk is better for babies than cow's milk, which is fine for calves. Mother's milk is full of antibodies, is easy to digest, and (supposedly) prevents colic. (I believed this until my sister-in-law had a very colicky baby, even though she was nursing. It turned out that the cow's milk products she herself was eating were showing up in her milk and affecting the baby. When you make the milk yourself, you have to watch what goes into it.)

But given all that, I'm not absolutely sure that I'd nurse another child. And I'm not alone. Many mothers who love nursing and extol its advantages don't do it the second time around. Sometimes because they don't want to be so tied down. (Nursing does take *time*. And obviously you have to be where the baby is.) Sometimes because they want to get out more, and they're shy about breastfeeding a baby in public. And sometimes simply because they don't want to walk around again with big breasts that often drip with milk whenever a child cries or they make love. (This is one of the biggest thrills of nursing, but it can also be a burden.)

To say that nursing has its pros (many) and cons (few) is probably obvious. Not so obvious is the fact that you can often compromise to include the best of both worlds. For example, it's simply not true that you can't work and nurse, or that the father of a breastfed infant can't take over the night shift once in a while. Many babies (Peter included) took well to breast and bottle alike. There's no reason to feel guilty about giving substitute bottles if it doesn't interfere with your milk. And especially not if the choice is between an occasional (or even daily) bottle and not nursing at all. Many babies nurse only at breakfast and bedtime, taking bottles during the day while Mommie works. Of course, you can't take a two-week business trip and nurse (unless you take the baby with you), but you probably can get around much more than you think.

The nicest thing about nursing is the peace and quiet it brings to your otherwise fretful day. It's the reward that makes all the rest worth it. You can put your feet up and love your baby all you like, all the while knowing that you're doing your best for him. Indeed, it's one of the few chores of motherhood that you can do sitting down. One mother said she read her first book in eleven years while nursing. I would watch TV, or talk to a friend on the phone, or sit outside and watch the sunset. There's a calmness about nursing that heals many kinds of wounds—physical and emotional. That's why so many mothers find it so hard to give up. For all the advice on how to wean babies, I think it's weaning the mothers that's the problem.

An added attraction is that you can eat practically all you want and not gain weight. It was the only time in my life that I was thin.

Nursing becomes a problem if you have a physical problem. Many mothers do develop cracked nipples or milk-flow problems or other difficulties—all of which usually disappear in the first month. And most of which are manageable. Books on breastfeeding are full of good advice. The three bits I found invaluable were (1) prepare while you're pregnant by toughening up your nipples (to prevent cracks); (2) always use a lap pad (those loose bowel movements); and (3) take an occasional glass of port or dark beer to relax you and baby alike.

Some problems are not so easily solved:

"My husband didn't want me to nurse. He said my tits were his. He was jealous. My mother wondered why I wasn't nursing, so I told her. She couldn't understand. But my father understood right away."

Some husbands are jealous not only in a sexual sense, but also because they feel left out. If giving the baby an occasional bottle is important to Daddy, I'd let him do it. But there are other ways he can establish an intimacy of his own that are more important. Perhaps you can show him how.

Sometimes nursing is simply an annoyance. Many women don't like the feel of it. They say it's like a mouse nibbling at the nipple. A not painful, but not pleasant sensation. Others are embarrassed by the very idea. And still others are embarrassed because they think other people will be embarrassed. More than one nursing mother has gone back to the bottle because friends and neighbors made her feel conspicuous.

One disadvantage to nursing that you can do something about is frequent night feedings. Breastfed babies generally do feed more often and are older before they sleep through the night. However, you don't need to get up to warm a bottle, and if you have a cooperative child who doesn't always need a diaper change, you don't even need to get out of bed:

"The solution with Cassie was to have her sleep in bed with us. At first I was afraid of rolling over on her, but it was really glorious. Eventually, my body adjusted to the every-hour feedings, even though I was the kind of person who always needed to have ten hours' sleep a day. I got to the point where I could get a full night's sleep and nurse her even every half-hour, and still feel completely refreshed the next day. If I'd have had to get physicaly, completely out of bed, I don't think I could have done it."

So there's more than one way to nurse a baby. Indeed, what is missing in most nursing literature today is compromise. You don't have to worry if you're not doing everything exactly by the book. Or if your baby isn't gaining a certain number of ounces every day. Or if you go out and give the baby an occasional bottle. If you skip a day or even a week, you don't have to stop nursing completely. You can keep up your milk supply with a breast pump—or even easier, you can express it manually. I thought I would never be able to nurse because my baby was separated from me for so many days and because he started life on a bottle. But I never had a problem. Some mothers have started nursing after as long as a month.

Of course, not everybody is in favor of nursing. The way some people object to it, you'd think it was a newfangled idea. And you're not likely to get good advice from people with prejudices. All the more reason not to listen to pediatricians who tell you to give nursing up after one or two months (that's when it starts getting good); or that the baby isn't getting enough to eat (if he isn't, you'll make more milk); or that if you skip a day, you have to stop. Read the books and arm yourself with information. Go to La Leche League meetings. If you run into an all-or-nothing approach, put in a word for women who need to compromise. And in the end, do what suits you best. But don't give up before you try. Don't be put off by rhetoric and irrational fears. You might be putting off one of the nicest parts of having a baby.

AND BABY MAKES THREE

"Coming home the first time was like coming home to your nest and your baby," said one mother. "It was just me and my husband, and we played some music, and I nursed the baby. I think it was the nicest time of my whole life."

For all the bad times, coming home is the best of times. To snuggle in the warmth of your own nest with your new baby. To kiss tiny fingers and tiny toes and watch your red, wrinkled prune ripen into a full-blown baby. Pretty soon the cord falls off, and the head looks less pointy, and giving him a bath isn't a bother at all. Before you know it, he's smiling and cooing and loving you back. You have the privilege of looking on as a new person unfolds. And there's always something to look forward to: the first laugh, the first tooth, the first hug, the first step. Every day is full of potential, packed with promises. For a mother, every month is a milestone. One morning you leave him safely in the center of the living-room floor, and then turn around to find him suddenly, surprisingly, behind you. When did he learn to crawl?

"The first three months are the worst. But as your baby grows, so does your confidence and pride. It's fun watching all the new things she learns. You start seeing things in a fresh, new way as you see things through your baby's eyes, and you realize that this person has never seen these things before. Such delight in something as simple as the pattern of leaves blowing in the sunshine."

Or the first lick of ice cream. Or the first feel of sand on her toes at the beach. Or the first snow.

As the years go by, you forget the bad parts. Or at least you put them in perspective as unimportant. Or as one mother chided me, "I forgot all the bad parts until I read this questionnaire."

Before you know it, you're wishing you had a baby around again. But be careful not to wish your life away.

First you wish you were pregnant, and then you wish you had a big belly to show off. But when the belly gets to be a burden, you wish for labor to come. And as soon as it comes, you wish it were over. You wish for the baby, and then you wish it were older. You wish your children toilet trained and off to school. You wish them grown up. And then you get what you wish, and your children are gone, and you've wished motherhood away.

The time it takes to have a baby is so fleeting, so full of everything, that maybe there isn't opportunity to savor it until it's over. And when it's over, you're left with your photographs and your memories and your regrets that you didn't appreciate it all the more at the time. You forget how busy you were and how tired. You remember only how wonderful it was to be a mother. And is.

So savor every morsel of motherhood as it comes along.

Especially if, like most women today, you're only having one or two or even three children. In the course of a lifetime, that's not so many times to do something as precious as making a baby. It's important to make it count.

About the Author

K.C. Cole has been writing for several years about education, health, science, business, travel, marriage, mothering and step-mothering for such publications as THE SATURDAY RE-VIEW, OMNI, THE SMITHSONIAN, PEOPLE, GLAM-OUR, NEWSDAY, THE NEW YORK NEWS, THE WASHINGTON POST, and THE NEW YORK TIMES. She has also been an editor at both THE SATURDAY REVIEW and NEWSDAY, and a consultant on health and education for the Ford Foundation, the Robert Wood Johnson Foundation and the Department of Health and Human Services. Her favorite subjects are her husband, also a writer and editor, her step-daughters, and her son, Peter.

INDEX

C. J. SANSOM estudió en la Universidad de Birmingham, donde se licenció, y también cursó un doctorado en Historia. Tras pasar por varios empleos, trabajó como abogado hasta que decidió dejarlo todo para escribir a tiempo completo. Además de *Invierno en Madrid*, C. J. Sansom ha escrito una serie de novelas de tema histórico, cuyo protagonista es Matthew Shardlake, abogado inglés del siglo XVI, de las cuales Ediciones B ha publicado *La piedra del corazón*. La cadena de librerías Waterstone's eligió a C. J. Sansom «uno de los veinticinco novelistas del futuro».

ZETA

Título original: *Winter in Madrid*
Traducción: M.ª Antonia Menini
1.ª edición: enero 2012

© C. J. Sansom, 2005
© Ediciones B, S. A., 2012
    para el sello Zeta Bolsillo
    Consell de Cent, 425-427 - 08009 Barcelona (España)
    www.edicionesb.com

Printed in Spain
ISBN: 978-84-9872-592-6
Depósito legal: B. 39.145-2011

Impreso por LIBERDÚPLEX, S.L.U.
Ctra. BV 2249 Km 7,4 Polígono Torrentfondo
08791 - Sant Llorenç d'Hortons (Barcelona)

Invierno en Madrid

C. J. SANSOM

ZETA

*En memoria de los miles de hijos
de padres republicanos que desaparecieron
en los orfelinatos de la España franquista*

Nota histórica

Casi tres cuartos de siglo después de su final, la Guerra Civil española sigue siendo un tema controvertido.

En los primeros años del siglo XX, el oligárquico régimen monárquico español ya se enfrentaba con la creciente resistencia de los reformistas republicanos de la clase media, los nacionalistas catalanes y vascos y, sobre todo, las depauperadas clases obreras tanto rurales como urbanas. Un ciclo de resistencia y opresión alimentó una lucha de clases y una polarización únicas en la Europa ajena a Rusia.

En 1931, el rey Alfonso XIII salió de España y se proclamó la Segunda República. Una serie de gobiernos desafortunados, primero liberal-socialistas y después conservadores, se fueron sucediendo hasta que, en 1936, una coalición radical del ala izquierda alcanzó el poder en las urnas. Los trabajadores empezaron a asumir el mando de la situación y se hicieron con el control de las propiedades y las instituciones locales.

Jamás se sabrá si el gobierno del Frente Popular habría alcanzado el éxito en su gestión, pues en 1936 tuvo lugar el siempre temido levantamiento militar, apoyado por las fuerzas conservadoras y con el importante respaldo económico de Juan March. Sin embargo, el golpe inicial fracasó: muchos militares se mantuvieron leales al gobierno legalmente constituido y, en las ciudades más importantes, el alzamiento fue derrotado. Los rebeldes conquistaron el control de algo más de un tercio del territorio continental español; no así el de sus regiones industriales.

Es posible que, sin la intervención extranjera, el alzamiento hubiera sido enteramente derrotado; pero Hitler y Mussolini enviaron inmediatamente aviones al general Franco, permitiéndole con ello aerotransportar tropas de elite desde la colonia española de Marruecos al continente e iniciar la marcha sobre Madrid. Entre tanto el gobierno británico, dominado por los conservadores, ejerció presión sobre Francia para que negara su ayuda a la República y cerrara la frontera. A consecuencia de ello, la República se vio obligada a solicitar ayuda a la única potencia dispuesta a ayudarla, la Unión Soviética. La zona republicana tuvo que depender de Stalin y sus «asesores», los cuales exportaron su aparato de terror junto con las armas. Todavía pervive en España un mito, fomentado por el régimen de Franco, según el cual el ejército se levantó en armas para impedir un golpe comunista; cuando, en realidad, el Partido Comunista Español antes de 1936 era minúsculo, y la tradición entre republicanos, socialistas y anarquistas, fuertemente antiautoritaria. El ascenso al poder de los comunistas fue una consecuencia directa de la presión británica sobre Francia, con el fin de que ésta se mantuviera al margen del conflicto.

La consiguiente guerra civil duró tres años y devastó España. Unos doscientos cincuenta mil hombres murieron en combate y otros doscientos mil en la campaña de terror llevada a cabo por ambos bandos, muchos de ellos apolíticos con «lealtades sospechosas» que acabaron en el lado equivocado de las líneas.

Cuando terminó la guerra, con la victoria de los nacionales en abril de 1939, no hubo reconciliación sino tan sólo constantes ejecuciones y desapariciones mientras Franco llevaba a efecto la «limpieza» de España. Para la mayoría de los españoles, los años cuarenta fueron una pesadilla casi tan grande como la de los años de la Guerra Civil, pues los efectos de la sequía se agravaron como consecuencia la destrucción de buena parte de las infraestructuras durante la guerra, de la política de autosuficiencia económica fascista de Franco y del caótico y corrupto sistema de distribución. El propio Franco soñaba con soluciones tales como gigantescas reservas de oro y manufactura de petróleo a partir de la hierba.

El régimen de Franco propiamente dicho estuvo dividido desde el principio entre los fascistas de la Falange, cuyas bandas armadas Franco había elegido como aliadas durante la Guerra Civil y que se acabaron convirtiendo en el único partido político de España, y los monárquicos, los tradicionales conservadores españoles. Los monárquicos acostumbraban a ser probritánicos y antialemanes, pero la Inglaterra que ellos admiraban era la de la aristocrática casa de campo; despreciaban a los falangistas por «vulgares» y, en cualquier caso, se mostraban todavía menos compasivos con los padecimientos de los españoles corrientes que la Falange. Y en la Guerra Civil actuaron con tanta violencia como ésta. El propio Franco estaba situado en un punto intermedio entre ambas fuerzas. Hábil estratega político, su capacidad para equilibrar los bandos que integraban su régimen lo ayudó a mantenerse en el poder durante casi cuarenta años. Pero, tras la derrota de Hitler, la Falange fue siempre un socio menor de su coalición.

En 1939-1940 el principal dilema con que se enfrentaba Franco era el de la posibilidad de entrar en guerra con Hitler, como quería la Falange. El propio Franco soñaba con ampliar su imperio hispanoafricano con las colonias de la Francia derrotada; pero los monárquicos deseaban mantenerse neutrales y consideraban la entrada en guerra una peligrosa aventura que traería como consecuencia la consolidación del poder de la Falange. Al final, como de costumbre, la postura de Franco fue pragmática. En su calidad de hijo de un oficial de la Armada, conocía el poderío de la Armada británica, que estaba ejerciendo un bloqueo contra España y podía desviar fácilmente la entrada de suministros. Por consiguiente, sólo podía entrar en guerra cuando Gran Bretaña estuviera a punto de ser derrotada y en caso de que semejante circunstancia se diera en algún momento. Cuando pareció que así había ocurrido en junio de 1940, Franco le hizo ofertas a Hitler, pero la respuesta del Führer fue muy cauta. En otoño de 1940, cuando a Hitler le convino que Franco entrara en guerra principalmente para apoderarse de Gibraltar, la batalla de Inglaterra ya había terminado en una derrota alemana y Franco se dio cuenta de que Gran Bretaña no estaba ni mucho menos acabada.

El encuentro entre Hitler y Franco en la frontera francoespañola en octubre de 1940 sigue siendo objeto de controversia. Los apologistas de Franco sostienen que su hábil diplomacia mantuvo a España al margen de la guerra; en cambio, sus detractores señalan que habría entrado en guerra si las condiciones hubieran sido adecuadas. Este último punto de vista parece ser el que más se acerca a la verdad; sin embargo, en 1940 Hitler no estaba en condiciones de facilitar la cantidad de ayuda alemana que Franco habría necesitado para impedir que el bloqueo británico llevara a España al borde de la inanición y, tal vez, a una renovada revolución. Las insistentes demandas de Franco dieron lugar a que el Führer abandonara hastiado el encuentro de Hendaya. Posteriormente, las negociaciones entre Franco y el Eje se siguieron llevando a cabo, pero cualquier perspectiva real de entrada en guerra de España fue disminuyendo gracias al constante control de los mares ejercido por la Marina británica.

En mayo de 1940, Churchill, primer ministro británico de la nueva coalición en tiempo de guerra, despidió a sir Samuel Hoare del Gabinete y lo envió a España como embajador en Misión Especial con la orden de mantener a Franco al margen de la guerra. Hoare era un ministro conservador y un destacado pacificador. Vanidoso, amanerado y arrogante, pero hábil administrador y político, sus aptitudes, su prestigio y su historial de experto apaciguador de dictadores lo convertían en una elección acertada, pese a la decepción sufrida por el hecho de no haber visto cumplida su esperada ambición de convertirse en virrey de la India. Churchill no apreciaba ni confiaba en Hoare y es posible que eligiera a su amigo Alan Hillgarth como funcionario encargado de las operaciones secretas en España (incluido el soborno de los monárquicos potencialmente afines), en parte para vigilar a Hoare. No cabe duda de que Hillgarth informaba directamente a Churchill.

Como embajador en otoño e invierno de 1940-1941, Hoare siguió un camino previsible. Franco y su principal ministro, el profalangista Serrano Súñer lo trataban con desdén; pero él logró establecer vínculos con los monárquicos y obtener importante información a través de ellos. Insistía en que, aparte de los sobornos, las actividades secretas en España se limitaran a la recogida de información; según él, no tendría que haber agentes del SOE —Special Operation Executive, es decir, de la Dirección de Operaciones Especiales— encargados de prender fuego a Europa, y rechazaba las propuestas de acercamiento de la oposición clandestina del ala izquierda, señalando que el de Franco era el Gobierno establecido, por cuyo motivo todos los esfuerzos británicos se tendrían que concentrar aquí. Éste me parece un argumento muy endeble: la amenaza de apoyo a la oposición habría conferido, sin duda, más recursos a Gran Bretaña. No obstante, el punto de vista de Hoare, como el de muchos conservadores británicos, coincidía emocionalmente con el de los aristocráticos monárquicos antirrevolucionarios. Hoare defendió con éxito una política de no asociación con la izquierda española, sembrando de este modo las semillas de la política aliada de la posguerra encaminada a dejar el régimen de Franco en su sitio.

Sin embargo, los puntos de vista de Hoare fueron cambiando a medida que la guerra seguía su curso y, para cuando terminó su servicio como embajador en 1944, ya se había convertido en un firme opositor a la idea de dejar el régimen de Franco en su sitio, abogando en su lugar por un programa de propaganda y sanciones económicas. Pero el pensamiento de Churchill ya había evolucionado en la dirección opuesta. Ahora éste creía que Franco era un baluarte contra el comunismo, por lo que convenía dejarlo en su sitio. Hoare no pudo modificar la opinión de Churchill que, en última instancia, resultó decisiva.

Mi interpretación de los personajes de Hillgarth y Hoare es personal; puede parecer dura, pero creo que coincide con los datos conocidos. Todos los demás personajes británicos y españoles son imaginarios, excepto algunas de las más destacadas figuras de la historia española de aquellos años que hacen breves apariciones. Azaña, el extravagante Millán Astray y, como es natural, el propio Franco.

La imagen que presento de España en 1940 es muy lúgubre, pero está basada mayoritariamente en relatos de observadores contemporáneos. Aunque el campo de prisioneros de las afueras de Cuenca es imaginario, hubo muchos auténticos. No creo que mi imagen de la Iglesia española en aquel período sea injusta; sus miembros estuvieron implicados de lleno en la política de un régimen violento en su fase más brutal, y los que, como el padre Eduardo, tenían dificultades para conciliarlo con su conciencia parece que fueron más bien escasos.

La visión arcaica del general Franco de una España católica y autoritaria murió con él en 1975. Los españoles dieron inmediatamente la espalda a su legado y abrazaron la democracia. El pasado se hundió en el «pacto del olvido». Tal vez ése fuera el precio de una transición pacífica a la democracia. Sólo ahora, a medida que va desapareciendo la generación de los años cuarenta, la situación empieza a cambiar y los historiadores vuelven a interesarse una vez más por los primeros años del régimen franquista, descubriendo muchas nuevas historias de horror que no serán muy del agrado de los apologistas del régimen, pero que a nosotros nos recuerdan las penalidades que tuvieron que sufrir los españoles de a pie no sólo durante la Guera Civil, sino también después de la victoria.

He tratado de ser lo más respetuoso posible en la tarea de acompasar los acontecimientos de la novela a las fechas históricas. Sin embargo, en dos ocasiones las he alterado ligeramente para satisfacer las exigencias del argumento. He retrasado un par de días la visita de Himmler a Madrid y he adelantado en un año la fundación de La Barraca (1931). También me he inventado la asistencia de Franco al concierto que ofreció Herbert von Karajan en Madrid, que en realidad tuvo lugar el 22 de mayo de 1940.

Prólogo

Valle del Jarama, España, febrero de 1937

Bernie llevaba horas semiinconsciente a los pies de la loma.

El Batallón Británico había sido transportado al frente dos días atrás, atravesando la yerma meseta castellana en una vieja locomotora. Aunque en el batallón había unos cuantos veteranos de la Primera Guerra Mundial, casi todos los soldados eran muchachos pertenecientes a la clase trabajadora que ni siquiera habían conocido la experiencia del Cuerpo de Instrucción de Oficiales de que había disfrutado Bernie, y mucho menos las superficiales nociones que poseían otros hombres educados en exclusivas escuelas privadas. Incluso aquí, en su propia guerra, la clase trabajadora se encontraba en inferioridad de condiciones.

La República mantenía una fuerte posición en lo alto de una colina que bajaba en acusada pendiente hacia el valle del Jarama, salpicado por pequeños altozanos y cubierto de olivares. Muy a lo lejos se distinguía la borrosa mancha de Madrid, la ciudad que había resistido a los fascistas desde el levantamiento de los generales del verano anterior. Madrid, donde estaba Barbara.

El ejército de Franco ya había cruzado el río. Allí abajo estaban las tropas coloniales marroquíes, muy duchas en el arte de utilizar todos los pliegues del terreno como protección. El batallón había recibido la orden de situarse en posición de defensa de la colina. Sus fusiles eran viejos, se registraba escasez de municiones y muchas armas ni siquiera se encontraban en condiciones de disparar debidamente. Se habían fabricado a partir de cascos de acero franceses de la Primera Guerra Mundial que, según los veteranos, no estaban hechos a prueba de balas.

Pese al intenso fuego del batallón, los moros iban ascendiendo poco a poco por la loma a medida que avanzaba la mañana, centenares de silenciosos y mortíferos fardos envueltos en sus grises capas cada vez más cercanos, agazapándose entre los olivos. De pronto se inició el ataque de la artillería desde las posiciones franquistas; la tierra amarilla que rodeaba al batallón se abrió en enormes cráteres y sembró el terror entre los soldados novatos. Por la tarde se recibió la orden de retirada. Todo se convirtió en un caos. Mientras corrían, Bernie vio que el terreno entre los olivos estaba sembrado de libros que los soldados habían sacado de sus macutos en un intento de aligerar el peso: poesía, manuales marxistas y textos pornográficos de los tenderetes callejeros de Madrid.

Aquella noche los supervivientes del batallón se tumbaron exhaustos en una vieja y hundida carretera de la meseta. No se tenían noticias sobre el resultado de la batalla en otras zonas del frente. Bernie se quedó dormido de puro agotamiento.

Por la mañana, el comandante del Estado Mayor ruso dio orden de que los restos del batallón reanudaran el avance. Bernie vio al capitán Wintringham discutiendo con él mientras las cabezas de ambos se perfilaban contra el frío cielo, que pasaba del rosa púrpura al azul con los primeros rayos de sol. El batallón estaba agotado y el enemigo lo superaba en número; los moros se habían atrincherado e iban armados con ametralladoras. Pero el ruso se mostraba inflexible y su rostro permanecía absolutamente inmóvil.

Los hombres recibieron la orden de formar, apretujados contra el borde de la hundida carretera. Al amanecer, los franquistas habían reanudado los disparos y el fragor ya era impresionante: sonoros disparos de fusil e incesantes ráfagas de ametralladora. Cuando aguardaba la orden de avanzar, Bernie estaba tan cansado que ni siquiera era capaz de pensar. La frase «estoy rendido, estoy rendido» le martilleaba una y otra vez la cabeza siguiendo el ritmo de un metrónomo. Muchos de los hombres estaban demasiado agotados para hacer otra cosa que no fuera mirar ciegamente al frente; otros temblaban de miedo.

Wintringham se puso personalmente al frente de la carga y cayó casi de inmediato, abatido por un disparo en la pierna. Bernie pegó un respingo y experimentó una sacudida, mientras las balas llovían por doquier y él contemplaba cómo los hombres con quienes se había adiestrado se desplomaban a su alrededor entre aullidos o leves suspiros, tras ser alcanzados por los disparos. Cuando apenas había avanzado cien metros, el desesperado impulso de caer y besar el suelo se volvió tan apremiante que Bernie se arrojó al amparo de un viejo y poderoso olivo.

Permaneció mucho rato apoyado contra el tronco nudoso, mientras las balas estallaban y silbaban a su alrededor y él contemplaba los cuerpos de sus compañeros, cuya sangre empapaba y teñía de negro la tierra pálida. Torció el cuerpo, tratando de pegarse al suelo.

Entrada la mañana cesaron los disparos, aunque Bernie los oyó en las primeras líneas. A su derecha vio una alta y escarpada loma cubierta de maleza. Decidió echar una corta carrera para alcanzarla. Se levantó, y echó a correr doblado casi por la mitad cuando oyó un disparo y sintió un punzante dolor en el muslo derecho. Notó la sangre que le resbalaba por los pantalones, pero no se atrevió a mirar a su alrededor. Impulsándose con los codos y la pierna sana, se arrastró desesperadamente hacia la protección de la loma mientras la antigua herida del brazo le provocaba un agudo dolor. Otra bala sacudió la tierra a su alrededor, pero no le impidió llegar a la loma. Se tumbó al abrigo de la pequeña colina y se desmayó.

Cuando volvió en sí ya era por la tarde y permanecía tumbado en una alargada sombra, mientras el calor del día se iba disipando. Había caído en la pendiente de la colina y no veía más que unos cuantos palmos de tierra y piedras. Se sintió agobiado por una sed espantosa. Todo permanecía inmóvil y en silencio. Se oía el canto de un pájaro en uno de los olivos, pero también el murmullo de unas voces lejanas en algún lugar. Hablaban en español y, por consiguiente, debían de ser franquistas, a no ser que las tropas republicanas de más al norte hubieran conseguido abrir una brecha, lo cual le costaba creer tras el percance sufrido por su sección. Él también permaneció inmóvil, con la cabeza hundida en la tierra polvorienta, consciente del entumecimiento de su pierna derecha.

Recuperaba el sentido intermitentemente y seguía oyendo el murmullo de las voces más adelante y a su izquierda. Al poco rato despertó del todo, se le despejó de pronto la cabeza y notó que la garganta le abrasaba. Ahora ya no se oían las voces, sólo el canto de un pájaro; seguramente no era el mismo de antes.

Bernie pensaba que España sería muy calurosa; recordaba de su visita con Harry seis años atrás un calor sofocante y seco. Pero, en febrero, aunque los días eran aceptablemente templados, al anochecer hacía frío, y él no se creía capaz de pasar la noche allí a la intemperie. Notaba que los piojos le corrían por el espeso vello del vientre. Habían infestado el campamento base, y Bernie no soportaba el picor. Le estaba ocurriendo algo muy curioso: podía resistir el dolor de la pierna, pero el deseo de rascarse le resultaba insoportable. Por lo poco que sabía, bien podía encontrarse rodeado de soldados nacionales que, tomando su forma inmóvil por un cadáver, le pegarían un tiro al menor movimiento. Levantó un poco la cabeza rechinando los dientes mientras esperaba el impacto de una bala de un momento a otro. Nada. Por delante de él sólo se extendía la ladera desnuda de la colina. Se volvió con rigidez. El dolor le traspasaba la pierna como un cuchillo y tuvo que apretar la mandíbula para ahogar un grito. Se incorporó sobre el codo y miró a su alrededor. Media pernera estaba desgarrada y la oscura sangre coagulada le cubría todo el muslo. Ahora no sangraba. La bala debía de haber pasado rozando la arteria, pero si se movía demasiado, posiblemente volviera a sangrar.

A su izquierda vio dos cuerpos con el uniforme de la Brigada, los dos boca abajo. Uno de ellos estaba demasiado lejos para verlo, pero el otro era McKie, el joven minero escocés. Con sumo cuidado y tratando de no mover la pierna, volvió a incorporarse sobre los codos y miró hacia la cumbre de la colina.

A unos cien metros por encima de él, asomado al borde, divisó un tanque alemán, uno de los que Hitler había regalado a Franco. Un brazo colgaba inerte de la torreta. Los franquistas debían de haber subido con tanques y uno de ellos se había detenido justo antes de precipitarse cuesta abajo. Se mantenía en precario equilibrio y el morro asomaba casi hasta la mitad; desde el lugar donde permanecía tumbado, Bernie distinguía los tubos y los tornillos de la parte inferior y las pesadas planchas blindadas de las bandas de rodamiento. Podía caérsele encima en cualquier momento; tenía que moverse.

Empezó a apartarse muy despacio. El dolor le apuñalaba la pierna y, tras recorrer un par de metros, se vio obligado a detenerse, sudando y jadeando. Ahora distinguía mejor a McKie. El disparo le había arrancado un brazo, que ahora descansaba a unos pocos metros de distancia. La brisa le alborotaba suavemente el cabello castaño, tan desgreñado en la muerte como solía estar en vida, pero el rostro ya aparecía mucho más blanco que de costumbre. Los ojos de McKie estaban cerrados y su semblante, gracioso a fuerza de feo, mostraba una apacible y serena expresión. Pobre muchacho, pensó Bernie mientras las lágrimas le escocían en los ojos.

La primera vez que había visto cadáveres, hombres traídos de la línea de combate madrileña y extendidos en hileras en la calle, Bernie se había mareado de horror. Sin embargo, cuando el día anterior libraron batalla, sus remilgos se disiparon. «No queda más remedio cuando estás bajo el fuego enemigo —le había dicho su padre en una de las insólitas ocasiones en que habló del Somme—, todos los sentidos se ponen en estado de alerta para sobrevivir. No ves, vigilas como vigila un animal. No oyes, escuchas como escucha un animal. Te conviertes en un ser tan centrado y despiadado como un animal.» Pero su padre sufría largos períodos de depresión y se pasaba las noches sentado en el pequeño despacho de la trastienda, con la cabeza inclinada bajo la débil y amarillenta luz de la lámpara, tratando de olvidar las trincheras.

Bernie recordaba las bromas de McKie acerca de la independencia de Escocia bajo el socialismo, mientras soñaba entre risas con verse libre del inútil idioma inglés. Se pasó la lengua por los labios resecos. Si salía de allí con vida, y aunque consiguieran crear un nuevo mundo libre, ¿recordaría en sueños aquel momento en que la brisa alborotaba el cabello de McKie?

Oyó un chasquido, un pequeño sonido metálico. Miró hacia arriba; el tanque se mecía ligeramente y el largo cañón se perfilaba contra el cielo cada vez más oscuro, balanceándose lentamente arriba y abajo. Sus movimientos al pie de la loma no podían haber bastado para desplazar el tanque, pero el caso es que el vehículo se estaba moviendo.

Bernie trató de incorporarse y el dolor le volvió a apuñalar la pierna herida. Siguió reptando y pasó junto al cuerpo de McKie. Ahora la herida le dolía más, notaba que la sangre le manaba de nuevo por la pierna. La cabeza le daba vueltas; le horrorizaba pensar que si se desmayaba, el tanque podía resbalar cuesta abajo y le aplastaría el cuerpo tumbado boca abajo. Tenía que permanecer consciente. Justo delante de él había un charco de agua sucia. A pesar del peligro, su sed era tan grande que hundió la cabeza en él y tomó un buen sorbo. Sabía a tierra y le entraron ganas de vomitar. Levantó la cabeza y se estremeció al ver el reflejo de su rostro: cada pliegue quedaba disimulado con una capa de barro sobre la desaliñada barba, y sus ojos eran los de un loco. De repente le pareció oír la voz de Barbara, recordó sus delicadas manos acariciándole el cuello. «¡Qué guapo eres! —le había dicho una vez—. Demasiado para mí.» ¿Qué diría si lo viera en ese momento?

Se oyó otro crujido, esta vez más fuerte. Levantó la mirada y descubrió que el tanque se estaba resbalando lentamente hacia delante.

Un pequeño desprendimiento de tierra y guijarros bajaba muy despacio por la cuesta de la colina.

—Oh, Dios mío —musitó—. Dios mío.

Se incorporó a medias y trató de seguir avanzando.

Sonó un fuerte chirrido y el tanque cayó rodando por la pendiente con un poderoso fragor. Bernie salió indemne por los pelos. Al llegar abajo, el largo cañón se hundió en la tierra y el vehículo blindado se detuvo, estremeciéndose como un gigantesco animal herido. El observador salió disparado de la torreta y cayó despatarrado en la trinchera, boca abajo. Tenía el cabello rubio ceniza: un alemán. Bernie cerró los ojos y emitió un jadeo de alivio.

Otro sonido lo indujo a volverse y mirar hacia arriba. Cinco hombres permanecían alineados al borde de la colina, atraídos por el estruendo. Tenían los rostros tan sucios y agotados como Bernie. Eran nacionales; vestían el uniforme de combate verde oliva de las tropas de Franco. Levantaron los fusiles y le apuntaron. Uno de los soldados desenfundó una pistola y le quitó el seguro, produciendo un leve chasquido. Se adelantó y empezó a bajar por la pendiente.

Bernie se apoyó en una mano y levantó la otra en un cansado gesto de súplica.

El franquista se detuvo a un metro de distancia. Era alto y delgado, y llevaba un bigotito como el del Generalísimo. Su duro rostro revelaba una expresión enojada.

—Me entrego —anunció Bernie.

No le quedaba otra salida.

—¡Cabrón comunista!

El hombre hablaba con acusado acento andaluz.

Bernie aún estaba tratando de descifrar las palabras, cuando el franquista levantó la pistola y le apuntó a la cabeza.

PRIMERA PARTE

OTOÑO

1

Londres, septiembre de 1940

En Victoria Street había caído una bomba que había abierto un enorme cráter y derribado la fachada de varias tiendas. La calle había sido acordonada y los hombres del ARP, el equipo de precaución contra incursiones aéreas, con la ayuda de voluntarios, habían formado una cadena y retiraban cuidadosamente cascotes de uno de los edificios dañados. Harry comprendió que tenía que haber alguien allí debajo. Los esfuerzos del equipo de rescate, viejos y jóvenes cubiertos de un polvo que los envolvía como un sudario, parecían inútiles en comparación con las enormes montañas de ladrillos y yeso. Depositó la maleta en el suelo.

Mientras el tren se acercaba a la estación Victoria, había visto otros cráteres y otros edificios destrozados. Se había sentido curiosamente alejado de la destrucción, cosa que le venía ocurriendo desde que se iniciaran las grandes incursiones diez días atrás. Allá abajo, en Surrey, a su tío James casi le había dado un ataque al ver las fotografías en el *Telegraph*. Harry apenas había reaccionado a la imagen del congestionado y enfurecido rostro de su tío ante aquel nuevo ejemplo del terror alemán. Su mente había conseguido apartarse de la furia.

Pero no se podía apartar del cráter de Westminster que, de repente, había aparecido ante sus ojos. Tuvo la impresión de regresar a Dunkerque: los cazabombarderos alemanes sobrevolando su cabeza, el estallido en la costa arenosa. Apretó los puños, clavándose las uñas en las palmas de las manos mientras respiraba hondo. El corazón le empezó a latir con fuerza, pero no se puso a temblar; ahora podía controlar sus reacciones.

Un vigilante del ARP se acercó a él. Era un cincuentón de duro rostro, con un fino bigotito gris y una espalda muy tiesa, enfundado en un uniforme negro cubierto de polvo.

—No puede pasar —le dijo en tono perentorio—. La calle está cerrada. ¿No ve que nos ha caído una bomba?

Le miró con recelosa expresión de reproche, sin duda preguntándose por qué razón un treintañero aparentemente sano no iba vestido de uniforme.

—Perdone —dijo Harry—. Acabo de subir del campo. No me había dado cuenta de que fuera tan grave.

Ante el refinado acento de escuela privada con el que Harry habló, casi todos los *cockneys* habrían utilizado un tono servil; pero no así aquel hombre.

—No hay escapatoria en ningún sitio —dijo con voz áspera—. Esta vez no. La cosa no puede durar mucho ni en la ciudad ni en el campo, se lo digo yo. —El vigilante miró fríamente a Harry—. ¿Está de permiso?

—Me han dado de baja por invalidez —contestó Harry bruscamente—. Mire, tengo que ir a Queen Anne's Gate. Asunto oficial.

Los modales del vigilante cambiaron de repente. Tomó a Harry del brazo y lo obligó a volverse.

—Suba por Petty France. Aquí sólo cayó una bomba.

—Gracias.

—No hay de qué, señor. ¿Estuvo usted en Dunkerque?

—Sí.

—Hubo mucha sangre y destrucción allá abajo en la Isla de los Perros, en pleno barrio de los Docklands. Yo estuve en las trincheras la última vez, sabía que la cosa se repetiría y que esta vez todo el mundo sufriría las consecuencias, no sólo los soldados. Tendrá ocasión de volver a combatir, ya lo verá. A clavar la bayoneta en el vientre de un tudesco, a retorcerla y volverla a sacar, ¿eh?

Esbozó una extraña sonrisa, retrocedió y se cuadró, mientras un extraño fulgor se encendía en sus pálidos ojos.

—Gracias.

Harry se cuadró a su vez y dio media vuelta para cruzar hacia Gillingham Street. Frunció el ceño. Las palabras del hombre le habían causado una profunda repugnancia.

En Victoria, el ajetreo había sido como el de cualquier lunes normal; al parecer, las noticias según las cuales en Londres las cosas seguían como de costumbre eran ciertas. Mientras recorría las anchas calles georgianas, observó que todo estaba tranquilo bajo el sol otoñal. De no ser por las cintas adhesivas de color blanco que se cruzaban sobre las ventanas para protegerlas de las explosiones, todo estaba como antes de la guerra. De vez en cuando, pasaba algún hombre de negocios con bombín y seguía habiendo niñeras que empujaban cochecitos infantiles. Las expresiones de la gente eran normales, e incluso alegres. Muchas personas se habían dejado las máscaras antigás en casa, aunque Harry llevaba la suya en una caja cuadrada colgada del hombro en bandolera. Sabía que el desafiante buen humor de que hacía gala casi todo el mundo ocultaba el temor a una invasión; pero él prefería la ficción de que todo era normal a las cosas que le hacían recordar a cada momento que ahora vivían en un mundo donde los restos del ejército británico se arremolinaban sumidos en el caos en una playa francesa y los trastornados veteranos de las trincheras paseaban por las calles, presagiando alegremente la llegada de un apocalíptico fin del mundo.

Sus pensamientos regresaron a Rookwood, como le solía ocurrir últimamente. El viejo patio del colegio en un día primaveral, los profesores con sus togas y birretes paseando bajo los olmos, los chicos que se cruzaban con ellos con sus *blazers* azules o sus blancos uniformes de críquet. Era una huida al otro lado del espejo, lejos de la locura. Pero más tarde o más temprano el doloroso y pesado pensamiento siempre conseguía insinuarse: ¿cómo demonios era posible que todo hubiera cambiado de aquello a esto?

El hotel St Ermin's había sido lujoso en otros tiempos, pero ahora su elegancia se había esfumado; la araña de cristal del vestíbulo estaba cubierta de polvo y se respiraba en el aire olor a repollo y betún. Unas acuarelas de venados y lagos de las Tierras Altas de Escocia cubrían las paredes revestidas de paneles de madera de roble. En algún lugar, un reloj de péndulo emitía un soñoliento tictac.

No había nadie en el mostrador de recepción. Harry pulsó el timbre y apareció un corpulento calvo enfundado en un uniforme de conserje.

—Buenos días, señor —dijo con el relajado y relamido tono propio de alguien que lleva toda la vida sirviendo—. Confío en no haberle hecho esperar.

—Tengo una cita a las dos y media con una tal señorita Maxse. Teniente Brett.

Siguiendo las instrucciones de su interlocutor del Foreign Office, Harry pronunció el nombre de la mujer como «Macksie».

El hombre asintió con la cabeza.

—Acompáñeme, si es tan amable.

Pisando en silencio la mullida y polvorienta alfombra, guió a Harry hasta un salón lleno de sillones y mesitas de café. Estaba desierto, salvo por un hombre y una mujer que había sentados junto a un mirador.

—El teniente Brett, señora.

El recepcionista se inclinó y se retiró.

Ambos se levantaron. La mujer le tendió la mano. Tenía cincuenta y tantos años, era menuda y de complexión delicada y vestía un elegante traje sastre de color azul. Tenía el cabello gris fuertemente rizado y un anguloso e inteligente rostro. Sus penetrantes ojos grises se cruzaron con los de Harry.

—¿Cómo está usted?, encantada de conocerlo. —Su autoritaria voz de contralto le hizo recordar a Harry a una directora de escuela de niñas—. Marjorie Maxse. Me han hablado mucho de usted.

—Nada malo, espero.

—Todo lo contrario. Permítame que le presente a Roger Jebb.

El hombre estrechó la mano de Harry con un fuerte apretón. Tenía aproximadamente la misma edad que la señorita Maxse, un alargado y bronceado rostro y un ralo cabello negro.

—¿Le apetece un poco de té? —preguntó la señorita Maxse.

—Gracias.

En una mesa había una tetera de plata y unas tazas de porcelana. Junto con una bandeja de panecillos, varios tarros de mermelada y lo que parecía nata de verdad. La señorita Maxse empezó a servir el té.

—¿Algún problema para venir? Tengo entendido que anoche cayeron una o dos bombas por aquí.

—Victoria Street está cerrada.

—Es un fastidio. Y eso va a seguir así durante algún tiempo. —Habla como si se estuviera refiriendo a unos días de lluvia. Sonrió—: Para la primera entrevista preferimos reunirnos aquí con la gente nueva. El director es un viejo amigo nuestro y, por consiguiente, no nos van a molestar. ¿Azúcar? —Siguió hablando con el mismo tono familiar—. Tome un panecillo, son exquisitos.

—Gracias.

Harry lo untó con nata y mermelada. Levantó los ojos y observó que la señorita Maxse lo estaba estudiando atentamente; ésta le dirigió una sonrisa cordial sin avergonzarse lo más mínimo.

—¿Qué tal se encuentra ahora? Le dieron de baja por invalidez, ¿no es cierto? ¿Después de Dunkerque?

—Sí. Una bomba cayó a seis metros de distancia. Levantó un montón de arena. Tuve suerte; eso me salvó de lo peor de la explosión.

Ahora vio que Jebb también lo escrutaba con unos ojos grises como el pedernal.

—Tengo entendido que sufrió una buena neurosis de guerra —dijo bruscamente Jebb.

—Fue muy poca cosa —dijo Harry—. Ahora ya estoy bien.

—Por un segundo, se le quedó el rostro blanco, allá fuera —dijo Jebb.

—Bueno, fue bastante más que un segundo —contestó Harry serenamente—. Y me temblaban constantemente las manos. Mejor que lo sepa.

—Y su oído también resultó afectado, ¿verdad?

La señorita Maxse formuló la pregunta en voz muy baja, pero Harry la oyó.

—Eso también se ha normalizado prácticamente. Sólo una leve sordera en el oído izquierdo.

—Es una suerte —comentó Jebb—. La pérdida de capacidad auditiva causada por una explosión suele ser permanente. —Se sacó un sujetapapeles del bolsillo y empezó a doblarlo con aire ausente, sin dejar de mirar a Harry.

—El médico dijo que tuve mucha suerte.

—La pérdida auditiva significa el término del servicio activo, naturalmente —terció la señorita Maxse—. Aunque sea leve. Eso tiene que ser duro. Se incorporó de inmediato el pasado mes de septiembre, ¿verdad?

Se inclinó hacia delante, sosteniendo la taza de té con ambas manos.

—Sí. Sí, en efecto. Disculpe, señorita Maxse, pero es que no sé nada...

Ella volvió a sonreír.

—Claro. ¿Qué le dijeron los del Foreign Office cuando lo llamaron?

—Simplemente que algunas personas de allí pensaban que quizás habría algún trabajo que yo pudiera hacer.

—Bien, ahora ya no dependemos del FO. —La señorita Maxse esbozó una alegre sonrisa—. Somos el Servicio de Inteligencia.

Soltó una sonrisa cantarina como abrumada por el extraño carácter de la situación.

—¡Ah! —dijo Harry.

La voz de la señorita Maxse adquirió un tono más serio.

—Nuestra tarea es decisiva, extremadamente decisiva. Ahora que Francia ha caído, el continente o bien está aliado con los nazis o bien depende de ellos. Ya no hay relaciones diplomáticas normales.

—Ahora el frente somos nosotros —añadió Jebb—. ¿Fuma?

—No, gracias. No fumo.

—Su tío es el coronel James Brett, ¿verdad?

—Sí, señor, en efecto.

—Sirvió conmigo en la India. ¡Allá por el año 1910, tanto si lo cree como si no! —Jebb soltó una áspera carcajada—. ¿Cómo está?

—Ya retirado.

«Pero, a juzgar por este bronceado, usted sigue en la brecha —pensó Harry—. La policía india, tal vez.»

La señorita Maxse posó la taza sobre la mesa y juntó las manos.

—¿Le gustaría trabajar para nosotros? —preguntó.

Harry volvió a experimentar el viejo cansancio de siempre; pero también otra cosa, una chispa de interés.

—Sigo estando dispuesto a participar en el esfuerzo bélico, por supuesto.

—¿Se siente en condiciones de enfrentarse a una tarea agotadora? —preguntó Jebb—. Ahora en serio. Si le parece que no, tiene que decirlo. No hay de qué avergonzarse —añadió con aspereza.

La señorita Maxse esbozó una alentadora sonrisa.

—Creo que sí —contestó cautelosamente Harry—. Ya he vuelto prácticamente a la normalidad.

—Estamos reclutando a mucha gente, Harry —dijo la señorita Maxse—. Puedo llamarle Harry, ¿verdad? A algunas personas, porque creemos que son adecuadas para la clase de trabajo que hacemos, y a otras, porque nos pueden ofrecer algo especial. Bueno, pues usted era especialista en lenguas modernas antes de incorporarse a nuestro servicio. Se graduó en Cambridge y después una beca en el King's hasta que estalló la guerra.

—Sí, en efecto.

Sabían muchas cosas acerca de él.

—¿Cómo es su español? ¿Fluido?

Aquella pregunta era sorprendente.

—Yo diría que sí.

—Su especialidad es la literatura francesa, ¿verdad?

Harry frunció el entrecejo.

—Sí, pero sigo practicando el español. Pertenezco a un Círculo Español en Cambridge.

Jebb asintió con la cabeza.

—Integrado principalmente por miembros del mundo académico, ¿no? Obras de teatro españolas y cosas por el estilo.

—Sí.

—¿Algún exiliado de la Guerra Civil?

—Uno o dos. —Harry sostuvo la mirada de Jebb—. Pero el Círculo no es de carácter político. Tenemos el acuerdo tácito de evitar la política.

Jebb depositó el sujetapapeles sobre la mesa, torturado ahora hasta quedar convertido en unos fantásticos bucles, y abrió su cartera de documentos. Sacó una carpeta de cartón con una cruz roja diagonal en la parte anterior.

—Me gustaría que volvamos al año 1931 —dijo—. Su segundo curso en Cambridge. Fue a España aquel verano, ¿verdad? Con un amigo de su colegio, Rookwood.

Harry volvió a fruncir el entrecejo. ¿Cómo podían saber todo aquello?

—Sí.

Jebb abrió la carpeta.

—Un tal Bernard Piper, más tarde miembro del Partido Comunista. Fue a combatir en la Guerra Civil española. Se dio por desaparecido y se cree que resultó muerto en la batalla del Jarama, 1937. —Sacó una fotografía y la depositó encima de la mesa. Una hilera de hombres con arrugados uniformes militares en la pelada ladera de una colina. Bernie ocupaba el centro, más alto que los demás, con el cabello rubio muy corto, sonriendo a la cámara como un chiquillo.

Harry miró a Jebb.

—¿Fue tomada en España?

—Sí. —Entornó los duros ojos—. Y usted fue a ver si lo encontraba.

—A petición de su familia, porque yo hablaba español.

—Pero no tuvo suerte.

—Hubo diez mil muertos en el Jarama —dijo Harry fríamente—.

No todos fueron identificados. Probablemente Bernie se encuentra en una fosa común en algún lugar de las afueras de Madrid. Señor, ¿le puedo preguntar de dónde ha sacado toda esta información? Creo que tengo derecho a...

—La verdad es que no lo tiene; pero, puesto que lo pregunta, aquí conservamos las fichas de todos los miembros del Partido Comunista. Da lo mismo; ahora Stalin ha ayudado a Hitler a masacrar Polonia.

La señorita Maxse esbozó una sonrisa conciliadora.

—Nadie lo asocia a usted con ellos.

—Eso espero —dijo Harry.

—¿Diría usted que tiene alguna tendencia política determinada?

No era la clase de pregunta que uno espera que le formulen en Inglaterra. Los conocimientos que tenían de su vida, de la historia de Bernie, le molestaban. Titubeó antes de contestar:

—Supongo que, en todo caso, soy una especie de *tory* liberal.

—¿No tuvo la tentación de ir a combatir en defensa de la República española, como Piper? —preguntó Jebb—, ¿en la cruzada contra el fascismo?

—Que yo sepa, antes de la Guerra Civil España era un maldito caos y tanto la derecha como los comunistas se aprovecharon de ello. Tropecé con algunos rusos en el treinta y siete. Eran unos cerdos.

—Eso de ir a Madrid en plena Guerra Civil debió de ser toda una aventura —dijo con entusiasmo la señorita Maxse

—Fui con la idea de intentar encontrar a mi amigo. Por su familia, tal como he dicho.

—En la escuela eran ustedes amigos íntimos, ¿verdad? —preguntó Jebb.

—¿Ha estado usted haciendo preguntas en Rookwood? —La idea lo enfurecía.

—Sí —Jebb asintió con la cabeza sin disculparse.

De repente, Harry abrió los ojos como platos.

—¿Todo eso es por Bernie? ¿Acaso está vivo?

—Nuestra ficha sobre Bernard Piper está cerrada —dijo Jebb en tono inesperadamente amable—. Que nosotros sepamos, murió en el Jarama.

La señorita Maxse se incorporó en su asiento.

—Tiene usted que comprender, Harry, que para tener claro si puede trabajar para nosotros tenemos que saberlo todo sobre su persona. Pero creo que estamos satisfechos. —Jebb asintió con la cabeza, y ella prosiguió—: Creo que ha llegado el momento de que vayamos al grano. Normalmente, no nos lanzaríamos en picado como lo estamos haciendo, pero es una cuestión de tiempo, ¿comprende? De urgencia. Necesitamos obtener información acerca de alguien. Y creemos que usted está en situación de ayudar. Podría ser muy importante.

Jebb se inclinó hacia delante.

—Todo lo que le digamos a partir de ahora es estrictamente confidencial, ¿está claro? Es más, debo advertirle de que, como haga cualquier comentario al respecto fuera de esta habitación, sufrirá graves consecuencias.

Harry lo miró a los ojos.

—De acuerdo.

—Esto no tiene nada que ver con Bernie Piper. Se trata de otro antiguo compañero suyo de escuela que también estableció ciertas conexiones políticas muy interesantes. —Jebb volvió a rebuscar en su cartera y depositó otra fotografía sobre la mesa.

Era un rostro que Harry no esperaba volver a ver en su vida. Sandy Forsyth debía de tener treinta y un años, unos cuantos meses más que él, pero aparentaba bastantes menos. Lucía un poblado bigote a lo Clark Gable y el cabello, perfectamente engominado, mostraba entradas en la frente. Su rostro era más mofletudo de lo que lo recordaba y le habían salido unas cuantas arrugas, pero los ojos penetrantes, la nariz aguileña y la boca ancha de labios delgados seguían siendo los mismos. Era una fotografía preparada; Sandy sonreía a la cámara con expresión de astro cinematográfico, medio enigmático y medio provocativo. No era un hombre apuesto, pero el fotógrafo había conseguido que lo pareciera. Harry volvió a levantar la vista.

—Yo no lo llamaría amigo íntimo —dijo en voz baja.

—Fueron ustedes amigos durante un tiempo, Harry —dijo la señorita Maxse—. Un año antes de que lo expulsaran. Después de aquel asunto relacionado con el señor Taylor. Hemos hablado con él, ¿sabe?

—El señor Taylor... —Harry titubeó momentáneamente—. ¿Cómo está?

—Muy bien, por ahora —contestó Jebb—. Pero no gracias a Forsyth. Bueno, pues cuando lo expulsaron, ¿se despidieron ustedes como amigos? —Señaló a Harry con el sujetapapeles—: Eso es muy importante.

—Sí. De hecho, yo era el único amigo que Forsyth tenía en Rookwood.

—Jamás hubiese imaginado que tendrían ustedes tantas cosas en común —dijo la señorita Maxse con una sonrisa.

—En muchos sentidos no teníamos demasiadas.

—Forsyth no era muy buena pieza, ¿verdad? No acababa de encajar. Pero usted siempre fue muy buen compañero con él.

Harry suspiró.

—Sandy también tenía su lado bueno. Aunque... —Hizo una pausa.

La señorita Maxse le dirigió una sonrisa alentadora.

—A veces me preguntaba por qué quería ser amigo mío. Porque casi todas las personas con las que se relacionaba eran... bueno, un poco malas piezas, para utilizar su expresión.

—¿No le parece a usted que quizás hubiera algo de tipo sexual, Harry?

El tono de la señorita Maxse era tan ligero y despreocupado como cuando hablaba de las bombas. Por un instante, Harry la miró con asombro y después soltó una carcajada.

—Por supuesto que no —respondió.

—Lamento importunarlo, pero estas cosas ocurren en las escuelas privadas. Enamoramientos, ya sabe.

—No hubo nada de todo eso.

—Cuando Forsyth se fue —dijo Jebb—, ¿siguieron ustedes en contacto?

—Nos carteamos durante un par de años. Cada vez menos, a medida que pasaba el tiempo. Desde que Sandy se fue de Rookwood, no hemos tenido demasiado en común. —Harry suspiró de nuevo—. En realidad, no estoy muy seguro de por qué me siguió escribiendo durante tanto tiempo. Tal vez para impresionarme... me hablaba de clubes y de chicas y cosas por el estilo.

Jebb asintió con la cabeza, instándolo a seguir adelante.

—En su última carta —continuó Harry— me decía que estaba trabajando para un corredor de apuestas de Londres. Me hablaba de caballos dopados y de resultados amañados como si todo aquello tuviese mucha gracia.

Harry recordó de pronto la otra cara de Sandy: los paseos por los Downs en busca de fósiles, las largas conversaciones. Pero ¿qué quería aquella gente?

—Sigue usted creyendo en los valores tradicionales, ¿verdad? —preguntó la señorita Maxse con una sonrisa—. En lo que Rookwood representa.

—Supongo que sí. Aunque...

—¿Sí?

—Me pregunto cómo ha llegado el país a esta situación. —Harry la miró a los ojos—. No estábamos preparados para lo que ocurrió en Francia. Me refiero a la derrota.

—Los franceses, esos cobardes, nos decepcionaron —masculló Jebb.

—A nosotros también nos obligaron a retirarnos, señor —dijo Harry—. Yo estuve allí.

—Tiene razón. No estábamos debidamente preparados —dijo la señorita Maxse con tono enfático—. Quizá fuimos demasiado honestos en Múnich. Después de la Gran Guerra no podíamos creer que alguien deseara meterse en otra. Pero ahora sabemos que Hitler siempre lo quiso. No estará contento hasta que no tenga toda Europa bajo su yugo. La Nueva Era del Oscurantismo, como la llama Winston.

Hubo un momento de silencio, tras el cual Jebb carraspeó.

—Bueno, Harry. Quiero hablar de España. Cuando Francia cayó el pasado mes de junio y Mussolini nos declaró la guerra, esperábamos que Franco fuera el siguiente. Hitler ha ganado la Guerra Civil para él y, como es natural, Franco quiere Gibraltar. Con ayuda de los alemanes, podría conquistarlo desde tierra, y entonces nosotros tendríamos vedado el acceso al Mediterráneo.

—Ahora mismo, España está arruinada —dijo Harry—. Franco no podría ganar otra guerra.

—Pero podría dejar pasar a Hitler. Hay divisiones de la Wehrmacht esperando en la frontera francoespañola. Los falangistas quieren entrar en guerra. —Jebb inclinó la cabeza—. Por otra parte, los generales leales a la monarquía desconfían de la Falange y temen una revuelta popular en caso de que entren los alemanes. No son fascistas, simplemente quieren derrotar a los rojos. Es una situación incierta, Franco podría declarar la guerra cualquier día de éstos. La gente de nuestra embajada en Madrid tiene los nervios a flor de piel.

—Franco es precavido —apuntó Harry—. Muchos piensan que si hubiera sido más audaz habría podido ganar la guerra mucho antes.

Jebb soltó un gruñido.

—Espero que tenga usted razón. Sir Samuel Hoare ha sido enviado allí como embajador para tratar de mantenerlos al margen de la contienda.

—Eso he oído.

—Su economía está arruinada, como usted dice. Esta debilidad es nuestra mejor carta, porque la Marina británica sigue controlando lo que entra y lo que sale.

—El bloqueo.

—Por suerte, los americanos no se oponen. Estamos autorizando la entrada de suficiente petróleo como para permitir que España siga funcionando, en realidad algo menos. Y acaban de sufrir otra mala cosecha. Tratan de importar trigo y de conseguir préstamos en el extranjero para pagarlo. Según nuestros informes, en las fábricas de Barcelona la gente se desmaya de hambre.

—Suena casi tan grave como durante la Guerra Civil. —Harry sacudió la cabeza—. Lo han pasado muy mal.

—Ahora nos llega de España toda clase de rumores. Franco está explorando todos los medios posibles para alcanzar la autarquía económica, buena parte de ellos totalmente descabellados. El año pasado un científico austriaco descubrió la manera de fabricar petróleo sintético a partir de extractos vegetales, y él le entregó dinero para que desarrollara la idea. Todo fue un timo, naturalmente. —Jebb volvió a soltar una carcajada que más parecía un ladrido—. Después dijeron que habían hallado unas grandes reservas de oro en Badajoz. Otro engaño. Pero ahora nos aseguran que han descubierto unos depósitos de oro en la sierra, cerca de Madrid. Tienen a un ingeniero con experiencia en Sudáfrica trabajando para ellos, un tal Alberto Otero. Y lo mantienen todo en secreto, lo cual nos induce a pensar que algo de cierto debe de haber en ello. Los científicos afirman que es geológicamente posible.

—¿Y eso haría que España no dependiera tanto de nosotros?

—No tienen reservas de oro para respaldar su moneda. Durante la guerra Stalin hizo que las reservas de oro se enviaran a Moscú. Y, como es natural, se las quedó. Por eso les resulta tan difícil comprar en el mercado libre. En estos momentos están tratando de conseguir de nosotros y de los yanquis créditos a la exportación.

—O sea que, si los rumores son ciertos, dependerían menos de nosotros.

—Exactamente. Por eso se muestran más favorables a entrar en guerra. Cualquier cosa podría inclinar la balanza.

—Intentamos llevar a cabo allí una operación muy arriesgada —señaló la señorita Maxse—. Debemos calcular cuántas sanciones aplicar y cuántos incentivos ofrecer. Cuánto trigo dejar que pase, cuánto petróleo.

Jebb asintió con la cabeza.

—El caso, Brett, es que el hombre que presentó a Otero al régimen fue Sandy Forsyth.

—¿Está en España? —Harry abrió los ojos como platos.

—Sí. No sé si vio usted unos anuncios en la prensa hace un par de años, sobre las giras por los campos de batalla de la Guerra Civil.

—Los recuerdo. Los nacionales organizaban recorridos para los ingleses. Un alarde propagandístico.

—Forsyth consiguió introducirse, no sé cómo. Fue a España como guía turístico. Los de Franco le pagaban muy bien. Después se quedó en el país y participó en toda una serie de negocios, supongo que algunos de ellos bastante turbios. Al parecer es un hombre de negocios muy hábil, aunque algo... impresentable. —Jebb torció la boca en una mueca de desagrado y después miró fijamente a Harry—. Ahora cuenta con algunos contactos importantes.

Harry respiró hondo.

—¿Puedo preguntar cómo ha averiguado usted todo eso?

Jebb se encogió de hombros.

—A través de sinuosos y escurridizos confidentes que trabajan fuera del ámbito de nuestra embajada. Pagan a funcionarios de segunda a cambio de información. Madrid está lleno de espías, pero ninguno de ellos ha establecido contacto directo con Forsyth. No tenemos agentes en la Falange, y Forsyth actúa en colaboración con el sector falangista del Gobierno. Dicen que es muy listo y que enseguida se olería algo raro en caso de que apareciera un desconocido y empezara a hacer preguntas.

—Sí. —Harry asintió con la cabeza—. Sandy es listo.

—Pero ¿y si usted se dejara caer por Madrid? —dijo la señorita Maxse—. Por ejemplo, como traductor adscrito a la embajada. Podría topar con él en un café, como ocurre a menudo, y renovar una vieja amistad.

—Queremos que usted averigüe qué está haciendo —dijo directamente Jebb—. Y que procure que se pase a nuestro bando.

O sea que era eso. Querían que espiara a Sandy, como había hecho muchos años atrás el señor Taylor en Rookwood. A través de la ventana, Harry contempló el cielo azul donde los globos de barrera flotaban cual gigantescas ballenas grises.

—¿Qué le parece? —preguntó suavemente la señorita Maxse.

—Sandy Forsyth está trabajando con la Falange. —Harry meneó la cabeza—. Y no es que necesite ganar dinero, precisamente... Su padre es obispo de la Iglesia anglicana.

—A veces, cuenta tanto la emoción como la política, Harry. Ambas cosas van juntas, en ocasiones.

—Es verdad. —Harry recordó a Sandy entrando sin resuello en el estudio, de vuelta de una de sus ilegales correrías de apuestas, y abriendo la mano para mostrar un arrugado billete de cinco libras. «Mira qué le he sacado a un primo»—. Trabaja con la Falange —continuó en tono pensativo—. Creo que siempre fue una oveja negra; pero, a veces..., un hombre puede hacer algo contra las normas y crearse una mala fama que luego empeora su situación.

—No tenemos nada en contra de las ovejas negras —dijo Jebb—. Las ovejas negras suelen ser inmejorables agentes. —Soltó una risita de complicidad.

Otro recuerdo de Sandy le vino a la mente a Harry. Miraba hacia el lado opuesto de la mesa del estudio y hablaba en un amargo susurro: «Sabes cómo son, cómo nos controlan, lo que hacen cuando nosotros intentamos escapar.»

—Veo que le gusta participar en el juego —dijo la señorita Maxse—. Es lo que esperábamos. Pero no podemos ganar esta guerra jugando limpio. —Sacudió la cabeza con expresión de tristeza—. No contra este enemigo. Habrá que matar, eso usted ya lo sabe. Y también habrá que engañar, me temo. —Esbozó una sonrisa de disculpa.

Harry sintió que en su interior se arremolinaban sentimientos encontrados, mientras el pánico empezaba a apoderarse de él. La idea de regresar a España lo entusiasmaba y lo horrorizaba. Había oído cosas muy malas por boca de exiliados españoles en Cambridge. En los Noticiarios Documentales había visto a Franco dirigirse a multitudes enfervorizadas que lo saludaban brazo en alto; pero se decía que, detrás de todo aquello, se ocultaba un mundo de denuncias y detenciones nocturnas. ¿Y Sandy Forsyth estaba metido en aquel fregado? Volvió a estudiar la fotografía.

—No estoy seguro —dijo muy despacio—. Quiero decir que no estoy seguro de poder hacerlo.

—Le hemos facilitado instrucción —dijo Jebb—. Ha sido un cursillo acelerado, porque las autoridades quieren una respuesta lo antes posible. —Miró a Harry—. Me refiero a personas del más alto nivel.

Una parte de Harry habría querido echarse atrás en aquel preciso instante, regresar a Surrey y olvidarse de todo. Pero se había pasado los últimos tres meses luchando contra aquel aterrorizado impulso de esconderse.

—¿Qué clase de instrucción? —preguntó—. No estoy muy seguro de poder engañar a nadie.

—Es más fácil de lo que usted piensa —replicó la señorita Maxse—. Si cree en la causa por la que miente. Y, hablando claro, usted tendría que mentir y engañar. Pero nosotros le enseñaríamos todas las malas artes.

Harry se mordió el labio inferior. Por un rato reinó el silencio en la estancia.

—No esperaríamos que usted se lanzara en frío.

—De acuerdo —dijo Harry—. Quizá logre convencer a Sandy. No puedo creer que sea un fascista.

—El principio será lo más duro —dijo Jebb—. Conseguir ganarse su confianza. Será entonces cuando todo le parecerá extraño y difícil y cuando más necesidad tendrá de fingir.

—Sí. Sandy es alguien que las ve venir a distancia.

—Lo imaginamos.

La señorita Maxse se volvió hacia Jebb. Éste titubeó momentáneamente y, después, asintió.

—Muy bien, pues —dijo en tono expeditivo la señorita Maxse.

—Habrá que actuar con rapidez —dijo Jebb—. Tomar algunas disposiciones y organizar las cosas. Tendrá usted que ser debidamente examinado, claro. ¿Va usted a quedarse esta noche?

—Sí. Iré a casa de mi primo.

Jebb volvió a mirar incisivamente a Harry.

—¿Ningún nexo aquí, aparte de su familia?

—No —contestó Harry, meneando la cabeza.

Jebb sacó una pequeña agenda.

—¿Número?

Harry se lo dio.

—Alguien le llamará mañana. No salga, por favor.

—De acuerdo, señor.

Los tres se levantaron de sus asientos. La señorita Maxse estrechó cordialmente la mano de Harry.

—Gracias, Harry —dijo.

Jebb lo miró con una sonrisita tensa.

—Prepárese para la sirena de esta noche. Se esperan más incursiones aéreas.

Arrojó el retorcido sujetapapeles a una papelera.

—Por Dios —dijo la señorita Maxse—. Eso es propiedad del Estado. Es usted un manirroto, Roger. —Volvió a mirar a Harry con una sonrisa de despedida—. Le estamos muy agradecidos, Harry. Esto podría ser muy importante.

Fuera de la estancia, Harry se detuvo un momento. Una pesada sensación de tristeza se le instaló en el estómago. Malas artes: ¿qué demonios significaba aquello? Las palabras lo hicieron temblar. Advirtió que, de manera semiinconsciente, estaba tratando de escuchar, como Sandy solía hacer tras las puertas de los profesores, con la oreja sana pegada a la puerta, para captar lo que Jebb y la señorita Maxse pudieran estar diciendo. Pero no consiguió oír nada. Al volverse, vio que estaba allí el recepcionista, cuyas pisadas habían sido amortiguadas por la alfombra polvorienta. Esbozó una sonrisa nerviosa y dejó que el hombre lo acompañara a la puerta. ¿Ya estaría adquiriendo los hábitos de un... qué: fisgón, espía, traidor?

2

Normalmente, el trayecto hasta la casa de Will, en Harrow, duraba menos de una hora; pero aquel día le llevó media tarde, pues el metro se detenía y volvía a ponerse en marcha a cada momento. En las estaciones, pequeños grupos de gente permanecían acurrucados en el suelo de los andenes con el rostro lívido a causa del miedo. Harry había oído que algunos habitantes del bombardeado distrito del East End se habían instalado en las estaciones de metro.

La idea de «espiar» a Sandy Forsyth le produjo una desagradable sensación de incredulidad. Contempló los pálidos y cansados rostros de sus compañeros de viaje y pensó que cualquiera de ellos podría ser un espía... ¿Cómo iba a saberlo por el aspecto de la gente? La fotografía acudía una y otra vez a su mente: la confiada sonrisa de Sandy, el bigote a lo Clark Gable. El tren siguió avanzando lentamente por los túneles.

Rookwood le había otorgado a Harry una identidad. Su padre, que era abogado, había quedado destrozado en la batalla del Somme cuando él tenía seis años, y su madre había muerto durante la epidemia de gripe del invierno en que había terminado la Primera Guerra, tal como la gente empezaba a llamar la última guerra. Harry aún conservaba la fotografía y la contemplaba a menudo. Su padre, posando delante de la iglesia con chaqué, se parecía mucho a él: moreno, robusto y con aire de persona seria y responsable. Rodeaba con el brazo a su esposa, rubia como el primo Will, y tenía una rizada cabellera que le caía sobre los hombros, bajo un sombrero eduardiano de ala ancha. Ambos miraban sonrientes a la cámara. La imagen se había tomado con un sol radiante y estaba ligeramente sobreexpuesta, lo cual creaba unos halos de luz alrededor de sus cabezas. Harry apenas se acordaba de ellos; al igual que el mundo de la fotografía, ambos se habían desvanecido como un sueño.

Al morir su madre, Harry se había ido a vivir con su tío James, el hermano mayor de su padre, un oficial del ejército profesional que había resultado herido en las primeras batallas de 1914. Tenía una herida en el estómago que, aunque casi no se le notaba, le provocaba constantes molestias estomacales que le habían agriado un carácter ya muy áspero de por sí, el cual constituía una perenne fuente de preocupación para tía Emily, su aprensiva y angustiada esposa. Cuando Harry se fue a vivir con ellos en su bonita casa de un pueblo de Surrey, tenían sólo cuarenta y tantos años pero ya parecían mucho mayores, como una pareja de jubilados inquietos y quisquillosos.

Se mostraban afectuosos con él, pero Harry siempre se había sentido un intruso. No tenían hijos y siempre daban la impresión de no saber qué hacer con él. Tío James le daba unas palmadas en la espalda que casi lo tumbaban y le preguntaba con entusiasmo a qué iba a jugar aquel día, mientras su tía se preocupaba constantemente por si comía bien o no.

De vez en cuando se iba a casa de tía Jenny, hermana de su madre y madre de Will. Ésta había querido mucho a su hermana y le dolía recordarla; pero lo abrumaba, tal vez con cierto remordimiento, a base de paquetes de comida y giros postales cuando iba a la escuela.

En su infancia, a Harry le había dado clase un maestro particular, un profesor jubilado al que su tío conocía. Se pasaba casi todo el tiempo libre, vagando por las calles y los bosques de los alrededores del pueblo. Allí conoció a los chicos del lugar, hijos de campesinos y de veterinarios; pero, aunque jugaba a indios y vaqueros y cazaba conejos con ellos, siempre se mantenía un poco apartado. Harry *el Presumido*, lo llamaban.

—Di «horrible», Harry —lo pinchaban—. Ogib... ble, ogib... ble.

Un día de verano en que Harry regresó a casa del campo, tío James lo llamó a su estudio. Tenía apenas doce años. Había otro hombre de pie en la estancia, junto a la ventana, iluminado directamente por el sol de tal manera que, al principio, no fue más que una alta sombra enmarcada por motas de polvo.

—Quiero presentarte al señor Taylor —dijo tío James—. Enseña en mi vieja escuela. Mi *alma mater*, como suele decirse. Eso es latín, ¿verdad?

Y, para asombro de Harry, su tío rió nerviosamente como un niño. El hombre se adelantó y estrechó con firmeza la mano de Harry. Era alto y delgado y vestía de oscuro. El cabello negro empezaba a ralear desde su nacimiento en pico sobre la despejada frente, y sus perspicaces ojos grises lo estudiaban desde detrás de unos quevedos.

—¿Cómo estás, Harry? —La voz sonaba muy seca—. Ya veo que eres un poco golfillo, ¿verdad?

—Se está volviendo un poco salvaje —dijo tío James en tono de disculpa.

—Eso ya lo arreglaremos si vienes a Rookwood. ¿Te gustaría ir a una escuela privada, Harry?

—No lo sé, señor.

—El informe de tu maestro es bueno. ¿Te gusta el rugby?

—Nunca he jugado, señor. Yo juego al fútbol con los chicos del pueblo.

—El rugby es mucho mejor. Un juego de caballeros.

—Rookwood fue la escuela de tu padre, y también la mía —explicó tío James.

Harry levantó la mirada.

—¿De mi padre?

—Sí. Tu *pater*, como dicen en Rookwood.

—¿Sabes qué significa *pater*, Harry? —preguntó el señor Taylor.

—Significa padre en latín, señor.

—Muy bien —dijo el señor Taylor, sonriendo—. Creo que el muchacho será apto, Brett.

Hizo otras preguntas. Era muy amable; pero su aire autoritario, propio de una persona que espera obediencia de los demás, hizo que Harry se pusiera sobre aviso. Al cabo de un rato, lo mandaron retirarse de la estancia, mientras el señor Taylor proseguía la conversación con su tío. Cuando tío James lo volvió a llamar, el señor Taylor ya se había ido. Su tío le pidió que se sentara y lo miró con la cara muy seria, acariciándose el bigote canoso.

—Tu tía y yo creemos que ha llegado el momento de que acudas al internado, Harry. Es mejor que quedarte aquí con un par de vejestorios como nosotros. Además, debes relacionarte con chicos de tu clase, y no con los del pueblo.

Harry no tenía ni idea de cómo era una escuela privada. Le vino a la mente la imagen de un enorme edificio lleno de una luz radiante como la de la fotografía de sus padres dándole la bienvenida.

—¿Qué te parece, Harry? ¿Crees que te gustaría?

—Sí, tío, me gustaría.

Will vivía en una calle de chalets de falso estilo Tudor. Un nuevo refugio antiaéreo, una alargada construcción de hormigón, se levantaba incongruentemente al borde del césped.

Su primo ya estaba en casa y le abrió la puerta. Se había cambiado de ropa y se había puesto un jersey vistoso y largo. Miró jovialmente a Harry a través de los cristales de sus gafas.

—¡Hola, Harry! ¿Todo bien, entonces?

—Muy bien, gracias. —Harry le estrechó la mano—. ¿Y tú cómo estás, Will?

—Pues aguantando, como todo el mundo. ¿Qué tal el oído?

—Casi normal. Un poquito sordo de uno.

Will hizo pasar a Harry al recibidor. Una mujer alta y delgada de cabello grisáceo y alargado rostro, torcido en una mueca de reproche, salió de la cocina secándose las manos con una servilleta de té.

—Muriel. —Harry se esforzó por esbozar una sonrisa cordial—. ¿Cómo estás?

—Voy tirando. No te doy la mano porque he estado guisando. He pensado que podríamos saltarnos la merienda y cenar directamente.

»Me las he ingeniado para conseguir un bistec. He conseguido llegar a un acuerdo con el carnicero. Bueno, pues, sube al piso de arriba, querrás lavarte las manos.

Harry ya había ocupado anteriormente el dormitorio de la parte de atrás. Había una espaciosa cama de matrimonio y pequeños adornos sobre unos tapetitos en la mesa del tocador.

—Vamos —dijo Will—. Refréscate y bajas.

Harry se lavó la cara en el pequeño lavabo y se estudió en el espejo mientras se secaba. Estaba engordando: su recia figura empezaba a acumular grasa a causa de la reciente falta de ejercicio, y el mentón cuadrado se le había redondeado. La gente le decía que tenía un rostro atractivo, a pesar de que él siempre había pensado que sus regulares facciones bajo el cabello rizado y castaño eran un poco demasiado anchas para ser hermosas. Últimamente, le habían salido unas arrugas alrededor de los ojos. Trató de conseguir que su rostro adoptara un gesto lo más inexpresivo posible. ¿Podría Sandy leerle el pensamiento tras semejante máscara? Era lo que se solía hacer en la escuela para ocultar los propios sentimientos... Éstos sólo se revelaban por medio de una boca fuertemente apretada o una ceja enarcada. La gente buscaba las pequeñas señales. Ahora tenía que aprender a no dejar traslucir nada, ninguna emoción. Se tumbó en la cama recordando la escuela y a Sandy Forsyth.

A Harry la escuela le gustó desde el principio. Con sede en una mansión del siglo XVIII, en plena campiña de Sussex, el colegio de Rookwood había sido fundado por un grupo de hombres de negocios que comerciaban en Ultramar, con el propósito de facilitar la educación a los hijos de los oficiales de sus barcos. Los apellidos de La Casa reflejaban su pasado naval: Raleigh, Drake y Hawkins. Ahora estudiaban allí los hijos de funcionarios de la Administración y de aristócratas de segunda junto con un grupo de becarios, financiados por medio de donaciones.

El colegio y sus costumbres ordenadas le otorgaron una sensación de pertenencia y de propósito. Tal vez la disciplina fuera dura, pero raras veces se utilizaba el castigo de copiar líneas, y no digamos la palmeta. Se le daban bien casi todas las asignaturas, especialmente el francés y el latín... de hecho, casi todos los idiomas se le daban bien. Los deportes también le gustaban: el rugby y, especialmente, el críquet con su ritmo pausado; el año anterior había sido capitán del equipo juvenil.

A veces paseaba solo por el llamado Big Hall, donde colgaban las fotografías de las promociones de sexto curso de cada año, y permanecía de pie ante la foto de 1902, donde el rostro juvenil de su padre lo miraba desde una doble hilera de «prefectos»; es decir, los alumnos especialmente nombrados para ejercer autoridad sobre sus compañeros, que posaban muy tiesos para la posteridad con sus birretes. Después se volvía a contemplar la lápida situada detrás del escenario dedicado a los caídos de la Gran Guerra, cuyos nombres figuraban en ella labrados en letras doradas. Al ver también allí el nombre de su padre, asomaban a sus ojos unas ardientes lágrimas que él se apresuraba a enjugar por temor a que alguien lo viera. El día en que llegó Sandy Forsyth en 1925, Harry empezaba el cuarto curso. Aunque los chicos seguían pasando la noche en un gran dormitorio común, contaban desde el año anterior con unos estudios, unas pequeñas estancias para dos o tres alumnos con sillones anticuados y mesas rayadas. Los amigos de Harry eran generalmente los más serios y tranquilos, y él se alegraba de compartir un estudio con Bernie Piper, uno de los becarios. Piper entró, mientras él deshacía el equipaje.

—Hola, Brett —le dijo—. Ya sé que tendré que soportar el olor de tus calcetines todo el año que viene.

Bernie era hijo de un tendero del East End y, cuando llegó a Rookwood, hablaba con un cerrado acento *cockney*. Poco a poco, éste se había ido transformando en el pausado acento de la clase alta que utilizaban los demás chicos, aunque el gangueo de Londres se dejaba sentir durante algún tiempo cada vez que regresaba de las vacaciones.

—¿Has tenido un buen verano?

—Un poco aburrido. Tío James estuvo enfermo mucho tiempo. Me alegro de estar de vuelta.

—Tendrías que haberlo pasado despachando a la gente en la tienda de mi padre. Entonces no sabrías lo que es aburrirse.

Otro rostro apareció en la puerta: un corpulento muchacho moreno. Depositó en el suelo una elegante maleta y se apoyó contra la jamba de la puerta con aire de desdeñosa indiferencia.

—¿Harry Brett? —preguntó.

—Sí.

—Soy Sandy Forsyth. El chico nuevo. Me han asignado este estudio. —Arrastró la maleta por el suelo y se quedó mirando a los otros dos. Tenía unos ojos castaños grandes y perspicaces y se advertía cierta dureza en sus rasgos.

—¿De dónde vienes? —le preguntó Bernie.

—Braildon. En Hertfordshire. ¿Habéis oído hablar de él?

—Sí —contestó Harry—. Dicen que es un buen colegio.

—Pues sí. Eso dicen.

—Este de aquí tampoco está mal.

—¿No? Tengo entendido que la disciplina es muy severa.

—Te muelen a palos nada más verte —convino Bernie.

—Y tú, ¿de dónde vienes? —preguntó Forsyth.

—Wapping —contestó orgullosamente Bernie—. Soy uno de los proletarios aceptados por la clase dominante.

El semestre anterior, Bernie se había declarado socialista ante la desaprobación general.

Forsyth enarcó las cejas.

—Apuesto a que lo tuviste más fácil que yo.

—¿Qué quieres decir?

—Soy más bien un chico malo.

El recién llegado se sacó del bolsillo una cajetilla de Gold Flakes y extrajo un cigarrillo. Bernie y Harry miraron hacia la puerta abierta.

—No se puede fumar en los estudios —dijo rápidamente Harry.

—Podemos cerrar la puerta. ¿Queréis uno?

Bernie soltó una carcajada.

—Aquí te dan con la palmeta por fumar. No merece la pena.

—Vale. —El nuevo miró de repente a Bernie con una ancha sonrisa en los labios, que dejaron al descubierto unos dientes grandes y blancos—. Entonces ¿eres un rojo?

—Soy socialista, si es a eso a lo que te refieres.

El chico nuevo se encogió de hombros.

—En Braildon teníamos un foro de discusión y, el año pasado, uno de quinto habló en favor del comunismo. Se armó un buen jaleo.

Se rió, y Bernie soltó un gruñido y lo miró con desagrado.

—Yo quería dirigir un debate en favor del ateísmo —dijo Forsyth—, pero no me dejaron. Porque mi padre es obispo. ¿Adónde tiene que ir uno aquí si le apetece fumar?

—Detrás del gimnasio —contestó Bernie fríamente.

—Muy bien, pues. Hasta luego. —Forsyth se levantó y se marchó.

—Hijo de puta —masculló Bernie en cuanto se hubo ido.

Horas después, a Harry le pidieron por primera vez que espiara a Sandy. Se encontraba en el estudio cuando se presentó un fámulo, uno de los estudiantes que sirven a los de los cursos superiores, anunciando que el señor Taylor quería verle.

Taylor era el profesor de su curso aquel año. Tenía fama de ser muy duro; los chicos de los cursos inferiores le tenían pánico. Al ver su alta y delgada figura cruzando el patio con su expresión severa de costumbre, Harry recordó el día en que el profesor había acudido a la casa de tío James; apenas habían vuelto a hablar desde entonces.

El señor Taylor se encontraba en su estudio, una cómoda estancia con alfombras y retratos de antiguos directores en la pared; le encantaba la historia del colegio. Tenía el escritorio cubierto de exámenes para corregir. El profesor permanecía de pie enfundado en su toga negra, revolviendo papeles.

—¡Ah, Brett! —dijo en tono cordial, y levantó un largo brazo para invitar a Harry a entrar. Taylor se estaba quedando calvo a ritmo acelerado y ahora el puntiagudo nacimiento del cabello no era más que un aislado mechón oscuro bajo una pelada coronilla—. ¿Ha tenido unas buenas vacaciones? ¿El tío y la tía están bien?

—Sí, señor.

—Este año está usted en mi clase. He recibido muy buenos informes, así que espero grandes cosas de usted.

—Gracias, señor.

El profesor asintió con la cabeza.

—Quería hablarle de los estudios. Hemos colocado al chico nuevo con usted en lugar de Piper. Forsyth. ¿Ya lo conoce?

—Sí, señor. No creo que Piper lo sepa.

—Será informado. ¿Qué tal se lleva con Forsyth?

—Muy bien, señor —contestó Harry intentando sonar imparcial.

—No sé si ha oído usted hablar de su padre, el obispo.

—Forsyth lo ha comentado.

—Forsyth viene de Braildon. Sus padres pensaron que Rookwood, con su fama de... bueno... disciplina sería más apropiado para él. —Taylor esbozó una sonrisa benévola que provocó la aparición de unas arrugas profundas en sus enjutas mejillas—. Le hablo con toda franqueza. Usted es un chico formal, Brett; creemos que podría llegar a tener madera de prefecto algún día. Vigile a Forsyth, si es tan amable. —Hizo una pausa—. Llévelo por el recto y estrecho camino.

Harry dirigió una rápida mirada al profesor. Era una advertencia muy rara; una de las deliberadas ambigüedades que utilizaban los profesores a medida que los chicos crecían. Se esperaba que éstos las entendieran. Oficialmente, no estaba bien visto que los chicos se espiaran mutuamente; pero Harry sabía que muchos profesores utilizaban a determinados alumnos como fuente de información. ¿Qué le estaba pidiendo Taylor que hiciera? Comprendió instintivamente que no le gustaría hacerlo; la sola idea lo ponía nervioso.

—No dude que contribuiré a que se comporte como es debido, señor —dijo con cierto recelo.

Taylor lo miró incisivamente.

—Y dígame si hay algún problema. Queremos ayudar a Forsyth a desarrollarse en la dirección apropiada. Es muy importante para su padre.

Estaba más claro que el agua. Harry no dijo nada, y el señor Taylor frunció levemente el entrecejo.

Después ocurrió algo asombroso. Un ser minúsculo se movió entre los papeles del escritorio del señor Taylor; Harry lo vio por el rabillo del ojo. Taylor soltó un repentino grito y se apartó de un salto. Para sorpresa de Harry, el profesor se quedó casi encogido, sin querer mirar una enorme araña doméstica que correteaba rápidamente por su secante. El insecto se detuvo encima de un texto de latín y permaneció absolutamente inmóvil.

Taylor se volvió para mirar a Harry con el rostro completamente congestionado. Sus ojos se desviaron momentáneamente hacia el escritorio y después apartó la mirada con un estremecimiento.

—Brett, hágame el favor de librarme de esta cosa. Se lo ruego. —En la voz del profesor se advertía un tono de súplica.

Presa de la curiosidad, Harry se sacó el pañuelo y tendió la mano hacia la araña. La cogió y la sujetó con delicadeza.

—Ah... gracias, Brett. —Taylor tragó saliva con dificultad—. Yo... creo... que no... tendría que haber semejantes arácnidos en los estudios. Transmiten enfermedades. Mátela, mátela, por favor —se apresuró a añadir.

Harry titubeó y después la apretó entre el índice y el pulgar. El débil chasquido que emitió el insecto lo indujo a hacer una mueca.

—Deshágase de ella. —Por un instante, los ojos de Taylor lo miraron trastornados tras los quevedos de montura dorada—. Y no le hable a nadie de esto, ¿entendido? Puede retirarse —añadió bruscamente.

En casa de Will, la sopa de la cena era de lata, llena de verduras descoloridas. Muriel se disculpó mientras la repartía.

—No he tenido tiempo de preparar otra cosa, lo siento. Como comprenderás, ahora no dispongo de una asistenta que me ayude. He de encargarme de cocinar, atender a los niños, las libretas de racionamiento y todo lo demás.

Se apartó un mechón de cabello del rostro y miró a Harry con expresión desafiante. Los hijos de Muriel y Will, un delgado chiquillo moreno de nueve años y una niñita de seis, observaban a Harry con gran interés.

—Debe de ser difícil —dijo Harry solemnemente—. Pero la sopa está muy rica.

—¡Está buenísima! —exclamó Ronald.

Su madre suspiró. Harry no comprendía por qué razón Muriel había tenido hijos; seguramente, porque eso era lo que había que hacer.

—¿Qué tal va el trabajo? —preguntó a su primo, para romper el silencio.

Will trabajaba en el departamento de Oriente Próximo del Foreign Office.

—Podría haber problemas en Persia. —Aquellos ojos tras los gruesos cristales de las gafas parecían preocupados—. El sah se está inclinando por Hitler. ¿Qué tal te fue en la reunión? —preguntó con exagerada indiferencia.

Había llamado a Harry unos días antes para decirle que unas personas relacionadas con el Foreign Office habían contactado con él y querían hablar, aunque no tenía idea de qué se trataba. Por su manera de hablar, Harry comprendió que ya había adivinado quiénes eran aquellas «personas». Se preguntó si Will habría hablado de él en el despacho, si habría comentado algo acerca de un primo que había estudiado en Rookwood y hablaba español y si alguien le habría pasado la información a la gente de Jebb. ¿O acaso había en alguna parte una especie de gigantesco fichero sobre los ciudadanos que los espías solían consultar?

Estuvo casi a punto de contestar: «Quieren que vaya a Madrid», pero recordó que no tenía que hacerlo.

—Por lo visto, tienen algo para mí. Eso significa que tendré que irme al extranjero. Algo ultrasecreto.

—Hablar demasiado cuesta vidas —dijo solemnemente la niña.

—Cállate, Prue —la reprendió Muriel—. Tómate la sopa.

Harry esbozó una sonrisa tranquilizadora.

—No es peligroso. No es como lo de Francia.

—¿Mataste a muchos alemanes en Francia? —preguntó Ronnie, alzando un poco la voz.

Muriel posó ruidosamente la cuchara en el plato.

—Te he dicho que no hagas esa clase de preguntas.

—Pues no, Ronnie —contestó Harry—. Pero ellos, en cambio, mataron a muchos de los nuestros.

—Ya se lo haremos pagar, ¿verdad? Y los bombardeos, supongo que también.

Muriel lanzó un profundo suspiro. Will se dirigió a su hijo.

—¿Te he dicho alguna vez que conocí a Von Ribbentrop, Ronnie?

—¡Anda! ¿Lo conociste? ¡Tendrías que haberlo matado!

—Entonces no estábamos en guerra, Ronnie. Simplemente era el embajador alemán. Siempre decía lo que no debía; lo llamábamos el Indiscreto.

—¿Y cómo era?

—Un estúpido. Su hijo estudiaba en Eton, y una vez Von Ribbentrop fue a verlo allí. Se plantó en el patio con el brazo en alto y gritó: «*Heil*, Hitler!»

—¿En serio? Eso en Rookwood no se lo habrían permitido. Espero ir allí el año que viene, ¿lo sabías, primo Harry?

—Quizá no podamos permitirnos pagar la matrícula, Ronnie.

—Eso, si es que todavía sigue allí —intervino Muriel—. Si no lo han requisado o no lo ha destruido una bomba.

Harry y Will la miraron en silencio. Ella se llevó la servilleta a los labios y se levantó.

—Voy por los bistecs —anunció—. Estarán resecos, los dejé debajo del grill —añadió mirando a su marido—. ¿Qué vamos a hacer esta noche?

—No iremos al refugio, a menos que suene la sirena, claro —contestó él.

Muriel abandonó la estancia. Prue se había puesto nerviosa. Harry observó que sostenía un osito de peluche en el regazo y que lo estrechaba con fuerza. Will suspiró.

—Cuando empezaron las incursiones, adquirimos la costumbre de ir al refugio después de cenar. Pero algunas personas de allí... ¿cómo diría?, son un poco vulgares; a Muriel no le gustan y se siente muy incómoda. Prue se asusta. O sea que nos quedamos en casa, a no ser que suenen las sirenas. —Volvió a lanzar un suspiro, mirando a través de la cristalera que daba al jardín. El crepúsculo daba paso a la noche y una clara luna llena se elevaba en el cielo—: Es una luna de bombardeo. Puedes irte, si quieres.

—No te preocupes —dijo Harry—. Me quedaré con vosotros.

El pueblo de su tío estaba situado en el «trayecto de los bombarderos», que discurría desde el Canal hasta Londres; las sirenas sonaban a cada momento al paso de los aparatos por encima de sus cabezas, pero ellos no les prestaban atención. Harry no soportaba el turbulento aullido de Winnie. Le recordaba el ruido que emitían los bombarderos que caían en picado: cuando regresó a casa después de Dunkerque, cada vez que se disparaban las sirenas apretaba tanto los dientes y los puños que éstos se le quedaban blancos.

—Si la cosa dura toda la noche, nos levantaremos y nos iremos al refugio —dijo Will—. Está al otro lado de la calle.

—Sí, ya lo he visto.

—Ha sido terrible. Diez días seguidos te dejan tremendamente agotado, y cualquiera sabe lo que va a durar todo eso. Muriel está pensando en llevar a los niños al campo. —Will se levantó y corrió las pesadas cortinas opacas que se utilizaban contra los bombardeos. Se oyó un ruido de cristales rotos procedente de la cocina, seguido de un grito de rabia. Will salió corriendo—. Será mejor que vaya a echarle una mano a Muriel.

Las sirenas rugieron a la una de la mañana. Empezaron en Westminster y, mientras otros barrios las seguían, el quejumbroso gemido se fue extendiendo hacia los suburbios. Harry despertó de un sueño en el que corría por las calles de Madrid y, entrando y saliendo rápidamente de las tiendas y los bares, preguntaba si alguien había visto a su amigo Bernie. Pero hablaba en inglés, no en español, y nadie le entendía. Se levantó y se vistió rápidamente, como le habían enseñado a hacer en el ejército. Tenía la mente despejada y centrada, y no sentía miedo alguno. No supo por qué había preguntado por Bernie y no por Sandy. Alguien había llamado del Foreign Office a las diez, pidiéndole que al día siguiente fuera a una dirección de Surrey.

Descorrió ligeramente la cortina. A la luz de la luna, unas sombras borrosas corrían por la calle en dirección al refugio. Los enormes haces de los proyectores atravesaban el cielo hasta donde alcanzaba la vista.

Salió al pasillo. La luz estaba encendida y Ronnie se encontraba allí de pie en pijama y bata.

—Prue está asustada —dijo—. No quiere venir. —Miró hacia la puerta abierta del dormitorio de sus padres.

Se oían los sollozos aterrorizados de una criatura.

Ni siquiera en aquel momento en que los gemidos de las sirenas resonaban en sus oídos Harry se atrevía a invadir el dormitorio de Will y Muriel; pero, haciendo un esfuerzo, lo consiguió. Ambos iban en bata. Muriel estaba sentada en la cama con rulos en el pelo. Acunaba en sus brazos a su llorosa hija, emitiendo tranquilizadores murmullos. Harry no la hubiera creído capaz de semejante dulzura. De uno de los brazos de la niña permanecía colgando el osito. Will las miraba sin saber qué hacer; con el ralo cabello de punta y las gafas torcidas, parecía casi más vulnerable que todos ellos. Las sirenas seguían sonando; Harry notó que le empezaban a temblar las piernas.

—Tendríamos que irnos —dijo bruscamente.

Muriel lo miró.

—¿Y a ti quién te ha preguntado nada?

—Prue no quiere ir al refugio —explicó Will en voz baja.

—Está oscuro —gimoteó la niña—. Allí está todo muy oscuro, ¡por favor, dejad que me quede en casa!

Harry se acercó y cogió a Muriel por el huesudo codo. Era lo que había hecho el cabo en la playa tras la caída de la bomba, lo había levantado y acompañado con sumo cuidado al bote. Muriel lo miró con expresión de asombro.

—Tenemos que irnos. Los bombarderos se están acercando. Will, tenemos que llevárnoslos.

Su primo sujetó a Muriel por el otro brazo y ambos la levantaron dulcemente. Prue había hundido la cabeza en el pecho de su madre, sollozando y sujetando fuertemente al osito por el brazo. El peluche miró a Harry con sus ojos de vidrio.

—Bueno, ya puedo caminar sola —dijo Muriel con evidente mal humor.

Ambos la soltaron. Ronnie bajó ruidosamente por la escalera y los demás lo siguieron. El muchacho apagó la luz y abrió la puerta principal de la casa.

Resultaba extraño estar en un Londres nocturno sin farolas. Ahora no había nadie fuera, pero la sombra oscura del refugio se veía al otro lado de la calle, bajo la luz de la luna. Se oía un ruido lejano de artillería antiaérea y de algo más, un zumbido sordo y pesado procedente del sur.

—Mierda —dijo Will—. ¡Vienen hacia aquí! —De repente, se quedó perplejo—. Pero si es a los muelles adonde se dirigen, a los muelles.

—Quizá se hayan perdido. —«O pretenden socavar la moral de los ciudadanos», pensó Harry. Ya no le temblaban las piernas. Tenía que asumir el mando de la situación—. Vamos —añadió—. Crucemos la calle.

Echaron a correr, pero Muriel tenía dificultades por la niña que llevaba en brazos. En mitad de la calle, Will se volvió para ayudarla y resbaló. Se desplomó ruidosamente y soltó un grito. Ronnie, que marchaba en cabeza, se detuvo y se volvió para mirar.

—¡Levántate, Will! —gritó histéricamente Muriel.

Will intentó levantarse, pero cayó hacia atrás. Prue, con el osito todavía colgando de su brazo, se puso a gritar.

Harry se arrodilló al lado de Will.

—Me he torcido el tobillo. —En el rostro de Will se mezclaban el dolor y el temor—. Déjame, acompaña a los demás al refugio.

A su espalda, Muriel estrechaba con fuerza a la llorosa Prue, que soltaba incesantes reniegos en un lenguaje que Harry jamás hubiera imaginado que ella conociera.

—¡Maldito Hitler de mierda, me cago en su puta madre!

La sirena seguía aullando. Los aviones casi ya estaban encima de sus cabezas. Harry oyó el silbido de las bombas que caían, cada vez más fuerte y rematado por una súbita y sonora detonación. Vio un destello de luz a unas cuantas calles de distancia y percibió un momentáneo azote de aire caliente contra su bata. Era algo muy parecido a lo de Dunkerque. Las piernas le volvían a temblar y notaba un sabor seco y ácido en el paladar, pero la mente muy despejada. Tenía que conseguir que Will se levantara.

Se oyó otro silbido y una detonación más cercana, mientras el suelo se estremecía bajo sus pies por efecto de los impactos. Muriel dejó de soltar maldiciones y se quedó allí plantada, con los ojos y la boca muy abiertos. Inclinó el escuálido cuerpo envuelto en la bata para proteger a su hija, que seguía llorando. Harry la tomó del brazo y la miró a los ojos llenos de terror. Después, le habló muy despacio y con claridad.

—Tienes que llevar a Prue al refugio, Muriel. Ahora mismo. Mira, allí está Ronnie; no sabe qué hacer. Tienes que acompañarlos. Yo me encargaré de Will.

La vida retornó a los ojos de Muriel. Ésta se volvió en silencio y echó a andar rápidamente hacia el refugio, alargando la otra mano para que Ronnie la tomara. Harry se inclinó y tomó la mano de Will.

—Vamos, muchacho, levántate. Baja la pierna sana y apoya el peso del cuerpo en ella.

Consiguió levantar a su primo, mientras se oía otra fuerte detonación a no más de una calle de distancia. Hubo otro breve destello amarillo y una onda expansiva estuvo casi a punto de derribarlos al suelo, pero Harry rodeó a Will con el brazo y consiguió evitar que perdiera el equilibrio. Harry percibió una sensación de presión y un quejumbroso silbido en el oído malo. Will se inclinó hacia él y avanzó a saltitos con la pierna sana, mirándolo con una sonrisa a través de los dientes fuertemente apretados.

—No vayas a saltar ahora por los aires —dijo—. ¡Los fisgones se pondrán furiosos!

«O sea que ha adivinado quiénes son los que buscan mi colaboración», pensó Harry. Cayeron más bombas; unos destellos amarillos iluminaron la calle, pero ahora parecían más lejanos.

Alguien lo estaba observando todo desde el refugio y mantenía la puerta ligeramente entornada. Unos brazos se alargaron para sujetar a Will y todos cayeron a la vez por la abarrotada oscuridad. Harry fue acompañado a un asiento, donde se encontró sentado al lado de Muriel. Apenas podía distinguir su silueta delgada, todavía inclinada sobre Prue. La chiquilla seguía sollozando. Ronnie también estaba acurrucado junto a ella.

—Perdona, Harry —dijo Muriel en voz baja—. Pero es que ya no podía aguantar. Cada día pienso en lo que podría ocurrirles a mis hijos. A cada momento, constantemente.

—Tranquila —dijo él—. No pasa nada.

—Siento haberme derrumbado. Tú nos has ayudado a resistir.

Levantó un brazo para tocar a Harry, pero lo dejó caer como si el esfuerzo fuera excesivo.

Harry apoyó la punzante cabeza contra la pared rasposa de hormigón. Los había ayudado, había asumido el control de la situación, no se había venido abajo. Unos meses atrás lo habría hecho.

Recordó la primera vez que había visto la playa de Dunkerque, cuando había subido a una duna y había contemplado desde allí las columnas de hombres negras e interminables adentrándose en un mar salpicado de barcos. Los había de todos los tamaños... Vio una embarcación de placer junto a un dragaminas. También había restos humeantes de naufragios. Los bombarderos alemanes rugían por encima de su cabeza, bajando en picado y arrojando las bombas sobre barcos y hombres. La retirada había sido tan rápida y caótica que el horror y la vergüenza de toda la situación resultaron casi imposibles de soportar. A Harry le habían ordenado que ayudara a los hombres a formar en fila en la playa para la evacuación. Sentado ahora en el refugio, experimentó una vez más la sorda vergüenza que se suele sentir en semejantes circunstancias, la comprensión de la derrota total.

Muriel musitó algo. Estaba sentada junto a su oído malo y él volvió la cabeza hacia ella.

—¿Cómo?

—¿Te encuentras mal? Estás temblando de arriba abajo. —Le temblaba la voz. Harry abrió los ojos. La oscuridad estaba salpicada por los puntos rojos de los cigarrillos encendidos. Los ocupantes del refugio permanecían en silencio, tratando de oír lo que ocurría fuera.

—Sí. Es que... me lo ha vuelto a recordar todo. La evacuación.

—Lo sé —murmuró ella.

—Creo que ahora ya se han ido —dijo alguien.

Se abrió una rendija en la puerta y alguien asomó la cabeza. Una ráfaga de aire frío traspasó el tufo a sudor y orines.

—Es terrible lo mal que huele aquí dentro —dijo Muriel—. Por eso no me gusta venir. No lo puedo soportar.

—A veces la gente no puede evitarlo... Cuando tiene miedo pierde el control.

—Supongo que sí.

La voz de Muriel se serenó. Harry pensó que deseaba verle la cara.

—¿Estáis todos bien? —preguntó.

—Bien —contestó Will, detrás de Muriel—. Has hecho un buen trabajo ahí fuera, Harry. Gracias, muchacho.

—Los soldados... ¿perdían el control? —preguntó Muriel—. ¿En Francia? Debió de ser espantoso.

—Sí. A veces. —Harry recordó el olor mientras se acercaba a la hilera de hombres en la playa. Llevaban varios días sin lavarse. Le vino una vez más a la mente la voz del sargento Tomlinson.

—Tenemos suerte... Las cosas van más rápido ahora que los botes pueden acercarse. Algunos pobres desgraciados llevan tres días aquí. —Era un sujeto alto y fornido de cabello rubio y rostro grisáceo por el agotamiento. Miró hacia el mar, sacudiendo la cabeza—. Fíjese en aquellos imbéciles de allí, harán zozobrar la embarcación.

Harry siguió su mirada hasta el final de la cola. Los hombres permanecían dentro del agua, que les llegaba hasta los hombros. A la cabeza de la cola, algunos se amontonaban en una embarcación de pesca y su peso ya la estaba escorando hacia un lado.

—Será mejor que bajemos —dijo Harry.

Tomlinson asintió con la cabeza, y ambos se dirigieron hacia la orilla. Harry vio a los pescadores discutiendo con los hombres que seguían amontonándose a bordo.

—Creo que hemos tenido suerte de que la disciplina no se haya venido abajo por completo.

Tomlinson se volvió hacia él, pero su respuesta se perdió. El fragor de un bombardero que pasaba justo por encima de sus cabezas ahogó el débil silbido de las bombas que iban cayendo. Después se oyó un rugido que hizo que Harry experimentara la sensación de que le estallaba la cabeza mientras sus pies se levantaban del suelo en medio de una nube de arena teñida de rojo.

—Y, de repente, desapareció —dijo Harry en voz alta—. Sólo trozos. Pedazos.

—¿Cómo dices? —preguntó Muriel, perpleja.

Harry cerró con fuerza los ojos, tratando de borrar las imágenes.

—Nada, Muriel. No pasa nada, perdona.

Sintió que la mano de Muriel buscaba la suya y la apretaba. Se la notó áspera, dura y reseca a causa del trabajo. Parpadeó para reprimir las lágrimas.

—Lo hemos conseguido esta noche, ¿eh?

—Sí, gracias a ti.

Se oyó el murmullo de la señal de que había pasado el peligro. Todo el refugio pareció lanzar un suspiro de alivio y relajarse. Se abrió la puerta de par en par y la silueta del que actuaba como jefe se perfiló contra un cielo estrellado iluminado por el resplandor de los incendios.

—Se han ido, chicos —dijo—. Ya podemos volver a casa.

3

El avión despegó de Croydon al amanecer. A Harry lo habían acompañado en coche hasta allí, directamente desde el centro de instrucción del SIS, el servicio secreto de espionaje. Era la primera vez que viajaba en avión. Se trataba de un vuelo civil ordinario, y los demás pasajeros eran hombres de negocios ingleses y españoles. Hablaban animadamente entre sí, sobre todo acerca de las dificultades que la guerra había representado para el comercio y la industria, mientras sobrevolaban el Atlántico, antes de girar al sur para evitar el territorio de la Francia ocupada por los alemanes. Harry experimentó un momento de temor cuando el aparato despegó, y se dio cuenta de que las vías de ferrocarril que podía ver allá abajo, y que parecían más pequeñas que las del tren de juguete de Ronnie, eran de verdad. Pero se le pasó en cuanto penetraron en un banco de nubes, grises como la densa niebla que había al otro lado de la ventanilla. Las nubes y el zumbido de los motores se fueron volviendo tan monótonos que Harry se retrepó en su asiento. Pensó en su instrucción, en las tres semanas de entrenamiento a que lo habían sometido hasta aquella mañana, antes de montarlo en un automóvil y llevarlo al aeropuerto.

La mañana siguiente al bombardeo Harry había sido trasladado desde Londres a una mansión en la campiña de Surrey, donde había pasado tres semanas. Nunca supo su nombre, ni siquiera dónde estaba ubicada exactamente. Era un conjunto de edificios victorianos de ladrillo rojo, típicos del período entre mediados del siglo XIX y principios del XX; algo en la disposición de las estancias, los suelos sin alfombras y un olor leve e indefinible lo inducían a pensar que aquello había sido anteriormente un colegio.

Las personas que lo adiestraban eran en su mayoría jóvenes. Transmitían entusiasmo y afán de aventura, y su energía y rapidez de reacción conseguían captar la atención y la mirada y asumir el mando de la conversación. A veces, a Harry le recordaban a esos vendedores incansables. Le enseñaron los principios generales de la labor de espionaje: introducción de cartas en los buzones, cómo saber si a uno lo vigilan, cómo enviar un mensaje en caso de que se tenga que huir. Eso a él no iba a ocurrirle, le aseguraron a Harry: gozaba de protección diplomática, lo que representaba un útil subproducto de su tapadera.

De lo general pasaron a lo particular: cómo abordar a Sandy Forsyth. Le hicieron interpretar lo que ellos llamaban comedias de rol, en las que un antiguo policía de Kenia desempeñaba el papel de Sandy: un Sandy receloso que dudaba de su historia; un Sandy hostil y bebedor que preguntaba qué coño estaba haciendo Brett allí, porque siempre le había caído mal; un Sandy que era espía; un Sandy que era un fascista encubierto.

—Usted no sabe cómo reaccionará ante su presencia; tiene que estar preparado para todas las posibilidades —dijo el policía—. Tiene que adaptarse a sus estados de ánimo; averiguar lo que siente y piensa.

Tendría que actuar en absoluta coherencia con su historia, le dijeron, y ésta debía resultar impecable. Eso sería muy fácil. Podría ser totalmente sincero acerca de su vida hasta el momento en que había recibido la llamada telefónica del Foreign Office. En la tapadera que habían utilizado, habían llamado buscando a un traductor para sustituir a un hombre de Madrid que había tenido que irse inesperadamente. Harry se lo aprendió todo de memoria, pero ellos le dijeron que seguía habiendo un problema. No con su cara ni con su voz, sino que se advertía un titubeo, casi una especie de desgana cuando contaba su historia. Un agente tan hábil como parecía ser Forsyth tal vez adivinara que estaba mintiendo. Harry trabajó su papel y, poco tiempo después, ellos se dieron por satisfechos.

—Claro que cualquier variación en el tono también sería atribuible a su pequeña sordera —dijo el policía—, que puede afectar a la voz. Aproveche para comentarle también las crisis de pánico que sufrió después de Dunkerque.

Harry se mostró sorprendido.

—Eso es cosa del pasado, ya no las sufro.

—Usted continúa sintiéndolas, ¿verdad? Logra reprimirlas, pero las presiente, ¿no es cierto? —El agente consultó la carpeta que sostenía sobre las rodillas; Harry tenía su propia carpeta de cuero con una cruz

roja y la palabra «secreto» encima—. Bueno, siga trabajando con eso...
un momento de desconcierto, como, por ejemplo, detenerse para pedirle que le repita algo, lo puede ayudar. Le da tiempo para pensar y presentarse a sus ojos como un inválido, y no ya como alguien de quien tener miedo.

Harry sabía que la información sobre sus crisis de pánico procedía de la extraña mujer que un día lo había entrevistado. Jamás le dijo quién era, pero Harry intuyó que era una especie de psiquiatra. Había en ella algo de la apremiante impaciencia propia de los espías. La mirada de sus ojos azules era tan penetrante que, por un instante, Harry se asustó.

Ella le tomó la mano y le pidió jovialmente que se sentara junto a la mesita.

—Tengo que hacerle unas cuantas preguntas de tipo personal, Harry. ¿Le puedo llamar Harry?

—Sí... Mmm...

—Señorita Crane, llámeme señorita Crane. Parece que ha llevado una vida muy normal, Harry. No como muchos de los que pasan por aquí, se lo aseguro. —Soltó una carcajada.

—Sí, creo que en efecto se puede considerar una vida corriente.

—Pero eso de perder a sus dos progenitores siendo tan joven no debe de haber sido nada fácil. Pasar de un tío y una tía a otra tía hasta llegar al internado.

El comentario le molestó de repente.

—Mi tío y mi tía siempre han sido muy buenos conmigo. Y fui muy feliz en el colegio. Rookwood es una institución privada, no un simple internado.

La señorita Crane lo miró inquisitivamente.

—¿Dónde reside la diferencia?

A Harry le sorprendió el ardor de su propia voz al decir:

—Un internado suena a un lugar donde lo aparcan a uno para meterle en cintura. En cambio, Rookwood, una escuela privada en la que perteneces a la comunidad, se convierte en parte de ti, modela tu personalidad.

Ella siguió mirándolo con una sonrisa; sin embargo, su comentario fue brutal:

—Pero no es lo mismo que tener unos padres que te quieren, ¿verdad?

Harry advirtió que su cólera daba paso ahora a un profundo cansancio. Bajó la mirada al suelo.

—Hay que afrontar las cosas como vienen, sacarles el mejor partido. Seguir adelante contra viento y marea.

—¿Por su cuenta? ¿Hay alguna novia... alguien?

Harry frunció el entrecejo, preguntándose si a continuación la mujer empezaría a aludir a su vida sexual, tal como había hecho la señorita Maxse.

—En este momento, no. Hubo alguien en Cambridge, pero no dio resultado.

—¿Y eso por qué?

—Laura y yo nos cansamos el uno del otro, señorita Crane. No fue ningún drama.

La mujer cambió de tema.

—¿Y después de Dunkerque? Me refiero a la neurosis de guerra, cuando descubrió que sufría crisis de pánico y los ruidos fuertes lo asustaban. ¿También entonces decidió seguir adelante contra viento y marea?

—Sí, a pesar de que ya no era soldado. Y no lo volveré a ser.

—¿Y eso le duele?

Harry la miró.

—¿A usted no le dolería?

—Estamos aquí para hablar de usted, Harry —dijo ella.

Harry lanzó un suspiro.

—Sí, decidí seguir adelante contra viento y marea.

—¿Estuvo tentado de no hacerlo? ¿De retirarse y... convertirse en un discapacitado?

Harry la volvió a mirar. Qué perspicacia la suya.

—Sí, sí, supongo que sí. Pero no lo hice. Así es la vida últimamente, ¿verdad? —contestó con aspereza—. Incluso cuando ves que todo lo que dabas por sentado, todo aquello en lo que creías, queda reducido a pedazos. —Suspiró—. Creo que el espectáculo de la retirada general en aquella playa, el caos, me afectó casi tanto como la granada que estuvo a punto de matarme.

—Pero seguir adelante contra viento y marea debió de ser una empresa muy solitaria.

Su voz se suavizó repentinamente. Harry notó que los ojos se le llenaban de lágrimas.

—Aquella noche en el refugio, fue todo muy extraño —dijo—. Muriel, la mujer de Will, me tomó de la mano. Jamás nos habíamos caído bien, siempre pensé que me tenía manía, pero me tomó de la mano. Y, sin embargo...

—¿Sí?

—Se la noté muy seca, muy fría, y eso... me entristeció.

—Quizá porque no era la mano de Muriel la que usted quería.

Harry la miró.

—No, tiene usted razón —dijo con asombro—. Pero la verdad es que no sé la mano de quién quería.

—Todos necesitamos la mano de alguien.

—¿De veras? —Harry soltó una carcajada—. Eso queda muy lejos de mi misión.

Ella asintió con la cabeza.

—Es que estoy tratando de conocerlo, Harry, simplemente tratando de conocerlo.

Harry despertó de sus ensoñaciones cuando el avión se inclinó hacia un lado. Se agarró al brazo del asiento y miró a través de la ventanilla, después se inclinó hacia delante y miró de nuevo. Habían vuelto a salir a la luz del sol y sobrevolaban España. Harry contempló el paisaje castellano, un mar amarillo y ocre salpicado de campos de labranza. Cuando el aparato descendía en círculo, distinguió unas carreteras blancas y desiertas, varias casas de tejado rojo y algunas ruinas dispersas de la Guerra Civil. Experimentó una mezcla de emoción y temor, seguía sin poder creer que, efectivamente, había regresado a Madrid.

Mirando a través de la ventanilla, vio a una media docena de guardias civiles en el exterior del edificio de la terminal que controlaba la pista. Harry reconoció sus uniformes verde oscuro y las fundas de pistola amarillas ajustadas a sus cinturones. Seguían luciendo sus siniestros y arcaicos tricornios de cuero redondos, con dos alitas en la parte de atrás, negros y lustrosos como el carapacho de un escarabajo. La primera vez que había estado en España, en 1931, los guardias civiles, desde siempre partidarios de la derecha, se encontraban bajo la amenaza de la República y el temor y la rabia se notaba en las duras facciones de sus rostros. Cuando regresó en 1937, en plena Guerra Civil, ya no estaban. Ahora habían regresado, y Harry notó la boca seca mientras contemplaba sus rostros y sus frías e inmóviles expresiones.

Se unió a los pasajeros que se dirigían a la salida. Un seco calor lo envolvió al bajar por la escalerilla e incorporarse a la fila que cruzaba la asfaltada pista de aterrizaje. El edificio del aeropuerto no era más que un bajo almacén de hormigón con la pintura desconchada. Uno de los guardias civiles se acercó y se situó a su lado.

—Por allí, por allí —ordenó autoritariamente, señalando una puerta con una placa que decía «Inmigración».

Harry llevaba pasaporte diplomático, por cuyo motivo lo hicieron pasar rápidamente tras haber marcado con tiza sus maletas sin echarles ni un vistazo. Miró a su alrededor en el desierto vestíbulo. Se respiraba olor a desinfectante, la nauseabunda sustancia que siempre se había utilizado en España.

Una figura solitaria que leía un periódico apoyada contra una columna lo saludó con la mano y se le acercó.

—¿Harry Brett? Simon Tolhurst, de la embajada. ¿Qué tal el vuelo?

Era aproximadamente de la misma edad que Harry, alto y rubio y con modales amistosos y cordiales. Tenía una complexión parecida a la de Harry, con cierta tendencia a la obesidad; aunque, en su caso, el proceso ya había llegado algo más lejos.

—Muy bien. Casi todo el rato nublado, pero sin demasiadas turbulencias.

Harry observó que Tolhurst lucía una corbata de Eton cuyos vistosos colores contrastaban con su chaqueta blanca de hilo.

—Lo llevaré a la embajada, tardaremos aproximadamente una hora. No utilizamos chóferes españoles, son todos espías al servicio del Gobierno. —Soltó una carcajada y bajó la voz, a pesar de que no había nadie cerca—. Tuercen tanto las orejas hacia atrás para escuchar que piensas que se les van a juntar en la nuca. Demasiado evidente.

Tolhurst lo acompañó al exterior y lo ayudó a colocar la maleta en la parte de atrás de un viejo Ford impecablemente abrillantado. El aeropuerto estaba en plena campiña, rodeado de campos de labranza. Harry contempló el áspero paisaje de tonos marrones. En el campo que se extendía al otro lado de la carretera vio a un campesino trabajando la tierra con un arado de madera, como hacían sus antepasados. En la distancia, las desiguales cumbres de la sierra de Guadarrama se elevaban sobre un cielo intensamente azul, envuelto por la trémula luz del bochorno. Harry notó que el sudor le cosquilleaba las sienes.

—Mucho calor para ser el mes de octubre —dijo.

—Hemos tenido un verano tremendamente caluroso. Las cosechas han sido muy malas; están muy preocupados por la situación alimentaria. Aunque eso a nosotros nos puede beneficiar... porque es menos probable que entren en guerra. Será mejor que nos demos prisa. Tiene usted una cita con el embajador.

Tolhurst se adentró en una carretera larga y desierta flanqueada por unos polvorientos álamos cuyas hojas, que amarilleaban en las copas, semejaban antorchas gigantescas.

—¿Cuánto tiempo lleva usted en España? —preguntó Harry.

—Cuatro meses. Vine cuando ampliaron la embajada y enviaron a sir Sam. Antes estuve una temporada en Cuba. Una situación mucho más relajada. Lo pasé muy bien. —Meneó la cabeza—. Me temo que éste es un país tremendo. Usted ya ha estado aquí otras veces, ¿verdad?

—Antes de la Guerra Civil y después, muy brevemente, durante la misma. En Madrid en ambas ocasiones.

Tolhurst volvió a menear la cabeza.

—Es un lugar más bien siniestro, si quiere que le diga la verdad.

Mientras circulaban por la pedregosa carretera llena de baches, hablaron de la guerra relámpago y ambos se mostraron de acuerdo en que, por el momento, Hitler había renunciado a sus planes de invasión. Tolhurst le preguntó a Harry en qué colegio había estudiado.

—Conque Rookwood, ¿eh? Buen sitio, o eso creo. Qué tiempos aquellos, ¿verdad? —añadió en tono nostálgico.

—Sí —reconoció Harry, esbozando una sonrisa triste.

Contempló la campiña. En el paisaje se advertía una nueva desolación. Sólo se cruzaron de vez en cuando con algún campesino con carro y asno, y sólo una vez con un camión del ejército que se dirigía al norte, un grupo de soldados jóvenes y fatigados que miraban con aire ausente desde la parte de atrás del vehículo. Las aldeas también estaban desiertas. Ahora hasta los ubicuos y esqueléticos perros de antaño habían desaparecido y sólo quedaban unas pocas gallinas picoteando en torno a las puertas cerradas. En la plaza de un pueblo había unos grandes carteles de Franco en todas las agrietadas y despintadas paredes, con los brazos confiadamente cruzados mientras su mofletudo rostro miraba el infinito con una sonrisa en los labios. ¡HASTA EL FUTURO! Harry respiró hondo. Vio que los carteles cubrían otros más antiguos cuyos bordes destrozados asomaban por debajo. Reconoció la mitad inferior del viejo lema ¡NO PASARÁN! Pero habían pasado.

Al final, llegaron a los acomodados barrios residenciales del norte. A juzgar por el aspecto de los elegantes edificios, cualquiera hubiera dicho que la Guerra Civil jamás había tenido lugar.

—¿El embajador vive en este barrio? —preguntó Harry.

—No, sir Sam vive en la Castellana. —Tolhurst soltó una carcajada—. En realidad, la situación es un poco embarazosa. Vive al lado del embajador alemán.

Harry se volvió hacia él, boquiabierto.

—¡Pero si estamos en guerra!

—España es un país «no beligerante». Pero todo está lleno de alemanes. La escoria campa a sus anchas. La embajada alemana de aquí es la más grande del mundo. No nos hablamos con ellos, claro.

—¿Cómo acabó el embajador al lado de los alemanes?

—Era el único edificio de gran tamaño disponible. Se toma a guasa lo de mirar con cara de pocos amigos a Von Stohrer al otro lado de la valla del jardín.

Llegaron al centro de la ciudad. Casi todos los edificios habían perdido la pintura y estaban más ruinosos de lo que Harry recordaba, pese a que muchos de ellos debían de haber sido impresionantes en otros tiempos. Por todas partes había carteles de Franco con el símbolo del yugo y las flechas de la Falange. Casi toda la gente iba muy desaliñada, mucho más de lo que él recordaba, y la mayoría estaba delgada y parecía profundamente cansada. Muchos hombres de rostro demacrado y curtido por la intemperie caminaban por las aceras enfundados en monos de trabajo. Y las mujeres iban envueltas en chales negros cubiertos de parches y remiendos. Hasta los escuálidos chiquillos descalzos que jugaban en las polvorientas cunetas tenían una expresión de temor en el rostro chupado. En cierto modo, Harry había esperado ver desfiles militares y concentraciones falangistas como los que se veían en los noticiarios, pero la ciudad estaba más tranquila de lo que había imaginado, y también más sucia. Vio a monjas y curas entre los viandantes; como los guardias civiles, ellos también habían regresado. Los pocos hombres de aspecto adinerado que había por la calle llevaban chaqueta y sombrero a pesar del calor.

Harry se volvió hacia Tolhurst.

—Cuando yo estuve aquí en el treinta y siete, llevar chaqueta y sombrero en días calurosos era ilegal. Amaneramientos burgueses.

—Pues ahora no se puede salir sin chaqueta si uno lleva camisa. Un detalle para recordar.

Los tranvías circulaban, pero los pocos coches que había debían sortear carros tirados por asnos y bicicletas. Harry se volvió bruscamente cuando captó su atención un emblema conocido: una cruz negra con los brazos doblados en ángulo recto.

—¿Ha visto usted eso? ¡La maldita cruz gamada ondeando junto a la bandera española en aquel edificio!

Tolhurst asintió con la cabeza.

—Tendrá que acostumbrarse a eso. No son sólo las esvásticas... los alemanes dirigen la policía y la prensa. Franco no oculta su deseo de que ganen los nazis. Fíjese en aquello.

Se habían detenido en un cruce. Harry vio un trío de chicas llamativamente vestidas y maquilladas. Al ver su mirada, sonrieron y volvieron provocativamente la cabeza.

—Hay putas por todas partes. Tenga mucho cuidado, casi todas están enfermas de gonorrea y algunas son espías del Gobierno. El personal de la embajada tiene prohibido acercarse a ellas.

Un guardia urbano con casco les hizo señas de que pasaran.

—¿Usted cree que Franco entrará en guerra? —preguntó Harry.

Tolhurst se pasó una mano por el cabello rubio y se lo dejó de punta.

—Sabe Dios lo que hará. La atmósfera es terrible; la prensa y la radio son furibundamente proalemanas. La semana que viene Himmler vendrá en visita de Estado. Pero usted tendrá que comportarse con toda la normalidad que pueda. —Hinchó los carrillos y esbozó una sonrisa triste—. Casi todo el mundo tiene hecha la maleta por si hay que largarse a toda prisa. ¡Vaya, hombre, un gasógeno!

Señaló un viejo y enorme Renault que avanzaba más despacio que los carros tirados por asnos. En la parte posterior llevaba una especie de caldera achaparrada que escupía nubes de humo por una pequeña chimenea. Desde allí unos tubos iban a parar a la parte inferior del vehículo. El conductor, un burgués de mediana edad, hizo caso omiso de las miradas de la gente que se había detenido en la acera para mirar. Un tranvía se acercó ruidosamente y el hombre tuvo que dar un tremendo bandazo para esquivarlo, mientras el pesado automóvil se tambaleaba hasta casi volcar.

—¿Qué demonios es eso? —preguntó Harry.

—La revolucionaria respuesta española a la escasez de petróleo. Utiliza carbón o leña en lugar de petróleo. Va muy bien, a menos que uno quiera subir una cuesta. Tengo entendido que en Francia también lo utilizan. No hay muchas posibilidades de que los alemanes estén interesados en este diseño.

Harry estudió a la gente. Algunas personas sonreían al ver el extravagante vehículo, pero a Harry le llamó la atención que nadie se riera o hiciera comentarios en voz alta, como sin duda habrían hecho los madrileños en otros tiempos ante semejante espectáculo. Pensó una vez más en lo callados que estaban todos; el murmullo de las conversaciones que él recordaba también había desaparecido.

Llegaron al distrito de la Ópera, desde donde se distinguía a lo lejos el Palacio Real, que destacaba visiblemente en medio de la pobreza general con sus blancos muros iluminados por el sol.

—¿Allí vive Franco? —preguntó Harry.

—Allí recibe a la gente, pero su residencia es el Palacio de El Pardo, a las afueras de Madrid. Teme que lo asesinen. Se desplaza por todas partes en un Mercedes blindado que Hitler le envió.

—Entonces ¿sigue habiendo oposición?

—Nunca se sabe. A fin de cuentas, Madrid fue tomada hace sólo dieciocho meses. En cierto modo, sigue siendo una ciudad tan ocupada como París. Aún hay resistencia en el norte, por lo que nos dicen, y grupos de republicanos que se ocultan en el campo. «Los vagabundos», los llaman.

—Dios mío —dijo Harry—. Lo que ha sufrido este país.

—Puede que todavía no haya dejado de sufrir —observó Tolhurst en tono sombrío.

Enfilaron una calle de grandes edificios decimonónicos en la fachada de uno de los cuales ondeaba la tranquilizadora bandera del Reino Unido. Harry recordó haber acudido a la embajada en 1937 para interesarse por Bernie, a quien daban por desaparecido. Los funcionarios no se habían mostrado demasiado serviciales con él, habida cuenta de la escasa simpatía que les inspiraban las Brigadas Internacionales. Una pareja de la Guardia Civil vigilaba la entrada. Había varios automóviles aparcados delante de la puerta, por lo que Tolhurst se detuvo un poco más arriba.

—Vamos a sacar su maleta —dijo.

Harry miró con recelo a los guardias mientras subía. Después advirtió que alguien le tiraba de la pernera del pantalón por detrás. Se volvió y vio a un escuálido chiquillo vestido con los harapos de una capa militar, sentado en una especie de trineo de madera con ruedas.

—Señor, por favor, ¿no tendrá dos perras gordas?

Harry observó que el niño no tenía piernas.

—Por el amor de Dios —suplicó el chico, alargando la otra mano y sin dejar de tirar de las vueltas de su pantalón.

Uno de los guardias civiles bajó rápidamente por la calle dando palmadas.

—¡Largo de aquí! ¡Largo de aquí!

Al oír los gritos, el chiquillo apoyó las manos en los adoquines y empujó el carrito hacia atrás en dirección a una calle lateral. Tolhurst tomó a Harry del hombro.

—Tendrá usted que ser más rápido, amigo. Los mendigos no suelen llegar tan lejos, pero en el centro abundan como las palomas. Aunque, en realidad, no es que haya muchas palomas ahora; se las han comido todas.

El guardia civil que había ahuyentado al chiquillo los escoltó hasta la puerta de la embajada.

—Gracias por su asistencia —dijo ceremoniosamente Tolhurst.

El hombre inclinó la cabeza, pero Harry vio una mirada de desprecio en sus ojos.

—Los niños causan una impresión algo fuerte al principio —dijo Tolhurst, mientras hacía girar el tirador de la enorme puerta de madera—. Pero hay que acostumbrarse a ello. Ahora ha llegado el momento de que conozca usted a su comité de recepción. Los peces gordos lo están esperando.

Tolhurst parecía un poco celoso, pensó Harry mientras el otro lo acompañaba al caluroso y oscuro interior.

El embajador permanecía sentado tras un enorme escritorio en una estancia imponente en cuyo techo había unos ventiladores que en verano emitían un suave zumbido. Había grabados del siglo XVIII en las paredes, y el suelo de mosaico estaba cubierto por unas alfombras mullidas. Una ventana daba a un patio interior lleno de plantas en macetas, donde unos hombres en mangas de camisa conversaban sentados en un banco.

Harry reconoció a sir Samuel Hoare de haberlo visto en los noticiarios. Había sido ministro con Chamberlain, un pacificador despedido con la llegada al poder de Churchill. Era un hombre menudo de rasgos severos y delicadamente angulosos y cabello ralo y blanco, enfundado en un chaqué con una flor azul en el ojal. El embajador se levantó y se inclinó sobre el escritorio para tenderle la mano.

—Bienvenido, Brett. —El apretón fue sorprendentemente fuerte. El embajador miró por un instante a Harry con unos ojos fríos y azules, antes de llamar por señas a otro hombre—. El capitán Alan Hillgarth, nuestro agregado naval —añadió—. Es el máximo responsable de nuestros Servicios Especiales.

Hoare pronunció las últimas palabras con un leve tono de desagrado.

Hillgarth era un cuarentón alto y misteriosamente apuesto, con unos grandes ojos pardos, de expresión dura pero provistos de una cierta malicia casi infantil que también se advertía en su boca ancha y sensual. Harry recordó que Sandy leía en Rookwood relatos de aventuras escritos por un tal Hillgarth. Trataban de espías y de aventuras en los más remotos y atrasados rincones de Europa. A Sandy Forsyth le encantaban, pero Harry los encontraba un poco embrollados.

El capitán le estrechó cordialmente la mano.

—Hola, Brett. Responderá directamente ante mí con Tolhurst aquí presente.

—Siéntese, por favor, siéntense todos. —Hoare le indicó a Harry un sillón.

—Nos alegramos mucho de verlo —dijo Hillgarth—. Hemos recibido informes acerca de su instrucción. Parece ser que usted lo captaba todo razonablemente bien.

—Gracias, señor.

—¿Preparado para contarle su historia a Forsyth?

—Sí, señor.

—Le hemos conseguido un apartamento. Tolhurst le acompañará más tarde por los alrededores. Bien, ¿ya conoce las instrucciones? ¿Lo han puesto al corriente de la tapadera que deberá utilizar?

—Sí, señor. Me han contratado como intérprete tras la marcha por enfermedad del anterior.

—El bueno de Greene —dijo Hillgarth, soltando una repentina carcajada—. Todavía no sabe por qué razón lo enviaron tan rápido de vuelta a casa.

—Un buen intérprete —terció Hoare—. Conocía el oficio. Brett, tendrá usted que ser muy cuidadoso con lo que diga. Aparte de su... mmm... otro trabajo, llevará a cabo tareas de intérprete por cuenta de algunos altos funcionarios, y ha de saber que aquí las cosas son delicadas. Muy delicadas. —Lo miró con dureza.

Harry se sintió intimidado. No acababa de creer que estuviera hablando con un hombre al que había visto en los noticiarios. Respiró hondo.

—Lo sé, señor —dijo—. Recibí instrucción en Inglaterra. Lo traduciré todo a un lenguaje lo más diplomático posible y jamás añadiré comentarios por mi cuenta.

Hillgarth asintió con la cabeza.

—Hará una sesión con el subsecretario de Comercio y conmigo el jueves que viene. Me hago cargo.

—Sí, maestro —masculló Hoare—. No queremos disgustarlo.

Hillgarth sacó una pitillera de oro y le ofreció un cigarrillo a Harry.

—¿Fuma?

—No, gracias.

Hillgarth encendió el suyo y exhaló una nube de humo.

—No queremos que tropiece con Forsyth de inmediato, Brett. Tómese unos cuantos días para instalarse y para que lo conozcan en el ambiente. Y acostúmbrese a que lo vigilen y lo sigan... El Gobierno espía a todo el personal de la embajada. Casi todos los espías son bastante inútiles, se les ve a un kilómetro de distancia, aunque ahora empiezan a llegar hombres muy bien preparados de la Gestapo. Observe si alguien le pisa los talones e informe a Tolhurst. —Sonrió como si todo aquello fuera una aventura, de una manera que a Harry le recordó a la gente de la escuela de instrucción.

—Así lo haré, señor.

—Bueno —continuó Hillgarth—. Hablemos de Forsyth. Usted lo conoció muy bien durante un tiempo en el colegio, pero no ha vuelto a verlo desde entonces. ¿Correcto?

—Sí, señor.

—¿Cree que a pesar de ello podría mostrarse receptivo con usted?

—Así lo espero, señor. Pero la verdad es que no sé qué ha estado haciendo desde que dejamos de escribirnos. De eso hace diez años. —Harry miró hacia el patio. Uno de los hombres de allí los estaba mirando.

—¡Esos malditos pilotos! —exclamó Hoare—. ¡Estoy harto de que vengan aquí a fisgonear!

Agitó autoritariamente la mano, y los hombres se levantaron y desaparecieron por una puerta lateral.

Harry observó que Hillgarth le dirigía a Hoare una mirada rápida de desagrado antes de volverse de nuevo hacia él.

—Son unos pilotos que tuvieron que saltar en paracaídas sobre Francia —dijo Hillgarth con una clara indirecta—. Algunos de ellos han venido a caer aquí.

—Sí, sí, lo sé —replicó Hoare en tono malhumorado—. Tenemos que seguir.

—Por supuesto, embajador —dijo Hillgarth con ceremoniosa formalidad antes de volverse de nuevo hacia Harry—. Bueno, pues tuvimos noticias de Forsyth por primera vez hace un par de meses. Tengo un agente en el Ministerio de Industria de aquí, un joven administrativo que nos informó de que todos estaban muy nerviosos por algo que ocurría en el campo, a unos ochenta kilómetros de Madrid. Nuestro hombre no tiene acceso a los documentos, pero oyó un par de conversaciones. Yacimientos de oro. Muy grandes. Geológicamente comprobados. Sabemos que están enviando equipos de minería al lugar. También se habla de mercurio y otras sustancias químicas; pero tienen escasez de medios.

—A Sandy siempre le había interesado la geología —dijo Harry—. En el colegio era muy aficionado a la geología y siempre andaba por allí en busca de huesos de dinosaurio.

—¿De veras? —dijo Hillgarth—. Eso no lo sabía. Jamás obtuvo un título oficial, que nosotros sepamos; pero está trabajando con un hombre que sí los tiene: Alberto Otero.

—¿El que adquirió experiencia en Sudáfrica?

—Exacto. —Hillgarth asintió con la cabeza—. Ingeniero de minas. Creo que le facilitaron a usted algunas lecturas sobre la minería de oro en su país.

—Sí, señor.

Le había producido una sensación muy extraña bregar con aquellos complicados textos por la noche, en su pequeño dormitorio.

—Como es natural, por lo que a Forsyth se refiere, usted no sabe nada sobre el oro. Está usted en la inopia al respecto.

—Sí, señor. —Harry hizo una pausa—. ¿Sabe usted cómo se conocieron Forsyth y ese tal Otero?

—No. Tenemos muchas lagunas. Sólo sabemos que, cuando trabajaba como guía turístico, Forsyth entró en contacto con el Auxilio Social, la organización de la Falange que se encarga de gestionar lo que aquí pasa por bienestar social. —Hillgarth enarcó las cejas—. Es lo más corrupto que hay. Cuantiosas ganancias y muy pocas prestaciones.

—¿Sigue Forsyth en contacto con su familia?

Hillgarth negó con la cabeza.

—Su padre lleva años sin saber nada de él.

Harry recordó la única vez que había visto al obispo; éste había acudido al colegio después del castigo de Sandy para interceder en favor de su hijo. Desde el aula, Harry lo había visto en el patio y lo había reconocido por la camisa roja episcopal que asomaba bajo el traje. Su aspecto era recio y aristocrático, nada que ver con el de Sandy.

—¿Forsyth era partidario de los nacionales? —preguntó Harry.

—Creo que era más bien partidario de las cuantiosas ganancias —contestó Hillgarth.

—Usted no era partidario de los republicanos, ¿verdad? —preguntó Hoare, mirando a Harry con expresión inquisitiva.

—Yo no era partidario de ninguno de los dos bandos, señor.

Hoare soltó un gruñido.

—Creo que ésta era la gran línea divisoria antes de la guerra, entre los partidarios de los rojos en España y los de los nacionales. Me sorprende que un hispanista no fuera partidario de ninguno de los dos bandos.

—Pues yo no lo era, señor. Pensaba que representaba una desgracia para ambos.

«Es un matón cascarrabias de mucho cuidado», pensó Harry.

—Jamás logré entender que hubiera gente capaz de pensar que una España roja pudiera ser algo menos que un desastre.

Hillgarth parecía molesto por la interrupción. Se inclinó hacia delante.

—Forsyth no debía de hablar español cuando vino aquí, ¿verdad?

—No, aunque seguramente lo aprendió enseguida. Es listo. Por eso lo odiaban los profesores en el colegio. Era brillante, pero no daba golpe.

Hillgarth enarcó una ceja.

—¿Odiar? Me parece una palabra muy fuerte.

—Pues creo que llegaron a ese extremo.

—Bien, según nuestro hombre está metido en el departamento de minería del Estado. Se encarga de asuntos sucios por cuenta de ellos; negocia suministros y cosas por el estilo. —Hillgarth hizo una pausa y continuó—: El sector de la Falange domina el Ministerio de Minas. Les encantaría que España pudiera pagar la importación de alimentos, en lugar de tener que suplicarnos préstamos a nosotros y a los norteamericanos. Lo malo es que no contamos con agentes infiltrados allí dentro. Si usted pudiera tratar directamente con Forsyth, sería una ayuda inestimable. Queremos averiguar si hay algo en estas historias que se cuentan sobre el oro.

—Sí, señor.

Hubo un momento de silencio en el transcurso del cual el suave zumbido del ventilador de techo se convirtió de repente en un ruido molesto; al cabo, Hillgarth prosiguió:

—Forsyth trabaja para una empresa que él mismo ha organizado.

Nuevas Iniciativas. Figura en la lista de la Bolsa de Madrid como compañía proveedora de suministros. Las acciones han ido subiendo y los funcionarios del Ministerio de Minas las han comprado. La empresa tiene un pequeño despacho cerca de la calle Toledo; Forsyth acude allí casi a diario. Nuestro hombre no ha conseguido averiguar su domicilio particular, lo cual es un fastidio... Simplemente sabemos que vive cerca de la calle Vigo con una putilla. Casi todos los días sale a la hora de la siesta a tomarse un café en un bar de la zona. Allí es donde nosotros queremos que establezca usted contacto con él.

—¿Va solo?

—En el despacho sólo están él y una secretaria. Siempre se toma esa media hora para salir por la tarde.

Harry asintió con la cabeza.

—En el colegio le gustaba salir solo —dijo.

—Hemos estado vigilándolo. Es algo que te destroza los nervios... Temo que Forsyth descubra a nuestro hombre. —Hillgarth le pasó a Harry un par de fotografías de una carpeta que había encima del escritorio—. Le sacó éstas.

La primera imagen mostraba a Sandy bronceado y bien vestido, bajando por una calle en compañía de un oficial del ejército. Sandy inclinaba la cabeza para oír las palabras de éste con expresión solemne. En la segunda, caminaba tranquilamente con la chaqueta desabrochada, fumándose un pitillo. Su sonrisa denotaba seguridad y perspicacia.

—Parece que le van bien las cosas.

Hillgarth asintió con la cabeza.

—Bueno, dinero no le falta —dijo. Volvió a la carpeta—. El apartamento que le hemos conseguido se encuentra a un par de manzanas de su despacho. Linda con una zona más bien pobre, pero con la escasez de viviendas que hay ahora, resultará verosímil que albergue a un joven diplomático.

—Sí, señor.

—Me han dicho que su apartamento no está nada mal. Pertenecía a un funcionario comunista durante la República. Probablemente ya le habrán pegado un tiro. Instálese allí, pero no vaya todavía al café.

—¿Cómo se llama, señor?

—Café Rocinante.

Harry esbozó una sonrisa irónica.

—El nombre del caballo de Don Quijote.

Hillgarth asintió y miró fijamente a Harry.

—Voy a darle un consejo —dijo con una sonrisa. El tono era cordial; la mirada, dura—. Se le ve demasiado serio, como si cargara sobre los hombros el peso del mundo. Anímese un poco, hombre, sonría. Tómeselo como una aventura.

Harry parpadeó. Una aventura. Espiar a un antiguo compañero que colaboraba con los fascistas.

El embajador soltó una carcajada áspera.

—¡Una aventura! Dios nos libre. Cualquiera diría que hay demasiadas aventuras en este país. —Miró a Harry con expresión jovial—. Preste atención, Brett. Parece que lo tiene todo muy claro, pero ándese con muchísimo cuidado. Acepté sus servicios porque es importante que averigüemos lo que ocurre; pero no quiero que malogre ningún plan.

—No estoy muy seguro de haberle entendido, señor.

—Este régimen está dividido en dos. Casi todos los generales que ganaron la Guerra Civil son personas muy sensatas que admiran a Inglaterra y quieren que España se mantenga al margen de la guerra. Mi misión es tender puentes y fortalecer su influencia sobre Franco. No quiero que llegue a oídos del Generalísimo que tenemos espías por ahí husmeando en uno de sus proyectos preferidos.

Hillgarth asintió con la cabeza.

—Entiendo —dijo Harry. «Hoare no me quiere aquí de ninguna manera —pensó—. Estoy atrapado en medio de un maldito embrollo político.»

Hillgarth hizo ademán de levantarse.

—Bueno, tenemos una ceremonia en honor a los Héroes Navales de España. Será mejor que icemos la bandera, ¿no le parece, embajador?

Hoare asintió con la cabeza y Hillgarth se levantó, mientras Tolhurst y Harry hacían lo propio. Hillgarth cogió la carpeta y se la entregó a Harry. La carpeta llevaba una cruz roja en la parte anterior.

—Tolhurst lo acompañará a su apartamento. Tome el expediente de Forsyth y échele un buen vistazo, pero mañana tráigalo de nuevo. Tolhurst le indicará dónde firmar para retirarlo.

Cuando abandonaban la estancia, Harry se volvió hacia Hoare. Vio que el embajador miraba a través de la ventana, con expresión de desagrado, a los pilotos, que estaban de regreso en el jardín.

4

Fuera del despacho del embajador, Tolhurst esbozó una sonrisa de disculpa.

—Siento lo de Sam —dijo en voz baja—. No suele estar presente durante la instrucción de un nuevo agente, pero es que está nervioso por culpa de este trabajo. Se atiene a una norma: la recogida de información secreta está autorizada, no así el espionaje, y tampoco el antagonismo con el régimen. Hace unas semanas vinieron unos socialistas pidiendo ayuda para las guerrillas que luchan contra Franco. Algo tremendamente peligroso para ellos. Los mandó a freír espárragos.

A Harry no le gustaba Hoare, pero le seguía escandalizando el hecho de que Tolhurst lo llamara Sam.

—¿Porque quiere mantener buenas relaciones con los monárquicos? —preguntó.

—Exacto. Después de la Guerra Civil, éstos aborrecen con toda su alma a los rojos, como es lógico.

Tolhurst enmudeció al salir a la calle, y los guardias civiles los saludaron al pasar. Abrió la puerta del Ford e hizo una mueca al tocar la manija ardiente de la puerta.

En cuanto se pusieron en marcha, reanudó la conversación.

—Dicen que Churchill envió a Sam aquí para quitárselo de encima —confesó jovialmente—. No lo soporta, y tampoco se fía de él. Por eso puso al capitán al frente del espionaje. Es un viejo amigo de Winston. Desde la época en que formaba parte del Gobierno.

—¿Acaso no tendríamos que estar todos en el mismo bando?

—Hay mucha política interna.

—Y que lo diga.

Tolhurst sonrió con ironía.

—Sam es un amargado. Quería ser virrey de la India.

—Las luchas internas no pueden facilitar el trabajo de nadie.

—Tal y como están las cosas, muchacho —Tolhurst lo miró con expresión muy seria—, más le vale conocer la situación.

Harry cambió de tema.

—Recuerdo de cuando estaba en el colegio ciertos libros de aventuras de un tal Alan Hillgarth. ¿No será el mismo?

Tolhurdst asintió con la cabeza.

—El mismo que viste y calza. No están nada mal, ¿verdad? ¿Leyó el que está ambientado en el Marruecos español? *The War Maker*. Franco es uno de los protagonistas. Novelado, claro. No sabe cuánto lo admiraba el capitán.

—No lo he leído. Sé que a Sandy Forsyth le encantaban.

—¿De veras? —preguntó Tolhurst con interés—. Se lo diré al capitán. Le hará gracia.

Atravesaron el centro de la ciudad por un laberinto de callejuelas de edificios de cuatro pisos. Era última hora de la tarde y el calor empezaba a amainar. Unas sombras largas se proyectaban sobre la calle mientras Tolhurst circulaba con cuidado sobre los adoquines. Las casas de vecindad llevaban años abandonadas y el revoque se desprendía de los ladrillos como la carne se desprende de un esqueleto. Había varios edificios bombardeados, montones de piedras cubiertos de malas hierbas. No había otros coches circulando, y los viandantes contemplaban el vehículo con curiosidad. Un asno que tiraba de un carro subió a la acera para apartarse del camino y a punto estuvo de derribar al hombre que llevaba las riendas. Harry vio que éste trataba de recuperar el equilibrio y soltaba un juramento.

—Me pregunto cómo se les ocurrió reclutarme —dijo con fingida indiferencia—. Simple curiosidad. No se preocupe si no puede decírmelo.

—Bueno, no es ningún secreto. Estaban buscando antiguos contactos de Forsyth y un profesor de Rookwood lo mencionó a usted.

—¿El señor Taylor?

—Ignoro su nombre. Cuando se enteraron de que usted hablaba español, se sintieron en el séptimo cielo. Fue entonces cuando se les ocurrió la idea del intérprete.

—Comprendo.

—Un auténtico golpe de suerte. —Tolhurst sorteó un boquete abierto en la calle por una bomba—. ¿Sabía usted que nuestra embajada de aquí fue el primer pedazo de territorio británico en ser alcanzado por una bomba alemana?

—¿Cómo? ¡Ah!, ¿quiere decir durante la Guerra Civil?

—Cayó accidentalmente en el jardín cuando los alemanes bombardearon Madrid. Sam lo ha arreglado. También tiene sus cualidades. Es un organizador de primera, la embajada funciona como un reloj. Hay que reconocer los méritos de la Rata Rosa.

—¿De quién?

Tolhurst esbozó una sonrisa confidencial.

—Es su apodo. Sufre crisis de pánico. Cree que España está a punto de entrar en guerra y que a él le pegarán un tiro; hay que convencerlo de que no huya a Portugal. ¿Sabe que la otra tarde entró un murciélago en su despacho y él se escondió debajo de la mesa, pidiendo a gritos que alguien lo sacara de allí? Ya puede usted imaginarse lo que piensa Hillgarth. Pero, cuando está en vena, Sam es un diplomático excelente. Le encanta exhibirse como representante del rey-emperador. Los monárquicos se pirran por cualquier cosa que tenga que ver con la realeza, naturalmente. ¡Ah!, ya hemos llegado.

Tolhurst había entrado en una plaza polvorienta en cuyo centro, sobre un pedestal, se elevaba la estatua de un soldado manco con prendas dieciochescas, y donde también había varias tiendas con los escaparates medio vacíos cubiertos de manchas de moscas. La plaza estaba rodeada de casas de vecindad, y las ventanas tras los oxidados balcones de hierro forjado tenían las persianas cerradas para protegerse del calor de la tarde. El lugar debió de tener cierto estilo en otros tiempos. Harry estudió los edificios a través de la ventanilla. Recordó un cuadro que había comprado en una tienda de un barrio humilde en 1931: una ruinosa casa de vecindad como aquéllas, con una sonriente muchacha asomada a una ventana mientras abajo un gitano le dedicaba una serenata. Lo había colgado en su habitación de Cambridge. Los edificios ruinosos tenían un aire romántico que, naturalmente, a los victorianos les encantaba. Pero la cosa cambiaba cuando uno tenía que vivir en ellos.

Tolhurst señaló una callejuela que conducía al norte y cuyos edificios se encontraban aún en peor estado.

—Yo que usted, no me metería por allí. Es el barrio de La Latina, que lleva, cruzando el río, al de Carabanchel.

—Lo sé —dijo Harry—. Cuando estuve aquí en 1931 solíamos visitar a una familia de Carabanchel.

Tolhurst lo miró con curiosidad.

—Los nacionales lo bombardearon de mala manera durante el asedio, ¿verdad? —preguntó Harry.

—Sí, y desde entonces han dejado que se pudriera. Piensan que el lugar está lleno de enemigos. Me han dicho que hay gente que se muere de hambre y jaurías de perros asilvestrados en los edificios en ruinas. Han mordido a mucha gente y han transmitido la rabia.

Harry miró hacia el fondo de la larga y desierta calle.

—¿Qué más necesita saber usted? —preguntó Tolhurst—. Los ingleses no tienen muy buena fama en general. Es cosa de la propaganda. Aunque la gente se limita a mirarlos con desprecio.

—¿Qué hacemos con los alemanes si topamos con ellos?

—Cortarles la cabeza a los muy cabrones, eso es todo. Procure no saludar por la calle a nadie con pinta de inglés —añadió Tolhurst, abriendo la puerta del vehículo—. Lo más seguro es que pertenezca a la Gestapo.

Fuera el aire estaba lleno de polvo, y una brisa suave levantaba pequeñas espirales del suelo. Sacaron la maleta de Harry del automóvil. Una anciana escuálida vestida de negro cruzó la plaza sujetando con una mano el enorme fardo de ropa que sostenía sobre la cabeza. Harry se preguntó a qué bando habría pertenecido durante la Guerra Civil o si habría sido una de las miles de personas apolíticas atrapadas en medio. Su rostro, surcado por unas arrugas profundas, mostraba una estoica expresión de cansancio. Era una de las muchas personas que habían conseguido sobrevivir... por los pelos.

Tolhurst entregó a Harry una cartilla marrón.

—Sus raciones. La embajada recibe raciones diplomáticas y nosotros las distribuimos. Son mejores que las que recibimos en casa. Y mucho mejores que las que reciben aquí. —Sus ojos siguieron a la anciana—. Dicen que la gente arranca raíces de hortalizas para comérselas. Se pueden comprar cosas en el mercado negro, claro, pero resultan muy caras.

—Gracias. —Harry se guardó la cartilla en el bolsillo.

Tolhurst se acercó a una de las casas, sacó una llave y ambos entraron en una portería oscura con las paredes agrietadas y desconchadas. Goteaba agua en algún lugar y se respiraba un rancio olor a orina. Ambos subieron por unos peldaños de piedra hasta llegar al segundo piso, donde se toparon con las puertas de tres apartamentos. Dos chiquillas jugaban con unas muñecas maltrechas en el rellano.

—Buenas tardes —dijo Harry, pero ellas apartaron la mirada.

Tolhurst abrió una de las puertas.

Era una vivienda de tres habitaciones como las que Harry recordaba haber visto y en las cuales solían alojarse familias de diez miembros apretujados en medio de la mugre. La habían limpiado y olía a cera. Estaba amueblada como un hogar de la clase media, llena de armarios y sofás viejos y mullidos. No había cuadros en las paredes, pintadas de amarillo mostaza, sólo unos cuadrados blancos en los lugares que habían ocupado en otro tiempo. Las motas de polvo danzaban en un rayo de sol.

—Es grande —dijo Harry.

—Pues sí, mucho mejor que la caja de zapatos donde vivo yo. Precisamente, el que ocupaba el único funcionario del Partido Comunista que había por aquí. Es una pena ver a la gente tan apretujada. Estuvo un año desocupado cuando a él se lo llevaron. Después, las autoridades recordaron que tenían este piso y lo pusieron en alquiler.

Harry recorrió con un dedo la película de polvo que cubría la mesa.

—Por cierto, ¿qué es eso de que Himmler va a venir aquí?

Tolhurst lo miró con expresión muy seria.

—Toda la prensa fascista habla de ello —dijo—. Una visita de Estado la semana que viene. —Sacudió la cabeza—. Jamás te acabas de acostumbrar a la idea de que quizá tengamos que echar a correr. Ha habido muchas falsas alarmas.

Harry asintió con la cabeza.

«No es valiente —pensó—; o no lo es más que yo.»

—¿O sea que usted responde directamente ante Hillgarth? —preguntó.

—Exacto. —Tolhurst golpeó con el pie la pata de un escritorio ornamentado—. Pero no me dedico exactamente a misiones secretas, soy el administrador. —Soltó una carcajada casi como para justificarse—. Simon Tolhurst, burro de carga general. Búsqueda de apartamentos, mecanografiado de informes, comprobación de gastos. —Hizo una pausa—. Por cierto, procure llevar una relación cuidadosa de todo lo que gaste. En Londres son muy cicateros con los gastos. —Tolhurst contempló a través de la ventana el patio de luces con sus cuerdas de tender la ropa entre los balcones, y después se volvió de nuevo hacia Harry—. Dígame —preguntó con curiosidad—, ¿es Madrid muy distinto de como era cuando usted estuvo aquí bajo la República?

—Sí. La situación de entonces ya era mala, pero ahora todo parece mucho peor. E incluso más pobre.

—Puede que mejoren las cosas. Al menos, eso creo, ahora que hay un gobierno fuerte.

—Quizá.

—¿Se enteró de lo que dijo Dalí, según el cual España es un país de campesinos que necesitan mano dura? En Cuba ocurrió lo mismo; no saben manejar la democracia. Todo se va a la mierda.

Tolhurst sacudió la cabeza como si todo aquello fuera superior a sus fuerzas. Harry experimentó una punzada de cólera ante su ingenuidad; sin embargo, después pensó que la tragedia que allí se había producido también era superior a la suya. Bernie era el único que tenía todas las respuestas, pero su bando había perdido y Bernie estaba muerto.

—¿Café? —le preguntó a Tolhurst—. Si es que hay.

—Ya lo creo que hay. La casa está muy bien abastecida. También hay teléfono; pero tenga cuidado con lo que diga, estará intervenido por ser usted miembro del cuerpo diplomático. Lo mismo le digo de las cartas que escriba a Inglaterra: están censuradas. Por consiguiente, cuidado con las cartas a la familia o a la novia. ¿Tiene a alguien allí? —preguntó Tolhurst con cierto recelo.

—No. —Harry negó con la cabeza—. ¿Y usted?

—No. No me permiten salir mucho de la embajada. —Tolhurst lo miró con curiosidad—. ¿Qué le llevó a Carabanchel cuando estuvo aquí?

—Vine con Bernie Piper, mi compañero de escuela comunista —contestó Harry con ironía—. Estoy seguro de que consta en mi expediente.

—Ah, sí —contestó Tolhurst, y se ruborizó ligeramente.

—Trabó amistad con una familia de allí. Era buena gente; quién sabe qué habrá sido de ellos ahora. —Harry suspiró—. Voy por el café.

Tolhurst consultó su reloj.

—La verdad es que prefiero irme. Tengo que comprobar algunos malditos gastos. Venga mañana a las nueve a la embajada, lo pondremos al corriente de las tareas de los traductores.

—¿Sabrán los demás traductores que trabajo para Hillgarth?

—No, por Dios —respondió Tolhurst—. Son miembros auténticos del cuerpo diplomático, simples artistas del circo de Sam. —Sonrió y tendió una sudorosa mano a Harry—. No se preocupe, mañana lo repasaremos todo.

Harry se aflojó el cuello de la camisa y la corbata y experimentó los efectos de una agradable corriente de aire jugueteando sobre el círculo de sudor que le rodeaba el cuello. Se sentó en un sillón de cuero y echó un vistazo al expediente de Forsyth. No había gran cosa: unas cuantas fotografías más, detalles acerca de su trabajo en colaboración con el Auxilio Social, sus contactos en la Falange. Sandy vivía en una casa muy grande y se gastaba un montón de dinero en la compra de artículos en el mercado negro.

A sus oídos llegó la voz chillona de una mujer que llamaba a sus hijos. Dejó el expediente, se acercó a la ventana y miró hacia el oscuro patio de abajo, donde jugaban unos niños. Abrió las ventanas y el consabido olor de comida mezclado con el hedor a podrido le cosquilleó en la nariz. Vio a la mujer asomada a la ventana: era joven y guapa, pero iba de luto por su marido. Volvió a llamar a sus hijos, y éstos corrieron al interior del edificio.

Harry se volvió de nuevo hacia la habitación. Estaba muy mal iluminada y parecía llena de rincones oscuros; los espacios antaño ocupados por cuadros o carteles destacaban cual espectrales cuadrados. Se preguntó qué habría colgado en ellos. ¿Imágenes de Stalin y Lenin? La silenciosa y sosegada atmósfera resultaba un tanto opresiva. El comunista habría sido detenido tras la entrada de Franco en Madrid, y después se lo habrían llevado y fusilado en algún sótano. Harry encendió la luz pero no pasó nada. Con la luz del pasillo ocurrió lo mismo; probablemente, un corte de corriente.

El hecho de tener que espiar a Sandy le había causado una cierta inquietud, pero ahora la furia que experimentaba era cada vez más profunda. Sandy trabajaba con los falangistas, una gente que quería declarar la guerra a Inglaterra.

—¿Por qué, Sandy? —preguntó.

El sonido de su voz en medio del silencio lo sobresaltó. De repente, se sintió solo. Se encontraba en un país hostil, trabajando por cuenta de una embajada que parecía un semillero de rivalidades. Tolhurst era extremadamente amable, pero Harry sospechaba que le transmitiría a Hillgarth sus impresiones acerca de él y que le encantaba estar al tanto de todo. Pensó en el consejo de Hillgarth acerca de que se lo tomara todo como una aventura; y se preguntó, como se había preguntado varias veces en el transcurso de su período de instrucción, si sería el hombre adecuado para aquella tarea y si estaría a la altura de lo que se esperaba de él. No había hecho ningún comentario sobre sus dudas: era un trabajo importante y ellos necesitaban que lo hiciera. Pero por un instante sintió que el pánico se agazapaba en los más recónditos rincones de su mente.

«Esto no va a dar resultado», se dijo. Había una radio encima de una mesa de rincón. El panel de cristal del centro se iluminó; habría vuelto la luz. Recordó cuando estaba en casa de su tío durante las vacaciones de Rookwood, jugando con la radio del salón por la noche. Al girar el dial, escuchaba voces de países lejanos: Italia, Rusia, los ásperos gritos de Hitler desde Alemania. Pensaba que ojalá pudiera entender las voces que iban y venían, tan lejanas, interrumpidas por silbidos y crujidos. Allí había empezado su interés por los idiomas. Hizo girar el dial en busca de la BBC, pero sólo consiguió encontrar una emisora española, que ofrecía música militar.

Se dirigió al dormitorio. La cama estaba recién hecha y se tumbó en ella, súbitamente cansado; había sido un día muy largo. Ahora que ya se habían ido los niños que jugaban, le volvió a llamar la atención el silencio del exterior, como si Madrid estuviera envuelto en un sudario. Era una ciudad ocupada, había dicho Tolhurst. Percibió el zumbido de la sangre en sus oídos; lo notaba más fuerte en el oído malo. Pensó que tenía que deshacer la maleta, pero dejó que su mente regresara a 1931, a su primera visita a Madrid. Él y Bernie, ambos de veinte años, habían acabado cerca de la estación de Atocha un día de julio con sus mochilas a la espalda. Recordó que, al salir de la estación y dejar atrás el olor a hollín que la impregnaba, había visto bajo la luz radiante del sol la bandera roja, amarilla y morada de la República ondear en el ministerio de la acera de enfrente, contra un cielo azul cobalto tan brillante que lo había obligado a cerrar los ojos.

Cuando Sandy Forsyth fue expulsado ignominiosamente de Rookwood, Bernie regresó al estudio y reanudó su amistad con Harry: dos muchachos reposados y estudiosos que preparaban su ingreso en Cambridge. Por aquel entonces, Bernie solía reservarse sus puntos de vista políticos. En el último curso consiguió formar parte del equipo de la llamada Rugby Union y disfrutó de la rápida brutalidad de aquel deporte. Harry prefería el críquet; cuando alcanzó el primer once, fue uno de los momentos más trascendentales de su vida.

Siete alumnos de sexto de aquel año eran candidatos al ingreso en

Cambridge. Harry quedó segundo y Bernie primero, ganador del premio de cincuenta libras donado por un ex alumno. Bernie dijo que era más dinero del que jamás hubiera imaginado ver, y mucho menos poseer. En otoño ambos se fueron a Cambridge, pero a distintos colegios; motivo por el cual sus caminos se separaron y Harry entró a formar parte de un serio y estudioso grupo de alumnos, mientras que Bernie se incorporaba a los grupos socialistas, cansados de los estudios. Seguían viéndose de vez en cuando para tomar una copa, aunque de forma cada vez más esporádica. Harry llevaba más de un mes sin ver a Bernie cuando éste entró en sus dominios una mañana de verano, a finales de su segundo curso.

—¿Qué vas a hacer estas vacaciones? —preguntó Bernie en cuanto Harry hubo terminado de preparar el té.

—Me iré a Francia. Ya está decidido. Pasaré el verano viajando por allí para mejorar mis conocimientos de francés. En principio, mi primo Will y su mujer iban a acompañarme, pero ella se ha quedado embarazada. —Harry suspiró; se había llevado una decepción, y el hecho de viajar solo lo ponía nervioso—. ¿Tú volverás a trabajar en la tienda?

—No. Pasaré un mes en España. Allí están ocurriendo cosas extraordinarias.

Harry había elegido el español como segunda lengua y sabía que en abril de ese año la monarquía había caído. Se había proclamado la República con un gobierno de liberales y socialistas empeñados, según decían ellos, en llevar la reforma y el progreso a uno de los países más atrasados de Europa.

—Quiero verlo —dijo Bernie con el rostro iluminado por el entusiasmo—. Esta nueva Constitución es una Constitución del pueblo; se acabaron los terratenientes y la Iglesia. —Miró a Harry con expresión pensativa—. Pero a mí tampoco me apetece ir a España solo. He pensado que a lo mejor a ti te gustaría venir. A fin de cuentas, hablas el idioma. ¿Por qué no ir también a ver España, verla directamente en lugar de leer a viejos y polvorientos dramaturgos españoles? Yo podría ir a Francia primero si tú no quieres ir solo —añadió—. Me gustaría visitarla. Y después podríamos ir juntos a España —concluyó con una sonrisa.

Bernie siempre había sido muy convincente.

—Pero España es bastante primitiva, ¿verdad? ¿Cómo nos vamos a orientar allí?

Bernie se sacó del bolsillo un maltrecho carnet del Partido Laborista.

—Esto nos va a ser muy útil. Te presentaré a la hermandad socialista internacional.

Harry esbozó una sonrisa.

—¿Puedo cobrar como intérprete?

Había comprendido que aquél era el motivo por el cual Bernie quería que lo acompañara y experimentó una inesperada tristeza.

Subieron al transbordador de Francia en julio. Pasaron diez días en París y después viajaron al sur en tren, pernoctando por el camino en albergues baratos. Fueron unos días perezosos y agradables en el transcurso de los cuales recuperaron el viejo compañerismo que los había unido en Rookwood. Bernie estudiaba a marchas forzadas una gramática española en su afán de conversar con la gente en su idioma. Transmitió a Harry parte de su entusiasmo por lo que él llamaba «la nueva España», y ambos miraron con ansia por la ventanilla cuando el tren entró en la estación de Atocha aquella calurosa mañana estival.

Madrid era un lugar emocionante y extraordinario. De paseo por el centro, ambos pudieron ver edificios engalanados con banderas socialistas y anarquistas, carteles de manifestaciones y convocatorias de huelgas cubriendo las desconchadas paredes de los viejos edificios. En cada rincón se veían iglesias quemadas, lo que hacía temblar a Harry pero provocaba en Bernie siniestras sonrisas de placer.

—No es precisamente el paraíso de los obreros —dijo Harry, enjugándose el sudor de la frente.

El calor era insoportable, un calor que ninguno de aquellos dos muchachos ingleses había imaginado que pudiera existir. Se encontraban en la ardiente y polvorienta Puerta del Sol. Los vendedores ambulantes, con sus carros tirados por asnos, sorteaban los tranvías mientras unos desarrapados limpiabotas permanecían tumbados a la sombra junto a las paredes de los edificios. Unas ancianas envueltas en negras manteletas caminaban con paso cansino; semejaban unos pajarracos polvorientos y hediondos.

—Pero, Harry, por Dios, esta gente lleva siglos de opresión —dijo Bernie—. En buena medida a manos de la Iglesia. Casi todos esos templos quemados estaban llenos de oro y plata. Se tardará mucho tiempo en volver a la normalidad.

Consiguieron habitación en el segundo piso de un hotel ruinoso, en una callejuela adyacente a la Puerta del Sol. En el balcón del edificio de enfrente solían descansar unas prostitutas que dirigían, entre risas, comentarios obscenos al otro lado de la calle. Harry se ruborizaba y se apartaba, pero Bernie les contestaba a gritos, diciéndoles que no tenían dinero para semejantes lujos.

El calor seguía causando estragos; durante las horas más calurosas del día, se quedaban tumbados en las camas del hostal con las camisas desabrochadas, leyendo o dormitando mientras saboreaban la menor brisa que se pudiera filtrar por la ventana. Después, a última hora de la tarde, salían a dar una vuelta por la ciudad antes de pasarse la noche en los bares.

Una noche entraron en un bar del barrio de La Latina llamado El Toro, en el que se anunciaba baile flamenco. Bernie lo había visto, lleno de optimismo y esperanza, en el periódico *El Socialista* que había conseguido que Harry le tradujera. Al llegar allí, se asombraron al ver las cabezas de toro que adornaban las paredes. Los demás clientes, que eran obreros, miraron a Bernie y Harry con curiosidad mientras se daban divertidos codazos los unos a los otros. Los muchachos pidieron un grasiento cocido y se sentaron en un banco, bajo el anuncio de una huelga y junto a un corpulento sujeto moreno de bigotes caídos. Todos los murmullos de las conversaciones cesaron de golpe cuando dos hombres enfundados en ajustadas chaquetas y tocados con negros sombreros redondos se acercaron al centro del local guitarra en mano. Los siguió de inmediato una mujer ataviada con una ancha falda roja y negra, un ceñido y largo corpiño y una mantilla en la cabeza. Todos tenían el rostro enjuto y una piel tan oscura que a Harry le hicieron recordar a Singh, su compañero indio de Rookwood. Los hombres se pusieron a tocar y la mujer empezó a cantar con tal vehemencia que captó la atención de Harry pese a que no podía seguir sus palabras. Interpretaron tres canciones, cada una de ellas acogida con grandes aplausos. Después, uno de los hombres pasó el sombrero.

—Muy bien —le dijo Harry—, muchas gracias —añadió, depositando unas monedas en el sombrero.

El corpulento sujeto que tenían al lado les dijo algo en español.

—¿Qué ha dicho? —le preguntó Bernie a Harry en voz baja.

—Dice que cantan sobre la opresión de los terratenientes.

El obrero los estudiaba con divertido interés.

—Eso está muy bien —le dijo Bernie en un titubeante español.

El corpulento individuo asintió con la cabeza en un gesto de aprobación. Después les tendió la mano. Era dura y callosa.

—Pedro Mera García —dijo el hombre—. ¿De dónde son ustedes?

—Inglaterra. —Bernie se sacó del bolsillo la tarjeta del partido—. Partido Laborista inglés.

Pedro esbozó una amplia sonrisa.

—Bienvenidos, compañeros.

Así empezó la amistad entre Bernie y la familia Mera. A éste lo consideraban un camarada, mientras que el apolítico Harry les parecía un primo ligeramente retrasado. Hubo una noche de principios de septiembre que Harry recordaría en particular. Había refrescado al caer el sol y Bernie estaba sentado en el balcón en compañía de Pedro, su mujer Inés y su hijo mayor, Antonio, que tenía la misma edad que Harry y Bernie y que, como su padre, era un activista del sindicato de la construcción. En el salón, Harry le había estado enseñando a la pequeña Carmela, de tres años, unas cuantas palabras en inglés. Su hermano Francisco, de diez años, delgado y tuberculoso, lo observaba todo con sus cansados ojos pardos, mientras que Carmela permanecía sentada en el brazo del sillón de Harry repitiendo aquellas extrañas palabras con fascinada solemnidad.

Al final, la niña se cansó y se fue a jugar con sus muñecas. Harry salió al pequeño balcón y miró hacia el otro lado de la plaza, donde una agradable brisa levantaba el polvo del suelo. De abajo le llegó el sonido de unas voces. Un vendedor de cerveza pregonaba su mercancía. Las palomas, que volaban en círculo bajo un cielo cada vez más oscuro, eran como destellos blancos recortándose contra las tejas rojas de los techados.

—Échame una mano, Harry —le pidió Bernie—. Quiero preguntarle a Pedro si el Gobierno ganará mañana el voto de confianza.

Harry hizo la pregunta y Pedro asintió con la cabeza.

—Tendría que ganarlo. Pero el presidente busca cualquier pretexto para echar a Azaña. Está de acuerdo con los monárquicos en que hasta la más miserable de las reformas que el Gobierno trata de llevar adelante constituye un ataque a sus derechos.

Antonio soltó una carcajada amarga.

—¿Qué harán si alguna vez los desafiamos de verdad? —El muchacho sacudió la cabeza—. La propuesta de ley para una reforma agraria carece de fondos que la respalden, porque Azaña no quiere subir los impuestos. La gente está furiosa y se siente decepcionada.

—Ahora que en España tenéis la República —dijo Bernie—, no puede haber vuelta atrás.

Pedro asintió con la cabeza.

—Creo que los socialistas tendrían que abandonar el Gobierno, celebrar elecciones y ganar por amplia mayoría. Entonces ya veremos.

—Pero ¿las clases dirigentes os permitirían gobernar? ¿No sacarán el ejército a la calle?

Pedro le pasó un cigarrillo a Bernie, que había empezado a fumar desde su llegada a España.

—Que lo intenten —dijo Pedro—. Que lo intenten y ya veremos lo que les damos nosotros.

Al día siguiente, Harry y Bernie decidieron asistir a la votación de confianza en las Cortes. Había mucha gente en los alrededores del edificio de las Cortes; pero, gracias a Pedro, ambos habían conseguido unos pases. Un asistente los acompañó por una escalera de mármol hasta una tribuna situada encima del hemiciclo. Los bancos azules estaban llenos de diputados con traje y levita. El líder de la izquierda liberal, Azaña, hablaba con voz sonora y apasionada mientras agitaba uno de sus cortos brazos. Dependiendo de cuáles fueran sus tendencias políticas, los diarios lo retrataban como un monstruo con cara de rana o como el padre de la República; pero Harry pensaba que su aspecto era de lo más vulgar. Hablaba con ardor y pasión. Insistió en un dato y después se volvió hacia los diputados que tenía a su espalda, quienes aplaudieron y expresaron a gritos su aprobación. Azaña se pasó la mano por el cabello ralo y blanco y siguió adelante, enumerando los logros de la República. Harry miró hacia abajo e identificó a los políticos socialistas cuyos rostros había visto en los periódicos: el rechoncho y obeso Prieto; Largo Caballero, con su aspecto sorprendentemente burgués. Por una vez, Harry se dejó arrastrar por la emoción.

—Menudo entusiasmo el suyo, ¿verdad? —dijo en voz baja a Bernie.

—Todo es un maldito embuste —replicó Bernie con expresión de desprecio—. Míralos. Millones de españoles quieren una vida digna y ellos les montan... este circo. —Contempló el agitado mar de cabezas del hemiciclo—. Hace falta algo más fuerte que todo esto si queremos que se imponga el socialismo. Venga, salgamos de aquí.

Aquella noche se fueron a un bar del centro. Bernie estaba tan cínico como furioso.

—Lo que hace la democracia —dijo en tono de enfado— es atraer a la gente hacia el corrupto sistema burgués. Lo mismo ocurre en Inglaterra.

—Pero tendrán que pasar muchos años para que España se convierta en un país moderno —apuntó Harry—. Y ¿cuál es la alternativa? ¿La revolución y el derramamiento de sangre como en Rusia?

—Los obreros tendrán que asumir el mando de la situación. —Bernie miró a Harry, luego suspiró—. Vamos —añadió—, será mejor que volvamos al hostal. Ya es muy tarde.

Subieron por la calle dando trompicones, ambos con unas cuantas copas de más.

La habitación era sofocante, por lo que Bernie se quitó la camisa y salió al balcón. Las dos prostitutas, envueltas en unas batas vistosas, bebían en la casa de enfrente. Lo llamaron.

—¡Eh, inglés! ¿Por qué no vienes a jugar con nosotras?

—¡No puedo! —contestó Bernie alegremente—. ¡No tengo dinero!

—¡Nosotras no queremos dinero! ¡Siempre decimos: «si el rubio viniera a jugar»!

Las mujeres rieron, Bernie también rió y se volvió hacia Harry.

Harry se sentía incómodo y algo avergonzado.

—¿Te apetece?

Llevaban varias semanas bromeando sobre la posibilidad de salir con alguna furcia española, pero había sido un simple farol y al final no lo habían hecho.

—No. Por Dios, Bernie, podrías pillar algo.

Bernie lo miró sonriendo.

—¿Tienes miedo? —Se pasó una mano por el espeso cabello rubio, flexionando el brazo musculoso.

Harry se ruborizó.

—No quiero hacerlo con un par de putas borrachas —dijo—. Además, es a ti a quien llaman, no a mí.

Los celos aletearon en su interior como hacían algunas veces. Bernie tenía algo que a él le faltaba: energía, audacia, pasión por la vida. No era sólo su aspecto.

—También te habrían llamado a ti si hubieras salido al balcón.

—No vayas —insistió Harry—. Podrías pillar algo.

Los ojos de Bernie brillaban de emoción.

—Ya lo creo que iré. Venga. Es tu última oportunidad. —Bernie soltó una carcajada y después lo miró sonriendo—. Tienes que aprender a vivir, Harry, muchacho. Aprende a vivir.

Dos días después abandonaron Madrid. Antonio Mera los ayudó a llevar el equipaje a la estación.

Hicieron transbordo de tranvías en la Puerta de Toledo. Era media tarde, la hora de la siesta, y las calles soleadas estaban desiertas. Un camión pasó lentamente con la capota de lona alegremente pintada y las palabras «La Barraca» escritas en el lateral.

—El nuevo teatro de García Lorca para el pueblo —explicó Antonio. Era un joven alto y moreno, tan corpulento como su padre. Esbozó una sonrisa y añadió—: Quiere llevar a Calderón a los campesinos.

—Eso es bueno, ¿no? —dijo Harry—. Yo pensaba que la educación era lo único que la República había reformado.

Antonio se encogió de hombros.

—Han clausurado los colegios de los jesuitas, pero los nuevos no son suficientes. La historia de siempre: los partidos de la burguesía no quieren cargar con impuestos a los ricos para sufragarlos.

Un poco más adelante se oyó una especie de estallido semejante al petardeo de un automóvil. El sonido se repitió otras dos veces, más cerca. Un muchacho no mayor que Harry y Bernie salió corriendo de una calle lateral. Vestía pantalón de franela y camisa de color oscuro, ambas prendas de aspecto demasiado caro para Carabanchel. Su rostro, deformado por una expresión de terror, estaba empapado de sudor, y tenía los ojos desmesuradamente abiertos. Bajó a toda prisa por la calle y se perdió en una callejuela.

—¿Qué ha sido eso? —preguntó Harry.

Antonio respiró hondo.

—Quién sabe. Podría ser uno de los fascistas de Redondo.

Aparecieron otros dos jóvenes vestidos con camiseta y pantalones de obrero. Uno de ellos sostenía un pequeño objeto de color oscuro en una mano. Harry se quedó mirándolo boquiabierto al percatarse de que era una pistola.

—¡Allí abajo! —gritó Antonio, indicando el lugar por donde el joven había huido—. ¡Se fue por allí!

—¡Gracias, compañero!

El muchacho levantó la pistola a modo de saludo y los dos se alejaron a toda prisa. Conteniendo la respiración, Harry esperó más disparos, pero no hubo ninguno.

—Lo iban a matar —susurró, escandalizado.

Antonio lo miró por un instante con expresión de culpa y frunció el entrecejo.

—Era de las JONS. Tenemos que impedir que los fascistas echen raíces.

—¿Quiénes eran los otros?

—Comunistas. Han jurado acabar con ellos. Que tengan suerte.

—Tienen razón —convino Bernie—. Los fascistas son unas sabandijas, lo peor de lo peor.

—Era sólo un muchacho que corría —protestó Harry—. No iba armado.

Antonio soltó una carcajada amarga.

—¡Pero vaya si tienen armas! Lo que ocurre es que los obreros españoles no se rendirán como los italianos.

Llegó el tranvía, el habitual tranvía con su tintineo de todos los días, y los tres subieron a bordo. Harry estudió a Antonio. Parecía cansado; aquella noche tenía otro turno de trabajo en la fábrica de ladrillos. «Bernie tiene más cosas en común con él que conmigo», pensó Harry con tristeza.

Harry se tumbó en la cama con lágrimas en los ojos. Recordó que, en el tren de regreso, Bernie le había dicho que no pensaba volver a Cambridge. Se había hartado de vivir al margen del mundo real y quería volver a Londres, donde estaba la verdadera lucha de clases. Harry pensaba que cambiaría de idea, pero no lo había hecho; en otoño ya no regresó a Cambridge. Mantuvieron correspondencia durante un tiempo, pero las cartas de Bernie acerca de las huelgas y las manifestaciones antifascistas le eran en cierto modo tan ajenas como las de Sandy Forsyth sobre las carreras de galgos; por lo que, al cabo de algún tiempo, las cartas también fueron disminuyendo paulatinamente.

Harry se levantó. Estaba inquieto. Necesitaba salir de la habitación porque el silencio le atacaba los nervios. Se lavó, se cambió de camisa y bajó por la escalera húmeda.

La plaza seguía tan tranquila como antes. Se respiraba en el aire un ligero olor que él recordaba, orina procedente de los desagües en mal estado. Pensó en el cuadro que tenía en la pared, en el barniz romántico que éste otorgaba a la pobreza y la necesidad. En 1931 era joven e ingenuo, pero su aprecio por el cuadro había perdurado a lo largo de los años, la muchacha que miraba sonriendo al gitano de abajo; al igual que Bernie, confiaba en que España progresara. Pero la República se había hundido en el caos, después había estallado la Guerra Civil y ahora el fascismo había alcanzado el poder. Harry dio varias vueltas por el barrio y se detuvo en una panadería. Apenas había nada a la vista, sólo unas cuantas barras de pan, pero no aquellos pastelitos pegajosos que tanto les gustaban a los españoles. Una tarde Bernie se había zampado cinco, después se había comido una paella y, por la noche, se había puesto espectacularmente enfermo.

Un par de obreros pasaron por su lado mirándolo con hostilidad. Fue consciente de su chaqueta de corte impecable y su corbata. Vio una iglesia en la esquina de la plaza; también la habían quemado, probablemente en 1936. La fachada ornamentada todavía se mantenía en pie, pero el techo había desaparecido; a través de las ventanas cubiertas de maleza se podía ver el cielo. Un letrero de gran tamaño escrito a lápiz decía que la misa se celebraba en la casa parroquial de la puerta de al lado y que las confesiones se oían en el mismo lugar. El anuncio terminaba con un «¡Arriba España!».

Harry ya se había orientado. Subiendo la cuesta, llegaría a la Plaza Mayor. De camino se encontraba El Toro, el bar donde él y Bernie habían conocido a Pedro. Un antiguo local frecuentado por socialistas. Siguió adelante, mientras sus pisadas resonaban en la angosta calle y una brisa agradable y vespertina lo refrescaba. Se alegró de haber salido.

El Toro seguía donde siempre, con el rótulo de la cabeza de toro colgando todavía en el exterior. Harry vaciló un momento antes de entrar. En los nueve años transcurridos, el local no había cambiado: cabezas de toro en las paredes, viejos carteles en blanco y negro de corridas manchados de amarillo por la nicotina y los años. Los socialistas eran contrarios a las corridas de toros, pero el tabernero era muy aficionado y su vino era muy bueno, por lo que ellos se lo perdonaban.

Sólo había unos cuantos parroquianos, unos ancianos tocados con boina. Éstos miraron a Harry con cara de pocos amigos. Ya no estaba el joven y dinámico tabernero que Harry recordaba, yendo incansablemente de un lado a otro detrás de la barra. Su lugar lo ocupaba ahora un fornido individuo de mediana edad de rostro cuadrado y macizo. El hombre ladeó la cabeza con expresión inquisitiva.

—¿Señor?

Harry pidió una copa de vino tinto y rebuscó en el bolsillo las desconocidas monedas en las que figuraba grabado, como en todo lo demás, el emblema falangista del yugo y las flechas. El barman le colocó la copa delante.

—¿Alemán? —preguntó.

—No. Inglés.

El hombre enarcó las cejas y se volvió. Harry fue a sentarse en un banco. Tomó un ejemplar abandonado del *Arriba*, el periódico de la Falange, editado en papel fino y arrugado. En la primera plana, un guardia de fronteras español estrechaba la mano a un oficial alemán en una carretera de los Pirineos. El artículo hablaba de eterna amistad, de cómo el Führer y el Caudillo decidirían juntos el futuro del Mediterráneo occidental. Harry bebió un sorbo de vino; era más áspero que el vinagre.

Estudió la imagen, la impresionante celebración del Nuevo Orden. Recordó que en una ocasión le había dicho a Bernie que él defendía los valores de Rookwood. Probablemente sus palabras habían sonado un tanto ampulosas. Bernie rió con impaciencia y dijo que Rookwood era un campamento de instrucción para la elite capitalista. Quizá lo fuera, pensó Harry, pero en cualquier caso se trataba de una elite mejor que la de Hitler. No obstante, sus palabras seguían siendo ciertas. Recordó un noticiario que había visto acerca de las cosas que ocurrían en Alemania: unos ancianos judíos limpiaban las calles con cepillos de dientes en medio de las burlas de la gente.

Levantó los ojos. El barman conversaba tranquilamente con un par de ancianos que lo miraban sin disimulo. Hizo un esfuerzo por apurar el contenido de la copa y se levantó.

—Adiós —dijo antes de salir, pero no obtuvo respuesta.

Había más gente en la calle, en especial trajeados oficinistas de clase media que regresaban a casa. Pasó por debajo de un arco y se encontró en la Plaza Mayor, el centro del viejo Madrid donde solían celebrarse festivales y pronunciamientos. Las dos grandes fuentes estaban secas, pero alrededor de la enorme plaza seguía habiendo cafés con mesitas donde unos cuantos empleados de oficina permanecían sentados tomando café o coñac. Pero incluso allí los escaparates estaban casi vacíos y la pintura de los viejos edificios medio desconchada. Los mendigos estaban acurrucados junto a algunos de los portales ornamentados. Una pareja de guardias civiles recorría el perímetro de la plaza.

Harry permaneció de pie sin saber qué hacer, preguntándose dónde se podría tomar un café. Las farolas, que proyectaban una luz débil y blanca, ya empezaban a encenderse. Harry recordó lo fácil que era perderse por las callejuelas o entrar en una taberna. Dos mendigos se habían levantado y se dirigían a él. Dio media vuelta.

Mientras abandonaba la plaza, observó que una mujer que caminaba delante se detenía en seco, dándole la espalda. Se trataba de una mujer elegantemente vestida de blanco con un sombrerito encasquetado sobre el cabello pelirrojo. Él también se detuvo, asombrado. Seguro que era Barbara. El cabello y los andares no podían ser sino suyos. La mujer reanudó la marcha, dobló rápidamente la esquina de una calle lateral apurando el paso y su figura se desvaneció, convertida en una borrosa mancha blanca en plena oscuridad.

Harry echó a correr tras ella, pero se detuvo indeciso en la esquina sin saber si seguirla. Era imposible que fuese Barbara, seguro que no seguía viviendo allí. Además, Barbara jamás hubiera vestido semejante clase de ropa.

5

Aquella mañana Barbara había despertado, como de costumbre, al dar las siete en el reloj de la iglesia de la acera de enfrente. Salió del sueño rodeada por el calor del cuerpo de Sandy, que dormía a su lado con el rostro apoyado sobre su hombro. Se movió, y él emitió un murmullo suave como el de un niño. Entonces lo recordó, y una punzada de remordimiento la traspasó de parte a parte. Aquel día se tenía que reunir con el contacto de Markby; la culminación de todas las mentiras que le había estado contando.

Él se volvió sonriendo, con los ojos medio adormilados.

—Buenos días, cariño.

—Hola, Sandy —le dijo, acariciándole la barba áspera de la mejilla.

Sandy lanzó un suspiro.

—Será mejor que me levante. Tengo una reunión a las nueve.

—Desayuna como Dios manda, Sandy. Dile a Pilar que te prepare algo.

Sandy se restregó los ojos.

—No te preocupes, me tomaré un café por el camino. —Se inclinó con una pícara sonrisa en los labios—. Te dejo con tu desayuno a la inglesa. Te puedes comer todas las palomitas de maíz.

Le dio un beso, se levantó y abrió el armario que había junto a la cama. Mientras él elegía la ropa que se iba a poner, Barbara contempló su tórax musculoso y su vientre plano. Sandy no hacía ejercicio ni se cuidaba en las comidas; era un milagro que conservase la figura, pero lo cierto es que la conservaba. Él captó su mirada y esbozó aquella media sonrisa suya a lo Clark Gable.

—¿Quieres que vuelva a la cama?

—Tienes que irte. ¿Qué te espera esta mañana, el comité judío?

—Sí. Han llegado cinco mil nuevas familias. Sólo con lo que pudieron llevarse de Francia.

—Ten cuidado, Sandy. No molestes al régimen.

—Franco no se cree su propia propaganda antijudía. Tiene que seguirle la corriente a Hitler.

—Me gustaría que me dejaras ayudarte. Tengo mucha experiencia en el trato con los refugiados.

—Son cosas de tipo diplomático. No es trabajo para una mujer; ya sabes cómo son los españoles en esto.

Ella lo miró muy seria y volvió a sentirse culpable.

—Lo que estás haciendo es una buena labor, cariño.

Sandy sonrió.

—Quiero expiar mis pecados —dijo—. Volveré tarde, tengo una reunión en el Ministerio de Minas que durará toda la tarde. —Se acercó a la mesa del tocador. Desde lejos y sin las gafas, el rostro de él se convirtió para Barbara en una mancha borrosa. Sandy colgó en el respaldo de una silla el traje que había elegido y se dirigió hacia el cuarto de baño. Ella alargó la mano para coger un cigarrillo y se quedó tumbada fumando mientras él tomaba una ducha. Sandy regresó a la habitación, se afeitó y se vistió. Se acercó de nuevo a la cama y se inclinó para darle un beso, ahora con las mejillas más suaves.

—Eso está muy bien para algunos —dijo.

—Eres tú quien me enseñó a ser perezosa, Sandy.

Barbara lo miró con una triste sonrisa en los labios.

—¿Qué vas a hacer hoy?

—No gran cosa. Pensaba acercarme al Prado más tarde.

Se preguntó si Sandy se habría percatado del leve temblor de su voz al decir aquella mentira, pero él se limitó a acariciarle la mejilla con la mano antes de encaminarse hacia la puerta y convertirse de nuevo en una mancha borrosa.

Había conocido a Markby en el transcurso de una cena que ambos habían ofrecido tres semanas atrás. Casi todos los invitados eran funcionarios del Gobierno que iban acompañados de sus esposas; cuando las mujeres se levantaran de la mesa, los hombres se ocuparían de sus asuntos y quizá se entonara algún himno falangista. Pero también estaba Terry Markby, un reportero del *Daily Express* a quien Sandy había conocido en uno de los bares frecuentados por gente de la Falange. Era un hombre tímido de mediana edad, vestido con un esmoquin que le iba demasiado grande. Se lo veía incómodo, y Barbara se compadeció de él. Le preguntó en qué trabajaba y él se inclinó hacia ella y en voz baja contestó:

—Trato de averiguar algo sobre estos campos de concentración para presos republicanos. —Hablaba con un marcado acento de Bristol—. Beaverbrook no habría aceptado esa clase de reportajes durante la Guerra Civil, pero ahora es distinto.

—He oído rumores —dijo ella cautelosamente—. Pero, si hubiera habido algo así, estoy segura de que la Cruz Roja lo habría descubierto. Yo trabajaba para ellos, ¿sabe? Durante la Guerra Civil.

—¿En serio? —Markby la miró con asombro. Barbara sabía que aquella noche se había mostrado más torpe e inepta que de costumbre y que incluso había cometido errores en español. Cuando entró en la cocina para supervisar las tareas de Pilar, los cristales de las gafas se le empañaron y, al salir, se los limpió con el dobladillo y vio que Sandy la miraba con expresión de reproche.

—Pues sí —contestó con cierta aspereza—. Y, si hubieran desaparecido muchas personas, ellos se habrían enterado.

—¿En qué lado del frente estaba usted?

—En ambos, en distintos períodos.

—Fue algo tremendo.

—Era una guerra civil, español contra español. Hay que comprenderlo para poder entender las cosas que ocurrieron aquí.

El periodista hablaba en tono pausado. Sentada a su otro lado, Inés Vilar Cuesta encabezaba una enérgica petición de medias de nailon por parte de las señoras.

—Muchos han sido detenidos tras la victoria de Franco. Sus familiares pensaron que habían sido fusilados, pero un número importante de ellos fueron trasladados a campos. Y se hicieron muchos prisioneros durante la guerra, hombres dados por desaparecidos y presuntamente muertos. Franco los está utilizando como mano de obra forzada.

Barbara frunció el entrecejo. Había intentado decirse a sí misma durante mucho tiempo que, ahora que Franco había ganado, se le tenía que apoyar en la tarea de reconstruir España. Pero cada vez le resultaba más difícil cerrar los ojos ante lo que allí ocurría; sabía que lo que le estaba diciendo el periodista podía tener algo de verdad.

—¿Hay pruebas? —preguntó—. ¿Quién se lo ha dicho?

El hombre sacudió la cabeza.

—Lo siento, pero no se lo puedo decir. No estoy autorizado a revelar mis fuentes. —Miró alrededor con expresión de hastío—. Y mucho menos aquí.

Ella titubeó y después bajó la voz hasta convertirla en un susurro.

—Conozco a alguien que fue dado por desaparecido y se cree que ha muerto. Mil novecientos treinta y siete, en el Jarama. Un brigadista internacional inglés.

—¿Del bando republicano?

Markby enarcó una pálida ceja.

—Jamás compartí sus puntos de vista políticos. No me interesa la política. Pero está muerto —añadió categóricamente—. Nunca encontraron su cuerpo. El Jarama fue espantoso, miles de muertos. Miles.

Incluso en aquellos momentos, después de tres años, se le encogía el estómago sólo de pensarlo.

Markby ladeó la cabeza con expresión pensativa.

—Me consta que casi todos los prisioneros extranjeros fueron enviados a casa. Pero tengo entendido que algunos escaparon de la red, por así decirlo. Si usted pudiera facilitarme su nombre y su graduación, quizá consiguiese averiguar algo. Los prisioneros de guerra están en un campo aparte, cerca de Cuenca.

Barbara miró a sus invitados. Las mujeres se habían congregado alrededor de un alto funcionario de la Dirección General de Abastecimiento, e insistían en que les consiguiera medias de nailon. Aquella noche vio la cara más desagradable de la Nueva España, voraz y corrupta. Sandy, a la cabecera de la mesa, los miraba a todos con una sonrisa sarcástica en los labios. Era un reflejo de la clase de seguridad que la educación privada le otorgaba a uno. A Barbara le llamó la atención el hecho de que, pese a sus treinta y un años, su engominado cabello negro peinado hacia atrás y su bigote, Sandy ofreciese el aspecto de alguien diez años mayor. Era una imagen que él cultivaba con esmero. Se volvió hacia Markby, respirando hondo.

—Es inútil. Bernie está muerto.

—Pues, si estuvo en el Jarama, no es probable que sobreviviera. Aunque nunca se sabe. Con probar no se pierde nada. —Markby la miró sonriendo.

Tenía razón, pensó Barbara, aunque sólo hubiera una mínima posibilidad.

—Se llamaba Bernard Piper —dijo rápidamente—. Era un soldado. Pero no...

—¿Qué?

—Alimente falsas esperanzas.

Él la estudió con la mirada inquisitiva propia de un periodista.

—Jamás lo haría, señora Forsyth. Es sólo una remota posibilidad. Pero merece la pena echar un vistazo.

Ella asintió con la cabeza. Markby contempló al grupo de invitados en el que los esmóquines y los vestidos de alta costura se mezclaban con uniformes militares, y volvió a mirar a Barbara con perspicaz interés.

—Ahora se mueve usted en otros ambientes.

—Me enviaron a trabajar a la zona nacional después de que Bernie... Después de su desaparición. Allí conocí a Sandy.

Markby señaló con la cabeza a los invitados.

—Puede que a los amigos de su marido no les guste que usted ande buscando a un prisionero de guerra.

Barbara titubeó.

—No —dijo.

Markby le dirigió una sonrisa tranquilizadora.

—Ya me encargaré yo. Veré si puedo averiguar algo. *Entre nous*.

—Dudo que pueda sacar un reportaje de todo eso —dijo ella, sosteniéndole la mirada.

Él se encogió de hombros.

—Cualquier cosa con tal de ayudar a un compatriota —repuso.

Esbozó una sonrisa dulce e ingenua, aunque de ingenuo no tenía nada. Si localizaba a Bernie, pensó Barbara, y la historia se divulgaba, sería el final de todo lo que ella había conseguido allí. Se escandalizó al darse cuenta de que lo único que le importaba era que Bernie estuviera vivo.

Se levantó y se puso la bata de seda que Sandy le había regalado por Navidad. Abrió la ventana; otro día caluroso con el jardín lleno de flores. Le resultó extraño pensar que, en cuestión de seis semanas, el invierno volvería a estar allí con sus nieblas y sus heladas.

Tropezó con una silla, soltó una maldición y sacó las gafas que guardaba en el cajón del tocador. Se miró en el espejo. Sandy insistía en que prescindiera de ellas siempre que pudiese y que se aprendiera debidamente la disposición de la vivienda para no tropezar con las cosas.

—Sería muy divertido, cariño —le decía—, pasear tranquilamente por ahí saludando a la gente sin que nadie supiera que eres un poco corta de vista.

Sandy no soportaba que llevase gafas; pero aunque a ella tampoco le gustaban, seguía poniéndoselas cuando estaba a solas. Las necesitaba, sencillamente.

—Menuda idiotez —musitó mientras se quitaba los rulos y se pasaba el peine por el espeso cabello cobrizo y ondulado.

Aquel peluquero era muy bueno, ahora iba siempre bien peinada. Se aplicó cuidadosamente el maquillaje, máscara para realzar sus claros ojos verdes y polvos para acentuar los pómulos. Todo aquello se lo había enseñado Sandy. «Puedes decidir tu aspecto, ¿sabes? —le había dicho—. Conseguir que la gente te vea tal como tú quieres. Si es que quieres.» Al principio, ella no se lo acababa de creer, pero él había insistido y, al final, había resultado que tenía razón: por primera vez en su vida había empezado a poner en duda su fealdad. Hasta con Bernie le había costado averiguar qué había visto en ella, pese a las incesantes muestras de cariño que él le ofrecía. Las lágrimas asomaron a sus ojos. Parpadeó rápidamente para contenerlas. Aquel día necesitaba ser fuerte y tener la mente despejada.

No se reuniría con el contacto de Markby hasta última hora de la tarde. Primero iría a El Prado. No soportaba quedarse encerrada en casa todo el día, esperando. Se puso su mejor vestido de calle, el blanco con estampado de rosas.

Llamaron a la puerta y apareció Pilar. La chica tenía un redondo rostro de expresión enfurruñada y un ensortijado cabello negro que pugnaba por escapar de debajo de su cofia de sirvienta. Barbara se dirigió a ella en español:

—Por favor, Pilar, prepare el desayuno. Hoy quiero un buen desayuno: tostadas, zumo de naranja y huevos, por favor.

—No hay zumo, señora, ayer no había naranjas en las tiendas.

—No importa. Dígale a la asistenta que salga más tarde a ver si encuentra algunas, por favor.

La chica se retiró. Barbara pensaba que ojalá sonriera alguna vez. Pero quizás hubiese perdido a algún familiar en la guerra, como le ocurría a casi todo el mundo. En ocasiones Barbara creía percibir una pizca de desprecio cuando Pilar la llamaba «señora», como si supiera que ella y Sandy no estaban realmente casados. Se decía que eran figuraciones suyas. No tenía experiencia con la servidumbre y, al llegar a la casa, se había sentido muy incómoda con Pilar, nerviosa y con ganas de complacer. Sandy le había dicho que tenía que impartir las órdenes con claridad y precisión y mantener las distancias. «Lo prefieren así, cariño.» Recordó lo que le había dicho María Herreira sobre la conveniencia de no fiarse jamás de las criadas: todas eran chicas de pueblo, y la mitad, rojas. Sin embargo, María era una mujer muy amable que trabajaba como voluntaria en el cuidado de ancianos por cuenta de la iglesia. Encendió otro cigarrillo y bajó a desayunar las palomitas de maíz que Sandy le conseguía como por arte de magia en un Madrid sometido a racionamiento y medio muerto de hambre.

Al estallar la guerra en 1936, Barbara llevaba tres años trabajando en el cuartel general de la Cruz Roja, en Ginebra. Estaba adscrita a la sección de Desplazados, donde se buscaba el rastro de miembros desaparecidos de familias de la Europa oriental desgarradas por la Primera Guerra Mundial y todavía desaparecidos. Comparaba nombres y documentos, escribía cartas a ministerios de Interior, desde Riga hasta Budapest. Conseguía poner en contacto a tantas personas con sus familias que la tarea merecía la pena. Aun en el caso de que todos los parientes hubieran muerto, al menos las familias lo sabían con certeza.

Al principio, el trabajo le encantaba: era un cambio respecto a su labor como enfermera en Birmingham. Lo había conseguido, en parte, gracias a su trabajo en la Cruz Roja británica. Pero al cabo de cuatro años se empezó a cansar. Tenía veintiséis años, no tardaría en llegar a los treinta y temía acabar fosilizándose entre fichas perfectamente ordenadas y la imperturbable monotonía de los suizos. Fue a entrevistarse con un funcionario en un bonito despacho que daba a las tranquilas y azules aguas del lago.

—En España la situación es muy grave —le dijo el funcionario—. Hay miles de personas que se han quedado en una zona mientras que sus familiares se encuentran en la otra. Estamos enviando material médico y tratando de organizar intercambios. Pero es una guerra salvaje. Los rusos y los alemanes están empezando a intervenir.

La miró con expresión cansada por encima de las gafas. Todas las esperanzas en el sentido de que la Primera Guerra Mundial hubiera sido verdaderamente la destinada a acabar con todas las contiendas se disipaban progresivamente. Primero, Mussolini en Abisinia, y ahora, España.

—Me gustaría trabajar sobre el terreno, señor —dijo Barbara con firmeza.

Llegó a un Madrid insoportablemente caluroso en septiembre de 1936. Franco avanzaba en el sur; las tropas coloniales marroquíes, transportadas por la aviación de Hitler a través del estrecho de Gibraltar, se encontraban a poco más de cien kilómetros de distancia. La ciudad estaba llena de refugiados y familias desplazadas que arrastraban los fardos enormes de sus pertenencias por las calles o bien se apretujaban en carros tirados por asnos. Ahora podía contemplar directamente el caos de la guerra. Jamás olvidaría al anciano de mirada aterrorizada que pasó por su lado aquel primer día, llevando a cuestas todo lo que tenía: un colchón sucio echado sobre los hombros y un canario en una jaula de madera. Simbolizaba a todos los refugiados, a los desplazados, a quienes habían quedado atrapados en mitad de la guerra.

Los milicianos rojos se trasladaban al frente en camiones y autocares. Eran madrileños corrientes cuyo uniforme consistía en el mono de trabajo azul oscuro que llevaban todos los obreros y el pañuelo rojo al cuello. Agitando sus anticuadas armas al pasar, lanzaban el grito de desafío de la República: «¡No pasarán!» Barbara, que creía en la paz por encima de todo, sentía deseos de llorar por ellos. Al principio, también por ella misma, porque estaba asustada: por el caos, por los relatos de las atrocidades de pesadilla cometidas por ambos bandos, por los aviones fascistas que habían empezado a aparecer en el cielo, induciendo a la gente a detenerse a mirar y, en ocasiones, a salir corriendo en busca de la seguridad del metro. Una vez vio caer varias bombas en serie mientras una nube de humo se elevaba al oeste de la ciudad. El bombardeo de la población civil era algo que Europa llevaba años temiendo; y ahora estaba ocurriendo.

La oficina de la Cruz Roja se había instalado en un pequeño despacho en el centro de Madrid, un oasis de cordura en el que media docena de hombres y mujeres, casi todos ellos suizos, se encargaban de repartir material médico y de organizar intercambios de niños refugiados. Aunque Barbara no hablaba español, su francés era excelente y se alegraba de hacerse entender.

—Necesitamos ayuda en los intercambios de refugiados —le dijo el director, Doumergue, en su segundo día de trabajo—. Centenares de niños han sido separados de sus familias. Hay todo un grupo de Burgos que se encontraba en un campamento de verano de la sierra de Guadarrama... Queremos intercambiarlos por unos cuantos niños de Madrid atrapados en Sevilla.

Doumergue era un suizo muy serio y tranquilo, joven, de rostro mofletudo y expresión de fatiga. Barbara sabía que había sufrido crisis de pánico, algo impropio de ella. «Babs, nuestro puntal», solían llamarla en Birmingham. Se apartó de la frente un mechón rebelde de cabello pelirrojo.

—Pues claro —repuso—. ¿Qué necesita que haga?

Aquella tarde fue a visitar a los niños al convento donde estaban alojados, para anotar sus datos. La acompañaba Monique, la intérprete de la Cruz Roja. Era una mujer menuda y bonita, vestida con una falda pulcra y una blusa perfectamente planchada. Al cruzar la Puerta del Sol, pasaron por delante de unos carteles enormes del presidente Azaña, de Lenin y de Stalin.

—Así están las cosas ahora —dijo—. Sólo Rusia ayudará a la República. Que Dios los ayude.

La plaza estaba llena de altavoces y la voz de una mujer subía y bajaba, puntuada por los minúsculos chirridos del micrófono. Barbara preguntó qué estaban diciendo.

—Es Dolores Ibárruri, *la Pasionaria*. Está diciendo a las amas de casa que, si vienen los fascistas, tienen que calentar aceite y arrojarlo desde los balcones sobre sus cabezas.

Barbara se estremeció.

—Si por lo menos los dos bandos comprendieran que todo será destruido.

—Es demasiado tarde para eso —contestó Monique en tono cansado.

Entraron en el convento por una sólida puerta de madera abierta en un alto muro levantado para proteger a las monjas del mundo exterior. La habían echado abajo y, al otro lado del pequeño patio, unos milicianos montaban guardia junto a la entrada con los fusiles al hombro. El edificio había sido incendiado. No había cristales en las ventanas, y unas negras nubes de hollín se elevaban desde las paredes. Se respiraba en el aire un nauseabundo olor a quemado.

Barbara se detuvo en el patio.

—¿Qué ha pasado? Yo creía que los niños estaban con las monjas...

—Las monjas han huido. Y los curas también. Los que pudieron.

El populacho quemó casi todos los conventos y las iglesias en julio. —Monique la miró inquisitivamente—. ¿Eres católica?

—No, no, la verdad es que no soy nada. Todo esto me impresiona un poco, sencillamente.

—La situación no es tan grave en la parte de atrás. Las monjas dirigían un hospital, hay unas camas.

El vestíbulo había sido incendiado y saqueado, y, entre las imágenes rotas había esparcidas hojas arrancadas de los breviarios.

—¡Qué mal debieron de pasarlo las monjas! —exclamó Barbara—. Encerradas aquí dentro, mientras entraba el populacho y lo quemaba todo.

Monique se encogió de hombros.

—La Iglesia apoya a los nacionales. Y llevan siglos viviendo a costa de la gente. En Francia ocurrió lo mismo.

Monique encabezó la marcha, bajando por un estrecho pasillo lleno de ecos, y abrió una puerta. Al otro lado había una sala de hospital con unas veinte camas. Las paredes estaban desnudas, unas manchas más claras en forma de cruz revelaban los lugares de los que se habían retirado los símbolos religiosos. Unos treinta niños de aproximadamente diez años, sucios y atemorizados, permanecían sentados en las camas. Una francesa alta con uniforme de enfermera se acercó a toda prisa a ellas.

—Ay, Monique, has venido. ¿Se sabe cuándo podremos enviar a los niños de vuelta a casa?

—Todavía no, Anna. Tomaremos sus datos y después acudiremos al ministerio. ¿Los ha examinado el médico?

—Sí. —La enfermera suspiró—. Todos están bastante bien, aparte de asustados. Proceden de hogares religiosos... Se asustaron mucho cuando vieron que habían quemado el convento.

Barbara contempló sus caritas tristes, casi todas ellas surcadas de lágrimas.

—Si alguno se encuentra mal, yo soy enfermera...

—No —dijo Monique—. Ya está aquí Anna. Lo mejor que podemos hacer por ellos es llevarlos al lugar de donde proceden.

Se pasaron una hora anotando sus datos. Algunos estaban aterrorizados, y la enfermera tuvo que persuadirlos de que hablaran. Al final, lo consiguieron. Barbara tosió por efecto del humo.

—¿No se les podría trasladar a otro sitio? —le preguntó a Monique—. Este humo es muy malo para ellos.

Monique negó con la cabeza.

—Hay miles de refugiados en esta ciudad, y cada día son más. Tuvimos suerte de que un funcionario se tomara la molestia de encontrar un sitio para estos niños.

Fue un alivio salir otra vez al exterior a pesar del ardiente sol. Monique saludó con la mano a un miliciano.

—Salud —contestó éste.

Monique le ofreció a Barbara un cigarrillo y la miró inquisitivamente.

—Es así en todas partes —le dijo.

—No puedo soportarlo. Yo era enfermera antes de trasladarme a Ginebra. —Bárbara exhaló una nube de humo—. Pero es que... estos niños, ¿volverán a ser lo que eran cuando regresen a sus casas?

—Nadie en España volverá a ser jamás lo que era —contestó Monique en un súbito arrebato de furia y desesperación.

En noviembre de 1936 Franco ya había llegado a las afueras de Madrid. Pero sus fuerzas tuvieron que detenerse en la Casa de Campo, el antiguo bosque real situado justo al oeste de la ciudad. Ahora la aviación rusa protegía la ciudad y caían menos bombas. Se habían levantado unas cercas provisionales de tablas para cubrir los edificios bombardeados y en ellas se exhibían más retratos de Lenin y Stalin. Había pancartas en todas las calles. ¡NO PASARÁN! La determinación de resistir era aún más fuerte que en verano y Barbara la admiraba, aunque se preguntaba cómo podría sobrevivir al frío invernal. Con sólo una carretera de acceso a la ciudad todavía abierta, las provisiones ya empezaban a escasear. Barbara casi deseaba que Franco tomara Madrid de una vez para que así terminara la guerra, a pesar de las terribles historias que se contaban acerca de las atrocidades cometidas por los nacionales. En el bando republicano también abundaban; pero las de Franco, fríamente sistemáticas, parecían peores.

A los dos meses, Barbara ya se había acostumbrado en la medida en que una persona podía habituarse a semejante situación. Se había anotado muchos éxitos, había conseguido el intercambio de docenas de refugiados, y ahora la Cruz Roja intentaba negociar intercambios de prisioneros entre la zona republicana y la nacional. Se enorgullecía de la rapidez con que aprendía español. Pero los niños seguían en el convento... su caso había caído en una especie de abismo burocrático. Pese a que llevaba semanas sin cobrar, Anna, la enfermera, había permanecido en su puesto. Por lo menos, los niños no se darían a la fuga; les daban miedo las hordas rojas que había al otro lado de los muros del convento.

Un día Barbara y Monique se pasaron toda una tarde en el Ministerio del Interior, tratando una vez más de conseguir el intercambio de niños. Cada vez hablaban con un funcionario distinto, y el de ese día era aún menos servicial que los anteriores. Llevaba la chaqueta negra de cuero que lo identificaba como comunista pero que a él le sentaba un poco rara, porque era grueso y de mediana edad y tenía pinta de empleado de banca. Se pasó el rato fumando cigarrillos sin ofrecerles ninguno a ellas.

—No hay calefacción en el convento, camarada —dijo Barbara—. Con el frío que se avecina, los niños enfermarán.

El hombre soltó un gruñido. Se inclinó y cogió una sobada carpeta de entre el montón que tenía encima del escritorio. La leyó, dando caladas al pitillo, y después miró a las mujeres.

—Son niños pertenecientes a acaudaladas familias católicas. Si vuelven, les harán preguntas acerca de los dispositivos militares que tenemos aquí.

—Apenas han salido del edificio. Les da miedo hacerlo.

Barbara se sorprendió de la soltura con que hablaba español cuando estaba alterada. El funcionario esbozó una sonrisa siniestra.

—Sí, porque a los rojos nos temen. No me gusta la idea de que vuelvan a casa. La seguridad lo es todo. —Dejó la carpeta nuevamente en su sitio—. Todo.

Mientras abandonaban el ministerio, Monique meneó la cabeza con desesperación.

—La seguridad. La eterna excusa para las peores atrocidades.

—Tendremos que echar mano de otro plan de acción. ¿Y si desde Ginebra se pudieran poner en contacto con el ministro?

—Lo dudo.

Barbara suspiró.

—Habrá que intentarlo. Tendré que organizar el envío de más provisiones para ellos. Dios mío, qué cansada estoy. ¿Vamos a tomar algo?

—No, tengo que hacer la colada. Nos vemos mañana.

Barbara vio alejarse a Monique. Se dejó arrastrar por una oleada de cansancio. Era consciente de lo lejos que estaba de la confraternidad, la solidaridad que reinaba entre los habitantes de la ciudad. Decidió irse a un bar cercano a la Puerta del Sol en el que a veces se reunían súbditos ingleses, personal de la Cruz Roja, periodistas y diplomáticos.

El bar estaba casi desierto, no había ningún conocido. Pidió una copa de vino y fue a sentarse a una mesa del rincón. No le gustaba sentarse sola en los bares, pero tal vez más tarde entrara algún conocido.

Al cabo de un rato, oyó la voz de un hombre que hablaba el típico inglés de las escuelas privadas, con vocales largas y perezosas. Levantó los ojos y vio su rostro reflejado en el espejo que había detrás de la barra. Le pareció el hombre más atractivo que jamás hubiera visto.

Lo estudió con disimulo. El forastero permanecía de pie junto a la barra, hablando un titubeante español. Vestía una camisa barata y un mono de trabajo y llevaba un brazo en cabestrillo. Era un veinteañero de hombros anchos y cabello rubio oscuro. Tenía un rostro largo y ovalado, unos ojos muy grandes y una boca fuerte de labios carnosos. Se le veía incómodo por el hecho de encontrarse solo en aquel lugar. Su mirada se cruzó con la de Barbara a través del espejo, y entonces ella apartó la suya y experimentó un sobresalto cuando el camarero se le acercó envuelto en su delantal blanco y le preguntó si quería otra copa. El hombre sostenía la botella en la mano, y ella le golpeó involuntariamente el codo con el suyo; eso hizo que la botella se le cayera ruidosamente sobre la mesa y el vino se derramara sobre sus pantalones.

—Ay, perdón. Ha sido culpa mía, perdone.

El camarero parecía molesto. Quizá fuese el único par de pantalones que tenía. Empezó a secarse con una servilleta.

—Cuánto lo siento. Le pagaré la limpieza, yo...

A Barbara se le atragantaron las palabras y olvidó sus conocimientos de español. Después, oyó a su lado la pausada voz del inglés.

—Disculpe, ¿es usted inglesa? ¿Puedo ayudarla en algo?

—No... no, no se preocupe.

El camarero se tranquilizó y ella se ofreció a pagarle la botella junto con la limpieza de los pantalones; entonces el hombre se retiró más calmado para ir por otra copa. Barbara miró muy nerviosa al inglés.

—Qué estúpida soy. Siempre he sido muy torpe.

—Son cosas que pasan —dijo él, tendiéndole una mano de dedos largos bronceados por el sol. La muñeca, cubierta por un fino vello rubio, reflejaba la luz y brillaba como el oro. Barbara vio que tenía el otro brazo escayolado desde más arriba del codo hasta la muñeca. El muchacho tenía unos ojos grandes y de color aceituna oscuro, como si fuera español—. Bernie Piper —añadió, estudiándola con curiosidad—. Está usted muy lejos de casa.

—Barbara Clare. Pues sí, me temo que en efecto estoy muy lejos. Colaboro con la Cruz Roja.

—¿Le importa que me siente? Hace semanas que no hablo inglés con nadie.

—Bueno, yo... no, siéntese, por favor.

Y así empezó todo.

Alguien de la oficina del *Daily Express* en Madrid había llamado a Barbara tres días antes, diciéndole que había un hombre que tal vez pudiera ayudarla. Se llamaba Luis y podría reunirse con ella en un bar de la parte antigua de la ciudad el lunes por la tarde. Ella había pedido hablar con Markby, pero no estaba. Mientras colgaba el auricular, Barbara se preguntó si el teléfono estaría intervenido; Sandy le había dicho que no, pero ella había oído que intervenían los teléfonos de todos los extranjeros.

Después del desayuno, regresó a su habitación. El escritorio con espejo era una pieza del siglo XVIII que ella y Sandy habían comprado en el Rastro la primavera anterior. Seguramente procedía del saqueo de alguna lujosa mansión de Madrid al principio de la guerra. Allí estaba la fotografía de Bernie, tomada poco antes de su marcha al frente en un estudio fotográfico con meridianas y palmeras en macetas. Bernie aparecía de pie y de uniforme, con los brazos cruzados, sonriendo a la cámara.

Estaba bellísimo. Era una palabra que solía utilizarse para describir a las mujeres, pero es que allí el bello era él. Llevaba mucho tiempo sin contemplar la fotografía; el hecho de verla le seguía haciendo daño; lloraba la pérdida de Bernie tan profundamente como siempre. Y se sentía culpable por que Sandy la hubiera rescatado y ayudado a reponerse, pero lo suyo con Bernie había sido diferente. Lanzó un suspiro. No tenía que abrigar demasiadas esperanzas. No tenía que hacerlo.

Todavía se asombraba de que Bernie se hubiera interesado por ella; debía de parecer un monstruo en aquel bar, con el cabello rizado y alborotado y aquel jersey viejo y holgado. Se quitó las gafas y pensó que sin ellas habría resultado bastante atractiva. Volvió a ponérselas. Como de costumbre, incluso en medio de sus preocupaciones por Bernie, el mero hecho de pensar que era atractiva desencadenó un recuerdo, uno de los peores. Por regla general, trataba de apartarlos, pero esta vez no lo hizo, a pesar de que siempre la dejaba con la sensación de encontrarse al borde de un precipicio. Millie Howard y su pandilla de niñas de once años formando un círculo a su alrededor en el patio del colegio y cantando: «Cuatro ojos con ricitos, cuatro ojos con ricitos.» De no haber llevado las gafas que la identificaban como algo diferente y de no haber reaccionado ruborizándose con lágrimas en los ojos, ¿habría llegado a producirse aquel tormento que había durado tanto tiempo? Cerró los ojos. Y entonces vio a su hermana mayor, la resplandeciente Carol, que había heredado el cabello rubio de su madre y su rostro en forma de corazón, cruzando el salón de su casita de Erdington para ir a reunirse con uno más de sus pretendientes. Pasaba en medio de un revuelo de faldas, dejando una estela de perfume. «Qué guapa está, ¿verdad?», le decía su madre a su padre, mientras Barbara se moría de celos y tristeza. Poco antes se había derrumbado y le había revelado a su madre el acoso a que la sometían las otras niñas en el colegio.

—La belleza no lo es todo, cariño —le había dicho su madre—. Tú eres mucho más inteligente que Carol.

La mano le temblaba cuando se encendió un cigarrillo. Ahora su madre y su padre, Carol y su apuesto marido contable se encontraban bajo las incursiones aéreas. La guerra relámpago se había extendido más allá de Londres. En la edición censurada del *Daily Mail* que había comprado en la estación, había tenido noticias, con una semana de retraso, de las primeras incursiones sobre Birmingham. ¡Y ella sentada en una bonita casa, lamiéndose todavía las viejas heridas mientras su familia corría a los refugios antiaéreos! Era un comportamiento tan mezquino que se avergonzó. A veces se preguntaba si no tendría algún problema mental, si no estaría un poco chiflada. Se levantó y se puso la chaqueta y el sombrero. Visitaría el Prado y después iría a ver qué sabía aquel hombre. Se alegró de sentirse tan decidida.

El Museo del Prado tenía casi todas las paredes vacías; buena parte de los cuadros habían sido descolgados para que estuvieran más protegidos durante la guerra, y, hasta el momento, sólo unos cuantos habían vuelto a su sitio. El ambiente era frío y húmedo. Tomó un desayuno frugal en el pequeño café y se pasó un rato fumando hasta que llegó la hora de marcharse.

Sandy había observado que algo raro le ocurría; la víspera le había preguntado si se encontraba bien. Ella le había contestado que se aburría, y era cierto: desde que se habían instalado en la casa ella disponía de largas horas muertas. Entonces Sandy le preguntó si le gustaría trabajar como voluntaria; porque, en ese caso, quizás él pudiera encontrarle algo. Barbara respondió que sí para despistarlo, y él asintió con la cabeza, aparentemente satisfecho, y se fue al estudio a trabajar un poco más.

Sandy ya llevaba seis meses trabajando en lo que él llamaba su «proyecto de Ministerio de Minas». A menudo trabajaba hasta muy tarde y con frecuencia lo hacía en casa, mucho más duro de lo que Barbara hubiera visto jamás. Unas veces sonreía con un brillo de emoción en los ojos, como si guardara un maravilloso secreto; a Barbara no le gustaba aquella sonrisita enigmática. Otras veces se le veía distraído y preocupado. Decía que el proyecto era confidencial, que no le estaba permitido hablar de él. Y en ocasiones hacía misteriosas excursiones al campo. Colaboraba con un geólogo, un hombre apellidado Otero, que había visitado la casa en un par de ocasiones y que a Barbara le producía cierta desconfianza. Temía que ambos estuvieran implicados en algo ilegal; media España parecía estar trabajando en el estraperlo. Sandy tampoco hablaba demasiado de sus actividades en el comité de ayuda a los refugiados judíos de Francia. Barbara se preguntaba si Sandy creía que sus tareas de voluntario lo apartaban de la imagen que él quería proyectar de sí mismo como próspero y duro hombre de negocios, pese a que aquella faceta de su personalidad, la del hombre deseoso de ayudar a los necesitados, era precisamente la que le había atraído de él.

A las cuatro de la tarde dejó el Prado y se dirigió al centro. Mientras caminaba por las callejuelas sofocantes y polvorientas que olían a estiércol, vio que las tiendas empezaban a abrir después de la siesta. Los tacones de sus cómodos zapatos resonaban sobre los adoquines. Al doblar una esquina, vio a un anciano con una camisa gastada y sucia que trataba de subir a la acera un carro lleno de latas de aceite de oliva. Sujetaba el carro por las lanzas en un intento de sortear el alto bordillo. Detrás de él se alzaba un edificio recién pintado, encima de cuya puerta había un letrero con el yugo y las flechas. Mientras Barbara contemplaba la escena, dos jóvenes de camisa azul aparecieron en el umbral. Se inclinaron ante ella pidiéndole disculpas por impedirle el paso y le preguntaron al viejo si podían ayudarlo. El hombre soltó las lanzas con alivio y ellos tiraron del carro y lo subieron a la acera.

—Se me ha muerto el burro —les dijo el hombre—. Y no tengo dinero para comprarme otro.

—Muy pronto en España todo el mundo tendrá un caballo. Denos tiempo, señor.

—Lo tenía desde hacía veinte años. Me lo comí cuando se murió. Pobre *Héctor*, tenía una carne muy dura. Gracias, camaradas.

—De nada.

Los falangistas le dieron al viejo unas palmadas en la espalda y entraron de nuevo en la casa. Barbara bajó de la acera para permitirle el paso. Se preguntó si ahora las cosas empezarían a ir mejor. No lo sabía; después de cuatro años en España, se seguía sintiendo una forastera y había muchas cosas que no entendía.

Sabía que en la Falange había muchos idealistas que sinceramente deseaban mejorar la vida de los españoles; pero que muchos más se habían afiliado para aprovechar la ocasión de obtener beneficios ilícitos. Contempló una vez más el emblema del yugo y las flechas que, al igual que las camisas azules, le recordaba que los de la Falange eran fascistas, hermanos gemelos de los nazis. Vio que uno de los falangistas la miraba a través de la ventana, y apuró el paso.

El bar era un lugar oscuro y astroso. El obligatorio retrato de Franco, cubierto de manchas de grasa, colgaba detrás de la barra junto a la cual dos jóvenes charlaban tranquilamente. Una corpulenta mujer vestida de negro y con el pelo blanco lavaba vasos en el fregadero. Uno de los hombres iba con muleta; había perdido media pierna y llevaba los bajos de la pernera toscamente cosidos. Todos miraron a Barbara con curiosidad. Por regla general, únicamente las putas entraban solas en los bares, no las elegantes extranjeras con costosos vestidos y sombreritos redondos en la cabeza.

Un joven sentado a una mesa de la parte de atrás levantó una mano. Mientras ella se acercaba, el joven se levantó con una reverencia y le estrechó la mano con un fuerte y seco apretón.

—¿Señora Forsyth?

—Sí —contestó ella en español, procurando no levantar la voz—. ¿Es usted Luis?

—En efecto. Tome asiento, por favor. Permítame que le traiga un café.

Mientras él se dirigía a la barra, Barbara lo estudió. Era un treintañero alto y delgado de cabello oscuro y rostro alargado y triste. Llevaba unos pantalones muy gastados y una chaqueta vieja cubierta de lamparones. Sus mejillas estaban cubiertas de una barba áspera, al igual que las de los otros hombres que se encontraban en el café; había escasez de cuchillas de afeitar en la ciudad. Caminaba como un soldado. Regresó con dos cafés y una bandeja con lo que parecían unas bolas de carne. Ella tomó un sorbo e hizo una mueca. Él la miró con una sonrisa irónica en los labios.

—Me temo que no es muy bueno.

—No se preocupe. —Barbara echó un vistazo a algo semejante a unas albóndigas pequeñas y marrones de las que asomaban unos delicados huesecillos—. ¿Qué son?

—Lo llaman pichones, pero yo creo que es otra cosa. No sé muy bien el qué. No lo recomendaría.

Barbara miró a Luis mientras comía, sacándose los huesecitos de la boca. Había decidido no decir nada y dejar que fuera él quien empezara. Se revolvió nerviosamente en su asiento y estudió aquel rostro de ojos grandes y oscuros.

—El señor Markby me ha contado que trata usted de localizar a un hombre que fue dado por desaparecido en el Jarama. Un inglés —precisó él en tono pausado.

—Sí, es cierto.

El joven asintió con la cabeza.

—Un comunista.

Con un estremecimiento de temor, Barbara se preguntó si sería un policía, si Markby la habría traicionado o lo habrían traicionado a él. Hizo un esfuerzo por conservar la calma.

—Mi interés es personal, no político. Era... era mi... mi novio antes de que yo conociera a mi marido. Pensé que había muerto.

Luis volvió a revolverse en su asiento y carraspeó.

—Usted vive en la España nacional y me han dicho que está casada con un hombre que tiene amigos en el Gobierno. Y, sin embargo, busca a un comunista que participó en la guerra. Perdone, pero me parece muy raro.

—Yo trabajaba en la Cruz Roja; éramos un organismo neutral.

Él esbozó una sonrisa amarga.

—Tuvo suerte. No hay ningún español que haya podido ser neutral durante mucho tiempo. —La miró detenidamente—. O sea que no es contraria a la Nueva España.

—No. El general Franco venció, y eso es lo que hay. Gran Bretaña no es enemiga de España. —«Al menos por el momento», pensó.

—Perdone —dijo Luis extendiendo las manos en un repentino gesto de disculpa—. Es que he de proteger mi propia situación, tengo que andarme con cuidado. ¿Su marido no sabe nada de esta... búsqueda?

—No.

—Pues procure que todo siga igual, señora. Si sus investigaciones trascendieran, podrían causarle problemas.

—Lo sé —reconoció Barbara. El corazón le empezaba a latir de emoción. Si él no tuviera ninguna información, no se habría mostrado tan precavido y cauteloso. Pero ¿de cuánto estaría al corriente? ¿Dónde lo habría encontrado Markby?

Luis volvió a mirarla con interés.

—Supongamos que usted encuentra a este hombre, señora Forsyth. ¿Qué desearía hacer en tal caso?

—Desearía que lo repatriaran. En su calidad de prisionero de guerra, tendrían que devolverlo a casa. Eso es lo que dice la Convención de Ginebra.

Luis se encogió de hombros.

—No es así como el Generalísimo ve las cosas. No le gustaría que un hombre que vino a nuestro país para combatir contra españoles fuera devuelto a casa sin más. Y, en caso de que se insinuara públicamente la existencia de prisioneros de guerra en España, puede que semejantes prisioneros desaparecieran. ¿Me comprende?

Ella lo miró directamente a los ojos, profundos e impenetrables.

—¿Qué es lo que sabe? —le preguntó.

Él se inclinó hacia delante. Un olor áspero a carne escapaba de su boca. Barbara hizo un esfuerzo para no echarse hacia atrás.

—Mi familia es de Sevilla —dijo—. Cuando las tropas de Franco tomaron la ciudad, mi hermano y yo fuimos reclutados y nos pasamos tres años luchando contra los rojos. Después de la victoria, parte del ejército se disolvió, pero algunos de nosotros tuvimos que quedarnos, y a Agustín y a mí nos destinaron a servicios de guardia en un campo cerca de Cuenca. ¿Sabe usted dónde está eso?

—Markby me lo comentó. De camino a Aragón, ¿verdad?

Luis asintió con la cabeza.

—Así es. Donde están las famosas «casas colgadas».

—¿Las qué?

—Son unas casas viejas construidas justo al borde de una garganta que discurre al lado de la ciudad y que parecen colgar por encima de ella. A algunos les parecen preciosas. —Suspiró—. Cuenca está en la zona más elevada de la meseta... te mueres de calor en verano y te congelas de frío en invierno. Ésta es la única época del año soportable; la nieve y las heladas no tardarán en llegar. Yo pasé dos inviernos allí y le aseguro que tuve más que suficiente.

—¿Cómo es ese campo?

Luis se revolvió de nuevo en su asiento y bajó la voz hasta convertirla en un susurro.

—Un campo de trabajos forzados. Uno de los campos que no existen oficialmente. Éste era para los prisioneros de guerra republicanos. A unos ocho kilómetros de Cuenca, allá arriba, en Tierra Muerta.

—¿Dónde?

—En una zona de colinas peladas al pie de los montes de Valdemeca. Así es como la llaman.

—¿Cuántos prisioneros?

Luis se encogió de hombros.

—Unos quinientos, más o menos.

—¿Extranjeros?

—Unos cuantos. Polacos, alemanes, gente cuyos países no desean que vuelva.

Ella le sostuvo la mirada con firmeza.

—¿Cuándo lo encontró el señor Markby? ¿Cuándo le contó usted todo esto?

Luis vaciló y se rascó las ásperas mejillas.

—Perdone, señora, eso no se lo puedo decir. Sólo le diré que algunos veteranos sin trabajo contamos con nuestros lugares de reunión y algunos tienen unos contactos que el Gobierno preferiría que no tuvieran.

—¿Con periodistas extranjeros, por ejemplo, para venderles historias?

—No puedo decirle más —contestó él. Pareció lamentarlo sinceramente y volvió a recuperar su anterior aspecto de persona muy joven.

Ella asintió con la cabeza, respiró hondo y notó que se le formaba un nudo en la garganta.

—¿Cómo eran las condiciones en el campo?

Luis sacudió la cabeza.

—No muy buenas. Unas barracas de madera rodeadas por una alambrada de púas. Tiene que comprenderlo; a esa gente jamás la pondrán en libertad. Trabajan en canteras y arreglan carreteras. No hay suficiente comida. Muchos mueren, que es lo que el Gobierno quiere que ocurra con todos.

Barbara se esforzó por conservar la calma. Tenía que comportarse como si Luis fuese un funcionario extranjero que estuviera hablándole de un campo de refugiados sobre el cual ella necesitaba información. Sacó una cajetilla de cigarrillos y se la ofreció.

—¡Cigarrillos ingleses! —Luis encendió uno y saboreó el humo, cerrando los ojos. Cuando volvió a mirarla, la expresión de su rostro era dura e implacable—. ¿Era fuerte su brigadista, señora Forsyth?

—Sí, lo era. Un hombre fuerte.

—Sólo los fuertes sobreviven.

Barbara sintió que las lágrimas asomaban a sus ojos y parpadeó para contenerlas. Era la clase de cosa que él le habría dicho si la estuviera engañando; habría intentado apelar a sus emociones. Y, sin embargo, su relato sonaba a verdadero. Hurgó en su bolso, sacó la fotografía de Bernie y la deslizó sobre la mesa hacia Luis, que la estudió un momento y negó con la cabeza.

—No recuerdo su rostro, pero ahora no tendría el mismo aspecto. No estábamos autorizados a hablar con los prisioneros, sólo a darles órdenes. Pensaban que sus ideas podían contaminarnos. —La miró detenidamente a los ojos—. Pero nosotros, los soldados, los admirábamos, sobre todo por su manera de seguir adelante pese a todo.

—¿No recuerda el nombre de Bernie Piper?

Luis sacudió la cabeza y volvió a estudiar la fotografía.

—Recuerdo a un extranjero rubio que era uno de los comunistas. A casi todos los prisioneros ingleses los devolvieron a casa... su Gobierno trató de recuperarlos. Pero algunos de los que fueron dados por desaparecidos acabaron en Cuenca. —Volvió a deslizar la fotografía sobre la mesa—. A mí me licenciaron esta primavera, pero mi hermano se quedó. —Luis miró a Barbara de modo significativo—. Puede conseguir información si se lo pido. Pero tendría que visitarlo, ya que censuran la correspondencia. —Guardó silencio.

Ella le preguntó sin rodeos:

—¿Cuánto costará?

Luis esbozó una sonrisa triste.

—Es usted muy directa, señora. Creo que, por trescientas pesetas, Agustín podría decirnos si ese hombre era un prisionero del campo o no.

Trescientas. Barbara tragó saliva con dificultad, pero no permitió que su rostro dejara traslucir nada.

—¿Cuánto tardaría? He de saberlo cuanto antes. Si España entra en guerra, tendré que irme.

Él asintió con la cabeza, con aire súbitamente práctico.

—Deme una semana. Visitaré a Agustín el próximo fin de semana. Pero ahora necesitaré un poco de dinero, un anticipo.

Ella enarcó las cejas, y Luis se ruborizó de repente con expresión avergonzada.

—Es que no tengo dinero para el tren.

—Ah, comprendo.

—Necesitaré cincuenta pesetas. No, no saque la cartera aquí, démelas fuera.

Barbara miró hacia la barra. El cojo y su amigo estaban profundamente enzarzados en una conversación y la dueña atendía a otro cliente; pero intuyó que todos estaban pendientes de ella. Respiró hondo.

—¿Y qué haremos si Bernie está allí? Ustedes no podrán liberarlo.

Luis se encogió de hombros.

—Quizá fuera posible, pero en cualquier caso es muy difícil. —Hizo una pausa—. Muy caro.

De modo que era eso. Barbara lo miró y pensó que quizá no sabía nada y le había dicho a Markby lo que éste quería escuchar, y que ahora le estaba repitiendo la misma historia a aquella inglesa rica.

—¿Cuánto? —preguntó Barbara.

Luis sacudió la cabeza.

—Cada cosa a su tiempo, señora. Primero, comprobemos si se trata de él.

Barbara asintió con la cabeza.

—Para usted es cuestión de dinero, ¿verdad? Deberíamos saber por dónde vamos.

Luis frunció levemente el entrecejo.

—Usted no es pobre —observó.

—Puedo conseguir dinero. Un poco.

—Yo sí soy pobre. Como todo el mundo lo es ahora en España. ¿Sabe usted la edad que yo tenía cuando me reclutaron? Dieciocho. Perdí los mejores años de mi vida. —Lo dijo con amargura; después suspiró y bajó los ojos un momento para al instante volver a fijarlos en los de ella—. No he tenido trabajo desde que dejé el ejército en primavera, sólo un poco en las carreteras, y muy mal pagado. Mi madre está enferma en Sevilla y yo no puedo hacer nada para ayudarla. Si tengo que ayudarla, señora, si tengo que buscar una información muy difícil de encontrar, comprenderá usted que... —Apretó fuertemente los labios y la miró con expresión desafiante.

—Muy bien —se apresuró a decir Barbara en tono conciliador—. Si usted consigue averiguar qué sabe Agustín, le daré lo que me pide. Lo conseguiré como sea.

Probablemente le sería fácil conseguir las trescientas, pero era mejor que él no lo supiese.

Luis asintió con la cabeza. Miró alrededor y después contempló a través de la ventana la calle envuelta en las sombras del ocaso. Acto seguido, volvió a inclinarse hacia delante.

—Iré a Cuenca este fin de semana —dijo—. Volveré a reunirme aquí con usted dentro de una semana, a las cinco de la tarde. —Se levantó y se inclinó ante ella. Barbara observó que su chaqueta tenía un agujero enorme en el codo.

Fuera, él volvió a estrecharle la mano y ella le entregó cincuenta pesetas. Mientras se alejaba, Barbara acarició la fotografía de Bernie. Pero no podía hacerse demasiadas ilusiones, tenía que andarse con cuidado. Su mente daba vueltas sin cesar. El hecho de que Bernie hubiera sobrevivido, cuando miles de hombres habían muerto, y de que Markby hubiera encontrado la manera de llegar hasta él sería una increíble coincidencia. Y, sin embargo, Markby había conseguido averiguar que todos los extranjeros eran enviados a Cuenca; después había buscado a un guardia de allí... Lo único que haría falta serían dinero y contactos entre los miles de soldados dados de baja que estaban en Madrid. Tenía que volver a ponerse en contacto con Markby y preguntarle. En caso de que Luis dijera que Bernie estaba vivo, ella podría armar un escándalo en la embajada. ¿Podría? Decían que la embajada trataba desesperadamente de mantener a Franco al margen de la guerra. Recordaba lo que le había dicho Luis acerca de los prisioneros que podrían desaparecer en caso de que se hicieran averiguaciones inoportunas.

Cruzó la Plaza Mayor apurando el paso para llegar al centro antes de que oscureciera. Y, de pronto, se detuvo en seco. La guerra había terminado en abril de 1939. En caso de que Luis hubiera abandonado el ejército aquella primavera de 1940, era imposible que hubiese pasado dos inviernos en el campo.

6

Llovía a cántaros desde hacía veinticuatro horas. Era una lluvia persistente que caía en vertical desde un cielo sin viento, para arremolinarse y gorgotear sobre los adoquines. También hacía más frío. Harry había encontrado un edredón en el apartamento y lo había extendido sobre la amplia cama de matrimonio.

Aquella mañana tenía que acudir al Ministerio de Comercio con Hillgarth, su primera salida en calidad de intérprete. Se alegraba de poder hacer algo finalmente.

Lo habían integrado en la vida de la embajada. El jefe del departamento de traducción, Weaver, había examinado sus conocimientos de español en su despacho. Era un hombre alto y delgado, de aspecto aristocrático.

—Muy bien —dijo, utilizando un lánguido tono de voz tras haber pasado media hora conversando con Harry—. Podrá hacerlo.

—Gracias, señor —dijo Harry sin la menor inflexión de voz.

Le molestaba la altiva indolencia de Weaver, que suspiró y añadió:

—Al embajador no le gusta que la gente de Hillgarth intervenga en las tareas habituales, pero qué le vamos a hacer. —Miró a Harry como si éste fuera un animal exótico.

—Sí, señor —contestó Harry.

—Lo acompañaré a su despacho. Hemos recibido unos comunicados de prensa con los que ya puede empezar a trabajar.

Acompañó a Harry a un pequeño despacho. Un escritorio maltrecho ocupaba casi todo el espacio y había varios comunicados de prensa españoles amontonados encima del papel secante. Llegaban con regularidad, y Harry se pasó los tres días siguientes muy ocupado. No volvió a ver a Hillgarth, pero Tolhurst aparecía de vez en cuando por el despacho para ver qué tal le iba.

Tolhurst le caía bien, por su modestia y sus comentarios irónicos; no así la mayoría del personal de la embajada, que despreciaba a los españoles: la desolada pobreza que Harry había visto y que tanto lo deprimía parecía divertir a algunos. Casi todas las tiendas de alimentación de Madrid ostentaban en su exterior unos letreros que rezaban «No hay...». «No hay...» patatas, lechuga, manzanas, lo que fuera. La víspera, en la cantina, Harry había oído que dos miembros del personal del agregado cultural se tomaban a broma el que todavía no hubiera heno para los pobres asnos, y había experimentado un inesperado arrebato de cólera. Sin embargo, bajo aquella insensibilidad, Harry adivinaba el temor de que Franco se incorporara a la guerra. Todo el mundo analizaba los periódicos a diario. En aquellos momentos, la visita de Himmler era objeto de una inquietud generalizada: ¿llegaría sencillamente para discutir cuestiones de seguridad, o habría algo más?

Hillgarth pasó a recogerlo a las diez por su apartamento en un impresionante automóvil norteamericano, un Packard conducido por un chófer inglés. Harry se había puesto su chaqué, que había planchado cuidadosamente la noche anterior; Hillgarth volvía a vestir su uniforme de capitán.

—Vamos a ver al subsecretario de Comercio, el general Maestre —explicó Hillgarth, contemplando la lluvia con los ojos entornados—. Tengo que confirmar qué petroleros serán autorizados a entrar por parte de la Royal Navy. También quiero hacerle alguna pregunta sobre Carceller, el nuevo ministro del ramo.

Tamborileó un momento con los dedos sobre el brazo del asiento, pensativo. La víspera se había anunciado toda una serie de cambios en el gabinete; Harry había traducido los correspondientes comunicados de prensa. Los cambios favorecían a la Falange: el cuñado de Franco Serrano Súñer había sido nombrado ministro de Asuntos Exteriores.

—Maestre no tiene nada de malo —añadió Hillgarth—. Pertenece a la vieja escuela. Es primo de un duque.

Harry miró por la ventanilla. La gente caminaba inclinada bajo la lluvia, los obreros con sus monos de trabajo y las mujeres con la cabeza cubierta por los perennes chales negros. Nadie tenía prisa; ya estaban todos empapados. Tolhurst le había dicho que era imposible encontrar paraguas, incluso en el mercado negro. Al pasar por delante de una panadería, Harry observó que un grupo de mujeres vestidas de negro esperaba bajo la lluvia. Muchas iban acompañadas de escuálidos chiquillos, y a través de la cortina de agua Harry vio los hinchados vientres propios de la desnutrición. Las mujeres se apiñaban delante de la puerta, aporreándola y llamando a gritos a alguien que se encontraba al otro lado.

Hillgarth soltó un gruñido.

—Corren rumores de que han traído patatas. Seguramente el hombre tiene unas pocas y las guarda para el mercado negro. El organismo encargado del abastecimiento ofrece tan poco a los productores de patatas que éstos no quieren vendérselas. Por eso la Junta de Abastos se queda con parte de la cosecha antes de que ellos las revendan.

—¿Y Franco lo permite?

—No puede impedirlo. La Junta es un organismo de la Falange. Corrupto hasta la raíz. Habrá carestía como no se anden con cuidado. Pero es lo que tienen las revoluciones: la escoria siempre asciende a lo más alto.

Pasaron por delante del edificio de las Cortes, cerrado y desierto, y entraron en el patio del Ministerio de Comercio. Un guardia civil les hizo señas desde el otro lado de la entrada.

—¿Y esto es una revolución? —preguntó Harry—. Más bien parece... no sé cómo llamarlo... una ruina.

—Pues es una revolución en toda regla, al menos para los falangistas. Quieren un estado como el de Hitler. Tendría usted que ver con qué gente hemos de tratar. Se le ponen a uno los pelos de punta. A su lado, los libros que yo escribía parecen un juego de niños.

En un despacho de paredes revestidas de madera, bajo un enorme retrato de Franco los esperaba un hombre vestido con uniforme de general, con la raya del pantalón impecablemente planchada. Tenía cincuenta y pocos años y era alto y bien plantado. En su rostro moreno brillaban unos ojos castaño claro. El ralo cabello negro estaba cuidadosamente peinado para disimular la calva. Un hombre más joven vestido de paisano permanecía a su lado con semblante inexpresivo.

El militar sonrió y estrechó cordialmente la mano de Hillgarth, hablándole en español con su bien timbrada voz. Su compañero más joven tradujo sus palabras.

—Mi querido capitán, me alegro de verlo.

—Y yo de verlo a usted, mi general. Hoy seguramente podremos entregarle los certificados.

Hillgarth miró a Harry, y éste repitió sus palabras en español.

—Muy bien. Entonces ya se podría dar por resuelto el asunto.
—Maestre le dedicó a Harry una breve sonrisa—. Veo que tiene usted
un nuevo intérprete. Espero que al señor Greene no le haya ocurrido
nada malo.

—Tuvo que regresar a casa por problemas familiares.

El general Maestre asintió con la cabeza.

—Vaya, cuánto lo siento. Espero que su familia no haya sido víctima de los bombardeos.

—No. Asuntos personales.

Se sentaron alrededor del escritorio. Hillgarth abrió su cartera de
documentos y sacó los certificados que iban a permitir que determinados petroleros entrasen escoltados por la Marina británica. Hillgarth
y Maestre los estudiaron y comprobaron fechas, rutas y tonelaje. Harry
traducía las palabras de Hillgarth al castellano, y el joven español traducía las respuestas de Maestre al inglés. Harry tuvo un pequeño problema con uno o dos términos técnicos, pero Maestre se mostró amable y comprensivo con él. Aquel militar no se parecía a lo que Harry
esperaba que fuera un alto cargo del régimen de Franco.

Al final, Maestre recogió los documentos y soltó un suspiro teatral.

—Ay, capitán, si usted supiera cómo se enfadan algunos de mis
colegas por el hecho de que España tenga que pedir permiso a la Marina británica para importar artículos de primera necesidad. Es un insulto a nuestro orgullo, ¿sabe?

—Inglaterra está en guerra, señor; tenemos que asegurarnos de que
nada importado por un país neutral sea vendido posteriormente a Alemania.

El general le pasó los certificados a su traductor.

—Fernando, encárguese de enviarlos al Ministerio de Marina.

El joven pareció vacilar por un instante, pero Maestre lo miró enarcando las cejas y entonces hizo una reverencia y se retiró. El general se
relajó de inmediato.

—Así me lo quito de encima —dijo en un inglés perfecto. Al ver que
Harry lo miraba boquiabierto, sonrió y añadió—: Pues sí, señor Brett,
hablo inglés. Estudié en Cambridge. Este joven está aquí para impedir
que diga cosas que no debo. Uno de los hombres de Serrano Súñer. El
capitán ya sabe a qué me refiero.

—Lo sé perfectamente, señor subsecretario. Brett también estudió
en Cambridge.

—¡No me diga! —Maestre lo miró con interés y después sonrió con expresión nostálgica—. Durante la guerra, cuando luchábamos contra los rojos en la Meseta, en medio del calor y las moscas, yo solía recordar mis días en Cambridge: las frías aguas del río, los soberbios jardines, todo tan tranquilo y majestuoso. Necesitas estas cosas en la guerra para conservar la cordura. ¿En qué colegio estuvo usted?

—En el King's, señor.

Maestre asintió con la cabeza.

—Yo estuve un año en Peterhouse. Me pareció maravilloso. —Sacó una pitillera de oro—. ¿Fuma usted?

—No, gracias.

—¿Alguna noticia sobre el nuevo ministro? —preguntó Hillgarth.

Maestre se echó hacia atrás en su asiento y exhaló una nube de humo.

—No se preocupe por Carceller —dijo—. Tiene muchas ideas falangistas... —Hizo una mueca de desdén—. Pero en el fondo es un pragmático.

—Sir Sam se alegrará de ello.

El general asintió lentamente con la cabeza. Después se volvió hacia Harry con una sonrisa cortés.

—Bien, joven, ¿cómo ve usted España?

Harry titubeó.

—Llena de sorpresas —respondió.

—Pasamos por delante de una larga cola de mujeres que esperaba a la entrada de una panadería —intervino Hillgarth—. Se habían enterado de que allí tenían patatas.

Maestre sacudió la cabeza con expresión de desaliento.

—Estos falangistas serían capaces de provocar una carestía en el Jardín del Edén. ¿Conoce usted el nuevo chiste, Alan? Hitler se reúne con Franco y le pregunta cómo matar de hambre a Inglaterra para que se rinda, porque con los submarinos alemanes no tienen suficiente. Franco le contesta: «*Mein Führer*, yo les enviaré mi Junta de Abastos. En tres semanas pedirán a gritos firmar la rendición.»

Hillgarth y Maestre rieron y Harry los imitó sin estar muy convencido. Maestre lo miró, inclinando levemente la cabeza.

—Disculpe, señor, los españoles tenemos cierto sentido negro del humor. Así es como podemos hacer frente a nuestros problemas; aunque no tendría que hacer bromas sobre las dificultades de Inglaterra.

—Bueno, vamos tirando —comentó Hillgarth, conciliador.

—Me han dicho que, cuando le preguntaron a la reina si sus hijos abandonarían Londres a causa de los bombardeos, ella contestó... ¿Qué fue lo que dijo?... ¡Ah, sí!: «No se irán sin mí, yo no me iré sin el rey, y el rey no se irá».

—Sí, en efecto.

—Una mujer extraordinaria. —Maestre miró a Harry con una sonrisa—. Qué estilo. Tiene duende.

—Gracias, señor.

—Y ahora a los italianos les están pegando una paliza en Grecia. La tortilla acabará por volverse. Juan March lo sabe muy bien. —El general enarcó una ceja al mirar a Hillgarth y después se volvió de nuevo hacia Harry—. Señor Brett, dentro de diez días daré una fiesta en honor de mi hija, que cumple dieciocho años. Es mi única hija. En estos momentos hay tan pocos jóvenes apropiados... No sé si a usted le apetecería venir. Estaría muy bien que Milagros conociera a un joven de Inglaterra. —El general sonrió con inesperada ternura al mencionar el nombre de su hija.

—Gracias, señor. Si... mmm... los compromisos de la embajada lo permiten...

—¡Estupendo! Estoy seguro de que sir Sam podrá prescindir de usted por una noche. Me encargaré de que le envíen una invitación. Y eso de los Caballeros de San Jorge ya lo discutiremos más tarde, capitán.

Hillgarth miró rápidamente a Harry y después sacudió imperceptiblemente la cabeza en dirección a Maestre.

—Sí, más tarde.

El general titubeó, luego asintió enérgicamente con la cabeza y estrechó la mano de Harry.

—Y ahora siento mucho tener que dejarlos. Ha sido un gran placer conocerlo. Hay una ceremonia en el palacio: el embajador italiano va a imponer una nueva condecoración al Generalísimo. —Soltó una carcajada—. Demasiados honores; tantos que *Il Duce* lo abruma.

Había dejado de llover. Hillgarth cruzó con semblante pensativo el aparcamiento.

—Este nombre que Maestre ha mencionado, Juan March, ¿lo conoce?

—Es un hombre de negocios español. Contribuyó a financiar a Franco durante la guerra. Un estafador, según tengo entendido.

—Bueno, pues olvídese de que ha oído su nombre, ¿de acuerdo? Y olvídese también de los Caballeros de San Jorge; es un asunto privado en el que está implicada la embajada. ¿De acuerdo?

—No diré nada, señor.

—Buen chico. —Hillgarth pareció aliviado—. Tiene usted que ir a esa fiesta y relajarse un poco. Conocerá a unas cuantas señoritas. Bien sabe Dios la poca vida social que hay en Madrid. Los Maestre son una familia importante. Emparentada con los Astor.

—Gracias, señor, puede que vaya. —Harry se preguntó de qué clase de fiesta se trataría.

El chófer esperaba dentro del coche, leyendo un ejemplar del *Daily Mail* de una semana de antigüedad. En el momento de subir al automóvil, Harry echó un vistazo a la primera plana. Las incursiones aéreas alemanas se alejaban de Londres y Birmingham había sufrido un duro bombardeo. Se trataba de la ciudad natal de Barbara. Harry recordó a la mujer que había visto unas noches antes. No podía ser ella. A esas alturas seguro que ya había regresado a casa. Confiaba en que estuviera a salvo.

—La hija de Maestre es muy guapa —dijo Hillgarth mientras iban de camino a la embajada—. Una auténtica belleza española... ¡se lo digo yo!

De pronto, ambos se vieron lanzados hacia delante cuando el vehículo experimentó la brusca sacudida de un frenazo. Estaban girando en la calle Fernando el Santo, donde se encontraba la sede de la embajada. La calle, habitualmente tranquila, estaba llena de gente que gritaba desaforadamente. El chófer perdió los estribos:

—Pero ¿qué demonios es eso?

Eran falangistas, la mayoría de ellos jóvenes con brillantes camisas azules y boinas rojas, que gritaban brazo en alto a modo de saludo fascista. Agitaban unas pancartas en las que se leía: «¡Gibraltar español!»

Los guardias civiles que siempre montaban guardia ante la embajada habían desaparecido.

—¡Abajo Inglaterra! —gritaban—. ¡Viva Hitler, viva Mussolini, viva Franco!

—¡Oh, no! —exclamó Hillgarth en tono de cansancio—. Otra manifestación, no.

Alguien de entre los manifestantes señaló el vehículo con el dedo, y los falangistas que estaban más cerca de ellos se volvieron y les gritaron sus consignas, mirándolos con rostros desencajados mientras extendían y doblaban los brazos como si fueran metrónomos. Una piedra se estrelló contra el capó.

—Siga adelante, Potter —dijo Hillgarth con firmeza.

—¿Está seguro, señor? Esto tiene mala pinta.

—No es más que puro espectáculo. Le digo que siga, hombre.

El chófer avanzó muy lentamente entre los manifestantes y el muro de la embajada. La mitad de ellos eran adolescentes que vestían el uniforme de la Falange Juvenil, copia del de las Juventudes Hitlerianas, sólo que sus camisas eran azules en lugar de pardas y las chicas llevaban unas faldas amplias, mientras que los chicos iban en pantalón corto. Uno de estos últimos tenía un tambor que empezó a aporrear enérgicamente. Su gesto enardeció a la muchedumbre y algunos muchachos alargaron los brazos y empezaron a zarandear el automóvil. Otros siguieron su ejemplo, mientras que Hillgarth y Harry brincaban en el interior y el vehículo seguía avanzando muy despacio. Harry experimentó una sensación de repugnancia: eran poco más que niños.

—Suélteles un bocinazo —ordenó Hillgarth.

Sonó la bocina y un falangista un poco más veterano se abrió paso entre los manifestantes e hizo señas a los jóvenes de que se apartaran del vehículo.

—¿Lo ve? —dijo Hillgarth—. Sencillamente se estaban dejando llevar por un exceso de entusiasmo.

Un muchacho alto y corpulento de unos diecisiete años se entregó a un paroxismo de furia y, abriéndose paso entre la multitud, se situó al lado del vehículo y empezó a lanzar insultos en inglés a través de la ventanilla:

—¡Muerte al rey Jorge! ¡Muerte al cerdo judío de Churchill!

Hillgarth rió, pero Harry se echó hacia atrás asqueado ante la ridiculez de los silbidos que otorgaban a los manifestantes una apariencia aún más desagradable.

—¿Dónde están los guardias civiles? —preguntó.

—Les habrán aconsejado que se vayan a dar un paseo, supongo. Éstas son las huestes de Serrano Súñer. Bueno, Potter, acérquese a la entrada. Cuando bajemos, Brett, procure mantener el tipo. No les haga caso.

Harry siguió a Hillgarth y puso un pie en la acera. Los gritos arreciaron, y se sintió expuesto al peligro y repentinamente asustado. El corazón le empezó a latir con fuerza. Los falangistas proferían gritos contra ellos desde el otro lado del automóvil mientras el joven enfurecido seguía aullando en inglés.

—¡Que se hundan los barcos ingleses! ¡Muerte a los judíos bolcheviques!

Otra piedra voló desde el otro lado de la calle y rompió un cristal de la puerta de la embajada. Harry retrocedió y tuvo que reprimir el impulso de agacharse.

Hillgarth cogió el tirador de la puerta.

—Maldita sea, está cerrada.

La sacudió y entonces vio moverse una figura en el oscuro interior, hasta que apareció Tolhurst corriendo agachado hacia la puerta. Una vez allí, éste empezó a manipular torpemente el pestillo.

—¡Vamos, Tolly! —le gritó Hillgarth—. Manténgase firme, por el amor de Dios, ¡no son más que una pandilla de gamberros!

De pronto, el chófer gritó:

—¡Miren allí!

Harry volvió la cabeza y distinguió algo que volaba por los aires. Sintió un fuerte golpe en el cuello y se tambaleó. Él y Hillgarth levantaron los brazos, mientras un objeto de color blanco giraba alrededor de sus cabezas casi asfixiándolos en medio de los gritos de júbilo de la multitud. Por un instante, Harry vio volar una especie de arena roja por el aire.

Se abrió la puerta de la embajada y Hillgarth entró agachado. Tolhurst tendió la mano, cogió a Harry del brazo y lo atrajo hacia el interior con una fuerza sorprendente. Cerró nuevamente la puerta y los miró boquiabierto. Harry se pasó las manos por el cuello y los hombros pero no encontró heridas ni magulladuras, sólo un polvillo blanco. Se apoyó contra un escritorio y respiró hondo. Hillgarth se olfateó la manga y soltó una carcajada.

—¡Harina! ¡No es más que harina!

—¡Desvergonzados hijos de puta! —exclamó Tolhurst.

—¿Está Sam al corriente de todo eso? —El rostro de Hillgarth reflejaba una intensa emoción.

—Ahora mismo está llamando al Ministerio del Interior, señor. ¿Están ustedes bien?

—Sí. Vamos, Brett, tenemos que limpiarnos.

Soltando otra risita, Hillgarth se encaminó hacia una puerta interior. Fuera, la multitud seguía riéndose de su hazaña y el enloquecido joven insistía en sus desvaríos. Tolhurst miró a Harry.

—¿Se encuentra bien?

Harry todavía temblaba.

—Sí... sí, perdón.

Tolhurst lo cogió del brazo.

—Venga, lo acompañaré a mi despacho. Allí tengo un cepillo para la ropa.

Harry se dejó llevar.

El despacho de Tolhurst era aún más pequeño que el de Harry. Sacó un cepillo del cajón de su escritorio.

—De todos modos, aquí tengo un traje de recambio. Le irá un poco grande, pero creo que lo ayudará a salir del paso.

—Gracias.

Harry eliminó con el cepillo buena parte de la harina. Se encontraba mejor y había recuperado la calma, aunque seguía oyendo los gritos procedentes de la calle. Tolhurst miró por la ventana.

—Vendrá la policía y los dispersará enseguida. Serrano Súñer ha conseguido dejar clara su postura. Y sir Sam le está echando una bronca por teléfono.

—¿La manifestación no le ha provocado una crisis de pánico?

Tolhurdst sacudió la cabeza.

—No, hoy está en plena forma, no hay ni rastro de pánico. Uno nunca sabe cómo va a reaccionar.

—Yo he sufrido un amago de pánico al caérseme encima toda esta harina —dijo Harry, mirando tímidamente alrededor—. No sabía lo que era. Por un instante me vi de nuevo en Dunkerque. Lo siento, habrá pensado que soy un cobarde.

Tolhurst pareció sentirse un tanto incómodo.

—No —dijo—. De ninguna manera. Sé lo que es la neurosis de guerra, mi padre la sufrió al final de sus días. —Vaciló por un instante y agregó—: El año pasado no permitieron que el personal de la embajada se alistara, ¿sabe? Me temo que suspiré aliviado. —Encendió un cigarrillo—. No soy precisamente lo que se dice un héroe. Me encuentro más a gusto sentado detrás de un escritorio, si he de serle sincero. No sé cómo me las habría arreglado con lo que usted tuvo que sufrir.

—Uno nunca sabe lo que es capaz de hacer hasta que llega el momento.

—Supongo que es así.

—El capitán Hillgarth parece muy valiente.

—Sí, creo que le encanta el peligro. Hay que admirar semejante valor, ¿no cree?

—Ésta fue una pequeña crisis de pánico comparada con la que tuve hace un par de meses.

Tolhurst asintió con la cabeza.

—Bien. Muy bien. —Se volvió hacia la ventana—. Vamos a ver qué hacen. No hay pan y, sin embargo, arrojan harina. Apuesto a que la han sacado de los almacenes del Auxilio Social; la Falange es la responsable de la alimentación de los pobres.

Harry se situó a su lado y contempló el agitado mar de camisas azules.

—Menos mal que no hay patatas, ¿eh?

—¿Sabe que enviamos a Londres unas muestras del pan del racionamiento para que las analizaran? Los científicos dijeron que no eran aptas para el consumo humano; la harina estaba adulterada nada menos que con serrín. Y, sin embargo, ellos se permiten el lujo de arrojarnos a nosotros harina blanca de la buena.

—Seguro que los peces gordos de la Falange no comen serrín.

—Eso por descontado.

—Gritaban consignas antisemitas. No sabía que la Falange fuera partidaria de todo eso.

—Ahora sí. Lo hacen, como Mussolini, para complacer a los nazis.

—Cabrones —masculló Harry con repentina furia—. Después de Dunkerque solía preguntarme qué sentido tenía seguir adelante con los combates; pero luego ves estas cosas... El fascismo es así. Arroja a unos matones que son prácticamente críos contra personas inocentes. Después bombardea a la población civil y ametralla a los soldados que se baten en retirada. Santo Dios, cuánto los aborrezco.

Tolhurst asintió con la cabeza.

—Pues sí. Pero aquí no tenemos más remedio que tratar con ellos. Por desgracia. —Señaló hacia abajo con un dedo—. Mire a ese idiota.

El chico que profería insultos en inglés se había apoderado de una de las pancartas que rezaban «Gibraltar español» y paseaba arriba y abajo por delante de la embajada con jactanciosa arrogancia militar, mientras la multitud lo jaleaba. Era un muchacho alto y apuesto, perteneciente probablemente a una familia de clase media.

Se abrió la puerta e irrumpió la figura nervuda del embajador. Parecía furioso.

—¿Está usted bien, Brett?

—Sí, señor, gracias. Sólo era harina.

—¡No toleraré que mi personal sea atacado! —La voz de Hoare temblaba de cólera.

—Estoy bien, señor, lo digo en serio.

—Sí, sí, sí, pero es el principio. —El embajador respiró hondo—. Creo que Stokes lo anda buscando, Tolhurst —añadió, señalando la puerta con la cabeza.

—Sí, señor. —Tolhurst se marchó de inmediato.

El embajador miró a través de la ventana, soltó un bufido y se volvió de nuevo hacia Harry. Lo observó de manera calculadora.

—Hillgarth me ha hablado de la reunión de esta mañana. Maestre es un bocazas. Las cosas que ha dicho acerca de Juan March y los Caballeros de San Jorge no debe usted comentarlas con nadie. Lo que hacemos aquí tiene multitud de facetas. Constituyen la base de lo que necesitamos saber, ¿comprende?

—Sí, señor, ya le he dicho al capitán que no comentaría nada.

—Buen chico. Me alegro de que esté bien. —Hoare le dio a Harry una palmada en el hombro y contempló con desagrado la harina que le había quedado en la mano—. Dígale a Tolhurst que mande limpiar todo esto.

Una vez a solas, Harry se sentó. Se sentía terriblemente cansado y le zumbaban los oídos. Volvió a recordar Dunkerque, después de que la bomba cayera a su lado. Había tratado de incorporarse. La arena que lo cubría estaba caliente y húmeda. No podía pensar debidamente, no podía ordenar sus pensamientos. Notó que alguien le tocaba el hombro y abrió los ojos. Un pequeño y vigoroso cabo permanecía inclinado sobre él.

—¿Se encuentra bien, señor?

Harry apenas podía oírlo, algo raro le ocurría en los oídos. Se incorporó. Tenía el uniforme cubierto de arena ensangrentada y, a su alrededor, toda una especie de grumos rojos. Se percató de que era Tomlinson.

Dejó que el cabo lo arrastrara por la playa hasta el agua. El agua estaba helada, y él se puso a temblar de la cabeza a los pies.

—Tomlinson —dijo. Apenas podía oír su propia voz—. Qué trocitos tan pequeños...

El cabo lo cogió por los hombros, lo obligó a dar la vuelta y lo miró a los ojos.

—Vamos, señor, vamos al bote.

El cabo lo obligó a adentrarse un poco más en el agua. Otros hombres vestidos de caqui chapoteaban a su alrededor. Después, Harry levantó los ojos y vio el casco de madera marrón del bote. Le parecía muy alto. Dos hombres se inclinaron hacia abajo y lo agarraron por los brazos. Notó que volvía a elevarse en el aire y se desmayó.

Fue consciente de las voces que seguían gritando en el exterior. Se levantó y se acercó de nuevo a la ventana. Ahora el chico permanecía en posición de firmes con la pancarta al lado, lanzando improperios contra la embajada. Harry captó las palabras.

—¡Muerte a los enemigos de España! ¡Muerte a los ingleses! ¡Muerte a los judíos!

El chico se detuvo en mitad de la frase. Abrió la boca y se ruborizó. Harry vio una mancha pequeña, oscura y redonda en la entrepierna de su pantalón corto. La mancha fue aumentando de tamaño y entonces Harry distinguió un brillante riachuelo que le bajaba por el muslo. Se había excitado hasta el extremo de orinarse encima. El chico se quedó rígido, mientras palidecía intensamente a causa del terror. Alguien gritó:

—¡Lucas! ¡Lucas, continúa!

El muchacho, sin embargo, no se atrevía a moverse; de pronto, el que había quedado atrapado por la multitud era él. Harry miró hacia abajo.

—Te lo tienes bien merecido, pequeño hijo de puta —dijo en voz alta.

7

Poco después, los falangistas se dispersaron. Al final, el chico que se había orinado encima también tuvo que dar media vuelta y retroceder para reunirse con sus camaradas. Los otros le miraron los pantalones empapados y apartaron rápidamente los ojos. De todos modos, ya se estaban cansando; guardaron sus tambores y sus pancartas y se fueron. Harry se apartó de la ventana sacudiendo la cabeza. Se sentó al escritorio de Tolhurst, agradecido por el silencio. Tolhurst había sido sumamente amable. Le había sorprendido la fuerza de sus manos al arrastrarlo hacia dentro; debía de haber algo de músculo debajo de tanta grasa.

Miró alrededor. Un maltrecho escritorio, un viejo archivador y un armario. Había polvo en los rincones. El retrato del rey colgaba en la pared, pero no vio ninguna fotografía de carácter personal. Pensó en la fotografía de sus propios padres que ahora tenía en el apartamento. ¿Vivirían los padres de Tolhurst, se preguntó, o acaso la guadaña de la muerte también los había segado en la Gran Guerra? Cerró los ojos y, por un instante, volvió a ver la playa. La apartó de inmediato de sus pensamientos. Había actuado bien; no mucho antes, un incidente como aquél lo habría inducido a esconderse aterrorizado bajo una mesa.

Recordó el tiempo que había pasado en el hospital de Dover, el desengaño y la desesperación. Se había quedado parcialmente sordo y las enfermeras tenían que hablarle a gritos para que las oyera. Apareció un médico y le hizo unas pruebas. Éste pareció mostrarse satisfecho. Se inclinó junto a la cama.

—Seguramente recuperará el oído —dijo—. El tímpano no ha sufrido daños graves. Ahora tiene que descansar, ¿comprende? Túmbese aquí y descanse.

—¡Qué remedio! —contestó Harry levantando la voz, pero enseguida recordó que era él y no el médico quien estaba sordo, y entonces volvió a bajarla—. Si me levanto de la cama, me pongo a temblar.

—Es la conmoción. Eso también mejorará.

Y así había sido gracias a la determinación que lo sacó de la cama y de la sala y después lo indujo a salir al jardín. Pero ni su recuperación ni la victoria de las Fuerzas Aéreas en la batalla de Inglaterra pudieron sanar su sensación de airada vergüenza ante la retirada de Francia. Por primera vez en su vida, Harry ponía en tela de juicio lo que le habían enseñado en Rookwood, que las normas de allí eran buenas y acertadas e Inglaterra era un país destinado a gobernar el mundo. Ahora los fascistas ganaban en todas partes. Siempre los había odiado, del mismo modo que en la escuela siempre había odiado a los tramposos y a los matones. Eso le ofrecía algo a que aferrarse. Si los invadieran, él lucharía cuanto pudiera incluso por aquella Inglaterra rota y desgarrada. Por eso había respondido a esa llamada inoportuna de los espías, que le proponían trasladarse a España. Dio un brinco cuando se abrió la puerta y volvió a aparecer Tolhurst con un montón de papeles bajo el brazo.

—¿Sigue ahí, Brett?

—Sí. Estaba mirando la trifulca. Uno de ellos se ha meado encima.

—Le ha estado bien empleado al muy cabrón. ¿Ahora ya se encuentra bien?

—Sí, estoy bien. Sólo necesitaba un minuto para reponerme. —Harry se levantó. Se miró el traje, todavía sucio de harina—. Tendría que cambiarme.

Tolhurst abrió el armario y sacó un arrugado traje oscuro y un sombrero de paño.

—Siempre digo que tengo que llevármelo para pasarle la plancha —dijo Tolhurst a modo de disculpa.

—No se preocupe. Gracias. Creo que me iré a casa, a menos que me necesiten para alguna otra cosa. Abajo no me queda ningún trabajo que hacer.

Tolhurst asintió con la cabeza.

—Muy bien. Por cierto, la semana que viene habrá un cóctel para algunos de los funcionarios más jóvenes de la embajada. En el Ritz. Últimamente, se ha convertido en lugar de reunión de los nazis; haremos acto de presencia. ¿Por qué no va?

—Gracias. Me gustaría. Gracias, Tolhurst.

—Ah, me puedes llamar Tolly. Todo el mundo lo hace.

—Entonces tú llámame Harry.

—De acuerdo. Por cierto, si te vas a casa, no cojas el metro, ha habido otro corte de corriente.

—El paseo me sentará bien.

—Me encargaré de que te limpien la chaqueta.

—Gracias otra vez... mmm... Tolly.

Harry dejó a Tolhurst con su trabajo. Fuera seguía sin llover, pero un viento frío y áspero soplaba desde las montañas. Se puso el sombrero y se estremeció levemente al percibir la humedad pegajosa de la vieja brillantina Brylcreem. Se encaminó hacia el centro de la ciudad. En la Puerta del Sol vio un grupo de mendigos gitanos apretujados en un portal.

—Una limosna —le pidieron a gritos—. Una limosna, por el amor de Dios.

Siempre había habido mendigos en España, pero ahora estaban por todas partes. Si uno los miraba a los ojos, se levantaban y lo seguían, de modo que al final uno procuraba no fijarse en ellos directamente. Durante su período de instrucción le habían hablado de la visión periférica. «Utilícela para averiguar si lo siguen; es asombroso lo mucho que uno puede llegar a ver sin que la gente se entere de que la están observando.»

En la calle Toledo, un restaurante había sacado la basura a la calle. Los cubos estaban volcados y el contenido se había esparcido por la acera. Una familia rebuscaba entre los desperdicios en busca de comida. Había una anciana, una mujer más joven que parecía su hija y dos chiquillos de vientre hinchado. La joven quizás hubiera sido guapa en otros tiempos, pero ahora su cabello negro estaba grasiento y enmarañado y sus pálidas mejillas mostraban las típicas manchas rojas de la tuberculosis. Una niña recogió una piel de naranja, se la acercó a la boca y empezó a chuparla con ansia. La vieja tomó un hueso de gallina y se lo guardó en el bolsillo. Los viandantes volvían la cabeza para evitarlos; al otro lado de la calle, una pareja de guardias civiles los miraba desde la entrada de una tienda. Un sacerdote elegantemente vestido de negro apuró el paso y apartó la mirada.

La joven estaba inclinada hurgando en la basura, cuando una súbita ráfaga de viento le levantó el negro vestido por encima de la cabeza. Ella soltó un grito y se incorporó agitando los brazos para sujetarlo. No llevaba ropa interior y su escuálido cuerpo había quedado repentinamente al descubierto con su impresionante palidez, sus prominentes costillas y sus pechos fláccidos. La vieja se acercó a ella corriendo y trató de alisarle el vestido.

Los guardias civiles cobraron vida. Cruzaron rápidamente la calle y agarraron a la mujer. Uno de ellos tiró del vestido y se lo rasgó, pero consiguió volverlo a bajar y cubrir a la mujer. Ella cruzó los brazos sobre el pecho, temblando violentamente.

—¿Qué haces? —le gritó a la cara uno de los guardias—. ¡Puta!

Era un sujeto alto de mediana edad, con bigote negro. La expresión de su rostro reflejaba furia e indignación.

—Ha sido un accidente. —La anciana se restregaba las manos—. Usted mismo lo ha visto, el viento... Por favor, ha sido un accidente.

—¡Pues estos accidentes no pueden permitirse! —le gritó el guardia a la cara—. Hace un par de minutos ha pasado un sacerdote. —Tiró del brazo de la joven—. ¡Queda detenida por ofensa a la moral pública!

Ella se llevó las manos a la cara y rompió a llorar. La anciana permanecía de pie en actitud de súplica ante el guardia civil, juntando las manos como si rezara.

—Mi hija —imploró—. ¡Mi hija!

El guardia más joven parecía sentirse incómodo, pero el de más edad aún estaba furioso. Apartó a la mujer de un empujón.

—¡Los demás, fuera de aquí! ¡Esos cubos de basura son propiedad privada! ¿Por qué no te buscas un trabajo? ¡Vete!

La anciana reunió a los niños y se quedó allí temblando, mientras los guardias civiles se llevaban medio a rastras a su hija. Asqueado, Harry los vio desaparecer entre los altos edificios de piedra.

Fue entonces cuando vio al hombre. Un sujeto bajito y delgado vestido con una chaqueta oscura y una camisa blanca sin cuello, que se escondió en la entrada de una tienda al advertir que Harry lo miraba. Éste se volvió y reanudó la marcha fingiendo no haberlo visto.

Más adelante, un policía municipal de casco blanco dirigía el tráfico desde el centro de la calle; los peatones estaban obligados a esperar a que él les permitiera cruzar a la acera opuesta, pero muchos se adelantaban a la señal aprovechando una distracción del guardia, exponiéndose a ser atropellados o a pagar una multa de dos pesetas. Harry se detuvo y miró a derecha e izquierda. El hombre estaba muy cerca, a diez pasos por detrás de él. Tenía el rostro pálido, cuadrado, de facciones sorprendentemente delicadas. Al advertir que Harry miraba en su dirección, vaciló por un instante; pero de inmediato reanudó la marcha y pasó rápidamente por su lado con la cabeza inclinada.

Harry cruzó la calle, entre un carro tirado por un asno y un antiguo modelo de la marca Ford. Quienquiera que fuese aquel hombre, no lo estaba haciendo muy bien. Experimentó una fría punzada de inquietud, pero enseguida recordó que le habían advertido que alguien lo seguiría, como a todos los funcionarios de la embajada. Y puesto que él era un funcionario novato, quizás el espía también lo fuese.

No volvió a mirar hacia atrás hasta que llegó al portal de su casa, aunque le costó no hacerlo. Se sentía tan furioso como asustado. Cuando al final se volvió, el que lo seguía ya había desaparecido. Subió la escalera y en el momento en que abría la puerta dio un respingo al oír una voz procedente del interior.

—¿Eres tú, Harry?

Tolhurst estaba sentado en el sofá del salón.

—Perdona que haya entrado sin permiso, chico —continuó—. ¿Te he asustado? Es que he recibido un mensaje de Hillgarth, y quería que te lo transmitiese cuanto antes. Acababas de irte, de modo que decidí venir.

—Muy bien. —Harry se acercó a la ventana y miró hacia la calle—. Dios mío, no me lo puedo creer, está allí. Me están siguiendo, ven a ver.

—Bueno, pero no corras la cortina. —Tolhurst se puso a su lado y ambos contemplaron al joven de abajo. Paseaba arriba y abajo, rascándose la cabeza y mirando los números de las casas.

Tolhurst soltó una carcajada.

—Algunas de estas personas no sirven para nada —dijo.

—Espía por espía —susurró Harry.

—Es lo que suele hacerse. —Tolhurst lo miró con expresión muy seria—. Oye, ha habido un cambio de planes. El capitán Hillgarth quiere que pases ahora mismo a la acción con Forsyth; acude al Café Rocinante mañana por la tarde y mira a ver si puedes establecer contacto. Antes, a las nueve de la mañana, preséntate en la embajada para recibir instrucciones. —Lo miró fijamente y añadió—: ¿De acuerdo?

Harry respiró hondo.

—Sí —dijo, esbozando una sonrisa irónica—. Para eso he venido, ¿no?

—Muy bien. —Tolhurst señaló con la cabeza hacia la ventana—. Procura despistar a ese tipo.

—¿A qué se ha debido el cambio de planes?

—Hitler va a visitar Francia, donde mantendrá una importante reunión con Pétain. Corren rumores de que después vendrá aquí. Por cierto, todo esto es secreto.

—Eso significa que Franco podría estar a punto de entrar en guerra —apuntó Harry con tono grave.

Tolhurst asintió con la cabeza.

—Al menos, se mueve en esa dirección. Tenemos que averiguar cuanto podamos acerca de todo.

—Sí —dijo Harry, resignado—, lo comprendo.

—Será mejor que vuelva a la embajada y le diga a Hillgarth que he conseguido hablar contigo. —Tolhurst contempló las paredes desnudas—. ¿Por qué no cubres todos estos espacios vacíos? Tenemos montones de cuadros en la embajada, si quieres unos cuantos. —Enarcó las cejas—. Seamos optimistas y pensemos que no a todos nos van a pegar un puntapié o algo peor.

Cuando Tolhurst se hubo marchado, Harry regresó a la ventana. Había comenzado a llover de nuevo y el cristal estaba cubierto de gotas. El hombre había desaparecido; probablemente se hubiese escondido cerca, a la espera de que él saliese. Pensó en la pobre mujer que había sido detenida. ¿Adónde la llevarían? Lo más seguro era que la encerrasen en un calabozo maloliente. En aquel incidente pareció cristalizar todo lo que había visto los últimos días. Harry cayó en la cuenta de que había dejado de ser neutral; aborrecía lo que Franco estaba haciendo.

A su mente volvió a acudir Sandy y el encuentro del día siguiente. Se imaginó los tanques alemanes cruzando los Pirineos para dar comienzo a una nueva guerra en España. Se preguntó de dónde habría sacado la embajada aquella información. Quizá tuviera algo que ver con aquello que habían estado hablando Hillgarth y Maestre. Juan March, el millonario sin escrúpulos, había financiado a Franco durante la Guerra Civil; pero cabía la posibilidad de que, aun así, fuera pro inglés como Maestre. Se preguntó qué eran los Caballeros de San Jorge, quizás una especie de clave. Hoare le había dicho que no pensara más en ello, pero ¿por qué a él y a Hillgarth les preocupaba tanto que él lo supiera? Se encogió de hombros. Bueno, sería mejor que empezara a prepararse mentalmente para su tarea, que se preparara para reunirse con Sandy, aquel Sandy que sacaba provecho del infierno español.

¿Cómo sería ahora? Recordó el año en que había compartido un estudio con Sandy, aquel año tan extraño.

El incidente de la araña en el estudio de Taylor había sido el comienzo de un período muy difícil. Todo era inestable e incómodo. Bernie había sido trasladado a otro estudio, pero había conservado la amistad con Harry. Bernie y Sandy se odiaban. Por nada en concreto; era algo visceral, instintivo. En el colegio abundaban las luchas encarnizadas y las rivalidades entre chicos, pero aquello era más inquietante porque no se manifestaba por medio de peleas y discusiones, sino de frías miradas y comentarios sarcásticos. Y, sin embargo, Bernie y Sandy eran muy parecidos en muchos sentidos. Compartían el desprecio que les inspiraba Rookwood, sus creencias y el sistema, algo que a Harry le resultaba muy doloroso.

Bernie se guardaba su socialismo prácticamente sólo para él, porque sabía que a casi todos los chicos sus ideas les habrían resultado no sólo censurables, sino incomprensibles. En clase lo hacía todo muy bien y era listo, como necesariamente tenían que serlo los becarios para poder ingresar en Rookwood. Jugaba al rugby con mucha agresividad y había conseguido formar parte del equipo juvenil. Pero de vez en cuando dejaba traslucir lo que pensaba acerca de Rookwood y se lo comentaba a Harry con implacable desprecio.

—Nos están preparando para formar parte de la clase dominante —le dijo una tarde a Harry. Hacía un tiempo desapacible y todos se encontraban en el estudio de Harry. Harry y Bernie estaban sentados a la mesa, mientras Sandy leía junto al fuego—. Para gobernar aquí a los obreros y a los nativos en las colonias.

—Alguien tiene que gobernar —señaló Harry—. Yo tenía pensado presentar una instancia a la Oficina Colonial cuando saliera de aquí. Puede que mi primo me eche una mano.

—¡Pero qué dices!

Bernie soltó una carcajada amarga.

—Ser inspector de un distrito es un trabajo tremendamente duro. Mi tío tiene un amigo que estuvo muchos años en Uganda, el único blanco en muchos kilómetros a la redonda. Regresó con malaria. Allí algunos se dejan la vida.

—Y otros se forran —replicó desdeñosamente Bernie—. Tendrías que escucharte, Harry. «Puede que mi primo me eche una mano.» «El amigo de mi tío.» Ninguna de las personas de mi entorno tiene primos o tíos que puedan echarle una mano para que acaben gobernando África.

—Y los socialistas saben llevar mejor las cosas, ¿verdad? Gente como esos idiotas de MacDonald y Snowden.

—Ésos son unos traidores. Son débiles. Necesitamos un tipo de socialismo más fuerte, como el que tienen en Rusia.

Sandy levantó la vista y soltó una carcajada.

—¿Tú crees que en Rusia están mejor que aquí? Probablemente estén igual, o peor.

Harry frunció el entrecejo.

—¿Cómo va a ser Rookwood igual que Rusia?

Sandy se encogió de hombros.

—Es un sistema basado en tremendas mentiras. Dicen que te están educando, pero lo que en realidad hacen es inculcarte una serie de cosas que quieren que asimiles, como hacen los rusos con toda su propaganda. Nos dicen cuándo tenemos que irnos a la cama, cuándo levantarnos, cómo hablar y cómo pensar. A las personas como tú, todo eso les da igual; pero Piper y yo somos distintos. —Miró a Bernie con perversa ironía.

—Dices muchas tonterías, Forsyth —contestó Bernie—. Crees que salir a escondidas de noche para ir a tomarte unas copas con Piers Knight y sus compinches te hace distinto. Yo quiero libertad para mi clase. Y nuestra hora está a punto de llegar.

—Y supongo que yo iré directo a la guillotina.

—Puede que sí.

Sandy se había juntado con un grupo de alumnos de cuarto y quinto que se reunían para beber en un local de la ciudad y, según decían ellos, para ligar con chicas.

Bernie decía que eran todos unos vagos y Harry se mostraba de acuerdo, aunque, después de los intentos de Taylor de reclutarlo como espía, empezaba a ver las cosas un poco desde la perspectiva de Sandy, la oveja negra, el chico al que había que vigilar; no era una situación precisamente envidiable. Sandy trabajaba lo menos posible; su actitud ante los profesores y ante sus deberes escolares era de mal disimulado desprecio.

Aquel semestre Harry adquirió la costumbre de dar largos paseos en solitario. El hecho de recorrer varios kilómetros por los bosques de Sussex le despejaba la mente. Una húmeda tarde de noviembre dobló un recodo y vio a Sandy Forsyth en cuclillas en el sendero examinando una piedra redonda que sostenía en las manos. Sandy alzó la vista.

—Hola, Brett —dijo.

—¿Qué estás haciendo? Tienes la chaqueta manchada de tiza.

—No importa. Fíjate en esto. —Sandy se incorporó y le pasó la piedra a Harry. A primera vista, parecía un trozo de pedernal; pero después Harry observó que estaba cubierta de círculos concéntricos que formaban una espiral.

Sandy esbozó una sonrisa, pero no era cínica como de costumbre, sino de felicidad.

—Es un amonites. Una criatura fosilizada. Antes todo eso era un mar lleno de bichos como éste, nadando por ahí. Cuando murió, se hundió en el fondo y, con el paso de muchos años, se convirtió en una roca. No te puedes imaginar cuántos. Millones.

—No sabía que los fósiles fueran así. Pensaba que eran muy grandes, como los dinosaurios.

—Bueno, también había dinosaurios. Los primeros fósiles de dinosaurio los encontró cerca de aquí, hace cien años, un hombre llamado Mantell. —Sandy sonrió con ironía—. El hombre no estaba muy bien visto en ciertos ambientes. Los fósiles eran un desafío a la idea de la Iglesia, según la cual la tierra sólo tenía unos cuantos miles de años de antigüedad. Mi padre sigue pensando que fue Dios quien puso directamente los fósiles para poner a prueba la fe de los hombres. Es un anglicano de lo más tradicional.

Harry jamás había visto a Forsyth en semejante estado. Su rostro aparecía iluminado por un emocionado interés, tenía el uniforme manchado de tiza y el espeso cabello negro, por regla general cepillado pulcramente, se le había puesto de punta y formaba unos pequeños penachos.

—Suelo venir aquí a la caza de fósiles. Éste es uno de los buenos. No se lo digo a nadie... pensarían que soy un empollón.

Harry estudió la piedra, limpiando con los dedos el barro acumulado en las espiras del caparazón.

—Es impresionante. —Le parecía precioso, pero en Rookwood no se utilizaban semejantes términos.

—Ven conmigo alguna vez, si te apetece —dijo Sandy con cierto recelo—. Me estoy haciendo una colección. Tengo una piedra con una mosca dentro, debe de rondar los trescientos millones de años. Los insectos y las arañas son tan antiguos como los dinosaurios, mucho más antiguos que nosotros. —Hizo una pausa y se ruborizó ligeramente ante semejante exhibición de entusiasmo.

—¿De veras?

—Pues sí. —Sandy dirigió la mirada más allá de las lomas onduladas—. Seguirán aquí cuando nosotros hayamos desaparecido.

—A Taylor le dan miedo las arañas.

Sandy se echó a reír.

—¿Cómo dices?

—Lo descubrí una vez. —Harry se ruborizó. No debería haberlo
dicho.

—Viejo imbécil. Pues yo iré a buscar fósiles cuando me largue de
este sitio de mala muerte, haré expediciones a lugares como Mongolia.
Quiero vivir aventuras lejos de aquí —añadió, sonriendo.

Y, de esta manera, ambos se hicieron más o menos amigos. Salían
a dar largos paseos en busca de fósiles y Harry adquiría conocimientos acerca de la vida que pulsaba y se mecía en los antiguos mares que
inundaban los lugares donde ellos se encontraban ahora. Sandy sabía
un montón de cosas. Una vez encontró el diente de un dinosaurio, un
iguanodonte, enterrado en la falda de una cantera.

—Hay muy pocos —dijo con entusiasmo—. Y valen mucho dinero. Lo entregaré al Museo de Historia Natural cuando lleguen las vacaciones.

El dinero era muy importante para Sandy. Su padre le daba unas
generosas asignaciones, pero él quería más.

—Eso significa que puedes hacer lo que quieras con tu vida —decía—. Cuando sea mayor, ganaré un dineral.

—¿Buscando huesos de dinosaurio? —preguntó Harry.

Exploraban una de las viejas herrerías que salpicaban los alrededores
del bosque.

Sandy estudió el horizonte y los desnudos árboles marrones. Era
un día de principios de invierno, frío y desapacible.

—Primero acumularé una fortuna.

—Me parece que yo no pienso mucho en el dinero.

—Piper diría que eso es porque te sobra. Aquí todos tenemos dinero. Pero es de nuestras familias. Yo me lo quiero ganar por mi propia cuenta.

—A mí el dinero me lo dejó mi padre. Ojalá lo hubiera conocido,
pero lo mataron en la guerra.

Sandy volvió a mirar el horizonte.

—Mi padre fue capellán en el frente occidental. Decía a todos aquellos soldados que Dios estaba con ellos antes de que salieran de las trincheras. Mi hermano Peter sigue sus pasos, ahora está estudiando en el colegio de Teología y después se incorporará al ejército. Fue delegado de los alumnos en Braildon, delegado de Deportes y Premio Extraordinario de Griego y todo eso. —El rostro de Sandy se ensombreció—. Pero es un imbécil, tan imbécil con su religión como Piper con su socialismo. Todo eso son tonterías. —Se volvió para mirar a Harry con los ojos iluminados por un extraño y ardiente fulgor—. Mi madre se largó cuando yo tenía diez años, ¿sabes? No hablan mucho de eso, pero yo creo que fue porque no podía seguir aguantando todas estas bobadas. Solía decir que quería un poco de diversión en la vida. Recuerdo que me compadecí de ella, porque sabía que la pobre jamás la tuvo.

Harry se sintió incómodo.

—¿Y dónde está ahora? —preguntó.

Sandy se encogió de hombros.

—No lo saben. O no lo quieren decir. —Esbozó una sonrisa—. Ella tenía razón, hay que divertirse un poco en la vida. ¿Por qué no vienes conmigo y con los de mi pandilla? Nos reunimos con unas chicas en la ciudad —añadió, enarcando las cejas.

Harry vaciló.

—¿Y qué hacéis? —preguntó, con cierto recelo—. Cuando estáis con ellas, quiero decir.

—De todo.

—¿De todo? ¿De verdad?

Sandy se echó a reír, se levantó de un salto de la roca en la que estaba sentado y le dio a Harry una palmada en el brazo.

—Bueno, en realidad, no. Pero algún día lo haremos, y yo quiero ser el primero.

Harry dio un puntapié a una piedra.

—No quiero meterme en líos, no merece la pena.

—Vamos. —Harry se sintió dominado por la fuerza de la personalidad de Sandy—. Yo lo organizo todo, me aseguro de que salgamos cuando no haya nadie a la vista, nunca vamos a ningún sitio en el que podamos encontrarnos con los profesores... o en el que, en caso de que topáramos con ellos, estuvieran más preocupados que nosotros de que alguien los viera.

Sandy se echó a reír.

—¿Un tugurio de mala muerte? No sé si me apetece.

—No van a descubrirnos. En Braildon me pillaron saltándome las normas y ahora procuro tener más cuidado. Es divertido saber que intentan pillarte y tú los engañas.

—¿Por qué te expulsaron de Braildon?

—Estaba en la ciudad, y un profesor me vio salir de un pub. Me denunció y me soltaron el sermón de siempre, que por qué no podía ser como mi hermano, que si él era mucho mejor que yo... —La furia volvió a asomar a los ojos de Sandy—. Pero se lo hice pagar.

—¿Qué hiciste?

Sandy volvió a sentarse y se cruzó de brazos.

—Aquel profesor, Dacre, era joven y tenía un coche de color rojo. Al volante se sentía el amo del mundo. Yo sé conducir; una noche salí a escondidas y saqué el automóvil del garaje del profesor. Hay una colina muy escarpada cerca del colegio. Subí hasta arriba, salté del coche en marcha y dejé que cayese por el precipicio. —Sonrió—. Fue impresionante. Se estrelló contra un árbol y el morro se aplastó como si fuera de cartón.

—¡Dios mío! Pero eso es muy peligroso.

—No si sabes hacerlo. Lo malo es que, cuando salté del coche, me arañé la cara con una rama. Me vieron y ataron cabos. Pero mereció la pena, y conseguí que me echaran de Braildon. No creía que me fueran a aceptar en ningún otro sitio; sin embargo, mi padre tiró de unos cuantos hilos y me trajeron aquí. Mala suerte.

Harry hundió la punta del zapato en la tierra.

—Creo que es ir demasiado lejos. Destruir el automóvil de otra persona...

Sandy lo miró fijamente a los ojos.

—Hay que hacer a los demás lo que ellos te hacen a ti.

—Eso no es lo que dice la Biblia.

—Es lo que digo yo. —Sandy se encogió de hombros—. Vamos, será mejor que regresemos; más nos valdrá estar presentes cuando pasen lista; de lo contrario, tendremos problemas con nuestros amables profesores, ¿no te parece?

Durante el camino de vuelta apenas hablaron. El sol otoñal se fue ocultando muy lentamente, mientras teñía de rosa los charcos que salpicaban los embarrados senderos. Llegaron a la carretera desde la que se divisaban los altos muros del colegio. Sandy se volvió hacia Harry.

—¿Sabes de dónde procede el dinero con que se creó este colegio y se financian las becas para alumnos como Piper?

—De unos comerciantes de hace un par de siglos, ¿verdad?

—Sí, pero ¿sabes a qué clase de negocio se dedicaban?

—¿Sedas, especias y cosas por el estilo?

—Comercio de esclavos. Eran negreros. Capturaban a los negros en África y los enviaban por barco a América. Encontré un libro en la biblioteca. —Sandy hizo una pausa—. Es curioso la de cosas que puedes descubrir si te fijas. Cosas que la gente quiere mantener en secreto y que podrían ser muy útiles. —Volvió a esbozar su sonrisa enigmática.

Los problemas empezaron unas semanas más tarde en la clase de Taylor. Los alumnos tenían que hacer una traducción del latín y Sandy se la saltó. Lo llamaron para que leyera su escrito y metió tantas veces la pata que sus compañeros se echaron a reír. Otro chico se habría muerto de vergüenza; Sandy, en cambio, se quedó allí sentado riéndose junto al resto de la clase.

Taylor se enfureció. Se acercó a Sandy con el rostro congestionado por la cólera.

—Usted ni siquiera ha intentado hacer la traducción, Forsyth. Tiene la misma capacidad que cualquier otro alumno de esta clase, pero ni siquiera se ha tomado la molestia.

—No, señor —repuso Sandy con seriedad—. Es que me ha parecido muy difícil.

Taylor enrojeció aún más de ira.

—Usted cree que semejante insolencia quedará impune, ¿no es cierto? Hay muchas cosas que usted cree que puede hacer sin sufrir ningún castigo, pero lo estamos vigilando.

—Gracias, señor —dijo Sandy con frialdad.

La clase volvió a reír, pero Harry se percató de que Sandy había ido demasiado lejos. No se podía provocar a Taylor de aquella manera.

El profesor regresó al estrado y cogió la palmeta.

—Esto es una insolencia desvergonzada, Forsyth. ¡Haga el favor de acercarse!

Sandy apretó los labios. Estaba claro que no se lo esperaba. Los castigos físicos delante de la clase eran muy raros.

—No me parece justo, señor —dijo.

—Ya decidiré yo lo que es justo.

Taylor se acercó a Sandy y lo sacó de su sitio agarrándolo por el cuello de la camisa. Sandy no era alto pero sí muy fuerte, así que Harry se preguntó por un instante si opondría resistencia, pero no fue así, y se dejó arrastrar hasta la parte delantera del aula. Sin embargo, sus ojos reflejaban una furia que Harry jamás le había visto, mientras se inclinaba sobre el escritorio de Taylor y éste descargaba la palmeta una y otra vez.

Al terminar la clase, Harry se acercó a Sandy, que permanecía inclinado sobre la mesa. Estaba muy pálido y jadeaba.

—¿Te encuentras bien?

—Me encontraré mejor... después. —Sandy hizo una pausa y añadió—: ¿Lo ves, Harry? ¿Te das cuenta de cómo nos controlan?

—No tendrías que haberlo provocado.

—Me vengaré —masculló Sandy.

—No digas tonterías. ¿Cómo vas a vengarte de él?

—Ya encontraré la manera.

Los alumnos del colegio comían sentados alrededor de unas mesas largas a cuya cabecera se sentaba el profesor de la clase. Una tarde, al cabo de una semana del incidente, Harry observó que Sandy y Taylor no estaban presentes.

A Sandy tampoco se le vio aquella noche, y otro profesor dio la clase a la mañana siguiente. Éste anunció que Alexander Forsyth ya no regresaría al colegio; lo habían expulsado por agredir al señor Taylor, que se tomaría un período de baja por enfermedad. Los chicos lo acribillaron a preguntas; pero el profesor, con una mueca de hastío, dijo que era algo demasiado desagradable para comentarlo. Aquella mañana, a través de la ventana de la clase, Harry vio al obispo Forsyth entrar en el patio con expresión de contrariedad. Sentado a su lado, Bernie le dijo en voz baja:

—No sé qué habrá hecho Forsyth, pero, en cualquier caso, estaremos mejor sin él.

A la hora del almuerzo, todos los chicos se preguntaron muy nerviosos qué habría ocurrido. Harry se saltó la comida y subió al dormitorio. Encontró a Sandy guardando cuidadosamente su colección de fósiles en una maleta.

—Hola, Brett —dijo Sandy con su acostumbrada sonrisa—. ¿Te has enterado de lo que ha pasado?

—Dicen que te vas. ¿Qué has hecho? No quieren explicárnoslo.

Sandy se sentó en la cama sin dejar de sonreír.

—La mejor venganza que te puedas imaginar. En realidad, fuiste tú quien me dio la idea. Arañas.

—¿Cómo?

—¿Recuerdas aquel día que salimos a buscar fósiles y te dije que los insectos y las arañas eran más antiguos que los dinosaurios?

Harry experimentó una sensación de desaliento. Recordaba que Taylor le había pedido que espiara a Sandy, aunque eso se lo había guardado para sí. A partir de aquel momento, Taylor se había mostrado muy distante con él.

—¿Has estado alguna vez en las buhardillas? —continuó Sandy—. Están llenas de telarañas —añadió con una amplia sonrisa en los labios—. Y donde hay telarañas, hay arañas. Elegí las más grandes y llené con ellas una lata de galletas. Y ayer fui al estudio de Taylor mientras él estaba en la sala de los profesores. —Se echó a reír—. Las puse por todas partes. En los cajones, en la pitillera de su escritorio, hasta en sus viejas y malolientes zapatillas. Después me fui al estudio de al lado. Ya sabes que está desocupado desde que el viejo Henderson se retiró en Navidad. Y allí me senté a esperar. Sabía que Taylor regresaría sobre las cuatro para corregir exámenes. Quería oírlo gritar.

Harry apretó los puños. Sandy había echado mano de la información que él le había facilitado y ahora se sentía parcialmente culpable.

—¿Y gritó? —preguntó.

Sandy se encogió de hombros.

—No. Me equivoqué. Lo oí salir al pasillo y cerrar la puerta, pero no hubo ningún ruido, sólo silencio. Yo pensé, vamos, cabrón, a estas alturas ya tienes que haberlas encontrado. Después oí que se abría su puerta y unas pisadas como de alguien que estuviera borracho y, a continuación, un ruido sordo. Luego se oyó una especie de gemido que parecía el maullido de un gato. El gemido se intensificó y se convirtió en una especie de crujido que hizo que otros profesores salieran de sus estudios. Oí que Jevons preguntaba. «¿Qué ocurre?» Y después la voz de Taylor. «Mi estudio está lleno de bichos.» Entonces Williams entró en el estudio y se puso a gritar que todo estaba lleno de arañas.

—Pero, hombre, Sandy, ¿por qué lo hiciste?

Sandy lo miró sin pestañear.

—Por venganza, naturalmente. Juré que me las pagaría. En cualquier caso, después oí a Taylor decir que se sentía mareado. Williams sugirió que lo llevaran al estudio vacío, y entonces abrió la puerta y todos se me quedaron mirando. —Sandy sonrió—. Merecía la pena sólo por ver la cara de Taylor. Se había mareado, estaba muy pálido y tenía toda la túnica manchada de vómito. Entonces Williams me agarró y me dijo: «Te hemos pillado, pequeño cerdo.» —Sandy cerró la maleta y se levantó—. El director dijo que Taylor había estado en la guerra y que aquello lo había impresionado mucho, porque había visto un cadáver o no sé qué lleno de arañas. ¿Cómo iba yo a saberlo? —Sandy volvió a encogerse de hombros—. De todos modos, eso se acabó, me voy a casa. Papá suplicó y trató de convencerlos, pero no hubo nada que hacer. No importa, Harry, no tienes por qué enfadarte. No dije nada de que tú me habías contado lo de las arañas. Me negué a explicar cómo me había enterado.

—No es eso. Es que me parece una salvajada. Y fui yo quien la hizo posible.

—No sabía que se iba a volver loco. De todos modos, a él lo han enviado a no sé qué hospital y a mí me han expulsado. Así es la vida. Yo ya sabía que más tarde o más temprano iba a pasar algo. —Sandy le dirigió una mirada extraña. Por un instante, Harry vio lágrimas en sus ojos—. Es mi destino ¿comprendes? Mi destino es ser un mal chico. No habría podido evitarlo, por mucho que lo hubiese intentado.

Harry se incorporó desorientado; se había quedado dormido en el sofá. Y había soñado que quedaba atrapado en su estudio y fuera llovía a cántaros y Sandy y Bernie y otros muchos chicos aporreaban la cristalera y le pedían a gritos que los dejara entrar. Se estremeció; hacía frío y se había hecho casi de noche. Se levantó y descorrió las cortinas. Los edificios y las calles estaban tan silenciosos que no podía evitar sentirse nervioso. Contempló la plaza desierta donde la estatua del manco era como una vaga sombra bajo la pálida y tenue luz de una farola. No había el menor movimiento. Harry se percató de que no había visto ni un solo gato desde que había llegado; seguramente se los habían comido todos, como las palomas. Tampoco se veía ni rastro de su vigilante; a lo mejor, por la noche le permitían regresar a casa.

De repente, se preguntó si en Rookwood estarían enterados de lo que le había ocurrido a Bernie. En caso afirmativo, lo más probable era que no se hubieran sorprendido ni lo hubieran lamentado. Y el destino de Sandy, o lo que lo impulsaba a actuar, lo había dejado varado en aquel lugar, donde al día siguiente él empezaría a espiarlo, después de todo. Harry recordó que Jebb le había dicho que había sido Taylor quien les había facilitado su nombre, y entonces él esbozó una triste sonrisa ante aquella ironía. Tal y como giraban las ruedas de los acontecimientos, quizás hubiera algo de verdad en lo que se decía acerca del destino.

8

Aquella misma tarde Barbara salió a dar un largo paseo. Estaba nerviosa y preocupada, como le venía ocurriendo desde su encuentro con Luis. El tiempo era bueno después de la lluvia, pero todavía frío, por lo que, por primera vez desde la llegada de la primavera, se había puesto el abrigo.

Se fue al parque del Retiro; lo habían remozado desde el final de la guerra y habían plantado nuevos árboles para sustituir los que se habían cortado durante el sitio para que sirvieran de combustible. El parque volvía a ser lugar de encuentro para las mujeres respetables de Madrid.

Había refrescado y sólo las mujeres más valientes y solitarias se sentaban a conversar en los bancos. Barbara reconoció a la esposa de uno de los amigos de Sandy y la saludó con un movimiento de la cabeza, pero siguió adelante en dirección al zoo situado en la parte de atrás del parque; quería estar sola.

El zoo estaba casi desierto. Se sentó cerca del foso de los leones marinos, encendió un cigarrillo y se los quedó mirando. Había oído decir que los animales habían sufrido terriblemente durante el sitio; muchos habían muerto de hambre, pero ahora había un nuevo elefante donado por el Generalísimo. Sandy era aficionado a los toros, pero por mucho que él le hablara de la habilidad y el valor que todo ello suponía, Barbara no soportaba ver aquel animal fuerte y enorme atormentado hasta morir, los caballos moribundos y cubiertos de sangre, dando coces en la arena. Había visto un par de corridas y se negaba a volver. Sandy se había reído y le había dicho que no lo comentara delante de sus amigos españoles; la considerarían una inglesa sentimental de la peor clase.

Retorció el asa de su bolso de piel de cocodrilo. Unos pensamientos angustiosos a propósito de Sandy acudían incesantemente a su mente.

No era justo; aquel engaño lo ponía en peligro y podía destruir su carrera en el caso de que se llegara a descubrir lo que ella estaba haciendo. Se debatía entre el sentimiento de culpabilidad y la cólera que le producía la existencia limitada que llevaba desde hacía tiempo y la manera en que Sandy pretendía dirigirlo todo.

Al día siguiente de su reunión con Luis, había acudido al despacho del *Express* en la Puerta del Sol y había preguntado por Markby. Le dijeron que se había ido al norte para informar de que algunos oficiales alemanes cruzaban la frontera con Francia para comprar de todo.

Tal vez tuviera que interrogar a Luis. ¿Por qué le había dicho que había permanecido dos inviernos en Cuenca? ¿Acaso los estaba engañando tanto a ella como a Markby a cambio de dinero? A lo largo de toda la entrevista se había mostrado nervioso y preocupado, pero muy firme a la hora de exigir el dinero que quería.

Se acercó una mujer envuelta en un abrigo de piel con un niño de unos ocho años al lado que vestía el uniforme de un pequeño «flecha», la sección más joven de la Falange Juvenil. Al ver los leones marinos, se apartó de su madre y se dirigió corriendo al foso, apuntando a los animales con su fusil de madera.

—¡Bang! ¡Bang! —gritó—. ¡Muerte a los rojos, muerte a los rojos!

Barbara se estremeció. Sandy le había dicho que los de la Falange Juvenil eran una especie de *boy-scouts* españoles, pero a veces ella tenía sus dudas.

Al verla, el niño se acercó ella y levantó el brazo haciendo el saludo fascista.

—¡Buenos días, señora! ¡Viva Franco! ¿La puedo ayudar en algo?

—No, gracias, estoy muy bien —repuso Barbara.

La mujer tomó al niño de la mano.

—Vamos, Manolito, el elefante está por allí. —Sacudió la cabeza, mirando a Barbara—. Qué agotadores son los niños, ¿verdad?

Barbara sonrió con recelo.

—Pero son el regalo que nos hace Dios —añadió la mujer.

—¡Vamos, mamá, a los elefantes, a los elefantes!

Barbara los vio alejarse. Sandy no quería tener hijos; a sus treinta años, probablemente ya no los tuviera jamás. Hubo un tiempo en que habría deseado tener un hijo de Bernie. Su mente regresó a aquellos días de otoño con él, en el Madrid rojo. Sólo habían pasado cuatro años, pero parecía otra era.

Aquella primera noche en el bar, Bernie se le había antojado una criatura extraordinaria y exótica. No era sólo su belleza. La incongruencia entre su refinado acento de ex alumno de colegio privado y su tosco uniforme de soldado había contribuido a acrecentar la sensación de irrealidad.

—¿Cómo se hizo esa herida en el brazo? —le preguntó ella.

—Me alcanzó un francotirador en la Casa de Campo. Se me está curando muy bien; no es más que una muesca en el hueso. Estoy de permiso por enfermedad, vivo en casa de unos amigos en Carabanchel.

—¿No es el barrio que bombardean los nacionales? Tengo entendido que ha habido combates por allí.

—Sí, en la zona más apartada de la ciudad. Pero la gente que vive más allá no quiere irse. —Bernie sonrió—. Son extraordinarios y tremendamente fuertes. Conocí a la familia cuando estuve aquí hace cinco años. El hijo mayor está con la milicia de la Casa de Campo. Su madre le lleva comida caliente todos los días.

—¿Nunca le han entrado deseos de volver a casa?

—¿A mí? No. Me quedaré hasta que todo termine —respondió Bernie con expresión seria—. Hasta que convirtamos Madrid en la tumba del fascismo.

—Parece ser que los rusos van a enviar más pertrechos.

—Sí. Conseguiremos repeler a Franco. Y usted, ¿qué está haciendo aquí?

—Trabajo en la Cruz Roja. Ayudo a localizar a personas desaparecidas, negocio intercambios. Sobre todo, de niños.

—Cuando yo estuve en el hospital, el material sanitario procedía de la Cruz Roja. Sólo Dios sabe lo mucho que lo necesitaban. —La miró fijamente a los ojos y añadió—: Pero ustedes también facilitan material a los fascistas, ¿verdad?

—Tenemos que hacerlo. Estamos obligados a ser neutrales.

—No olvide cuál fue el bando que se levantó para acabar con un gobierno libremente elegido.

Ella cambió de tema.

—¿En qué parte del brazo lo alcanzaron?

—Por encima del codo. Me han asegurado que pronto quedará como nuevo. Y entonces volveré al frente.

—Un poco más arriba y le habrían dado en el hombro. Ahí la cosa ya podría ser más complicada.

—¿Es usted médico?

—Enfermera. Aunque llevo años sin ejercer. Ahora soy una burócrata —respondió Barbara, y soltó una carcajada.

—No lo desprecie, el mundo necesita organización.

Ella volvió a reír.

—Me parece que eso jamás se lo he oído decir a nadie. No importa lo útil que sea el trabajo que haces, la palabra burocracia siempre inspira recelo.

—¿Cuánto tiempo lleva en la Cruz Roja?

—Cuatro años. Ahora no voy mucho a Inglaterra.

—¿Tiene familia allí?

—Sí, pero hace dos años que no los veo. No tenemos demasiadas cosas en común. Y usted, ¿a qué se dedicaba antes de venir a España?

—Bueno, antes de irme trabajaba como modelo de escultor.

Barbara estuvo a punto de derramar el vino.

—¿Como qué?

—Posaba para algunos escultores de Londres. No se preocupe, no es nada vergonzoso. Es un trabajo como cualquier otro.

—Se debe de pasar mucho frío —comentó ella por decir algo.

—Sí. Hay estatuas con piel de gallina por todo Londres.

En ese momento se abrió la puerta ruidosamente y entraron unos milicianos vestidos con monos de trabajo, entre ellos varias chicas del Batallón de Mujeres. Todos se agruparon alrededor de la barra entre gritos y empujones. Bernie se puso muy serio.

—Nuevos reclutas que mañana mismo marcharán hacia el frente —dijo—. ¿Quiere ir a algún otro sitio? ¿Qué le parecería ir al Café Gijón? Tal vez coincidamos con Hemingway.

—¿No es ese que está cerca de la central telefónica que los nacionales tratan constantemente de bombardear?

—No tema, es un sitio bastante seguro.

Se acercó una miliciana que no debía de tener más de dieciocho años y pasó un brazo por los hombros de Bernie.

—¡Salud, compañero! —Lo estrechó con más fuerza y dijo a sus camaradas algo que los hizo reír y vitorearla. Barbara no entendió nada, pero Bernie se ruborizó.

—Mi amiga y yo tenemos que irnos —dijo en tono de disculpa.

La miliciana puso cara de decepción. Bernie cogió a Barbara por el brazo con la mano sana y la condujo hacia la salida, abriéndose paso entre la gente.

Fuera, en la Puerta de Sol, siguió sujetándola por el brazo. Barbara notó que se le aceleraba el pulso. El sol poniente arrojaba un resplandor rojizo sobre los carteles de Lenin y Stalin. Los tranvías cruzaban ruidosamente la plaza.

—¿Ha entendido lo que decían? —preguntó Bernie.

—No, mis conocimientos de español no dan para mucho.

—Pues quizá sea mejor así. Los milicianos son bastante desinhibidos. —Bernie se echó a reír un tanto avergonzado—. ¿Cómo se las arregla en su trabajo si no domina el idioma?

—Bueno, tenemos intérpretes. Y mi español va mejorando. Me temo que en el despacho formamos una pequeña Babel. Franceses y suizos, en su mayoría. Yo hablo francés.

Entraron en la calle Montera. Un tullido alargó la mano desde un portal.

—Por solidaridad —dijo.

Bernie le entregó una moneda de diez céntimos.

Mientras cruzaban la Gran Vía, oyeron un rugido sordo por encima de sus cabezas. Alarmada, la gente miró hacia arriba. Algunas personas dieron media vuelta y echaron a correr. Barbara miró muy nerviosa alrededor.

—¿No tendríamos que buscar un refugio antiaéreo?

—No se preocupe. Es sólo un avión de reconocimiento. Venga.

El Café Gijón, un lugar de reunión de bohemios radicales antes de la guerra, era un local extremadamente moderno, con su típica decoración estilo *art déco*. Casi todas las paredes estaban revestidas de espejos. Junto a la barra se apretujaban los oficiales.

—No veo a Hemingway —dijo ella con una sonrisa.

—No importa. ¿Qué va a tomar?

Barbara pidió una copa de vino blanco y se sentó a una mesa. Mientras Bernie se acercaba a la barra, movió la silla buscando una posición donde no hubiera espejos, pero los muy condenados estaban por todas partes. No soportaba ver su imagen reflejada. Bernie regresó, sosteniendo en el brazo sano una bandeja con dos copas.

—Sujétela, si es tan amable.

—Sí, perdón.

—¿Le ocurre algo?

—No. —Barbara jugueteó con sus gafas—. Es que no me gustan demasiado los espejos.

—¿Y eso?

Ella apartó la mirada.

—La verdad es que no lo sé. ¿Es usted admirador de Hemingway?

—En realidad, no. ¿Usted lee mucho?

—Pues sí, dispongo de mucho tiempo por las noches. A mí tampoco me gusta Hemingway. Creo que le encanta la guerra, y yo la aborrezco. —Levantó la vista, preguntándose si habría sido demasiado vehemente; pero él se limitó a ofrecerle un cigarrillo, mirándola con una alentadora sonrisa en los labios—. Han sido un par de años muy malos para alguien que trabaja en la Cruz Roja. Primero Abisinia, y ahora, esto.

—La guerra no acabará hasta que el fascismo sea derrotado.

—¿Hasta que Madrid se convierta en su tumba?

—Sí.

—Y habrá otras muchas tumbas.

—No podemos huir de la historia —dijo Bernie, citando una frase.

—¿Es usted comunista? —le preguntó Barbara de repente.

Bernie sonrió y levantó su copa.

—Sección Central de Londres. —Sus ojos brillaron con un destello de picardía—. ¿Se sorprende?

Ella se echó a reír.

—¿Después de dos meses aquí? ¡Ya estoy curada de espantos!

Dos días más tarde, fueron a dar una vuelta por el Retiro. Habían colocado una pancarta sobre la verja principal. ¡NO PASARÁN!, rezaba. Los combates eran cada vez más encarnizados, y las tropas de Franco habían penetrado por la zona universitaria, al norte de la ciudad, pero las habían repelido. Los rusos enviaban más armamento. Barbara había visto una hilera de tanques bajando por la Gran Vía y levantando los adoquines de la calzada en medio de los vítores de la multitud. Al caer el sol las calles permanecían a oscuras para protegerlas de los bombardeos nocturnos, pero se podían ver los incesantes fogonazos blancos de artillería desde la Casa de Campo, en medio de retumbos y rugidos semejantes a los truenos de una tormenta interminable.

—Siempre he aborrecido la idea de la guerra, ya desde pequeña —le dijo Barbara a Bernie—. Perdí a un tío mío en el Somme.

—Mi padre también estuvo allí. Nunca ha sido el mismo desde entonces.

—De pequeña solía ver a personas que habían pasado por todo aquello, ¿sabe? Su comportamiento parecía normal, pero se las veía marcadas.

Bernie ladeó la cabeza.

—Ésa es una manera de pensar muy sombría para una niña pequeña.

—Pues yo siempre lo pensaba. —Barbara se echó a reír como si quisiera disculparse—. Me pasaba muchas horas sola.

—¿Es hija única como yo?

—No, tengo una hermana cuatro años mayor que yo. Está casada y lleva una vida muy tranquila en Birmingham.

—Todavía se le nota un poco el acento.

—Oh, no, no me lo diga.

—Es bonito —dijo Bernie, imitando su tono—. Mis padres son unos londinenses de clase obrera. Es muy duro ser hijo único. Depositaron muchas esperanzas en mí, sobre todo cuando me dieron la beca para ir a estudiar a Rookwood.

—De mí nadie esperó nunca nada.

Bernie la miró con curiosidad y, de repente, hizo una mueca y se sujetó el brazo herido con el otro.

—¿Le duele?

—Un poco. ¿Le importa que nos sentemos?

Ella lo ayudó a acomodarse en un banco. A través del tejido áspero de su gabán, su cuerpo se notaba duro y firme, y Barbara se sintió inmediatamente atraída por él.

Encendieron sendos cigarrillos. Estaban sentados delante del estanque, y el agua que brillaba a la luz de la luna constituía un reclamo para los bombarderos. Un leve olor a podrido se elevaba desde el barro que había en el fondo. Un árbol había sido talado allí cerca y unos hombres lo estaban cortando a hachazos; hacía frío y escaseaba el combustible. Al otro lado del estanque, seguía en pie la estatua de Alfonso XII con su enorme columnata de mármol; muy cerca de allí, la boca de un gigantesco cañón antiaéreo representaba un extraño contraste.

—Si aborrece la guerra —dijo Bernie, reanudando la conversación—, seguro que es antifascista.

—Odio todas esas tonterías nacionalistas acerca de la raza superior. El comunismo también es algo demencial... La gente no quiere tenerlo todo en común con los demás, no es natural. Mi padre es propietario de una tienda. Pero ni es rico ni explota a nadie.

—Mi padre también regenta una tienda, pero no es el propietario. He ahí la diferencia. El partido no está en contra de los tenderos ni de otros pequeños comerciantes, reconocemos que la transición al comunismo va a ser muy larga. Por eso pusimos fin a lo que los ultrarrevolucionarios hacían aquí. A lo que somos contrarios nosotros es al gran capital, a los que apoyan el fascismo. Gente como Juan March.

—¿Y ése quién es?

—El máximo financiador de Franco. Un hombre de negocios sin escrúpulos natural de Mallorca que ganó millones con el sudor de la frente de los demás. Corrupto hasta la médula.

Barbara apagó el cigarrillo.

—No se puede decir que todo lo malo corresponde a un bando en esta guerra. ¿Qué me dice de todas las personas que desaparecieron, que fueron detenidas de noche por las fuerzas de seguridad y a las que jamás se volvió a ver? Y no me niegue que eso esté pasando. Nosotros atendemos constantemente a mujeres angustiadas que se presentan en nuestras oficinas diciendo que sus maridos han desaparecido. Nadie les informa de dónde están.

—Los inocentes quedan atrapados en la guerra —repuso Bernie con serenidad.

—Precisamente. Miles y miles de ellos. —Bárbara volvió la cabeza. No quería discutir con él, por nada del mundo lo hubiera querido. Notó una cálida mano sobre la suya.

—No discutamos —pidió Bernie.

El contacto fue como una descarga eléctrica, pero Barbara apartó la mano y se la metió en el bolsillo. No lo esperaba; creía que él la había invitado a salir por segunda vez porque se sentía solo y no conocía a ningún otro inglés. «A lo mejor, necesita una mujer, una inglesa —pensó—; de lo contrario, ¿por qué me habría mirado?» Notó que se le aceleraba el pulso.

—¿Barbara? —Bernie se inclinó hacia delante, tratando de que sus miradas se cruzasen. Inesperadamente, hizo una mueca, bizqueó y sacó la lengua. Ella rió y lo apartó—. No quería disgustarla —añadió—. Perdone.

—No... es que... No me coja la mano. Seré su amiga, pero no haga eso.

—De acuerdo. Disculpe.

—Sería mejor que no habláramos de política. Cree que soy una estúpida, ¿verdad?

Bernie negó con la cabeza.

—No. Ésta es la primera conversación decente que mantengo con una chica desde hace siglos.

—No conseguirá convertirme, ¿sabe?

Bernie la miró con expresión desafiante.

—Deme tiempo —dijo.

Al cabo de un rato, se levantaron y continuaron andando. Bernie le habló de la familia en cuya casa se hospedaba, los Mera.

—Pedro, el padre, es capataz de una obra. Gana diez pesetas al día. Tienen tres hijos y viven en un apartamento de dos habitaciones. Pero la acogida que nos dispensaron a mi amigo Harry y a mí cuando estuvimos aquí en el treinta y uno fue algo nunca visto. Inés, la esposa de Pedro, me cuidó cuando salí del hospital; no quiso ni oír hablar de que me fuera a otro sitio. Es indomable, una de esas mujeres españolas menudas que son puro fuego. —Bernie clavó sus grandes ojos en Barbara y añadió con una sonrisa—: Podría presentárselos, si quiere. Les encantaría conocerla.

—¿Sabe que nunca he tratado con una familia española corriente? —Barbara suspiró—. A veces, si la gente me mira por la calle, creo que hay algo que no les gusta. No sé el qué. Quizá me esté volviendo un poco paranoica.

—Va usted demasiado bien vestida.

Ella se miró el viejo abrigo con incredulidad.

—¿Yo?

—Sí. Es un buen abrigo y además lleva un broche.

—Es viejo. Y en cuanto al broche, no es más que vidrio de colores. Lo compré en Ginebra.

—Aun así, se considera una ostentación. La gente de aquí está viviendo un infierno. Ahora la solidaridad lo es todo, tiene que serlo.

Barbara se quitó el broche.

—Pues fuera con él. ¿Así le parece mejor?

—Está muy bien. Una persona entre tantas.

—Claro que usted, por ir de uniforme, siempre debe de conseguir lo mejor.

—Soy un soldado. —Bernie pareció ofendido—. Visto de uniforme para demostrar mi solidaridad.

—Disculpe. —Barbara se maldijo por haber vuelto a meter la pata. ¿Por qué demonios se interesaba Bernie por ella?—. Hábleme de ese colegio al que asistió.

Bernie se encogió de hombros.

—Rookwood hizo de mí un comunista. Al principio, me encantaba: lleno de hijos del Imperio, el críquet, un juego de caballeros, el viejo y querido himno de la institución... Pero muy pronto comprendí lo que había debajo de todo eso.

—¿Se sintió a disgusto allí?

—Aprendí a ocultar mis sentimientos. Eso es lo único que te enseñan. Cuando me fui y regresé a Londres, me pareció... una liberación.

—Pues no le queda el menor acento de Londres.

—No, ésta es la única cosa que Rookwood me arrebató para siempre. Si ahora intento hablar *cockney*, sueno estúpido.

—Pero debió de tener amigos allí, ¿verdad? —No se lo imaginaba sin ningún amigo.

—Tenía a Harry —contestó Bernie—, que estuvo aquí conmigo hace cinco años. Me caía bien. Tenía el corazón donde hay que tenerlo. Ahora hemos perdido el contacto —añadió con tristeza—. Seguimos caminos distintos. —Hizo una pausa y se apoyó contra el tronco de un árbol—. Muchas personas excelentes acaban abrazando la ideología burguesa.

—Supongo que me considera una burguesa.

—Usted es otra cosa. —Bernie le guiñó el ojo.

Noviembre dio paso a diciembre, y unas lluvias frías y torrenciales bajaron desde la sierra de Guadarrama. Los fascistas habían quedado incomunicados en la Casa de Campo. Habían intentado abrir una brecha por el norte, pero allí también los habían repelido. El fuego de mortero seguía como siempre; en cambio, la crisis de desesperación ya se había superado. Ahora había bombarderos rusos en el cielo, unos rápidos monoplanos de morro achaparrado gracias a los cuales, en caso de que se aproximara algún bombardero alemán, éste era inmediatamente perseguido y obligado a alejarse. A veces se producían combates aéreos sobre la ciudad. Muchos decían que los rusos se habían apoderado de todo y que la República estaba a merced de ellos. Ahora los funcionarios gubernamentales se mostraban más antipáticos que antes y, en ocasiones, hasta parecían asustados. Los niños de los orfelinatos habían sido trasladados, de la noche a la mañana, a un campamento del Estado situado en algún lugar de las afueras de Madrid, por supuesto sin consultar con la Cruz Roja.

Bernie seguía viéndose con Barbara, la cual se pasaba casi todas las tardes con él en el Gijón o bien en algunos de los bares del centro. Los fines de semana se iban a pasear por la zona oriental de la ciudad, más segura, y a veces salían al campo que se extendía más allá. Ambos compartían el mismo sentido irónico del humor y se reían hablando de libros y de política y de sus infancias solitarias, cada una a su manera.

—La tienda en que trabaja mi padre es una de las cinco que posee el propietario —le explicó Bernie a Barbara un día. Estaban sentados en el murete divisorio de un campo de labranza de las afueras, aprovechando el sol en un día insólitamente templado. Las nubes se perseguían unas a otras y sus sombras se cernían sobre los campos. Costaba creer que el frente se encontrara a escasos kilómetros de distancia—. El señor Willis vive en Richmond, en una casa enorme, y le paga una miseria a mi padre. Sabe que éste jamás podría conseguir otro trabajo, ya que la guerra lo dejó muy... tocado. Mi madre es la que se encarga de casi todo, con la ayuda de una chica.

—Supongo que, en comparación con eso, yo estaba mejor —dijo Barbara—. Mi padre tiene un taller de reparación de bicicletas en Erdington. Siempre le ha ido muy bien. —Sintió la tristeza que siempre la embargaba al recordar su infancia; casi nunca hablaba de ella, pero de pronto se lo estaba contando todo a Bernie—. Cuando nació mi hermana, soñó con un hijo que algún día pudiera hacerse cargo del negocio, pero me tuvo a mí. Y después mi madre ya no pudo tener más hijos. —Encendió un cigarrillo.

—¿Se lleva bien con su hermana? A menudo he pensado que me habría gustado tener una.

—No. —Barbara volvió el rostro—. Carol es muy guapa y siempre le ha encantado exhibirse. Sobre todo, delante de mí. —Miró a Bernie, y éste le dirigió una sonrisa de aliento—. Pero yo era más inteligente, la que pudo seguir estudiando.

Se mordió el labio inferior al pensar en los recuerdos que aquellas palabras le hacían evocar, y después volvió a mirarlo y decidió que lo mejor era seguir adelante. Por mucho que le doliera, le contó que había sido víctima del acoso de sus compañeras desde el primer día de clase hasta el último, a los catorce años.

—El primer día se burlaron de mis gafas y mis rizos, y yo me puse a llorar —continuó—. Así empezó todo, ahora lo comprendo. Supongo que eso me señaló como alguien a quien se podía atormentar y hacer llorar. Allí donde fuera, las niñas se burlaban de mí. —Lanzó un profundo suspiro y se estremeció—. Las niñas pueden ser muy crueles.

De pronto Barbara se sintió fatal y pensó que no debería habérselo contado, que había sido una estupidez. Bernie levantó la mano como para tomar la suya, pero después la dejó caer de nuevo.

—En Rookwood ocurría lo mismo —dijo—. Si tenías algo que se salía un poco de lo corriente y no contraatacabas, te elegían como víctima. Empezaron conmigo cuando llegué, a causa de mi acento; «plebeyo», me llamaban. Tumbé a unos cuantos y la cosa se resolvió. Pero me pareció curioso que esas cosas ocurrieran precisamente en las escuelas privadas. —Sacudió la cabeza—. Y en los colegios de chicas también, ¿eh?

—Sí. Ojalá les hubiera dado una paliza, pero estaba demasiado bien educada. —Barbara arrojó lejos el cigarrillo—. Tanto sufrimiento sólo porque llevaba gafas y tenía una pinta un poco rara. —Se levantó bruscamente y dio unos pasos, contemplando la ciudad que, desde allí, era una mancha lejana y borrosa. En su extremo más alejado se divisaban unos minúsculos resplandores que parecían señales indicadoras justo en los lugares que los fascistas bombardeaban.

Bernie se acercó a ella y le ofreció otro cigarrillo.

—No es verdad.

—¿No es verdad el qué?

—Que tenga una pinta un poco rara. Es una tontería. Además, me gustan esas gafas.

Barbara se enfureció, como siempre cuando alguien le hacía un cumplido. Simplemente pretendían que ella se sintiera más a gusto con su aspecto. Se encogió de hombros.

—Bueno, al final me largué —dijo—. Querían que me quedara en aquel infierno y que fuera a la universidad, pero me negué. Tenía catorce años. Trabajé como mecanógrafa hasta que tuve edad suficiente para estudiar enfermería.

Bernie permaneció un rato en silencio. Barbara habría preferido que no la mirara tanto.

—¿Cómo ingresó en la Cruz Roja? —le preguntó él.

—A la escuela solían ir personas que ofrecían charlas los miércoles por la tarde. Una mujer nos habló de la labor que llevaba a cabo la Cruz Roja, ayudando a los refugiados de Europa. La señorita Forbes... —Barbara sonrió—. Era una mujer fornida de mediana edad, con el cabello canoso y un estúpido sombrero con flores; pero era tan amable y se esforzó tanto por hacernos comprender lo importante que era aquel trabajo que decidí unirme a ellos, al principio como voluntaria juvenil. Yo había perdido la confianza en el género humano, y ellos me la devolvieron. Al menos en parte. —Las lágrimas asomaron a sus ojos.

—¿Y acabó en Ginebra?

—Sí —respondió Barbara—. Porque también necesitaba alejarme de casa. —Exhaló una larga nube de humo y miró a Bernie—. ¿Qué pensaron sus padres cuando usted decidió unirse como voluntario a las Brigadas Internacionales?

—Sufrieron otra decepción. Como cuando dejé la universidad. —Bernie se encogió de hombros—. A veces me siento culpable por haberlos abandonado.

«Para trabajar por el partido —pensó Barbara—. Y para ser modelo de escultor.» Se lo imaginó momentáneamente sin ropa y bajó la mirada al suelo.

—No querían que viniera aquí, claro —continuó Bernie—, no lo entendían. —La miró de nuevo a los ojos—. Pero era preciso que viniera. Cuando vi los noticiarios, las colas de refugiados... Tenemos que destruir el fascismo, tenemos que hacerlo.

La llevó a ver a la familia Mera, pero la visita no fue un éxito. Barbara no los entendía a causa de su acento y se sentía incómoda entre tanto desorden.

Acogieron a Bernie como a un héroe, y ella imaginó que éste habría protagonizado algún acto de valentía en la Casa de Campo. Bernie compartía una habitación de aquella vivienda de alquiler con uno de los hijos, un escuálido muchacho de quince años con un pálido y demacrado rostro de tuberculoso.

En el camino de vuelta a casa, Barbara comentó que Bernie corría peligro al compartir una habitación con él. Él replicó con uno de sus ocasionales estallidos de cólera.

—No pienso tratar a Francisco como si fuera un leproso. Con buena alimentación y medicamentos apropiados, la tuberculosis se puede curar.

—Lo sé. —Barbara se avergonzó de sí misma.

—La clase obrera española es la mejor del mundo. Saben lo que es luchar contra la opresión y no temen hacerlo. Practican la verdadera solidaridad entre ellos y son internacionalistas; creen en el socialismo y trabajan por él. No son unos materialistas voraces, como casi todos los sindicalistas británicos. Son lo mejor de España.

—Lo siento —se disculpó Barbara—. Es que... no comprendía lo que decían y... bueno, me estoy comportando como una burguesa, ¿verdad? —Lo miró muy nerviosa, pero la cólera de Bernie ya se había desvanecido.

—Al menos, usted empieza a entenderlo, y eso ya es más de lo que la mayoría de la gente puede hacer.

Barbara habría comprendido que Bernie la quisiera sólo como amiga. Sin embargo, él intentaba tomarle la mano una y otra vez, y en un par de ocasiones había intentado besarla. ¿Por qué la quería a ella, pudiendo elegir a quien le diera la gana?, se preguntaba Barbara. Sólo se le ocurría pensar que, a pesar de su internacionalismo, él prefería a una inglesa. Temía que Bernie le hubiera dicho que su aspecto no tenía nada de malo sólo para llevársela a la cama. Sabía que los hombres no se andaban con muchos remilgos. Una vez ya la habían atrapado de aquella manera y eso constituía su peor recuerdo, un recuerdo que la avergonzaba. Sus anhelos y la confusión que experimentaba la estaban consumiendo.

A Bernie se le estaba curando el brazo; le habían quitado la escayola, pero aún lo llevaba en cabestrillo, y además debía presentarse cada semana en el cuartelillo.

Cuando se recuperara del todo, decía, lo trasladarían a un nuevo campo de instrucción para voluntarios ingleses, en el sur. Ella temía la llegada de aquel día.

—Me he ofrecido para echar una mano con los nuevos combatientes llegados de Inglaterra —prosiguió él—. Pero me han dicho que ya lo tienen todo resuelto. —Bernie frunció el ceño—. Creo que temen que mi maldito acento de escuela privada provoque el rechazo de los chicos de la clase obrera que están viniendo.

—Pobre Bernie —dijo Barbara—. Atrapado entre dos clases.

—Yo nunca he estado atrapado —replicó él con amargura—. Sé dónde están mis lealtades de clase.

Un sábado de principios de diciembre ambos fueron a dar un paseo por los barrios residenciales del norte. Era una zona de viviendas para ricos, enormes mansiones con jardín privado. Hacía mucho frío y la víspera había caído una ligera nevada. Al fundirse, la nieve había dejado una atmósfera gélida y húmeda, aunque aún quedaban algunas manchas blancas en los tejados.

Muchos habitantes de los barrios residenciales habían huido a la zona nacional o habían sido encarcelados, y algunas casas permanecían cerradas. Otras, en cambio, habían sido invadidas por ocupantes ilegales y los jardines aparecían plagados de malas hierbas o se habían convertido en huertos de hortalizas; cerdos y gallinas campaban a su antojo en algunos de ellos. Aunque el desorden la molestaba profundamente, Barbara ya empezaba a ver las cosas con los ojos de Bernie: evidentemente aquella gente necesitaba vivienda y comida.

Se detuvieron ante la verja de una enorme mansión en cuyas ventanas colgaba la colada. Una jovencita de unos quince años ordeñaba una vaca atada a un árbol en el centro de un césped salpicado de boñigas.

Al ver el gabán militar de Bernie, la chica se enderezó y lo saludó con el puño en alto.

—Habrán perdido sus casas por culpa de la artillería o los bombardeos de Franco —observó Bernie.

—Me pregunto dónde estarán los antiguos propietarios.

—Se han ido, eso es lo único que cuenta.

Al oír un rugido, los dos levantaron la vista hacia el cielo. Un gigantesco bombardero alemán sobrevolaba la zona, escoltado por un par de pequeños cazas. Tres aparatos rusos, con el morro pintado de rojo, volaban en círculo a su alrededor, dejando unas largas estelas de humo blanco en el cielo azul. Barbara echó la cabeza atrás para verlos mejor. Era una hermosa exhibición, hasta que uno caía en la cuenta de lo que estaba ocurriendo allí arriba. Al final de la calle se levantaba una iglesia neogótica del siglo XIX. Una pancarta colgaba sobre una puerta que estaba abierta: «Establo de la Revolución.»

—Venga —dijo Bernie—. Vamos a echar un vistazo.

El interior había sido destruido; casi todos los bancos se habían retirado y las vidrieras de colores estaban rotas. Las imágenes habían sido sacadas de sus hornacinas y arrojadas al suelo; unas balas de paja se amontonaban en un rincón. La parte de atrás de la iglesia había sido vallada para albergar un rebaño de ovejas. Los animales estaban todos apretujados y, cuando la pareja se acercó, se apartaron atemorizados y empezaron a balar, emparejándose entre sí y mirando de soslayo con sus extraños ojos desmesuradamente abiertos. Bernie intentó calmarlos murmurando palabras tranquilizadoras.

Barbara se acercó al montón de imágenes rotas. Una cabeza de yeso de la Virgen con los ojos llenos de lágrimas pintadas la miró con expresión de reproche desde el suelo y le evocó el convento donde se alojaban los niños. De pronto fue consciente de la presencia de Bernie a su lado.

—Las lágrimas de la Virgen —dijo, soltando una risita cohibida.

—La Iglesia siempre ha apoyado a los opresores. Al alzamiento de Franco lo llaman «cruzada» y bendicen a los soldados fascistas. No se puede reprochar que la gente esté furiosa.

—Yo jamás he entendido a la Iglesia, con todos sus dogmas. Es triste.

Sintió que Bernie le rodeaba el cuerpo con el brazo bueno y la obligaba a volverse. Se llevó tal sorpresa que no le dio tiempo a reaccionar cuando él se inclinó hacia delante. Notó el contacto de su mejilla y luego una cálida sensación de humedad mientras él la besaba. Después retrocedió un poco, tambaleándose.

—Pero ¿qué demonios estás haciendo?

Él la miró avergonzado, con un mechón de cabello rubio cayéndole sobre la frente.

—Tú lo deseabas —dijo—. Lo sé. Barbara, dentro de unas semanas estaré en el campo de instrucción. Puede que jamás vuelva a verte.

—¿Y qué quieres? ¿Un poco de sexo con una inglesa? ¡Pues conmigo no cuentes! —Levantó la voz y el eco resonó por todo el templo. Las ovejas se asustaron y empezaron a balar en tono quejumbroso.

Bernie se acercó a ella.

—¡Sabes muy bien que no es eso! —contestó, también a gritos—. Ya conoces mis sentimientos, ¿o acaso estás ciega?

—Ciega con mis estúpidas gafas, ¿verdad?

—¿No ves que te quiero? —exclamó él.

—¡Mentiroso!

Salió corriendo de la iglesia y bajó por el sendero. Mientras cruzaba la verja, resbaló sobre una placa de nieve y se desplomó sollozando contra el muro de piedra. Bernie se acercó y le apoyó una mano en el hombro.

—¿Por qué iba a mentir? ¿Por qué? Te quiero. Y tú sientes lo mismo, lo he visto, ¿por qué no quieres creerme?

Ella se volvió para mirarlo.

—Porque soy fea y torpe y... ¡No! —Se cubrió el rostro con las manos y rompió a llorar con desconsuelo.

Un niño que pasaba caminando descalzo con un cerdito en brazos se detuvo a mirarlos.

—¿Por qué te aborreces tanto? —preguntó Bernie con dulzura.

Ella sentía deseos de ponerse a gritar. Se enjugó las lágrimas, lo apartó de un empujón y echó a andar calle abajo. De repente, el niño se puso a gritar.

—¡Miren! ¡Miren!

Barbara se volvió; el niño se había colocado el cerdito, que no paraba de chillar, bajo el brazo, mientras con el otro señalaba muy nervioso hacia lo alto. Arriba, en el cielo, uno de los cazas alemanes había sido alcanzado y caía en picado. Se oyó una fuerte detonación en algún lugar, no muy lejos de allí, y el niño vitoreó. Tras echar una rápida mirada hacia el cielo, Bernie echó a correr tras ella.

—Barbara, espera. —Logró alcanzarla y le cortó el paso—. Escúchame, por favor. El sexo me da igual, me trae sin cuidado; pero te quiero, te quiero.

Ella meneó la cabeza.

—Dime que tú no sientes lo mismo —insistió él—, y ahora mismo me voy.

A la mente de Barbara acudió la imagen de una docena de chiquillas gritando a su espalda en el patio de recreo: «Cuatro ojos con ricitos, pelitos de zanahoria!»

—Lo siento, es inútil, no puedo... no.

—No lo entiendes, no te das cuenta...

Barbara se volvió para mirarlo y, al ver el dolor y la tristeza reflejados en su rostro, se le encogió el corazón. Después dio un respingo al oír un silbido procedente de lo alto. Levantó la mirada. El segundo caza alemán había sido alcanzado y caía sobre ellos. Ya se encontraba espantosamente cerca: las llamas brotaban de su costado formando una larga lengua de color rojo amarillento. Cayó a plomo; Barbara vio las hélices que todavía giraban, brillantes como las alas de un insecto. Bernie también miraba hacia arriba. Ella lo apartó de su lado de un empujón y, mientras él se tambaleaba hacia atrás, el aire se llenó de un rugido sobrecogedor. Barbara vio que el alto muro de la casa ante la que pasaban se le venía encima. De pronto sintió un dolor terrible e insoportable cuando algo le golpeó la cabeza.

Sólo permaneció un instante sin sentido. Cuando volvió en sí, fue consciente del dolor de cabeza y trató desesperadamente de recordar lo que había ocurrido y dónde estaba. Abrió los ojos y vio a Bernie inclinado sobre ella, pero desenfocado, pues había perdido las gafas. Había ladrillos y polvo a su alrededor. Bernie lloraba sin apartar los ojos de ella. Barbara jamás había visto llorar a un hombre.

—Barbara, Barbara, ¿cómo estás? ¡Oh, Dios mío!, pensaba que habías muerto. ¡Te quiero, te quiero!

Ella permitió que la incorporara. Después apoyó el rostro en su pecho y se echó a llorar; ambos estaban sentados en el suelo, llorando en mitad de la calle. Oyó pisadas a su alrededor, de gente que había salido de las casas y se congregaba en torno a ellos.

—¿Cómo están? —preguntó alguien—. ¡Dios mío, miren eso!

—Estoy bien —contestó Barbara—. Mis gafas, ¿dónde están mis gafas?

—Aquí —contestó Bernie en un susurro.

Se las alcanzó, y ella se las puso. Vio que el muro del jardín se había derrumbado y no los había alcanzado por los pelos, aunque toda la calle estaba sembrada de ladrillos. Uno de ellos debía de haberla alcanzado. Las llamas y el humo negro salían por todas las ventanas de la mansión y la cola del aparato asomaba por el tejado hundido. Barbara distinguió una cruz gamada de color negro. La habían tapado con pintura amarilla, pero igualmente se veía. Se llevó la mano a la cabeza y la retiró manchada de sangre. Una anciana envuelta en un chal negro la rodeó con su brazo.

—Es sólo un corte, señorita. ¡Ay!, se ha salvado de milagro.

Barbara alargó una mano hacia Bernie, que estaba lívido y se acariciaba el brazo herido. Los abrigos de ambos estaban cubiertos de polvo blanco.

—¿Te encuentras bien? —le preguntó.

—La explosión me ha tirado al suelo. Me he lastimado un poco el brazo. Pero, ¡oh, Dios mío!, pensaba que estabas muerta. Te quiero, por favor, créeme. ¡Ahora tienes que creerme! —Bernie volvió a echarse a llorar.

—Sí —dijo ella—, te creo. Perdóname, perdóname, por favor.

Ambos se fundieron en un abrazo.

El grupito de españoles, unos refugiados que tal vez tres meses atrás jamás habían salido de sus pueblos, permanecía a su lado contemplando los restos del aparato que asomaban por el tejado de la mansión en llamas.

Mientras contemplaba los leones marinos sentada en el banco, Barbara volvió a recordar el abrazo de Bernie. Cuánto le debió de doler el brazo herido mientras la estrechaba con fuerza. Consultó su reloj, el relojito de pulsera de la marca Dior que Sandy le había regalado. En su mente no había resuelto nada, simplemente se había emocionado recordando el pasado. Ya era hora de regresar a casa, Sandy la estaría esperando.

Sandy ya estaba en casa cuando ella regresó, había dejado el coche aparcado en el camino particular de la casa. Se quitó el abrigo. Pilar subió trotando desde el sótano y se quedó de pie en el recibidor con las manos cruzadas, como siempre hacía cuando Barbara regresaba a casa.

—No necesito nada, Pilar. Gracias.

—Muy bien.

La chica inclinó la cabeza y regresó a la cocina de abajo. Barbara sacudió los pies para quitarse los zapatos. Tenía los pies doloridos tras haberse pasado toda la tarde caminando.

Subió al estudio de Sandy. Éste solía trabajar largas horas allí arriba, examinando papeles y efectuando llamadas por teléfono. La estancia se encontraba en la parte de atrás de la casa y tenía una pequeña ventana que apenas dejaba entrar la luz. Sandy la había llenado de adornos y obras de arte elegidas por él mismo. Un cuadro expresionista con una distorsionada figura que conducía un asno a través de un asombroso paisaje desértico dominaba la estancia iluminada por una lámpara de pared.

Ahora estaba sentado detrás de su escritorio, envuelto en una maraña de papeles, pasando un lápiz por el margen de una columna de cifras. No la había oído acercarse y su rostro ofrecía el aspecto que a veces tenía cuando pensaba que nadie podía verlo: vehemente, calculador y, en cierto modo, depredador. En su mano libre sostenía un cigarrillo cuya larga cola de ceniza amenazaba con desprenderse de su extremo.

Ella lo estudió con una nueva mirada crítica. Llevaba el cabello todavía alisado hacia atrás con una gomina tan espesa que se podían ver las huellas del peine a través de él. Tanto el cabello engominado como el bigotito recto estaban de moda en los círculos falangistas. Al verla, esbozó una sonrisa.

—Hola, cariño. ¿Has tenido un buen día?

—No ha estado mal. He ido al Retiro esta tarde. Está empezando a hacer frío.

—Llevas las gafas puestas.

—Por Dios, Sandy, no puedo salir a la calle sin ellas y que me atropellen. Me las tengo que poner, sería estúpido no hacerlo.

Él la miró un instante y después volvió a sonreír.

—En fin. El viento te ha coloreado las mejillas. Parecen dos rosas.

—¿Y tú qué has hecho? ¿Has trabajado mucho?

—Sólo unos números para mi proyecto del Ministerio de Minas. —Apartó los papeles de la línea visual de Barbara y después tomó su mano en la suya—. Tengo una buena noticia. Ya sabes que me comentaste tu deseo de trabajar como voluntaria. Hoy he hablado con un hombre del Comité Judío cuya hermana es un pez gordo del Auxilio Social. Buscan enfermeras. ¿Te gustaría trabajar con los niños?

—No lo sé. Sería... una manera de hacer algo. —Una manera de apartar su mente de Bernie, del campo de Cuenca, de Luis.

—La mujer con quien tenemos que hablar es una marquesa. —Sandy arqueó las cejas. Fingía despreciar la esnobista adoración de la aristocracia que practicaba la clase alta española en tanta medida como la inglesa, pero Barbara sabía que le encantaba alternar con aquella gente—. Alicia, marquesa de Segovia. El sábado asistirá al concierto que se da en la Ópera; tengo entradas. —Sonrió y se sacó un par de entradas grabadas en letras doradas.

Barbara se sintió culpable.

—Oh, Sandy, siempre piensas en mí.

—No sé cómo será este concierto, pero también habrá algo de Strauss.

—Oh, gracias, Sandy. —Su generosidad la hacía sentirse avergonzada. Notó que las lágrimas asomaban a sus ojos y se levantó precipitadamente—. Será mejor que le diga a Pilar que empiece a preparar la cena.

—Muy bien, cariño. Yo todavía tengo para una hora.

Barbara bajó a la cocina, poniéndose los zapatos por el camino. No estaría bien que Pilar la viera caminar descalza.

La pintura de las paredes de la cocina era de un desagradable color mostaza, no blanca como la del resto de la casa. La chica estaba sentada a una mesa que había al lado de la vieja y enorme cocina económica. Contemplaba una fotografía. Mientras se la acercaba a la pechera del vestido y se levantaba, Barbara vislumbró fugazmente la imagen de un joven enfundado en un uniforme republicano. Era peligroso llevar encima una fotografía como aquélla; en caso de que le pidieran la documentación y un guardia civil la encontrara, le harían preguntas. Barbara fingió no haberla visto.

—Pilar, ¿podría empezar a preparar la cena? Hoy tenemos pollo al ajillo, ¿verdad?

—Sí, señora.

—¿Tiene todo lo que necesita?

—Sí, señora. Gracias. —Había frialdad en los ojos de la chica.

Barbara habría querido explicarse, decirle que sabía lo que era aquello, que ella también había perdido a alguien. Pero no podía ser. Asintió con la cabeza y subió al piso de arriba para vestirse para la cena.

9

El Café Rocinante se encontraba en una callejuela de las inmediaciones de la calle Toledo. Al salir de la embajada, Harry vio al pálido joven español pisándole una vez más los talones. Soltó una maldición... Habría deseado volverse, pegarle un grito y arrearle un guantazo. Dobló un par de esquinas y consiguió despistarlo. Siguió adelante rebosante de satisfacción; pero, en cuanto vio el café y cruzó la calle, sintió que el corazón se le salía del pecho. Respiró hondo varias veces mientras abría la puerta. Repasó todo lo que habían preparado en Surrey con vistas a aquel primer encuentro. «Dé por sentado que se mostrará desconfiado —le habían dicho—; procure parecer cordial e ingenuo como corresponde a un recién llegado a Madrid. Muéstrese receptivo y dispuesto a escuchar.»

El café estaba muy oscuro; la luz natural que penetraba a través de la pequeña y polvorienta ventana sólo contaba con la ayuda de unas cuantas bombillitas de quince vatios distribuidas por las paredes. Casi todos los parroquianos eran hombres de mediana edad de la clase media, tenderos y pequeños comerciantes. Permanecían sentados a las mesitas, bebiendo café o chocolate y hablando, sobre todo, de negocios. Un escuálido muchacho de diez años se paseaba entre las mesas vendiendo los cigarrillos de una bandeja que llevaba atada alrededor del cuello con una cinta. Harry se sentía incómodo y miraba con disimulo en torno a sí para no llamar la atención. O sea que aquello era ser espía. Notaba una especie de silbido y de sordo zumbido en el oído malo.

Aparte de un par de mujeres de mediana edad que comentaban lo caras que se estaban poniendo las cosas en el mercado de estraperlo, sólo había otra mujer fumando en soledad con una taza de café vacía delante. Era una treintañera delgada y nerviosa, envuelta en un vestido desteñido. Miraba constantemente a los restantes clientes y sus ojos se movían con la rapidez de un rayo de una mesa a otra. Harry se preguntó si sería alguna especie de confidente. Llamaba demasiado la atención, pero la verdad es que también la llamaba su «espía».

Vio inmediatamente a Sandy, sentado solo a una mesa leyendo un ejemplar del *ABC*. En la mesa había una taza de café y un enorme cigarro apoyado en un cenicero. Si no hubiera visto las fotografías, no lo habría reconocido. Con su impecable traje a medida, su bigote y su cabello engominado peinado hacia atrás, poco le quedaba del compañero de colegio que Harry recordaba. Estaba más grueso, aunque no de grasa sino de músculo, y ya tenía unas cuantas arrugas en el rostro. Sólo le llevaba a Harry unos cuantos meses, pero aparentaba cuarenta años. ¿Cómo podía parecer tan mayor?

Se acercó a la mesa. Sandy no levantó la mirada y él se quedó allí de pie un instante, sintiéndose un poco ridículo. Carraspeó y entonces Sandy dejó el periódico y lo miró con semblante inquisitivo.

—¿Sandy Forsyth? —Harry fingió sorprenderse—. Eres tú, ¿verdad? Soy Harry Brett.

Sandy se quedó momentáneamente en blanco, pero enseguida cayó en la cuenta. Se le iluminó todo el rostro y esbozó la ancha sonrisa que Harry recordaba, dejando al descubierto unos blancos dientes cuadrados.

—¡Harry Brett! Eres tú. ¡No puedo creerlo! ¡Después de tantos años! Pero, Dios mío, ¿qué estás haciendo aquí? —Se levantó y estrechó con firmeza la mano de Harry. Harry respiró hondo.

—Trabajo como intérprete en la embajada.

—¡Dios bendito! Sí, claro, te matriculaste en idiomas en Cambridge, ¿verdad? ¡Menuda sorpresa! —Se inclinó hacia delante y le dio una palmada en el hombro—. Jesús, has cambiado muy poco. Siéntate, ¿te apetece un café? ¿Qué haces en el Rocinante?

—Vivo muy cerca de aquí, a la vuelta de la esquina. Decidí salir a dar un paseo.

Se le hizo un nudo momentáneo en la garganta al soltar la primera mentira; pero, al ver la ingenua y jovial expresión de sorpresa en el rostro de Sandy, comprendió que éste se había tragado la trola. Experimentó una punzada de remordimiento, y después, de alivio al ver la alegría de Sandy, aunque ello no contribuyera precisamente a facilitarle las cosas.

Sandy chasqueó los dedos y un anciano camarero envuelto en una chaqueta blanca cubierta de lamparones se acercó de inmediato. Harry pidió chocolate caliente. El humo del cigarro se elevó en espirales desde la boca de Sandy, mientras éste estudiaba a Harry.

—Bueno, bueno, hay que ver. —Sandy meneó la cabeza—. Han pasado... ¿cuántos?... quince años. Me asombra que me hayas reconocido.

—Bueno, un poco sí que has cambiado. Al principio, no estaba seguro...

—Años atrás pensé que me habías olvidado.

—Esos días jamás se olvidan.

—Te refieres a Rookwood, ¿eh? —Sandy meneó la cabeza—. Has engordado un poco.

—Creo que sí. Te veo en muy buena forma.

—El trabajo me mantiene alerta. ¿Recuerdas aquellas tardes buscando fósiles? —Sandy volvió a sonreír con una expresión repentinamente rejuvenecida—. Fueron para mí los mejores momentos en Rookwood. Los mejores. —Lanzó un suspiro y su rostro pareció cerrarse mientras se reclinaba contra el respaldo de su asiento. Seguía sonriendo, pero su mirada revelaba un cierto recelo—. ¿Cómo terminaste trabajando para el Gobierno de su majestad?

—Me hirieron en Dunkerque.

—Sí, claro, la guerra. —Sandy hablaba como si fuera algo que ya hubiera olvidado y no tuviera nada que ver con él—. Nada grave, espero.

—No, ahora ya estoy bien. Me ha quedado un pequeño problema de oído. Sea como fuere, después ya no quise regresar a Cambridge. El Foreign Office estaba buscando intérpretes y me aceptaron.

—Conque Cambridge, ¿eh? ¿O sea que, al final, no te presentaste a la Oficina de Colonias? —Sandy soltó una carcajada—. Sueños juveniles. ¿Recuerdas que tú ibas a ser un funcionario territorial en Bongolandia y yo un cazador de dinosaurios? —Ahora la expresión de Sandy se había vuelto a relajar y mostraba un semblante risueño. Alargó la mano hacia el cigarro y le dio una larga calada.

—Pues sí. Es curioso cómo cambian las cosas. —Harry procuró que su tono sonara relajado—. ¿Y tú qué haces aquí? He notado una especie de sacudida al verte. Yo a éste lo conozco, he pensado, pero ¿quién es? Y entonces te he reconocido. —Ahora las mentiras le salían con la mayor fluidez.

Sandy dio otra calada a su cigarro y exhaló nuevas volutas de áspero humo.

—Vine a parar aquí hace tres años. Hay muy buenas oportunidades de negocios. Estoy aportando mi granito de arena a la reconstrucción de España. Aunque no descarto marcharme a otro sitio dentro de un tiempo.

El anciano camarero se acercó y depositó una tacita de chocolate delante de Harry. Sandy le hizo una seña al pequeño que vendía cigarrillos Lucky Strike a la flaca.

—¿Te apetece un cigarro? Le daremos una alegría a Roberto. Tiene un par de habanos escondidos por aquí dentro. Un poco secos, pero no están mal.

—Gracias, no fumo.

Harry miró a la mujer. Ni siquiera se molestaba en disimular que vigilaba a los clientes. Su rostro demacrado ofrecía un aspecto un tanto oficinesco.

—Tú nunca caíste, ¿verdad? Recuerdo que jamás te reunías detrás del gimnasio con nosotros, los chicos malos.

Harry se echó a reír.

—Nunca me gustó. Las dos veces que lo probé, me mareé. —Alargó la mano hacia la tacita de chocolate y observó que no le temblaba.

—Vamos, Brett, tú lo censurabas. —Ahora la voz de Sandy había adquirido un matiz irónico—. Siempre fuiste un hombre de Rookwood de la cabeza a los pies. Siempre cumplías las normas.

—Es posible. Pero llámame Harry, hombre.

Sandy sonrió.

—Como en los viejos tiempos, ¿eh? —Ahora la sonrisa de Sandy era auténticamente cordial.

—Sea como fuere, Sandy, la última vez que supe de ti aún estabas en Londres.

—Necesitaba largarme. Algunas personas del ambiente de la hípica llegaron a la conclusión de que yo no les gustaba. Mal asunto, lo de las carreras de caballos. —Sandy miró a Harry—. Fue entonces cuando perdimos el contacto, ¿verdad? Lo sentí mucho porque me encantaba recibir tus cartas. —Lanzó un suspiro—. Tenía un proyecto muy bueno, pero a algunos peces gordos les molestaba. De todas maneras, aprendí unas cuantas lecciones. Después, un conocido mío de Newmarket me comentó que la gente de Franco buscaba personas para trabajar como guías turísticos de los campos de batalla de la Guerra Civil. Personas con unos antecedentes adecuados para conseguir unas cuantas divisas y buscar en Gran Bretaña un poco de apoyo a los nacionales.

Y así me pasé un año acompañando a viejos coroneles de Torquay en un recorrido por los campos de batalla del norte. Más tarde, me metí en un par de negocios. —Sandy extendió los brazos—. Y acabé quedándome. Llegué a Madrid el año pasado, inmediatamente después de la entrada del Generalísimo.

—Comprendo. —«Mejor no hacer demasiadas indagaciones», pensó Harry. Demasiado prematuro—. ¿Sigues en contacto con tu padre?

El rostro de Sandy se endureció.

—Ya no. Mejor así, porque nunca nos llevamos bien. —Sandy guardó silencio un instante y después volvió a sonreír—. En fin. ¿Tú cuánto tiempo llevas en Madrid?

—Sólo unos días.

—Pero tú ya habías estado aquí antes, ¿verdad? Viniste con Piper después de la escuela.

Harry lo miró asombrado. Sandy soltó una risita y lo señaló con el extremo del cigarro.

—¿A que no sabías que yo lo sabía?

A Harry le dio un vuelco el corazón. ¿Cómo se habría enterado?

—Pues sí. En tiempos de la República. Pero ¿cómo...?

—Y después regresaste, ¿verdad? —Harry lanzó un suspiro de alivio al ver que Sandy lo miraba con semblante risueño, lo cual no habría sido posible de haber conocido éste el verdadero propósito de su presencia allí—. Viniste para intentar averiguar su paradero tras haber sido dado por desaparecido en el Jarama y entonces conociste a su novia. Barbara.

—Ahora Sandy rió de buena gana—. No te sorprendas tanto. Lo siento. Es sólo que conocí a Barbara en Burgos cuando trabajaba como guía, la Cruz Roja la envió allí cuando Piper se fue al oeste. Ella me lo contó todo.

Así que era eso. Harry lanzó un suspiro y se volvió a reclinar contra el respaldo de su asiento.

—Le escribí a través de la oficina de la Cruz Roja en Madrid, pero jamás obtuve respuesta. Seguramente las cartas no se llegaron a enviar.

—Probablemente, no. Por aquel entonces, todo era muy caótico en la República.

—Pero ¿cómo demonios os conocisteis vosotros dos? Menuda casualidad.

—No tanta. Había muy pocos ingleses en el Burgos del treinta y siete. Fue una coincidencia que ambos nos encontráramos en la zona nacional, supongo. Nos conocimos en una fiesta organizada por la Texas

Oil para los exiliados. —Sandy sonrió de oreja a oreja—. De hecho, nos fuimos a vivir juntos. Ahora está conmigo, vivimos en una casa de la calle Vigo. Seguro que no la reconocerías.

—El otro día me pareció verla cruzando la Plaza Mayor.

—¿De veras? ¿Qué estaría haciendo allí? Quizá buscando alguna tienda donde hubiera algo que mereciera la pena comprar.

Sandy sonrió.

«Esto es una complicación —pensó Harry—. Barbara.» ¿Cómo demonios se habría liado con Sandy?

—¿Sigue trabajando con la Cruz Roja? —preguntó.

—No, ahora es ama de casa. Lo de Piper la afectó mucho, pero ya está bien. Intento convencerla de que trabaje un poco como voluntaria.

—El hecho de que mataran a Bernie la dejó destrozada. Jamás averiguamos dónde estaba su cuerpo.

Sandy se encogió de hombros.

—A los rojos les daba igual lo que les ocurriera a sus hombres. En todas aquellas ofensivas fallidas que ordenaron los rusos. Sólo Dios sabe cuántos de ellos quedaron enterrados en la sierra. Pero ahora Barbara está bien. Estoy seguro de que se alegrará de verte. El martes tendremos un par de invitados, ¿por qué no vienes tú también?

Era la clase de acceso que a Harry le habían dicho que intentara conseguir, ofrecido en bandeja.

—¿No será perjudicial... para Barbara? No quisiera despertarle... malos recuerdos.

—Le encantará verte. —Sandy bajó la voz—. Por cierto, siempre decimos a todo el mundo que estamos casados; aunque no sea cierto. Es más fácil, estos del Gobierno son unos puritanos.

Harry se fijó en que Sandy lo miraba a la espera de su reacción. Sonrió, inclinando la cabeza.

—Entiendo —dijo con torpeza.

—Durante la Guerra Civil todo el mundo vivía a salto de mata; claro, nadie sabía el tiempo que le quedaba. —Sandy sonrió—. Sé que Barbara agradeció mucho la ayuda que tú le prestaste.

—¿De veras? Ojalá hubiera podido hacer algo más. Pero gracias, iré con mucho gusto.

Sandy se inclinó hacia delante y le dio otra palmada en el hombro.

—Y ahora, cuéntame algo más de ti. ¿Cómo están aquellos ancianos tíos tuyos?

—Pues como siempre. Ellos no cambian.

—¿No te has casado?

—No. Hubo alguien, pero no salió bien.

—Pues aquí hay montones de señoritas muy guapas.

—De hecho, estoy invitado a una fiesta la semana que viene, por parte de uno de los subsecretarios al que serví como intérprete. Los dieciocho años de su hija.

—Ah, ¿y quién es? —preguntó Sandy con interés.

—El general Maestre.

Sandy entornó los ojos.

—Nada menos que Maestre. Te estás moviendo en ambientes muy exclusivos. ¿Qué tal es?

—Muy amable. ¿Lo conoces?

—Me lo presentaron brevemente una vez. Tenía muy mala fama durante la Guerra Civil. —Sandy hizo una pausa como de reflexión—. Vas a tener ocasión de conocer a mucha gente del Gobierno en tu profesión.

—Supongo que sí. Yo voy simplemente donde me mandan.

—Me han presentado a Carceller, el nuevo jefe de Maestre. He tratado con algunas personas del Gobierno. Incluso he conocido al Generalísimo —añadió Sandy con orgullo—. Durante una recepción que ofreció a hombres de negocios extranjeros.

«Quiere impresionarme», pensó Harry.

—¿Y cómo es?

Sandy se inclinó hacia delante y bajó la voz.

—No como tú te imaginas al verlo pavonearse en los noticiarios. Parece más un banquero que un general. Pero es listo, como buen gallego. Seguirá aquí cuando gente como Maestre lleve tiempo desaparecida. Y dicen que es el hombre más duro del mundo. Firma las sentencias de muerte mientras se toma el café de la noche.

—¿Y si ganamos nosotros la guerra? Seguro que Franco cae, aunque no se haya aliado con Hitler. —Le habían dicho que se mantuviera al margen de la política, pero Sandy había sacado el tema a colación. Era una oportunidad para averiguar lo que éste opinaba del régimen.

Sandy meneó confiadamente la cabeza.

—No entrará en guerra. Le da demasiado miedo el bloqueo naval. El régimen no es tan fuerte como parece; si los alemanes marcharan sobre España, los rojos empezarían a salir de sus escondrijos. Y, si ganamos nosotros —Sandy se encogió de hombros—, Franco nos será muy útil. No hay nadie más anticomunista que él. —Sonrió con ironía—. No te preocupes, no estoy ayudando a un enemigo de Inglaterra.

—Lo dices muy seguro.

—Es que lo estoy.

—Pues aquí la situación parece desesperada. La pobreza. Se respira una atmósfera auténticamente sombría.

Sandy se encogió de hombros.

—España es así. Como siempre ha sido y siempre será. Necesitan mano dura.

Harry inclinó la cabeza.

—Jamás habría imaginado que te gustara la idea de recibir órdenes de una dictadura, Sandy.

Sandy se echó a reír.

—Lo de aquí no es una auténtica dictadura. Es demasiado caótico para eso. Hay muy buenas oportunidades de negocio si mantienes alerta los cinco sentidos. Tampoco es que tenga intención de quedarme aquí para siempre.

—Podrías irte a otro sitio.

Sandy se encogió de hombros.

—Quizás el año que viene.

—Aquí parece que la gente está al borde de la inanición.

Sandy lo miró con la cara muy seria.

—Las dos últimas cosechas han sido desastrosas a causa de la sequía. Y la mitad de las infraestructuras fueron destruidas en la guerra. Gran Bretaña tampoco está ayudando mucho, francamente. Sólo se autoriza la entrada de la gasolina necesaria para mantener el transporte en marcha. ¿Has visto los gasógenos?

—Sí.

—Todo eso es una pesadilla burocrática, naturalmente; pero el mercado triunfará. Personas como yo les mostramos el camino. —Sandy miró a Harry a los ojos—. Y eso les servirá de ayuda. Porque yo quiero ayudar de verdad a esta gente.

La mujer los miraba. Harry se inclinó sobre la mesa y dijo en voz baja:

—¿Has visto a la de aquella mesa? Se ha pasado el rato mirándonos desde que yo entré. Temo que sea una confidente.

Sandy se quedó momentáneamente en blanco y después echó la cabeza hacia atrás y soltó una carcajada. Los demás clientes se volvieron para mirarlos.

—¡Oh, Harry, Harry, eres increíble!

—¿Cómo? ¿Qué quieres decir?

—Es una puta, Harry. Siempre está aquí, buscando negocio.

—¿Cómo?

—Tú te pasas el rato mirándola, cruzas la mirada con la suya y después apartas los ojos, y la pobre chica está que no se aclara. —Sandy la miró sonriendo. La mujer no comprendió sus palabras, pero se ruborizó al ver la burlona expresión de sus ojos.

—De acuerdo, pues no lo sabía. Pero no tiene pinta de puta.

—Muchas no la tienen. Probablemente es la viuda de algún republicano. Muchas se tienen que prostituir para llegar a fin de mes.

La mujer se levantó. Rebuscó en su bolso, dejó unas monedas encima de la mesa y salió. Sandy la vio alejarse sin dejar de sonreír en plan de guasa ante su visible azoramiento.

—De todos modos, hay que vigilar —añadió Sandy—. Hace poco tuve la sensación de que me seguían.

—¿De veras?

—No estoy seguro. Pero después pareció que se largaban. —Sandy consultó su reloj—. Bueno, tengo que regresar a mi despacho. Deja que te invite.

—Gracias.

Sandy volvió a sonreír, meneando la cabeza.

—No sabes cuánto me alegro de verte. —Su voz denotaba sincero afecto—. Ya verás cuando se lo diga a Barbara. ¿Puedo ir a recogerte a la embajada el martes?

—Sí. Pregunta por el departamento de traducción.

Ya en la calle, Sandy le estrechó la mano a Harry.

—Inglaterra ha perdido la guerra, ¿sabes? Yo tenía razón... todas aquellas ideas de Rookwood, todo aquello del Imperio y de que si *noblesse oblige* y de que hay que participar en el juego, no son más que bobadas. Le pegas una patada y todo se desploma. La gente que se crea sus propias oportunidades, que se hace a sí misma, es el futuro. —Meneó la cabeza—. En fin. —Casi pareció lamentarlo.

—Aún no ha terminado.

—No del todo. Pero casi. —Sandy esbozó una sonrisa compasiva, después dio media vuelta y se fue.

10

Las puertas del Teatro de la Ópera estaban abiertas de par en par y la luz de las arañas de cristal llegaba hasta la plaza de Isabel II. Aquella noche de octubre era muy fría, y los guardias civiles acunaban las armas en sus brazos alrededor de la plaza, entre las sombras del anochecer. Una alfombra roja cubría los peldaños de la entrada y bajaba hasta el bordillo de la acera, a la espera del Generalísimo. El resplandor de las luces indujo a Barbara a parpadear mientras se acercaba del brazo de Sandy.

La noche anterior había llegado un poco más lejos en su engaño a Sandy. Tenía unos ahorros en Inglaterra y había escrito a su banco para que le enviaran el dinero a España. También se había vuelto a pasar por la oficina del *Express* y les había pedido que enviaran un telegrama a Markby diciéndole que necesitaba hablar con él, pero allí nadie sabía dónde estaba.

Esperó en el salón a que Sandy regresara a casa. Había pedido a Pilar que encendiera la chimenea y ahora la estancia resultaba cómoda y acogedora, con una botella de su whisky preferido y un vaso en una mesita al lado de su sillón. Se sentó a esperar, como hacía casi todas las noches.

Sandy regresó a las siete. Barbara se había quitado las gafas al oír sus pisadas; pero, aun así, vio que estaba muy contento por algo. Sandy la besó cariñosamente.

—Mmm. Me encanta este vestido que llevas puesto. Realza la blancura de tu piel. Oye, ¿a que no te imaginas a quién me he encontrado hoy en el Rocinante? No lo adivinarías ni en un millón de años. Esto es Glenfiddich, ¿verdad? Delicioso. Jamás lo adivinarías. —Su entusiasmo era propio de un colegial.

—No lo sabré si no me lo dices.

—Harry Brett.

Se quedó tan sorprendida que tuvo que sentarse.

Sandy asintió con la cabeza.

—Ni yo mismo me lo podía creer. Apareció en persona. Resultó herido en Dunkerque, y ahora lo han enviado aquí.

—Dios bendito. ¿Está bien?

—Eso parece. Le tiembla un poco la mano. Pero es el mismo Harry de siempre. Muy serio y ceremonioso. No sabe cómo interpretar lo que está ocurriendo en España.

Sandy sonrió, meneando comprensivamente la cabeza. Barbara lo miró. Harry. El amigo de Bernie. Hizo un esfuerzo por sonreír.

—Erais buenos amigos en el colegio, ¿verdad?

—Sí. Es un buen chico.

—Pues mira, es la primera persona de Inglaterra de quien hablas con afecto.

Sandy se encogió de hombros.

—Lo he invitado para el martes por la noche. Me temo que Sebastián vendrá con la muy inaguantable de Jenny. ¿Te pasa algo?

Barbara se había ruborizado intensamente.

—Sí, es que ha sido una sorpresa. —Tragó saliva.

—Puedo cancelar la invitación, si lo prefieres. Si eso te trae malos recuerdos.

—No, no, será maravilloso volver a verle.

—Bueno, entonces subo arriba a cambiarme.

Abandonó la estancia. Barbara cerró los ojos, recordando aquellos terribles días después de que a Bernie lo hubieran dado por desaparecido. Entonces Harry la había ayudado, pero había sido Sandy quien la había salvado. Volvió a avergonzarse de su conducta.

El vestíbulo estaba prácticamente lleno y se oía el murmullo de conversaciones animadas. Barbara miró alrededor. Todo el mundo lucía sus mejores galas; hasta las mujeres vestidas de riguroso luto iban ataviadas con prendas de seda negra, y algunas se habían puesto unas mantillas de encaje que les caían sobre la frente. Los hombres iban de etiqueta, vestidos con uniforme militar o bien con el uniforme de la Falange. Había también algún que otro eclesiástico con sotana o ropajes morados. Barbara se había puesto un vestido blanco de noche con un broche verde que realzaba el color de sus ojos, y una estola blanca de piel.

El vestíbulo se había restaurado para la primera representación después de la Guerra Civil. Las paredes y las columnas blancas y estriadas estaban recién pintadas y los asientos se habían vuelto a tapizar elegantemente de rojo. Sandy se encontraba en su elemento, mirando con una sonrisa a sus amistades. Saludó con una inclinación de cabeza a un coronel cuando éste pasó por su lado en compañía de su mujer.

—Saben montar un espectáculo cuando quieren —dijo en voz baja.

—Supongo que eso es señal de que las cosas empiezan a normalizarse.

Sandy leyó el programa.

—Tocan obras de Weber, Wagner, Brahms y Strauss. Al parecer, el director es una joven promesa alemana de poco más de treinta años. Se llama Herbert von Karajan y ha dirigido la Filarmónica de Berlín. Vete a saber, tal vez desean celebrar las buenas relaciones entre el régimen español y el alemán, ahora que Franco se reúne con Hitler en Hendaya. Por cierto —dijo, cambiando de tema—, tenemos que ir un día de éstos a ver los jardines de Aranjuez, ¿no te parece?

—Será bonito.

El teatro empezaba a llenarse. La orquesta ensayaba y unos retazos de música traspasaban el aire. La gente levantaba los ojos hacia el vacío palco real.

—El Generalísimo aún no ha llegado —dijo Sandy en voz baja.

Hubo un revuelo de actividad cuando dos soldados acompañaron a una pareja vestida de noche hasta sus asientos en un palco de allí cerca. Ambos eran muy altos, la escultural mujer llevaba el cabello rubio suelto y el hombre era calvo y de nariz aguileña. Lucía un brazalete con la cruz gamada en la manga de su traje de etiqueta. Barbara reconoció su rostro de haberlo visto en los periódicos. Von Stohrer, el embajador alemán.

Sandy le dio un codazo con disimulo.

—No mires, cariño.

—Aborrezco este emblema.

—España es neutral, cariño. No hagas caso. —La tomó del brazo y le indicó, sentada allí cerca, a una mujer alta y de mediana edad vestida de negro que conversaba tranquilamente con otra mujer—. Es la marquesa. Vamos a presentarnos. —La acompañó pasillo abajo—. Por cierto —añadió en un susurro—, no le hables para nada de su marido.

Los braceros de una de sus fincas se lo dieron de comer a los cerdos en el treinta y seis. Muy desagradable.

Barbara se estremeció levemente. Sandy solía hablar con indiferente ligereza acerca de los horrores que había sufrido la gente durante la Guerra Civil.

Sandy se inclinó ante la marquesa. Barbara no sabía cómo saludarla y optó por hacerle una reverencia que fue acogida con una leve sonrisa. La marquesa debía de tener unos cincuenta años, con un afable rostro que debió de ser bonito en otros tiempos pero que ahora aparecía surcado por unas arrugas de tristeza.

—Señora —dijo Sandy—, permítame que me presente. Alexander Forsyth. Ésta es mi esposa, Barbara. Disculpe la impertinencia, pero el señor Cana me dijo que estaba usted buscando voluntarias para su orfelinato.

—Sí, ya me lo comentó. Tengo entendido que es usted enfermera, señora.

—Me temo que llevo años sin ejercer mi profesión.

La marquesa la miró con la cara muy seria.

—Esas habilidades jamás se olvidan. Muchos de los niños de nuestro orfelinato están enfermos o resultaron heridos durante la guerra. Hay muchos huérfanos en Madrid. —La marquesa meneó tristemente la cabeza—. Sin progenitores ni casa ni escuela, muchos de ellos se dedican a mendigar por las calles.

—¿Dónde está el orfelinato, señora?

—Cerca de la calle de Atocha, en un edificio que nos ha cedido la Iglesia. Las monjas nos echan una mano con la enseñanza, pero necesitamos más ayuda médica. La atención sanitaria les lleva todavía mucho tiempo.

—Naturalmente.

—¿Cree usted que nos podría ayudar, señora?

Barbara pensó en los descalzos pilluelos de rostro desencajado que solía ver vagando por las calles.

—Sí, me gustaría.

La marquesa se llevó una mano a la barbilla.

—Disculpe que se lo pregunte, señora, pero usted es inglesa. ¿Y católica?

—No, no, me temo que no. Fui bautizada en el credo anglicano. —Barbara soltó una avergonzada carcajada. Sus padres jamás habían ido a la iglesia. ¿Qué pensaría la marquesa si supiera que ella y Sandy no estaban casados?

—Tal vez haya que convencer a las autoridades religiosas. Pero necesitamos enfermeras, señora Forsyth. Hablaré con el obispo. ¿Podría telefonearla?

Sandy extendió los brazos.

—Lo entendemos perfectamente.

—Veré qué se puede hacer. Sería estupendo que usted nos pudiera ayudar. —La marquesa inclinó la cabeza para dar a entender que la entrevista había terminado. Barbara le hizo otra reverencia y siguió a Sandy por el pasillo.

—Lo hará —dijo Sandy—. La marquesa tiene mucha influencia.

—No entiendo por qué mi religión tiene que ser un problema. La Iglesia de Inglaterra no es nada de lo que uno tenga que avergonzarse.

Sandy se volvió para mirarla súbitamente enojado.

—Porque a ti no te educaron en el meollo de lo que es eso —replicó—. Y no tuviste que aguantar a esos hipócritas un día sí y otro también. Por lo menos, con los católicos sabes qué terreno pisas.

Barbara había olvidado que la Iglesia era para Sandy como un nervio en carne viva. Como la mención de su familia, era un tema capaz de provocar su enfado repentino.

—Bueno, bueno, perdona.

Sandy había vuelto la cabeza y estaba mirando a un hombre medio calvo que se encontraba muy cerca de ellos vestido con uniforme de general y los estudiaba con expresión de reproche. El general enarcó levemente las cejas y se alejó. Sandy tuvo la sensación de haber caído en una trampa y se volvió hacia Barbara con semblante enfurecido.

—Mira lo que has hecho —murmuró—. Me has dejado en ridículo delante de Maestre. Lo ha oído.

—¿Qué quieres decir? ¿Quién es Maestre?

—Un enemigo de mi proyecto del Ministerio de Minas. No importa. Perdona. Mira, cariño, tú ya sabes que el tema de la Iglesia me ataca los nervios. Vamos, quieren que nos sentemos.

Unos lacayos vestidos con uniformes del siglo XVIII se abrieron paso entre la gente, instando a todo el mundo a ocupar sus asientos. Ahora el teatro ya estaba lleno. Sandy llegó a su fila situada hacia el medio de platea y se colocó junto a un hombre vestido con uniforme de la Falange. Barbara lo reconoció. Otero, uno de los socios de negocios de Sandy. Era algo así como ingeniero de minas. Tenía un rostro redondo de burócrata, pero sus ojos color verde aceituna miraban por encima de la almidonada camisa azul con penetrante dureza. No le gustaba.

—Alberto —dijo Sandy, apoyando la mano en su hombro.

—Hola, amigo. Señora.

Se oyó un murmullo entre los presentes. Al fondo de la sala se abrió una puerta y un grupo de lacayos se inclinó ante una pareja de mediana edad. Barbara había oído decir que Franco era un hombre bajito, pero ahora se sorprendió al ver lo menudo e incluso frágil que parecía. Vestía uniforme de general con un fajín ancho rojo alrededor de la amplia cintura. La calva de la coronilla le brillaba bajo las luces. Doña Carmen, que caminaba a su espalda, era ligeramente más alta que su marido y lucía una tiara de brillantes sobre el cabello negro azabache. Su rostro alargado y altivo estaba hecho como a medida para la regia expresión que exhibía. En cambio, el pétreo rostro del Generalísimo tenía un algo de artificial, con aquella boca pequeña tan apretada bajo el bigotito y aquellos ojos tan sorprendentemente grandes mirando directamente hacia delante mientras avanzaba con aire marcial ante el escenario.

Los falangistas mezclados entre el público se pusieron en pie y lo saludaron brazo en alto. «¡Jefe!», gritaron. El resto del público y los componentes de la orquesta hicieron lo propio. Sandy rozó ligeramente a Barbara con el codo. Ella lo miró, no esperaba tener que hacer eso, pero él le volvió a tocar el codo con insistencia. Se puso en pie a regañadientes y levantó el brazo, sin poder asociarse a los gritos.

—¡Je-fe! ¡Je-fe! ¡Fran-co! ¡Fran-co!

El Generalísimo no correspondió a los saludos y siguió avanzando como un autómata hasta llegar a una puerta del otro extremo. Los lacayos la abrieron y la pareja desapareció al otro lado. Los gritos arreciaron y la gente saludó brazo en alto, mirando hacia el palco real mientras Franco y doña Carmen hacían nuevamente su aparición y contemplaban por un instante la platea. Ahora doña Carmen sonreía; en cambio, el rostro de Franco seguía tan frío e inexpresivo como antes. Éste alzó levemente un brazo y los gritos cesaron de inmediato. El público se sentó. El director de orquesta extranjero se levantó y se inclinó en dirección al palco real.

A Barbara le gustaba la música clásica. Cuando vivía en Inglaterra, la prefería al jazz que tanto entusiasmaba a su hermana y, a veces, acudía a algunos conciertos en compañía de sus padres. Jamás había prestado atención a la música romántica alemana, y de hecho el nombre de Weber no le sonaba de nada, pero le gustó. Vio que la gente se relajaba, sonreía y asentía con la cabeza.

Pronto pasaron a Wagner. El alegro fue subiendo hasta alcanzar el clímax, e inmediatamente empezó el adagio. Ahora la música era más lenta y el sonido transmitía una tristeza pura y fluida. La gente rompió a llorar por todo el teatro, primero una o dos mujeres, y después más y más, y también algunos hombres. Se oían ahogados sollozos en todos los rincones. Casi todos los presentes habían perdido a alguien en la Guerra Civil y aquella música parecía hablarles a todos de batallas y de héroes, sí, pero también de muerte y melancolía. Barbara miró a Sandy; él le dedicó una sonrisa tensa y avergonzada.

Levantó la vista hacia el palco real. Carmen Polo mostraba un semblante apacible y sosegado. En cambio, el Generalísimo fruncía levemente el entrecejo. De pronto, Barbara observó una trémula contracción muscular alrededor de su boca. Pensó que él también se iba a echar a llorar, pero después los rasgos se volvieron a relajar y ella se percató de que el Generalísimo había reprimido un bostezo. Apartó la mirada con una súbita y violenta sensación de repugnancia.

En un momento dado perdió la noción del tiempo, pero más tarde el sonido de un piano le hizo evocar a Barbara una desierta y desolada llanura. Sabía que el tal Luis era probablemente un embustero, pero también cabía la posibilidad de que Bernie estuviera encarcelado en algún lugar mientras ella permanecía allí sentada. Sus dedos se doblaron con fuerza alrededor de la estola, hasta hundirse en la suave piel.

Las notas de piano se intensificaron para dar paso a los violines con los que la música alcanzó un clímax desgarrador. Barbara sintió que algo se quebraba y se desbordaba en su interior, y también rompió a llorar, mientras las lágrimas le bajaban por las mejillas. Sandy la miró inquisitivamente y después le tomó la mano y se la oprimió con recelo.

Cuando terminó la música, hubo un prolongado momento de silencio antes de que el público estallara en ensordecedores aplausos que se prolongaron durante varios minutos. Las lágrimas brillaban en el rostro del director de orquesta. Sandy se volvió hacia Barbara:

—¿Te ocurre algo?

—No. Perdona.

Sandy lanzó un suspiro.

—Antes no debería haber perdido los estribos. Pero tú ya sabes que ciertas cosas me atacan los nervios.

Barbara percibió un velado tono de irritación por debajo de sus tranquilizadoras palabras.

—No es eso. Es que... todo el mundo ha perdido muchas cosas. Todo el mundo.

—Lo sé. Anda, sécate las lágrimas. Ya estamos en el descanso. ¿Te quedas aquí? Si quieres, pido que te traigan un brandy.

—No, estoy bien. Te acompaño. —Barbara miró alrededor y vio que Otero la estudiaba con curiosidad. Él captó su mirada y esbozó una rápida e hipócrita sonrisa.

—Buena chica —dijo Sandy—. Vamos, pues.

En la barra, Sandy le pidió una tónica con ginebra. Era fuerte, pero ella lo necesitaba. Notó que se le encendían las mejillas mientras bebía. Otero se reunió con ellos en compañía de su mujer, la cual era sorprendentemente joven y agraciada.

—Qué música más triste, ¿verdad? —le dijo ésta a Barbara.

—Sí, pero muy bonita.

Otero se arregló el nudo de la corbata.

—Un gran director. Tiene que sentirse muy orgulloso de haber tocado en presencia del Generalísimo.

—Sí, ¿lo ha visto usted? —le preguntó con entusiasmo la mujer de Otero a Barbara—. Yo estaba deseando verlo. Un genio de la cabeza a los pies.

—Sí —dijo Barbara, esbozando una tensa sonrisa.

Oyó que Otero hablaba en voz baja con Sandy.

—¿Alguna noticia sobre los últimos judíos?

—Sí. Harán lo que sea con tal de evitar que los envíen de nuevo a Vichy.

—Muy bien. Necesitamos exhibir algo más. Yo puedo conseguir que parezca un hecho positivo.

Otero se dio cuenta de que Barbara estaba escuchando y le dirigió otra de sus miradas penetrantes.

—Bueno, señora Forsyth —dijo—. No sé si este Von Karajan conseguirá ser recibido por el Generalísimo. Al parecer, tuvo un problema y se equivocó en un concierto de gala el año pasado y Hitler juró que no volvería a dirigir.

—Estoy segura de que la música al menos le habrá encantado —contestó ella en tono imparcial.

Un hombre se abrió paso entre la gente. Era el general cuya mirada había inquietado previamente a Sandy. Otero apretó los labios, y sus ojos penetrantes miraron parpadeando alrededor; pero Sandy inclinó la cabeza y miró al militar con una cordial sonrisa en los labios.

—General Maestre.

El general lo miró fríamente a los ojos.

—Señor Forsyth —dijo—. Y mi viejo amigo el capitán Otero... que pertenece a la Falange.

—Sí, señor. —Maestre asintió con la cabeza.

—Tengo entendido que su proyecto marcha viento en popa. Material de construcción requisado por aquí y sustancias químicas por allá.

—Sólo pedimos lo que necesitamos, señor. —Se advertía un tono de desafío en la voz de Otero—. El propio Generalísimo lo ha...

—Aprobado. Sí, lo sé. Un proyecto para ayudar a España en su camino hacia la prosperidad. Y para que usted gane dinero, naturalmente.

—Soy un hombre de negocios, señor —dijo Sandy, con una sonrisa en los labios.

—Sí. Usted nos ayuda y, al mismo tiempo, se hace rico.

—Así lo espero, señor.

Maestre asintió lentamente un par de veces con la cabeza. Estudió un momento a Barbara con los ojos entornados, después inclinó bruscamente la cabeza y se retiró. Mientras se volvía, Barbara le oyó pronunciar en voz baja la palabra «sinvergüenza».

Otero miró a Sandy; Barbara intuyó que el falangista estaba asustado.

—No te preocupes —le dijo Sandy—. Todo está controlado. Mira, mañana hablamos de eso.

Otero vaciló un instante.

—Algo va mal —murmuró—. Vamos —dijo bruscamente a su mujer. —Ambos se incorporaron al goteo de personas que se dirigía lentamente hacia la salida. Sandy se acodó en la barra, haciendo girar entre sus dedos el pie de su copa vacía con expresión pensativa.

—¿Qué es todo eso? —preguntó Barbara—. ¿Qué ha querido decir con eso de que algo va mal?

Sandy se acarició el bigote.

—Es una vieja, a pesar de toda su parafernalia falangista.

—¿Qué has hecho para incomodar al general? Aquí no se incomoda a un general así como así.

Sus ojos entornados la miraron con expresión pensativa.

—Maestre forma parte del comité de suministros para nuestro proyecto del Ministerio de Minas. Es un monárquico. —Sandy se encogió de hombros—. Todo política. Intrigas encaminadas a asegurarse el puesto.

—¿Al general no le gusta vuestro proyecto porque cuenta con el apoyo de la Falange?

—Exacto. Pero, a la hora de la verdad, Maestre no pinta nada porque nosotros contamos con la bendición de Franco.

Sandy se levantó, alisándose las solapas.

—¿Qué decía Otero sobre los judíos?

Sandy volvió a encogerse de hombros.

—Eso también es confidencial. Tenemos que mantener en secreto las actividades del comité. Si los alemanes se enteraran, se armaría un follón.

—Me desagrada que se agasaje a los nazis.

—Les encanta que los halaguen. Pero eso es todo lo que hay. Juegos diplomáticos. —Ahora la voz de Sandy denotaba impaciencia. Apoyó una mano en la parte inferior de su espalda—. Vamos, ahora viene Strauss. Procura olvidar la guerra. Nos queda muy lejos.

11

El día en que el avión alemán se estrelló contra la casa de la calle Vigo, Barbara y Bernie tomaron un tranvía y regresaron al pequeño y bonito apartamento de Barbara, situado en las inmediaciones de la calle Mayor donde ambos se abrazaron, cubiertos de polvo. Ya en el apartamento, se sentaron el uno al lado del otro en la cama de Barbara, tomados de la mano.

—¿Seguro que estás bien? —le preguntó Bernie—. Estás más blanca que la cera.

—Es sólo un corte. El polvo hace que parezca peor de lo que es. Tendría que darme un baño.

—Pues hazlo. Entre tanto, yo prepararé la comida. —Bernie le apretó la mano.

Cuando Barbara salió del cuarto de baño, él ya había preparado la comida. Comieron garbanzos con chorizo sentados a la mesita. Ambos guardaron silencio, todavía bajo los efectos del shock. A media comida, Bernie alargó la mano bajo la mesa y tomó la de Barbara.

—Te quiero —le dijo—, te quiero de verdad. Lo digo en serio.

—Yo también a ti. —Barbara respiró hondo—. Yo... yo no te podía creer. Cuando era jovencita... es tan difícil de explicar...

—¿El acoso en la escuela?

—Parece una tontería; pero, cuando la cosa se prolonga a lo largo de los años, con estas constantes humillaciones... ¿por qué los niños se ensañan con la gente, por qué necesitan a alguien a quien odiar? A veces, me escupían. Sin ningún motivo, simplemente porque era yo.

Bernie le volvió a apretar la mano.

—¿Por qué aceptas la opinión que ellos tienen de ti? ¿Por qué no aceptas la mía en su lugar?

Barbara rompió a llorar. Bernie rodeó la mesa, se arrodilló a su lado y la abrazó con fuerza. Ella experimentó una sensación de liberación.

—Sólo he estado una vez con un hombre —dijo en voz baja.

—Ahora no tienes por qué hacerlo. Nunca he querido nada que tú no quisieras. Jamás.

Ella lo miró a los ojos color aceituna oscuro. El pasado pareció alejarse y desvanecerse por el pasillo de su mente. Sabía que regresaría; pero, por ahora, estaba muy lejos. Lanzó un profundo suspiro.

—Lo quiero. Lo quise desde el día en que te conocí. Quédate conmigo, no vuelvas a Carabanchel esta noche.

—¿Seguro que ahora no necesitas irte a dormir?

—No. —Barbara se quitó las gafas. Él la miró sonriendo y se las quitó dulcemente de las manos.

—Me gustan —le dijo con dulzura—. Te dan un aire más inteligente.

Ella le devolvió la sonrisa.

—O sea que no me elegiste simplemente para convertirme al comunismo.

Él meneó la cabeza sonriendo.

Se despertó en mitad de la noche sintiendo en el cuello la caricia de sus dedos. Estaban a oscuras y ella sólo podía distinguir el perfil de su cabeza, pero notaba la presión de su cuerpo contra el suyo.

—No puedo creer que esté ocurriendo —dijo en un susurro—. Y mucho menos contigo.

—Te quise desde el primer día que te vi —dijo Bernie—. Jamás he conocido a nadie como tú.

Ella soltó una carcajada nerviosa.

—¿Como yo? ¿Y eso qué significa?

—Viva, compasiva y sensual; aunque tú finjas no serlo.

Las lágrimas asomaron a sus ojos.

—Pensaba que eras demasiado guapo para mí. Eres el hombre más guapo que he visto en mi vida. Pensaba que, si alguna vez estuviéramos los dos juntos desnudos —añadió bajando la voz—, me moriría de vergüenza.

—Pero qué tonta eres. Qué tonta. —Bernie la volvió a estrechar entre sus brazos.

No les parecía decoroso ser tan felices en la ciudad sitiada. Los combates seguían en el norte, y el bando republicano ofrecía resistencia a las fuerzas de Franco. El Gobierno había huido a Valencia y Madrid estaba gobernado por unos comités que, según decían, estaban controlados por los comunistas. Los altavoces instalados en el centro de la ciudad advertían a los ciudadanos de la posible presencia de traidores entre ellos.

Barbara seguía trabajando en el intercambio de prisioneros y en las investigaciones acerca de personas desaparecidas; pero, junto con la sensación de impotencia ante el caos reinante, experimentaba en su fuero interno una cálida sensación como de alivio. «Le quiero —se decía, y después, casi con asombro, añadía—: y él me quiere a mí.»

Él la esperaba todos los días a la salida del trabajo para irse juntos a su casa, al cine o a un café. Los médicos decían que el brazo de Bernie se estaba recuperando muy bien. En cuestión de aproximadamente un mes volvería a ser apto para el servicio. Él había vuelto a pedir que le permitieran ayudar al partido con nuevos reclutamientos para las Brigadas Internacionales, pero le habían dicho que ya tenían suficiente gente.

—Ojalá no tuvieras que volver al frente —le había dicho ella una noche.

Faltaban pocos días para Navidad y, a la salida del cine, se habían ido a sentar un rato en un bar del centro. Habían visto un documental soviético acerca de la modernización del Asia central y, después, una película de gánsteres protagonizada por Jimmy Cagney. Así era el desordenado mundo en el que ahora vivían. Algunos días las tropas nacionales de la Casa de Campo disparaban su artillería contra la Gran Vía cuando la gente salía de los cines, pero no aquella noche.

—Soy un soldado del Ejército Republicano —contestó Bernie—. Tendré que volver cuando me lo digan. De lo contrario, me podrían fusilar.

—Ojalá pudiéramos regresar a casa. Lejos de todo esto. Es lo que durante muchos años hemos temido en la Cruz Roja. Una guerra en la que no se diferencia entre soldados y civiles. Una ciudad llena de gente atrapada en medio. —Barbara lanzó un suspiro—. Hoy he visto a un anciano por la calle con pinta de haber ejercido una profesión liberal. Llevaba un grueso abrigo, pero muy polvoriento y gastado, y buscaba con disimulo algo que comer en los cubos de la basura. Al ver que yo lo miraba, se ha muerto de vergüenza.

—Dudo que lo esté pasando peor que los pobres. Seguro que le dan las mismas raciones. ¿Por qué iba a ser peor para él por el simple hecho de pertenecer a la clase media? Esta guerra se tiene que combatir. No queda más remedio.

Ella tomó su mano y lo miró a los ojos.

—Si ahora te permitieran regresar a casa conmigo, ¿lo harías?

Bernie bajó la mirada.

—Tengo que quedarme. Es mi deber.

—¿Para con el partido?

—Para con la humanidad.

—A veces pienso que ojalá tuviera tu fe. Entonces puede que no lo pasara tan mal.

—No es cuestión de fe. Me gustaría que intentaras comprender el marxismo, que es precisamente el que deja al descubierto los huesos de la realidad. ¡Oh, Barbara!, no sabes cuánto desearía que vieras las cosas con claridad.

Ella soltó una carcajada cansina.

—No, eso jamás se me ha dado muy bien. No vuelvas al frente, Bernie, por favor. Si ahora te vas, no estoy muy segura de poder resistirlo. Ahora, no. Por favor, por favor, volvamos a Inglaterra. —Alargó la mano y tomó la suya—. Tienes un pasaporte británico, te podrías ir. Podrías acudir a la embajada.

Bernie guardó silencio un instante.

Después, Barbara oyó que una voz de fuerte acento escocés lo llamaba por su nombre.

Se volvió y vio a un joven rubio saludándolo con la mano desde la barra donde permanecía acodado en compañía de un grupo de hombres uniformados y con aspecto cansado.

—¡Piper! —El escocés levantó su vaso—. ¿Qué tal el brazo?

—Muy bien, McNeil. ¡Mucho mejor! Pronto volveré.

—¡No pasarán!

Bernie y el soldado intercambiaron el saludo del puño cerrado. Luego Bernie se volvió hacia Bárbara y bajó la voz.

—No puedo hacerlo, Barbara. Te quiero, pero no puedo. Además, no tengo pasaporte, lo tuve que entregar al ejército. Y... —Lanzó un suspiro.

—¿Qué?

—Me avergonzaría toda la vida. —Señaló con la cabeza a los soldados de la barra—. No los puedo dejar. Sé que a una mujer le resulta difícil comprenderlo, pero no puedo. Tengo que volver aunque no quiera.

—¿Y tú no quieres?

—No. Pero soy un soldado. Lo que yo quiera no importa.

Los combates en la Casa de Campo se hallaban en punto muerto, una guerra de trincheras como la del Frente Occidental en la Gran Guerra. Sin embargo, todo el mundo decía que Franco reanudaría la ofensiva en primavera, probablemente en algún lugar de los descampados al sur de la ciudad. Seguían produciéndose muchas bajas; Barbara veía cada día a los heridos que eran devueltos desde el frente en carros o camiones. El estado de ánimo de la población había cambiado, y el ardiente afán otoñal de combate estaba dando paso al desánimo. Por si fuera poco, había escasez de alimentos; la gente ofrecía un aspecto enfermizo, y a todo el mundo le salían forúnculos y sabañones. Barbara se avergonzaba de la calidad de los artículos alimenticios de la Cruz Roja que compartía con Bernie. Su felicidad se alternaba con el temor a perderlo, y también con la rabia que sentía por el hecho de que él hubiera entrado en su vida y la hubiera transformado para acabar finalmente alejándose de ella sin más. A veces, la rabia se convertía en un cansancio desesperado y temeroso.

Dos días más tarde, ambos se dirigían a pie desde el apartamento de Barbara a su lugar de trabajo. Era un día frío y despejado, con un tímido sol y escarcha en las aceras. Las colas para el racionamiento diario empezaban a las siete; una larga cola de mujeres vestidas de negro aguardaba en el exterior de las oficinas del Gobierno de la calle Mayor.

Repentinamente, las mujeres dejaron de hablar y miraron hacia el principio de la calle. Barbara vio acercarse un par de carros tirados por caballos. Al pasar éstos por su lado, respiró el olor alquitranado de la pintura recién aplicada y vio que los carros contenían unos pequeños ataúdes de color blanco destinados a los niños cuyas almas aún no estaban manchadas, según las prácticas católicas todavía en vigor. Las mujeres los contemplaron en desolado silencio. Una de ellas se santiguó y después se echó a llorar.

—La gente ya ha llegado al límite de sus fuerzas —dijo Barbara—. No podrá resistir mucho tiempo. ¡Tantos muertos! —Y rompió a llorar allí mismo, en mitad de la calle. Bernie la rodeó con su brazo, pero ella lo rechazó—. ¡También te veo a ti en un ataúd! ¡A ti!

Bernie la sujetó por los hombros, la mantuvo a distancia y la miró a los ojos.

—Si Franco entra en Madrid, habrá una matanza. Y yo no los abandonaré. ¡No pienso hacerlo!

Llegó el día de Navidad. Comieron un grasiento estofado de cordero en el apartamento de Barbara y después subieron al dormitorio de arriba. Allí permanecieron un rato charlando, tumbados en la cama el uno en brazos del otro.

—Ésta no es la Navidad que yo esperaba —dijo Barbara—. Pensaba que estaría en Birmingham y que iría con papá y mamá a ver a mi hermana y su familia. Siempre me pongo nerviosa a los dos días y me entran ganas de largarme.

Él la estrechó con fuerza.

—¿Por qué te inculcaron este mal concepto de ti misma?

—No lo sé. Simplemente ocurrió.

—Tendrías que estar dolida con ellos.

—Jamás comprendieron por qué me fui a trabajar con la Cruz Roja. —Deslizó un dedo por su pecho—. Les habría gustado verme casada y con hijos como Carol.

—¿Te gustaría tener hijos?

—Sólo cuando ya no haya guerras.

Bernie encendió un par de cigarrillos para los dos, buscando a tientas en medio de la oscuridad. Su rostro estaba muy serio bajo el rojizo resplandor.

—Yo he decepcionado a mis padres. Creen que he arrojado por la borda todo lo que Rookwood me enseñó. Ojalá jamás hubiera ganado la maldita beca.

—¿No obtuviste ningún beneficio del colegio?

Bernie rió con amargura.

—Como decía Calibán, me enseñaron la lengua y, por consiguiente, sé soltar maldiciones.

Barbara buscó su corazón y apoyó la mano para percibir los suaves latidos.

—Puede que eso sea lo que nos ha unido. Dos decepciones. —Hizo una pausa—. Tú crees en el destino, ¿verdad, Bernie?

—No. En el destino histórico.

—¿Y cuál es la diferencia?

—Tú puedes influir en el destino, puedes ponerle obstáculos o acelerar su curso. Puedes hacer lo que quieras para modificar el curso del destino.

—Ojalá mi destino estuviera a tu lado. —Notó que el pecho le subía y bajaba bruscamente al respirar hondo.

—Barbara.

—¿Qué?

—Tú sabes que ya estoy prácticamente recuperado. Dentro de un par de semanas me enviarán al nuevo campo de instrucción de Albacete. Me lo dijeron ayer.

—¡Oh, Dios mío! —Barbara se hundió en el desánimo.

—Lo siento. Esperaba el momento adecuado para decírtelo; pero no lo hay, ¿verdad?

—No.

—Creo que antes no me importaba vivir, pero ahora sí. Ahora que vuelvo al frente.

Durante las dos semanas que siguieron a la marcha de Bernie, Barbara no recibió ninguna noticia. Acudía al trabajo y pasaba el día como podía; pero, cuando regresaba a su apartamento y él no estaba allí, el silencio parecía resonar como un eco, como si él ya hubiera muerto.

La primera semana de febrero se recibió la noticia de una ofensiva fascista al sur de Madrid. Pretendían rodear rápidamente la capital y dejarla completamente aislada, pero les cerraron el paso junto al río Jarama. La radio y la prensa hablaron de la heroica defensa gracias a la cual el avance de Franco había quedado interrumpido antes de empezar. Las Brigadas Internacionales habían desempeñado un papel destacado en los combates. Dijeron que había habido numerosas bajas.

Todas las mañanas, antes de acudir al trabajo, Barbara pasaba por el cuartel general del ejército en la Puerta del Sol. Al principio, el personal se mostraba receloso; pero, cuando ella volvió al segundo día y al tercero, empezaron a mostrarse más amables con ella. Barbara descuidó su aspecto, adelgazó, tenía unas ojeras oscuras bajo los ojos y su dolor resultaba claramente visible para todo el mundo.

El cuartel general era un lugar caótico. Los funcionarios uniformados iban de un lado para otro con papeles en las manos, mientras los teléfonos sonaban por todas partes. Barbara se preguntó si algunas de aquellas líneas telefónicas estarían conectadas con el frente, si habría alguna conexión entre uno de aquellos ruidosos timbrazos y el lugar donde Bernie se encontraba en aquellos momentos. Ahora lo hacía constantemente, establecía conexiones mentales. «El mismo sol nos ilumina a los dos, la misma luna, sostengo en mis manos el libro que él sostenía en las suyas, me acerco a la boca el tenedor que él se acercaba a la suya...»

Se registraron fuertes combates en la segunda y la tercera semanas de febrero, pero ella seguía sin recibir noticias. Tampoco había recibido ninguna carta, aunque ya le habían dicho que las comunicaciones eran difíciles. Hacia finales de febrero, los combates disminuyeron y la situación se volvió a estancar. Barbara abrigó la esperanza de recibir noticias.

Se enteró el último día de febrero, un frío día de principios de primavera. Había acudido como de costumbre al cuartel general antes de ir al trabajo, y esta vez un funcionario uniformado le dijo que esperara en una sala contigua. Comprendió de inmediato que le iban a dar una mala noticia. Se sentó en un pequeño y mísero despacho con un escritorio, una máquina de escribir y un retrato de Stalin en la pared. Se preguntó, de manera totalmente improcedente: «¿Cómo consigue mantener arreglados estos bigotes tan grandes?»

Se abrió la puerta y entró un hombre enfundado en un uniforme de capitán. Sostenía un papel en la mano y la expresión de su rostro era sombría. Barbara sintió que un escalofrío le recorría el cuerpo, como si hubiera caído a unas aguas oscuras a través de un agujero. No se levantó para estrechar la mano del hombre, se limitó a permanecer sentada donde estaba.

—Señorita Clare. Buenas tardes. Tengo entendido que ha venido usted aquí muchas veces.

—Sí. Para tener noticias. —Tragó saliva—. Ha muerto, ¿verdad? El militar levantó una mano.

—No lo sabemos con certeza. No con certeza. Pero figura en la lista de desaparecidos presuntamente muertos. El Batallón Británico estuvo enzarzado en duros combates el día trece.

—Desaparecidos presuntamente muertos —repitió ella, sin la menor inflexión en la voz—. Sé lo que eso significa. Simplemente no se ha encontrado el cuerpo.

El hombre no contestó, se limitó a inclinar la cabeza.

—Combatieron espléndidamente bien. Durante dos días enteros, ellos solos impidieron el avance fascista. —El capitán hizo una pausa—. Muchos no pudieron ser identificados.

Barbara notó que se caía de la silla. Mientras se desplomaba, empezó a llorar sin remedio y se comprimió contra las tablas del suelo sólo porque debajo de ellas se encontraba la tierra, la tierra donde ahora Bernie estaba enterrado.

12

El comedor del Ritz estaba iluminado por resplandecientes arañas de cristal. Harry tomó asiento a la larga mesa reservada para el personal de la embajada. Tolhurst se sentaba a su lado; al otro, Goach, el anciano que lo había instruido en cuestiones de protocolo, se acomodó cuidadosamente en su asiento. Era calvo, lucía unos grandes bigotes blancos de guías caídas, tenía una voz muy suave y utilizaba un monóculo sujeto por un largo hilo de color negro. El cuello de su esmoquin estaba salpicado de caspa.

A Harry le apretaba el cuello de pajarita cuando miraba alrededor de la mesa; un par de docenas de miembros del personal de la embajada habían acudido allí para hacer acto de presencia. A la cabecera de la mesa se sentaba Hoare en compañía de su esposa lady Maud, una corpulenta mujer de aspecto anodino. A su otro lado estaba Hillgarth, con su uniforme de marino resplandeciente de medallas.

Harry había informado a Hillgarth tras su encuentro con Sandy. Tolhurst también había estado presente en la reunión. Hillgarth se había mostrado satisfecho de sus progresos, especialmente de la invitación a cenar, y le había manifestado su interés por Barbara.

—Procure conseguir que le hable un poco más de sus negocios —le había dicho Hillgarth—. ¿No sabe quiénes serán los otros invitados?

—No. No lo pregunté. No quería mostrarme demasiado insistente.

Hillgarth asintió con la cabeza.

—Muy bien. ¿Y qué me dice de su pareja? ¿Podría tener conocimiento de sus planes?

—No lo sé.

Harry frunció el entrecejo.

—Ustedes eran simplemente amigos, ¿verdad? —preguntó bruscamente Hillgarth.

—Sí, señor. Pero es que no quiero mezclarla en el asunto, a menos que no haya más remedio. Aunque creo que podría ser necesario —añadió—. Es curioso que terminaran juntos... Sandy no se llevaba bien con Bernie.

—Me pregunto si se interesó por la chica porque ésta era la novia de su enemigo —terció Tolhurst con expresión pensativa.

—No lo sé. —Harry meneó la cabeza—. Cuando yo conocí a Sandy, éste era sólo un niño. Ha cambiado. Todo en él parecía falso, ostentoso. Excepto su alegría al verme, ésa sí fue auténtica. —Harry volvió a fruncir el entrecejo.

—Aprovéchela. —Hillgarth miró a Harry con la cara muy seria—. Lo que usted está haciendo es importante. El negocio del oro encaja dentro de un cuadro mucho más amplio, la cuestión de cómo podemos manejar al régimen. Reviste una gran importancia.

Harry miró a Hillgarth a los ojos.

—Lo sé, señor.

El camarero depositó delante de él un menú de color blanco de proporciones considerables. Los platos podrían ser de antes de la guerra. Harry se preguntó si en el Ritz de Londres tendrían todavía platos tan buenos como aquéllos. Aquella mañana había recibido una carta de Will. Lo iban a trasladar a un nuevo puesto en el campo, allá por los Midlands; Muriel estaba encantada de poder alejarse de las bombas, aunque temía que pudieran entrar ladrones en la casa. Las noticias de su país habían llenado a Harry de una añoranza casi insoportable. Levantó la vista del menú lanzando un suspiro y se quedó de piedra al ver a cuatro militares vestidos con uniformes grises tomando asiento a la mesa, un poco más allá de los bien trajeados madrileños. Las voces ásperas y cortantes de los militares resultaron inmediatamente reconocibles.

—Aquí están los alemanes —dijo Tolhurst en voz baja—. Asesores militares. Los de la Gestapo visten de paisano. —Uno de los alemanes captó la mirada de Harry, arqueó una ceja y apartó los ojos—. Es que el Ritz se ha convertido en una guarida de alemanes e italianos —añadió Tolhurst—. Por eso a sir Sam le gusta dar muestras de patriotismo de vez en cuando. ¿Preparado para mañana? —preguntó en un susurro—. ¿Para la cena con nuestro amigo?

—Sí.

—No sé si la chica sabrá algo —dijo Tolhurst, mientras en sus ojos se encendía un destello de curiosidad.

—Pues no lo sé, Tolly.

Harry miró hacia el fondo de la mesa. La cena de aquella noche también tenía su agenda oculta. Habían recibido instrucciones de mostrarse animados y relajados y de no dar a entender su preocupación por los cambios en el Gabinete. Todo el mundo bebía sin recato y soltaba carcajadas sonoras. Era como una cena en un club de rugby. Los secretarios de embajada, allí presentes para llenar el cupo, parecían sentirse un tanto incómodos.

Los camareros, con sus blancas chaquetas almidonadas, empezaron a servir el vino y la comida. La comida era excelente, la mejor que Harry había saboreado desde su llegada al país.

—Se están recuperando los antiguos niveles de calidad —dijo Goach, rozándolo con el codo.

Harry se preguntó qué edad tendría; decían que llevaba en la embajada desde los tiempos de la guerra americano-española. Habían transcurrido cuarenta años. Al parecer, no había nadie que supiera más que él acerca del protocolo español.

—Por lo menos en el Ritz, a juzgar por la comida —contestó Harry.

—Bueno, y en otros lugares también. Están volviendo a abrir los teatros, el Teatro de la Ópera. Recuerdo la conversación que tuve allí con el antiguo rey. Fue encantador. Te hacía sentir a gusto. —Goach suspiró—. Creo que el Generalísimo desearía restaurar la monarquía, pero la Falange no quiere. Menudo desastre. El jueves le arrojaron harina, ¿verdad?

—Sí, en efecto.

—Maldita gentuza. Tenía la típica mandíbula de los Habsburgo, ¿sabe? Prominente.

—¿Cómo?

—El rey Alfonso. Pero sólo un poco. Gajes de la realeza. El duque de Windsor pasó por Madrid el pasado mes de junio. Cuando huyó de Francia. —Goach meneó la cabeza—. Lo hicieron pasar rápidamente por la embajada y lo enviaron a Lisboa. Sin recepción oficial ni nada. Pero, hombre, por Dios, un ex rey. —Volvió a menear tristemente la cabeza.

Harry miró de nuevo alrededor de la mesa. Se preguntó qué habría pensado Bernie de todo aquello.

—¿En qué piensas? —preguntó Tolhurst.

Harry se volvió para mirarlo.

—A veces tengo la sensación de encontrarme en el País de las Maravillas —dijo en voz baja—. No me sorprendería ver aparecer un conejo blanco vestido.

Tolhurst lo miró perplejo.

—¿Qué quieres decir?

Harry se echó a reír.

—Aquí no tienen ni idea de cómo es la vida ahí afuera. —Señaló con la cabeza hacia la ventana—. ¿Tú nunca piensas en toda la maldita miseria que se ve por la ciudad, Simon?

Tolhurst frunció el entrecejo con expresión pensativa.

En medio de la conversación, Harry captó la enérgica voz del embajador.

—Esta bobada de las Operaciones Especiales es una locura. Tengo entendido que utilizan a republicanos españoles exiliados para adiestrar a los soldados británicos en la guerra política. Malditos comunistas.

—Van a prender fuego a toda Europa —replicó Hillgarth.

—Pues sí, una de las típicas frases de Winston. Retórica pura. —Hoare levantó la voz—. Sé cómo son los rojos, estaba en Rusia cuando cayó el zar.

Hillgarth bajó la voz, pero Harry lo oyó.

—Muy bien, Sam. Estoy de acuerdo contigo. No es momento para eso.

Tolhurst salió de su ensimismamiento.

—Supongo que ya estoy acostumbrado. La pobreza. En Cuba ocurre lo mismo.

—Pues yo no me acostumbro —dijo Harry.

Tolhurst reflexionó un instante.

—¿Has estado alguna vez en una corrida de toros?

—Estuve una vez en el treinta y uno. No me gustó. ¿Por qué?

—La primera vez que fui, me puse enfermo, con toda aquella sangre cuando pican al toro, la aterrorizada expresión de su rostro todavía ensangrentado cuando después llevaron la cabeza al restaurante. Pero tuve que ir; formaba parte de la vida diplomática. La segunda vez ya no lo pasé tan mal; pensé, bueno, es sólo un animal. La tercera vez empecé a valorar la habilidad y la valentía del matador. Cuando eres diplomático, tienes que cerrar los ojos ante la parte negativa de un país, ¿comprendes?

«O cuando eres un espía», pensó Harry. Con el tenedor, trazó una línea sobre el mantel blanco.

—Pero así es como siempre se empieza, ¿verdad? Nos anestesiamos para protegernos y, de esta manera, dejamos de ver la crueldad y el sufrimiento.

—Supongo que, si empezamos a pensar en todas estas cosas tan horribles, acabamos imaginando que nos ocurren a nosotros. Lo sé, porque a mí me sucede algunas veces —dijo Tolhurst, soltando una carcajada nerviosa.

Harry miró a uno y otro lado de la mesa y observó el carácter forzado de las sonrisas y el áspero tono de las carcajadas.

—Creo que no estás solo —dijo.

Alguien situado al otro lado de Tolhurst lo agarró del brazo y empezó a contarle en voz baja que dos funcionarios habían sido sorprendidos juntos en un armario de material de escritorio.

—¿Julian, marica? No me lo puedo creer.

Harry se volvió de nuevo hacia Goach.

—Está bueno el salmón.

—Excelente.

—¿Cómo? —Harry no había captado la respuesta del anciano. En medio de la gente, su sordera podía seguir siendo un problema. Por un instante, se sintió desorientado.

—He dicho que es excelente —repitió Goach—. Verdaderamente excelente.

Harry se inclinó hacia delante.

—Usted lleva mucho tiempo en el servicio diplomático, señor. El otro día oí un comentario acerca de los Caballeros de San Jorge. ¿Tiene alguna idea de lo que eso significa? Pensé que, a lo mejor, era una especie de jerga de la embajada.

Goach se ajustó el monóculo y frunció el entrecejo.

—No creo, Brett; jamás he oído hablar de semejante cosa. ¿Dónde oyó el comentario?

—En algún lugar de la embajada. Me pareció extraño.

Goach meneó la cabeza.

—Lo siento, no tengo ni idea. —Miró a Hoare un instante y, después, dijo—: El embajador es un buen hombre. Pese a todos los defectos que pueda tener, conseguirá mantener a España al margen de la guerra.

—Así lo espero —dijo Harry. A continuación, añadió—: Si España se mantiene al margen y nosotros ganamos, ¿qué ocurrirá después con el país?

Goach soltó una leve carcajada.

—Primero ganemos la guerra. —Reflexionó un momento—. Aunque, si Franco se mantiene al margen y consigue controlar el elemento fascista del Gobierno, creo que tendríamos motivos para estarle agradecidos, ¿no le parece?

—¿Usted cree que en el fondo es un monárquico?

—Estoy seguro. Si analiza usted cuidadosamente sus discursos, verá que le interesa todo lo relacionado con las tradiciones españolas y sus antiguos valores.

—¿Y sus gentes?

Goach se encogió de hombros.

—Siempre han necesitado mano dura.

—Pues eso ya lo tienen.

Goach inclinó la cabeza y bajó la vista a su plato. Se escucharon unas risotadas desde el otro extremo de la mesa, seguidas de unas sonoras carcajadas de los alemanes que no tenían la menor intención de pasar inadvertidos.

13

El martes Barbara acudió a una nueva cita con Luis. Era un día espléndido, tranquilo y apacible, y las hojas de los árboles caían suavemente al suelo. Barbara iba a pie, porque la Castellana estaba cerrada al tráfico; el *Reichsführer* Himmler bajaría más tarde por allí en su camino hacia el Palacio Real para celebrar su encuentro con el Generalísimo.

Tuvo que cruzar la Castellana. La cruz gamada ondeaba en todos los edificios y colgaba de unas cuerdas tendidas de uno a otro extremo de la calle. Las banderas rojas con la cruz de brazos doblados en ángulo recto contrastaban fuertemente con los edificios grises. Unos guardias civiles jalonaban la calle a intervalos, algunos de ellos acunando unas metralletas en sus brazos. Cerca de allí, un grupo de las Juventudes Falangistas permanecía alineado a lo largo del bordillo de la acera, sosteniendo en sus manos unas banderitas con la cruz gamada. Barbara apuró el paso y desapareció en el laberinto de calles que conducían al centro.

Cuando ya estaba cerca del café, el corazón le empezó a palpitar con fuerza. Luis ya había llegado, Barbara lo vio a través de la ventana. Permanecía sentado en la misma mesa, sosteniendo en sus manos una taza de café. La expresión de su rostro era sombría. Barbara reparó una vez más en su andrajoso aspecto; llevaba la misma chaqueta raída y calzaba unas alpargatas baratas de suela de esparto. Respiró hondo y entró. La propietaria la saludó con la cabeza desde debajo del retrato de Franco; estaba por todas partes, ahora incluso en los sellos.

Luis se levantó, esbozando una sonrisa de alivio.

—Buenos días, señora. ¡Pensaba que no iba a venir!

—Lo siento —contestó ella, sin responder a su sonrisa—. He tenido que venir a pie y he tardado más de lo que pensaba. Por la visita de Himmler.

—No importa. ¿Un café?

Barbara dejó que fuera a por una taza de aguachirle. Encendió un cigarrillo, pero esta vez no le ofreció ninguno a él. Respiró hondo y lo miró a los ojos.

—Señor Luis, antes de seguir adelante con el asunto, hay algo que quiero preguntarle.

—Faltaría más.

—La última vez usted me dijo que había dejado el ejército en primavera.

—Sí, en efecto. —Luis la miró perplejo.

—Pero también me dijo que se había pasado dos inviernos allí. ¿Eso cómo es posible? Cuenca estaba en manos de los rojos, hasta la rendición del año pasado.

Luis tragó saliva. Después esbozó una sonrisa triste.

—Mire, señora, yo le dije que pasé dos inviernos en la meseta, no en Cuenca. El año anterior, yo me encontraba en otra zona. Un puesto en Teruel. ¿Recuerda el nombre?

—Sí, claro. —Había sido una de las batallas más salvajes de la guerra. Barbara trató de recordar exactamente qué palabras había utilizado Luis.

—Teruel se encuentra a más de cien kilómetros de Cuenca, pero sigue estando prácticamente en la meseta. Alta y fría. Durante la batalla, a muchos hombres se les congelaron las extremidades y hubo que sacarlos de las trincheras para amputarles los pies. —Ahora Luis parecía casi enfadado.

Barbara volvió a respirar hondo.

—Comprendo.

—Usted temía que yo no le dijera la verdad —dijo bruscamente Luis.

—Tengo que asegurarme, señor Luis. Me arriesgo mucho. Tengo que estar segura de todo.

Luis asintió lentamente con la cabeza.

—Muy bien. Lo comprendo. Sí, es bueno que tenga cuidado. —Extendió los brazos—. Pregúnteme lo que se le ocurra y siempre que quiera.

—Gracias. —Barbara encendió otro pitillo.

—Fui a Cuenca el último fin de semana —dijo Luis—. Tal como le prometí.

Barbara asintió con la cabeza y volvió a mirarlo a los ojos. Eran inescrutables.

—Permanecí en la ciudad hasta que Agustín fue a verme. Me confirmó que en el campo hay un prisionero llamado Bernie Piper. Lleva allí desde que lo abrieron.

Barbara bajó la cabeza para que Luis no viera la impresión que le había causado la mención del nombre de Bernie. Tenía que conservar la calma y el control. Sabía, por su labor con los refugiados, hasta qué extremo se aferraban las personas a las esperanzas, por pequeñas que éstas fueran.

Levantó la vista y miró fijamente a Luis.

—Como usted comprenderá, señor, necesitaré pruebas. Necesito que su hermano le diga algo más acerca de él. Cosas que yo no le he dicho ni a usted ni a Markby, cosas que usted no podría saber. No que es rubio, por ejemplo; eso lo puede ver usted en la fotografía.

Luis se apoyó contra el respaldo de la silla, frunciendo los labios.

—No es una petición absurda —dijo Barbara—. Millares de brigadistas internacionales murieron en la guerra, y usted sabe lo escasas que son las posibilidades de que hayan sobrevivido. Necesito pruebas antes de poder seguir adelante.

—Y yo soy pobre y me podría estar inventando una historia. —Luis volvió a asentir con la cabeza—. No, señora, no es absurda. En qué mundo vivimos. —Reflexionó un instante—. Entonces ¿se supone que debo pedir a Agustín que me diga todo lo que sabe sobre este hombre y, luego, facilitarle los detalles a usted?

—Sí.

—¿Ha vuelto a hablar con el señor Markby?

—No. —Lo había intentado, pero aún estaba fuera.

Luis se inclinó hacia delante.

—Volveré a Cuenca; aunque no puedo ir muy a menudo a visitar a mi hermano, porque la gente podría sospechar. —Ahora el joven se había puesto en tensión. Se frotó la frente con la mano—. Supongo que podría decir que nuestra madre ha empeorado. No se encuentra muy bien. —Levantó la vista—. Pero el tiempo puede ser importante, señora Clare, si usted quiere que hagamos algo. Ya conoce los rumores que circulan. Si España entrara en guerra, usted se tendría que ir. Y su brigadista, si fuera comunista, podría ser entregado a los alemanes. Es lo que ocurrió en Francia.

Cierto, pero Barbara se preguntó si Luis la quería asustar para que se diera prisa.

—Si usted tuviera que hacer algo —repitió—. ¿Quiere decir —Barbara bajó la voz—... «escapar»? —Sintió los fuertes latidos de su corazón.

Luis asintió con la cabeza.

—Agustín cree que se puede hacer. Pero será peligroso. —Se inclinó hacia delante y bajó la voz—. Permítame explicarle cómo funciona el campo. Está cercado por una alambrada de púas. Hay atalayas con ametralladoras.

Barbara se estremeció involuntariamente.

—Perdone, señora, pero le tengo que explicar cuál es la situación.

—Lo sé. Siga.

—Es imposible que alguien del interior del campo pueda salir. Pero hay destacamentos de obreros forzados que salen todos los días... para arreglar carreteras, instalar tuberías y trabajar en una cantera de lo alto de las colinas. Piper se ha pasado algún tiempo trabajando en la cantera. Si Agustín pudiera conseguir un puesto de vigilante en aquel destacamento de prisioneros, quizá consiguiera ayudar a su amigo a escapar. Quizá se podría inventar una excusa para escoltar a Piper hasta un lugar un poco apartado; allí, Piper podría simular un ataque contra Agustín y escapar. —Luis frunció el entrecejo—. Eso es todo lo que hemos podido planear hasta ahora.

Barbara asintió con la cabeza. Al menos, parecía factible.

—Ésta es la única manera que se nos ocurre. Pero, cuando se descubra la fuga, Agustín será interrogado. Si se sabe la verdad, será fusilado. Lo hará sólo por dinero. —Luis la miró con semblante muy serio—. Hablando con toda franqueza.

Barbara asintió y procuró respirar hondo varias veces para que se le calmara el corazón sin que Luis se diera cuenta.

—El período de servicio de Agustín termina en primavera y él no quiere verse obligado a renovarlo. A algunos de allí les gusta este trabajo, pero a Agustín no. Lo hace sólo para mantener a nuestra madre en Sevilla.

—¿Cuánto, entonces?

—Dos mil pesetas.

—Eso es mucho —dijo Barbara, a pesar de ser menos de lo que ella temía.

—Agustín tiene que arriesgar su vida.

—Si aceptara, tendría que conseguir el dinero de Inglaterra. No sería fácil, dadas las restricciones monetarias. —Barbara volvió a respirar hondo—. Pero, si usted pudiera convencerme de que Bernie se encuentra en este campo, entonces ya veríamos.

—Tendríamos que concretar la cuestión del dinero, señora.

—No. Primero necesito una prueba. —Dio una calada al cigarrillo y lo miró a través de una nube de humo—. Otra visita a Cuenca no será peligrosa. Le pagaré el precio del billete. —Y entonces pensó: «¿Te volveré a ver?»

Luis titubeó un instante y después asintió con la cabeza. Barbara dio gracias a Dios por sus años de negociaciones con funcionarios corruptos. Luis se reclinó contra el respaldo de la silla con aire cansado. Barbara pensó: «Está menos acostumbrado que yo a esta clase de cosas.»

—¿Le dijo algo Agustín acerca de él... de Bernie, de cómo está? —Se le trabó la lengua al pronunciar el nombre.

—Está bien. Pero los inviernos son muy duros para los prisioneros. —Luis la miró con el semblante muy serio—. Si lo hacemos, usted tendría que desplazarse a Cuenca y llevárselo a la embajada británica en Madrid. ¿Dispone de automóvil?

—Sí, sí, eso ya lo arreglaré.

Luis la miró inquisitivamente.

—¿Su marido sabe algo?

—No. —Barbara levantó la cabeza—. Yo sólo quiero rescatar a Bernie y llevarlo a la embajada británica para que ellos lo puedan enviar a casa.

—Muy bien. —Luis lanzó un suspiro cansado.

Barbara encendió otro cigarrillo y le ofreció uno a él.

—¿Entonces nos volveremos a ver? —preguntó—. ¿La semana que viene?

—A la misma hora. —Luis la miró como avergonzado—. Me tendrá que pagar el precio del billete ahora.

Volvieron a salir a la calle para la entrega del dinero. Cuando Barbara le entregó el sobre, Luis soltó una carcajada amarga.

—Antes los españoles éramos un pueblo orgulloso. Hay que ver las cosas que tenemos que hacer ahora. —Dio media vuelta y apuró el paso hasta que su andrajosa figura se perdió calle arriba.

Barbara se topó con más calles cortadas en su camino de vuelta a casa y tuvo que bajar por la calle de Fernando el Santo y pasar por delante de la embajada británica. Contempló el edificio. Probablemente, Harry Brett se encontraba allí dentro; lo vería aquella misma noche. Harry, el amigo de Bernie.

Al final de la calle, unos guardias civiles impedían a los peatones el paso a la Castellana.

—Disculpe, señora. No se puede pasar hasta dentro de una hora. Medidas de seguridad.

Inclinó la cabeza y retrocedió. Un pequeño grupo de personas se había congregado en las inmediaciones. Calle arriba, unas voces juveniles lanzaron vítores al paso de un Mercedes negro que circulaba a poca velocidad escoltado por soldados motorizados. En la cubierta del motor ondeaba un banderín con la cruz gamada. Barbara distinguió en la parte de atrás un rostro pálido y mofletudo aparentemente separado del cuerpo por efecto del uniforme negro y la gorra. Un destello de sol se reflejó en los cristales de las gafas y a Barbara le pareció que, por un instante, Heinrich Himmler se volvía para mirarla. Después, el vehículo desapareció en medio de un remolino de hojas otoñales. Se oyeron nuevos vítores de las Juventudes Falangistas situadas más adelante. Barbara se estremeció y dio media vuelta.

14

Harry bajó por la Castellana, donde las banderas nazis que ondeaban en los edificios destacaban a través de la niebla que cubría la ciudad. Vestía abrigo y sombrero; ahora ya estaban a finales de octubre y las noches eran más frías. Se dirigía a la parada del tranvía para trasladarse a la calle Vigo del barrio de la Arganzuela donde estaba invitado a cenar en casa de Sandy y Barbara.

Aquella tarde, él y Tolhurst habían vuelto a hablar un poco más acerca de Barbara.

—Ha sido un golpe de suerte —le había dicho Tolhurst—. Jamás supimos dónde vivía Forsyth, ¿sabes? Nuestra fuente nos informó de que vivía con una chica, pero pensamos que debía de ser alguna putilla española.

—Me gustaría saber cómo acabó Barbara arrejuntándose con Sandy. —Harry meneó la cabeza—. Me pareció que iba por mal camino cuando la vi en el treinta y siete. Después le escribí, pero no me contestó o no recibió mis cartas.

—No le interesaba la política, ¿verdad? No se le contagiaron las ideas de aquel novio rojo que tenía, ¿no es cierto?

—No. Trabajaba en la Cruz Roja y era una persona de temperamento muy práctico y juicioso. No sé qué pensará ahora del régimen.

Lo averiguaría aquella noche. Mientras caminaba, Harry experimentó un repentino cansancio al pensar en la tarea que le esperaba. Pero se había comprometido, tenía que seguir.

Oyó unas pisadas a su espalda, un ruido débil a través de la niebla. Demonios, otra vez el sujeto que le pisaba los talones. No había visto al hombre durante el fin de semana, pero ahora parecía que ya había vuelto. Giró rápidamente a la izquierda y después a la derecha. Vio el portal abierto de un edificio de apartamentos, pero no así al portero que debía de estar por allí cerca. Eran unos apartamentos de clase media muy bien cuidados, el aire olía a líquido de fregar los suelos. Harry entró, se situó detrás de la puerta y atisbó. Oyó unas pisadas, un repiqueteo y el crujido de unas hojas secas. Un instante después apareció el joven que le había estado pisando los talones. Permaneció de pie y miró arriba y abajo en medio de la calle desierta, frunciendo el entrecejo de su rostro pálido y delicado. Harry escondió rápidamente la cabeza. Esperó unos minutos y volvió a salir. En la calle no había nadie, excepto una mujer que paseaba su perro envuelta en un abrigo de pieles. La mujer le dirigió una mirada recelosa. Desanduvo el camino, meneando la cabeza. La verdad era que aquel hombre no lo estaba haciendo demasiado bien.

El espía no lo había asustado; pero, aun así, mientras subía por el camino particular de Sandy media hora más tarde, experimentó aquella momentánea embriaguez que algunas veces se apoderaba de él. No le había comentado a Sandy sus crisis de pánico después de lo de Dunkerque, a pesar de que los espías le habían dicho que semejante detalle no lo podría perjudicar. El orgullo le había impedido hacerlo, pensaba. La casa era un enorme chalet rodeado de un amplio jardín. Harry permaneció de pie un momento en el peldaño de la entrada, para serenarse; luego respiró hondo y llamó al timbre.

Una joven sirvienta le abrió la puerta. Era agraciada, pero de aspecto ligeramente tristón. Lo acompañó a través de un pasillo decorado con varias piezas de porcelana china que descansaban encima de dos mesitas, hasta llegar a un salón espacioso con la chimenea encendida. Todo era cómodo y muy caro.

Sandy se acercó y le estrechó la mano con un firme apretón. Su esmoquin estaba inmaculado y el cabello le brillaba a causa de la gomina.

—Harry, cuánto me alegro de que hayas podido venir. Bueno, a Barbara ya la conoces.

Se encontraba de pie, fumando junto a la repisa de la chimenea con una copa de vino en la mano. Estaba completamente distinta. Sus viejos cárdigans y su despeinado cabello habían sido sustituidos por un costoso vestido de seda que realzaba la belleza de su tez y de su figura; su rostro había adelgazado, e iba impecablemente maquillada para acentuar sus pómulos pronunciados, sus brillantes ojos verdes y su largo cabello de puntas rizadas. A pesar de los cambios, se la veía tensa y cansada; lo cual no le impidió esbozar una sonrisa cordial en el momento de estrecharle la mano.

—Harry, ¿cómo estás?

—Muy bien. Has cambiado mucho.

—Jamás he olvidado lo amable que fuiste conmigo hace tres años. Entonces me encontraba fatal.

—Hice simplemente lo que pude. Eran tiempos muy duros.

—Sandy me ha dicho que intentaste escribirme. Lo siento, pero jamás recibí tus cartas. La Cruz Roja me trasladó a Burgos. Necesitaba alejarme de Madrid después de... —Hizo un gesto con la mano.

—Sí. Te escribí a Madrid, y supongo que las cartas no se entregaban a través de las líneas del frente.

—La culpa es mía —dijo Barbara—. Tendría que haber procurado mantener el contacto.

—Muchas veces me preguntaba qué tal estarías. Tengo entendido que ya no trabajas en la Cruz Roja, ¿verdad?

—No, lo dejé cuando conocí a Sandy. La verdad es que tuve que hacerlo porque no estaba en condiciones. Pero puede que muy pronto me dedique a algún trabajo de voluntariado con unos huérfanos.

Harry meneó la cabeza sonriendo.

—Y entonces te encontraste con Sandy. Estupendo.

—Sí. Él me ayudó a recuperarme.

Sandy se acercó a ella y le rodeó los hombros con el brazo, estrechándola en ademán protector. A Harry le pareció que Barbara se echaba un poco hacia atrás.

—Y tú, Harry —añadió Barbara—, ¿cómo estás? Sandy me dijo que estuviste en Dunkerque.

—Sí, pero ahora ya estoy bien. Sólo me ha quedado una pequeña sordera.

—¿Qué tal van las cosas en casa? Recibo cartas de mi familia, pero no me explican muy bien qué tal lo lleva la gente. Los periódicos españoles dicen que la situación es bastante mala.

—La gente resiste muy bien. La batalla de Inglaterra fue una inyección de moral.

—Me alegro. Estando tan lejos, no me preocupaba demasiado la falsa guerra; pero, desde que empezaron los bombardeos... supongo que tú en la embajada te enteras de todo. Aquí todos los periódicos están censurados.

Sandy se echó a reír.

—Sí, hasta censuran los desfiles de moda del *Daily Mail*. Si les parece que los vestidos son demasiado escotados, les ponen encima una franja negra.

—Bueno, la situación es muy dura, pero no tanto como los periódicos de aquí dan a entender. El estado de ánimo de la gente es asombroso, Churchill ha conseguido unir a todo el mundo.

—Toma una copa de vino —dijo Sandy—. Comeremos algo más tarde, cuando lleguen los demás. Oye, ¿por qué nos os reunís los dos una tarde para charlar un poco más acerca de la situación en vuestro país? A Barbara le sentará bien.

—Pues sí; sí, lo podríamos hacer.

Barbara inclinó la cabeza en señal de asentimiento, pero Harry percibió una cierta desgana en su voz.

—Estaría muy bien. —Harry se volvió hacia Sandy—. ¿Tú qué haces ahora exactamente? El otro día no me lo acabaste de explicar.

Sandy esbozó una ancha sonrisa.

—Bueno, toco varias teclas.

Harry miró a Barbara sonriendo.

—Sandy se ha abierto camino en el mundo.

—Pues sí. —A Barbara pareció molestarle la mención de los negocios. Harry se alegró. Si no supiera nada, no tendría nada que contar.

—Ahora mismo me ocupo, sobre todo, de un proyecto respaldado por el Gobierno —contestó Sandy—. Extracción de minerales. Todo muy aburrido, simples tareas de exploración. Pero requiere cierta organización.

—Así que explotación de minas, ¿eh? —dijo Harry. Debía de ser lo del oro. Seguía estando de suerte. Se le aceleraron los latidos del corazón. «Tranquilo —se dijo—, tómatelo con calma»—. Recuerdo que en el colegio querías ser paleontólogo. Los secretos de la tierra, solías decir.

Sandy se rió.

—Bueno, ahora no se trata de dinosaurios. —Sonó el timbre de la puerta—. Disculpa. Tengo que ir a recibir a Sebastián y Jenny. —Se retiró.

Barbara permaneció en silencio un instante y después sonrió con cierta inseguridad.

—Me alegro de volver a verte.

—Y yo a ti también. Tienes una casa muy bonita.

—Sí, creo que he caído de pie. —Barbara hizo una pausa y después se apresuró a preguntar—: ¿Crees que Franco entrará en guerra?

—Nadie lo sabe. Corren toda suerte de rumores. Si ocurre, será de repente.

Ambos se callaron cuando Sandy apareció en compañía de una pareja muy bien vestida. El hombre tenía treinta y tantos años, era bajito y delgado y resultaba muy atractivo desde un moreno y sureño punto de vista español. Vestía el uniforme de la Falange, atuendo militar oscuro y camisa azul. La mujer era más joven y también muy atractiva, rubia y de facciones redondeadas y suaves y expresión arrogante.

—Harry —dijo Sandy en español—, permíteme presentarte a Sebastián de Salas, un colega mío. Sebastián, te presento a Harry Brett.

El español estrechó la mano de Harry.

—Encantado, señor. Hay muy pocos ingleses en Madrid. —Se volvió hacia su acompañante—. Jenny ve a muy pocos compatriotas suyos.

—¡Hola! —La voz de la mujer era cortante como el cristal, y sus duros ojos miraban con expresión de complacencia. Se volvió para dirigirle a Barbara una fría y ceremoniosa sonrisa—. Hola, Babs, qué vestido más bonito.

—¿Te apetece una copa de vino? —El tono de Barbara era tan frío como el suyo.

—Más bien prefiero un *gin-tonic*. Me he pasado toda la tarde en el club de golf.

—Vamos todos —dijo Sandy jovialmente—. A sentarse.

Los cuatro se acomodaron en unos mullidos sillones.

—Bueno, Harry, ¿usted a qué se dedica? —preguntó Jenny de repente.

—Soy traductor en la embajada.

—¿Ha conocido a alguien interesante?

—Sólo a un subsecretario.

—Jenny es una aristócrata, Harry —explicó Sandy—. Y Sebastián, también.

El español soltó una carcajada como de disculpa.

—Más bien pequeño. Tenemos un castillito en Extremadura, pero se está desmoronando.

—No te rebajes, Sebastián —dijo Jenny—. Yo soy prima de lord Redesdale. ¿Lo conoce?

—No. —Harry hubiera deseado reírse. Aquella mujer era ridícula.

Jenny tomó la copa que Barbara le ofrecía.

—Vaya, muchas gracias. Mmm, delicioso —dijo, apoyándose en De Salas.

—¿Cuánto tiempo lleva usted en Madrid, señor Brett? —preguntó De Salas.

—Algo más de una semana.

—¿Y qué le parece España?

—Veo que la Guerra Civil ha provocado... muchos trastornos.

—Pues sí. —De Salas asintió tristemente con la cabeza—. La guerra hizo mucho daño y ahora nos enfrentamos con las malas cosechas. La gente lo está pasando muy mal. Pero nos esforzamos por mejorar la situación. El camino es arduo, pero ya hemos dado el primer paso.

—Sebastián pertenece a la Falange, como puedes ver —dijo Sandy en tono neutral, pero mirando a Harry con cierta guasa. De Salas sonrió y Harry lo miró con una sonrisa imparcial. Sandy apoyó una mano en el brazo de Barbara—. Barbara, ve a ver qué hace Pilar, ¿te importa?

Barbara inclinó la cabeza y se retiró. «La esposa obediente», pensó Harry. La idea le dolió por una razón inexplicable.

—Señor Brett —dijo De Salas cuando Barbara se retiró—: ¿puedo preguntarle una cosa? El caso es que me temo que muchos ingleses no comprendan lo que es la Falange.

—A menudo resulta difícil comprender la política de los países extranjeros —contestó cuidadosamente Harry, recordando los gritos de la horda que había rodeado el vehículo y al chico que se había mojado los pantalones.

—En Inglaterra tienen ustedes una democracia, ¿verdad? Por eso luchan ustedes, por el sistema.

—Sí.

«Estupendo —pensó Harry—, va directamente al grano.»

De Salas sonrió.

—Comprenda, por favor, que no es mi intención ofenderlo.

—No, desde luego.

—La democracia ha funcionado bien en Inglaterra y en Estados Unidos, pero no funciona en todas partes por igual. En España, la democracia trajo el caos y los derramamientos de sangre bajo la República. —De Salas sonrió con tristeza—. No todos los países son aptos para sus libertades, se rompen en pedazos. A veces, la vía autoritaria resulta ser la única válida.

Harry asintió, recordando que tenía que evitar la política en la medida de lo posible.

—Lo comprendo perfectamente. Es sólo que supongo que cabría preguntarse a quién deberían rendir cuentas los gobernantes.

De Salas se echó a reír y extendió las manos.

—Pues mire, señor, las rinden a toda la nación. A toda la nación representada por un solo partido. Eso es lo bonito de nuestro sistema. Oiga, ¿sabe usted por qué la Falange viste camisas azules?

—No me digas que es porque todos los demás colores ya estaban ocupados —terció Sandy riéndose.

—Porque el azul es el color de los monos de los obreros. Nosotros representamos a todo el mundo en España. La Falange es un camino intermedio entre el socialismo y el capitalismo. Ha dado resultado en Italia. Sabemos lo dura que es ahora la vida en España, pero haremos justicia a todo el mundo. Denos tiempo —añadió De Salas, sonriendo con la cara muy seria.

—Así lo espero —dijo Harry. Estudió a De Salas. Su expresión era abierta y sincera. «Se lo cree», pensó Harry.

Barbara regresó.

—Ya podemos pasar —dijo.

Sandy se levantó y se situó entre Harry y De Salas, apoyando una mano en los hombros de cada uno de ellos.

—Tendríamos que reanudar esta charla en otro momento. Pero ahora cambiemos de tema, ¿eh?, por deferencia a las señoras. —Les dirigió a los dos una paternal sonrisa y Harry se preguntó cómo podía ser que pareciera un hombre de mediana edad, mucho mayor de lo que era. Antes se había compadecido de Sandy, pero ahora éste le empezaba a resultar ligeramente repulsivo.

En el comedor se había dispuesto un bufet frío. Los cinco se llenaron los platos y se los llevaron a la mesa de madera de roble. Sandy abrió otra botella de vino. Jenny tenía consigo la botella de ginebra.

—Sandy —dijo De Salas—, deberías haber invitado a una señorita para el señor Brett.

—Sí, Sandy, nos falta una persona —convino Jenny—. Malas maneras.

—No ha habido tiempo.

—No se preocupen —dijo Harry—. Seguramente tendré ocasión de conocer a muchas señoritas el jueves que viene. Me han invitado a mi primera fiesta española.

—¿Y dónde va a ser? —preguntó De Salas.

—En casa del general Maestre. Su hija cumple dieciocho años.

De Salas miró a Harry con renovado interés.

—Conque en casa de Maestre, ¿eh?

—Sí. Intervine como intérprete en una reunión entre él y uno de nuestros diplomáticos.

De repente, Sandy habló en tono perentorio.

—No, Sebastián, nada de negocios esta noche.

De Salas asintió con la cabeza y se volvió hacia Barbara.

—¿Cómo van sus planes de trabajar con los huérfanos, señora? ¿La marquesa la ayudó?

—Sí, gracias. Espera poder organizar algo.

—Me alegro. ¿Le gustará volver a trabajar como enfermera?

—Me gustaría hacer algo útil. En realidad, lo considero un deber.

—Jenny también es enfermera, como Barbara —explicó De Salas a Harry—. La conocí cuando vino aquí para ayudar durante la guerra.

—¿Cómo? —Jenny levantó la cabeza con el rostro arrebolado. Harry vio que estaba bebida—. No lo he entendido. ¿Por qué soy como Barbara?

—Estaba diciendo que tú fuiste enfermera.

—¡Ah, sí! ¡Sí! —Jenny se rió—. Aunque no soy propiamente una enfermera. Nunca estudié. Pero, cuando vine, me encomendaron la tarea de ayudar en las operaciones. Después de la batalla del Jarama. Menos mal que no soy aprensiva.

Barbara inclinó la cabeza sobre su plato. Sandy le dirigió una mirada solícita.

—Harry —dijo después—, prueba este estupendo tinto. Me ha costado un riñón. Un escándalo.

De Salas miró a Harry con una sonrisa.

—Supongo que la embajada cuenta con sus propias provisiones.

—Recibimos raciones. No están demasiado mal.

De Salas preguntó:

—¿Es cierto que hay muchas privaciones en Inglaterra? ¿Y que los alimentos están racionados?

—Sí. Pero todo el mundo recibe lo suficiente.

—¿De veras? Pues no es lo que se lee por aquí. —De Salas se inclinó hacia delante, sinceramente interesado—. Pero dígame, por favor, porque de veras me interesa. ¿Por qué siguen ustedes adelante con la guerra? Ya los derrotaron en Francia, ¿por qué no rendirse ahora?

No había manera de que abandonara el tema. Harry miró a Barbara.

—Eso es lo que piensan todos los españoles —le dijo ésta.

—Hitler les ha ofrecido a ustedes la paz. Y yo he visto tantos muertos en España que desearía que cesaran las matanzas en Europa.

Sandy se inclinó hacia delante.

—Tiene razón, ¿sabes? Inglaterra tendría que rendirse ahora que tienen unas buenas condiciones sobre la mesa. No es que no sea patriota, Harry, sólo quiero lo mejor para los intereses de mi país. Llevo fuera casi cuatro años y, a veces, las cosas se ven más claras desde lejos. E Inglaterra no puede ganar.

—La gente está firmemente decidida.

—A defender la democracia, ¿eh? —dijo De Salas sonriendo con tristeza.

—Sí.

—Quizás Hitler nos permitiría conservar la democracia —apuntó Sandy—. A cambio de nuestra renuncia a seguir luchando.

—No tiene un historial muy bueno en este sentido —dijo Harry, repentina y visiblemente dominado por la cólera. Él había luchado contra los alemanes, mientras que Sandy se había quedado allí sentado ganando dinero. Si Sandy había acompañado a la gente en recorridos por los antiguos campos de batalla, Harry había combatido en uno auténtico.

—Ya no queda demasiada democracia en Inglaterra, por lo que me cuentan —terció Jenny, levantando la voz—. A Oswald Mosley lo metieron en chirona simplemente por haberse puesto al frente del partido equivocado.

Barbara le lanzó una mirada rebosante de veneno. De Salas carraspeó.

—Creo que quizá nos estamos acalorando demasiado —dijo con torpeza.

La fiesta no duró demasiado. De Salas no tardó en decir que tenían que marcharse y se retiró llevándose a rastras a una Jenny que casi no se tenía en pie.

—No la vuelvas a invitar, Sandy, por favor —dijo Barbara cuando se fueron.

Sandy arqueó las cejas, mirando a Harry mientras se encendía un cigarro.

—Jenny se pasó toda la Guerra Civil trabajando aquí como enfermera. Antes era bastante alocada, al parecer se fugó del colegio de Roedean. Por lo visto, no sabe adaptarse a la paz, se pasa la vida borracha. Sebastián está pensando en quitársela de encima.

—Es asquerosa —dijo Barbara. Se volvió hacia Harry—. Perdona, no he estado muy amable esta noche.

—Pero don Sebastián parece bastante civilizado —dijo Harry—. A su manera.

—Sí. —Sandy asintió con la cabeza—. El fascismo español no es como el nazismo, Harry, tienes que recordarlo. Se parecen más bien a los italianos. Yo, por ejemplo, llevo a cabo una labor de beneficencia con refugiados judíos. Sin embargo, hay que hacerlo con cierta discreción, porque temen molestar a los alemanes; pero la verdad es que las autoridades hacen la vista gorda. —Miró a Harry con una sonrisa—. No hagas caso de lo que antes he dicho acerca de la rendición británica. Ha sido una simple... conversación. Aquí es el tema del día, como puedes imaginar. Les encantaría que terminara la guerra; ya ha habido demasiados derramamientos de sangre, como bien ha dicho Sebastián.

Barbara se encendió un cigarrillo.

—Estoy de acuerdo en que aquí no tienen esas ideas nazis sobre la pureza racial. Pero son todos bastante brutos.

Sandy enarcó las cejas.

—Pensaba que estabas de acuerdo en que, al final, Franco había puesto un poco de orden.

Barbara se encogió de hombros.

—Puede ser. Voy a decirle a Pilar que recoja, Sandy, y después subo arriba. Os dejo con vuestras copas. Perdona, Harry, no estoy muy brillante esta noche. Me duele un poco la cabeza. —Lo miró con una leve sonrisa en los labios—. Te llamaré, a ver si nos vemos.

—Sí, por favor. Si me llamas a la embajada, seguramente me encontrarás. Cualquier día de esta semana quizá.

—Quizá.

Harry volvió a percibir cierta desgana en su voz. «¿Por qué?», se preguntó.

Una vez solos, Sandy llenó sendos vasos de whisky y se encendió un cigarro. Al parecer, su aguante era tremendo. Harry lo había observado beber despacio para mantener la cabeza despejada.

—¿Le ocurre algo a Barbara?

Sandy hizo un gesto como de rechazo con la mano.

—Bueno, no. Simplemente está cansada y preocupada por lo que ocurre en Inglaterra. Los bombardeos y todo lo demás. Oye, cuando te llame, llévala a comer a un buen restaurante. Aquí está demasiado sola.

—De acuerdo.

—España es un lugar muy curioso, pero hay muchas oportunidades de negocios. —Sandy se echó a reír—. Mejor será no decir que me conoces cuando acudas al baile de la niña de Maestre. El Gobierno es un nido de rivalidades, y el bando en el que yo trabajo y el de Maestre no se llevan bien.

—¿Ah, no? —Harry hizo una pausa y después preguntó con la mayor inocencia—. Maestre es monárquico, ¿verdad?

Los ojos entornados de Sandy lo miraron a través del humo del cigarro con expresión calculadora.

—Pues sí, en efecto. Menudos fanáticos están hechos. —Sandy miró a Harry con la cara muy seria—. Por cierto, ¿recuerdas lo que dije en el café acerca de la posibilidad de salir de España?

—Sí.

—No le comentes nada a Barbara, por favor. En caso de que decida irme, tardaré algún tiempo en hacerlo. Yo se lo diré cuando llegue el momento.

—Pues claro. Entendido.

—Todavía tengo algunos negocios que terminar aquí. Y dinero que ganar. —Sandy miró a Harry con una sonrisa—. Confío en que tengas invertido tu dinero en cosas seguras.

Harry vaciló. El rostro de Sandy había vuelto a recuperar su expresión calculadora

—Sí. Mis padres me dejaron algún dinero, y mi tío lo invirtió en valores seguros. Lo tengo todo donde él lo colocó. A veces pienso que demasiado seguro. —Se echó a reír en tono dubitativo. En realidad, pensaba que el dinero nunca estaba demasiado seguro, pero quería ver adónde quería ir a parar Sandy.

—El dinero siempre puede generar más dinero si sabes dónde invertirlo.

—Sí, supongo que sí.

Para decepción de Harry, Sandy se levantó.

—En cualquier caso, quiero enseñarte una cosa. Acompáñame arriba.

Harry lo siguió hasta un pequeño y cómodo estudio del piso de arriba, lleno a rebosar de obras de arte.

—Mi refugio. Subo aquí para trabajar tranquilo.

La mirada de Harry se desplazó hacia el escritorio cubierto de carpetas de cartón y papeles, pero no alcanzó a ver qué eran.

—Fíjate en eso. —Sandy encendió la pequeña lámpara que iluminaba la figura del hombre tumbado de cualquier manera sobre el caballo distorsionado, cruzando el desierto medio muerto de cansancio—. Creo que es un Dalí —dijo—. ¿No te parece asombroso?

—Inquietante —dijo Harry.

Casi todas las piezas que se exhibían en la estancia tenían cierto carácter perturbador. La mano de una mujer que asomaba desde una manga de encaje exquisitamente labrada en plata; un jarrón japonés con una cruenta escena guerrera pintada con unos colores extraordinarios.

—En el Rastro puedes encontrar las cosas más sorprendentes —dijo Sandy—. Cosas que los rojos sacaron de las casas de los ricos durante la guerra. Aquí está, eso es lo que quiero enseñarte. —Abrió un cajón del escritorio y sacó una bandeja. Estaba llena de fósiles de piedras con los huesos de extrañas criaturas atrapados en su interior—. Mi colección. Las mejores piezas, en cualquier caso. —Señaló una piedra oscura—. ¿La recuerdas?

—Dios mío, sí. El amonites.

—Me lo pasaba muy bien con nuestras cazas de fósiles... Como dije el otro día, son las únicas cosas buenas que recuerdo de Rookwood.

Esbozó una torpe sonrisa, y Harry se sintió extrañamente conmovido y repentinamente culpable por lo que estaba haciendo.

—Y ahora —dijo Sandy—, echa un vistazo a esto. —Se arrodilló y levantó la tapa de una alargada y plana caja de madera que descansaba junto al escritorio. Dentro había una piedra ancha y plana de color blanco—. La encontré allá abajo por Extremadura hace unos meses. —Incrustados en la piedra se podían ver los huesos de una pata muy larga cuyos tres dedos terminaban en unas garras curvadas. Una garra era mucho más grande que las otras dos y tan larga como la mano de un hombre—. Bonita, ¿verdad? Principios del Cretáceo, más de cien millones de años de antigüedad. —Un sincero asombro le iluminó el rostro; por un instante, volvió a ser un colegial.

—¿Qué especie es?

—Eso es lo más interesante. Creo que puede ser un nuevo ejemplar. Cuando vuelva a casa, la voy a llevar al Museo de Historia Natural. Si todavía sigue en pie. —Sandy contempló el fósil—. Por cierto, otra cosa cuando veas a Barbara. Le dije que no era muy amigo de Piper, pero lo que no le dije fue que no nos llevábamos bien en absoluto. Preferí no decírselo.

—Lo comprendo.

—Gracias. —Sandy esbozó una sonrisa avergonzada—. Aborrecía tanto aquel colegio.

—Lo sé. Pero te ha ido muy bien. —Harry se echó a reír—. ¿Recuerdas que, cuando te fuiste, me dijiste que pensabas que estabas destinado a ser siempre el chico malo, el perdedor?

Sandy se rió.

—Sí. Me dejaba machacar por los muy hijos de puta. Recibí una educación mucho mejor en las pistas de las carreras de caballos. Allí aprendí que tú mismo puedes crearte tu propio futuro y ser lo que tú quieras.

—A veces yo mismo me lo pregunto.

—¿Qué?

—Si Rookwood nos daba una imagen distorsionada del mundo. Una imagen complaciente.

Sandy asintió con la cabeza.

—Como te dije en el café, el mundo pertenece a la gente que puede alargar la mano y apoderarse de la vida. Jamás tendríamos que permitir que el pasado nos frenara. Y eso que se llama el destino no existe.

Miró inquisitivamente a Harry. Éste contempló a su vez la extremidad del dinosaurio. Observó que las garras estaban curvadas; como si, en el momento de morir, la criatura hubiera estado a punto de atacar.

15

A la mañana siguiente, Harry presentó su informe a Hillgarth. Éste se mostró encantado con sus progresos. Le dijo que procurara volver a reunirse con Sandy lo antes posible, que intentara encauzar la conversación de forma que éste le hablara del oro y que también tratara de conseguir información de Barbara cuando se reuniera con ella.

Ya era casi la hora de comer cuando regresó a su despacho. Había estado traduciendo un discurso del gobernador de Barcelona, pero descubrió que alguien se lo había llevado de su escritorio. Fue a ver a Weaver.

—Se lo he tenido que pasar a Carne —dijo lánguidamente Weaver—. No sabía cuánto tiempo estaría usted reunido con los espías y era algo que se tenía que hacer. —Lanzó un suspiro—. Ahora ya podrá tomarse el resto del día libre, si quiere.

Harry abandonó el edificio y regresó a casa a pie. Sabía que los otros dos traductores estaban molestos por sus constantes ausencias del trabajo, por lo que la frialdad entre ellos era cada vez mayor. «Que se vayan a tomar por saco», pensó Harry. Eran unos estirados sujetos estilo Foreign Office que a él lo traían sin cuidado. Sin embargo, cada vez era más consciente de su soledad; aparte de Tolhurst, no tenía amigos en la embajada.

Al llegar a casa, se comió unos fiambres y después, como no le apetecía quedarse solo en el apartamento toda la tarde, se puso un atuendo más informal y salió a dar un paseo. El tiempo seguía siendo húmedo y frío y una ligera niebla oscurecía el final de la calle. Se detuvo en la plaza sin saber adónde ir y luego bajó por la calle que conducía al barrio de La Latina, más allá del cual se encontraba Carabanchel, un lugar que Tolhurst había calificado de mala zona aquella primera tarde.

Recordó a los Mera, los amigos de Bernie, y se preguntó si todavía estarían en algún sitio de por allí.

Mientras atravesaba La Latina, pensó en Barbara. No le entusiasmaba demasiado la tarea que tenía por delante, eso de hacer preguntas inquisitivas acerca de las actividades de Sandy sin que se notara en exceso. Barbara había cambiado tanto que prácticamente resultaba irreconocible. Pese a lo cual, él comprendió que no era feliz. Se lo había comunicado a Hillgarth, pero después se había arrepentido de haberlo hecho.

Bajó hasta la Puerta de Toledo. Más allá se encontraba Carabanchel. Dudó unos momentos y después cruzó el puente y se adentró en el populoso barrio de las altas casas de vecindad. Aquella fría y húmeda tarde el barrio estaba casi desierto y sólo se veían unos pocos viandantes. «Cuánto debimos de llamar la atención aquí Bernie y yo en el treinta y uno, tan pálidos e ingleses con nuestras camisas blancas», pensó. Algunos edificios parecían a punto de derrumbarse y estaban apuntalados con tablones de madera; en las calles abundaban los baches y las losas rotas y, de vez en cuando, se veía algún que otro cráter de bomba así como muros medio derruidos asomando por encima de montones de cascotes cual dientes rotos. Harry se echó hacia atrás al ver que una enorme rata salía de un edificio bombardeado y cruzaba corriendo la calzada por delante de él.

De pronto, oyó el sonido regular de unas pisadas a su espalda y soltó una maldición por lo bajo. Otra vez su espía, probablemente debía de estar esperando en las inmediaciones de su apartamento. En su inquietud, había olvidado comprobar su posible presencia; no había ejercido bien su oficio. Entró en el portal del edificio más próximo. La puerta estaba cerrada y él alargó la mano hacia el pomo y se perdió en un oscuro zaguán. Caía agua desde algún sitio y se respiraba un fuerte olor a orines. Entornó la puerta y dejó sólo un resquicio para mirar alrededor.

Vio pasar al pálido joven arrebujado en su abrigo. Esperó unos minutos y luego salió y dobló la esquina de una calle. El lugar le resultaba familiar. Un grupito de hombres de mediana edad lo miró fríamente al pasar por delante de la esquina donde ellos conversaban. Recordó con una punzada de tristeza lo amable que era la gente nueve años atrás.

Dobló la esquina de una plaza. Dos lados de la plaza habían sido bombardeados y reducidos a escombros, los edificios se habían derrumbado y un caos de muros destrozados se elevaba por encima de un mar de ladrillos rotos y empapados jirones de ropa de cama. La maleza había crecido entre las piedras, unos altos y ásperos hierbajos de color verde oscuro. Unos huecos cuadrados en el suelo, llenos de espumajosa agua de color verdoso señalaban la antigua ubicación de los sótanos. La plaza estaba desierta y las casas que quedaban en pie ofrecían un aspecto abandonado, con todas las ventanas rotas.

Harry jamás había visto una destrucción de semejante calibre; los cráteres de las bombas de Londres parecían pequeños en comparación con todo aquello. Se acercó un poco más para contemplar la destrucción. La plaza debía de haber sido objeto de intensos bombardeos. Cada día se recibían noticias acerca de nuevas incursiones aéreas en Inglaterra... ¿Ofrecería Londres ahora el mismo aspecto que aquella plaza?

Después vio un rótulo en una esquina, Plaza del General Blanco, y experimentó una terrible sacudida en el estómago. Era la plaza donde vivía la familia Mera. Volvió a mirar a su alrededor para tratar de orientarse y entonces se dio cuenta de que el bloque de viviendas donde vivía la familia había desaparecido y ahora sólo quedaban los escombros. Permaneció allí en pie, boquiabierto de asombro. Percibió un repentino movimiento y se sobresaltó cuando un perro pegó un brinco y saltó a lo alto de lo que quedaba de una pared y se lo quedó mirando desde allí. Era un pequeño mestizo de color canela y rabo de pelo rizado; debía de haber sido la mascota de alguien, pero ahora estaba muerto de hambre y se le marcaban las costillas a través del pelaje medio comido por la sarna.

El animal soltó dos ladridos secos y entonces una docena de formas emergieron desde detrás de los muros y a través de la maleza, unos perros flacos y sarnosos de todas las formas y tamaños. Algunos no eran más grandes que el mestizo, pero había tres o cuatro de gran tamaño, incluido un pastor alemán. Los perros se juntaron para mirarlo. Harry retrocedió recordando lo que Tolhurst le había dicho el primer día acerca de los perros asilvestrados y la rabia. Miró angustiado alrededor, pero, además de los perros, no había la menor señal de vida en la brumosa y devastada plaza. El corazón le empezó a latir con fuerza al tiempo que notaba un silbido en el oído malo.

Los perros avanzaron hacia él sobre los escombros y se desplegaron lentamente en abanico en medio de un silencio pavoroso. El pastor alemán, que debía de ser el jefe, se adelantó y le enseñó los dientes. Con qué facilidad aquel levantamiento del labio podía convertir un perro en un animal salvaje.

No tienes que manifestar temor. Eso es lo que se decía de los perros.

—¡Vete! —le gritó al perro.

Para su alivio, los perros se detuvieron a unos diez metros de distancia de él. El pastor alemán le volvió a enseñar los dientes.

Harry retrocedió sin apartar los ojos de ellos. Estuvo a punto de tropezar con un ladrillo roto y agitó los brazos para no perder el equilibrio. Mirando al pastor alemán a los ojos, se agachó para recoger el ladrillo. Los perros se pusieron tensos.

Lo arrojó contra el pastor alemán, soltando un grito. Alcanzó al animal en una de sus sarnosas caderas y éste se retorció emitiendo un aullido.

—¡Vete! —le volvió a gritar Harry.

Los perros vacilaron un instante, pero después dieron media vuelta y echaron a correr en pos de su jefe.

La jauría se detuvo lejos de su alcance y se lo quedó mirando en actitud vigilante. A Harry le temblaban las piernas. Recogió otro fragmento de ladrillo y se retiró muy despacio. Los perros se quedaron donde estaban. Se detuvo en el extremo más alejado de la plaza con la espalda apoyada contra una pared. Un maltrecho cartel republicano seguía fijado a la misma, un soldado con casco de acero que saltaba ante el fuego de artillería.

Harry volvió lentamente sobre sus pasos sin apartarse de las paredes, vigilando por si hubiera algún movimiento desde el cráter de la bomba. Los perros habían desaparecido entre los escombros, pero él sintió su mirada y no volvió la espalda hasta llegar a la calle que desembocaba en la plaza. Se apoyó contra la pared, respirando afanosamente. De pronto, oyó un grito, un alarido de puro terror. Lo siguió otro todavía más fuerte. Dudó un instante y después corrió de nuevo a la plaza.

Su espía se encontraba al borde del cráter de la bomba. Los perros lo habían rodeado y se le habían echado encima. Un mestizo de gran tamaño lo sujetaba por la espinilla y lo sacudía para derribarlo al suelo mientras el hombre volvía a gritar. La pernera de su pantalón y el hocico del perro estaban manchados de sangre. Mientras Harry contemplaba la escena, uno de los perros más pequeños pegó un brinco y apresó el brazo del hombre, haciendo que se tambaleara. El hombre se desplomó, soltando otro grito. Entonces el pastor alemán se le arrojó al cuello. El hombre consiguió cubrirse la garganta con el brazo, pero el pastor alemán le apresó el brazo. La jauría emitió unos gruñidos de excitación y el hombre estuvo casi a punto de desaparecer debajo de ellos.

Harry cogió otro trozo de ladrillo y lo arrojó. Cayó entre los perros y éstos se apartaron enseñando los dientes sin dejar de gruñir. Cruzando la plaza medio agachado, recogió piedras y fragmentos de ladrillo y los arrojó con ambas manos, sin dejar de gritar contra los perros. Una vez más, apuntó especialmente al jefe, el pastor alemán. Los perros vacilaron y Harry pensó que ahora irían también por él, pero el pastor alemán retrocedió y echó a correr. Renqueaba; el ladrillo que Harry le había arrojado anteriormente le debía de haber hecho un poco de daño. Los otros perros lo siguieron y se perdieron una vez más entre la maleza.

El hombre permanecía tumbado, despatarrado sobre los adoquines rotos, apretando el brazo contra la garganta. Miró a Harry con la boca abierta, respirando entre jadeos sonoros. La pernera del pantalón estaba rasgada y cubierta de sangre.

—¿Se puede levantar? —le preguntó Harry. El hombre lo miró con los ojos desorbitados a causa del terror—. Tenemos que irnos de aquí —añadió dulcemente Harry—. Podrían volver, ahora ya han probado su sangre. Vamos, yo lo ayudo.

Sujetó al hombre por las axilas y lo ayudó a levantarse. Era muy liviano, sólo piel y huesos. Apoyando el peso del cuerpo en una pierna, el hombre puso el otro pie en el suelo y lo volvió a levantar, haciendo una mueca. El pastor alemán había regresado y los observaba desde lo alto de una montaña de escombros. Harry le pegó un grito y el perro se retiró una vez más. Después, ayudó al hombre a abandonar la plaza, echando la vista hacia atrás a cada pocos segundos. Cuando ya se encontraban a un par de calles de distancia, lo dejó en el peldaño de la entrada de una casa de vecindad. Una mujer los miró desde una ventana y después cerró las persianas.

—Gracias —dijo el espía casi sin resuello—. Gracias, señor.

La pierna le seguía sangrando y ahora también había sangre en los pantalones de Harry. Éste pensó en la rabia... Si los perros estuvieran infectados, el espía moriría.

—Pensaba que lo había despistado —dijo Harry.

El espía lo miró horrorizado.

—¿Lo sabe? —Abrió enormemente los ojos. Era todavía más joven de lo que Harry pensaba, poco más que un niño. Ahora su pálido rostro estaba blanco como la cera a causa del sobresalto y el temor.

—Lo sé desde hace algún tiempo. Pensé que me había librado de usted.

El hombre lo miró con tristeza.

—Siempre lo pierdo. Lo perdí cuando salió esta mañana. Más tarde lo vi cerca de su apartamento, pero se me volvió a escapar antes de llegar a la plaza. —Miró a Harry con una leve sonrisa en los labios—. En eso es usted mejor que yo.

—¿Cómo se llama?

—Enrique. Enrique Roque Casas. Habla usted muy bien el español, señor.

—Soy traductor. Aunque supongo que eso usted ya lo sabe.

El joven pareció avergonzarse.

—Me ha salvado la vida. Créame, señor. Yo no quería hacer este trabajo, pero necesitamos el dinero. Ahora me avergüenzo. —Se apoyó la mano en la pierna y la retiró cubierta de sangre. Le empezaban a castañetear los dientes.

—Vamos, lo acompañaré a casa. ¿Dónde vive?

La respuesta fue un susurro que él no pudo captar, le silbaba el oído malo. Inclinó el sano hacia él y repitió la pregunta.

—A unas pocas calles de aquí, cerca del río. En Madre de Dios... había oído hablar de esos perros, pero lo olvidé. No quería tener que informar de que lo había vuelto a perder. La verdad es que no están muy satisfechos conmigo. —Ahora Enrique estaba temblando y ya empezaba a experimentar los efectos del choque.

—Vamos —dijo Harry—. Póngase mi abrigo.

Se lo quitó y rodeó con él aquellos escuálidos hombros. Sujetándolo, Harry siguió las instrucciones de Enrique a través de las angostas callejuelas, sin prestar atención a las miradas de los viandantes. «Esto es ridículo», pensó, pero no podía abandonar sin más al muchacho; se encontraba en estado de choque y necesitaba que le examinaran la pierna.

—Bueno, ¿entonces para quién trabaja? —le preguntó bruscamente.

—Para el Ministerio de Asuntos Exteriores, señor. El jefe de nuestro bloque me consiguió el trabajo. Me dijeron que tenía que seguir a un diplomático británico y comunicarles adónde iba.

—Ya.

—Mandan seguir a todos los diplomáticos, menos a los alemanes. Incluso a los italianos. Dijeron que usted era traductor, señor, y que probablemente sólo iría a la embajada y a los buenos restaurantes de la ciudad; pero yo lo tenía que seguir y anotarlo todo.

—Puede que consiguieran alguna información útil. Si yo acudiera a un burdel, por ejemplo, me podrían someter a chantaje.

Enrique asintió con la cabeza.

—Sé cómo funciona la cosa, señor.

«Lo sabes demasiado bien», pensó Harry.

Se detuvieron ante una ruinosa casa de vecindad.

—Ésta es mi casa, señor —dijo Enrique.

Harry abrió la puerta de un empujón y entró en el húmedo y oscuro zaguán.

—Vivimos en el primer piso —dijo Enrique—. Si usted me pudiera ayudar...

Harry lo ayudó a subir el tramo de escalera. Enrique sacó una llave y abrió la puerta con mano temblorosa. La puerta daba a un recibidor pequeño y oscuro. Se respiraba en el aire un penetrante olor a moho. Enrique abrió otra puerta y entró renqueando en un saloncito. Harry lo siguió y se quitó el sombrero. Debajo de una mesilla ardía un brasero, pero la estancia seguía estando muy fría. Un par de sillas de madera arañadas rodeaban una mesa junto a la cual permanecía sentado un delgado chiquillo de unos ocho años, dibujando una y otra vez al pastel unas oscuras formas en un ejemplar del periódico *Arriba*. Al ver a Harry, el niño se levantó de un salto y se acercó corriendo a una combada cama individual que había en un rincón. La rodeaban unas cortinas que en aquel momento estaban descorridas. Una anciana de fino cabello gris, arrugado rostro torcido hacia un lado en una siniestra mueca y ojo semicerrado, descansaba en ella recostada sobre unas almohadas. El niño se encaramó a la cama de un salto y se acurrucó contra el costado de la anciana. Harry se sorprendió al ver el temor y la rabia que reflejaba su rostro.

La anciana se incorporó apoyándose en un brazo.

—Enrique, ¿qué ha pasado, quién es éste? —Hablaba arrastrando muy despacio las palabras, y Harry se dio cuenta de que había sufrido un ataque.

Enrique pareció recuperar el dominio de sí mismo. Se acercó y besó a la mujer en la mejilla mientras le daba al niño una palmada en la cabeza.

—Tranquila, mamá. He sufrido un accidente, unos perros me atacaron y este hombre me ha acompañado a casa. Por favor, señor.

Acercó una de las desvencijadas e inseguras sillas de madera y Harry se sentó. La silla chirrió bajo su peso. Enrique volvió a acercarse renqueando a la anciana. Se sentó en la cama y tomó su mano.

—No te preocupes, mamá, no pasa nada. ¿Dónde está Sofía?

—Ha ido a comprar.

La anciana se inclinó hacia delante para acariciar al niño. Éste había hundido el rostro en su brazo izquierdo, muy blanco y arrugado. El niño se incorporó y señaló la pierna de Enrique.

—¡Sangre! —chilló—. ¡Sangre!

—Tranquilo, Paquito, es sólo un corte, no es nada —dijo Enrique, tratando de serenarlo.

La anciana acarició la cabeza del chiquillo.

—No es nada, niño. —Después miró a Harry—. ¿Extranjero? —le preguntó a su hijo en voz baja—. ¿Es alemán?

—Soy inglés, señora.

Ella lo miró con inquietud y Harry comprendió que sabía con qué se ganaba la vida su hijo. Harry contempló los pantalones desgarrados y manchados de Enrique.

—Habría que lavar esta pierna.

La anciana asintió con la cabeza.

—Agua, Enrique, trae agua.

—Sí, mamá.

Enrique inclinó la cabeza y se acercó renqueando a la puerta. Harry se levantó para echarle una mano, pero Enrique rechazó su ayuda con un gesto de la mano.

—No. Quédese aquí, señor, por favor. Ya ha hecho suficiente.

Tomó un cubo que había en un rincón y se retiró dejando a Harry allí sin saber qué hacer. Éste pensó que ya podría marcharse, pero no quería parecer grosero. Recordó cómo el pastor alemán había tirado del brazo del espía, en un intento de morderle la garganta, y se estremeció.

La mujer y el niño lo miraban fijamente desde la cama. Era difícil leer la expresión del rostro de la anciana, pero la del niño reflejaba rabia y temor. Harry esbozó una torpe sonrisa. Miró alrededor. Todo estaba muy limpio, pero, si la mujer se pasaba allí todo el día, era lógico que no se pudiera evitar aquel olor a moho que se respiraba en el aire. Había unas flores secas en unos jarrones y unos cuadros baratos de escenas campestres en las paredes destinados a alegrar un poco la estancia. Sin embargo, Harry observó que la pared de debajo de la ventana presentaba unas oscuras estrías de hongos en la parte donde el agua goteaba desde un antepecho podrido sobre una manta doblada. Apartó la mirada. Vio también unas cuantas fotografías prendidas en la pared. La anciana señaló una de ellas con el dedo.

—Mi boda —graznó.

Harry asintió cortésmente y se levantó para echarle un vistazo, mientras el niño se ponía tenso al verle cruzar el cuarto. La fotografía mostraba a una joven pareja de pie ante el pórtico de una iglesia y, a su lado, un joven y sonriente sacerdote. A juzgar por la ropa, la fotografía parecía corresponderse más o menos con la época de la boda de sus padres. La mujer sonrió con la mitad del rostro que todavía podía mover.

—Días más felices —dijo en un susurro.

—Sí, más felices, señora.

—Por favor, tome asiento, señor.

Harry volvió a sentarse. La mujer acarició el cabello del niño. Éste miraba a Harry con semblante asustado.

Se abrió la puerta y entró una muchacha envuelta en un grueso abrigo, con una bolsa de la compra. Era una veinteañera menuda y morena, con la cara en forma de corazón y grandes ojos castaños. Al ver a Harry, se detuvo en seco. Éste se levantó.

—¿Qué ha pasado? —preguntó bruscamente la chica—. ¿Quién es usted?

—Tranquila —dijo la anciana—. Es que unos perros han atacado a Enrique. Este hombre lo ha acompañado a casa. Tu hermano ha ido por un poco de agua.

La chica dejó la bolsa en el suelo, frunciendo el entrecejo con inquietud.

—Siento haberla asustado —dijo Harry.

—¿De dónde es usted?

—Soy inglés. Me llamo Harry Brett. Trabajo en la embajada.

La chica lo miró boquiabierta de asombro.

—Entonces... ¿usted es el que...?

—Pues... sí. —O sea que la chica también sabía con qué se ganaba la vida su hermano.

—¿Y ahora qué es lo que ha hecho? —preguntó mirando a Harry con dureza. Acto seguido, dio media vuelta y abandonó la estancia.

—Mi hija —dijo la anciana sonriendo—. Mi Sofía, corazón de mi vida.

Se oyeron unas voces en la escalera; la de la chica, enojada, la de Enrique y un murmullo como de disculpa. Éste entró renqueando, seguido de la chica, que llevaba el cubo de agua. Enrique se sentó en una silla frente a Harry y la chica sacó unas tijeras de un cajón y miró al niño.

—Paquito, ve a la cocina, anda. Enciende el horno para calentar.

El niño obedeció, se levantó de la cama y se retiró, dirigiéndole a Harry una última mirada de temor.

—Creo que lo de la pierna es lo peor —dijo Harry—. Pero también lo han mordido el brazo. ¿La puedo ayudar?

La chica levantó la cabeza.

—Ya me las arreglo yo sola. —Después se volvió hacia su hermano—. Tendrás que buscarte otros pantalones en algún sitio. —Empezó a cortar la pernera, mientras Enrique se mordía el labio para ahogar un grito de dolor. La pierna estaba hecha un desastre, llena de señales de mordeduras que se alargaban hasta formar desgarros allí donde los perros habían tirado violentamente de la carne. La chica le quitó la chaqueta a su hermano y cortó la manga de la camisa, dejando al descubierto otras mordeduras. Sacó un frasco de yodo de un cajón—. Esto te va a picar mucho, Enrique; pero, si no lo hacemos, las heridas se te van a infectar.

—¿Hay alguna señal de rabia? —preguntó Enrique con voz trémula.

—Eso no se puede saber —contestó ella en un susurro—. ¿Alguno de los perros se comportaba de una manera extraña, se tambaleaba o parpadeaba?

—Uno se tambaleaba, el pastor alemán —contestó Enrique con inquietud—. ¿Verdad, señor?

Sofía miró a Harry con semblante preocupado.

—Es que yo le había arrojado una piedra cuando antes me había querido atacar a mí. Por eso se tambaleaba. Ninguno de los perros parecía enfermo.

—Menos mal —dijo Sofía.

—Esos perros son un peligro —dijo Harry—. Habría que sacrificarlos.

—Sería un milagro que el Gobierno hiciera algo por nosotros. —Sofía siguió lavándole la pierna a su hermano. Harry observaba con asombro su habilidad y su fría profesionalidad.

—Sofía iba para médico —graznó la anciana desde la cama.

Harry se volvió para mirarla.

—¿De veras? —preguntó con fingido interés.

Sofía no levantó la vista.

—La guerra acabó con mis estudios. —Empezó a cortar un trozo de tela en tiras.

—¿No convendría que a su hermano lo viera un médico?

—No podemos permitirnos ese gasto —contestó secamente—. Procuraré mantener las heridas limpias.

Harry vaciló.

—Yo lo podría pagar. A fin de cuentas, lo he rescatado y tendría que encargarme de él hasta el final.

La chica lo miró.

—Hay otra cosa que usted podría hacer por nosotros, señor, algo que no le costaría dinero.

—Cualquier cosa que yo pueda hacer...

—No diga nada. Mi hermano me ha dicho en la escalera que usted ya llevaba algún tiempo sabiendo que él lo seguía. Sólo lo hacía porque necesitamos el dinero.

Harry miró a Enrique; allí sentado con sus improvisados vendajes parecía un muchacho muy cansado y asustado.

—El jefe del bloque, el representante de la Falange responsable de este edificio, sabía que lo estábamos pasando muy mal y dijo que le podría conseguir un trabajo a Enrique. No nos hizo mucha gracia cuando nos enteramos de lo que era, pero necesitamos el dinero.

—Lo sé —dijo Harry—. Ya me lo ha dicho su hermano.

La chica entornó los párpados.

—¿O sea que usted le preguntó a qué se dedicaba?

—¿Acaso usted no lo hubiera hecho?

La chica frunció los labios.

—Quizá. —No le quitaba los ojos de encima. Estaba muy seria, pero su expresión no era de súplica; Harry intuyó que no era una persona capaz de suplicar nada.

—Menos mal que Ramón no estaba abajo —dijo Enrique.

—Sí, eso nos da una oportunidad. Podemos decir que Enrique fue atacado por unos perros, pero no que usted estaba presente; incluso puede que le paguen hasta que se ponga mejor.

—Y, cuando ya esté mejor, usted no tendrá que preocuparse de que alguien lo siga, señor, porque sabrá que soy yo —añadió Enrique—. Diré que sólo pasea por las calles para tomar el aire; cosa que, de hecho, es lo único que le he visto hacer.

Harry se echó a reír y meneó la cabeza. Enrique también se rió muy nervioso. Sofía frunció el entrecejo.

—Lo siento mucho —dijo Harry—. Lo siento de veras, pero es que todo ha sido muy extraño.

—Éste es el mundo en el que vivimos constantemente —replicó la chica con aspereza.

—Pero usted sabe que yo no he provocado la situación —dijo Harry—. De acuerdo, no diré nada.

—Gracias. —Sofía lanzó un suspiro de alivio. Sacó una cajetilla barata de cigarrillos y le pasó uno a Enrique antes de ofrecerle la cajetilla a Harry.

—No, gracias, no fumo.

Enrique dio una larga calada. Se oyó un sonoro ronquido desde la cama; la anciana se había quedado dormida.

—¿Cómo se encuentra? —preguntó Harry.

La chica miró tiernamente a su madre.

—Se pasa todo el rato durmiendo. Sufrió un ataque cuando papá murió combatiendo con los milicianos.

Harry asintió con la cabeza.

—¿Y Paquito es su hermanito?

—No. Vivía en el piso de enfrente con sus padres. —La chica miró al niño sin pestañear—. Eran activistas sindicales. Un día del año pasado, al volver a casa, vi la puerta del piso abierta y sangre por las paredes. Se habían llevado a sus padres y a él lo habían dejado. Lo acogimos en casa para que no lo llevaran a las monjas.

—Desde entonces, no anda muy bien de la cabeza —añadió Enrique.

—Lo siento.

—Sofía trabaja en una vaquería —prosiguió diciendo Enrique—. Pero no es suficiente para mantenernos a los cuatro, señor, por eso acepté este trabajo.

Harry respiró hondo.

—No diré nada. Lo prometo. Puede estar tranquilo.

—Pero, por favor, señor —añadió Enrique, en un intento de hacerse el gracioso—. No me vuelva a llevar a aquella plaza.

Harry sonrió.

—No lo haré.

Experimentaba una extraña sensación de parentesco con Enrique; otro como él, obligado por las circunstancias a trabajar a regañadientes como espía.

—Es un sitio un poco raro para que un diplomático vaya a pasear por aquel lugar —terció Sofía, mirándolo con perspicacia.

—Es que allí vivía una familia que yo conocía. Hace años, antes de la Guerra Civil. Vivían en la plaza donde ahora están los perros. Su casa fue bombardeada. —Harry suspiró—. No sé qué habrá sido de ellos.

—Allí ya no queda nadie —dijo Sofía. Miró a Harry con curiosidad—. ¿O sea que usted conocía España antes de... todo esto?

—Sí.

Ella asintió con la cabeza, pero no dijo más. Harry se levantó.

—No diré nada de Enrique. Y, por favor, permítanme que pague la atención de un médico.

Sofía apagó el pitillo.

—No, gracias, ya ha hecho usted suficiente.

—Se lo ruego. Envíeme la cuenta. —Sacó un trozo de papel, anotó su dirección y se la entregó. Ella se levantó y la cogió. Entonces Harry cayó en la cuenta de que Enrique ya sabía dónde vivía.

—Ya nos veremos —dijo Sofía en tono evasivo—. Gracias, señor... Brett, así es como se dice, ¿verdad? —añadió, acentuando la erre.

—Sí.

—Brett. —La chica asintió con la cabeza, mirándolo con semblante muy serio—. Yo me llamo Sofía —añadió, tendiéndole una mano cálida y delicada muy bien proporcionada—. Estamos en deuda con usted, señor. Adiós.

Era una despedida. Para su sorpresa, Harry se dio cuenta de que no deseaba marcharse. Le apetecía quedarse y averiguar algo más acerca de sus vidas. Pero se levantó y recogió su sombrero.

—Adiós.

Abandonó el apartamento y bajó por la escalera a oscuras hasta la calle. Mientras regresaba a la Puerta de Toledo, advirtió que le temblaban un poco las piernas y que le volvían a zumbar los oídos. Volvieron a su mente la plaza en ruinas y los perros. ¿Habrían muerto todos los miembros de la familia Mera?, se preguntó. ¿Como Bernie?

16

Harry había conocido a Barbara a través de los padres de Bernie. Había pasado la Pascua de 1937 con su tía y su tío. Entonces se encontraba en el primer año de su beca y, desde que se fuera a Cambridge cuatro años atrás, apenas los había visto; curiosamente, este detalle hacía que ellos lo echaran mucho de menos, por lo que, en las pocas visitas que él les hacía, lo recibían con inmenso cariño, ansiosos de escuchar sus noticias.

Una tarde de finales de abril sonó el teléfono en el recibidor de la vieja y espaciosa casa. Tío James entró en el salón donde Harry leía el *Telegraph*. Parecía preocupado.

—Era la madre de tu amigo Bernie Piper —dijo—. El chico con quien estuviste en España.

Harry llevaba cinco años sin saber nada de Bernie.

—¿Ha ocurrido algo?

—Costaba entenderla, se le trababa la lengua; no creo que tenga mucha costumbre de hablar por teléfono. Al parecer, el chico se fue a España a combatir en el bando de los rojos —añadió tío James, haciendo una mueca de desagrado—. Ha recibido una carta en la que se les comunica que su hijo ha desaparecido en acto de servicio. Pregunta si tú los podrías ayudar. A mí todo eso me parece un lío. En realidad, le he dicho que no estabas en casa.

Harry experimentó un estremecimiento en la boca del estómago. Recordaba a la madre de Bernie, una mujer nerviosa con pinta de pajarillo. Bernie lo había llevado a verla en Londres poco antes de que ambos se fueran a España en 1931; quería que Harry la convenciera de que ambos estarían seguros. La mujer había creído en sus palabras, que no en las de su hijo; puede que representara para ella la respetable solidez de Rookwood que Bernie había rechazado.

—No tienen teléfono. Pregunta si podrías ir a verla. Menuda cara. —Tío James hizo una pausa—. Pero, bueno, la pobre mujer debe de estar desesperada.

Harry subió al tren con destino a Londres a la mañana siguiente. Recordó el camino a la pequeña tienda de ultramarinos en la Isla de los Perros, entre las callejuelas por las que deambulaban harapientos hombres sin empleo. La tienda ofrecía el aspecto de siempre: verduras en cajas abiertas en el suelo, artículos baratos enlatados en los estantes. El padre de Bernie permanecía sentado detrás del mostrador. Era tan alto y fuerte como Bernie y debía de haber sido muy guapo en sus tiempos, pero ahora estaba pálido y encorvado y su mirada era triste y apagada.

—Eres tú —le dijo a Harry—. Hola. Madre está allí dentro. —Señaló con la cabeza una cristalera que había detrás del mostrador. No siguió a Harry al interior de la vivienda.

Edna Piper permanecía sentada junto a la mesa del saloncito. Su rostro chupado bajo el desgreñado cabello se iluminó al ver entrar a Harry. Se levantó y estrechó su mano en un huesudo apretón.

—Arry, Arry, ¿cómo estás?

—Muy bien, gracias, señora Piper.

—Me dio mucha pena que Bernie perdiera el contacto contigo y malgastara el tiempo con aquella gente de Chelsea... —La señora Piper dejó la frase sin terminar—. ¿Sabías que se había ido a combatir a España?

—No. Creo que llevo años sin saber nada de Bernie. Perdimos el contacto.

La mujer suspiró.

—Es como si jamás hubiera ido al colegio, dejando aparte su manera de hablar. Siéntate, por favor. ¿Te apetece una taza de té?

—No. No, gracias. ¿Qué... qué ha ocurrido? Me temo que mi tío no me lo supo explicar muy bien.

—Hace un mes recibimos una carta de la embajada británica. Decía que había habido una batalla en febrero y que Bernie había desaparecido en acto de servicio. Era una carta tan corta y tan fría. —Se le llenaron los ojos de lágrimas—. Su padre dice que eso significa que ha muerto, pero que no encontraron su cuerpo.

Harry estaba sentado frente a la señora Piper. Encima de la mesa había un sobre con un vistoso sello español. La señora Piper lo tomó y empezó a darle vueltas en las manos.

—Bernie entró un día del pasado mes de octubre y dijo que se iba a luchar contra los fascistas. Me miró con aire desafiante porque sabía que yo iba a protestar. Pero el más afectado fue su padre. Aunque a Bernie ni se le ocurrió pensarlo, yo vi que se hundía como si se hubiera quedado sin aire cuando nos lo dijo. Esto acabará con él. —Miró a Harry con semblante desolado—. A veces los hijos crucifican a sus padres, ¿sabes?

—Lo siento.

—Tú los perdiste a los dos, ¿verdad?

—Sí.

—Pete no lo podrá resistir, está seguro de que Bernie ha muerto. —Sostuvo en alto la carta—. ¿Le quieres echar un vistazo? Es de una chica inglesa a la que Bernie conoció allá abajo.

Harry extrajo la carta del sobre y la leyó. Estaba fechada tres semanas atrás.

Apreciados señor y señora Piper.

Ustedes no me conocen, pero Bernie y yo estábamos muy unidos y por eso quería escribirles. Sé que la embajada les ha escrito diciendo que Bernie ha desaparecido y ha sido dado por muerto. Yo aquí trabajo en la Cruz Roja y quería que ustedes supieran que trabajo duro para tratar de averiguar algo más, si cabe la posibilidad de que todavía esté vivo. Aquí es muy difícil obtener información, pero yo lo seguiré intentando. Bernie siempre fue una persona maravillosa.

Sinceramente suya,

BARBARA CLARE

—No sé qué quiere decir —comentó la señora Piper—. Habla de que, a lo mejor, está vivo, y después de que Bernie siempre fue una persona maravillosa, como si hubiera muerto.

—Es como si esperara contra toda esperanza —dijo Harry. Le pareció que el corazón se le caía a los pies; por primera vez, pareció darse cuenta de que Bernie había desaparecido. Volvió a dejar la carta.

—Bernie nos había escrito por Navidad hablándonos de ella. Decía que había conocido a una chica inglesa allá abajo. Debe de estar destrozada. No quiero ni imaginármela ahí sola.

—¿Han contestado ustedes a su carta?

—Al momento, pero no ha habido respuesta. —La mujer lanzó un profundo suspiro—. No creo que las cartas lleguen siempre a su destino. Estaba pensando... tú hablas español, ¿verdad? ¿Y conoces el país?

—No he estado en España desde el treinta y uno —contestó Harry en tono vacilante.

—¿Tú de qué bando estás? —preguntó ella de repente.

Harry meneó la cabeza.

—De ninguno. Creo que todo eso es una tragedia.

—Han estado aquí los del Comité de Ayuda a las familias de los miembros del Batallón Británico de las Brigadas Internacionales; pero yo no quiero dinero, sólo quiero a Bernie. —La señora Piper lo miró a los ojos—. ¿Tú podrías ir allí para localizar a esta chica y averiguar lo que ha ocurrido? —La mujer se inclinó hacia delante y tomó una mano de Harry entre las suyas—. Es mucho pedir, pero los dos erais muy buenos amigos. Si pudieras averiguarlo con certeza, averiguar si hay alguna esperanza...

Dos días después de su visita a la señora Piper, Harry subió al tren con destino a Madrid. Había conseguido reservar habitación en un hotel. El agente de viajes le había dicho que estaría lleno de periodistas; eran los únicos que viajaban a España en aquellos momentos.

A través de la ventanilla del tren Harry veía letreros por todas partes que proclamaban la guerra de los «trabajadores». Era una tibia y serena primavera castellana, pero la gente se mostraba amargada y como a la defensiva. Cuando llegó a Madrid, se sorprendió de lo distinto que estaba todo en comparación con lo que él había visto durante su primera visita. Carteles de gran tamaño, soldados y milicianos por todas partes, gente con semblante nervioso y preocupado pese a la propaganda que tronaba a través de los altavoces instalados en el centro. En los periódicos no se hablaba de otra cosa más que del intento de golpe en Barcelona por parte de unos traidores «trotskistas-fascistas».

Se registró en el hotel, muy cerca de la Castellana. Tenía la dirección de Barbara, pero primero quería orientarse un poco. Aquella tarde fue a dar un paseo y atravesó el barrio de La Latina para dirigirse a Carabanchel. Recordó haber bajado por allí con Bernie en 1931 para ir a ver a los Mera, el calor de aquel verano y lo despreocupados y alegres que ambos se sentían entonces.

Cuanto más al sur se desplazaba, menos gente había. Muchas calles estaban cerradas por barricadas, unas toscas estructuras de adoquines con un pequeño hueco para los peatones; las calles, privadas de sus adoquines, eran unos barrizales. Se oía el ruido de la artillería y, de vez en cuando, silbidos y detonaciones a lo lejos. Harry dio media vuelta. Se preguntó, con una sensación de mareo en el estómago, si los Mera estarían todavía en Carabanchel.

Aquella noche en su hotel conoció a un periodista, un individuo cínico y culto llamado Phillips. Le preguntó qué había ocurrido en Barcelona.

—Los rusos están imponiendo su control. —Soltó una carcajada—. Trotskistas una mierda. No hay ninguno.

—¿O sea que es cierto? ¿Los rusos se han apoderado de la República?

—Vaya si es cierto. Ahora lo gobiernan todo; tienen sus propias cámaras de tortura en un sótano de la Puerta del Sol. Guardan un as en la manga, ¿comprende? En caso de que el Gobierno los desafíe, Stalin podrá decir: «Muy bien, pues ahora interrumpimos los envíos de armas.» Hasta ha conseguido que envíen el oro del Banco de España a Moscú. Y tardarán mucho en volver a verlo.

Harry meneó la cabeza.

—Me alegro de que nosotros seamos partidarios de la no intervención.

Phillips soltó otra carcajada.

—No intervención, un cuerno. Si Baldwin hubiera permitido que los franceses entregaran armas a la República el año pasado, no habrían querido a los rusos ni regalados. La culpa es nuestra. Al final, la República perderá; los alemanes y los italianos lo están inundando todo de armas y de hombres.

—Y entonces, ¿qué ocurrirá?

Phillips saludó brazo en alto a la romana.

—*Sieg heil*, amigo mío. Otra potencia fascista. Bueno, será mejor que me vaya a la cama. Mañana tengo que elaborar un informe desde la Casa de Campo, mala suerte. Ojalá me hubiera traído mi sombrero de hojalata.

Al día siguiente, Harry se presentó en el cuartel general de la Cruz Roja y preguntó por la señorita Clare. Lo acompañaron a un despacho donde un suizo de aire agobiado permanecía sentado detrás de una mesa de caballete llena de papeles. Ambos se hablaron en francés. El funcionario lo miró con la cara muy seria.

—¿Conoce personalmente a la señorita Clare?

—No, yo conocía a su amigo. Sus padres me han pedido que me ponga en contacto con ella.

—Está muy afectada. La hemos dado de baja por enfermedad, pero no sabemos si sería mejor que volviera a Inglaterra.

—Comprendo.

—Una lástima, ha sido un pilar de fortaleza en esta oficina. Pero no se irá, no piensa hacerlo hasta que averigüe con toda certeza qué le ha ocurrido a su novio, dice. Sin embargo, puede que jamás lo sepa con certeza. —El hombre hizo una pausa—. Siento haber recibido una queja de las autoridades. Clare se está poniendo pesada. Y nosotros necesitamos mantener buenas relaciones con las autoridades. Si usted pudiera ayudarla a ver las cosas con cierta perspectiva...

—Haré todo lo que pueda. —Harry suspiró—. Aunque aquí parece que no hay demasiada perspectiva, que digamos.

—En efecto. Más bien poca.

La dirección correspondía a un bloque de apartamentos. Harry llamó a la puerta y oyó unas pisadas como de alguien que arrastrara los pies. Se preguntó si se habría equivocado de apartamento, parecían las pisadas de una anciana; pero quien le abrió la puerta fue una joven de estatura elevada, desgreñado cabello pelirrojo y rostro hinchado y congestionado.

—¿Sí? —preguntó sin interés.

—¿La señorita Clare? Usted no me conoce. Me llamo Brett, Harry Brett. —Ella lo miró sin comprender—. Soy un amigo de Bernie.

Al oír el nombre, la joven cobró vida.

—¿Hay alguna noticia? —preguntó con ansia—. ¿Tiene usted alguna noticia?

—Me temo que no. Los padres de Bernie recibieron su carta y me han pedido que venga a ver qué se puede hacer.

—Ah. —La joven volvió a hundirse de inmediato, pero sostuvo la puerta abierta—. Pase.

El apartamento estaba revuelto y desordenado y, en el aire, se respiraba un fuerte olor a humo de tabaco. Ella frunció el entrecejo con expresión perpleja.

—Conozco su nombre de algún sitio.

—Rookwood. Estuve allí con Bernie.

Ella sonrió con semblante repentinamente cordial.

—Claro. Harry. Bernie hablaba de usted.

—¿De veras?

—Decía que usted era su mejor amigo en el colegio. —Barbara hizo una pausa—. Aunque él aborrecía aquel colegio.

—¿Todavía?

Barbara lanzó un suspiro.

—Todo estaba relacionado con sus ideas políticas. Y ahora parece ser que sus malditas ideas políticas han acabado con él. Perdone, mis modales son horribles. —Retiró unas prendas de ropa de un sillón—. Siéntese. ¿Le apetece un café? Me temo que es bastante malo.

—Gracias, me encantará.

Le preparó un café y se sentó frente a él. Una vez más, la vida parecía haber huido de ella. Se hundió en el sillón, fumando unos fuertes cigarrillos españoles.

—¿Ha ido a la Cruz Roja? —preguntó.

—Sí. Me dijeron que estaba usted de baja por enfermedad.

—Ahora ya han pasado casi dos meses. —Barbara meneó la cabeza—. Quieren que regrese a Inglaterra, dicen que seguramente Bernie ha muerto. Yo también lo creía al principio, pero ahora no estoy segura, no puedo estar segura hasta que alguien me diga dónde está el cuerpo.

—¿Ha hecho algún progreso?

—No. Se están cansando de mí, me han dicho que no vuelva. Incluso se han quejado al viejo Doumergue. —Barbara encendió otro cigarrillo—. Había un comisario a quien Bernie conocía de los combates en la Casa de Campo, un comunista que trabajaba en el cuartel general del ejército. El capitán Duro. Era muy amable; trataba de averiguar todo lo que podía, pero se fue de repente la semana pasada. Lo trasladaron o algo por el estilo. Ha habido muchos cambios últimamente. Pregunté si podía ir allí, a las líneas del frente; pero, naturalmente, me dijeron que no.

—Quizá sería mejor regresar a casa.

—No tengo nada por lo que regresar a casa. —Su mirada se perdió como si la hubiera dirigido hacia dentro; pareció olvidarse de la presencia de Harry. Éste se compadeció inmensamente de ella.

—Venga a comer a mi hotel —le dijo.

Ella esbozó una rápida y triste sonrisa y asintió con la cabeza.

Se pasó con ella buena parte de los dos días siguientes. Barbara quería saberlo todo acerca de Bernie, y eso parecía animarla un poco a ratos; aunque constantemente volvía a hundirse en aquella profunda y retraída tristeza de ojos vidriosos. Vestía faldas viejas y blusas sin planchar y no llevaba maquillaje; su aspecto la traía sin cuidado.

Al segundo día Harry acudió a la embajada británica, pero allí le dijeron lo que todo el mundo decía «desaparecido y dado por muerto», lo cual significaba que no habían encontrado ningún cuerpo identificable. Regresó al apartamento de Barbara sin el menor deseo de contarle lo que le habían dicho. Le había prometido visitar el cuartel general del ejército al día siguiente, quizás allí tuvieran más interés por un hombre. Después, ya no sabía qué otra cosa podría hacer. Estaba seguro de que Bernie había muerto.

Llamó al timbre y volvió a escuchar las cansinas pisadas. Barbara abrió la puerta y se apoyó en ella, mirándolo fijamente. Estaba bebida.

—Pasa —le dijo.

Había una botella de vino semivacía encima de la mesa y otra en la papelera. Barbara se dejó caer en una silla junto a la mesa.

—Toma una copa —dijo—. Bebe conmigo, Harry.

Éste dejó que le escanciara una copa. Barbara levantó la suya.

—Por la maldita revolución.

—La maldita revolución.

Le explicó lo que le habían dicho en la embajada. Barbara posó su copa y su rostro volvió a adquirir la ensimismada expresión de costumbre.

—Siempre estaba tan lleno de vida. Era tan divertido. Tan guapo. —Levantó los ojos—. Me decía que algunos chicos de la escuela se enamoraban locamente de él. Y eso a él no le gustaba.

—No. No, no le gustaba.

—¿Tú te enamoraste de él?

—No. —Harry sonrió tristemente. Recordó la noche en que Bernie se había ido de putas—. Pero a veces le envidiaba la guapura.

—¿Tienes alguna novia allá en Inglaterra?

—Sí. —Harry vaciló—. Una buena chica. —Llevaba unos cuantos meses saliendo con Laura; se sorprendió al darse cuenta de que apenas había pensado en ella desde su llegada a Madrid.

—Dicen que siempre hay alguien para todo el mundo, y es cierto; pero no te dicen que, a veces, te lo vuelven a arrebatar. Se esfuma. Desaparece. —Barbara se comprimió la frente con el puño y rompió a llorar en ásperos y desgarradores sollozos—. Me estoy engañando, ¿verdad? Se ha ido.

—Me temo que eso parece —contestó serenamente Harry.

—Pero mañana irás al cuartel general del ejército por mí, ¿verdad? Pregunta a ver si está el capitán Duro. Y si no tienen más noticias, yo... me daré por vencida. Tendré que aceptarlo.

—Lo haré. Te lo prometo.

Barbara meneó la cabeza.

—Normalmente no me pongo en este plan. Te he escandalizado, ¿verdad?

Harry se inclinó sobre la mesa y tomó su mano.

—Lo siento —le dijo con dulzura—. Lo siento con toda mi alma.

Barbara le apretó la mano, apoyó la cabeza en ella y lloró con desconsuelo.

El soldado de la entrada del cuartel general del ejército no quería franquearle el paso, pero Harry le explicó lo que quería en español y eso facilitó las cosas. Dentro, le dijo a un sargento que había acudido allí para informarse acerca de un soldado desaparecido en el Jarama. Dio el nombre de Bernie y el del comunista que había ayudado a Barbara. El sargento le dijo que lo consultaría con un oficial y lo acompañó a un pequeño despacho sin ventana. Harry se sentó a esperar junto a una mesa. Contempló un retrato de Stalin que colgaba en la pared, con los ojillos entornados, grandes bigotes y una sonrisa que parecía una mueca. Había también un mapa de España en el que unas líneas trazadas a lápiz señalaban las zonas cada vez más reducidas que conservaba la República.

Entró un español con uniforme de capitán, sujetando en la mano una carpeta. Era bajito y moreno, y su rostro cansado ostentaba una barba de dos días. Lo acompañaba otro capitán alto y fuerte y con la cara muy pálida. Ambos se sentaron frente a él. El español inclinó brevemente la cabeza a modo de saludo.

—Tengo entendido que está usted haciendo indagaciones acerca de un tal capitán Duro.

—No, no; estoy tratando de averiguar el paradero de un voluntario inglés, Bernie Piper. Su novia ha estado aquí y dice que el capitán Duro la ha estado ayudando mucho.

—¿Me permite su pasaporte, si es tan amable?

Harry se lo entregó. El español lo abrió, lo estudió a contraluz. Después soltó una especie de gruñido y lo guardó en la carpeta.

—¿Me lo podría devolver, por favor? —dijo Harry—. Lo necesito. —El capitán cruzó los brazos encima de la carpeta y se volvió hacia su compañero. El otro inclinó la cabeza.

—Habla usted muy bien el español, señor. —Su acento era extranjero, gutural.

—Es mi especialidad... soy lector... en Cambridge.

—¿Quién lo ha enviado aquí?

Harry frunció el entrecejo.

—Los padres del soldado Piper.

—Pero su mujer ya ha estado aquí. Consta en las fichas que desapareció y se le dio por muerto. Eso significa que murió, pero no se encontró el cuerpo. Después esta mujer de la Cruz Roja ha estado viniendo aquí día tras día, y ahora usted. Y hablan siempre del capitán Duro.

—Mire, nosotros queremos saber, eso es todo. —Ahora Harry ya empezaba a enfadarse—. El soldado Piper vino a combatir por la República, ¿no le parece que es lo menos que se nos debe?

—¿Usted es partidario de los nacionales, señor?

—No, no lo soy. Soy inglés, somos neutrales. —Harry se estaba empezando a poner nervioso. Observó que ambos oficiales iban armados con revólveres. El oficial extranjero le arrebató bruscamente la carpeta a su compañero.

—La señorita Barbara Clare, que ha estado aquí muchas veces, veo que pidió permiso para visitar el campo de batalla. Es una zona de acceso limitado. Y ella, que trabaja en la Cruz Roja, debería saberlo. Allí han declinado cualquier responsabilidad por sus investigaciones.

—Ella no venía en nombre de la Cruz Roja. Verá, Bernie Piper era su... bueno, su amante.

—Y usted, ¿qué relación tiene con él?

—Fuimos compañeros de escuela.

El capitán soltó una carcajada, un áspero sonido desde lo más profundo de su garganta.

—¿Y a eso lo llama usted una relación?

—Bueno, mire —dijo Harry—, yo he venido aquí de buena fe para interesarme por un soldado desaparecido. Pero, si ustedes no me van a ayudar, quizá será mejor que me vaya —añadió, haciendo ademán de levantarse.

—Siéntese. —El oficial extranjero se levantó y le propinó un fuerte empujón en el pecho. Harry perdió el equilibrio y cayó de bruces al suelo, aterrizando dolorosamente sobre la pelvis. El oficial lo miró fríamente cuando se levantó—. Siéntese en aquella silla.

A Harry se le aceleraron los latidos del corazón. Recordó lo que el periodista le había dicho acerca de las cámaras de tortura de la Puerta del Sol. El oficial español contempló la escena con semblante preocupado. Se inclinó y susurró algo al oído a su compañero. Éste meneó la cabeza con impaciencia, sacó una cajetilla de cigarrillos y se encendió uno. Harry miró la cajetilla; el texto estaba escrito con caracteres cirílicos.

El oficial sonrió.

—Pues sí, soy ruso. Ayudamos a nuestros camaradas españoles en asuntos de seguridad. Necesitan ayuda; hay espías fascistas y trotskistas por todas partes. Haciendo preguntas. Inventándose mentiras.

Harry procuró que no le temblara la voz.

—Yo he venido aquí para interesarme por un amigo...

—El soldado Piper no vino aquí a través de los procedimientos establecidos de las Brigadas Internacionales. Se presentó sin más en Madrid el pasado mes de noviembre. Eso no es normal.

—Yo no sé nada de eso. Llevo años sin ver a Bernie.

—¿Y, sin embargo, ahora viene aquí a preguntar por él?

—Sus padres me lo han pedido.

El ruso se inclinó hacia delante.

—¿Y quién le ha dicho a usted que preguntara por el capitán Duro?

Harry respiró hondo. Se encontraba en un sótano de una ciudad extranjera bajo la ley marcial. No podría salir de allí, a no ser que lo autorizaran a hacerlo.

—La señorita Clare. Dice que el capitán Duro la atendió la primera vez que ella vino aquí para hacer indagaciones. Ya se lo he dicho, conoció a Bernie en la Casa de Campo. El capitán intentó averiguar algo más. Pero después dijeron que lo habían trasladado. Y ya no hubo nadie más que pudiera ayudarla.

—Ahora nos empezamos a aclarar. En realidad, el capitán Duro no fue trasladado. Fue detenido por saboteador. Le oyeron decir que habríamos tenido que negociar con los rebeldes de Barcelona. —El oficial se reclinó contra el respaldo de su asiento—. Negociar con los saboteadores trotskistas-fascistas.

—Mire, la verdad es que yo no sé nada de todo eso. Sólo voy a permanecer tres días en el país.

—La ficha del soldado Piper dice que, tras resultar herido en los combates de la Casa de Campo, se ofreció para atender a los voluntarios que llegaban desde Inglaterra. Pero se consideró que era un burgués, un sentimental que probablemente no aprobaría algunas de las duras medidas que aquí se imponen. Se consideró que se le debería permitir recuperarse para enviarlo posteriormente al frente. Tenía madera de soldado de a pie, no era la clase de hombre de acero como la que aquí necesitamos ahora.

Harry miró al ruso.

—Esta gente se deja seducir fácilmente por el trotskismo-fascismo. —El ruso se volvió hacia su compañero. El español se inclinó hacia él; Harry captó las palabras «Cruz Roja». El ruso frunció el entrecejo—. Eso ya lo discutiremos fuera. —Se volvió para mirar a Harry—. Usted, señor Brett, se queda aquí.

Harry notó que un escalofrío le recorría toda la espalda y sintió frío a pesar del bochorno que reinaba en la estancia.

Los oficiales se retiraron. Harry oyó un murmullo de voces. Pensó con inquietud en lo que iba a ocurrir en caso de que se lo llevaran a alguna parte. Barbara lo esperaba en el apartamento. Parecía más calmada, después del estallido de la víspera; esperaba que no le hubiera vuelto a dar a la botella. Saldría en su busca en caso de que él no regresara. Le sudaban las manos. Se dijo a sí mismo que tenía que calmarse.

Las voces del pasillo sonaban más fuerte. Oyó los gritos del ruso.

—¿Quién manda aquí?

Unas pisadas se alejaron y se hizo el silencio, un espeso silencio que casi se podía tocar con las manos. Recordó a los chicos en la escuela, cuando hablaban excitados acerca de las distintas clases de tortura. Lo que hacían el potro, las empulgueras, las nuevas torturas con descargas eléctricas.

Se abrió la puerta y entró el oficial español, solo y con la cara muy seria. Le entregó a Harry su pasaporte.

—Deles las gracias a sus contactos de la Cruz Roja —dijo fríamente—. Dé gracias porque nosotros necesitamos sus medicinas. Puede irse. Lárguese ahora mismo, antes de que el otro cambie de idea. —Miró a Harry a los ojos—. Dispone de veinticuatro horas para abandonar España.

De regreso en el apartamento, Harry le contó a Barbara lo ocurrido. Tenía que abandonar España de inmediato, y convendría que ella también lo hiciera; jamás debería regresar al cuartel general del ejército. Pensó que, a lo mejor, ella no le creería, pero le creyó.

—Sabemos lo que ocurre —dijo en voz baja—. En la Cruz Roja, quiero decir. Las detenciones y las desapariciones. —Meneó la cabeza—. Simplemente, lo había olvidado. Sólo pensaba en averiguar algo acerca de Bernie. He sido muy egoísta. Siento que hayas tenido que pasar por todo esto.

—Yo me ofrecí voluntariamente a hacerlo. Puede que los dos hayamos sido unos ingenuos.

—Pues yo tengo menos excusa, llevo nueve meses aquí.

—Barbara, tendrías que regresar a Inglaterra.

—No. —Barbara se levantó, animada por una nueva determinación—. Regresaré al trabajo, le contaré a Doumergue lo ocurrido. Veré si puedo conseguir un traslado.

—¿Estás segura de que lo podrás soportar?

—Me encontraré mejor trabajando, eso me ayudará a salir adelante.

Harry hizo el equipaje y después regresó al apartamento de Barbara para cenar. A ninguno de los dos le apetecía cenar fuera.

—Necesitaba un poco de esperanza —dijo ella—. No podía aceptar que Bernie hubiera muerto.

—¿Qué vas a hacer ahora?

Barbara esbozó una valerosa sonrisa.

—Convenceré a Doumergue de que me traslade a otro sitio. Voy a ayudar a organizar los suministros médicos en Burgos.

—¿En la zona nacional?

—Sí. —Soltó una sonrisa incierta—. Veré el otro lado de la historia. En Burgos no hay combates, queda muy por detrás del frente.

—¿Y lo podrás soportar? ¿Eso de trabajar con la gente contra la cual luchaba Bernie?

—Bueno, los nacionales y los comunistas no son mejores los unos que los otros. Lo sé muy bien, yo sólo quiero hacer mi trabajo, ayudar a la gente que se ha quedado atrapada en medio. Así reviente toda la maldita política. Ya todo me da igual.

Harry la miró, preguntándose si tendría fuerzas para cumplir su propósito.

—¿Sientes la presencia de Bernie? —preguntó ella de repente—. ¿Aquí, en el apartamento?

—No. —Harry esbozó una azorada sonrisa—. Yo no siento nada de todo eso.

—A veces experimento una especie de calor, como si él estuviera aquí. Supongo que eso demuestra que está muerto.

—Pase lo que pase, conservas unos cuantos recuerdos muy buenos. Y eso será un consuelo con el tiempo.

—Supongo. ¿Y tú?

Harry la miró sonriendo.

—Vuelta a casa, a las costumbres de siempre.

—Parece una buena vida. ¿Eres feliz?

—Me conformo, supongo. Quizás eso es lo máximo que podemos esperar.

—Yo siempre quise más. —Por un instante, los ojos de Barbara se perdieron en la distancia—. Bueno, tendré que hacer un esfuerzo para trabajar en Burgos. —Sonrió—. ¿Me escribirás?

—Sí, claro.

—Háblame de Cambridge, mientras yo esté hasta la coronilla de formularios. —Volvió a esbozar su triste y fugaz sonrisita de costumbre.

17

La casa del general Maestre era una mansión del siglo XVIII situada en una zona residencial al norte de la ciudad. El general envió un automóvil para recoger a Harry y Tolhurst, un impresionante Lincoln americano; circulaban a gran velocidad por la Castellana, donde ya se habían retirado las banderas nazis. Himmler se había ido, pero la víspera los periódicos habían publicado una noticia aún más sensacional. Hitler y Franco se habían reunido en la ciudad de Hendaya, en la frontera con Francia, para una ronda de conversaciones de seis horas de duración. La prensa vaticinaba que España no tardaría en entrar en guerra.

—En realidad, la reunión no fue bien, o eso es lo que dice Sam —les había dicho Hillgarth a Harry y Tolhurst aquella tarde.

Los había convocado para una reunión en el despacho de Tolhurst. Vestido aquel día de paisano, mostraba una expresión de profundo cansancio. Permanecía sentado con las piernas cruzadas y no paraba de mover el pie libre.

—El embajador tiene una fuente en el entorno de Franco. Dice que Franco le comunicó a Hitler que él sólo entraría en guerra en caso de que Hitler le garantizara enormes cantidades de suministros. Sabe que nosotros no permitiríamos pasar nada a través del bloqueo. Bueno, esperemos que así sea.

Tomó un ejemplar del *ABC* que descansaba sobre el estrecho escritorio de Tolhurst; el Generalísimo había sido sorprendido en el momento de bajar del tren real para saludar a Hitler, con una ancha sonrisa en los labios y un brillo de emoción en los ojos.

—Franco está que bebe los vientos por Hitler, quiere formar parte del Nuevo Orden. —Hillgarth meneó la cabeza y después miró inquisitivamente a sus dos subordinados—. Van ustedes esta noche a la fiesta, ¿verdad? Intenten averiguar a través de Maestre qué tal lo está haciendo el nuevo ministro de Comercio. El otro día Carceller pronunció un discurso profascista. Puede que Maestre no dure mucho más como subsecretario. En ese caso, habremos perdido a un amigo.

—¿Leyó usted el informe de nuestro hombre en Gerona, señor? —preguntó Tolhurst—. ¿Trenes cargados de alimentos rumbo a la frontera francesa, con las palabras «Alimentos para nuestros amigos alemanes» pintadas en los costados?

Hillgarth asintió con la cabeza. Se revolvió en su asiento, y dejó de mover el pie.

—Ha llegado el momento de que se concentre en Forsyth, Brett. Averigüe algo más acerca del maldito oro. ¿Y qué me dice de esa tal Clare, qué pinta en todo eso?

—No creo que Barbara sepa nada.

Hillgarth lo miró con perspicacia.

—Bueno, averígüelo —dijo en tono perentorio—. Usted la conoce.

—No muy bien. Pero el lunes comeremos juntos. —La había llamado la víspera; Barbara había aceptado la invitación tras dudar un instante. Harry se sentía culpable pero, al mismo tiempo, lleno de curiosidad acerca de su relación con Sandy. «El hecho de ser espía despierta la curiosidad», pensó—. Creo que la mejor línea de actuación consiste en seguir indagando sobre lo que dijo Sandy a propósito de las oportunidades de negocios —añadió—. Eso me puede ayudar a formarme una idea de lo que está haciendo.

—¿Cuándo lo volverá a ver?

—Tenía previsto organizar algo cuando me reuniera con Barbara. El pie de Hillgarth volvió a moverse a sacudidas.

—Eso no puede esperar. Ya tendría que haber organizado algo cuando habló con la mujer.

—No conviene que se nos vea demasiado interesados —terció Tolhurst.

Hillgarth agitó una mano con impaciencia.

—Necesitamos esta información. —Se levantó bruscamente—. Me tengo que ir. Encárguese de ello.

—Sí, señor.

—Está preocupado —dijo Tolhurst, mientras se cerraba la puerta—. Será mejor que organices cuanto antes una reunión con Forsyth.

—De acuerdo. Pero Sandy es muy listo.

—Nosotros lo tenemos que ser más que él.

El baile tenía un tema morisco. Los dos guardias marroquíes que flanqueaban la entrada principal lucían turbantes y largas capas de color amarillo y empuñaban unas lanzas. Harry contempló sus impasibles rostros morenos al pasar por su lado, recordando la terrible fama de los moros durante la Guerra Civil. Dentro, el amplio vestíbulo estaba adornado con tapices moriscos y los hombres vestían de esmoquin. La mampara que separaba el vestíbulo del salón había sido retirada para crear una sala de enormes proporciones. La sala estaba llena de gente. Un sirviente español, pero vestido con fez y caftán, tomó sus nombres e hizo señas a un camarero del otro extremo de la sala para que les sirviera bebidas.

—¿Conoces a alguien? —preguntó Harry.

—A una o dos personas. Mira, allí está Goach. —El anciano experto en protocolo estaba de pie en un rincón, conversando animadamente con un clérigo de elevada estatura vestido con ropajes morados—. Es católico, ¿sabes? Le encantan los monseñores.

—Fíjate en el disfraz de los criados. Se deben de morir de calor.

Tolhurst se inclinó hacia él.

—Hablando de cuestiones marroquíes, mira allí abajo.

Harry siguió la dirección de su mirada. En el centro del salón, Maestre permanecía de pie en compañía de otros dos hombres vestidos como él, de uniforme. Uno era un teniente. El otro, un general como Maestre, era una figura extraordinaria. De cierta edad, delgado y con el cabello cano, conversaba con tal vehemencia que amenazaba con salpicar a sus interlocutores con el contenido de la copa que sostenía en la mano. La otra manga colgaba vacía. Su cadavérico rostro surcado por una cicatriz tenía un solo ojo, mientras que la cuenca vacía del otro aparecía cubierta con un parche de color negro. Cuando se rió, dejó al descubierto una boca casi desdentada.

—Millán Astray —dijo Tolhurst—. Es inconfundible. El fundador de la Legión. Astray es profascista y está como una cabra, pero sus viejos soldados lo adoran. Franco sirvió a sus órdenes, y lo mismo hizo Maestre. Es el jefe de los novios de la muerte.

—¿Los qué?

—Así se llaman los soldados de la Legión. Comparados con ellos, los de la Legión Extranjera francesa parecen unos catequistas. —Tolhurst se inclinó hacia delante y bajó la voz—. El capitán me contó una historia acerca de Maestre. Unas monjas de una orden religiosa dedicada al cuidado de enfermos llegaron a Marruecos durante la rebelión de las tribus del Rif. Corre el rumor de que Maestre y algunos de sus hombres las recibieron en el muelle de Melilla y les regalaron una enorme cesta de rosas... con las cabezas de dos jefes rebeldes marroquíes en el centro.

—Parece un cuento chino. —Harry volvió a mirar a Maestre. Los gestos de Millán Astray eran todavía más violentos que antes y Maestre daba la impresión de estar un poco nervioso; pero, aun así, mantenía la cabeza cortésmente inclinada hacia él para escucharle.

—Se la contó el propio Maestre al capitán Hillgarth. Al parecer, las monjas ni siquiera parpadearon. La Legión tiene cierta predilección por las cabezas, y antes solían desfilar con ellas clavadas en las puntas de las bayonetas. —Tolhurst meneó la cabeza con semblante inquisitivo—. Y las malas lenguas afirman que ahora la mitad del Gobierno está integrada por ex legionarios. Es lo único que mantiene unidos a los bandos monárquico y falangista. El pasado en común.

Millán Astray había posado su copa y estrechaba el hombro del otro compañero de Maestre sin dejar de charlar animadamente con él. Harry observó que hasta aquella mano carecía de dedos. Maestre captó la mirada de Harry y murmuró algo a Millán Astray. El anciano asintió con la cabeza y Maestre y el teniente se acercaron a Harry y Tolhurst. Por el camino, Maestre le dijo algo en voz baja a una mujer menuda y regordeta ataviada con un vestido de flamenca y largos guantes blancos, y entonces ella los siguió.

Maestre le tendió la mano a Harry con una cordial sonrisa de bienvenida en los labios.

—Ah, señor Brett. Cuánto me alegro de que haya podido venir. Y usted debe de ser el señor Tolhurst.

—Sí, señor. Gracias por invitarme.

—Siempre me alegro de poder saludar a los amigos de la embajada. Debería estar atendiendo a los invitados, pero recordaba viejos tiempos en Marruecos. Mi mujer, Elena. —Harry y Tolhurst se inclinaron ante ella—. Y mi mano derecha de entonces, el teniente Alfonso Gómez.

El otro hombre les estrechó la mano y se inclinó rígidamente. Era bajito y rechoncho, con una cara muy seria de color caoba y unos ojos de mirada penetrante.

—¿Son ustedes ingleses? —preguntó.

—Sí, de la embajada.

La señora Maestre sonrió.

—Me han dicho que estuvo usted en Eton, ¿no es cierto, señor Tolhurst?

—Un lugar excelente —dijo Maestre, asintiendo con gesto de aprobación—. Donde se educan los caballeros ingleses, ¿verdad?

—Así lo espero, señor.

—¿Y usted, señor Brett? —preguntó la señora Maestre.

—Estudié en otro colegio público, señora. Rookwood. —Observó que Gómez lo miraba como si lo estuviera evaluando.

La señora Maestre asintió con la cabeza.

—¿Y a qué se dedica su familia?

Harry se desconcertó ante el carácter directo de la pregunta.

—Pertenezco a una familia con antecedentes militares.

La mujer asintió satisfecha con la cabeza.

—Estupendo, como nosotros. ¿Y dice que es lector en Cambridge? —preguntó, estudiándolo con mirada inquisitiva.

—Sí. En tiempos de paz. Pero sólo como adjunto... no como titular.

Maestre asintió con semblante complacido.

—Cambridge. Qué bien lo pasé allí, como ya sabe el señor Brett. Fue allí donde nació mi amor por Inglaterra.

—Tiene que conocer a mi hija —dijo la señora Maestre—. Jamás ha conocido a un inglés. Sólo italianos, y no son una buena influencia.

Enarcó las cejas y se estremeció levemente.

—Sí, ustedes los jóvenes acompañen a Elena —añadió Maestre. Mientras Harry pasaba por su lado, le rozó levemente el brazo y le dijo en voz baja, mirándolo muy serio con sus perspicaces ojos castaños—. Esta noche está entre amigos. Aquí no hay alemanes ni camisas azules, a no ser por Millán Astray, que es una excepción. Hoy en día tiene poco que hacer, lo hemos invitado por cortesía.

Harry y Tolhurst siguieron a la señora Maestre, que se abría camino entre los invitados, en medio de un revuelo de faldas. Al fondo, tres muchachas permanecían de pie con expresión cohibida, sosteniendo en sus manos unas altas copas de vino de cristal. Dos de ellas lucían vestidos de flamenca; la tercera, bajita y regordeta como su madre, de piel aceitunada y rostro redondo de marcadas facciones, llevaba un vestido de noche de seda blanca. La señora Maestre dio unas palmadas y las muchachas levantaron los ojos. Harry recordó por un instante a las cantaoras flamencas que bailaban en El Toro la vez que él y Bernie habían estado allí nueve años atrás. Pero aquéllas vestían de negro.

—¡Milagros! —dijo la señora Maestre—. Tendrías que hablar con nuestros invitados. Señor Brett, señor Tolhurst, mi hija Milagros y sus amigas Dolores y Catalina. —Acto seguido, se volvió rápidamente hacia un hombre que pasaba por su lado en aquel momento—. ¡Marqués! ¡Ha venido! —Tomó al hombre del brazo y se lo llevó.

—¿Es usted de Londres? —le preguntó Milagros a Harry con una tímida sonrisa en los labios. Parecía nerviosa e incómoda.

—De muy cerca de allí. Un lugar llamado Surrey. Simon es de Londres, ¿verdad?

—¿Cómo?... Ah, sí. —Tolhurst se había puesto colorado y estaba empezando a sudar. Un mechón de cabello le caía sobre la frente y él se lo apartó de manera tan brusca que a punto estuvo de derramar el contenido de su copa.

Las amigas de Milagros intercambiaron unas miradas y se echaron a reír.

—He visto fotografías de su rey y su reina —dijo Milagros—. Y de las princesas, ¿cuántos años tienen ahora?

—La princesa Isabel tiene catorce años.

—Es muy guapa, ¿no le parece?

—Sí, sí que lo es. —Pasó un camarero y les volvió a llenar las copas. Harry miró con una sonrisa a Milagros, tratando de buscar algo que decirle—. O sea que hoy cumple usted dieciocho años.

—Sí, hoy me presentan en sociedad. —Lo dijo con un cierto tono de añoranza; por su infancia, tal vez. Miró a Harry un instante y después sonrió y pareció relajarse—. Mi padre dice que es usted traductor. ¿Lleva mucho tiempo dedicado a eso?

—No, antes era profesor de universidad.

Milagros volvió a sonreír con tristeza.

—Yo no era muy lista en el colegio. Pero ahora esa época ya pasó.

—Sí —dijo alegremente una de sus amigas—. Ahora es la época de encontrar marido. —Ambas se rieron y Milagros se ruborizó. Harry se compadeció de ella.

—Por cierto —terció Tolhurst de repente—. Su nombre, Milagros; y el suyo, Dolores. Suenan un poco raro en inglés. Nosotros a las niñas no les ponemos nombres religiosos. —Se rió, y las chicas lo miraron fríamente.

—Algunas se llaman Charity, Caridad —dijo Harry, tratando de arreglar el estropicio.

—¿Tiene calor, señor Simon? —preguntó Dolores con picardía—. ¿Quiere un pañuelo para la frente?

El rubor de Tolhurst se intensificó.

—No, no, estoy bien. Yo...

—Mira, Dolores —dijo Catalina con entusiasmo—, allí está Jorge. Vamos.

Las dos muchachas se retiraron entre risas y se acercaron a un apuesto joven vestido con uniforme de cadete. Milagros pareció avergonzarse.

—Disculpen, mis amigas no han sido muy amables.

—No se preocupe —dijo Tolhurst un tanto avergonzado—. Yo... mmm... me voy a buscar algo que comer. —Se retiró con la cabeza gacha.

Harry sonrió tristemente.

—Creo que llevaba algún tiempo sin asistir a un acontecimiento tan importante como éste.

La muchacha sacó un abanico y empezó a agitarlo frente a su cara.

—Pues yo igual, no ha habido ninguna fiesta desde que regresamos a Madrid el año pasado. Pero ahora las cosas empiezan a normalizarse. De todos modos, resulta un poco raro después de tanto tiempo.

—Pues sí. Sí, en efecto. También es mi primera fiesta desde hace bastante.

Desde Dunkerque. Harry se sentía curiosamente apartado, como si una pared de cristal se interpusiera entre él y los demás invitados a la fiesta. A través del oído malo le resultaba difícil captar las palabras en medio de la cacofonía del ruido que lo rodeaba.

Milagros lo miró con la cara muy seria. Harry volvió la cabeza para poder inclinar el oído sano hacia ella.

—No sabe cuánto espero que España se pueda mantener al margen de la guerra de Europa —dijo la chica—. ¿Usted qué cree, señor?

—Yo también lo espero.

Milagros lo volvió a examinar.

—Disculpe la pregunta, pero ¿es usted soldado? En mi familia son soldados desde hace varias generaciones. No podemos evitar darnos cuenta cuándo un hombre se siente cohibido como su amigo. En cambio, usted se mantiene firme como un soldado.

—Es usted muy inteligente. Estuve en el ejército hasta hace muy pocos meses.

—Papá estuvo en Marruecos cuando yo era pequeña. Era un lugar terrible. Me alegré de volver a casa. Pero después vino la Guerra Civil. —La muchacha sonrió, haciendo un esfuerzo por mostrarse alegre—. Y usted, señor, ¿estuvo mucho tiempo en el ejército?

—No. Sólo me incorporé cuando empezó la guerra.

—Dicen que los bombardeos de Londres son terribles.

—Sí, vivimos tiempos difíciles. —Recordó la caída de las bombas.

—Es una pena. Y eso que Londres dicen que es muy bonita. Con tantos museos y galerías de arte.

—Sí, han guardado los cuadros para que no sufran los efectos de la guerra.

—En Madrid tenemos el Prado. Ahora están volviendo a colocar los cuadros. Yo jamás los he visto, pero me gustaría ir. —Miró a Harry con una alentadora sonrisa en los labios, aunque también con cierta turbación, y él pensó: «Quiere que la lleve.» Se sintió halagado, pero la muchacha era muy joven, poco más que una niña.

—Bueno, la verdad es que a mí también me gustaría ir, sólo que ahora estoy muy ocupado...

—Sería muy bonito. Tenemos teléfono, podría usted llamar a mi madre para ponernos de acuerdo...

Catalina y Dolores regresaron, rodeadas por un grupo de cadetes. Milagros frunció el entrecejo.

—Milagros, quiero presentarte a Carlos. Ya ha ganado una medalla, ha estado combatiendo contra los bandidos rojos del norte...

—Disculpe, será mejor que vaya en busca de Simon.

Inició la huida, hinchando los carrillos de alivio. Era una buena chica. Pero sólo una niña. Tomó otra copa de la bandeja de un camarero que pasaba por su lado. Sería mejor que procurara no pasarse. Pensó en Sofía, como ya había hecho varias veces. Se la veía rebosante de vida y energía. No le había dicho nada a nadie acerca del espía. Cumpliría su promesa.

Tolhurst se encontraba en el centro del salón, conversando con Goach, el cual lo miraba con una ligera expresión de desagrado a través de su monóculo. «Pobre Tolly», pensó Harry de repente. Con su imponente figura, debería haber resultado muy atractivo; pero siempre había en él un no sé qué de lánguido y desgarbado.

Goach se animó al ver acercarse a Harry.

—Buenas noches, Brett. Me parece que será mejor que vigile. El general y su mujer andan en busca de un buen partido para Milagros.

Me lo dijo el hermano del general. Monseñor Maestre. —Señaló con la cabeza hacia el lugar donde el clérigo conversaba con un par de ancianas. En su rostro enjuto y sus modales autoritarios, Harry descubrió un parecido con Maestre.

—¿Lo conoce, señor?

—Sí, es todo un erudito. Especialista en liturgia de la Iglesia durante el período de la Reconquista. —Goach sonrió e inclinó la cabeza cuando, al oír mencionar su nombre, el monseñor se acercó.

—Ah, George —dijo el clérigo en español—, ya he conseguido unas cuantas suscripciones más. —Su mirada se desplazó hacia Harry y Tolhurst, tan rápida e incisiva como la de su hermano.

—Espléndido, espléndido. —Goach hizo las presentaciones—. Monseñor está al frente de una iniciativa para la reconstrucción de todas las iglesias quemadas de Madrid. El Vaticano ha prestado una gran ayuda, pero la tarea es enorme y se necesita mucho dinero.

Monseñor Maestre meneó la cabeza tristemente.

—En efecto. Pero lo vamos consiguiendo. Sin embargo, nada puede sustituir a nuestros mártires, a nuestros sacerdotes y monjas asesinados. —Se volvió hacia Harry y Tolhurst—. Recuerdo, durante el período más negro de nuestra guerra, que algunas iglesias inglesas nos enviaron sus objetos de oro y plata para compensar lo que habíamos perdido. Fue un gran consuelo, nos hizo sentir que no habíamos sido olvidados.

—Me alegro —dijo Harry—. Debieron de ser unos tiempos muy duros.

—Usted no sabe, señor, las cosas que nos hicieron. Mejor que no lo sepa. Queremos reconstruir las iglesias de La Latina y Carabanchel. —El clérigo miró a Harry con la cara muy seria—. La gente de allí necesita una guía, algo a lo que aferrarse.

—Hay una iglesia quemada cerca de donde yo vivo —dijo Harry—, en la parte alta de La Latina.

El rostro del monseñor se endureció.

—Sí, y las personas que lo hicieron tienen que saber que no han podido destruir la autoridad de la Iglesia de Jesucristo. Que hemos regresado más fuertes que nunca.

Goach asintió con la cabeza.

—Muy cierto.

Una sonora carcajada indujo a monseñor Maestre a fruncir el entrecejo.

—Lástima que mi hermano haya invitado a Millán Astray. Es tan inculto. Y, encima, falangista. Son todos tan poco religiosos. —Enarcó las cejas—. Los necesitábamos durante nuestra guerra, pero ahora... bueno, gracias a Dios que el Generalísimo es un auténtico cristiano.

—Algunos falangistas lo convertirían en su dios —dijo Goach en voz baja.

—Sin duda.

Harry miró a uno y a otro. Ambos hablaban sin pelos en la lengua. Pero allí todos eran monárquicos, excepto Millán Astray. Ahora el general mutilado peroraba en presencia de un grupo de cadetes; todos parecían estar muy pendientes de sus palabras.

El clérigo tomó a Goach del brazo.

—Venga conmigo, George, le quiero presentar al secretario del obispo. —Saludó a Harry y Tolhurst con una reverencia y se retiró con Goach en medio de un revuelo de faldas rojas.

—Pensaba que nunca iba a terminar. ¿Qué tal te ha ido con la señorita?

—Quería que la llevara al Prado. —Harry miró hacia el lugar donde Milagros conversaba de nuevo con sus amigas. Ella captó su mirada y le dedicó una sonrisa incierta. Se sintió culpable; su repentina retirada debía de haberle parecido una grosería.

—Aquí hay un montón de bomboncitos. —Tolhurst se limpió los cristales de las gafas en la manga—. Supongo que he sido un poco estúpido, burlándome de sus nombres. Pero es que no sé qué me ocurre, no acabo de cogerles el tranquillo a las chicas, al menos en sociedad. —Se tambaleaba ligeramente, algo más que un poco borracho—. Pero es que, verás, estuve tanto tiempo en Cuba que me acostumbré a las putas. —Se rió—. Me gustan las putas, lo malo es que te olvidas de cómo hay que hablar con las chicas respetables. —Miró a Harry—. ¿Entonces la señorita Maestre no es tu tipo?

—No.

—No es una Vera Lynn, ¿verdad?

—Es joven. La pobre chica teme el futuro.

—¿Acaso no lo tememos todos? Oye, hay un tipo en el gabinete de prensa que conoce una casa de putas cerca del Teatro de la Ópera...

Harry le dio un ligero codazo para que se callara. Maestre se estaba volviendo a acercar a ellos con una ancha sonrisa en los labios.

—Señor Brett, espero que Milagros no lo haya abandonado.

—No, no. Puede estar orgulloso de ella, mi general.

Maestre miró hacia el lugar donde las chicas se hallaban profundamente enzarzadas en una conversación con otros cadetes y meneó la cabeza con indulgencia.

—Me temo que no pueden resistir la tentación de alternar con un joven oficial. Ahora las chicas sólo viven para este día. Tiene usted que perdonarlas.

«Debe de pensar que Milagros me ha plantado», pensó Harry.

Maestre tomó un sorbo, se secó el bigotito y los miró.

—Caballeros —dijo—. Ustedes dos conocen al capitán Hillgarth, ¿verdad? Él y yo somos buenos amigos.

—Sí, señor. —El rostro de Tolhurst adquirió de inmediato una expresión de solícito interés.

—Debería saber —añadió Maestre— que reina un profundo malestar en el Gobierno por la cuestión de Negrín. No fue una buena idea que Inglaterra concediera asilo político al primer ministro republicano. Estos rumores que se escuchan en el Parlamento británico molestan sobremanera a nuestros amigos. —El general meneó la cabeza—. A veces, ustedes los ingleses dejan que aniden las víboras en su pecho.

—Es complicado —dijo Tolhurst con la cara muy seria—. No sé cómo se enteraron en la Cámara de los Comunes de que sir Samuel había recomendado que Negrín fuera invitado a marcharse, pero los laboristas están indignados.

—Ustedes pueden controlar su Parlamento, ¿no es cierto?

—Más bien no —contestó Tolhurst—. Estamos en una democracia —añadió en tono de disculpa.

Maestre extendió las manos, sonriendo perplejo.

—Pero Inglaterra no es una república decadente como era Francia, ustedes tienen una monarquía y una aristocracia, comprenden el principio de autoridad.

—Se lo diré al capitán Hillgarth —dijo Tolhurst—. Por cierto, señor —añadió—, el capitán preguntaba qué tal van las cosas con el nuevo ministro.

Maestre asintió con la cabeza.

—Dígale que no hay ningún motivo de preocupación a este respecto —contestó en un suave susurro.

Se acercó la señora Maestre y le dio a su marido unos golpecitos en el brazo con su abanico.

—Santiago, ¿ya estás otra vez hablando de política? Esto es el baile de cumpleaños de nuestra hija. —Meneó la cabeza—. Tienen que perdonarle.

Maestre la miró sonriendo.

—Claro, cariño, tienes toda la razón.

La mujer miró con una radiante sonrisa a Harry y Tolhurst.

—Tengo entendido que Juan March está en Madrid. Si ha vuelto definitivamente, seguro que organizará algunas fiestas.

—A mí me han dicho que sólo ha sido una visita breve —replicó Maestre.

Harry lo miró. Otra vez Juan March. El nombre que Hillgarth le había ordenado olvidar, junto con el de los Caballeros de San Jorge.

La señora Maestre miró a sus invitados exultante de felicidad.

—Es el hombre de negocios más próspero de España. Tuvo que marcharse bajo la República, naturalmente. Sería bueno que regresara. No se pueden ustedes imaginar qué triste era la vida en la zona nacional durante la guerra. Pero así tenía que ser, claro. Y, cuando volvimos... —Una sombra cruzó fugazmente por su rostro.

—La casa estaba medio en ruinas —dijo Maestre—. El mobiliario se había utilizado como leña. Todo estaba roto o destrozado. Las familias que la República instaló aquí ni siquiera sabían usar el retrete; pero lo peor de todo fue lo que ocurrió con las propiedades de nuestra familia, fotografías vendidas en el Rastro sólo porque estaban enmarcadas en plata. Ahora ya pueden ustedes comprender por qué razón el hecho de que se haya ofrecido una residencia en Londres a Negrín ha provocado el enfado de la gente. —Maestre miró por un instante con expresión de profunda ternura hacia el otro extremo del salón donde estaba su hija—. Milagros es una chica muy sensible, no lo pudo soportar. Y ahora no es feliz. Me temo que sea una planta demasiado delicada para florecer ahora en España. A veces hasta llego a pensar que quizá podría ser más feliz en el extranjero. —Rodeó con el brazo los hombros de su mujer—. Creo que tendríamos que abrir el baile, querida. Pediré a la orquesta que empiece a tocar. —Miró a Harry con una sonrisa—. Sólo lo mejor para Milagros. Le diré que les conceda un baile. Discúlpennos. —Y se retiró con su mujer.

—Dios mío —dijo Tolhurst—, con lo mal que a mí se me da el baile.

—Este Juan March —dijo Harry en tono imparcial— debe de ser un hombre muy importante, ¿verdad?

—Más bien diría que sí. Tiene millones. Un sujeto sin escrúpulos, empezó como contrabandista. Ahora vive en Suiza, se llevó todo el dinero antes de que empezara la Guerra Civil. Partidario de la monarquía. Probablemente, sólo ha venido para arreglar sus asuntos. —Tolhurst hablaba con ligereza, pero Harry vio en su rostro una expresión de alerta que lo indujo a cambiar de tema—. Terrible, lo de las pérdidas de los Maestre; todas las familias de las clases media y alta lo pasaron tremendamente mal. Una cosa que hay que decir en favor de este régimen es que, por lo menos, protege a la gente de... ¿cómo diría?... de nuestra clase.

—Sí, supongo que sí. Nuestra clase. He estado pensando, ¿sabes? En cierta manera, creo que el hecho de que ambos seamos ex alumnos de Rookwood ahora significa más para Sandy que para mí. Él sigue abrigando sentimientos al respecto, aunque sólo sean sentimientos de odio.

—¿Y tú?

—Pues ya no lo sé, Tolly.

Cuatro hombres vestidos de esmoquin aparecieron con instrumentos musicales en compañía de la señora Maestre, seguidos por un grupo de sirvientes en caftán que empujaban un pequeño escenario de madera. Los invitados aplaudieron y lanzaron vítores. Harry vio que Milagros le hacía señas con su abanico desde el otro extremo del salón. Harry levantó su copa. A su lado, Tolhurst lanzó un suspiro.

—Ay, Dios mío —dijo éste—. Ya estamos.

18

A Barbara no le apetecía reunirse con Harry. Éste había sido amable con ella tres años atrás y a ella le había resultado agradable contemplar un jovial rostro inglés; pero el hecho de volver a ver al mejor amigo de Bernie le parecía, en cierto modo, algo así como tentar al destino. Había considerado la posibilidad de decírselo a Harry, pero lo veía tan afectuoso con Sandy que no le parecía correcto. Además, Harry había cambiado. Se observaba en él una tristeza enfurecida, inexistente tres años atrás. Lo tendría que mantener todo en secreto. Ahora Harry estaba allí y Sandy se había encariñado con él, lo cual la obligaría a afrontar la situación y a engañar también a Harry. Era la segunda persona a la que engañaba, y esta vez se trataba del mejor amigo de Bernie.

El sábado se había enterado, a través de la BBC, de un gran bombardeo alemán sobre Birmingham. Cerca de doscientas personas habían resultado muertas. Se quedó horrorizada, sentada junto a la radio. No le había dicho nada a Sandy. Éste la habría consolado, pero ella no lo habría podido soportar, no se lo merecía. Se había pasado dos días preocupada, pero aquella mañana había recibido un telegrama de su padre, informándola de que todos estaban bien y de que las incursiones aéreas habían tenido lugar en el centro de la ciudad. Se puso a llorar de alivio.

Tenía que volverse a reunir con Luis en cuestión de dos días. Temía que el dinero de su banco de Inglaterra no llegara a tiempo. Por más que hubiera dudado del relato de Luis después de su primer encuentro con él, ahora se mostraba más inclinada a creerle. Si éste se presentara en el café con la prueba que ella le había pedido, la cosa estaría resuelta. Se había estado diciendo a sí misma que eso era lo que ella quería creer y que no tenía que abrigar demasiadas esperanzas. Pero ¿y si fuera verdad? ¿Ayudar a Bernie a escapar de la cárcel de un campo de prisioneros y llevarlo a la embajada? En los últimos tiempos había comprendido que, entre el conjunto de sentimientos que Sandy le inspiraba, había un elemento de temor, temor a la crueldad que sabía que formaba parte de él.

La víspera había hecho algo que unas pocas semanas atrás le habría parecido inconcebible. Sandy había salido con unos amiguetes y ella había entrado en su estudio para averiguar cuánto dinero tenía. Se dijo que jamás se atrevería a robarle; pero, en caso de que sus ahorros no llegaran a tiempo, quizá pudiera sacarle dinero con una mentira. Siempre y cuando él tuviera suficiente. Como casi todos los hombres, Sandy no creía que el dinero fuera algo acerca de lo cual las mujeres tuvieran que estar informadas.

Con el corazón galopando en el pecho, consciente de que estaba cruzando para siempre una especie de frontera, Barbara buscó la llave del escritorio que Sandy tenía en su estudio. La guardaba en el dormitorio, en el cajón de los calcetines... Ella lo había visto guardarla allí algunas veces, cuando se iba a la cama después de haberse pasado la noche trabajando. La encontró al fondo del cajón, en el interior de un calcetín doblado. La miró, vaciló un instante y después se dirigió a su estudio.

Algunos cajones estaban cerrados, pero no todos. En uno encontró dos libretas del banco. Una era una cuenta de una sucursal de un banco español que contenía mil pesetas; en ella figuraban ingresos y reintegros regulares que ella supuso que correspondían a sus gastos. Para su sorpresa, la segunda era de un banco argentino. Había varios ingresos pero ningún reintegro y el total era de casi un millón de pesos argentinos; a saber lo que sería. Como es natural, no había manera de que ella pudiera retirar directamente el dinero. Las cuentas estaban exclusivamente a nombre de Sandy. Experimentó una curiosa sensación de alivio.

Abandonó el estudio, deteniéndose en la puerta para asegurarse de que Pilar no estuviera por allí.

Mientras volvía a dejar la llave en su sitio, se dio cuenta de que algo más duro que el acero estaba penetrando en su interior, algo cuya existencia jamás había sospechado.

Había acordado reunirse con Harry en un restaurante de las inmediaciones del Palacio Real, un pequeño local muy tranquilo que servía buena comida procedente del mercado negro. Llegaba con retraso. Su asistenta se había puesto muy nerviosa, porque los guardias civiles le habían pedido la documentación mientras se dirigía al trabajo y ella la había olvidado. Barbara había tenido que escribir una carta, confirmando que la chica trabajaba para ella. Unos cuantos hombres de negocios y algunas parejas acomodadas ocupaban las mesas restantes. Harry se levantó para saludarla.

—Barbara, ¿cómo estás? —Parecía pálido y cansado.

—Pues no del todo mal.

—Hace frío.

—Sí, el invierno está a la vuelta de la esquina.

El camarero tomó su abrigo y dejó los menús delante de ellos.

—Bueno, ¿y tú qué tal? —le preguntó ella jovialmente—. ¿Cómo es la embajada?

—Un poco aburrida. Me dedico, sobre todo, a actuar como intérprete en reuniones con funcionarios. —Se le veía nervioso e incómodo.

—¿Cómo están los tuyos? ¿Bien?

—Mi tío y mi tía están bien. Allí abajo, en Surrey, casi no parece que haya guerra. La familia de mi primo lo pasó un poco mal en Londres. —Hizo una pausa y la miró con cara muy seria—. Tengo entendido que Birmingham ha sido castigada.

—Sí. Me enviaron un telegrama diciéndome que están todos bien.

—Pensé en ti cuando me enteré. Habrás estado terriblemente preocupada.

—Pues sí, y supongo que habrá más incursiones. —Bárbara lanzó un suspiro—. Pero tú las sufriste durante mucho más tiempo en Londres, ¿verdad?

—Hubo una cuando yo estuve allí hace un mes, en casa de mi primo Will. Pero ahora él está a salvo en el campo, haciendo no sé qué trabajo secreto.

—Debe de ser un alivio.

—Pues sí.

Barbara encendió un cigarrillo.

—Creo que mis padres están procurando seguir adelante, como todo el mundo. ¿Qué otra cosa pueden hacer? Papá y mamá apenas dicen nada en sus cartas.

—¿Cómo está el padre de Sandy, el obispo?

—Pues mira, no tengo ni la menor idea. No se han puesto en contacto desde que Sandy llegó aquí. Él jamás habla de su padre ni de su hermano. Es triste. —Barbara estudió a Harry. Había cambiado de aspecto y se le veía muy tenso. Era muy guapo cuando ella lo había conocido tres años atrás, aunque no fuera su tipo. Ahora parecía mayor, estaba más grueso y tenía más arrugas alrededor de los ojos. «Toda una generación de hombres está envejeciendo a marchas forzadas», pensó. Titubeó un poco, pero luego preguntó—: ¿Y tú cómo estás ahora? Te veo un poco cansado.

—Bueno, estoy bien. Tuve una neurosis de guerra, ¿sabes? —añadió Harry de repente—. Padecía unas crisis de pánico espantosas.

—Lo siento.

—Pero ahora ya estoy mucho mejor, llevo bastante tiempo sin sufrir ninguna.

—Por lo menos, estás haciendo algo útil en la embajada.

Harry esbozó una sonrisa tensa.

—Te veo muy distinta de la última vez que nos vimos —dijo.

Barbara se ruborizó.

—Sí, con todos aquellos viejos jerséis. Entonces, en el estado en que me encontraba, me importaba un bledo mi aspecto. —Lo miró con una cálida sonrisa en los labios—. Tú me ayudaste.

Harry se mordió el labio clavando en ella sus ojos azules y, por un instante, Barbara pensó: «Oh, Dios mío, ha adivinado algo.» Después, él le preguntó.

—¿Qué tal se vive aquí? Madrid se encuentra en un estado lamentable. Con tanta pobreza y miseria y con todos estos mendigos. Está peor que durante la Guerra Civil.

Barbara suspiró.

—La Guerra Civil destrozó España y, en especial, Madrid. La cosecha ha vuelto a ser mala y ahora tenemos un bloqueo que limita los suministros de importación. Por lo menos, eso es lo que dicen los periódicos. Aunque no sé... —Barbara sonrió con tristeza—. La verdad es que ya no sé qué creer.

—El silencio es lo que no puedo soportar. ¿Recuerdas lo ruidoso que era Madrid? Es como si le hubieran arrebatado a la gente toda la energía y la esperanza.

—Así es la guerra.

Harry la miró con la cara muy seria.

—¿Sabes lo que temo? Este año hemos impedido que Hitler invadiera Inglaterra; pero, si lo volviera a intentar el año que viene, es posible que perdiéramos. Lucharíamos como fieras, lucharíamos en las playas y en las calles tal como dijo Churchill, pero podríamos perder.

Me imagino Gran Bretaña terminando como España, un país destrozado y arruinado, gobernado por una pandilla corrupta de fascistas. Eso
nos podría ocurrir a nosotros.

—¿De veras? Sé que la disciplina es muy dura, pero hay personas
como Sebastián de Salas que quieren reconstruir el país de verdad.
—Barbara hizo una pausa y se pasó una mano por la frente—. Oh, Dios
mío —dijo—. Los estoy defendiendo. Es que todas las personas que
conozco están de su parte, ¿sabes?

Se mordió el labio. Debería haber comprendido que, en caso de que
se reuniera con Harry, toda su confusión y todo su temor aflorarían a
la superficie. Pero quizá fuera bueno para ella enfrentarse con ciertas
cosas; siempre y cuando no se tocara el tema de Bernie.

—¿Qué piensa Sandy de ellos? —preguntó Harry.

—Piensa que España está mejor que si hubieran ganado los rojos.

—¿Y tú estás de acuerdo?

—¿Quién sabe? —replicó ella con repentina emoción.

Harry sonrió.

—Perdona, hablo más de la cuenta. Cambiemos de tema.

—¿Echamos un vistazo al menú?

Eligieron los platos y el camarero les llevó una botella de vino.
Harry lo cató y asintió con la cabeza.

—Muy bueno.

—Casi todo el vino de ahora es malísimo, pero aquí tienen una
bodega muy buena.

—El bueno se consigue cuando uno se puede permitir el lujo de
pagarlo, ¿verdad?

Barbara levantó los ojos al oír el amargo tono de su voz.

—Pronto empezaré a trabajar en un orfelinato —dijo.

—¿Vuelves a tu trabajo de enfermera?

—Sí, quería hacer algo positivo. En realidad, me lo aconsejó el propio Sandy.

Harry asintió con la cabeza y comentó, tras un breve titubeo:

—Lo veo bien. Parece alguien muy próspero.

—Pues sí. La organización se le da muy bien. Es un hombre de
negocios.

Hicieron una pausa mientras el camarero les servía la sopa y después Harry dijo:

—Sandy siempre supo abrirse su propio camino. Incluso en el colegio. Se nota que es un triunfador. —Miró a Barbara a los ojos—. Ahora

está trabajando en eso del Ministerio de Minas, lo comentó la otra noche, ¿verdad?

Barbara se encogió de hombros.

—Sí, pero yo no sé gran cosa de eso. Dice que es un asunto confidencial. —Sonrió con tristeza—. Me he convertido en una pequeña ama de casa; no me interesan los asuntos de negocios.

Harry asintió con la cabeza. Se abrió la puerta del restaurante y aparecieron tres jóvenes vestidos con el uniforme de la Falange. Se abrió una puerta al fondo, y por ella entró un hombre bajito y rechoncho vestido con una levita cubierta de lamparones que miraba con una sonrisa nerviosa a los visitantes de la camisa azul.

—Buenas tardes, señor —dijo alegremente uno de ellos. Debía de tener aproximadamente la edad de Harry, alto, delgado y con el consabido bigotito—. Una mesa para tres, por favor. —El *maître* inclinó la cabeza y los acompañó a una mesa libre.

—Espero que no armen demasiado jaleo —dijo Barbara en voz baja.

El falangista miró alrededor y, acto seguido, se acercó a la mesa que ellos ocupaban y, con una amplia sonrisa en los labios, les tendió la mano.

—Ah, ¿visitantes extranjeros? —dijo—. ¿Alemanes?

—No, ingleses —contestó Barbara con una sonrisa nerviosa. El falangista retiró la mano sin dejar de sonreír.

—Vaya, conque ingleses —dijo, asintiendo alegremente con la cabeza—. Por desgracia, muy pronto se tendrán que marchar; el Generalísimo se va a incorporar a la cruzada del Führer contra Inglaterra. Muy pronto recuperaremos Gibraltar.

Barbara miró nerviosamente a Harry. Éste mostraba un semblante frío e impasible. El jefe de los falangistas se inclinó ante ellos en una reverencia burlona y fue a reunirse con sus compañeros. Harry tenía el rostro arrebolado a causa de la furia.

—Tranquilo —le dijo ella—. No los provoques.

—Ya lo sé —musitó Harry—. Hijos de puta.

El camarero se acercó presuroso con los platos principales y su mirada se desplazó nerviosamente de ellos a los falangistas, pero éstos ya estaban ocupados con sus menús.

—Terminemos cuanto antes y larguémonos de aquí —dijo Barbara—. Antes de que empiecen a beber.

Terminaron rápidamente el resto de la comida. Harry le detalló la fiesta de los Maestre y después volvió a encauzar la conversación hacia Sandy, como si le apeteciera seguir hablando de él.

—Me enseñó una garra de dinosaurio que ha encontrado.

Barbara sonrió.

—Está entusiasmado con sus fósiles. Y cuando está así es como un chiquillo, un encanto.

—En el colegio decía que los fósiles eran la clave de los secretos de la tierra.

—Eso es muy propio de Sandy. —Cuando terminaron de comer, Barbara vio que los falangistas estaban empezando a beber y se reían ruidosamente—. Será mejor que nos vayamos.

—Sí, claro. —Harry pidió la cuenta con una seña. El camarero se la entregó enseguida, sin duda alegrándose de poder librarse de ellos cuanto antes, no fuera a ser que los falangistas empezaran a armar alboroto. Pagaron y se pusieron los abrigos. Una vez fuera, Harry añadió en tono dubitativo—: Me preguntaba si te importaría que fuéramos a ver un momento el Palacio Real, está aquí mismo, justo al otro lado de la calle. Jamás lo he visto de cerca.

—Sí, claro. Vamos. Tengo tiempo de sobra.

Cruzaron la calle. Brillaba un poco el sol, pero la tarde era muy fría. Barbara se abrochó el abrigo. Se detuvieron ante la verja. Estaba cerrada y fuera montaban vigilancia unos guardias civiles. Harry contempló los muros blancos y ornamentados.

—No han pintado «Arriba España» al lado —dijo.

—La Falange no quiso tocar el palacio. Es el símbolo de los monárquicos. Éstos esperan que Franco permita algún día el regreso de la monarquía.

Hizo una pausa para encender un pitillo. Harry llegó al final de la calle. Al otro lado de la verja había una acusada pendiente que bajaba hasta los jardines del palacio. Más allá se podía ver la Casa de Campo, un enmarañado paisaje pardo verdoso.

Barbara se reunió con él.

—El campo de batalla —dijo Harry en voz baja.

—Sí. Y parece que todavía está todo hecho un desastre. Aunque la gente ya vuelve a pasear por allí. Quedan todavía muchas granadas sin detonar, pero se han señalado unos caminos seguros.

Harry miró más allá de los jardines.

—Me gustaría ir a verlo. ¿Te importa?

Barbara titubeó. No quería recordar la guerra ni el sitio.

—¿Mejor no? —preguntó Harry con dulzura.

Barbara respiró hondo.

—No, vamos. Quizá conviene que lo vea.

Estaba a sólo dos paradas de tranvía. Se apearon y echaron a andar por una corta alameda. Otras personas caminaban en la misma dirección, un joven soldado con su novia y dos mujeres de mediana edad vestidas de negro. Rodearon una pequeña loma y se encontraron de repente ante un erial de terreno desgarrado, punteado aquí y allá por tanques quemados y piezas de artillería rotas y oxidadas. Muy cerca de allí, un muro de ladrillo acribillado a balazos era lo único que quedaba de un edificio. La hierba primaveral había vuelto a crecer en buena parte del terreno, pero numerosos cráteres de granada llenos de agua salpicaban el paisaje y largas hileras de trincheras cortaban la tierra cual si fueran heridas abiertas. Unos caminos permitían cruzar el devastado paisaje, y pequeños letreros de madera colocados a intervalos regulares advertían a los visitantes de la conveniencia de no apartarse de ellos por el peligro que suponían las granadas sin detonar. En la distancia, el blanco palacio destacaba con la nitidez de un espejismo.

Barbara temía que la contemplación de aquel lugar la afectara profundamente, pero sólo experimentó tristeza. Le recordaba las fotografías de la Gran Guerra. Harry, en cambio, parecía más afectado y estaba muy pálido. Ella le tocó ligeramente el brazo.

—¿Te encuentras bien?

Harry respiró hondo.

—Sí. Por un momento, me ha hecho recordar Dunkerque. Allí también había piezas de artillería por todas partes.

—¿Quieres que regresemos? Quizás hubiera sido mejor no venir.

—No. Sigamos. Aquí hay un camino. —Caminaron un rato en silencio.

—Dicen que en el norte todavía es peor —dijo Barbara—. Donde se libraron los combates de la batalla del Ebro. Millares de tanques abandonados.

Más adelante, a la izquierda, las dos mujeres vestidas de negro seguían otro camino fuertemente abrazadas la una a la otra.

—Cuántas viudas —dijo Barbara, sonriendo tristemente—. Yo estaba en el mismo barco que ellas, sola y desamparada hasta que me tropecé con Sandy.

—¿Y eso cómo fue? —preguntó Harry.

Barbara interrumpió la marcha para encender otro pitillo.

—La Cruz Roja me envió a Burgos, naturalmente. Todo era muy distinto de Madrid. Para empezar, estaba muy por detrás de la línea del frente. Es una ciudad muy triste, llena de enormes edificios medievales. En la Cruz Roja local había muchos generales retirados y respetables damas españolas. De hecho, todos eran amabilísimos y mucho menos paranoicos que los republicanos. Pero podían permitirse el lujo de serlo. Ya entonces sabían que iban a ganar.

—Te debió de resultar extraño trabajar con los enemigos de Bernie.

Era la primera vez que mencionaba su nombre. Barbara lo miró e inmediatamente apartó los ojos.

—Yo no compartía sus puntos de vista políticos, tú lo sabes. Era neutral. En la Cruz Roja eso no tiene connotaciones negativas; no ser ni chicha ni limoná se considera positivo, aliviar el sufrimiento ajeno es lo que cuenta. Eso la gente no lo entiende. Bernie no lo entendía. —Barbara se volvió y lo miró a los ojos—. ¿Crees que hice mal? —preguntó de repente—. ¿Irme a vivir con un hombre que es partidario del régimen? Sé que Sandy y Bernie no eran amigos en el colegio.

—No —dijo Harry sonriendo—. Yo también soy neutral por naturaleza.

Barbara experimentó una oleada de alivio al oír su respuesta; no hubiera podido soportar que Harry censurara su conducta. Lo miró y hubiera deseado gritarle: «¡Quizás esté vivo, quizás esté vivo!» Pero se mordió la lengua.

—Tú recuerdas en qué estado me encontraba, Harry. No me importaba la política, realizar mi trabajo me costaba un esfuerzo enorme. Era como si estuviera envuelta en una espesa niebla gris. Tenía que guardar silencio sobre Bernie, naturalmente. No podía esperar que quienes estaban en el bando nacional se mostraran encantados de que yo hubiera salido con alguien contra el cual ellos habían combatido.

—No.

Cruzaron unos tablones de madera tendidos sobre una trinchera. Al fondo se veían unas botas viejas y un montón de latas oxidadas de sardinas con la etiqueta escrita en caracteres cirílicos. Y al borde de la trinchera, un letrero ostentaba una flecha que señalaba en ambas direcciones. «NOSOTROS» y «ELLOS». En la distancia, las dos mujeres seguían caminando muy despacio, todavía abrazadas la una a la otra.

—¿Y entonces conociste a Sandy? —preguntó Harry, interrumpiendo sus pensamientos.

—Sí. —Barbara lo miró con la cara muy seria—. Él me salvó, ¿sabes?

—Me contó que estuvo por allí, haciendo recorridos turísticos por los campos de batalla.

—Sí. Yo me encontraba muy sola en Burgos. Y entonces lo conocí en una fiesta y él… no sé cómo decirte, me prestó su apoyo. Y me dio fuerzas para continuar.

—Qué casualidad, conocer a otro antiguo alumno de Rookwood.

—Sí. Aunque, en realidad, todos los ingleses que se encontraban en el bando nacional acababan conociéndose tarde o temprano. No éramos muchos. —Barbara sonrió—. Sandy dijo que fue el destino.

—Antes creía en el destino. Pero me dijo que ya no.

—Pues yo creo que sigue creyendo, aunque no lo quiera. Es un hombre complicado.

—Sí, lo es. —Habían llegado a otra trinchera—. Cuidado con esos tablones. Dame el brazo.

La tomó de la mano y la guió hasta el otro lado. Otra vez los letreros de «nosotros» y «ellos» señalaban en distintas direcciones.

—Ha sido muy bueno conmigo —dijo Barbara—. Sandy.

—Perdona. —Harry se volvió hacia ella—. No te he oído. Sigo estando un poco sordo de este oído. —La miró con expresión momentáneamente perdida y desconcertada.

—He dicho que Sandy ha sido muy bueno conmigo. Me ha convencido de que me dedique a esta tarea de voluntaria porque sabe que necesito algo nuevo. —Se preguntó con amargura: «¿Será la sensación de culpa la que me induce a defenderlo de esta manera?»

—Bien —dijo Harry en tono precavido y neutral.

Barbara pensó con repentino asombro: «Sandy no le gusta. Pero entonces, ¿por qué ha reanudado su amistad con él?»

—Está intentando ayudar a unos judíos que huyeron de Francia.

—Sí. Ya me lo comentó.

—Durante la invasión alemana, muchos de ellos vinieron aquí huyendo con nada más que lo puesto. Ahora quieren pasar a Portugal y, desde allí, a América. Les tienen pánico a los nazis. Hay un comité que intenta ayudarlos, y Sandy forma parte de él.

—Hace poco hubo una manifestación de la Falange ante la embajada, donde se gritaban lemas antisemitas a pleno pulmón.

—El régimen tiene que seguir la línea de los nazis, pero permite que el comité de Sandy siga actuando siempre y cuando sea discreto.

A lo lejos, las dos mujeres se habían detenido. Una de ellas lloraba mientras la otra la abrazaba. Barbara volvió a mirar a Harry.

—Sandy y yo no estamos verdaderamente casados, ¿te lo dijo?

Harry titubeó antes de contestar.

—Sí.

Ella se ruborizó.

—A lo mejor piensas que eso es terrible. Pero es que nosotros... no estábamos preparados para dar el paso.

—Lo comprendo —dijo Harry en tono avergonzado—. No son tiempos normales.

—¿Tú sigues con aquella chica... cómo se llamaba?

—Laura. Eso terminó hace siglos. Estoy soltero, de momento. —Harry contempló el Palacio Real a lo lejos—. ¿Crees que te vas a quedar en España? —preguntó.

—No lo sé. No sé qué nos deparará el futuro.

Harry se volvió para mirarla.

—Yo aborrezco todo esto —dijo con repentina vehemencia—. Aborrezco lo que ha hecho Franco. Antes tenía una idea de España, el romanticismo de sus tortuosas callejuelas y sus decrépitos edificios. Y no sé por qué; quizá porque, cuando vine aquí en el treinta y uno, se respiraba esperanza, incluso entre las personas que no tenían nada como la familia Mera. ¿Te acuerdas de ellos?

—Sí. Pero mira, Harry, aquellos sueños, el socialismo... todo eso ha terminado...

—La semana pasada estuve en la plaza donde ellos vivían; la habían bombardeado o cañoneado. Su apartamento ha desaparecido. Había un hombre... —hizo una pausa y después siguió adelante con un destello de rabia en los ojos—... un hombre que fue atacado por unos perros asilvestrados. Yo lo ayudé y lo acompañé a su casa. Vive en un pequeño apartamento con su madre, que ha sufrido un ataque, y no creo que esté recibiendo la menor atención médica, un chiquillo que se volvió medio loco cuando se llevaron detenidos a sus padres y una hermana, una chica muy inteligente, que tuvo que abandonar sus estudios de medicina para trabajar en una vaquería. —Harry respiró hondo—. Ésta es la nueva España.

Barbara lanzó un suspiro.

—Lo sé, tienes razón. Me siento culpable por la manera en que vivimos en medio de todo esto. No se lo digo a Sandy, pero así es.

Harry asintió con la cabeza. Ahora parecía más calmado, su cólera había desaparecido. Barbara estudió su rostro. Adivinaba que su rabia y su desilusión obedecían a algo más que a su encuentro con una pobre familia, pero no comprendía qué podía ser.

De repente, sonrió.

—Perdona que te haya dicho todo esto. No me hagas caso, es que estoy un poco cansado.

—No, haces bien en recordármelo. —Barbara sonrió—. Pero no parece que sigas siendo tan neutral como antes.

Harry soltó una carcajada amarga.

—No. Puede que no. Las cosas cambian.

Habían llegado al Manzanares, el pequeño río que discurría al oeste de la ciudad. Más adelante, había un puente y unas escaleras que conducían a los jardines del palacio.

—Podemos regresar al palacio desde aquí —dijo Barbara.

—Sí, será mejor que regrese a la embajada.

—¿Seguro que estás bien, Harry? —le preguntó ella de repente—. Pareces... no sé... preocupado.

—Estoy bien. Verás, es todo esto de Hendaya y lo demás. En la embajada, todo el mundo está nervioso. —Sonrió—. Tenemos que volver a comer juntos. Podríais venir a mi apartamento. Ya llamaré a Sandy.

19

Sandy estaba en casa cuando Barbara regresó. Se encontraba en el salón, leyendo el periódico y fumando uno de aquellos enormes cigarros suyos que llenaban la estancia de un humo denso y espeso.

—¿Acabas de llegar? —le preguntó.

—Sí. Hemos ido a dar un paseo por la Casa de Campo.

—¿Y qué habéis ido a hacer allí? Todavía está lleno de bombas sin detonar.

—Ahora es un lugar seguro. A Harry le apetecía ir.

—¿Cómo estaba?

—Un poco deprimido. Creo que lo de Dunkerque lo afectó más de lo que él reconoce.

Sandy sonrió a través de la niebla del humo.

—Tiene que encontrar a una chica.

—Quizá.

—¿Qué quieres hacer el jueves? ¿Una cena?

—¿Cómo? —preguntó ella, mirándolo perpleja.

—Es el tercer aniversario del día en que nos conocimos. ¿Acaso lo habías olvidado? —dijo Sandy, aparentemente dolido.

—No... no, claro que no. Vamos a cenar a algún sitio, sería bonito. —Barbara sonrió—. Sandy, estoy un poco cansada, creo que voy a tumbarme un rato arriba antes de cenar.

—De acuerdo, me parece muy bien.

Barbara adivinó que estaba molesto por el hecho de que ella hubiera olvidado la fecha del aniversario. Pero la había olvidado por completo.

Cuando abandonó la estancia, vio que Pilar se acercaba por el pasillo. Ésta la miró con aquellos ojos suyos tan negros e inexpresivos.

—¿Quiere que encienda el fuego, señora? Hace un poco de frío.

—Pregúntele al señor Forsyth, a ver qué le parece, Pilar. Está en el salón.

—Muy bien, señora.

La chica enarcó levemente las cejas; los asuntos domésticos correspondían a la señora. Pero a Barbara le importaban un bledo. Un profundo cansancio se había apoderado de ella mientras regresaba a casa de su encuentro con Harry, necesitaba tumbarse un rato. Subió y se tumbó en la cama. Cerró los ojos, pero en su mente se arremolinaban toda suerte de imágenes. La visita de Harry a Madrid tras la desaparición de Bernie, el final de la esperanza de que Bernie pudiera estar vivo y, después, Burgos. Burgos, donde había conocido a Sandy.

Había llegado a la capital de la zona nacional en mayo de 1937, cuando ya se acercaba el verano y una brillante luz azulada iluminaba los vetustos edificios de color pardo oscuro. Cruzar las líneas era imposible. Tendría que haber viajado de Madrid a Francia y después cruzar de nuevo la frontera con la España nacional. Por el camino, había leído un discurso del doctor Martí, el venerable delegado de la Cruz Roja a los miembros españoles. «No elijan ningún bando —había dicho éste—, busquen desde un punto de vista exclusivamente clínico la mejor manera de ayudar.» Y esto era lo que ella tenía que seguir haciendo, pensó. El hecho de trasladarse a la España de Franco no era una traición a Bernie; iba allí a hacer su trabajo, como había hecho en la zona republicana.

La pusieron a trabajar en la sección encargada de intentar enviar mensajes entre miembros de familias que la guerra había separado a ambos lados del frente. Buena parte de su labor consistía en tareas de carácter administrativo, muy ligeras comparadas con el trato directo con los prisioneros y los niños. Sabía, por su manera solícita de tratarla, que sus compañeros estaban al corriente de lo ocurrido con Bernie. Le molestaba que fueran tan amables y compasivos, ella que siempre asumía el mando de las situaciones y era una organizadora nata. Así que acabó tratándolos, a su vez, con irritable aspereza.

Jamás les hablaba de Bernie y nunca se habría atrevido a mencionarlo a los españoles que conocía en el trabajo, funcionarios y enfermeras de la clase media y coroneles retirados de la Cruz Roja Española que siempre se le mostraban corteses y hacían gala de una exagerada educación que la inducía a echar de menos el trato informal reinante en la zona republicana; aunque, en las reuniones y recepciones a las que tenía que asistir, a veces también manifestaban desprecio y rabia por las tareas que estaba llevando a cabo.

—No estoy de acuerdo con el intercambio de soldados capturados —le dijo un día un soldado veterano de la Cruz Roja Española—. Los niños sí, los mensajes entre familias separadas sí; pero intercambiar un caballero español por un perro rojo... ¡eso jamás! —terminó diciendo con tal furia que una rociada de su saliva le salpicó la barbilla.

Ella dio media vuelta, se fue al retrete y vomitó.

En el transcurso del verano se fue dando cuenta de que cada vez se sentía más deprimida y más aislada de las personas que la rodeaban, como si se viera envuelta en una fina niebla gris. El verano dio paso al otoño, y unos fríos vientos empezaron a soplar a través de las angostas y oscuras calles donde la gente permanecía sentada en los cafés con los hombros encorvados y donde unos camiones llenos de sombríos soldados circulaban sin descanso. Se entregó en cuerpo y alma a su trabajo, a su deseo de hacer algo, de conseguir algún resultado positivo, y por la noche regresaba muerta de cansancio a su pequeño apartamento.

Durante unos cuantos días de octubre compartió su apartamento con Cordelia, una enfermera voluntaria de Inglaterra que estaba en Burgos de permiso. Era una inglesa perteneciente a una familia aristocrática que había sido novicia en un convento pero al final había descubierto que no tenía vocación.

—Por eso he venido aquí, para intentar hacer un poco el bien —explicó, mientras una seria expresión se dibujaba en su amable y poco agraciado rostro.

—Supongo que yo también he hecho lo mismo —replicó Barbara.

—Por todas las personas que han sido perseguidas por sus creencias religiosas.

Barbara recordó la iglesia convertida en establo que ella y Bernie habían visitado el día en que se estrelló el avión, con las ovejas asustadas y apretujadas en un rincón.

—La gente está siendo perseguida por toda suerte de creencias en ambas zonas.

—Tú estuviste en la zona roja, ¿verdad? ¿Cómo era?

—Sorprendentemente parecida a lo de aquí en muchos sentidos. —Miró a Cordelia a los ojos—. Allí tenía un novio, un brigadista internacional inglés que resultó muerto en el Jarama.

Su intención había sido escandalizar a Cordelia, pero ésta se limitó a asentir con la cabeza con semblante afligido.

—Rezaré por él y le encenderé una vela.

—No lo hagas —dijo Barbara—. A Bernie no le habría gustado. —Hizo una pausa—. Llevo varios meses sin pronunciar su nombre en voz alta. Reza si quieres, eso no puede hacer ningún daño; pero no le enciendas una vela.

—Lo querías mucho.

Barbara no contestó.

—Tendrías que procurar salir un poco —dijo Cordelia—. Pasas demasiado tiempo aquí.

—Estoy demasiado cansada.

—En la iglesia a la que acudo van a organizar una cena de recogida de fondos...

Barbara meneó la cabeza.

—No pienso recurrir a la religión, Cordelia.

—Yo no me refería a eso. Quería decir simplemente que no tendrías que quedarte anclada en el pasado.

—No estoy anclada. Procuro no pensar en él; pero los sentimientos siempre están ahí, por mucho que yo intente reprimirlos. La... —miró a Cordelia a la cara y después gritó—: ¡la maldita rabia que llevo dentro! ¡Mira que abandonarme así, sin más, para dejarse matar de esta maldita manera, el muy cabrón! —Rompió a llorar mientras su cuerpo se estremecía con los gemidos y los sollozos—. Ya está, te he escandalizado —añadió entre lágrimas—, te quería escandalizar. —Soltó una carcajada histérica mientras una mano indecisa se apoyaba en su hombro.

—Suéltalo todo —le oyó decir a Cordelia—. Tienes que procurar sacarlo como sea. Lo sé. Tengo un hermano, se fue por el mal camino, yo lo quería mucho y también me enfadé con él, me puse muy furiosa. No te entierres en todo eso, no lo hagas.

Unas veces, dejaba que Cordelia la llevara consigo; pero se negaba a asistir a las ceremonias de la iglesia. Otras, se sentía torpe y desmañada y no se molestaba en hablar; aunque, de vez en cuando, conocía a alguien amable o con quien le apetecía conversar, y entonces la niebla gris parecía disiparse un poco. El último día de octubre, poco antes de que venciera el permiso de Cordelia, ambas acudieron a una fiesta organizada por un alto ejecutivo de la Texas Oil, la compañía que suministraba combustible a Franco. No se sentía a gusto; era una deslumbrante recepción en el mejor hotel de Burgos donde los ruidosos americanos iban de un lado para otro, disfrutando de las atenciones que les dispensaban los invitados españoles. Pensó en lo que hubiera dicho Bernie, la conspiración capitalista internacional, exhibiéndose con sus plumas de pavo real o algo por el estilo. Cordelia conversaba con un cura español. De pie en un rincón, fumando y bebiendo un vino muy malo, Barbara la observaba. Cordelia no tardaría en marcharse, su permiso estaba a punto de expirar. Barbara había acabado encariñándose con ella; si bien apenas tenían nada en común, excepto la certeza de no estar hechas para ser unas esposas y madres al uso. Mientras la miraba, comprendió que la iba a echar mucho de menos, como también echaría de menos su desinteresada bondad. De repente, se sintió desaliñada entre todas aquellas damas tan bien vestidas y decidió escabullirse discretamente. Cuando dio media vuelta para marcharse, se percató de que había un hombre a su lado. No lo había visto acercarse. La miró con una sonrisa, dejando al descubierto unos dientes grandes y blancos.

—¿Eran usted y su amiga las que hablaban el inglés que he oído hace un rato?

Barbara sonrió indecisa.

—Sí —contestó, presentándose.

El hombre le pareció un poco vulgar, a pesar de su hermosa sonrisa. Le explicó que se llamaba Sandy Forsyth y que trabajaba como guía para turistas ingleses que recorrían los campos de batalla. Su manera de hablar arrastrando las sílabas como hacía la clase alta le hizo recordar la de Bernie.

—Todo es pura propaganda —le explicó—. Les enseño los campos de batalla y les explico los detalles militares, pero suelto muchas cosas acerca de las atrocidades cometidas por los rojos. Suelen ser unos carcamales bastante memos, muy interesados en cuestiones militares. Son increíblemente ignorantes. Uno me preguntó si era cierto que los vascos tenían seis dedos.

Barbara se rió. Animado por su interés, él le contó la historia del autocar lleno de ancianos turistas ingleses detenidos al borde de la carretera a causa de una avería, pero demasiado finos para vaciar sus vejigas a punto de estallar en los arbustos de los alrededores, que se aguantaron plantados junto al autocar en medio de angustias atroces. Ella se volvió a reír. Llevaba meses sin que nadie la hiciera reír. El hombre la miró sonriendo.

—No sé por qué, pero sabía que le podría contar esta historia sin que usted se escandalizara; aunque, en realidad, no resulta muy apropiada para las damas.

—Soy enfermera, llevo más de un año en España, a ambos lados del frente. Ya nada me escandaliza.

Sandy asintió con la cabeza, mirándola con interés. Le ofreció un cigarrillo y ambos pasaron un rato estudiando a los invitados.

—Bueno —dijo Sandy—, ¿qué opina usted de la Nueva España y sus amigos?

—Supongo que todo parece muy civilizado después de lo de Madrid. Pero se respira una atmósfera excesivamente militar. Un lugar muy duro. —Miró a Cordelia todavía enfrascada en su conversación con el cura—. Puede que la Iglesia ejerza una influencia moderadora.

Sandy exhaló una nube de humo.

—No crea. La Iglesia sabe muy bien lo que le conviene; dejará que el régimen haga lo que le dé la gana. Estas gentes van a ganar, ¿sabe?, cuentan con las tropas y el dinero necesario. Lo saben, y se les nota en la cara. Es sólo cuestión de tiempo.

—¿Usted cree?

—Sí.

—¿Es usted católico?

—No, por Dios.

—Aquella amiga mía lo es. Pero sí, tiene usted razón. Van a ganar.

Barbara suspiró.

—Mejor que la alternativa.

—Tal vez.

—Puede que me quede aquí cuando todo termine. Estoy harto de Inglaterra.

—¿No tiene vínculos familiares?

—No. ¿Y usted?

—Más bien tampoco.

—¿Le apetece salir a tomar algo cualquier noche de éstas? Ahora estoy sin trabajo, en busca de empleo; pero aquí se siente uno muy solo.

Ella lo miró con asombro, no se lo esperaba.

—Sin compromiso —añadió Sandy—. Sólo para tomar unas copas. Traiga a su amiga Cordelia, si quiere.

—Muy bien, de acuerdo. ¿Por qué no?

Pese a constarle que a Cordelia no le gustaría Sandy.

Cuando llegó la noche de la cita, no le apetecía ir. Cordelia no podía acompañarla porque tenía que asistir a otra ceremonia en la iglesia, y ella se sentía cansada y deprimida después del trabajo. Pero había acordado ir y fue.

Se reunieron en un bar pequeño, tranquilo y oscuro muy cerca de la catedral. Sandy le preguntó qué tal le había ido en el trabajo. La pregunta la molestó un poco; se lo había preguntado como si ella trabajara en un despacho o una tienda.

—No muy bien, la verdad. Me han asignado la tarea de intentar evacuar a unos niños al otro lado del frente. Casi todos ellos son huérfanos. Y eso siempre resulta terriblemente desagradable. —Apartó el rostro mientras las lágrimas asomaban inesperadamente a sus ojos—. Perdone —añadió—. He tenido una jornada muy larga y este nuevo trabajo me trae... muy malos recuerdos.

—¿Quiere hablar de ello? —le preguntó él con amable curiosidad.

Decidió contárselo. Cordelia tenía razón, de nada servía reprimirlo.

—Cuando trabajaba en Madrid, conocí a un hombre... un inglés de las Brigadas Internacionales. Estuvimos juntos el pasado invierno. Después, él se fue al Jarama. Desaparecido y dado por muerto.

Sandy asintió con la cabeza.

—Lo siento de veras.

—Sólo han pasado nueve meses y cuesta mucho superarlo. —Barbara lanzó un suspiro—. Es una historia muy corriente en estos momentos en España, lo sé.

Él le ofreció un cigarrillo y se lo encendió.

—¿Uno de los voluntarios?

—Sí, Bernie era comunista. Aunque, en realidad, no pertenecía a la clase obrera; le habían concedido una beca para estudiar en un colegio privado, y hablaba con el mismo acento que usted. Más tarde averigüé que el partido lo consideraba ideológicamente sospechoso por sus complicados orígenes de clase. No era lo bastante duro.

Se fijó en Sandy y le sorprendió ver que éste se había reclinado en su asiento, desde donde la estudiaba con una mirada penetrante e inquisitiva.

—¿En qué colegio estudió? —preguntó en voz baja.

—Un sitio llamado Rookwood, en el condado de Surrey.

—¿Su apellido no sería Piper, por casualidad?

—Sí. —Ahora la sorprendida era ella—. Pues sí, exactamente. ¿Acaso usted...?

—Yo estudié en Rookwood durante algún tiempo. Conocí a Piper. No mucho, pero lo conocí. ¿Supongo que no le habló de mí? —Sandy soltó una extraña carcajada que sonó como un ladrido forzado—. La oveja negra de la clase.

—No. No hablaba demasiado de su colegio. Sólo decía que no se encontraba a gusto allí.

—No. En eso coincidíamos, recuerdo.

—¿Eran ustedes amigos? —A Barbara le dio un vuelco el corazón; era como si una parte de Bernie hubiera regresado.

Sandy titubeó.

—Más bien no. Como ya le he dicho, no lo conocía muy bien. —Meneó la cabeza—. Pero qué coincidencia, Dios mío.

—Es algo así como el destino —dijo Barbara sonriendo—. Conocer a alguien que lo conoció.

El hecho de que Sandy hubiera conocido a Bernie, aunque no hubieran sido amigos, fue lo que atrajo a Barbara. Ambos adquirieron la costumbre de reunirse todos los jueves en el bar para tomarse unas copas. Al final, acabó esperando con ansia aquellas citas. Cordelia había regresado al frente y aquéllas eran ahora las únicas noches que tenía libres. Se fue una mañana, después de darle a Barbara un rápido abrazo y negarse a que ésta la ayudara a llevar las maletas a la estación. Barbara le agradeció que la hubiera ayudado a recuperarse un poco; pero Cordelia sonrió y le dijo que habría hecho lo mismo por cualquier otra persona, pues así se lo exigía su fe y su amor a Dios. Aquella respuesta impersonal le dolió y la hizo volver a sentirse muy sola. Averiguó que Sandy también conocía a Harry y había sido amigo suyo, ya que no de Bernie. En cierto modo, su actitud la desconcertaba. Era enigmático y apenas hablaba de sí mismo. En aquellos momentos no tenía ninguna gira turística a la vista, pero aun así se quedó en Burgos tratando de montar algún negocio, le dijo. Aunque nunca le reveló de qué clase. Iba siempre impecablemente vestido. Barbara se preguntaba si tendría novia en algún sitio, pero él jamás hacía el menor comentario al respecto. Se le llegó a pasar por la cabeza la posibilidad de que fuera marica, aunque no lo parecía.

Un jueves de diciembre, Barbara se dirigió a toda prisa al café bajo una lluvia torrencial que caía implacable desde un cielo encapotado. Al llegar, Sandy ya estaba allí, sentado a la mesa de siempre con un hombre vestido con un uniforme falangista. Ambos estaban inclinados el uno hacia el otro con las cabezas muy juntas y, aunque Barbara no pudo oír lo que decían, adivinó que estaban discutiendo. Se quedó indecisa mientras las gotas de lluvia se deslizaban por su chubasquero hasta caer al suelo. Al verla, Sandy le hizo señas de que se acercara.

—Perdona, Barbara, estaba terminando un asunto de negocios.

El falangista se levantó y la miró. Era un hombre de mediana edad y rostro extremadamente severo. Miró a Sandy desde arriba.

—El negocio tiene que ser para los españoles, señor —dijo—. Negocio español, beneficios españoles.

El hombre saludó a Barbara inclinando levemente la cabeza, dio media vuelta y se retiró haciendo sonar sus tacones sobre las tablas del suelo. Sandy lo miró con semblante enfurecido. Barbara se sentó, algo desconcertada. Sandy se calmó y soltó una carcajada incierta.

—Disculpa —le dijo—. Un plan que yo tenía para un trabajo se ha ido a pique. Aquí parece que no tienen mucha vista para los negocios. —Lanzó un suspiro—. No importa. Supongo que tendré que volver a las giras turísticas. —Fue por una copa para Barbara y regresó a la mesa.

—Quizá convendría que pensaras en la posibilidad de regresar a casa —le dijo Barbara—. Yo he estado pensando en lo que voy a hacer cuando termine la guerra. No creo que me apetezca regresar a Ginebra.

Sandy meneó la cabeza.

—Yo no quiero volver —dijo tranquilamente—. Allí no tengo a nadie. Inglaterra me resulta asfixiante.

—Entiendo lo que quieres decir. —Barbara levantó su copa—. Brindemos por el desarraigo.

Sandy la miró sonriendo.

—Por el desarraigo. Mira, aquella primera noche en que nos conocimos pensé, esta chica se mantiene al margen observándolo todo. Como yo.

—¿De veras?

—Sí.

Barbara suspiró.

—Es que no me gusto demasiado —dijo—. Por eso me mantengo apartada.

—¿Porque estás enojada con Bernie?

—¿Con Bernie? No, no es eso. Él hizo que me gustara un poquito a mí misma. Durante algún tiempo.

Sandy la miró muy serio.

—No tienes que dejarles a los demás la tarea de hacer que te gustes a ti misma. Lo sé porque antes yo también era así.

—¿Tú? —Barbara lo miró con asombro. Siempre se le veía tan confiado, tan seguro de sí mismo.

—Sólo antes de tener la edad suficiente para pensar por mí mismo.

Barbara respiró hondo.

—Yo lo pasé muy mal en la escuela. Sufrí acoso escolar. —Hizo una pausa, pero él se limitó a asentir con la cabeza, animándola a seguir. Y entonces le contó la historia—. A veces me parece oír sus voces, ¿sabes? No, no las oigo, eso significaría que estoy loca; pero sí las recuerdo. Cuando estoy cansada y cometo errores en mi trabajo. Me digo que soy fea, la cuatro ojos con ricitos que no sirve para nada. Y eso me ocurre cada vez más a menudo desde que Bernie murió. —Inclinó la cabeza—. Nunca hablo de eso. Sólo Bernie lo sabía.

—Entonces, me considero privilegiado porque me lo has dicho.

—Presiento que te puedo contar cosas —dijo Barbara sin levantar la cabeza—. No sé por qué.

—Mírame —dijo Sandy en voz baja—. Mírame, no tengas miedo.

Ella levantó la cabeza y sonrió con valentía, parpadeando para reprimir las lágrimas.

—Diles que se vayan a la mierda —dijo Sandy—. Cuando las oigas, diles que están equivocadas y que tú se lo vas a demostrar. No exteriormente, sino dentro de tu cabeza. Es lo que yo hice. Con mis padres y mis profesores, que me decían que iba a terminar muy mal.

—¿Y dio resultado? Sí, lo debió de dar... porque tú crees en ti mismo, ¿verdad?

—No queda más remedio. Tienes que decidir lo que quieres ser y lanzarte. No prestes atención a la opinión que tengan los demás de ti. La gente siempre anda buscando a alguien a quien humillar. Eso hace que se sienta segura.

—No todo el mundo. Yo, no.

—Bueno, pues casi todo el mundo. ¿Te puedo decir una cosa?

—Si quieres.

—¿No te ofenderás?

—No.

—No sacas el mejor partido de ti misma. Es como si no quisieras que los demás te respetaran. Esfuérzate un poco con la ropa que vistes, con tu cabello; podrías ser una mujer muy atractiva.

Barbara volvió a bajar la cabeza.

—Eso es lo otro que pensé la noche en que nos conocimos.

Notó que las puntas de sus dedos rozaban las de los de Sandy y se hizo un momento de silencio. Recordaba con toda claridad la escena en la iglesia. El beso de Bernie. Apartó la mano y levantó los ojos.

—No estoy... no estoy preparada para esto. Después de Bernie, no creo que jamás pueda...

—Vamos, Barbara —le dijo él con dulzura—. No me digas que crees en esta idea tan romántica de que sólo hay una persona para cada cual.

—Pues me parece que lo creo. —Quería irse de allí, el torbellino de emociones que se agitaba en su interior le provocaba mareos. Sandy levantó una mano.

—De acuerdo, pues olvídalo.

—Sólo quiero que seamos amigos, Sandy.

—Necesitas a alguien que cuide de ti, Barbara —dijo Sandy sonriendo—. Siempre he querido tener a alguien de quien cuidar.

—No, Sandy. No. Simplemente amigos.

Sandy asintió con la cabeza.

—Está bien. Está bien. Pero, de todos modos, deja que te cuide un poco.

Ella apoyó la cabeza en la mano y se cubrió el rostro. Fuera la lluvia seguía cayendo con fuerza.

El otoño se convirtió en invierno. Corrían rumores de una nueva ofensiva nacional que pondría fin a la guerra. Durante algún tiempo, Burgos se llenó de soldados italianos; pero, después, éstos volvieron a desaparecer.

Sandy cumplió su palabra; dejó de hacerle insinuaciones románticas. Ella no sentía por él lo mismo que había sentido por Bernie, era imposible. Sin embargo, y muy a pesar suyo, la emocionaba e ilusionaba que otro hombre la encontrara atractiva. Se daba cuenta de que una parte, una pequeña parte, de su pena había sido por sí misma, por el hecho de haber perdido en un santiamén su única oportunidad de amar. Como si la declaración de Sandy hubiera abierto la puerta de algo, Barbara empezó a pensar en él como hombre, un hombre alto y fuerte.

A mediados de diciembre llegó la noticia de que los republicanos se habían adelantado a la ofensiva de Franco y lanzado la suya propia en Teruel, muy hacia el este. El tiempo era frío, las calles de Burgos estaban cubiertas de nieve y en la oficina les habían dicho que a algunos soldados les habían tenido que amputar los pies congelados en el mismo campo de batalla. La oficina de la Cruz Roja se encontraba de nuevo en plena actividad.

—Lo tendrías que dejar —le dijo Sandy cuando ambos se reunieron aquel jueves por la noche—. Te está dejando rendida.

La miró con preocupación, pero también con aquel atisbo de impaciencia que ella le había visto en los últimos tiempos. La semana anterior, por primera vez, Sandy había intentado tomarle la mano al salir del bar. Habían bebido más que de costumbre, porque él se había pasado el rato pidiendo más vino. Ella había retirado la mano.

Barbara suspiró.

—Es mi trabajo. Incluso he anulado el permiso de Navidad para poder echar una mano.

—Pensaba que ibas a regresar a casa. A Birmingham, ¿no?

—Ésa era mi intención. Pero la verdad es que no me apetecía, me alegro de tener un pretexto. —Barbara lo miró—. ¿Y tú? Nunca hablas de tu familia, Sandy; lo único que yo sé es que tienes un padre y un hermano.

—Y una madre en algún lugar, si es que vive todavía. Ya te lo dije, rompí con ellos. Pertenecen al pasado. —La miró—. Pero me iré un par de semanas de todos modos.

—Ah, ¿sí? —Se le cayó el alma a los pies; confiaba en que se quedara con ella por Navidad.

—Una oportunidad de negocio. Importación de automóviles desde Inglaterra. No les gusta que los de fuera intervengan en sus negocios, eso ya lo he captado; pero necesitarán a alguien que domine el inglés para poder hacerlo. Y ahora me voy a San Sebastián a echarle un vistazo.

Barbara recordó al falangista con quien Sandy había discutido.

—Comprendo. Parece una buena oportunidad. Pero es una mala época del año para viajar y las carreteras estarán llenas de soldados, con esta batalla que...

—Las del norte, no. Intentaré estar de vuelta para el día de Navidad.

—Sí. Sería bonito que lo pudiéramos celebrar juntos.

—Lo intentaré.

Pero no pudo ser. La llamada a la oficina que ella esperaba jamás tuvo lugar. La afectó más de lo que imaginaba. El día de Navidad salió a dar una vuelta sola por las calles nevadas, contemplando envidiosa las casas con pesebres en los jardines y la gente que entraba y salía de las ceremonias en las numerosas iglesias de Burgos. Experimentó una repentina y enfurecida impaciencia contra sí misma. ¿Por qué no había aceptado lo que Sandy le ofrecía? ¿A qué esperaba? ¿A que llegara la vejez? Pensó en Bernie y la tristeza le volvió a atenazar el corazón; pero Bernie ya no estaba.

Sandy la llamó al despacho dos días después de Navidad.

—Perdona que haya tardado tanto —le dijo.

Barbara sonrió al oír su voz.

—¿Cómo ha ido?

—Muy bien. Estás hablando con un hombre que dispone de un permiso de importación firmado por el mismísimo ministro de Comercio. Oye, ¿quieres que nos veamos en el bar esta noche? Ya sé que no es jueves.

Ella se echó a reír.

—Sí, estaría bien. ¿A la hora de siempre?

—Nos vemos a las ocho. Tomaremos un poco de champán para celebrar el acuerdo.

Barbara se había puesto su nuevo abrigo, el verde que Sandy había elegido para ella porque decía que combinaba muy bien con el color de su cabello. Se presentó allí antes que ella, como de costumbre, con un paquete de gran tamaño envuelto en papel de regalo de vistosos colores sobre la mesa. La miró sonriendo.

—Un tardío regalo de Navidad. Para disculparme por haber permanecido tanto tiempo fuera.

Barbara lo abrió. Dentro había un broche en forma de flor, con unas piedrecitas verdes que brillaban en los pétalos.

—Oh, Sandy —dijo ella—. Es precioso. ¿Y esto...?

Él la miró sonriendo.

—Unas esmeraldas. Pero pequeñitas.

—No tendrías que haberlo hecho, te habrá costado un dineral.

—No, si sabes dónde buscar.

—Gracias. —A Barbara le temblaba el labio—. No soy digna de él.

—Pues yo digo que sí. —Sandy alargó la mano y tomó la suya. Esta vez, ella no la retiró.

La miró a los ojos.

—Quítate las gafas —le dijo—. Quiero verte sin ellas.

20

El miércoles, después de su paseo con Harry, Barbara acudió a su tercera cita con Luis. Era un cálido y soleado día de otoño. Mientras bajaba por la Castellana, oyó el crujir de las hojas secas bajo sus pies y notó el leve pero penetrante olor a humo de unas hojas que alguien debía de estar quemando en alguna parte. Barbara paseaba mucho últimamente; eso la ayudaba a pensar y, además, cada vez le gustaba menos quedarse en casa.

No le había llegado el dinero de Inglaterra y ya empezaba a perder las esperanzas de recibirlo alguna vez. Si Luis le facilitara la prueba que ella le había pedido para confirmar la presencia de Bernie en el campo, de algún sitio lo tendría que sacar.

Luis ya estaba en el café. Fumaba una buena marca de cigarrillos, y Barbara se preguntó si parte del dinero que ella le había entregado para el billete de tren a Cuenca la habría gastado en tabaco; no sabía lo que costaba el billete. Como es natural, sólo tenía su palabra de que había estado allí.

Luis se levantó y estrechó su mano tan educado como siempre, y después fue a la barra a buscarle una taza de café. El local estaba muy tranquilo; el veterano cojo con la pernera cosida permanecía acodado solo en la barra.

Barbara encendió un cigarrillo, mirando deliberadamente la cajetilla de Luis.

—¿Estuvo usted en Cuenca? —preguntó.

—Sí, señora. —Luis la miró sonriendo—. Me volví a reunir con Agustín en la ciudad. —Se inclinó hacia delante—. Agustín ha conseguido echar un vistazo a la ficha de Bernie, pero le aseguro que no fue nada fácil. Me facilitó muchos detalles.

Barbara asintió con la cabeza.

—Sí.

—Nació en un lugar de Londres llamado la Isla de los Perros. Vino a combatir por la República en 1936 y sufrió una herida leve en el brazo en una de las batallas de la Casa de Campo. —Barbara sintió que se le aceleraban los latidos del corazón. No había manera de que Luis o Markby supieran algo de aquella herida si no era echando un vistazo a una ficha oficial—. Cuando se recuperó, lo enviaron al Jarama, donde resultó herido y hecho prisionero.

—¿Herido? —preguntó Barbara bruscamente—. ¿De gravedad?

—No fue nada serio. Una herida superficial en el muslo. —Luis la miró sonriendo—. Por lo visto, tenía buena estrella.

—No tan buena, Luis, si acabó en el campo de prisioneros.

—Agustín me lo describió —siguió diciendo Luis—. Es un hombre de estatura elevada, hombros anchos y cabello rubio. Probablemente muy guapo, me dijo Agustín; aunque ahora, como es natural, lleva barba de dos días y tiene piojos. —Barbara hizo una mueca—. Tiene fama de ser un hombre difícil y de espíritu indomable. Agustín le ha dicho que tenga cuidado, que es posible que lleguen mejores tiempos, pero de momento sólo eso. —Luis la miró con una sonrisa burlona en los labios—. Dice que su hombre tiene duende. Cree que tiene voluntad de fugarse. Y muchos en el campo han perdido la voluntad o la fuerza necesaria para hacerlo. —El corazón de Barbara latía violentamente en el pecho. Ahora sabía que todo era verdad, estaba segura. Luis ladeó la cabeza—. ¿Está usted satisfecha, señora? ¿Cree que le he dicho la verdad?

—Sí. Sí, lo creo. Gracias, Luis. —Respiró hondo—. Todavía no he recibido el dinero de mi banco de Inglaterra. Cuesta recibir dinero de fuera del país.

Él la miró con la cara muy seria.

—Es importante que todo se haga antes de que llegue el mal tiempo. Los inviernos son muy duros allá arriba y empiezan muy pronto. Ya hará frío.

—Y la situación diplomática puede cambiar. Lo sé. Insistiré, hoy mismo les volveré a escribir. ¿Le parece que nos volvamos a reunir aquí dentro de una semana? Para entonces, tendré el dinero como sea. Si lo recibiera antes, ¿hay alguna manera de contactar con usted?

—No tengo teléfono, señora. ¿Quiere que la llame yo?

Barbara lo miró, indecisa.

—Mejor no. No quiero que mi marido descubra nada, bastante preocupado está ya por mí.

—Entonces hasta dentro de una semana. Pero tendremos que empezar con los preparativos. Pronto estaremos en noviembre.

—Sí, lo sé.

Mientras hablaba, pensó: «Ya no hay tiempo para que les vuelva a escribir. ¿Y si le pidiera un préstamo a Harry?» Sabía que éste tenía dinero. Pero era un diplomático, podría ser peligroso para él...

Hizo un esfuerzo por regresar de nuevo al presente.

—¿El plan sigue siendo el mismo? —le preguntó a Luis—. ¿Agustín lo ayuda a fugarse y yo lo recojo en Cuenca?

—Sí. Puede haber alguna manera de conseguirle ropa de paisano para que no llame tanto la atención. Agustín lo está estudiando. Entonces de usted dependería, señora, sacarlo de allí y llevárselo a la embajada.

—Puede que eso no sea tan fácil. He pasado por allí y siempre hay guardias civiles en la entrada.

—Eso lo tendrá que resolver usted, señora —dijo Luis con una triste sonrisa en los labios. Parecía que la cosa ya no le interesaba; en cuanto Barbara recogiera a Bernie, el problema dejaría de ser suyo.

—Le pagaré una parte cuando hayamos elaborado un plan definitivo, y el resto, cuando todo esté hecho —dijo Barbara—. A todos nos interesa que la empresa llegue a buen puerto.

Luis la miró.

—Usted ya se encargará de que así sea, lo sé.

Barbara volvió a pensar en Harry. Si ella pudiera trasladar a Bernie a Madrid y esconderlo en algún sitio. Lanzó un suspiro. Se dio cuenta de que Luis la estaba mirando con curiosidad.

—¿Qué ocurre? —le preguntó.

—Disculpe la indiscreción, señora, pero ¿este asunto no tendrá consecuencias para usted y su marido? Si el señor Piper consigue llegar a la embajada, es probable que el asunto pase a dominio público. Por lo menos, se presentarán quejas ante nuestro Gobierno. Y su marido trabaja con el Gobierno, ¿no es cierto? Usted misma me lo dijo en nuestra primera reunión.

—Sí, Luis —dijo Barbara en un susurro—. Puede que haya consecuencias. Tendré que afrontarlas.

Luis la miró con semblante muy serio.

—Es usted una mujer muy valiente al poner en peligro su futuro de esta manera.

Ella lo estudió. Su rostro ofrecía un aspecto muy tenso y cansado. En realidad, era poco más que un muchacho obligado a manejar cosas terribles a una edad excesivamente temprana, como le ocurría a la mitad de los hombres del mundo en aquellos momentos.

—¿Qué harán usted y su hermano, Luis, cuando esto termine y su hermano abandone el Ejército?

Luis sonrió tristemente.

—Sueño con ir a recoger a mi madre a Sevilla y llevarla a vivir al campo, cerca de Madrid, donde quizá podría cultivar verduras y hortalizas. Es algo que siempre me ha gustado, y una gran ciudad necesita verduras y hortalizas, ¿no cree? Así todos volveremos a ser una familia. —Su rostro se ensombreció—. La familia es importante para los españoles y la guerra separó a muchas... usted, que viene de Inglaterra, no puede comprender lo dolorosa que resulta toda esta situación. Por eso tengo que hacer lo imposible con tal de estar juntos otra vez. ¿Lo comprende, señora?

—Sí. Y espero que lo consiga.

—Yo también. —Luis inclinó un momento la cabeza, cerró los ojos y después los volvió a abrir con una sonrisa en los labios—. Hasta la semana que viene, señora.

—Para entonces ya habré conseguido el dinero como sea.

Aquella noche, a la hora de cenar, Sandy le dijo que había reservado mesa en el Ritz para celebrar su aniversario la noche del día siguiente.

—Ah —dijo ella, sorprendida.

—¿Qué tiene eso de malo? —le preguntó él. Aún no le había perdonado el olvido—. Es el hotel más caro de Madrid.

—Lo sé, Sandy. Sólo que estará lleno de alemanes y de sus compinches italianos. Y tú sabes que no soporto verlos.

—Una oportunidad para hacer acto de presencia —dijo Sandy sonriendo.

Barbara se preguntó si Sandy habría elegido deliberadamente el Ritz para provocar su enfado. Lo miró y recordó su ternura la primera vez que se habían visto. ¿Adónde habría ido a parar todo aquello? Se dio cuenta de que lo que disgustaba a Sandy era su malestar ante la vida que él había elegido para ella, un malestar que llevaba mucho tiempo creciendo en su interior pero que, en realidad, sólo había aflorado a la superficie a partir de aquella cena con Markby.

—¿Recuerdas la primera Navidad después de nuestro primer encuentro? —le preguntó Sandy, mirándola con una expresión dura y burlona en los ojos.

—Sí. Cuando te fuiste por un asunto de negocios y no pudiste regresar hasta pasada la Navidad.

—Exactamente —dijo Sandy sonriendo—. Sólo que sí hubiera podido. Pero comprendí que, si no regresaba, tú te darías cuenta de lo mucho que me necesitabas. Y no me equivoqué.

Ella lo miró, sintiéndose primero escandalizada, y después, tremendamente furiosa.

—O sea que me manipulaste —dijo muy despacio—. Manipulaste mis sentimientos.

Él la miró desde el otro lado de la mesa, ahora con la cara muy seria.

—Yo sé lo que quiere la gente, Barbara, lo intuyo. Es un don muy útil en los negocios. Veo lo que hay bajo la superficie. A veces, eso es muy fácil. Los judíos, por ejemplo, sólo quieren sobrevivir, tiemblan y se estremecen en su desesperado afán de sobrevivir. Lo que quieren las personas con quienes yo trabajo suele ser dinero, aunque a veces es otra cosa. Yo trato de complacerlas en lo que sea. Tú me querías a mí y querías seguridad, lo que ocurre es que no acababas de darte cuenta. Yo te ayudé a que lo sacaras a la superficie. —Sandy inclinó la cabeza y levantó su copa.

—¿Y tú, Sandy? ¿Qué es lo que quieres?

Él la miró sonriendo.

—Éxito, dinero. Saber que puedo estar a la altura de las circunstancias y conseguir que la gente me dé lo que yo quiero.

—A veces eres una mierda, Sandy. ¿Lo sabes? —dijo ella.

Jamás le había hablado en semejantes términos, y él la miró momentáneamente desconcertado. Después, la expresión de su rostro se endureció.

—Últimamente no cuidas mucho tu aspecto, ¿sabes? Estás hecha un desastre. Espero que el hecho de trabajar en ese orfelinato te ayude a serenarte un poco.

Las palabras la azotaron con fuerza y ella se dio cuenta de que Sandy las había elegido para golpearla donde más le dolía. Algo frío y duro acudió a su mente mientras pensaba, «no contestes, hay que guardar las apariencias de momento». Se levantó, dejando cuidadosamente la servilleta sobre la mesa, y abandonó la estancia. Le temblaban las piernas.

SEGUNDA PARTE

PRINCIPIOS DE INVIERNO

21

El psiquiatra era un hombre alto y delgado, con gafas y cabello plateado. Vestía un traje gris de raya diplomática. Bernie llevaba tres años y medio sin ver a nadie vestido con traje de calle, sólo los monos de los prisioneros y los prácticos uniformes de los guardias, ambos de un triste color verde aceituna.

Al médico lo habían instalado en el cuarto situado bajo la barraca del comandante, detrás de una mesa rayada procedente de los despachos de arriba. Bernie pensó que no le habían dicho para qué se usaba aquel cuarto. El hecho de haberlo colocado allí era muy propio del macabro sentido del humor de Aranda.

Agustín, uno de los guardias, estaba esperando a Bernie cuando su cuadrilla de trabajo regresó de la cantera, con órdenes de conducirlo ante el comandante.

—No tienes por qué preocuparte, no hay ningún problema —le dijo el guardia en voz baja, mientras cruzaban el patio. Bernie había inclinado la cabeza para darle las gracias. Agustín era uno de los mejores, un joven desaliñado que sólo aspiraba a vivir tranquilo. El sol brillaba muy bajo y un frío viento soplaba desde las montañas. Bernie llevaba la cuenta de los días y sabía que estaban a uno de noviembre; el invierno ya se les estaba echando encima y los pastores empezaban a bajar sus rebaños desde los altos pastos. Trabajar en la cuadrilla de la cantera resultaba muy duro, pero por lo menos uno podía captar un poco el sentido de los ritmos del mundo exterior. Se estremeció, envidiándole a Agustín la gruesa capa que llevaba sobre el uniforme.

El comandante Aranda permanecía sentado tras su escritorio. Levantó los duros ojos hacia Bernie, mientras una expresión burlona se dibujaba en su rostro alargado y hermoso adornado con un poblado bigote negro.

—Ah, Piper —le dijo—, tengo una visita para usted.

—¿Señor? —Bernie se cuadró rígidamente, como Aranda esperaba que hiciera. Un espasmo de dolor le traspasó el brazo; le dolía la vieja herida tras haberse pasado el día acarreando piedras.

—¿Recuerda que, en San Pedro de Cardeña, un psiquiatra efectuó una evaluación de su estado?

—Sí, mi coronel.

Había sido una farsa grotesca, una broma de mal gusto. San Pedro de Cardeña era un abandonado monasterio medieval situado a las afueras de Burgos. Miles de presos republicanos habían sido amontonados allí dentro después de la batalla del Jarama. Un día les habían entregado unos largos cuestionaros para que los rellenaran. Les dijeron que era para un proyecto sobre la psicología del fanatismo marxista. Doscientas preguntas que oscilaban entre su reacción a ciertos colores y su grado de patriotismo.

El comandante encendió un cigarrillo y lo estudió con sus fríos ojos color avellana a través de una espiral de humo. Aranda llevaba casi un año al frente del campo de Tierra Muerta. Era un coronel veterano de la Guerra Civil y antes lo había sido en la Legión. Disfrutaba siendo cruel, y ni siquiera Bernie se habría atrevido a mostrarse insolente con él. Como siempre, el comandante iba vestido impecablemente, el uniforme planchado y las rayas del pantalón rectas como el filo de una navaja. Los prisioneros conocían todas las arrugas y las curvas de su rostro hermoso y bronceado con bigote encerado. Cuando fruncía el entrecejo o hacía pucheros como un chiquillo, seguro que alguien estaba a punto de recibir una tanda de azotes.

Aquella tarde, sin embargo, mostraba un semblante risueño. Le arrojó a Bernie una bocanada de humo, y éste experimentó de inmediato su antigua ansia de fumar y se inclinó ligeramente hacia delante para respirar otra vaharada.

—Están haciendo un estudio complementario sobre algunos prisioneros de especial interés. El doctor Lorenzo le espera abajo. Por cierto, Piper, procure colaborar con él, ¿vale?

—Sí, mi comandante.

El corazón de Piper latía con fuerza cuando Agustín lo acompañó al cuarto del sótano y abrió una pesada puerta de madera. Bernie jamás había estado allí, pero había oído describir gráficamente la estancia.

El rostro del psiquiatra era frío.

—Puede retirarse —le dijo éste a Agustín.

—Estaré fuera, señor.

El psiquiatra señaló con la mano una silla de acero colocada ante el escritorio.

—Siéntese.

Bernie se dejó caer en ella. En un rincón había una estufa de petróleo, así que en el cuarto hacía calor. El psiquiatra recorrió con una pluma plateada las columnas de un cuestionario. Bernie reconoció su propia letra. Los piojos de su barba se empezaron a mover, estimulados por el calor.

El psiquiatra levantó los ojos.

—¿Es usted Piper, Bernard, inglés, de treinta y un años de edad?

—Sí.

—Yo soy el doctor Lorenzo. Hace tres años, cuando estaba en San Pedro, contestó usted a un cuestionario. ¿Lo recuerda?

—Sí, doctor.

—El propósito del estudio era establecer los factores psicológicos que pueden inducir a las personas a abrazar el marxismo. —Su voz era uniforme y monótona—. Casi todos los marxistas son personas ignorantes de la clase obrera, con escasa inteligencia y cultura. Queremos volver a examinar a las personas que no se ajustaban a estos criterios. Usted, por ejemplo. —El psiquiatra estudió detenidamente a Bernie.

—Lo que lleva a las personas hacia el marxismo es muy sencillo —dijo serenamente Bernie—. La pobreza y la opresión.

El psiquiatra asintió con la cabeza.

—Sí, eso es lo que yo esperaba que usted me dijera. Y, sin embargo, es posible que usted no haya estado sometido a ninguna de estas cosas; veo que estudió usted en una escuela privada inglesa.

—Mis padres eran pobres. Yo conseguí una plaza en Rookwood gracias a una beca.

Los ojos de Bernie se desviaron hacia un rincón de la estancia donde había un objeto alto, cubierto con una lona. Lorenzo golpeó bruscamente la superficie del escritorio con la pluma de plata.

—Preste atención, por favor. Hábleme de sus padres... ¿a qué se dedicaban?

—Trabajaban en una tienda propiedad de otra persona.

—¿Y quizás usted se compadecía de ellos? ¿Los quería mucho?

Una imagen de su madre acudió a la mente de Bernie, de pie en el salón retorciéndose las manos. «Bernie, Bernie, ¿por qué te tienes que ir a esta guerra tan horrible?»

Se encogió de hombros.

—Que yo sepa, a estas alturas ya podrían estar muertos.

—¿Les escribiría si pudiera?

—Sí.

Lorenzo hizo otra anotación.

—Este colegio, este Rookwood que le permitió establecer contacto con chicos de una cultura superior. Me interesa el hecho de que usted rechazara aquellos valores.

Bernie se rió amargamente.

—Allí no hay cultura. Y su clase era enemiga de la mía.

—Ah, sí, la metafísica marxista. —El psiquiatra asintió con la cabeza y lo miró con expresión pensativa—. Nuestros estudios revelan que, cuando las personas inteligentes y privilegiadas se sienten atraídas por el marxismo, se debe a un defecto de carácter. No comprenden los valores más elevados como la espiritualidad o el patriotismo. Son seres antisociales y agresivos por naturaleza. El comandante me dice que usted, Piper, rechaza, por ejemplo, los intentos de rehabilitación del campamento, ¿verdad?

Bernie se rió por lo bajo.

—¿Se refiere a la instrucción religiosa obligatoria?

Lorenzo lo estudió como a una rata de laboratorio en el interior de una jaula.

—Sí, parece que usted odia el cristianismo. Una religión que predica el amor y la reconciliación. Sí, esto está muy claro.

—Nos dan también otras lecciones.

El doctor Lorenzo lo miró, perplejo.

—¿Qué quiere decir?

—Esto es un cuarto de torturas. Este armario que hay a su espalda seguramente está lleno de porras y de cubos para ahogamientos simulados.

Lorenzo meneó suavemente la cabeza.

—Fantasías.

—Pues entonces retire la lona de esa cosa que tiene a su espalda —dijo Bernie—. Hágalo. —Se percató de que su tono era cada vez más insolente y se mordió el labio. No quería que le presentaran una queja a Aranda.

El psiquiatra emitió un leve gruñido de hastío, se levantó y retiró la lona. Las facciones de su rostro se endurecieron al ver la alta estaca de madera con el asiento de metal, las correas de sujeción, el aro para el cuello y el pesado tornillo de latón con sus correspondientes manijas en la parte posterior.

—Las ejecuciones, doctor. Ha habido seis desde mi llegada aquí. Los colocan en fila en el patio y nos obligan a mirar.

El psiquiatra volvió a sentarse. Su voz no se había alterado. Miró fijamente a Bernie y después meneó la cabeza.

—Usted es un antisocial —dijo en tono pausado—. Un psicópata. —Volvió a menear la cabeza—. Los hombres como usted jamás se rehabilitan; sus mentes son anormales, incompletas. Por desgracia, el garrote es necesario para mantener a raya a individuos como usted. —Hizo una anotación en su cuestionario y después levantó la voz para llamar a Agustín—. ¡Guardia! Ya he terminado con este hombre.

Agustín acompañó a Bernie fuera de la estancia. El sol ya se había ocultado tras el horizonte, y un resplandor rojizo bañaba las barracas de madera que bordeaban el patio de tierra. No tardarían en encenderse los reflectores de la atalaya que se levantaba por encima de la alambrada de púas. Pegado al barracón del rancho había un poste enorme de más de metro ochenta del que colgaban unas cuerdas. Parecía un símbolo, pero no lo era: ataban a él a los hombres como castigo. Bernie deseó haber mencionado aquel detalle al psiquiatra.

Ya había llegado la hora de pasar lista; trescientos prisioneros empezaban a formar alrededor de la pequeña plataforma de madera que había en el centro. Agustín se detuvo y se echó el pesado fusil al hombro.

—Esta noche tengo que llevar a otros cinco al loquero —dijo—. Va a ser una noche muy larga.

Bernie lo miró con asombro. Los guardias tenían prohibido hablar con los prisioneros.

—El médico parecía enfadado —añadió Agustín.

Bernie lo miró, pero el guardia mantenía el enjuto rostro apartado.

—Ten cuidado —dijo Agustín en voz baja—. Ya vendrán tiempos mejores, Piper. Ahora no puedo decir más. Pero ten cuidado. Procura que no te castiguen, o te maten.

Bernie permanecía de pie junto a su amigo Vicente. El rostro chupado del abogado, enmarcado por una desgreñada mata de cabello gris y una enmarañada barba, ofrecía un aspecto ojeroso y cansado. Miró con una sonrisa a Bernie y después sufrió un acceso de tos mientras, desde lo más hondo de su pecho, se escuchaba una especie de gorgoteo líquido. Vicente sufría infecciones pulmonares desde el verano; parecía que se recuperaba, pero éstas lo volvían a atacar, cada vez con más saña. Algunos guardias le permitían encargarse de trabajos más ligeros a cambio de su ayuda en la tarea de rellenar impresos; sin embargo, aquella semana el sargento encargado de la cuadrilla de la cantera era Ramírez, un hombre brutal que había obligado a Vicente a pasarse todo el día cargando piedras. Parecía que a duras penas podía tenerse en pie.

—¿Qué te ha pasado? —preguntó a Bernie en un susurro.

—Hay un psiquiatra que anda entrevistando a unos cuantos hombres de San Pedro. Me ha dicho que soy un psicópata antisocial.

Vicente sonrió con ironía.

—Eso demuestra lo que yo siempre he dicho, que eres un buen hombre, aunque seas bolchevique. Si alguien de aquí te dice que eres normal, ya puedes empezar a preocuparte. Te has perdido la cena.

—Resistiré —dijo Bernie.

Tendría que disfrutar de una buena noche de sueño para estar en condiciones de trabajar al día siguiente. El arroz que les daban a los prisioneros era espantoso, las barreduras de algún almacén de arroz valenciano mezcladas con polvo arenoso; pero, para poder trabajar, uno tenía que comer todo lo que pudiera.

Pensó en lo que Agustín le había dicho. No lo entendía. ¿Tiempos mejores? ¿Se habría producido algún cambio político en España? El comandante les había dicho que Franco se había reunido con Hitler y que España no tardaría en entrar en guerra; pero, en realidad, ellos no sabían nada de lo que ocurría fuera de allí.

Aranda salió de su barraca. Sostenía en la mano su fusta de montar y se golpeaba la pierna con ella. Aquella tarde estaba sonriendo y, al verlo, todos los prisioneros se tranquilizaron ligeramente. Subió a la plataforma y empezó a pronunciar nombres con su voz clara y enérgica.

La tarea de pasar lista duró media hora, en cuyo transcurso los hombres se mantuvieron en la rígida posición de firmes. Hacia el final, alguien de unas filas más allá se desplomó. Unos compañeros se inclinaron para ayudarlo.

—¡Dejadlo! —gritó Aranda—. ¡Vista al frente!

Al final, el comandante levantó el brazo e hizo el saludo fascista.

—¡Arriba España!

Los primeros días del cautiverio de Bernie en San Pedro muchos prisioneros se negaban a responder; pero, tras el fusilamiento de unos cuantos, optaron por obedecer y contestar con voz áspera y apagada. Bernie había revelado a sus compañeros una palabra inglesa que sonaba casi como «arriba», así que ahora muchos contestaban «*Grieve* —es decir, "pobre", "triste"— España».

Los prisioneros recibieron la orden de romper filas. El hombre que se había desplomado fue levantado del suelo por sus compañeros y conducido de nuevo a su barraca. Era uno de los polacos. Se movía levemente. Al otro lado de la alambrada de púas, una figura borrosa envuelta en largas y negras vestiduras contemplaba la escena.

—El padre Eduardo —musitó Vicente—. Viene por su presa.

Los prisioneros observaron cómo el joven sacerdote cruzaba la verja y se acercaba a la barraca del polaco mientras su larga sotana levantaba pequeños remolinos de polvo en el patio. El último rayo de sol brillaba en los cristales de sus gafas.

—Hijoputa —murmuró Vicente—. Viene a ver si puede aterrorizar a otro buen ateo, amenazándolo con las penas del infierno para que acepte recibir la extremaunción.

Vicente era un viejo republicano de izquierdas, miembro del partido de Azaña. Había ejercido la abogacía en Madrid, ofreciendo ayuda casi gratuita a los pobres de Madrid hasta su incorporación a la milicia en 1936. «Fue un gesto romántico —le había dicho a Bernie—. Era demasiado viejo. Pero hasta los españoles más racionalistas como yo son románticos en su fuero interno.»

Como todos los miembros del partido, Vicente sentía un odio visceral hacia la Iglesia. Era casi una obsesión para los republicanos de izquierdas; una distracción liberal burguesa, decían los comunistas. Vicente despreciaba a los comunistas y decía que habían destruido la República. Eulalio, jefe de los comunistas en la barraca de Bernie, no aprobaba la amistad entre Bernie y Vicente.

—En este campo sólo tus convicciones te ayudan a seguir adelante —le había advertido Eulalio a Bernie en cierta ocasión—. Si se te las comen, pierdes también la fuerza, te rindes y mueres.

Bernie se había encogido de hombros y le había dicho a Eulalio que acabaría convirtiendo a Vicente, pues en el abogado maduraban las semillas de una visión clasista. No sentía el menor respeto por Eulalio, y tampoco lo había votado cuando los veinte comunistas de la barraca lo habían elegido como jefe. Eulalio estaba obsesionado por el control y no soportaba la disidencia. Durante la guerra, la presencia de aquellas personas había sido necesaria, pero allí la situación era otra. Al término de la Guerra Civil, los partidos que integraban la República se odiaban los unos a los otros, pero en el campo los prisioneros tenían que colaborar para sobrevivir. Sin embargo, Eulalio procuraba mantener la identidad propia de los comunistas. Les decía que seguían siendo la vanguardia de la clase obrera y que algún día volverían a tener su oportunidad.

Un par de días atrás, Pablo, uno de los comunistas, le había susurrado al oído a Bernie:

—Procura no mantener demasiado trato con el abogado, compañero. Eulalio se lo está tomando muy a pecho.

—Que se vaya a tomar por culo. De todas maneras, ¿quién es él para impedírmelo?

—¿Por qué arriesgarte, Bernardo? Es obvio que el abogado no tardará en morir.

Treinta prisioneros entraron arrastrando los pies en la desnuda barraca de madera y se tumbaron en los jergones que cubrían las tablas de madera de sus camas, cada uno de ellos envuelto en una manta marrón del ejército. Bernie había elegido la litera situada al lado de la de Vicente al morir su último ocupante. Lo había hecho, en parte, como desafío a Eulalio, el cual permanecía tumbado en su litera de la fila del otro lado, mirándolo fijamente.

Vicente volvió a toser. Se le congestionó la cara y se reclinó hacia atrás entre jadeos.

—Estoy muy mal. Mañana tendré que decir que estoy enfermo.

—No puedes. Ramírez está de servicio y sólo conseguirás que te den una paliza.

—No sé si podré trabajar un día más.

—Vamos, si aguantas hasta que vuelva Molina, él te encomendará una tarea más fácil.

—Lo intentaré.

Guardaron silencio un instante, después del cual Bernie se incorporó sobre un codo y habló en voz baja.

—Oye, antes el guardia Agustín me ha dicho algo muy raro.

—¿Ese taciturno de Sevilla?

—Sí.

Bernie repitió las palabras del guardia. Vicente frunció el entrecejo.

—¿Qué habrá querido decir?

—Vete tú a saber. ¿Y si los monárquicos hubieran derribado la Falange? Nosotros no nos habríamos enterado.

—No estaríamos mejor bajo los monárquicos. —Vicente reflexionó un momento—. ¿Ya vendrán tiempos mejores? ¿Para quién? A lo mejor, se refería sólo a ti y no a todo el campo.

—¿Y por qué me iban a hacer un favor a mí?

—No lo sé. —Vicente volvió a tumbarse con un suspiro que inmediatamente se transformó en un acceso de tos. Se le veía muy enfermo y desdichado.

—Mira —dijo Bernie para distraerlo—, yo le planté cara al muy hijoputa del matasanos. Me dijo que era un degenerado porque no se me podía convertir al catolicismo. ¿Recuerdas la escena de las pasadas Navidades? La del muñeco.

Vicente emitió un sonido a medio camino entre una carcajada y un gruñido.

—¿Cómo iba a olvidarla?

Había sido un día muy frío, con nieve acumulada en el suelo. Los prisioneros fueron obligados a salir al patio donde el padre Jaime, el mayor de los dos sacerdotes que prestaban servicio en el campo, permanecía de pie envuelto en una capa pluvial de color verde y amarillo. Con todas sus galas en medio de aquel desolado patio nevado, parecía un visitante de otro mundo. A su lado, el joven padre Eduardo, vestido con su sotana negra como de costumbre, parecía sentirse algo incómodo, con su rostro redondo enrojecido por el frío. El padre Jaime sostenía entre sus manos un muñeco infantil de madera envuelto en un pañolón. El muñeco llevaba un círculo plateado pintado alrededor de la frente que, por un instante, desconcertó a Bernie hasta que éste se dio cuenta de que pretendía simular una aureola.

Como siempre, el rostro del padre Jaime mostraba una expresión contrariada y arrogante; y su nariz aguileña, con los tiesos pelillos encima, aparecía arrugada, como si le molestara algo más que el olor a rancio que despedían los hombres. Aranda ordenó a los hombres formar en trémulas filas y después subió a la plataforma, golpeándose la pierna con la fusta.

—Hoy celebramos la Epifanía —anunció mientras su aliento formaba unas nubes grises en la gélida atmósfera—. Hoy adoramos al Niño Jesús que vino a la Tierra para salvarnos. Si le rendís homenaje, puede que el Señor se compadezca de vosotros e ilumine vuestras almas con su luz. Cada uno de vosotros besará la imagen de Cristo Jesús que el padre Jaime sostiene en sus manos. No os preocupéis si la persona que tenéis delante está enferma de tuberculosis, el Señor no permitirá que os contagiéis.

El padre Jaime frunció el entrecejo ante la falta de seriedad del tono del comandante. El padre Eduardo se miró los pies. Entonces el padre Jaime alzó el muñeco en gesto amenazador, como si fuera un arma.

Uno a uno, los hombres se aproximaron arrastrando los pies y lo besaron. Algunos no acercaron del todo los labios a la madera y el sacerdote los llamó severamente al orden.

—¡Otra vez! ¡Besa como es debido al Niño Jesús!

Hubo un anarquista que se negó. Tomás, el constructor naval de Barcelona. Se situó delante del sacerdote, mirándolo a los ojos. Era un hombre corpulento, así que el padre Jaime reculó un poco hacia atrás.

—No pienso besar su símbolo de superstición —dijo—. ¡Le escupo!

Y así lo hizo, dejando un reguero de saliva blanca en la frente de madera de la imagen. El padre Jaime lloró como si el niño fuera de verdad. Uno de los guardias le soltó a Tomás un guantazo que lo derribó al suelo. El padre Eduardo hizo ademán de acercarse a él, pero la mirada severa del padre Jaime se lo impidió. El sacerdote de mayor edad limpió con un pañuelo blanco la frente del muñeco.

Aranda brincó de la plataforma y se dirigió a grandes zancadas al lugar donde el hombre permanecía tumbado en el suelo.

—¡Has insultado a Nuestro Señor! —gritó—. ¡La Virgen del Cielo llora porque has escupido a su hijo!

Las palabras eran de indignación, pero el tono seguía siendo de guasa. Aranda tomó la fusta y empezó a azotar metódicamente al anarquista Tomás, empezando por las piernas y terminando con un golpe en la cabeza que lo hizo sangrar. Ordenó a un par de guardias que se lo llevaran y después se volvió hacia el padre Jaime. El sacerdote se había echado hacia atrás, abrazando al muñeco contra su pecho como para protegerlo de la escena.

Aranda inclinó la cabeza.

—Disculpe el insulto, padre. Siga, se lo ruego. Vamos a conducir a estos hombres a la religión, aunque en ello nos vaya la vida, ¿verdad?

Aranda hizo una seña al siguiente hombre de la fila. Bernie se alegró de ver un poco de miedo y cólera en los ojos del padre Jaime mientras el prisionero se acercaba arrastrando los pies e inclinaba la cabeza hacia el muñeco. Nadie más opuso resistencia.

—Recuerdo cómo olía el muñeco —le dijo Bernie a Vicente—. A pintura y saliva.

—Esos escarabajos negros son todos iguales. El padre Jaime es un bruto, pero este Eduardo es más taimado. Ahora estará en la barraca del polaco enfermo, tratando de averiguar si está a punto de morir y si es lo bastante débil para dejarse convencer de que acepte la absolución.

Bernie lo negó con un movimiento de la cabeza.

—Eduardo no es tan taimado. ¿Recuerdas que intentó conseguir que asignaran un médico al campo? ¿Y las cruces para el cementerio?

Pensó en la ladera de la loma, fuera del campo, donde se enterraba a los que morían en sepulcros anónimos. Cuando llegó al campo en verano, el padre Eduardo pidió cruces para señalar la localización de las tumbas. El comandante lo había prohibido; quienes estaban en el campo habían sido condenados por los tribunales militares a varias décadas de prisión, pero en la práctica ya estaban muertos. Algún día, el campo se clausuraría, y tanto las barracas como la alambrada de púas se retirarían sin dejar en la desnuda colina azotada por el viento la menor huella de su existencia.

—¿Qué importan las cruces? —replicó Vicente—. Más símbolos de superstición. La bondad del padre Eduardo es falsa, todo lo que hace tiene un fin. Los escarabajos negros son todos iguales, intentan obligarte a hacer lo que ellos quieren cuando te estás muriendo y te encuentras en tu momento de máxima debilidad.

Fuera ya había oscurecido. En la barraca, algunos jugaban a las cartas o se remendaban los uniformes raídos a la mortecina luz de unas velas de sebo. Bernie cerró los ojos y trató de dormir. Pensó en la paliza que le habían propinado a Tomás; el anarquista había muerto unos días después. Y él mismo había corrido peligro con el psiquiatra aquella tarde. Había tenido suerte de que, por lo visto, el hombre lo considerara un simple ejemplar. Una parte de Bernie deseaba protagonizar un gesto de rebeldía como el de Tomás, pero el resto de su ser quería vivir. Si lo mataban, ellos alcanzarían su definitiva e irrevocable victoria.

Al final, se quedó dormido. Tuvo un sueño muy extraño. Entraba en la barraca con todo un grupo de colegiales de Rookwood a cuyo frente se encontraba el señor Taylor. Los chicos examinaban los jergones de madera y después se situaban alrededor de la mesa hecha con viejas cajas de embalar que había colocada en el centro. Decían que, si aquel era su nuevo dormitorio, pues muy bien, a ellos les daba igual. «No sean tan conformistas —les replicaba Taylor en tono de reproche—. Éste no es el estilo de Rookwood.»

Se despertó sobresaltado. La barraca estaba completamente a oscuras y él no podía ver nada. Tenía frío. Empujó la fina manta hacia abajo para cubrirse los pies. Era la primera noche auténticamente fría. Septiembre y octubre eran los meses más fáciles. El calor sofocante del verano se iba desvaneciendo cada semana en unos pocos pero bienvenidos grados y la temperatura, por la noche, era lo bastante agradable para que uno pudiera dormir a gusto. Sin embargo, ahora ya había llegado el invierno.

Permaneció despierto en la oscuridad, prestando atención a las toses y los murmullos de los demás hombres. Se oían unos crujidos cuando algunos se movían inquietos en sus jergones, quizá también a causa del frío. Pronto habría heladas cada mañana; por Navidad, la gente se empezaría a morir.

Oyó un susurro procedente de la litera de al lado.

—Bernardo, ¿estás despierto? —Vicente volvió a toser.

—Sí.

—Presta atención.

La voz sonaba apremiante. Bernie se volvió, pero no vio nada en medio de la espesa oscuridad.

—No creo que aguante todo el invierno —dijo Vicente.

—Pues claro que aguantarás.

—Si no aguantara, quiero que me prometas una cosa. Al final vendrán los escarabajos negros e intentarán darme la absolución. No se lo permitas. Puede que mi determinación se debilite, sé que a muchos les ocurre. Sería una traición a todo aquello por lo que he vivido. Por favor, impídeselo de la manera que sea.

Bernie sintió el escozor de las lágrimas en sus ojos.

—Muy bien —contestó en un susurro—. Si alguna vez se plantea esta situación, te prometo que lo haré.

Vicente alargó el brazo, encontró el de Bernie y lo apretó con su escuálida mano.

—Gracias —le dijo—. Eres un buen amigo. Tú me ayudarás a cumplir mi último desafío.

22

El uno de noviembre amaneció muy húmedo y frío en Madrid. El apartamento de Harry ofrecía un aspecto sombrío, a pesar de las acuarelas de paisajes ingleses que había pedido prestadas a la embajada para cubrir las paredes desnudas.

A veces pensaba en el comisario desaparecido. Se preguntó qué clase de comisario habría sido Bernie si hubiera vivido y su bando hubiera ganado la guerra. Su misión había consistido en alentar a Barbara a que le hablara de Sandy cuando ambos se reunían y, en tales ocasiones, apenas habían mencionado el nombre de Bernie; lo cual le producía una extraña sensación de vergüenza, como si lo hubieran tachado de sus vidas. «Bernie habría sido un comisario muy competente», pensó; poseía la dureza y la furia necesarias para ello, junto con una conciencia social profunda y compasiva. Sin embargo, no se lo imaginaba convertido en uno de aquellos individuos de quienes había oído hablar y que durante la Guerra Civil condenaban a los soldados a ser fusilados por protestar.

De pie junto a la ventana, se tomó una taza de té de la marca Liptons facilitado por la embajada. Había encendido el brasero y un agradable calor se difundía por toda la estancia desde el pequeño recipiente metálico situado bajo la mesa. La lluvia caía muy despacio desde los balcones de la acera de enfrente. Le había resultado muy desagradable hacer preguntas a Barbara acerca de Sandy y sonsacarle información, y en cambio le había alegrado descubrir que ésta no sabía aparentemente nada. Debía de ser porque él no era gran cosa como espía.

Aquella mañana había actuado como intérprete en una sesión celebrada en el Ministerio del Interior y después se había vuelto a reunir con Sandy en el Café Rocinante. Lo había telefoneado al día siguiente de su paseo con Barbara por la Casa de Campo. Le dijo que en la embajada no tenía mucho trabajo y le preguntó si le apetecería volver a quedar. Sandy había aceptado encantado.

Bajó por la calle para dirigirse al café. Miró atentamente alrededor como de costumbre, pero no se veía la menor señal de que Enrique hubiera sido sustituido por otro espía más eficiente.

Cuando llegó, Sandy ya estaba en el Rocinante, sentado a una mesa y con un pie apoyado en un bloque de madera mientras un desarrapado chiquillo de diez años le lustraba los zapatos. Sandy lo llamó agitando el brazo.

—¡Estoy aquí! Perdona que no me levante.

Harry se sentó. El local estaba muy tranquilo aquella tarde; a lo mejor, la gente se había quedado en casa por la lluvia y la niebla.

—Qué tiempo más desagradable, ¿verdad? —dijo Sandy alegremente—. Es como si estuviéramos en casa.

—Perdona el retraso.

—No te preocupes. He llegado hace unos minutos. Me temo que ya está aquí el invierno.

El niño se sentó en cuclillas mientras Sandy inspeccionaba sus zapatos.

—Muy bien, niño —dijo Sandy, entregándole una moneda al chiquillo, que inmediatamente desvió sus grandes y tristes ojos hacia Harry.

—¿Le limpio los zapatos, señor?

—No, gracias.

—Vamos, Harry, son sólo cinco céntimos.

Harry asintió con la cabeza y el niño colocó el bloque de madera bajo sus pies y empezó a sacar brillo a los zapatos negros que él mismo se había lustrado apenas una hora antes. Sandy llamó al camarero por señas, y ambos pidieron café. El niño terminó con los zapatos de Harry, éste le entregó una moneda y entonces el chiquillo pasó a otros clientes, preguntándoles con un triste y lastimero tono de voz:

—¿Limpiabotas?

—Pobre criatura —dijo Harry.

—La semana pasada intentó venderme unas postales guarras. Una cosa horrorosa, unas prostitutas maduras que se remangaban las bragas. Como no se ande con cuidado, los guardias civiles lo pillarán.

El camarero les sirvió los cafés. Sandy estudió a Harry con semblante pensativo.

—Dime una cosa —preguntó—, ¿qué te pareció Barbara cuando la viste?

—Bien. Fuimos a dar un paseo por la Casa de Campo.

Pero lo cierto era que no le había parecido bien en absoluto; había en ella un no sé qué de cerrado y reservado que jamás le había visto anteriormente, pero no tenía la menor intención de comentárselo a Sandy. Era una lealtad que podía permitirse el lujo de no traicionar.

—¿No te pareció inquieta o preocupada?

—Pues la verdad es que no.

Sandy encendió un cigarro.

—Hay algo en ella desde hace unas semanas. Me dice que no es nada, pero yo no estoy tan seguro. —Sandy miró sonriendo a Harry—. En fin, puede que este trabajo de voluntaria la esté agotando demasiado. ¿Te ha hecho algún comentario al respecto?

—Sí. Y me pareció bueno.

—También tuvisteis un encuentro con la Falange en el restaurante.

Sandy arqueó las cejas.

Harry hizo un gesto de asentimiento con la cabeza.

—Una pequeña muestra de grosería.

Sandy se rió.

—Hitler dijo una vez que el fascismo podía convertir un gusano en un dragón. Es lo que les ha ocurrido a unos cuantos gusanos de aquí. Bueno, hay que dejarles soltar su fuego y su humo. Aunque cansa un poco. —Sonrió con repentino afecto—. Resulta agradable ver de vez en cuando un apacible rostro inglés.

—Te debe de resultar extraño trabajar con esta gente. Trabajas sobre todo con el Ministerio de Minas, ¿verdad? Me lo comentabas el otro día.

Sandy asintió con la cabeza y se pasó una mano por el bigote.

—Exacto. Al final, todas aquellas excursiones a la caza de dinosaurios me fueron muy útiles, ¿sabes? Más útiles que el latín con que nos llenaban la cabeza. Sé algo de geología... conocí hace algún tiempo a un ingeniero de minas en el teatro y acabamos yendo directamente al grano.

—Ah, ¿sí? —«Éste es Otero», pensó Harry, procurando disimular su interés.

—La política económica de Franco se orienta a convertir España en un país lo más autosuficiente posible, para no tener que estar a merced de las potencias extranjeras. Conceptos típicamente fascistas. O sea que, si tú te dedicas a prospecciones mineras, las oportunidades son ilimitadas. Hasta te subvencionan los gastos si tú ofreces experiencia a cambio. —Sandy hizo una pausa, estudiando tan intensamente a Harry que, por un instante, éste temió que su amigo supiera algo—. ¿Recuerdas cuando la otra noche te dije que te podría hacer algunas sugerencias sobre negocios?

—Sí.

—Aquí se puede ganar mucho dinero si sabes dónde invertir.

Harry hizo un movimiento afirmativo con la cabeza para animarlo a seguir adelante.

—Yo he ahorrado una parte considerable de mi asignación a lo largo de los años. Algunas veces he pensado que me gustaría hacer algo con mi dinero, en lugar de guardarlo simplemente en el banco.

Sandy se inclinó hacia delante y le dio una palmada en el brazo.

—Entonces soy tu hombre. Me encantaría ayudarte a ganar un poco de dinero. Especialmente, en el sector de la explotación minera, en agradecimiento por haberme acompañado a todas aquellas expediciones a la caza de fósiles. —Sandy bajó la cabeza—. No te aburrían, ¿verdad?

—No, al contrario. Me gustaban.

—A mí me siguen fascinando. Las cosas que hay ocultas en la tierra. —Sandy miró a Harry con expresión juiciosa—. Veré qué puedo hacer. Tendré que andarme con un poco de cuidado; los falangistas del ministerio hacen una excepción conmigo, pero no les gustan los británicos. —En sus labios se dibujó una sonrisa—. Ya se me ocurrirá algo. Me gustaría que vieras el éxito que he tenido. —Hizo una pausa y le dirigió a Harry una de sus perspicaces miradas de siempre—. Tú tenías ciertas dudas al respecto, ¿a que sí?

—Bueno...

—Lo leí en tu cara, Harry. Te preguntabas qué hacía yo con esta gente. Barbara se lo sigue preguntando, también lo he visto en su cara. Pero no hay que tener remilgos en los negocios.

—Lleva tiempo comprender... lo complicadas que pueden ser las cosas aquí.

Sandy le dirigió una mirada rápida e irónica.

—Vaya si lo son. ¿Fuiste a aquella fiesta en casa del general Maestre?

—Sí. Tengo que acompañar a su hija al Prado. —La tendría que llamar aquella noche; lo había estado aplazando.

—¿Buena chica?

—Muy joven. Todos eran monárquicos en la fiesta. No les gustaba la Falange en absoluto.

—Ellos lo que quieren es una monarquía autoritaria en la que los aristócratas corten el bacalao como hace cincuenta años. Pero todo se volvería a derrumbar.

—Son proaliados.

—No los interpretes mal, Harry. Son más duros que una piedra. Todos combatieron al lado de Franco en la guerra; Juan March, el compinche de los monárquicos, financió la rebelión inicial.

—Últimamente oigo mucho este nombre.

—La Falange cree que está conspirando con los monárquicos y que mantiene vínculos con los Aliados. Dicen que está sobornando a los generales y que compra su apoyo a la idea de mantener España al margen de la guerra.

Y entonces Harry lo vio, fue como si se hubiera encendido una luz en su cerebro. Soborno. De eso habían estado hablando Hillgarth y Maestre aquel día. Los Caballeros de San Jorge eran una clave para designar a los soberanos, la moneda en cuyo reverso figuraba san Jorge matando al dragón. Les pagarían en soberanos. Respiró hondo.

—¿Te ocurre algo? —le preguntó Sandy.

—No. Es que... acabo de recordar una cosa. —Tomó un sorbo de café e hizo un esfuerzo por regresar al presente—. Por cierto —añadió, por decir algo—, ¿has tenido noticias de tu hermano últimamente?

—Llevo nueve años sin saber nada de él. Cuando me echaron de Rookwood, mi padre ya no me quiso ni ver. Dijo que pertenecía a la categoría de los perdidos, no comprendía que alguien pudiera hacer algo tan perverso como lo que yo hice. —Sandy soltó una sorda carcajada—. Colocar arañas en el despacho de un profesor. Dios mío, si supiera algunas de las cosas que han estado ocurriendo aquí. Sea como fuere, cuando me marché de casa, ya jamás volví a tener noticias de papá ni de Peter, el hijo perfecto. —En su voz se advertía un tono de amargura—. Estoy seguro de que Pete se está comportando como un heroico capellán militar en algún sitio.

Sandy encendió un cigarro.

—Perdona, no quería...

—No te preocupes. Mira, en cuanto al otro asunto, deja que hable con una o dos personas, a ver qué se puede hacer.

—Estaría muy bien. —Harry titubeó—. ¿Me podrías decir algo más al respecto?

Sandy sonrió, meneando la cabeza.

—Todavía no. Cuestión de confidencialidad. —Consultó su reloj—. Ya es hora de que me vaya. Tengo una reunión con mi Comité Judío.

—Barbara me comentó que estabas haciendo un trabajo con los refugiados.

—Sí, no dejan de cruzar los Pirineos. Intentan pasar a Portugal, por si Franco entra en guerra y los entrega de nuevo a Hitler. Algunos de ellos se encuentran en muy malas condiciones cuando llegan... procuramos asearlos y los ayudamos con los papeles. —Esbozó una sonrisita, como si se avergonzara de sus obras benéficas—. Me gusta ayudarlos; supongo que porque siempre me he sentido un poco como un judío errante. —Se incorporó—. Bueno, ahora sí que me tengo que ir. Invito yo. Pero tenemos que volver a vernos. Siempre suelo estar aquí a esta hora.

Harry inició el camino de regreso a casa. El ambiente seguía siendo frío y húmedo. La conversación entre Maestre y Hillgarth volvía incesantemente a su mente, junto con la seca orden de Hillgarth de que se olvidara de Juan March y de los Caballeros de San Jorge. ¿Sería posible que la embajada también estuviera implicada en una operación de soborno de ministros? Le parecía una posibilidad descabellada; y, por si fuera poco, peligrosa en caso de que Franco lo descubriera.

Meneó la cabeza; notaba una sensación de presión en el oído malo, otra vez aquel zumbido débil y molesto. A lo mejor, era cosa de la humedad. Volvió a recordar a la señorita Maxse diciéndole que no podían ganar aquella guerra jugando limpio. ¿Qué otra cosa había dicho acerca de las personas que se mezclaban con políticas extremistas? «A veces, es tanto cuestión de sentimiento como de política.» Sandy siempre había disfrutado asumiendo riesgos... ¿sería por eso por lo que había acabado allí? Pensó una vez más en el asunto de los judíos. Sandy tenía su lado bueno. Ayudaba a la gente siempre que podía, como cuando lo había instruido en el tema de los fósiles o como ahora, que parecía estar gobernando la vida de Barbara.

Tendría que regresar a la embajada para informar acerca de sus progresos. Les entusiasmaría la idea de que él pudiera participar en uno de los proyectos de Sandy. Cierto que podía tratarse de otra cosa que no tuviera nada que ver con el oro. Pero él seguía pensando en los Caballeros de San Jorge y preguntándose qué podría significar todo aquello. ¿Y si fracasaran, y si los falangistas consiguieran convencer a

Franco y España entrara en guerra? Personas como Maestre podrían correr peligro; tal vez por eso éste deseaba sacar a su hija del país a la menor oportunidad.

Se dio cuenta de que había llegado casi sin querer hasta la Puerta de Toledo. Entonces se detuvo y se quedó un momento contemplando los carros y los destartalados automóviles que pasaban. Algunos de ellos parecían llevar veinte años circulando, y quizás así fuera. Pasó un gasógeno traqueteando. No había tenido noticias de Sofía sobre la conveniencia de buscar a un médico para Enrique, y ya había transcurrido más de una semana. ¿Y si Enrique enfermara de rabia? Harry había oído decir que los chinos sustentan una creencia según la cual, si alguien salva la vida de una persona, quedaba unido a ella para siempre; pero él sabía que era Sofía la que lo inducía a pensar en aquella familia. Titubeó, después cruzó la calle y bajó hacia el barrio de Carabanchel.

La calle de Sofía, como todas las demás de aquella zona, permanecía desierta y en silencio. Empezaba a caer la noche cuando se detuvo ante la casa de vecindad. Dos niños que empujaban una vieja carretilla arriba y abajo cual si fuera un aro se detuvieron a mirarlo. Iban descalzos y tenían los pies enrojecidos por el frío. Harry se avergonzó de su grueso abrigo y de su sombrero de ala ancha.

Franqueó el oscuro portal, dudó un momento y después subió los húmedos peldaños y llamó a la puerta. Mientras lo hacía, se abrió la puerta del otro piso del rellano y apareció una anciana. Tenía un rostro redondo y arrugado y unos ojos fríos y penetrantes. Harry se quitó el sombrero.

—Buenas tardes.

—Buenas tardes —contestó recelosamente la mujer, justo en el momento en que Sofía abría la puerta de su apartamento.

Lo miró asombrada con sus grandes ojos castaños abiertos de par en par.

—Ah, señor Brett.

Harry volvió a quitarse el sombrero.

—Buenas tardes. Perdone que la moleste, sólo quería saber cómo estaba Enrique.

Sofía miró hacia la vecina que seguía estudiando a Harry con descaro.

—Buenas tardes, señora Ávila —le dijo en tono perentorio.

—Buenas —musitó la anciana.

Cerró la puerta de su apartamento y bajó presurosa los peldaños.

Sofía se la quedó mirando momentáneamente y, después, se volvió hacia Harry.

—Pase, señor, por favor —le dijo con la cara muy seria y sin la menor sonrisa en los labios.

Harry la siguió al húmedo y frío salón. La anciana de la cama utilizaba la mano sana para jugar a las damas con el niño. Al ver a Harry, éste se echó hacia atrás y le empezaron a temblar los hombros. La anciana lo rodeó con el brazo sano.

—Buenas tardes —le dijo Harry—. ¿Cómo está?

—Bastante bien, señor, muchas gracias.

Enrique estaba sentado junto a la mesa con la pierna vendada apoyada en un almohadón. Su rostro alargado y chupado mostraba un aspecto febril. Al ver a Harry, se le iluminó el rostro.

—Cuánto me alegro de verlo, señor.

Se inclinó hacia delante y le estrechó la mano.

—¿Cómo va la pierna?

—Bastante mal, todavía. Sofía me la limpia, pero parece que no mejora.

Su hermana lo miró avergonzada.

—Necesita tiempo —dijo.

Sobre la mesa descansaban unos dibujos infantiles. Harry les echó un vistazo y abrió los ojos asombrado. Dos guardias civiles con sus uniformes verdes y sus correas amarillas exactamente del mismo color que los de verdad fusilaban a una mujer de cuyo cuerpo brotaban pequeños chorros de color rojo. Al lado, se podía ver el dibujo de otro guardia civil ahorcado en una farola y a un chiquillo tirando de la cuerda para levantarlo en el aire. Pero el dibujo estaba tachado con unos gruesos trazos negros.

—Los ha hecho Paco —explicó Sofía dulcemente—. Hace estos dibujos, pero después los tacha y se pone muy triste. Sólo mamá lo puede calmar. De tanto ruido como metió esta mañana, pensé que iba a venir la señora Ávila.

Harry miró al niño. No se le ocurría nada que decirle.

—Señor Brett —dijo Sofía con cierto titubeo—. ¿Podría hablar con usted en la cocina?

—Pues claro.

Harry la siguió a una estancia de suelo de hormigón cuyas paredes estaban forradas de armarios baratos. Empezaba a oscurecer; Sofía accionó el interruptor y se encendió una bombilla de pocos vatios que iluminó la estancia con un débil resplandor amarillento. Todo estaba muy limpio, aunque los platos se amontonaban en el fregadero. Sofía siguió la dirección de su mirada.

—Ahora tengo que guisar y limpiar para todos.

—No... yo no quería...

—Siéntese, por favor.

Le indicó a Harry una silla junto a la mesa de la cocina y ella se sentó frente a él con las manos cruzadas delante. Después lo miró con expresión pensativa.

—No esperaba que regresara —le dijo.

Harry la miró sonriendo.

—No he recibido la factura del médico.

—Esperaba que la pierna de Enrique se curara sola. —La joven lanzó un suspiro—. Pero la infección no cede. Creo que sí, que necesita un médico.

—Mi ofrecimiento sigue en pie.

Ella frunció el entrecejo.

—Disculpe, señor, pero ¿por qué tiene usted que ayudarnos? ¿Después de que Enrique lo espiara?

—Me sentí obligado de alguna manera. Por favor, no son más que los honorarios de un médico; en eso la puedo ayudar. Me lo puedo permitir.

—Como la vieja del piso de al lado se entere de que recibo dinero de diplomáticos extranjeros, ya sé yo lo que va a pensar.

Harry se ruborizó. ¿Eso era lo que Sofía pensaba también?

—Disculpe, no quería ponerla en un apuro. —Harry se dispuso a levantarse—. Sólo quería ayudarla.

—No, ya lo veo. Quédese, por favor. —El tono de Sofía era de disculpa. Se sentó y encendió un cigarrillo—. Pero es una sorpresa que un extranjero nos ofrezca ayuda, después de lo que hizo Enrique. —Se mordió el labio—. Creo que mi hermano necesita un poco de esa nueva penicilina.

—Pues entonces, deje que la ayude. Veo que la situación es... difícil.

Sofía sonrió, y después se le iluminó el rostro.

—Muy bien. Muchas gracias.

—Vaya en busca de un médico, compre las medicinas que su hermano necesita y después envíeme la factura de los gastos.

Ella lo miró avergonzada.

—Perdone, señor Brett, usted ha salvado la vida de mi hermano y yo ni siquiera le he dado las gracias como es debido.

—No se preocupe.

—Hoy en día, todo el mundo sospecha de todo el mundo. —Sofía se levantó—. ¿Le apetece un café? No es muy bueno, no será como ése al que usted está acostumbrado.

—Sí, gracias.

Llenó una tetera negra de gran tamaño en el fregadero.

—Esta bruja que ha visto usted en el rellano, ahora que Enrique está enfermo, quiere que entreguemos a Paquito al orfelinato de la iglesia. Pero no lo haremos, no son buenos sitios.

—Ah, ¿no?

Estaba a punto de decirle que conocía a alguien que iba a trabajar como voluntaria en uno de ellos, pero decidió no hacerlo. Sofía le ofreció una taza de café. Harry la miró. ¿De dónde sacaba tanta serenidad y tanta energía? Su cabello negro azabache adquiría reflejos castaños cuando le tocaba la luz.

—¿Lleva mucho tiempo trabajando en la embajada? —preguntó Sofía.

—En realidad, sólo unas cuantas semanas. Dejé el ejército por invalidez.

—¿O sea que usted combatió? —preguntó otra vez, con un nuevo tono de respeto en la voz.

—Sí. En Francia.

—¿Y qué le pasó?

—Sufrí una lesión en el oído cuando estalló una granada. Ya estoy mejor. —Sin embargo, la presión en la cabeza aún no había desaparecido.

—Tuvo suerte.

—Sí. Supongo que sí. —Harry titubeó—. También sufrí neurosis de guerra. Ahora ya no.

Ella preguntó tras dudar un poco:

—O sea que usted ha luchado contra los fascistas.

—Sí. Sí, en efecto. —La miró—. Y lo volvería a hacer.

—Sin embargo, muchos admiran al Generalísimo. Durante la Guerra Civil conocí a un voluntario, un chico inglés. Me dijo que muchos ingleses piensan que Franco es un digno caballero español.

—Pues yo no, señorita.

—Era de Leeds, ese chico. ¿Conoce usted Leeds?

—No, yo soy del norte.

—Mi padre lo conoció en las batallas de la Casa de Campo. Los dos murieron allí.

—Lo siento. —Harry se preguntó si habría sido su amante.

—Ahora tenemos que sacar todo el provecho que podamos de la situación.

Sofía sacó un pitillo y lo encendió.

—¿No hay ninguna posibilidad de que usted reanude sus estudios de medicina?

Ella denegó con la cabeza.

—¿Teniendo que atender a mamá y a Paquito? ¿Y también a Enrique?

—Con un tratamiento, quizá pueda volver a trabajar.

—Sí, pero esta vez en otra cosa. —Arrojó con rabia la ceniza del cigarrillo a un platito de postre—. Le dije que no debería haber aceptado este trabajo. —Volvió a mirar a Harry con perspicacia—. ¿Cómo puede ser que hable usted tan bien el español?

—Soy profesor, lector, en Inglaterra; al menos, lo era antes de que estallara la guerra. Nuestra guerra —añadió—. Visité España en 1931, ya se lo dije; supongo que fue entonces cuando nació mi interés.

Ella sonrió con tristeza.

—Nuestro tiempo de esperanza.

—El amigo con quien yo vine aquí en 1931 regresó para combatir en la Guerra Civil. Resultó muerto en el Jarama.

—¿Usted también era partidario de la República?

—Bernie, sí. Era un idealista. Yo era neutral.

—¿Y ahora?

Harry no contestó. Sofía sonrió.

—En cierto sentido, me recuerda usted al chico de Leeds; su cara reflejaba el mismo desconcierto. —Sofía se levantó—. Y ahora voy a buscar a un médico. Ahora mismo.

Harry la acompañó de nuevo al salón.

—Enrique, he estado hablando con el señor Brett —le dijo Sofía a su hermano—, voy a buscar a un médico. Ahora mismo.

Enrique lanzó un suspiro de alivio.

—Gracias a Dios. Mi pierna no es muy agradable de ver. Gracias, señor. Mi hermana es una pesada.

La anciana trató de incorporarse.

—Es usted muy amable con nosotros.

—De nada —contestó tímidamente Harry.

El niño lo miró con expresión atemorizada. Harry volvió a mirar alrededor, respirando el olor a moho de la atmósfera mientras contemplaba las manchas de humedad bajo la ventana. Se avergonzó de su riqueza y de la seguridad de que él disfrutaba.

—La señora Ávila volvía a fisgonear cuando llegó el señor Brett —le dijo Sofía a su madre.

—Esa beata —musitó la anciana, arrastrando las palabras—. Cree que, si les cuenta suficientes detalles a los curas, Dios la convertirá en una santa.

Sofía se ruborizó.

—¿Le importaría salir usted primero, señor Brett? Si nos ven salir juntos, correrán rumores.

—Claro —dijo Harry algo azorado.

Enrique se incorporó.

—Gracias una vez más, señor.

Harry se despidió de todos y regresó muy despacio a la parada del autobús de la Puerta de Toledo. Miró al suelo para evitar los baches y los desagües sin tapa que arrojaban un nauseabundo olor a la calle. Si uno no iba atento, se podía romper una pierna.

Le entristeció pensar que ahora quizá sólo recibiría la cuenta de los honorarios de un médico y ya no habría nada más. Ellos no esperarían que regresara. Pero, en cierto modo, él ya había decidido volver a ver a Sofía.

23

El lunes siguiente fue un día de mucho ajetreo en la embajada. Harry había acordado reunirse con Milagros Maestre en el Prado a las cuatro, pero tuvo que traducir al español un comunicado de prensa de la embajada acerca de las victorias británicas en el norte de África y llegó con un cuarto de hora de retraso.

La había llamado el fin de semana. No le apetecía, pero no tenía más remedio que hacerlo; habría sido una grosería. Tolhurst le había dicho que Maestre se ofendería y ellos no podían permitírselo. Milagros parecía encantada, así que aceptó la invitación de inmediato.

Harry ya había visitado el Prado anteriormente, una tarde de 1931 con Bernie. Entonces el museo le había parecido un hervidero de actividad; en cambio, ahora, el enorme edificio estaba muy tranquilo. Compró la entrada y cruzó el vestíbulo principal. Apenas había visitantes, menos que los vigilantes que paseaban lentamente por las salas haciendo tintinear las llaves que llevaban al cinturón mientras el eco de sus pisadas resonaba con un rumor sordo. Había muy poca luz, y aquella triste tarde de invierno el edificio producía una impresión de sombrío abandono.

Casi bajó corriendo los peldaños del café donde acababa de reunirse con Milagros. Ella estaba sola, sentada al fondo del café. Harry se sorprendió al ver a un hombre sentado frente a ella. El hombre se volvió y Harry reconoció en él al acompañante de Maestre en el baile, el teniente Gómez. En su rostro severo y cuadrado se observaba una mueca de contrariedad. Milagros sonrió con alivio.

—Ah, señor Brett —dijo Gómez en tono de reproche—. Ya empezábamos a temer que no viniera.

—Les pido disculpas, me han entretenido en la embajada. —Harry se volvió para mirar a Milagros—. Le ruego que me perdone.

—No se preocupe —dijo ella—. Por favor, Alfonso, no es nada.

Lucía un costoso abrigo de pieles y se acababa de ondular el cabello castaño con una permanente. Pese a que iba vestida como una mujer de más edad, Harry reparó una vez más en la apariencia infantil de su rostro mofletudo .

Gómez soltó un gruñido, apagó el cigarrillo y se levantó.

—Les dejo. Milagros, la veré en la entrada a las cinco y media. Buenas tardes, señor Brett.

Su mirada era muy fría cuando le estrechó la mano. Harry recordó el cesto de rosas con aquellas cabezas de marroquíes en el centro que, según decían, Maestre había regalado a las monjas. Se preguntó si Gómez habría estado presente.

Se sentó frente a Milagros.

—Me temo que lo he ofendido.

Milagros denegó con la cabeza.

—Don Alfonso me protege demasiado. Me lleva a todas partes, es mi dama de compañía, mi carabina. ¿Las chicas de Inglaterra todavía tienen carabinas?

—No. Más bien no.

Milagros sacó una cajetilla de cigarrillos del bolsillo. Unos cigarrillos de calidad, Lucky Strike, no los ponzoñosos pitillos que fumaba Sofía. No sabía por qué, pero se había pasado todo el fin de semana pensando en Sofía.

—¿Usted fuma, señor Brett?

Harry sonrió.

—No, gracias. Y llámeme Harry, por favor.

Milagros exhaló una larga columna de humo.

—Ah, así está mejor. No les gusta que fume, consideran que soy demasiado joven —explicó, ruborizándose—. Piensan que no es apropiado para una chica seria.

—Todas las mujeres que yo conozco fuman.

—¿Le apetece un café?

—Ahora no, gracias. Quizá cuando hayamos visto los cuadros, ¿le parece?

—Me parece muy bien. Pues entonces, me termino el pitillo. —Milagros esbozó una sonrisa nerviosa—. Me encanta que me vean fumar en público. —Exhaló una nube de humo azulada, apartando el rostro para no arrojársela a Harry a la cara.

A Harry no le importaba visitar galerías de arte, siempre y cuando no tuviera que permanecer en ellas mucho rato; pero la verdad era que tampoco le entusiasmaban. La impresión de cavernoso vacío del Prado se fue intensificando progresivamente a medida que recorrían las salas en las que sólo se escuchaba el eco de sus pisadas. Casi todas ellas estaban vacías. Unos espacios en blanco en las zonas de las paredes antaño ocupadas por cuadros robados o desaparecidos durante la Guerra Civil. En los rincones, unos guardias uniformados de negro permanecían sentados en sillas, leyendo el *Arriba*.

Milagros era todavía más ignorante en arte que Harry. Se detenían delante de algún cuadro, él o ella hacían algún comentario grandilocuente y seguían adelante.

En la sala de Goya, el horror oscuro de las Pinturas Negras pareció poner muy nerviosa a Milagros.

—Pinta cosas muy crueles —dijo la muchacha en voz baja mientras contemplaba el *Aquelarre*.

—Había visto muchas cosas de la guerra. Bueno, creo que ahora ya lo hemos visto casi todo... ¿le apetece un café?

Ella le sonrió con gratitud.

—Oh, sí. Gracias.

Las salas estaban muy frías; en cambio, en la cafetería hacía demasiado calor. Cuando él llevó de la barra a la mesa dos tazas de pésimo café, Milagros ya se había quitado el abrigo y en torno a ella se percibía el intenso aroma almizcleño de un perfume muy caro. Se lo había aplicado en exceso. Harry se compadeció repentinamente de ella.

—Me gustaría ver las galerías de arte de Londres —dijo la joven—. Me gustaría ver todo lo que hay en Londres. Mi madre dice que es una gran ciudad.

—¿La conoce?

—No, pero lo sabe todo de ella. A mis padres les encanta Inglaterra.

A los españoles no les gustaba que sus hijas salieran con extranjeros. Harry lo sabía; pero, en aquellos momentos, un lugar como Inglaterra debía de ser un destino muy apetecible a los ojos de alguien como Maestre. Contempló el rostro serio y mofletudo de la muchacha.

—Todos los países parecen mejores desde lejos.

—Quizá. —Milagros parecía abatida—. Pero tiene que ser mejor que España; aquí todo es tan sucio y miserable, tan inculto.

Harry pensó en Sofía y en su familia mutilada, que vivían en aquel pobre apartamento.

—Su padre tiene una casa muy bonita.

—Pero todo es muy inseguro. Tuvimos que huir de Madrid durante la guerra, ¿sabe? Ahora tenemos esta nueva guerra que se cierne sobre nosotros. ¿Y si lo volvemos a perder todo? —La muchacha pareció entristecerse momentáneamente, pero después volvió a sonreír—. Hábleme más de Inglaterra. He oído decir que la campiña es preciosa.

—Sí, todo es muy verde.

—¿Hasta en verano?

—Especialmente en verano. Hierba verde y árboles gigantescos.

—Antes Madrid estaba lleno de árboles. Cuando volvimos, los rojos los habían cortado todos para hacer leña. —Milagros lanzó un suspiro—. Yo me sentía más a gusto en Burgos.

—Ahora la situación también es bastante insegura en Inglaterra. —Harry la miró sonriendo—. Recuerdo que en el colegio no había nada más bonito que un largo partido de críquet en una tarde estival.

Evocó las verdes canchas de juego, a los chicos con sus uniformes blancos de críquet y el sonido del bate y la pelota. Era un sueño tan lejano como el mundo de la fotografía en la que sus padres habían quedado atrapados.

—He oído hablar del críquet. —Milagros soltó una carcajada nerviosa que le otorgó, más que nunca, el aspecto de regordeta colegiala—. Aunque no sé cómo se juega. —Bajó la mirada—. Perdone, esta tarde... es que tampoco sé nada de pintura.

—Como yo, la verdad —contestó Harry, un poco avergonzado.

—Tenía que pensar en algún sitio adonde ir. Pero, si usted quiere, otro día podemos ir al campo; lo podría acompañar a ver la sierra de Guadarrama en invierno. Alfonso nos llevaría en coche.

—Sí, sí, tal vez.

Milagros se había vuelto a ruborizar; no cabía ninguna duda, se estaba enamorando de él. «Vaya por Dios», pensó Harry. Consultó el reloj de la pared.

—Ya es hora de marcharnos —dijo—. Alfonso estará esperando. No conviene que lo hagamos enfadar.

La boca de Milagros tembló levemente.

—No.

El viejo soldado esperaba en la escalinata del Prado, vuelto de cara al Ritz del otro lado de la calle, con un cigarrillo en los labios. Empezaba a oscurecer. Se volvió y, esta vez, miró con una sonrisa a Harry.

—Ah, justo a tiempo. ¿Lo ha pasado bien, Milagros?

—Sí, Alfonso.

—Tiene que comentarle a su madre los cuadros que ha visto. El automóvil está a la vuelta de la esquina. —El militar le dio a Harry un apretón de manos—. Puede que volvamos a vernos, señor Brett.

—Sí, teniente Gómez.

Harry estrechó la mano de Milagros. La chica lo miró expectante, pero él no le dijo nada acerca de la posibilidad de volver a verse. El rostro de Milagros reflejó decepción y Harry se sintió culpable; pero no tenía la menor intención de engañarla. Se los quedó mirando mientras ambos se alejaban. ¿Por qué se habría encaprichado aquella chica de él? No tenían nada en común.

—Vaya por Dios —añadió en voz alta.

Harry había quedado con Tolhurst para tomar unas copas en el Café Gijón. Pasó por delante del edificio cerrado de las Cortes y, después, del ministerio donde había conocido a Maestre y cuya calle patrullaban unos guardias armados con metralletas. Se subió el cuello del abrigo. El tiempo había vuelto a refrescar; después del sofocante calor del verano y de un otoño fallido, parecía que el invierno se acercaba.

La Gran Vía se había rebautizado con el nombre de «Avenida de José Antonio Primo de Rivera», en memoria del fundador de la Falange; pero era exactamente como Harry la recordaba en 1937: una larga arteria comercial. Las tiendas ya volvían a abrir después de la pausa de la siesta, y la luz amarillenta se derramaba sobre la acera. Incluso allí los escaparates estaban muy mal surtidos. Había oído hablar del Gijón, pero jamás había estado en él. Al entrar en el local adornado con espejos, vio a varias personas repartidas por las mesas. Había individuos con pinta de artistas con barba y bigotes extravagantes, pero no cabía duda de que todos debían de ser partidarios del régimen como lo era Dalí.

—El fascismo es el sueño convertido en realidad —decía un joven, entusiasmado, a su compañero—, lo surrealista hecho realidad.

«Y que lo digas», pensó Harry.

Tolhurst estaba sentado a una mesa, con su corpachón comprimido contra la pared. Harry lo saludó con la mano, después se acercó a la barra para pedir un brandy y se reunió con él.

—¿Qué tal ha ido la cita? —le preguntó Tolhurst.

Harry tomó un sorbo de brandy.

—Esto está mejor. Bastante mal, en realidad. La chica es muy simpática pero es... cómo diría yo... sólo una niña. Llevaba carabina. El ex ordenanza o lo que sea de Maestre.

—Aquí tienen unas ideas muy anticuadas sobre las mujeres. —Tolhurst lo miró fijamente—. Procura no perderla de vista; es un nexo con Maestre.

—Quiere que vayamos a dar una vuelta por la sierra de Guadarrama.

—Ah —Tolhurst lo miró sonriendo—. Tú y ella solos, ¿eh?

—Con Gómez como chófer.

—Ah, bueno. —Tolhurst se chupó los carrillos mofletudos—. Santo cielo, a veces pienso que ojalá pudiera volver a casa. La echo de menos.

—¿Echas de menos a tu familia?

Tolhurst encendió un cigarrillo y contempló cómo el humo se elevaba hacia el techo en espiral.

—No exactamente. Mi padre está en el ejército y llevo siglos sin verlo. —Suspiró—. Yo siempre quise vivir en Londres y disfrutar de la refinada existencia de allí. Jamás lo conseguí... primero el colegio y, después, el servicio diplomático. —Volvió a suspirar—. Probablemente ahora ya es demasiado tarde. Con los bombardeos y las ciudades a oscuras, toda esta clase de vida tiene que haber desaparecido. —Meneó la cabeza—. ¿Has echado un vistazo a los periódicos? Siguen comentando lo mucho que congenió Franco con Hitler en Hendaya. Y Sam está en plan muy conciliador; le ha dicho a Franco que Gran Bretaña estaría encantada de que España les arrebatara Marruecos y Argelia a los franceses.

—¿Qué? ¿Como colonias españolas?

—Pues sí. Está alentando los sueños imperiales de Franco. Supongo que comprende su manera de pensar. Francia está acabada como potencia.

Tolhurst comentaba lo que «Sam» hacía como si fuera el confidente del embajador, era típico de él; aunque Harry sabía que probablemente se limitaba a repetir los chismes que circulaban por la embajada.

—Contamos con el bloqueo —dijo Harry—. Podríamos privarlos de sus suministros de alimentos y petróleo como quien cierra el grifo. Quizá ya va siendo hora de que lo hagamos. Para advertirlos sobre sus coqueteos con Hitler.

—No es tan sencillo. Si los dejamos sin nada que perder, puede que se unan a los alemanes y tomen Gibraltar.

Harry bebió otro trago de brandy.

—¿Recuerdas la noche del Ritz? Le oí decir a Hoare que aquí no puede haber el menor apoyo británico para operaciones especiales. Tengo presente un discurso que pronunció Churchill poco antes de que yo me fuera. La supervivencia de Gran Bretaña enciende destellos de esperanza en la Europa ocupada. Podríamos ayudar a la gente de aquí en lugar de dar coba a sus dirigentes.

—Calma —dijo Tolhurst, soltando una carcajada nerviosa—. El brandy se te está subiendo a la cabeza. Si Franco cayera, los rojos volverían. Y serían peores que antes.

—¿Y qué piensa el capitán Hillgarth? Aquella noche en el Ritz me pareció que estaba de acuerdo con sir Sam.

Tolhurst se removió muy inquieto en su asiento.

—Pues mira, Harry, si quieres que te diga la verdad, le molestaría bastante saber que alguien oyó sus comentarios.

—No lo hice a propósito.

—Aun así, yo de eso no sé nada —añadió Tolhurst en tono cansado—. Yo sólo soy el burro de carga. Arreglo las cosas, recibo información de las fuentes y controlo sus gastos.

—Dime una cosa —le preguntó Harry—, ¿tú has oído hablar alguna vez de los «Caballeros de San Jorge»?

Tolhurst entornó los ojos.

—¿Dónde has oído eso? —preguntó en tono precavido.

—Maestre utilizó esa expresión el primer día que fui con Hillgarth para hacer de intérprete. Se refiere a los soberanos, ¿verdad, Tolly? —Tolhurst no contestó, se limitó a fruncir los labios. Harry siguió adelante, sin preocuparse por los protocolos que pudiera estar infringiendo—. Hillgarth también habló de Juan March. ¿Estamos implicados en una operación de soborno a los monárquicos? ¿Es éste el caballo por el que estamos apostando para mantener a España fuera de la guerra? ¿Por eso Hoare no quiere mantener ningún tipo de trato con la oposición?

—Mira, Harry, no conviene que seamos demasiado fisgones. —La voz de Tolhusrt sonaba tranquila como al principio—. No nos corresponde a nosotros pensar en... bueno... los planes de acción. Y, por el amor de Dios, a ver si bajas un poco la voz.

—Entonces estoy en lo cierto, ¿verdad? Te lo leo en la cara. —Harry se inclinó hacia delante y murmuró en tono decidido—. ¿Y si todo fracasa y se viene abajo, y Franco se entera? Entonces nos hundiríamos en la miseria y lo mismo les ocurriría a Maestre y sus compinches.

—El capitán ya sabe lo que hace.

—¿Y si la cosa da resultado? Estaremos atados a estos cabrones para siempre. Gobernarán España por siempre jamás.

Tolhurst respiró hondo. Estaba furioso y tenía la cara arrebolada por la emoción.

—Por Dios, Harry, ¿cuánto tiempo llevas dándole vueltas a todo eso?

—El otro día adiviné qué podían ser los Caballeros de San Jorge. —Se reclinó contra el respaldo de su asiento—. No te preocupes, Tolly, no diré nada.

—Más te vale no hacerlo, si no quieres ser acusado de alta traición. Es lo que pasa cuando se contratan los servicios de gente perteneciente al mundo académico —dijo Tolhurst—. Sois demasiado entrometidos. —Soltó una carcajada para intentar recuperar el tono amistoso—. No te lo puedo decir todo —añadió—. Eso lo tienes que comprender. Pero Sam y el capitán ya saben lo que hacen. Tendré que decirle al capitán que has descubierto todo esto. ¿Seguro que no se lo has dicho a nadie más?

—Te lo juro, Tolly.

—Entonces, toma otro trago y olvídate de todo.

—De acuerdo —dijo Harry, pensando que ojalá hubiera resistido el impulso de hacerle la pregunta a Tolhurst.

Tolhurst se levantó con cierta dificultad e hizo una mueca cuando la esquina de la mesa se le clavó en el vientre. Harry fijó la vista en el vaso. Experimentó un momento de pánico. Sus creencias acerca del mundo y del lugar que ocupaba en él se volvían a mover como arena bajo sus pies.

24

El dinero llegó el 5 de noviembre, la víspera del día en que Barbara tenía concertada su nueva cita con Luis. Ya desesperaba de recibirlo y se había preparado para suplicarle a Luis que esperara. A medida que su preocupación iba en aumento, Barbara comprendió que estaba cada vez más nerviosa y retraída. Sandy empezaba a preguntarse con toda claridad qué le ocurría. Aquella mañana se había hecho la dormida mientras él se vestía; porque estaba despierta, mirando la almohada mientras recordaba que era el día de Guy Fawkes, en que Gran Bretaña conmemoraba la detención de Guy Fawkes el año 1605 por su intento de hacer saltar por los aires las Cámaras del Parlamento. Aquel año no habría fuegos artificiales en Inglaterra; ya tenían suficiente con las explosiones reales de todas las noches. La BBC informaba de que no se habían registrado más incursiones en la región de los Midlands; en cambio, Londres seguía siendo bombardeada casi cada noche. Los periódicos de Madrid señalaban que buena parte de la ciudad había quedado reducida a escombros, pero ella se decía a sí misma que todo era propaganda.

Cuando Sandy se fue, Barbara bajó a buscar las cartas. Vio un sobre mecanografiado encima del felpudo con la cabeza del rey de Inglaterra en el sello, en lugar de la de Franco y su fría mirada. Lo rasgó para abrirlo. En frío tono oficial, el banco le comunicaba que había transferido sus ahorros a la cuenta que ella había abierto en Madrid. Más de 5.000 pesetas. Comprendió el tono de reproche que emanaba de la misiva por el hecho de haber sacado el dinero al extranjero en tiempo de guerra.

Regresó a la habitación y dejó la carta en su escritorio. Ahora guardaba en él dos guías de Cuenca que había estudiado cuidadosamente. Cerró el escritorio.

Se vistió a toda prisa; tenía que estar en el orfelinato a las nueve. Era su segunda mañana de trabajo allí. La víspera se había presentado con la ropa de costumbre, pero sor Inmaculada le había dicho que era una lástima que ensuciara un buen vestido. A Barbara le pareció un alivio volver a ponerse una falda vieja y un jersey holgado. Consultó su reloj. Ya era hora de irse.

Barbara había acordado acudir al orfelinato dos veces por semana, pero ya no estaba muy segura de poder seguir. Había trabajado como enfermera anteriormente, aunque jamás en condiciones como aquéllas.

Recordó con añoranza los pasillos impecablemente fregados del Hospital Municipal de Birmingham mientras se acercaba al orfelinato. Pasó un gasógeno, y el humo maloliente que se escapaba de la pequeña chimenea la hizo toser. Llamó a la puerta y le abrió una monja.

El edificio del siglo XIX era un antiguo monasterio construido alrededor de un patio central con un claustro de columnas. Los muros del claustro estaban cubiertos de carteles anticomunistas. Un ogro fiero con una gorra de la estrella roja se cernía sobre una joven madre y sus hijos; la hoz y el martillo en un montaje con una calavera y la leyenda: «Esto es el comunismo.» La víspera le había preguntado a sor Inmaculada si no temía que los carteles asustaran a los niños. La alta monja había denegado tristemente con la cabeza.

—Casi todos los niños proceden de familias rojas. Hay que recordarles que vivían a la sombra del demonio. Si no, ¿de qué otra manera se podrían salvar sus almas cándidas?

Cuando llegó Barbara, sor Inmaculada, que llevaba una palmeta metida entre el hábito y el cinturón, estaba terminando de pasar lista con una voz clara y bien timbrada que resonaba por todo el patio. Cincuenta niños y niñas de entre seis y doce años permanecían de pie en fila sobre el suelo de hormigón. La monja bajó la tablilla.

—¡Ya os podéis retirar! —ordenó, levantando inmediatamente el brazo para hacer el saludo fascista—. ¡Viva Franco!

Los niños contestaron en un coro desigual mientras movían vagamente los brazos arriba y abajo. Barbara recordó el concierto y a Franco reprimiendo un bostezo. Se dirigió al dispensario; «España Reconquistada para Cristo», decía una leyenda pintada encima de la puerta.

Su primera tarea del día consistía en examinar el estado de salud de los niños recién llegados por si alguno de ellos necesitaba asistencia médica. En el interior del frío dispensario, con camas de hierro e instrumentos de acero colgados en las paredes, la esperaba la señora Blanco. Era una anciana cocinera retirada, una beata cuya vida giraba en torno a la iglesia. Tenía unos apretados rizos grises y llevaba un delantal de color marrón; su rostro mofletudo estaba arrugado y, a primera vista, parecía amable.

—Buenos días, señora Forsyth. Ya tengo preparada el agua caliente.

—Gracias, señora. ¿Cuántos tenemos hoy?

—Sólo dos. Traídos por la Guardia Civil. Un niño sorprendido robando en una casa y una chiquilla que andaba perdida por ahí. —La mujer meneó la cabeza piadosamente.

Barbara se lavó las manos. Los niños que llegaban al orfelinato vivían casi todos como salvajes y ejercían el robo y la mendicidad. La mendicidad era una molestia y, cuando la policía los pillaba, los solía entregar a las monjas.

La señora Blanco hizo sonar una campanilla y una monja hizo pasar a un niño de unos ocho años envuelto en un grasiento abrigo marrón demasiado grande para él. Sor Teresa era joven y tenía un rostro cuadrado de campesina.

—A esta pequeña fiera la pillaron robando —dijo en tono de amonestación.

—Qué niño más malo —comentó tristemente la señora Blanco—. Quítate la ropa, niño, que te vea la enfermera.

El niño se desvistió con aire malhumorado y se quedó en cueros: le asomaban las costillas a través de la piel y los brazos parecían palillos. Inclinó la cabeza y Barbara lo examinó. Olía a sudor rancio y a orina; su piel estaba fría como la de un pollo desplumado.

—Está muy delgado —dijo en voz baja—. Y tiene liendres, naturalmente. —El niño tenía en la muñeca un corte largo y enrojecido que supuraba—. Qué corte más feo, niño —le dijo con dulzura—. ¿Cómo te lo hiciste?

El niño levantó la cabeza y la miró con sus grandes ojos asustados.

—Un gato —contestó en voz baja—. Entró en mi sótano y entonces yo quise agarrarlo y me arañó.

Barbara sonrió.

—Gato malo. Te pondremos un poco de ungüento. Después te daremos algo de comer, ¿te parece bien? —El niño asintió con la cabeza—. ¿Cómo te llamas?

—Iván, señora.

La señora Blanco apretó los labios.

—¿Quién te puso este nombre?

—Mis padres.

—¿Y dónde están tus padres ahora?

—Los guardias civiles se los llevaron.

—Iván es un mal nombre, un nombre ruso, ¿lo sabías? Las monjas ya te buscarán otro mejor.

El niño inclinó la cabeza.

—Creo que eso es todo —dijo Barbara.

Hizo una anotación en una tarjeta y se la entregó a la señora Blanco, la cual se retiró con el niño. Sor Teresa se retiró por la otra puerta para ir en busca del siguiente niño.

La beata regresó a los pocos minutos, limpiándose las manos en el delantal oscuro.

—Señor, qué mal olía.

Fuera hubo alboroto. Barbara oyó unos gritos estridentes antes de que la puerta se abriera de golpe. Sor Teresa llevaba a rastras a una escuálida niña morena de unos once años de edad, que forcejeaba violentamente con ella. La monja tenía el rostro arrebolado y, con la toca ladeada, parecía que estuviera borracha.

—Madre de Dios, se resiste más que un cerdo. —Sor Teresa inmovilizó a la niña sujetándola por los brazos y la obligó a estarse quieta—. Basta, si no quieres que te dé con la palmeta. Lleva el diablo dentro. Vivía en una casa abandonada de Carabanchel... los guardias civiles la tuvieron que perseguir por las calles.

Barbara se agachó ante la niña. Ésta respiraba afanosamente, sus labios entreabiertos mostraban una dentadura estropeada y sus ojos parecían tremendamente asustados. Llevaba un sucio vestido azul y sostenía en la mano un burrito peludo, tan sucio y destrozado que apenas se distinguía lo que era.

—¿Cómo te llamas? —le preguntó Barbara amablemente.

La niña tragó saliva.

—¿Usted es monja?

—No, soy una enfermera. Sólo te quiero examinar para ver si te hace falta un médico.

La niña la miró con expresión implorante.

—Por favor, déjeme ir. No quiero que me conviertan en sopa.

—¿Cómo?

—Las monjas convierten a los niños en sopa y después se la dan de comer a los soldados de Franco. Por favor, por favor, pídales que me dejen ir.

Sor Teresa se echó a reír.

—Ya ve usted quién la ha educado.

La señora Blanco miró a la niña frunciendo el entrecejo.

—Éstas son las mentiras perversas que contaban los rojos. Eres una niña mala por decir estas cosas. Ahora quítate la ropa, que te vea la enfermera. ¡Y dame eso! —Alargó la mano hacia el burrito peludo, pero la niña lo agarró con más fuerza—. Te digo que me lo des. ¡A mí no me desafíes, rojita!

Agarró el juguete y tiró de él. El burrito se rompió por la mitad y el relleno blanco salió volando. La beata perdió el equilibrio y la niña pegó un brinco y huyó chillando. Después corrió a esconderse bajo una cama y allí se quedó acurrucada, con la cabeza del burrito —lo único que quedaba de él— apretada contra su rostro mientras seguía aullando sin descanso. La señora Blanco arrojó el resto del juguete al suelo.

—Pequeña bruja del demonio...

—¡Quieta! —le gritó Barbara severamente.

La beata pareció ofenderse. Sor Teresa cruzó los brazos y contempló la escena con interés mientras Barbara se agachaba ante la niña.

—Perdona —le dijo en un susurro—. Ha sido un accidente. A lo mejor yo te puedo arreglar el burro.

La niña restregó la cabeza del peluche contra su mejilla.

—*Fernandito, Fernandito*... ella me lo ha matado.

—Dámelo. Yo te lo volveré a coser. Te lo prometo. ¿Cómo te llamas?

La niña la estudió con recelo, no estaba acostumbrada a ser tratada con amabilidad.

—Carmela —contestó en voz baja—. Carmela Mera Varela.

Barbara se estremeció. Mera. El apellido de los amigos de Bernie. Los que vivían en Carabanchel. Recordó sus visitas allí tres años atrás... el corpulento y cordial progenitor, la madre agobiada de trabajo, el chico enfermo de tuberculosis. Y también había una niña pequeña que entonces debía de tener unos ocho años.

—¿Tienes... tienes familia?

La niña denegó con la cabeza y se mordió el labio.

—Lanzaron una granada muy grande —dijo—. Después busqué un sótano vacío para mí y *Fernandito*. —La niña rompió a llorar en atormentados sollozos.

Barbara alargó la mano, pero la niña se escabulló, llorando con desconsuelo. Barbara se levantó.

—Dios mío, debe de llevar años viviendo a la intemperie. —Sabía que no podía decir que la conocía, que conocía a su familia. Una familia roja.

—¿Le parece que nos la llevemos? —preguntó fríamente la señora Blanco.

Barbara volvió a agacharse.

—Carmela, te prometo que las monjas no te van a hacer daño. Te darán de comer, te pondrán ropa abrigada. No te ocurrirá nada si haces lo que te mandan, pero se enfadarán si no obedeces. Si lo haces, te prometo que te arreglaré el burro, te lo coseré. Pero tienes que ser obediente y salir de aquí. —Esta vez la niña dejó que Barbara tirara de ella para sacarla de debajo de la cama—. Muy bien, Carmela. Ahora estate quieta y quítate la ropa para que yo te examine. Eso es, muy bien, dame a *Fernandito*, yo cuidaré de él. —Los brazos y las piernas de la niña estaban cubiertos de eczema; Barbara se preguntó cómo habría logrado sobrevivir—. Está muy desnutrida. ¿De dónde sacas la comida, Carmelita?

—Pido limosna. —Una mirada de desafío apareció en sus ojos—. Robo cosas.

—¡Hala! —dijo bruscamente sor Teresa—. Vístete, que vamos a apuntarte en el registro. Y basta ya de bromas. Te darán un poco de comida si te portas bien. De lo contrario, probarás el bastón.

La niña volvió a ponerse el vestido. Sor Teresa apoyó firmemente una mano rechoncha y enrojecida en su hombro. Mientras se la llevaban, Carmela se volvió hacia Barbara y le dirigió una mirada de angustia.

—Te traeré a *Fernandito* dentro de uno o dos días —le dijo Barbara—. Te lo prometo. —La puerta se cerró a su espalda.

La señora Blanco soltó un bufido.

—Esto es una basura.

Se inclinó y recogió del suelo el resto del relleno de *Fernandito*. Lo comprimió todo en una bola apretada y lo arrojó a una papelera, junto con la otra mitad del burro peludo. Barbara se acercó, lo volvió a sacar todo y se lo guardó en el bolsillo.

—Le he prometido arreglarlo.

La beata resopló.

—Es una porquería. No le permitirán conservarlo, ¿sabe? —Se acercó un poco más a Barbara y la miró con los ojos entornados—.

Señora Forsyth, con toda mi caridad me pregunto si es usted adecuada para el trabajo que estamos llevando a cabo aquí. Ahora no podemos permitirnos el lujo del sentimentalismo en España. Quizá convendría que lo comentara con sor Inmaculada. —Con un movimiento brusco y arrogante de su ensortijada cabeza, la mujer abandonó el dispensario.

Aquella tarde, en casa, Barbara trató de recomponer el burro. Estaba sucio y grasiento, y tuvo que poner mucho cuidado en volver a colocar debidamente el relleno para que no acabara convertido en un objeto sin forma. Utilizó el hilo más fuerte que tenía, pero no estuvo muy segura de que pudiera resistir el constante maltrato de un niño. No podía dejar de pensar en Carmela. ¿Pertenecería a aquella familia, los amigos de Bernie? ¿Habrían muerto todos los demás?

Pilar entró para atizar el fuego y miró a Barbara con extrañeza. Barbara pensó que debía de tener una pinta muy rara, sentada allí en el suelo del salón vestida de aquella manera, cosiendo un juguete infantil con frenética concentración.

Cuando terminó, colocó el burro en el suelo. No había hecho un mal trabajo. Se preparó una tónica con ginebra, encendió un cigarrillo y se sentó a mirarlo. Tenía la expresión humilde y paciente de un burro de verdad.

A las siete entró Sandy. Se calentó las manos a la vera del fuego y la miró sonriendo. Barbara no se había tomado la molestia de encender la lámpara del techo y, exceptuando el charco de luz procedente de la lámpara de lectura en el cual se arremolinaba el humo de su cigarrillo, la estancia estaba en penumbra.

Sandy parecía contento y satisfecho.

—Hace mucho frío en la calle —dijo. Después miró al burro con asombro—. ¿Qué demonios es eso?

—Es *Fernandito*.

Sandy frunció el entrecejo.

—¿Quién?

—Pertenece a una niña del orfelinato. Se rompió cuando me la llevaron al dispensario.

Sandy soltó un gruñido.

—Creo que será mejor que no te tomes demasiado a pecho lo de estos niños.

—Pensé que te sería útil que yo trabajara allí. Por la conexión con la marquesa. —Barbara alargó la mano hacia la botella de ginebra que descansaba sobre la mesa de costura y se preparó otro trago. Sandy la miró.

—¿Cuántos te has tomado?

—Sólo uno. ¿Quieres?

Sandy tomó un vaso y se sentó frente a ella.

—Pasado mañana me volveré a reunir con Harry Brett. Creo que voy a poder introducirlo en algo.

Barbara suspiró.

—No lo metas en ningún asunto turbio, por lo que más quieras. A él no le gustaría. Trabaja en la embajada, tienen que andarse con cuidado.

—Es sólo una oportunidad de negocios. —Sandy la miró inquisitivamente.

—Si tú lo dices. —No solía hablar con él en aquel tono, pero estaba muy cansada y deprimida.

—Parece que no sientes demasiado interés por Harry —dijo Sandy—. Pensé que se había portado muy bien contigo cuando Piper murió.

Ella lo miró fijamente sin contestar. Por un instante, había visto en sus ojos una expresión desagradable, algo cruel y amenazador. Con sus facciones marcadas iluminadas por la lumbre, ofrecía el aspecto de un hombre disoluto de mediana edad. Él se revolvió en la silla y luego sonrió.

—Le he dicho que tú te reunirías con nosotros después. Sólo nosotros tres.

—De acuerdo.

Sandy la miró de nuevo sonriendo.

—Harry es un tipo muy curioso —añadió, con tono pensativo—. A veces, no sabes en qué está pensando. Arruga la frente en silencio y te das cuenta de que le está dando vueltas a algo.

—A mí siempre me ha parecido muy sincero. ¿Quieres que encienda la lámpara del techo?

Los ojos oscuros de Sandy se clavaron en ella.

—¿Qué te ocurre últimamente, Barbara? Pensé que el trabajo de enfermera te animaría un poco, pero te veo más abatida que nunca.

Ella lo estudió. No parecía que sospechara nada, estaba simplemente irritado.

—Si vieras las cosas que yo veo en el orfelinato, tú también estarías abatido. —Barbara lanzó un suspiro. ¿O no lo estaría? Puede que no.

—Vas a tener que dejarlo. Tengo muchas cosas en la cabeza en estos momentos.

—Es que estoy cansada, Sandy.

—Estás descuidando mucho tu aspecto. Fíjate en este jersey raído que llevas puesto.

—Me lo pongo para el orfelinato.

—Bueno, pero ahora no estás en el orfelinato. —Barbara se dio cuenta de que estaba muy molesto con ella—. Me recuerdas la vez que te conocí. Y te tienes que volver a hacer la permanente. Comprendo por qué aquellas niñas te llamaban cuatro ojos con ricitos. Y, además, te sigues poniendo las gafas.

La intensidad de su dolor y su rabia la dejó asombrada. Cuando hacía enfadar a Sandy, éste raras veces contraatacaba con semejante violencia. Sabía cómo herirla. Tuvo que hacer un esfuerzo para controlar el temblor de su voz. Se levantó.

—Voy arriba a cambiarme —dijo.

Sandy la miró con una sonrisa radiante en los labios.

—Eso ya está mejor. Tengo que leer unos papeles... dile a Pilar que cenaremos a las ocho.

Barbara abandonó el salón. Mientras subía al piso de arriba, pensó: «Cuando saque a Bernie de aquí, regresaré a Inglaterra. Lejos de este lugar horrible, lejos de él.»

Luis no estaba en el café cuando ella llegó al día siguiente. Miró a través de la luna que daba a la calle y sólo vio a unos cuantos obreros acodados en la barra. Era una tarde grisácea, muy fría y desapacible.

Se acercó a la barra y pidió un café. La gorda la miró inquisitivamente.

—¿Otro trabajito, señora? —le preguntó, guiñándole el ojo.

Barbara se ruborizó sin decir nada.

—Su amigo es muy guapo, ¿verdad, señora? Aquí tiene su café.

Una pareja de ancianos permanecía sentada a una mesa, contemplando sus tazas vacías. Ya estaban allí la otra vez, pensó Barbara mientras se sentaba a su mesa de costumbre y encendía un cigarrillo. Los estudió. No parecían espías, simplemente una pareja de ancianos que se había ido a pasar un rato en el café porque allí se estaba calentito. Tomó un sorbo de su café; sabía a aguachirle caliente. Ya llevaba diez minutos esperando con creciente nerviosismo, cuando finalmente apareció Luis. Éste entró casi sin resuello y la miró como disculpándose. Pidió un café en la barra y se le acercó presuroso.

—Discúlpeme, señora, es que me he cambiado de casa.

—No se preocupe. ¿Tiene alguna noticia?

Luis asintió con la cabeza y se inclinó hacia ella con expresión anhelante.

—Sí. Hemos hecho progresos. Agustín ya ha conseguido que lo incluyan en los turnos de guardia de la cantera. En el momento oportuno, se pondrá de acuerdo con su amigo para que éste pida ir al lavabo diciendo que... —carraspeó como si le diera vergüenza—... tiene diarrea. Le propinará a Agustín un golpe en la cabeza, le robará las llaves de las esposas y escapará.

—¿Van esposados? —Era uno de los horrores que había imaginado.

—Pues sí, tendrá que ir al lavabo esposado.

Barbara lo pensó un momento y después asintió con la cabeza.

—Muy bien. —Encendió otro pitillo y le ofreció la cajetilla a Luis—. ¿Cuándo? Cuanto más se prolongue la espera, tanto mayor será el peligro. Y no simplemente a causa de la situación política. Es que ya no aguanto más, mi... marido... se ha dado cuenta de que no soy la misma.

Luis se revolvió en su asiento.

—Me temo que ahí está el problema. Agustín tiene tres semanas de permiso a partir de la semana que viene. No regresará hasta principios de diciembre. Habrá que esperar hasta entonces.

—¡Pero si todavía falta un mes! ¿No puede cambiar la fecha del permiso?

—Por favor, señora, baje la voz. Piense en lo sospechoso que resultaría si Agustín cancelara de repente el permiso que tenía previsto desde hace varios meses y, estando de servicio, se registrara una fuga.

—Todo esto me parece muy mal. ¿Y si España entra en guerra, y si yo me tengo que ir?

—Llevan desde junio diciendo que vamos a entrar y hasta ahora no ha ocurrido nada, ni siquiera después de la entrevista de Franco con Hitler. Le prometo, señora, que se hará lo antes posible, cuando Agustín regrese al trabajo. Y todo será más fácil cuando los días sean más cortos... la oscuridad favorecerá la fuga de su amigo.

—Se llama Bernie... Bernie. ¿Por qué no puede utilizar su nombre?

—Sí, claro, Bernie.

Barbara reflexionó cuidadosamente.

—¿Cómo se podrá trasladar desde el campo de prisioneros hasta Cuenca? Irá vestido de paisano.

—Todo es territorio abrupto y rural hasta llegar a la garganta de Cuenca, con sitios de sobra donde esconderse. Y hay un lugar de Cuenca en el que usted se podrá reunir con él. Todo eso lo arreglará Agustín.

—¿Cuál es la distancia entre el campo de prisioneros y Cuenca?

—Unos ocho kilómetros. Pero, mire, señora, su Bernie es un prisionero fuerte como el que más. Están acostumbrados al trabajo duro y a las largas caminatas invernales. Lo conseguirá.

—¿Qué sabe Bernie? ¿Sabe que yo estoy intentando ayudarlo?

—Todavía no. Así es más seguro. Agustín sólo le dijo que ya llegarán tiempos mejores. No le quita el ojo de encima.

—Poco lo podrá vigilar desde Sevilla.

—Eso es inevitable. Lo siento, pero no podemos hacer nada más.

—Muy bien. —Barbara suspiró y se pasó una mano por la cara. ¿Cómo podría resistir las semanas que tenía por delante?

—Ahora ya está todo arreglado, señora. —Luis la miró con intención—. Acordamos que yo cobraría la mitad cuando todo estuviera arreglado.

Barbara denegó con la cabeza.

—No exactamente, Luis. Yo le dije que le pagaría la mitad cuando hubiéramos elaborado un plan. Eso significa cuando yo sepa cómo y cuándo se llevará a efecto el plan.

Vio un destello de furia en sus ojos.

—Su amigo tendrá que pegarle a mi hermano un fuerte golpe en la cabeza para que ellos se crean la historia. Después, Agustín se tendrá que quedar quizá varias horas en Tierra Muerta para darle ocasión de escapar. Y ya hay nieve en los picos de la sierra.

Barbara lo miró desde lo alto de su estatura superior.

—Cuando tenga una fecha, Luis. Una fecha.

—Pero...

Se calló de golpe. Dos guardias civiles acababan de entrar en el local con sus tricornios y sus capas cortas brillando cual carapachos de insectos. Las armas resultaban visibles en las fundas amarillas que llevaban al cinto. Se acercaron a la barra.

—¡Mierda! —exclamó Luis por lo bajo. Hizo ademán de levantarse, pero Barbara apoyó una mano en su brazo.

—Siéntese. ¿Qué van a pensar si nos largamos en cuanto ellos aparecen?

Luis volvió a sentarse. La vieja atendió a los guardias, comentándoles el frío que hacía.

—Demasiado frío para irnos directamente a casa después del servicio, señora. —Tomaron sus cafés y se sentaron. Uno de ellos miró con curiosidad a Barbara y después le murmuró algo a su compañero. Ambos se echaron a reír.

—Vamos, señora, vámonos ahora mismo. —Luis temblaba de inquietud.

—De acuerdo. Pero muy despacio.

Se levantaron y salieron a la calle. Ambos lanzaron un suspiro de alivio cuando la puerta se cerró a su espalda.

—Me ha decepcionado con eso del dinero, señora —dijo Luis con expresión enfurruñada—. Ciertas cosas escapan a mi control.

«¿Se habrá cambiado de casa confiando en el dinero que pensaba cobrar?», se preguntó Barbara. Habría sentido mucho que así fuera.

—Cuando yo tenga una fecha, usted tendrá el dinero.

Luis se encogió de hombros con gesto airado.

—Regresaré a Cuenca este fin de semana, veré a Agustín antes de que se vaya a Sevilla. Podemos volver a reunirnos dentro de una semana.

Y después, para asombro de Barbara, le estrechó de nuevo la mano con aquella rígida formalidad tan propia de él antes de dar media vuelta y perderse en la tarde gris. «Más semanas —pensó Barbara—, más semanas de lo mismo.» Apretó los puños. Mientras se alejaba, evitó mirar a los guardias civiles a través de la luna del local, pero observó que los ancianos mantenían las cabezas inclinadas sobre sus tazas de café y miraban furtivamente a los guardias con expresión atemorizada. Ellos también les tenían miedo; no vigilaban a nadie.

25

Ya habían caído las primeras nieves sobre los picos de la sierra de Valdemeca, allá lejos hacia el noreste. Aquella mañana habían visto por primera vez una blanca capa de escarcha en el patio del campo, una finísima piel de hielo en los pequeños charcos. Los primeros rayos de sol iluminaron la nieve de las lejanas montañas, tiñéndola de un delicado color rosa que a Bernie le pareció hermoso mientras permanecía de pie envuelto en su delgado mono de trabajo, a la espera de que Aranda pasara su lista de la mañana.

A su lado, Vicente se sonó la nariz con la manga e hizo una mueca al ver en ella unos trazos de moco de intenso color amarillo. Algo le ocurría a su nariz; le dolía mucho la cabeza y soltaba constantes mucosidades.

Aranda salió de su barraca con su gabán y sus guantes y se dirigió a la plataforma. Una vez allí, se quitó los guantes, se sopló las manos y miró con semblante enfurecido a los prisioneros. Una brisa gélida soplaba desde la sierra, y alborotaba con sus ásperos dedos el cabello de los prisioneros mientras la voz sonora de Aranda los iba llamando por sus nombres. Había media docena de nuevos prisioneros, republicanos que habían huido a Francia tras la victoria de Franco y habían sido devueltos por los nazis. Ahora contemplaban su nueva prisión sin el menor interés. Uno de ellos dijo que el presidente catalán Companys había sido devuelto a Madrid y enviado a Barcelona para acabar siendo fusilado en el castillo de Montjuïc. En la barraca del comedor, Bernie se sentó con algunos de los comunistas a la hora del desayuno. Pablo, un ex minero de Asturias, se desplazó un poco para hacerle sitio en el banco.

—Buenos días, camarada. Hoy hace frío, ¿no?

—Mucho frío. Este invierno ha llegado muy pronto.

Bernie se fue comiendo a cucharadas el líquido puré de garbanzos. Eulalio lo miró desde el fondo de la mesa. Su sarna había empeorado y su cara estaba cubierta de ronchas rojas en las zonas donde se había rascado. Una mancha dura y enrojecida en la muñeca revelaba que la enfermedad había alcanzado la fase de la formación de costras y pústulas bajo las cuales se ocultaban los ácaros y los huevos.

—Compañero Piper, veo que hoy has decidido unirte a nosotros.

—Verás, compañero, a mí me gusta moverme un poco por ahí, de esta manera te enteras de más noticias.

Eulalio lo miró con sus duros y penetrantes ojos grises.

—¿Y de qué noticias te has enterado por ahí?

—Pues de que uno de los guardias le ha dicho a Guillermo que la piedra de la cantera es para un monumento que Franco está empezando a construir en la sierra de Guadarrama. Al parecer, quiere que sea su sepulcro; tardarán veinte años en terminarlo.

—Si está en la sierra de Guadarrama, ¿por qué quieren piedra caliza de aquí?

—Más apropiada para los adornos monumentales, dice Guillermo.

Eulalio soltó un gruñido.

—A mí todo eso me suena a propaganda. Los guardias siembran todas estas historias para hacernos creer que Franco siempre estará aquí. Deberías analizar un poco lo que te dicen, camarada.

—Ya lo hago, camarada Eulalio.

Bernie le devolvió la gélida mirada. Con su calva abombada y los pelillos que tenía en el cuello, Eulalio le recordaba a las lagartijas que se veían en verano escabulléndose entre las rocas. Eulalio sonrió fríamente.

—Confío en que analices muy especialmente lo que te diga este burgués de Vicente.

—Lo hago. Y él analiza a su vez lo que yo le digo.

—¿Sigues en la cuadrilla de la cantera? —le preguntó Pablo, cambiando de tema.

—Toda esta semana. Preferiría estar en la barraca de la cocina contigo.

El guardia tocó el silbato.

—Vamos, a ver si termináis. ¡Ya es hora de trabajar!

Bernie recogió con la cuchara lo último que le quedaba del puré y se levantó. Con la boca torcida en una mueca de dolor, Eulalio se rascaba las costras de la muñeca.

Los prisioneros formaron largas filas en el patio. Ahora el sol asomaba por encima de las pardas y las yermas colinas, y el ambiente era un poco más cálido; el hielo de los charcos se empezaba a fundir. Se abrieron las verjas y la cuadrilla de Bernie salió, formando una larga fila mientras los guardias armados con fusiles ocupaban sus posiciones a cada pocos metros. El sargento Ramírez bajó muy despacio a lo largo de la fila, contemplando con rostro enfurruñado a los prisioneros. Era un gordinflón de cincuenta y tantos años con un desordenado bigote gris, un rubicundo rostro y una bulbosa nariz de borracho. Ofrecía un aspecto decrépito; pero era muy peligroso, un volcán ardiente en cuyo interior se agitaban toda suerte de odios reconcentrados. Era un viejo soldado profesional, de esos que por regla general solían ser los más crueles, pues normalmente los reclutas preferían tomarse la vida con más calma. Bajo su gabán, se distinguía el bulto de su látigo metido en el cinturón. Llegó al principio de la fila, tocó el silbato y los prisioneros iniciaron el ascenso a las colinas.

Era un paseo de casi cinco kilómetros. El nombre de Tierra Muerta le iba que ni pintado: un territorio raso y pedregoso, unos pocos campos de labranza protegidos por chaparros y arañados en las hondonadas abiertas entre las colinas. Pasaron por delante de una familia de labriegos que trabajaba la tierra pedregosa con un arado de bueyes. Los labriegos no levantaron la vista al paso de la columna; por acuerdo tácito, los prisioneros eran invisibles.

Un poco más allá, coronaron una colina y Ramírez tocó el silbato para anunciar un descanso de cinco minutos. Vicente se sentó en una roca. Estaba muy pálido y respiraba con jadeos entrecortados y ásperos. Bernie miró al guardia más próximo y se sorprendió de que fuera Agustín, el hombre que una semana atrás le había hecho aquel extraño comentario tras su visita al psiquiatra.

—Hoy me encuentro muy mal, Bernardo —dijo Vicente—. Tengo la cabeza a punto de estallar.

—Molina regresa la semana que viene... él dejará que te lo tomes con más calma. —Bernie se inclinó un poco más hacia él—. Trabajaremos juntos, así podrás descansar.

—Eres bueno, para ser un viejo burgués —dijo el abogado en un intento de dárselas de gracioso. Estaba sudando, y la humedad le brillaba en la frente arrugada—. Empiezo a preguntarme de qué sirve seguir luchando. Al final, los fascistas nos van a matar a todos. Eso es lo que quieren, matarnos a trabajar.

—Serán derrotados. Tenemos que resistir.

—Han ganado en todas partes. Aquí, en Polonia, en Francia. Inglaterra será la siguiente. Y Stalin ha firmado un pacto de no agresión con Hitler porque se muere de miedo.

—El camarada Stalin firmó ese pacto con Hitler para ganar tiempo.

Era lo que Eulalio había dicho al enterarse a través de los guardias del pacto nazi-soviético. Bernie no podía aceptar la idea de que aquella guerra contra el fascismo se tuviera que llamar ahora guerra entre potencias imperialistas. Fue entonces cuando empezó a poner en duda por vez primera la línea de conducta del partido.

—El camarada Stalin. —Vicente se rió con una carcajada hueca que acabó convirtiéndose en un acceso de tos.

Muy a lo lejos, allí donde la Tierra Muerta bajaba suavemente hasta perderse en la brumosa distancia, Bernie divisó un espectáculo extraordinario. Por encima de una capa de niebla blanca se distinguía un peñasco en cuya ladera se levantaban unas casas con las ventanas iluminadas por unos radiantes rayos de sol. Parecían muy cercanas, como si flotaran sobre la niebla. Era una jugarreta que la luz gastaba allí algunas veces, como un espejismo del desierto. Bernie le dio un suave codazo a Vicente.

—Mira allí, amigo mío, ¿no te parece un espectáculo por el que merece la pena vivir? Un panorama como éste no se ve muy a menudo.

Vicente atisbó en la distancia.

—No veo nada, no llevo las gafas. ¿Hoy se puede ver Cuenca?

—Se pueden ver nada menos que las casas colgadas; es como si flotaran sobre la niebla que se levanta desde la garganta de más abajo. —Bernie lanzó un suspiro—. Es como contemplar otro mundo.

Delante de ellos, Ramírez tocó el silbato.

—¡En marcha! —gritó Agustín.

Bernie ayudó a Vicente a ponerse en pie. Mientras reanudaban su camino, Agustín se situó a su lado, acompasando el paso al suyo. Bernie observó que aquel hombre lo estudiaba con disimulo. Se preguntó si estaría interesado en su trasero; cosas que ocurrían en el campo.

La cantera era un inmenso y profundo corte excavado en la ladera de la colina. Se habían pasado varias semanas trabajando allí día tras día, arrancando enormes pedazos de piedra caliza y partiéndolos en trozos de tamaño más reducido que después se llevaban en camiones. Bernie se preguntó si la historia sobre el monumento de Franco sería cierta; a veces se preguntaba, como Vicente, si la extracción de piedras de la cantera no sería una simple excusa para matarlos a todos poco a poco a trabajar en aquel desierto.

Agustín y otro guardia encendieron una hoguera delante del cobertizo levantado a la entrada de la cantera, pero Ramírez no se acercó al calor como lo habría hecho Molina. Permaneció de pie sobre un montón de rocas, con las manos a la espalda mientras uno de los guardias montaba la ametralladora. Otros guardias empezaron a repartir los picos y las palas que se guardaban en el cobertizo. No había la menor posibilidad de que los prisioneros utilizaran las herramientas para atacarlos... el fuego de la ametralladora los habría abatido en menos que canta un gallo.

Bernie y Vicente encontraron un montón de bloques de piedra caliza en el que trabajar, parcialmente oculto por un saliente rocoso que se proyectaba hacia fuera. Allí trabajarían hasta la puesta del sol con sólo una breve pausa a mediodía para comer y beber. Ahora, por lo menos, los días eran cada vez más cortos; en verano, la jornada laboral duraba trece horas. El estruendo y el fragor de la piedra contra el metal resonaban en todos los rincones.

Una hora más tarde, Vicente tropezó y se dejó caer pesadamente sobre las piedras. Volvió a sonarse la nariz, se manchó la manga con un hilillo de mucosidad que parecía pus y emitió un gemido de dolor.

—No puedo seguir —dijo—. Llama al guardia.

—Descansa un poco.

—Es demasiado peligroso, Bernardo. Hay que llamar al guardia cuando alguien está enfermo.

—Calla esa boca burguesa.

Vicente permaneció sentado, respirando entre jadeos. Bernie siguió con su tarea, prestando atención por si oía unas pisadas detrás del saliente. Le dolían los pies dentro de aquellas botas viejas y cuarteadas y había alcanzado el primer grado de la sed cotidiana en el que la lengua se movía incesantemente alrededor de la boca en busca de humedad.

El soldado apareció sin previo aviso, asomando por detrás del saliente con demasiada rapidez para que Bernie pudiera decirle a Vicente que se levantara. Era Rodolfo, un curtido veterano de las guerras de Marruecos.

—¿Qué haces? —gritó—. ¡Tú! ¡Levántate ahora mismo! —Vicente se levantó temblando.

Rodolfo se acercó a Bernie.

—¿Por qué permites que este hombre eluda sus obligaciones? ¡Eso es un sabotaje!

—Es que se acaba de poner enfermo, señor cabo. Ahora mismo lo iba a llamar.

Rodolfo sacó el silbato del bolsillo y empezó a tocarlo con fuerza. Vicente encorvó la espalda, presa de la desesperación.

Se oyó el crujido sobre la tierra de unos pies calzados con botas y apareció Ramírez. Inmediatamente después, Agustín se acercó corriendo a su espalda. Ramírez miró enfurecido a Bernie y Vicente.

—¿Qué coño pasa aquí?

Rodolfo enseguida levantó el brazo haciendo el saludo fascista.

—He sorprendido al abogado aquí sentado sin hacer nada —dijo—. Y el inglés lo estaba mirando tan tranquilo.

—Por favor, mi sargento —dijo Vicente—. Me he sentido indispuesto. Y Piper estaba a punto de llamar al guardia.

—Conque indispuesto, ¿eh?

A Ramírez se le salían los ojos de las órbitas a causa de la rabia. Con la mano enguantada, abofeteó el rostro de Vicente. El sonido resonó en la cantera como un disparo de fusil, mientras el abogado se desplomaba convertido en un guiñapo. Ramírez se volvió para mirar a Bernie.

—Y tú lo dejabas holgazanear, ¿verdad? Inglés comunista, hijo de la grandísima puta. —Dio un paso al frente para acercársele un poco más—. Tú eres uno de esos que mentalmente no se sienten derrotados, ¿verdad? Me parece que necesitas pasarte un día en la cruz.

Ramírez se volvió hacia Rodolfo, el cual sonrió e inclinó la cabeza con expresión sombría. Bernie apretó los labios. Pensó en el daño que le haría el estiramiento en la vieja herida del hombro... bastante le dolía ya después de una jornada de trabajo. Estudió los ojos de Ramírez. Algo en su aspecto debía de haber provocado el enojo del militar. Con una rapidez superior a la que la mirada habría podido seguir, éste sacó el látigo y azotó a Bernie en el cuello. Bernie lanzó un grito y se tambaleó mientras la sangre le brotaba entre los dedos.

Agustín se adelantó y rozó nerviosamente el brazo de Ramírez.

—Mi sargento.

Ramírez se volvió con impaciencia.

—¿Qué?

Agustín tragó saliva.

—Mi sargento, el psiquiatra está estudiando a este hombre. Creo... creo que al comandante no le gustaría que sufriera algún daño.

Ramírez frunció el entrecejo.

—¿Estás seguro? ¿Éste?

—Seguro, mi sargento.

Ramírez hizo pucheros como un niño al que acabaran de arrebatar una golosina, y asintió con la cabeza a regañadientes.

—Muy bien. —Se inclinó sobre Bernie y le arrojó a la cara un fétido aliento que apestaba a ajo rancio—. Que te sirva de advertencia. Y tú... —señaló a Vicente con un gesto de la mano—... vuelve al trabajo. —Luego se alejó, con Rodolfo a la zaga. Agustín los siguió apurando el paso, sin volverse para mirar a Bernie.

Aquella noche, mientras los hombres permanecían tumbados en sus literas a la espera de que apagaran las luces, Vicente se volvió hacia Bernie. El abogado se había pasado casi toda la tarde durmiendo.

—¿Te encuentras mejor? —le preguntó Bernie.

Vicente lanzó un suspiro.

—Por lo menos, he descansado. —A la tenue luz de la vela, su rostro estaba arrugado y ojeroso—. ¿Y tú?

Bernie se tocó cuidadosamente la larga herida del cuello. Se la había lavado y confiaba en que no se le infectara.

—Todo irá bien.

—¿Qué ocurrió esta mañana? —preguntó Vicente en voz baja—. ¿Por qué te soltaron?

—No lo sé, me he pasado todo el día tratando de averiguarlo. —La indulgencia de Ramírez era la comidilla de todo el campo; a la hora de la cena, Eulalio también se lo había preguntado, mirándolo con recelo—. Agustín le dijo que me estaba tratando el psiquiatra, pero yo creo que al psiquiatra le importa un bledo el estado en que yo me encuentre.

—A lo mejor, Agustín te quiere en su cama.

—Lo he pensado, pero no creo. No me mira de esa manera.

—Pues a mí alguien me ha mirado así al entrar —dijo Vicente en voz baja—. Lo he visto.

—¿El padre Eduardo? Sí, yo también lo he visto.

Bernie había tenido que ayudar al abogado en la última etapa del camino de regreso desde la cantera, sujetándolo para ayudarlo a caminar. Mientras atravesaban el patio, había visto al joven sacerdote saliendo de la barraca de las clases. Se había detenido y los había seguido con la mirada mientras ambos avanzaban renqueando en dirección a su barraca.

—Ahora ya me tiene fichado —dijo Vicente—. Para él sería un buen trofeo.

26

El despacho de Sandy estaba situado en una mísera plaza llena de tiendas y de pequeños almacenes que anunciaban excedentes de quiebras. Caía una fría y fina llovizna. Desde el refugio de su quiosco, un viejo vendedor de periódicos contemplaba con aire melancólico a Harry mientras éste cruzaba la plaza. Al otro lado, unos hombres que descargaban cajas de un carro lo miraron con curiosidad. Que Harry supiera, en aquellos momentos no lo seguía nadie; pero, aun así, se sentía desprotegido. En el dintel de una puerta de madera maciza sin pintar figuraba una hilera de timbres eléctricos. Y una placa de madera al lado del de arriba decía «Nuevas Iniciativas». Harry pulsó el timbre y esperó.

Sandy lo había llamado a la embajada.

—Perdona que haya tardado tanto; pero, a propósito de esta oportunidad de negocio... ¿podríamos reunirnos en mi despacho y no en el café? Quiero enseñarte unas cosas. Barbara se reunirá después con nosotros para tomar un café.

Aquella mañana Harry se había reunido con Tolhurst y Hillgarth en el despacho de Tolhurst para ponerlos al corriente. Hillgarth estaba de muy buen humor, y su rostro melancólico aparecía relajado y satisfecho.

—¿A ver si será el oro? —preguntó, con expresión risueña.

—Ha estado muy evasivo al respecto —contestó Harry cautelosamente.

Hillgarth se pasó un dedo por la raya de los pantalones y frunció el entrecejo con aire pensativo.

—Sabemos que Franco trata de negociar el envío de suministros alimenticios de Argentina. Digo yo que querrán cobrar, ¿verdad Tolly?

—Sí, señor.

Hillgarth hizo un gesto afirmativo con la cabeza y se reclinó contra el respaldo de su asiento.

—Ofrezca lo que ofrezca, creo que usted debería picar el anzuelo. —Soltó una risita suave—. No, no exactamente; aquí el anzuelo es usted, y él es el pescado. Muy bien, Tolly. El dinero.

Tolhurst abrió una carpeta y miró con la cara muy seria a Harry.

—Estás autorizado a ofrecer una inversión de hasta dos mil libras en cualquier proposición significativa de negocio de Forsyth. Si pide más, puedes recurrir a nosotros una vez más. Te facilitaremos el dinero, pero tú tendrás que enseñarle a Forsyth tu propia libreta de ahorro para demostrarle que dispones de fondos.

—Aquí la tengo —dijo Harry, empujando la pequeña cartilla de cartulina sobre la mesa.

Hillgarth la estudió con cuidado.

—Eso es mucho dinero.

—Recibí el capital de mis padres al cumplir los veintiún años. No gasto mucho.

—Tendría usted que vivir un poco. Cuando yo tenía su edad, dirigía una mina de estaño en Bolivia... qué no habría yo dado entonces por cinco mil libras.

—Es bueno que Brett las haya conservado —dijo Tolhurst—. A Londres no le gustan las libretas de ahorro falsas.

Los grandes ojos castaños de Hillgarth seguían clavados en Harry. Éste se revolvió un poco en su asiento, recordando que no les había dicho nada sobre Enrique. Había sido una estúpida testarudez por su parte, pero no lo había hecho. ¿Qué mal podía haber en ello?

—Maestre me dice que su hija tiene el corazón destrozado porque usted no se ha vuelto a poner en contacto con ella desde que la acompañó al Prado —dijo Hillgarth.

Harry titubeó antes de contestar.

—Preferiría no volver a verla, con toda franqueza.

Hillgarth se encendió un Gold Flake, y estudió a Harry por encima del encendedor.

—Una señorita encantadora, me deja usted de piedra.

—Es poco más que una niña.

—Lástima. Nos podría ser muy útil desde un punto de vista diplomático.

Harry no contestó. Ya estaba engañando a Sandy y a Barbara, ¿tenía que engañar también a Milagros?

—Supongo que alguien podría decir que es usted un agente ideal, Brett —dijo Hillgarth en tono pensativo—. Incorruptible. No persigue a las mujeres, no le interesa el dinero. Y ni siquiera bebe demasiado, ¿verdad?

—Nos tomamos unas cuantas copas la otra noche —dijo Tolhurst jovialmente.

—Casi todos los agentes son corruptibles. Quieren algo, aunque sólo sea emoción. Pero eso a usted tampoco le entusiasma, ¿verdad?

—Lo hago por mi país —dijo Harry. Sabía que sus palabras sonaban ampulosas y excesivas, pero le daba igual—. Porque me dijeron que sería útil para el esfuerzo bélico. Es otra forma de servir.

Hillgarth movió muy despacio la cabeza en gesto afirmativo.

—Eso es bueno, me parece estupendo. La lealtad. —Hillgarth lo pensó un poco—. ¿Hasta dónde estaría usted dispuesto a llegar por lealtad?

Harry titubeó, pero los modales despectivos de Hillgarth le habían caído tan mal que se envalentonó.

—No lo sé, señor, dependería de lo que se me pidiera.

Hillgarth asintió con la cabeza.

—¿Habría límites?

—Dependería de lo que se me pidiera —repitió Harry.

—Dudo que Forsyth tenga límites. ¿Usted qué cree?

—Sandy sólo te deja ver lo que él quiere que veas. La verdad es que no sé qué sería capaz de hacer. —Harry hizo una pausa—. Probablemente casi todo. —«Como usted», pensó.

—Bueno, ya veremos. —Hillgarth volvió a reclinarse en su asiento—. En cuanto a hoy, a ver qué es lo que le ofrece; dígale que está de acuerdo y después preséntenos su informe.

—Pero no te lances sin más, Harry —añadió Tolhurst—. Finge dudar y estar preocupado por tu dinero. Dile que necesitas saberlo todo antes de comprometerte.

—Sí —convino Hillgarth—. Ésta es la línea que hay que seguir. La manera de conseguir que le enseñe algo más.

Abrió la puerta una mujer regordeta de cincuenta y tantos años con la cara arrugada y el cabello gris recogido en un moño.

—¿Sí? —preguntó.

—Tengo una cita con el señor Forsyth. Me llamo Brett.

Lo acompañó, subiendo un angosto tramo de escaleras hasta un pequeño despacho con una máquina de escribir sobre un escritorio maltrecho. Llamó con los nudillos a una puerta y apareció Sandy, sonriendo de oreja a oreja. Vestía un traje de raya diplomática, con un pañuelo rojo en el bolsillo superior de la chaqueta.

—¡Harry! Bienvenido a Nuevas Iniciativas. —Miró sonriendo a la secretaria, y ésta se ruborizó inesperadamente—. Ya veo que conoces a María, prepara el mejor té de Madrid. Dos tés y dos cafés, María.

La secretaria se retiró de inmediato.

—Vamos.

Sandy acompañó a Harry a una estancia sorprendentemente espaciosa. Una mesa de gran tamaño atestada de mapas y papeles ocupaba toda una pared. Harry se sorprendió al ver relucientes botes metálicos parecidos a termos apilados, también, sobre la mesa. Por encima de la mesa destacaba una reproducción de un lienzo del siglo XIX. Un mar tropical rebosante de vida salvaje, con unos reptiles gigantescos que se atacaban entre sí con sus mandíbulas ensangrentadas mientras en el cielo de arriba unos pterodáctilos circunvolaban la escena. Al otro lado, tras un enorme escritorio de madera de roble, dos hombres vestidos de paisano permanecían sentados fumando.

—A Sebastián de Salas ya lo conoces, claro —dijo Sandy.

—Buenas tardes. —De Salas se levantó e inclinó la cabeza mientras estrechaba la mano de Harry. El otro hombre era bajito, tenía el rostro muy pálido y vestía un traje que le sentaba muy mal. En contraste con la pulcritud de De Salas, parecía un oficinista desastrado.

—Alberto Otero, el cerebro de nuestro equipo.

Otero se levantó brevemente y estrechó la mano de Harry en un húmedo apretón. Estudió a Harry con semblante inexpresivo y sin la menor sonrisa en los labios.

—Ya veo que te ha llamado la atención mi cuadro —dijo Sandy—. *Antiguo condado de Dorset*, de Henry de la Beche. Pintado en 1830, cuando la gente empezaba a descubrir los dinosaurios.

—Naturalmente, todo es falso —terció severamente Otero—. Los animales están muy desproporcionados.

—Sí, Alberto. Pero tú imagínate lo que debió de pensar la gente al darse cuenta de que, en otros tiempos, su precioso paisaje inglés había estado lleno de reptiles gigantes. —Forsyth sonrió y se acomodó junto a De Salas. Sentado frente a ellos, Harry se dio cuenta de que los tres lucían idénticos bigotitos, el distintivo de la Falange.

Sandy se reclinó en su asiento, cruzando los brazos sobre la barriga.

—Mira, Harry, tú tienes un poco de dinero para invertir y nosotros tenemos un proyecto que necesita más capital. Pero Alberto quiere saber algo más acerca de los fondos disponibles. —Sandy guiñó el ojo—. Son muy precavidos, estos españoles. Y les sobra razón.

—Tengo algo de dinero en el banco —dijo Harry—. Aunque no quisiera invertir demasiado en un solo proyecto.

De Salas hizo un movimiento afirmativo con la cabeza, pero Otero conservó su semblante inexpresivo.

—¿Puedo preguntar cuál es su procedencia? —inquirió éste—. No quisiera parecer impertinente, pero tenemos que saberlo.

—Por supuesto. Es el capital de la testamentaría de mis padres. Murieron cuando yo era pequeño.

—Harry es un soso —dijo Sandy—. No gasta demasiado.

—¿Dónde está el dinero ahora?

—En mi banco de Inglaterra. —Harry sacó la libreta de ahorro—. Pueden echar un vistazo, no me importa. Pensé que les interesaría verlo.

Otero examinó la libreta.

—¿Y qué me dice de las restricciones monetarias?

—No tienen aplicación en este caso —dijo Sandy—. Personal de la embajada, ¿no es así, Harry?

—Estoy autorizado a invertir en un país neutral.

De Salas lo miró sonriendo.

—¿Y no le importaría invertir aquí? Estoy pensando en la situación política. Más bien discrepábamos a este respecto la última vez que nos vimos.

—Apoyo a mi país contra Alemania. No tengo nada contra España. Se tiene que construir su propio futuro, como usted mismo dijo.

—Cuando hay dinero de por medio, ¿verdad, señor? —Sebastián miró con una sonrisa a Harry, una sonrisa conspiradora pero también ligeramente despectiva.

—¿Y si España entra en guerra? —preguntó Otero—. Eso inmovilizaría cualquier inversión británica que se hubiera efectuado aquí.

—En la embajada están bastante convencidos de que Franco no entrará en guerra. Lo bastante para que yo me atreva a correr el riesgo.

Otero hizo una ligera señal de asentimiento con la cabeza.

—¿Hasta qué extremo es fiable su información? ¿Eso es lo que piensa el embajador?

Semejante información habría valido un montón de dinero, y Harry lo sabía.

—Yo oigo simplemente lo que dicen otros traductores. Como es lógico, no tengo acceso a ningún material secreto. —Dejó que en su voz se insinuara una nota de arrogancia—. Y ni se me ocurriría soltar una sola palabra en caso de que lo tuviera. Yo sólo sé lo que dice la gente en general; probablemente los mensajeros españoles sepan lo mismo.

Sebastián levantó una mano.

—Por supuesto, señor Brett. Disculpe mi curiosidad.

—Harry es leal al rey —dijo Sandy sonriendo.

Otero lo miró inquisitivamente.

—En caso de que le facilitáramos información acerca de este asunto que tenemos entre manos, tendría usted que mantenerlo en un plano absolutamente confidencial.

—Por supuesto.

—No quisiéramos que se comentara en ningún otro sitio. Y mucho menos en la embajada. ¿Cree que allí podrían estar interesados?

—No veo por qué razón —contestó Harry con la mayor inocencia—. En caso de que se trate verdaderamente de un negocio, claro. —Adoptó una expresión preocupada—. Porque no será nada de tipo ilegal, ¿verdad?

Otero sonrió.

—Todo lo contrario. Pero es un tema que podría despertar... un interés considerable.

—Claro que no le diré nada a nadie. —Harry titubeó un instante—. Lo prometo.

—Ni siquiera a Barbara —añadió Sandy—. Palabra de caballero, ¿eh?

—Pues claro.

Sebastián de Salas sonrió.

—Sandy nos ha hablado de las relaciones de honor entre los compañeros de estudios de los colegios públicos. Es una especie de código, ¿verdad?

—Que Harry jamás quebrantaría —añadió Sandy.

—¿Un código de honor como el que reina entre los soldados de la Legión?

—Sí —contestó Harry—. Sí, eso es.

Otero estudió un poco más a Harry y después se volvió para mirar a Sandy.

—Muy bien. Queda bajo su responsabilidad, Forsyth.

—Respondo por Harry —dijo Sandy sonriendo.

—¿Cuánto tenía pensado invertir? —le preguntó Otero a Harry.

—Depende. Depende de lo que se me ofrezca.

Llamaron con los nudillos a la puerta y entró María con una bandeja. Les sirvió el té y el café. En medio del silencio, Harry se sintió inesperadamente presa del temor. Notaba las axilas húmedas de sudor. Le estaba resultando muy difícil mantener la ficción con tres personas concentradas en él. La secretaria se retiró y cerró suavemente la puerta a su espalda.

—De acuerdo. —Sandy abrió un cajón de su escritorio. Todos se lo quedaron mirando mientras sacaba una ampolla de cristal llena de un polvo amarillo. Tomó una hoja de papel y le echó cuidadosamente encima una pequeña cantidad del contenido de la ampolla—. Ya está. ¿Qué creen ustedes que es? Adelante, cojan un poco.

Harry se pasó el polvo entre los dedos. Sabía lo que era, pero fingió ignorarlo.

—Es como aceitoso.

Otero soltó una carcajada que más bien parecía un ladrido y meneó la cabeza. Sandy sonreía satisfecho.

—Es oro, Harry. Oro español. Procede de un campo situado a cierta distancia de aquí. Alberto llevaba años buscando por allí, tomando muestras, y esta primavera va y saca el gordo. España tiene algunos pequeños yacimientos de oro, pero éste es grande. Muy grande.

Harry dejó caer nuevamente los granos sobre el papel.

—¿Éste es el aspecto que tiene el oro cuando lo extraen de la tierra?

Otero se levantó y se acercó a la mesa. Tomó uno de los botes, lo llevó al escritorio y abrió la tapa. Estaba lleno de una tierra blanda de color amarillo anaranjado.

—Esto es el mineral. Se le aplica mercurio y ácido para separar el oro. Dos botes como éste producirían aproximadamente el contenido de la ampolla; el contenido en oro es muy elevado. ¿Se imagina lo que podría valer todo un yacimiento de este mineral? ¿Veinte yacimientos?

Harry se pasó suavemente la tierra grumosa entre los dedos. «Ya está —pensó—. Lo he conseguido.»

—Estos botes van al Ministerio de Minas para su análisis. —Sandy se volvió hacia De Salas—. Es donde trabaja Sebastián, nuestro contacto de allí.

De Salas asintió con la cabeza.

—Como usted sabe, señor Brett, la política económica de España se basa en la autosuficiencia. El Ministerio de Minas concede licencias a empresas privadas para explorar yacimientos. Después, si se encuentran depósitos minerales explotables y los laboratorios del Gobierno se muestran satisfechos con las pruebas, la empresa recibe una licencia de explotación.

—Y las acciones suben —añadió Sandy.

—¿Y eso es lo que hace Nuevas Iniciativas?

—Exacto. Nosotros tres somos los principales accionistas. Técnicamente, Sebastián no debería ser un miembro de la empresa porque es funcionario del Ministerio de Minas; pero aquí nadie se preocupa por estas cosas. Además, él ha conseguido que algunos compañeros suyos inviertan.

—¿Y están satisfechos con su mineral?

—Ha habido demoras —contestó De Salas—. Por desgracia, hay política de por medio. ¿Se ha enterado de lo del fracaso de Badajoz?

—Algo he oído decir.

Sandy asintió con la cabeza.

—El año pasado se informó de la existencia de enormes depósitos de oro, pero al final resultó que allí no había nada. Después de que el Generalísimo hubiera anunciado al país en su discurso radiofónico de Navidad que España muy pronto tendría todo el oro que necesitaba. —Sandy sonrió tristemente—. Fue muy embarazoso... como lo de aquel científico austriaco que afirmaba poder fabricar petróleo a partir de la hierba. El Generalísimo buscaba tan desesperadamente todas estas cosas que se volvió, ¿cómo diría?, un poco crédulo. Ahora ha pasado al otro extremo y se ha vuelto excesivamente precavido. Hay un comité que estudia todas las concesiones de importantes depósitos mineros. Las personas que forman parte de él no congenian políticamente con el Ministerio de Minas. Nos ven como un nido de falangistas.

—Pero, si hay auténticos recursos, todo el mundo tendría que estar interesado en desarrollarlos, ¿no?

—Eso es lo que cabría esperar, Harry —convino Sandy—. Lo que cabría esperar.

Otero se encogió de hombros.

—Ciertas personas alargan las cosas y ordenan que se hagan nuevas pruebas, a pesar de que ya se han llevado a cabo suficientes análisis para satisfacer a cualquier cliente razonable. Pruebas hechas con muestras obtenidas en el mismo emplazamiento y en presencia de inspectores del Gobierno.

—Es posible que te podamos mostrar los informes —dijo Sandy—. En plan estrictamente confidencial, naturalmente.

—A mí las pruebas no me importan —prosiguió diciendo Otero—. Es más, por de pronto, he estado efectuando reconocimientos en zonas adyacentes que ofrecen un potencial todavía mejor. Cuando hayamos superado toda esta carrera de obstáculos burocráticos y la cosa pase a dominio público, todo el que esté asociado a esta empresa se va a hacer pero que muy rico. Pero todo cuesta dinero, señor. Obtener muestras, hacer pruebas... e incluso un territorio aledaño que queremos comprar. El precio es superior al que en estos momentos nos podemos permitir.

—No es simplemente una cuestión política —terció De Salas—. A estos generales que integran el comité les gustaría que nos arruináramos, exigiéndonos una prueba tras otra hasta dejarnos en la situación de tener que venderlo todo a otra empresa de prospección. Controlada por ellos, claro.

—En última instancia, todo se reduce al vil metal. —Sandy enarcó las cejas—. Unas quinientas libras, por ejemplo, nos podrían ser muy útiles en este momento. Podríamos costear más prospecciones, preparar muestras y adquirir los derechos de estas nuevas tierras. Si ellos vieran que disponemos de recursos financieros, creo que los obstáculos desaparecerían y entonces ya podríamos empezar a ganar una fortuna.

—¿Quinientas? —repitió Harry—. Eso es mucho dinero. Parece un poco... arriesgado.

—No es arriesgado —dijo fríamente Otero—. Como ya le he dicho, tengo informes que certifican la calidad de nuestro mineral.

Harry fingió reflexionar, frunciendo los labios. El corazón le latía muy rápido, pero ya no tenía miedo. Olfateaba el éxito.

—Estos informes, ¿están escritos en lenguaje profano?

—Por supuesto —contestó De Salas, riéndose—. Los tienen que entender los del comité.

—Tienes que venir aquí a leerlos —dijo Sandy—. No los podemos sacar del despacho, pero nosotros te guiaremos en su lectura.

—Es usted un privilegiado, señor Brett —dijo Otero con la cara muy seria—. Muy pocas personas saben algo al respecto.

Harry respiró hondo. De perdidos al río.

—Me gustaría ver la zona. No quisiera hacer las cosas a ciegas.

Otero denegó lentamente con la cabeza.

—La localización es algo muy confidencial, señor. No estoy preparado para llegar tan lejos, no.

—Pero seguramente el Gobierno sabe dónde está.

—Sí, Harry. —La voz de Sandy sonó repentinamente impaciente—. Pero sólo a nivel de estricta confidencialidad.

—Es que, si voy a formar parte de este... —Harry extendió las manos.

—Eso habría que discutirlo. —Sandy se acarició el bigote, mirando de De Salas a Otero. No se les veía muy contentos.

—De acuerdo —dijo Harry.

No era el momento de insistir. Se alegró de haber provocado en ellos una inquietud visible. Y de haber borrado del rostro de Sandy la complaciente sonrisa que lo iluminaba. En caso de que se negaran a enseñárselo, seguiría con ellos de todos modos, pero el hecho de ver el emplazamiento habría sido un auténtico golpe de efecto.

Llamaron con los nudillos a la puerta. Sandy levantó la vista, todavía irritado, y María asomó la cabeza.

—¿Qué?

—Ha llegado la señora Forsyth, señor. Está fuera.

Sandy se pasó una mano por el cabello.

—Ha venido muy temprano. Mira, Harry, eso lo tendremos que discutir. ¿Por qué no te llevas tú solo a Barbara a tomar ese café? Te llamaremos más tarde.

—Como quieras.

—Muy bien pues. Salgo un momento contigo a saludar. —Sandy se levantó y los españoles hicieron lo propio.

—Hasta nuestro próximo encuentro —dijo De Salas estrechándole la mano seguido por Otero, el cual volvió a dirigirle otra de sus frías miradas.

Sandy lo acompañó fuera. Barbara estaba sentada junto al escritorio de María, la cabeza tocada con un pañuelo estampado empapado de lluvia. Estaba muy pálida y parecía preocupada.

—Hola, Harry.

—¡Llegas muy temprano! —Sandy señaló con impaciencia el pañuelo de la cabeza—. ¿Y por qué te has puesto eso? Como si no tuvieras suficientes sombreros.

Harry lo miró, sorprendiéndose de su tono de voz. Al ver aquella mirada, Sandy sonrió y tomó a Barbara del brazo.

—Mira, cariño, ha habido un cambio de planes. Hemos celebrado una reunión y ahora tengo que discutir ciertas cosas con unos amigos. ¿Por qué no os vais tú y Harry a tomar un café juntos?

—Sí, me parece muy bien. —Barbara le dirigió a Harry una rápida sonrisa.

—Después te acompañará a casa, ¿verdad, Harry? Buen chico. Mañana te llamo. —Sandy le guiñó el ojo a Harry—. Veré qué puedo hacer con Otero.

Fuera seguía lloviendo y el ambiente era frío y desapacible. Barbara se arregló el pañuelo de la cabeza.

—No le gusta que me ponga estas cosas —dijo—. Cree que son demasiado vulgares. —Sonrió con una tensa frialdad que Harry jamás había visto en su rostro—. ¿Qué habéis estado haciendo... te intenta liar con alguno de sus proyectos?

Harry soltó una carcajada forzada.

—Hay una posibilidad de inversión.

—Oye, ¿te importa que no vayamos a tomar café? Prefiero volver a casa, creo que estoy a punto de pillar un resfriado.

—Claro que no. —Echaron a andar muy despacio. Harry contempló su pálido y tenso rostro—. ¿Te ocurre algo, Barbara?

—No, la verdad es que no. —Barbara lanzó un profundo suspiro—. He ido al cine después de comer para pasar el rato hasta la hora de reunirme contigo. Han dado el noticiario, ya sabes cómo son, pura propaganda proalemana. —Se estremeció con un suspiro—. Han dado la noticia del bombardeo, «Gran Bretaña de rodillas». Han pasado unas imágenes del centro de Birmingham.

—Lo siento. ¿Tan grave ha sido?

—Horrible. Algunos sectores de la ciudad estaban ardiendo. Toda aquella gente muerta en la última incursión aérea y ellos regocijándose de lo ocurrido. —Barbara se detuvo de golpe—. Dios mío, perdona, estoy un poco mareada.

Harry miró alrededor en busca de algún café, pero no había ninguno a la vista, sólo una de las grandes iglesias que salpicaban la ciudad. Sujetó a Barbara por el brazo.

—Ven, vamos a sentarnos un poco aquí dentro. —Subió con ella las gradas.

El interior del templo estaba frío y oscuro, sólo el ornamentado altar cubierto de pan de oro aparecía iluminado. En los bancos en penumbra unas figuras borrosas permanecían sentadas con los hombros encorvados, algunas de ellas murmurando oraciones. Harry acompañó a Barbara a un banco vacío. Había lágrimas en sus mejillas. Barbara se quitó las gafas y se sacó un pañuelo del bolsillo.

—Perdona —dijo en un susurro.

—Lo comprendo. Yo también estoy preocupado por mi primo Will.

—¿El que está casado con una fiera?

—Sí. Aunque, poco antes de marcharme, descubrí su otra faceta. Nos vimos atrapados en una incursión aérea y tuve que acompañarla a un refugio. Estaba muerta de miedo por sus hijos. No pensaba que los quisiera tanto.

Barbara suspiró.

—Aquí vi algunas incursiones aéreas durante la Guerra Civil, claro, pero verlas en Inglaterra... —Se mordió el labio—. Las cosas ya jamás volverán a ser lo mismo después de todo esto, ¿verdad? ¿En ningún sitio?

Harry contempló la seriedad de su semblante intensamente pálido en medio de la penumbra.

—No. No creo que lo vuelvan a ser.

—Tendría que estar allí. En Inglaterra. Hubo un tiempo en que buscaba seguridad después de lo de Bernie... —hizo una pausa—... cuando él se fue. Sandy me la ofreció o, por lo menos, yo lo creí. Pero no hay seguridad en ninguna parte, ya no. —Hizo otra pausa—. Y ni siquiera estoy segura de si la deseo.

Harry sonrió con tristeza.

—Me temo que yo sí. No soy un héroe. Si te soy sincero, lo que de veras quisiera es largarme corriendo a casa y disfrutar de una vida tranquila.

—Pero no lo harás, ¿verdad? —Barbara lo miró sonriendo—. Eso sería contrario a tu sentido del honor.

—Es curioso que esta palabra haya surgido en la conversación que acabo de mantener con Sandy. El honor de los colegios privados. Como es natural, eso jamás significó nada para él.

Ambos guardaron silencio un instante. Sus ojos se habían adaptado a la penumbra y Harry observó que casi todas las personas que rezaban eran pobres mujeres vestidas de negro. Algunas sólo tenían un trozo de trapo negro para cubrirse la cabeza. Barbara contempló en una capilla lateral la imagen de Jesús crucificado con la sangre pintada manando de sus heridas.

—Qué religión tan rara —dijo con amargura—. Sangre y tortura;

no es de extrañar que los españoles acabaran matándose los unos a los otros. La religión es una maldición, en eso Sandy tiene razón.

—Pensaba que servía para refrenar los excesos de la gente.

Barbara soltó una carcajada amarga.

—Pues aquí sirve para todo lo contrario, y creo que siempre ha servido para lo mismo. —Volvió a ponerse las gafas—. ¿Recuerdas aquella familia amiga de Bernie? ¿Los Mera?

—Sí, yo estaba con él cuando conoció a Pedro Mera. De hecho, fui a ver... fui a ver si podía localizar su apartamento. —Harry titubeó un poco, no quería decirle a Barbara lo que había descubierto en Caraban-chel.

—¿De veras?

—Sí. ¿Por qué... acaso los has visto? —Harry la miró con ansia.

Barbara se mordió el labio.

—¿Sabes que trabajo como voluntaria en un orfelinato de la Igle-sia? —dijo serenamente.

—Sí.

—Aquello es un infierno. Tratan a los niños como animales. Hace un par de días llevaron allí a Carmela, la hijita de Pedro e Inés. Vi-vía a la intemperie, como una salvaje. Creo que todos los demás han muerto.

—Dios mío. —Harry recordó a la chiquilla, que lo miraba solem-nemente mientras él intentaba enseñarle unas cuantas palabras en in-glés. A su hermano Antonio, testigo de cómo los comunistas habían echado a los fascistas con su ayuda y la de Bernie; a Pedro, el corpu-lento y campechano progenitor; a Inés, la incansable y abnegada ma-dre—. ¿Todos?

—Creo que sí. —Barbara buscó en el interior de su bolso y sacó el maltrecho burro de lana, remendado con un costurón alrededor de la parte central—. La bruja que trabaja conmigo se lo quitó de las manos y lo rompió. Creo que era la última posesión que le quedaba a Carmela. Le prometí que se lo arreglaría, pero esta mañana cuando se lo iba a devolver me han dicho que había hecho varios intentos de fuga y que la han trasladado a un hogar especial para niños rebeldes. Ya te puedes imaginar lo que eso significa. La monja que se encarga de estos menes-teres no me ha querido revelar su paradero; ha dicho que no era asunto mío. Sor Inmaculada. —El tono de su voz reflejaba una dolorosa amar-gura.

—¿Y no te puedes enterar?

—¿Cómo? ¿Cómo, si no me lo quieren decir? —Barbara levantó la voz, lanzó un suspiro y apretó los labios—. Ya sé, voy a dejar al burro *Fernandito* como ofrenda al Señor. Quizás Él cuide de Carmela. Quizá. —Se levantó y se acercó con el juguete a la barandilla de la capilla lateral. Lo arrojó con gesto airado sobre las flores que había ante el Crucificado, después regresó y volvió a sentarse junto a Harry—. No pienso regresar al convento. A Sandy no le gustará, pero tendrá que aguantarse.

—Tú y Sandy... —Harry vaciló—. ¿Va todo bien entre vosotros?

Barbara sonrió con tristeza.

—Eso vamos a dejarlo, Harry. Venga, salgamos de este panteón.

Harry la miró con la cara muy seria.

—Barbara, si alguna vez necesitas... bueno... algún tipo de ayuda, siempre podrás acudir a mí.

Ella le rozó la mano. Una anciana que pasaba por su lado chasqueó la lengua en gesto de reproche.

—Gracias, Harry, pero estoy bien, simplemente he tenido un mal día.

Harry observó que la anciana agarraba a un cura de la manga y los señalaba con el dedo.

—Vamos, Barbara —dijo—. Nos van a detener por inmoralidad en lugar sagrado.

Una vez fuera, Barbara se enojó consigo misma por su momentánea debilidad. Tenía que ser fuerte.

Al salir de la iglesia, dejó que Harry la acompañara a un bar. Le preguntó cuáles eran las últimas noticias de la embajada sobre la posible entrada en guerra de Franco. Harry le dijo que en la embajada se creía que la reunión de Franco con Hitler había sido un fracaso. Era un alivio.

Al llegar a casa, se preparó un té y se sentó sola en la cocina, pensando y fumando. Pilar tenía la tarde libre y no estaba. Barbara se alegró, pues jamás se sentía a gusto con la chica cerca. En la previsión meteorológica de la radio, el locutor anunció más frío en Madrid y nevadas en la sierra de Guadarrama. Contempló el jardín barrido por la lluvia y pensó: «Eso significa que en Cuenca también nevará.» Ahora no se podía hacer más que esperar a que el hermano de Luis se tomara su permiso. Volvió a pensar en Harry. Habría deseado contarle algo acerca de Bernie, no soportaba la idea de que siguiera pensando que su viejo amigo había muerto y habría querido decirle la verdad; pero Harry también era amigo de Sandy y lo que ella tenía intención de hacer era ilegal. Era peligroso decirle algo, era peligroso decírselo a cualquiera.

Al cabo de un rato, se fue al salón y le escribió una carta a sor Inmaculada, comunicándole en términos fríamente corteses que sus obligaciones domésticas le impedirían seguir trabajando por más tiempo en el orfelinato. Ya estaba terminando cuando entró Sandy. Parecía cansado. La miró sonriendo mientras posaba en el suelo el maletín, que emitió un tintineo como si contuviera algún objeto metálico. Se acercó y le apoyó una mano en el hombro.

—¿Cómo estás, cariño? Mira, perdóname por el arrebato de furia del despacho. He tenido un mal día. Acabo de pasar una hora en el Comité de Judíos. —Se inclinó y la besó en el cuello.

En otro momento, semejante gesto la hubiera ablandado, pero ahora sólo fue consciente del cosquilleo de los pelos de su bigote. Se apartó, y él frunció el entrecejo.

—¿Qué ocurre? Ya te he pedido perdón.

—Es que yo también he tenido un mal día.

—¿A quién le escribes?

—A sor Inmaculada. Le digo que ya no voy a volver al orfelinato. No soporto ver cómo tratan a esos niños.

—Pero eso no se lo habrás dicho en la carta, ¿verdad?

—No, Sandy, he dicho obligaciones domésticas. No te preocupes, no habrá ningún problema con la marquesa.

Sandy se apartó.

—No hace falta que me contestes así.

Barbara respiró hondo.

—Perdona.

—Bueno, ¿y ahora qué piensas hacer? Te conviene hacer algo.

«Necesito un mes para ayudar a Bernie a salir y escapar de allí», pensó Barbara.

—Pues no lo sé. ¿Podría echar una mano con tus refugiados? ¿Los judíos?

Sandy tomó un trago de whisky y denegó con la cabeza.

—Son muy tradicionales. No les gusta que las mujeres les digan lo que tienen que hacer.

—Yo creía que casi todos ejercían profesiones liberales.

—Pero, aun así, son muy tradicionales. —Sandy cambió de tema—. ¿Qué te ha estado contando Harry?

—Hemos hablado de la guerra. No cree que Franco entre en ella.

—Sí, eso es lo que me ha dicho a mí. Es muy astuto en cuestión de negocios, ¿sabes? —Sandy sonrió con aire pensativo—. Mucho más de lo que imaginaba. —Volvió a mirar a Barbara—. Pero verás, cariño, yo creo que te equivocas en esto del orfelinato. Hay que hacer las cosas a su manera. Donde fueres... Te lo he dicho muchas veces.

—Sí, es cierto. Pero yo no pienso volver allí, Sandy, no quiero participar en la manera que ellos tienen de tratar a los niños.

¿Por qué la provocaba y la hacía enfadar tanto últimamente, cuando ella más necesitaba que todo pareciera normal y se mantuviera en equilibrio? Barbara sabía que él había notado algo raro. Ahora incluso evitaba hacer el amor con él y, cuando él insistía y ella cedía, le resultaba imposible fingir placer.

—Esos niños son muy salvajes —dijo Sandy—. Tú misma lo has dicho. Necesitan disciplina, no animales de juguete.

—Por Dios, Sandy, a veces pienso que tienes una piedra por corazón. —Las palabras se le escaparon sin que ella pudiera evitarlo.

El rostro de Sandy se congestionó de rabia y éste hizo ademán de acercarse a ella. Apretó los puños y Barbara se estremeció mientras el corazón le latía con fuerza en el pecho. Siempre había sabido que Sandy podía ser cruel y perverso cuando estaba enojado, pero hasta aquel momento jamás había temido ninguna acción violenta de él. Respiró hondo. Sandy consiguió controlarse y habló fríamente.

—Yo te he hecho —dijo—. No lo olvides. No eras nada cuando yo te encontré; un desastre, porque a ti lo único que siempre te ha preocupado es lo que la gente piensa de ti. En lugar de corazón, tú lo que tienes es un revoltijo de sensiblería empalagosa. —La miró con rabia, y entonces comprendió claramente por primera vez qué era lo que siempre había querido de ella y en qué había consistido la relación entre ambos desde el principio. Control. Poder.

Barbara se levantó y abandonó la estancia.

27

Cuando Harry regresó a casa tras haber dejado a Barbara, encontró dos cartas esperándolo. Una era una nota garabateada de Sandy, entregada directamente en mano. Decía que había convencido a Otero y De Salas de que le permitieran visitar la mina y que él mismo acudiría a recogerlo a su casa tres días más tarde, el domingo a primera hora de la mañana, para acompañarlo al lugar. Estaba a sólo tres horas de camino por carretera.

Abrió la otra carta; la dirección estaba escrita en una caligrafía pulcra y menuda que él no reconoció. Era de Sofía e incluía una factura de tratamiento y medicinas extendida por un médico del centro de la ciudad, junto con una carta en español.

Estimado señor Brett:

Le incluyo la factura del médico. Sé que los honorarios son razonables. Enrique ya está mejor. Pronto podrá volver a trabajar y entonces las cosas serán más fáciles para todos nosotros. Le da las gracias, y mamá también. Usted le salvó la vida a Enrique y nosotros siempre recordaremos con gratitud lo que usted hizo.

Harry sufrió una decepción ante el ceremonioso tono de la carta en el cual parecía encerrarse una despedida.

Le dio vueltas un par de veces entre sus manos; después, se sentó y escribió una respuesta:

Me alegro de que Enrique ya esté mejor y mañana mismo pagaré los gastos del médico. Me gustaría volver a verla para entregarle la factura y, de paso, invitarla a tomar un café. Me encantó hablar con usted, porque raras veces tengo ocasión de conversar con españoles de manera informal. Espero que pueda venir.

Sugería que ambos se reunieran dos días más tarde en un café que él conocía cerca de la Puerta del Sol a las seis en punto, pues sabía que ella empezaba a trabajar muy temprano.

Cerró la carta. La echaría al correo cuando saliera.

Lo de la factura era un pretexto y ella así lo interpretaría. Bueno, ¿contestaría o no? Se volvió hacia la mesita del teléfono y marcó el número de la embajada. En recepción, pidió que le comunicaran al señor Tolhurst que necesitaba hablar con él sobre el previsto comunicado de prensa relativo a las importaciones de fruta. Era la clave que ambos habían acordado para cuando él tuviera alguna noticia sobre Sandy. Al principio pensaba que aquellas claves eran estúpidas y melodramáticas, pero ahora había comprendido que eran necesarias porque todos los teléfonos estaban pinchados.

El recepcionista se puso de nuevo al aparato para decirle que el señor Tolhurst estaba disponible, por si quisiera hablar con él en aquel momento. No le extrañaba. Tolly se pasaba muchas tardes en la embajada. Harry cogió el abrigo y volvió a salir.

Tolhurst se mostró enormemente encantado cuando Harry le explicó lo ocurrido. Dijo que se lo comunicaría a Hillgarth que, en aquel momento, se encontraba en una reunión pero tendría interés en saberlo. A los pocos minutos, regresó emocionado al pequeño despacho.

—El capitán está muy contento —dijo—. Si hay mucho oro, me parece que se pondrá directamente en contacto con Churchill, y entonces éste dispondrá un endurecimiento del bloqueo para que sólo se permita la entrada de los suministros que se puedan pagar con oro. —Tolhurst se frotó las manos.

—¿Qué va a decir sir Sam a todo eso?

—Lo que a Churchill le importa es lo que piensa el capitán. —Un arrebol de placer iluminó el rostro de Tolhurst mientras éste pronunciaba el nombre del primer ministro arrastrando aristocráticamente las sílabas.

—Preguntarán por qué se ha endurecido el bloqueo.

—Y probablemente nosotros se lo diremos. Para que sepan que no nos pueden ocultar nada. Y le pegaremos un puñetazo en el ojo al sector de la Falange. Tú dijiste que convendría que practicáramos una política más firme, Harry. Puede que lo consigamos.

Harry asintió con expresión pensativa.

—Eso hará que Sandy se encuentre en apuros. Y puede que acabe teniendo problemas muy serios.

Comprendió que había estado tan concentrado en su misión que apenas había pensado en lo que podría ocurrirle a Sandy. Experimentó una punzada de remordimiento.

Tolhurst le guiñó el ojo.

—No necesariamente. El capitán también se guarda algo en la manga.

—¿Qué? —Harry lo pensó un poco—. ¿No será que vais a intentar reclutarlo?

Tolhurst meneó la cabeza.

—No te lo puedo decir, todavía no. —Esbozó una sonrisa engreída que irritó a Harry—. Por cierto, el otro asunto, lo de los Caballeros de San Jorge, no se lo habrás dicho a nadie más, ¿verdad?

—Por supuesto que no.

—Es importante que no lo hagas.

—Lo sé.

A la mañana siguiente, Harry acompañó a uno de los secretarios de embajada a otra sesión de interpretación con Maestre, con el cual se tenían que revisar unos certificados. El joven intérprete de la Falange también estaba presente y volvieron a repetir la comedia de fingir que Maestre no hablaba inglés. La actitud del general español para con Harry era visiblemente fría y éste comprendió que Hillgarth tenía razón; el hecho de que no se hubiera vuelto a poner en contacto con Milagros se había interpretado como un desaire. Pero él no iba a fingir que quizás hubiera algo entre él y la chica simplemente para que los espías estuvieran contentos. Se alegraba de que fuera viernes, fin de semana. Cuando regresó a casa, encontró una respuesta de Sofía encima del felpudo, sólo un par de líneas accediendo a reunirse con él la tarde del día siguiente. Harry se sorprendió de la emoción que experimentó en su fuero interno.

El café era un local pequeño, alegre y moderno. De no ser por el retrato de Franco colgado en la pared detrás de la barra, habría podido estar en cualquier lugar de Europa. Llegó con cierto adelanto, pero Sofía ya estaba allí, sentada al fondo del local con una taza de café entre sus manos. Vestía el abrigo largo de color negro que llevaba la noche en que él había acompañado a Enrique a su apartamento, algo raído como él pudo ver bajo las luces del local. Su rostro de duendecillo sin asomo de maquillaje estaba muy pálido. Parecía mucho más joven y vulnerable. Levantó los ojos con una sonrisa al verlo acercarse.

—Espero no haberla hecho esperar demasiado —dijo Harry.

—Yo he llegado antes de lo previsto. Es usted muy puntual. —Había algo distinto en su sonrisa. Era sincera y amistosa, pero se advertía en ella cierta perspicacia.

—Voy a buscarle otro café. —Fue a pedir las consumiciones.

—Enrique está mucho mejor —dijo la chica, mientras él se sentaba—. La semana que viene empezará a buscar trabajo.

Harry sonrió con ironía.

—Un trabajo distinto.

—Sí, claro. Algún trabajo de tipo manual, si lo encuentra.

—¿Le pagó el ministerio... mientras estuvo enfermo?

Por un instante, la sonrisa de Sofía adquirió un aire un tanto cínico.

—No.

—Tengo la factura. —Harry había visitado el consultorio y había pagado los gastos médicos tal como había prometido hacer.

—Gracias.

Sofía dobló cuidadosamente el papel y se lo guardó en el bolsillo.

—Si su hermano tiene algún otro problema, yo tendría mucho gusto en ayudarlo.

—Creo que ahora ya está todo arreglado.

—Muy bien.

—Le decía en mi carta que usted le salvó la vida. Siempre le estaremos agradecidos.

—Faltaría más. —Harry sonrió, pero, de repente, se quedó sin saber qué otra cosa decir.

—¿Ha sido... —Sofía enarcó ligeramente las cejas— sustituido?

—No, gracias a Dios. Ahora me dejan en paz. Es que yo no soy nada importante, ¿sabe? Un simple traductor.

Sofía encendió un pitillo y después se reclinó en su asiento para estudiarlo. Su expresión era inquisitiva, pero ni hostil ni recelosa. Lejos de su apartamento, se la veía mucho más relajada.

—¿Regresará usted a Inglaterra? —preguntó—. Por Navidad, quiero decir.

—Navidad. —Harry se rió—. Ni siquiera lo había pensado.

—Faltan sólo seis semanas. Creo que, en Inglaterra, ustedes la celebran por todo lo alto.

—Sí, pero dudo que vaya a casa. En la embajada nos necesitan a todos. Ya sabe usted cómo son las cosas. En el mundo diplomático. —Harry se preguntó cómo era posible que conociera aquel detalle acerca de la Navidad inglesa. Quizás a través de aquel chico de Leeds que había conocido durante la Guerra Civil. Se preguntó una vez más si habría sido su amante. ¿Cuántos años tendría? ¿Veinticinco? ¿Veintiséis?

—O sea que no la podrá celebrar con sus padres.

—Mis padres han muerto.

—Qué pena.

—Mi padre murió en la Primera Guerra. Y mi madre murió en la epidemia de gripe que hubo poco después.

Sofía asintió con la cabeza.

—Sí, España no participó en la Primera Guerra, aunque después sufrimos la epidemia. Es una pena perder al padre y a la madre.

—Tengo tías, un tío y un primo. Él me mantiene informado de lo que ocurre en casa.

—¿Las incursiones aéreas?

—Sí. Son graves, pero menos de lo que la propaganda de aquí quiere dar a entender. —Vio que ella miraba rápidamente alrededor al oír sus palabras y se maldijo a sí mismo por haber olvidado que se encontraban en un país lleno de espías donde uno tenía que vigilar lo que decía—. Perdón.

Sofía volvió a esbozar la sonrisa irónica de antes, extrañamente seductora.

—Nadie nos puede oír. He elegido a propósito una mesa del fondo.

—Comprendo.

—¿Y no tiene a nadie más en su país? —preguntó ella—. ¿Una esposa quizá?

Aquella pregunta tan directa lo pilló desprevenido.

—No. A nadie. Nadie en absoluto.

—Perdone mi pregunta. Le debo de haber parecido una descarada. Estará pensando, no es la clase de preguntas que hacen las españolas.

—A mí no me importa la franqueza —dijo Harry, contemplando los grandes ojos castaños de Sofía—. Para variar del ambiente que se respira en la embajada. Hace un par de semanas estuve en una fiesta ofrecida por un ministro del Gobierno para celebrar los dieciocho años de su hija. Las normas de etiqueta resultaban asfixiantes. Pobre chica —añadió.

Sofía exhaló una nube de humo.

—Yo vengo de otra tradición distinta.

—Ah, ¿sí?

—De la tradición republicana. Mi padre y los familiares que lo precedieron eran republicanos. Los extranjeros ricos piensan que España es la de las iglesias antiguas, las corridas de toros y las mujeres con mantilla; pero aquí existe otra tradición completamente distinta. En mi familia pensábamos que las mujeres tenían que ser iguales. A mí me educaron en la creencia de que valía tanto como un hombre. Al menos, mi madre. Mi padre tenía unas ideas más anticuadas. Pero a veces tenía la amabilidad de avergonzarse de ellas.

—¿A qué se dedicaba?

—Trabajaba en un almacén. Por muy poco dinero, como yo.

—Creo que la familia que tuve ocasión de conocer cuando estuve aquí en 1931 también formaba parte de esta tradición. Aunque yo no lo veía en estos términos. —Pensó en la historia que le había contado Barbara, la de Carmela y su burrito.

—Usted los apreciaba —dijo Sofía.

—Sí, eran buena gente —contestó Harry sonriendo—. ¿Su familia también era socialista?

Sofía negó con la cabeza.

—Teníamos amigos socialistas, anarquistas y republicanos de izquierdas. Pero no todos se afiliaron al partido. Los partidos hablaban de utopías comunistas y anarquistas, pero lo único que quiere la mayoría de la gente es paz, pan en la mesa y dignidad. ¿No cree?

—Sí.

Sofía se inclinó hacia delante y clavó sus penetrantes ojos en Harry.

—Usted no sabe lo que fue para nosotros el advenimiento de la República, lo que eso significó. De repente, teníamos importancia. Yo obtuve una plaza en la Facultad de Medicina. También tenía que trabajar mucho en un bar, pero todo el mundo estaba muy esperanzado; al final habría cambios, la posibilidad de vivir con dignidad. —Sofía sonrió de repente—. Perdone, señor Brett, pero me dejo arrastrar por la lengua. Casi nunca tengo oportunidad de hablar de aquellos tiempos.

—No se preocupe. Me ayuda a comprender.

—¿Comprender el qué?

—España. —Harry vaciló—. A usted.

Ella bajó la mirada a la mesa, alargó la mano hacia la cajetilla de cigarrillos y encendió otro. Cuando levantó la vista, sus ojos reflejaban incertidumbre.

—A lo mejor, tiene que abandonar España antes de lo previsto. Si Franco entra en guerra.

—Esperamos que no lo haga.

—Todo el mundo dice que Inglaterra le dará a Franco todo lo que pida con tal de que se mantenga al margen de esta maldita guerra. Y entonces, ¿qué será de nosotros?

Harry lanzó un suspiro.

—Supongo que mis jefes dirían que tenemos que hacer lo que sea para mantener a España fuera de la guerra, pero... no tenemos muchas cosas de las que enorgullecernos, lo sé.

Sofía sonrió inesperadamente.

—Perdone, lo veo muy triste. Usted ha hecho tanto por ayudarnos y yo aquí, discutiendo con usted, le ruego que me perdone.

—No se preocupe. ¿Le apetece otro café?

Sofía denegó con la cabeza.

—No, creo que ya tengo que volver. Mi madre y Paco me esperan. Voy a ver si encuentro un poco de aceite de oliva.

Harry vaciló. Había visto un anuncio en el periódico de la tarde y había decidido preguntárselo, a menos que aquella tarde hubiera terminado mal.

—¿Le gusta el teatro? —preguntó de repente, con tal torpeza que Sofía lo miró, momentáneamente desconcertada—. Disculpe —se apresuró a añadir—: pero es que mañana por la noche se estrena *Macbeth* en el teatro Zara. No sé si a usted le apetecería ir. Me gustaría ver la obra en español.

Ella lo miró indecisa con sus grandes ojos castaños.

—Gracias, señor, pero será mejor que no.

—Es una lástima —dijo Harry—. Es que me gustaría... que fuéramos amigos. No tengo amigos españoles.

Sofía sonrió denegando con la cabeza.

—Ha sido muy agradable conversar con usted, señor, pero vivimos en mundos muy distintos.

—¿Tan distintos somos? ¿Soy demasiado burgués?

—Todos vestirán sus mejores galas para el Zara. Yo no tengo ropa como la suya. —Sofía lanzó un suspiro y lo volvió a mirar—. Hace unos cuantos años, eso no me hubiera preocupado.

Harry sonrió.

—¿Entonces?

—Sólo tengo un vestido que podría llevar.

—Venga, se lo ruego.

Ella le devolvió la sonrisa.

—De acuerdo, señor Brett —dijo ruborizándose—. Pero sólo como amigos, ¿eh?

28

Había llovido mucho la semana anterior, una lluvia fría que a veces se transformaba en aguanieve. Por el camino de la cantera, los prisioneros chapoteaban a través de un barro pegajoso y rojizo; cada día el límite de la nieve en las lejanas montañas bajaba un poco más.

Aquella mañana había amanecido muy húmeda y cruda. La cuadrilla de trabajo formaba en fila junto a la cantera, moviendo los pies para conservar el calor mientras un par de zapadores del ejército colocaba cuidadosamente unos cartuchos de dinamita en una enorme grieta que discurría a lo largo de una cara rocosa de siete metros. El sargento Molina, de vuelta de su permiso, hablaba con el conductor de un camión del ejército que había transportado los explosivos desde Cuenca.

Bernie pensó en Agustín. Días atrás, éste se había ido de permiso y lo había hecho mientras se pasaba la lista de la mañana; Bernie lo había visto cruzar el patio con una mochila a la espalda. Los ojos de Agustín se cruzaron brevemente con los suyos un segundo antes de que éste apartara rápidamente la cabeza. Se abrió la verja y Agustín desapareció, subiendo por el camino de Cuenca.

—Ésta es una carga muy fuerte —murmuró Pablo. Ahora el compañero comunista de Bernie trabajaba con él en la cuadrilla de la cantera. Era un antiguo minero de Asturias, un experto en explosivos—. Tendríamos que apartarnos más, saltarán astillas por todas partes.

—Tendrían que haberte encomendado a ti la colocación de las cargas, amigo mío.

—Tendrían miedo de que las colocara debajo de su camión, como hicimos el treinta y seis en Oviedo.

—Anda que si les pudiéramos meter mano, ¿eh, Vicente?

—Pues sí.

El abogado permanecía medio tumbado sobre una roca al lado de sus compañeros. Aquella mañana había estado ayudando a Molina con el trabajo de oficina —el sargento, un gordinflón holgazán ascendido a un cargo superior a sus capacidades, apenas sabía escribir y el abogado era para él como una bendición de Dios—; pero lo habían hecho esperar junto a los demás mientras se colocaban las cargas. Vicente se sostenía la cabeza entre las manos. El estado de su nariz había empeorado. Las secreciones habían cesado, pero ahora parecía que el veneno se le había quedado atrapado en los senos nasales. No podía respirar por la nariz y el hecho de aspirar el aire o tragar le resultaba muy doloroso.

—¡Apartaos! ¡Todavía más! —gritó Molina.

La cuadrilla se retiró arrastrando los pies mientras los zapadores regresaban al camión; Molina y el conductor se reunieron con ellos detrás del camión.

Se oyó una sorda explosión y Bernie retrocedió, pero no volaron astillas por el aire. En su lugar, toda la cara rocosa se vino abajo y se desintegró como un castillo de arena alcanzado por una ola. Una nube de polvo se abrió en abanico hacia fuera y los hizo toser. Una pequeña manada de ciervos que habitaba en Tierra Muerta bajó brincando aterrorizada por la ladera.

Mientras el polvo se iba posando en el suelo, vieron que el derrumbamiento había dejado al descubierto una cueva de aproximadamente un metro y medio de altura detrás de la cara de la roca. Estaba claro que la grieta se ensanchaba por detrás y penetraba en la ladera de la colina. Los zapadores se acercaron a la cueva. Sacaron unas linternas y, agachándose con cuidado, entraron a través de la abertura. Hubo un momento de silencio, después se oyó un repentino grito y los dos hombres volvieron a salir, corriendo hacia el camión con expresión aterrada. Los prisioneros y los guardias contemplaron la escena con asombro.

Los zapadores hablaron con Molina en tono apremiante. El rollizo sargento se echó a reír.

—Pero ¿qué decís? ¡No puede ser! ¡Estáis locos!

—¡Es verdad! ¡Es verdad! ¡Vaya a verlo!

Molina frunció el entrecejo visiblemente desconcertado y después se dirigió con los zapadores al lugar donde se encontraban Bernie y los demás. El sargento le hizo una seña a Vicente y éste se levantó medio atontado.

—Bueno, abogado, tú eres un hombre instruido, ¿no? Quizá tú puedas entender lo que dice este loco. —Señaló al zapador que tenía más cerca, un muchacho con la cara picada de acné—. Dile lo que has visto.

El chico tragó saliva.

—En la cueva hay pinturas. Unos hombres que persiguen animales, ciervos y hasta elefantes. ¡Parece una locura, pero lo hemos visto!

Un destello de interés iluminó el rostro de Vicente.

—¿Dónde?

—¡En la pared, en la pared!

—Algo muy parecido se encontró en Francia hace unos años. Pinturas rupestres realizadas por hombres prehistóricos.

El joven soldado se santiguó.

—Es como estar viendo las paredes del infierno.

A Molina le brillaron los ojos.

—¿Podrían ser valiosos? —preguntó.

—Creo que sólo para los científicos, mi sargento.

—¿Las podríamos ver? —preguntó Bernie—. Yo tengo un título de la Universidad de Cambridge —añadió, mintiendo como un bellaco.

Molina lo pensó un momento y luego asintió con la cabeza. Bernie y Vicente lo acompañaron a la cueva. Los zapadores se quedaron donde estaban. Molina señaló bruscamente al hombre que había hablado.

—Enséñaselo.

El hombre tragó saliva y, a continuación, tomó la linterna de su compañero para pasársela a Bernie antes de encabezar a regañadientes la marcha hacia la entrada de la cueva. Los prisioneros contemplaban la escena con interés.

La cueva era estrecha y estaba tan llena de polvo que Vicente se puso a toser dolorosamente. Unos tres metros más allá, la cueva se abría a una amplia caverna circular. Ante ellos, bajo la luz de las linternas, vieron unas figuras en la pared, unos hombres delgados como palillos que perseguían a unos animales enormes, unos elefantes peludos de altas cabezas abombadas, rinocerontes y venados. Pintados en vivos colores rojo y negro, los animales parecían brincar y danzar a la luz de las linternas. Las pinturas llenaban toda una pared de la cueva.

—Vaya —dijo Bernie en voz baja.

—Es como en Francia —murmuró Vicente—. Vi las pinturas en una revista. Pero no tenía idea de que las imágenes pudieran parecer tan reales. Ha hecho usted un hallazgo importante, señor.

—¿Quién las pintó? —preguntó muy nervioso el soldado—. ¿Por qué pintar figuras en la oscuridad?

—Eso nadie lo sabe, soldado. A lo mejor, era para sus ceremonias religiosas.

Muy impresionado, el zapador recorrió con la luz de su linterna las paredes de la cueva que lo rodeaban e iluminó las estalagmitas y la roca desnuda.

—Pero aquí no se podía entrar —dijo con inquietud.

Bernie señaló unas rocas amontonadas de cualquier manera en un rincón de la cueva.

—Esto puede que fuera una entrada que quedó bloqueada con el tiempo.

—Y todo esto lleva miles de años en la oscuridad —musitó Vicente—. Es más antiguo que la Iglesia católica, más antiguo que Jesucristo.

Bernie estudió las pinturas.

—Son preciosas —dijo—. Es como si las hubieran acabado de pintar ayer. Mira, un mamut peludo. Cazaban mamuts —añadió riéndose con asombro.

—Tengo que salir —dijo el zapador, regresando con sus ruidosas pisadas a la entrada.

Bernie arrojó un último haz de luz sobre un grupo de estilizados hombres que perseguían a un venado enorme, y dio media vuelta.

Al salir, el zapador y Vicente se fueron a hablar con Molina. Un guardia le indicó a Bernie con un movimiento del fusil que regresara junto a los demás prisioneros que formaban filas irregulares, muchos de ellos temblando en medio del frío y la humedad del aire.

—¿Qué pasó? —le preguntó Pablo a Bernie.

—Unas pinturas rupestres —contestó Bernie—. Pintadas por hombres prehistóricos.

—¿De verdad? ¿Y cómo son?

—Sorprendentes. Tienen miles de años de antigüedad.

—La época del comunismo primitivo —dijo Pablo—. Antes de que se crearan las clases sociales. Habría que estudiarlas.

Vicente cruzó el terreno irregular, emitiendo unos ásperos jadeos que sonaban a papel de lija.

—¿Qué ha dicho Molina? —preguntó Bernie.

—Que presentará un informe al comandante. Nos van a desplazar al otro lado de la colina; quieren colocar cargas en otro sitio. —Volvió a sufrir un acceso de tos y la frente se le quedó empapada de sudor—. Ah, es como si estuviera ardiendo. Si al menos tuviera un poco de agua.

Un soldado trepó hasta la boca de la cueva. Se santiguó y permaneció de pie a la entrada, montando guardia.

Aquella noche, a la hora de cenar, el estado de Vicente se agravó. A la mortecina luz de las lámparas de petróleo, Bernie vio que temblaba y sudaba profusamente. Cada vez que se tragaba una cucharada de puré de guisantes pegaba un respingo.

—¿Cómo te encuentras?

Vicente no contestó. Soltó la cuchara y se sostuvo la cabeza entre las manos.

Se abrió la puerta de la barraca del rancho y entró Aranda, seguido por Molina. El sargento parecía asustado. Detrás de ellos entró el padre Jaime, alto y serio en su sotana, con el cabello gris acero peinado hacia atrás desde la frente despejada. Los hombres sentados alrededor de las mesas de tresillo se revolvieron con inquietud mientras Aranda los miraba con semblante severo.

—Hoy en la cantera —empezó diciendo Aranda con su bien timbrada voz— la cuadrilla del sargento Molina ha hecho un descubrimiento. El padre Jaime desea dirigiros la palabra a este respecto.

El sacerdote inclinó la cabeza.

—Los garabatos de unos hombres de las cavernas en las paredes de roca son cosas paganas realizadas antes de que la luz de Cristo iluminara el mundo. Hay que evitarlos y huir de ellos. Mañana se colocarán otras cargas en la cueva y las pinturas serán destruidas. Cualquiera que tan siquiera las mencione será castigado. Eso es todo.

El cura saludó con la cabeza a Aranda, dirigió una mirada de desprecio a Molina y se retiró a toda prisa, seguido por los oficiales.

Pablo se inclinó hacia Bernie.

—Será cabrón. Eso forma parte del patrimonio de España.

—Son como los godos y los vándalos, ¿eh, Vicente?

Vicente emitió un gemido y resbaló hacia delante golpeándose la cabeza contra la mesa. Su plato de hojalata cayó ruidosamente al suelo, haciendo que un guardia se acercara a toda prisa.

Era Arias, un joven recluta despiadadamente brutal.

—¿Qué pasa aquí? —preguntó, sacudiendo a Vicente por el hombro.

El abogado emitió un gemido.

—Se ha desmayado —explicó Bernie—. Está enfermo, necesita que lo atiendan.

Arias soltó un gruñido.

—Llevadlo a su barraca. Vamos, cógelo. Ahora tendré que salir, con el frío que hace. —Se pasó el poncho por la cabeza, protestando.

Bernie levantó a Vicente. Era muy liviano, un puro saco de huesos. El abogado trató de mantenerse en pie, pero le temblaban demasiado las piernas. Bernie lo sujetó mientras abandonaban la barraca del rancho, seguidos por el guardia. Cruzaron el patio chapoteando entre los charcos donde el hielo que se estaba condensando brillaba bajo la luz de los reflectores de las atalayas. Una vez en la barraca, Bernie colocó a Vicente en su jergón. Empapado de sudor y en estado semiinconsciente, éste jadeaba sin apenas poder respirar. Arias estudió el rostro del abogado.

—Creo que ha llegado la hora de llamar al cura para éste.

—No, no es tan grave —dijo Bernie—. Ya ha estado así otras veces.

—Yo tengo que llamar al cura cuando un hombre parece que está a punto de morir.

—Sólo está indispuesto. Llame al padre Jaime si quiere, pero ya ha visto usted que está de muy mal humor.

Arias vaciló.

—Bueno. Déjalo y volvamos a la barraca del rancho.

Cuando los hombres regresaron a la barraca después de cenar, Vicente se había despertado, pero su aspecto era peor que nunca.

—¿Qué ha pasado? —preguntó—. ¿Me he desmayado?

—Sí. Ahora tienes que descansar.

—Me arde la cabeza. Está llena de veneno.

Tumbado en la litera del otro lado, Eulalio los miraba con su rostro amarillento y sarnoso monstruosamente iluminado por la luz de una vela de sebo.

—¡Ay, compañero! Tú has visto las pinturas de los hombres prehistóricos. ¿Cómo eran? Unos hombres estupendos, ¿eh? Los primeros comunistas.

—Sí, Eulalio, eran unos hombres estupendos. Cazaban unos elefantes peludos.

Eulalio lo miró inquisitivamente.

—¿Cómo iban a ser peludos unos elefantes? No me vaciles, Piper.

El día siguiente era domingo, y la obligatoria ceremonia religiosa se celebró en la barraca que hacía las veces de iglesia, con un lienzo blanco extendido sobre la mesa de tresillo que servía de altar. Durante la celebración, los prisioneros permanecieron sentados como de costumbre, muchos de ellos medio dormidos. El padre Jaime habría pedido al guardia que los sacudiera para despertarlos, pero aquel día el celebrante era el padre Eduardo y éste los dejó dormir. Los sermones de Jaime solían estar llenos de venganzas y llamas infernales; mientras que Eduardo, en tono casi de súplica, hablaba más bien de la luz de Cristo y del gozo que el arrepentimiento llevaba aparejado. Bernie lo estudió cuidadosamente.

Después de la celebración, el sacerdote estaba a disposición de quienquiera que deseara hablar con él. Pocos solían hacerlo. Bernie esperó mientras los prisioneros iban saliendo y después le dijo algo en voz baja al guardia. El soldado lo miró extrañado y después lo acompañó a una pequeña estancia al fondo de la barraca.

Bernie se sintió cohibido al entrar en la habitación del sacerdote. El padre Eduardo se había quitado las vestiduras de oficiante y se había vuelto a poner la sotana negra. Su rostro mofletudo parecía muy joven, como el de un niño al que acabaran de lavar la cara. Miró a Bernie con una sonrisa nerviosa y le indicó la silla que había ante su escritorio.

—Buenos días. Siéntate, por favor. ¿Cómo te llamas?

—Bernie Piper. Barraca 8.

El sacerdote consultó la lista.

—Ah, sí, el inglés. ¿En qué puedo ayudarte, hijo mío?

—Tengo en mi barraca a un amigo que está muy enfermo. Vicente Medina.

—Sí, conozco a este hombre.

—Si fuera posible que lo atendiera un médico, quizá se podría hacer algo por él.

El sacerdote denegó tristemente con la cabeza.

—Las autoridades no permitirán la entrada de ningún médico aquí. Yo lo he intentado, lo siento.

Bernie asintió con la cabeza. Ya se lo esperaba. Repasó las palabras que había ensayado durante la ceremonia.

—Señor, ¿usted cree que las conversiones forzadas son un error?

El sacerdote vaciló un instante.

—Sí. La Iglesia enseña que una conversión al cristianismo que no sea auténtica, sino tan sólo una simple sucesión de palabras, carece de validez.

—Vicente es un viejo republicano de izquierdas. Usted sabe que son unos ateos empedernidos.

El rostro del padre Eduardo se puso tenso.

—En efecto. Mi iglesia fue quemada por el populacho en 1931. La policía recibió la orden de no intervenir; Azaña, el republicano de izquierdas, dijo que todas las iglesias de España no valían lo que la vida de un republicano.

—Ahora Vicente ya no puede hacer ningún daño. —Bernie respiró hondo—. Pido que ustedes lo dejen morir en paz cuando llegue el momento. No intenten administrarle la extremaunción. Dadas sus creencias, eso no sería más que una burla.

El padre Eduardo lanzó un suspiro.

—¿Tú crees que tratamos de influir en los moribundos para que acepten convertirse a la fuerza?

—¿No es eso lo que hacen?

—Qué malos te debemos de parecer. —El padre Eduardo miró detenidamente a Bernie. Los gruesos cristales de las gafas aumentaban el tamaño de sus ojos de tal manera que éstos parecían flotar detrás de las lentes—. ¿A ti no te educaron como católico, Piper?

—No.

—Veo que eres comunista.

—Sí. —Bernie hizo una pausa—. Pero los cristianos creen en el perdón, ¿verdad?

—Eso es lo más importante de nuestra fe.

—Entonces, ¿por qué no perdonan a Vicente lo que pueda haber hecho su partido y lo dejan en paz?

El padre Eduardo levantó una mano.

—Es que tú no lo entiendes en absoluto. —Su voz volvió a adquirir el tono anterior de súplica—. Por favor, trata de comprenderlo. Si un hombre muere tras haber negado a la Iglesia, va al infierno. En cambio, si se arrepiente y pide perdón, aunque sólo sea al final y después de haber llevado la peor vida posible, Dios lo perdonará. Cuando un hombre se encuentra en su lecho de muerte, se nos ofrece la última oportunidad de salvar su alma. Es entonces cuando un hombre se encuentra al borde de la eternidad. A veces, puede realmente ver su vida y sus pecados por primera vez y elevar sus ojos a Dios.

—Es entonces cuando un hombre se encuentra en su momento de máxima debilidad y de terror. Ustedes saben aprovecharlo. ¿Y si un hombre recibe los sacramentos por simple temor?

—Sólo Dios puede saber si está sinceramente arrepentido.

Bernie se dio cuenta de que había perdido. Había subestimado hasta qué extremo el sacerdote estaba hundido en la superstición. Su natural compasión era sólo una trémula emoción superficial.

—Tiene usted respuesta para todo, ¿verdad? —preguntó en tono abatido—. ¿No cree que eso es torcer interminablemente la lógica?

El padre Eduardo sonrió con tristeza.

—Yo podría decir lo mismo de tu credo. El edificio que construyó Karl Marx.

—Mis creencias son científicas.

—¿De veras? Me he enterado de lo de la cueva que descubrieron en las colinas con pinturas prehistóricas. Unas figuras de hombres que perseguían a animales ya extinguidos, ¿no es cierto?

—Sí. Probablemente su valor es incalculable y ustedes las van a destruir.

—La decisión no ha sido mía. Pero tú crees que aquellas personas vivían como comunistas, ¿verdad? El comunismo primitivo, la primera fase de la dialéctica histórica. Como ves, me conozco muy bien a mi Karl Marx. Pero es sólo una creencia, tú no puedes saber cómo vivían aquellas personas. Vosotros también vivís de la fe; una falsa fe.

Era como el psiquiatra. Bernie habría deseado hacerle daño al sacerdote, provocar su enfado como había hecho con el médico.

—Esto no es un juego intelectual. Nos encontramos en un lugar en el que a los enfermos se les niega la asistencia médica y en el que un Gobierno apoyado por su Iglesia los mata a trabajar.

El sacerdote lanzó un suspiro.

—Tú no eres español, Piper, ¿cómo vas a comprender realmente la Guerra Civil? Yo tenía amigos, sacerdotes, que quedaron atrapados en la zona republicana. Fueron fusilados, arrojados a precipicios, torturados.

—Y por eso ahora se vengan de nosotros. Yo creía que los cristianos eran mejores que el común de los mortales. —Bernie soltó una carcajada amarga—. ¿Qué dice la Biblia? Por sus frutos los conoceréis.

El padre Eduardo no se enfadó, más bien se entristeció y pareció hundirse en el dolor.

—¿Qué piensas tú que supone para el padre Jaime y para mí —preguntó serenamente— el hecho de trabajar aquí entre personas que mataron a nuestros amigos? ¿Por qué crees que lo hacemos? Por caridad, para intentar salvar a los que nos odian.

—Usted sabe que, si es el padre Jaime el que va a ver a Vicente, disfrutará con lo que hace. ¿Su venganza quizá? —Bernie hizo ademán de levantarse—. ¿Puedo irme con su permiso?

El padre Eduardo levantó una mano y después la dejó caer con aire cansado sobre el escritorio.

—Sí. Vete. —Bernie se levantó—. Rezaré por tu amigo —dijo el padre Eduardo—. Por su restablecimiento.

Aquella noche Eulalio ordenó una reunión de la célula. Los diez comunistas se congregaron alrededor del jergón de Pablo, al fondo de la barraca.

—Tenemos que fortalecer nuestro credo marxista —dijo Eulalio. Bernie lo miró a la cara mientras utilizaba aquella palabra. Vio que estaba muy serio—. El descubrimiento de estas pinturas me ha dado que pensar. Tendríamos que organizar aulas acerca de la valoración marxista de la historia y el desarrollo de la lucha de clases a lo largo de los años. Algo que nos volviera a unir; lo necesitamos, ahora que se nos echa encima otro invierno.

Uno o dos hombres asintieron con la cabeza, pero otros adoptaron una expresión de hastío. Habló Miguel, un viejo tranviario de Valencia.

—Hace demasiado frío para permanecer sentados por ahí en medio de la oscuridad.

—¿Y si los guardias se enteran? —preguntó Pablo—. ¿O si alguien se lo dice?

—¿Quién dirigirá estas aulas? —preguntó Bernie—. ¿Tú? —Comprendió que la reunión se estaba volviendo en contra de Eulalio; éste tendría que haber hecho la sugerencia antes de que las frías noches obligaran a los hombres a encerrarse corriendo en sí mismos.

La escamosa cabeza se volvió en dirección a Bernie, con los ojos encendidos por la furia.

—Sí. Yo soy el jefe de la célula.

—El camarada Eulalio tiene razón —dijo Pepino, un joven obrero del campo de rostro enjuto—. Tenemos que recordar lo que somos.

—Pues yo, por de pronto, no tengo la energía necesaria para escuchar las lecciones del camarada Eulalio acerca del materialismo histórico.

—Ya está decidido, camarada —dijo Eulalio en tono amenazador—. He sido elegido y las decisiones las tomo yo. Éste es el centralismo democrático.

—No, no lo es; yo aceptaré tus órdenes, contrarias a la opinión de este grupo, cuando un Comité Central legalmente constituido del Partido Comunista Español me lo diga. No antes.

—Ya no existe ningún Comité Central —dijo tristemente Pepino—. Al menos, no en España.

—Exacto.

—Tendrías que cuidar tu lenguaje, inglés —dijo Eulalio en voz baja—. Conozco tu historia. Un hijo de obreros que estudió en un colegio aristocrático, un arribista.

—Y tú eres un *petit bourgeois* ávido de poder —replicó Bernie—. Crees que sigues siendo capataz de fábrica. Soy leal al partido, pero tú no eres el partido.

—Te puedo expulsar de esta célula.

Bernie se rió por lo bajo.

—Menuda célula.

Enseguida comprendió que no tendría que haberlo dicho, los pondría a todos en su contra; pero es que la cabeza le daba vueltas a causa del agotamiento y la rabia. Se levantó y se tumbó en su jergón. Alguien les gritó que se callaran, la gente quería dormir. Poco después, oyó el crujido del jergón de Eulalio en el momento en que éste se tumbaba. Le oyó rascarse y sintió sus ojos clavados en él.

—Vamos a tener que estudiar tu caso, camarada —dijo Eulalio en un susurro.

Bernie no contestó. Oía los jadeos ásperos y los gorgoteos de la respiración de Vicente y hubiera deseado romper a llorar de rabia y dolor. Recordó las palabras de Agustín que tanto lo habían desconcertado. Tiempos mejores. «No —pensó—, fuera lo que fuera lo que me querías decir, te equivocaste.»

Aquella noche no pudo dormir. Permaneció tumbado sin dar vueltas en su litera en medio del frío, con la mirada perdida en la oscuridad. Recordó cómo, en Londres, las teorías del Partido Comunista sobre la lucha de clases le habían parecido una revelación, la explicación definitiva del mundo. Al principio, cuando dejó Cambridge, había ayudado a sus padres en la tienda, pero la depresión de su padre y la decepción y las quejas de su madre por el hecho de que hubiera arrojado por la borda todo lo que significaba Cambridge lo asfixiaban de tal manera que decidió irse de casa y buscar alojamiento cerca de allí.

Lo sacaba más que nunca de quicio el contraste entre la opulencia de Cambridge y la pobreza desolada y despreciable del East End donde los parados holgazaneaban por las esquinas de las calles y ya se empezaban a advertir los ligeros movimientos de un fascismo doméstico. Millones de personas estaban en paro, y el Partido Laborista no hacía nada. Se mantenía en contacto con los Mera; la República había sido una decepción y el Gobierno se negaba a subir los impuestos para financiar las reformas, pues tal cosa habría despertado la cólera de las clases medias. Un amigo lo había acompañado a un mitin del Partido Comunista y enseguida había comprendido que allí estaba la verdad y que aquello era explicar en serio cómo funcionaban realmente las cosas.

Estudió a Marx y a Lenin; su dura prosa, tan distinta de cualquier otra cosa que hubiera leído anteriormente, le planteó al principio una cierta dificultad; pero, cuando comprendió los análisis que ellos hacían, descubrió que allí estaba la inexorable realidad de la lucha de clases. Más dura que el hierro, le dijo su instructor del partido. Bernie trabajó con gran denuedo por el partido, vendiendo el *Daily Mail* a la entrada de las fábricas bajo la lluvia, actuando como encargado del orden en los mítines que se organizaban en locales semidesiertos. Muchos de los socios locales del partido eran gente de la clase media, bohemios, intelectuales y artistas. Sabía que, para muchos de ellos, el comunismo era un capricho, un acto de rebelión; pero, al mismo tiempo, se daba cuenta de que se sentía más a gusto con ellos que con los obreros. Con su acento de la escuela privada, éstos lo consideraban uno de los suyos; y precisamente uno de ellos, un escultor, le consiguió su trabajo como modelo. No obstante, una parte de él seguía sintiéndose desarraigada y solitaria. Ni proletaria ni burguesa, sino tan sólo un híbrido inconexo.

En julio del treinta y seis, el ejército español se alzó contra el gobierno del Frente Popular y estalló la Guerra Civil. En otoño los comunistas empezaron a pedir voluntarios y él fue a King Street y se apuntó.

Tuvo que esperar. La formación de las Brigadas Internacionales, los itinerarios y los puntos de reunión estaban llevando mucho tiempo. Empezaba a perder la paciencia; hasta que, tras otra visita infructuosa al cuartel general del partido, desobedeció al partido por primera y única vez en su vida. Hizo la maleta y, sin decir ni una palabra a nadie, se fue a la estación Victoria y subió al tren que enlazaba con el barco.

Llegó a Madrid en noviembre; Franco había llegado a la Casa de

Campo pero, de momento, contenía su avance y los ciudadanos de Madrid mantenían a raya al ejército español. Aunque el tiempo era frío y desapacible, los ciudadanos que cinco años atrás se mostraban tristes y abatidos parecían haber cobrado nueva vida, y se advertía por todas partes un fervor revolucionario y un entusiasmo ardiente. Los tranvías y los camiones llenos de obreros con monos azules de trabajo y pañuelos rojos al cuello pasaban por las calles en su camino hacia el frente, con las palabras «¡Abajo el Fascismo!» pintadas en tiza en los costados.

Tendría que haberse presentado en la sede central del partido, pero ya era muy tarde cuando el tren llegó y se fue directamente a Carabanchel. Un grupo de mujeres y niños montaba una barricada en una esquina de la plaza de los Mera, levantando para ello los adoquines de la calzada. Al ver a un forastero, alzaron las manos haciendo el saludo del puño cerrado.

—¡Salud, compañero!

—¡Salud! ¡Hermanos proletarios, uníos! —«Algún día —pensó Bernie—, eso ocurrirá en Inglaterra.»

Le había escrito a Pedro y ellos sabían que iría, aunque no cuándo. Inés abrió la puerta del apartamento; parecía cansada y abatida, y un desgreñado cabello entrecano le enmarcaba el rostro. Se le iluminó el semblante al verlo.

—¡Pedro! ¡Antonio! —llamó—. ¡Ya está aquí!

Sobre la mesa del salón había un fusil desmontado, un arma de apariencia muy antigua con una boca enorme. Pedro y Antonio examinaban las distintas piezas. Iban sin afeitar y cubiertos de polvo, con sus monos de trabajo sucios de tierra. Francisco, el hijo tuberculoso, permanecía sentado en una silla sin apenas haber crecido después de cinco años, pálido y delgado como siempre. La pequeña Carmela, que ahora tenía ocho años, estaba sentada sobre sus rodillas.

Pedro se limpió las manos con un trozo de papel de periódico y corrió a abrazarlo.

—¡Bernardo! Menudo día para llegar. —Respiró hondo—. Mañana Antonio se va al frente.

—Estoy intentando limpiar este viejo fusil que me han dado —dijo Antonio con orgullo.

Inés frunció el entrecejo.

—¡Pero ahora no sabe cómo armarlo!

—A lo mejor, yo te puedo ayudar.

Bernie había estado en el Cuerpo de Instrucción de Oficiales de

Rookwood. Y recordaba haber irritado a los demás alumnos diciendo que los conocimientos militares quizá les fueran útiles cuando estallara la revolución. Así pues, ayudó a sus amigos a recomponer el fusil, después despejaron la mesa e Inés sirvió cocido.

—¿Has venido para ayudar a matar a los fascistas? —preguntó Carmela, mirándolo con unos ojos llenos de emoción y curiosidad.

—Sí —contestó Bernie, acariciándole la cabeza. Después se volvió para mirar a Pedro—. Mañana me tendría que presentar en la sede central del partido.

—¿Los comunistas? —Pedro denegó con la cabeza—. Ahora estamos en deuda con ellos. Si al menos los británicos y los franceses hubieran accedido a vendernos armas.

—Stalin sabe cómo librar una guerra revolucionaria.

—Mi padre y yo nos hemos pasado toda la tarde cavando trincheras —dijo Antonio con la cara muy seria—. Después me han entregado este fusil y me han dicho que duerma bien esta noche y me presente mañana para mi incorporación a la acción.

Bernie contempló el rostro chupado y juvenil de Antonio y respiró hondo.

—¿Crees que podría haber un fusil para mí?

Antonio lo miró con la cara muy seria.

—Sí. Necesitan cuantos más hombres mejor, con tal de que sepan sostener un fusil.

—¿Cuándo te tienes que presentar?

—Al amanecer.

—Iré contigo. —Bernie experimentó una extraña y jubilosa sensación de emoción y temor. Apretó la mano de Antonio y se echó a reír; al final, ambos acabaron riéndose histéricamente.

Pero Bernie estaba asustado cuando se levantó con Pedro y Antonio al amanecer. Al salir, oyó a lo lejos el fuego de artillería. Se estremeció en la fría y grisácea mañana. Antonio le había dado un pañuelo rojo; llevaba la chaqueta y los pantalones con los que había llegado, pero ahora acompañados por el pañuelo rojo alrededor del cuello.

En la Puerta del Sol, unos oficiales enfundados en uniformes caqui invitaban a los hombres a formar en fila y los acompañaban a los tranvías que permanecían alineados uno detrás de otro. Mientras se alejaban del centro de la ciudad, los hombres se empezaron a poner en tensión, sujetando los fusiles entre las rodillas. Cuando el tranvía se detuvo ruidosamente delante de la entrada de la Casa de Campo, Bernie oyó el fragor del fuego de artillería. El corazón le latía violentamente cuando el sargento les ordenó a gritos que bajaran.

Entonces Bernie vio los cuerpos. Media docena de muertos yacían en fila en el suelo, todavía con los pañuelos rojos anudados alrededor del cuello. No era la primera vez que veía un cadáver —su abuela había permanecido en el cuarto de atrás de la tienda antes del funeral—; pero aquellos hombres cuyos rostros estaban tan inmóviles y pálidos como el de su abuela eran jóvenes. Un chico presentaba un orificio negro en la frente con una gotita de sangre debajo que parecía una lágrima. El corazón le golpeó en el pecho como un martillo, y notó un sudor frío en la frente mientras seguía a Pedro y Antonio para incorporarse al desorganizado grupo de milicianos.

Pedro fue acompañado a un destacamento destinado a la labor de cavar trincheras; mientras que Bernie, Antonio y otros veinte hombres, algunos con fusiles y otros sin ellos, recibían la orden de seguir a un sargento hasta una trinchera a medio cavar donde unos hombres con azadas interrumpieron su labor para permitirles el paso. Unos sacos terreros se habían amontonado en el lado que miraba a la Casa de Campo, desde donde se escuchaban esporádicos disparos. Todo era muy caótico. Los hombres corrían de un lado para otro mientras unos camiones se deslizaban y patinaban sobre el barro. Otros hombres permanecían apoyados en los sacos terreros con expresión perpleja.

—Jesús —le dijo Bernie a Antonio—. Esto no es un ejército.

—Pues es lo único que tenemos —dijo Antonio—. Toma, guárdame esto, voy a echar un vistazo. —Había una escalera de mano al lado de Antonio y, antes de que Bernie se lo pudiera impedir, el chico empezó a trepar por ella.

—Déjalo, insensato, te van a dar. —Bernie recordó a su padre diciéndole que así era como muchos miles de nuevos reclutas habían muerto en el Frente occidental: asomando la cabeza para mirar al otro lado.

Antonio apoyó los brazos sobre los sacos terreros.

—No te preocupes, no me pueden ver. Dios mío, ellos tienen cañones de campaña y todo lo que quieran al otro lado. Aquí no se mueve nada...

Bernie soltó un reniego, posó el fusil en el suelo y subió por la escalera de mano, agarrándose a la cintura de Antonio.

—¡Baja te digo!

—Bueno, hombre, ya voy.

Bernie subió otro peldaño y agarró a Antonio por el hombro, y fue entonces cuando el francotirador disparó. La bala no le dio a Antonio en la cabeza por muy poco, pero alcanzó a Bernie en el brazo. Éste lanzó un grito y ambos rodaron juntos escalera abajo hasta llegar al suelo de la trinchera. Bernie vio que la sangre le traspasaba el tejido de la chaqueta y se desmayó.

Un comisario español lo fue a visitar al hospital de campaña.

—Eres un necio —le dijo—. Deberías haberte presentado primero en el Quinto Regimiento; allí te habrían dado un poco de instrucción.

—Mis amigos me dijeron que en la Casa de Campo se necesitaban todos los hombres posibles, lo siento.

El comisario soltó un gruñido.

—Pues ahora te pasarás varias semanas fuera de combate. Y te tendremos que alojar en algún sitio cuando salgas de aquí.

—Mis amigos de Carabanchel cuidarán de mí.

El hombre lo miró de soslayo.

—¿Son del partido?

—Socialistas.

El comisario soltó otro gruñido.

—¿Cómo van los combates?

—Los vamos conteniendo. Estamos formando un regimiento que aporte un poco de disciplina.

Bernie cambió de posición en la litera para calentarse un poco las piernas. En la cama de al lado Vicente dormía emitiendo un terrible gorgoteo. Recordó sus semanas de convalecencia en Carabanchel. Sus intentos de convertir a los Mera al comunismo habían resultado infructuosos. Decían que los rusos estaban destruyendo la República y que hablaban de colaboración con la burguesía progresista pero al mismo tiempo traían su policía secreta y sus espías. Bernie les dijo que los rumores que corrían sobre la brutalidad rusa eran exagerados y que, en la guerra, uno tenía que ser duro. Pero no era fácil discutir con un veterano como Pedro, con treinta años de lucha de clases a su espalda. A veces, dudaba y no sabía si lo que se decía acerca de los rusos era mentira o no; pero procuraba apartar aquellos pensamientos de su mente porque eran una distracción y, en medio de aquella lucha, tenía que concentrarse.

Pero las dudas volvían en mitad de la fría noche. Necesitaban hombres duros, decían, pero, en caso de que ganaran, ¿el poder iría a parar a las manos de hombres como Eulalio? El cura Eduardo había dicho que el marxismo era una ideología equivocada. Él jamás había comprendido debidamente lo que era el materialismo dialéctico y sabía que muchos comunistas tampoco lo entendían porque era algo muy difícil de comprender. Pero el comunismo no era un credo como el catolicismo... estaba enraizado en una comprensión de la realidad, del mundo material.

Se agitaba y daba vueltas en la cama. Procuraba no pensar en Barbara, le dolía demasiado; pero aquel rostro seguía regresando a sus pensamientos. Los recuerdos que tenía de ella estaban siempre impregnados de remordimiento. La había abandonado. La imaginaba de nuevo en Inglaterra o quizás en Suiza, rodeada de gobiernos fascistas. Le solía decir que ella no entendía nada, pero aquella noche se empezaba a preguntar hasta qué punto él comprendía. Procuraba evocar una imagen antigua y consoladora que a veces acudía a su mente cuando no podía dormir, la escena de un viejo noticiario del partido que había visto en Londres: unos tractores que rodaban por los interminables trigales rusos, seguidos de obreros que entonaban cantos mientras recolectaban las mieses a manos llenas.

ros hinmos, nos queda todavía media hora hasta la mina...

29

Sandy se reunió con Harry en la puerta de su casa a primera hora de la mañana. Era un día frío y despejado, el oblicuo sol brillaba en un cielo claro y azul. Sandy bajó de su Packard y le estrechó la mano a Harry. Vestía un grueso abrigo de lana de camello y una bufanda de seda, y la luz del sol arrancaba destellos de su cabello engominado. Se le veía feliz y rebosante de entusiasmo por el hecho de haber salido de casa tan temprano.

—¡Qué mañana tan estupenda! —dijo, contemplando el cielo—. No solemos disfrutar de muchas mañanas como ésta en invierno. —Abandonaron Madrid en dirección noroeste para subir a la sierra de Guadarrama—. ¿Te apetece venir a cenar a casa un día de éstos? —preguntó Sandy—. Sólo Barbara y nosotros dos. La sigo viendo un poco extraña. Puede que eso la anime.

—Me parece muy bien. —Harry respiró hondo—. Me alegro de que me hayas incluido en este proyecto.

—Faltaría más —contestó Sandy, sonriendo con expresión condescendiente.

Subieron hasta el final de la carretera de montaña; por encima de ellos, las cumbres más altas ya estaban cubiertas de nieve. Después bajaron de nuevo a la desnuda y parda campiña, cruzaron Segovia y giraron al oeste hacia Santa María la Real. Había muy poco tráfico y el campo estaba desierto y en silencio. Harry recordó el día de su llegada y el desplazamiento en automóvil a Madrid en compañía de Tolhurst.

Al cabo de una hora, Sandy enfiló un polvoriento sendero de carros que serpeaba entre las lomas.

—Ahora me temo que tendremos que prepararnos para unos cuantos brincos, nos queda todavía media hora hasta la mina.

En el sendero, las huellas de los cascos de los asnos quedaban tapadas por los surcos profundos de vehículos pesados. El automóvil empezó a experimentar sacudidas, pero Sandy circulaba con absoluta confianza y seguridad.

—No hago más que pensar en Rookwood desde que volvimos a encontrarnos —dijo en tono pensativo—. Piper se trasladó de nuevo a nuestro estudio cuando a mí me expulsaron, ¿verdad? Me lo dijiste en una carta.

—Sí.

—Apuesto a que debió de pensar que había ganado.

—No lo creo. Apenas volvió a mencionar tu nombre, que yo recuerde.

—No me sorprende que se hiciera comunista, siempre había sido un poco fanático. Me miraba como si nada le hubiera gustado más en esta vida que empujarme contra una pared para que me pegaran un tiro. —Sandy meneó la cabeza—. Los comunistas siguen siendo el verdadero peligro para el mundo, ¿sabes? Es contra Rusia contra lo que tendría que combatir Inglaterra, no contra Alemania. Pensaba que eso es lo que ocurriría después de lo de Múnich.

—El fascismo y el comunismo son malos de por sí, tanto el uno como el otro.

—Quita, hombre, por Dios. Por lo menos, con las dictaduras de derechas la gente como nosotros está a salvo; siempre y cuando sigamos las directrices del partido. Aquí apenas hay impuestos sobre la renta, aunque reconozco que el hecho de tener que bregar con la burocracia puede ser un engorro. No obstante, el Gobierno tiene que enseñarle a la gente quién es el que manda. Eso es lo que ellos piensan: conseguir que todo el mundo cumpla estas normas, enseñarles a los españoles el orden y la obediencia.

—Pero la burocracia es completamente corrupta.

—Esto es España, Harry. —Sandy lo miró con afectuosa ironía—. En el fondo, sigues siendo un hombre de Rookwood, ¿verdad? ¿Sigues creyendo en todos aquellos códigos de honor?

—Antes creía en ellos. Ahora ya no sé ni lo que soy.

—En los viejos tiempos, yo te admiraba por eso, ¿sabes? Pero son cosas del colegio, Harry, no es la vida real. Supongo que la vida académica también nos protegía mucho.

—Sí, es verdad, tienes toda la razón. Aquí se me han abierto mucho los ojos acerca de ciertas cosas.

—El mundo real, ¿eh?

—Más bien, sí.

—Ahora todos necesitamos seguridad con vistas al futuro, Harry. Yo te puedo ayudar a conseguirla si tú me lo permites. —Había algo así como una petición de beneplácito en el tono de voz de Sandy—. Y no hay nada más seguro que el oro, sobre todo en los tiempos que corren. Bueno, ya hemos llegado.

Más adelante, una alta alambrada de púas rodeaba una amplia extensión de terreno ondulado. En la tierra amarilla se habían perforado unos grandes hoyos, algunos de ellos parcialmente llenos de agua. Cerca de allí descansaban dos excavadoras mecánicas. El camino terminaba ante una verja con una cabaña de madera en la parte interior. A cierta distancia se podían ver otras dos cabañas, una de ellas bastante grande, y también un fortín de piedra de gran tamaño. Un letrero junto a la verja decía: «Nuevas Iniciativas S. A. Prohibida la entrada. Con el patrocinio del Ministerio de Minas.» Sandy hizo sonar la bocina y un escuálido anciano salió precipitadamente de la cabaña a abrir la verja. El hombre saludó a Sandy mientras el vehículo cruzaba la entrada y se detenía. Ambos bajaron del automóvil. Un viento frío cortaba las mejillas de Harry, que se encasquetó mejor el sombrero.

Sandy se volvió hacia el vigilante.

—¿Todo bien, Arturo?

—Sí, señor Forsyth. Ha venido el señor Otero, está en el despacho. —El tono del vigilante era de respeto. «El que habría cabido esperar de un empleado más joven para con el jefe», pensó Harry. Aunque le resultaba extraño imaginarse a Sandy como un jefe al frente de una plantilla de empleados.

En un pliegue de las colinas se distinguía una finca de considerable tamaño rodeada de álamos. Unas cabezas de ganado negro pastaban en los campos circundantes. Sandy señaló en la distancia.

—Ése es el terreno que queremos comprar. Alberto ha estado allí en el más absoluto secreto y ha tomado algunas muestras. Por cierto, se alegra mucho de tu visita. Yo lo convencí. Temía confiar en alguien que trabaja en la embajada; pero yo le dije que tu palabra era tu garantía, le aseguré que no dirías nada.

—Gracias. —Harry experimentó una punzada de remordimiento. Procuró concentrarse en lo que Sandy le estaba diciendo.

—El filón de oro llega justo hasta debajo de la finca y allí es todavía más abundante. El ganadero cría toros de lidia. No es demasiado listo, ni siquiera se ha enterado de lo que hacemos aquí. Creo que lo podríamos convencer de que vendiera. —Sandy soltó una repentina carcajada mientras contemplaba los campos—. ¿No te parece maravilloso? Lo tenemos todo allí. A veces, ni yo mismo me lo creo. Y nos haremos con la propiedad de esta finca, no te quepa la menor duda. Le he dicho al ganadero que le pagaremos en efectivo para que se pueda ir a vivir con su hija a Segovia. —Se volvió para mirar a Harry—. Por regla general, se me da muy bien eso de convencer a la gente de que haga las cosas a mi manera, averiguar qué es lo que le interesa y colocárselo delante como un cebo —añadió, esbozando una nueva sonrisa.

Harry se agachó para recoger del suelo un puñado de tierra. Era muy parecida a la tierra de los botes del despacho de Sandy. Se notaba fría al tacto y se deshacía entre los dedos.

—Vamos a tomar un café en el despacho. Así nos calentamos un poquito. —Acompañó a Harry a la cabaña más cercana—. Hoy no hay nadie aquí, sólo el personal de seguridad.

El despacho era de una simplicidad espartana. Un escritorio y unas cuantas sillas plegables. Había un cuadro de una bailaora de flamenco colgado en una pared y una fotografía de Franco presidía el escritorio, detrás del cual permanecía sentado Otero leyendo un informe. Se levantó al ver entrar a Harry y a Sandy y estrechó sonriendo la mano de Harry. Su comportamiento era más cordial que unos cuantos días atrás.

—Bienvenido, señor Brett, le agradezco que se haya tomado la molestia de venir hasta aquí. ¿Café para los dos?

—Gracias, Alberto —contestó Sandy—. Aquí fuera se nos han estado congelando los cojones. Siéntate, Harry.

El geólogo se acercó a un rincón donde había una tetera para calentar agua y un hornillo de gas. Sandy se sentó junto a una esquina del escritorio y encendió un pitillo. Tomó el documento que Otero había estado leyendo.

—¿Es éste el informe sobre las últimas muestras?

—Sí. Los resultados son buenos. La sección junto al río es una de las mejores. Usted perdone, señor Brett, pero sólo tenemos leche en polvo.

—No se preocupe. Veo que es una zona muy grande.

—Sí. Pero los terrenos que tenemos han sido exhaustivamente inspeccionados. —Otero se volvió para mirar a Harry—. Las nuevas muestras corresponden a la finca de aquí cerca. —Otero distribuyó las tazas de café y se volvió a sentar—. Todo eso me exaspera. No podemos iniciar labores intensivas hasta que el ministerio nos conceda su autorización. Según la legislación española, los minerales del subsuelo pertenecen al Gobierno y es cuestión de establecer nuestros derechos de explotación, nuestra comisión. El ministerio nos sigue pidiendo más muestras que cuestan más dinero, y necesitamos fondos para poder comprar la finca. En principio, contamos con el respaldo del Generalísimo; pero el ministerio le sigue diciendo que tenga cuidado y él sigue su consejo después del fracaso de Badajoz del año pasado.

—Si Madrid da su visto bueno y ustedes compran la finca, ¿cuánto podrían ganar? Digamos, en un año...

Sandy soltó una carcajada.

—La gran pregunta.

Otero asintió con la cabeza.

—No se puede decir exactamente, pero para mí que unos veinte millones de pesetas. Y, en cuanto la finca estuviera en pleno rendimiento, ¿quién sabe... treinta, cuarenta?

—Eso es más de un millón de libras el primer año —dijo Sandy—. Si tú adquirieras un tres por ciento de las acciones, serían quince mil libras por una inversión de quinientas. Y treinta mil, si invirtieras mil.

Harry tomó un sorbo de café. Era amargo, con unos grumos de leche en polvo que flotaban en la superficie.

Sandy y Otero lo miraron en silencio, mientras unas espirales de humo se escapaban de sus cigarrillos.

—Eso es mucho dinero —dijo Harry al final.

Otero se rió.

—Ustedes, los ingleses, siempre infravalorándolo todo.

—Y Harry, más que nadie. —Sandy soltó una carcajada y se levantó—. Ven, te vamos a enseñar las excavaciones.

Lo acompañaron al terreno, le mostraron de qué manera las mínimas variaciones de color de la tierra indicaban distintos contenidos de oro. Todo el terreno estaba salpicado por pequeños hoyos circulares; Otero explicó que allí se habían recogido las muestras.

Aparecieron unas nubes que se perseguían unas a otras en el cielo.

—Vamos a echar un vistazo al laboratorio —dijo Sandy—. ¿Qué tal va tu oído últimamente? Parece que bien, ¿no?

—Sí, ya casi se ha normalizado.

—Harry resultó herido en Dunkerque, Alberto. En la batalla de Francia.

—¿En serio?

El geólogo inclinó la cabeza con interés. Llegaron a la cabaña del laboratorio y entraron. Se respiraba en el aire el olor áspero y penetrante de una sustancia química. Unos bancos largos estaban cubiertos por filtros de vidrio, grandes bateas de metal y bandejas llenas de un líquido claro y de una tierra de color amarillo.

—Ácido sulfúrico —explicó Sandy—. ¿Recuerdas las clases de química en el colegio? No toques ninguno de estos recipientes.

Lo acompañaron en un recorrido por todo el lugar, mientras Otero le explicaba los procesos de extracción del oro a partir del mineral. A Harry no le interesó demasiado. Mientras se retiraban, éste volvió a ver el fortín y observó que las ventanitas estaban protegidas por barrotes.

—¿Qué es eso?

—Aquí guardamos el mineral destinado a la segunda fase del proceso de purificación. Es demasiado valioso para dejarlo por ahí. La llave está en el despacho, pero echa un vistazo a través de los barrotes, si quieres.

El interior estaba oscuro; sin embargo, Harry pudo distinguir más material de laboratorio. Había también toda una serie de grandes recipientes, casi todos ellos a rebosar de tierra amarilla molida hasta dejarla convertida en una especie de polvillo.

Regresaron al despacho donde Otero, cordial como al principio, preparó más café.

—Yo tengo experiencia con los yacimientos de oro de África del Sur —dijo Otero—. Era el lugar adonde iban los geólogos cuando yo era joven. Allí aprendí un poco de inglés, aunque ahora ya se me ha olvidado.

Otero esbozó una sonrisa como de disculpa.

—¿Y cómo es este lugar en comparación?

Otero se sentó.

—Mucho más pequeño, naturalmente. Los yacimientos de Witwatersrand son los más grandes del mundo. Pero allí la calidad del mineral es inferior y las vetas se encuentran a mucha mayor profundidad. Aquí, en cambio, la calidad es muy alta y el mineral se encuentra en la superficie o muy cerca de ella.

—¿En cantidad suficiente como para darle a España unos importantes depósitos de oro?

—¿Quiere decir suficiente para que suponga un cambio significativo para el país? Pues sí.

Sandy miró a Harry por encima del borde de su taza.

—¿Qué dices ahora?

—Me interesa. Pero me gustaría consultarlo con el director de mi banco de Londres, escribirle sólo en términos muy generales acerca de una inversión en un yacimiento de oro con reservas comprobadas, no diré dónde, en comparación con otro tipo de inversiones, etc.

—Tendríamos que echar un vistazo a la carta —dijo Sandy—. Te lo digo en serio, se trata de un proyecto muy confidencial.

Otero lo miró con la perspicacia que Harry recordaba.

—Como ya dijimos, nadie en la embajada tiene por qué saberlo. Una carta a Inglaterra podría ser abierta por el censor.

—No, si la envío por valija diplomática. Pero no me importa que ustedes la lean antes de que yo la envíe, si quieren.

—El director del banco seguramente te dirá que es una inversión arriesgada —le advirtió Sandy.

Harry sonrió.

—Pero yo no estoy obligado a aceptar su consejo. —Meneó la cabeza—. El tres por ciento de un millón.

—El primer año. —Sandy hizo una pausa para dejar que sus palabras surtieran el debido efecto.

Harry pensó: «Quizá todo eso podría haber sido mío si yo no los estuviera espiando.» Experimentó el repentino impulso de echarse a reír. Sandy se levantó y se dio unas palmadas en las rodillas.

—Bueno, pues. Yo me tengo que ir. Ceno esta noche con Sebastián.

Otero sonrió una vez más mientras estrechaba la mano de Harry.

—Espero que se una usted a nosotros, señor. Es el momento adecuado para invertir. Mil libras nos serían muy útiles para impedir que el ministerio nos machaque. Y, en cuanto a usted... —agitó la mano en el aire— las posibilidades... —Enarcó las cejas...

Mientras Harry y Sandy se dirigían al automóvil, se abrió la verja y apareció otro hombre, menudo y delgado. Para su asombro, Harry reconoció en él al antiguo ordenanza de Maestre, el acompañante de Milagros.

—Teniente Gómez —dijo sin pensar—. Buenos días.

—Buen día —musitó Gómez. Su rostro conservaba la impasible expresión propia de un militar; pero la atormentada e inquisitiva mirada de sus ojos hizo que Harry se detuviera en seco y que a éste se le helara el corazón al darse cuenta de que había cometido un error, y muy grave, por cierto.

—¿Os conocéis? —preguntó Sandy en tono cortante.

—Sí, nos conocimos en una... una recepción hace algún tiempo, ¿verdad?

—Sí, señor, en una recepción nos conocimos.

Gómez se volvió y abrió la verja manteniendo la cabeza apartada mientras pasaba el vehículo. A través del espejo retrovisor, Sandy lo vio regresar a su cabaña.

—Es nuestro portero —explicó—. Acaba de entrar a nuestro servicio. —Hablaba tranquilamente y como quien no quiere la cosa—. ¿Cómo lo conociste?

—Pues en una recepción, una fiesta.

—¿Conociste a un portero en una fiesta?

—Era un criado o algo por el estilo. Un sirviente de la familia. A lo mejor, lo sorprendieron robando cucharas. —Harry soltó una carcajada.

Sandy frunció el entrecejo y permaneció un momento en silencio.

—¿Fue en la fiesta del general Maestre de la que me hablaste? ¿En honor de su hija?

«Mierda —pensó Harry—, mierda.» Qué rápido era Sandy; la fiesta de Maestre era la única de la que él le había hablado y Sandy no tenía más remedio que haberla recordado, siendo Maestre su enemigo. Sandy seguía mirando al portero a través del espejo retrovisor.

—Pues sí. Cuando más tarde acompañé a la hija de Maestre al Prado, él la fue a recoger. Supongo que lo habrán despedido.

—Tal vez. —Sandy hizo una pausa—. Nos vino recomendado, dijo que era un veterano que se había quedado sin trabajo.

—Si lo despidieron, se comprende que no tuviera referencias.

—¿Has vuelto a ver a la hija? —preguntó Sandy con aparente indiferencia.

—No. Ya te dije que no era mi tipo. He conocido a otra persona —añadió para apartar a Sandy del tema. Pero Sandy se limitó a asentir con la cabeza. Ahora fruncía el entrecejo con semblante pensativo. Harry pensó: «Maestre ha colocado a Gómez aquí como espía y yo lo acabo de traicionar. Mierda. Mierda.»

Atravesaron una aldea. Sandy se detuvo ante un bar. Fuera había dos asnos atados a una verja.

—¿Esperas un minuto, Harry? —dijo—. Tengo que hacer una llamada rápida, se me ha olvidado una cosa.

Harry esperó mientras Sandy entraba en el bar. Los asnos atados a la verja le hicieron recordar el Lejano Oeste. Tiroteos al amanecer. ¿Qué le harían a Gómez? Era mucho lo que estaba en juego. Tragó saliva. ¿Lo habría enviado Maestre allí para espiar? Un par de chiquillos andrajosos se habían detenido a contemplar el impresionante automóvil americano. Él les hizo señas para que se fueran, y los niños dieron media vuelta y echaron a correr, resbalando con los pies descalzos entre el barro.

Sandy volvió a salir con una expresión fría y reconcentrada, que le hizo recordar a Harry el día en que lo habían castigado en clase y empezó a planear su venganza contra Taylor. Abrió la puerta del vehículo y subió sonriendo con semblante más relajado.

—Cuéntame algo más de esta chica —dijo, mientras ponía en marcha el motor.

Harry le contó la historia de la salvación de un desconocido del ataque de unos perros y del encuentro con su hermana. Las mejores mentiras son las que más se acercan a la verdad. Sandy sonrió asintiendo con la cabeza, pero la fría expresión de su rostro cuando regresaba al vehículo se quedó grabada en la mente de Harry. Habría llamado a Otero, lo habría llamado con toda seguridad. Supo que se había equivocado con respecto a Sandy, se había equivocado al pensar que éste no tenía ni idea de las barbaridades que podían ocurrir, como, por ejemplo, lo de Dunkerque. Pero vaya si la tenía, y él mismo podía cometer barbaridades. Era como en el colegio, le importaba todo un bledo.

30

Habían acordado que, a la vuelta de la mina, Harry acudiría directamente a la embajada para presentar su informe. Le pidió a Sandy que lo dejara en la puerta de su casa, alegando que tenía que traducir un documento. En cuanto el vehículo dobló la esquina, Harry tomó un tranvía para dirigirse a la calle de Fernando el Santo.

Tolhurst estaba en su despacho, leyendo un ejemplar cuatro días atrasado del *Times*. Se había producido un corte de electricidad y él se había puesto un jersey grueso con un dibujo muy llamativo para protegerse del frío. El jersey le confería una apariencia más juvenil, como de regordete colegial.

—¿Cómo ha ido? —le preguntó con ansia.

—Existe una mina, eso seguro. —Harry se sentó y respiró hondo—. Pero algo ha fallado.

El rostro redondo de Tolhurst pareció encogerse.

—¿Cómo? ¿Sandy desconfía de ti?

—No es eso. Me acompañó en un recorrido por la mina. Está más allá de Segovia; abarca un territorio muy amplio, aunque la producción parece ser que se encuentra en una fase muy inicial. Otero estaba allí y esta vez se mostró muy amable conmigo.

—¿Y qué más?

—Cuando ya nos íbamos, salió el vigilante para abrirnos la verja y yo lo reconocí. Es un tal Gómez. Trabaja para Maestre; ¿recuerdas que lo conocimos en la fiesta?

—Sí, era su antiguo ordenanza o algo por el estilo.

—Lo saludé sin pensar. Él me reconoció, pero yo comprendí que estaba asustado.

—Mierda. ¿Y cómo reaccionó Forsyth?

—Captó de inmediato el detalle y me preguntó dónde había conocido a Gómez.

—¿Y tú se lo dijiste?

—Sí; lo siento, Simon, me... me quedé en blanco, no conseguí inventarme ninguna trola en aquel momento. Dije que Gómez trabajaba para Maestre y que quizá lo habían despedido. Fue lo único que se me ocurrió.

—Maldita sea. —Tolhurst cogió un lápiz y empezó a darle vueltas entre las manos. Harry estaba furioso consigo mismo, horrorizado ante las consecuencias que su fallo pudiera tener para Gómez—. Supe que Sandy estaba preocupado. Se detuvo en un pueblo, dijo que tenía que hacer una llamada. Salió con la cara muy seria. Debió de llamar a Otero. ¿Cómo puede Maestre estar metido en todo eso, Simon?

Tolhurst se mordió el labio.

—Pues no lo sé, pero está metido en todas las batallas de monárquicos contra falangistas. Sabíamos que formaba parte del comité de evaluación de la mina de oro, pero el capitán no ha conseguido sonsacarle nada más. Es muy hermético en todo lo que él considera intereses nacionales de España.

«O sea que los Caballeros de San Jorge sólo te llevarán hasta un determinado punto», pensó Harry.

—No tendrías que haber saludado a alguien que sabías que trabajaba para él —dijo severamente Tolhurst—. Tendrías que haber adivinado que quizá se trataba de una tapadera.

—Jamás me había visto obligado a pensar tan rápido. Lo siento. Estaba totalmente concentrado en el emplazamiento de la mina y en tratar de interpretar bien el papel de un inversor auténtico.

Tolhurst soltó el lápiz.

—Forsyth comprenderá que Maestre no puede haber despedido sin más a un antiguo ordenanza suyo al que, encima, utilizaba para acompañar a su hija. Por Dios, Harry, menudo lío has armado. Se lo tendré que decir al capitán. Ahora mismo está reunido con sir Sam, hay una valija diplomática que tiene que salir esta misma noche. Espera aquí.

Tolhurst se retiró y él se quedó allí, mirando tristemente a través de la ventana. Bajó por la calle un mendigo montado en un burrito con los pies casi rozando el suelo a ambos lados. Unos pesados fardos de leña iban atados al lomo del animal. Harry pensó en las tremendas cargas que las bestias de pequeño tamaño se veían obligadas a soportar; parecía que estuviera a punto de rompérsele el espinazo.

Fuera se oyeron unas rápidas pisadas. Harry se levantó en el momento en que Tolhurst, con semblante muy serio, abría la puerta para franquearle la entrada a Hillgarth. Lo acompañaba el embajador. Hoare, con el rostro enjuto congestionado por la furia, se dejó caer en el asiento de Tolhurst, mirando ceñudo a Harry.

—Es usted un maldito insensato, Brett —empezó diciendo Hillgarth—. Pero ¿cómo se le ha ocurrido?

—Disculpe, señor, yo no sabía que Maestre...

Hoare se dirigió a Hillgarth en un tono cortante como el cuchillo.

—Alan, le advertí que esta operación era muy arriesgada. Siempre se lo digo, nada de operaciones encubiertas; tendríamos que habernos limitado a recoger información y nada más. Nosotros no somos el maldito SOE, la Dirección de Operaciones Especiales. Pero no, ¡usted y Winston tenían que montarse sus propias historias! Ahora puede que hayamos puesto en peligro nuestras relaciones con todo el sector monárquico por culpa de este idiota. —El embajador señaló a Harry con el gesto de quien espanta un molesto insecto.

—Vamos, Sam, Maestre nos habría dicho algo si hubiera puesto en práctica su propio plan.

—¿Y por qué iba a hacerlo? ¿Por qué? Es su maldito país. —Hoare se acercó a la frente una mano trémula de rabia—. Maestre es una de nuestras mejores fuentes. He sudado sangre durante estos últimos cinco meses para convencer a los monárquicos de que tenemos intereses comunes y de que Inglaterra no constituye una amenaza para ellos. He intentado convencer a Winston de que hiciera algún gesto amistoso a propósito de Gibraltar para expulsar a la chusma de Negrín. Y usted ya sabe qué otras cosas he hecho también. Y ahora se enterarán de que habíamos montado una operación secreta que choca con una de las suyas, pese a todas mis promesas de apoyo.

—Si le ocurre algo a este Gómez —dijo Hillgarth—, no se podrá relacionar con nosotros.

—¡No sea necio! Si Maestre tenía a un hombre en el lugar, seguro que éste habrá metido las narices en sus papeles. Eso es lo primero que haría. ¿Y si hubiera alguna nota acerca de un posible inversor en este proyecto llamado señor H. Brett, traductor adscrito al Servicio Diplomático de su majestad? —El rostro enjuto de Hoare se aflojó como si estuviera profundamente cansado—. Supongo que será mejor que llame a Maestre y lo advierta de que intente limitar los daños.

—Disculpe, señor —se atrevió a decir Harry—. Si hubiera sabido...

Hoare lo miró con rabia mientras el labio superior se le curvaba sobre unos pequeños dientes muy blancos.

—¿Si lo hubiera sabido? Saber las cosas no es ningún maldito asunto suyo, su misión es mantenerse alerta y parar las pelotas. —Se volvió hacia Hillgarth—. Será mejor que aborte este proyecto. Envíe a este maldito insensato a casa, que se vaya a luchar contra los italianos en el norte de África. Yo dije que, si tuviéramos que hacerlo, lo mejor habría sido abordar directamente a Forsyth y tratar de sobornarlo sin tantas historias de espías y misterios.

Hillgarth tomó serenamente la palabra, aunque en su voz se percibiera un cierto tono de cólera reprimida.

—Señor embajador, decidimos que este camino sería demasiado peligroso, a menos que supiéramos cuánto valía para él el proyecto. Ahora ya lo sabemos, sabemos lo importante que es. Y la tapadera de Brett aún no ha quedado al descubierto; si éste le dijera a Forsyth que conoce al hombre de Maestre, puede que ganara credibilidad.

—Tengo que llamar a Maestre. Hablaremos más tarde. —Hoare se levantó y Tolhurst se apresuró a abrirle la puerta. El embajador le dirigió una mirada asesina al pasar por su lado—. Debería haberlo comprendido, Tolhurst. Hillgarth, lo necesito para esta llamada.

Tolhurst cerró lentamente la puerta a su espalda.

—Será mejor que te vayas a casa, Harry. Se pasarán toda la noche discutiendo.

—Esta noche pensaba ir al teatro. *Macbeth*. ¿Puedo?

—Supongo que sí.

—Tolly, ¿qué ha querido decir Hoare con eso de que deberías haberlo comprendido?

Tolhurst esbozó una sonrisa irónica.

—Yo soy tu vigilante, Harry. Controlo de cerca todo lo que haces, informo al capitán Hillgarth. Todos los espías inexpertos tienen un vigilante y yo soy el tuyo.

—Ah. —Harry ya lo sospechaba, pero el hecho de saberlo le produjo una sensación de profunda decepción.

—Siempre dije que lo estabas haciendo muy bien; Hillgarth empezaba a perder la paciencia, pero yo le decía que estabas manejando el asunto de Forsyth con sumo cuidado. Y hasta ahora, lo has hecho muy bien. Pero no te puedes permitir ningún error, no en este trabajo.

—Ah.

—No pensaba que pudieras cometer un fallo tan garrafal. Eso es lo malo. Si un sujeto te cae simpático, acabas siendo parcial. —Tolhurst le dirigió a Harry una mirada de resentimiento—. Será mejor que te vayas. Apártate de la vista de Hillgarth. Te llamaré cuando te necesitemos.

Harry llegó tarde al teatro. Se había pasado horas caminando de un lado a otro de su apartamento, pensando en su error, en la cólera de Hoare y Hillgarth, en la revelación de que, en cierto modo, Tolhurst había sido su espía. «No estoy hecho para eso —pensó—; jamás quise hacerlo.» Si lo enviaran a casa, no lo lamentaría, aunque fuera una vergüenza y un descrédito para él. Se alegraría de no volver a ver a Sandy jamás. Pero no podía quitarse de la cabeza a Gómez, el súbito terror que había visto en los ojos del viejo soldado.

Se dijo que todo aquello no lo iba a llevar a ninguna parte. Consultó el reloj y experimentó un sobresalto al darse cuenta de lo tarde que era. Tras haberse pasado tanto tiempo pensando en Sofía, se dio cuenta de que aquel día apenas había pensado en ella. Se cambió a toda prisa, tomó el abrigo y el sombrero y salió corriendo.

Sofía ya lo estaba esperando cuando él llegó al teatro, una figura diminuta tocada con una boina y enfundada en su viejo abrigo negro, de pie a la sombra de la entrada mientras elegantes parejas subían los peldaños del teatro. No llevaba bolso de mano; puede que no se pudiera permitir el lujo de tenerlo. Al verla tan menuda y vulnerable, el corazón le dio un vuelco en el pecho. Cuando se le acercó, vio que un mendigo, un anciano en una silla de ruedas de fabricación casera, la estaba atosigando.

—Ya le he dado todo lo que puedo —dijo ella.

—Por favor, sólo un poquito más. Para que pueda comer mañana.

Harry se le acercó corriendo.

—Sofía —dijo casi sin resuello—. Siento llegar con retraso. —Ella lo miró con alivio. Harry dio cincuenta céntimos al mendigo y éste se alejó en su silla de ruedas—. Ha habido un... pequeño conflicto en el trabajo. ¿Lleva mucho rato esperando?

—No, pero es que, por el hecho de verme aquí, ese hombre pensaba que tenía dinero.

—Vaya por Dios, ¿qué puedo decir? —Harry la miró sonriendo—. Me alegro de verla.

—Y yo a usted.

—¿Cómo está Enrique?

Sofía volvió a sonreír.

—Casi curado.

—Muy bien. —Harry carraspeó—. ¿Entramos?

Le ofreció tímidamente el brazo y ella lo aceptó. El calor de aquel cuerpo contra el suyo lo reconfortó.

Sofía había hecho un gran esfuerzo. Se había rizado elegantemente las puntas del cabello y se había aplicado polvos en la cara y carmín en los labios. Estaba muy guapa. El público que llenaba el vestíbulo lo integraban burgueses muy bien vestidos, y las mujeres lucían pendientes y collares de perlas. Sofía los estudió con expresión de divertido desprecio.

Harry había conseguido unas localidades situadas hacia el centro de la platea llena a rebosar. Alguien en la embajada había dicho que la vida cultural empezaba a renacer y que quien se lo podía permitir estaba evidentemente deseoso de salir una noche.

Sofía se quitó el abrigo. Debajo lucía un largo vestido blanco de corte impecable que realzaba su piel morena, con un escote más pronunciado de lo que en aquellos momentos se consideraba correcto. Harry apartó rápidamente la mirada. Ella lo miró sonriendo.

—Ah, qué calor hace aquí, ¿cómo lo consiguen?

—Calefacción central.

En el entreacto se fueron a tomar unas copas al bar. Sofía se sentía incómoda entre los apretones de la gente y tosió al primer sorbo de vino.

—¿Se encuentra bien?

Ella rió con una carcajada nerviosa que contrastaba con su habitual confianza.

—Perdón, es que no estoy acostumbrada a tanta gente. Cuando no estoy en casa, estoy en la vaquería. —Sonrió con ironía—. Ahora estoy más acostumbrada a las vacas que a las personas.

Una mujer la miró, enarcando las cejas.

—¿Y qué tal se está allí? —Harry sabía que las callejuelas de Madrid estaban llenas de pequeñas vaquerías, unos lugares muy poco saludables y con muy poco espacio.

—El trabajo es muy duro; pero, por lo menos, me dan leche para la familia.

—Debe de estar hasta el moño.

—Pero nos ayuda a ir tirando. Los hombres del organismo del

Gobierno vienen cada día a llevarse sus cien litros que, una vez bautizados para el racionamiento, se convierten en doscientos.

—Terrible —dijo Harry, meneando la cabeza.

—Es usted un hombre muy extraño —le dijo ella.

—¿Por qué?

—Su interés por mi vida. Una vaquería maloliente dista mucho de aquello a lo que está usted acostumbrado, supongo. —Sofía se inclinó hacia delante—. Fíjese en todas estas personas que hablan de las cosas que han comprado en el mercado negro y de sus problemas con la servidumbre. ¿No son éstas las cosas de que suelen hablar las personas de su clase? —En su rostro se había vuelto a dibujar la leve sonrisa burlona de antes.

—Sí. Pero yo ya estoy harto.

Sonó un timbre y regresaron a la sala. Durante el segundo acto, Harry se volvió un par de veces para mirarla, pero Sofía estaba tan enfrascada en la representación que no le correspondió con una sonrisa como él esperaba. Llegaron al momento en que lady Macbeth camina como en sueños, torturada por el remordimiento del asesinato que ella ha instado a cometer a su marido. «¿Cómo jamás podré lavar mis manos?» Harry experimentó un repentino arrebato de pánico al pensar que quizá sería el culpable de la muerte de Gómez y tendría las manos manchadas de sangre. Emitió un jadeo y se agarró con fuerza a los brazos de la butaca; Sofía se volvió para mirarlo. Al término de la función, sonó el himno nacional a través de los altavoces. Harry y Sofía se pusieron en pie, pero no se unieron a las numerosas personas que levantaron el brazo haciendo el saludo fascista.

Al salir al frío de la calle, Harry volvió a sentirse un extraño, más extraño de lo que jamás se hubiera sentido en muchos meses. Le volvían a zumbar los oídos, el corazón le latía muy rápido y se dio cuenta de que le temblaban las piernas. Suponía que era una reacción tardía a todo lo que había ocurrido aquel día. Mientras se dirigían a la parada del tranvía trató de entablar conversación, consciente de que le temblaba la voz. No tomó a Sofía del brazo; no quería que ésta notara su temblor.

—¿Le ha gustado la obra?

—Sí —contestó Sofía, sonriendo—. No sabía que Shakespeare pudiera ser tan apasionado. Todos los asesinos reciben su justo castigo, ¿verdad?

—Sí.

—No ocurre lo mismo en el mundo real. —Harry no la había oído debidamente y ella tuvo que repetir lo que había dicho.

—Pues no, la verdad.

Llegaron a la parada del tranvía. Ahora Harry temblaba de pies a cabeza y ansiaba desesperadamente apartarse del frío y húmedo aire nocturno. No había ningún tranvía detenido en la parada. Tampoco había gente esperando, lo cual significaba probablemente que un tranvía acababa de marcharse. Necesitaba sentarse. Maldijo su temor; si tenía que experimentarlo, ¿por qué no en el apartamento, cuando estuviera solo?

—¿Le ocurre algo? —oyó que Sofía le preguntaba.

De nada hubiera servido fingir, ahora se notaba todo el rostro empapado de sudor frío.

—No me encuentro demasiado bien. Perdone, es que de vez en cuando me dan estos pequeños ataques, desde que estuve en los combates de Francia. Ya se me pasará, no se preocupe; perdone, es una tontería.

—No es una tontería. —Sofía lo miró, preocupada—. Es algo que les ocurre a los hombres en la guerra, lo vi aquí. Debería coger un taxi, lo acompañaré a su casa. No conviene que espere en medio del frío.

—Ya se me pasará, se lo aseguro. —No soportaba exhibir su debilidad de aquella manera, no lo soportaba en absoluto.

—No, voy a buscar un taxi. —De repente, Sofía había asumido el mando de la situación, como había hecho en su casa—. ¿Puede quedarse aquí un momento mientras yo me acerco a la esquina? He visto unos cuantos taxis esperando.

—Sí, pero...

—Sólo será un minuto. —Ella le rozó el brazo, lo miró sonriendo y se alejó. Harry se apoyó en el frío poste de la parada, inspirando hondo a través de la nariz y espirando por la boca como le habían enseñado a hacer en el hospital. Momentos después, se acercó un taxi.

Sentado en medio del calor del vehículo, enseguida se sintió mejor. Miró a Sofía con una triste sonrisa.

—Menuda manera de terminar la velada, ¿eh? Deje que pague yo el taxi para que la lleve a casa.

—No, quiero asegurarme de que se encuentra bien. Está muy pálido —dijo Sofía, estudiándolo con mirada profesional.

Al llegar a su destino, el taxi los dejó. Harry temía necesitar la ayuda de Sofía para subir la escalera, pero ahora ya se encontraba mucho mejor y subió sin ningún problema. Abrió la puerta y ambos pasaron al salón.

—Siéntese en aquel sofá —le dijo ella—. ¿Tiene un poco de alcohol?

—Hay algo de whisky en aquel aparador.

Ella fue por un vaso a la cocina y le preparó un trago. El whisky le hizo experimentar como una especie de pequeña sacudida. Sofía lo miró sonriendo.

—Bueno, ya le está volviendo el color a la cara. —Encendió el brasero y se sentó en el otro extremo del sofá, mirándolo.

—Beba usted también —le dijo Harry.

—No, gracias. No me gusta demasiado. —Estudió la fotografía de los padres de Harry.

—Son mi madre y mi padre.

—Es una fotografía muy bonita.

—Su madre me enseñó la fotografía de su boda el día que acompañé a Enrique a casa.

—Sí. Ella, papá y tío Ernesto.

—Su tío era sacerdote, ¿verdad?

—Sí, en Cuenca. No hemos sabido nada de él desde que empezó la Guerra Civil. Puede que haya muerto; Cuenca estaba en la zona republicana. ¿Le importa que fume, Harry?

—Claro que no. —Harry tomó el cenicero de la mesita auxiliar y se lo pasó. Observó que la mano le seguía temblando ligeramente.

—¿Fue muy grave? —preguntó Sofía—. La guerra en Francia, quiero decir.

—Sí, una granada estalló justo a mi lado y mató al hombre que estaba conmigo. Me quedé sordo durante algún tiempo y sufría unos tremendos ataques de pánico. Últimamente, me encuentro mucho mejor. Luché contra ellos y pensé que los había derrotado, pero esta noche han vuelto.

—Quizá no se cuida usted lo bastante.

—Me encuentro bien. No me puedo quejar, recibo buenas raciones y vivo en este apartamento tan grande.

—Sí, es bonito. —Sofía miró alrededor—. Pero la atmósfera resulta un poco triste.

—La verdad es que para mí es demasiado grande. Me paseo constantemente de un lado para otro. Pertenecía a un funcionario comunista.

—Aquella gente se daba muy buena vida. —Sofía suspiró.

—A veces, me parece sentir su presencia. —Harry soltó una tímida carcajada.

—Ahora Madrid está lleno de fantasmas.

Todas las luces se apagaron y los sumieron en la más completa oscuridad, salvo por el resplandor del brasero. Ambos soltaron una exclamación y después Sofía explicó:

—Es sólo un corte de electricidad.

—Vaya, hombre, lo que faltaba.

Ambos se echaron a reír.

—Tengo unas velas en la cocina —dijo Harry—. Deme una cerilla para que vea un poco e iré por ellas. ¿A no ser que usted prefiera volver a casa?

—No —contestó Sofía—. Es bueno hablar un rato.

Harry encendió las velas y las colocó en unos platitos. Las velas iluminaron la estancia con una trémula luz amarilla. Allí donde lo iluminaba la luz, Harry observó una vez más que el cabello de la chica no era totalmente negro, sino que tenía unos reflejos castaños. Tenía un rostro muy triste.

—Siempre nos cortan la luz —dijo—. Ya nos hemos acostumbrado.

Harry permaneció en silencio un instante y después dijo:

—He visto aquí más penalidades de las que jamás hubiera imaginado.

—Sí. —Sofía volvió a suspirar—. ¿Recuerda a nuestra beata, la señora Ávila? Ayer vino a vernos. Dice que el cura está preocupado, y teme que no estemos cuidando debidamente a Paco; quiere que lo dejemos ir al orfelinato. El cura no vino personalmente porque nosotros no vamos a la iglesia. Naturalmente, ésta es la verdadera razón de que quieran apartarnos de Paco. Pero no lo van a conseguir. —Su expresión se endureció por un instante—. Enrique pronto podrá volver a trabajar. Puede que haya trabajo para él en la vaquería.

—Yo tengo una amiga, una inglesa, que trabajó durante algún tiempo en uno de esos orfelinatos. Dijo que era un mal sitio. Y se fue.

—Pues yo he oído hablar de niños que se suicidan. Eso es lo que yo temo que ocurra con Paco. Siempre tiene miedo. Apenas habla y sólo lo hace con nosotros.

—¿Hay alguien que pudiera... no sé cómo decirlo... ayudarlo?

Sofía se rió amargamente.

—¿Quién? Sólo estamos nosotros.

—Lo siento.

Sofía se inclinó hacia delante mientras sus grandes ojos brillaban a la luz de las velas.

—No tiene por qué sentirlo. Ha sido muy amable. Se preocupa por los demás. Los forasteros y los ricos de aquí cierran los ojos ante la manera en que vive la gente. Y los que no tienen nada están abatidos y se muestran apáticos. Es bueno conocer a alguien que se preocupa. —Sonrió levemente—. Aunque eso lo entristezca. Es usted un hombre bueno.

Harry pensó en Gómez y en el terror de sus ojos. Denegó con la cabeza.

—No, no lo soy. Quisiera serlo, pero no lo soy. —Se sujetó la cabeza entre las manos, lanzó un profundo suspiro y la miró. La muchacha lo miraba sonriendo. Entonces él alargó la mano y tomó la suya—. La buena es usted —dijo.

Ella no apartó la mano y la mirada de sus ojos se suavizó. Harry se inclinó muy despacio hacia ella y le rozó los labios con los suyos. El vestido de Sofía emitió un leve crujido cuando ésta se inclinó hacia delante para besarlo, un beso profundo y prolongado con un fuerte y apasionante sabor a tabaco. Harry se apartó.

—Perdón —dijo—. Usted está sola en mi apartamento y yo no quería...

Sofía sonrió, denegando con la cabeza.

—No. Me alegro. No me costó demasiado comprender lo que sentía. Y llevo pensando en usted desde que visitó nuestra casa y se sentó en el salón con aquella expresión tan desconcertada, pero con deseo de ayudarnos. —La muchacha bajó la cabeza—. No quería sentir lo que siento, ya bastante complicadas son nuestras vidas. Por eso no llamé al médico al principio. Pobre Enrique —añadió sonriendo—. Ya ve usted lo egoísta que soy.

Harry se inclinó hacia delante y le tomó la mano. Era pequeña y cálida y estaba llena de vida.

—Es usted la persona menos egoísta que he conocido. —Algo en él seguía dudando, no podía creer lo que estaba ocurriendo.

—Harry —dijo ella.

—Pronuncia mi nombre como nadie —dijo él, soltando entre dientes una pequeña carcajada.

—Es más fácil de pronunciar que la manera en que los ingleses dicen David.

—¿El chico de Leeds?

—Sí. Estuvimos juntos algún tiempo. En la guerra hay que aprovechar las oportunidades que se presentan. A lo mejor lo escandalizo. Los católicos dirían que soy una mujer inmoral.

—Eso, nunca. —Harry vaciló, pero después se inclinó hacia ella y la volvió a besar.

31

Barbara había oído decir que, cuando se amaba a una persona y después se la dejaba de amar, a veces el amor se convertía en odio. Sandy le había dicho que tenía el corazón lleno de una sensiblería empalagosa, pero no era verdad. Ahora estaba lleno de hastío.

Tenía que ocultar sus sentimientos. Era miércoles y se había vuelto a reunir con Luis; Agustín regresaría de su permiso en cuestión de tres semanas, el 4 de diciembre. En cuanto lo hiciera, Luis se trasladaría a Cuenca para disponer todo lo necesario. La fecha de la fuga dependería de los horarios de los guardias, aunque lo más seguro es que se pudiera hacer antes de Navidad. Durante el tiempo que faltaba, ella tendría que procurar que Sandy no sospechara nada.

La casa, con sus estancias espaciosas y su mobiliario costoso e impecablemente limpio, le resultaba cada vez más opresiva. A veces, experimentaba el impulso de descolgar los relucientes espejos de las paredes y estrellarlos contra las enceradas tablas del suelo. Mientras iba de acá para allá, recorriendo con creciente nerviosismo las habitaciones o contemplando a través de las ventanas el jardín invernal, empezó a preguntarse si se estaría volviendo un poco loca.

Después de su discusión acerca del orfelinato, Barbara había vuelto a mostrarse extremadamente amable y sumisa. El domingo siguiente a la discusión, Sandy salió de buena mañana en su coche; asuntos de negocios, alegó. Barbara salió a dar un paseo y compró unas rosas de Andalucía en una lujosa floristería. Costaban mucho dinero, pero eran las preferidas de Sandy. Las llevó a la mesa en un jarrón. Sandy tomó una y olió su perfume.

—Muy bonitas —dijo secamente—. ¿Entonces ya se te ha pasado el enfado? —Seguía estando de muy mal humor.

—Las peleas son absurdas —contestó ella muy tranquila.

—Tu carta a sor Inmaculada ha provocado cierta perplejidad. Una o dos personas me han preguntado si no estaré dando cobijo a una subversiva.

—Mira, Sandy, no te quiero causar problemas con tus socios en los negocios. ¿Por qué no me ofrezco como voluntaria en otro sitio, quizás en algún hospital militar?

Sandy soltó un gruñido.

—Casi todos están dirigidos por la Falange. No quiero que ahora te pelees con ellos.

—Basta con que no vea maltratar a los niños, eso es todo.

La miró con sus ojos sombríos y gélidos.

—Casi todos los niños son maltratados. Así es la vida. A no ser que tengas suerte, como mi hermano. Tú fuiste maltratada y yo también.

—Pero no de esta manera.

—El maltrato es siempre el mismo. —Sandy se encogió de hombros—. Hablaré con Sebastián acerca del hospital militar.

—Gracias. —Barbara procuró fingir agradecimiento. Sandy soltó un gruñido y se inclinó sobre su plato.

No había vuelto a mantener relaciones sexuales con ella desde la pelea. La tarde siguiente, Barbara bajó a la cocina para hablar con Pilar y, desde la escalera, la oyó reírse. Sandy estaba allí apoyado en la mesa, fumando un cigarrillo con una sonrisa lasciva en los labios. Pilar lavaba los platos en el fregadero. Al ver a Barbara, la chica se puso colorada como un tomate y bajó la cabeza.

—Le traigo la lista de la compra, Pilar —dijo Barbara fríamente—. Se la dejo aquí encima de la mesa.

Más tarde no dijo nada, pero él sí lo hizo. Estaban sentados en el salón, cuando él se reclinó en su asiento acunando en sus manos un vaso de whisky con una sonrisa en los labios.

—Buena chica, Pilar. Aunque a veces es un poco descarada.

Barbara siguió enhebrando una aguja en silencio. «Lo hace para castigarme —pensó—, como si ahora me importara.»

—Hay que ver cómo os gusta coquetear con las criadas —dijo alegremente—. Supongo que es una fantasía, una cosa de las escuelas privadas.

—Si tú supieras cuáles son mis fantasías —dijo él—, no te gustarían. —Algo en su tono de voz indujo a Barbara a mirarlo bruscamente. Él le dirigió una fría mirada y tomó otro trago de whisky.

—Tengo que ir a buscar un patrón que mamá me ha enviado —dijo Barbara.

Acto seguido, abandonó la estancia y se quedó en el pasillo respirando afanosamente. A veces, necesitaba apartarse de él. Y pensaba: «Me paso una hora sentada con él y después salgo unos cuantos minutos. De esta manera, me acerco una hora más al momento en que me iré para siempre.»

Subió al dormitorio. No necesitaba el patrón para nada, pero pensó que sería mejor que lo recogiera. Ya allí, abrió el cajón de su escritorio y acarició su libreta de ahorro. Se alegraba de que el escritorio tuviera una buena cerradura; siempre se guardaba la llave en el bolsillo.

Respiró hondo una vez más. Tendría que bajar para intentar suavizar la situación. Le podría preguntar qué tal iban las cosas con Harry; si Harry se iba a incorporar al proyecto, fuera el que fuera. Pero, en el caso de que él insistiera en seguir utilizando a Pilar para burlarse de ella, dejaría que lo hiciera. Fingiría estar dolida y, de esta manera, tendría otra excusa para no hacer el amor cuando él se le volviera a acercar.

Para su alivio, aquella noche Sandy no volvió a mencionar a Pilar. Cuando ella le preguntó por Harry, le contestó que lo había vuelto a invitar a cenar el jueves de la otra semana. Después se levantó, diciendo que tenía que clasificar unos papeles en su estudio. Barbara lanzó un suspiro de alivio cuando la puerta se cerró a su espalda.

Poco después, oyó sonar el teléfono un par de veces y enmudecer de golpe. Sandy debía de haber contestado a través del supletorio de su estudio. Se había puesto ligeramente nerviosa; al poco rato, se volvió a sobresaltar al oír el timbre de la puerta. «Quién demonios será —pensó—, ya es muy tarde.» Dejó la labor.

Oyó que Pilar subía de la cocina y, después, el repiqueteo de sus tacones sobre el mosaico del suelo. Al cabo de un minuto, la chica llamó con los nudillos y entró en el salón. Por muy poco que le importara lo que Sandy pudiera hacer en aquellos momentos, Barbara experimentó una punzada de cólera.

—¿Quién es? —preguntó.

Pilar no quería mirarla a la cara.

—Disculpe, señora, es un hombre que quiere ver al señor Forsyth. Parece un poco... —vaciló— extranjero. Ya sé que al señor Forsyth no le gusta que lo molesten en su estudio.

—Voy a ver quién es. —Barbara se levantó y pasó por delante de la chica. Una ráfaga de aire la azotó desde el recibidor; Pilar había dejado la puerta de la entrada abierta de par en par. Un anciano menudo con un abrigo manchado y un sombrero viejo y flexible esperaba en el umbral. Llevaba unas gafas rotas sujetas sobre el caballete de la nariz con esparadrapo. Se quitó el sombrero.

—Perdón, señora, ¿está el señor Forsyth en casa?

Hablaba español muy despacio y con gran esfuerzo, con un marcado acento francés. Barbara le contestó en este idioma.

—Sí. ¿En qué puedo servirlo?

En el rostro del anciano se dibujaron unas arrugas de alivio.

—Ah, habla usted francés. Mi español es muy deficiente. Perdone que la moleste. Me llamo Blanc, Henri Blanc, y tengo que entregarle una cosa al señor Forsyth.

Rebuscó en el interior de su abrigo y sacó una bolsita de lona que emitió un sonido metálico. Barbara lo miró perpleja.

—Disculpe —dijo el hombre—. Tengo que explicarme. Soy uno de los refugiados que el señor Forsyth ha estado atendiendo.

—Ah, comprendo. —Eso explicaba la ropa raída y el acento francés. Era uno de los judíos. Sujetó la puerta para que no se cerrara—. Pase, por favor.

El anciano meneó la cabeza.

—No, no; se lo ruego. No quiero molestar a estas horas. Es que hoy me han dicho que ya tengo mi permiso de traslado a Lisboa. —Sonrió, sin poder disimular su alegría—. Me voy con mi familia mañana a primera hora. —Volvió a ofrecerle el paquete—. Acéptelo, por favor. Dígale que es de máxima calidad, tal como le dije. Llevan en nuestra familia mucho tiempo, pero merece la pena para poder trasladarnos a Lisboa.

—Muy bien. —Barbara tomó el paquete—. Tiene que haber caminado mucho... ¿seguro que no quiere entrar un minuto? —Estudió sus zapatos, los tacones estaban casi totalmente gastados; probablemente, había caminado con ellos desde Francia.

—No, gracias. Tengo que regresar —contestó el hombre, sonriendo—. Pero estaba obligado a cumplir mi promesa. Dele las gracias al señor Forsyth de mi parte. Hemos estado muy preocupados; dicen que los alemanes están enviando a los refugiados republicanos desde Francia y tenemos miedo de que nos pidan a nosotros a cambio. Pero ahora estaremos a salvo gracias a su marido. —Alargó la mano para estrechar la suya, se volvió a poner el sombrero, dio media vuelta y se alejó renqueando ligeramente por el camino particular.

Barbara cerró la puerta. Vio una sombra en lo alto de la escalera del sótano y se dio cuenta de que Pilar había estado escuchando. ¿Sería eso lo que tendría que aguantar a partir de ahora?

—Pilar —llamó, levantando la voz—, ¿me puede preparar una taza de chocolate, por favor?

La sombra pegó un brinco y la chica contestó.

—Sí, señora.

Sus pisadas bajaron rápidamente los peldaños de la escalera de la cocina. Barbara se quedó en el vestíbulo, sopesando la bolsa que sostenía en las manos. No eran monedas, sino algo más liviano. Regresó al salón y tiró de la cinta que cerraba la bolsa. Vació el contenido en la palma de su mano. Había sortijas y collares, un par de broches y algunos objetos de extraña forma que parecían tener una función religiosa. Todos eran de oro, de claro y reluciente oro. Frunció el entrecejo, perpleja.

Pensó que sería mejor que le entregara la bolsa a Sandy. Subió lentamente los peldaños. La calefacción central silbaba y gorgoteaba en el silencioso pasillo. Una luz se filtraba por debajo de la puerta del estudio. Lo oyó hablar, aún debía de estar al teléfono. Estaba a punto de llamar con los nudillos, pero algo en el tono de su voz le impidió hacerlo. Le recordaba su voz de antes, cuando le había mencionado sus fantasías.

—Ya tendría que haber cantado. Lleváis con él todo el día. ¿Qué le habéis hecho? —Una pausa y después de nuevo la voz de Sandy—. Estos viejos soldados de Marruecos aguantan mucho. ¿Sigue diciendo que Gómez es su verdadero apellido? Bueno, supongo que tiene su lógica, han tenido que crear documentación falsa para un nombre falso, y eso es territorio de la Gestapo. —Más silencio, un par de gruñidos en respuesta a lo que el hombre del otro extremo de la línea estaba diciendo y de nuevo la voz de Sandy, cortante e irritada—: Lo dejo en vuestras expertas manos. —Otra pausa antes de añadir—: Hay sitios de sobra por Santa María. Oye, te tengo que dejar. Tengo aquí los papeles de Brett. No, él confía en mí. Sí. Adiós. —Se oyó un clic cuando colgó el aparato.

Las frases resonaban en la cabeza de Barbara. «¿Qué le habéis hecho?» «Territorio de la Gestapo.» Y, en cierto modo, Harry estaba implicado en todo aquello. Se quedó allí con el corazón latiéndole con fuerza en el pecho. Oyó que Sandy abría un cajón de su escritorio y después un gruñido. Tragó saliva y se apartó de la puerta, apretando la bolsa de lona en su mano. Se la daría más tarde.

En el salón, Pilar había dejado la taza de chocolate encima de la mesa de costura. Se sentó pesadamente con la bolsa en el regazo. Pero ¿en qué demonios andaría Sandy metido? Recordó las burlas sobre sus fantasías. «Sería capaz de cualquier cosa —pensó—; jamás he llegado a conocerlo realmente.» Volvió a tragar saliva y depositó la bolsa encima de la mesa de costura. La contempló en silencio con el cuerpo en tensión y el oído atento a sus pisadas al otro lado de la puerta.

32

Sofía y Harry paseaban muy despacio entre la muchedumbre del Rastro. Era domingo, un día frío y nublado, y el principal mercadillo callejero de Madrid estaba lleno a rebosar de gente. Los destartalados tenderetes de madera, con sus toldos, se derramaban por las angostas callejuelas que rodeaban la plaza de Cascorro, atestados de toda suerte de baratijas... vulgares adornos, piezas de maquinaria rotas, canarios en jaulas de madera. Harry habría deseado tomar a Sofía de la mano, pero tal cosa estaba prohibida por inmoral; a no ser que la pareja estuviera casada. Varias parejas de guardias permanecían en los portales, vigilando a la gente con sus miradas frías y duras.

Había transcurrido exactamente una semana desde que ambos hicieran el amor en el apartamento de Harry. Desde entonces, se las habían arreglado para verse casi a diario. Harry disponía de mucho tiempo; no había recibido más instrucciones de los espías. Sofía acudía a su apartamento por la noche y se iba muy pronto, porque empezaba a trabajar muy temprano en la vaquería.

Él, por su parte, se alegraba de estar enamorado por primera vez, de que su mundo tranquilo y ordenado se hubiera trastocado de arriba abajo. Cuando recibió la última carta de Will sobre los problemas que éste tenía para conseguir una asistenta para su casa de campo y escolarizar a los niños, se sintió tremendamente alejado del mundo de su primo; pero, al mismo tiempo, experimentó un cálido torrente de amor hacia él.

Sin embargo, había secretos entre ellos. Harry no deseaba otra cosa que poder hablarle a Sofía de su trabajo como espía y de lo mucho que lo odiaba, o del amigo de la embajada que había resultado ser su vigilante. Pero no podía y no debía. Sofía tampoco había dicho nada a su familia acerca de sus relaciones. Decía que no era el momento oportuno. Cuando a primera hora de la noche dejaba a su madre y a Paco al cuidado de Enrique, le decía a éste que iba a ver a una de las chicas de la vaquería. No le importaba mentir a su hermano. Harry pensaba que quizá familias tan unidas como la de Sofía sólo podían soportar aquella estrecha intimidad a base de secretos.

Aquél era el día en que Sofía libraba en la vaquería. Se las había arreglado para que Enrique se quedara en casa al cuidado de su madre y de Paco.

Habían hecho el amor en el apartamento de Harry y después ella había sugerido la visita al Rastro. Mientras se abrían paso entre la multitud, Harry le dijo en voz baja:

—Nunca hueles a leche. ¿Por qué no hueles a leche?

Ella se echó a reír.

—¿Y a qué huelo?

—Simplemente, a ti. A limpio.

—Cuando entré a trabajar allí, me prometí a mí misma no acabar oliendo como los demás. Allí hay una ducha más fría que el hielo con un suelo de hormigón y un desagüe roto de metal en el que tienes que procurar no caer, pero yo me ducho todos los días.

—Nunca permitirás que nadie te doblegue, ¿verdad?

—No —contestó ella sonriendo—. Eso espero.

Prosiguieron su paseo entre la gente, riéndose de algunos de los objetos extravagantes que había a la venta, hasta llegar a la parte del mercado donde se vendían artículos de alimentación. Casi todos los tenderetes estaban prácticamente vacíos, sólo algunas verduras secas aquí y allá. En un tenderete de carne vendían despojos cuyo olor Harry pudo percibir a dos metros de distancia, pero aun así había cola para comprar. Sofía se percató de su mueca de desagrado.

—Ahora la gente lo compra todo —dijo—. Las raciones no serían suficientes ni para dar de comer a un perro.

—Lo sé.

—Todo el mundo está desesperado. Por eso Enrique aceptó aquel trabajo, ¿sabes? En el fondo es muy bueno; no habría aceptado ser espía.

—No sé si el hecho de ser un mal espía te convierte en un hombre mejor.

—Puede que sí. Las personas que saben engañar a los demás no pueden ser muy buenas, ¿no crees? Él es más feliz trabajando como barrendero.

—¿Cómo tiene la pierna?

—Muy bien. Se sigue cansando por las noches, pero mejorará. La señora Ávila está decepcionada. Ahora que hay más ingresos en la familia, ya no tiene excusa para acudir al cura y decirle que no nos podemos permitir atender a Paco.

Harry la miró.

—¿Cómo era tu tío el cura? —preguntó.

Sofía sonrió con tristeza.

—Mi madre y mi padre se trasladaron de Tarancón a Madrid para encontrar trabajo cuando yo era pequeña, y tío Ernesto se fue a una parroquia de Cuenca. Aunque mis padres eran republicanos, se mantenían en contacto con él porque la familia lo es todo en España. Cada verano de mi infancia íbamos a pasar unos días con tío Ernesto. Recuerdo lo mucho que me llamaba la atención su sotana. —Sofía se rió—. Solía preguntarle a mi madre por qué tío Ernesto llevaba vestido. Pero era muy bueno. Me permitía limpiar los candeleros de la iglesia. Dejaba marcadas las huellas de los dedos en ellos, y él decía que no importaba. Después debía de dejar que les sacara brillo alguna de sus beatas. —Miró a Harry—. Desde que terminó la guerra, mamá lleva diciendo que alguno de nosotros tendría que ir a Cuenca para averiguar si está vivo. Pero, aunque nos lo pudiéramos permitir, no lo considero una buena idea. He oído contar historias terribles acerca de lo que les ocurrió a los curas y a las monjas de allí.

—Lo siento.

Aprovechando el gentío que los rodeaba, ella le tomó la mano un momento.

—Por lo menos, yo tenía una familia que me cuidaba. No me enviaron a un colegio como a ti.

La calle se ensanchaba ante ambos. Allí reinaba un especial ajetreo y Harry vio un número insólito de personas elegantemente vestidas alrededor de un tenderete, examinando atentamente la mercancía con el entrecejo fruncido. Una pareja de la Guardia Civil vigilaba desde un portal.

—¿Qué es lo que pasa aquí? —preguntó Harry.

—Aquí es donde acaban todos los objetos que sacaron de las casas de los ricos en 1936 —contestó Sofía—. Las personas que se los llevaron necesitaban el dinero para comprar comida y por eso ahora los venden a los propietarios de los tenderetes. Los madrileños ricos vienen aquí, a ver si encuentran los bienes heredados de sus familias.

Pasaron por delante de los tenderetes. Había jarrones y vajillas, figuras de porcelana e incluso un viejo gramófono con brazo de plata. Harry leyó la inscripción que figuraba en él: «A don Juan Ramírez Dávila, de sus compañeros del Banco de Santander, 12-07-1919.» Una anciana rebuscaba entre un montón de broches y collares de perlas.

—Jamás lo encontraremos, Dolores —murmuró su marido en tono cansado—. Tienes que olvidarlo.

Harry tomó una figura de mujer vestida al estilo dieciochesco, con la nariz desportillada.

—Algunas de estas cosas debieron de significar mucho para alguien en otros tiempos.

—Pero se compraron con dinero robado a la gente —replicó Sofía con aspereza.

Pasaron por delante de una mesa con un montón de fotografías encima. La gente se apretujaba alrededor y rebuscaba entre las fotografías con semblante triste y afligido, incluso desesperado.

—¿Y todo eso de dónde viene? —preguntó Harry.

—A las fotografías les quitaban los marcos cuando las vendían. La gente viene aquí en busca de fotografías de sus familiares.

Algunas de las imágenes eran recientes y otras tenían medio siglo de antigüedad. Fotografías de bodas, retratos familiares en blanco y negro o sepia. Un joven vestido de militar, sonriendo a la cámara; una pareja joven sentada delante de una taberna con las manos entrelazadas. Harry comprendió que muchas de aquellas personas ya debían de haber muerto. No era de extrañar que aquella gente buscara con tal ansia. Puede que allí encontraran la única imagen que quedaba de un hijo o un hermano perdido.

—Cuántos han muerto —dijo en voz baja—. Cuántos.

Sofía se inclinó hacia él.

—Harry, ¿conoces a aquel hombre de allí? Nos está mirando.

Harry se volvió y contuvo bruscamente la respiración. El general Maestre se encontraba ante el tenderete de los objetos de porcelana, con su mujer y su hija Milagros. Vestía de paisano, un abrigo grueso y un sombrero de paño. Sin el uniforme, sus rasgos curtidos por la intemperie parecían duros y más viejos. La señora Maestre examinaba un candelabro de plata, pero el general seguía mirando a Harry con expresión ceñuda. Milagros también lo miraba con unos ojos cuya infinita tristeza se extendía a todos los rasgos de su rostro mofletudo. Los ojos de Harry se cruzaron con los suyos y entonces ella se ruborizó y bajó la cabeza. Harry saludó con un movimiento de la cabeza al general. Éste enarcó levemente las cejas antes de inclinar bruscamente la suya en respuesta al saludo.

—Es un alto cargo del Gobierno, el general Maestre —murmuró Harry.

—¿Y de qué lo conoces? —preguntó Sofía con un tono de voz repentinamente cortante, mirándolo con los ojos muy abiertos.

—Tuve que hacer una traducción para él. Es una situación muy violenta, porque una vez salí con su hija por obligación. Ven, será mejor que nos vayamos.

Pero había tanta gente alrededor del tenderete de las fotografías que tuvieron que salir por el otro lado, en dirección al lugar donde se encontraba Maestre. El general se adelantó, le cortó el paso a Harry y lo saludó sin sonreír.

—Señor Brett, buenos días. Milagros se preguntaba si había desaparecido usted de la faz de la tierra.

—Lo lamento, mi general, pero he estado tan ocupado que...

Maestre miró a Sofía y ésta le correspondió con una fría mirada de enojo.

—Milagros esperaba que usted la volviera a llamar —prosiguió diciendo el general—. Aunque ahora ya lo ha dejado correr. —Se volvió para mirar a su familia—. A mi mujer le gusta venir aquí, a ver si encuentra alguna parte de los tesoros robados a nuestra familia. Pero yo le digo que acabará pillando algo en medio de todas estas putas de los barrios bajos.

Enarcó las cejas mirando a Sofía y después sus ojos recorrieron de arriba abajo su viejo abrigo negro, tras lo cual dio media vuelta para reunirse de nuevo con su mujer y con Milagros, que fingía estar absorta en la contemplación de una pastorcita de porcelana de Dresde. Sofía lo siguió con la mirada, respirando afanosamente con los puños apretados. Harry le rozó el hombro.

—Sofía, perdona...

Ella le apartó la mano y se volvió de cara a la gente. La aglomeración le impedía caminar más rápido, por lo que sólo podía arrastrar los pies y Harry le dio inmediatamente alcance.

—Sofía, Sofía, perdona. —Suavemente la obligó a volver el rostro para mirarlo—. Es un cerdo, un bruto, por haberte insultado de esta manera.

Para su asombro, ella soltó una carcajada áspera y amarga:

—¿Tú crees que las personas como yo no estamos acostumbradas a los insultos de las personas como él? ¿Crees que me importa lo que diga este viejo de mierda?

—¿Entonces?

Sofía meneó la cabeza.

—Bueno, es que tú no lo entiendes; hablamos de estas cosas pero tú no lo entiendes.

Harry buscó sus manos y las tomó en las suyas. La gente los miraba, pero a él le daba igual.

—Quiero entenderlo.

Sofía respiró hondo y se zafó de su presa.

—Será mejor que sigamos caminando, estamos ofendiendo la moralidad pública.

—De acuerdo. —Se situó a su lado y Sofía levantó los ojos hacia él.

—He oído hablar de este hombre. El general Maestre. El suyo era uno de los nombres más temidos durante el asedio. Dicen que en un pueblo mandó reunir en la plaza principal a todas las esposas de los concejales socialistas y ordenó a los moros atarlas y cortarles los pechos en presencia de sus maridos. Sé que hubo mucha propaganda falsa, pero yo atendí como enfermera a un hombre de aquel pueblo y me dijo que era verdad. Y cuando tomaron Madrid el año pasado, Maestre tuvo un destacado papel en la tarea de acorralar a los subversivos. No sólo a los comunistas, sino también a gente que sólo quería vivir en paz y disfrutar de una parte de su país. —Harry vio que estaba llorando, y que las lágrimas le rodaban por las mejillas—. La limpieza, la llamaban. Noche tras noche, oías los disparos procedentes del cementerio del este. Y a veces todavía se oyen. Tomaron esta ciudad como si fueran un ejército de ocupación, y así es como la siguen ocupando. Y la Falange presumiendo y buscando camorra por toda nuestra ciudad...

Habían llegado a una zona más tranquila. Sofía se detuvo de golpe, respiró hondo y se enjugó el rostro con un pañuelo. Harry se la quedó mirando. No sabía qué decirle. Ella le tocó el brazo.

—Sé que tratas de entenderlo —le dijo—. Pero después te veo hablando con aquel personaje. Has venido a visitar este... infierno... desde otro mundo, Harry. Te quedarás algún tiempo aquí y después te irás. Llévame a tu apartamento, Harry, hagamos el amor. Al menos, podemos hacer el amor. Ahora ya no quiero seguir hablando.

Siguieron caminando en silencio hasta llegar a la plaza de Cascorro, donde empezaba el mercado. Mientras se abrían paso para cruzar la plaza, Harry pensó: «¿Y si pudiera sacarla de aquí y llevármela a Inglaterra?» Pero ¿cómo? Ella jamás dejaría a su madre, a Enrique y a Paco; ¿y cómo iba a sacarlos también a ellos? Sofía caminaba delante de él, señalando el camino a través de la muchedumbre, fuerte e indómita, pero menuda y vulnerable en aquella ciudad gobernada por los generales que Hoare y Hillgarth manejaban a su antojo por medio de los Caballeros de San Jorge.

33

En Tierra Muerta el tiempo había empeorado. Una mañana el campo amaneció enteramente cubierto de nieve, incluso los tejados inclinados de las atalayas. La nieve era tan abundante en el camino de montaña que conducía a la cantera que hasta penetraba a través de las grietas de las viejas botas que calzaban los prisioneros. Bernie recordó a su madre cuando él era chico, diciéndole que procurara no mojarse nunca los pies en invierno, pues era la manera más segura de pillar un resfriado. Se rió en voz alta y Pablo se volvió para mirarlo con extrañeza.

Los hombres se detuvieron a hacer un breve descanso en el pliegue de las colinas desde el cual, si las condiciones eran apropiadas, se podía divisar Cuenca a lo lejos. Aquel día no se podía ver nada, sólo un atisbo del pardo peñasco de la garganta que se abría entre las lomas blancas y el cielo frío y lechoso.

—¡Vamos, cabrones holgazanes! —gritó el guardia.

Los hombres se levantaron rápidamente para que la circulación fuera restablecida y volvieron a colocarse en fila.

Vicente se estaba muriendo. Las autoridades habían visto ya suficientes muertes para saber cuándo alguien estaba a punto de morir, motivo por el cual habían cejado en su empeño de intentar hacerle trabajar. Los últimos dos días se los había pasado tumbado en su jergón de la barraca, entrando y saliendo de la conciencia. Siempre que se despertaba, pedía agua y decía que le ardían la cabeza y la garganta.

Aquella noche un fuerte viento empezó a soplar desde el oeste, llevando consigo una intensa corriente de aire cálido que fundió la nieve. A la mañana siguiente, seguía lloviendo a cántaros y el viento empujaba la lluvia a través del patio en cortinas verticales. A los hombres se les comunicó que aquel día no habría cuadrillas de trabajo. «A los guar-días no les gusta salir en días como éste», pensó Bernie. La tormenta no cesaba y los hombres se quedaron en sus barracas, jugando a las cartas, cosiendo o leyendo versículos católicos o ejemplares del *Arriba*, que era lo único que se les permitía leer.

Bernie sabía que el grupo comunista había celebrado una reunión dos días atrás para discutir su situación. Desde entonces lo evitaban, incluso Pablo; pero no le habían comunicado su decisión. Bernie adivinaba que estaban esperando a que muriera Vicente para concederle un breve período de indulgencia.

El abogado se pasó casi toda la mañana durmiendo, se despertó hacia mediodía. Bernie estaba tumbado en su jergón, pero se incorporó y se inclinó hacia él. Ahora Vicente estaba muy delgado y tenía los ojos profundamente hundidos en el interior de unas cuencas oscuras.

—Agua —graznó.

—Voy por ella, espera un momento.

Bernie se puso su viejo y remendado gabán del ejército y salió a la lluvia del exterior, haciendo una mueca cuando los proyectiles de aguanieve le azotaron el rostro. Las barracas no disponían de agua corriente, y él había limpiado cuidadosamente su cubo de mear y lo había dejado fuera toda la noche para que se llenara de agua de lluvia. Lo trasladó al interior de la barraca, recogió un poco de agua en un recipiente de hojalata y después levantó cuidadosamente la cabeza del abogado para darle de beber. Eulalio, tumbado en el catre del otro lado, soltó una carcajada gutural.

—Ay, inglés, ¿es que estás dando tus orines de beber al pobre hombre?

Vicente volvió a reclinarse; hasta el esfuerzo de beber lo dejaba agotado.

—Gracias.

—¿Cómo estás?

—Me duele mucho. Ojalá terminara todo de una vez. No hago más que pensar: «Se acabó la cantera, se acabaron las funciones dominicales.» Estoy muy cansado. Preparado para el silencio infinito.

Bernie no contestó. Vicente sonrió con gesto cansado.

—Precisamente ahora soñaba con el primer día que llegamos aquí. ¿Recuerdas aquel camión? ¿Los brincos que pegaba?

—Sí.

Tras su captura, Bernie se había pasado muchos meses en la prisión de San Pedro de Cardeña, donde lo habían sometido a las primeras pruebas psiquiátricas. Para entonces, casi todos los prisioneros ingleses habían sido repatriados a través de vías diplomáticas, menos él. Después, a finales de 1937, lo habían trasladado junto con un grupo de prisioneros españoles y extranjeros considerados políticamente peligrosos al campo de Tierra Muerta. Bernie se preguntaba si su condición de miembro del partido habría sido la causa de que la embajada no hubiera solicitado su puesta en libertad; seguro que su madre habría intentado sacarlo de allí al enterarse de que había sido hecho prisionero.

Los trasladaron a Tierra Muerta en unos viejos camiones del ejército donde Vicente fue esposado a su lado en el banco. Éste le preguntó a Bernie de dónde era y muy pronto ambos se enzarzaron en una discusión acerca del comunismo. A Bernie le gustaba el ácido sentido del humor de Vicente y siempre había sentido debilidad por los burgueses intelectuales.

A los pocos días de su llegada a Tierra Muerta, Vicente fue en su busca. El abogado había sido adscrito al despacho para ayudar a la administración a aligerar la montaña de papeles relacionada con el traslado de prisioneros al nuevo campo. Bernie estaba sentado en un banco del patio. Vicente se sentó a su lado y bajó la voz.

—¿Recuerdas que me dijiste que los demás prisioneros ingleses se habían ido a casa y que tú pensabas que tu embajada no quería tomarse ninguna molestia contigo porque eras comunista?

—Sí.

—Pues ése no es el motivo. Hoy he echado un vistazo a tu expediente. Los ingleses creen que has muerto.

Bernie lo miró asombrado.

—¿Cómo?

—Cuando te capturaron en el Jarama, ¿qué ocurrió exactamente?

Bernie arrugó la frente.

—Me pasé un rato inconsciente. Y después una patrulla fascista se hizo cargo de mí.

—¿Te preguntaron lo de siempre? ¿Nombre, nacionalidad, filiación política?

—Sí, el sargento que me capturó tomó unas cuantas notas. Era un cabrón. Estaba a punto de pegarme un tiro, pero su cabo lo convenció de que no lo hiciera porque yo era extranjero y podría haber problemas.

Vicente asintió lentamente con la cabeza.

—Creo que fue más cabrón de lo que tú te imaginas. Las embajadas de los prisioneros de guerra siempre tenían que ser informadas de su captura. Pero, según tu expediente, te apuntaron como español. Un tribunal militar te condenó a veinticinco años de prisión bajo un nombre español, junto con todo un grupo de prisioneros. Las autoridades no descubrieron el error hasta más tarde y entonces decidieron dejar las cosas como estaban.

La mirada de Bernie se perdió en la distancia.

—¿Entonces mis padres me creen muerto?

—Debieron de darte por desaparecido y presuntamente muerto los de tu propio bando. Supongo que el sargento que te capturó facilitó detalles falsos, precisamente para que tu embajada no fuera informada de que habías sido capturado. Con toda la mala intención.

—¿Y por qué jamás hubo una rectificación?

Vicente extendió las manos.

—Probablemente, por simple inercia burocrática. Cuanto más tardaran en notificarlo, más probable sería que tu embajada armara un escándalo. Sospecho que te convertiste en un estorbo, una anomalía. Y por eso te han enterrado aquí.

—¿Y si ahora dijera algo?

Vicente meneó la cabeza.

—No serviría de nada. —Lo miró con la cara muy seria—. Puede que te pegaran un tiro para eliminar la anomalía. Aquí no tenemos ningún derecho, no somos nada.

Vicente se pasó el resto del día durmiendo, despertando de vez en cuando y pidiendo agua. Al anochecer, el padre Eduardo entró en la barraca. Bernie lo vio cruzar el patio en medio del viento y la lluvia, envuelto en una gruesa capa negra. Entró chorreando agua sobre las tablas desnudas.

El padre Jaime se habría acercado directamente al lecho del enfermo sin prestar atención a los demás, pero el padre Eduardo siempre trataba de establecer contacto con los prisioneros. Miró alrededor con una sonrisa nerviosa en los labios.

—Vaya, menuda tormenta —dijo.

Algunos hombres se lo quedaron mirando fríamente; otros volvieron a su lectura o a su costura. A continuación, el cura se dirigió al jergón de Vicente. Bernie se levantó y le impidió el paso.

—Él no quiere verlo, padre —dijo en tono pausado.

—Tengo que hablar con él. Es mi deber. —El sacerdote se inclinó un poco más—. Mira, Piper, el padre Jaime quería venir, pero yo le he dicho que consideraba que este hombre me correspondía a mí. ¿Prefieres que lo vaya a buscar? No quisiera hacerlo; pero, si me impides el paso, tendré que comunicárselo. Él es el sacerdote de mayor antigüedad.

Bernie se apartó a un lado sin decir nada. Se preguntó si habría sido mejor que estuviera allí el padre Jaime; a Vicente tal vez le hubiera resultado más fácil oponer resistencia a aquel hombre tan brutal.

El ruido había despertado al abogado. Éste levantó la vista mientras el sacerdote se inclinaba hacia él. Unas gotas de agua cayeron desde la capa del cura sobre la sábana de arpillera.

—¿Eso es agua bendita, padre?

—¿Cómo estás?

—No muerto todavía. Bernardo, amigo mío, ¿me quieres dar un poco más de agua?

Bernie introdujo el recipiente en el cubo y se lo pasó a Vicente. Éste bebió con avidez. El sacerdote contempló con desagrado el cubo de los meados.

—Hijo, estás muy enfermo —dijo—. Debes confesar tus pecados.

Se hizo un silencio absoluto en la barraca. Todos los prisioneros miraban y escuchaban con sus rostros convertidos en círculos borrosos de color blanco bajo la pálida luz de las velas. Todo el mundo sabía que Vicente aborrecía a los curas, sabía que se acercaba aquel momento.

—No. —Vicente consiguió incorporarse un poco. La luz brilló en la barba grisácea de dos días de sus mejillas y en sus ojos cansados y enfurecidos—. No.

—Si mueres sin confesión, tu alma irá derecha al infierno. —El padre Eduardo estaba nervioso y sus dedos retorcían un botón de su sotana. Sus gafas reflejaban la luz de la vela y convertían sus tristes ojos en dos pequeñas hogueras.

Vicente se pasó la lengua por los labios resecos.

—No hay infierno —dijo entre jadeos—. Sólo... silencio. —Se volvió a reclinar, agotado por el esfuerzo.

El padre Eduardo lanzó un suspiro y dio media vuelta. Inclinándose hacia Bernie, le habló en voz baja. Emanaba de él un leve perfume a incienso y óleo sagrado.

—Creo que a este hombre le quedan tan sólo uno o dos días. Volveré mañana. Pero, dime, ¿este cubo de los orines es lo único que tienes para darle de beber?

—Lo he limpiado.

—Aun así, tener que utilizar eso... ¿Y de dónde sacas el agua?

—Es agua de lluvia.

—La lluvia no durará eternamente. Oye, tengo un grifo en la iglesia y también un cubo. Ven mañana y te daré un poco de agua.

—No se va a ganar su confianza de esta manera.

—¡No quiero verlo sufrir más de lo debido! —replicó el padre Eduardo, súbitamente enojado—. Vengas o no vengas, como quieras; pero hay agua, si quieres.

Dio media vuelta y abandonó a grandes zancadas la barraca para regresar a la tormenta del exterior. Bernie se volvió de nuevo hacia Vicente.

—Se ha ido.

El abogado sonrió amargamente.

—He sido fuerte, ¿verdad, Bernardo?

—Sí. Sí lo has sido. Perdona que no se lo haya podido impedir.

—Has contribuido a distraerlo. Sé que sólo tengo la nada por delante. Y lo acepto. —Vicente emitió un jadeo entrecortado—. Intentaba reunir suficientes gargajos para escupirle. Como vuelva, lo haré.

Aquella noche el viento viró al este y volvió a nevar. A la mañana siguiente, hacía un frío espantoso. El viento había amainado, la nieve formaba una espesa capa, los ruidos del campo estaban amortiguados y los pies de los hombres hacían crujir la nieve mientras éstos se colocaban en fila para el acto de pasar lista. A Aranda no le gustaba el frío; se paseaba por allí con un pasamontañas que contrastaba poderosamente con el inmaculado uniforme que vestía.

Estaban a domingo y no había ninguna cuadrilla de trabajo. Después del acto de pasar lista, a algunos prisioneros les encomendaron la tarea de quitar la nieve del patio y amontonarla contra las barracas. Vicente se había despertado con una sed ardiente. Bernie había dejado el cubo fuera antes de irse a dormir y ahora estaba lleno de nieve. Lo miró. Tardaría siglos en fundirse en la gélida barraca y, cuando lo hiciera, sólo habría una cuarta parte de agua en el cubo. Permaneció un momento temblando en la gélida mañana; las viejas heridas del hombro y el muslo le dolían intensamente. Miró hacia la barraca que albergaba la iglesia, con una cruz pintada en la parte lateral. Dudó y echó a andar hacia ella.

Aranda permanecía de pie a la entrada de su barraca, contemplando la actuación de la cuadrilla quitanieves. Miró a Bernie, mientras éste pasaba por delante de él. Bernie atravesó la iglesia y llamó con los nudillos a la puerta del despacho. Dentro ardía una estufa de gran tamaño y la cálida atmósfera era como un bálsamo. El padre Jaime permanecía de pie junto a ella, calentándose las manos mientras el padre Eduardo trabajaba sentado tras el escritorio. El cura de más edad miró a Bernie con recelo.

—¿Qué quieres?

—Este hombre y yo hemos mantenido unas cuantas discusiones —explicó el padre Eduardo.

El padre Jaime enarcó sus pobladas cejas.

—¿Éste? Es un comunista. ¿Ha hecho la confesión?

—Todavía no.

El padre Jaime arrugó la nariz con gesto de desagrado.

—Me he dejado el misal en mi habitación. Tengo que ir a buscarlo. Aquí la atmósfera no es lo que era. —Pasó como una exhalación y cerró ruidosamente la puerta a su espalda.

—Decirle una mentira a su superior, ¿no es un pecado venial o algo por el estilo?

—No ha sido una mentira. Hemos hablado, ¿no? —El padre Eduardo lanzó un suspiro—. Eres implacable, ¿verdad, Piper?

—He venido por el agua.

—Allí la tienes.

El padre Eduardo le señaló el grifo que había en un rincón. Debajo había un cubo limpio de acero.

Bernie lo llenó y después se volvió de nuevo hacia el padre Eduardo.

—Le creo capaz de haber echado una gota de agua bendita en el fondo del cubo y de haberlo bendecido después.

El padre Eduardo meneó la cabeza.

—Sabes muy poco sobre lo que nosotros creemos. Sabes lanzar dardos que hieren, pero no hace falta ser muy listo para eso.

—Por lo menos, yo no amargo las últimas horas de la gente, padre. Adiós. —Bernie dio media vuelta y se fue.

Ahora el patio ya estaba casi limpio de nieve. Los hombres amontonaban las paletadas contra el muro de la barraca del comandante. A medio cruzar el patio, Bernie oyó un grito.

—¡Oye, tú! ¡Inglés! —Aranda bajó los peldaños de su barraca y se acercó a él. Bernie dejó el cubo en el suelo y se cuadró. El comandante se detuvo delante de él y lo miró con semblante enfurecido—. ¿Qué hay en este cubo?

—Agua, mi comandante. Tenemos a un hombre enfermo en mi

barraca. El padre Eduardo me dijo que podía sacar un poco de agua del grifo de la iglesia.

—Ese marica de mierda. Cuanto antes muera el abogado, mejor.

Bernie adivinó que Aranda estaba aburrido y quería provocar su reacción. Bajó la vista al suelo.

—No creo en la blandura. —Aranda propinó un puntapié al cubo con su bota y el agua se derramó sobre la tierra—. Yo digo: «¡Viva la muerte!» Devuélvele este cubo al cura maricón. Ya hablaré yo después de eso con el padre Jaime. ¡Andando!

Bernie recogió el cubo y regresó lentamente a la barraca. Estaba furioso, pero también aliviado. De buena se había librado. Aranda estaba deseando hostigar a alguien.

Le contó al sacerdote lo que Aranda había dicho.

—Dice que presentará una queja contra usted al padre Jaime.

—Es un hombre muy duro. —El padre Eduardo se encogió de hombros.

Bernie dio media vuelta para retirarse.

—Espera —le dijo el cura, mirando todavía a través de la ventana—. Está regresando a su barraca. —Se volvió hacia Bernie—. Mira, lo conozco muy bien. Ahora irá a calentarse junto a la estufa, en la parte de atrás de la barraca. Vuelve a llenar el cubo y vete rápido, no te verá.

Bernie lo miró con los ojos entornados.

—¿Por qué está usted haciendo todo esto?

—Vi a tu amigo pidiendo desesperadamente agua y quería ayudar. Eso es todo.

—Entonces, déjelo en paz. No le amargue sus últimas horas por la probabilidad de uno contra un millón de que se arrepienta.

El sacerdote no contestó. Bernie volvió a llenar el cubo y abandonó la barraca sin decir ni una sola palabra más. El corazón le latía violentamente en el pecho cuando cruzó el patio. Como Aranda viera que lo había desobedecido, se pondría hecho una fiera.

Llegó sano y salvo a la barraca y cerró la puerta a su espalda. Se acercó al jergón de Vicente.

—Agua, amigo mío —dijo—. Cortesía de la Iglesia.

El sacerdote regresó aquella tarde. Casi todos los hombres que se encontraban en forma, hartos de permanecer encerrados, habían salido fuera a jugar un inconexo partido de fútbol en el patio. Vicente deliraba; al parecer, se imaginaba de vuelta en su despacho de Madrid y pedía repetidamente a alguien que le llevara una carpeta y abriera la ventana porque hacía demasiado calor. Estaba empapado de sudor a pesar del intenso frío que reinaba en la barraca. Bernie se sentó a su lado, secándole el rostro de vez en cuando con una esquina de la sábana. En la cama del otro lado, Eulalio permanecía tumbado fumando en silencio. Ahora raras veces salía de la barraca.

Bernie oyó un murmullo junto a su codo y se volvió. Era el padre Eduardo; debía de haber entrado sigilosamente.

—Está soñando, padre —dijo Bernie en voz baja—. Déjelo, ya está muy lejos de aquí.

El cura depositó una caja encima de la cama, una caja con los santos óleos, supuso Bernie. Se le aceleraron los latidos del corazón; había llegado el momento. El padre Eduardo se inclinó hacia delante y le tocó la frente a Vicente. El abogado hizo una mueca, se echó hacia atrás y abrió lentamente los ojos. Respiró hondo y emitió un estertor.

—Mierda. Otra vez usted.

El padre Eduardo respiró hondo.

—Creo que se acerca su hora. Se ha estado deslizando hacia el sueño y puede que la próxima vez ya no regrese. Pero incluso ahora, señor Vicente, Dios lo acogerá en la vida eterna.

—No lo escuches —le dijo Bernie.

Vicente esbozó un rictus espectral a modo de sonrisa, dejando al descubierto unas pálidas encías.

—No te preocupes, compadre. Dame un poco de agua. —Bernie ayudó a Vicente a beber. Éste ingirió muy despacio unos sorbos, sin quitarle los ojos de encima al sacerdote, y después se volvió a reclinar entre jadeos.

—Por favor. —Se advertía en la voz del padre Eduardo un tono de súplica—. Tiene una oportunidad de alcanzar la vida eterna. No la desprecie.

Vicente empezó a emitir unos gorgoteos a través de la garganta. El sacerdote volvió a hablar.

—Si no aprovecha esta última oportunidad, tendrá que ir al infierno. Eso es lo que está escrito.

La garganta de Vicente estaba trabajando. Gorgoteó y farfulló algo, y Bernie comprendió lo que intentaba hacer. El sacerdote se inclinó hacia delante y Vicente respiró hondo, pero la mucosidad que había estado intentando escupir le resbaló de nuevo al interior de la garganta. Tosió y después se empezó a asfixiar, emitiendo unos jadeos en su desesperado intento por respirar. Se incorporó con el rostro congestionado a causa del esfuerzo y trató de aspirar un poco de aire. Bernie se inclinó hacia él y le dio unas palmadas en la espalda. A Vicente se le desorbitaron los ojos mientras experimentaba un acceso de náuseas y vomitaba. De pronto, un espasmo le recorrió todo el cuerpo devastado y volvió a caer sobre el jergón. Un gorgoteo prolongado y chirriante se escapó de su garganta, una especie de sonido de terrible cansancio. Bernie vio que la expresión huía de sus ojos. Había muerto. El cura cayó de rodillas y empezó a rezar.

Bernie se quedó sentado en la cama. Le temblaban las piernas. Al cabo de un minuto, el padre Eduardo se levantó y se santiguó. Bernie lo miró con frialdad.

—Estaba intentando escupirle, ¿no se ha dado cuenta?

El cura denegó con la cabeza.

—Usted lo amenazó con el infierno, y él trató de soltarle un escupitajo y se atragantó con él. Usted le ha provocado esta muerte.

El sacerdote contempló el cuerpo de Vicente y después meneó la cabeza y dio media vuelta para abandonar la barraca. Bernie le gritó a su espalda.

—No se preocupe, padre, no está en el infierno. ¡Acaba de salir de él!

Vicente fue enterrado al día siguiente. Puesto que no había recibido los últimos sacramentos, no se pudo celebrar ninguna ceremonia por la Iglesia. Vicente se habría alegrado. Bernie caminó con paso cansino a través de la nieve, siguiendo a la cuadrilla que llevaba el cadáver cosido en el interior de una vieja sábana hasta la ladera de la colina donde estaban las sepulturas. Contempló cómo lo bajaban a una tumba muy poco profunda que había sido cavada aquella misma mañana.

—Adiós, compañero —murmuró serenamente. Se sentía muy solo.

El guardia que los acompañaba se santiguó e indicó a Bernie con un movimiento del fusil que regresara al campo. La cuadrilla del entierro empezó a llenar la tumba, luchando con la tierra congelada. Se puso otra vez a nevar, unos copos blancos y pesados. Bernie pensó: «El padre Eduardo estará pensando que te quemas en el fuego eterno, pero la verdad es que te van a encajonar en hielo.» El chiste hubiera hecho gracia a Vicente.

Aquella tarde Bernie estaba apoyado contra la pared de la barraca fumando un cigarrillo que le había regalado amablemente un miembro de la cuadrilla del entierro, cuando Pablo se le acercó. Parecía un poco incómodo.

—Me han enviado para hablar contigo en nombre de la célula del partido —dijo. «Porque tú eras mi amigo —pensó Bernie—, para demostrarme que Eulalio es el que mete en cintura a todo el mundo.»—. Se te ha considerado culpable de un incorregible individualismo burgués y de resistencia a la autoridad —dijo Pablo, mirándolo muy envarado—. Se te expulsa del partido y se te advierte de que, si hicieras algún intento de sabotear nuestra célula, se tomarán medidas.

Bernie ya sabía lo que eso significaba; una navaja clavada en la oscuridad, como ya había ocurrido anteriormente entre los prisioneros.

—Soy un comunista leal y siempre lo he sido —dijo—. No acepto la autoridad de Eulalio como dirigente nuestro. Algún día presentaré mi causa al Comité Central.

Pablo bajó la voz.

—¿Por qué armas jaleo? ¿Por qué eres tan terco? Eres muy terco, Bernardo. La gente dice que te hiciste amigo del abogado sólo para fastidiarnos.

Bernie sonrió amargamente.

—Vicente era un hombre honrado. Y yo lo admiraba.

—¿A qué vino todo aquel alboroto con el cura? Estas cosas provocan problemas. Es inútil discutir con los curas. Eulalio tiene razón, eso es puro individualismo burgués.

—Pues entonces, ¿qué hacemos? ¿Cómo podemos resistir?

—Debemos mantenernos fuertes y unidos. Algún día el fascismo caerá.

Pablo hizo una mueca y se rascó la muñeca. A lo mejor, era sarna... éste era el riesgo que se corría cuando uno permanecía demasiado rato con Eulalio.

—Otra cosa, Eulalio quiere que te vayas de la barraca. Quiere que pidas un traslado, que digas que no puedes seguir aquí después de la muerte de tu amigo.

Bernie se encogió de hombros.

—Puede que no me lo concedan.

—Eulalio dice que te tienes que largar.

—Lo pediré, camarada.

Bernie subrayó amargamente la última palabra. Pablo dio media vuelta y Bernie lo vio alejarse. «Y, si no me conceden el traslado —pensó—, como probablemente ocurrirá, Eulalio dirá que causaré más problemas si me quedo. Lo tiene todo preparado.» Miró a través de la valla hacia la colina donde Vicente estaba enterrado, un tajo alargado de color marrón en la nieve. Pensó que no le importaría reunirse con él bajo tierra. Pero después apretó los labios. Mientras siguiera con vida, lucharía. Eso era lo que tenía que hacer un verdadero comunista.

34

Se respiraba una atmósfera inquietante alrededor de la mesa del comedor. Sandy y Barbara fumaban sin cesar y encendían nuevos pitillos entre plato y plato. Sandy se mostraba insólitamente taciturno y se hundía en pequeños silencios, mientras que los intentos de conversación de Barbara sonaban nerviosos e inseguros, y una o dos veces ésta había mirado a Sandy de una manera muy rara. A Harry le dio la impresión de que ambos estaban muy lejos el uno del otro, singularmente desconectados. El ambiente lo estaba poniendo nervioso y le hacía sentirse incómodo. No podía dejar de estudiar el rostro preocupado y un tanto enfurruñado de Sandy y de preguntarse qué le habría ocurrido a Gómez. «¿Qué le habéis hecho?»

Los espías sabían que lo habían vuelto a invitar a cenar en casa de Sandy y que aquella tarde se había entrevistado con Hillgarth. Éste llevaba más de una semana sin verlo. El despacho del capitán estaba en la parte de atrás de la embajada, una zona que Harry jamás había visitado. Una secretaria extremadamente profesional lo acompañó a una estancia espaciosa de techo alto abovedado. Varias fotografías enmarcadas de buques de guerra colgaban en las paredes; en un estante, junto a los anuarios *Whitaker's Almanac* y *Jane's Fighting Ships*, había varios ejemplares encuadernados de las novelas de Hillgarth. Harry recordó uno o dos títulos que había visto leer a Sandy en el colegio. *La princesa y el perjuro* y *El belicista*.

Hillgarth permanecía sentado a un enorme escritorio de madera de roble. Su rostro mostraba una expresión dura y ceñuda y sus grandes e inquisitivos ojos reflejaban toda la cólera que sentía, por más que el tono de su voz fuera sereno y pausado.

—Tenemos problemas con Maestre —empezó diciendo—. Está

furioso. Él y algunos de sus compinches monárquicos espiaban aquella maldita mina, y Gómez trabajaba para ellos. Es una lástima que usted haya delatado a su hombre. De todos modos, Maestre ya no estaba muy contento con usted por el hecho de haber dejado plantada a su hija. Es el final de la operación que estaban llevando a cabo.

—¿Puedo preguntar qué le ocurrió a Gómez, señor? ¿Está...?

—Maestre lo ignora. Pero no espera volver a verlo. Gómez había trabajado muchos años a su servicio.

—Comprendo. —A Harry se le encogió el estómago.

—Al menos, parece que Forsyth no sospecha de usted. —Hillgarth lo miró fijamente—. Así que siga engañándolo, acceda a invertir y manténgame al tanto de aquellos informes de los que hablaron cuando los reciba. Eso es lo que yo quiero ver.

—Sí, señor.

—Sir Sam está ejerciendo presión en Londres. Puede que se anule esta operación. En caso de que así sea o de que algo falle, tengo un plan de emergencia para Forsyth. —Hillgarth hizo una pausa—. Intentaremos reclutarlo. No le podemos ofrecer lo mismo que él espera conseguir con esta mina, pero es posible que podamos ejercer otra clase de presiones. ¿Sigue estando enemistado con su familia?

—Por completo.

Hillgarth soltó un gruñido.

—O sea, que por ahí no hay nada que nos pueda servir. En fin, ya veremos. —El capitán miró incisivamente a Harry—. Lo veo preocupado. ¿No le gusta la idea de que apretemos las tuercas a Forsyth? Tenía la impresión de que usted lo despreciaba.

Harry no dijo nada. Hillgarth siguió adelante sin quitarle los ojos de encima.

—La verdad es que usted no está hecho para este tipo de trabajo, ¿verdad, Brett?

—No, señor —contestó Harry en tono abatido—. Hice simplemente lo que me pidieron que hiciera. Siento muchísimo lo que le ocurrió al teniente Gómez.

—Es comprensible. Pero nosotros necesitamos que siga haciendo lo que ha hecho hasta ahora, de momento. Después lo enviaremos a casa. Seguramente, muy pronto. —Hillgarth esbozó una media sonrisa—. Confío en que eso sea un alivio, ¿eh?

Pilar llevó a la mesa el plato principal: una paella con mejillones, gambas y anchoas sobre un lecho de arroz. Depositó la bandeja sobre la mesa y se retiró sin mirar a nadie. Barbara tomó una cuchara de servir y llenó los platos.

—Es todo un lujo conseguir pescado fresco —dijo Sandy, aparentemente animado por el aroma del plato. Miró a Harry con una sonrisa—. Cada vez hay menos.

—¿Y eso?

—Los pescadores reciben una asignación de combustible para sus embarcaciones, pero los precios del petróleo en el mercado negro son tan astronómicos que ellos lo venden a cambio de enormes ganancias y no se molestan en salir a pescar. Ésos son los efectos que produce nuestro bloqueo, ¿comprendes?

—¿Y el Gobierno no los puede obligar a que utilicen el combustible para pescar?

Sandy rió.

—No. Aunque aprueben leyes, no pueden obligar a nadie a cumplirlas. Y, además, la mitad de los ministros están metidos hasta el cuello.

—¿Cómo va ese proyecto en el que vas a invertir? —preguntó Barbara, dirigiéndole a Harry otra mirada muy rara.

—Bueno...

Sandy lo interrumpió.

—Despacio. De momento, no hay ninguna novedad.

Barbara miró un instante de uno a otro.

—Ayer recibí una carta de Will —dijo Harry—. Ahora se lo pasa muy bien viviendo en el campo.

—Su mujer debe de estar encantada de haberse alejado de las incursiones aéreas —terció Barbara.

—Sí, todo eso ha sido demasiado para ella. —Harry la miró con la cara muy seria—. ¿Te has enterado de lo de Coventry?

Barbara dio una larga calada al cigarrillo. Tras los cristales de las gafas, sus ojos parecían cansados y estaban rodeados por unas ojeras que Harry jamás le había visto anteriormente.

—Sí. Quinientos muertos, según los informes. Todo el centro de la ciudad arrasado.

—Los reportajes del *Arriba* son exagerados —dijo Sandy—. Siempre hacen que los bombardeos parezcan peores de lo que son. Los alemanes les dicen lo que tienen que escribir.

—Pero eso lo dijeron en la BBC.

—Y vaya si es verdad —convino Harry.

—Coventry se encuentra a sólo veinticinco kilómetros de Birmingham —dijo Barbara—. Cada vez que escucho la BBC, temo enterarme de que ha habido más incursiones. Deduzco de sus cartas que mi madre ya empieza a sufrir los efectos de la tensión. —Lanzó un suspiro y miró a Harry con una sonrisa triste en los labios—. Resulta extraño ver que tus padres se han convertido de repente en unos ancianos atemorizados.

—Tendrías que ir a verlos —dijo Sandy.

Ella lo miró con asombro.

—¿Por qué no? Llevas años sin verlos. Se acerca la Navidad. Sería una bonita sorpresa para ellos.

Barbara se mordió el labio.

—Es que... no me parece el momento adecuado —dijo.

—No veo por qué no. Yo te podría encontrar plaza en un avión.

—Lo pensaré.

—Como quieras. —Harry miró a Barbara. Se preguntó por qué no quería ir a su casa.

Ella se volvió para mirarlo.

—¿Y tú qué, Harry, te van a conceder vacaciones por Navidad?

—No creo. Quieren tener a los traductores disponibles por si hubiera alguna emergencia.

—Supongo que te gustaría ver a tu tío y a tu tía.

—Pues sí.

—Sandy dice que te has echado novia —dijo Barbara con falsa jovialidad—. ¿A qué se dedica?

Harry se arrepintió de habérselo comentado a Sandy en el coche el día que ambos habían visitado la mina.

—Pues... trabaja en el sector lácteo.

—¿Y cuánto tiempo llevas con ella?

—No mucho.

Harry pensó en la víspera, que había transcurrido en el apartamento de Carabanchel. Sofía le había revelado inesperadamente que su familia estaba al corriente de las relaciones entre ambos. Harry se había preguntado cómo reaccionarían. Enrique y su madre lo habían recibido encantados; pero Harry suponía que era porque pensaban que Sofía había pescado a un hombre rico, aunque fuera extranjero. Paco se había mostrado más tranquilo y relajado y hasta había hablado con él por primera vez. Y él, por su parte, se había sentido extrañamente privilegiado.

—La tendrás que traer a cenar —dijo Barbara alegremente—. Formaremos dos parejas.

—Por eso no vas a casa por Navidad —dijo Sandy, señalando a Harry con el dedo—. Qué guardado te lo tenías, pillín. —Se secó la boca con la servilleta—. ¿Dónde está la pimienta? A Pilar se le ha olvidado.

—Voy por ella —dijo Barbara—. Perdón. —Abandonó la estancia. Sandy miró a Harry con la cara muy seria.

—Quería librarme un momento de ella —dijo—. Me temo que hay un problema en el asunto de la mina.

El corazón de Harry se puso a latir con fuerza.

—¿Qué ha ocurrido?

—Sebastián teme que un extranjero invierta en el negocio. Creo que no va a poder ser.

Parecía sinceramente apenado.

—Qué lástima. —O sea que, al final, no habría ningún informe que presentarle a Hillgarth—. Me sorprende, porque yo pensaba que era Otero el que más dudas tenía.

Sandy jugueteó con su vaso de vino.

—Teme que a este comité de supervisión no le guste la idea de un inversor inglés. Nos están sometiendo... —hizo una pausa— a mucha presión.

—¿El comité del general Maestre?

—Sí. Nos vigilan más de cerca de lo que nosotros pensábamos. Creemos que saben algo de ti.

Harry quería preguntar por Gómez, pero no se atrevió.

—Entonces, ¿seguís teniendo problemas por falta de fondos?

Sandy asintió con la cabeza.

—El comité está insinuando más o menos la posibilidad de asumir ellos la dirección del proyecto. Y, en ese caso, adiós beneficios. La gente del comité ganará una fortuna, claro.

—Lo siento.

—Bueno, supongo que algo sacaremos. Lamento haberte dejado en la estacada. —Sandy miró a Harry con aquellos ojos castaños tristes y líquidos como los de un perro. Con cuánta rapidez podía cambiar su expresión.

—No te preocupes. Quizá sea mejor que no participe. No estoy muy seguro de que fuera el tipo de negocio más apropiado para mí.

—Menos mal que te lo tomas así. Es una pena, quería hacer algo por ti, en... bueno, en recuerdo de los viejos tiempos.

Sonó el teléfono en el vestíbulo y Harry experimentó un sobresalto. Oyó unas pisadas y la voz de Barbara hablando en inglés. Momentos después, ésta regresó con semblante angustiado.

—Harry, en la embajada quieren hablar contigo. Dicen que es urgente. —Lo miró con inquietud—. Espero que no sean malas noticias de Inglaterra.

—¿Les diste nuestro número? —Sandy lo miró incisivamente.

—Tuve que hacerlo, esta noche estoy de servicio. Me tendré que ir si hay algo urgente que traducir. Disculpadme. —Salió al vestíbulo. Un braserillo colocado bajo la mesita del teléfono le calentó los pies, arrojando un resplandor amarillo sobre el mosaico del suelo. Descolgó el teléfono.

—Dígame. Harry Brett.

Contestó una cultivada voz de mujer.

—Ah, señor Brett, me alegro de que hayamos podido localizarlo. Tengo una llamada en espera, una tal señorita Sofía Roque Casas. —La mujer vaciló—. Dice que es urgente.

—¿Sofía?

—Está esperando. ¿Quiere atender la llamada?

—Sí, por favor, pásemela.

Se oyó un clic y, por un instante, Harry temió que se hubiera cortado la comunicación; pero enseguida se escuchó la voz de Sofía. Le pareció raro oírla en el vestíbulo de la casa de Sandy.

—Harry, Harry, ¿eres tú? —Su voz, normalmente serena, parecía asustada.

—Sí, Sofía, ¿qué es lo que ocurre?

—Es mamá. Creo que ha sufrido otro ataque. Enrique ha salido y yo estoy sola. Paco se encuentra fatal, lo ha visto todo. Harry, ¿puedes venir? —Tenía voz de llorar.

—¿Un ataque?

—Creo que sí. Ha perdido el conocimiento.

—Voy enseguida. ¿Dónde estás?

—Tuve que caminar dos manzanas para encontrar un teléfono. Perdona, no sabía qué hacer. Oh, Harry, está muy mal.

Harry reflexionó un momento.

—De acuerdo. Vuelve al apartamento, iré lo antes posible. ¿Cuándo regresará Enrique?

—Muy tarde. Ha salido con unos amigos.

—Mira, ahora estoy en la calle Vigo. Pediré un taxi y llegaré en cuanto pueda. Vuelve con tu madre y Paco.

—Por favor, date prisa; por favor, date prisa. —Era terrible oírla tan asustada—. Sabía que vendrías —añadió Sofía.

Después se oyó un clic mientras ella colgaba el aparato.

Se abrió la puerta del salón y Barbara asomó la cabeza.

—¿Qué ocurre? Has dicho que alguien había sufrido un ataque, ¿verdad? ¿Es tu tío?

Harry respiró hondo.

—No, es la madre de Sofía, mi... mi novia. —Siguió a Barbara al comedor—. Ha llamado a la embajada y ellos me la han pasado aquí. Está sola con su madre y un chiquillo que tienen a su cuidado. Me tengo que ir para allá.

Sandy lo miró con curiosidad.

—¿No pueden llamar a un médico?

—No se lo pueden permitir.

Debió de haber utilizado un tono desabrido, porque Sandy levantó la mano diciendo.

—Bueno, chico, bueno.

—¿Puedo pedir un taxi desde aquí? —Para trasladarse a casa de Sandy, Harry había cogido un tranvía.

—Tardará siglos a estas horas de la noche. ¿Dónde viven?

Harry vaciló antes de contestar.

—En Carabanchel.

—¿En Carabanchel? —Sandy enarcó las cejas.

—Sí.

De repente, Barbara intervino en tono decidido.

—Yo te llevo. Si esta pobre mujer ha sufrido un ataque, quizá la pueda ayudar.

—Sofía estudió medicina. Pero tú la puedes ayudar. ¿Te importa?

—Es peligroso circular en coche por allá abajo —dijo Sandy—. Podemos pedir un taxi.

—No me ocurrirá nada. —Barbara se encaminó hacia la puerta—. Ven, voy por las llaves.

Harry la siguió. Al llegar al umbral, se volvió. Sandy permanecía sentado a la mesa. Se le veía furioso y malhumorado. Jamás le había gustado que lo dejaran de lado.

La noche era fría y despejada. Barbara condujo rápido y con pericia por el centro de la ciudad y entre las callejuelas oscuras de los barrios obreros. Parecía alegrarse de haber salido. Miró a Harry con curiosidad.

—No pensaba que Sofía fuera de Carabanchel.

—¿Esperabas que fuera alguien de la clase media?

—Supongo que, subconscientemente, sí. —Barbara sonrió con tristeza—. Bien sé yo que el hecho de enamorarse de alguien es algo imprevisible. —Volvió a mirarlo con expresión inquisitiva—. ¿Tiene algo de especial?

—Sí. —Harry vaciló—. Al principio me pregunté si no sería... no sé, por una especie de sentimiento de culpa o algo por el estilo, eso de querer averiguar cómo viven los españoles corrientes. —Soltó una tímida carcajada.

—¿Un deseo de identificarte con la manera de vivir de los nativos?

—Algo así. Pero es simplemente... simplemente amor, ¿sabes?

—Lo sé. —Barbara vaciló—. ¿Y qué piensan en la embajada?

—No se lo he dicho. Quiero reservarme una parte de mi vida para mí mismo. Ya estamos, la siguiente calle.

Aparcaron ante el bloque de apartamentos de Sofía, entraron rápidamente y subieron corriendo por la oscura escalera. Sofía los había oído subir y esperaba en la puerta. Una luz amarillenta se derramaba por el rellano. Se oía desde dentro el llanto histérico de un niño. Sofía estaba muy pálida y un lacio y desgreñado cabello le enmarcaba el rostro. Miró a Barbara.

—¿Quién es?

—Barbara, la mujer de un amigo mío. Estábamos cenando juntos. Es enfermera y quizá te pueda ayudar.

Sofía encorvó los hombros.

—Demasiado tarde. Mamá ha muerto. Ya había muerto cuando regresé después de haberte llamado.

Los hizo pasar. La anciana yacía en la cama. Le habían cerrado los ojos y su blanco rostro ofrecía un aspecto sereno y tranquilo. Paco se había arrojado sobre el cadáver y lo abrazaba con fuerza, sollozando entre lastimeros gemidos. El niño levantó la cabeza al oírlos entrar y miró a Barbara con expresión atemorizada. Sofía se le acercó y le acarició el cabello.

—Tranquilo, Paco, esta señora es amiga de Harry. Ha venido a ayudarnos. No es de la Iglesia. Anda, apártate. —Lo apartó delicadamente del cadáver y lo abrazó. Ambos se sentaron en la cama, llorando. Harry se sentó a su lado y rodeó a Sofía con el brazo.

Paco se levantó y miró a Barbara, todavía asustado. Ésta se le acercó y, muy suavemente, le tomó aquellas sucias manitas entre las suyas.

—Hola, Paco —le dijo—. ¿Te puedo llamar Paco? —El niño asintió en silencio—. Mira, Paco, Sofía está muy disgustada. Tienes que procurar comportarte como un chico mayor. A ver si puedes, ya sé que es difícil. Mira, ven a sentarte aquí conmigo. —Paco permitió que lo apartara suavemente de la cama. Barbara lo sentó en una desvencijada silla y acercó otra para sentarse a su lado.

Sofía, abrazada fuertemente a Harry, contemplaba el cadáver de su madre.

—Ya pensaba que podía ocurrir y que quizá fuera lo mejor para ella, pero es muy duro. Tendría que pedir que vengan por ella, no sé, una ambulancia tal vez, no podemos dejarla aquí.

—¿Enrique no querrá verla? —le preguntó Harry.

—Será mejor que no. —Sofía se levantó y fue en busca de su abrigo, colgado tras la puerta.

—Ya voy yo —dijo Harry.

Barbara se levantó.

—No, tú quédate aquí con Sofía. De camino, he visto una cabina telefónica no lejos de aquí.

—No conviene que vaya sola —le dijo Sofía.

—He estado en sitios peores. Por favor, déjeme ir. —Barbara hablaba en tono enérgico y profesional, con deseo de ayudar—. No tardo ni un minuto.

Se fue antes de que pudieran protestar y sus pisadas resonaron escalera abajo. Sofía tomó la mano de Paco y lo acompañó para que se sentara de nuevo en la cama con ellos. Contempló el rostro inmóvil de Elena.

—Estaba muy cansada últimamente —murmuró Sofía—. Y de pronto, esta noche después de cenar lanzó un grito tremendo, como un gemido muy fuerte. Cuando me acerqué, ya había perdido el conocimiento. Después, cuando regresé de llamarte, ya había muerto. Dejé al pobre Paco solo con ella. —Besó la cabeza del niño—. No tendría que haberlo hecho. Me tendría que haber quedado aquí.

—Hiciste lo que pudiste.

—Mejor así —repitió en tono apagado—. A veces, mojaba la cama. Le dolía tanto hacerlo que se echaba a llorar. —Meneó la cabeza—. Tendrías que haber conocido a mamá antes de que se pusiera enferma, era tan fuerte que cuidaba de todos nosotros. Mi padre no quería que fuera a la universidad, pero mamá siempre me apoyó. —Contempló la fotografía de su madre vestida de novia, de pie entre su marido y su hermano, el cura, los tres mirando con una sonrisa a la cámara.

Harry la estrechó con fuerza en sus brazos.

—Pobre Sofía. No sé cómo has podido resistirlo. —Ella correspondió a su abrazo. Al final, se oyeron unas pisadas en la escalera—. Barbara ya está aquí —dijo Harry—. Algo habrá arreglado.

Sofía lo miró.

—¿La conoces bien?

Harry la besó en la frente.

—Desde hace mucho tiempo. Pero es sólo una amiga.

Barbara entró con el rostro arrebolado a causa del frío.

—He conseguido hablar con el hospital. Van a dar aviso a la morgue y enviar a alguien, pero puede que tarden un ratito. —Se sacó un trozo de papel del bolsillo del abrigo—. He pasado por una bodega y he comprado un poco de brandy para todos. Pensé que nos vendría bien.

—Muy bien hecho —dijo Harry.

Sofía fue por unas copas y Barbara sirvió una generosa medida para todos. Paco sintió curiosidad y pidió probarlo, y ellos le dieron un poco, mezclado con agua.

—Uy —exclamó el pequeño, haciendo una mueca—. ¡Es asqueroso! —Se quebró la tensión y todos se echaron a reír de una manera un tanto histérica.

—No está bien que nos riamos —dijo Sofía en tono culpable.

—A veces no queda más remedio que hacerlo —dijo Barbara. Miró alrededor, contemplando las paredes manchadas de humedad y los muebles maltrechos y, al darse cuenta de que Sofía la estaba estudiando, bajó los ojos avergonzada.

—¿Es usted enfermera, señora? —preguntó Sofía—. ¿Trabaja aquí como enfermera?

—No, ahora no. Estoy... estoy casada con un hombre de negocios inglés. Fue compañero de colegio de Harry.

—Barbara trabajó como voluntaria en uno de los orfelinatos de la Iglesia —explicó Harry—. Pero no lo pudo resistir.

—No, era un lugar horrible —dijo Barbara, mirando con una sonrisa a Sofía—. Harry me dice que estudió usted medicina.

—Sí, antes de que estallara la Guerra Civil. ¿Tienen ustedes mujeres médico en Inglaterra?

—Algunas. No muchas.

—En mi curso de la universidad éramos tres. A veces los profesores no sabían qué pensar de nosotras. Comprendías que se avergonzaban de ciertas cosas que tenían que enseñarnos.

—¿Impropias de una dama? —preguntó Barbara, sonriendo.

—Sí. Aunque, en la guerra, todo el mundo las veía.

—Lo sé. Estuve algún tiempo en Madrid, trabajando para la Cruz Roja. —Barbara se volvió hacia Paco—. ¿Tú cuántos años tienes, niño?

—Diez.

—¿Vas al colegio?

Paco denegó con la cabeza.

—No pudo adaptarse —explicó Sofía—. Además, las nuevas escuelas no sirven para nada, están llenas de ex soldados nacionales sin experiencia docente. Yo intento darle clase en casa.

Se oyeron pisadas en la escalera, unas fuertes pisadas masculinas. Sofía contuvo bruscamente la respiración.

—Debe de ser Enrique. —Se levantó—. Déjenme hablar con él a solas. ¿Quieren acompañar a Paco a la cocina, por favor?

—Vamos, jovencito. —Barbara tomó al niño de la mano y Harry la siguió. Éste encendió la estufa. Barbara señaló un libro que había sobre la mesa para distraer a Paco, mientras se oía desde fuera un murmullo de voces. El libro tenía unas tapas verdes, con la imagen de un niño y una niña que iban a la escuela—. ¿Qué es este libro? —Paco se mordió al labio, prestando atención a las voces del exterior. Harry había oído la voz de Enrique, un grito repentino y doloroso—. ¿Qué es? —insistió Barbara, en un intento de distraerlo.

—Mi viejo libro del colegio. De cuando iba al colegio, antes de que se llevaran a papá y mamá. Me gustaba.

Barbara lo abrió y lo empujó hacia él sobre la mesa. Oyeron que alguien lloraba fuera, el llanto de un hombre. Paco volvió a mirar hacia la puerta.

—Enséñamelo —le dijo dulcemente Barbara—. Sólo unos minutos. Es bueno dejar a Enrique y Sofía juntos un ratito. Recuerdo el libro —añadió—. Los Mera me lo enseñaron una vez. Carmela tenía un ejemplar. —Se le llenaron los ojos de lágrimas y Harry comprendió que, pese a su fingida alegría, estaba al límite de sus fuerzas. Se volvió hacia Paco—. Mira todos los apartados. Historia, geografía, aritmética.

—A mí me gustaba la geografía —dijo Paco—. Mira los dibujos, todos los países del mundo.

Fuera volvía a reinar el silencio. Harry se levantó.

—Voy a ver cómo están. Tú quédate con Paco. —Apretó afectuosamente el hombro de Barbara y regresó a la habitación principal. Enrique estaba sentado en la cama con Sofía. Miró a Harry con una amarga expresión que éste jamás le había visto y que afeaba su pálido rostro surcado por las lágrimas.

—Ya ve usted todos nuestros dramas familiares, inglés.

—Lo siento mucho, Enrique.

—Harry no tiene la culpa —dijo Sofía.

—Si al menos nos viera con un poco de dignidad. Antes teníamos dignidad, ¿lo sabe usted, señor?

Llamaron a la puerta. Sofía suspiró.

—Debe de ser la ambulancia. —Pero, mientras se encaminaba hacia la puerta, ésta se abrió y apareció el rostro chupado de la señora Ávila. Llevaba la cabeza envuelta en un chal negro y se sujetaba fuertemente los extremos.

—Perdón, pero he oído que alguien lloraba, ¿ha ocurrido algo?... ¡Oh! —La mujer vio el cuerpo en la cama y se santiguó—. ¡Oh, pobre señora Roque! ¡Pobre señora! Pero ahora está en paz con Dios. —Después miró a Harry con curiosidad.

Sofía se levantó.

—Señora Ávila, quisiéramos estar solos, por favor. Esperamos a que vengan a llevarse a nuestra madre.

La beata miró alrededor.

—¿Dónde está Paco, pobrecito?

—En la cocina. Con otra amiga.

—Aquí tendría que haber un sacerdote en estos momentos —dijo la anciana en tono halagüeño—. Voy a avisar al padre Fernando.

Algo pareció romperse con un chasquido en el interior de Sofía. Harry lo percibió casi físicamente, como si hubiera sonado un crujido en la estancia. Sofía se levantó y se acercó a ella a grandes zancadas. La anciana era más alta; pero, aun así, se echó hacia atrás.

—Óigame bien, buitre del demonio, ¡aquí no queremos que venga el padre Fernando! —La voz de Sofía se elevó hasta casi convertirse en un grito—. Por mucho que intente introducirlo en nuestra casa, por mucho que intente apoderarse de Paco, ¡jamás lo conseguirá! ¡No es bienvenida aquí, ¿comprende?! Y ahora, ¡largo!

La señora Ávila se irguió en toda su estatura mientras el pálido rostro se le teñía de arrebol.

—¿Así es como recibes a una vecina que viene a ayudarte? ¿Así es como correspondes a la caridad cristiana? El padre Fernando tiene razón, sois enemigos de la Iglesia...

Enrique se levantó de la cama y se acercó a la señora Ávila con los puños apretados. La beata retrocedió.

—¡Pues vaya y denúncienos al cura si quiere, bruja maldita! ¡Usted, que disfruta de todo un apartamento para usted sola porque su cura es amigo del jefe de la finca!

—A mi padre lo mataron los comunistas —replicó la beata temblando—. No tenía a donde ir.

—¡Pues yo escupo a su padre! ¡Fuera de aquí! —Enrique levantó un puño. La señora Ávila lanzó un grito y abandonó a toda prisa el apartamento, cerrando estrepitosamente la puerta a su espalda. Enrique se sentó a los pies de la cama, respirando con entrecortados jadeos. Sofía se sentó a su lado, agotada. Barbara salió y se quedó en la puerta de la cocina—. Lo siento —dijo Enrique—. No tendría que haberle gritado así.

—No importa. Si nos denuncia, diremos que estábamos abrumados por la pena.

Enrique agachó la cabeza y juntó las huesudas manos sobre las rodillas. Desde algún lugar del exterior, Harry oyó una especie de aullido que fue en aumento hasta dar la impresión de proceder de una docena de lugares a la vez.

—¿Qué demonios es eso? —preguntó Barbara con voz trémula.

Sofía levantó la mirada.

—Los perros. Los perros asilvestrados. A veces, en esta época del año aúllan por el frío. Señal de que el invierno ha llegado de verdad.

TERCERA PARTE

FRÍO GLACIAL

35

Una gruesa capa de nieve cubría Tierra Muerta desde hacía casi un mes. Había llegado temprano y se había quedado; los guardias decían que, en Cuenca, la gente comentaba que era el invierno más frío que tenían desde hacía muchos años. Unos días claros y gélidos alternaban con copiosas nevadas, y el viento siempre soplaba desde el noreste. Algunas noches, los pequeños venados de las colinas que captaban el olor de la comida, bajaban y se detenían a escasa distancia del campo. Cuando se acercaban demasiado, los guardias de las atalayas los mataban a tiros y de esta manera disponían de carne de venado para comer.

Ahora, a principios de diciembre, ya se había abierto un trillado camino a través de los ventisqueros entre el campo y la cantera. Cada mañana la cuadrilla de trabajo subía arrastrando los pies a las colinas, donde el panorama de interminables paisajes blancos sólo quedaba interrumpido por las finas ramas desnudas de las carrascas.

Bernie se sentía muy solo. Echaba de menos a Vicente y ahora ningún comunista le dirigía la palabra. Por la noche permanecía silenciosamente tumbado en su jergón. Incluso en Rookwood había tenido siempre a alguien con quien hablar. Pensó en Harry Brett; a veces Vicente le recordaba a Harry, bondadoso y con principios, pese a su irremediable pertenencia a la clase media.

A los prisioneros les resultaba muy difícil resistir el mal tiempo. Todo el mundo estaba resfriado o tosía; ya había habido nuevas muertes y más cortejos fúnebres hasta el anónimo cementerio. Bernie notó que la antigua herida del brazo le estaba causando molestias; a media tarde, el hecho de sostener el pico en la cantera le resultaba extremadamente doloroso. La herida de la pierna del Jarama, que había cicatrizado con gran rapidez y jamás le había vuelto a dar problemas, ahora le volvía a doler.

No había conseguido cambiar de barraca, como Eulalio le había ordenado que hiciera. Había presentado la petición semanas atrás, pero no se había producido ningún cambio. De pronto, una tarde en que regresaba de la cantera le dijeron que Aranda lo quería ver.

Bernie permaneció de pie en la caldeada barraca ante el comandante. Aranda estaba sentado en su sillón de cuero, con su fusta de montar apoyada contra el costado del sillón. Para asombro de Bernie, el comandante lo miró sonriendo y lo invitó a tomar asiento. Después, sacó una carpeta y se puso a hojear su contenido.

—Tengo el informe del doctor Lorenzo —le dijo jovialmente—. Dice que eres un psicópata antisocial. Según él, todos los izquierdistas cultos padecen una forma innata de locura antisocial.

—¿En serio, mi comandante?

—A mí, personalmente, me parece una tontería. En la guerra, tu bando combatió por vuestros intereses y nosotros lo hicimos por los nuestros. Ahora poseemos España por derecho de conquista. —Aranda enarcó una ceja—. ¿Qué dices a eso, eh?

—Estoy de acuerdo con usted, mi comandante.

—Muy bien. O sea que estamos de acuerdo. —Aranda sacó un cigarrillo de una pitillera de plata y lo encendió—. ¿Te apetece uno? —Bernie vaciló, pero Aranda le ofreció la pitillera—. Vamos, cógelo, te lo ordeno. —Bernie extrajo un cigarrillo y Aranda le ofreció un encendedor de oro. El comandante se reclinó en su asiento y el cuero chirrió—. A ver, ¿qué es eso de que ahora quieres cambiar de barraca?

—Desde que murió mi amigo el mes pasado, me cuesta estar allí.

—También he oído decir que te has apartado de tus amigos comunistas. Y, muy especialmente, de Eulalio Cabo. Es un hombre fuerte y, en cierto modo, hasta lo admiro. —El comandante sonrió—. No te sorprendas tanto, Piper. Tengo oídos entre los prisioneros. —Bernie guardó silencio. Sabía que había confidentes en casi todas las barracas. En la suya se sospechaba de un pequeño vasco, un católico que asistía a los oficios religiosos. Había muerto de neumonía dos semanas atrás—. No es fácil ser prisionero y, encima, no gozar de la simpatía de los demás hombres. Tus amigos comunistas te han abandonado, ¿por qué no vengarte un poquito? —El comandante enarcó las cejas—. Podrías tener todos los cigarrillos que quisieras, y otros privilegios. Te podría sacar de la cuadrilla de la cantera. Debe de hacer mucho frío allí arriba; yo, estas mañanas, me quedo congelado de sólo salir al patio. Si tú te convirtieras en mi confidente entre los prisioneros, yo no te pediría demasiado. sólo un poco de información de vez en cuando. Tener amigos en el campo enemigo facilita mucho la vida.

Bernie se mordió el labio. Pensó que, si se negaba, habría problemas. Contestó muy despacio, procurando que su voz sonara lo más respetuosa posible.

—No daría resultado, mi comandante. Eulalio ya me considera un traidor. Me vigila.

Aranda lo pensó.

—Sí, ya lo veo; pero quizá los problemas con los comunistas serían una buena excusa para que tú te buscaras otros amigos. De esta manera, podrías averiguar cosas.

Bernie vaciló.

—Mi comandante, usted ha hablado antes de la batalla entre nuestros dos bandos...

—Me vas a decir que no puedes cambiar tus lealtades —dijo Aranda sin dejar de sonreír, pero ahora con los párpados entornados. Bernie guardó silencio—. Pensaba que me ibas a decir eso, Piper. Vosotros, los ideólogos, os buscáis muchos problemas. —Aranda meneó la cabeza—. Bueno, pues ya te puedes retirar; ahora estoy ocupado.

Bernie se levantó. Se sorprendió de haber salido tan bien parado. Sin embargo, a veces Aranda esperaba y te pillaba más tarde. El cigarrillo ya se había consumido, por lo que Bernie se inclinó hacia delante para apagar la colilla en el cenicero. Casi esperaba que el comandante levantara la fusta y lo azotara en el rostro, pero Aranda no se movió. Esbozó una sonrisa cínica, regodeándose en el temor que le había provocado, y después levantó la mano haciendo el saludo fascista.

—¡Arriba España!

—¡*Grieve* España! —Bernie abandonó la barraca y cerró la puerta. Le temblaban las piernas.

Eulalio se había puesto enfermo. De la sarna, estaba cada vez peor, y ahora sufría una dolencia estomacal y tenía diarrea casi todos los días. Se estaba consumiendo, se había quedado en los puros huesos y se veía obligado a caminar con un bastón; pero, cuanto más debilitado tenía el cuerpo, tanto más brutal y autoritario se volvía.

Pablo había ocupado el jergón de Vicente, aunque tenía orden de no dirigirle la palabra a Bernie. Apartó la cabeza cuando Bernie regresó de su visita a Aranda y se tumbó en su jergón. Eulalio había estado hablando con los demás comunistas al fondo de la barraca, pero ahora se acercó a Bernie fuera del resplandor de la luz de la vela, golpeando el suelo de madera con el bastón. Se detuvo al pie del jergón.

—¿Qué quería Aranda de ti? —Su voz era un resuello gutural. Bernie contempló el rostro amarillento cubierto de sarna.

—Era por mi petición de cambiar de barraca. Me ha dicho que no.

Eulalio lo miró con recelo.

—Te trata con mucha amabilidad. Como a todos los confidentes. —Hablaba en voz alta, y otros hombres se volvieron para mirarlos.

Bernie también levantó la voz.

—Me ha pedido que informara, Eulalio. Me ha dicho que, si lo hago, me trasladará. ¿Crees que lo haría, ahora que tú ya me tienes aislado? Le he dicho que un comunista no informa.

—Tú no eres un comunista —dijo Eulalio, respirando afanosamente—. Ten cuidado, Piper, te estamos vigilando. —Dicho lo cual, regresó renqueando a su camastro.

Al día siguiente, Bernie estaba trabajando con un grupo en la limpieza de la zona antaño ocupada por la cueva. Habían hecho detonar una enorme carga de dinamita en su interior, la habían destruido por completo y dejado en su lugar una gigantesca montaña de escombros. El grupo había recibido órdenes de clasificarlos en trozos de distintos tamaños y de desmenuzar los que fueran demasiado grandes para poder manejarlos. Un camión llegaría por la tarde y se los llevaría; al monumento de Franco, según decían los rumores.

Pablo trabajaba al lado de Bernie. De repente, dejó el pico a un lado y recogió algo.

—¡Ay, fíjate en esto! —exclamó.

Bernie se volvió, preguntándose qué habría inducido a Pablo a romper la prohibición de hablar con él. Mirando al guardia que tenía más cerca para asegurarse de que éste no lo estuviera observando, se inclinó hacia el lugar donde Pablo sostenía un trozo de piedra aplanado en sus manos agrietadas. La superficie era de color rojo oscuro; en ella figuraba pintada la cabeza de un mamut de color rojo que miraba a dos hombres delgados como palillos y armados con lanzas a punto de atacar.

—Mira —murmuró Pablo—, algo ha sobrevivido.

Bernie acarició la superficie suavemente con los dedos. El tacto era como el de cualquier otra piedra, pero la pintura se remontaba a muchos miles de años de antigüedad.

—Es preciosa —dijo en un susurro.

Pablo asintió con la cabeza y se guardó el trozo de piedra en el bolsillo del viejo poncho de hule que llevaba puesto.

—Lo esconderé. Algún día, enseñaré a la gente lo que aquí destruyeron.

—Pero ten cuidado —le dijo Bernie en voz baja.

La vida en la prisión, Bernie lo sabía muy bien, resultaba más llevadera gracias a las pequeñas victorias contra los captores; aunque, a veces, semejantes victorias podían costar muy caras.

Al menos, las jornadas en la cantera eran muy cortas. El silbato sonaba a las cuatro y media cuando empezaban a caer las sombras del atardecer. Había sido uno más de los muchos días fríos, claros y desapacibles que vivían en aquella época del año. Un sol rojo de enorme tamaño se había ocultado en el horizonte, tiñendo las lejanas montañas de un rosado resplandor. El montón de escombros ya casi había desaparecido; dejaba tan sólo un mellado boquete en la ladera de la colina. Mientras el camión enviado para recoger la carga de piedra bajaba traqueteando por el camino de montaña, los hombres devolvieron sus herramientas e iniciaron el lento y cansado regreso al campo.

Aquel día no se veía Cuenca; había demasiada neblina. Últimamente, la divisaban casi todos los días. Bernie se preguntó si los guardias no estarían mandando descansar a la columna en aquel lugar con el deliberado propósito de atormentar a los hombres con una visión lejana de la libertad. A veces, pensaba en las casas colgadas. ¿Cómo debía de ser vivir en una de ellas y contemplar el desfiladero desde tu ventana? ¿Daba vértigo? Aquellos días, teniendo tan poca gente con quien hablar, su mente parecía regresar cada vez más a menudo al pasado. Hasta los que no eran comunistas lo evitaban; suponía que Eulalio les habría dicho que era un confidente.

En el patio, los hombres se incorporaron con gesto cansino a la fila para el acto de pasar lista. El sol, que casi rozaba el horizonte, arrojaba un resplandor rojizo sobre el patio, las barracas y las atalayas. Aranda subió al estrado y empezó a pronunciar nombres. A medio camino, Bernie oyó delante de él un repentino clic, como de algo que hubiera caído al suelo. Vio a Pablo llevarse la mano a los pantalones y bajar la vista. El trozo de piedra se había abierto camino a través del deshilachado tejido de los pantalones y ahora descansaba en el suelo. Uno de los guardias se acercó rápidamente a él. Desde el estrado, Aranda levantó bruscamente la vista.

—¿Qué pasa aquí?

El guardia se agachó y recogió la piedra. La miró, clavó los ojos en Pablo y después subió al estrado. Él y Aranda inclinaron la cabeza sobre la piedra. Pablo los observó con el rostro muy pálido.

Obedeciendo a un movimiento de la cabeza de Aranda, el guardia volvió a bajar. Él y otro guardia sacaron a Pablo de la fila y le ataron las manos a la espalda. Aranda sostuvo la piedra en alto.

—¡Tenemos entre nosotros a un coleccionista de recuerdos! —gritó—. Este hombre ha encontrado un fragmento de aquellas blasfemas pinturas de la cantera y se lo ha quedado. ¿Alguien más se ha llevado alguna pinturita a su barraca? —Miró hacia la silenciosa hilera de prisioneros—. ¿No? Bueno, pues esta noche todos vosotros seréis registrados y las barracas también. —Meneó tristemente la cabeza—. ¿Por qué no aprendéis a hacer lo que os decimos? Tendré que imponer un castigo ejemplar a este hombre. Que esta noche permanezca incomunicado. Mañana todos lo volveréis a ver. —Los guardias se llevaron a Pablo en volandas.

—Eso significa la cruz —murmuró alguien.

Aranda reanudó el acto de pasar lista, pronunciando los nombres con su voz áspera y bien timbrada.

Aquella noche en la barraca, después del registro, Eulalio se acercó al jergón de Bernie. Lo acompañaban cuatro de los restantes comunistas. Se sentó en el camastro vacío de Pablo. Eulalio cruzó las manos sobre la empuñadura del bastón. Bajo la piel reseca se podían ver los tendones moviéndose sobre los huesos.

—Me han dicho que hoy has estado hablando con Pablo en la cantera. ¿Les has dicho tú a los guardias que él se había llevado aquel fragmento de piedra? Se lo has dicho, ¿eh? —Bernie se incorporó y miró a Eulalio a los ojos.

—Tú sabes que no es cierto, Eulalio. Todo el mundo ha visto lo que ha ocurrido... se le cayó del bolsillo.

—Y tú, ¿qué le estabas diciendo? Él tiene prohibido hablar contigo.

—Me enseñó el trozo de piedra que había encontrado. Le dije que tuviera cuidado. Pregúntaselo a él.

—Creo que lo has delatado.

—Se le cayó del bolsillo —dijo Miguel, el viejo tranviario—. Vamos, camarada, todos lo hemos visto.

Eulalio dirigió una mirada perversa a Miguel. Bernie se rió.

—¿Lo ves?, la gente empieza a ver lo que realmente eres, hijo de puta. Un hombre que saca beneficio de lo que le van a hacer a Pablo.

—Déjalo, Eulalio —dijo Miguel.

El viejo dio media vuelta y los otros tres lo siguieron vacilando. Bernie miró a Eulalio con una sonrisa en los labios.

—A medida que se te va marchitando el cuerpo, Eulalio, te transparenta el corazón.

Eulalio se levantó con gran dificultad, agarrando el bastón.

—Voy a acabar contigo, cabrón —dijo en voz baja.

—Si antes no te mueres —le replicó Bernie a su espalda, mientras el otro se alejaba renqueando.

A la mañana siguiente, después del acto de pasar lista, los prisioneros recibieron la orden de permanecer en su sitio sin romper filas. Bernie observó que Agustín se había vuelto a incorporar al servicio. Parecía que tuviera frío de pie allí fuera... debía de ser un cambio tremendo después de haber estado en Sevilla. El hombre cruzó momentáneamente la mirada con la suya y apartó la vista; parecía que lo estuviera estudiando. Bernie se volvió a preguntar si estaría interesado en su trasero, si aquél sería el motivo de que lo hubiera ayudado aquella mañana en la colina. «Tiempos mejores», le había dicho Agustín. Ahora Bernie estuvo casi a punto de reírse en voz alta.

Dos guardias sacaron a Pablo de la barraca donde había permanecido incomunicado y lo llevaron a rastras hasta la cruz que había junto a la barraca del rancho. Bernie vio suspirar a Agustín, como si estuviera cansado. Colocaron a Pablo al lado de aquella cosa mientras la respiración se les congelaba en el aire. Aranda se acercó a ellos a grandes zancadas, golpeándose el muslo con la fusta. Lo acompañaban el padre

Jaime y el padre Eduardo, ambos envueltos en unas gruesas capas negras. Habían permanecido junto a él en el estrado durante el acto de pasar lista. El padre Jaime, frío y ceñudo; el padre Eduardo, con la cabeza inclinada. Los tres se detuvieron ante Pablo. Aranda se volvió para dirigirse a los prisioneros.

—Vuestro camarada Pablo Jiménez se va a pasar un día en la cruz, como castigo por su operación de contrabando. Pero primero tenéis que ver esto.

El comandante se sacó del bolsillo el trozo de piedra pintada y lo depositó en el suelo. El padre Jaime dio un paso al frente. Sacó un pequeño martillo del bolsillo, se agachó y empezó a golpear el trozo de piedra. Éste se hizo añicos y las astillas volaron en todas direcciones. El padre Jaime le hizo una seña con la cabeza al padre Eduardo y éste recogió los fragmentos. El padre Jaime se volvió para guardar el martillo en el bolsillo y miró a los hombres con una mueca de satisfacción en su inflexible semblante.

—Así es como la Iglesia militante se ha venido enfrentando con el paganismo desde sus primeros tiempos —dijo, levantando la voz—. ¡A golpes de martillo! Recordadlo... si es que algo puede penetrar en vuestras duras e impías molleras. —Dicho lo cual, se alejó a grandes zancadas seguido por el padre Eduardo, que sostenía en sus manos ahuecadas los fragmentos de piedra.

Los guardias tomaron los brazos de Pablo y los ataron con cuerdas al palo horizontal de la cruz. Lo ataron de manera que sólo las puntas de los pies rozaran el suelo y después dieron un paso atrás. Pablo se aflojó un segundo y luego se volvió a incorporar, apoyándose en los dedos de los pies. La tortura de la cruz consistía en la incapacidad del hombre de respirar con los brazos extendidos por encima de él, a no ser que tuviera la fuerza de elevarse. Al cabo de unas cuantas horas en semejante posición, cualquier movimiento suponía un calvario; pero era la única manera de poder respirar. Subiendo y bajando dolorosamente, subiendo y bajando.

Aranda estudió la posición de Pablo y asintió con semblante satisfecho. Miró a los prisioneros con una torva sonrisa, gritó un «¡Rompan filas!» y regresó a grandes zancadas a su barraca. Los guardias distribuyeron a los hombres en sus distintos grupos de trabajo. Agustín estaba en la cuadrilla de Bernie. Mientras cruzaban la verja, se le acercó.

—Quiero hablar contigo —le dijo en voz baja—. Es importante. Sal de tu barraca esta noche después de cenar, como si fueras a mear. Yo te esperaré en la parte de atrás.

—¿Qué quieres? —le replicó Bernie en un susurro airado.

A juzgar por la inquieta expresión de su rostro, no parecía que el hombre se lo quisiera follar.

—Más tarde. Tengo que decirte una cosa. —Agustín se apartó.

A última hora de la tarde, empezó a caer una copiosa nevada y los guardias ordenaron a los hombres que interrumpieran el trabajo. En el camino de vuelta, Agustín permaneció al otro extremo de la fila, evitando mirar a Bernie. Al regresar al campo, vieron a Pablo todavía atado a la cruz con la nieve arremolinándosele alrededor de la cabeza.

—Mierda —murmuró el hombre que caminaba al lado de Bernie.

—Aún está aquí.

Pablo estaba pálido e inmóvil y, por un instante, Bernie pensó que había muerto; pero después lo vio elevarse empujando el suelo con los dedos de los pies. Respiró hondo y exhaló el aire en medio de un prolongado y chirriante gemido. Los guardias cerraron las verjas y dejaron que los prisioneros regresaran por su cuenta a sus barracas. Bernie y algunos otros se acercaron a Pablo.

—Agua —graznó éste—. Agua, por favor.

Los hombres se agacharon y empezaron a recoger puñados de nieve, acercándoselos para que bebiera. Fue un proceso muy lento. De pronto, se abrió la puerta de la barraca de Aranda y una luz amarilla atravesó la espesa cortina de copos de nieve. Los hombres se pusieron tensos, temiendo que saliera el comandante y les ordenara alejarse; pero el que salió fue el padre Eduardo. Vio al grupo alrededor de la cruz, titubeó un instante y después se acercó a ellos. Los prisioneros se hicieron a un lado para dejarle pasar.

—Yo creía que eran los romanos los que crucificaban a los inocentes —dijo alguien en voz alta.

El padre Eduardo se detuvo un instante y después reanudó la marcha, levantando la mirada hacia Pablo.

—He hablado con el comandante —dijo—. Muy pronto te van a bajar.

La única respuesta de Pablo fue otro ruidoso jadeo mientras se elevaba, empujando una vez más el suelo con los dedos de los pies. El cura se mordió el labio y dio media vuelta para retirarse.

Bernie le cortó el paso. El padre Eduardo lo miró parpadeando, pues tenía los cristales de las gafas cubiertos por una fina capa de nieve fundida.

—¿Es eso lo que usted quiere decir, cura, cuando habla de los cristianos que comparten los sufrimientos de Cristo en la cruz?

El padre Eduardo se volvió y se alejó muy despacio con la cabeza inclinada. Mientras luchaba contra la nieve que se arremolinaba a su alrededor, alguien le gritó a su espalda.

—¡Hijo de puta!

Un manotazo en la espalda sobresaltó a Bernie. Se volvió y vio a Miguel.

—Bien hecho, Bernardo —dijo éste—. Creo que has avergonzado al muy cabrón.

Sin embargo, mientras contemplaba la espalda del padre Eduardo perdiéndose en la distancia, Bernie también se avergonzó. Jamás se hubiera atrevido a insultar al padre Jaime de aquella manera, ninguno de los hombres lo habría hecho. Había elegido al representante más débil, al que más fácilmente podía herir; y, en ese caso, ¿qué clase de valor era el suyo?

Bernie abandonó la barraca después de cenar, alegando que tenía que mear y su cubo ya estaba lleno. Les estaba permitido hacerlo hasta que se apagaban las luces. Agustín lo había puesto nervioso, pero necesitaba averiguar qué quería de él. Dejó a Pablo tumbado en el jergón de al lado, tapado por una gruesa capa de mantas ofrecidas por los demás hombres, pues estaba congelado y le dolían tremendamente los hombros. Bernie había colocado su manta encima de las demás. El rostro de Pablo estaba muy pálido. Miguel le murmuró a Bernie:

—Es joven y vigoroso, con un poco de suerte lo superará. —Estaba claro que había decidido hacer caso omiso de las órdenes de Eulalio para desairarlo; es probable que otros imitaran su ejemplo.

Fuera había cesado de nevar. Bernie rodeó la barraca para dirigirse a la parte de atrás, donde la luz de la luna arrojaba una sombra alargada. En el interior de la sombra, Bernie vio el rojo resplandor de una colilla de cigarrillo. Se acercó a Agustín. El guardia apagó el cigarrillo aplastándolo con el pie.

—¿Qué coño quieres? —le preguntó Bernie con aspereza—. Llevas siglos mirándome a hurtadillas.

Agustín lo miró fijamente.

—Tengo un hermano en Madrid que también era guardia, ¿lo recuerdas? Alto y delgado como yo, se llama Luis.

Bernie frunció el entrecejo.

—Se fue hace varios meses, ¿verdad? ¿Qué tiene que ver conmigo?

—Se fue a Madrid en busca de trabajo; en Sevilla no hay. Allí entró en contacto con un periodista inglés que conoce a una amiga tuya. —Agustín vaciló, mirando a Bernie, y después añadió—: Han planeado una fuga para ti.

—¿Qué? —Bernie se lo quedó mirando—. ¿Y quién es esta amiga?

—Una inglesa. La señora Forsyth.

Bernie meneó la cabeza.

—¿Quién? Yo no conozco a ninguna señora Forsyth. En el colegio conocía a un chico que se llamaba Forsyth, pero no era amigo mío.

Agustín levantó la mano.

—Tranquilo, hombre, por el amor de Dios. Esta mujer está casada con tu compañero del colegio. Tú la conociste en Madrid durante la guerra. Su nombre era entonces Barbara Clare.

Bernie se quedó boquiabierto de asombro.

—¿Barbara sigue en España? ¿Y está casada con Sandy Forsyth?

—Sí. Es un hombre de negocios que vive en Madrid. Él no sabe nada, Barbara se lo ha ocultado. Ella es la que nos paga. Mi trabajo aquí está a punto de terminar y no quiero volver a firmar para otro período de servicio. Odio este lugar. El frío y el aislamiento.

—Santo Dios. —Bernie miró a Agustín—. ¿Cuánto tiempo lo lleváis planeando?

—Muchas semanas. No ha sido fácil. Te he estado vigilando desde que regresé. Tienes que andarte con cuidado, te has creado muchos enemigos. No es bueno pasar el invierno en el campo. Todo el mundo tiene frío y evita salir, y el cerebro empieza a inventarse maldades.

Bernie se pasó la mano por la barba enmarañada.

—Barbara. ¡Oh, Dios mío, Barbara! —Experimentó una repentina sensación de debilidad y tuvo que apoyarse contra la pared de la barraca—. Barbara. —Pronunció el nombre en un susurro mientras las lágrimas le humedecían los ojos. Después respiró hondo y se acercó un poco más a Agustín, el cual se echó ligeramente hacia atrás—. ¿Es eso verdad? ¿De veras es cierto?

—Lo es.

—¿Se casó con Forsyth? —Rompió a reír sin dar crédito—. ¿Y él sabe algo de esto?

—No, sólo ella.

Bernie respiró hondo.

—¿Cómo se hará? ¿Cuál es el plan?

Agustín se inclinó hacia él.

—Ya te lo diré.

36

Hacía mucho frío en Madrid desde principios de diciembre, y el día 6 al despertar Harry se encontró con la ciudad cubierta por una espesa capa de nieve. Le resultó extraño ver nieve allí. Ésta ocultaba parcialmente la fealdad y las cicatrices de la guerra; pero, mientras se dirigía a pie a la embajada contemplando los rostros angustiados y enrojecidos de los viandantes, se preguntó cómo podría la población medio muerta de hambre resistir la situación en caso de que ésta se prolongara.

La nevada había sido tan fuerte que los tranvías no circulaban; Harry atravesó una ciudad extraña y silenciosa con todos los sonidos amortiguados bajo un cielo gris pizarra que prometía más nieve. Al cruzar la Castellana, vio un gasógeno detenido en mitad de la calle que vomitaba espesas nubes de humo mientras el conductor trataba desesperadamente de ponerlo en marcha. Un viejo pasó lentamente con un asno cargado con latas de aceite de oliva. Las botas agrietadas del hombre estaban empapadas.

—Hace mal tiempo —le dijo Harry.

—Sí, muy malo.

Tenía que ver a Hillgarth a las diez; no es que deseara precisamente aquel encuentro, y encima ahora iba a llegar tarde. A lo largo de las dos semanas transcurridas desde que la cena quedara interrumpida por la llamada de Sofía, Harry había seguido adelante con su «turno de vigilancia» sobre Sandy, con quien se había reunido un par de veces en el café y en cuya casa había vuelto a cenar; pero ya no había podido averiguar nada más. Sandy ya no le había vuelto a mencionar la mina de oro y, al preguntarle qué tal iban las cosas por allí, Sandy contestaba que la situación era «difícil» y rápidamente cambiaba de tema. Parecía preocupado, y sólo haciendo un gran esfuerzo conseguía conservar su habitual afabilidad. En su más reciente reunión en el café, le había preguntado a Harry cómo iba todo en Inglaterra, si el mercado negro era muy grande y cuánto negocio hacían los traficantes del mercado negro. A su vez, Harry le había preguntado si pensaba regresar a casa; pero él se había limitado a encogerse de hombros. Harry habría deseado que todo terminara de una vez, estaba harto del engaño y las mentiras. La idea de que Gómez tal vez hubiera sido asesinado no se apartaba jamás de sus pensamientos.

Barbara seguía dando la impresión de estar muy alterada y se mostraba muy distante con él. Sin embargo, cuando lo acompañó a la puerta tras su visita de unos días atrás, le preguntó cómo estaba Sofía. Ésta había expresado su deseo de volver a ver a Barbara y Harry había apuntado la posibilidad de que los tres se reunieran a almorzar algún día. Tras dudarlo un instante, Barbara había accedido.

A los espías no les había gustado enterarse de la existencia de Sofía. Tolhurst lo había interrogado sobre la llamada de la chica a la embajada; Harry adivinó que todas las llamadas relacionadas con él eran comunicadas automáticamente a Tolhurst.

—Nos tenías que haber informado de que habías conocido a una putita española —le dijo—. ¿Cómo os conocisteis?

Harry le contó la historia del rescate del hermano del ataque de los perros, y omitió el detalle de quién era Enrique.

—Podría ser una espía —dijo Tolhurst—. Aquí nunca se es lo bastante precavido con las mujeres. Dijiste que ya no te seguían. No obstante, si os conocisteis por casualidad...

—Por pura casualidad. Además, Sofía es enemiga del régimen.

—Sí, Carabanchel era un barrio rojo. Pero allí abajo no son muy amigos nuestros. Ten cuidado, Harry, es lo único que te digo.

—Le he dicho que soy traductor. No me pregunta nada acerca de mi trabajo.

—¿Es guapa? ¿Ya te la has metido entre las sábanas?

—Vamos, Tolly, no es una de tus pelanduscas —replicó Harry con repentina exasperación.

Una expresión ofendida se dibujó en el rostro de Tolhurst. Éste se apartó un mechón de cabello de la cara y se ajustó la corbata blanca de Eton.

—Calma, chico. —Enarcó una ceja—. Pero no te impliques demasiado.

Habían quitado la nieve de delante de la embajada. No hacía viento, y la bandera británica colgaba como sin vida del asta. Harry pasó por delante de la pareja de guardias civiles de la entrada, arrebujados en sus capas. Una vez más, la reunión iba a tener lugar en el despacho de Tolhurst. Hillgarth ya estaba allí, aquel día enfundado en su uniforme de la Armada, sentado detrás del escritorio fumando Players. Tolhurst permanecía de pie, estudiando unos documentos. En la pared, el enjuto y sombrío rostro del rey miraba desde su retrato.

—Buenos días, Harry —lo saludó Tolhurst.

—Buenos días. Lamento el retraso, pero hoy no circulan los tranvías a causa de la nieve.

—Bueno —dijo Hillgarth—. Quiero revisar la situación con Forsyth. He estado examinando los informes de sus reuniones recientes. Ya no habla de la mina de oro, pero usted dice que parece preocupado.

—Sí, señor, lo está.

Hillgarth tamborileó con los dedos sobre la mesa.

—No podemos obtener ninguna información de Maestre acerca de la mina. Ahora sabemos que forma parte de este comité de vigilancia, aunque él no va a decir nada al respecto. Por muchas cosas que le ofrezcamos a cambio. —Hillgarth arqueó las cejas, mirando a Harry—. Seguimos sin tener noticias del tal Gómez. De lo cual se nos acusa. Sobre todo a usted, Harry. —Hillgarth encendió otro cigarrillo y exhaló un torrente de humo—. Será mejor que se mantenga apartado de él a partir de ahora.

—Lo vi en el Rastro hace un par de semanas. No estuvo muy amable.

—Me lo imagino. —Hillgarth reflexionó un instante—. Dígame, ¿cree usted que Forsyth u otra persona podría estar activamente implicado en algún tipo de juego sucio?

—Podría ser —contestó Harry muy despacio—. En caso de que pensara que sus intereses corren peligro.

Hillgarth asintió con la cabeza.

—Necesitamos averiguar datos sobre esta mina, con cuántos recursos de oro cuenta el régimen. El único camino que nos queda es Forsyth. —Hillgarth miró a Harry con expresión inquisitiva—. Me gustaría ofrecerle una oportunidad de redimirse. Barajamos la posibilidad de reclutarlo, dado que Maestre no se dejará sobornar. Dígaselo, Tolly.

Tolhurst lo miró más serio que una lechuza.

—Ésta es información clasificada, Harry. ¿Recuerdas que me preguntaste acerca de los Caballeros de San Jorge? —Harry asintió con la cabeza—. Nuestro Gobierno dispone de grandes sumas destinadas a sobornar a gente aquí en España. A destacados monárquicos bien relacionados con el régimen y a cualquier otra persona que ejerza influencia sobre el Gobierno y pueda abogar en favor de que España no entre en guerra.

—Casi todas las embajadas cuentan con fondos para sobornos —terció Hillgarth—. Pero esto, a distinta escala. No es sólo la antipatía por los fascistas lo que induce a Maestre a facilitarnos información; a él y a otros personajes de alto rango. Si Forsyth se pasara a nuestro bando, podríamos hacerle llegar fondos y ofrecerle protección diplomática si fuera necesario. He llegado a la conclusión de que es la única manera de averiguar algo acerca del oro. Las acciones de su empresa están cayendo en picado. Supongo que Maestre y su comité le están apretando las tuercas. Quieren arrebatarle el control del oro a la Falange.

—Estaría muy bien, señor.

—Londres quiere saber si hay oro, y cuánto. Están ejerciendo presión sobre Sam; pero, de momento, éste ni siquiera consigue concertar una cita con Franco. El Generalísimo se está tomando toda suerte de molestias para tratarnos con el mayor desdén posible y complacer así a los alemanes. Y lo que hemos conseguido averiguar acerca de la personalidad de Forsyth nos induce a pensar que éste se tirará de cabeza a nuestro bando si su proyecto tropieza con dificultades. —Hillgarth se inclinó hacia delante—. ¿Usted qué piensa, Harry?

Harry reflexionó un momento.

—Si tiene problemas, creo que podría hacerlo.

Al final, había acabado por despreciar a Sandy, pero pensaba que la perspectiva de que Hillgarth le arrojara un salvavidas sería un alivio para él.

—Si necesita un plan de fuga, se conformará con menos dinero —terció Tolhurst—. No conviene estirar demasiado el presupuesto.

Harry miró a Hillgarth con la cara muy seria.

—Pero no sé hasta qué extremo se pueden fiar ustedes de Sandy. Siempre le hace el juego a alguien.

Hillgarth sonrió.

—Ah, sí, de eso ya me he dado cuenta. De hecho, creo que Forsyth podría convertirse en un espía excelente. Alguien aficionado a tener secretos; puede que disfrute con la emoción del peligro. ¿Qué tal le suena eso?

—Yo diría que bien, siempre y cuando el peligro no se acerque demasiado. Tal vez debería estar asustado —contestó Harry, mirando a Hillgarth a los ojos—. Podríamos estar contratando a alguien implicado en un asesinato.

El capitán inclinó la cabeza.

—No sería el primero, no podemos ser remilgados.

Hubo una pausa de silencio. Tolhurst la rompió.

—¿Tiene Forsyth alguna preferencia política?

—Creo que apoya cualquier sistema que le dé mano libre para ganar dinero. Por eso le gusta Franco. Odia a los comunistas, naturalmente. —Harry hizo una pausa—. Pero tampoco es leal a Gran Bretaña, ni poco ni mucho.

—Su padre es obispo, ¿verdad? —preguntó Hillgarth—. Por regla general, los hijos de los clérigos acostumbran a ser personas inestables.

—Sandy cree que la Iglesia y todas sus antiguas tradiciones están hechas a propósito para asfixiar a personas como él.

—Y no le falta razón. —Hillgarth asintió con la cabeza y luego juntó las puntas de los dedos de las manos delante de sí—. Entonces, eso es lo que vamos a hacer: vuelva a reunirse con Forsyth; dígale, simplemente, que hay alguien en la embajada que tiene un ofrecimiento que hacerle. No revele demasiado, sólo anímelo a venir. Puede decirle que tiene contactos con el servicio secreto si cree que eso le podría resultar útil. Si consigue hacerlo, podría borrar la pizarra y regresar a casa con un triunfo en el bolsillo.

Harry asintió con la cabeza.

—Haré lo que pueda. Hoy voy a comer con Barbara. Puedo intentar organizar algo. —«Menos mal que es lo último que me piden», pensó.

—Muy bien. ¿Qué tal es la mujer de Forsyth?

—No creo que sean muy felices.

—¿Sigue sin saber nada acerca del negocio?

—Sí. Estoy prácticamente seguro de que él no le cuenta nada.

—Temíamos que usted se hubiera empezado a encariñar con ella, hasta que se lió con esa lechera —dijo Hillgarth, haciéndole a Harry un repentino e inoportuno guiño.

Mientras se dirigía a pie al centro a la hora del almuerzo, Harry pensó en la entrevista. La indiferente manera con que Hillgarth había despachado la desaparición de Gómez y la posible intervención de

Sandy en el asunto lo habían dejado helado. ¿Acaso no sabían lo que significaba para una persona normal el hecho de tener que hacer aquel trabajo? Unas pequeñas brigadas de obreros limpiaban sin orden ni concierto las aceras con palas y escobas. Harry buscó la posible presencia de Enrique entre ellos, pero no lo vio.

Barbara le había propuesto reunirse con él y Sofía en el Café Gijón. La elección del lugar le había parecido un poco rara; sabía que Barbara solía ir allí con Bernie durante la Guerra Civil, pero ahora apenas mencionaba su nombre. «Pobre Bernie —pensó—, por lo menos no tuvo que ver en qué se había convertido España.»

La barra estaba llena de prósperos madrileños que se quejaban de la nieve mientras tomaban café. Se respiraba en el aire un húmedo olor a grasa. Harry se llevó su taza de café con leche a un desierto rincón del local. Se dio cuenta de que había llegado muy temprano.

Sandy y los espías se llevarían muy bien, pensó. Bueno, él los dejaría con lo suyo y se iría a casa. «Pero ¿a casa para hacer qué?», se preguntó. Vuelta a Cambridge, más solo que la una. Se miró la cara en los espejos. Había adelgazado desde su llegada allí, lo cual le parecía de perlas. «¿Y si me pudiera llevar a Sofía?», se preguntó. ¿Habría alguna manera? Tendría que cargar también con Paco, porque ella jamás lo abandonaría. Si pudiera llevárselos a los dos a Inglaterra... ¿Y si no diera resultado? Una parte de su mente también le decía que estaba loco, que sólo la conocía desde hacía seis semanas.

El barman le había dejado el cambio en un platito. Una de las nuevas monedas de cinco pesetas con el busto de Franco. Volvió a pensar en Hillgarth, hablando como si tal cosa de la posibilidad de reclutar a alguien... que quizá fuera un asesino, contándole de qué manera había sobornado a los monárquicos. Hoare había dicho que había sudado sangre para intentar convencer a los monárquicos de que él y ellos hablaban el mismo lenguaje. «Pero también había sudado oro», pensó Harry. Gente como Maestre que hablaban del honor de España y de las tradiciones que preservaban; pero que, al mismo tiempo, aceptaban sobornos de un enemigo en potencia. Y Gran Bretaña, a la que sólo interesaba España por su valor estratégico... aunque ganaran la guerra, España quedaría en poder de Franco y volvería a ser olvidada.

Se inclinó sobre su taza de café con leche. Pensó que quizá fuera mejor que Hitler invadiera España. Hasta Sandy decía que el régimen era muy débil; quizás el pueblo volviera a alzarse contra los alemanes tal como se había alzado contra Napoleón. Pero entonces Gran Bretaña perdería Gibraltar y quedaría todavía más debilitada. Recordó la imagen que había visto el primer día, unos soldados alemanes y españoles saludándose en la frontera. El Führer y el Caudillo sellando su eterna amistad tras la victoria de ambos en Europa. La idea era espantosa. Volvió a estudiar su tenso rostro en el espejo. Les prestaría aquel último servicio, intentaría reclutar a Sandy para ellos.

Experimentó un sobresalto al notar el roce de una mano en su hombro. Era Sofía, envuelta en su viejo abrigo negro y con el rostro arrebolado por el placer de verlo, comprendió Harry presa de una cálida emoción.

—¿En qué estabas pensando? —preguntó ella, con una sonrisa en los labios.

—Nada. Unos problemas del trabajo. Anda, siéntate.

—¿Aún no ha llegado Barbara?

—No. —Harry consultó su reloj y se extrañó de que ya fuera casi la una—. Se está retrasando. Voy a pedirte un café.

—De acuerdo —dijo ella, tras dudar un instante.

Había habido entre ambos algunas discusiones por el hecho de que Harry lo pagara todo y hasta le hiciera regalos.

—Tengo dinero —le había dicho él—, puede que no me lo merezca, pero lo tengo. ¿Por qué no gastarme una parte contigo?

—La gente dirá que soy una mantenida —había contestado ella, ruborizándose.

Harry se había dado cuenta de que Sofía no estaba tan libre como quería creer de lo que ella llamaba «las sensibilidades burguesas».

—Tú sabes que no es cierto, y eso es lo que importa.

Pero Sofía no permitía que le diera dinero para la familia, alegando que ya se las arreglaría ella sola. Harry habría deseado que le dejara hacer algo más; sin embargo, también admiraba su orgullo. Fue a pedirle un café.

—¿Cómo está Paco?

—Muy callado y tranquilo. Hoy Enrique está con él; tiene el día libre.

Con Elena muerta y Sofía y Enrique trabajando, ahora el chiquillo se tenía que quedar solo en el apartamento casi todos los días. Pero se negaba a salir, a no ser que alguno de los mayores lo acompañara.

—Le han gustado los lápices de colores que le regalaste ayer. Quiere saber cuándo volverá la señora pelirroja. Lo dejó muy impresionado. La llama «la señora buena».

—Le podríamos preguntar si le importaría ir a verlo.

—Estaría muy bien. —Sofía arrugó la frente—. Tengo miedo de que algún día Paco le abra la puerta a la señora Ávila. Sé que ella llama. Le tengo dicho que no abra. Las llamadas lo asustan, le recuerdan la vez que se llevaron a sus padres. Pero yo temo que un día le abra la puerta y ella se lo lleve porque está solo.

—No le abrirá la puerta si le tiene miedo.

—Pero así no podemos seguir, dejándolo constantemente solo en casa.

—No —convino Harry.

—No quiero perderlo. —Sofía lanzó un suspiro—. ¿Crees que somos unos tontos, cargando con un peso como éste? A veces Enrique cree que sí, lo sé, pero él también quiere mucho a Paco.

Harry pensó: «Ha perdido a su madre, ahora teme perder al niño y, si a mí me envían a casa, también me perderá.» Frunció el entrecejo.

—¿Qué ocurre, Harry?

—Nada. —Levantó la vista y, al ver acercarse a Barbara con el pañuelo que le cubría la cabeza y las gafas punteados de copos de nieve, levantó la mano para saludarla.

—Perdón por el retraso. Fuera ha empezado a nevar otra vez.

—En mi vida había visto cosa igual —dijo Sofía—. La sequía en verano y ahora esto.

Harry se levantó y recogió el abrigo de Barbara.

—¿Pedimos el menú del almuerzo?

Barbara levantó una mano.

—No, verás. Lo lamento muchísimo, pero no me puedo quedar. Tengo una cita en la otra punta de la ciudad y los tranvías no circulan. Tendré que ir a pie. Pídeme sólo un café, si no te importa.

—De acuerdo. —Harry estudió a Barbara. Había algo serio y decidido en su manera de comportarse. Fue a pedir otro café. Al volver, Sofía y Barbara estaban enzarzadas en una conversación muy seria.

—Barbara dice que Paco necesita que lo vea un médico —le dijo Sofía.

—Pues sí, quizás un médico pueda ofrecer alguna idea sobre la mejor manera de ayudarlo. Yo podría colaborar en los gastos... —Se mordió la lengua al ver que Sofía fruncía el entrecejo. No tendría que haber hablado de dinero delante de Barbara.

—Si yo pudiera echar una mano al pobre chiquillo —dijo Barbara—. Pero comprendo que es difícil.

—¿Ya has empezado a trabajar en el hospital militar? —le preguntó Harry, cambiando de tema.

—Sí, por lo menos es mejor que el orfelinato. Aunque las heridas de guerra son tremendas. Todo lo que la Cruz Roja trató de evitar. —Barbara suspiró—. En fin, ahora es demasiado tarde para pensar en eso. —Miró a Harry—. Es probable que, al final, vuelva a casa por Navidad.

—¿A Inglaterra?

—Sí, ¿recuerdas que Sandy me lo sugirió y yo pensé, «bueno, por qué no»? Por lo menos veré qué tal están realmente por allí.

—¿Y después te permitirán regresar a España? —preguntó Sofía—. Supongo que sí, porque tu marido trabaja aquí.

Barbara titubeó.

—Supongo.

«Pero es que Sandy no es su marido», pensó Harry. De pronto, se le ocurrió una cosa.

—A lo mejor sucede lo contrario, ¿verdad? Quiero decir que, si un inglés tuviera... digamos... una novia española, probablemente le pondrían pegas para llevársela a Inglaterra. En cambio, estando casados, los dejarían entrar a los dos.

—Sí —dijo Barbara—. Por lo menos, así era antes de la guerra. Recuerdo todas aquellas normas de la Cruz Roja. Para trasladar a los refugiados de un país a otro. —Se quedó momentáneamente en blanco—. Hace menos de cinco años. Y parece toda una vida.

Sofía bajó la voz.

—Y sigue habiendo el peligro de que Franco declare la guerra.

Barbara se quitó las gafas empañadas por el vapor y las limpió con su pañuelo. Sin ellas, su rostro resultaba más atractivo, pero también más vulnerable. Removió cuidadosamente su café y después los miró.

—Seguramente no volveré —dijo, sin la menor inflexión en la voz—. No creo que Sandy y yo podamos seguir juntos.

—Lo siento —dijo Harry—. Supe que no eras feliz.

Barbara dio una calada a su cigarrillo.

—Estoy muy en deuda con él. Me ayudó a recuperarme después... después de lo de Bernie. Sin embargo, creo que ya no me gusta el papel que me asignó. —Se rió avergonzada—. Perdona que te haya soltado todo esto tan de repente. Pero es que no tengo a nadie con quien hablar, ¿sabes? ¿Tiene sentido lo que digo?

—Llega un momento en la vida en que uno se tiene que enfrentar con las cosas —dijo Harry—. Y quitarse la venda de los ojos. —Meneó la cabeza mirando a Sofía—. Ésta es la impresión que me ha dado España. Me ha hecho comprender que el mundo es más complicado de lo que yo pensaba.

Barbara lo miró con aquella extraña manera suya tan perspicaz e incisiva.

—Vaya si lo es.

Hubo unos momentos de silencio.

—¿Le has dicho que no vas a volver? —le preguntó Sofía.

—No. De todos modos, ya no le importa. Tengo un... un pequeño asunto que resolver aquí y después espero poder irme por Navidad.

—Sandy podría tener algún problema con sus negocios —señaló Harry en tono dubitativo.

—¿Sabes algo? —le preguntó Barbara.

Harry vaciló.

—Me iba a introducir en... en una de sus empresas. Pero todo se ha quedado en agua de borrajas.

—¿Qué empresa?

—No sé. Apenas sé nada.

Barbara hizo un movimiento afirmativo con la cabeza.

—Siento parecer desleal —dijo—, pero te he estado observando cuando estabas con él. En realidad, ahora ya no te gusta, ¿verdad? Simplemente conservas la relación por el tema del colegio.

—Bueno... algo así.

—Es curioso, pero él busca tu aprobación. —Barbara se volvió hacia Sofía—. Aquí en España no hay nada comparable a los vínculos que se crean entre hombres que estudiaron en esas escuelas privadas inglesas. —Soltó una carcajada un poco histérica y Sofía se sintió incómoda. Harry pensó: «Está al borde de un ataque de nervios.» Barbara se mordió el labio—. Lo vais a mantener en secreto, ¿verdad? Perdona.

—Faltaría más.

Sofía la miró sonriendo.

—Paco pregunta constantemente por ti. No sé si podrás ir a verlo antes de marcharte a Inglaterra.

Barbara le devolvió la sonrisa.

—Me encantaría. Gracias. A lo mejor, lo podríamos llevar a algún sitio que le guste.

Harry respiró hondo.

—Tengo que hablar con Sandy de un asunto relacionado con aquel negocio. ¿Sabes si hoy estará en su despacho?

—Supongo que sí. —Barbara consultó el reloj—. ¡Oh, Dios mío, me tengo que ir! No os he dejado comer, contándoos todas mis penas. ¡Cuánto lo siento!

—No te preocupes. Oye, a ver si me llamas y organizamos algo para que vayas a ver a Paco.

—Lo haré. Me ha encantado veros a los dos.

Barbara se inclinó para besar a Sofía en la mejilla al estilo español y después se levantó y se encaminó hacia la salida, luego se detuvo un momento para anudarse el pañuelo alrededor de la cabeza. Harry la miró, pero pensando en el matrimonio. ¿Se atrevería a dar aquel paso? ¿Y Sofía lo aceptaría? En la embajada averiguaría más detalles; pero primero tendría que intentar reclutar a Sandy para que Hillgarth le permitiera apuntarse aquel triunfo.

Barbara abrió la puerta y se volvió para despedirse rápidamente con la mano antes de perderse en medio del remolino de los copos de nieve.

37

Barbara se maldijo en su fuero interno mientras se alejaba calle abajo. No era su intención soltarlo todo de aquella manera. Sin embargo, al verlos a ellos dos sentados allí con aquel aire tan doméstico y en cierto modo tan seguro, no lo había podido evitar.

Tras haber escuchado furtivamente aquella llamada, había temido durante un tiempo que Harry pudiera estar implicado en alguna de las muchas cosas horribles en las que Sandy andaba metido. Pero, cuando más tarde lo vio, supo que no era así; más bien, otros lo utilizaban a él como rehén. Menos mal que el negocio se había ido a pique, fuera lo que fuera. Se sentía culpable cada vez que veía a Harry, porque éste seguía pensando que Bernie había muerto. Precisamente aquel día estaba citada con Luis y esperaba discutir los planes efectivos para la fuga de Bernie. Sabía que Agustín ya había regresado de su permiso de vacaciones. Le había sugerido a Harry que se reunieran en el Café Gijón porque, ahora que la posibilidad de ver a Bernie estaba tan cerca, quería volver a visitar todos los lugares en los que ambos habían estado juntos, lugares que durante tanto tiempo ella había evitado. Tres años transcurridos en campos de prisioneros. «¿Cómo estará? ¿Cómo reaccionará al verme?» Se dijo que no tenía que esperar nada, ambos habrían cambiado hasta extremos irreconocibles. Lo único que tenía que esperar era sacarlo de allí.

La nieve caía copiosamente, cubría los automóviles y los abrigos de quienes deambulaban entre la tormenta cual blancos fantasmas. Se le fundía a través del pañuelo de la cabeza, y pensó que debería haber llevado sombrero. El viento le arrojaba la nieve contra los cristales de las gafas y se las tenía que limpiar con las manos enguantadas.

Pasó por delante de una pareja de la Guardia Civil que montaba guardia a la entrada de un edificio del Gobierno; con sus gruesas capas y sus tricornios cubiertos de nieve, parecían muñecos de nieve con unas máscaras siniestras pintadas encima. Era la primera vez que la contemplación de un guardia civil le provocaba risa.

Se daba cuenta de que últimamente se sentía muy a menudo al borde de la histeria, pero cada vez le resultaba más difícil reprimir sus sentimientos. Quizá le faltara muy poco para irse. Desde la noche, dos semanas atrás, en que había escuchado la conversación telefónica, había estado intentando analizar las palabras de Sandy. «Estos viejos soldados de Marruecos aguantan mucho. ¿Sigue diciendo que Gómez es su verdadero apellido?» Había tratado de buscar una docena de interpretaciones distintas, pero siempre acababa en lo mismo: alguien estaba siendo torturado. Y empezó a pensar: «Como se entere de lo que estoy haciendo, puede que yo también corra peligro.»

Cuando Sandy bajó del estudio después de la llamada, Barbara le entregó la bolsa que el viejo judío le había entregado, pero él pareció no darle importancia. La dejó en el suelo, junto a su silla, y se quedó allí sentado contemplando el fuego de la chimenea sin prestarle la menor atención. Estaba más preocupado que nunca: el sudor le brillaba en el negro bigote. A partir de aquella noche, se había mostrado cada vez más reservado. Ya apenas le prestaba atención, aunque eso a ella le daba igual. Si pudiera aguantar hasta liberar a Bernie y después huir a Inglaterra. Quizá Sandy jamás se enterara de lo que había hecho.

Dos noches atrás, Sandy había regresado a casa muy tarde. A pesar de que bebía mucho, raras veces se emborrachaba. Tenía un extraordinario autocontrol. Aquella noche, en cambio, entró en el salón tambaleándose y miró alrededor con la expresión de quien lo ve todo por primera vez.

—¿Qué miras? —le preguntó a Barbara con voz pastosa.

A Barbara el corazón le empezó a galopar en el pecho.

—Nada, cariño. ¿Te encuentras bien? —Siempre en actitud conciliadora, su estrategia instintiva. Dejó su labor de punto. Ahora se pasaba la tarde haciendo calceta, los rítmicos movimientos la tranquilizaban.

—Pareces una vieja, todo el día con tu maldita calceta —dijo él—. ¿Dónde está Pilar?

—Es su noche libre, ¿no lo recuerdas? —Probablemente quería acostarse con ella; le estaría bien empleado a Pilar, tener que aguantar que él la sobara en semejante estado.

—Ah, sí, es verdad. —Una lujuriosa sonrisa se le dibujó en los labios mientras se acercaba al mueble bar para prepararse un whisky. Después, se sentó frente a ella y tomó un buen trago—. Esta noche vuelve a hacer un frío de cojones.

—La escarcha ya ha matado un montón de plantas en el jardín.

—Plantas —repitió Sandy en tono burlón—. Plantas. Hoy he tenido un día fatal. Algo muy importante que tenía entre manos se ha ido al carajo, a la puta mierda. —Se volvió a mirarla con su ancha sonrisa de siempre—. ¿Te imaginas que fuéramos pobres, Barbara?

—Pero no es para tanto, ¿verdad?

—¿Que no? Pobre Barbara. —Se rió para sus adentros—. Pobre Barbara, eso fue lo que pensé de ti cuando nos conocimos. —La sonrisa le tembló a Barbara en los labios. Si se quedara dormido. Si se cayera al fuego de la chimenea. Sandy la volvió a mirar, esta vez con la cara muy seria—. No seremos pobres —dijo—, yo no permitiré que eso ocurra. ¿Lo entiendes?

—Pues claro, Sandy.

—Me recuperaré. Siempre lo hago. Nos quedaremos en esta casa. Tú, yo y Pilar. —Una chispa se encendió en sus ojos—. Ven a la cama. Anda, te voy a enseñar de qué estoy hecho todavía.

Barbara respiró hondo. Recordó el plan de echarle en cara su relación con Pilar para mantenerlo a raya, pero ahora estaba demasiado asustada.

—Has bebido mucho, Sandy.

—Pero eso a mí no me detiene. Vamos.

Se levantó, se acercó a ella haciendo eses y le estampó un húmedo beso de cerveza en la boca. Barbara reprimió el instinto de apartarse y dejó que la levantara, la rodeara con un brazo y la acompañara al piso de arriba. Al llegar al dormitorio, Barbara confió en que Sandy se desplomara en la cama, pero ahora parecía que estaba más controlado. Empezó a desnudarse mientras ella se quitaba la ropa, muerta de asco en su fuero interno. Se quitó la camisa y dejó al descubierto el cuerpo musculoso que tanto la excitaba en otros tiempos, pero que ahora sólo le recordaba a un animal fuerte y perverso. Consiguió dominar su repugnancia mientras él la penetraba, emitiendo unos pequeños gruñidos que parecían de desesperación. Después se apartó de ella y, al cabo de un minuto, se puso a roncar. Barbara se preguntó cómo había podido aguantarlo y cómo no se había echado a llorar y no lo había apartado a golpes. Por miedo, suponía. El miedo te puede aplastar, pero también te puede conferir fuerza y capacidad de control. Se dirigió sigilosamente al cuarto de baño, cerró la puerta y, víctima de unos violentos mareos, empezó a vomitar.

El pequeño café estaba lleno de gente que había entrado huyendo de la nieve; todas las sillas estaban ocupadas, y los clientes permanecían de pie en doble fila junto a la barra. La atmósfera olía a moho. La anciana iba de la barra a la cafetera automática con las tazas de café en la mano. Los cristales de las ventanas estaban empañados por el vapor y hasta el retrato de Franco aparecía cubierto por una húmeda película. Los cristales de las gafas de Barbara se cubrieron inmediatamente de vaho. Se los limpió en la manga del abrigo y miró alrededor en busca de Luis. Su mesa de costumbre estaba ocupada, pero lo vio en el rincón del fondo, apretujado contra la pared, sentado a una mesa para dos con el abrigo doblado sobre el respaldo de la otra silla. Contemplaba su taza de café con semblante cansado y abatido. Levantó la mirada y su expresión se transformó en una sonrisa al verla abriéndose paso entre la gente para reunirse con él. Barbara se sentó y se quitó el empapado pañuelo de la cabeza, pasándose una mano por el cabello mojado.

—Esta nieve es terrible —dijo.

Luis se inclinó sobre la mesa.

—¿Le importa no tomar café? Es que hay tanta gente en la barra.

—Si quiere, podemos ir a otro sitio A algún otro sitio más tranquilo...

—Hoy será lo mismo en todas partes. —Se advertía una aspereza insólita en sus modales.

—¿Qué ocurre? —le preguntó ella, preocupada.

—No ocurre nada. Es que toda esta gente me pone nervioso. —Luis bajó la voz—. Todo está preparado. ¿Trae el dinero?

—Sí. Setecientas pesetas cuando usted me diga dónde y cuándo. El resto cuando él esté fuera.

Luis asintió con la cabeza, aliviado. Barbara extrajo sus cigarrillos y le ofreció un Gold Flake.

—Gracias. Y ahora, escúcheme bien, por favor. —Se inclinó un poco más hacia ella y habló con una voz que no era más que un áspero murmullo—. Acabo de regresar de Cuenca. Ayer estuve con Agustín. Le ha hablado a su amigo de la fuga. Le ha dicho que es usted la que lo ha organizado.

—¿Y cómo reaccionó? —preguntó ansiosamente Barbara—. ¿Qué dijo?

Luis asintió con la cara muy seria.

—Se puso muy contento, señora. Se alegró mucho.

Barbara vaciló.

—¿Sabe que yo estoy... estoy con otro?

—Agustín no me lo dijo.

Barbara se mordió el labio.

—Bueno; entonces, ¿cuál es el plan?

—La fuga tendrá lugar el catorce de diciembre. Sábado.

«Ocho días —pensó Barbara—, ocho días más.»

—¿No podríamos hacerlo antes?

—Ése será un buen día. Empezarán las fiestas de Navidad; las condiciones en el campo de prisioneros y en la ciudad empezarán a relajarse. Agustín no quiere que los hechos ocurran demasiado cerca de su regreso y yo estoy de acuerdo en que podría resultar sospechoso. Además, con un poco de suerte, la nieve ya habrá desaparecido para entonces. Un hombre corriendo podría destacar demasiado en la nieve.

—Seguramente ya habrá desaparecido para entonces. Las fuertes nevadas no son habituales en esta época.

—Esperemos que no.

—¿Y será tal como usted ha dicho? ¿Una fuga de la cuadrilla de trabajo?

—Sí. El señor Piper fingirá tener diarrea, Agustín se adentrará entre los arbustos con él, recibirá un golpe en la cabeza lo bastante fuerte para provocarle una magulladura y el señor Piper le quitará las llaves de las esposas y huirá. Después, echará a correr colina abajo hacia Cuenca. Su amigo recorrerá cierta distancia y se ocultará entre árboles y arbustos hasta que oscurezca, y entonces se dirigirá a la ciudad.

—¿Y en Cuenca no lo buscarán? ¿No comprenderán que es allí adonde ha ido?

—Sí. En realidad, es el único sitio adonde puede ir; en la otra dirección, sólo hay yermos y montañas. De manera que sí, lo buscarán en la ciudad. —Luis sonrió—. Pero allí tenemos un lugar donde esconderlo.

—¿Dónde?

—Hay unos matorrales en la carretera, cerca del puente que hay junto al desfiladero, en el otro extremo de la ciudad. Se ocultará allí hasta que llegue usted con ropa para cambiarse.

Barbara respiró hondo.

—Muy bien.

—Tendrá usted que dirigirse a Cuenca en automóvil el día catorce y estar allí a las tres de la tarde. Es importante que esté allí antes de que oscurezca... una mujer caminando sola por la ciudad podría ser interrogada. Hay un lugar fuera de la ciudad, un lugar apartado donde usted podrá dejar el automóvil. —Luis la miró con la cara muy seria—. Agustín se ha pasado todos los días libres recorriendo las calles y los alrededores de Cuenca para asegurarse de que todo vaya bien.

—Entonces, ¿tendré que esperar en la ciudad a que oscurezca?

Luis meneó la cabeza.

—No. Tenemos un lugar donde podrá esperar, un lugar que usted podrá decir que ha venido a visitar en caso de que alguien le hiciera preguntas. La catedral. Es allí adonde tendrá que llevar después a su amigo. Una vez se haya cambiado de ropa en el matorral, cruzarán el puente como una pareja de turistas ingleses que ha ido a ver la catedral. Allí dentro se podrá afeitar —lleva barba— y asearse.

—¿Y si hubiera alguien allí?

Luis meneó la cabeza.

—Un sábado de invierno no habrá visitantes en la catedral. Sólo alguien que los ayudará.

—¿Agustín? ¿Estará allí?

—No. —Luis sonrió con ironía—. Pero a veces acude a las celebraciones del domingo en la catedral de Cuenca. Es una excusa para ir a la ciudad... Creen que se ha vuelto muy devoto. Allí hay un vigilante al servicio de la iglesia que se encarga de echarle un vistazo a todo. Se ha ofrecido a ayudarnos.

—¿Un empleado de la iglesia? —preguntó bruscamente Barbara—. ¿Y por qué nos iba a ayudar?

—Por dinero, señora. —Una impaciente expresión de cólera se dibujó por un instante en el rostro de Luis—. Su anciana mujer está enferma y no tienen dinero para pagar a un médico. O sea que la ayudará por el mismo motivo por el que la ayudamos nosotros. Quiere trescientas pesetas.

Barbara respiró hondo.

—Muy bien.

—O sea que diríjase por carretera a Cuenca el día catorce y procure estar allí a las tres. Deje el coche donde yo le diré y vaya a la catedral. El viejo, que se llama Francisco, la estará esperando. Aguarde allí hasta que oscurezca y, después, diríjase a las casas colgadas. ¿Sabe dónde están?

—Sí. He estado estudiando un plano y una guía. Seguramente podría ir con los ojos cerrados.

—Muy bien. Lleve un poco de ropa para su amigo, un traje, a poder ser.

—De acuerdo. Elegiré la talla grande. Bernie es alto y de complexión muy fuerte.

Luis meneó la cabeza.

—Después de tres años en el campo, no. Bastará con un traje para un hombre delgado. Y artículos para afeitar.

—¿Qué le parece un sombrero? ¿De ala ancha para ocultar el rostro y el cabello rubio?

—Sí. Eso iría muy bien.

—Puedo conseguir la ropa —dijo Barbara—. Diré que son regalos de Navidad. Lo del automóvil ya es otra historia; mi... mi marido quizá lo necesite.

Luis arrugó el entrecejo.

—Eso lo tendrá que resolver usted, señora.

—Sí, claro, encontraré la manera. ¿Y qué hago cuando llegue a las casas colgadas?

—Junto a Tierra Muerta se encuentra la garganta de un río. Es muy profunda. No se puede trepar por ella. Al otro lado de la garganta está la ciudad vieja que conduce a la carretera de Madrid. Allí hay un gran puente de hierro para peatones tendido sobre la garganta. En el lado de la ciudad están las casas colgadas, y en el lado contrario, la carretera. Un poco más allá, a lo largo de la carretera, verá la arboleda donde su amigo estará esperando.

—¿Y si hubiera guardias en el puente? ¿Y si supieran que se ha fugado un prisionero?

—Podría ser. Los del campo habrán llamado a la ciudad. Si así fuera, espere en la catedral. El señor Piper cruzará el desfiladero más abajo y se dirigirá allí. Después tendrán ustedes que regresar al automóvil y fingir ser un matrimonio inglés que está pasando el día en Cuenca. Y recuerde que andarán buscando a un prisionero, no a un hombre impecablemente afeitado y vestido con traje de paisano. Con un poco de suerte, no habrá bloqueo de carreteras, no pensarán que se haya ido en coche. —Luis miró a Barbara con sus profundos y duros ojos verde aceituna—. Su aspecto de persona acomodada será su mejor disfraz, señora.

—¿Cuánto ha dicho usted que distaba Cuenca del campo? ¿Ocho kilómetros?

—Sí.

—¿Él estará en condiciones de caminar tanto? —preguntó Barbara con voz trémula.

—Supongo que sí. Con el frío que hace, muchos se ponen enfermos en el campo; pero, de momento, su amigo está bien. Y todo es cuesta abajo.

—¿Y si lo descubren por el camino?

—Esperemos que no —contestó Luis en tono cortante. Tomó otro cigarrillo de la cajetilla que descansaba sobre la mesa—. Tenemos que confiar en que no haya nieve y no brille la luna. —Encendió el cigarrillo y dio una calada profunda—. Tendrá que moverse con cuidado y ocultarse en la sombra.

Barbara se sintió repentinamente abrumada por las dudas.

—¿Y si lo atrapan...?

—Él lo ha querido así, señora.

—Sí. —Barbara se mordió el labio—. Sí, correrá el riesgo, lo sé. Tengo que hacerlo por él.

Luis la miró con curiosidad.

—Cuando lo tenga a su lado, ¿qué hará usted?

El rostro de Barbara se puso tenso.

—Lo acompañaré a la embajada británica. Es ciudadano británico; tendrán que aceptarlo. Ya enviaron a casa a todos los demás brigadistas internacionales.

—¿Y usted?

—Ya veremos. —Barbara no tenía intención de revelarle sus planes.

—Confío en que me pague el resto del dinero cuando regrese.

—Me volveré a reunir con usted el día dieciséis —dijo Barbara—. Aquí, a mediodía. ¿Y si se produce algún cambio en el plan, si le cambian el turno a Agustín, o Bernie se pone enfermo o algo por el estilo?

—Agustín me enviará un mensaje y yo la llamaré a usted a casa. Me tendrá que dar su número.

—Eso es peligroso. —Barbara lo pensó un momento—. Si no estoy en casa, diga que llama de la panadería por lo del pastel de Navidad y que volverá a llamar. Yo enseguida me pondré en contacto con usted. ¿De acuerdo? —Anotó el número en la cajetilla de cigarrillos y se la entregó. Luis sonrió, siempre encantado de que le regalaran cigarrillos; pero, de repente, la miró con aire muy cansado.

—Lo han planeado todo muy bien —dijo Barbara—. Usted y su hermano.

Luis evitó mirarla a los ojos.

—No nos dé las gracias —dijo—. No nos dé las gracias, por favor.

—¿Por qué no?

—Lo hemos hecho por dinero. Necesitamos dinero para nuestra madre. —Otra vez el mismo cansancio en su rostro. Ambos guardaron silencio un instante.

—Dígame —preguntó Barbara—, ¿ha tenido alguna otra noticia de aquel periodista? ¿Markby?

Luis meneó la cabeza.

—No, contactó conmigo a través de un amigo; quería hacer un reportaje sobre los campos de prisioneros, pero ya no supe nada más de él. Creo que ha regresado a Inglaterra.

—He intentado llamarle varias veces, pero siempre estaba fuera.

—Los periodistas. Son gente sin raíces. —Luis contempló su café y después carraspeó—: Señora...

—Sí, claro. —Barbara abrió el bolso y le entregó un sobre abultado por debajo de la mesa.

Él lo tomó, permaneció inmóvil un instante y después hizo una señal afirmativa con la cabeza. Barbara observó que los hombros de su raída chaqueta estaban mojados; comprendió que no tenía abrigo.

—Gracias —dijo Luis—. Y ahora le sugiero que nos reunamos aquí el viernes, día once, para discutir los preparativos definitivos. Para asegurarnos de que todo marcha como la seda.

—De acuerdo. —Se sentía alborozada. Estaba ocurriendo, iba a ocurrir.

Luis se metió el sobre en el bolsillo y miró a hurtadillas a los clientes que lo rodeaban para asegurarse de que no lo estaban observando. Barbara se sintió súbitamente oprimida y agobiada. Estaba deseando irse de allí. Se levantó.

—¿Nos vamos?

—Yo me quedaré un ratito, hasta que deje de nevar. Hasta la semana que viene, señora. —Después la miró y añadió inesperadamente—: Es usted una buena mujer.

Barbara rió.

—¿Yo? No lo creo. Simplemente causo problemas.

Luis meneó la cabeza.

—No. Eso no es cierto. Adiós, señora.

—Hasta luego.

Se abrió paso hasta la puerta. Fue un alivio respirar una vez más el frío aire del exterior. La nieve empezaba a amainar. Encendió un cigarrillo y se dirigió al centro. Ahora había muy pocas personas en la calle. Todos los que podían se habían quedado en casa. La gente no quería correr el riesgo de estropearse los zapatos; aunque pudiera encontrar otros que los sustituyeran, los precios estaban por las nubes.

Cruzó la Plaza Mayor. Las palmeras cubiertas de nieve ofrecían un aspecto extraño. Al lado de una de las fuentes, un vendedor de periódicos permanecía en pie junto a su quiosco. Le llamó la atención un titular garabateado en una cartelera: «Veterano de guerra torturado y asesinado en Alcalá. El Terror Rojo, bajo sospecha.»

Compró un ejemplar del *Ya*, el periódico católico. Se acercó a la entrada de una tienda cerrada y examinó la primera plana. Bajo la fotografía de un hombre de complexión delgada vestido con uniforme del ejército en posición de firmes, leyó:

> El cuerpo del teniente Alfonso Gómez Romero, de 59 años, fue descubierto ayer en una acequia de drenaje cerca del pueblo de Paloblanco, a las afueras de Santa María la Real. El teniente Gómez, veterano de las guerras de Marruecos que en 1936 participó en la liberación de Toledo, fue salvajemente torturado. Lo hallaron con las manos y los pies quemados y el rostro desfigurado. Se sospecha de una de las bandas del Terror Rojo que actúan en distintas zonas de la sierra. El subsecretario de Comercio coronel Santiago Maestre Miranda, patrón y antiguo jefe del teniente Gómez, declaró que eran amigos y compañeros desde hacía treinta años y que él se encargaría personalmente de que los asesinos fueran detenidos. «No hay seguridad ni protección para los enemigos de España», dijo.

Barbara sintió flojera en las rodillas y pensó que se iba a desmayar. Un sacerdote que pasaba por delante de la tienda la miró con curiosidad. Ahora ya lo sabía. Sandy había mencionado el apellido de Gómez por teléfono y ella había oído mencionar el nombre de Maestre como adversario de los amigos de la Falange de Sandy. Estaba implicado en la tortura y el asesinato de aquel hombre. Sandy había dicho que tendrían que resolver el asunto, queriendo decir con ello «asesinar». Y aquél era el hombre al que ella estaba engañando para salvar a su enemigo de la infancia. Se agarró al tirador de la puerta cerrada y respiró hondo varias veces, para no desmayarse.

38

Tras su encuentro con Barbara y Sofía, Harry regresó a la embajada. Llamó al despacho de Sandy desde la pequeña estancia en la que había un teléfono privado a disposición de los espías. La secretaria le pasó la llamada.

—¿Sandy? Hola, soy Harry. Mira, quisiera reunirme contigo. Hay algo que me gustaría comentarte.

Percibió un tono de impaciencia en la voz de Sandy.

—Es que estoy muy ocupado, Harry. ¿Qué te parece después del fin de semana?

—Es un poco urgente.

—De acuerdo. Mañana es sábado, pero yo vendré al despacho. Me reuniré contigo en el café. —Harry captó un suspiro inmediatamente reprimido—. ¿A las tres en punto?

—Gracias.

A continuación, Harry se dirigió al registro con la intención de averiguar detalles acerca de los visados de entrada para Gran Bretaña. Al regresar a su despacho, Tolhurst lo esperaba apoyado en su escritorio, leyendo un ejemplar del *Ya*.

—Hola, Harry. —Su voz sonaba seca y preocupada.

—He llamado a Forsyth —le dijo Harry—. Mañana nos reuniremos en el café.

—Muy bien. —Tolhurst le pasó el periódico—. Tendrías que ver esto.

Harry leyó la información sobre Gómez y dejó el periódico encima del escritorio.

—O sea que lo han matado —dijo en tono sombrío.

Tolhurst asintió con la cabeza.

—Eso parece. Lo sospechábamos. Ya no hay ningún problema para reclutar a Forsyth. —Su voz sonaba fría y distante. Harry recordó su primer encuentro con él. Tolhurst, el gordito simpático. Ahora veía su otra cara.

—¿Pese a constaros su implicación en este asunto? —preguntó.

—Presunta implicación, Harry, presunta. Y nosotros no somos la policía.

—No. Está bien, Tolly, intentaré ponerme en contacto con él.

Tolhurst sonrió.

—Buen chico —dijo, con un vestigio de su antigua cordialidad—. Por cierto, ¿qué tal va el oído?

—Bien. Creo que, en parte, era una cuestión psicológica; como las crisis de pánico. —No había vuelto a sufrir ninguna desde aquella noche en el teatro. Al parecer, el hecho de estar con Sofía lo había curado.

—Me parece estupendo —dijo Tolhurst—. Bueno, me voy volando. Que haya suerte.

Cuando Tolhurst se retiró, Harry se sentó para echar otro vistazo a la noticia y leyó lo que le habían hecho a Gómez. Pobre desgraciado. ¿Y Sandy estaría presente? No, pensó Harry con amargura. Eso se lo habría dejado a otros.

Sofía parecía cansada cuando llegó aquella noche a su apartamento. Tenía unas marcadas ojeras oscuras bajo los ojos.

—¿Te encuentras bien? —le preguntó Harry mientras tomaba su abrigo.

Ella esbozó una sonrisa de niña valiente. A veces parecía muy joven.

—No quiero volver a la vaquería. Estoy harta de las vacas —dijo—. Es muy aburrido. Y no sabes cuánto aborrezco el olor de la leche.

—Siéntate. Ahora mismo sirvo la cena. He preparado un cocido.

Tenía puesto el tocadiscos y Vera Lynn cantaba *When the lights go on again all over the world* en tono nostálgico; pero Sofía lo siguió a la cocina y se apoyó contra la pared, contemplando cómo mezclaba el contenido de las cacerolas que había puesto a hervir en los fogones.

—Eres el primer hombre que conozco que sabe cocinar.

—Cuando uno vive solo, aprende. No hay más remedio.

Ella inclinó la cabeza.

—Te veo preocupado. ¿Tienes algún problema en el trabajo?

Harry respiró hondo.

—No. Pero, mira, tengo que decirte una cosa.

—¿Qué? —preguntó ella, poniéndose inmediatamente en guardia. Harry comprendió que, desde hacía mucho tiempo, cualquier noticia era para ella una mala noticia.

—Espera a que nos sentemos. —Había comprado un tinto muy bueno y, en cuanto se sentaron, le llenó la copa a Sofía. La luz mortecina de la lámpara del techo iluminaba la mesa, dejando el resto de la estancia en penumbra—. Sofía —dijo—. La embajada me quiere enviar a casa.

Sofía pareció encogerse y su rostro palideció.

—Pero ¿por qué? Seguro que te necesitan, aquí nada ha cambiado, a no ser que... —respiró hondo bruscamente—. A no ser que Franco esté a punto de declarar la guerra. ¡Oh, Dios mío!, os van a evacuar a todos...

Harry levantó una mano.

—No, no es eso. Soy yo; ellos... creen que me pueden sacar mejor partido en casa.

—Harry —dijo ella en un suave susurro—. ¿Estás en apuros?

—No, lo digo en serio. Simplemente... había estado haciendo otro trabajo aparte de la traducción y ahora ya está casi terminado.

Sofía arrugó la frente.

—¿Qué clase de trabajo?

Harry vaciló antes de contestar.

—Agente secreto. —Se mordió el labio—. Por favor, no te puedo decir nada más. Ni siquiera te lo tendría que haber dicho. Pero eso ya está a punto de terminar. Me alegro, porque lo odio.

—¿Agente secreto contra este régimen?

—Sí.

—Muy bien. Me alegro. —Sofía respiró hondo—. ¿Y cuándo te vas?

—No estoy seguro. Puede que antes de que finalice el año. —La miró a los ojos—. Sofía, ¿vendrás conmigo? No hace falta que me contestes ahora; pero, mira, me he pasado toda la tarde pensándolo. ¿Recuerdas lo que dijo Barbara sobre los extranjeros que podían entrar en Inglaterra siempre y cuando estuvieran casados con un ciudadano británico?

Ella lo miró con la cara muy seria.

—Harry, no me pidas eso —dijo, con voz trémula—. No podría dejar aquí a Paco. Enrique puede cuidar de sí mismo, pero no de Paco. La beata se lo llevaría. —Alargó la mano y tomó la de Harry—. No me pidas que elija...

—También he estado pensando en eso. Si hubiera alguna manera de adoptar a Paco...

Ella meneó la cabeza con aire cansino.

—No puedo. Ahora es la Iglesia la que se encarga de estas cosas y jamás lo permitiría.

—No. En España, no; en Inglaterra. Si decimos que lo hemos estado cuidando desde que murieron sus padres y que nos lo podríamos llevar a Inglaterra, es posible que lo pudiéramos adoptar... Creo que hay alguna manera. Verás, si hago bien este último trabajo que tengo entre manos, me ganaré el favor de la gente de la embajada. Puede que ellos nos ayuden.

Ella lo miró fijamente a los ojos.

—¿Es peligroso eso que estás haciendo?

—No, ¡qué va! —Harry se rió—. De verdad que no, te lo juro. Trato de sonsacar información a unos hombres de negocios. No hay ningún peligro. Olvídate de eso. ¿Qué dices, Sofía?

—¿Y cómo estaría Paco en Inglaterra? Un idioma desconocido, las bombas. Tengo que pensar en Paco.

Harry no pudo evitar sentirse dolido por el hecho de que el niño pareciera ser más importante que él.

—Podríamos ir a Cambridge —dijo—. Allí no hay bombas. Viviríamos muy bien; en Inglaterra se puede conseguir casi todo si tienes dinero. Y yo tengo lo suficiente. Paco estaría a salvo, ya no habría más llamadas a la puerta. Luego intentaría sacar también a Enrique, aunque eso tal vez resultara más difícil.

—Sí, Paco tendría más oportunidades en Inglaterra. A no ser que lleguen los alemanes, que también podrían venir aquí. Dicen que éste es el peor momento; pero España tardará muchos años, décadas, en recuperarse de lo que ha hecho Franco. Si es que alguna vez puede recuperarse. —Sofía miró a Harry con asombro—. ¿Y tú te llevarías a Paco, asumirías esa responsabilidad?

—Sí, yo tampoco lo quiero dejar. Creo que le vendría muy bien recibir la atención sanitaria que necesita.

Sofía asintió con la cabeza.

—Debe de haber muchos médicos en Cambridge.

—Montones. Si pudiéramos sacar a Paco, ¿querrías... te querrías casar conmigo? Tú... no has dicho lo que piensas al respecto. Si... si no quieres...

Sofía lo estudió.

—¿Aceptarías una vida conmigo y con Paco? ¿Sabiendo cómo es Paco?

—Sí, claro. Es la única responsabilidad que ahora me interesa. Sofía, ¿quieres casarte conmigo?

Sofía se levantó y se acercó a él. Se arrodilló y lo besó, después separó la boca de la suya y lo miró sonriendo.

—Sí, sí quiero. Aunque no sé si estás loco.

Harry soltó una sonora carcajada de alivio y alegría.

—Puede que un poco, pero quiero estarlo. Me he pasado el día entero pensando en qué hacer, desde que me dijeron que me iban a mandar a casa...

Ella se inclinó hacia delante y apoyó un dedo en sus labios.

—Algo se te ocurrirá, seguro. Sí, Harry, me casaré contigo.

—Ya sé que nos conocemos desde hace sólo unas pocas semanas, pero en los tiempos que corren hay que aprovechar las cosas buenas mientras se pueda.

—Han sido las mejores pocas semanas de mi vida. —Sofía se arrodilló a su lado en el suelo y él se inclinó para abrazarla—. Tenía que pensar en Paco —dijo Sofía—, no podía abandonarlo, ¿comprendes? —Su voz se convirtió en un susurro—. Es lo único que he podido salvar de todas las esperanzas que antaño teníamos.

—Lo comprendo, Sofía. Quizás en Inglaterra puedas volver a estudiar para médico.

—Antes tengo que aprender el inglés. Y eso será muy duro. Pero estoy dispuesta a todo, siempre y cuando sea contigo. Y pensar que no nos habríamos conocido de no ser por Enrique. —Sofía meneó la cabeza—. Qué casualidad tan frágil y extraña.

La prostituta que, al principio, Harry había tomado por espía se encontraba en el Café Rocinante cuando él se presentó en el local a la tarde siguiente. Sandy aún no había llegado. La mujer estaba sentada a su mesa del fondo del local en compañía de un hombre de negocios gordinflón que hablaba español con fuerte acento alemán. El hombre presumía del dinero que había ganado desde su llegada a España y de la cantidad de tratos que había cerrado. La mujer sonreía y asentía con la cabeza, pero la expresión de su rostro era distante. Permanecía sentada en ángulo recto con respecto a la mesa y exhibía unas piernas bien torneadas a pesar de su edad. Harry vio que se había pintado una raya en la parte posterior para simular que llevaba medias de nailon; pero, por la manera en que la luz se reflejaba en sus piernas, se veía que no llevaba ningún tipo de media. Debía de morirse de frío, caminando por la calle entre la nieve.

El alemán vio que Harry lo estaba mirando y arqueó las pobladas cejas. Harry tomó asiento lo más lejos posible de ellos. Una ráfaga de aire frío le azotó el rostro cuando se abrió la puerta y entró Sandy. Llevaba un grueso abrigo negro y un sombrero de ala flexible y tenía los hombros cubiertos por una fina capa de nieve, pues acababa de ponerse otra vez a nevar. Mientras esperaba allí, sabiendo lo que Sandy había hecho, Harry se preguntó si sentiría miedo cuando lo volviera a ver; pero la verdad es que sólo sintió rabia y repugnancia.

Sandy se acercó a la mesa y se detuvo un momento para intercambiar unos comentarios acerca del tiempo con un conocido. Harry levantó un brazo para llamar al viejo camarero que se encontraba de pie en un rincón, charlando con el limpiabotas. El chico era nuevo; puede que el anterior se hubiera ido o se hubiera muerto de frío en la puerta de algún otro local.

—Hola, Harry —dijo Sandy, tendiéndole la mano. Tenía los dedos helados.

—Hola. ¿Café?

—Creo que mejor chocolate en un día como éste. —Sandy miró al camarero que se acercaba a toda prisa—. Un café con leche y un chocolate, Alfredo.

Harry estudió el rostro de Sandy. Sonreía cordialmente como siempre, pero su aspecto era tenso y cansado. Encendió un cigarrillo.

—¿Qué tal van las cosas? —le preguntó.

—No tan bien como antes. ¿Qué es este asunto tan urgente? Estoy intrigado.

Harry respiró hondo.

—Pues resulta, Sandy, que comenté en la embajada que un amigo mío inglés tenía ciertos problemas con sus negocios. Hay un par de personas que tendrían mucho gusto en hablar contigo. Quizá les podrías hacer un trabajo.

Sandy lo miró con dureza. Casi se podía escuchar el ruido de las ruedas de los engranajes al girar. Sacó un cigarrillo de la pitillera y lo encendió.

—Eso me suena a servicio secreto —dijo en tono cortante. Santo Dios, qué rápido era. Harry no contestó, y Sandy entornó los ojos—.

¿Son espías? —Sandy se detuvo y emitió un pequeño jadeo de asombro—. ¿Eres un espía, Harry? —preguntó en voz baja. Dudó un instante y añadió—: ¡Santo cielo! Lo eres, ¿verdad? Supongo que lo de la traducción es una buena tapadera. ¿Has estado revolviendo las papeleras de Franco? —Rió con incredulidad, miró a Harry y se volvió a reír.

—Ahora mismo no te puedo decir nada más, Sandy, lo lamento. Es que... he visto que las cosas no te estaban yendo demasiado bien y me gustaría echarte una mano. —Con qué facilidad le estaban saliendo las mentiras—. Sólo una reunión de tanteo con un par de personas de la embajada, sin compromiso.

—Supongo que me quieren contratar, ¿verdad? —Sandy siguió hablando con el tono reposado que había estado utilizando hasta aquel momento. Apareció el camarero y Sandy tomó la bandeja que éste sostenía en sus manos—. Ah, muy bien, Alfredo. ¿Azúcar, Harry? —Se entretuvo un buen rato en organizar las consumiciones, buscando tiempo para pensar. Se reclinó en su asiento, exhalando una nube de humo, y después le dio a Harry un juguetón puntapié en la espinilla—. ¿Seguro que no me puedes decir nada más, muchacho?

—Lo siento.

De repente, un espasmo, una expresión de angustia se dibujó en el rostro de Sandy y éste miró a Harry con los ojos muy abiertos.

—¡Dios!, supongo que eso no tendrá nada que ver con el oro, ¿verdad?

Por primera vez, Harry experimentó una sacudida de temor.

—No te puedo decir más.

Sandy volvió a reclinarse en su asiento. Procuró que su semblante no dejara traslucir la menor emoción, pero no pudo borrar la angustiada expresión de sus ojos.

—Se rumorea que la embajada británica está llena de espías —espetó—. Hay más espías allí que en ninguna otra embajada, exceptuando la alemana. Y no es que yo haya estado en la embajada alemana, pero conozco a gente que sí. Tengo entendido que Hoare está furioso porque Franco le sigue diciendo que está demasiado ocupado para recibirlo, mientras que Von Stohrer entra y sale de El Pardo y se pasea por allí como Pedro por su casa. —Harry no contestó. Sandy respiró hondo—. En fin, parece que estamos en tiempo de cambios. Mi hermano ha muerto, ¿sabes?

Harry levantó la vista.

—¿De veras? Lo siento.

—Recibí una carta hace una semana. Estaba en Egipto, una granada italiana alcanzó su tienda. —Sandy esbozó una sonrisa irónica—. Probablemente apuntaba contra Archibald Wavell... muy propio de los italianos, haberle dado al capellán por equivocación.

—Lo siento, Sandy. Es una mala noticia.

Sandy volvió a encogerse de hombros.

—Llevaba años sin verlo. Nunca me llevé bien con Peter, tú lo sabes.

—¿Te escribió tu padre?

—No, un viejo amigo mío lo leyó en el periódico y me envió una carta. Mi viejo y querido padre no me escribiría aunque supiera dónde estoy. Me ha borrado, estoy destinado a acabar en el fuego del infierno. En cambio, Peter estará en el Cielo, a salvo en los brazos de Dios. —Sandy soltó una amarga carcajada—. Te veo un poco incómodo, Harry. Tú no te creerás todas estas idioteces religiosas, ¿verdad?

—No. Y menos después de todo lo que he visto aquí.

Sandy se reclinó contra el respaldo del asiento, dando caladas al cigarrillo con semblante pensativo; después soltó una áspera y amarga carcajada.

—A veces, todo parece muy divertido.

—¿A qué te refieres?

—A la vida. La muerte. Todas estas imbecilidades. Fíjate en aquella puta de allí, con sus medias de nailon pintadas. Miles de años de evolución nos han llevado hasta aquí. Muchas veces pienso que los dinosaurios eran más emocionantes. Duraron ciento sesenta millones de años. —Sandy apuró su taza de chocolate—. Tú me has estado espiando durante todo este tiempo, ¿verdad, Harry?

—Ya te lo he dicho, de momento no te puedo contar nada más.

Sandy meneó la cabeza.

—Yo buscaba tu aprobación, ¿sabes? Lo mismo hacía en Rookwood. No sé por qué. Me pareció muy raro que regresaras aquí. Muy raro... —La mirada de Sandy se perdió un momento a media distancia y, después, éste volvió a mirar a Harry con dureza—. Quería ayudarte a ganar un poco de dinero, tú lo sabes. Mi viejo amigo Harry. Peor para mí, ¿eh? —Harry no contestó; no tenía nada que decir. Sandy hizo un gesto afirmativo con la cabeza—. Iré a ver a tus amigos del servicio secreto. ¿Tienes el número? —Empujó su cajetilla de cigarrillos hacia Harry. Éste anotó el número que lo conduciría hasta Tolhurst. Sandy se lo guardó en el bolsillo y después esbozó una extraña media sonrisa, torciendo la boca—. A lo mejor, tengo una noticia que los deja de piedra.

—¿Cuál?

Sandy inclinó la cabeza.

—Ya lo verás. Por cierto, no le he comentado a Barbara lo de mi hermano. No quiero que se ponga a llorar. Tú tampoco le digas nada, si la ves.

—De acuerdo.

—¿Sabe que eres un espía, Harry?

—No. No sabe nada, Sandy.

Sandy asintió con la cabeza.

—Por un momento, me he preguntado si no sería eso lo que le ocurre. —Volvió a esbozar la extraña media sonrisa de antes—. Qué curioso, cuando era pequeño quería ser bueno. Pero nunca supe muy bien cómo hacerlo. Y, si no eres bueno, los buenos se te echan encima como fieras. Por consiguiente, más te vale ser malo. —Contempló un momento la taza vacía y después alargó la mano hacia el abrigo—. Muy bien. Vamos allá.

Ambos se encaminaron hacia la puerta. Sandy apartó al vendedor de cigarrillos con un gesto de la mano. Se quedaron en la puerta... la nieve seguía cayendo y los ventisqueros se amontonaban contra los muros de los edificios. Al otro lado de la calle, la gente, arrebujada en sus abrigos, bajaba las gradas de un templo al término de una ceremonia religiosa, mientras que un sacerdote estrechaba la mano de los feligreses en la entrada.

Sandy se puso el sombrero.

—Bueno, ya estamos otra vez con la nieve.

—Pues sí.

—Procura que no te sorprendan revolviendo papeleras. Nos vemos, Harry. —Sandy dio media vuelta bruscamente, envuelto en su abrigo. Harry respiró hondo y salió bajo la nevada para ir a decirle a Tolhurst que la presa había mordido el anzuelo.

39

El taxi se abrió tortuosamente camino a través de Carabanchel. Se había producido un corte de electricidad y las calles estaban oscuras como la boca del lobo, excepto la pálida luz de las velas que brillaba en las ventanas de los altos bloques de apartamentos. El vehículo avanzaba a sacudidas sobre las accidentadas calzadas cubiertas de nieve. Un carro detenido junto al bordillo apareció ante los globos gemelos de los faros delanteros mientras el taxista se desviaba bruscamente para esquivarlo.

—¡Mierda! —murmuró el hombre—. Esto es como un viaje al infierno, señor.

Cuando Harry lo había parado en la Puerta del Sol, el taxista se había negado a llevarlo a Carabanchel en mitad de un corte de electricidad. Al caer la noche, cesó la nevada y salió la luna; sin la luz de las farolas y con sólo el débil resplandor de las velas en las ventanas, era como circular a través de las ruinas de una ciudad muerta y abandonada a los elementos.

Aquella mañana, Harry había sido llamado al despacho de Tolhurst. El corte de electricidad había afectado a la calefacción central y la regordeta figura de Tolhurst aparecía envuelta de nuevo en unos gruesos jerséis.

—Forsyth ya ha llamado —le dijo éste—. Debe de estar interesado.

—Muy bien. —«Hecho», pensó Harry, «misión cumplida».

—Nos gustaría que estuvieras presente cuando lo entrevistemos.

—¿Cómo? —Harry frunció el entrecejo—. ¿Es necesario?

—Creemos que podría ayudar. Es más, nos gustaría que la reunión tuviera lugar en tu apartamento.

—Yo creía que eso era todo, por lo que a mí respecta.

—Y lo será. Esto es lo último. Sé que estás deseando dejarlo. —El tono de Tolhurst era de reproche y casi de ofensa—. El capitán dice que después ya te podrás ir, probablemente habrá plaza para ti en el avión que lleva a la gente a casa por Navidad. Pero cree que Forsyth estaría más dispuesto a aceptar en tu territorio. A veces estos pequeños detalles pueden influir, ¿sabes? Y, en caso de que negara haberte dicho alguna cosa, tú estarías presente para contradecirlo.

Harry se puso furioso y notó que se le hacía un apretado nudo en el estómago.

—Eso será muy humillante. Para él y para mí. Por lo menos, que sea en tu despacho, no nos obligues a echarnos mutuamente en cara ciertas cosas.

Tolhurst meneó la cabeza.

—Lo lamento, órdenes del capitán. —Harry guardó silencio. Tolhurst lo miró con tristeza—. Siento que las cosas no hayan salido todo lo bien que esperábamos. Es lo malo de esta clase de trabajo: una palabra fuera de lugar, y estás hundido.

—Lo sé. —Harry lo estudió—. Oye, Tolly, tú sabes que he estado saliendo con esta chica, ¿verdad?

—Sí.

—Quiero casarme con ella. Y llevármela a Inglaterra.

Tolhurst arqueó las cejas.

—¿A esta pequeña lechera?

Harry se enfureció. Pero tenía que intentar que Tolhurst se pusiera de su parte. Procuró que se le calmara la voz.

—Ha accedido a casarse conmigo.

Tolhurst arrugó la frente.

—No sé qué decirte, ¿estás seguro de lo que haces? Si te la llevas a Inglaterra, tendrás que cargar con ella para siempre. —Se rascó la barbilla—. No la habrás metido en algún lío, ¿verdad?

—No. Aunque hay un niño que ella y su hermano han estado cuidando, un huérfano de guerra. Nos gustaría llevárnoslo.

Tolhurst miró a Harry con cara de lechuza sabionda.

—Bueno, ya sé que las cosas no han sido fáciles para ti, pero ¿te parece el momento apropiado para tomar decisiones de este calibre? Si no te importa que te lo diga.

—Mira, Tolly, es lo que yo quiero. ¿Me puedes ayudar? Con los de inmigración, quiero decir.

—No sé. Tendré que hablar con el capitán.

—¿Lo harás? Por favor, Simon, sé que sería una gran responsabilidad; pero es lo que yo quiero, ¿comprendes?

Tolhurst volvió a acariciarse la barbilla.

—¿Tienen la chica o su hermano algún tipo de simpatía política?

—No, son contrarios al régimen, pero eso no tiene nada de extraño.

—En esta clase de personas, no. —Tolhurst tamborileó con los dedos sobre el escritorio.

—Si pudieras hacer todo lo posible, Tolly, te estaría eternamente agradecido.

Tolhurst lo miró complacido.

—De acuerdo. Lo intentaré.

Harry y Sofía habían acordado que él acudiría a cenar al apartamento de Carabanchel y entonces les comunicarían sus planes a Paco y Enrique. Cuando el taxi lo dejó finalmente ante el edificio de Sofía, Harry abrió la puerta con la llave que ella le había dado. Subió con cuidado por la escalera, que estaba a oscuras; no se veía nada y tuvo que encender una cerilla. Éste había sido uno de los consejos de Tolhurst. llevar siempre cerillas por si hubiera cortes de electricidad.

Llamó y, cuando Sofía le abrió, una pálida luz inundó el rellano. Se había puesto el vestido que llevaba la noche en que habían ido al teatro. A su espalda, había velas en todos los rincones de la estancia; la suave luz ocultaba las manchas de humedad de las paredes y el desastroso estado de los maltrechos muebles. La cama de su madre seguía donde siempre, empujada contra la pared. Harry se inclinó hacia delante y la besó. Parecía cansada.

—Hola —le dijo ella en un susurro.

—¿Dónde están Paco y Enrique?

—Han salido por un poco de café. No tardarán en volver.

—¿Saben algo de lo nuestro?

—Paco ha adivinado que algo ocurre. Ven, quítate el abrigo.

La cama de su madre estaba cubierta con una colcha de retazos limpia, y la mesa, con un mantel blanco. El brasero llevaba un buen rato encendido y la estancia estaba bien caldeada. Se sentaron en la cama, el uno al lado del otro. Harry le dijo a Sofía que había hablado con un compañero acerca de la cuestión de los visados.

—Creo que hará todo lo que pueda. Podría ser antes de Navidad.

—¿Tan pronto?

Harry asintió con la cabeza, y ella meneó la suya.

—Será muy duro para Enrique.

—Le podemos enviar dinero. De esta manera, por lo menos, podrá conservar el apartamento. —Harry le tomó la mano entre las suyas—. ¿Estás segura de lo que haces?

—Sí. —Sofía lo miró—. ¿Y qué hay de ese trabajo tuyo del que me hablaste? ¿Ya está a punto de terminar?

—Sí. Pero ¿tú no crees que sería mejor esperar a que tengamos la certeza de que podemos hacerlo antes de decírselo?

Sofía meneó enérgicamente la cabeza.

—No. No podemos esperar a decírselo en el último momento, cuando ya estemos a punto de irnos. Tienen que saber ahora lo que queremos hacer.

—Me alegro.

Se oyeron unas pisadas en la escalera. Entró Enrique con Paco. Parecía cansado; en cambio, Paco a su lado mostraba un insólito arrebol en las mejillas. Enrique le estrechó la mano a Harry.

—Buenas tardes. Madre de Dios, menudo frío hace hoy. —Se volvió hacia Sofía—. Mira, hemos encontrado un poco de café. Algo es algo. —Con una insólita sonrisa en los labios, Paco se sacó un frasco de extracto de achicoria de debajo del abrigo y lo sostuvo en alto como si fuera un trofeo.

Sofía preparó la cena. Garbanzos con chorizo. Comieron juntos sentados alrededor de la mesa, mientras Enrique comentaba su trabajo como barrendero encargado de retirar la nieve y hablaba de las mujeres ricas que se empeñaban en lucir zapatos de tacón a pesar de la nieve y se pegaban a cada momento unos morrones impresionantes. Cuando terminaron de comer, Sofía apartó su plato a un lado y tomó la mano de Harry.

—Tenemos algo que deciros.

Enrique los miró, perplejo. Paco, cuya cabeza a duras penas rebasaba el nivel de la mesa, frunció el entrecejo con semblante preocupado.

—Le he pedido a Sofía que se case conmigo —dijo Harry—. Pronto regresaré a Inglaterra y Sofía me ha dicho que vendrá conmigo, siempre y cuando nos llevemos a Paco.

A Enrique se le aflojó la cara. Miró a Sofía.

—¿Y yo me quedaré aquí solo? —Después se encogió de hombros e hizo un esfuerzo por sonreír—. Bueno, ¿qué iba a hacer yo en Inglaterra? Apenas sé leer y escribir. Tú siempre fuiste la inteligente.

Paco los había estado mirando a uno y a otro. Al oír las palabras de Enrique, su rostro se puso tenso.

—¡No! ¡No! ¡Yo no quiero dejar a Enrique, no! —Se abrazó al cuello de Enrique y hundió el rostro en su hombro, mientras de su boca salían unos desesperados gritos de protesta. Enrique lo levantó.

—Me lo llevo a la cocina —dijo, sujetándolo y retirándose con él de la estancia.

Mientras se cerraba la puerta de la cocina, Sofía lanzó un suspiro.

—Enrique es muy valiente. Ahora esto, justo después de lo de mamá.

Harry le tomó la mano y la apartó de su rostro.

—Cuando estemos bien instalados, quizá podríamos conseguir que se reuniera con nosotros... —Interrumpió la frase al oír una insistente llamada a la puerta. Sofía se levantó con semblante cansado.

—Como sea otra vez la señora Ávila... —Se encaminó hacia la puerta y la abrió de par en par.

Era Barbara. Su rostro estaba muy pálido y había estado llorando.

—¿Estás bien? —preguntó bruscamente Harry—. ¿Qué ha ocurrido?

—¿Puedo entrar? ¡Por favor! Fui a tu apartamento y después pensé que, a lo mejor, estarías aquí. Perdonad, es que no tenía ningún otro sitio adonde ir. —Parecía desesperada y asustada.

Sofía la miró un momento y después tomó su mano.

—Pase. —La acompañó a una silla y Barbara se dejó caer pesadamente en ella.

—Toma un poco de vino —le dijo Harry—. Tienes cara de estar helada.

—Gracias. Lo siento, ¿estabais cenando?

—Ya hemos terminado —dijo Sofía—. Paco está disgustado y Enrique se lo ha llevado un momento a la cocina.

Barbara se mordió el labio.

—Mejor que no se entere de por qué he venido. —Sacó una cajetilla del bolso, se la ofreció a Sofía y encendió un pitillo. Después, lanzó un suspiro de alivio—. Es bueno estar con amigos. No tenéis ni idea.

—¿Qué ha pasado? ¿Por qué estás tan alterada?

Barbara juntó fuertemente las manos sobre la mesa y respiró hondo.

—Tú ya sabes que Sandy y yo no nos llevamos muy bien últimamente. Y sabes que he estado hablando de la posibilidad de volver a casa.

—Sí.

Barbara tragó saliva.

—Hace poco oí una conversación telefónica que él mantenía en su estudio. Fue por casualidad. No estaba escuchando furtivamente, pero lo que él decía me sonó muy raro. Hablaba con alguien acerca de tus inversiones; después, preguntó a la persona del otro extremo de la línea qué le había hecho a un hombre... —Barbara se estremeció—... y dijo que éste aguantaba mucho. No me lo podía quitar de la cabeza. Mencionaron un nombre. Un tal Gómez. —Harry abrió los ojos como platos mientras Barbara se sacaba del bolso un ejemplar del *Ya*—. Y anteayer por la tarde veo esto. —Sofía se inclinó hacia delante para leer la información. Harry se reclinó en su asiento y miró a Barbara, mientras la cabeza le daba vertiginosas vueltas.

Sofía levantó la vista.

—¿Estás diciendo que guarda relación? —preguntó en tono apremiante.

Se abrió la puerta de la cocina y Enrique asomó la cabeza con semblante inquisitivo. Sofía se levantó y entró en la cocina con él. Barbara permaneció hundida en su asiento, mientras Harry la miraba. Sofía regresó.

—Les he pedido que se queden en la cocina. —Volvió a sentarse—. Señora Barbara, ¿está segura de lo que dice? La veo... usted me perdonará... muy alterada.

Barbara meneó enérgicamente la cabeza.

—Todo coincide. —Barbara levantó la voz—. Sandy está implicado en la tortura y el asesinato de un hombre. Cuando leí el periódico, no quise volver a casa. Pero me obligué a hacerlo. Le dije que me dolía mucho la cabeza y que me tenía que ir a la cama. Ahora ni siquiera soporto hablar con él. —Por un instante, todo su cuerpo se estremeció—. Lo oí reírse en el pasillo con la chica, se acuesta con ella. Tuve un miedo tan grande tumbada allí en la cama, jamás en mi vida he estado tan asustada. Hoy he salido muy de mañana para ir al hospital militar; pero después... no me he sentido con ánimos de regresar a casa. Debería hacerlo, lo sé, pero simplemente no pude.

—Barbara —dijo Harry en tono pausado. Carraspeó porque, por un instante, no le salió la voz—. Lo sé todo.

—¿Cómo? —Barbara lo miró sin saber qué decir. Sofía clavó los ojos en él.

Harry apoyó las manos sobre la mesa.

—Trabajo en el servicio secreto. Soy un espía. Yo soy el culpable de la muerte de este hombre.

Barbara lo miró con horror y estupefacción.

—Me dijiste que lo que hacías no era peligroso —dijo Sofía en un tono más duro y cortante que un látigo.

—Jamás habría querido hacerlo. Jamás.

Se lo contó todo a las dos. Su reclutamiento en Londres, sus reuniones con Sandy, su visita a la mina, el error que le había costado la vida a Gómez. Ellas lo escucharon en horrorizado silencio. Desde la cocina, se oían los ocasionales sollozos de Paco y los tranquilizadores murmullos de Enrique.

—¿Una mina de oro? —preguntó Barbara, en cuanto él terminó su relato. Lo miró a los ojos—. Eres un cabrón, Harry. —No levantó la voz, habló más bien en un triste susurro—. Te has pasado estos dos últimos meses viniendo a cenar a casa o reuniéndote a almorzar conmigo, cuando en realidad no dejabas de espiar a Sandy. ¡Y, probablemente, también a mí!

—¡No! No, cuando vine a España, no tenía ni idea de que tú estabas con él. No soportaba engañarte y, si quieres que te diga la verdad, no soportaba todo este asunto. ¡No lo soportaba! —dijo en voz tan alta y amargada que Sofía lo miró con asombro.

—¿Pues qué me dices del peligro que yo corría? —prosiguió diciendo Barbara—. ¡Tú sabías lo de Gómez y no me advertiste!

—No lo supe con certeza hasta el viernes. Pero te dije que era mejor que volvieras a Inglaterra.

—¡Gracias, Harry, muchísimas gracias! —Barbara se quitó las gafas y se pasó las manos por el rostro—. Oí mencionar tu nombre cuando escuché sin querer a Sandy hablando por teléfono. Jamás habría imaginado que pudieras estar implicado en un asesinato. Y, resulta que, durante todo este maldito tiempo, actuabas como espía.

Harry miró a Sofía. Ésta mantenía el rostro apartado.

—Ya todo ha terminado, te suplico que me creas, por favor. Mira, me han echado por lo de Gómez. Y yo me alegro. —Respiró hondo—. Ahora están tratando de contratar a Sandy. —Contemplando los escandalizados rostros de ambas mujeres, pensó: «¡Dios mío!, pero ¿qué les he hecho?»

Sofía lo volvió a mirar.

—Ese tal Gómez estuvo en Toledo, donde por las calles corría la roja sangre republicana y donde los moros cortaban cabezas como trofeos. No tienes que lamentar la muerte de un hombre como ése. —Barbara se volvió para mirarla. Estaba escandalizada. Sofía la miró a los ojos—.

Tendría que regresar a Inglaterra, señora, lejos de aquí. Podría alojarse en un hotel hasta que consiguiera pasaje para un barco o un avión. —Sofía miró a Harry—. Nosotros la vamos a ayudar, ¿verdad, Harry?

—Sí, claro. —Harry asintió enérgicamente con la cabeza, alegrándose de aquel «nosotros»—. Sofía tiene razón, Barbara, tendrías que regresar a casa cuanto antes.

—¿Acaso crees que no lo sé? —Para asombro de Harry, Barbara soltó una carcajada áspera y amarga—. Pero, de momento, no puedo volver a casa. ¡Dios mío! Tú no sabes de la misa la media.

Algo en el tono de su voz dejó helado a Harry.

—¿Qué quieres decir?

Barbara respiró hondo y echó los hombros hacia atrás.

—No sabes lo de Bernie. Bernie está vivo. Está en un campo de trabajo cerca de Cuenca y yo estoy implicada en un plan con un ex guardia aquí, en Madrid, para sacarlo. Para rescatarlo. El sábado que viene, dentro de seis días. —Barbara hizo una pausa y miró a Harry—. Ahora te toca a ti escandalizarte, ¿verdad?

Harry se había quedado boquiabierto. Barbara volvió a reírse con aquel tono estridente e histérico que él ya le había oído anteriormente. Harry tuvo una visión de Bernie caminando entre risas por una calle de Madrid, con sus ojos verdes rebosantes de entusiasmo y picardía.

Sofía parecía perpleja.

—¿Quién es Bernie? ¿Se refiere a aquel amigo tuyo que vino a combatir aquí?

—Sí. —Harry miró a Barbara a los ojos—. Dios mío, ¿es eso cierto?

—Vaya si lo es.

Sofía lo miraba con sus grandes ojos castaños llenos de emoción. «Maldita sea —pensó Harry—, lo he estropeado todo. Ahora no me perdonará mi manera de tratar a Barbara.»

—Eso es lo que hay —terminó diciendo Barbara—. Tengo que quedarme aquí hasta el sábado.

—Pero, aun así, podría dejar a este hombre —le dijo Sofía.

—No. Me buscaría, no me soltaría así, sin más. Se armaría un alboroto tremendo. Él no tiene que saberlo. —Apretó los labios—. Como se entere, es capaz de conseguir que sus amigos le hagan algo a Bernie, por despecho.

—¿Y si usted encontrara a alguien que pudiera ir a Cuenca? —Sofía miró inquisitivamente a Harry—. ¿Nosotros, quizá?

Barbara la miró sorprendida.

—¿Por qué ibas a correr este peligro? —dijo Barbara, pasando al tuteo.

—Porque significaría ayudar a alguien que luchó por nosotros. Y sería hacer algo contra estos miserables que ahora nos gobiernan. —Sofía miró a Harry—. Yo mantengo mis lealtades. Son importantes.

—No daría resultado —dijo Barbara—. Si apareciera un desconocido para reunirse con Luis, el ex guardia, éste echaría a correr; y bastante nervioso está ya. —Les reveló el plan, desde su primera entrevista con el periodista, en octubre. Ellos la escucharon en silencio. Al final, Barbara dijo en voz baja—: No, tendré que regresar junto a Sandy. Fingiré estar enferma, diré que tengo la gripe y pediré una habitación separada. A él le dará igual; seguramente, meterá a la chica en nuestra cama.

—Esta semana va a ser muy dura —dijo Harry—. Tener que fingir constantemente con Sandy.

—¡Bien lo sabes tú! —contestó Barbara en tono airado—. Casi me da pena, ver cómo lo habéis tratado. —Lanzó un suspiro y se sostuvo la cabeza con las manos—. No, me equivoco —añadió más tranquila—. Él se lo buscó —dijo, levantando la vista—. Creo que lo podré resistir, si con ello consigo sacar a Bernie de allí. —Volvió a mirar el periódico—. Fue la impresión que me llevé al enterarme de lo de este hombre, no me lo he podido quitar de la cabeza.

Sofía contemplaba las fotografías de la pared de su madre y su padre y de su tío, el cura.

—No tendrías que ir sola a Cuenca —le dijo—. Una extranjera sola llamará la atención. Es una ciudad muy apartada.

—¿La conoces?

—Estuve allí muchas veces de niña. Nosotros somos de Tarancón, que está al otro lado de la provincia; pero tenía un tío allí. No tendrías que ir sola —repitió.

Barbara lanzó un suspiro.

—Ni siquiera tengo coche para ir, a no ser que me pueda llevar el de Sandy. Éste es el otro inconveniente.

—Ahí yo te podría echar una mano —dijo Harry—. Podría sacar un vehículo de la embajada.

—¿Y eso no va contra las normas?

Harry se encogió de hombros. No le importaba. Si Bernie estuviera vivo...

Sofía se inclinó hacia delante.

—Harry y yo te podríamos llevar. Sí, seguro que daría resultado. Harry podría ser un diplomático que acompaña a dos amigas a una excursión. Un vehículo con matrícula diplomática.

Sofía lo miró. El corazón de Harry empezó a latir con fuerza. Pensó que aquello era una locura. Si los pillaban, Sofía se quedaba sin poder salir de España. A él y a Barbara los podrían expulsar, pero Sofía... La miró. Adivinó que ella quería que dijera que sí para redimirse. Y, en caso de que Bernie estuviera vivo, de que consiguieran sacarlo de allí... Se volvió para mirar a Barbara.

—¿Estás segura de que Luis sabe lo que tiene entre manos?

—Claro que lo estoy —contestó Barbara con impaciencia—. ¿Crees que no lo he puesto todo en duda durante estas últimas semanas? Luis no es tonto, él y su hermano lo han preparado todo minuciosamente.

—Muy bien, pues —dijo Harry—, iré contigo. Pero tú no, Sofía; tienes demasiado que perder.

Barbara se sorprendió.

—¿Y si la embajada se enterara? Te podrías meter en un buen lío, ¿verdad? Sobre todo, teniendo en cuenta... lo que has estado haciendo hasta ahora.

Harry respiró hondo.

—Que se vayan todos al carajo. Tú tienes razón, Sofía, en eso que has dicho acerca de la lealtad. Tú me has ayudado a perder muchas de mis viejas lealtades, ¿lo sabías?

La cólera se encendió en los ojos de Sofía.

—Las tenías que perder.

—Supongo que mi lealtad a Bernie es la más antigua de todas. —Harry meneó la cabeza—. Había oído rumores acerca de estos campos secretos.

Barbara fruncía el entrecejo por la concentración.

—Podríamos traer a Bernie en coche y dejarlo en una cabina telefónica cerca de la embajada. Entonces ellos enviarían a alguien a recogerlo, ¿verdad?

Harry lo pensó un momento.

—Sí, lo harían.

—Él podría decir que un conductor lo había recogido en Cuenca y nadie tendría que saber que tú participaste en su rescate.

—Sí. Sí, podría dar resultado. —Harry lanzó un suspiro. Se enfrentaba con la posibilidad de perderlo todo, pero tenía que hacerlo. Por Sofía. Y por Bernie. Bernie, vivo...

—Yo también iré —dijo Sofía con determinación—. Os serviré de guía.

—No —dijo Harry, apoyando una mano en su brazo—. No, no debes hacerlo.

—Escúchame, Harry, será mucho menos peligroso si vamos todos juntos. Te lo digo yo, que conozco la ciudad. Podremos ir directamente a donde tenemos que ir sin consultar planos ni llamar la atención.

—Sofía, piensa...

Sofía se incorporó en su asiento. Su voz sonaba tranquila, pero ahora brillaba en sus ojos un extraño fulgor.

—Me sentía culpable por el hecho de abandonar mi país. No te lo había dicho, pero así era. Ahora, en cambio, se me ofrece la oportunidad de hacer algo. Algo contra ellos.

40

De vez en cuando, los hombres eran obligados a pasar una tarde en la iglesia viendo películas de propaganda. El año anterior habían visto una filmación del desfile de la victoria de Franco: cien mil hombres desfilando delante del Caudillo mientras los aparatos de la Legión Cóndor sobrevolaban la zona. Habían visto películas sobre el resurgimiento de España, sobre los batallones de las Juventudes Falangistas que contribuían a las labores del campo, sobre un obispo que bendecía la reapertura de unas fábricas en Barcelona. Y, más recientemente, habían visto la película de la entrevista en Hendaya en la que Franco, con el rostro radiante de felicidad, pasaba revista a una guardia de honor en compañía de Hitler.

El tiempo frío seguía en toda su intensidad. Los venados, en su desesperado afán de encontrar algo que comer, se acercaban al campo atraídos por el olor de la comida. Los guardias disponían de más carne de la que necesitaban y ahora disparaban contra los venados simplemente para matar el aburrimiento.

Los prisioneros entraron arrastrando los pies en la iglesia, alegrándose de poder disfrutar por lo menos del calor de la estufa. Se sentaron en unas duras sillas de madera, revolviéndose y tosiendo mientras un par de guardias colocaba debidamente el viejo proyector. Sobre la pared se había extendido una pantalla ante la cual Aranda permanecía de pie, enfundado en su uniforme impecablemente planchado, sosteniendo entre sus manos un ligero bastón mientras miraba con impaciencia al operador. Encogido en su chaqueta, Bernie se frotaba el hombro. Estaban a 9 de diciembre; faltaban cinco días para la fuga. Procuró no mirar a Agustín, que estaba de servicio en la entrada.

A una señal del operador, Aranda se adelantó sonriendo.

—Muchos de vosotros, los prisioneros extranjeros, estaréis deseando ver alguna imagen del mundo exterior. Así que nuestro Noticiario Español se enorgullece de presentar una película sobre los acontecimientos de Europa. —Señaló la pantalla con el bastón—. Os voy a ofrecer... Alemania Victoriosa.

«Es todo un actor —pensó Bernie—; todo lo que hace, desde esto hasta torturar a la gente, gira en torno al hecho de que él tiene que ser el centro del escenario.» Procuró que su mirada no se cruzara con la de Aranda, como llevaba haciendo desde su negativa a convertirse en confidente.

La película empezaba con un noticiario de las tropas alemanas entrando en Varsovia, pasaba a los tanques que cruzaban la campiña francesa y después a Hitler, contemplando París. Bernie jamás había visto nada de todo aquello; el alcance de lo ocurrido era aterrador. De repente, apareció en la pantalla la ciudad de Londres, humeante tras el bombardeo.

—Sólo Gran Bretaña no se ha rendido. Huyó del campo de batalla de Francia, y ahora Churchill espera malhumorado en Londres negándose a luchar y a rendirse con honor, en la creencia de que está a salvo porque Gran Bretaña es una isla. Pero la venganza llega desde el cielo y destruye las ciudades de Gran Bretaña. Ojalá Churchill hubiera seguido el ejemplo de Stalin y firmado una paz beneficiosa tanto para él como para Alemania.

Las imágenes pasaban de un Londres en llamas a un despacho donde el ministro de Asuntos Exteriores soviético Molótov permanecía sentado a un escritorio firmando un documento, mientras Von Ribbentrop sonreía y Stalin le daba una palmada en la espalda. La contemplación de todas aquellas imágenes le causó a Bernie una fuerte impresión. A menudo se había preguntado por qué razón Stalin había firmado el año anterior un pacto con Hitler —lo cual parecía una locura—, en lugar de unirse a los Aliados. Los comunistas decían que sólo Stalin conocía las realidades concretas y que había que confiar en su criterio, pero el hecho de verlo celebrar el pacto con Von Ribbentrop, a Bernie le había producido escalofríos.

—Pese a haber pactado con Alemania, Rusia no sólo ocupa la mitad de Polonia, sino que mantiene un floreciente comercio con Alemania y recibe divisas a cambio de materias primas.

Se mostraba la imagen de un enorme tren de mercancías controlado en una frontera y a unos soldados alemanes protegidos con cascos de acero que examinaban unos manifiestos de carga con unos rusos envueltos en gabanes. La filmación pasaba a ensalzar las hazañas alemanas en los países ocupados; la atención de Bernie se perdió mientras Vidkun Quisling daba la bienvenida en Oslo a una compañía de ópera alemana.

Aquella tarde, en la cantera, Bernie se había quejado ante Agustín de su diarrea. Había sido una prueba para dejar claro que tenía un problema.

—Entonces será mejor que te vayas a los arbustos —le había contestado Agustín, levantando la voz para que todos lo oyeran. Encadenó los pies de Bernie y lo acompañó al otro lado de la colina. Desde allí, el territorio descendía cuesta abajo y se podía contemplar un panorama de blancas y onduladas colinas. Era un día nublado y la luz ya empezaba a menguar.

Bernie miró a Agustín. Su rostro enjuto mostraba la expresión sombría y preocupada de siempre; pero sus ojos estudiaban el paisaje con perspicacia.

—Primero dirígete a aquel pliegue de la colina —le dijo Agustín en voz baja, señalándolo con el dedo—. Hay un camino que podrás distinguir a través de la nieve. Yo he estado por allí abajo en mis días libres. Verás unos cuantos árboles... escóndete entre ellos hasta que oscurezca. Después sigue recto cuesta abajo por los caminos de ovejas. Al final, llegarás a la carretera que bordea el desfiladero.

Bernie contempló el inmenso espacio nevado.

—Verán las huellas de mis pisadas.

—Puede que, para entonces, la nieve ya haya desaparecido. Y, aunque no fuera así, si te largas a última hora de la tarde, ellos no podrán iniciar una búsqueda como Dios manda antes de que oscurezca. Les va a ser más difícil seguir tus huellas. Los guardias enviarán a alguien al campo de abajo para dar la alarma; pero, para cuando Aranda haya enviado a una partida en tu búsqueda, tú ya estarás casi a punto de llegar a Cuenca.

Bernie se mordió el labio. Se imaginó corriendo cuesta abajo, el sonido de un disparo y a sí mismo desplomándose. El final de todo.

—Veremos cómo está el tiempo el sábado.

Agustín se encogió de hombros.

—Puede que ésta sea tu única oportunidad. —Consultó el reloj y miró muy nervioso alrededor—. Ya tendríamos que estar de vuelta. Estudia el paisaje, Piper. Si regresamos aquí por segunda vez antes del día acordado, es posible que a alguien le parezca raro. —Se volvió a echar el fusil al hombro y le dirigió a Bernie una triste mirada de angustia.

Bernie le sonrió con picardía.

—A lo mejor, piensan que nos estamos casando, Agustín.

Agustín arrugó el entrecejo, indicándole con un brusco movimiento del fusil que regresara a la cantera.

La película seguía adelante, mostrando a unos ingenieros alemanes ocupados en la tarea de modernizar unas fábricas polacas. Los prisioneros despedían el húmedo olor propio de las personas que no se lavan. Algunos de ellos se habían quedado dormidos en medio del insólito calor que los envolvía, mientras que otros permanecían sentados con la mirada perdida en la distancia. Siempre ocurría lo mismo durante las películas de propaganda y las ceremonias en la iglesia: sensación de hastío, desdicha y malhumor. ¿Podía el padre Eduardo creer en serio que aquellas ceremonias tenían algún valor? Eran como las películas. Otra forma de venganza y de castigo. Bernie miró a Pablo, sentado unas sillas más allá en la fila. Desde la crucifixión, éste parecía más introvertido, tenía los ojos hundidos en las órbitas y le dolían mucho los brazos. A veces, parecía que ya se hubiera dado por vencido. Su expresión era la misma que la de Vicente hacia el final de su vida. Eulalio trataba a Pablo con sorprendente amabilidad. Le fallaban las fuerzas y había conseguido que éste le echara una mano en sus actividades cotidianas; Bernie dudaba de la eficacia de darle a Pablo algo que hacer para evitar que se hundiera en la depresión.

El padre Eduardo también se había sentido muy afectado por la crucifixión. Bernie lo había visto mirar a Pablo mientras éste cruzaba el patio cubierto de nieve, arrastrando penosamente los pies. El sacerdote se mostraba taciturno y preocupado, y su rostro reflejaba un profundo dolor mientras sus ojos seguían tristemente a Pablo. Ahora Bernie esquivaba al padre Eduardo, que se sentía todavía culpable de haber participado en su tormento; aunque, la víspera, el cura se había acercado a él en el patio después de pasar lista.

—¿Cómo está Pablo Jiménez? —preguntó—. Comparte contigo la barraca.

—Nada bien.

El sacerdote miró a Bernie a los ojos.

—Lo siento muchísimo.

—Eso se lo tendría que decir a él.

—Ya lo hice. O, por lo menos, lo intenté; pero no me hizo caso.

Quería que tú también lo supieras. —El padre Eduardo se alejó arrastrando los pies, con la cabeza hundida entre los hombros como un anciano.

Se oyó un zumbido y un clic y la pantalla se quedó en blanco. Un guardia encendió las lámparas de petróleo y Aranda se situó ante ellos, con las manos cruzadas a la espalda y una sonrisa en los labios. «Se divierte humillándonos», pensó Bernie.

—Bueno, caballeros, ¿les ha impresionado la película? —preguntó—. Demuestra lo cobardes, miedicas y acojonados que están los comunistas. Prefieren firmar un tratado con sus enemigos, los alemanes, antes que luchar. Son tan poco combatientes como los holgazanes de los británicos. —Agitó el bastón que sostenía en la mano—. Vamos, quiero oír lo que pensáis. ¿Quién tiene algo que decir?

Responder a aquellos desafíos verbales era un juego muy peligroso. Aranda podía etiquetar cualquier respuesta que no le gustara como una insolencia e imponer el correspondiente castigo al hombre que la hubiera formulado. Pese a lo cual, Eulalio, sentado al lado de Pablo, se levantó dolorosamente de su asiento con la ayuda de su bastón. Ahora la piel de su rostro mostraba el color amarillento propio de la ictericia y contrastaba fuertemente con las rojas estrías de la sarna. Pero Eulalio jamás se daría por vencido.

—El camarada Stalin es más listo de lo que usted cree, mi comandante. —Su voz sonaba como un resuello y tuvo que hacer una pausa para respirar—. Espera a que las potencias imperialistas se desgasten con la guerra. Entonces, cuando el Imperio Británico y Alemania hayan combatido entre sí hasta quedar extenuados, los obreros de ambos países se levantarán y la Unión Soviética les prestará su apoyo.

Aranda estaba encantado. Contempló con una sonrisa en los labios el devastado rostro de Eulalio.

—Pero Gran Bretaña se encuentra al borde de la derrota, mientras que Alemania es más poderosa que nunca. No seguirán combatiendo hasta llegar a un punto muerto, sino que Alemania se alzará simplemente con la victoria. —Señaló con el bastón a Bernie—. ¿Qué piensa nuestro comunista inglés?

Ahora todo dependía de su capacidad de no meterse en líos. Bernie se levantó.

—No lo sé, mi comandante.

—Tú ya has podido deducir de la película que Gran Bretaña no se enfrentará en buena lid a Alemania. Tú no esperas que los combates se prolonguen hasta que las clases dominantes de Gran Bretaña y Alemania se destruyan entre sí como ha dicho tu camarada, ¿verdad? —Eulalio se volvió para mirarlo con expresión desafiante. Bernie no dijo nada. Aranda sonrió y, después, para alivio de Bernie, le hizo señas de que volviera a sentarse—. Los británicos saben que serán derrotados, por eso se quedan en casa. Pero la primavera que viene, el canciller Hitler invadirá el país y todo habrá terminado. —Aranda miró con una sonrisa a los prisioneros—. Y entonces, ¿quién sabe?, quizá dirija su atención a Rusia.

Más tarde, en la barraca, Bernie estaba tumbado en su jergón, meditando. La gruesa capa de nieve llevaba varias semanas cubriendo la tierra. Aquella situación no podía prolongarse por mucho tiempo. Pero sólo faltaban cinco días. Oyó el golpeteo de un bastón y levantó la vista. Ahora Eulalio no podía caminar sin ayuda, y Pablo le sujetaba el otro brazo. Se detuvo al pie del jergón y miró a Bernie con los ojos tan vivos y penetrantes como siempre bajo la luz de la vela, la única parte de su cuerpo que no se había encogido ni había sido devorada por la enfermedad.

—Esta noche apenas has tenido nada que decirle al comandante, Piper.

—De nada sirve discutir con locos.

—Gran Bretaña sigue combatiendo en el mar. Sigue siendo un poderoso enemigo para Alemania.

—Así lo espero.

—Porque Gran Bretaña y Alemania pueden acabar debilitándose la una a la otra hasta el extremo de que los trabajadores se sientan con ánimos para sublevarse, ¿no crees? Ya has visto cómo el camarada Stalin ha engañado a Alemania, haciéndole creer que es amigo suyo.

—Si se hubiera unido a Francia y Gran Bretaña el año pasado, puede que Alemania hubiera sido derrotada.

—¿O sea que estás de acuerdo con Aranda en que el camarada Stalin es un cobarde?

—No sé por qué firmó el pacto. Y tú tampoco lo sabes.

—Tiene razón. Ésta es una guerra imperialista.

—Es una guerra contra el fascismo. Por eso combatí en el treinta y seis. Vete, Eulalio, no quiero discutir con un enfermo.

Bernie miró a Pablo. Tenía el rostro contraído por el dolor y mantenía una mano apoyada en la barandilla de la litera, mientras con la otra sujetaba a Eulalio.

—Algún día —dijo Eulalio en un sereno susurro—, cuando los soviéticos hayan ganado, lamentarás no haber conservado la fe. Yo no estaré allí para denunciarte como enemigo de la clase obrera, pero otros sí lo harán. —Señaló a Pablo con un brusco movimiento de la cabeza—. Esta gente conservará mi memoria.

—Sí, camarada. —Bernie se levantó del jergón. Tenía que acabar con aquella situación como fuera—. Disculpa, tengo que ir a mear.

Se encaminó hacia la puerta y dobló la esquina de la barraca para hacer sus necesidades. Contempló a través de la alambrada de púas el paisaje blanco del otro lado. «Que no salga la luna esa noche», pensó. De pronto, se sobresaltó y estuvo casi a punto de lanzar un grito al percibir una mano en su hombro. Giró en redondo. Era Agustín.

—¿Qué coño estás haciendo? —le preguntó en un susurro áspero.

—Llevo una hora esperando, a ver si sales. —Agustín respiró hondo—. Han cambiado los turnos. Me han obligado a librar el sábado. No lo podremos hacer.

41

Hillgarth y Tolhurst tenían que estar en el apartamento de Harry a las siete, mientras que Sandy se presentaría allí a las siete y media. Al decirle a Harry que él acompañaría a Hillgarth, el rostro de Tolhurst se había iluminado de orgullo.

—El capitán me ha pedido que esta vez le eche una mano porque yo lo sé todo al respecto —explicó, hinchándose como un pavo, como si a Harry le importara.

Cuando a última hora de la tarde Harry regresó a casa desde la embajada, en el apartamento hacía un frío espantoso. No había vuelto a nevar, pero quedaban una espesa capa de escarcha y varios dedos de hielo en la ventana. Encendió el brasero, se dirigió a la cocina y depositó las llaves en el platito donde solía dejarlas. Las llevaba en el abrigo y el metal estaba frío. Recordó un verso de *Ricardo III*, en cuya producción teatral escolar había participado. La escena en la que Gloucester quiere asegurarse de que el duque de Clarence ha muerto y le responden que el duque está «más frío que una llave».

Fue al salón y enderezó una acuarela torcida en la pared. La espera era lo peor. Habría que esperar mucho entre aquel momento y el sábado en que se irían a Cuenca.

La estancia conservaba el leve aroma del perfume de Sofía. Era curioso que el perfume oliera a almizcle cuando hacía calor y despidiera un aroma intenso y penetrante cuando el tiempo era frío. La víspera, ambos habían permanecido casi todo el rato sentados, hablando del rescate. Lo que iban a hacer era un delito muy grave. En caso de que los descubrieran, él disfrutaría de inmunidad diplomática y Barbara de protección; pero Sofía era española, lo cual podría significar una larga sentencia de cárcel. Harry se había pasado media velada tratando de disuadirla de que los acompañara, pero ella se había mostrado inflexible.

—Bastante peligro corrí durante el sitio —dijo—. Si voy a abandonar mi país, que por lo menos pueda hacer una buena obra y rescatar a una persona.

—Bernie es importante para mí... no podría hacer otra cosa. Pero tú no le debes nada.

—Yo estoy en deuda con todas las personas que vinieron a ayudar a la República. Quiero hacer algo antes de irme —dijo, sonriendo con tristeza—. ¿Te suena muy romántico, muy español y muy estúpido?

—No, no. Es una cosa muy limpia.

Se preguntó, por un instante, si ella querría ver si él también era capaz de hacer algo limpio después de las sucias actividades en las que se había visto implicado y de todas las traiciones que había cometido. Harry le había dicho a Barbara que la ayudaría; en parte, porque el corazón le había dado un vuelco de alegría en el pecho al enterarse de que Bernie estaba vivo y, en parte, para compensar sus mentiras, pero también para demostrarle a Sofía que era capaz de hacer una buena obra. Algo había cambiado entre ellos; un ligero alejamiento por parte de Sofía y un leve titubeo por la suya que sólo un amante habría podido detectar.

Ella, en cambio, no había vacilado al manifestarle él su intención de casarse en la embajada. Sería una ceremonia civil porque él no era católico, pero la embajada podía celebrar una boda de acuerdo con la legislación inglesa. Tolhurst había soltado alguna que otra palabrita en determinados departamentos y había allanado el terreno.

—Lo único que me preocupa —dijo Harry— es saber si Barbara será lo bastante fuerte para resistirlo.

—Yo creo que sí. Hasta ahora lo ha llevado todo ella sola. Este Bernie debe de ser alguien muy especial. Casi todos los comunistas españoles eran mala gente.

—Era mi mejor amigo. Bernie nunca te dejaba en la estacada, era más fuerte que una roca. —«No como yo», pensó Harry—. No sabes con cuánta firmeza defendía su socialismo. —Rió por lo bajo—. Y eso no estaba nada bien visto en Rookwood, te lo aseguro. —Sonrió con ironía—. No conviene que Paco estudie en una de esas escuelas privadas. O bien te rebelas o bien te dejan convertido en un sonámbulo para toda la vida.

El estridente sonido del timbre de la puerta despertó a Harry de sus ensoñaciones. Hillgarth y Tolhurst estaban en la puerta, tocados con unos sombreros de paño y envueltos en gruesos abrigos. Debajo, vestían unos elegantes trajes de calle. Hillgarth se frotó las manos.

—Por Dios bendito, Brett, pero qué frío hace aquí.

—Tarda un poco en calentarse. ¿Les apetece tomar algo?

Preparó whisky para Hillgarth y brandy para Tolhurst y para él. Consultó el reloj: las siete menos cuarto. Tolhurst se sentó muy nervioso en el sofá. Hillgarth se puso a pasear por la estancia, estudiando los cuadros.

—¿Son de la embajada?

—Sí, no había nada en las paredes cuando vine.

—¿Encontraste algún recuerdo del comunista que había vivido aquí? —Tolhurst sonrió—. ¿Alguna consigna de Moscú en la parte de atrás de las sillas?

—No, nada de todo eso.

—Seguro que los de Franco lo limpiaron a conciencia. Por cierto, han dejado de seguirte, ¿verdad?

—Sí. Desde hace unas semanas.

—Debieron de llegar a la conclusión de que eras demasiado jovencito. —Santo Dios, pensó Harry, la de cosas que les estaba ocultando; y eso no era nada comparado con lo que iba a hacer el sábado. No tenía que pensar en ello, tenía que conservar la cabeza fría. Fría como una llave—. Por cierto —dijo Tolhurst—, tu prometida tiene que ir mañana a la embajada para una entrevista. Sólo para un examen político, para asegurarnos de que no es una agente de Franco. Te puedo asesorar sobre lo que tendrá que decir.

—De acuerdo. Te lo agradezco.

—El chiquillo no planteará ningún problema, seguramente —añadió Tolhurst—; pero ella tendrá que demostrar que lo ha tenido a su cargo. —Miró a Harry con su habitual cara de lechuza.

—Recoge sus raciones de alimentos y lo lleva haciendo desde hace un año y medio.

Tolhurst asintió con la cabeza.

—Creo que eso bastará.

Hillgarth miró a uno y a otro, sosteniendo la copa en sus manos.

—Tendría usted que estarle muy agradecido a Tolly, Brett. Media tarde de ayer se la pasó en el departamento de inmigración.

Volvió a escucharse el agudo sonido del timbre. Por un segundo, los tres permanecieron en silencio como haciendo acopio de todos sus recursos. Después, Hillgarth dijo:

—Vaya a abrir, Brett.

Con una sonrisa en los labios, Sandy esperaba en la puerta en posición relajada.

—Hola, Harry. —Miró por encima del hombro de éste—. ¿Ya están aquí?

—Sí, pasa.

Lo acompañó al salón. Sandy saludó a Hillgarth y Tolhurst con una inclinación de cabeza y luego miró alrededor.

—Bonito apartamento. Veo que tienes unos cuantos cuadros ingleses.

Hillgarth se le acercó y le tendió la mano.

—Soy el capitán Alan Hillgarth. Le presento a Simon Tolhurst.

—Encantado de conocerles.

—¿Qué vas a tomar, Sandy? —le preguntó Harry.

—Whisky, por favor. —Observó la botella del aparador—. ¡Ah!, veo que tienes Glenfiddich. No sé si tu proveedor es el mismo que yo tengo. ¿Un pequeño local dedicado al mercado negro detrás del Rastro?

—Más bien suministros de la embajada —explicó Hillgarth—. Directamente de Inglaterra. Ventajas del oficio.

—Comodidades hogareñas, ¿eh? —Sandy miró a Harry con su ancha sonrisa de siempre mientras éste le ofrecía el vaso.

Harry se revolvió inquieto en su fuero interno.

—¿Nos sentamos? —preguntó Hillgarth.

—Por supuesto. —Sandy se sentó y le ofreció la pitillera de plata a Hillgarth. Después, se reclinó en su asiento—. ¿En qué puedo servirlo?

—Lo hemos estado vigilando, Forsyth —dijo Hillgarth en tono pausado—. Estamos al corriente de su participación en la mina de los alrededores de Segovia; sabemos que es un gran proyecto y que usted ha tenido problemas con el comité del general Maestre. Creemos que su sector monárquico quiere arrebatarles el control de este importante recurso a los falangistas del Ministerio de Minas.

El rostro de Sandy se quedó en blanco mientras éste miraba a Hillgarth. Harry pensó: «Sandy se dará cuenta de que todo esto sólo se habrá podido averiguar a través de mí.» Hillgarth lo tendría que haber advertido de que irían directamente al grano.

—Las acciones de su empresa, Nuevas Iniciativas —añadió Hillgarth, mirando a Sandy a los ojos—, están bajando.

Sandy se inclinó hacia delante, sacudió cuidadosamente la ceniza de su cigarrillo en el cenicero, volvió a reclinarse en su asiento y enarcó una ceja.

—Eso es para usted el mercado bursátil.

—Y, como es natural, las cosas se habrán complicado considerablemente tras descubrirse el cadáver del teniente Gómez.

Sandy mantuvo un semblante inexpresivo y no dijo nada. Fueron sólo unos segundos, pero parecieron durar una eternidad. Después, miró a Tolhurst antes de volverse para mirar nuevamente el rostro de Hillgarth.

—Veo que está usted muy bien informado —dijo en un pausado susurro—. ¿O sea que Harry me ha estado espiando? ¿Mi viejo compañero del colegio? —Se volvió muy despacio para mirar a Harry. Sus grandes ojos castaños reflejaban una profunda tristeza—. Lo has estado fisgoneando todo, ¿verdad?

—La información es correcta, ¿no es cierto? —lo interrumpió Hillgarth.

Sandy se volvió para mirarlo.

—Una parte podría serlo.

Hillgarth se inclinó hacia delante.

—No juegue conmigo, Forsyth. Muy pronto va a necesitar un refugio. Si el Estado se hace cargo de la explotación de la mina, se quedará usted sin un céntimo. Incluso alguien podría acusarlo del asesinato de Gómez.

Sandy inclinó la cabeza.

—Yo no tengo la culpa de que a algunas de las personas con quienes trabajo se les fuera la mano.

—Nuestra fuente nos dice que usted fue el instigador.

Sandy ingirió un buen trago de whisky sin mediar palabra. Hillgarth se reclinó contra el respaldo de su asiento. Tolhurst se había pasado todo el rato mirando con cara de lechuza a Sandy. Si con ello pretendía ponerlo nervioso, su propósito falló... Sandy ni siquiera pareció darse cuenta.

—Todo eso está fuera de nuestra jurisdicción —añadió Hillgarth, agitando una mano—. Pero la verdad es que tampoco nos interesa. Simplemente queríamos decirle que, si se encuentra usted en dificultades, quizá podría considerar la posibilidad de cambiar de actividad. Y trabajar para nosotros.

—¿Qué clase de trabajo sería?

—Espionaje. Lo devolveríamos a Inglaterra. Pero, primero, nos lo tendría que decir todo acerca de la mina. Para eso enviamos a Brett. ¿Qué extensión tiene; cuánto falta para iniciar la producción? ¿Otorgará a España las reservas de oro necesarias para adquirir productos alimenticios en el extranjero? De momento, el país depende de nuestros préstamos y de los de Estados Unidos, lo cual nos permite ejercer cierta presión.

Sandy asintió muy despacio.

—¿O sea que, si les dijera todo lo que sé sobre la mina, me sacarían ustedes de aquí?

—Sí. Lo enviaríamos a Inglaterra y, si usted quisiera, lo adiestraríamos y lo enviaríamos a trabajar a algún otro sitio en el que sus conocimientos pudieran resultar útiles. Tal vez a Latinoamérica. Creemos que el lugar podría ser muy indicado para usted. La paga sería buena. —Hillgarth se inclinó levemente hacia delante—. Si se encuentra a gusto con su trabajo de aquí, perfecto. Pero, si quiere salir, primero tendremos que averiguarlo todo acerca de la mina. Lo que se dice todo.

—¿Es una promesa?

—Lo es.

Sandy ladeó la cabeza mientras movía el vaso que sostenía en la mano para agitar su contenido. Hillgarth añadió en tono tranquilo y reposado:

—De usted depende. Puede asociarse a nosotros o regresar a su mina de oro. Pero el juego es muy peligroso, por rentable que pueda haber parecido al principio.

Para asombro de Harry, Sandy echó la cabeza hacia atrás y soltó una carcajada.

—Me has estado espiando y no te has enterado. Es para troncharse. Jamás lo adivinaste.

—¿Qué? —preguntó Harry, perplejo.

—¿Qué? —repitió Sandy, imitando su tono de voz—. ¿Sigues estando un poco sordo o la historia no era más que una tapadera?

—No —contestó Harry—. Pero ¿qué quieres decir? ¿Adivinar el qué?

—Pues que no hay ninguna mina de oro —contestó Sandy en un suave susurro teñido de un ligero tono de desprecio—. Nunca la hubo.

Harry se incorporó bruscamente en su asiento.

—Pero yo la vi.

Sandy miró a Hillgarth y no a Harry cuando contestó.

—Vio una extensión de territorio, un poco de material y unas cabañas. Bueno, el terreno es del tipo que podría contener yacimientos de oro, sólo que no los contiene. —Soltó otra carcajada y meneó la cabeza—. ¿Alguno de ustedes ha oído hablar alguna vez de eso que se llama aplicación de sal?

—Yo sí —dijo Hillgarth—. Se toma una muestra de un determinado tipo de terreno y se colocan en ella unos granos de oro, para que parezca mineral de oro. —Se quedó boquiabierto—. Dios bendito, ¿eso es lo que han estado haciendo?

Sandy asintió con la cabeza.

—Ni más ni menos. —Sacó otro cigarrillo—. Casi merece la pena haber sido traicionado por Brett para ver la cara que ustedes ponen ahora.

—Yo también he trabajado en el sector de la minería —dijo Hillgarth—. La aplicación de sal es una tarea difícil, hay que ser un experto geólogo para eso.

—Cierto. Tanto como mi amigo Alberto Otero. Trabajó en África del Sur y me contó algunos de los malabarismos que se han hecho por allí. Yo sugerí la posibilidad de hacer lo mismo en España, donde el Gobierno anda buscando desesperadamente oro y el Ministerio de Minas está lleno de falangistas que tratan de aumentar su influencia. Descubrió el lugar apropiado y compramos la tierra. Ya he conseguido establecer algunos contactos útiles con el ministerio.

—¿Se refiere a De Salas? —preguntó Tolhurst.

—Sí, De Salas. Tuvo muchas dificultades para mantener a raya a Maestre. Él también cree que la mina es auténtica y que servirá para que España se convierta en un gran país fascista. —Sandy se volvió para mirar a Hillgarth con una sonrisa en los labios—. En nuestros laboratorios mezclamos polvo de oro de excelente calidad con la llamada «mena» y después lo enviamos todo a los laboratorios del Gobierno. Llevamos seis meses haciéndolo. Ellos siguen pidiendo más muestras y nosotros se las proporcionamos.

Hillgarth entornó los párpados.

—Necesitarían ustedes una considerable cantidad de oro para poder hacerlo. El precio en el mercado negro es muy elevado. Cualquier compra importante sería objeto de comentario.

—No, si formas parte de un comité que ayuda a unos pobres y desgraciados judíos a huir de Francia. A éstos sólo les está permitido traer lo que puedan llevar en su equipaje de mano, y la mayoría trae oro. Nosotros nos quedamos con él a cambio de visados para Lisboa; después, Alberto lo funde y lo convierte en minúsculos granos de oro.

Tenemos todo el oro que necesitamos y nadie se entera. En realidad, lo de los judíos fue idea mía. —Exhaló una nube de humo—. Cuando supe que los judíos de Francia se estaban trasladando a Madrid para huir de los nazis, pensé que quizá los podría ayudar. Es probable que Harry no se lo crea, pero yo me compadecía de ellos, de esa gente a la que parece que nunca le sale nada a derechas y siempre anda errante por el mundo. Pero, para conseguirles visados, necesitaba dinero y lo único que ellos tenían era oro. Eso me indujo a comentarle a Otero el sempiterno valor del oro que siempre hace que a la gente se le iluminen los ojos de codicia. De ahí surgió toda la idea.

Sandy miró con una sonrisa a Hillgarth, todavía reacio a mirar a Harry.

O sea que todo había sido un engaño, pensó Harry. Todo aquello, el trabajo, las traiciones y la muerte de Gómez no había servido de nada. Pura prestidigitación.

Hillgarth se pasó un buen rato mirando a Sandy. Después, soltó una sonora risotada.

—Dios bendito, Forsyth, pero qué listo es usted. Ha tenido engañado a todo el mundo. —Sandy inclinó la cabeza—. ¿Qué pensaba hacer? ¿Esperar a que las acciones de la compañía subieran lo suficiente para después endilgárselas a alguien y desaparecer?

—La idea era ésta. Pero alguien del Ministerio de Minas ha estado haciendo correr la voz de que es muy probable que la empresa sea adquirida por otra. Su táctica más reciente para hacerse con el control. Un puñado de taimados cabrones. —Sandy volvió a reírse—. Sólo que los pobres no saben que no van a controlar nada, simplemente un par de fincas inservibles. Pero entonces va Maestre y nos coloca un espía. Tenía las llaves de todos los despachos... a poco listo que fuera, habría acabado descubriendo la verdad.

—O sea que podía usted llegar a quedarse sin un céntimo. —Los ojos de Hillgarth eran duros como piedras—. Y puede que con precio sobre su cabeza.

—En cualquier momento. O bien apuñalado en una oscura callejuela. No me gusta tener que vigilarme constantemente la espalda.

—Ha estado jugando a un juego muy peligroso.

—Sí. Pensé que Harry podría ser una ventaja. —Seguía sin querer mirar a Harry—. Sabía que tenía dinero y que, si invirtiéramos más dinero y compráramos más tierras, seríamos más fuertes y resultaría más difícil comprarnos nuestra parte. Harry también habría obtenido unos buenos beneficios. Yo me habría encargado de que así fuera y le habría aconsejado cuándo vender. Después, cuando nos enteramos de lo de Gómez, temimos que éste hubiera averiguado que todo era una impostura; pero no fue así, pues no ocurrió nada más. Gómez no era muy listo. Pero Maestre sigue urdiendo intrigas para apoderarse del oro. Ya es hora de dejarlo. —Finalmente, Sandy se volvió para mirar a Harry. Su rostro inexpresivo estaba lleno de rabia y dolor—. Yo confiaba en ti, Harry, eras la última persona del mundo en quien todavía confiaba. —Esbozó una leve sonrisa—. Pero no importa. Todo se ha resuelto de la mejor manera. —Se reclinó un momento contra el respaldo de su asiento con semblante pensativo. Harry observó una ligera sacudida espasmódica por encima de su ojo izquierdo. Estaba avergonzado, demasiado avergonzado para contestar, a pesar de lo que Sandy había hecho. Sandy miró de nuevo a Hillgarth—. Usted es el Alan Hillgarth que escribía novelas de aventuras, ¿verdad?

—Pues sí.

—Y ahora lo hace en la vida real, ¿eh? Yo leía sus libros en el colegio. Es como yo, le gusta la aventura. —Hillgarth no contestó—. Sólo que usted daba un toque romántico a las cosas. ¿Recuerda aquella novela cuyo argumento transcurría en el Marruecos español? No mostraba cómo eran realmente las guerras coloniales. La violencia.

Hillgarth lo miró sonriendo.

—Lo que realmente ocurría no habría superado la censura.

Sandy asintió con la cabeza.

—Creo que tiene usted razón. Hay censores por todas partes, ¿verdad? Unos censores que nos hacen creer que el mundo es mejor y más seguro de lo que realmente es.

—Volvamos a los negocios, Forsyth. Creo que usted nos podría seguir siendo muy útil. ¡Qué barbaridad!, alguien capaz de montar semejante malabarismo. Pero, si lo sacamos de esta apurada situación, tendrá que aceptar nuestras condiciones. Para empezar, todo esto se lo tendría que revelar a ciertas personas de Londres. Lo escoltaremos en su vuelo de regreso. ¿Lo ha entendido?

Sandy dudó un instante, pero después inclinó la cabeza.

—Perfectamente.

—Muy bien, pues. Preséntese en la embajada mañana a las diez. Está viviendo con una inglesa, ¿verdad?

—Sí.

—¿Qué sabe ella acerca de la mina?

Sandy esbozó una cínica media sonrisa.

—Nada. Nada en absoluto. —Volvió a mirar a Harry—. Barbara es una pardilla, ¿verdad, Harry?

Hillgarth soltó un gruñido.

—Le tendrá que decir por qué regresa a Inglaterra.

—Bueno, supongo que le encantará regresar a casa. Además, dudo mucho que sigamos demasiado tiempo juntos. No es un factor que debamos tener en cuenta.

—Bien. —Hillgarth se levantó y miró a Sandy.

—Eso es todo de momento. Creo que tiene madera para convertirse en un buen agente, Forsyth. —Lo miró sonriendo—. Pero no nos vaya a tomar el pelo.

Sandy inclinó la cabeza, se levantó y le tendió la mano a Hillgarth. Éste se la estrechó.

—¿Y qué hará con su casa? —preguntó Tolhurst.

—La había alquilado a uno de los ministerios. En realidad, el alquiler es gratuito. —Sandy le tendió la mano a Tolhurst, el cual se la estrechó tras un leve titubeo. Harry también se levantó. Sandy lo miró un instante, después dio media vuelta y se encaminó hacia la puerta. Tolhurst lo acompañó.

Hillgarth miró a Harry.

—Es frío como un témpano. El trabajo que nos ha costado esta mina. Supongo que no nos habrá mentido, ¿verdad?

—Creo que ha dicho la verdad —contestó Harry en un susurro.

—Sí. Si todo este maldito montaje hubiera sido verdad, habría sido un tira y afloja tremendo y él lo hubiera aprovechado. Supongo que por eso ha confesado de inmediato que era falso. Probablemente ha pensado que era sólo cuestión de tiempo que se descubriera la verdad. —Hillgarth reflexionó un momento.

Tolhurst regresó a la estancia y se sentó.

—Sir Sam se pondrá furioso, señor. Tantos medios malgastados, la enemistad de Maestre, y todo por una mina que jamás existió. ¡Dios mío!

—Sí, tendré que buscar el momento oportuno para decírselo. —Hillgarth meneó la cabeza y después se echó a reír—. Mira que engañar al mismísimo Franco. Pero bueno, hay que reconocer que Forsyth tiene un par de cojones. —Por primera vez, miró amablemente a Harry—. Siento haber tenido que destapar su papel, pero no había más remedio para poder hablar de la mina.

Harry vaciló momentáneamente y después dijo:

—No se preocupe, señor, ya nada me sorprende; ya ni siquiera me sorprende la cuestión de los Caballeros de San Jorge, eso de que el Gobierno estuviera dispuesto a sobornar en masa a los monárquicos.

—Harry —dijo Tolhurst avergonzado, mientras Hillgarth arqueaba las cejas. Pero Harry siguió adelante, todo había terminado y ya nada le importaba.

—Lo único que me pregunto es por qué había que sobornarlos —añadió con amargura—. No quieren combatir en una guerra contra nosotros y saben que a nosotros nos importa un carajo lo que le hagan a la gente de aquí.

Harry pensaba que Hillgarth iba a perder los estribos y, en parte, lo deseaba; pero el capitán se limitó a esbozar una sonrisita de desprecio.

—Váyase, Brett. Arregle las cosas con su novieta y después ya puede regresar a casa. Deje España en manos de quienes saben lo que hay que hacer.

42

Aquella tarde Barbara se quedó en casa cuidándose un resfriado. Lo tenía de verdad... lo había pillado la víspera y, con la nariz que no paraba de gotearle y los ojos enrojecidos, no le había sido difícil exagerar los síntomas y simular que tenía la gripe. Había apuntado la posibilidad de dormir en uno de los dormitorios de reserva para minimizar el riesgo de contagiárselo a Sandy y éste se había mostrado de acuerdo. Se le veía más preocupado que nunca y ahora casi ni prestaba atención a lo que ella decía.

Le había comentado que no regresaría a casa hasta muy tarde y ella se había pasado todo el rato en la cama, fingiendo tener la gripe también con Pilar. Puso la radio, tratando de sintonizar con la BBC; pero la recepción era mala. Después se sentó junto a la ventana y contempló la calle cubierta de nieve. El ambiente era indudablemente más cálido y el agua de la nieve goteaba desde las ramas de los árboles. Una franja de verdor ya había asomado bajo el olmo del jardín de la parte anterior de la casa. Experimentó una oleada de alivio. En caso de que desapareciera la nieve, el rescate de Bernie sería más fácil.

Al día siguiente, acudiría con Harry y Sofía a su última reunión con Luis. Habían acordado que ella se reuniría primero con él; pues Barbara temía que, si ella se presentara con otras dos personas, Luis huyera despavorido. Cuando ella le hubiera explicado la situación a Luis, aparecerían los otros. No veía ningún motivo para que él pusiera reparos. Sofía tenía razón: el hecho de tenerlos a ella y a Harry a su lado no podía sino aumentar sus posibilidades de éxito. Les estaba muy agradecida, pero, al mismo tiempo, se sentía traicionada por Harry; qué cuestiones tan complejas habían resultado ocultarse bajo aquella superficie tan aparentemente tranquila.

Sus reflexiones quedaron interrumpidas por una llamada con los nudillos a la puerta del dormitorio. Se levantó de un brinco y cerró la ventana. Mientras se acercaba a la puerta, se sonó ruidosamente la nariz y trató de adoptar la fatigada expresión de una inválida. Pilar estaba fuera con su enfurruñado rostro de costumbre y un cabello más rizado que nunca asomando por debajo de la pequeña cofia.

—¿Puedo hablar un momento con usted, señora?

—Claro que sí. Pase —dijo Barbara en tono cortante. La chica no podía esperar otra cosa; ni ella ni Sandy se habían molestado en ocultar lo que estaban haciendo. Barbara permaneció de pie en el centro de la estancia, frente a Pilar—. ¿Qué ocurre?

Pilar entrelazó las manos delante de su blanco delantal. Sus ojos reflejaban una cólera malhumorada. «Las personas siempre aborrecen a aquellos a quienes han ofendido», pensó Barbara. Suponía que eso permitía mantener a raya el remordimiento.

—Quería anunciarle mi despedida, señora.

Fue una sorpresa.

—Ah, ¿sí?

—Me gustaría irme a finales de la semana que viene, si a usted le parece bien.

No era mucho tiempo para buscar a otra persona, pero Barbara estaría encantada de no volver a verle el pelo. La asistenta externa ya se las arreglaría. Se preguntó qué habría ocurrido. ¿Pilar se habría peleado con Sandy?

—Esto es muy precipitado, Pilar.

—Sí, señora; mi madre se ha puesto enferma en Zaragoza y tengo que ir a cuidarla.

Era una mentira descarada. Barbara sabía que los padres de la chica eran madrileños. No pudo resistir la tentación de soltarle un alfilerazo.

—Espero que no se haya sentido a disgusto trabajando para mi marido y para mí.

—No, señora —contestó Pilar, sin dejar de mirarla con sus enfurecidos ojos semientornados—. Mi madre se ha puesto enferma en Zaragoza —repitió.

—En tal caso, tiene que reunirse con ella. Váyase esta misma noche, si quiere. Le pagaré hasta el final de la semana.

Pilar pareció tranquilizarse.

—Se lo agradezco, señora, me iría muy bien.

—Vaya a hacer la maleta, que yo mientras tanto le preparo el dinero.

—Gracias. —Pilar hizo una reverencia y abandonó rápidamente la estancia. Barbara tomó la llave del escritorio donde guardaba el dinero. «Que se vaya con viento fresco», pensó.

Pilar hizo la maleta y se fue en menos de una hora. Desde la ventana, Barbara la vio alejarse subiendo por el camino con su pesada y maltrecha maleta, mientras sus zapatos dejaban unas profundas huellas marcadas en la nieve que se fundía rápidamente. Se preguntó adónde iría la chica. Bajó a la cocina. Estaba hecha un desastre, con los platos amontonados en el fregadero y el suelo sin barrer. Barbara pensó que debería haber hecho algo al respecto, pero no quiso molestarse. Se quedó allí sentada, fumando un cigarrillo mientras contemplaba con indolencia la caída de la noche. Después, para pasar el rato, preparó un cocido para la cena.

Ya eran más de las diez cuando oyó las pisadas de Sandy. Éste entró en el salón. Barbara subió muy despacio los peldaños del sótano, confiando en poder llegar a su habitación sin que Sandy la oyera, pero él la llamó a través de la puerta entornada del salón.

—Barbara, ¿eres tú?

Se detuvo en los peldaños.

—Sí.

—Sube un momento. —Se encontraba junto a la chimenea apagada, fumando con el abrigo y el sombrero todavía puestos—. ¿Cómo estás? —preguntó. Parecía un poco bebido. Sus apagados ojos reflejaban una tristeza que ella jamás había visto anteriormente.

—Aún no se me ha pasado el resfriado.

—Hace mucho frío en esta habitación. ¿Por qué no ha encendido Pilar la chimenea?

Barbara respiró hondo.

—Pilar se ha ido, Sandy. Ha subido a verme esta tarde para anunciarme que se iba. Su madre se ha puesto enferma en Zaragoza, o eso me ha dicho.

Sandy se encogió de hombros.

—En fin. —Miró a Barbara—. He estado con ciertas personas de la embajada británica. Y después me he ido a tomar una copa.

—¿Y eso por qué? —Naturalmente, ya lo sabía. Harry le había dicho que lo querían reclutar.

—Siéntate —le dijo Sandy. Ella se sentó en el borde del sofá. Sandy encendió otro cigarrillo—. Dime una cosa, cuando te reunías con Brett, ¿él te hizo alguna vez preguntas sobre mí? ¿Sobre mi trabajo?

«¡Oh, Dios mío! —pensó ella—, sabe lo de Harry. Por eso lo llama Brett.»

—Algunas veces cuando venía al principio. Poco podía yo decirle.

Sandy asintió con expresión pensativa y después dijo:

—Harry no es un traductor en absoluto, sino un espía. Ha estado espiando mis actividades empresariales por cuenta del maldito servicio secreto.

Barbara fingió sorprenderse.

—¿Cómo? ¿Seguro que no te equivocas? ¿Y por qué te iba a espiar?

—Yo estaba implicado en un proyecto importante. —Sandy meneó la cabeza con semblante enfurecido—. Pero ahora eso ya terminó. Estoy acabado.

—¿Cómo? Pero ¿por qué?

—Tenía demasiados enemigos. Los jefes de Brett me ofrecen un salvavidas, pero... Harry me engañó. Debería haberme dado cuenta —dijo, hablando más consigo mismo que con ella—. Debería haber permanecido alerta. Pero yo confiaba en él. Y, probablemente, ellos lo sabían.

—¿Quiénes? ¿Quién lo hizo?

—¿Cómo dices? Pues sus jefes, los taimados fisgones. —Volvió a menear la cabeza—. Debería haberme dado cuenta. Debería haberme dado cuenta. No hay que bajar nunca la guardia —murmuró—, no hay que confiar nunca en nadie. —Sus ojos estaban desenfocados y Barbara creyó ver en ellos el atisbo de unas lágrimas.

—¿Estás seguro de que es eso? —preguntó Barbara—. ¿Por qué... por qué iba él a espiarte?

—Él mismo me lo dijo. —Sandy hablaba en tono pausado y sin la menor inflexión en la voz—. O más bien me lo dijeron sus jefes delante de él. Comprendí que no quería que yo lo supiera. Ellos se habían estado interesando por mis actividades empresariales. Y ahora quieren que trabaje para ellos. —Meneó una vez más la cabeza—. El goteo de información y las normativas y la quejumbrosa hipocresía. Y las bombas. Eso si no me meten entre rejas o me rematan de un golpe en la cabeza cuando regrese a casa. Con escolta. —Miró inquisitivamente a Barbara—. Tú quieres volver, ¿verdad?

—Sí —contestó ella con cierto titubeo—. Pero ¿y tus negocios?

—Ya te lo he dicho, eso se acabó. —Sus labios se movieron momentáneamente—. Todo ha terminado. Lo más importante que jamás había hecho en mi vida.

Barbara experimentó el repentino e insensato impulso de soltarlo todo, de hablarle de Bernie y de su liberación. Era la tensión, no podía soportar la tensión ni un minuto más. Pero Sandy dijo bruscamente:

—Voy arriba, tengo que ordenar unas cosas. Después saldré un rato a dar una vuelta.

—¿A estas horas de la noche?

—Sí. —Sandy dio media vuelta y abandonó la estancia.

Barbara se acercó al mueble bar y se sirvió un whisky solo, se sentó y encendió un cigarrillo. O sea que Harry había sido desenmascarado. Seguro que no le había gustado. Pero quizá se lo tenía bien merecido.

Sonó el estridente timbre del teléfono en el vestíbulo.

—Vaya por Dios —musitó Barbara—. Y ahora, ¿quién llama? —Esperó a que contestara Pilar, pero recordó que la chica ya no estaba. El timbre seguía sonando. ¿Por qué no se ponía Sandy desde el supletorio de arriba? Salió al vestíbulo y levantó el auricular.

—¿Señora Forsyth? —Reconoció de inmediato la voz de Luis, áspera y casi sin resuello. Miró angustiada alrededor, temiendo que Sandy apareciera en lo alto de la escalera y preguntase quién era.

—Sí —contestó en voz baja—. ¿Qué pasa? ¿Por qué llama aquí?

—Disculpe, señora, tenía que hacerlo. —Luis hizo una pausa—. ¿Puedo hablar sin peligro?

—Sí. Pero si oye un clic, será él desde el supletorio; entonces deje de hablar. —Barbara conversaba en un desesperado murmullo—. ¿Qué ocurre? Sea rápido.

—Me acabo de enterar a través de Agustín. Tenemos un acuerdo para que él me pueda llamar al bar al que yo acudo por las noches...

—Sí, sí; pero, por favor, dese prisa.

—Han cambiado los turnos del personal. Agustín no estará el sábado con Piper en la cantera de la prisión.

—¿Cómo? ¡Oh, Dios mío!

—Tendrá que ser el viernes, ¿puede trasladarse a Cuenca la víspera? El plan será el mismo. Reunirse con Piper a las siete en los matorrales que hay junto al puente. Agustín se ha ido a Cuenca para hablar con el viejo de la catedral.

—Sí, sí, de acuerdo, sí. —Barbara arrugó el entrecejo. ¿Podría Harry tomarse el viernes libre en la embajada?

—Ya sé que mañana nos tenemos que reunir, pero quería que usted lo supiera lo antes posible, señora. En caso de que usted tuviera que cambiar algún otro plan.

—Muy bien, sí, de acuerdo. Nos vemos mañana.

—Adiós.

Se oyó un clic y el teléfono enmudeció, sólo el zumbido del tono de marcar llenaba su oído. Colgó el auricular. Regresó al salón, pero no lograba calmarse. Salió y subió al piso de arriba. El pasillo estaba a oscuras y ella recordó su temor infantil a la oscuridad en lo alto de la escalera cada vez que subía a su habitación. De repente pensó en Carmela y en el burrito peludo que había dejado en la iglesia.

Un haz de luz se filtraba por debajo de la puerta de su dormitorio. Sandy estaba allí dentro, abriendo y cerrando cajones. ¿Qué estaría haciendo?

Regresó al salón y se sentó a beber y a fumar. Al cabo de un rato, oyó las pisadas de Sandy en la escalera. Se puso tensa a la espera de que él entrara en la estancia, pero entonces oyó cerrarse la puerta principal y, a continuación, el ruido de la puesta en marcha del motor del coche. El vehículo se alejó. Barbara subió corriendo a su dormitorio del piso de arriba. Sandy había recogido algunas prendas, un traje y una camisa. Miró por la ventana: todo aparecía envuelto en una espesa niebla, y la débil luz de las farolas de la calle traspasaba la mortecina bruma amarillenta. ¿Adónde habría ido? ¿Qué andaría haciendo? El tiempo no era seguro para conducir.

Se pasó horas sentada junto a la ventana, fumando sola en casa.

43

Todo estaba tranquilo en el restaurante de las inmediaciones del Palacio Real. Barbara le pidió un café al bajito y rechoncho propietario del local; adivinó que el hombre la recordaba del día en que ella había estado allí con Harry. Habían transcurrido tan sólo unas semanas, aunque parecían toda una vida.

Eran sólo las dos de la tarde; Harry y Sofía aún tardarían una hora en llegar, pero Barbara no aguantaba en la casa desierta y había salido. Sandy aún no había regresado. La asistenta había llegado a las nueve y Barbara le había ordenado limpiar la cocina. Después empezó a pasear por las silenciosas estancias en las que no se oía el menor sonido, aparte de sus pisadas y el incesante goteo de la lluvia en el exterior. La nieve ya casi había desaparecido. Entró en el estudio de Sandy. Todo parecía normal, todos los cuadros y los objetos de decoración estaban en su sitio. Abrió el cajón del escritorio donde él guardaba sus libretas de ahorro. Estaba vacío. «Se ha ido para siempre —pensó—, me ha abandonado.» Se sintió extrañamente abatida y desamparada. Trató de librarse de aquella sensación, diciéndose a sí misma que no fuera tonta, que eso era lo que ella quería. Pensó con una extraña indiferencia que, muy poco tiempo atrás, el hecho de que Sandy se acostara con la sirvienta, y ya no digamos de que la abandonara a ella, la habría dejado absolutamente hundida y habría confirmado los peores conceptos que tenía de sí misma.

El restaurante se empezaba a llenar de clientes cuando llegaron Harry y Sofía. Ambos estaban muy serios.

—¿Todo bien? —les preguntó ella.

—Sí. —Harry se sentó—. Sólo que Sandy se tendría que haber presentado esta mañana para una entrevista en la embajada y no ha aparecido.

Barbara lanzó un suspiro.

—Creo que se ha ido. Se ha largado. —Les contó lo que había ocurrido la víspera—. Ahora se entienden algunas de las cosas tan raras que decía. Creo que se ha ido con Pilar.

—Pero ¿adónde se pueden haber ido? —preguntó Sofía.

—A Lisboa, quizá —dijo Harry—. Anoche nos habló de no sé qué comité de ayuda a los judíos refugiados de Francia; aceptaban oro a cambio de visados para Portugal.

—Conque era eso —dijo Barbara—. Por eso los ayudaba.

—Fundían las joyas familiares de esa gente para obtener el oro que utilizaban para falsear las muestras. —Harry le contó lo que había averiguado la víspera: que la mina de oro era un timo.

Barbara se lo quedó mirando un segundo y después suspiró.

—Entonces todo era una impostura —dijo—. Absolutamente todo.

—Supongo que Sandy se habrá ido con pasaporte falso.

—Dios mío.

—Hillgarth dijo que casi lo esperaba, porque no pensaba que Sandy fuera una persona dispuesta a doblegarse y a recibir órdenes.

—No —dijo Barbara—, es verdad. —Lanzó un suspiro—. O sea que se acabó. Me pregunto qué va a hacer ahora.

Harry se encogió de hombros.

—Montar algún negocio en algún sitio, supongo. Tal vez en América. No sé por qué no ha querido aprovechar la ocasión que se le ofrecía de regresar a Inglaterra.

—Había dicho algo de que eso lo asfixiaría. Y temía ir a parar a la cárcel.

—No creo que eso hubiera ocurrido. Querían utilizar sus... habilidades. —Harry hizo una mueca—. Y, sin embargo... él dijo que todo empezó porque quería ayudar realmente a los judíos. Aunque parezca mentira, yo le creo.

Barbara guardó silencio.

—¿Qué ocurrirá con la casa? —preguntó Sofía.

—Sandy la consiguió a través de un ministerio sin pagar alquiler. Supongo que la querrán recuperar. Entre tanto, yo acamparé allí. No será por mucho tiempo.

Se acercó el camarero y Harry y Sofía pidieron café. Faltaba todavía casi una hora para la cita con Luis; el café se encontraba a quince minutos a pie. Sofía miró inquisitivamente a Barbara.

—¿Cómo llevas el que Sandy se haya marchado?

Barbara encendió un cigarrillo.

—De todos modos, yo lo hubiera dejado a él dentro de unos días. Me pregunto cuánto durará Pilar. Lo debían de tener preparado desde hace algún tiempo. —Exhaló una nube de humo.

—Eso nos facilita las cosas a nosotros —dijo Sofía en tono dubitativo.

—Sí. —Barbara respiró hondo—. Pero es que hay otro problema. Anoche llamó Luis. Han cambiado el turno de su hermano; se tendrá que adelantar un día. Tendrá que ser el viernes.

Sofía frunció el entrecejo.

—¿Y por qué le han cambiado el turno en el último minuto?

—En el campo se cambian los turnos. No pregunté. Estaba en el vestíbulo, temiendo que de un momento a otro bajara Sandy —explicó Barbara con cierta irritación en la voz—. Se lo podemos preguntar a Luis cuando lo veamos.

Harry se acarició la barbilla.

—Tendré que cambiar la reserva del coche. Había conseguido uno para el sábado, uno de los pequeños Fords que la embajada pone a disposición de los miembros de menor antigüedad del personal; dije que quería hacer una excursión por el campo el fin de semana. Pero supongo que no habrá ningún problema, diré que he cambiado de idea. Mañana estoy de servicio... han organizado un fiestorro de Navidad para los traductores en la Real Academia y a mí no me apetece ir, por eso me he ofrecido para quedarme de guardia en el despacho. Pero el viernes tengo el día libre.

—Y yo me pondré enferma en la vaquería el viernes, en lugar del sábado.

Barbara la miró.

—Siento haber perdido antes los estribos, supongo que todos estamos un poco nerviosos.

Sofía asintió, sonriendo.

—No te preocupes.

Hubo unos minutos de silencio. Harry sonrió y tomó la mano de Sofía.

—Nos han concedido una autorización especial. Nos casamos el diecinueve. De mañana en una semana. Después nos iremos a Inglaterra en avión el veintitrés. Hemos conseguido un visado para Paco.

—Qué bien —dijo Barbara sonriendo—. Me alegro muchísimo.

—Paco figura con nuestro apellido en el formulario —dijo Sofía—. Se me hace extraño verlo. Francisco Roque Casas.

—Gracias a Dios que un niño puede salir de aquí. ¿Cómo está?

—La verdad es que no entiende demasiado lo que significa eso de marcharse. —Una sombra se dibujó en el rostro de Sofía—. Le entristece que Enrique no vaya con nosotros.

—¿No ha habido manera de arreglarlo?

—No. —Harry meneó la cabeza—. Lo volveremos a intentar desde Inglaterra. Pero creo que será imposible, mientras haya guerra. Tuvimos suerte de encontrar pasaje para el avión.

—Me alegro mucho por vosotros.

—¿Tú has reservado algo?

—No. Confío en la suerte, no pienso planear nada hasta que Bernie haya entrado en la embajada británica y esté todo listo para su vuelta a casa. Me preocupa que pueda haber problemas porque es comunista. Por lo que tú me has dicho acerca de Hoare, no me sorprendería que lo devolviera a los españoles.

Harry meneó enérgicamente la cabeza.

—No, Barbara, la embajada lo tiene que acoger. Independientemente de lo que Hoare quiera hacer, él es un prisionero de guerra ilegalmente detenido según la legislación internacional. Y yo me imagino que las autoridades españolas no armarán ningún escándalo. Les daría mala imagen. Pero tú tienes que mantenerte al margen. —Harry reflexionó un momento—. Y no lo acompañes a la puerta principal. Si se ha fugado, los guardias civiles de la entrada podrían haber recibido la orden de vigilar y detenerlo; no estará en territorio británico hasta que se encuentre realmente en el interior de la embajada.

—Lo acompañaré a una cabina telefónica del centro de Madrid. Desde allí podrá llamar a la embajada y pedir que vayan a recogerlo. Podrá decir que robó la ropa y que paró un automóvil en la carretera pidiendo que lo llevara a Madrid, como acordamos. Eso no lo podrán refutar.

Harry se echó a reír. Barbara pensó que era la primera risa de auténtico placer que le oía desde que ambos se habían vuelto a encontrar.

—Será la comidilla de toda la embajada al día siguiente; yo puedo decir que nos conocimos en la escuela y después lo ayudaré a regresar a Inglaterra. —Harry meneó la cabeza con asombro—. Hasta puede que lo haga en el mismo avión que nosotros.

—Está todo perfectamente cronometrado —dijo Sofía—. Pero recuerda que las cosas pueden fallar y que, a lo mejor, tendremos que improvisar. —Volvió a mirar a Barbara—. ¿Te encuentras bien? ¿Estás resfriada?

—No es nada. Hoy ya estoy mejor —contestó Barbara. Le sorprendió ver que ahora Sofía parecía haber asumido el mando de la situación.

—Tengo un arma —dijo Sofía—. Por si acaso.

Harry se inclinó hacia delante.

—¿Un arma? ¿Y de dónde la has sacado?

—Era de mi padre, de la Guerra Civil. Lleva en casa desde entonces. —Sofía se encogió de hombros—. Hay muchas armas en Madrid, Harry.

Barbara se horrorizó.

—Pero ¿por qué llevar un arma?

—Por si tenemos que echar a correr. Como ya he dicho, puede que tengamos que improvisar.

Barbara denegó enérgicamente con la cabeza.

—Las armas empeoran las cosas, crean más peligro...

—Es sólo por si hubiera una emergencia. Yo no quiero utilizarla.

—¿Tienes balas? —preguntó Harry en tono vacilante.

—Sí, y sé disparar. A las mujeres las adiestraron a disparar durante la guerra.

—¿Me dejas que la lleve yo? —preguntó Harry—. Yo también sé disparar.

Sofía vaciló antes de contestar.

—De acuerdo. —Mirando a Barbara, añadió—: Esto que estamos haciendo no es una acción muy pacífica, que digamos.

—Está bien, está bien, lo sé. —Barbara se pasó una mano por la frente. El hecho de llevar armas iba en contra de sus creencias; pero Sofía tenía razón, era ella la que conocía la vida de allí.

—Sigo pensando que tú no tendrías que ir —le dijo Harry a Sofía—. Tú corres más peligro que cualquiera de nosotros dos.

—Facilitará las cosas —dijo ella con firmeza—. Cuenca es una antigua ciudad medieval; y no es fácil orientarse en ella. —Se volvió hacia Barbara—. ¿No es hora de que vayas a reunirte con el guardia?

—Sí. Dadme un cuarto de hora y después seguidme. —Cuando se levantó, le temblaban las piernas.

La tarde era húmeda y desapacible y las calles estaban mojadas de barro y aguanieve. Aún quedaban vestigios de la niebla de la víspera y algunas tiendas ya tenían la luz encendida. En los escaparates, había algunos motivos navideños, y los Reyes Magos rodeaban la cuna con sus regalos. Barbara se preguntó qué clase de Navidad le iba a ofrecer Sandy a Pilar en Lisboa.

El Real Madrid disputaba un partido y había muy poca gente junto a la barra del café, escuchando la radio. Luis estaba sentado junto a su mesa de costumbre. Hoy su nerviosismo irritó a Barbara.

—Anoche me asustó —le dijo bruscamente mientras se sentaba.

—Se lo tenía que decir.

—¿Y por qué este cambio de turno?

Él se encogió de hombros.

—Son cosas que pasan. Uno de los guardias se puso enfermo y hubo que cambiarlo todo. Será exactamente el mismo plan, sólo que el viernes en lugar del sábado.

—Viernes, trece —dijo Barbara, soltando una frágil carcajada.

Luis la miró sin comprender.

—Se considera un día de mala suerte en Inglaterra.

—Jamás lo había oído decir. —Luis esbozó una leve sonrisa—. Aquí en España el día de mala suerte es el martes y trece, señora; así que no se preocupe por eso.

—No importa. Oiga, ¿la nieve también se estará fundiendo en Cuenca?

—Creo que sí. La radio dijo que todo el país está en época de deshielo. —Luis miró alrededor y después se inclinó hacia delante—. La fuga será a las cuatro, como dijimos. Su amigo ya tendría que haber alcanzado el puente a las siete. Si hay una fuerte nevada y él no está allí a las nueve, o en la catedral en caso de que el puente esté vigilado, significará que hemos decidido anularlo todo a causa del mal tiempo.

—O que lo han atrapado.

—En cualquiera de los dos casos, usted no podrá hacer nada. Si él no aparece, tendrá usted que regresar a Madrid. No se quede a pasar la noche en Cuenca... los datos de todos los clientes de los hoteles van a parar a la Guardia Civil y una inglesa sola llamaría la atención. ¿Entiende?

—Sí, claro que lo entiendo. —Barbara le ofreció un cigarrillo a Luis y dejó la cajetilla de Gold Flakes encima de la mesa.

—Puede que tengamos suerte. A pesar de ser viernes y trece. La nieve se quedará en las cumbres de las montañas, pero en la parte más baja de Tierra Muerta ya habrá desaparecido.

—He tenido suerte en otro sentido —dijo Barbara, mirándolo a los ojos—. Aquí en Madrid hay un viejo amigo inglés de Bernie y él me facilitará un automóvil. Me acompañará hasta allí con su novia española. Ella conoce Cuenca.

—¿Cómo? —Luis la miró horrorizado—. Pero, señora, esto tenía que ser un secreto. ¿A cuánta gente se lo ha dicho?

—Sólo a ellos dos. Son de confianza. Conozco a Harry desde hace años.

—Señora, usted tenía que ir sola, el trato era éste. Eso complica las cosas.

—No es cierto —contestó serenamente Barbara—. Las facilita. Tres personas de excursión no llamarán tanto la atención como una mujer sola. Y, en cualquier caso, yo no habría podido conseguir un automóvil sin la ayuda de Harry. ¿Por qué tiene tanto miedo? —Luis estaba absolutamente desconcertado. A través de la luna del local, Barbara vio a Harry y Sofía cruzando la calle—. Es absurdo discutir, estarán aquí en menos de un minuto.

—¡Mierda! —exclamó Luis, dirigiéndole una enfurecida mirada de hombre atrapado—. Me lo tendría que haber dicho.

—Es que a ellos no se lo dije hasta hace tres días.

—¡Primero tenía que haber hablado conmigo! Bajo su responsabilidad, señora. —Miró a Harry y Sofía con rabia al verlos entrar en el café. La gente soltó un grito, alguien había marcado un gol.

Harry y Sofía se acercaron. Luis les estrechó la mano sin sonreír.

—Luis no está muy contento —les explicó Barbara—. Pero yo le he dicho que ya está todo decidido.

Luis se inclinó hacia delante.

—Esto es una empresa muy arriesgada —dijo en tono enojado.

—Lo sabemos —contestó Harry, adoptando una actitud serena y razonable—. ¿Por qué no repasamos las cosas y vemos si el hecho de que seamos tres complica de alguna manera la situación? Nos dirigimos a Cuenca por carretera, llegamos allí sobre las cuatro y dejamos el automóvil en algún sitio, ¿verdad?

Luis asintió con la cabeza.

—Agustín se pasó toda una tarde pateándose las calles para buscar el mejor lugar. Hay una granja colectiva abandonada en las afueras de la ciudad y un campo protegido de la carretera por una hilera de árboles, justo un poco más allá de un letrero donde dice que está usted a punto de entrar en Cuenca. Tendría que dejar el coche en el campo, allí nadie lo verá. —Luis volvió a inclinarse hacia delante—. Es importante dejar el automóvil allí porque es el escondrijo más cercano a la ciudad. Pocas personas tienen automóvil en Cuenca; el suyo podría llamar la atención de los guardias civiles si lo dejara aparcado en una calle.

Harry asintió con la cabeza.

—Sí, es lógico.

Luis miró a Barbara con los ojos entornados.

—Agustín ha invertido mucho trabajo en todo esto. Y, si falla, lo podrían fusilar.

—Lo sabemos, Luis —dijo Barbara serenamente.

—Y después, ¿qué hacemos? —preguntó Harry—. ¿Subimos a pie hasta la ciudad vieja y la catedral?

—Sí. Ya habrá oscurecido cuando ustedes lleguen allí. Esperen en la catedral hasta las siete, después crucen el puente hasta el otro lado del desfiladero y quédense entre los árboles. A aquellas horas de una noche invernal habrá muy poca gente por allí, si es que hay alguien. Pero el viejo, Francisco, sólo espera a la señora Forsyth.

—Ya se lo explicaremos —dijo Harry—. Creo que tendría que ser yo quien recogiera a Bernie. Vosotras dos podríais esperar en la catedral.

—No —replicó Barbara rápidamente—. Tengo que ser yo, él me espera sólo a mí.

Luis levantó las manos.

—A eso me refería yo. Veo que no se ponen de acuerdo ni siquiera en eso.

—Eso ya lo decidiremos más tarde —dijo Harry—. Barbara, ¿tienes la ropa?

—Toda empaquetada. Él se cambia detrás de los arbustos, cruzamos el puente en dirección a la catedral y, desde allí, regresamos al automóvil.

Harry asintió con la cabeza.

—Como dos parejas que hubieran pasado el día fuera. Muy verosímil.

—¿Es de confianza ese viejo de la catedral? —preguntó Sofía.

—Necesita dinero desesperadamente. Tiene a la mujer enferma.

—La catedral. —Sofía titubeó—. Supongo que, como en todas las catedrales de la zona republicana, habrá una lista con los nombres de todos los sacerdotes que fueron asesinados durante la República.

Luis la miró perplejo.

—Supongo que sí. ¿Por qué?

—Un tío mío era sacerdote allí.

—Lo siento, señorita. —Luis miró a Harry—. ¿Por qué está usted en España, señor? ¿Es un hombre de negocios, como el marido de la señora Forsyth?

—Sí, sí, en efecto —mintió Harry con la cara muy seria.

«Qué bien se te da mentir», pensó Barbara.

—¿Su marido sigue sin saber nada? —le preguntó Luis.

—Nada.

Luis miró de uno a otro y después se encogió de hombros.

—Bueno, pues la responsabilidad es suya, digo yo. ¿Y al día siguiente me reuniré con usted, señora?

—Sí. Según lo previsto.

—¿Y su hermano? —preguntó Harry—. ¿Dejará que le arreen un estacazo en la cabeza y después se atendrá a la historia?

—¡Claro que sí! Ya se lo he dicho, ¡lo podrían fusilar por colaborar en una fuga!

—Muy bien —dijo Harry—. Eso es todo, pues. Solucionado. No veo ningún problema.

—Y después usted y su hermano volverán a Sevilla —dijo Sofía.

Luis exhaló una nube de humo.

—Sí. Y olvidaremos el ejército y la guerra y el peligro.

—¿A ustedes los reclutaron cuando los fascistas tomaron Sevilla al principio de la guerra? —preguntó Sofía.

—Sí. —Luis la miró fijamente—. No se nos ofrecía ninguna otra alternativa. Si te negabas, te pegaban un tiro.

—Eso quiere decir que llegaron con Franco a Madrid en 1936. Con los moros.

La voz de Luis se endureció.

—Ya se lo he dicho, señorita, no se nos ofrecía ninguna otra alternativa. Yo participé en el sitio aquel invierno, al otro lado de la línea de donde usted seguramente se encontraba. No hay prácticamente ninguna calle de España que no haya tenido gente en ambos bandos.

—Es cierto, Sofía —dijo Harry—. Piensa en vosotros y en vuestro tío.

Se oyó un grito de decepción entre la gente. El partido había terminado; el Real Madrid acababa de perder. Los hombres que se encontraban junto a la barra se fueron distribuyendo por las mesas.

—Si no tienen más preguntas, yo me voy —dijo Luis.

—Creo que ya lo hemos repasado todo. —Harry miró inquisitivamente a las mujeres y éstas asintieron en silencio.

Luis se levantó.

—Pues entonces, les deseo buena suerte.

—No me gusta este hombre —dijo Sofía en cuanto se fue.

Harry tomó su mano.

—Lo que ha dicho de la guerra es verdad. La gente no podía elegir en qué bando luchar.

—Nunca ha fingido hacerlo por otro motivo que no fuera el dinero —dijo Barbara—. Si me quería engañar, ya habría agarrado el dinero que yo le he dado, que es mucho, por cierto, y habría desaparecido.

—Es verdad.

Los hombres de la mesa de al lado se pusieron a hablar en voz alta.

—El Real Madrid lo está haciendo pero que muy mal.

—Es que ha tenido mala suerte, hombre —replicó su amigo—. ¿Has oído que se acerca otra helada? Volverá a hacer más frío. Y hasta puede que nieve.

Barbara se mordió el labio inferior, pensando: «Viernes y trece.» Hasta los mejores planes necesitaban contar con un poco de suerte.

44

A la mañana siguiente, Harry y Sofía bajaron a pie por la Castellana camino de la embajada. Harry habría deseado darle el brazo, pero había una pareja de la Guardia Civil por allí cerca.

El tiempo había vuelto a refrescar de la noche a la mañana; se veían trozos de hielo negro en las aceras y aguanieve congelada en las cunetas. La gente que iba al trabajo caminaba arrebujada en sus abrigos. Pero no había nevado y el cielo matinal era de un claro azul eléctrico.

—¿Lo sabrás hacer? —le preguntó Harry a Sofía.

—Sí. —Sofía lo miró sonriendo—. Es sólo cuestión de rellenar formularios, y a eso los españoles estamos muy acostumbrados. Ayer contesté a las preguntas políticas.

Había que preparar ciertos documentos para la ceremonia de la boda y aquella mañana tenía una entrevista con el abogado de la embajada. El hombre quería verla a ella sola; pero después Sofía acudiría al despacho de Harry.

—Mañana a esta hora estaremos camino de Cuenca —dijo Harry.

—¿Estás seguro de que el embajador enviará a Bernie de vuelta a Inglaterra?

—Tiene que hacerlo. No puede actuar ilegalmente.

—Pues aquí lo harían. Lo hacen constantemente.

—Inglaterra es distinta —dijo Harry—. No es un lugar perfecto, pero en ese sentido es distinto.

—Así lo espero.

—Que en recepción me llamen cuando hayan terminado contigo. Te enseñaré mi despacho. Hoy las horas pasan muy despacio. ¿Cuándo tienes que estar en la vaquería?

—A las doce. Hoy tengo turno de tarde.

—He recibido una carta de Will. Nos ha alquilado una casa. Está en las afueras de Cambridge y tiene cuatro dormitorios. —Sofía se rió meneando la cabeza ante la idea de semejante lujo—. Podemos entrar a vivir cuando queramos. Después, yo empezaré a buscarme trabajo en la enseñanza y me encargaré de conseguir un médico para Paco.

—Y yo iré a clases de inglés.

Harry la miró sonriendo.

—Procura portarte bien. No seas descarada con el profesor.

—Lo intentaré. —Sofía contempló los altos edificios de la Castellana que la rodeaban y el claro cielo azul de Madrid.

—Se me hace extraño pensar que dentro de un par de semanas estaremos tan lejos.

—Al principio, Inglaterra te parecerá muy rara. Tendrás que acostumbrarte a nuestra formalidad, a nuestra manera de hablar siempre con rodeos.

—Tú no lo haces.

—No lo hago contigo. Bueno, aquí está la embajada. ¿Ves la bandera?

Harry anotó el nombre de Sofía en el registro y esperó con ella hasta que apareció el abogado, un sujeto campechano y simpático que se presentó y les estrechó la mano antes de llevarse a Sofía. Mientras Harry los veía alejarse, se abrió otra puerta y apareció Weaver.

—Hola, Brett, irá a la Real Academia, ¿verdad? Será mejor que nos demos prisa o llegaremos tarde.

—Estoy de servicio.

—¡Ah, claro!, lo había olvidado. Hay tantas fiestas en esta época del año. Mañana tiene el día libre, ¿verdad?

—Pues sí, he pedido un automóvil para ir a dar una vuelta por el campo.

—Hace un poco de frío para eso, ¿no? Pero, en fin, que lo pase bien. Nos vemos la semana que viene.

Tolhurst estaba sentado a su escritorio con un montón de carpetas al lado. Había montones de hojas de papel llenas de cálculos anotados con su pulcra y redonda caligrafía.

—¿Gastos de los agentes?

—Sí, los tengo que tener todos listos antes de Navidad. ¿Vas a ir mañana a la recepción de la embajada norteamericana? Supongo que estará bien.

—No, tengo el día libre. Llevaré a Sofía a dar una vuelta por el campo. —Harry volvió a experimentar una chispa del antiguo afecto que había sentido por él—. Oye, Tolly, en cuanto a la boda, te agradezco tu ayuda.

—¡Ah!, bueno, faltaría más.

—Siento que las cosas no dieran resultado con Forsyth. —Tolhurst entrelazó las manos sobre su prominente estómago. Estaba cada vez más grueso.

—Bueno, por lo menos, sabemos que no tienen oro.

—¿Alguna noticia más a este respecto? —preguntó tímidamente Harry.

—Según el capitán, Sam estaba considerando la posibilidad de comunicarle a Maestre que la mina era un timo. Él sabe hasta qué extremo estábamos implicados en este asunto; pero, por lo menos, le habríamos facilitado una información que él habría podido utilizar. Que el ridículo lo hagan los falangistas.

—Ya. —A Harry ya nada le importaba.

Tolhurst lo miró sonriendo.

—Tengo entendido que estás a punto de irte.

—Sí, después de la boda.

—¿Ya tenéis padrino? —preguntó Tolhurst.

—Le hemos pedido al hermano de Sofía que lo sea.

Harry sabía que Tolhurst esperaba que se lo pidieran a él. Tolhurst, su vigilante. Harry le estaba agradecido por su ayuda en la cuestión de la boda, pero la idea ni siquiera se le había pasado por la cabeza.

—¿Y tú regresarás a Inglaterra por Navidad? —le preguntó, para cambiar de tema.

—No —contestó Tolhurst en tono malhumorado—. Me quedo de servicio. Estaré por ahí, por si surgiera algún problema con nuestros agentes. —Sonó el teléfono. Tolhurst levantó el auricular y asintió con la cabeza—. Son los de recepción. Han terminado con tu chica. Dice que todo ha ido bien y que te espera abajo.

—Pues voy para allá.

Tolhurst lo miró.

—Por cierto, ¿has visto por ahí a la señorita Clare? ¿La chica de Forsyth?

—Ayer estuve tomando un café con ella —contestó cautelosamente Harry.

—Parece que Forsyth se ha largado en toda regla. Supongo que ahora la mujer regresará a Inglaterra.

Llamaron a la puerta y entró un anciano secretario vestido con levita. Parecía nervioso. Miró a Harry a través de unos quevedos de oro.

—¿Es usted Brett?

—Sí.

—El embajador desea verle en su despacho.

—¿Cómo? ¿A propósito de qué?

—Si es usted tan amable de acompañarme, señor. Es urgente.

Harry miró a Tolhurst, pero éste se limitó a encogerse de hombros con semblante perplejo.

Harry dio media vuelta y siguió al secretario, bajando por el pasillo. Estaba al borde del pánico. ¿Habrían descubierto algo sobre Cuenca?

El secretario hizo pasar a Harry al despacho de Hoare. No había vuelto a visitar aquella lujosa estancia desde su llegada. El embajador permanecía de pie tras su escritorio, vestido con traje de calle. Su enjuto rostro estaba arrebolado por la cólera. Miró a Harry con expresión ceñuda.

—¿Es el único que hay aquí? —preguntó bruscamente al secretario.

—Sí, señor embajador.

—No comprendo cómo han permitido que todos los traductores se fueran a esa recepción.

—El señor Weaver se acaba de marchar, señor, era el último. He intentado llamarlo a la Real Academia, pero sus teléfonos comunican.

Hoare le dirigió a Harry una gélida mirada.

—Bueno, pues me tendré que conformar con usted. ¿Por qué no ha ido a la recepción?

—Mi novia está aquí ultimando la documentación para nuestra boda.

Hoare soltó un gruñido. Mandó retirarse al secretario con un irritado gesto de la mano.

—¿Dónde está su traje de calle? —le preguntó a Harry en tono cortante.

—En casa.

—Pues tendrá que pedir uno prestado de los que hay aquí. Y ahora, escúcheme bien. Llevo semanas tratando de conseguir una entrevista con el Generalísimo. Pero él me hace esperar, se niega a verme mientras Von Stohrer y los italianos entran y salen de allí cada cinco minutos como Pedro por su casa. —La voz de Hoare rebosaba de furia—. Pero, de pronto, recibo noticias de que me quiere ver esta misma mañana. Tengo que ir. Hay cuestiones importantes que plantear y necesito hacer sentir mi presencia. —El embajador hizo una pausa—. Yo leo el español, naturalmente, pero hablar no se me da tan bien.

Harry experimentó el impulso de echarse a reír de alivio por el hecho de que no hubiera ningún problema y por la pose de Hoare; todo el mundo sabía que apenas hablaba una palabra de español.

—Sí, señor.

—Por consiguiente, voy a necesitar un traductor. Me gustaría que usted se preparara en cuestión de media hora, por favor. Nos vamos a El Pardo. Usted ha traducido para subsecretarios, ¿verdad?

—Sí, señor. Y también he traducido algunos discursos de Franco.

Hoare meneó la cabeza con gesto irritado.

—No se refiera a él en estos términos. Usted quiere decir el generalísimo Franco. Es el jefe de Estado. —El embajador volvió a menear la cabeza—. Por eso necesitaba a un hombre experto. Vaya a prepararse. —Mandó retirarse a Harry con un gesto semejante al de quien espanta un insecto molesto.

Era largo, el trayecto hasta el palacio situado al norte de la ciudad del que Franco se había apropiado para convertir en su residencia. El vehículo se adentró en la campiña circulando por la carretera que bordeaba el curso del río Manzanares, cuyas frías aguas grises discurrían entre unas altas y boscosas riberas de árboles esqueléticos. Sentado en la parte de atrás con Hoare, Harry levantó la vista al cielo. Esperaba con toda su alma que no volviera a nevar hasta el día siguiente.

Tras elegir uno de los trajes de calle de repuesto que había en la embajada, Harry regresó al despacho de Hoare y bajó con él a recepción. Sofía, que lo esperaba sentada, los miró con asombro. Él se le acercó para explicarle rápidamente adónde se dirigía mientras Hoare esperaba con una irritada mirada de impaciencia. Al mencionarle el nombre de Franco, observó que Sofía apretaba los labios y sintió sus ojos clavados en ellos cuando abandonaban la embajada.

El embajador permanecía sentado hojeando una carpeta, y tomaba apuntes con una pluma estilográfica. Al final, Hoare se volvió para mirar a Harry.

—Cuando traduzca, asegúrese de que transmite el sentido exacto de mis palabras. Y no mire al Generalísimo a los ojos, se considera una impertinencia.

—Sí, señor.

Hoare soltó un gruñido.

—Hay fotografías de Hitler y Mussolini en su escritorio. No mire, simplemente ignórelas. —Hoare se pasó una mano por el ralo cabello—. Voy a tener que parecer muy duro con la propaganda de la prensa en favor del Eje. Pero usted mantenga el tono normal y hable sin la menor emoción en la voz, como un mayordomo. ¿Entendido?

—Sí, señor.

—Si el Generalísimo fuera un hombre razonable, me daría las gracias por la cantidad adicional de trigo que he convencido a Winston de que le permita recibir. Pero razonable es precisamente lo que no es. Todo esto ha sido repentino, muy repentino. —Hoare sacó un peine y empezó a alisarse el cabello.

Algunas imágenes acudieron a la mente de Harry: una mujer rebuscando en los cubos de la basura, detenida cuando el viento le había levantado la falda del vestido por encima de la cabeza; los perros asilvestrados atacando a Enrique; Paco agarrado al cadáver de la anciana. Ahora iba a conocer finalmente al creador de aquella nueva España.

El automóvil llegó a una pequeña aldea convertida en cuartel, con soldados por todas partes; los hombres miraron hacia el interior del vehículo, mientras éste circulaba bordeando un muro elevado. El chófer se acercó a una alta verja de hierro de doble hoja custodiada por soldados armados con ametralladoras. Entregó la documentación para que la examinaran y, acto seguido, la verja se abrió y el automóvil cruzó lentamente la entrada. Los guardias saludaron el paso del vehículo, brazo en alto.

El Palacio de El Pardo era un edificio de tres pisos construido en piedra amarilla, rodeado por extensos prados cubiertos de blanca escarcha. Unos miembros de la Guardia Mora armados con lanzas permanecían de pie junto a los peldaños que conducían a la entrada; uno de ellos bajó y les abrió la portezuela. Harry oyó desde algún lugar el triste lamento de un pavo real. Se estremeció; allí fuera el frío parecía todavía más intenso.

Un ayudante vestido de paisano los recibió en los peldaños y los acompañó a través de toda una serie de estancias decoradas con muebles del siglo XVIII, fastuosos pero cubiertos de polvo. A Harry se le aceleraron los latidos del corazón. Llegaron a una puerta más grande flanqueada por otros miembros de la Guardia Mora de rostros morenos e impasibles. Uno de ellos llamó con los nudillos a la puerta y el ayudante los hizo pasar.

El despacho de Franco era espacioso y estaba lleno de oscuros y pesados muebles que le otorgaban un aspecto tenebroso, a pesar de la luz solar que se filtraba a través de las altas ventanas. Las paredes estaban cubiertas de pesados tapices antiguos que mostraban escenas de batallas medievales. El Generalísimo permanecía en pie delante de un inmenso escritorio, con las fotografías de Hitler y Mussolini en lugar destacado y, para asombro de Harry, una del Papa. Franco vestía de general con una ancha faja roja alrededor de la voluminosa cintura. Su cetrino rostro mostraba una expresión altiva. Harry esperaba presencia, pero Franco no la tenía; con su calva, su papada y su bigotito grisáceo, le recordaba a Harry lo que Sandy le había dicho el primer día en el Café Rocinante: un director de banco. Y era bajito y menudo. Bajando la mirada tal como le habían aconsejado hacer, Harry observó que el Generalísimo calzaba zapatos con plataforma.

—Buenos días, Generalísimo —dijo Hoare. Al menos, hasta ahí llegaban sus conocimientos de español.

—Excelencia. —La voz de Franco sonaba estridente y chillona. Estrechó la mano de Hoare, ignorando la presencia de Harry.

El ayudante ocupó su posición al lado de Franco.

—Ha pedido usted una reunión, excelencia —dijo Franco en un suave murmullo.

—Me alegro de poder verlo, finalmente —dijo Hoare casi en tono de reproche. Había que reconocer que no estaba en absoluto intimidado—. El Gobierno de su majestad ha estado muy preocupado por el apoyo que recibe el Eje en la prensa. Prácticamente incitan al pueblo español a entrar en guerra.

Harry tradujo, esforzándose en mantener un tono de voz tranquilo y reposado. Franco se volvió para mirarlo. Sus grandes ojos castaños eran líquidos, pero en cierto modo inexpresivos. El Generalísimo se volvió para mirar de nuevo a Hoare y se encogió de hombros.

—Yo no soy responsable de la prensa, excelencia. No querrá usted que me entrometa, ¿verdad? —Franco miró a Hoare con una fría sonrisa en los labios—. ¿Acaso no son este tipo de cosas las que nos critican las potencias liberales?

—La prensa está controlada por la censura del Estado, mi general, como usted bien sabe. Y buena parte del material procede de la embajada alemana.

—Yo no me ocupo de la prensa. Tendría usted que hablar con el ministro de Interior.

—Lo haré sin falta. —La voz áspera de Hoare cortaba como un cuchillo—. Es una de las cuestiones que más graves considera mi Gobierno.

El Generalísimo meneó la cabeza y volvió a esbozar una fría sonrisa.

—¡Ah, excelencia!, me entristece que haya obstáculos a la amistad entre nuestros países. Ojalá ustedes concertaran la paz con Alemania. El canciller Hitler no desea la destrucción del Imperio Británico.

—Jamás permitiremos que los alemanes dominen Europa —replicó bruscamente Hoare.

—Pero si ya lo están haciendo, señor embajador, ya lo están haciendo. —Muy cerca había un antiguo y enorme globo terráqueo. Franco alargó una pequeña mano asombrosamente delicada y lo hizo girar suavemente—. Los ingleses son un pueblo orgulloso, lo sé; como nosotros, los españoles. Pero hay que afrontar la realidad. —El Generalísimo volvió a menear la cabeza—. Hace apenas dos años, cuando firmó los acuerdos de Múnich, pensé que su viejo amigo el señor Chamberlain se uniría a los alemanes y se volvería contra el verdadero enemigo, que son los bolcheviques. —Franco lanzó un suspiro—. Pero ahora ya es demasiado tarde.

Mientras Harry traducía, la furia hizo que Hoare se pusiera tenso.

—Es inútil seguir discutiendo —dijo éste en tono cortante—. Gran Bretaña jamás se rendirá.

Franco se incorporó y su fría mirada le recordó a Harry la expresión que mostraba en las monedas.

—En ese caso, me temo que serán ustedes derrotados.

—Quería analizar las importaciones de trigo —dijo Hoare—. Su Gobierno tendrá que solicitar certificados para que puedan pasar el bloqueo. Seguimos controlando los mares —añadió en tono iracundo—. Necesitamos garantías de que ninguna cantidad de trigo será reexportada a Alemania y de que su importe será íntegramente pagado por el Gobierno español.

Franco volvió a sonreír con auténtico regocijo.

—Lo será. Los argentinos han accedido a aceptar condiciones de crédito. A fin de cuentas, nosotros no tenemos reservas de oro ni somos un país productor de oro. —Se volvió lentamente para mirar a Harry y, pese a su sonrisa, algo en sus ojos le infundió temor—. Precisamente ayer estuve hablando con el general Maestre —añadió suavemente el Generalísimo. —«Oh, Dios mío», pensó Harry, «lo sabe.» Hoare se lo habría dicho a Maestre y Maestre se lo habría dicho a él. Y Hoare experimentó un sobresalto—. Confío en que todo pueda seguir adelante sin ningún contratiempo —añadió Franco—. De lo contrario... No quisiéramos considerar a Inglaterra un país enemigo, aunque siempre es cuestión de ver cómo actúa una potencia respecto a nosotros. En sus convenios abiertos y en los secretos. —Franco arqueó las cejas, mirando a Hoare, y el embajador se ruborizó.

Harry se preguntó qué habría dicho Franco si se hubiera enterado del asunto de los Caballeros de San Jorge. Se agarró a una mesa que tenía a su espalda para no tambalearse.

A bordo del automóvil que los llevaba de regreso a Madrid, Hoare estaba furioso. La reunión se había prolongado media hora más de lo previsto. Hoare había analizado los acuerdos comerciales y los rumores que corrían sobre el envío de camiones cargados de alimentos destinados al ejército alemán en Francia; pero, al final, había perdido la iniciativa. La actitud de Franco había sido la de una parte ofendida tratando con un negociador importuno.

—Ya verá cuando me reúna con Hillgarth —dijo Hoare, mirando a Harry enfurecido—. He sido humillado ahí dentro, ¡humillado! Por eso me ha llamado, para echarme en cara la maldita mina de oro. Y yo he tenido la mala suerte de que usted fuera el único traductor disponible. ¡Estas aventuras tienen que terminar! ¡Me han obligado a hacer el ridículo!

Hoare hablaba casi entre dientes y las enjutas facciones de su rostro parecían una máscara de furia. Harry advirtió que una gota de saliva aterrizaba en su rostro.

—Lo siento, señor.

—Maestre se lo tiene que haber dicho todo a Franco después de que Hillgarth le revelara que todo era una estafa. Maestre ha hecho quedar en ridículo a la Falange, pero a nosotros nos ha hecho quedar muchísimo peor. —Hoare respiró hondo—. Menos mal que pronto se irá. Tenemos que asegurarnos de que el Generalísimo sepa que usted se ha ido. Casarse con una española de clase tan baja... no sé cómo cree usted que eso lo podrá ayudar en su futura carrera, Brett. Es más, yo diría que ha sido un digno remate —añadió despectivamente el embajador.

Después apartó el rostro, abrió la cartera con un chasquido y sacó una carpeta. Harry vio pasar rápidamente a través de la ventanilla los primeros suburbios de Madrid. Mañana, a aquella hora, ya estarían a punto de llegar a Cuenca; y unos días después, ya se habrían ido de allí. «Váyase usted a la mierda —pensó Harry—, váyanse todos a la mierda.»

45

Seguía habiendo nieve en las cotas más altas de Tierra Muerta; sin embargo, por debajo de la cantera, casi toda se había fundido durante la breve fase de tiempo más templado que había convertido el patio del campo en un barrizal.

La víspera, durante la pausa de descanso en su camino hacia la cantera, Agustín se había situado al lado de Bernie mientras éste miraba colina abajo hacia Cuenca.

—¿Estás preparado para mañana? —le preguntó en un susurro. —Bernie asintió con la cabeza—. Mañana recoge una piedra afilada de gran tamaño y guárdatela en el bolsillo.

Bernie lo miró con asombro.

—¿Por qué?

Agustín respiró hondo. Parecía asustado.

—Para golpearme con ella. Me tienes que hacer un corte para que salga sangre, será más realista. —Bernie se mordió el labio y asintió con la cabeza.

Tumbado aquella noche en su jergón de la barraca, Bernie se frotó el hombro que le ardía de dolor después de la dura jornada de trabajo. La pierna también la tenía muy rígida; esperaba que no le fallara cuando, al día siguiente, tuviera que bajar por la ladera de la montaña. Bajar por la ladera de la montaña. Le parecía increíble y, sin embargo, era verdad. Miró hacia el jergón del otro lado. Eulalio había muerto en medio de grandes dolores dos noches atrás y los demás prisioneros se habían repartido sus mantas. Los comunistas de la barraca estaban tristes y abatidos.

Cuando amaneció, se sentía muy débil. Se levantó y miró a través de la ventana. Hacía más frío que nunca, pero seguía sin nevar. El corazón le empezó a latir con fuerza. Lo conseguiría. Ejercitó con cuidado la pierna rígida.

A la hora del desayuno, evitó mirar a los comunistas a los ojos. Volvió a avergonzarse de abandonar a los demás prisioneros. Pero no podía hacer nada por ellos. En caso de que consiguiera escapar, se preguntó si se alegrarían por él o bien lo condenarían. Si llegara a Inglaterra, contaría al mundo las condiciones en las que se encontraban allí, lo proclamaría desde los tejados.

Se colocó en fila con los demás en el patio cubierto de barro, para el acto de pasar lista. El ondulante barro se había congelado y una película de blanca escarcha lo cubría como si de un mar helado se tratara. Aranda tomó la lista. A veces, desde que Bernie se negara a convertirse en confidente, los ojos de Aranda se clavaban en él mientras pasaba lista: se detenía un instante y sonreía como si le tuviera reservada alguna jugarreta. Algún día lo atraparía por algo que hubiera hecho, pero aquél no era el más apropiado; Aranda pasó al siguiente nombre. Bernie lanzó un suspiro de alivio. «Has perdido la oportunidad, cabrón», pensó.

El padre Eduardo salió de la iglesia con aire cansado y abatido, como le solía ocurrir últimamente. A Bernie le pareció que su cabello pelirrojo oscuro presentaba casi el mismo tono que el de Barbara. Jamás lo había observado anteriormente, pese a lo mucho que la había estado recordando desde que supiera que ella estaba detrás de los planes de su fuga. El sacerdote se acercó a la verja y levantó el brazo en respuesta al saludo del guardia mientras éste le franqueaba el paso. Debía de ir a Cuenca. Ninguno de los curas se había presentado por Eulalio. Quizá no se habían atrevido. A diferencia del pobre Vicente, Eulalio era un hombre temido.

Al terminar el acto de pasar lista, la cuadrilla de la cantera se reunió ante la verja. Agustín no miró a Bernie. Se abrió la verja y la fila de hombres empezó a ascender por la ladera. Al principio, el camino ascendía entre una hierba de color marrón; después, unos dedos de nieve asomaron en las hondonadas y, al final, se elevaron por encima de la línea de las nieves perennes y todo el paisaje volvió a cubrirse de blanco. Agustín caminaba un poco por delante de Bernie; no quería que nadie recordara haberlos visto juntos antes de la fuga.

Bernie fue colocado en un grupo encargado de romper rocas de gran tamaño. Esperaba poder tomarse el día con calma para conservar las fuerzas; pero hacía tanto frío que, si dejaba de trabajar, enseguida se ponía a temblar. Entrada la mañana, encontró una piedra adecuada para golpear a Agustín; plana y redonda y con un canto cortante que haría salir sangre para que el golpe pareciera más grave de lo que era. Se la guardó en el bolsillo, apartando de su mente la imagen de Pablo en la cruz.

Durante la pausa del almuerzo, procuró tomar la mayor cantidad posible de garbanzos con arroz. Por la tarde, mientras trabajaba, contempló el cielo. Seguía despejado. El sol empezó a ponerse, arrojando un resplandor rosado sobre las laderas desiertas y las altas montañas blancas del este. El corazón se le aceleró antes de tiempo. De una u otra manera, aquélla sería la última vez que contemplaría aquel paisaje.

Al final, vio que Agustín, que se las había ingeniado para vigilar su sección, se acercaba un poco más. Era la señal de que había llegado el momento. Bernie respiró hondo y contó hasta tres, preparándose para la representación. Acto seguido, soltó el pico y se apretó el vientre gritando como si le doliera algo. Después, dobló el espinazo y volvió a gritar aún más fuerte. Los hombres con los que estaba trabajando se lo quedaron mirando. No había ningún otro guardia a la vista. Estaban de suerte.

—¿Qué ocurre, Bernardo? —le preguntó Miguel.

Agustín se descolgó el fusil del hombro y se acercó.

—¿Qué es lo que pasa aquí? —preguntó con aspereza.

—Tengo diarrea. ¡Ay!, no me aguanto.

—Aquí no lo hagas. Yo te acompaño detrás de los arbustos. —Agustín levantó la voz—. ¡Dios mío!, la de quebraderos de cabeza que nos dais. Quédate quieto para que te pueda encadenar.

«Sabe actuar», pensó Bernie. Agustín dejó el fusil en el suelo y sacó de la bolsa que llevaba colgada al cinto una larga y fina cadena con grilletes en los extremos. Con ella aseguró las piernas de Bernie.

—¡Rápido, por favor! —Bernie hizo una mueca de angustia.

—¡Vamos para allá!

Agustín recogió el fusil y le hizo señas para que echara a andar. Alcanzaron rápidamente el caminito que serpeaba alrededor de la colina. En cuestión de un minuto, ambos se perdieron de vista a la altura de los arbustos. Bernie jadeó de alivio.

—Lo hemos conseguido —dijo respirando afanosamente.

Agustín se agachó a toda prisa y le quitó los grilletes con los dedos trémulos. Arrojó la llave al suelo. Después soltó el fusil y se arrodilló sobre la nieve. Levantó la vista y miró a Bernie, dirigiéndole una aterrorizada mirada de súplica, ahora que se encontraba a su merced.

—No me matarás, ¿verdad? —Tragó saliva—. No me he confesado, tengo pecados sobre mi conciencia...

—No. Sólo un golpe en la cabeza. —Bernie se sacó la piedra del bolsillo y la levantó.

—Hazlo ahora —se apresuró a decirle Agustín—. ¡Ahora! Pero no demasiado fuerte.

Apretó los dientes y cerró los ojos. Por un instante, Bernie se mostró indeciso; le era difícil establecer con cuánta fuerza golpear. Después golpeó a Agustín con la piedra en la sien. Sin un sonido, el guardia rodó por el suelo y se quedó inmóvil. Bernie lo miró asombrado, no tenía intención de dejarlo sin sentido. Un riachuelo de sangre brotaba del corte de la cabeza donde la piedra lo había golpeado. Se arrodilló junto al guardia. Éste todavía respiraba.

Se levantó y miró hacia atrás, después hacia la pendiente de la ladera. Pensó en la posibilidad de llevarse el fusil de Agustín, pero habría sido un estorbo. Respiró hondo y echó a correr cuesta abajo entre la nieve medio fundida, consciente de lo mucho que destacaban la manchada chaqueta marrón y el mono verde sobre la blancura que lo rodeaba. Su espalda experimentó una sacudida, a la espera de una bala. Era como en el Jarama, el mismo temor de indefensión.

Pasó por debajo de la línea de las nieves perpetuas y se detuvo para contemplar la línea de huellas que había dejado más arriba, a su espalda. Se había desviado a la derecha y ahora echó correr hacia la izquierda, confiando en que el cambio de dirección engañara a los guardias. Había pliegues en las colinas, en ambos sentidos. Era terrible estar solo, correr por aquel paisaje desolado; inesperadamente, Bernie echó de menos las paredes protectoras de la barraca. De pronto, resbaló sobre un retazo de hierba congelada y empezó a rodar cuesta abajo entre gemidos y jadeos. Se golpeó el hombro y tuvo que ahogar un grito de dolor.

Se detuvo al fondo del primer pliegue de las colinas y se incorporó sin resuello. Miró hacia arriba. Nada. Nadie. Sonrió. Había llegado adonde quería más rápido de lo que había imaginado. Se levantó y corrió al socaire de la colina. Como le había dicho Agustín, un pequeño carrascal crecía en un lugar resguardado. Corrió a esconderse entre los árboles y se tumbó sobre un tronco, respirando afanosamente. «Bien hecho —pensó—. Hasta ahora, todo bien.»

Permaneció sentado y prestó atención; pero no se oía nada, sólo un silencio que parecía zumbarle en los oídos. Se puso nervioso, llevaba más de tres años sin experimentar un silencio tan absoluto. Aunque estuvo tentado de echar a correr, Agustín tenía razón; era mejor esperar hasta que oscureciera antes de seguir adelante. Molina enseguida se habría dado cuenta de que Agustín y él habían desaparecido. Echó la espalda hacia atrás y empezó a mover los dedos medio congelados de los pies. Poco después, le pareció oír unos débiles gritos en la distancia que luego ya no se volvieron a repetir.

En el cielo se elevó una media luna y salieron las estrellas. Bernie se sorprendió de ver que las estrellas aparecían repentinamente de una en una. Cuando el cielo estuvo completamente negro, Bernie se levantó. Hora de irse. De repente, se quedó helado. Había oído un crujido a escasos metros de la entrada del carrascal. «¡Oh, Dios mío! —pensó—, ¡Dios mío!» Lo volvió a oír, procedente del mismo lugar. Apretando los dientes, separó con sumo cuidado las ramas de un arbusto y miró. Un pequeño venado pastaba la áspera hierba muy cerca de allí. Era muy joven, quizá la madre hubiera muerto abatida por un disparo de los guardias. Ahora que la nieve había desaparecido, el venado volvería a trepar por la montaña en busca de alimento. De repente, Bernie se emocionó; las lágrimas asomaron a sus ojos al tiempo que él levantaba la mano para enjugarlas. El venado lo oyó, levantó la cabeza, se volvió y huyó bajando estrepitosamente por la pendiente. Bernie contuvo la respiración para escuchar. Si lo estuvieran persiguiendo y estuvieran cerca de allí, aquel ruido les habría llamado la atención. Pero el silencio no se quebró. Volvió a salir de entre los arbustos. Soplaba un viento gélido. Se agachó y volvió a sentirse tremendamente expuesto al peligro. Después, hizo un esfuerzo por levantarse y empezó a bajar una vez más por la ladera. Faltaban siete kilómetros.

Se sorprendió de la cantidad de cosas que podía ver a la luz de la luna en cuanto los ojos se acostumbraban a ella. Se mantuvo a la sombra, siguiendo los senderos abiertos por los pastores, y caminó cuesta abajo sin detenerse. Calculaba que habrían transcurrido casi dos horas desde que dejara a Agustín; pero no podía estar seguro. Siguió bajando y deteniéndose de vez en cuando para recuperar el resuello y prestar atención desde detrás de una de las pequeñas carrascas que ahora eran cada vez más frecuentes. El hombro lo estaba matando y los pies ya le empezaban a doler. Aunque era como si llevara una eternidad corriendo cuesta abajo, la pierna mala seguía aguantando.

Después, al llegar a la cumbre de una pequeña loma, vio las luces de Cuenca directamente delante de él y sorprendentemente cerca: los puntos amarillos de las ventanas iluminadas. Un grupito de luces destacaba por debajo de las demás: las casas colgadas construidas en el mismo borde del peñasco. Respiró hondo. Había tenido suerte de salir justo al otro lado de la ciudad.

Ahora decidió ir más despacio, buscando todas las sombras. Unas nubes aparecieron surcando el cielo por delante de la cara de la luna y él agradeció los minutos adicionales de oscuridad que éstas le ofrecieron. Entonces distinguió el desfiladero y los negros machones del puente de hierro que lo cruzaban. Parecía increíblemente frágil, con un camino de madera peatonal lo bastante ancho para que pudieran caminar por él tres personas a un tiempo. Vio que sólo había unas cuantas casas construidas al borde del peñasco del otro lado. Eran mucho más pequeñas de lo que había imaginado.

La carretera que discurría paralela al desfiladero se distinguía claramente unos cien metros más abajo. Bernie se agachó tras un arbusto. No se veía a nadie. Los del campo ya habrían telefoneado a la Guardia Civil; quizás enviaran efectivos para vigilar el puente. Sin embargo, aquél no era el único puente, recordó que le había dicho Agustín; había otros más allá, otros medios de entrar en la ciudad. En caso de que el puente principal estuviera vigilado, Barbara lo esperaría en la catedral.

Oyó unas voces y se quedó petrificado. Voces de mujer. Un grupo de cuatro mujeres envueltas en pañolones negros, acompañadas de dos asnos cargados con leña. Las miró mientras pasaban por debajo de él; no alcanzaba a distinguir sus rostros, pero las ásperas voces parecían de ancianas. Llevaba tres años sin ver a una mujer. Recordó a Barbara esperándolo en su cama, y el corazón le empezó a latir con fuerza mientras una cálida saliva le subía a la boca. Se la tragó y respiró hondo.

Las mujeres y sus asnos se alejaron. Cruzaron el puente y desaparecieron. Bernie abandonó su refugio y contempló la carretera de abajo. Un poco más allá del puente vio una arboleda junto a la carretera. Aquél debía de ser el lugar. Casi no había ningún sitio donde esconderse; ahora tendría que caminar a lo largo de la ladera visible de la colina, de cara a la ciudad del otro lado del desfiladero. Se apartó de su refugio y empezó a avanzar muy despacio, deteniéndose en cada carrasca.

Mientras salía de detrás de un árbol oyó un sonido por encima de su cabeza, como un chasquido metálico. Se arrojó al suelo, esperando un disparo. No ocurrió nada. Abrió los ojos: sólo se distinguía la ladera desierta. Ligeramente por encima de él distinguió otra carrasca más grande, aislada de las demás. Le pareció que el sonido procedía de allí; pero, si fuera un guardia civil o un guardia del campo, ya habría disparado. Siguió adelante, volviéndose a cada momento a mirar el árbol, y ya no se oyó nada más. A lo mejor, había sido otro venado o una cabra.

Alcanzó la arboleda y se refugió en ella. También había unos arbustos espesos cuyas rígidas ramas le azotaron las piernas.

Desde allí no podía ver la carretera, pero tenía que permanecer escondido. Oiría acercarse a Barbara. Ella sabría que estaba allí. Barbara. Se estremeció, consciente del frío, ahora que había dejado de moverse. Y, cansado, le temblaban las manos y los pies. Se frotó las manos y se las sopló. Tendría que aguantar. No podía hacer más que esperar; esperar a que Barbara acudiera a rescatarlo.

46

Aquella mañana, Harry se había despertado temprano. Por primera vez en varias semanas le volvían a zumbar los oídos; no obstante, al permanecer tumbado el zumbido desapareció. Descorrió las cortinas, vio que la calle estaba cubierta de blanco y se desanimó por un instante. «Maldita sea —pensó—, más nieve.» Pero entonces se dio cuenta de que sólo era escarcha, una gruesa capa blanca sobre las aceras y la calzada. Lanzó un suspiro de alivio.

Sofía llegó a las nueve, según lo previsto. Harry le preparó el desayuno. Ambos estaban un poco apagados, ahora que había llegado el momento.

—¿Has dormido bien? —le preguntó Sofía.

—No demasiado. Tengo el coche, un viejo Ford. Está fuera. ¿Y tú?

—Bien.

—¿Has conseguido inventarte alguna excusa?

—Enrique está enfadado por tener que quedarse en casa con Paco. Le dije que nos habíamos tomado el día libre y quería venir con el niño. —Sofía meneó la cabeza—. Me duele tener que mentirles.

Harry tomó su mano.

—A partir de hoy, basta de mentiras. Vamos, tenemos que comer un poco. —Llevó unos platos de huevos revueltos al salón.

—¿Cómo está Barbara? —preguntó Sofía, mientras desayunaban.

—Bien.

La víspera, tras haber recogido el automóvil en la embajada, Harry se había dirigido a casa de Barbara. Le había dicho que la noticia de la estafa de la mina de oro había llegado hasta el mismísimo Franco; ahora, lo más probable sería que las autoridades salieran en persecución de Sandy.

Se oyeron unas pisadas en la escalera. Ambos se pusieron tensos.

—Debe de ser ella —dijo Harry.

Barbara llevaba una mochila de gran tamaño y su pálido rostro parecía cansado.

—Perdonad que llegue un poco tarde —dijo, casi sin aliento—. Ha venido gente a las seis, cuando yo todavía estaba en cama. Una pareja de guardias civiles y alguien del Gobierno. Querían saberlo todo acerca de Sandy. Yo he interpretado el papel de la mujercita tonta y les he dicho que no sabía nada. —Se sentó y encendió un cigarrillo—. Les he dicho que se había largado hace un par de días. Me ha sido fácil engañarlos. Son de esos que no creen que las mujeres sirvan para nada. Se han llevado todo lo que había en su estudio, incluso su colección de fósiles. Casi lo he sentido por él.

Harry respiró hondo.

—Él se lo ha buscado, Barbara. —Harry descubrió que ya no sentía el menor afecto por Sandy. Éste no era más que un espacio en blanco.

—Pues sí —dijo Barbara, asintiendo con la cabeza—. Es verdad.

—Si ya lo tenemos todo, tendríamos que irnos —dijo Sofía. Fue por su abrigo y sacó una pesada pistola alemana, una Mauser. Se la entregó a Harry—. Llévala tú.

—De acuerdo. —Harry la examinó. Estaba limpia y lubricada, y las cámaras, cargadas. Se la guardó en el bolsillo. Barbara se estremeció levemente y miró a Sofía, que le devolvió serenamente la mirada. Harry se levantó—. Bueno, pues —dijo—. Lo repasamos todo en un momento y enseguida nos vamos.

Fuera hacía tanto frío que el mero hecho de respirar resultaba doloroso. Tuvieron que rascar la escarcha del parabrisas del Ford. Harry temía que el motor no arrancara, pero éste cobró vida de inmediato. La embajada británica cuidaba muy bien su parque automovilístico. Barbara y Sofía se acomodaron en la parte de atrás y se pusieron en marcha por la carretera de Valencia. Los tres estaban muy taciturnos; la cuestión de la pistola parecía haber levantado una barrera entre ellos. Al cabo de un rato, Sofía habló:

—Estoy pensando en lo que tendríamos que decir si alguien nos pregunta por qué hemos ido a una ciudad tan apartada como Cuenca. Podríamos decir que me habéis acompañado para averiguar alguna noticia acerca de mi tío. Esto también podría ser un motivo para visitar la catedral y examinar la lista de sacerdotes asesinados durante la guerra.

—¿Crees que el nombre de tu tío podría constar en ella? —preguntó Barbara.

—Si fue asesinado, sí. —Sofía apartó la cabeza y, a través del espejo retrovisor, Harry la vio parpadear para reprimir las lágrimas. Y, pese a ello, estaba dispuesta a utilizar la tragedia de su familia para ayudarlos. Harry experimentó un sentimiento de amor y admiración.

Se pasaron toda la mañana en la carretera. En muchos lugares, la carretera se encontraba en muy mal estado y los obligaba a circular más despacio. Había muy poco tráfico y muy pocas ciudades; estaban en el corazón seco de Castilla. A primera hora de la tarde, la tierra empezó a elevarse y las laderas escarpadas de las colinas quebraron el pardo paisaje. Los riachuelos helados bajaban por los declives, destacando como delgadas y blancas cuchilladas sobre el oscuro terreno. «Frío como una llave —pensó Harry—, frío como una llave.»

Sobre las tres de la tarde vislumbraron una línea de bajas montañas de redondeadas cumbres en el horizonte. La campiña empezó a cambiar: ahora había más tierras de labranza; retazos de un brillante color verde en las zonas de regadío. Una gran ciudad apareció a lo lejos, un revoltijo de edificios blanco grisáceos que trepaban por una ladera tan empinada que parecían haber sido construidos los unos encima de los otros, cada vez más cerca del cielo. Llegaron a un cartel indicador en el que se informaba a los automovilistas de que estaban a punto de entrar en Cuenca. Barbara se inclinó hacia delante y tocó el brazo de Harry para señalarle un camino que se apartaba de la carretera y se adentraba en un terreno baldío por donde serpeaba tras una arboleda que ocultaría el automóvil de la carretera.

—Ése debe de ser el sitio.

Harry asintió con la cabeza y enfiló el camino mientras el vehículo brincaba sobre los congelados surcos. Se detuvo tras la arboleda. Al otro lado, el prado se elevaba suavemente hacia el horizonte.

—¿Qué os parece? —preguntó.

—Nos pegaremos una caminata para volver —dijo Barbara.

—Tenemos que seguir el consejo de Luis. Dijo que era el escondrijo más cercano.

—De acuerdo.

Abrieron las puertas. Fuera, Harry se sintió repentinamente vulnerable y expuesto al peligro. Una brisa fría y cortante les alborotó el cabello mientras salían a la carretera. Harry se echó a la espalda la mochila con la ropa y la comida. Sofía se situó en el lado de la carretera que miraba a Cuenca.

—No veo la catedral —dijo Harry.

—Está justo en lo alto de la colina. Detrás se encuentra el desfiladero.

—¿Y Tierra Muerta está al otro lado del desfiladero? —preguntó Barbara.

—Sí. —Sofía respiró hondo y echó a andar en dirección a la ciudad. Los demás la siguieron, bajando por la larga y desierta carretera.

Sólo un par de carros y un automóvil pasaron por su lado antes de llegar al puente tendido sobre un turbulento río de agua gris verdoso. Para entonces, el sol invernal ya estaba muy bajo sobre el horizonte. Pasaron por entre las casas humildes y destartaladas de la ciudad nueva, más allá de la estación del tren. Había muy poca gente y nadie les prestó demasiada atención. Se mantenían en actitud vigilante, temiendo la presencia de patrullas de la Guardia Civil en las calles; sin embargo, sólo un par de perros sarnosos les plantó cara: los animales emitieron ladridos furiosos, pero se escabulleron a toda prisa al verlos acercarse. Sus ladridos le hicieron recordar a Harry la jauría asilvestrada de Madrid y lo indujeron a acariciar con la mano la Mauser que guardaba en el bolsillo para mayor seguridad.

A continuación, iniciaron el ascenso pisando unos adoquines gastados hacia un encumbrado desierto de piedra cada vez más alto, mientras empezaban a caer las primeras sombras del ocaso. Las estrechas callejuelas se enroscaban progresivamente, subiendo cada vez más arriba. Las interminables casas de vecindad de tres o cuatro plantas de altura y varios siglos de antigüedad estaban descoloridas y con el revoque desconchado. Los edificios de apartamentos que se elevaban por encima de sus cabezas se convertían, cuando ellos ascendían a la siguiente calle, en un mar de tejados contemplado desde arriba. Las malas hierbas crecían entre los agrietados azulejos, el único verdor entre tanta piedra. Unos finos jirones de humo se elevaban al cielo desde las chimeneas y el olor a humo de leña y a excrementos de animales era más intenso que en Madrid. Casi todas las ventanas tenían las persianas cerradas; pero, de vez en cuando, se vislumbraban en ellas unos rostros que los miraban y rápidamente se apartaban.

—¿Qué antigüedad tienen estos edificios? —le preguntó Harry a Sofía.

—No lo sé. Quinientos años, seiscientos. Nadie sabe quién construyó las casas colgadas.

Al llegar a una plazoleta situada a medio camino de la cuesta, se detuvieron para permitir el paso a un anciano que conducía un burro medio derrengado por el peso de la leña que llevaba encima.

—Gracias —dijo el hombre, mirándolos con curiosidad. Se detuvieron un momento para recuperar el resuello.

—Recuerdo todo esto —dijo Sofía—. A veces temía haberme extraviado.

—Todo está muy desolado —dijo Barbara.

El sol poniente arrojaba un frío resplandor sobre la calle, confiriendo un matiz rosado a los montículos de nieve congelada en las cunetas.

—No para una niña —dijo Sofía, sonriendo con tristeza—. Todas estas calles tan empinadas eran muy emocionantes. —Tomó a Harry del brazo y reanudaron su ascenso.

La vieja Plaza Mayor coronaba la cumbre de la colina en dos de cuyos lados se levantaban unos edificios municipales. El tercer lado caía en picado a la calle de abajo desde un pretil, pero el solar no estaba ocupado por ningún edificio y ofrecía con ello una despejada vista de la catedral que dominaba el cuarto lado con su enorme fachada cuadrada, tan sólida como amenazadora. Una ancha escalinata se elevaba en el lugar donde unos mendigos permanecían acurrucados en el profundo pórtico de una grandiosa entrada. Había un bar junto a la catedral, pero estaba cerrado; aparte de los mendigos, la plaza estaba desierta.

Permanecieron en pie delante del bar, mientras sus ojos recorrían rápidamente las ventanas cerradas que los rodeaban. Una anciana con un enorme fardo de ropa en la cabeza cruzó la plaza al tiempo que el eco de sus pisadas resonaba en medio del gélido crepúsculo.

—¿Por qué está todo tan tranquilo? —preguntó Harry.

—Esta ciudad siempre ha sido muy tranquila. En un día como éste, la gente se suele quedar en casa para calentarse. —Sofía contempló el cielo. Unas nubes lo cubrían desde el norte.

—Deberíamos entrar en la catedral. —Barbara contempló la puerta tachonada de color marrón junto a la cual se acurrucaban los mendigos, que los miraban en silencio—. Mejor que no nos vean.

Sofía asintió con la cabeza.

—Tienes razón. Tendríamos que buscar al vigilante. —Encabezó la marcha hacia la escalinata con los hombros encorvados y las manos profundamente hundidas en los bolsillos del viejo abrigo al pasar por delante de los mendigos; éstos alargaron las manos hacia ellos. Empujó la enorme puerta y ésta se abrió muy despacio.

La gigantesca catedral estaba desierta e iluminada tan sólo por la luz fría y amarillenta que se filtraba a través de las vidrieras de colores. El aliento de Harry formaba una nube en el aire delante de su rostro. Barbara se situó a su lado.

—Aquí parece que no hay nadie —murmuró.

Sofía avanzó muy despacio entre las altas columnas hacia el presbiterio donde un enorme cancel adornado con reluciente pan de oro se levantaba detrás de una alta reja. Contempló el cancel frunciendo el entrecejo; su figura, envuelta en el viejo abrigo negro, parecía más menuda de lo que era. Harry la rodeó con su brazo.

—Cuánto oro —dijo Sofía—. A la Iglesia jamás le ha faltado oro.

—¿Dónde está el vigilante? —preguntó Barbara, acercándose a ellos.

—Vamos a buscarlo. —Sofía se separó de Harry y bajó por la nave. Los demás la siguieron. La pesada mochila se clavaba en los hombros de Harry.

A la derecha, una inmensa vidriera de colores permitía el paso de una luz cada vez más pálida. Bajo la vidriera había un estrecho confesionario de madera oscura. La luz se fue apagando mientras ellos seguían avanzando por el templo. Harry experimentó una violenta sacudida al ver una figura de pie en una capilla lateral. Barbara se agarró a su brazo.

—¿Qué es eso?

Mirando con más detenimiento, Harry vio que era un retablo en tamaño natural de *La Última Cena*. El que le había provocado el sobresalto era Judas, un Judas sorprendentemente realista labrado en el acto de levantarse de la mesa. Su rostro, vuelto ligeramente hacia el Maestro al que estaba a punto de traicionar, resultaba brutalmente frío y calculador, con la boca entreabierta como si estuviera emitiendo un gruñido siniestro. A su lado, Jesús, vestido con una túnica blanca, permanecía sentado de espaldas a la nave.

—Impresionante, ¿verdad?

—Sí.

Harry miró a Sofía, que caminaba un poco por delante de ellos con las manos todavía tan profundamente metidas en los bolsillos que las costuras de los hombros amenazaban con abrirse. Sofía se detuvo y, cuando ellos la alcanzaron, se volvió y le dijo a Harry en voz baja:

—Mira, está allí, en aquel banco.

Un hombre permanecía sentado junto a una capilla de la Virgen, casi invisible en medio de la oscuridad. Se acercaron a él en silencio. De pronto, Harry oyó un áspero y repentino jadeo por parte de Sofía, que estaba contemplando una lápida nueva empotrada en el muro. En unas hornacinas laterales ardían unas velas y, delante de ellas, descansaba un ramillete de eléboros negros. Por encima de una lista de nombres, figuraba la inscripción «Caídos por Dios y por la Iglesia».

—Aquí está —dijo Sofía—. Mi tío. —Los hombros se le encorvaron. Harry la rodeó con su brazo. Era tan menuda, tan delicada.

Sofía volvió a apartarse.

—Tenemos que reunirnos con el vigilante —dijo en un susurro.

El hombre se levantó del banco al verlos acercarse. Era viejo, bajito y de complexión fuerte y vestía un traje gastado y una camisa raída. Los estudió a todos con unos penetrantes ojos azules que destacaban en un rostro hostil y desconfiado surcado por múltiples arrugas.

—¿Viene usted de parte de Luis, el hermano de Agustín? —le preguntó a Barbara.

—Sí. ¿Es usted Francisco?

—Me dijeron que esperara sólo a una inglesa. ¿Por qué han venido tres personas?

—Los planes han cambiado. Luis ya lo sabe.

—Agustín dijo que una sola persona. —Los ojos del anciano miraron nerviosamente a unos y a otros.

—Tengo el dinero —dijo Harry—. Pero ¿es seguro esperar y traer aquí a nuestro amigo?

—Creo que sí. Hoy no hay ninguna función vespertina. Hace frío. No ha venido nadie esta tarde, excepto la hermana del padre Belmonte. —Señaló brevemente con la cabeza la placa conmemorativa—. Con unas flores. Fue uno de los que murieron mártires por España —añadió con intención—. Cuando los sacerdotes fueron asesinados y las monjas violadas para dar gusto a los rojos.

«Es del bando nacional», pensó Harry.

—Aquí tenemos las trescientas pesetas.

El anciano alargó una mano.

—Pues démelas.

—Cuando llegue el hombre al que hemos venido a buscar. —Harry procuró que su voz sonara seca y autoritaria como la de un oficial del ejército—. Éste fue el trato.

Se metió una mano en el bolsillo y le mostró al viejo el fajo de billetes ladeando el cuerpo de manera que éste pudiera vislumbrar también fugazmente la pistola.

El hombre abrió los ojos como platos y asintió con la cabeza.

—Sí, sí.

Harry consultó el reloj.

—Hemos llegado antes de lo previsto. Tendremos que esperar un poco.

—Pues esperen. —El vigilante se volvió y regresó a su banco. Se sentó allí a vigilarlos.

—¿Nos podemos fiar de él? —preguntó Barbara en voz baja—. Se le ve muy hostil.

—Porque lo es —replicó Sofía en tono cortante—. Es partidario de los otros. ¿Crees que la Iglesia contrata a republicanos?

—El hermano de Luis se debe de fiar de él —dijo Harry—. Y le podrían pegar un tiro si esto fallara. —Se fueron a sentar en un banco desde el cual podían ver tanto al vigilante como la entrada—. Son las seis y diez —dijo Harry—. Sofía, ¿cuánto se tarda en llegar al puente desde aquí?

—No mucho. Unos quince minutos. Tenemos que esperar un cuarto de hora más. Yo te acompaño... rodearemos la iglesia por detrás y enseguida estaremos en el desfiladero y el puente.

Barbara respiró hondo.

—Déjame allí y vuelve, Sofía. Él espera que yo acuda sola.

—Lo sé. —Sofía se inclinó hacia delante y le apretó el brazo a Barbara—. Todo irá bien, todo irá bien.

Barbara se ruborizó ante aquel inesperado gesto.

—Gracias. Siento lo de tu tío, Sofía.

Sofía asintió tristemente con la cabeza.

Harry pensó en el anciano sacerdote fusilado ante un paredón. Se preguntó si unas imágenes parecidas pasarían también por la mente de Sofía. La volvió a rodear con el brazo.

—Sofía —dijo Barbara en voz baja—. Os quería decir una cosa... os agradezco mucho que hayáis venido. Ninguno de los dos tenía por qué hacerlo.

—Yo sí —dijo Harry—. Por Bernie.

—Y yo quisiera poder hacer algo más —terció Sofía con repentino ardor—. Me gustaría que se volvieran a levantar barricadas, porque esta vez yo empuñaría un arma. No tendrían que haber ganado. Mi tío tampoco habría muerto si ellos no hubieran empezado la guerra. —Se volvió para mirar a Barbara—. ¿Te parezco muy dura?

Barbara lanzó un suspiro.

—No. A veces es difícil, para alguien como yo, comprender todo lo que habéis sufrido.

Harry apretó la mano de Sofía.

—Tú te esfuerzas todo lo que puedes en ser dura; pero, en realidad, no lo quieres ser.

—No me ha quedado más remedio.

—Todo será distinto en Inglaterra.

Permanecieron sentados un rato en silencio. Después, Sofía levantó un poco la manga de la camisa de Harry para consultar el reloj.

—Las seis y media —dijo—. Ya tendríamos que irnos. —Miró al vigilante—. Tú quédate aquí, Harry, no le quites los ojos de encima. Dale la mochila a Barbara.

Harry no quería dejarla.

—Tendríamos que ir los tres juntos.

—No. Uno de nosotros se tiene que quedar aquí.

Harry le soltó la mano y ambas mujeres se levantaron. Después, de espaldas al vigilante, Harry extrajo el arma.

—Creo que es mejor que la llevéis. Por si hubiera algún problema. No para disparar, sino sólo para amenazar. —Se la ofreció a Sofía, sujetándola por la culata, pero Sofía vaciló; ahora no le apetecía llevarla. Barbara alargó la mano y la asió con delicadeza.

—Yo la llevo —dijo, guardándosela en el bolsillo. Harry le pasó la mochila y sonrió con ironía—. Es curioso, pero te da una sensación de seguridad. —Respiró hondo—. Vamos, Sofía.

Ambas mujeres se encaminaron hacia la salida. La puerta se abrió con un chirrido y se volvió a cerrar a su espalda. Harry experimentó la separación de Sofía como un dolor físico. Miró al viejo y percibió la hostilidad de sus ojos.

47

Fuera, ya estaba casi oscuro. Barbara se colocó la mochila con la ropa y la comida en el centro de la espalda. Pesaba mucho. Los mendigos ya no estaban. Las nubes tapaban la luna, pero las farolas de la calle ya estaban encendidas. Sofía encabezó la marcha hacia una callejuela que discurría por el lateral de la catedral. Conducía a una calle más ancha, con la parte posterior de la catedral a un lado. Al otro, más allá del pretil de piedra, la calle daba a un ancho y profundo desfiladero. Barbara miró al otro lado del precipicio. Algo más adelante, un puente peatonal sostenido por unos pilares de hierro cruzaba la garganta.

—O sea que ya estamos —dijo Barbara.

—Sí, el puente de San Pablo. Nadie lo vigila —dijo Sofía con emoción—. Las autoridades aún no se habrán enterado de la fuga.

—Eso si es que se ha fugado.

Sofía señaló las colinas.

—Mira, aquello es Tierra Muerta. Bajará por allí.

A su derecha, Barbara vio las luces de las casas construidas al borde del precipicio y los balcones colgados sobre el profundo abismo.

—Las casas colgadas —dijo Sofía.

—Impresionante.

De repente, Barbara se tensó al oír el rumor de unas fuertes pisadas acercándose por una calle lateral. Apareció un hombre envuelto en una larga capa negra y con una franja blanca en el cuello. Un sacerdote. Era joven, de unos treinta años, llevaba gafas y, bajo un cabello pelirrojo casi del mismo color que el suyo, mostraba un semblante redondo y risueño. Parecía preocupado; pero, al verlas, esbozó una sonrisa.

—Buenas tardes, señoras. Ya es tarde para pasear por la calle.

«Maldita sea», pensó Barbara. Sabía que los curas acostumbraban a interrogar a las mujeres por la calle y enviarlas a casa. Sofía bajó modestamente los ojos.

—Ya vamos de vuelta, señor.

El sacerdote miró a Barbara con curiosidad.

—Disculpe, señora, pero ¿es usted extranjera?

Barbara adoptó un tono jovial.

—Soy inglesa, señor. Mi marido trabaja en Madrid. —Era consciente del peso de la pistola contra su costado.

—¿Inglesa? —El cura la miró inquisitivamente.

—Sí, señor. ¿Ha estado usted en Inglaterra?

—Pues no. —El cura estaba a punto de añadir algo más, pero se abstuvo de hacerlo—. Está oscureciendo —añadió con dulzura, como si hablara con una niña—. Ya deberían regresar a casa.

—Estábamos a punto de hacerlo.

El sacerdote se volvió hacia Sofía.

—¿Es usted de Cuenca?

—No. —Sofía respiró hondo—. He venido a ver la placa conmemorativa de la catedral. Mi amiga me ha acompañado desde Madrid. Yo tenía un tío aquí, un sacerdote.

—Ah. ¿Lo martirizaron en el treinta y seis?

—Sí.

El cura asintió tristemente con la cabeza.

—Cuántos muertos. Hija mía, la veo un poco amargada, pero creo que tenemos que empezar a perdonar para que España pueda renacer. Ha habido demasiada crueldad.

—No es un sentimiento muy extendido —dijo Sofía.

El sacerdote sonrió con tristeza.

—No —convino. Se hizo una breve pausa y después el sacerdote preguntó como quien no quiere la cosa—: ¿Dónde se alojan?

Sofía vaciló.

—En el convento de San Miguel.

—Vaya. Yo también. Pero sólo por un par de noches. A lo mejor, las veré después a la hora de cenar. Soy el padre Eduardo Alierta.

Saludó con una inclinación de la cabeza y después se volvió hacia la calle que conducía a la catedral. Sus pisadas se perdieron lentamente. Las mujeres se miraron.

—Hemos tenido suerte —dijo Sofía—. Algunos curas se habrían empeñado en acompañarnos al convento.

—Si va al convento, descubrirá que allí nadie sabe nada de nosotras.

Sofía se encogió de hombros.

—A la hora de cenar ya nos habremos ido.

—Parecía triste. Casi todos los curas me parecen severos; pero él, en cambio, daba la impresión de estar triste.

—Casi toda España está triste —dijo Sofía—. Vamos.

Mientras se dirigían al puente, el corazón de Barbara se puso a palpitar con fuerza. Se notaba la boca seca y en su mente se agolpaban las imágenes de Bernie, pero de Bernie tal como era antes. ¿Cómo sería ahora? Se agarró al refuerzo metálico del puente y contempló el paso peatonal de abajo, unas tablas de madera tendidas sobre un retículo de hierro. El otro extremo del puente no era más que un perfil borroso en la oscuridad.

—Vuelve con Harry —le dijo a Sofía—. Regresaré dentro de una hora, espero.

—De acuerdo. —Sofía le dio un rápido abrazo—. Todo irá bien, ya verás. Dile al brigadista que una amiga española está deseando conocerlo.

—Se lo diré.

Sofía la besó en la mejilla e inmediatamente dio media vuelta y se alejó por el camino. Volvió una sola vez la vista atrás y después desapareció por la callejuela que había seguido el sacerdote.

Barbara se quedó sola en la calle desierta y silenciosa. Unas pulsaciones de emoción le latían en la garganta. Dio un paso adelante y se agarró a la barandilla. El metal estaba frío. Con la otra mano sujetó el arma que guardaba en el bolsillo. «Ten cuidado —se dijo—. No vayas a apretar el gatillo y herirte en la pierna. Ahora no.» Entró en el puente y avanzó muy despacio, por si hubiera hielo en las tablas del suelo. Seguía sin ver el otro lado del puente, sólo la mole de la colina algo más oscura que el cielo. Echó a andar. Una ligera brisa tremendamente fría soplaba por el valle del río. Todo estaba en silencio, no se escuchaba el menor ruido del río de abajo; desde arriba, sólo podía ver la negrura que se extendía bajo sus pies y alrededor del estrecho puente de hierro. Por un instante, experimentó una sensación de vértigo y la cabeza empezó a darle vueltas.

«¡Cálmate!» Respiró hondo un par de veces y siguió adelante. Notó algo frío en la mejilla y se dio cuenta de que había empezado a nevar ligeramente.

De pronto, oyó unas pisadas que cruzaban el puente desde el otro lado. Contuvo la respiración. ¿Sería Bernie? ¿Y si las hubiera visto a ella y a Sofía al otro lado y hubiera decidido cruzar el puente para reunir- se con ella? No, seguramente habría preferido permanecer escondido hasta que pudiera quitarse la ropa de presidiario; debía de ser alguien de la ciudad.

Las pisadas sonaban más cerca; ahora percibía las pequeñas rever- beraciones a través de las tablas de madera. Siguió adelante, aferrada a la barandilla mientras se esforzaba por conseguir que su rostro mostrara una expresión relajada.

Apareció una alta figura masculina envuelta en un grueso abrigo. Caminaba por el centro del puente sin tocar la barandilla. Poco a poco distinguió su rostro, vio los ojos que la miraban fijamente. El corazón se le paró un segundo antes de volver a palpitar.

Sandy se detuvo a unos tres metros de ella en el centro del puente, con una mano en el bolsillo del abrigo y la otra cerrada en puño al costado. Se había afeitado el bigote y su rostro ofrecía otro aspecto, mofletudo y amarillento. Sus labios se abrieron en la ancha sonrisa de costumbre.

—Hola, cariño —dijo—. ¿Te sorprende verme? ¿Esperabas a otro?

En el interior de la catedral, el anciano se levantó y se acercó con paso cansino a un interruptor de la pared. Un sonoro clic sobresaltó a Harry mientras se encendía una luz eléctrica sobre el altar y el blanco resplandor del sodio hacía palidecer el revestimiento dorado de la reja que había de- lante. Vio al anciano regresar a su asiento. Pensó que ojalá tuviera la pis- tola. Ya se había acostumbrado a su reconfortante presencia. Como en la guerra. Cruzó por su mente un rápido flash de la playa de Dunkerque.

Se levantó y empezó a pasear arriba y abajo para entrar un poco en calor. Si al menos Sofía se diera prisa; ahora ya tendría que estar de vuelta. Para ella había sido muy duro ver el nombre de su tío en la lá- pida conmemorativa.

Giró en redondo al oír el chirrido de la puerta. Quien acababa de entrar no era Sofía, sino un alto sacerdote pelirrojo. Harry se dejó caer en el banco más cercano, entrelazó las manos e inclinó la cabeza como si estuviera rezando. Vio a través de las rendijas de entre los dedos cómo el sacerdote se acercaba al altar mayor y se arrodillaba delante de él. Después el cura se santiguó y se acercó a Francisco. El anciano se le- vantó del banco muy nervioso. Harry juntó fuertemente las manos. ¿Y si el viejo se asustara y los traicionara?

—Buenas tardes, señor —dijo el cura amablemente—. Estoy de

visita en la ciudad y me quedaré un par de noches en el convento. Me gustaría quedarme un rato a rezar.

—Pues claro, padre.

—Está todo muy tranquilo esta tarde.

—Con este tiempo, hay muy pocos visitantes.

—La verdad es que hace mucho frío. Pero nunca demasiado para rezar.

El sacerdote se acercó a los bancos y eligió uno situado unas filas más adelante que la de Harry. Parecía preocupado y no daba muestras de haber reparado en la presencia del otro penitente en medio de la penumbra. Francisco volvió a sentarse. Sus ojos se desviaron rápidamente de Harry al sacerdote, el cual se había arrodillado y se cubría el rostro con las manos.

La puerta se volvió a abrir. Harry miró rápidamente al sacerdote, pero éste siguió rezando mientras entraba Sofía. Para su sorpresa, Sofía se dirigió rápidamente al feo confesionario situado bajo la vidriera y se pegó contra su costado para esconderse. Harry se levantó, perplejo. Se golpeó la rodilla contra el banco y apretó los dientes al oír el ruido y experimentar un intenso dolor. Se acercó muy despacio al confesionario para amortiguar con ello el eco de sus pisadas, consciente de que el sacerdote levantaría la vista en caso de que oyera correr a alguien en el recinto sagrado. Pero el sacerdote seguía rezando de rodillas.

—¿Qué ocurre? —preguntó en un susurro inquieto—. ¿Barbara se encuentra a salvo?

—Sí. La dejé en el puente. Pero es que nos cruzamos por el camino con este sacerdote pelirrojo. Le expliqué que nos alojábamos en el convento y que ya íbamos directamente para allá. No conviene que me vea aquí contigo. Y, cuando Barbara venga con Bernie...

—Tendré que decirle al viejo que se libre de él.

Sofía meneó enérgicamente la cabeza, con semblante atemorizado.

—No le va decir a un cura que abandone la catedral.

—Tendrá que hacerlo. —Harry le apretó el brazo para darle ánimos y bajó con paso decidido por la nave hasta el lugar donde se encontraba Francisco.

Barbara se detuvo en seco, sujetando con fuerza la barandilla.

—¿Se te ha comido la lengua un gato? —preguntó Sandy en tono burlón—. ¿Recuerdas la llamada que te hizo aquel guardia de la prisión?

Yo la escuché; levanté el auricular al mismo tiempo que tú. —Hablaba en tono amable y reposado—. Después abrí tu escritorio y vi todo lo que guardabas allí. El plano con los arbustos del puente marcados.

—Pero ¿cómo lo pudiste abrir?

—Me hice un duplicado de la llave del escritorio cuando lo compré. Siempre tengo duplicados de todo lo que compro que tenga cerradura. Especialmente, cuando es para otra persona. Una vieja costumbre. —Barbara no dijo nada; se limitó a mirarlo, respirando entre dolorosos jadeos—. ¿Desde cuándo sabes que Piper está vivo? —le preguntó Sandy—. ¿Cuánto tiempo llevas planeando todo esto?

—Un par de meses —contestó Barbara en un susurro. Estudió su rostro. ¿Qué se propondría hacer? Sus ojos la miraban con furia asesina. A pesar del frío, tenía la frente empapada de sudor.

Un músculo de su mejilla se contrajo involuntariamente.

—¿Brett también estaba metido en esto?

—No.

Bernie ignoraba que Harry estaba allí. Barbara contempló la mano que Sandy se había metido en el bolsillo. Vio un bulto. ¿Él también iba armado?

—Han estado en casa, buscándote —dijo. El corazón le palpitaba con tal fuerza que le costaba mucho evitar que le temblara la voz, pero tenía que hacerlo—. La policía. Se llevaron todo lo que guardabas en el despacho.

—Sí. Me imaginaba que lo habrían hecho. Tengo un pasaporte que me permitirá embarcar. Pertenecía a uno de los judíos franceses que se dirigían a Lisboa, pero ahora le he colocado mi fotografía y saldré por Valencia. Decidí pasar por aquí de camino.

Barbara asió el arma, rodeando el gatillo con los dedos.

—¿Dónde está Pilar? —preguntó.

Ahora su voz sonaba más firme.

—Se ha ido. Le pagué para que se largara. Sólo fue una pequeña diversión. Nada tan importante como tu manera de traicionarme. —Le arrojó la palabra en un sibilante susurro de rabia, respiró hondo y siguió burlándose de ella—. Pues vaya, el gusano se ha convertido en un dragón. Y pensar que soy yo quien te ha hecho. Debería haber dejado que te pudrieras en Burgos. —Barbara no contestó, se limitó a mirarlo en silencio. Sandy volvió la cabeza hacia el fondo del puente—. Él está por ahí, esperando carretera arriba entre unos árboles. Lo he visto. Lo esperaba escondido detrás del tronco de un árbol. Iba a matarlo. Quería que te lo encontraras muerto. Pero él me oyó cuando estaba encendiendo un puro detrás de un árbol y eso lo puso sobre aviso, así que me vine para acá. A fin de cuentas, no hay nada más peligroso que un hombre acorralado. No creo que nos esté viendo en este extremo del puente. —Sandy inclinó la cabeza hacia su bolsillo—. Por cierto, voy armado.

Barbara apenas podía distinguir la arboleda situada a unos cuantos cientos de metros carretera arriba. ¿Estaría Bernie realmente allí?

—¿Por qué, Sandy? —preguntó—. Quiero decir, ¿de qué sirve... de qué sirve eso ahora? Todo ha terminado.

Sandy seguía hablando en voz baja, pero el tono se había vuelto muy frío.

—En el colegio me trataba como un trozo de mierda, lo mismo que mi maldito padre. Hizo todo lo posible por apartar a Harry de mí. Y ahora ha conseguido que me traiciones y lo saques de la prisión. Bueno, pues ahora me vengaré. —Sandy volvió a sonreír; una sonrisa extraña, casi infantil—. Me vengaré; hablo en serio. —Barbara se echó involuntariamente hacia atrás. Ahora había en su voz algo de profundamente salvaje y trastornado—. No me mires de esta cochina manera —dijo—. ¿Acaso he hecho yo algo peor que lo que Piper y todos los demás ideólogos le hicieron a España, eh? ¿He hecho yo algo peor?

—Bernie no me ha hecho hacer todo esto, Sandy; la idea fue mía. Hasta hace muy poco, él ni siquiera lo sabía.

—Pero, aun así, he sido traicionado —dijo Sandy—. No permitiré que me vuelva a ocurrir. No permitiré que me dejen tirado como un trapo. Y, si éste es mi destino, lucharé hasta el final. Te juro que lo haré. —Sus ojos oscuros estaban a punto de saltársele de las órbitas. Barbara no contestó. Ambos se miraron un momento en silencio entre ocasionales copos de nieve. Sandy respiró hondo, cerró los ojos y, cuando habló, lo hizo en afable tono familiar—. ¿Cómo llegaste aquí? ¿En tren?

—Sí.

Sandy ignoraba que Harry y Sofía estuvieran allí, creía que Barbara estaba sola. Pero, desde la catedral, los otros no podían ayudarla.

—Supongo que en esta mochila llevas una muda de ropa para él.

—Sí.

—Pues, bueno, yo te voy a decir lo que puedes hacer. Puedes dar media vuelta y regresar por donde has venido. Puedes volver a Inglaterra. Después yo me encargaré de él. —Inclinó de nuevo la cabeza hacia el bolsillo—. Me encantaría liquidarte a ti también, pero un disparo desde aquí se podría oír. —Se inclinó hacia delante, haciendo visajes—. Simplemente, no olvides durante el resto de tu vida que yo te perdono, no olvides que el que ha ganado soy yo. —Pronunció las palabras casi entre dientes; parecía un niño tontito. Hizo señas con la cosa que guardaba en el bolsillo—. Y ahora, da media vuelta y echa a andar. —Barbara se soltó de la barandilla y respiró hondo—. Adelante —dijo Sandy, levantando la voz—. Ya. De lo contrario, te pego un tiro, me cago en la puta. Tres años me pasé construyéndote de la nada para que ahora me traiciones. Puta de mierda. Vamos, da la vuelta y camina.

Barbara se metió la mano en el bolsillo y extrajo la Mauser. La sujetó con ambas manos y extendió los brazos quitándole el seguro mientras le apuntaba contra el pecho.

—Arroja el arma por el puente, Sandy. —Se sorprendió de lo clara que le había salido la voz. Separó las piernas para conservar mejor el equilibrio—. Hazlo ya. Hazlo ahora mismo o te mato. —Mientras lo decía, supo con toda certeza que podría hacerlo si no le quedaba más remedio.

Sandy retrocedió y la miró con asombro.

—Tú... ¿tú tienes un arma?

—Saca la tuya del bolsillo, Sandy. Despacito.

Sandy apretó los puños.

—Puta.

—¡Arroja el arma al agua!

Sandy la miró a los ojos y después se sacó muy despacio la mano del bolsillo. «A ver si ahora la saca y me pega un tiro», pensó Barbara. Pero ella dispararía primero. No permitiría que Sandy acabara con Bernie, no lo permitiría.

Sandy sacó una piedra de gran tamaño. La miró, miró sonriendo a Barbara y se encogió de hombros.

—No tuve tiempo de conseguir un arma. Iba a machacarle el cerebro a Piper con esto. —Soltó la piedra al suelo del puente y ésta se desvió hacia un lado y se perdió en el vacío. No se oyó el menor ruido cuando llegó al agua de abajo, estaba demasiado lejos.

Barbara recorrió rápidamente con los ojos sus bolsillos restantes.

—Colócate las manos en la cabeza —dijo.

Su rostro se volvió a ensombrecer, pero hizo lo que ella le ordenaba.

—¿Qué vas a hacer? —le preguntó. Ahora había temor en su voz, algo que ella jamás había visto. Se alegró; él había comprendido que hablaba en serio. Pensó rápidamente.

—Vamos a cruzar de nuevo el puente para ir junto a Bernie.

—No. —El rostro de Sandy se aflojó—. Así, no.

Barbara le apuntó a la cabeza con el arma.

—Date la vuelta.

Sandy vaciló.

—Está bien.

Se volvió y echó a andar muy despacio para regresar por donde había venido. Barbara lo siguió a la distancia de un brazo, por si él se diera repentinamente la vuelta y tratara de agarrarla. Llegaron al final del puente y pisaron la hierba del borde de la carretera. Había dejado de nevar y la luna había asomado por detrás de las nubes.

—Quieto —dijo Barbara.

Sandy se detuvo. Estaba ridículo allí de pie, con las manos en la cabeza. Barbara tenía que pensar qué hacer ahora. Se volvió para mirar hacia la arboleda. «¿Bernie nos puede ver? —se preguntó—. ¿Qué vamos a hacer con Sandy?» Sabía que ella no le podría disparar a sangre fría, pero Bernie probablemente lo hiciera.

De pronto, oyó un repiqueteo de pisadas. Se volvió y vio a Sandy corriendo por el puente. Había actuado con la rapidez de un rayo en cuanto ella había apartado la vista.

—¡Quieto! —Sandy empezó a correr en zigzag de uno a otro lado del puente. Barbara trató de apuntar contra él, pero le fue imposible. Recordó lo que él había dicho anteriormente sobre el eco que provocaría un disparo desde aquel lugar. Barbara inclinó el arma mientras Sandy alcanzaba el otro lado del puente y echaba a correr volviéndose a cada momento mientras zigzagueaba colina arriba. Sandy desapareció entre los árboles. Barbara oyó el crujido y el susurro de las ramas.

Inclinó otra vez el arma. «Deja que se vaya —pensó—, no puedes correr el riesgo de disparar.» No iba armado y no podía ir a la ciudad y denunciarla a las autoridades... a él también lo andaban buscando.

Apuró el paso carretera arriba, mirando constantemente hacia la ladera de la colina y sintiéndose sola y expuesta al peligro. Contempló las luces de la ciudad al otro lado del desfiladero y distinguió la oscura mole de la catedral donde Harry y Sofía la estarían esperando. Encontró la arboleda. Todo estaba oscuro y en silencio. ¿Le habría mentido Sandy, estaría Bernie allí realmente? Levantó los ojos hacia la escarpada ladera e inició el ascenso. Se dio cuenta de que todavía sostenía el arma en la mano y se la guardó en el bolsillo. Sus pies resbalaban sobre la hierba congelada. Volvió la vista hacia la carretera y el puente, ambos todavía desiertos. Se preguntó dónde habría aprendido a decir aquellas cosas, «manos arriba» y «manos en la cabeza». Una década de películas, suponía, ahora todo el mundo conocía esas cosas.

—Bernie —gritó hacia los árboles en un susurro sonoro. No hubo respuesta—. Bernie —repitió un poco más alto.

Se oyó un murmullo de ramas desde el interior de la arboleda. Se puso tensa y volvió a sacar la pistola mientras un hombre aparecía de entre las sombras. Barbara vio una figura demacrada envuelta en un abrigo raído, una barba y una cojera de anciano. Creyó que era un vagabundo e hizo ademán de sacar el arma.

—Barbara —lo oyó llamarla, oyó su voz por primera vez en más de tres años. Se adelantó. Ella abrió los brazos y él se arrojó a ellos.

El anciano Francisco había sacado un rosario y pasaba nerviosamente las cuentas con sus inquietas manos. Harry se inclinó y acercó los labios a la peluda oreja del viejo.

—Tiene que pedirle al cura que se vaya. Vio a mis amigas en la calle. Ellas le dijeron que iban al convento. Si vuelven y él las ve, les hará preguntas.

—No le puedo decir a un sacerdote que está rezando a Nuestro Señor que se vaya de la catedral —contestó Francisco en un susurro enfurecido.

—Tiene que hacerlo. —Harry lo miró a los ojos—. De lo contrario, todos correríamos peligro. Y no habría dinero.

Francisco se pasó una mano callosa por la barba de las mejillas.

—Mierda —murmuró—. ¿Por qué tuve que meterme en esto?

Los bisbiseos del sacerdote habían cesado. Éste se había apartado las manos del rostro y permanecía arrodillado, contemplándose las palmas. No podía haber entendido las palabras pronunciadas en voz baja, pero tal vez el apremiante tono de voz de Harry hubiera llegado a sus oídos. «Maldita sea —pensó Harry—, maldita sea.» Habló de nuevo en susurros.

—Ahora no está rezando. Dígale que ha habido una emergencia familiar y que tiene que cerrar un rato la catedral.

El cura se levantó y se acercó a ellos mientras alrededor de sus piernas se escuchaba el frufrú de la capa negra. Francisco se levantó. El sacerdote lo miró sonriendo.

—¿Le ocurre algo, abuelo?

—Me parece que su mujer se ha puesto enferma —dijo Harry, procurando que su acento sonara más español—. Soy médico. Nos haría usted un gran favor, padre, si él pudiera cerrar la catedral e irse a casa junto a ella. Yo iré a buscar al otro vigilante.

El sacerdote le dirigió una mirada inquisitiva. Harry pensó en lo fácil que sería obligarlo a obedecer por la fuerza. Era joven, pero parecía un poco blandengue.

—¿De dónde es usted, doctor? No reconozco su acento.

—De Cataluña, padre. Pero vine a parar aquí después de la guerra. Francisco señaló a Harry.

—Padre, él tiene... tiene... —Pero no pudo seguir e inclinó la cabeza.

—Si usted quiere, puedo esperar a que vaya en busca del otro hombre.

Francisco tragó saliva.

—Por favor, padre, las normas dicen que la catedral se tiene que cerrar si no hay un vigilante.

—Es mejor que cerremos la catedral —dijo Harry—. Acompañaré a Francisco a su casa; la casa del deán nos viene de camino y podré avisar al otro hombre.

El cura asintió con la cabeza.

—Muy bien. De todos modos, ya tendría que estar en el convento. ¿Cómo se llama su esposa?

—María, padre.

—Muy bien. —El cura dio media vuelta—. Rezaré a la Virgen por su recuperación.

—Sí. Rece por nosotros. —Justo en aquel momento el anciano se vino abajo y se disolvió en un mar de lágrimas mientras se cubría el rostro con las manos. Harry le hizo una seña con la cabeza al cura.

—Yo cuidaré de él, padre.

—Vaya con Dios, abuelo.

—Vaya usted con Dios, padre. —La respuesta del vigilante fue un murmullo avergonzado. El sacerdote le tocó el hombro. Finalmente, se alejó por la nave central y salió a la plaza.

Francisco se enjugó el rostro sin mirar a Harry.

—Me ha hecho avergonzar, cabrón rojo. Me ha hecho avergonzar en este lugar sagrado.

Bernie y Barbara se abrazaron con fuerza. Ella percibió la aspereza del tejido de su abrigo que parecía de arpillera y respiró aquel repugnante olor; pero el cálido cuerpo que había debajo era el suyo.

—Bernie, Bernie —le dijo.

Él se apartó y la miró. Tenía el rostro enjuto sucio de tierra y la barba enmarañada.

—Dios mío —exclamó—. ¿Cómo lo has hecho?

—Tenía que hacerlo, tenía que encontrarte. —Barbara respiró hondo—. Pero debemos marcharnos de aquí. —Miró hacia lo alto de la colina—. Sandy ha estado aquí hace un rato.

—¿Forsyth? ¿Lo sabe?

—Sí. —Barbara le explicó rápidamente lo ocurrido. Bernie abrió enormemente los ojos cuando ella le dijo que Harry los esperaba en la catedral con su novia española.

—Harry y Sandy. —Bernie meneó la cabeza y rió sin dar crédito—. Y Sandy está por aquí arriba. —Levantó los ojos hacia lo alto de la colina—. Debe de estar loco.

—Se ha ido. No volverá mientras yo vaya armada.

—¿Tú con una pistola? ¡Oh, Barbara, lo que has hecho por mí! —Se le quebró la voz a causa de la emoción. Barbara respiró hondo. Ahora tenía que ser práctica. Sandy se había ido, pero había otros muchos peligros.

—Aquí tengo un poco de ropa. Te podrías cambiar y afeitarte la barba. No, no hay luz suficiente para eso, lo tendremos que hacer en la catedral. Pero cámbiate.

—Sí. —Bernie le tomó las manos—. ¡Dios mío!, has pensado en todo. —La estudió en medio de la oscuridad—. ¡Qué distinta te veo!

—Yo a ti también.

—La ropa. Y te has puesto perfume. Antes no lo hacías. Huele raro.

Barbara se agachó y empezó a sacar el contenido de la mochila. Era muy difícil ver algo allí entre los árboles; debería haber llevado una linterna.

—Aquí traigo un abrigo muy calentito.

—¿Habéis cruzado la ciudad?

—Sí. Estaba todo muy tranquilo.

—En estos momentos, el campo de prisioneros ya habrá comunicado la noticia por radio a la Guardia Civil.

—No vimos a ningún guardia.

—¿Lleváis automóvil?

—Sí, uno con matrícula diplomática. El de Harry. Está escondido fuera de la ciudad, te acompañaremos a la embajada. Están obligados a acogerte.

—¿Y eso no le supondrá ningún problema a Harry?

—No sabrán que ha intervenido. Te dejaremos fuera y tú podrás decir que robaste la ropa, que allanaste una morada o algo por el estilo y que después hiciste autoestop en la carretera.

Bernie la miró y rompió súbitamente a llorar.

—¡Oh, Barbara!, cuando ya pensaba que estaba acabado, van y me dicen que tú me salvarás. Y yo te abandoné para irme a la guerra. Barbara, no sabes cuánto lo siento...

—No, no. Vamos, cariño. Alguien podría venir. Te tienes que cambiar.

—De acuerdo.

Bernie empezó a desnudarse, soltando dolorosos gruñidos mientras se quitaba la camisa que tantos días había llevado encima, pegada con tierra a su cuerpo. En medio de la oscuridad, Barbara distinguió vagamente unas cicatrices y vislumbró el cuerpo que tanto había amado convertido ahora en piel y huesos.

A los pocos minutos, él se le plantó delante vestido con un traje de Sandy, un abrigo y un sombrero de paño que ella se había llevado de casa; se habían arrugado en la mochila, pero le otorgaban un aspecto verosímil y normal, dejando aparte su cara sucia y su barba de mendigo. Barbara le alisó un par de arrugas.

—Bueno —dijo en un susurro. De repente, experimentó un deseo salvaje de echarse a reír—. Estás pasable.

La media hora que siguió a la partida del sacerdote fue la más larga de la vida de Harry. Él y Sofía paseaban sin descanso, mirando de la puerta al viejo y viceversa. Se habían librado del cura por los pelos. Él y Sofía se sentían al borde de la felicidad, y quizá Paco también. «Que nada más salga mal», le rogó al Dios en que no creía.

Al final, la puerta volvió a abrirse. Sofía se puso tensa. El anciano también miró atemorizado mientras Barbara y Bernie entraban muy despacio en el templo; Barbara sostenía a Bernie, el cual cojeaba a causa del esfuerzo. Al principio, Harry no reconoció la escuálida figura con barba; pero enseguida corrió a su encuentro, seguido por Sofía.

—Bernie —le dijo en voz baja—. Bueno, parece que has pasado lo tuyo.

Bernie rió sin poderlo creer.

—Harry, eres tú. —Parpadeó varias veces, como si el nuevo mundo en el que se encontraba fuera demasiado para él y no lo pudiera asimilar—. Jesús, no me lo podía creer.

Harry sintió que las facciones de su rostro pugnaban por reprimir la emoción al contemplar aquel semblante de espantapájaros.

—Pero ¿qué demonios has estado haciendo? ¡Mira qué pinta tienes! Rookwood tendría algo que decir al respecto.

Bernie se mordió el labio y Harry comprendió que estaba al borde de las lágrimas.

—He estado librando una batalla, Harry. —Se inclinó hacia delante y lo abrazó a la española. Harry se relajó en aquel abrazo y ambos permanecieron un momento fuertemente abrazados antes de que Harry se apartara, un poco cohibido. Bernie se tambaleó levemente.

—¿Te ocurre algo? —le preguntó Sofía preocupada.

—Será mejor que me siente. —Bernie la miró sonriendo—. Tú debes de ser Sofía.

—Sí.

—Viva la República —dijo Bernie en voz baja.

—Viva la República.

—¿Eres comunista? —le preguntó Bernie.

—No —Sofía lo miró con la cara muy seria—. No me gustaron las cosas que hicieron los comunistas.

—Pensamos que eran necesarias. —Bernie lanzó un suspiro.

Barbara lo tomó del brazo.

—Vamos, te tienes que afeitar. Ve a la pila bautismal. —Le entregó un neceser de afeitado y él se encaminó cojeando hacia la pila. Harry se acercó al anciano. Francisco lo miró enfurecido y con el rostro surcado por las lágrimas. Harry le entregó el fajo de billetes.

—Su dinero, señor.

Francisco lo arrugó en su puño con gesto airado. Harry pensó que lo iba a arrojar al suelo, pero el hombre se lo guardó en el bolsillo y se apoyó contra la pared. Bernie regresó con la cara no muy bien afeitada, más envejecida, delgada y marcada por profundas arrugas, pero ahora ya reconocible como la suya.

—Tengo que sentarme —dijo—. Estoy hecho polvo.

—Sí, claro. —Barbara se volvió hacia los demás—. Está muy cansado, pero nos tenemos que ir de aquí cuanto antes.

—¿Ha ocurrido algo? —preguntó Sofía, cuyo áspero tono de voz indujo a Harry a levantar la vista. Barbara les contó lo de Sandy.

—Santo Dios —dijo Harry—. Se ha pasado de la raya. Está loco.

—En cualquier caso, medio loco de rabia.

—Tendríamos que irnos lo antes posible de aquí —dijo Sofía—. Temo que el cura diga en el convento que la catedral está cerrada y que envíen a alguien a la casa del viejo.

—Sí. —Harry miró hacia el lugar desde el cual Francisco los contemplaba con el rostro petrificado, y después apoyó la mano en el hombro de Bernie—. El vehículo se encuentra a pocos kilómetros de aquí. Fuera de la ciudad. ¿Crees que podrás caminar? Es todo cuesta abajo.

Bernie asintió con la cabeza.

—Lo intentaré. Si vamos despacio.

—Ya vuelves a tener aspecto de persona.

—Gracias. —Bernie levantó los ojos—. ¿Es cierto que Inglaterra sigue resistiendo?

—Sí. Los bombardeos son tremendos, pero resistimos. Bernie, nos tenemos que ir —le dijo Barbara.

—Muy bien. —Bernie se levantó haciendo una mueca.

«Está absolutamente agotado y consumido», pensó Harry.

—¿Qué decíais de un sacerdote? —preguntó Bernie.

—Sofía y Barbara se cruzaron con él mientras se dirigían al puente. Después entró en la catedral para rezar, pero yo conseguí que el vigilante se librara de él. Fue un momento muy desagradable. De pronto lo vi rezando arrodillado como si tuviera que pasarse allí toda la vida, con su sotana negra y su cabello pelirrojo.

—¿Cabello pelirrojo? —Bernie pensó un momento—. ¿Cómo era?

—Alto, joven. Un poco gordito.

Bernie respiró hondo.

—Dios mío, parece el padre Eduardo. Es uno de los curas del campo.

—Sí, ése era su nombre —dijo Barbara—. ¡Santo cielo! Pues no daba esta impresión.

—No es de ésos, es una especie de santo inocente o algo por el estilo. —Bernie apretó los labios—. Pero, como nos encuentre aquí, estamos perdidos. Pese a todo, nos denunciaría. —Respiró hondo—. Vamos. Vamos, nos tenemos que ir.

Harry tomó la mochila vacía y los cuatro se encaminaron hacia la puerta. Experimentó una abrumadora sensación de alivio al abandonar el templo. Se volvió para mirar al viejo; éste seguía sentado en su banco sosteniéndose la cabeza con las manos, una figura minúscula entre todos aquellos gigantescos monumentos a la fe.

48

El camino de vuelta a través de las empinadas y mal iluminadas callejuelas fue extremadamente lento. Bernie se sentía agotado. Las pocas personas que pasaban se volvían para mirarlos; Bernie se preguntó si, al verlo tambalearse de aquella manera, pensarían que estaba borracho. Y borracho se sentía efectivamente, intoxicado por el asombro y la felicidad.

Se había preguntado qué sentiría al ver a Barbara después de tanto tiempo. La mujer que había aparecido en la fría ladera de la colina era más dura y sofisticada, pero seguía siendo la misma Barbara de siempre; y él había percibido que conservaba todas las cosas que antaño apreciara en ella. Le parecía que había sido ayer la última vez que la había visto, que el Jarama y los últimos tres años no habían sido más que un sueño. Sin embargo, el dolor de su hombro era muy real y los pies hinchados en el interior de las botas viejas y cuarteadas lo estaban matando.

A medio camino de la pendiente, llegaron a una plazoleta con un banco de piedra bajo la estatua de un general.

—¿Me puedo sentar? —le preguntó Bernie a Barbara—. Sólo un minuto.

Sofía se volvió y los miró con la cara muy seria.

—¿No puedes continuar? —Contempló nerviosamente un bar situado a un lado de la plaza. Las ventanas estaban iluminadas y se oían voces que procedían del interior.

—Sólo cinco minutos —le suplicó Barbara.

Bernie se dejó caer en el banco. Barbara se sentó a su lado, mientras los otros dos esperaban a cierta distancia. «Como ángeles de la guarda», pensó Bernie.

—Perdón —dijo en voz baja—, es que estoy un poco aturdido. En cuestión de un minuto, me recupero.

Barbara le apoyó una mano en la frente.

—Tienes un poco de fiebre —dijo.

Sacó la cajetilla y le ofreció un cigarrillo. Él rió.

—Un cigarrillo como Dios manda. Gold Flake.

—Sandy solía conseguirlos.

Bernie tomó su mano y la miró a la cara.

—Traté de olvidarte —dijo—. En el campo.

—¿Y lo conseguiste? —preguntó ella, con una frivolidad forzada.

—No. Intentas olvidar las cosas buenas para que no te atormenten. Pero vuelven incesantemente a tu memoria. Como las fugaces visiones de las casas colgadas. Las veíamos a veces, cuando subíamos a la cantera. Flotando por encima de la niebla. Eran como una especie de espejismo. Me han parecido muy pequeñas cuando antes pasamos por delante de ellas.

—No sabes cuánto siento lo de Sandy —dijo Barbara—. Pero es que... cuando pensé que habías muerto, me derrumbé. Además, al principio, era muy cariñoso; o, por lo menos, lo parecía.

—Jamás tendría que haberte dejado. —Bernie le apretó la mano con fuerza—. Cuando Agustín me dijo que eras tú la que estabas organizando la fuga, cuando me dijo tu nombre, fue el mejor momento, el mejor. —Experimentó una oleada de emoción—. Jamás te volveré a dejar.

Se abrió la puerta del bar y, a través de ella, se filtró al exterior un olor a vino rancio y a humo de cigarrillos. Salieron dos obreros y echaron a andar cuesta arriba, mirando con asombro al cuarteto que había junto a la fuente. Harry y Sofía se acercaron a ellos.

—No podemos quedarnos aquí —dijo Harry—. ¿Puedes seguir?

Bernie asintió con la cabeza. Al levantarse, fue como si introdujera los pies en el fuego; pero procuró no hacer caso, ya estaban casi a punto de llegar.

Caminaron muy despacio sin apenas decir nada. Bernie descubrió que, pese al dolor de pies, sus sentidos parecían haberse agudizado: el ladrido de un perro, la contemplación de un árbol gigantesco en medio de la oscuridad, el aroma del perfume de Barbara; las mil y una cosas que le habían sido arrebatadas desde el año 1937. Dejaron atrás la ciudad, cruzaron el puente y bajaron por la larga y desierta carretera hasta el campo donde estaba el automóvil. Se había puesto a nevar, aunque no mucho; unos minúsculos copos que emitían un suave susurro al caer sobre la hierba. La ropa nueva mantenía a Bernie abrigado y su insólita suavidad constituía para él una nueva sensación.

—Ya casi estamos —le murmuró Barbara al final—. El automóvil está tras aquellos árboles.

Cruzaron la entrada y siguieron los surcos del camino mientras Bernie apretaba los dientes cada vez que sus botas resbalaban sobre el terreno accidentado. Harry y Sofía caminaban un poco adelantados y Barbara seguía acompañando a Bernie. Éste distinguió de repente la forma borrosa de un automóvil algo más allá.

—Yo conduciré —le dijo Barbara a Harry.

—¿Seguro?

—Sí. Tú nos has llevado a la ida. Bernie, siéntate detrás para estirar las piernas.

—De acuerdo. —Se apoyó contra el metal frío del Ford, mientras Barbara abría la puerta del piloto. Arrojó la mochila al interior y se deslizó hacia el asiento del copiloto para desactivar el dispositivo de apertura de las demás puertas. Harry abrió una puerta posterior y esbozó su tranquilizadora sonrisa de siempre.

—Su automóvil, señor.

Bernie le apretó el brazo.

De pronto, Sofía levantó la mano.

—Oigo algo —dijo en voz baja—. Entre los árboles.

—Será un ciervo —dijo Bernie, recordando el que le había pegado un susto en su escondrijo.

—Espera. —Sofía se apartó del automóvil y se acercó al carrascal. Los árboles arrojaban sombras alargadas y negras sobre la hierba. Los otros se la quedaron mirando. Se detuvo y atisbó entre las ramas.

—No oigo nada —murmuró Bernie. Miró hacia el interior del vehículo. Barbara se volvió para mirarlos inquisitivamente desde la parte anterior del automóvil.

—Anda, vamos —gritó Harry.

—Sí, ya voy. —Acto seguido, Sofía se apartó.

El rayo de luz de un reflector los iluminó desde los árboles. Una ametralladora empezó a escupir fuego desde la arboleda y Bernie vio volar unas ramitas por el aire mientras Sofía, iluminada por el reflector, pegaba un brinco y experimentaba unas sacudidas violentas, desgarrada por las balas. Unas salpicaduras de sangre volaron desde su pequeña figura cuando ésta cayó y alcanzó violentamente el suelo.

Harry quiso echar a correr hacia ella, pero Bernie lo agarró por el brazo y, con una fuerza insospechada, lo arrojó contra el costado del automóvil. Harry forcejeó un segundo, aunque enseguida dejó de hacerlo al ver aparecer por entre los árboles a una pareja de la Guardia Civil con sus negros tricornios brillando bajo la luz del reflector. El mayor de los guardias, un hombre de rostro severo, les apuntó con una pesada metralleta, mirándolos con frío e inexpresivo semblante. El otro, que era joven y parecía un poco asustado, no había echado mano al fusil, sino que empuñaba un revólver.

Bernie se quedó sin respiración. Jadeaba y trataba de respirar sin dejar de sujetar a Harry por los hombros. El guardia civil de mayor edad se acercó a Sofía y le levantó la cabeza con el pie, soltando un gruñido de satisfacción al ver que ésta caía exánime hacia atrás. Harry trató por segunda vez de soltarse, pero Bernie se lo impidió pese a lo mucho que le dolía el hombro.

—Demasiado tarde —dijo.

Se volvió para mirar hacia el automóvil. Barbara seguía inclinada sobre el asiento con expresión aterrorizada. Los guardias civiles se situaron a cierta distancia, apuntándoles con sus armas mientras dos hombres uniformados emergían de su escondrijo. Uno de ellos era Aranda, con su hermoso rostro iluminado por una sonrisa. El otro era mayor y más delgado, con unos mechones de cabello negro peinados hacia atrás sobre la calva y una siniestra expresión de satisfacción en su curtido rostro de soldado.

—Maestre —dijo Harry—. ¡Dios mío!, es el general Maestre. ¡Oh, Dios mío!, Sofía. —Se le quebró la voz mientras rompía en irreprimibles sollozos.

Los militares se acercaron a ellos caminando a grandes zancadas. Maestre miró a Harry con desprecio y dijo, levantando la voz:

—Señorita Clare, baje del vehículo.

Barbara salió. Parecía a punto de derrumbarse; se apoyó contra la puerta abierta, contemplando con expresión de profundo dolor el cuerpo de Sofía. Aranda miró a Bernie con una jovial sonrisa.

—Bueno, ya hemos vuelto a atrapar a nuestro pajarito.

Harry miró a Maestre.

—¿Cómo lo supo? ¿Fue Forsyth?

—No. —El subsecretario lo miró fríamente—. Este rescate lo organizamos nosotros, señor Brett. El coronel Aranda y yo somos viejos amigos, servimos juntos en Marruecos. Una noche en el transcurso de una reunión me habló de un prisionero inglés del campo de Tierra Muerta que tenía una novia inglesa que ahora vivía en Madrid. El nombre me sonó. —Se introdujo ambas manos en los bolsillos—. Tenemos fichas de todos los que estuvieron relacionados con la República y, cuando vi que la señorita Clare se estaba haciendo pasar por la esposa de Forsyth, mi amigo y yo decidimos ponerlo en un apuro. Hoy habría sido un buen día para forzar el desenlace... mañana se celebra una importante reunión sobre el destino de la mina de oro.

—¡Oh, no! —gimió Barbara.

Maestre extrajo un cigarrillo y lo encendió. Lanzó una nube de humo hacia el cielo y después volvió a mirar a Harry con dura concentración; como si lo odiara, pensó Bernie. Pero su voz seguía conservando un tono cortés y civilizado.

—Aunque, al final, resultó no haber ninguna mina de oro, ¿verdad? Ahora ya lo sabemos. —Harry no contestó. Parecía que ya ni siquiera lo escuchara. Trató de zafarse una vez más de la presa de Bernie; pero éste lo sujetó con fuerza, haciendo una mueca de dolor. Como intentara huir, lo más probable era que le pegasen un tiro. Maestre siguió adelante—. Sobornamos al periodista inglés Markby para que lo organizara; bueno, no ponga esta cara de asombro, señorita Clare, los ingleses también se dejan sobornar, y después el coronel Aranda consiguió que uno de nuestros antiguos guardias que estaba en el paro en Madrid desarrollara el proyecto. Sabía que él y su hermano necesitaban dinero para su madre.

—¿Luis? —preguntó Barbara—. ¿Luis trabajaba para ustedes? ¡Oh, Dios mío!

—Él y Agustín cobrarán dinero para atender a su madre, pero de nosotros. Aunque también les vamos a permitir que se queden con el dinero que usted les dio. —Maestre meneó la cabeza—. Luis intentó apartarse del proyecto un par de veces. Creo que el hecho de engañarla les dolía enormemente tanto a él como a su hermano. Pero tenemos que ser duros si queremos reconstruir España.

Maestre empezó a pasear arriba y abajo con su alta figura entrando y saliendo del rayo de luz del reflector donde los copos de nieve se arremolinaban cada vez en mayor número, cual soldado que comenta una exitosa campaña militar. La luz centelleaba en sus botones relucientes. Aranda lo miraba con una sonrisa en los labios. Un poco más allá, la nieve se posaba sobre el abrigo negro de Sofía y su cabello. Harry, que había dejado de sollozar, permanecía ahora desplomado entre los brazos de Bernie.

—Siempre tuvimos el propósito de practicar su detención aquí. Ahora Forsyth no importa y, además, ya teníamos previsto impedir su fuga. Pero sabíamos que usted levantaría revuelo en la embajada sobre el campo, señorita Clare, e incluso que podría llegar a implicar a sus amigos de la Cruz Roja. El señor Brett también estaba en el ajo, lo cual pondría en un apuro al embajador Hoare que ya ha provocado el enfado del Generalísimo con sus tareas de espionaje y con el hecho de que el inglés Forsyth había intentado engañarlo con el oro. Por cierto, atraparemos a Forsyth; todos los puertos y fronteras están vigilados. Y necesitamos a Hoare, necesitamos su ayuda para mantener a España al margen de la guerra y para que quienes siempre la han gobernado puedan arrebatarle el control a la chusma de la Falange.

—¿Qué va usted a hacer con nosotros? —Bernie notó el temblor de la voz de Barbara.

Maestre se encogió de hombros.

—De momento, mantenerla a usted encerrada. Lo mejor para todos sería que Piper recibiera un disparo durante un intento de fuga y que se informara de su muerte y de la del señor Brett, quizás en un accidente de carretera.

Aranda, que ya no sonreía, se acercó a Maestre.

—Los tendríamos que matar a todos ahora mismo —dijo.

Maestre meneó la cabeza.

—No. De momento, los mantendremos encerrados. Mañana se celebrará la importante reunión. Pero le doy las gracias, Manuel, por haber adelantado la fuga en un día. Los quería ver yo mismo en persona. —Maestre volvió a sonreír.

Todos se volvieron cuando Barbara lanzó un pequeño gemido y se desplomó al suelo. Aranda soltó una carcajada.

—Esta puta de mierda se ha desmayado. —Señaló con la cabeza al guardia civil más joven—. Despiértela. —El hombre se arrodilló a su lado. La sacudió por los hombros y ella emitió un gemido.

—¿Qué...?

—Se ha desmayado, señorita —le dijo el guardia con sorprendente amabilidad.

—¡Oh! ¡Oh, Dios mío! —Barbara se incorporó y dejó las manos colgando entre las rodillas. Bernie hizo ademán de acercarse a ella, pero el guardia civil le indicó con un movimiento de la pistola que retrocediera. Harry, libre de la presa de Bernie, se alejó tambaleándose. Se acercó muy despacio al cadáver de Sofía encorvado como un anciano, y pasó con expresión aturdida a través del rayo luminoso del reflector. El guardia civil de la metralleta giró en redondo hacia él, pero Maestre levantó una mano mientras Harry se arrodillaba junto a Sofía. Le acarició el cabello salpicado de nieve y después miró a Maestre.

—¿Por qué la ha matado? ¿Por qué?

—Quebrantó la ley. —Maestre agitó un dedo en gesto amenazador—. Y eso ahora no se va a tolerar. Hay que controlar a las personas subversivas y nosotros sabemos hacerlo. Y, ahora, vuelvan al automóvil.

—Asesinos —dijo Harry, acariciando el cabello de Sofía—. Asesinos.

—Y pensar que mi hija quería salir a pasear con usted —dijo Maestre—. Pequeño imbécil. Alfonso murió por su culpa.

Barbara se levantó y se apoyó en la puerta abierta del coche con la cara más pálida que la cera.

—Por favor —dijo en un débil susurro—. ¿Me puedo sentar dentro del automóvil? Estoy temblando.

—Parece que está indispuesta, mi general —dijo el joven guardia civil.

Maestre asintió con la cabeza, mirando despectivamente a Barbara mientras ésta subía al vehículo. El guardia civil más joven cerró la puerta. Aranda miró a Bernie con una sonrisa.

—Las inglesas no tienen agallas, ¿eh?

Maestre soltó un gruñido.

—Son gente débil y degenerada. Si ganaran la guerra, nosotros nos podríamos librar de la Falange; pero dudo mucho que sean capaces de hacerlo.

Bernie miró alrededor. Podía ver que la parte posterior de la cabeza de Barbara temblaba ligeramente. Harry seguía sollozando inclinado sobre Sofía mientras la nieve caía también ahora sobre él.

—Ya es hora de irse —dijo Maestre—. ¡Usted! —llamó a Harry—. ¡Vuelva al automóvil!

Harry se levantó y regresó lentamente junto a Bernie. Bernie lo sujetó por el brazo y lo miró. Ofrecía un aspecto espantoso y el rostro se le había aflojado a causa de la impresión.

Maestre le hizo una seña al guardia civil de la pistola.

—Vaya a nuestro vehículo. Avise al cuartelillo de que vamos para allá.

El guardia se cuadró.

—Regresaré dentro de un cuarto de hora, mi general. —Echó a correr hacia el vehículo. Su compañero permanecía inmóvil, apuntando todavía con su metralleta a Harry y Bernie.

Aranda, que ya había recuperado el buen humor, señaló a Bernie con un dedo.

—El general Maestre se ha desplazado especialmente desde Madrid para reunirse aquí conmigo. Naturalmente, sabíamos que estabais en la catedral; el vigilante y las autoridades eclesiásticas colaboraban con nosotros. Te he estado observando estas últimas semanas, esperaba castigarte por no haber accedido a ser mi confidente. He estado jugando contigo. Y aquí tienes tu castigo. —Soltó una carcajada—. ¿Sabes una cosa?, el padre Eduardo ha estado importunando a los guardias civiles con la historia de la desaparición de dos mujeres que no habían vuelto al convento donde se alojaban. Menudo bobalicón está hecho el pobre.

En realidad, Barbara no se había desmayado; si bien, al oírle decir al general que los iba a matar a todos, poco le había faltado. Eso le había dado la idea de fingir desplomarse para poder regresar al vehículo. Ahora los dos militares se encontraban situados justo detrás. Supuso que ellos no debían de pensar que sabía conducir, pocas españolas sabían. Contempló la escena a través del espejo retrovisor y empezó a calcular, procurando mantener los ojos apartados del cadáver de Sofía. Al ver que el guardia civil más joven regresaba a los árboles, pensó: «Ahora o nunca.» Era un riesgo que tenía que correr. De todos modos, lo más probable era que los mataran a todos, y ella no había llegado hasta allí para no llevarse a Bernie y compartir su vida con él. No lo volvería a dejar en sus manos.

Poco a poco, comprobando a través del espejo retrovisor que no la vigilaban, agarró la llave de contacto. Todo dependería de que el motor arrancara a la primera, pero era un buen automóvil; aquella mañana había arrancado sin problemas tras haberse pasado toda la noche a la intemperie. Si hiciera rápidamente marcha atrás, Bernie y Harry, que estaban apoyados contra el costado del vehículo, saldrían disparados hacia un lado; los militares serían alcanzados y, si el guardia civil de la metralleta le diera tiempo, podría desviarse y arrollarlo también a él. Miró al guardia civil. Éste mantenía los ojos clavados en Harry y Bernie, y su semblante era tan implacable e inexpresivo como antes.

Respiró hondo y giró lentamente la llave. El motor se encendió con un rugido y ella hizo marcha atrás. Notó que Harry y Bernie salían despedidos hacia un lado a causa del golpe y oyó que Bernie lanzaba un grito.

—¡No!

El militar más joven, el que se había estado burlando de Harry, consiguió saltar a un lado, pero cayó hacia atrás. Por una décima de segundo, Barbara vio a través del espejo retrovisor una expresión de indignado asombro en el rostro del otro militar, el coronel del campo de prisioneros. Después, éste cayó bajo el vehículo; Barbara oyó un grito y percibió un crujido cuando las ruedas le pasaron por encima.

El guardia civil permaneció de pie con una expresión de asombro en la cara y después se volvió y levantó la pesada metralleta para apuntar contra el automóvil. Sin embargo, aquellos pocos segundos le dieron a Barbara tiempo suficiente para cambiar de dirección; la esquina posterior del vehículo golpeó violentamente al hombre y la metralleta se le escapó de las manos y voló por los aires, rebotando ruidosamente sobre la capota mientras el hombre se desplomaba. Barbara accionó el freno de mano y saltó, extrayendo el arma del bolsillo de su abrigo. El motor seguía en marcha.

Harry y Bernie se estaban levantando de la hierba. Harry parecía aturdido, pero Bernie se mantenía alerta.

—¡Cuidado! —gritó.

El guardia civil, que se estaba incorporando medio atontado, alargó la mano hacia su pistola. Barbara no lo pensó, simplemente levantó la Mauser y disparó. Un rugido, un destello y enseguida brotó un chorro de sangre del pecho del hombre. El guardia se tambaleó hacia atrás y quedó tendido inmóvil en el suelo. Barbara contempló horrorizada lo que había hecho. Se volvió hacia el lugar donde Aranda yacía bajo el automóvil. También estaba muerto; sus ojos miraban hacia arriba con incredulidad y su boca abierta dejaba al descubierto unos blancos dientes en una definitiva mueca de rabia, mientras un riachuelo de sangre le bajaba por la barbilla.

—¡Oh, Dios mío! —exclamó Barbara.

Maestre se incorporó medio aturdido, con los mechones de cabello negro inicialmente peinados sobre la calva caídos ahora de una manera absolutamente absurda a un lado de su rostro.

—No me dispare —gritó con una nueva voz, áspera y aterrorizada. Levantó la mano como para protegerse de las balas—. Por favor, por favor.

Barbara dejó que Bernie la sujetara por el brazo y le quitara el arma de la mano. Éste apuntó a Maestre.

—Sube al automóvil —gritó a Barbara en tono apremiante por encima del hombro—. Ayuda a Harry a subir. ¿Sabes conducir?

—Sí.

—No disponemos de mucho tiempo —dijo Bernie—. El otro no tardará en regresar.

Maestre permanecía tumbado boca arriba sobre la hierba, apoyando el peso del cuerpo sobre los codos. Barbara observó cómo Bernie se le acercaba lentamente, apuntando el arma contra su cabeza. El general parpadeó para apartarse la nieve de los ojos. La nevada se había intensificado y ahora los copos se le posaban sobre el uniforme. A su lado, el cuerpo de Sofía se había convertido en un montículo blanco.

Barbara no soportaba la idea de oír otro disparo, de ver morir a otra persona.

—Bernie —dijo—, Bernie, no lo mates.

Bernie se volvió para mirarla y, justo en aquel momento, Barbara vio cómo la mano de Maestre se desplazaba hacia su bolsillo, rápida como una serpiente en pleno ataque.

—¡Cuidado! —gritó, mientras el general extraía un arma. Bernie se volvió y abrió fuego al mismo tiempo que Maestre. Tanto el general como Bernie cayeron hacia atrás. Barbara vio saltar volando la parte lateral del rostro de Maestre mientras su sangre y su cerebro brotaban como un chorro y Bernie se tambaleaba y se desplomaba contra el costado del automóvil. Oyó un grito animal y cayó en la cuenta de que era su propia voz.

—¡Bernie!

—¡Mierda! —gritó él—, ayúdame a subir al automóvil. —Le rechinaban los dientes a causa del dolor y se sujetaba el muslo mientras la sangre se escapaba a través de los dedos.

Harry había contemplado la escena con expresión aturdida, pero ahora parecía haberse recuperado. Miró a Bernie.

—Oh, no, Dios mío —gimió.

—Ayúdame a subirlo —le dijo Barbara. Harry se adelantó y entre los dos consiguieron colocar a Bernie en el asiento de atrás—. Conduce tú, Harry, por favor —le pidió—. Yo tengo que atenderlo. Nos tenemos que ir ahora mismo, antes de que regrese el otro guardia. ¿Podrás hacerlo?

Harry miró a Sofía más allá de donde Barbara se encontraba.

—Está muerta, ¿verdad? Ya nada podemos hacer por ella.

—Nada, Harry, ¿puedes conducir? —Barbara le sujetó la cabeza con las manos y lo miró a los ojos. Temía que el motor se volviera a calar.

Harry respiró hondo y clavó los ojos en ella.

—Sí, sí. Lo haré.

Bernie experimentaba un dolor pulsante en el muslo. No podía mover la pierna y sentía que la sangre se le escapaba a borbotones entre los dedos. Barbara se había quitado el abrigo y arrancaba el grueso forro. Desde el asiento de atrás, Bernie podía ver la parte posterior de la cabeza de Harry y sus manos firmemente agarradas al volante. Bajo el resplandor de los faros delanteros, la nieve caía en implacables remolinos.

—¿Adónde vamos? —preguntó.

—De regreso a Madrid, la embajada es nuestra única esperanza.

—Cuando vuelva el guardia civil, ¿no empezarán a dar la voz de alarma para que intenten detenernos?

—Tenemos que intentar regresar a Madrid. No hables, cariño. —Lo seguía llamando cariño, como en los viejos tiempos. Bernie la miró sonriendo y después hizo una mueca cuando ella sacó unas tijeras de manicura y le cortó la pernera del pantalón—. Te ha machacado la pierna, Bernie. Creo que la bala está alojada en el hueso. Te voy a vendar. Te llevaremos a un médico en Madrid. Procura incorporarte un poco. —Y sus manos frías y expertas empezaron a vendarle la pierna con las tiras del forro.

Cuando terminó, Bernie se dejó caer sobre el asiento. Tuvo que hacer un esfuerzo para no cerrar los ojos. Buscó su mano y se la apretó. Se pasó un rato desmayado; cuando volvió en sí, Barbara le seguía sujetando la mano. La nieve se arremolinaba ante las luces delanteras. Bernie se notaba la pierna entumecida. Barbara lo miró sonriendo.

—Recuerda una cosa por mí, Barbara —dijo—. ¿Recordarás una cosa?

—Te pondrás bien. Te lo prometo.

—Pero por si acaso. Recuerda una cosa.

—Lo que tú quieras.

—La gente, la gente normal, parece que haya perdido; pero algún día, algún día la gente ya no será manipulada y perseguida por los jefes y los curas y los soldados; algún día se liberará, vivirá con libertad y dignidad, como estaba destinada a vivir.

—Te pondrás bien.

—Por favor.

—Lo haré. Sí. Lo haré.

Cerró los ojos y se volvió a quedar dormido.

49

Harry conducía rápido y seguro como un autómata. Procuraba concentrarse en la mancha de luz creada por las luces delanteras del automóvil. Todo lo que había más allá de su blanco resplandor estaba oscuro como la boca del lobo. Al cabo de un rato dejó de nevar, pero seguía resultando muy difícil conducir por la accidentada carretera en medio de la oscuridad. Harry experimentaba la constante sensación de un terrible agujero negro en el estómago, como si a él también le hubieran pegado un tiro. La imagen del cuerpo de Sofía acribillado a balazos se le clavaba en el cerebro y le provocaba deseos de llorar; pero hacía un esfuerzo por apartarla a un lado y concentrarse en la carretera, la carretera, la carretera. A través del espejo retrovisor, podía ver el rostro angustiado de Barbara, inclinada sobre Bernie. Estaba dormido o inconsciente; pero, por lo menos, el rumor de su respiración pesada y afanosa significaba que todavía estaba vivo.

En cada pueblo o ciudad temía que aparecieran los guardias civiles y les ordenaran detenerse, pero apenas vieron un alma durante todo el viaje. Poco después de las once, llegaron a las afueras de Madrid y Harry aminoró la marcha mientras se dirigía a la embajada a través de las calles todavía cubiertas de nieve.

—¿Cómo está? —le preguntó a Barbara.

—Todavía inconsciente —contestó ella en voz baja—. Ya me preocupó al principio; pero es que ya estaba muy débil y ha perdido mucha sangre. —Levantó una mano manchada de sangre y consultó el reloj—. Has ido muy rápido.

—¿Por qué no nos habrán obligado a detenernos? —preguntó Harry, muy nervioso.

—No lo sé. A lo mejor aquel guardia civil ha tardado mucho en regresar.

—Llevaba una radio. Y aquí las fuerzas policiales son lo único que funciona. —Una idea a la que había estado dando vueltas en su mente durante todo el viaje afloró ahora a la superficie—. A lo mejor esperan a atraparnos aquí, en Madrid. —Harry miró a Barbara a través del espejo retrovisor. Estaba pálida y agotada.

—¿Dónde está la pistola?

—En el bolsillo de Bernie. No quiero molestarlo. El movimiento lo podría volver a hacer sangrar.

Harry vio pasar velozmente los altos edificios de las calles; se estaban acercando al centro de la ciudad.

—Puede que tengamos que abrirnos paso a tiros —dijo—. Deja que la lleve yo.

Barbara vaciló un instante y después palpó el bolsillo de Bernie. Le pasó la pistola a Harry, manchada de sangre negra reseca. Éste la acunó sobre sus rodillas. Tuvo un recuerdo fugaz de sí mismo sentado en la catedral con Sofía y, de repente, pegó un brinco y se desvió para evitar un gasógeno que avanzaba chisporroteando muy despacio por la calle. El conductor tocó enfurecido la bocina.

Al final, apareció ante sus ojos el edificio de la embajada. Harry pasó por delante de la entrada, despertando la curiosidad del único guardia civil que estaba de guardia, y después dobló la esquina para dirigirse al aparcamiento. Estaba casi desierto. Harry se detuvo junto a la puerta posterior. Estaban en territorio británico. En el primer piso, vio luz en una sola ventana protegida por una cortina; el funcionario de guardia. La cortina se movió y apareció una cabeza.

Harry se volvió hacia Barbara. En su blanco rostro destacaba una mancha de sangre.

—Alguien bajará dentro de un minuto. Vamos a sacar a Bernie. ¡Oh, Dios mío, qué mala cara tiene!

Bernie mantenía los ojos cerrados, su respiración era muy superficial y sus mejillas estaban más hundidas que nunca. Los pantalones de Bernie estaban fuertemente vendados con unas tiras anchas del forro del abrigo de Barbara.

—¿Lo puedes despertar? —preguntó.

—No estoy muy segura de que convenga moverlo.

—Pero es que tenemos que llevarlo dentro. Inténtalo.

Barbara comprimió el hombro de Bernie primero muy suavemente y, después, con más fuerza. Bernie soltó un gruñido, pero no se movió.

—Me tendrás que ayudar a llevarlo —dijo Barbara.

Harry descendió del vehículo. Abrió la puerta de atrás y sujetó a Bernie por los hombros. Se sorprendió de lo liviano que era su cuerpo. Barbara lo ayudó a colocarlo en posición sentada. La sangre rezumaba a través del vendaje improvisado y había manchado todo el asiento de atrás y la ropa de Barbara.

Se oyó el ruido de unos pestillos que alguien estaba descorriendo. Después se abrió una puerta y unas pisadas crujieron sobre la nieve. Al volverse, vieron la mirada de Chalmers, un hombre alto y delgado de treinta y tantos años con una nuez muy pronunciada. Incluso a aquella hora de la noche vestía un convencional traje de calle. Les iluminó la cara con una linterna y abrió los ojos como platos al ver sus ropas manchadas de sangre.

—¡Santo cielo!, ¿qué es eso? ¿Quiénes son ustedes?

—Soy Brett, uno de los traductores. Llevamos a un herido, necesita atención médica.

Chalmers concentró la luz de la linterna en Bernie.

—¡Dios mío! —Iluminó el interior del automóvil y contempló horrorizado la sangre que empapaba los asientos de atrás—. ¡Dios mío!, pero ¿qué ha pasado aquí? ¡Éste es uno de nuestros vehículos!

Harry ayudó a Barbara a arrastrar a Bernie hasta la puerta abierta. Gracias a Dios, todavía respiraba. Emitió otro gemido. Chalmers corrió tras ellos.

—¿Qué ha ocurrido? ¿Quién es? ¿Ha habido un accidente?

—Le han disparado. Es británico. Por Dios bendito, hombre, ¿quiere usted hacer el favor de decidirse de una vez y llamar a un médico? —Harry empujó la puerta y entraron tambaleándose. Se encontraban en un largo pasillo; Harry empujó la puerta del despacho más cercano y entraron. Él y Barbara depositaron a Bernie cuidadosamente en el suelo mientras Chalmers se acercaba al teléfono.

—Doctor Pagall —dijo éste—. Llamen al doctor Pagall.

—¿Cuánto tardará? —preguntó Harry lacónicamente mientras Chalmers colgaba el aparato.

—No mucho. Pero, por el amor de Dios, Brett, dígame qué ha ocurrido.

La imagen del cuerpo de Sofía cayendo con una espasmódica sacudida hacia atrás apareció de nuevo en su mente. Harry dio un respingo y respiró hondo. Chalmers lo miraba con curiosidad.

—Oiga, llame a Simon Tolhurst, Operaciones Especiales, su número está en la agenda. Déjeme hablar con él.

—¿Operaciones Especiales? Dios mío. —Chalmers frunció el entrecejo; a los funcionarios corrientes no les caían muy bien los espías. Marcó otro número y le pasó el aparato a Harry.

—¿Sí, dígame? —contestó una voz soñolienta.

—Soy Harry. Es una emergencia. Estoy en la embajada con Barbara Clare y un inglés que ha resultado herido de bala. No, no es Forsyth. Un prisionero de guerra. Sí, de la Guerra Civil. Está gravemente herido. Ha habido un... incidente. El general Maestre ha muerto de un disparo.

Tolhurst actuó con sorprendente rapidez y decisión. Le dijo a Harry que estaría allí de inmediato y que llamaría a Hillgarth y al embajador.

—Quédate donde estás —terminó diciendo.

«Como si pudiera ir a otro sitio», pensó Harry mientras colgaba el teléfono. Recordó a Paco y Enrique, que esperaban en casa. Se estarían preguntando dónde estaban él y Sofía. Aquello sería el final para Paco.

—Le dije que no viniera —murmuró.

Tolhurst y el médico llegaron al mismo tiempo. El médico era un español de mediana edad, todavía medio muerto de sueño. Se acercó a Barbara y ésta le explicó lo ocurrido. Tolhurst se tomó con sorprendente calma la imagen de Bernie tendido en el suelo con la ropa empapada de sangre y la de Barbara tan empapada como la suya.

—¿Es ésta la señorita Clare? —le preguntó a Harry en voz baja.

—Sí.

—¿Quién es este hombre?

Harry respiró hondo.

—Un brigadista internacional retenido ilegalmente en un campo de trabajos forzados durante tres años. Somos viejos amigos. Teníamos un plan para rescatarlo; pero falló.

—¡Qué barbaridad! —Tolhurst miró a Barbara—. Será mejor que los dos vengáis a mi despacho.

Barbara levantó la vista.

—No, soy enfermera; puedo ayudar.

El médico la miró con dulzura y le dijo amablemente:

—No, señorita, prefiero trabajar solo. —El médico había empezado a retirar el vendaje y Harry vio fugazmente un retazo de carne roja hecha papilla y hueso blanco. Barbara contempló la herida y tragó saliva.

—¿Lo podrá... lo podrá ayudar?

El médico levantó las manos.

—Trabajaré mejor si usted me deja solo. Por favor.

—Vamos, Barbara. —Harry la sujetó por el codo y la ayudó a levantarse. Abandonaron la estancia con Tolhurst y subieron por una escalera oscura. En todo el edificio se estaban encendiendo las luces y se oían murmullos mientras el personal del turno de noche se preparaba para hacer frente a la crisis.

Tolhurst encendió la luz de su despacho y les indicó unos asientos. «Ayer estuve aquí —pensó Harry—, justo ayer. En otro tiempo, otro mundo. Sofía estaba viva.» Tolhurst se sentó a su escritorio, con sus rasgos mofletudos serenados en una tensa expresión de alerta.

—Bueno, Harry. Dime exactamente qué ha ocurrido. ¿Qué demonios es eso de que Maestre ha muerto de un disparo?

Harry le contó la historia a partir del momento en que Barbara se había presentado en su casa para explicarle el plan hasta el rescate de aquella tarde. Tolhurst no paraba de mirar a Barbara. Ésta permanecía hundida en el sillón con sus empañados ojos perdidos en el espacio.

—¿Y todo esto lo hizo usted sin decirle nada a Forsyth? —le preguntó bruscamente Tolhurst en determinado momento.

—Sí —contestó Barbara con indiferencia.

Harry le habló de la emboscada en el claro del bosque.

—Dispararon contra Sofía —dijo, y por primera vez se le quebró la voz—. Le pregunté a Maestre por qué y me dijo que porque los españoles necesitaban mano dura.

Tolhurst respiró muy hondo. «Ayúdanos, Tolly —pensó Harry—, ayúdanos.» Y, a continuación, pasó a describirle cómo habían escapado mientras Tolhurst volvía a mirar a Barbara con incrédulo asombro.

—¿Usted pasó con el automóvil por encima de un hombre y mató a otro de un disparo?

—Sí —contestó Barbara, mirándolo a los ojos—. No me quedó más remedio.

—¿Y el arma la tiene aquí ahora? —preguntó Tolhurst.

—No. La tiene Harry.

Tolhurst alargó una mano.

—Dámela, muchacho, por favor.

Harry se metió la mano en el bolsillo y se la entregó. Tolhurst la guardó en el cajón de su escritorio, haciendo una mueca de desagrado al ver la sangre que la manchaba. Se limpió cuidadosamente los dedos con un pañuelo y después se inclinó hacia delante.

—Eso es muy grave —dijo—. Un subsecretario ministerial muerto y un funcionario de la embajada implicado. Y después de lo que Franco le dijo ayer a Hoare... mierda —añadió, meneando la cabeza.

—No ha sido un asesinato —afirmó rotundamente Barbara—. Ha sido en defensa propia. La única que ha sido asesinada es Sofía.

Tolhurst la miró frunciendo el entrecejo como si fuera una estúpida incapaz de comprender la importancia de la situación. Harry sintió que el peso de la decepción se añadía al dolor sordo y profundo que experimentaba; esperaba que Tolhurst los pudiera ayudar y, en cierto modo, ponerse de su parte. Pero, en realidad, ¿qué otra cosa habría podido hacer?

Tolhurst volvió bruscamente la cabeza al oír el timbre del teléfono de su escritorio. Levantó el auricular.

—Muy bien —dijo, respirando hondo—. El capitán y el embajador están aquí. Tendré que informarles de lo ocurrido. —Se levantó y abandonó la estancia.

Barbara miró a Harry.

—Quiero ver a Bernie —dijo con firmeza.

Harry vio una mancha de sangre en sus gafas.

—Me ha parecido que el médico sabía lo que hacía.

—Quiero verlo.

Harry experimentó un repentino arrebato de furia. ¿Por qué ella había sobrevivido y, en cambio, Sofía había muerto? Era curioso, ambos se habrían tenido que consolar el uno al otro y, sin embargo, él sólo sentía aquella furia terrible. Al inclinarse sobre Sofía, había observado que sus ojos inexpresivos estaban entornados y que sus labios entreabiertos mostraban un atisbo de sus blancos dientes fuertemente apretados en el momento en que le habían arrancado la vida. Parpadeó, tratando de borrar aquella imagen de su mente. Ambos permanecieron sentados en silencio. La espera les pareció interminable. De vez en cuando, oían voces cortantes y pisadas en el exterior del despacho. Harry volvió a notar un zumbido en su oído malo.

Se oyeron otras voces en el pasillo. El profundo timbre de voz de Hillgarth y la estridente jerigonza del embajador. Harry se puso tenso cuando la puerta se abrió. Hillgarth vestía traje de calle y, como de costumbre, estaba más fresco que una rosa, con el cabello negro alisado hacia atrás y los grandes ojos castaños más penetrantes que nunca. En cambio, Hoare era un completo desastre, con el traje puesto de cualquier manera, los ojos enrojecidos y el fino cabello blanco de punta. Miró a Harry hecho una furia y palideció intensamente al ver a Barbara cubierta de sangre. Se sentó al escritorio de Tolhurst, con éste a un lado y Hillgarth al otro.

Hillgarth miró a Barbara.

—¿Está usted herida? —le preguntó con sorprendente dulzura.

—No, estoy bien. Por favor, ¿cómo está Bernie?

Hillgarth no contestó, sino que se volvió muy despacio hacia Harry.

—Brett, Simon me dice que su novia ha muerto.

—Sí, señor. Los guardias civiles dispararon contra ella con una ametralladora.

—Lo siento muchísimo. Pero usted nos ha traicionado. ¿Por qué lo ha hecho?

—Dispararon contra ella con una ametralladora —repitió Harry—. Porque quebrantó la ley y hay que tener mano dura con la gente.

Hoare se inclinó hacia delante con una cara que era la viva imagen de la indignación y la furia.

—¡Y a usted también lo reclaman por asesinato, Brett! —El embajador se volvió y señaló a Barbara con el dedo—. ¡Y a usted también! —Ella lo miró con asombro. El embajador levantó la voz—. He telefoneado a uno de nuestros amigos del Gobierno. Lo saben todo al respecto, aquel guardia civil regresó al claro del bosque y se encontró con una carnicería. Sus superiores acudieron a El Pardo. Han tenido que despertar al Generalísimo. ¡Mierda! —gritó—. ¡Los tendría que entregar a los dos para que los llevaran al paredón y los fusilaran! —Le temblaba la voz—. ¡Un subsecretario del Gobierno muerto de un disparo!

—Fue Piper quien lo hizo —terció Hillgarth en un susurro—. A ellos no les interesan realmente Brett y la señorita Clare; Sam, Franco no quiere por nada del mundo que ahora se produzca un grave incidente diplomático. Piénselo bien, habrían podido detenerlos por el camino, pero les han permitido llegar hasta aquí.

Hoare volvió a dirigir su atención a Harry, parpadeando a ritmo sincopado a causa de un tic en la mejilla.

—¡Lo podría acusar de traición, joven, lo podría enviar a casa para que lo metieran entre rejas! —Se pasó una mano por el cabello—. ¡Yo habría sido virrey de la India, Winston prácticamente me lo había prometido! ¡Habría sido virrey en lugar de tener que enfrentarme con esta locura, estas imbecilidades, estos necios! Eso podría estar muy bien para este nuevo hombre de la oficina de Madrid en Londres... ¿cómo se llama...?

—Philby —dijo Hillgarth—. Kim Philby.

—¡Eso estaría muy bien para que lo manejara Philby! ¡Pero ahora Winston me va a echar la culpa a mí!

—Bueno, Sam —dijo Hillgarth en tono apaciguador.

—¿Cómo que bueno?

Barbara preguntó con un hilillo de voz.

—Por favor, ¿me pueden decir cómo está Bernie? Por favor. Esta sangre es suya, lo hemos traído desde Cuenca; por favor, díganme algo.

Hoare hizo un gesto de impaciencia.

—El médico ha dispuesto su envío al hospital, necesita una transfusión. Esperemos que tengan el equipo necesario porque, lo que es yo, no pienso enviarlo a una clínica privada. Si sale de ésta, quizá no pueda volver a utilizar la pierna izquierda, daño neurológico o algo parecido. —El embajador miró a Barbara frunciendo el entrecejo—. Y, si no sale, por lo que a mí respecta, ¡que tenga un buen viaje! ¡Un grave incidente diplomático por culpa de un terrorista rojo de mierda! Al menos, no tenemos que preocuparnos por la otra, la española que ha resultado muerta.

Barbara pegó un respingo hacia atrás en su asiento, como si acabaran de propinarle un puñetazo. Una momentánea expresión de satisfacción se dibujó en el rostro de Hoare, lo cual ejerció un efecto definitivo en Harry: todo el dolor, el pesar y la cólera se concentraron de golpe en su mente; por lo que, lanzando un grito, éste cruzó la estancia en dirección a Hoare y rodeó el huesudo cuello del embajador con sus manos. El hecho de apretar su piel reseca y de sentir cómo los tendones cedían bajo su presa, lo llenó de una inmensa sensación de liberación. El rostro de Hoare se congestionó y la boca se le abrió. Harry pudo contemplar directamente el fondo de la garganta del embajador de su majestad británica en Misión Especial ante la Corte del generalísimo Francisco Franco. Los brazos de Hoare se agitaron débilmente mientras éste trataba de agarrar los hombros de Harry.

De pronto, Harry oyó gritar a Barbara «¡Cuidado!» justo antes de recibir un fuerte golpe en el cuello. Miró aturdido alrededor y vio que había sido Tolhurst el que lo había golpeado; Tolhurst, que lo apartaba del embajador con una fuerza sorprendente y un rostro horrorizado. Hoare había caído hacia atrás en su sillón y ahora, con dos inflamadas ronchas rojas en su garganta, vomitaba en medio de unas fuertes náuseas.

Harry se mareó y notó que las piernas le flaqueaban. Mientras se desplomaba, captó en el rostro de Hillgarth una expresión extraña, algo que casi se habría podido definir como admiración. «A lo mejor, se piensa que todo esto no es más que una aventura», pensó antes de perder el conocimiento.

Epílogo

Croydon, mayo de 1947

La escuela se encontraba en un frondoso barrio residencial con edificios de falso estilo Tudor. Barbara bajó desde la estación a través de toda una serie de calles flanqueadas de árboles bajo un sol primaveral. Llevaba colgada del hombro la cartera de documentos en la cual guardaba los papeles correspondientes a la reunión. La zona de los agentes de bolsa, pensó. Pero hasta allí habían llegado las cicatrices: cráteres de bomba cubiertos de maleza.

Oyó la escuela antes de verla, una cacofonía de voces infantiles cada vez más fuerte. Caminó pegada a un alto muro de ladrillo, hasta llegar a una puerta con un rótulo de gran tamaño en la parte exterior y el nombre de Haverstock School en letras negras bajo un escudo de armas.

Avanzó entre apretujones hasta la entrada principal. Los chicos no le prestaron la menor atención; tuvo que apartarse a un lado para esquivar un partido de fútbol que se disputaba demasiado cerca de allí.

—Suelta el balón, Chivers —gritó alguien.

Todos hablaban con el típico acento de la clase alta, arrastrando las vocales. Barbara se preguntó cómo sería darles clase. En un rincón alejado, tenía lugar una pelea: dos muchachos rodaban por el suelo y se propinaban puñetazos mientras un grupo los jaleaba. Apartó los ojos.

Entró en un inmenso vestíbulo con vigas de madera de roble y un estrado al fondo. No había nadie; por lo visto, todo el mundo estaba fuera disfrutando del sol. Era un ambiente impresionante, muy distinto de los estrechos pasillos pintados de su antiguo instituto de enseñanza secundaria; aunque el penetrante aroma a desinfectante fuera el mismo en ambos casos. Una nueva lápida conmemorativa de la guerra en reluciente bronce se había colocado a un lado del escenario bajo la inscripción 1939-1945 por encima de una lista de nombres. La lista era más corta que la de la lápida de 1914-1918 del otro lado; pero bastante larga, de todos modos.

Harry le había indicado en su carta el camino de su aula. Encontró el pasillo y siguió las puertas numeradas hasta llegar a la 14A. Lo vio a través de una ventana, sentado a su escritorio corrigiendo exámenes. Llamó con los nudillos y entró.

Harry se levantó sonriendo.

—Barbara, cuánto me alegro de verte.

Llevaba una chaqueta de tweed con coderas de cuero como una caricatura de maestro de escuela, y había engordado considerablemente; ahora tenía papada y su cabello negro estaba salpicado de hebras grises; como, ella, rondaba ya los cuarenta.

Barbara le estrechó la mano.

—Hola, Harry. Dios mío, cuánto tiempo ha transcurrido, ¿verdad?

—Casi un año —dijo él—. Demasiado.

Barbara miró alrededor. Pósters de la torre Eiffel, tablas de verbos irregulares franceses, hileras de pupitres cubiertos de rayas.

—O sea que es aquí donde das clase.

—Pues sí, aquí vive el profesor de francés. Los profesores de francés tienen fama de ser unos blancos muy fáciles, ¿sabes?

—No me digas.

—En efecto. —Harry señaló la palmeta que descansaba en el otro extremo de su escritorio—. Por desgracia, a veces la tengo que utilizar para recordarles quién manda aquí. Anda, vamos a comer algo. Hay un pequeño pub muy agradable no muy lejos de aquí.

Abandonaron el edificio y regresaron al centro de la ciudad. Los árboles estaban en flor. Mientras pasaban junto a un cerezo, la cálida brisa hizo que se desprendiera una nube de pétalos blancos que flotó a su alrededor, recordándole a Barbara unos copos de nieve.

—¿Enseñas algo de español? —preguntó Barbara.

—No hay suficiente demanda. Sólo francés. Se limitan a aprender unas cuantas frases para salir del paso. —Con una sonrisa en los labios, Harry señaló la cartera que ella llevaba—. Aquí la experta en español eres tú. ¿A quién vas a recibir en el aeropuerto de Croydon?

—Pues a un grupo de hombres de negocios de Argentina. Han venido acompañando la gira europea de Eva Perón y, desde aquí, volarán a París para echar un vistazo a las oportunidades comerciales. Carne de vaca en conserva y productos cárnicos, no demasiado interesante que digamos.

A su regreso a Inglaterra en 1940, Barbara se había puesto a trabajar como intérprete y traductora de español. El dinero le había servido para cubrir gastos durante el largo período de convalecencia de Bernie. Le habían dicho que éste jamás volvería a caminar con normalidad; pero, con un enorme esfuerzo, él les había demostrado que se equivocaban. Cuando se habían casado en 1941, Bernie había podido avanzar por el pasillo sin ayuda de nadie y sin el menor atisbo de cojera, a pesar de la bala que tenía alojada en el fémur. Lo cual había aliviado el remordimiento de Barbara, pues ésta sabía que, de no haber gritado llamando a Bernie, Maestre no habría tenido tiempo de alargar la mano para empuñar su arma.

—¿Sigues trabajando con los refugiados? —le preguntó Harry.

—Sí. Ahora el trabajo es más bien de tipo teórico, la resistencia ya está prácticamente derrotada. En estos momentos, enseño inglés a un escritor de Madrid. —Miró a Harry—. ¿Alguna noticia de Paco y Enrique?

El rostro de Harry se iluminó con una sonrisa.

—Hace un mes recibí una carta, ahora ya no recibo noticias suyas tan a menudo. Paco empezará a trabajar en una granja.

—¿Cuántos años tiene ahora?

—Dieciséis. Nunca pensé que pudiera superarlo, pero lo ha conseguido. Enrique dice que no habla mucho, pero que disfruta con su trabajo.

—Enrique lo salvó.

—Sí.

Después de la matanza, Barbara, Bernie y Harry habían sido sacados de España en el primer avión. Nada más llegar a Inglaterra, Harry le había escrito una carta a Enrique; ni siquiera sabía si el hermano de Sofía había sido informado de lo que le había ocurrido a su hermana. Unas semanas después, recibió respuesta desde el norte de España. La Guardia Civil se había presentado para comunicarle a Enrique la muerte de Sofía y, aquella misma noche, Enrique había hecho un par de maletas, se había ido con Paco a la estación y había subido a un tren con destino al norte. Se había acogido a la benevolencia de unos parientes lejanos que tenían una pequeña granja cerca de Palencia. Éstos les habían ofrecido cobijo y, desde entonces, Paco y Enrique vivían allí. De vez en cuando, Harry les enviaba dinero. Apenas ganaban para vivir, pero Enrique decía que el campo era un lugar muy tranquilo y agradable, y que eso era lo que Paco necesitaba. Ahora el muchacho ya estaba mejor, pero Enrique pensaba que jamás abandonaría el pueblo. Se había librado del orfelinato, a diferencia de Carmela Mera. Ahora Carmela ya debía de ser una adolescente, pensó Barbara. En caso de que hubiera sobrevivido. Era una de las cosas en las que procuraba no pensar. Meneó la cabeza para que se le despejara la mente.

—Es una lástima dejar perder una lengua —le dijo a Harry—. Tendrías que practicar un poco.

—Bueno, ya tengo suficiente con el francés. —Harry la miró con una triste sonrisa en los labios—. Tuve que desprenderme de muchas cosas cuando en Cambridge se negaron a volver a concederme la plaza.

—Fue una injusticia.

—La venganza de Hoare —dijo categóricamente Harry—. Y eso que, por aquel entonces, andaban muy escasos de profesores.

—Sí. Y tampoco les gustó que Bernie intentara reunir documentos para publicar la verdad acerca de los campos de trabajos forzados de España.

—Bernie fue muy ingenuo. Debería haber comprendido que ellos incluirían esta historia en sus peticiones oficiales a las agencias de noticias, instándolas a no publicar artículos acerca de determinados temas por motivos de seguridad nacional.

—¿Has pensado en la posibilidad de volver a intentarlo? Porque ya han pasado casi siete años. —Barbara vaciló—. No creo que sigan conservando mis fichas.

Desde su regreso, se había pasado años recibiendo cartas abiertas y vueltas a cerrar de cualquier manera y, a veces, oía ruidos extraños al hablar por teléfono. A Harry le había ocurrido lo mismo.

—Will dice que, cuando estás en una lista negra, te quedas en ella. Además, me encuentro bastante a gusto en Haverstock.

—A veces me pregunto... —Barbara dejó la frase sin terminar.

—¿Qué?

—El hecho de ver la nueva lápida conmemorativa me lo ha hecho recordar. No sé si el nombre de Bernie figura en la lápida de Rookwood.

Bernie había sido llamado a filas en 1943, tras haber sido declarado apto. Con todas las lesiones sufridas, probablemente podría haberse librado de ser reclutado, pero ni siquiera lo intentó; quería volver a luchar contra el fascismo. Había muerto el Día D, el 6 de junio de 1944, abatido de un disparo cuando trataba desesperadamente de alcanzar la orilla en la playa de Juno. En el automóvil que lo llevaba a Madrid, le había dicho a Barbara que jamás la volvería a dejar, pero lo había hecho. Ahora ella comprendía que un hombre como él en los tiempos que corrían, siempre habría ido a luchar. Pero aun así, lo seguía echando de menos, tanto como al hijo que jamás habían tenido.

—¿Has visto las memorias que ha publicado Hoare? —preguntó Harry.

—Ah, pero ¿las ha publicado?

—Ahora bajo el nombre de vizconde de Templewood, claro, el título que le han otorgado. —Harry soltó una amarga carcajada—. Embajador en Misión Especial. Dice que Franco se mantuvo al margen de la guerra gracias exclusivamente a la firme diplomacia que él supo desarrollar. Naturalmente, no menciona a Hillgarth para nada. Las memorias del cobarde.

Ya habían llegado al pub, un local espacioso donde servían comidas. Estaba lleno de agentes de bolsa. Mientras acompañaba a Barbara a una mesa, Harry saludó con la cabeza a un par de personas acodadas en la barra.

—La comida no está mal. ¿A qué hora tienes que estar en el aeropuerto?

—No antes de las cuatro de la tarde. Dispongo de mucho tiempo.

Pidieron bistecs y pastel de riñón. La comida estaba demasiado cocida y correosa; pero, por lo visto, a Harry le daba igual.

—O sea que el trabajo te mantiene ocupada, ¿eh?

—Sí, el trabajo y los refugiados. —Barbara lo estudió; se había hecho un corte muy feo en la barbilla con la cuchilla de afeitar.

—¿Qué haces últimamente, aparte de dar clase? ¿Qué ocurrió con aquella profesora con la que habías hecho amistad?

Harry se encogió de hombros.

—Bueno, más bien lo dejamos. En realidad, no hago gran cosa, aparte de las clases.

—El trabajo también es mi vida, supongo. Y los refugiados. Había pensado estudiar a tiempo parcial para una licenciatura en español.

—Buena idea. Seguramente a ti te sería muy fácil.

—Tendría que reducir un poco mi actividad con los refugiados.

—Barbara se echó a reír—. Me he acabado convirtiendo en una de esas bienintencionadas mujeres solteras que se dedican a labores benéficas. Siempre pensé que terminaría así.

—Supongo que, por lo menos, nos quedan los recuerdos —dijo Harry. Con los ojos empañados, volvió a esbozar una sonrisa tensa—. Estoy pensando en dejar mi apartamento e irme a vivir a Haverstock. Ahora el hijo de Will está en Haverstock, ¿sabes? Ronnie. Un chico muy listo. Ya está casi en sexto grado. Se parece a su padre. Al final, no pudieron pagar la matrícula de Rookwood.

—¿Will y Muriel siguen en Italia?

—Sí. Echo de menos a Will, sobre todo desde la muerte de tío James. —Otra vez la sonrisa tensa—. A Muriel no le gusta. Roma es demasiado calurosa y polvorienta para ella. Quiere un destino en París.

Con el tenedor, Barbara empujó la espantosa comida por el plato.

—¿No crees que eso de irte a vivir a la escuela te hará sentir... bueno... un poco aislado del mundo?

—¿Y qué tiene el mundo de maravilloso? De todos modos, ahora me dedico a la enseñanza. Ya puesto en este plan, mejor seguir hasta el final. A veces, resulta un poco aburrido; pero ya estoy acostumbrado. De vez en cuando, puedes ayudar a un chico y sólo por eso ya merece la pena.

—Bernie solía decir que las escuelas privadas eran un mundo cerrado. Un mundo privilegiado.

Harry la miró incisivamente.

—Lo sé. Sofía tampoco lo habría aprobado.

Barbara respiró hondo.

—No, ninguno de los dos lo habría aprobado, pero no es eso lo que yo quería decir. Tú estabas furioso cuando regresamos de España, querías hacer cosas. Ahora es como si... bueno... como si te hubieras encerrado en ti mismo.

—¿Y qué otra cosa se puede hacer? —Otra vez la amarga sonrisa—. ¿Qué hemos hecho tú y yo?

—Por lo menos, yo ayudo a los refugiados. Al regresar, pensé que, a lo mejor, me podría dedicar a la política; había algo... algo que Bernie había dicho en el automóvil. —Le pareció oír una vez más las palabras en su mente y lanzó un suspiro—. Dejó caducar su carnet del Partido Comunista. Estaba decepcionado con ellos, pero seguía conservando los principios que siempre había tenido. Es que en España no podemos cambiar las cosas. Y supongo que, por lo menos aquí, las cosas van mejor con los laboristas.

Harry hizo una mueca.

—Ah, ¿sí? ¿Quiénes eran los dueños de todo antes de la guerra? La gente que estudió en sitios como Haverstock. ¿Y quiénes lo son ahora? Los mismos.

—Pues entonces —le dijo Barbara—, ¿por qué te quedas aquí? —Estaba enojada con él, allí sentado comiendo aquella comida vomitiva, con toda la pinta de un solterón polvoriento.

—Porque, en realidad, no se puede cambiar nada —contestó Harry en tono cansado—. Ellos son demasiado fuertes y, al final, acaban contigo.

—Yo no lo creo. Hay que luchar.

—Pues yo he perdido —se limitó a decir Harry.

Apenas hablaron durante el resto de la comida. Harry se disculpó por no poderla acompañar al autobús, tenía una clase. Se estrecharon la mano y prometieron volver a reunirse; pero Barbara comprendió en cierto modo que no lo harían, que aquélla sería la última vez. Probablemente sólo hablaban de Bernie y Sofía cuando estaban juntos, lo cual les provocaba más dolor y no menos, como habría cabido esperar conforme pasaban los años.

A bordo del autobús, notó que las lágrimas le escocían en los ojos, pero consiguió reprimirlas parpadeando. Abrió la cartera de documentos e hizo un esfuerzo por estudiar los detalles correspondientes a las personas con quienes iba a reunirse, sus nombres y las empresas que representaban. Señor Gómez, señor Barrancas, señor Grazziani. Muchos argentinos tenían apellidos italianos; descendientes de inmigrantes italianos, suponía.

En el aeropuerto se reunió con un representante de la Cámara de Comercio de Londres, un caballero alto y cortés con una corbata del club de polo de los Guards, el cual se presentó como Gore-Brown. Lo acompañaban unos seis hombres de negocios.

—Dios mío —dijo Barbara—, no sabía que habría tantos en su grupo. Sólo hay cuatro argentinos. Me temo que habrá que turnarse.

—Me han dicho que uno o dos hablan inglés. Creo que muchos argentinos lo hablan.

—Bueno pues, ya veremos cómo lo arreglamos. —Barbara adoptó el jovial y confiado tono de voz de solterona que solía utilizar con hombres como aquéllos. Esperaba salir airosa de aquella prueba con el difícil y sibilante acento argentino.

—Creo que el aparato está a punto de tomar tierra —dijo Gore-Brown—. Podríamos subir a verlo a la sala de espera.

—Sería estupendo —dijo uno de los hombres de negocios—, nunca he visto aterrizar un avión.

—Se ve que no ha estado usted en la RAF —dijo un rubicundo sujeto con bigote de guías enroscadas hacia arriba.

—Cinco años en acorazados, amigo. Derribé a unos cuantos, pero nunca he visto aterrizar ninguno.

Los componentes del grupo subieron entre risas la escalera que conducía a la cubierta de observación. Un amplio ventanal daba a la pista de aterrizaje. Había un par de aparatos cuyos pasajeros estaban desembarcando.

—Ya lo tenemos aquí —dijo el marino.

Barbara observó cómo un biplano de tamaño sorprendentemente pequeño se posaba en la pista y rodaba lentamente hacia ellos. Barbara sacó los papeles de la cartera de documentos. Gore-Brown se inclinó hacia ella.

—¿Cuál es el hombre de Fray Bentos? —le preguntó.

—Barrancas.

—Estupendo. Encárguese de colocarlo a mi lado. Aquí podría hacer un buen negocio. Estoy en el sector de la distribución. Se puede sacar mucho partido a la cuota de carne —añadió, guiñándole el ojo.

El aparato ya se había detenido. Un par de operarios vestidos con monos acercaron la escalerilla a la puerta. Ésta se abrió y un grupito de hombres bajó los peldaños. Todos estaban muy bronceados y llevaban sombrero y pesados abrigos. Inglaterra debía de parecerles muy fría, pensó Barbara. Entornó los párpados y se puso las gafas. Algo en el último hombre del grupo se le antojaba familiar. Se mantenía ligeramente apartado de los demás y miraba alrededor como si lo que estaba viendo le encantara. Barbara se aproximó al cristal y observó al otro lado de éste.

Gore-Brown se acercó a ella.

—Este último es Barrancas —dijo—. Me enviaron la fotografía. Creo que es uno de los que hablan inglés.

Pero su apellido, en realidad, no era Barrancas, y Barbara lo sabía. Conocía a aquel individuo rechoncho, ahora un poco más corpulento y con los hombros encorvados, aquel rostro de facciones marcadas y bigote a lo Clark Gable. Vio cómo Sandy Forsyth cruzaba la pista de aterrizaje para acercarse a ellos, sonriendo como un emocionado y curioso colegial mientras levantaba el rostro a la soleada tarde inglesa.

Agradecimientos

Estoy profundamente agradecido a varios amigos que leyeron el manuscrito de *Invierno en Madrid* y que abordaron conmigo las cuestiones más peliagudas de perspectiva política, histórica y cultural que planteaba el libro a partir de una variedad sorprendentemente amplia de puntos de vista. Mi gratitud a Roz Brody, Emily Furman, Mike Holmes, Caroline Hume, Jan King, Tony Macaulay, Charles Penny, Mari Roberts por su revisión del manuscrito original y William Shaw; a mi agente Antony Topping y a mi editora Maria Rejt en Macmillan. Gracias también a Will Stone, por su ayuda en las investigaciones en una circunstancia decisiva. Como siempre, doy las gracias a Frankie Lawrence por el mecanografiado y por la identificación de algún que otro gazapo.

Bibliografía seleccionada

Existen muchos libros en inglés acerca de la Guerra Civil española y sus orígenes. Después de más de sesenta años, creo que *El laberinto español* de Gerald Brenan sigue siendo el mejor acerca de los orígenes de la guerra. *La Guerra Civil española*, de Anthony Beevor, es la introducción más accesible a la guerra propiamente dicha.

Diplomacy and the Strategy of Survival. British Policy and Franco's Spain 1940-41 (Cambridge. Cambridge UP, 1986) es el principal relato teórico del período, aunque diría que subestima la importancia de las afinidades culturales entre los monárquicos españoles y las clases dominantes británicas. La monumental biografía *Franco* (Barcelona. Grijalbo, 1988) es también muy útil por lo que respecta a la política exterior del régimen en tiempo de guerra, si bien la cuestión de las condiciones domésticas en aquellos años está curiosamente ausente. El relato de Hoare de su período como embajador, escrito tras haberse convertido en vizconde de Templewood, *Embajador ante Franco en Misión Especial* (Madrid. Editorial Sedmay, 1977) es autocomplaciente y poco fidedigno en su relato de los acontecimientos de 1940-1941 (aunque muchos aspectos como, por ejemplo, el soborno de ministros, no se pudieran revelar en la época en que fue escrito); pero muestra la evolución de su pensamiento hacia una postura fuertemente antifranquista hacia el final de la guerra. *Churchill y Franco* (Barcelona. Editorial Debate, 2005,) de Richard Wigg, arroja una nueva e interesante luz acerca de la evolución de las perspectivas tanto de Churchill como de Hoare acerca de España a medida que avanza la guerra. *Philby Maestro de Espías* (Barcelona. Ediciones B, 1998), de Phillip Knightley, me abrió el mundo del espionaje en tiempo de guerra. La señorita Maxse es un personaje real; entrevistó a Philby para el Servicio Secreto de Inteligencia (SIS) en el hotel St Hermin's. *Dunant's Dream* (Londres. HarperCollins, 1998), de Caroline Moorhead, es una historia de la Cruz Roja realista e imparcial. El artículo de J. Bandrés y R. Llavona «Psychology in Spain», 1997, vol. I, n.º I, pp. 3-9) es un estremecedor relato sobre el abuso de la psiquiatría. En cuanto a los detalles de la estafa de la mina de oro, me basé en el relato de otra moderna estafa todavía más extraordinaria contada en *Bre-X. Gold Today, Gone Tomorrow* (Toronto. Knopf Canada, 1997), de V. Danielson y J. White.

Por lo que respecta a la batalla del Jarama, *English Captain* (Londres. Faber & Faber, 1939), de Tom Wintringham, narra la historia desde el gélido punto de vista de un estalinista de la clase alta; mientras que *Crusade in Spain* (Londres. Faber & Faber, 1974), de Jason Gurney, lo hace desde el de un comprometido y, más tarde, decepcionado voluntario.

Para los detalles sobre la vida en Madrid durante los primeros años de Franco me he basado principalmente en obras de periodistas y diplomáticos británicos y norteamericanos que estuvieron allí en aquel período. Aun reconociendo sus puntos de vista fuertemente antifranquistas, la imagen que nos ofrecen es impresionante. *Appeasement's Child* (Londres. Left Book Club, 1943), de T. Hamilton; *Report from Spain* (Nueva York, 1948), de E. J. Hughes, y *Masquerade in Spain* (Boston. Houghton Mifflin Company, 1948,) de C. Foltz, me fueron especialmente útiles. Las cartas de David Eccles, agregado de asuntos económicos en la embajada británica en 1940, *By Safe Hand, Letters of Sybil and David Eccles, 1939-42* (Londres. Bodley Head, 1983) ofrecen un relato realista y emocionante de la diplomacia y la vida diaria por parte de un hombre que, por muy curiosas que puedan parecer hoy en día sus ideas políticas, se compadecía profundamente de la situación del pueblo español. La historia de la mujer detenida cuando el viento le levantó la falda por encima de la cabeza está basada en un incidente que él describe, como la historia de Hoare que se esconde bajo una mesa para huir de un murciélago. El Café Rocinante está en deuda con el café de Doña Rosa en *La Colmena* de Camilo José Cela (Buenos Aires. Emecé, 1951).

Índice

OTROS TÍTULOS DE LA COLECCIÓN

Dulce prisionera

KAT MARTIN

Todos piensan que Velvet Moran es una rica heredera. La verdad es que necesita un esposo rico para pagar las enormes deudas de su padre. Velvet cree haber encontrado a su pareja ideal en Avery Sinclair, duque de Carlyle, pero no imagina que él también quiere casarse con ella por dinero.

Cuando se dirige a encontrarse con su prometido, es raptada por un hombre que le promete dejarla libre mediante el pago de un rescate. Pero Velvet sospecha que no se trata de un simple bandolero, y a pesar de mostrarse distante y hasta agresiva, no puede evitar sentirse atraída por su misterioso raptor. Y a él le ocurre lo mismo.

Kat Martin consigue en esta novela una sabia combinación de intriga e idilio. Desde el corazón de un bosque inglés hasta los lujosos salones de baile, pasando por la oscura sombra del patíbulo, esta maravillosa historia de amor tendrá en vilo a sus lectoras.